$\text{R-S} \int_a^b f\,dg$	Riemann–Stieltjes integral	
exp	exponential	
ln	natural logarithm	
sgn	signum	
$[x]$	greatest integer not exceeding x	
$\lvert \cdot \rvert$	absolute value	
$\lVert \cdot \rVert$	norm	
$< , >$	inner product	
$\mathbf{R}^+$	set of positive integers	
$\mathbf{R}$	set of real numbers	
$\mathbf{Q}$	set of rational numbers	
$\mathbf{N}$	set of natural numbers	
$\mathbf{Z}$	set of integers	
$\mathbf{F}$	a field	
$\mathbf{C}$	field of complex numbers	
$\mathbf{R}^2$	two-dimensional space (plane)	
$\mathbf{R}^k$	k-dimensional space	
$\mathbf{R}^3$	3-dimensional space	
$[a, b]$	closed interval	
(a, b)	open interval	
$(a, b]$	half-open interval (open at left)	
$[a, b)$	half-open interval (open at right)	
$+\infty$	infinity	
$-\infty$	minus infinity	
$\mathbf{C}[a, b]$	continuous function on $[a, b]$	
$\Re[a, b]$	family of R-integrable functions on $[a, b]$	
$\rho_p(\mathbf{x}, \mathbf{y})$	metric on the plane	
$\rho_p(f, g)$	metric on $\mathbf{C}[a, b]$	
$\prod$	product	
$\sum$	sum	
$\prod_{i=1}^{\infty} a_i$	infinite product	

$\sum_{n=1}^{\infty} a_n$	infinite series	
$\{a_n\}$	infinite sequence	
A'	complement of A	
A_{lm}	derived set of A	
$\overline{A}$	closure of A	
A°	inferior of A	
bd A	boundary of A	
Ext A	exterior of A	
$\square$	end of a proof, solution, or discussion	

GREEK LETTERS

Φ	PHI
Ψ	PSI
Σ	SIGMA
Π	PI
Γ	GAMMA
Δ	DELTA
α	alpha
β	beta
γ	gamma
δ	delta
ϵ	epsilon
σ	sigma
θ	theta
λ	lambda
ψ	psi
ϕ	phi
ζ	zeta
ξ	xi
π	pi
ρ	rho
ω	omega

FOUNDATIONS OF ANALYSIS

FOUNDATIONS OF ANALYSIS
The Theory of Limits

Herbert S. Gaskill

P. P. Narayanaswami

Memorial University of Newfoundland

1817

HARPER & ROW, PUBLISHERS, New York

Grand Rapids, Philadelphia, St. Louis, San Francisco,
London, Singapore, Sydney, Tokyo

Sponsoring Editor: Peter Coveney
Project Editor: Thomas R. Farrell
Cover Design: Wanda Lubelska Design
Text Art: Vantage Art, Inc.
Production Manager: Willie Lane
Compositor: House of Equations, Inc.
Printer and Binder: R. R. Donnelley & Sons Company

FOUNDATIONS OF ANALYSIS

Library of Congress Cataloging-in-Publication Data

Gaskill, Herbert S.
    Foundations of analysis: the theory of limits / Herbert S.
Gaskill, P.P. Narayanaswami.
        p. cm.
    Includes index.
    ISBN 0-06-044734-6
    1. Mathematical analysis. 2. Calculus. I.
Narayanaswami, P. P. II Title.
QA300.G29 1989   88-7627
515—dc19   CIP

88 89 90 91   9 8 7 6 5 4 3 2 1

This book is dedicated to mathematics,
a garden of infinite delights.

Contents

Preface   xi

Chapter **0**   **Basic Concepts   1**

0.1 Logic   2

0.2 Field Axioms   13

0.3 Order Axioms   21

0.4 Completeness Axiom   26

0.5 Completeness: Further Consequences   42

0.6 Absolute Value   48

Chapter **1**   **Limits of Sequences   54**

1.1 Sequences   54

1.2 Basic Limit Theorems   66

1.3 Monotonicity and Its Consequences   74

Chapter **2**   **Limits of Functions   83**

2.1 Functions, Limit at Infinity   83

2.2 Limit of a Function at a Real Number   95

2.3 Basic Limit Theorems   109

2.4 Monotone Functions   114

2.5 Continuity   120

2.6 Properties of Continuous Functions   134

Chapter **3**   **A Little Topology   139**

3.1 Basic Topological Concepts   141

3.2 Properties of **R** Associated with Closed Bounded Sets   152

3.3 The Cauchy Criterion   160

3.4 Limit Superior and Limit Inferior   166

3.5 Uniform Continuity   173

3.6 Continuous Functions Defined on Closed Bounded Sets   184

Chapter 4   Differentiation   188

4.1 Definition and Basic Facts   189

4.2 Continuity of the Derivative, the Differential, and the Chain Rule   206

4.3 The Mean Value Theorem   214

4.4 L'Hospital's Rule   223

Chapter 5   Integration   230

5.1 Motivation for Definition of the Riemann–Darboux Integral   231

5.2 Definition of the Riemann–Darboux Integral   233

5.3 The Problem of Computing an Integral   253

5.4 Properties of the Integral   264

5.5 The Relationship Between Integration and Differentiation   273

Chapter 6   Applications of Integration   284

6.1 Applications of the Integral Concept   284

6.2 Improper Riemann Integration   297

6.3 Riemann–Stieltjes Integration   312

Chapter 7   Infinite Series of Constants   328

7.1 Infinite Series and Its Convergence   329

7.2 Series of Nonnegative Terms and Tests for Their Convergence   344

7.3 Absolute Convergence   353

7.4 Series with Arbitrary Terms   370

7.5 Infinite Products   382

Chapter 8   Sequences of Functions   391

8.1 Pointwise Convergence of a Sequence of Functions   391

8.2 Uniform Convergence of Sequence of Functions   403

8.3 Consequences of Uniform Convergence   417

Chapter **9** **Infinite Series of Functions** **426**

9.1 Series of Functions, Pointwise and Uniform Convergence   426
9.2 Power Series   445
9.3 Taylor Series   459
9.4 Weierstrass's Approximation Theorem   472

Chapter **10** **Transcendental Functions** **482**

10.1 Exponential Function   483
10.2 Logarithmic Function and Power Function   491
10.3 Trigonometric Functions   497

Chapter **11** **Limits and Topology in the Plane** **510**

11.1 Geometry of Functions of Two Variables   510
11.2 Double Sequences   518
11.3 Properties of the Plane   526
11.4 Convergence of Sequences and Topology of the Plane   541
11.5 Limits and Continuity of Real-Valued Functions of Two Real Variables   552

Chapter **12** **Metric Spaces** **566**

12.1 Definition and Examples of Metric Spaces   566
12.2 Convergence in a Metric Space   578
12.3 Topology of Metric Spaces   586
12.4 Continuity in Metric Spaces   593
12.5 Compact Metric Spaces   598

Appendix on Set Theory **609**
Selected Readings **628**
Index **631**

Preface

To the Instructor

The book covers the essential elements of analysis and limiting processes on the real line including convergence of sequences and series, limits of functions, continuity, topology of the line, differentiation and integration. The book concludes by extending the ideas to the general setting of metric spaces after considering sequences and series of functions, limiting processes in the plane and the problem of approximating continuous functions with polynomials. It is intended that students attempting this book will have a minimum of one solid year of university-level calculus under their belts.

Level of Preparation

Twenty-five years ago several classic books on a similar theme were written aimed at introducing students to rigorous mathematics in the form of analysis. Even at that time, when most would agree that students were better prepared, it was recognized that students had tremendous difficulties achieving competence at rigorous mathematics. During the past twenty-five years, the level of preparedness in mathematics of students entering university has declined. The principal reasons for this decline are decreased skill at basic algebra and symbol manipulation. Facility in these two skills is an essential prerequisite for mathematicians, and lack thereof hampers mathematical development. Thus, the continuing decline in these fundamental skills exacerbates the difficulties faced by today's students attempting their first rigorous mathematics course. There are two plausible ways to address this problem.

The first is to reduce the level of material being presented to the student, and there are several books which have taken this approach in various areas of mathematics. In analysis, this approach can be accomplished in two ways: by carefully selecting the material presented to avoid the most (more) difficult material, or by carefully selecting the kinds of questions put to students to avoid presenting the student with those questions and/or problems which cannot be solved without extreme effort by weaker students. We have rejected both of these approaches because we believe them to be self-defeating to the stated objectives of the basic advanced calculus/first real analysis course, which are to produce mathematical sophistication combined with a thorough knowledge and understanding of limiting processes.

All major branches of modern mathematics have their roots in real analysis, and many apparently abstract questions are posed as analogies to simple questions about the real number system or a limiting process on the reals. We want students to understand this and to view real analysis as a cohesive whole which provides answers to a series of generic questions. To take a simple example, one always wants to know how a new limiting process behaves with respect to the algebraic operations on the underlying structure. Thus, each time a new limiting process is introduced, this question is posed, and plausible conjectures are generated based on previous knowledge. Later, it is suggested to the student that he or she review the previous theory and attempt to generate the questions and the answers. In this way, students are being encouraged to begin thinking like mathematicians and further develop their mathematical maturity.

In presenting the body of material contained herein, the main focus is on the epsilon-delta definition. We consider that a deep understanding of this definition and an accompanying ability to work with it are the foundation on which mathematical maturity can be developed. For this reason, we have stressed the use of this definition, from first principles, throughout the book. As indicated, the main tool for manipulating this definition is algebra.

Features

The second approach to the problem of lack of skill at symbol manipulations and basic algebra is to confront the problem head-on. This is the approach taken in this text. Specifically, we consistently stress the role of algebra and algebraic manipulation in the construction of proofs. Throughout, but especially early in the book, calculations are performed in great detail so that students will not be left with a feeling that mathematics is mysterious and understanding is beyond their abilities. In addition, each definition, proof, and example is followed by a **Discussion** section which presents material on intuition, on what thought processes might lead to the proof which was just presented, on what ideas a definition is trying to capture, and so forth. In this sense, the book has been written for students and not for colleagues. Colleagues can generate the material in discussions for themselves; it was expected that the students of twenty-five years ago could generate this material; it is recognized that most of today's students cannot.

In recognition of this, the book contains almost 3000 individual exercises. Some of these problems are very simple, requiring little more than the completion of the details of an argument or a simple calculation. Others are much more difficult in that they ask a student to 'sort out' a situation. In this latter regard by not supplying a specific statement to prove, we require students to act like mathematicians and find the desired results. Thus to solve a 'sort out' type problem, a student would have to structure an investigation to achieve the required end. An example of this type would be asking students to find a characterization of those situations in which a function is lower semicontinuous at a point at which it has a jump discontinuity.

A solutions manual is available which contains solutions to more than 500 exercises. The exercises chosen for presentation in the manual include a selection from simple to advanced. Solutions manuals are nice, but they can present a problem for the instructor because there may be nothing left for the student to solve. In this case, the problem is dealt with by making sure that plenty of exercises are left unsolved for the student to attempt—more than 2000. Thus, the effect of the solutions manual is to place in the students' hands another 500 or so worked examples.

Finally, we consider elementary real analysis to be one of the most beautiful areas of mathematics. We hope we have supplied you, the teacher, with a teaching tool which is worthy of the subject.

To the Student

This book is about the theory of limiting processes on the real line. While it does contain some other material in the last two chapters, in the main it is concerned only with the real line. This material forms the heart of mathematics, and in its present state of development, it brings to fruition more than two thousand years of mathematical work in geometry and algebra. As such it is an essential part of the training of any student of mathematics, whether pure or applied.

It is commonly said that mathematics is the only true deductive science. As working mathematicians, we know this is utterly false. Mathematical ideas, like any other ideas, are generated by mulling over observations. The simplest way to collect observations is to perform experiments. The way in which mathematics differs from other sciences is that the mathematician's experiments are thought experiments conducted by working out the details of simple examples related to the particular system or theory of interest. The intuitions gained as a result of these experiments must then be provable in a rigorous mathematical sense before they will be accepted as truth. Thus, there are two aspects to the mathematical process: generating insight via experiment and establishing insight as truth by means of constructing a rigorous proof of the statement.

Proofs in mathematics are not merely a bunch of statements put together to draw up the desired conclusion; rather, they are cleverly and delicately woven fabrics of thought, and hence must be understood as a single theme. Construction of proofs requires insight as to why the particular fact *should be true*. Thus, even though throughout this book you will be given problems of the form 'Show . . .', whence the true statement is known, you will not be able to generate the required proof of the statement without a fundamental understanding of the basic insight which is the essential reason why the given statement is true. Thus the first question which you should ask when confronting the problem 'Show . . .' is, Why should this be true? Or alternatively, what is the insight which led to this statement? To answer these questions you will be forced into performing the type of experiments which are essential to the generation of insight, and without which no proof would have ever been found.

In the text, each theorem is followed by a standard type of mathematical proof. Most proofs, examples, and definitions are followed by a section labeled **Discussion.** This section is an attempt to explain the essential piece of insight which is being captured by the theorem, example, or definition. It also may contain clues about which experiments are most relevant to the ideas. One effect of these sections should be to convince you that mathematics is not nearly so much the result of brilliance as it is of hard work!

Throughout the book, you will find the words **WHY?** and **HOW?,** which are invitations to the reader to supply a missing argument or a simple calculation. Also, phrases such as 'it is readily seen', 'it follow easily', and 'it is straightforward' are to be taken as warning signals, where you must stop and provide the appropriate reasoning in support of the conclusion which follows. In the early part of the book, proofs are given in detail, but as the subject unfolds the proofs may have 'gaps' to be filled by the student.

A list of references is provided at the end of the book. The titles can be found in most university libraries, and perusal of some of these texts may prove an aid in understanding the material presented herein.

The essence of our previous remarks has been succinctly captured by J. L. Kelley when he said, 'Mathematics is not a spectator sport.' With this in mind, we have supplied a goodly number of exercises for your attention. Your success will depend on the effort with which you attack these problems. All answers must be justified with a rigorous argument. Some are very difficult, and many cannot be done in five minutes but require much thought and work to generate the insight discussed above.

As an aid to you in dealing with the exercises, we have written a solutions manual covering Chapters 0–9. Roughly half of this manual deals with material in Chapters 0, 1, and 2—more than 250 solutions to exercises from these three chapters. The stress on the early chapters reflects our belief that it is essential for you to come to grips with the most basic material, that is, the reals and their structure, the supremum principle, limits of sequences, limits of functions, and continuity, if you are to succeed in mastering the material in later chapters.

Finally, to succeed in this endeavor, you will require the two most important attributes of working mathematicians, patience and persistence: patience so as not to hurry a solution whose time has not yet arrived; persistence to keep trying even when you believe that **you** have no hope of succeeding. It is these two qualities which finally see all research mathematicians through the day.

Acknowledgments

No book which is close to 10 years in the making could ever be completed without the support of others. We have had a great deal of help, and it is a real pleasure for us to thank those who helped us:

First and foremost, our wives, Cathy and Padma, who did so many different things to bring the book to fruition. Second, our department heads, John Burry and Bruce Shawyer, who from time to time reorganized our teaching loads to aid the cause. Third, our colleagues Renzo Piccinini, Don Rideout, Mike Clase, and Peter Hilton, who read early portions of the manuscript and were very encouraging. As well, we thank the many other of our colleagues who read bits and pieces and gave comments along the way.

It goes without saying that no book ever gets published if it doesn't have a publisher. In our case it is Harper & Row, and a good publisher they are, too. We have worked closely with seven members of the Harper & Row staff, all of whom have been very helpful. They ensured that we would produce the best possible book that was in us as authors, and for this we offer many thanks to Ann Trump, Judy Rothman, Peter Coveney, Thomas Farrell, Lauren Bahr, and Sheryl Trugman. And our special thanks to Allen Dykler, who initiated our relationship with Harper & Row.

As part of the generation process, Harper & Row had the book reviewed. Some eleven individuals participated in this process. Needless to say, we were pleased by their praise and chagrined by their criticisms. Mostly, their critical comments and their care helped to produce a better book, and for this we thank them. They are

John Cavalier, West Virginia Institute of Technology

The Rev. Gabriel Costa, Seton Hall University

Robert Fisher, University of Oklahoma

Chaitan Gupta, Northern Illinois University

Joe Howard, New Mexico Highlands University

Douglas Kelley, University of North Carolina at Chapel Hill

Steven Krantz, Washington University

Stanley Lukawecki, Clemson University

N. F. G. Martin, University of Virginia

P. D. Morris, Pennsylvania State University

R. E. Williamson, Dartmouth College

The manuscripts for this book were produced using Memorial University's UNIX-based text-processing facilities. Critical technical support for these facilities was supplied by Mike Rayment, John Rochester, Glen Hoffe, Mary Myrick, Randy Chafe, Marg Stevens, Gina Everson, Randy Dodge, and Brian Power. We thank you all and want it recognized that without the support of this system and your help this book would never have been completed. Finally, we thank Bob Garufy of House of Equations for the excellent job of typesetting.

HERBERT S. GASKILL
P. P. NARAYANASWAMI

Basic Concepts

This book is about limits and limiting processes and some five basic types of limiting processes and their interrelationships will be studied. But more than this, this book is about the heart of mathematics, and the structure which serves as the foundation not only for real analysis, but also for all of modern science. This structure is none other than the real numbers. It is a structure with which all readers of this text should be long since familiar. And it is in the theory of this structure that all the mainstream branches of modern mathematics have their roots.

This book is also about how to do mathematics and start thinking like a mathematician. It is about the kinds of questions that mathematicians ask and the methods mathematicians use to find answers to their questions. It is about the activities mathematicians undertake to develop their intuitive understanding of mathematical objects and conjectures related to such objects. Finally, it is about how mathematicians test their understanding by constructing rigorous proofs of their intuitively arrived at conjectures.

The purpose of this chapter is to lay a logical and axiomatic foundation on which we can build real analysis. This axiomatic foundation will precisely describe the real numbers. It will also provide a framework which we will use to capture the geometry of our intuitive ideas. Thus, we will consistently draw pictures and perform sample calculations to aid and encourage our intuition, since drawing pictures and performing sample calculations are well established methods by which mathematicians build intuition. We will also reason by analogy, taking ideas developed in a simple context and pushing them to their limit in a more complicated context. This too will develop our intuition. But as mathematicians, we will always test our intuition by constructing proofs from the axioms which we will adopt. For, it is by virtue of these proofs that we will convert intuitive ideas into incontrovertible facts.

0.1 LOGIC

This section presents the basic principles of logic which are indispensable to a working mathematician. Logic provides the methodology by which we will wield our axioms, and a minimal understanding of this methodology is essential to any working mathematician.

Mathematicians are primarily interested in two things: discovering and proving theorems. (Of course, this process does not take place in a vacuum, and the mathematician hopes that the theorems which he/she* discovers and proves will provide information about the objects he is curious about.) The statement of a theorem is a mathematical assertion or a formula, and so one requirement for mathematical success is an ability to manipulate these formulae in various ways. Generally, theorems tend to be rather complex statements. However, these can be broken down into basic units.

If we think of complex statements as being constructed from simple ones, then the constructions turn out to be simple and few in number. Suppose then that we let Φ and Ψ stand for two mathematical assertions, say, $x = 2$ and $y < 7$, respectively. Now we can construct new statements from Φ and Ψ as follows:

$$\Phi \ or^\dagger \ \Psi,$$
$$\Phi \ and \ \Psi,$$
$$not \ \Phi,$$
$$if \ \Phi, \ then \ \Psi,$$
$$\Phi \ if \ and \ only \ if \ \Psi.$$

Using the examples given for Φ and Ψ, the constructions yield the following mathematical assertions:

$$x = 2 \ or \ y < 7,$$
$$x = 2 \ and \ y < 7,$$
$$not \ (x = 2),$$
$$if \ x = 2, \ then \ y < 7,$$
$$x = 2 \ if \ and \ only \ if \ y < 7.$$

(We usually write $x \neq 2$ or $y \not< 7$ instead of *not* $(x = 2)$ or *not* $(y < 7)$.) These constructions carry the names **disjunction, conjunction, negation, implication,** and **logical equivalence,** respectively. Of these constructions, the implication construction is considered so important that it exists in several equivalent forms:

$$\Phi \ implies \ \Psi,$$
$$\Phi \ is \ necessary \ for \ \Psi,$$
$$\Psi \ is \ sufficient \ for \ \Phi.$$

---

* We will use 'he' and 'she' interchangeably throughout this book.

$\dagger$ In this first section, *or, and, if, then,* and other similar mathematical terms will be written in *italics* to remind the reader that they are being used with precise mathematical meanings and not their usual English meanings.

Again we stress that all of these statements are identical in meaning to: *if* Φ, *then* Ψ. Another statement related to this same implication is the **converse:**

if Ψ, *then* Φ.

Finally, a construction which is often used instead of logical equivalence, but which has the same meaning is

Φ *is necessary and sufficient for* Ψ.

The key question of importance to a mathematician is: *How does the truth of the complex whole depend on the truth of the constituent parts?* The answer to this question is determined by how we reason in the real world and also by the fact that the truth of a statement should depend *only on the truth values of the respective parts and not on the meaning of the respective parts.* The latter comment becomes clearer when we consider that a column of numbers whose sum we must find may represent bushels of wheat, gallons of gas or dollars and cents, but the outcome of the computation is independent of any meaning we attach to the numbers. It depends only on the individual magnitudes forming the sum. For this to be true of our logical analysis of statements, the truth of an *or* statement should depend only on the truth of the two disjuncts[†] and not on the meaning of the two disjuncts. With this principle in mind, if we think about reality, a disjunction is true exactly if one of the disjuncts is true or if both are; a conjunction is true exactly if both of the conjuncts are true; a negation is true exactly if the negated statement is false. The implication is more subtle and we treat it in detail.

A main feature of mathematics is the universal acceptance of the following law:

Law of the Excluded Middle

A given mathematical statement Φ is either true or false; there is no third alternative.

It is impossible to do much mathematics without accepting this principle, and so we adopt it and use it in an axiomatic fashion. With this in mind, consider the statement

If it rains tomorrow, then I will not go swimming,

in which a **hypothesis** about rain implies a **conclusion** about swimming. There are various factual outcomes which can happen tomorrow, and these are shown in a two-way table. Inside Table 0.1.1, we have put the **truth values** for the implication which are associated with these outcomes.

TABLE 0.1.1

	Rain	No rain
Do not swim	True	True
Swim	False	True

[†] The constituent parts of a disjunction (conjunction) are called disjuncts (conjuncts).

It is clear that if it really does rain and I don't swim, then the implication should be true; also, if it really does rain and I do swim, then the implication is false. The issue is: in any other case have I lied? In real life, we generally have almost no interest in the statement when the hypothesis is false. This is the tack we take in mathematics. By labeling as true those cases in which the hypothesis is false, we are agreeing that *the only time an implication can be false is when the hypothesis is true and the conclusion simultaneously false.* Thus, in proving the truth of an implication, we may take as an assumption the truth of the hypothesis. If under a true hypothesis, the conclusion is always true, then the implication is true. If under the same hypothesis there is an instance in which the conclusion is false, then the implication is false. Thus, we see that of the two choices for truth values for the other cases, choosing 'true' instead of 'false' is really agreeing to proceed as we do in reality; namely, ignore the cases when the hypothesis is false.

The logical equivalence construction is really an abbreviation. Thus, Φ *if and only if* Ψ stands for

$$\Phi \text{ implies } \Psi \text{ .and. } \Psi \text{ implies } \Phi.$$

(The periods are used in the above instead of parentheses to indicate the conjunction of two implications; we shall continue the practice of using periods, instead of parentheses to avoid the ambiguities which arise when a statement contains several logical connectives.) From this, we see that Φ is logically equivalent to Ψ if the truth of Φ implies the truth of Ψ, and the truth of Ψ implies the truth of Φ. While proving that two statements are logically equivalent, we will always proceed by writing out the two implications and proving them separately.

A key feature of this analysis is that it provides us with a method for testing whether two statements always yield the same truth value, and hence are logically equivalent. An example of this is the **contrapositive,** a statement form which is constructed from an implication in the following manner:

original implication: *if* Φ, *then* Ψ

contrapositive: *if (not* Ψ), *then (not* Φ).

To see that these statements are logically equivalent, we ask the question: under what conditions is each statement false? The original implication is false exactly when the hypothesis is true and the conclusion is false. This means that Φ is true and Ψ is false. But then *not* Ψ is true and *not* Φ is false, whence the contrapositive is also false. On the other hand, the only time the contrapositive is false is when its hypothesis is true and its conclusion is false. But this is exactly the situation just described. We conclude that an implication is false exactly when its contrapositive is false. Thus, an implication and its contrapositive are equivalent.

The contrapositive is a very useful form since the contrapositive of a statement is often much easier to prove than the original statement.

EXAMPLE 1 _____

Find the contrapositive of the statement

if $x = 2$, *then* $y < 7$.

Solution.   The contrapositive is

$$\text{if } y \not< 7, \text{ then } x \neq 2.\qquad \square^{\dagger}$$

One of the most important manipulational skills in mathematics is to be able to take a given mathematical statement and correctly write down its negation. The process of forming the negation is simplified if one has a working knowledge of some simple rules. These rules are easily established by considering how we negate disjunctions, conjunctions, negations, and implications.

The simplest statement to negate is a negation, that is, a statement of the form *not* Φ.

original statement: *not* Φ

negation: *not* (*not* Φ)

equivalent form: Φ.

The fact that the negation of the negation of a statement is equivalent to the original statement, namely, *not* (*not* Φ) is logically equivalent to Φ, is usually expressed as the principle of the **Double Negative.**

To negate a disjunction, we proceed as follows:

original statement: Φ *or* Ψ

negation: *not* (Φ *or* Ψ)

equivalent form: (*not* Φ) *and* (*not* Ψ).

The general rule to remember here is that when you negate an *or* statement you get an *and* statement. You may be familiar with this principle for sets where the complement of a union is the intersection of the complements. This is one of **De Morgan's Laws.**

The other De Morgan's Law concerns the negating of a conjunction:

original statement: Φ *and* Ψ

negation: *not* (Φ *and* Ψ)

equivalent form: (*not* Φ) *or* (*not* Ψ).

The fact that the negation of an *and* statement is an *or* statement is not too surprising once one has accepted the first De Morgan's Law and given some thought to the relationship of *and* and *or*.

The last construction to be negated is an implication:

original statement: *if* Φ, *then* Ψ

negation: *not* (*if* Φ, *then* Ψ)

equivalent form: Φ *and* (*not* Ψ).

The equivalent form is perhaps worth a bit of further explanation. Consider the assertion: *if* $x = 2$, *then* $y < 7$. We have already noted that this assertion is false only when the antecedent (hypothesis) is true and the conclusion is false. Now our equivalent form of the negation is: $x = 2$ *and* $y \not< 7$. Evidently, this latter is true

---

exactly when the antecedent (of the previous statement) is true and its conclusion is false. Thus, this form must be equivalent to the negation.

This tells us something very important about testing the truth or falsity of implications. If we want to disprove an implication, we are required to set up a situation in which the *hypothesis is true and the conclusion is false*. Thus, in the example above, if we want to disprove the assertion that *if* $x = 2$ *then* $y < 7$, we would have to produce a y which was greater than or equal to 7 while at the same time keeping x fixed at the value 2. The specific x and y which disprove the assertion form a **counter-example**.

EXAMPLE 2 _____

Find the negation of

$$\text{if } x^2 - y^2 \text{ is even, } then \ (x \neq 2 \ or \ y = 3).$$

Solution. The form of the statement is an implication in which the conclusion is a disjunction. Thus, the basic form of the negation obtained by using the rules for implication is

$$x^2 - y^2 \text{ is even } .and. \ not \ (x \neq 2 \ or \ y = 3).$$

This can be further simplified by using the rules for disjunctions, to obtain

$$x^2 - y^2 \text{ is even } .and. \ x = 2 \ and \ y \neq 3.$$

At this point, we see that the original statement is false exactly if each of these conjuncts can be made true simultaneously. □

In the above example, we have made use of parentheses. Parentheses in mathematical statements play the same role as punctuation in English. To remove them will generally introduce ambiguities and, at worst, will completely change the meaning of statements. Consider

$$not \ (x \neq 2 \ and \ y = 3),$$

and

$$not \ x \neq 2 \ and \ y = 3.$$

The meaning of the first statement is completely clear. While the meaning of the second is ambiguous, it would generally be taken to be the same as

$$(not \ x \neq 2) \ and \ y = 3,$$

which has a different meaning from the first statement. It is safe to say that unless one works in one of the specially developed parenthesis-free languages, such as reverse Polish notation which is employed on Hewlett-Packard calculators, the correct use of parentheses, and/or periods, is essential and should be cultivated.

We have already used the symbol '$=$' which stands for equality. The equality relation plays a fundamental role in mathematics as a *logical* tool. To fully specify this role requires a deeper excursion into the principles of logic than we intend to take.

However, there are certain minimal requirements which the equality relation must satisfy. We summarize these:

Equality Principles

Let x, y, and z denote arbitrary mathematical quantities. Then:

    (i) $x = x$;
    (ii) if $x = y$, then $y = x$;
    (iii) if $x = y$ and $y = z$, then $x = z$.

The notion of *mathematical quantity* is imprecise; however, it can be made precise with effort, but the details are again beyond the scope of this book. The reader should think of *mathematical quantities* as sets, numbers, functions, or anything else mathematicians ordinarily discuss. The basic point then becomes that any statement we would make about the number 5 is unchanged with respect to truth if we rephrase it in terms of $2 + 3$ or $4 + 1$ or any other convenient expression for 5. More generally: *the truth of any mathematical statement is unchanged by the replacement of any mathematical quantity occurring in the statement with any other equal quantity.*

    A key feature of mathematical statements which we have not yet discussed is their use of quantifiers. Mathematical statements consistently contain expressions like: *for all x, for every y, there is a w,* or *there exists a q.* These expressions are of two distinct types, but they have the same general purpose: namely, to **quantify** a variable. Phrases of the form *for every x, for each x,* or *for all x,* have the same function: they *universally quantify* the variable x. Hence, they are called **universal quantifiers.** Their intent is to assert that no matter what value we substitute for x, the given statement will be true.

    The other type of quantifier is the **existential quantifier.** True to its name, it acts to assert the *existence* of an individual which when substituted for x (the variable named) will make the statement true. Phrases used to denote existential quantification are: *for some x, there is an x* or *there exists an x.*

EXAMPLE 3 _____

> *There is an x, $x = \sqrt{2}$.*
> *For every x, if $x < 0$, then $x^2 > 0$.*
> *For all x, there exists y, $x - y = 0$.*
> *For all x, there exists y, $xy = 1$.*

Discussion. Whenever a mathematician writes statements such as those above, he intends them to be interpreted in some context. The context usually is determined by the structures being studied. We may want, for example, to study a general class of mathematical structures such as groups or fields or some particular field such as the real numbers, **R**, or the rational numbers, **Q**. In each case, the context of the study determines a set of legal substitutions for the variables which appear in the statements.

In the case of groups, we substitute elements from an arbitrary group; in the case of fields, an arbitrary element from an arbitrary field; and in the case of a particular field, an arbitrary element from the field in question. *The context will, in general, have a substantial effect on the truth of assertions.* The first assertion that the square root of 2 exists, is certainly true if the field under study is the real numbers. But it is false if we are studying the rational numbers, since as we shall later show, there is no rational number whose square is 2. □

As with many things, mathematicians have developed a set of standard symbols to denote quantification. We will not generally employ these symbols in this book, preferring the English expressions. However, since they are in common use, particularly by mathematics professors writing on blackboards, we introduce them. The English phrase 'for all' is represented by the symbol ∀, which, according to lore, was arrived at by turning an 'A' upside down. The English phrase 'there exists' is symbolically represented by ∃ which, by similar reasoning, was arrived at by reversing the letter 'E'. The examples above, when written using these symbols, yield:

EXAMPLE 4 _____

$$\exists\, x,\ x = \sqrt{2}.$$
$$\forall\, x,\ if\ x < 0,\ then\ x^2 > 0.$$
$$\forall\, x\ \exists\, y,\ x - y = 0.$$
$$\forall\, x\ \exists\, y,\ xy = 1. \qquad \square$$

The examples above are of a completely mathematical nature, which may suggest that quantifiers are not a part of our everyday thought and reasoning processes. Nothing could be further from the truth. We often make statements involving quantifiers. For example, the statement

All mathematicians are good citizens

involves a universal quantifier, whereas the statement

I knew a mathematician who was a spy

also involves a quantifier, but in an indirect way. The use of quantifiers in normal language is complicated by the fact that it usually involves hidden additional logical structure. For example, consider the initial statement about mathematicians. What it really asserts is that every member of the class of mathematicians belongs to the class of good citizens. Thus, it could be rephrased as

For all x, if x is a mathematician, then x is a good citizen.

Notice that this form of the statement contains an implication which was implied by the initial statement. Of course, we never actually speak this way, but this is what is meant. Similarly, the second example could be rephrased as

There exists x, (x is a mathematician and x is a spy).

Again, there is additional logical structure in the form of an 'and' statement.

As with other mathematical statements, it is essential to be able to negate statements containing quantifiers correctly. One useful device in the process is to write down the statement preceded by: *it is not true that*. We then carefully consider the meaning of the prefixed statement. For the first statement in Example 3, this procedure yields

It is not true that (there is an x, x = $\sqrt{2}$).

We would like to translate this into a simple statement in which all quantifiers precede the negation phrase, that is, *it is not true that*. Consider the meaning of the negated statement. Evidently, the only way the statement can be true will be that no matter what substitution we make for *x*, it is not the case that the substituted individual is the square root of 2. Thus, an equivalent statement is

For every x, x $\neq$ $\sqrt{2}$.

Notice that the negation symbol is now completely contained within the simplest basic assertion of the original statement, that is, $x = \sqrt{2}$ becomes, after negation, $x \neq \sqrt{2}$. Further, as the negation symbol is moved inside the existential quantifier, *the quantifier is changed to a universal quantifier.*

Consider now, the second assertion

For every x, if x < 0, then x^2 > 0.

This becomes, after negation,

It is not true that (for every x, if x < 0, then x^2 > 0),

which, in turn, becomes

There is an x, (x < 0 and x^2 $\ngtr$ 0).

Again, in the last statement, the negation symbol is now completely contained in the basic assertion. Notice that as the negation symbol moves inside the universal quantifier, *the quantifier is changed to an existential quantifier.* It seems apparent that of the two forms of the negation, the latter is much clearer in meaning, and so it is easier to see how to check its truth: we simply look for a number less than 0 whose square is not greater than 0.

The third and fourth of the sample statements are similar, so we consider only the last.

For all x, there exists y, xy = 1,

becomes, after negation,

It is not true that (for all x, there exists y, xy = 1),

becomes

There exists x, for all y, xy $\neq$ 1.

Again, we see that as the negation symbol is moved in, the type of quantification is reversed, that is, *for every* becomes *there exists* and *there exists* becomes *for every*. The name of the variable which is quantified is unchanged and *the order in which the variables are quantified is unchanged.* As before, it is much easier to decipher the meaning of the latter form than the former. Moreover, it is clear that to check the truth of the latter, we must produce a substitution for x such that no matter what we substitute for y, the product is not equal to 1. If the structure being discussed is, for example, the real numbers, then it is clear that substituting 0 for x will result in the obviously true statement

$$\text{For every } y, 0y \neq 1.$$

To conclude our discussion of this example, we point out that *changing the order in which variables are quantified in a statement will change the meaning of the statement.* To see this, let us consider the third statement of Example 3, again in the context of real numbers, together with the statement obtained from it by reversing the order in which the variables are quantified.

$$\text{For all } x, \text{ there exists } y, x - y = 0.$$
$$\text{There exists } y, \text{ for all } x, x - y = 0.$$

In the context of the real number system **R**, the first statement asserts that if we are given any arbitrary real number, then we can find another real number such that the difference of the two is 0. Note that the choice of y *depends* upon which x we were given in the first place. The second statement asserts that there is a *fixed* y such that no matter what value we choose for x, the difference will be 0. A little thought shows that while the first statement is clearly true, the second is definitely false.

In our consideration above on how to negate statements containing quantifiers, we argued based upon the meaning of particular statements. The use of meaning was illustrative. In fact, the methodology developed for negating statements containing quantifiers is completely independent of the meaning of these statements; rather, the methodology depends only on the *form* of the particular statement to be negated. Let us complete this discussion of negating statements involving quantifiers by again considering

$$\textit{All mathematicians are good citizens.}$$

As we have already remarked, this statement is equivalent to

$$\textit{For all } x, \text{ if } x \text{ is a mathematician, then } x \text{ is a good citizen.}$$

When we negate this statement, we must deal not only with the quantifier, but with the implication as well. Thus, the negation is

$$\textit{There exists } x, (x \text{ is a mathematician and } x \text{ is not a good citizen}).$$

Before concluding our section on logic, we want to discuss definitions as they occur in mathematics. The first important fact about definitions is that *they must be committed to memory, grasped thoroughly, and completely understood.* The reason for this is simple: in order to prove theorems, one must be able to think about the concepts involved or being discussed in these theorems. Thinking is a process which is internal to the brain, and in mathematics, there is evidence to suggest that much of the most creative work is done at a subconscious level. In any case, the brain must be supplied with the basic tools for the job. Definitions are these tools. Trying to do mathematics while picking all the relevant definitions from a book is about as efficient as a computer whose memory functions by printing out questions the answers to which are found and punched back in by a keypuncher with a high school education. In short, you must acquire the tools if you expect success. Need we add that the axioms and theorems also fall in this category?

The second aspect of definitions which must be understood is their purpose. Mathematical languages, as with any language, are filled with nouns, that is, words which denote or select out some class of objects. The word *sequence* in mathematics plays exactly the same role as the word *chair* in English. The difference is that *sequence* is defined in such a way that it is always possible to decide whether or not any given object is a *sequence,* and the result is a completely unambiguous *yes* or *no.* A little thought together with a visit to a modern furniture store will convince one that it is impossible to set down a completely unambiguous test for membership in the class of *chairs.* Thus, mathematical definitions achieve a level of *precision* which cannot be attained by ordinary languages. (Indeed, it is this very level of precision which is one of the really beautiful features of mathematics.) Thus, the role of a definition is to precisely delineate a class of objects in such a way that it is possible to decide for any object whether it is, or is not, a member of the class. To do this, the definition will generally enumerate the properties which define membership in the class. In consequence, to assert that an object satisfies a given definition is equivalent to asserting that an object has all the properties enumerated in the definition.

EXERCISES

1. Give a *precise* negation of the following statements:
    (a) all snakes are not poisonous;
    (b) some problems are not easy;
    (c) it is not the case that I am not hardworking;
    (d) there exists x, $x > 0$ and $f(x) = 4$;
    (e) for all x, $f(x) = 7$ implies $x > 0$;
    (f) there exists x, $(x = 0$ or $f(x) = x)$;
    (g) for all x, there exists y, $f(x,y) = 0$;
    (h) there exists x for all y there exists z, $(f(x) = 0$ and $g(x,y) = 1$ and $h(x,y,z) = 0)$.

2. Obtain the contrapositive equivalents of the following implications:
    (a) whenever the phone rings, I run to answer it;
    (b) if $x^2 + y^2$ is negative, the earth will not rotate;
    (c) it is necessary for you to eat in order to live;
    (d) if $x^2 \neq 3$ and $y^2 \geq 5$, then ω is not an irrational number;
    (e) if the sum of any two even integers is odd, then there is a rational number whose square root is 7;
    (f) a sufficient condition for getting good grades is to be a genius.

3. Construct a truth table (similar to Table 0.1.1) for the following statements:
    (a) I will take a vacation, if I have money, and I do not work;
    (b) a monotonic and bounded sequence will have a limit;
    (c) (P implies Q) .implies. R;
    (d) (P and not R) .implies. (not Q).

4. Let $f(x,y)$ stand for $x + y - xy$. Consider the eight statements:

(a) for all x for all y, $f(x,y) = 0$;
(b) for all y for all x, $f(x,y) = 0$;
(c) there exists y there exists x, $f(x,y) = 0$;
(d) there exists x there exists y, $f(x,y) = 0$;
(e) there exists y for all x, $f(x,y) = 0$;
(f) there exists x for all y, $f(x,y) = 0$;
(g) for all x there exists y, $f(x,y) = 0$;
(h) for all y there exists x, $f(x,y) = 0$.
Which of these are true statements?
Which of these statements are logically equivalent?

5. Repeat Exercise 4 with the function $f(x,y) = x^2 + y - xy$.

6. Show that the following statements are logically equivalent:
(a) P implies Q;
(b) not $(P$ and $($not $Q))$;
(c) $($not $P)$ or Q.

7. Specify the hypothesis and the conclusion for each of the statements in Exercise 2.

8. Obtain the converse statements of each of the implications in Exercise 2.

9. Supply counterexamples to show that each of the following statements is false:
(a) all animals are carnivorous;
(b) all birds can fly;
(c) $n^2 + n + 41$ is always a prime number;
(d) $(a + b + c)^n = a^n + b^n + c^n$ for all natural numbers n and all real numbers a, b, and c;
(e) $1^2 + 2^2 + \cdots + n^2 = (n + 1)^2$ for all n.

10. The following mathematical definitions can be found in various places in this book. Use the symbols $\forall$, $\exists$ respectively to denote the universal and the existential quantifier, that is,

$$\forall\, x\, P(x) \text{ stands for 'for all } x, \text{ the property } P(x) \text{ holds'}.$$
$$\exists\, x\, P(x) \text{ stands for 'there exists } x, \text{ for which } P(x) \text{ holds'}.$$

Rewrite the following statements using the symbols $\forall$ and $\exists$, and then obtain a *precise* negation of each of them.
(a) If $(x,y) \in F$ and $(x,z) \in F$, then $y = z$. (F is a function.)
(b) If $(x_1,y) \in F$, and $(x_2,y) \in F$, then $x_1 = x_2$. (F is one-to-one.)
(c) Given $y \in A$, there exists an $x \in \text{Dmn } F$ such that $y = F(x)$. (F is onto A.)
(d) If x, $y \in \text{Dmn } f$, then $x < y$ implies $f(x) \leqslant f(y)$. (f is monotonic increasing.)
(e) s is a function whose domain is the set $\mathbf{N}$ of natural numbers and the range is contained in the set $\mathbf{R}$ of all real numbers. (s is a sequence.)
(f) Given $\epsilon > 0$, there exists a real number $N > 0$ such that $n > N$ implies $|a_n - L| < \epsilon$. (The sequence $\{a_n\}$ converges to the limit L.)
(g) Given $\epsilon > 0$, there exists a real number $\delta > 0$ such that for all $x \in \text{Dmn } f$, $|x - c| < \delta$ implies $|f(x) - f(c)| < \epsilon$. (The function f is continuous at the real number c.)
(h) There exists a real number L such that given $\epsilon > 0$, we can find $\delta > 0$, satisfying
$$|h| < \delta \text{ implies } \left| \frac{f(x+h) - f(x)}{h} \right| < \epsilon. \ (f \text{ is differentiable at the point } x.)$$
(i) Given $\epsilon > 0$, there exists $N \in \mathbf{N}$ such that for all $x \in A$, $n > N$ implies $|f_n(x) - f_0(x)| < \epsilon$. (The sequence f_n of functions is uniformly convergent to the function f_0 on the set A.)
(j) Given $\epsilon > 0$, there exists $\delta > 0$ such that for all x, $y \in A$, $|x - y| < \delta$ .implies. $|f(x) - f(y)| < \epsilon$. (The function f is uniformly continuous on the set A.)

0.2 FIELD AXIOMS

The real numbers, which we will denote by **R**, have three important aspects: algebraic properties, order properties, and completeness properties. We want to specify a set of axioms to describe the real number system. Our axioms, therefore, will be divided into three groups: those dealing with algebra, those dealing with order, and those dealing with completeness.

The general purpose of a set of axioms is to lay down the basic properties of a class of objects to be studied. These initial properties, stated in the form of axioms, should be self-evident, since they will serve as the starting point for all future discussions. The basic objects for study, in this case the real numbers, are not defined. Instead, **number** is a primitive. Our axioms do not tell us what numbers are, rather, they tell us how numbers behave. The initial description of their behavior is contained in the axioms, and this description is augmented by the logical process of proving theorems. Thus, our overall intent is to build a rigorous description of **R** in the same way that Euclid's *Elements* builds a description of geometry.

One of the basic things we know we can do with numbers is to combine them in various ways to get new ones. Formally, this involves the notion of a binary operation.

Definition.   A **binary operation** on a set A is a function from $A \times A$ into A.

In the Appendix on Set Theory, there is a complete treatment of the essential set theory required to support our development. In particular, operations with sets are discussed and appropriate set-theoretic definitions for the fundamental concepts are given.

There are two principal binary operations used to combine numbers: **addition** and **multiplication.** The study of the properties associated with these operations, generally, is the realm of algebra. However, algebra is an essential tool in analysis and supplies a portion of the foundation on which to base our rigorous development.

Definition.   A **field** is a nonempty set **F** together with a binary operation $+\cdot$, a binary operation $\cdot$, and two distinct constants 0 and 1 in **F**, which satisfy the following axioms (for members $x,\ y,\ z \in$ **F**):

> **A1** For every x, and for every y, $x + y = y + x$ and $x \cdot y = y \cdot x$.
> **A2** For every x, for every y and for every z, $(x + y) + z = x + (y + z)$ and $(x \cdot y) \cdot z = x \cdot (y \cdot z)$.
> **A3** For every x, $x + 0 = x$ and $x \cdot 1 = x$.
> **A4** For every x, there exists y, $x + y = 0$.
> **A5** For every x, there exists y if $x \neq 0$, then $x \cdot y = 1$.
> **A6** For every x, for every y, for every z, $x \cdot (y + z) = (x \cdot y) + (x \cdot z)$.

The operations $+$ and $\cdot$ are called the **addition** and the **multiplication** in the field **F**.

Discussion.   These axioms are undoubtedly familiar to the reader. **A1** is the **commutative law** for $+$ and $\cdot$; **A2** is the **associative law**; **A3** asserts that 0 and 1 are the **additive** and **multiplicative identities,** respectively; **A4** asserts the existence of **addi-**

additive inverses; A5 asserts the existence of **multiplicative inverses** for elements other than 0; and **A6** is the **distributive law**. It is a convention that the constants 0 and 1 are not permitted to be equal. Thus, the set **F** must contain at least two distinct elements. We, of course, use the standard names for 0 and 1: namely, **zero** and **one**, respectively. These are not to be confused with the "usual" zero and "usual" one in the real number system, which we use in our day-to-day life. We emphasize that 0 is the only member of the field that does not possess a multiplicative inverse. As an immediate consequence of **A2**, either of the two equal members $(x + y) + z, x + (y + z)$ is unambiguously referred to as $x + y + z$, without using parentheses. A similar remark applies to $x \cdot y \cdot z$. (As we progress, when the context is clear, we will just write xy instead of $x \cdot y$.)

Note that even though we say that **F** is a field, to be more precise, we must refer to the field as the quintuple, $\{F, +, \cdot, 0, 1\}$, since each of these entities has a role to play in the definition of a field. □

In the bulk of this book we will be concerned with four familiar structures, **R**, the field of real numbers, **Q**, the subfield of rational numbers, **Z**, the collection of whole numbers or integers, and **N**, the collection of natural numbers or positive integers. (A **subfield** of a field **F** is a subset **G** of **F** which, with the field operations of **F**, satisfies the field axioms.) Of these structures, the first two are fields, whereas the integers fail to have multiplicative inverses and the positive integers fail to have additive inverses and a 0.

In the development being followed, **R** will simply be realized as a structure satisfying the required axioms and the natural numbers, integers, and rational numbers will be obtained as subsets of the real numbers. This process amounts to making a definition. What the student should understand is that the process of axiomatization, which may seem artificial and unfamiliar, is leading to the four mathematical structures with which all of us are familiar. What axiomatization adds, and is the only reason why we take this course, is a foundation from which all of the remainder of analysis can be obtained rigorously, and without which some truths would be unobtainable. In particular, the basic facts of arithmetic can be obtained (see for instance, Exercise 1) and it is the manipulation of these facts which is one of the primary tools of analysis.

EXAMPLE 1

Show the quintuple, $\{ \{0,1,2\}, \oplus, \otimes, 0,1 \}$, forms a field, where $\oplus$ denotes addition '*mod* 3' and $\otimes$ denotes multiplication '*mod* 3', namely, $x \oplus y$ (respectively, $x \otimes y$) is the remainder obtained when $x + y$ (respectively, $x \cdot y$) is divided by 3.

Solution. The following two tables define the two binary operations on $\{0,1,2\}$.

$\oplus$	0	1	2
0	0	1	2
1	1	2	0
2	2	0	1

$\otimes$	0	1	2
0	0	0	0
1	0	1	2
2	0	2	1

Because the underlying set is finite, the axioms may be checked by 'brute force'. □

Discussion. Once one has obtained the integers and their properties, one simply observes that the required properties follow as consequences of the arithmetic properties of integers. For example, suppose one wants to establish the axiom **A2** on associativity for $\otimes$. First one observes that for any three integers, $i, j, k, (i \cdot j) \cdot k = i \cdot (j \cdot k)$. One then proves that if m and n have the same remainder on division by 3, then $n \cdot i$ and $m \cdot i$ will also have the same remainder on division by 3. These two facts now yield the required result.

While examples of different algebraic structures will be discussed in the exercises, the thrust of our discussions will be concerned with **R**, **Q**, **N**, and **Z**. □

Our intent is to study analysis rather than algebra, so we do not want to delve into the consequences of the field axioms in great detail. However, the facts of arithmetic are essential to the program and the methods of obtaining them will illustrate the standard of rigor we intend to maintain.

For the remainder of this section, as well as section 0.3, unless otherwise stated, x, y, z will denote arbitrary members of a field **F**, and 0 and 1 will denote the fixed elements, zero and one, of the field **F**. We begin with the additive version of a theorem on cancellation. The multiplicative version is left to Exercise 5.

Theorem 0.2.1. For every x, y, z, if $x + y = x + z$, then $y = z$.

Note. We have used the phrase *for every* only once, but from the context, it is clearly intended that we mean *for every x, for every y, for every z.* We will abuse our notation in this way whenever the meaning remains clear.

Proof. Let $x, y,$ and z be fixed but arbitrary elements of **F** satisfying the hypothesis. By **A4**, there is a w in **F** such that $x + w = 0$. Now

$w + (x + y) = w + (x + z)$	by the Equality Principles, whence
$(w + x) + y = (w + x) + z$	by **A2**,
$(x + w) + y = (x + w) + z$	by **A1**,
$0 + y = 0 + z$	by choice of w,
$y + 0 = z + 0$	by **A1**,
$y = z$	by **A3**,

as desired. □

Discussion. We begin with some general comments and then follow with specifics. The proof above is really the sequence of statements on the left, together with the initial choice of w. Notice that each of the statements is an instance of an axiom, namely, the axiom listed or referred to on the right, or it is the result of an application of a principle of logic, as in the appeal to the Equality Principles. Thus, a proof is a sequence of statements, each of which is either an instance of an axiom or previously established theorem, and the last line of which is the result to be proved. In our case, the statement '$y = z$' is the mathematical equivalent of the statement of the theorem which is in English. The remarks on the right tell us how the statements are obtained from the axioms, and as such, they are an important aid to understanding the proof. These statements will, in later proofs, be omitted where they are obvious and minor gaps in the reasoning will result. However, it is important that the reader be able to supply all the missing reasons, and fill in all the gaps, since the ability to do so is an important test of understanding. Further, supplying the reasons and filling in any missing steps will make the proofs completely *convincing* and this, after all, is the point of a proof, *to convince the skeptic.*

The motivation for this proof is very simple. We want to conclude that $y = z$ from the hypothesis that $x + y = x + z$. In other words, we must try to eliminate x. Axiom **A4** guarantees the existence of a w, which 'cancels' x in the sense that $w + x = 0$. Also, **A3** states that the addition of 0 has no effect on the element. The above proof only formalizes these simple facts.

A particular feature of the proof is the use of the Equality Principles. Since the hypothesis of the theorem asserts

$$x + y = x + z,$$

we are permitted to substitute the right-hand side for the left-hand side in any expression and deduce equality between the original and resulting expressions. In particular, we start with the quantity $w + (x + y)$ and assert that it is equal to $w + (x + z)$, by replacing $x + y$ with the equal quantity $x + z$.   □

Remark.   We want to digress for a moment to discuss the general style and format of this book. It is traditional in that theorems are stated and proofs of these theorems are presented. It is an unfortunate fact that proofs can be very misleading. Proofs exist to establish once and for all, according to very high standards, that certain mathematical statements are irrefutable facts. What is unfortunate about this is that a proof, in spite of the fact that it is perfectly correct, does not in any way have to be enlightening. Thus, mathematicians, and mathematics students, are faced with two problems: the generation of proofs, and the generation of internal enlightenment. To understand a theorem *requires enlightenment*. If one has enlightenment, one knows in one's soul why a particular theorem must be true. Understanding why a theorem is true will almost always lead to a proof. Sometimes, one's own understanding of a theorem will be significantly different than that presented in someone else's proof of the same theorem. Thus, understanding may lead to an alternate proof of a given theorem.

One can be enlightened about proofs as well as theorems. Without enlightenment, one is merely reduced to memorizing proofs. With enlightenment about a proof, its flow becomes clear and it can become an item of astonishing beauty. In addition, the need to memorize disappears because the proof has become part of your soul.

What do the preceding comments have to do with the style and format of this book? First, as authors, we must confront the fact that we want to present the reader with correct proofs. Secondly, we want to create a situation of maximum possible enlightenment.

The first aim is achieved by presenting blocks of material which begin with the word 'Proof' and end with a '□'. They are correct mathematical proofs, and they contain 'the truth and nothing but the truth' so to speak. As such, there is no attempt to motivate within a proof, since motivational material is not generally recognized as appropriate content for proofs. (This may have something to do with why research papers in mathematics are difficult to read.) As well, so that enlightenment is as easy to come by as possible, we have, by design, sacrificed elegance in favor of what is sometimes rather mundane computation.

The second aim is approached by the inclusion of blocks of material which start with 'Discussion' and end with '□'. In these sections the motivation behind proofs is discussed. They also contain some of the words which we would say to our own students about the proof as we presented it in our classrooms. These are the sections which show how proofs are generated, and make clear that proofs do not spring full blown from the heads of rather strange fellows called mathematicians. In the final analysis, the discussion sections can only offer pointers toward the direction of enlightenment. They can only act as aids for starting the search. The real work must be done by you, the reader. What we promise is that you, the reader, will know when you have achieved enlightenment, and second that when you have achieved it, you will know why abstract mathematics has been the ultimate intellectual activity of mankind since before the time of Pythagoras and Archimedes.

In conclusion then, as you read a proof, know that some suggestions toward a fuller understanding exist in the following discussion section. Look there for help.

□

We turn now to proving that for a given member x, there is exactly one member y belonging to the field, which satisfies axiom **A4**. Similarly, if $x \neq 0$, there is a unique member y which answers axiom **A5**.

Theorem 0.2.2. The additive inverse of any element of **F** is unique. Likewise, the multiplicative inverse of a nonzero element of **F** is unique.

Proof. Let x be fixed and y and z be any two elements of **F** which witness **A4** for x. Then

$$x + y = x + z \qquad \text{since both sides are zero, whence}$$
$$y = z \qquad \text{by Theorem 0.2.1.}$$

Thus, the additive inverse is unique, as claimed. The proof for multiplicative inverses is left to the reader (Exercise 6). □

Notation. In the future, we will use $-x$ to denote the additive inverse of x. We use x^{-1} or $\frac{1}{x}$ to denote the multiplicative inverse of a nonzero x, as well as $\frac{y}{x}$ for $y \cdot \left(\frac{1}{x} \right)$. These notations are justified by the above theorem. Thus, it is clear that for any element x, we have $x + (-x) = (-x) + x = 0$, and for any nonzero x, $x \cdot \frac{1}{x} = \frac{1}{x} \cdot x = 1$. We emphasize that 0^{-1} does not exist in any field.

Theorem 0.2.3. For every x, $x \cdot 0 = 0$.

Proof. Let x be fixed, but arbitrary. Now

$$0 + 0 = 0 \qquad \text{by **A3**,}$$

$$x \cdot (0 + 0) = x \cdot 0 \qquad \text{by Equality Principles,}$$
$$x \cdot 0 + x \cdot 0 = x \cdot 0 \qquad \text{by } \mathbf{A6}.$$

Also,

$$x \cdot 0 + 0 = x \cdot 0 \qquad \text{by } \mathbf{A3},$$
$$x \cdot 0 = x \cdot 0 + 0 \qquad \text{by Equality Principle.}$$

It follows that

$$x \cdot 0 + x \cdot 0 = x \cdot 0 + 0 \qquad \text{by Equality Principle,}$$

whence

$$x \cdot 0 = 0 \qquad \text{by Theorem 0.2.1.} \qquad \square$$

Discussion. The key to this proof is the fact that $0 + 0 = 0$. Once we focus on this fact as a starting point, it is clear that we only have to multiply through on both sides by x, use the distributive law, and then cancel. This leaves the question of how one arrives at the above as an appropriate staring point. To get there, one must start by having a full internal grasp of the axioms. Without this, one cannot hope to succeed.

$\square$

Theorem 0.2.4.   For every x and y, $(-x) \cdot (-y) = x \cdot y$.

Proof. Let x and y be arbitrary, but fixed. We claim that $x \cdot y$ and $(-x) \cdot (-y)$ are both additive inverses of $(-x) \cdot y$. If this claim is true, then we are done, by Theorem 0.2.2 on the uniqueness of additive inverses. To establish the claim, note that

$$\begin{aligned} (-x) \cdot y + (-x) \cdot (-y) &= (-x) \cdot [y + (-y)] \qquad &\text{by } \mathbf{A6}, \\ &= (-x) \cdot 0 \qquad &\text{by the definition of } -y, \\ &= 0 \qquad &\text{by Theorem 0.2.3.} \end{aligned}$$

On the other hand,

$$\begin{aligned} (-x) \cdot y + x \cdot y &= [(-x) + x] \cdot y \qquad &\text{by } \mathbf{A1} \text{ and } \mathbf{A6}, \\ &= 0 \cdot y \qquad &\text{by } \mathbf{A1} \text{ and the definition of } -x, \\ &= y \cdot 0 = 0 \qquad &\text{by } \mathbf{A1}, \text{ and Theorem 0.2.3.} \end{aligned}$$

Thus, the claim is established. $\square$

Discussion. This proof seems rather 'slick'. It stems, however, from the fact that $-(-x) = x$. If we apply this idea to the above situation, we get

$$x \cdot y = -(-(x \cdot y)) = -((-\mathbf{x}) \cdot \mathbf{y}) = (-x) \cdot (-y)$$

Notice that the emboldened quantity is exactly the additive inverse of the quantity, $(-x) \cdot y$, which we chose to add to both sides and that it has the feature of a common factor with both $x \cdot y$ and $(-x) \cdot (-y)$. Finding the quantity $(-x) \cdot y$ is, in large part, a matter of experimentation. Experimental calculations are often useful in getting an intuitive 'feel' for the reasoning underlying a proof. Such calculations should be performed before actually attempting a formal proof. □

EXERCISES

1. Prove the following statements where the letters $a, b, c, \cdots$ stand for arbitrary members of a fixed field:

    (a) $-0 = 0$;

    (b) $-(-a) = a$;

    (c) $-a = (-1) \cdot a$;

    (d) $(-a) \cdot b = -(a \cdot b) = a \cdot (-b)$;

    (e) $1^{-1} = 1$;

    (f) $a \neq 0$ implies $\dfrac{a}{a} = 1$;

    (g) $a \neq 0$ and $a \cdot b = a \cdot c$ .implies. $b = c$ (can the restriction $a \neq 0$ be removed?);

    (h) $b \neq 0$ and $d \neq 0$ .implies. $\dfrac{a}{b} \cdot \dfrac{c}{d} = \dfrac{a \cdot c}{b \cdot d}$;

    (i) $b \neq 0$ and $c \neq 0$ .implies. $\dfrac{a}{b} = \dfrac{a}{b} \cdot \dfrac{c}{c}$;

    (j) $a \cdot b = 0$ .implies. $a = 0$ or $b = 0$;

    (k) $b \neq 0$ and $\dfrac{a}{b} = 0$ .implies. $a = 0$;

    (l) $c \neq 0$ implies $\dfrac{a+b}{c} = \dfrac{a}{c} + \dfrac{b}{c}$;

    (m) $b \neq 0$ and $d \neq 0$ .implies. $\dfrac{a}{b} + \dfrac{c}{d} = \dfrac{a \cdot d + b \cdot c}{b \cdot d}$;

    (n) $b \neq 0$ and $d \neq 0$ .implies. $\dfrac{a}{b} = \dfrac{c}{d}$ if and only if $a \cdot d = b \cdot c$.

2. If a, b, c are arbitrary members of a field $\mathbf{F}$, show that all the six expressions

$$a + b + c, a + c + b, b + a + c,$$
$$b + c + a, c + a + b, c + b + a$$

    represent the same element.

3. If a, b, c, d are arbitrary elements of a field $\mathbf{F}$, prove that

    (a) $(a + b) + (c + d) = (a + c) + (b + d) = a + [(b + c) + d]$;

    (b) $(a \cdot b)(c \cdot d) = (a \cdot d)(b \cdot c) = a \cdot [(b \cdot c) \cdot d] = [(a \cdot b) \cdot c] \cdot d$ [thus, the expressions like $a + b + c + d$ and $a \cdot b \cdot c \cdot d$ have unambiguous meaning, when parenthesis is not used];

    (c) $(a + b)(c + d) = a \cdot c + a \cdot d + b \cdot c + b \cdot d$.

4. Let a and b denote arbitrary elements of a field. Define

$$a - b = a + (-b).$$

    This definition of **subtraction** abuses our notation by using the '$-$' in two distinct ways, as a **unary operator** (the initial use) and now as a binary operation symbol. Prove that subtraction is not associative in any field in which $1 + 1 \neq 0$, but that a form of the distributive law holds. Further, show that if a, b, c, d are arbitrary members of a field $\mathbf{F}$:

    (a) $-(a - b) = -a + b = b - a$;

    (b) $(a - b) + (b - c) = a - c$;

    (c) $a - (b + c) = (a - b) - c$;

(d) $a - (b - c) = (a - b) + c$;

(e) $a - b = c - d$ if and only if $a + d = b + c$;

(f) $(a - b) \cdot (a + b) = a \cdot a - b \cdot b$.

5. State and prove the multiplicative version of Theorem 0.2.1 (see Exercise 1(g)).

6. Prove the remainder of Theorem 0.2.2.

7. Prove that if an element a of a field satisfies $a + x = x$ for every other x, then $a = 0$. Prove an analogous statement for the element 1.

8. If a and b are elements of a field such that $a \cdot a = b \cdot b$, prove that either $a = b$, or $a = -b$. Can you make a similar statement if the hypothesis was changed to $a \cdot a \cdot a = b \cdot b \cdot b$?

9. Show that the set $\{0,1\}$ with a suitable definition of addition and multiplication satisfies the definition of a field. Is subtraction associative in this field?

10. Show that the set $\mathbf{F} = \{0, 1, 2, \cdots, 18\}$ forms a field, if addition (denoted by $\oplus$) and multiplication (denoted by $\otimes$) are defined "modulo 19" (as in Example 1). Find the additive and multiplicative inverses of the elements 3, 10, 14, and 18. Are there elements in this field which are their own additive (multiplicative) inverses? Perform the following arithmetic in this field:

$$\frac{1}{4} \otimes \left[\frac{3}{5} \oplus \frac{10}{17} \right]$$

[This field is usually denoted by $\mathbf{Z}_{19}$.]

11. Show that $\mathbf{Z}_{12}$ is not a field, and the quadratic equation $x^2 - 5x + 6 = 0$ admits more than two solutions in $\mathbf{Z}_{12}$. Find all solutions.

12. Construct an example of a field $\mathbf{F} = \{ \mathbf{F}, +, \cdot, 0, 1 \}$ where

$$1 + (1 + (1 + (1 + (1 + (1 + 1))))) = 0.$$

13. Let $\mathbf{F} = \{\mathbf{F}, +, \cdot, 0, 1\}$ be a field, and let a and b denote two distinct, fixed elements of $\mathbf{F}$. If new operations of addition and multiplication are defined on $\mathbf{F}$ as follows:

$$x \oplus y = x + y - a, \qquad x \otimes y = a + \frac{(x - a)(y - a)}{b - a}$$

prove that one obtains a new field $\mathbf{F}_1$. What are the zero and one in the field $\mathbf{F}_1$?

14. Let $\mathbf{C}$ denote the set of all **complex numbers**, that is, elements of the form $a + bi$, where $a, b \in \mathbf{R}$ and i satisfies the identity $i \cdot i = -1$. Show that $\mathbf{C}$ is a field under the following addition and multiplication:

$$(a + bi) + (c + di) = (a + c) + (b + d)i,$$
$$(a + bi) \cdot (c + di) = (ac - bd) + (ad + bc)i.$$

Identify the zero and one in $\mathbf{C}$.

15. Let $\mathbf{F}$ be a given field, and let $\mathbf{C}_\mathbf{F}$ denote the product $\mathbf{F} \times \mathbf{F}$, namely, $\{(x,y) : x \in \mathbf{F} \text{ and } y \in \mathbf{F}\}$. Define addition and multiplication on $\mathbf{C}_\mathbf{F}$ as follows:

$$(a,b) + (c,d) = (a + c, b + d),$$
$$(a,b) \cdot (c,d) = (a \cdot c - b \cdot d, a \cdot d + b \cdot c).$$

Prove that $\mathbf{C}_\mathbf{F}$ is a field under the above field operations. What are the zero and one in $\mathbf{C}_\mathbf{F}$? Show that the element $(0,1)$ satisfies the equation $x \cdot x + 1 = 0$. [The field $\mathbf{C}_\mathbf{F}$ is referred to as the **field of complex numbers** over $\mathbf{F}$. If $\mathbf{F} = \mathbf{R}$, the resulting field $\mathbf{C}_\mathbf{F}$ is the field $\mathbf{C}$ of complex numbers.]

16. Let $\mathbf{F} = \{a + \sqrt{3}b : a, b \in \mathbf{Q}\}$. Define suitable addition and multiplication, so that $\mathbf{F}$ is a field.

17. For subsets A, B of a field $\mathbf{F}$, define the operations $+$ and $\cdot$ as follows:
$$A + B = \{a + b : a \in A \text{ and } b \in B\},$$
$$A \cdot B = \{a \cdot b : a \in A \text{ and } b \in B\}.$$
We also write $\{k\} \cdot A = kA$, $-1A = -A$, $A + (-B) = A - B$.
For arbitrary subsets A, B, C of a field $\mathbf{F}$, prove the following:
(a) $\mathbf{F} + \mathbf{F} = \mathbf{F} - \mathbf{F} = \mathbf{F}$;
(b) if $A \neq \varnothing$, then $A - A$ is not empty;
(c) $A \cdot \varnothing = \varnothing$;
(d) if $A \subseteq B$, $A + C \subseteq B + C$;
(e) $A \cdot (B + C) \subseteq A \cdot B + A \cdot C$.
Give an example to show that equality need not happen in (e).
If $A \cdot C = B \cdot C$, does it follow that $A = B$?

0.3 ORDER AXIOMS

We turn now to the second aspect of the real numbers: **order.** Much of man's initial concept of number arises in geometry where they are used to record and compare lengths. Thus, larger numbers correspond to longer lengths. Of course, we could start with numbers corresponding to the number of elements in a set, but this gives only the whole numbers, while the idea of length gives rise to not only rational numbers, but also irrationals such as $\sqrt{2}$ and π. As these geometrical ideas were developed over the centuries, mathematicians came to associate the real numbers with the **real number line.** Thus, we think of a line stretching to infinity in both directions, and the real numbers being assigned to points of the line. As we move along the line in one direction, we pass over the real numbers in a fixed order which is determined by the lengths they represent. Any set of axioms which we write down must make some attempt to capture these properties, and this is the thrust of the order axioms.

The basic feature of the picture is the fact that given a pair of real numbers, a and b, one lies 'to the left of' the other. Thus, we could think of a binary relation (see Appendix) which is characterized by the phrase 'to the left of'. Keeping this simple idea in mind, we proceed to write down statements which are obviously true for the geometric picture presented above.

Definition. An **ordered field** is a field $\mathbf{F}$, together with a binary relation, $<$, satisfying the following axioms (for x, y, z in $\mathbf{F}$):

O1 For every x, and for every y, exactly one of the following is satisfied:
$$x = y \text{ or } x < y \text{ or } y < x.$$
O2 For every x, for every y, and for every z
$$x < y \text{ and } y < z \text{ .implies. } x < z.$$

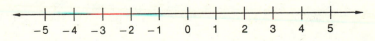

Figure 0.3.1   The real number line.

O3 For every x, for every y, and for every z
$$x < y \text{ implies } x + z < y + z.$$
O4 For every x, for every y, and for every z
$$0 < z \text{ and } x < y \text{ .implies. } z \cdot x < z \cdot y.$$

Discussion. The principal concept underlying these axioms is that of a binary relation. Recall that a binary relation is an arbitrary collection of ordered pairs. In this case, the ordered pairs are from $\mathbf{F} \times \mathbf{F}$. As a matter of convenience, we write $x < y$, instead of $(x, y) \in <$. These matters are discussed more fully in the Appendix.

The first axiom is known as the **Law of Trichotomy.** The second states the **transitive** property. The third allows us to add across an inequality, while preserving the inequality. The last gives the restricted situations in which multiplication preserves the inequality.

While we write $a < b$, we say 'a is **less than** b'. We define the binary relation $>$ (**greater than**) by

$$a > b \text{ if and only if } b < a.$$

We define $\leqslant$ (**less than or equal**) by

$$a \leqslant b \text{ .if and only if. } a < b \text{ or } a = b.$$

Similarly, the reader can define $\geqslant$ (**greater than or equal**) in the obvious way. We often write

$$a < b < c$$

to mean

$$a < b \text{ and } b < c.$$

The other relations, $\leqslant$, $>$, and $\geqslant$, can also be used this way, and the expression can be extended to four or more terms. We say that a is **positive** in case a is greater than 0, a is **negative** provided a is less than 0, and a is **nonnegative** if $a \geqslant 0$. We note that

$$a < b \text{ if and only if } (b - a) \text{ is positive.}$$

Let $\mathbf{F}$ (more precisely, $\{\mathbf{F}, +, \cdot, <, 0, 1\}$) denote an arbitrary ordered field. For the remainder of this section and the start of the next, our theorems and definitions relate to such an arbitrary ordered field. However, the reader should keep in mind that the motivation for proving these theorems is to establish the basic facts about the order properties of $\mathbf{R}$ and $\mathbf{Q}$, and these two structures should be thought of as the prime examples of ordered fields. Again, the facts established below and in the exercise will prove essential in the remainder of this text.

Theorem 0.3.1. For every x, if x is positive, then $-x$ is negative. If x is negative, then $-x$ is positive.

Proof. Fix x which is negative. By definition, $x < 0$. Now,

$$x + (-x) < 0 + (-x) \qquad \text{by } \mathbf{O3}, \text{ whence}$$
$$0 < -x \qquad \text{by } \mathbf{A3} \text{ and } \mathbf{A4}.$$

The fact that $-x$ is positive follows by definition. The rest of the theorem is left to Exercise 1. $\square$

Theorem 0.3.2. $0 < 1$.

Proof. By **O1**, exactly one of the following is true:

$$0 = 1; \ 0 < 1; \ 1 < 0.$$

The first possibility has already been discarded. Thus, it is enough to show that the last can also be discarded. Hence, we assume for the sake of argument that $1 < 0$. Now,

$$0 < -1 \qquad \text{by Theorem 0.3.1, whence}$$
$$(-1) \cdot 0 < (-1) \cdot (-1) \qquad \text{by } \mathbf{O4}.$$

It follows that

$$0 < 1 \cdot 1 \qquad \text{by Theorems 0.2.3 and 0.2.4, whence}$$
$$0 < 1 \qquad \text{by } \mathbf{A3}.$$

The last statement clearly contradicts our assumption that $1 < 0$ and so this assumption must, in fact, be false. The only other possibility is that $0 < 1$ as claimed. $\square$

Discussion. The proof above employs an **indirect argument** (proof by **contradiction**). We do not give a direct proof of the desired conclusion (in this case: $0 < 1$), but rather show that any other alternative leads to nonsense (in this case: $1 < 0$ and simultaneously $0 < 1$, a possibility denied by **O1**.) Such arguments are justified by our belief that our axioms are consistent, or simply put, that our axioms will not permit the logical production of nonsense. We shall, on occasion, employ this method of reasoning and the reader should study the above simple example, so that he may use the technique as well. He should note that to use the technique correctly, care must be taken to state clearly the nature of the contradiction. $\square$

Theorem 0.3.3. For every x, if $0 < x$, then $0 < \dfrac{1}{x}$.

Theorem 0.3.4. For every x, for every y, if $x < y$, then $x < \dfrac{x+y}{2} < y$, where $2 = 1 + 1$.

Theorem 0.3.5. For every x, for every y, if $0 < x < y$, then $0 < \dfrac{1}{y} < \dfrac{1}{x}$.

Proofs of the above are left to the reader (Exercises 2, 3, and 4). It should be noted that each of the above theorems is formalizing some fact that our intuition knows to be well established. It is also telling us that our axioms are leading us in directions which we want to go and, in this sense, they are 'correct'.

EXERCISES

1. Complete the proof of Theorem 0.3.1.

2. Prove Theorem 0.3.3.

3. Prove Theorem 0.3.4.

4. Prove Theorem 0.3.5.

5. Prove the following where $a, b, c, \ldots$ denote arbitrary elements of a fixed ordered field:
   (a) $a \neq 0$ implies $0 < a \cdot a$;
   (b) $a < 0$ and $0 < b$ .implies. $0 > a \cdot b$;
   (c) $a < 0$ and $b < 0$ .implies. $0 < a \cdot b$;
   (d) $0 \leqslant a$ and $0 \leqslant b$ .implies. $0 \leqslant a + b$;
   (e) $a \leqslant b$ and $b \leqslant a$ .implies. $a = b$;
   (f) $a < b$ if and only if $b - a$ is positive;
   (g) $0 < a < 1$ .implies. $a \cdot a < a$;
   (h) $1 < a$ implies $a < a \cdot a$;
   (i) $a < a + 1$;
   (j) $0 < a < b$ .implies. $a \cdot a < b \cdot b$;
   (k) $a \leqslant b$ and $c \leqslant d$ .implies. $a + c \leqslant b + d$;
   (l) $0 < a$ and $0 < b$ .implies. $\dfrac{1}{a + b} < \dfrac{1}{a}$;
   (m) $0 < b$ and $0 < c$ .implies. $\dfrac{a}{b} < \dfrac{a + c}{b}$;
   (n) $0 < a, b, c, d$ .implies. $\dfrac{a}{b} < \dfrac{c}{d}$ if and only if $a \cdot d < b \cdot c$;
   (o) $a \cdot a + 1 > 0$;
   (p) $ab < 0$ .implies. $(a < 0$ and $b > 0)$ or $(a > 0$ and $b < 0)$;
   (q) $ab > 0$ .implies. $(a > 0$ and $b > 0)$ or $(a < 0$ and $b < 0)$;
   (r) $a < b$ and $0 < k < 1$ .implies. $a < k \cdot a + (1 - k) \cdot b < b$;
   (s) $0 \leqslant a < b$ .implies. $\dfrac{a}{1 + a} < \dfrac{b}{1 + b}$;
   (t) $0 < b, d$ and $\dfrac{a}{b} < \dfrac{c}{d}$ .implies. $\dfrac{a}{b} < \dfrac{a + c}{b + d} < \dfrac{c}{d}$.

6. Prove the following statements for an ordered field $\mathbf{F}$:
   (a) $a + a = 0$ implies $a = 0$;
   (b) $a + a + a = 0$ implies $a = 0$;
   (c) $a \cdot a + b \cdot b \geqslant 0$, and $a \cdot a + b \cdot b > 0$ unless $a = b = 0$.

7. If a and b are arbitrary members of an ordered field $\mathbf{F}$, prove that either $\dfrac{a}{b} + \dfrac{b}{a} \geqslant 1 + 1$ or $\dfrac{a}{b} + \dfrac{b}{a} \leqslant (-1) + (-1)$. Hence or otherwise, prove that $a \cdot a \cdot a = b \cdot b \cdot b$ implies $a = b$.

8. If $x < \epsilon$ for every $\epsilon > 0$ in an ordered field, prove that $x \leqslant 0$.

9. If a and b are arbitrary elements of an ordered field $\mathbf{F}$ such that $a \leqslant b$, and for every $\epsilon > 0$, $a + \epsilon > b$, prove that $a = b$.

10. Show that if the equation $x \cdot x + 1 = 0$ has a solution in a field $\mathbf{F}$, then $\mathbf{F}$ can not be an ordered field.

11. Prove that there are no finite ordered fields.

12. Show that this field $\mathbf{C}$ of complex numbers can not be an ordered field.

13. Let **F** be ordered field. Consider the field C_F of all complex numbers over **F** (see Exercise 0.1.15)[†]. The **dictionary ordering** on C_F is defined by specifying $(a,b) > (c,d)$ when either $a > b$, or else, $a = b$ and $c > d$. Show that C_F is not an ordered field, under this ordering. Can there be any other ordering on C_F that makes it an ordered field?

14. Some authors define a field **F** to be ordered, if there exists a subset $P \subseteq F$ (called the set of **positive elements**) such that
    (a) $P \cap -P = \varnothing$ (here, $-P = \{-x: x \in P\}$);
    (b) $P \cup \{0\} \cup (-P) = F$;
    (c) $x, y \in P$ implies $x + y \in P$;
    (d) $x, y \in P$ implies $x \cdot y \in P$.
    Determine whether this set of axioms for an ordered field is equivalent to the one given in this section.

15. Let **F** denote the set of all **rational functions**, that is, expressions of the form

    $$\frac{a_n x^n + a_{n-1} x^{n-1} + \cdots + a_0}{b_m x^m + b_{m-1} x^{m-1} + \cdots + b_0} \qquad (*)$$

    where the a's and the b's are real numbers and $b_m \neq 0$. The field operations are the 'usual' addition and 'usual' multiplication of such expressions. Define an order in **F** by prescribing (*) to be positive if $a_n \cdot b_m > 0$. Verify that **F** is ordered field that contains the real numbers as a subfield. Arrange the following elements of **F** in ascending order of magnitude:

    $$\frac{x}{1}, \ \frac{1}{x}, \ \frac{x + 2}{x - 2}, \ \frac{2x - 1}{x - 3}, \ \frac{x}{1 - 3x}, \ \frac{x + 1}{x^2 - 2}.$$

    [NOTE: You may require the Principle of Induction (next section) to verify some of the field axioms.]

16. Let $Q_{\sqrt{2}}$ denote the set $\{a + b\sqrt{2} : a, b \in Q\}$, with the obvious field operations. Is it possible to prescribe an order in $Q_{\sqrt{2}}$ so that it is an ordered field?

17. In the ordered field **R**, of real numbers, obtain the solution set for the following inequalities:
    (a) $(3x + 1)(2x - 3) > 0$;
    (b) $7x(3x + 1) \geqslant 0$;
    (c) $\dfrac{3x + 11}{1 - 5x} > 0$;
    (d) $\dfrac{4x}{8 + 7x} \leqslant 0$;
    (e) $-\dfrac{1}{100} < 2x + 3 < \dfrac{1}{100}$;
    (f) $-0.001 \leqslant \dfrac{5x + 1}{2x} - \dfrac{11}{3} \leqslant 0.002$;
    (g) $-\epsilon < \dfrac{3x + 1}{2x} < \epsilon$, with $0 < \epsilon < \dfrac{1}{3}$;
    (h) $\dfrac{3x - 2}{2x} \geqslant \dfrac{1}{2}$ or $\dfrac{3x - 2}{2x} \leqslant -\dfrac{1}{2}$.

[†] Exercise x.y.z refers to Exercise z in section x.y. Exercise z refers to Exercise z in the current section.

0.4 COMPLETENESS AXIOM

So far, the axioms we have laid down are not enough to restrict our attention to the field **R** of all real numbers. The reason for this is that there are many structures which satisfy the axioms for an ordered field which are provably distinct from the real numbers. As an example, think of the familiar field, **Q**, the rational numbers. This field is precisely defined in Exercise 31, and it is well known (we leave the proof to the reader) that the rational numbers form an ordered field. To see that **Q** is distinct from the reals, **R**, we have only to write down the statement:

$$\text{There is an } x \text{ such that } x \cdot x = 1 + 1.$$

It has been known since the days of Pythagoras that there is no rational number whose square is 2 (we prove this later). However, there is such a real number (as we will show) and the two fields cannot, therefore, be the same.

Let us return to our geometric example of the real line (see Figure 0.4.1). Suppose we draw a line at right angles to the real line which crosses it. The two lines will intersect in a point, and this point should correspond to a real number. If we think of the rational 'subline' as being all those points which correspond to rational numbers, then the assertion about a number corresponding to a point of intersection will not be true. For example, consider the vertical line which intersects the real line at the square root of 2; since there is no rational number whose square is 2, all we get where this vertical line crosses the rational subline is a hole. A similar statement holds for any other irrational number, such as the square root of 5. To 'fill in the holes' in the rational subline, we need a definition and our last axiom. In this section, **F**, or more precisely $<\mathbf{F}, +, \cdot, <, 0, 1>$, will always refer to an ordered field.

Definition.   Let $S \subseteq \mathbf{F}$. Then, an element $b \in \mathbf{F}$ is called an **upper bound** for S, if for every $x \in S$, $x \leqslant b$. Further, b is called the **least upper bound** for S, if b is an upper bound for S, and for every other upper bound c of S, $b \leqslant c$.

If $S \subseteq \mathbf{F}$ has an upper bound, we say that S is **bounded above**. The least upper bound of a set S is often referred to as the **supremum** and we sometimes write **sup** S (or **l.u.b** S) to denote the supremum of S. If the supremum of S is a member of S, then the supremum is referred to as the **greatest member (maximum)** of S. In a similar manner, we can define **lower bound**, **greatest lower bound (infimum**, abbreviated as **inf**, or **g.l.b**), and **least member (minimum of S.)** Also, a set S is said to be **bounded** if it is bounded above as well as below.

Figure 0.4.1   Rational 'subline' has 'holes.'

Discussion. Think about what the words 'upper bound for S' should mean. The definition should say that a number is an upper bound if it is larger than every member of the set. This is exactly what the definition does say, except that we have allowed an upper bound to be equal to an element of the set. What should 'b is the least upper bound of S' mean? It should mean that there is no upper bound which is smaller (less) than b. But this is exactly what it does say. If follows that to show that b is not an upper bound, we must find a member of S which is greater than b. To show that b is not the least upper bound, we must show that it is not an upper bound, or find an upper bound which is less than b.

If b is the greatest member of S, then b is the supremum of S (**WHY?**)*. It is a special kind of supremum. Note that a set, even if it is bounded, need not possess a supremum (infimum) or greatest (least) element.   □

EXAMPLE 1 _____

Find upper bounds and the suprema of the following subsets of **R**, if they exist:

$$H_1 = \{x \in \mathbf{Q} \text{ and } x < 0\};$$
$$H_2 = \{0, 1, 2, 3\};$$
$$H_3 = \mathbf{Q}.$$

Solution. It is clear that 4 (where the symbols 1, 2, 3, 4 have their usual meaning) is an upper bound for both H_1 and H_2. The number 2, on the other hand, is an upper bound for H_1, but not H_2. The collection of all upper bounds for H_1 is $\{y : y \in \mathbf{R} \text{ and } 0 \leqslant y\}$. To see that no real number c which is less than 0 can be an upper bound for H_1, we have only to find a rational number x, such that $c < x < 0$. The proof of this fact is left to Exercise 36. It is immediate that 0 is the supremum of H_1. Note that $0 \notin H_1$. For H_2, 3 is easily seen to be an upper bound. Since $3 \in H_2$, there can be no upper bounds which are less than 3. It follows that 3 is the supremum of H_2. H_3 is the set of all rational numbers, **Q**. Evidently, this set has no upper bounds (**WHY?**). Since **Q** has no upper bounds, it has no least upper bound.   □

Discussion. The collection of rational numbers has no upper bounds, whence it has no least upper bound. This illustrates one of the reasons why a set can fail to have a supremum, namely, it has no upper bounds. The other reason a set can fail to have a supremum is that it has too many upper bounds. This question, of when a set fails to have a supremum, will be explored in Exercise 7.   □

We now prove the uniqueness of the supremum which will justify our use of the phrase 'the supremum' in the above definition.

---

*When (**WHY?**) or (**HOW?**) appears in the text, it requests the reader to provide an explanation. In this case, it asks the reader to justify why b must be the supremum of S. The following would do. As the greatest member of S, b is greater than or equal to every other member of S, and so is an upper bound for S. Since b is the greatest member of S, b is the supremum, by definition. □ It is not necessary to write this out, but it is necessary that the reader be able to construct the required fact or reasoning—as required by the next (**WHY?**)—in his head.

Theorem 0.4.1 . Let $H \subseteq \mathbf{F}$. If sup H exists, then it is unique.

Proof. Let b and c be two suprema of H. Then both must be upper bounds for H. If they are not equal, then we may assume that $b < c$ (**WHY?**). But this clearly means that either b is not an upper bound for H, or c is not the least upper bound. In either case, we contradict our assumptions about b and c.   □

Discussion. The straightforward proof, which is an indirect argument, uses the trichotomy law, as well as the definition of supremum.   □

An immediate consequence of this theorem is the fact that if there is an upper bound for H which is also a member of H, then there is only one such and it will be the least upper bound, as well as its greatest member. Thus, an upper bound for H is strictly greater than every member of H except possibly one.

The next theorem gives a useful characterization of the supremum.

Theorem 0.4.2 . Let H be a nonempty subset of $\mathbf{F}$ bounded above by an element $b \in \mathbf{F}$. Then, b is the supremum of H if and only if for every positive ϵ (epsilon) there is an $x \in H$ such that $b - \epsilon < x \leqslant b$.

Proof. We prove that the supremum has the property claimed; the converse is left to Exercise 3. Thus, let H be a nonempty subset of $\mathbf{F}$ and $b = \sup H$. Fix a positive ϵ. Now, $b - \epsilon < b$ (**WHY?**), and so $b - \epsilon$ is not an upper bound for H. This means that there is an $x \in H$ which will witness the fact that $b - \epsilon$ is not an upper bound. For such an x, we must have

$$b - \epsilon < x \leqslant b,$$

where the last inequality is obtained by virtue of the fact that b is an upper bound for H.   □

Discussion. As a general rule, the symbol 'ϵ' always denotes a fixed small positive quantity, say something smaller than 10^{-1000}, or even smaller. With this in mind, we draw a picture. Notice that as ϵ is fixed close to 0, the quantity, $b - \epsilon$, is fixed close to b on the left side (see Figure 0.4.2). The function of $b - \epsilon$ is to generate a witness to the fact that no number which is less than or equal to $b - \epsilon$ can be an upper bound for H. It does this by producing an x such that $x \in H$ and $b - \epsilon < x$. In the figure, $b - \epsilon$ has been chosen so that it witnesses that c is not an upper bound for H. Finally, as $b - \epsilon$ moves in on b, it clearly kills the chance of any number to the left of b being an upper bound for H. Thus, there is no upper bound which is less than b, whence b is the supremum.

The statement of Theorem 0.4.2 is an 'if and only if' statement. Thus, there are in fact two statements to be proved. We have proved only one of these and have left the other for the reader in Exercise 3.   □

Figure 0.4.2 b is the supremum of H.

The concepts of upper bound and supremum are the tools we needed to state the last definition leading to the completeness axiom.

Definition.   Let **F** be an ordered field. Then, **F** is **complete** (or **order-complete**) provided that for every nonempty subset S of **F** which is bounded above, there is an element $x_S \in$ **F** such that x_S is the supremum of S.

Completeness Axiom

The real numbers are a complete ordered field.

We now have our axioms for the real numbers; namely, **A1–A6, O1–O4,** and the Completeness Axiom. The first ten axioms, **A1–A6** and **O1–O4**, permit many realizations. For example, **Q** is one such realization, while **R** is another. It is an amazing fact, although we will not prove it here, that this axiom forces the real numbers to be unique! This result is a direct consequence of the last axiom which has a very special nature, distinct from all the others. The first ten axioms discuss the behavior of *numbers*. The last axiom describes the behavior of *sets of numbers*. This is a key difference, and we will now explore some of its more remarkable consequences. However, we first note that as a consequence of the uniqueness of the real numbers, the completeness axiom can be restated as follows:

Supremum Principle

Let S be a nonempty set of real numbers which is bounded above. Then there is a real number which is the supremum (least upper bound) of S.

For the remainder of this book, unless otherwise stated, we are working in the structure R satisfying the eleven axioms above.

We note that the approach we have taken has been nonconstructive, that is, we have laid down a set of eleven axioms and taken **R** to be any structure which satisfies these axioms. This leaves us with the question: Why should we believe that a structure exists which satisfies these axioms, much less a unique structure? One answer to this is that the real numbers with which we are all familiar satisfy these axioms and we are merely setting down the self-evident truths about **R** which we take as the place to start. While this deals with existence, it does not deal with uniqueness. Another approach is to obtain **R** constructively from Peano's Axioms. These axioms specify the structure **N**. While this approach may seem more satisfactory as a result of **N** being a simpler structure, one is still left with wondering why **N** should exist and be unique. Such a development can be found in the book, *Foundations of Analysis* by E. Landau, or in other texts on advanced calculus.

As noted in section 0.2, the main structures of interest in this text are **R, Q, Z,** and **N**. We have defined **R**. We turn now to the problem of identifying the positive integers (natural numbers) within the structure **R** and developing their essential properties.

Definition.   A subset S of $\mathbf{R}$ is **inductively closed** provided

    (i) $1 \in S$;
    (ii) if $x \in S$, then $x + 1 \in S$.

The collection of **natural numbers (positive integers)** is defined by

$$\mathbf{N} = \bigcap \{S : S \subseteq \mathbf{R} \text{ and } S \text{ is inductively closed}\}.$$

Discussion.   The purpose of this definition is to select out for special consideration those numbers which one usually uses to count. At the same time, we want to capture the very powerful properties associated with the structure inherent in the natural numbers, namely, the power associated with the induction axiom which is used as a proof technique. To accomplish these two goals, we must make sure that all of the counting numbers end up in $\mathbf{N}$, and at the same time ensure that no other numbers get into $\mathbf{N}$. Putting 1 in $\mathbf{N}$, and requiring closure under the "unary" operation of 'addition by one' (usually referred to as the **successor operation**), will guarantee that all the counting numbers are in $\mathbf{N}$. However, there are many inductively closed sets which contain numbers other than the counting numbers (**give an example!**). To ensure that we have only the counting numbers, we take an intersection over all possible such inductively closed sets. It is this intersection then, which yields $\mathbf{N}$. Thus, if we can prove that $\mathbf{N}$ itself is inductively closed, then it will follow that $\mathbf{N}$ is the smallest inductively closed subset of $\mathbf{R}$. This is done in the next theorem. □

Theorem 0.4.3.   The natural numbers, $\mathbf{N}$, form an inductively closed subset of the real numbers $\mathbf{R}$.

    Proof.   We first claim that $\mathbf{R}$, itself, is inductively closed. But this is obvious from the field axioms. Now 1 belongs to every inductively closed set, S, and so is in the intersection. Let x be an arbitrary member of $\mathbf{N}$. Then $x \in S$, where S is an arbitrary inductively closed set. Since S is inductively closed, $x + 1 \in S$, and hence to the intersection of all S, which is $\mathbf{N}$. Thus, the natural numbers are an inductively closed set, as claimed. □

Discussion.   We point out that in general, if each member of a family of sets possesses a property, say (P), it is not necessarily true that their intersection will also possess the property (P). In other words, the 'intersection' of all these sets need not be the smallest set with the property (P). The reader will find several such instances in subsequent chapters. This is the reason why we need a proof to convince that $\mathbf{N}$ itself is inductively closed. □

We shall use the standard notations for natural numbers, that is,

$$2 = 1 + 1; \quad 3 = 2 + 1; \quad 4 = 3 + 1; \quad \cdots$$

Principle of Mathematical Induction

Let M be any subset of the natural numbers which is inductively closed. Then $M = \mathbf{N}$.

Proof. By definition, M is one of the sets forming the intersection which is **N**. It is immediate that **N** is a subset of M and so equality follows. $\square$

The remainder of this section brings out the importance of the Principle of Mathematical Induction as a useful proof technique, and also as a tool for recursive definitions.

Theorem 0.4.4. The natural numbers have the following properties:

(i) Every natural number is greater than or equal to 1.
(ii) For every natural number, n, other than 1, there is a natural number m such that $n = m + 1$.
(iii) For every pair of natural numbers n and m, if $m < n$, then $m + 1 \leqslant n$.
(iv) Every nonempty subset of **N** has a least element.
(v) For every real number x there exists a natural number n such that $x < n$.

Proof. For (i), let

$$M = \{n : n \in \mathbf{N} \text{ and } 1 \leqslant n\}.$$

Observe that $1 \in M$, and if $n \in M$, then $n + 1 \in M$, as is easily shown from the order axioms (**HOW?**). Thus, M is inductively closed, so $M = \mathbf{N}$.

For (ii), set

$$M = \{n : n \in \mathbf{N} \text{ .and. } n = 1 \text{ or for some } m \in \mathbf{N}, n = m + 1\}.$$

It is easily checked that M is inductively closed, and so equals **N**. Since (i) is established, it is clear that $m \in \mathbf{N}$ implies $1 \neq m + 1$.

For (iii), let

$$M = \{n : n \in \mathbf{N} \text{ .and. for any } m \in \mathbf{N}, \; m < n \text{ implies } m + 1 \leqslant n\}.$$

Clearly, $1 \in M$ since there is no $m < 1$, so the statement '$m < n$ implies $m + 1 \leqslant n$' is always true.

Let $n \in M$ and consider the case for $n + 1$. Let $m \in \mathbf{N}$ and $m < n + 1$. If $m = 1$, then (i) asserts that $m = 1 \leqslant n$, so $m + 1 \leqslant n + 1$. Otherwise, we have

$$m < n + 1$$
$$m - 1 < n \qquad \text{by } \mathbf{A4} \text{ and } \mathbf{O3}.$$

Note that $m - 1 \in \mathbf{N}$ by (ii), since $m \neq 1$. Thus,

$$(m - 1) + 1 \leqslant n \qquad \text{since } n \in M$$
$$m \leqslant n \qquad \text{by } \mathbf{A2} \text{ and } \mathbf{A4}$$
$$m + 1 \leqslant n + 1 \qquad \text{by } \mathbf{O3}.$$

Hence, $n + 1 \in M$. Then M is inductively closed and so equals **N**.

To establish (iv), first note that we may assume that $1 \notin H$, the given arbitrary nonempty subset of **N**. We set

$$M = \{j : j \in \mathbf{N} \text{ and for all } n \in H, \; j < n\}.$$

By assumption, $1 \in M$. Further, if $j \in M$, and $k < j$ is a natural number, then $k \in M$ (**WHY?**). Evidently, $M \neq \mathbf{N}$, since H is a nonempty subset of **N**, and $M \cap H = \varnothing$.

It follows that M is not inductively closed, whence there is an $x \in M$ such that $x + 1 \notin M$. Let m witness this fact, that is, let $m \in M$ and $m + 1 \notin M$. Then $m + 1 \in H$ (**WHY?**), and in fact is the least element of H, as desired.

For (v), we assume for the sake of argument that there is a fixed real number x such that for every natural number n, $n \leqslant x$. Thus, **N** is bounded above, and hence by the supremum principle, **N** has a supremum; call it m. By Theorem 0.4.2, taking $\epsilon = \dfrac{1}{2}$, there is an $n \in \mathbf{N}$ such that

$$m - \frac{1}{2} < n \leqslant m,$$

whence

$$m < m + \frac{1}{2} < n + 1. \tag{WHY?}$$

Since $n + 1$ is also a natural number, this contradicts our choice of m as the supremum of **N**. Thus, our initial assumption of the existence of an upper bound for **N** was false. □

Discussion. Some of these arguments are rather complicated, so we examine the argument for (iii) in detail. Rather than consider every pair of natural numbers n and m, we use induction upon n. For each n, we prove the statement 'For all m, if $m < n$ then $m + 1 \leqslant n$'. We define M to be the set of all n for which this statement is true.

To show that $1 \in M$, we need only remark that there is no $m < 1$ (by (i)), and hence the condition 'if $m < 1$ then $m + 1 \leqslant 1$' is true by default.

Then we show that $n \in M$ implies $n + 1 \in M$. We take $m < n + 1$ and show that $m + 1 \leqslant n + 1$. We simply subtract 1 to get $m - 1 < n$, use the fact that $n \in M$ to get $m \leqslant n$, and add 1 to get $m + 1 \leqslant n + 1$. Because of the way M is defined, we must deal with the case $m = 1$ separately. Since $m - 1 = 0 \notin \mathbf{N}$, we cannot use the fact $n \in M$ to go from $m - 1 < n$ to $m \leqslant n$.

We have shown that M is inductively closed, and by the Induction Principle, $M = \mathbf{N}$. This completes the proof.

All these proofs have a common feature. We want to prove that a certain property holds for all natural numbers. The strategy is to define a set M which consists of all natural numbers enjoying that property. Once we establish that M is inductively closed, we can conclude that $M = \mathbf{N}$. The crucial steps are the correct formulation of the set M, and the ability to reason out that M is inductively closed.

The property (iv) of Theorem 0.4.4 is called the **well-ordering property** of natural numbers.

Property (v) is closely related to the **Archimedean Principle** which asserts that to every pair of positive real numbers, x and y, there is a natural number n such that $y < nx$ (Exercise 32). The Archimedean Principle is usually invoked to assert the existence of a natural number n such that $\dfrac{1}{n} < x$, where x is a fixed small positive number (Exercise 33). □

The properties of the natural numbers stated in the above theorem are sometimes given a slightly different formulation known as **Peano's Axioms.** More precisely, these axioms state that the set **N** of natural numbers possesses the following properties:

(a) $1 \in \mathbf{N}$;

(b) Each $n \in \mathbf{N}$, possesses an **immediate successor** n';

(c) $n' = m'$ implies $n = m$;

(d) For each $n \in \mathbf{N}$, the statement '$n' = 1$' is false;

(e) If $M \subseteq \mathbf{N}$ is such that $1 \in S$, and the statement ($n \in M$ implies $n' \in M$) is true for each n, then $M = \mathbf{N}$.

In fact, $n' = n + 1$, in our familiar notation.

Discussion. We want to emphasize here that these are consequences of our axioms and that a key axiom in the development is the axiom of completeness.

The other feature in Theorem 0.4.4 of overwhelming importance is the use of the Principle of Mathematical Induction as a technique for proving theorems. This is also stated in Peano's Axiom (e) above. Suppose we are interested in proving a certain statement $S(n)$ involving natural numbers for each $n \in \mathbf{N}$. If we can verify the truth of $S(1)$, for the case $n = 1$, and further, assuming the truth of $S(n)$, arrive at the truth of $S(n+1)$ by suitable reasonings, then we have proved the truth of $S(n)$ for each $n \in \mathbf{N}$. Let

$$M = \{n \in \mathbf{N} : S(n) \text{ is true}\}.$$

Clearly, $1 \in M$, since $S(1)$ is true. If $n \in M$, then $S(n)$ is true, so $S(n + 1)$ is also true, and hence, $n + 1 \in M$. Thus, M is an inductively closed subset of $\mathbf{N}$ and so $M = \mathbf{N}$. In other words, $S(n)$ is true for each $n \in \mathbf{N}$. Such a proof is known as **proof by induction**.

An important fact to remember while using induction is that after checking the truth of the statement $S(n)$ for the initial case $n = 1$, we are trying to show that the implication '$S(n)$ implies $S(n + 1)$' is always true. To do this, we proceed by assuming the truth of $S(n)$ and from there, derive the truth of $S(n + 1)$. If we did not assume the truth of $S(n)$, the implication is always true. (**WHY?**) There is a common misunderstanding of this fact. When we say 'assume $S(n)$ is true', we are only using it as a tool to justify the truth of the implication '$S(n)$ implies $S(n + 1)$'. We are *not* asserting that $S(n)$ is indeed true. In fact, at this stage of the game, we do not know whether $S(n)$ is true for a specific value of n. The assumption that $S(n)$ is true is called the **induction hypothesis**.

A second point to remember is that we need both of these conditions:

(i) $S(1)$ is true;

(ii) The implication '$S(n)$ implies $S(n + 1)$' is true

to conclude by Mathematical Induction that $S(n)$ holds for all n. Omitting one or the other may not prove what we want. These are illustrated in Exercises 17 and 18. Again, we need not start the induction with the initial case $n = 1$. We could, for example, prove a statement for $n \geqslant 3$, where the initial case to be checked will be for $n = 3$.   □

We will illustrate the use of the Principle of Induction, by proving the Binomial Theorem. But first, we require some definitions.

Definition. Let $n \in \{0\} \cup N$, the **nonnegative integers,** and x a fixed real number. We define x^n by:

> **(i)** if $n = 0$ and $x \neq 0$, then $x^0 = 1$;
> **(ii)** if $n = 1$, then $x^1 = x$;
> **(iii)** if $n > 1$, then $x^n = x \cdot x^{n-1}$.

(Note that 0^0 is not defined.)

Definitions such as that above are referred to as **recursive definitions.** To illustrate their use, let us calculate x^4:

$$x^4 = x \cdot x^3 = x \cdot (x \cdot x^2) = x \cdot (x \cdot [x \cdot x]).$$

Definition. For a nonnegative integer, n, we define **n!** (**n factorial**) by

> **(i)** $0! = 1$;
> **(ii)** for $n \geqslant 1$, $n! = n \cdot (n - 1)!$

We then set

$$\binom{n}{k} = \frac{n!}{k! \, (n - k)!}$$

where $0 \leqslant k \leqslant n$, and refer to this quantity as the n-**plus-first binomial coefficient.** (The quantity $\binom{n}{k}$ is the same as that resulting from counting the number of combinations of n things taken k at a time. Thus, the coefficient is often referred to as 'n-choose-k'.)

In what follows, we shall be using the Σ (**Sigma**) notation, which is formally defined in Exercise 19.

Theorem 0.4.5 (Binomial Theorem). For any nonzero x and y in $\mathbf{R}$ and any n in $\mathbf{N}$,

$$(x + y)^n = \sum_{k=0}^{n} \binom{n}{k} x^{n-k} y^k.$$

[Note that we have indicated the field multiplication by mere juxtaposition.]

Proof. Let x and y be any pair of fixed real numbers. For this fixed pair, let M be the collection of natural numbers for which the theorem is true. We will be done if we can show that $M = \mathbf{N}$. Clearly, the simplest way to do this is to show that M is inductively closed. Now $1 \in M$ (**WHY?**). Thus, we assume that n is a fixed natural number belonging to M. Now

$$(x + y)^{n+1} = (x + y) \cdot (x + y)^n \qquad \text{by definition,}$$

$$= (x + y) \cdot \sum_{k=0}^{n} \binom{n}{k} x^{n-k} y^k \qquad \text{since } n \in M,$$

$$= x \cdot \sum_{k=0}^{n} \binom{n}{k} x^{n-k} y^k + y \cdot \sum_{k=0}^{n} \binom{n}{k} x^{n-k} y^k \qquad \text{by distributivity,}$$

$$= \sum_{k=0}^{n} \binom{n}{k} x^{n+1-k}y^k + \sum_{k=0}^{n} \binom{n}{k} x^{n-k}y^{k+1}$$

as a result of the generalized distributive law (see Exercise 20). We now want to rename the index variable in the second sum. We call the new index j, and set $j = k + 1$. The second term of the sum now becomes

$$\sum_{j=1}^{n+1} \binom{n}{j-1} x^{n-(j-1)}y^j.$$

Notice that $n - (j - 1) = n + 1 - j$. Now we shift the index again (back from j to k), since we want the same index variable for both terms, this time leaving the range unchanged and changing only the name, to obtain the following formulation of the whole expression:

$$= \sum_{k=0}^{n} \binom{n}{k} x^{n+1-k}y^k + \sum_{k=1}^{n+1} \binom{n}{k-1} x^{n+1-k}y^k.$$

Observe that the coefficient of the first term of the first sum satisfies

$$\binom{n}{0} = 1 = \binom{n+1}{0}$$

and that the last term in the second sum satisfies

$$\binom{n}{n} = 1 = \binom{n+1}{n+1}.$$

Now the remaining terms occur in pairs, one for each sum, where the powers of x and y exactly match. Let us pick such a pair, with k arbitrary, but fixed and satisfying $1 \leqslant k \leqslant n$. We have

$$\binom{n}{k} x^{n+1-k}y^k + \binom{n}{k-1} x^{n+1-k}y^k = \left[\binom{n}{k} + \binom{n}{k-1} \right] x^{n+1-k}y^k.$$

Let us compute the coefficient:

$$\binom{n}{k} + \binom{n}{k-1} = \frac{n!}{(n-k)!\,k!} + \frac{n!}{(n-(k-1))!\,(k-1)!}$$

$$= \frac{n!}{(n-k)!\,k!} + \frac{n!}{(n+1-k)!\,(k-1)!}$$

$$= \frac{n![(n+1-k)!\,(k-1)! + (n-k)!\,k!]}{k!\,(n-k)!\,(n+1-k)!\,(k-1)!}$$

$$= \binom{n+1}{k}.$$

The details of the last step should be worked out in full by the reader. It is immediate from these calculations that

$$(x + y)^{n+1} = \sum_{k=0}^{n+1} \binom{n+1}{k} x^{n+1-k}y^k$$

as desired. Thus $n + 1 \in M$, whence $M = \mathbf{N}$ and we are done. $\square$

Discussion.   Aside from the fact that this is an important result which will be a useful tool in our future discussions, there are several points about the proof worth noting. The first is the use of the set M. Now the theorem is not really one single statement; rather, it is a collection of statements, one for each positive integer n. We use the set M to collect those n's for which the theorem is true (for that particular n). All proofs employing the Principle of Mathematical Induction can be written in this form and, indeed, the set M is there whether it is explicitly formulated or not. At this stage of your career, it will usually clarify your thinking to explicitly define M and use it appropriately. The other point is that the bulk of the proof is heavy algebraic manipulation. There is no escape from calculations of this type at almost any level in mathematics, and undoubtedly not in analysis. Algebra is certainly the most important tool in these discussions, and the reader would do well to sharpen his ability to manipulate expressions and be prepared to do so without the least trepidation.   □

EXERCISES

1. Define lower bound, greatest lower bound (infimum for subsets of **R**. Restate the Completeness axiom in terms of greatest lower bound, and prove the equivalence of the two forms.

2. Find two upper bounds, two lower bounds, the supremum, and the infimum for each of the following sets of real numbers (if such exist). You may assume Exercises 32–36, 40, where needed.

   (a) $\left\{ -1, 4, \dfrac{1}{2}, \dfrac{9}{2} \right\}$;

   (b) $\left\{ \dfrac{-1}{n} : n \in \mathbf{N} \right\}$;

   (c) $\{ -\pi \}$;

   (d) $\varnothing$;

   (e) $\mathbf{R}$;

   (f) $^{\dagger}(\mathbf{R} \sim \mathbf{Q}) \cup \mathbf{Z}$;

   (g) $\left\{ \dfrac{1 + (-1)^n}{2} : n \in \mathbf{N} \right\}$;

   (h) $\left\{ \dfrac{n + (-1)^n}{n} : n \in \mathbf{N} \right\}$;

   (i) $\left\{ n^{(-1)^n} : n \in \mathbf{N} \right\}$;

   (j) $\left\{ (-1)^n \left[\pi + \dfrac{1}{n} \right] : n \in \mathbf{N} \right\}$;

   (k) $\left\{ (-1)^n \left[\dfrac{1}{4} - \dfrac{8}{n} \right] : n \in \mathbf{N} \right\}$;

   $^{\dagger}A \sim B = \{ x : \in A \text{ and } x \notin B \}.$

(l) $\{x : x \in \mathbf{Q} \text{ and } x \leqslant \sqrt{3}\}$;

(m) $\left\{x + \dfrac{1}{x} : x \in \mathbf{R} \sim \{0\}\right\}$;

(n) $\left\{x + \dfrac{1}{x} : \dfrac{1}{2} < x < 2\right\}$;

(o) $\left\{\dfrac{x}{1 + x} : x > -1\right\}$;

(p) $\left\{\dfrac{3 + (-1)^n}{2^{n+1}} : n \in \mathbf{N}\right\}$;

(q) $\left\{\dfrac{1}{3^n} + \dfrac{1}{5^{n-1}} : n \in \mathbf{N}\right\}$;

(r) $\left\{\dfrac{1}{m} + \dfrac{1}{n} : m, n \in \mathbf{N}\right\}$;

(s) $\left\{\dfrac{1}{2^m} + \dfrac{1}{3^n} : m, n \in \mathbf{N}\right\}$;

(t) $\left\{n \sin \dfrac{n\pi}{2} + \dfrac{1}{n} \cos n\pi : n \in \mathbf{N}\right\}$;

(u) $\{\sin x \cos x : x \in \mathbf{R}\}$;

(v) $\left\{\dfrac{1}{1 + x^2} : x \in \mathbf{R}\right\}$;

(w) $\left\{\dfrac{x}{1 + x^2} : x \in \mathbf{R}\right\}$;

(x) $\left\{\dfrac{x}{y} + \dfrac{y}{x} : x, y \in \mathbf{R} \sim \{0\}\right\}$;

(y) $\{x \in \mathbf{R} : (x-a)(x-b)(x-c)(x-d) < 0, \ a < b < c < d\}$;

(z) $\left\{(x + y + z)(\dfrac{1}{x} + \dfrac{1}{y} + \dfrac{1}{z}) : x, y, z \in \mathbf{R} \sim \{0\}\right\}$.

3. Supply the proof of the missing part of the 'if and only if' statement in Theorem 0.4.2.

4. Fill in the missing details in the proof of Theorem 0.4.4.

5. Complete the algebraic manipulations in the proof of Theorem 0.4.5.

6. Show that a nonempty finite subset of $\mathbf{R}$ has a supremum, infimum, greatest member, and a least member. Can you make a similar statement for infinite subsets?

7. Let $A \subseteq \mathbf{R}$. Show if the supremum of A does not exist, then $A = \varnothing$ or A is not bounded above.

8. If A is a nonempty bounded set and $B = \{y : y \text{ is an upper bound for } A\}$, prove that $\inf B = \sup A$.

9. If $\sup A = \inf A$, what can you say about A?

10. If M is a nonempty, bounded set such that $\inf M > 0$, show that
$\sup \{\dfrac{1}{m} : m \in M\} = \dfrac{1}{\inf M}$.

11. If A and B are bounded sets and $A \subseteq B$, show that $\sup A \leqslant \sup B$ and $\inf A \geqslant \inf B$. If $\sup A = \sup B$ and $\inf A = \inf B$, must A and B be identical?

12. If A_i is a family of subsets of $\mathbf{R}$, and if $m_i = \sup A_i$ for each i, show that $\sup \cup A_i = \sup \{a_i\}$. Formulate and prove a similar statement for infimums.

13. For $A, B \subseteq \mathbf{R}$, recall the definitions of $-A$, $A + B$, and $A \cdot B$ from Exercise 0.2.17. Which of the following statements are true? Justify.
    (a) $\sup(-A) = -\inf A$;
    (b) $\sup(A + B) = \sup A + \sup B$;
    (c) $\inf(A + B) = \inf A + \inf B$;
    (d) $\sup(A \cdot B) = (\sup A) \cdot (\sup B)$;
    (e) $\inf(A \cdot B) = (\inf A) \cdot (\inf B)$;
    (f) $A \subseteq B$ implies $\sup A \leqslant \sup B$;
    (g) $A \subseteq B$ implies $\inf A \leqslant \inf B$;
    (h) $\sup(A \cap B) \leqslant$ minimum of $(\sup A, \sup B)$;
    (i) $\inf(A \cap B) \geqslant$ maximum of $(\inf A, \inf B)$.

14. Give examples of inductively closed subsets of $\mathbf{R}$, different from $\mathbf{N}$ and $\mathbf{Q}$.

15. Use mathematical induction to prove the following statements:
    (a) $\dfrac{1}{1 \cdot 2} + \dfrac{1}{2 \cdot 3} + \cdots + \dfrac{1}{n \cdot (n+1)} = \dfrac{n}{n+1}$, $(n \in \mathbf{N})$;
    (b) $1 \cdot 2 \cdot 3 + 2 \cdot 3 \cdot 4 + \cdots + n \cdot (n+1) \cdot (n+2) =$
    $$\dfrac{n(n+1)(n+2)(n+3)}{4}, \quad (n \in \mathbf{N});$$
    (c) $10^n - 3^n$ is always a multiple of 7;
    (d) **(Bernoulli's inequality)**: if $-1 \leqslant x$, $1 + nx \leqslant (1 + x)^n$ $(n \in \mathbf{N})$;
    (e) $(1 - x)^n \leqslant 1 - nx + \dfrac{n(n-1)}{2} x^2$ for $0 \leqslant x < 1$ and $n \geqslant 1$;
    (f) $\dfrac{(2n)!}{(n!)^2} \leqslant 4^{n-1}$ for $n \geqslant 5$;
    (g) $|\sin nx| \leqslant n |\sin x|$ for $n \in \mathbf{N}$ (assume standard properties of the sine function);
    (h) $a_1{}^2 + a_2{}^2 + \cdots + a_n{}^2 \geqslant 0$ unless $a_1 = a_2 = \cdots = a_n = 0$.

16. For each $n \in \mathbf{N}$, we define a real number a_n by:
    (a) $a_1 = \sqrt{2}$;
    (b) $a_{n+1} = \sqrt{2 + a_n}$.
    Show that for every m, $a_m \leqslant a_{m+1} \leqslant 2$. (In this exercise, assume the existence of square roots of positive real numbers, with the usual defining property. This assumption is justified by Theorem 0.5.2.)

17. Consider the statement
    $$P(n): 1 \cdot 1! + 2 \cdot 2! + \cdots + n \cdot n! = (n + 1)!$$
    Show that '$P(n)$ implies $P(n + 1)$' is always true. Is $P(n)$ true for all n? Justify.

18. What is the fallacy in the following argument by induction?

    Statement. Each group of n people have the same name.

    Proof. Let $S(n)$ denote the given statement. Trivially, for $n = 1$, a group consisting of 1 person has the same name. Assume the truth of $S(n)$. Consider a group consisting of $(n + 1)$ people. Omitting a particular individual, say X, we have a group of n people, so by induction hypothesis, all have the same name. Also, omitting a different individual Y, and adjoining X, we have a different group of n people, so all have the same name. So X

and Y, and hence all the $(n + 1)$ people have the same name. Thus, $S(n + 1)$ is valid, and hence by induction, $S(n)$ holds for all $n \in \mathbf{N}$. $\qquad\square$

19. Let m and n be integers with $m \leqslant n$, and f a function defined on the integers. Set

$$\sum_{k=m}^{n} f(k) = \begin{cases} f(m), & \text{if } n = m. \\ f(n) + \sum_{k=m}^{n-1} f(k), & \text{if } m < n. \end{cases}$$

(a) Show that $\sum_{k=1}^{n} a = n \cdot a$.

(b) Show that $\sum_{k=1}^{n} k = \dfrac{n(n+1)}{2}$.

(c) Show that $\sum_{k=1}^{n} f(k) = \sum_{k=0}^{n-1} f(k+1) = \sum_{k=(1+m)}^{n+m} f(k-m)$.

In the remaining exercises, the letters n, m, and k denote natural numbers.

20. Let $x_1, x_2, \ldots, x_n$ be n real numbers. Show that for any fixed real number y,

$$y \cdot \sum_{k=1}^{n} x_k = \sum_{k=1}^{n} y \cdot x_k.$$

21. Let x be any fixed real number other than 1. Show that

$$\sum_{k=0}^{n} x^k = \frac{1 - x^{n+1}}{1 - x}.$$

22. Show that for any n and m and any real x, $x^n \cdot x^m = x^{n+m}$.

23. Let $x \neq 0$ be a real number and $n \in \mathbf{N}$. Define $x^{-n} = \dfrac{1}{x^n}$. Show that $(x^n)^{-1} = (x^{-1})^n$, for every integer, n. Further, show that if $x \neq 0$ and $m,n \in \mathbf{Z}$, then $x^m x^n = x^{m+n}$.

24. Prove that there is a positive integer m such that $m \leqslant n$ implies $n^2 < 2^n$. [HINT: apply the binomial theorem to the expression $(1 + 1)^n$.]

25. Prove there is a positive integer m such that $m \leqslant n$ implies $n^3 < 2^n$.

26. Prove there is a positive integer m such that $m \leqslant n$ implies $n^4 < 2^n$.

27. Let x be an arbitrary positive number. Show that there is an m such that $m \leqslant n$ implies $n^2 < (1 + x)^n$.

28. Prove that the sum of two arbitrary positive integers is a positive integer.

29. Prove that the product of two positive integers is a positive integer.

30. Let $\mathbf{Z} = \{x : x = 0 \text{ or } x \in \mathbf{N} \text{ or } -x \in \mathbf{N}\}$. Prove that $\mathbf{Z}$, the set of **integers**, is closed under sums and products.

31. Let $\mathbf{Q} = \{x : x = \dfrac{m}{n} \text{ for some } m, n \in \mathbf{Z} \text{ such that } n \neq 0\}$. Prove that $\mathbf{Q}$, the set of **rational numbers**, (with the obvious field operations—see Exercise 0.2.1) is an ordered subfield of $\mathbf{R}$ which is contained in every subfield of $\mathbf{R}$.

Explain how you will plot a rational number $\dfrac{m}{n}$ as a point in the geometrical line.

Show further that if we identify the integer $m \in \mathbf{Z}$ with the member $\dfrac{m}{1} \in \mathbf{Q}$, then we have the inclusions: $\mathbf{N} \subset \mathbf{Z} \subset \mathbf{Q} \subset \mathbf{R}$.

32. Prove that the real numbers satisfy the **Archimedean Property:** For every pair of positive real numbers, x and y, there is an $n \in \mathbf{N}$ such that $y < n \cdot x$.

33. Show that for every positive real number, x, there is an $n \in \mathbf{N}$ such that $0 < \dfrac{1}{n} < x$.

34. For a nonempty subset A of $\mathbf{R}$, show that the following statements are equivalent:
(a) $a = \sup A$;

(b) for each $n \in \mathbf{N}$, $a - \dfrac{1}{n}$ is not an upper bound, but $a + \dfrac{1}{n}$ is always an upper bound for A.

35. Show that for every pair of positive real numbers x and y, there exists an n such that
$$0 < \frac{y}{n} < x.$$

36. Prove that between any two distinct real numbers lies a rational number.

37. Prove that if $x \in \mathbf{R}$, then $\sup \{q \in \mathbf{Q}: q < x\} = x$.

38. Given $x \in \mathbf{R}$, prove that there is a unique integer $n \in \mathbf{Z}$ satisfying $n \leqslant x < n + 1$. (the unique integer so determined is called the **integral part** of x, and is denoted by $[x]$.)

39. Prove that the sum of two rational numbers is rational. A real number is **irrational** if it is not rational. (For example, $\sqrt{2}$ is irrational; see Theorem 0.5.1.) What can be said about the sum of a rational with an irrational? Sum of two irrationals? What about products in all four combinations?

40. Prove that between any two distinct real numbers there is an irrational.

41. Prove that between any two real numbers a and b, there exist an infinite number of rational numbers and an infinite number of irrational numbers.

42. Assume $x \geqslant 0$. Prove that for each $n \geqslant 1$, there exists a finite decimal $r_n = x_0 \cdot x_1 x_2 \cdots x_n$ where $r_n \leqslant x < r_n + 10^{-n}$.

43. Prove that the Principle of Induction is equivalent to the well-ordering property of $\mathbf{N}$: every nonempty subset of $\mathbf{N}$ has a minimum (statement (iv) of Theorem 0.4.4.).

44. Prove the **Second Principle of Mathematical Induction:** Let S be a subset of $\mathbf{N}$ such that for each $n \in \mathbf{N}$, the inclusion $S_n \subseteq S$ implies that $n \in S$, where $S_n = \{m: m \in \mathbf{N} \text{ and } m < n\}$. Then $S = \mathbf{N}$. Use it to show that if $a_1 = 1$, $a_2 = 2$ and for $n \geqslant 1$, $a_{n+2} = a_n + a_{n+1}$, then $a_n < \left[\dfrac{7}{4}\right]^n$ for each n.

45. The **Fibonacci sequence** $\{u_n\}$ is defined inductively by $u_1 = u_2 = 1$, and for $n \geqslant 2$, $u_n = u_{n-1} + u_{n-2}$. Prove the following:

(a) $\displaystyle\sum_{i=1}^{n} u_i = u_{n+2} - 1$;

(b) $\displaystyle\sum_{i=1}^{n} u_i^2 = u_n u_{n+1}$;

(c) $u_n = \dfrac{\alpha^n - \beta^n}{\alpha - \beta}$, where α, β are the roots of the quadratic equation $x^2 - x - 1 = 0$;

(d) $\alpha^{n-2} \leqslant u_n \leqslant \alpha^{n-1}$ for all n.

46. In Exercise 19(b) above, you were asked to prove that the sum of the first n positive integers was given by $\dfrac{n(n+1)}{2}$. Consider the sum of the squares of the first n positive integers; show that this sum is given by a polynomial in n of degree 3. [HINT: Assuming the existence of the polynomial, use values for the sum to find its coefficients; then use induction to establish the formula.]

47. Find a formula for the sum of the cubes of the first n positive integers.

48. Find a formula for the sum of the fourth powers of the first n positive integers.

49. Consider the field $\mathbf{F}$ of rational functions described in Exercise 0.3.15.

(a) Prove that $\mathbf{F}$ does not possess the Archimedean Property.

(b) Show that there is a member of $\mathbf{F}$ that exceeds every member of the form $\dfrac{n}{1}$, $n \in \mathbf{N}$.

(c) Exhibit a member $g \in \mathbf{F}$, $g > 0$ satisfying for all $n \in \mathbf{N}$, $0 < g \leqslant \dfrac{1}{n}$.

(d) Show that $\mathbf{F}$ does not satisfy the Completeness Axiom, by constructing a nonempty bounded set without a supremum.

50. Set $t_n = \left(1 + \dfrac{1}{n}\right)^n$. Use the Binomial Theorem to show that

$$t_n = 1 + 1 + \frac{1}{2!}\left[1 - \frac{1}{n}\right] + \frac{1}{3!}\left[1 - \frac{1}{n}\right]\left[1 - \frac{2}{n}\right] + \cdots$$

$$+ \frac{1}{n!}\left[1 - \frac{1}{n}\right]\left[1 - \frac{2}{n}\right]\cdots\left[1 - \frac{n-1}{n}\right].$$

Conclude that if $n \geqslant m$, then

$$t_n \geqslant 1 + 1 + \frac{1}{2!}\left[1 - \frac{1}{n}\right] + \frac{1}{3!}\left[1 - \frac{1}{n}\right]\left[1 - \frac{2}{n}\right] + \cdots$$

$$+ \frac{1}{m!}\left[1 - \frac{1}{n}\right]\left[1 - \frac{2}{n}\right]\cdots\left[1 - \frac{m-1}{n}\right].$$

51. If C_k denotes the coefficient of x^k in the binomial expansion of $(1 + x)^n$, prove the following:

(a) $\displaystyle\sum_{k=0}^{n} C_k = 2^n$;

(b) $\displaystyle\sum_{k=0}^{n} (-1)^k C_k = 0$;

Compute: $\displaystyle\sum_{k=0}^{n} C_k^2$ and $\displaystyle\sum_{k=0}^{n} kC_k$.

52. Obtain the following factorizations:

(a) $x^3 + a^3 = (x + a)(x^2 - xa + a^2)$;

(b) $x^3 - a^3 = (x - a)(x^2 + xa + a^2)$;

(c) $x^4 - a^4 = (x - a)(x + a)(x^2 + a^2)$;

(d) $x^4 + a^4 = (x^2 - \sqrt{2}xa + a^2)(x^2 + \sqrt{2}xa + a^2)$;

(e) $x^n - a^n = (x - a)(x^{n-1} + ax^{n-2} + \cdots + a^{n-1})$;

(f) $x^n + a^n = (x + a)(x^{n-1} - ax^{n-2} + \cdots + a^{n-1})$ if n is odd.

53. Let $\mathbf{N} \times \mathbf{N} = \{(m,n) : m, n \in \mathbf{N}\}$. We prescribe the **dictionary ordering** on $\mathbf{N} \times \mathbf{N}$ (see Exercise 0.3.13). That is, $(k,l) > (m,n)$ if and only if either $k > m$ or else, $k = m$ and $l > n$. Prove that every nonempty subset of $\mathbf{N} \times \mathbf{N}$ possesses a least member with respect

to the dictionary ordering. Based on the above ordering, enunciate and prove a Principle of Induction on $\mathbf{N} \times \mathbf{N}$. Mr X. formulates a principle of induction on $\mathbf{N} \times \mathbf{N}$ as follows: Let $S \subseteq \mathbf{N} \times \mathbf{N}$ be such that $(1,1) \in S$ and $(k,l) \in S$ implies $(k+1, l+1) \in S$. Then $S = \mathbf{N} \times \mathbf{N}$.
Will your formulation be equivalent to that of Mr. X?

54. Prove that for any nonzero real numbers a, b, c, and $n \in \mathbf{N}$,

$$(a + b + c)^n = \sum_{i+j+k=n} \frac{n!}{i!\, j!\, k!} a^i b^j c^k, \quad 0 \leqslant i,\, j,\, k \leqslant n, \quad a,\, b,\, c \in \mathbf{R}, \quad n \in \mathbf{N}.$$

55. Define the product of n real numbers, $a_1 \cdot a_2 \cdots a_n$ (denoted by $\prod_{i=1}^{n} a_i$) recursively. Prove that if $0 < a_i < b_i$, $\prod_{i=1}^{n} a_i < \prod_{i=1}^{n} b_i$.

56. Prove the following identity involving binomial coefficients:

$$\binom{p}{0} \binom{q}{n} + \binom{p}{1} \binom{q}{n-1} + \cdots + \binom{p}{n} \binom{q}{0} = \binom{p+q}{n}.$$

[HINT: Consider $(1+x)^{p+q}$.]

0.5 COMPLETENESS: FURTHER CONSEQUENCES

In the last section, we used the Completeness Axiom to establish the basic properties of the positive integers, one of the most important being part (v) of Theorem 0.4.4 and its consequence, the Archimedean Property (see Exercises 0.4.32, 0.4.33). Completeness has two other effects, one **algebraic** and the other **geometric.** It is these effects which we explore now.

The subfield of rational numbers, $\mathbf{Q}$, was developed in the last section (see Exercise 0.4.31). It is straightforward that $\mathbf{Q}$ satisfies the order axioms. We show now that the rational numbers are not **algebraically complete,** in the sense that there is an algebraic equation which has no rational number as a solution.

Theorem 0.5.1.   There does not exist a rational number which satisfies the equation

$$x^2 = 2.$$

Proof.   Let us assume, for the sake of argument, that there is a rational number, $\dfrac{m}{n}$, whose square is 2. First note that we may take m and n positive and that we may also assume that m and n have no common factor (the reasons being implicit in Theorem 0.2.4 and the exercises following). The reader should prove that (Exercise 3): if $2 \cdot k = i \cdot j$, i, j, and k positive integers, then there is a positive integer k' such that $2 \cdot k' = i$ or $2 \cdot k' = j$. We now proceed. By choice of m and n,

$$\frac{m^2}{n^2} = 2$$

whence

$$m^2 = 2 \cdot n^2.$$

Evidently, $m \cdot m = 2 \cdot j$, where $j = n^2$. Thus for some positive integer k, we have $m = 2 \cdot k$, so

$$(2k) \cdot (2k) = 2 \cdot n^2$$

whence by cancellation,

$$2 \cdot k^2 = n^2.$$

It follows that for some k',

$$n = 2 \cdot k'. \qquad\qquad \textbf{(WHY?)}$$

But this means that m and n have a common factor of 2, contrary to the hypothesis! Thus, there can be no rational number whose square is 2. □

Discussion. Geometrically, we say that two line segments are **commensurable** provided their lengths are integral multiples of some fixed length d. As a consequence, when a line segment commensurable with the unit length is placed on the real line, with one end coinciding with the origin, the other end always lies on a rational point $\pm\dfrac{a}{b}$. To say that $\sqrt{2}$ is not a rational number amounts to saying that the diagonal of a square whose side is 1 unit is not commensurable with its side. Thus, if the diagonal is placed on the real line with one end coinciding with 0, the other end will not lie on a rational point. A geometrical proof of the above theorem using this concept can be found in *An Introduction to the Theory of Numbers* by G. H. Hardy and E. M. Wright. □

The above result can be generalized to show that positive integers which are not already perfect squares, that is, the squares of other integers, do not have rational square roots. If we assume for a moment that there is a real number whose square is 2, then we can establish the connection between algebraic completeness and completeness in the sense of our axiom. Let us define a set

$$B = \{x : x \in \mathbf{Q} \text{ and } x^2 \leqslant 2\}.$$

The point is that B is a nonempty set of rationals which does not have a rational number for a supremum; thus, $\mathbf{Q}$ does not satisfy the Completeness Axiom (Exercise 2). We will now use the Completeness Axiom to force the existence of real square roots for positive real numbers.

Theorem 0.5.2. Let x be a positive real number; then there exists a positive real number y such that $y^2 = x$.

Proof. Let x be a given positive real number. There are two cases to treat, $x < 1$ and $x \geqslant 1$; we treat the latter, and leave the former to Exercise 4. Since $1 = 1^2$, we assume $x > 1$. Let

$$B = \{z : 0 < z^2 \leqslant x\}.$$

Evidently, $1 \in B$. Further, note that if $z \in B$, then $z \leqslant x$, since $x < z$ implies

$$x < x^2 < x \cdot z < z^2 \qquad \text{by the order axioms,}$$

which contradicts $z \in B$. It follows that B is a nonempty subset of $\mathbf{R}$ which is bounded above by x. Thus, B has a supremum; call it m. We want to show that $m^2 = x$. To see this, suppose first that $x < m^2$. Let $a = m^2 - x$. Choose $n \in \mathbf{N}$ such that

$$\frac{1}{n} < \frac{a}{2m}.$$

(WHY does such an n exist?) Then $0 < \dfrac{2m}{n} < a$. Since m is the supremum of B, there exists a $z \in B$ such that

$$m - \frac{1}{n} < z < m; \qquad\qquad\qquad \textbf{(WHY?)}$$

evidently, for such a z, we have

$$x = m^2 - a < m^2 - \frac{2m}{n} < m^2 - \frac{2m}{n} + 1 = \left[m - \frac{1}{n} \right]^2 < z^2.$$

This contradicts the fact that $z \in B$; thus $m^2 \leqslant x$. Now suppose on the other hand that this last inequality is strict. Let $a = x - m^2$ and choose $n \in \mathbf{N}$ such that

$$\frac{1}{n} < \frac{a}{2m + 1}.$$

(WHY does this choice of n exist?) For such an n, we have

$$\left[m + \frac{1}{n} \right]^2 = m^2 + \frac{1}{n} \left[2m + \frac{1}{n} \right] \leqslant m^2 + \frac{1}{n}(2m + 1) < m^2 + a = x,$$

which contradicts the choice of m as sup B. Thus, $m = x^2$. $\square$

Discussion. The above proof exemplifies the type of calculations which occur over and over again in elementary analysis. It should be understood that such calculations are not carried out in an *a priori* fashion; rather, once the set B has been written down, our intuition tells us that m should have a certain desired property, in this case, $m^2 = x$. However, this intuition must be tested, and the test will in general be an algebraic manipulation employing the previously established facts. These facts must be in the head, rather than in the textbook at one's side, if one is to hope for success in these endeavors. Further, one should expect to do considerable experimentation before the right calculation is found. In this case, the key is the recognition that if ϵ is 'small', then the quantity $(w + \epsilon)^2$ should be 'close to' w^2. The calculations only formalize this intuition by finding a particular number, in this case $m - \dfrac{1}{n}$ which will witness this intuitive belief. To find the correct value for $\dfrac{1}{n}$, we simply perform suitable algebraic experiments; in the case at hand, we square $\left(m - \dfrac{1}{n} \right)$ and ask how small does $\dfrac{1}{n}$ have to be so that the quantity

$$\frac{2m}{n} - \left[\frac{1}{n} \right]^2 < a.$$

When the answer has been determined, we are ready to write out the proof. ☐

In principle, it might seem that if we add to **Q** all the solutions to polynomial equations that are real, then we should have all the real numbers. This turns out not to be the case, since it is known that there exist real numbers that do not satisfy any polynomial equation. An **algebraic number** is a real number that is a root of a polynomial equation with integer coefficients (see Exercise 10). Real numbers that are not algebraic numbers are called **transcendental numbers**. It turns out that the collection of transcendental numbers is much larger than the collection of algebraic numbers. The numbers e, π, e^π, $2^{\sqrt{2}}$ are some examples of transcendental numbers. The study of these numbers is a very fascinating one, since it is usually very difficult to establish the transcendental nature of some familiar numbers. The transcendentality of e, the base for natural logarithms, was demonstrated by Hermite in 1873. The fact that π is transcendental was proved by F. Lindemann in 1882. Using his result, one could show that $\dfrac{\pi}{2}$, $\pi + 1$, and $\sqrt{\pi}$ are transcendental. The first number that was proved transcendental was not e or π, but a number artificially constructed for this purpose by Liouville in 1844. The existence of a vast infinite supply of transcendentals was proved by Cantor in 1874. The difficulty of identifying a given number as algebraic or transcendental is illustrated by the fact that it is not yet known whether the numbers, π^π, $e\pi$, $e + \pi$ are algebraic or transcendental. The comforting result that any number of the form a^b, where a is an algebraic number different from 0 or 1, and b is an irrational algebraic number, is transcendental, was recently proved. This result is a culmination of a long effort to prove that the so-called **Hilbert number**, $2^{\sqrt{2}}$, is transcendental.

In any case, it is clear that completeness has important algebraic consequences. What about geometry?

If we think again of the real line being drawn as in Figure 0.3.1, then if we draw a line which intersects it, it divides the line into two parts which are almost disjoint; namely, those numbers to the left and those to the right (of course, there should be one in the middle). We can formalize this geometric idea as follows:

Definition. A **cut** (or more precisely, a **Dedekind cut**) of the real line is a pair of nonempty subsets L and R of **R** such that $L \cup R = \mathbf{R}$ and for every $x \in L$ and $y \in R$, $x < y$.

In terms of the geometry, L is the left-hand set and R is the right-hand set. Now the issue of substance here is whether there is a real number x which is in the middle.

The answer is, of course, yes. But this is not a consequence of the field and order axioms, since it may happen that our field is Q and our cut 'passes through' $\sqrt{2}$. Thus, some form of the Completeness Axiom is required. We state now a theorem of Dedekind which is equivalent to our axiom of completeness, but which grows out of an alternative development of the real numbers via the Peano Axioms and Dedekind cuts.

Theorem 0.5.3.   Let L and R define a cut of the real line. Then there is one and only one real number a such that for every $x \in L$ and every $y \in R$, $x \leqslant a \leqslant y$.

The proof of this theorem is left to Exercise 6. We want to emphasize that the historical development of the real numbers was from the positive integers to the rationals to the full reals, where the irrationals were obtained either as cuts of rationals (Dedekind) or as Cauchy sequences (Cantor) or as suprema of sets of rationals. These ideas are explored somewhat in the exercises but for a full treatment, we refer the reader to *Foundations of Analysis* by E. Landau. Historical perspective on these developments may be obtained by consulting *Mathematical Thought from Ancient to Modern Times* by M. Kline.

EXERCISES

1. Set $Q_x = \{y: y \in Q$ and $y \leqslant x\}$, where x is fixed but an arbitrary real number. Prove the following:
   (a) $x = y$ if and only if $Q_x = Q_y$;
   (b) x is the supremum of Q_x;
   (c) when $a = \sqrt{2}$, Q_a has no largest element and that $Q \sim Q_a$ has no least element [Note: $Q \sim Q_a$ denotes the relative complement of Q_a in Q];
   (d) if $R_x = \{y: y \in R$ and $y \leqslant x\}$, then for every x, $\sup R_x = \sup Q_x$.

2. Show that the set $B = \{x: x \in Q$ .and. $x \leqslant 0$ or $x^2 \leqslant 2\}$ does not possess a supremum in Q, and the set $Q \sim B$ has no infimum in Q.

3. Supply the missing details in the proof of Theorem 0.5.1.

4. Complete the proof of Theorem 0.5.2.

5. Supply a proof of Theorem 0.5.3.

6. Show that for any ordered field, Dedekind's Theorem (Theorem 0.5.3) is equivalent to the Completeness Axiom.

7. A natural number p is said to be a **prime number**, if it is divisible only by ± 1 and $\pm p$. Given any prime number p, show that there exists a unique irrational number x satisfying $x^2 = p$.

8. Prove **rational root theorem**: If the rational number $\dfrac{p}{q}$ is a root of the polynomial equation

$$a_n x^n + a_{n-1} x^{n-1} + \cdots + a_1 x + a_0 = 0,$$

where $n \geqslant 1$, a_i ($i = 1, 2, \cdots, n$) are integers, $a_n \neq 0$, and p and q have no common factors, then p divides a_0 and q divides a_n.

9. Use Exercise 8 to prove that the following real numbers are not rational:

$$\sqrt{6}, \quad (17)^{1/5}, \quad \sqrt{\frac{3 + \sqrt{5}}{7}}, \quad (3 + 5\sqrt{2})^{1/3}, \quad \sqrt{1 + 2\sqrt{2} + 3\sqrt{3}}.$$

10. Prove that every rational number is an algebraic number, but not conversely. (Recall that an algebraic number is a root of a polynomial equation of the form

$$a_n x^n + a_{n-1} x^{n-1} + \cdots + a_1 x + a_0 = 0,$$

where $n \geqslant 1$, a_i $(i = 1,2, \cdots ,n)$ are integers and $a_n \neq 0$.) Also, prove that the following numbers are algebraic numbers:

$$\sqrt{2} + 5^{1/3}, \quad \left[\frac{3 - 5\sqrt{6}}{7}\right]^{1/3}, \quad (2 + 3\sqrt{6})^{2/3}, \quad 2 + \sqrt{2} + \sqrt{3} + \sqrt{5}.$$

11. Let $0 \leqslant y$, a fixed real number. We say a nonnegative real number x is an **nth root** of y, (denoted $y^{1/n}$) provided $x^n = y$. Prove that cube and fourth roots exist for any nonnegative real number y. Further show that if $1 \leqslant y$, then

$$y^{1/4} \leqslant y^{1/3} \leqslant y^{1/2}.$$

12. State and prove the general result implicit in Exercise 11.

13. Let $x \geqslant 0$, $x \in \mathbf{R}$. For $m,n \in \mathbf{N}$, $n \neq 0$, define $x^{m/n} = (x^{1/n})^m$. Show that this definition makes sense for all rational powers of nonnegative real numbers except 0^0. Further show that for all $m,n \in \mathbf{N}$, $n \neq 0$

$$(x^{1/n})^m = (x^m)^{1/n}.$$

What can be said about order relations between the various rational powers?

14. If $a, b > 0$ and $\left[\dfrac{a}{b}\right]^2 < 2$, show that

(a) $2 < \left[\dfrac{a + 2b}{a + b}\right]^2$, and

(b) $\left[\dfrac{a + 2b}{a + b}\right]^2 - 2 < 2 - \left[\dfrac{a}{b}\right]^2.$

[Thus, if $\dfrac{a}{b}$ is an approximation for $\sqrt{2}$, then $\dfrac{a + 2b}{a + b}$ is a better approximation.]

15. Prove that Theorem 0.5.2 is false if the word 'real number' is replaced by 'rational number'. Where does the proof break down?

16. Prove that there exists a real number $c > 0$ such that for all integers p and q, with $q \neq 0$, we have

$$|q\sqrt{2} - p| > \frac{c}{q}.$$

More generally, let a be a positive integer and let $\alpha = \sqrt{a}$ be irrational. Show that there exists $c > 0$, such that for all integers p and q, with $q > 0$, we have

$$\left| q\alpha - p \right| > \frac{c}{q}.$$

0.6 ABSOLUTE VALUE

We begin this section with a brief treatment of notation. For real numbers a and b, define

$$[a,b] = \{x: a \leqslant x \leqslant b\} \quad \text{to be the \textbf{closed interval};}$$
$$(a,b) = \{x: a < x < b\} \quad \text{to be the \textbf{open interval}.}$$

One can of course use combinations of the two such as $(a,b]$ or $[a,b)$ (called **half-open intervals**, open at the left end, the right end, respectively) with their obvious meanings. We also introduce two symbols ∞, $-\infty$ (called **infinity, minus infinity**, respectively) with the property that for each real number x, we have the order relation $-\infty < x < \infty$, and make the following abbreviations:

$$[a,\infty) = \{x: a \leqslant x\}$$
$$(a,\infty) = \{x: a < x\}$$
$$(-\infty,b) = \{x: x < b\}$$
$$(-\infty,b] = \{x: x \leqslant b\}$$
$$(-\infty,\infty) = \{x: x \in \mathbf{R}\}$$

The reader should note that ∞ and $-\infty$ are not real numbers, and are used here only for convenience. Thus, at this stage, it is meaningless to talk about expressions like $\infty \pm a$, $\infty \pm -\infty$, $a \cdot \infty$, $\dfrac{\infty}{\infty}$, and so forth, where a is any real number.

Definition. Let x be an arbitrary real number. The quantity, **absolute value** of x, denoted by $|x|$, is defined by

$$|x| = \begin{cases} x, & \text{if } 0 \leqslant x \\ -x, & \text{if } x < 0. \end{cases}$$

Discussion. It is clear from the definition that the absolute value is always nonnegative. One should think of the absolute value of x as a measure of the 'size' of x. Another way to think of it is as the distance from x to the origin, 0, on the real line. In the remainder of this book, many of our calculations will contain absolute values. Often the problem will be to get rid of the absolute value signs. This can be done most simply by dividing the problem into cases as specified by the definition. □

EXAMPLE 1 _____

Find the set of all real numbers satisfying $|x - 6| < 3$.

Solution. According to the definition,

$$|x - 6| = \begin{cases} x - 6, & \text{if } 0 \leqslant x - 6 \\ -(x - 6), & \text{if } x - 6 < 0. \end{cases}$$

We may therefore divide the problem into two cases.

Case 1. $0 \leqslant x - 6$. Under this assumption the problem reduces to solving $x - 6 < 3$, which is clearly equivalent to $x < 9$. Thus the solution set under case 1 is $[6,9)$.

Case 2. $x - 6 < 0$. The basic inequality is $-(x - 6) < 3$, which is equivalent to $6 - x < 3$. This is the same as $3 < x$, whence the solution set under this case is $(3,6)$. Now the solution set for the whole inequality is the union of the two sets found under the two cases, which is $(3,9)$. $\square$

For two real numbers x and y, one of the most fundamental quantities is the absolute value of their difference: $|x - y|$. This nonnegative number may be thought of as the distance between the two numbers on the real line. Thus, if this quantity is small, the numbers are 'close together', while if it is large, they are 'far apart'. The absolute value is the algebraic tool for treating and manipulating that most fundamental geometric idea: **distance.**

EXAMPLE 2
_____

Give a geometric interpretation to the inequality $|x - 6| < 3$.

Solution. The quantity $|x - 6|$ is the distance between x and 6. This distance is required to be less than 3. From Figure 0.6.1 it is obvious that the inequality will be satisfied exactly if x is strictly between $6 - 3$ and $6 + 3$. Thus, the geometry of the situation leads directly to $(3,9)$ as the solution set. $\square$

Discussion. It is immediate that the geometry can lead us directly to the solution set. Indeed, the geometry makes the solution so simple, one wonders why we would bother with the original solution at all! The answer is that while the geometry can make it transparent what the solution set ought to be, the argument based on geometry does not constitute a proof that the purported solution set is in fact the solution set. Only a sequence of statements, each of which is an axiom or a previously established theorem can constitute a proof. *Statements about pictures can not be part of proofs.* But they can and must be at the heart of our intuition. Thus, geometry must be used to show us plausible directions in which to proceed; but the rigor of proof must always be used to keep us from false paths. $\square$

We now establish the basic properties of distance.

Theorem 0.6.1. Let x and y be arbitrary real numbers. Then

(i) $|x - y| = 0$ if and only if $x = y$, otherwise $|x - y| > 0$;
(ii) $|x - y| = |y - x|$;
(iii) for any z, $|x - y| \leqslant |x - z| + |z - y|$.

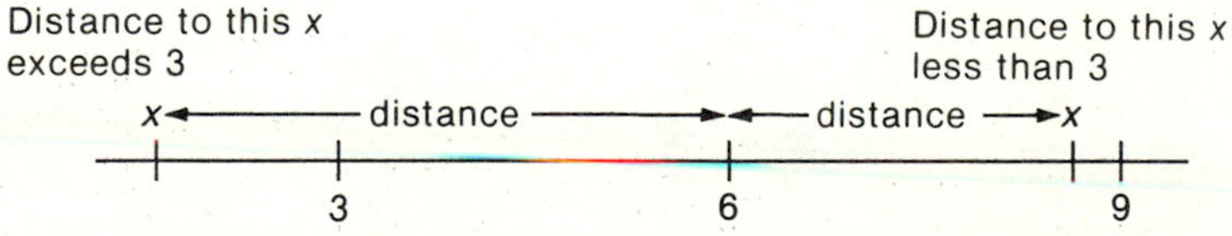

Figure 0.6.1 Geometrical interpretretation of $|x - 6| < 3$ (distance is measured from the number 6).

Proof.   By definition of absolute value, $0 \leqslant |x - y|$. Evidently, this quantity is 0 exactly when $x = y$. For (ii), we may assume without loss of generality that $x - y < 0$. But $-(x - y) = y - x > 0$, whence

$$|x - y| = -(x - y) = y - x = |y - x|$$

as desired. Now for (iii), fix an arbitrary z and consider

$$|x - y| = |(x - z) + (z - y)|.$$

We would like to split the term on the right in the obvious way while achieving the desired inequality. But the fact that

$$|(x - z) + (z - y)| \leqslant |x - z| + |z - y|$$

is an immediate consequence of our next more general theorem. $\square$

Discussion.   Part (iii) of this theorem is known as the **Triangle inequality**. The reason for this is that the inequality has the geometric interpretation which says that the distance between two points is less than or equal to the sum of the distances of the two points to any third point. $\square$

Theorem 0.6.2.   For any pair of real numbers x and y, $|x + y| \leqslant |x| + |y|$.

Proof.   Fix x and y two arbitrary real numbers. We may assume that $x \leqslant y$. Now if $0 \leqslant x$, or $y \leqslant 0$, then we have equality between the two terms. Thus, the situation of interest is when $x < 0 \leqslant y$. There are two possible cases under this assumption: $-x \leqslant y$ and $y < -x$. For the former, we have $x < -x$, whence

$$0 \leqslant x + y < -x + y = |x| + |y|.$$

Since $x + y$ is nonnegative we are done under this assumption. The other case follows by observing that

$$|x + y| = |-x + (-y)|$$

and using the fact just obtained. $\square$

Discussion.   This inequality in its most general form is referred to as **Minkowski's inequality**. It will prove to be very useful in the development of metric spaces (Chapter 12). $\square$

Theorem 0.6.3.   For any real numbers x and y, $\|x| - |y\| \leqslant |x \pm y|$.

Theorem 0.6.4 .   Let x and y be real numbers with $0 < x$, then

$$|y| < x \text{ .if and only if. } -x < y < x.$$

The proofs of these two theorems are left to Exercises 1 and 2. Before closing this section we would like to make several comments on the methods for dealing with inequalities. Theorem 0.6.2 is an essential fact which will be employed repeatedly throughout this book. In many instances it will be used in exactly the manner of

Theorem 0.6.1, namely a situation will be created in which a number z is added and subtracted inside an absolute value and an inequality deduced:

$$|(x - z) + (z - y)| \leqslant |x - z| + |z - y|.$$

Of course the 'z' which is added and subtracted is not chosen at random, but is determined by the situation. The point is that the reader should be prepared for this to happen and ready with the question: why that particular choice of 'z'?

Another observation is on the use of cases to get rid of the absolute value signs in the proof of 0.6.2. This analysis lacks the elegance of a proof which shrewdly employs the fact that $-|x| \leqslant x \leqslant |x|$, but we believe it is more natural in that a systematic analysis of the cases leads to the solution of the problem. We strongly believe that elementary real analysis has an internal consistency which will lead the practitioner to the successful solution of many problems if only he will allow the mathematics to guide him.

Lastly, we remark on the content of Theorem 0.6.1. What is it telling us about distance? It says that the distance between distinct points is positive; the distance between two points is independent of the direction in which it is measured; and finally that the distance between two points is not more than the sum of the distances from the two to any third point. All these are what is required by experience!

EXERCISES

1. Prove Theorem 0.6.3.

2. Prove Theorem 0.6.4.

3. Generalize Theorem 0.6.2 to arbitrary finite sums of real numbers: For $n \in \mathbf{N}$ show that $|\sum_{k=1}^{n} a_k| \leqslant \sum_{k=1}^{n} |a_k|$, where $a_1, a_2, \ldots, a_n$ are any real numbers.

4. Describe the following subsets of $\mathbf{R}$ and find the supremum and infimum of these sets. The domain of n is the set of natural numbers.
   (a) $\{x: |x + 3| < 4\}$ (what is the geometry of this inequality?);
   (b) $\{x: |x^2 - 2| < 4\}$;
   (c) $\{x: |1 - 2x| < x + 1\}$;
   (d) $\{x: |x + 2| + |3 - x| < 4\}$;
   (e) $\left\{ x: |x - 1| < \dfrac{1}{x} \right\}$;
   (f) $\left\{ x: \text{for all } n, \ x < \dfrac{1}{n} \right\}$;
   (g) $\left\{ x: x = \dfrac{n + 1}{n} \right\}$;
   (h) $\{x: |x^3| < 3\}$;
   (i) $\left\{ x: \left| \dfrac{x + 2}{x - 2} \right| < x \right\}$;

(j) $\{x: |5 - 2x| < |2x|\}$;

(k) $\left\{ x: \dfrac{1}{x + |x - 1|} < 2 \right\}$.

5. Show that $|x - a| < \epsilon$ if and only if $a - \epsilon < x < a + \epsilon$.

6. Find the general solution set in **R** for the following inequalities ($a, b, c, d \in \mathbf{R}$):
   (a) $|ax + b| < c$;
   (b) $|ax + b| > c$;
   (c) $|x^2 - (a + b)x + ab| < c$;
   (d) $|x^2 + (a + b)x + ab| \geqslant c$;
   (e) $|(x - a)(x - b)(x - c)| \leqslant d$;
   (f) $|(x + a)(x - b)(x + c)| > d$.

7. For each of the subsets of real numbers in Exercise 4, there is a subset of rationals obtained by adding the condition $x \in \mathbf{Q}$. Repeat Exercise 4 for these sets.

8. Establish the following inequalities for any real numbers x, y, and z:
   (a) $|x \cdot y| = |x| \cdot |y|$;
   (b) $\sqrt{x^2 + y^2} \leqslant x + y$, provided $x, y \geqslant 0$;
   (c) $\left| \dfrac{x}{y} \right| = \dfrac{|x|}{|y|}$, if $y \neq 0$;
   (d) $\dfrac{|x|}{1 + |x|} + \dfrac{|y|}{1 + |y|} \geqslant \dfrac{|x + y|}{1 + |x + y|}$;
   (e) $\left| \dfrac{x}{y} + \dfrac{y}{x} \right| \geqslant 2$ provided $x, y \neq 0$;
   (f) $|x + y| + |x - y| \geqslant |x| + |y|$;
   (g) $2|xy| \leqslant z^2 x^2 + \dfrac{1}{z^2} y^2$, if $z > 0$;
   (h) $|x| + |y| + |z| + |x + y + z| \geqslant |x + y| + |y + z| + |z + x|$.

9. State and prove a result for products which is similar to that in Exercise 3.

10. Show that any open interval of the form (a,b) can be expressed as: $\{x: |x - c| < d\}$, where c and d are fixed real numbers determined by a and b.

11. Show that a subset $S \subseteq \mathbf{R}$ is bounded if and only if there exists a real number $K > 0$, such that $|s| < K$ for all $s \in S$. Formulate a similar criterion for unboundedness.

12. By an **interval** I we mean a set of real numbers having the property that whenever $a, b \in I$, with $a < b$, then $(a,b) \subseteq I$. Show that an interval must have one of the following forms: $[a,b]$, $(a,b]$, $[a,b)$, (a,b), $(-\infty, a]$, $(-\infty, a)$, $[a, \infty)$, (a, ∞) or **R**.

13. Let x and y be arbitrary elements of an ordered field. The **maximum** and the **minimum** of the elements x and y are defined by

$$\max \{x, y\} = \begin{cases} x, & \text{if } y \leqslant x, \\ y, & \text{if } x < y \end{cases}$$

$$\min \{x, y\} = \begin{cases} x, & \text{if } x \leqslant y, \\ y, & \text{if } x < y \end{cases}$$

Prove the following:
(a) $\max \{x, -x\} = |x|$;
(b) $\min \{x, -x\} = -|x|$;

(c) $\max \{x, y\} = \dfrac{x + y + |x - y|}{2};$

(d) $\min \{x, y\} = \dfrac{x + y - |x - y|}{2};$

(e) $- \max \{x, y\} = \min \{-x, -y\};$

(f) If $x < y$, $- \max \{|x|, |y|\} \leqslant x < y \leqslant \max \{|x|, |y|\}$.

14. The **positive part** x^+ of x is defined to be $\max \{0, x\}$, and the **negative part** x^- is $\min \{0, x\}$. Show that $x = x^+ + x^-$, and $|x| = x^+ - x^-$.

15. The **signum** of a real number x is defined by

$$\operatorname{sgn} x = \begin{cases} 1, & x > 0 \\ 0, & x = 0 \\ -1, & x < 0 \end{cases}$$

Prove the following:

(a) $|x| = x \cdot \operatorname{sgn} x;$

(b) $\operatorname{sgn} x \cdot \operatorname{sgn} y = \operatorname{sgn}(xy);$

(c) $\dfrac{\operatorname{sgn} x}{\operatorname{sgn} y} = \operatorname{sgn}\left\{\dfrac{x}{y}\right\}$ if $y \neq 0.$

16. If A is a bounded set of real numbers and if $|a - b| < 1$ for all $a, b \in A$, show that $\sup A - \inf A \leqslant 1$.

Chapter 1

Limits of Sequences

Our purpose now is to begin the careful study of analysis. At this level, we will be following the paths of many eighteenth and nineteenth century mathematicians who concerned themselves with trying to understand such concepts as limit, continuity, and derivative. Their efforts were hampered by the fact that they had an imperfect understanding of the heart of the subject: namely, the structure of the real number system. In fact, it was the existence of the problems associated with trying to correctly define the fundamental concepts which forced mathematicians to come to terms with the structure of the real numbers, and it was only after a deep understanding of the properties of real numbers had been achieved that a full treatment of analysis was obtained. For us, Chapter 0 contains the prerequisite knowledge of the real number system; the reader would do well to remember that the essential facts required in the sequel are to be found in our work on the fundamental properties of real numbers.

1.1 SEQUENCES

The basic tool of analysis is the notion of a 'limit', and the simplest form of limit results from applying the concept to sequences.

Definition. A **sequence** is a function from the set **N** of all positive integers to a subset of the real numbers.

Discussion. A short treatment of the basic tools of set theory including the definitions of ordered pair, function, domain, and range may be found in the Appendix. If the reader is not completely familiar with these, he should study the Appendix with care. The important feature of a sequence is not so much that the domain of the function is the positive integers, but that the range inherits the sequential aspect of the integers.

integers. Thus, we can think of the sequence as moving from range point to range point according to the natural order of the integers.

When specifying sequences, instead of the usual functional notation, we write $\{a_n : n \in \mathbf{N}\}$ or more simply, $\{a_n\}$, by setting a_n to be the value of the function at the natural number $n \in \mathbf{N}$. We will often speak of the sequence

$$a_n = \text{the given functional expression in } n,$$

where this equation defines the nth **term** of the sequence which is simply the value of the sequence at the natural number n. The reader will notice that this notation emphasizes our interest in the range of the function, rather than in the function itself. Often, a sequence is specified by simply providing an explicit formula for the nth term. For example, the specification $a_n = \dfrac{2n}{n^2 + 1}$ is indeed an abbreviation for the function $f : \mathbf{N} \to \mathbf{R}$ defined by $f(n) = a_n$ for each $n \in \mathbf{N}$. On the other hand, a sequence can also be defined recursively. That is, the first term a_1 is specified, and using induction, the term a_{n+1} is described using the knowledge of the previous term a_n (or perhaps, using some a_k, for $k \leqslant n$). For example, a sequence $\{a_n\}$ could be specified by the following recurrence rule: $a_0 = a_1 = 1$, $a_2 = 2$ and for $n \geqslant 0$, $a_{n+3} = 2a_n - a_{n+1} + 3a_{n+2}$. The Fibonacci sequence in Exercise 0.4.45 is an example of such a sequence.   □

The next definition further establishes our identification of a sequence with the range of a function.

Definition.   A sequence, $\{a_n\}$, is said to be **bounded** provided the set $\{a_n : n \in \mathbf{N}\}$ is bounded, that is, there exists a real number B such that for all $n \in \mathbf{N}$, $|a_n| \leqslant B$. A sequence which is not bounded is said to be **unbounded.**

Discussion.   Notice that there is no mention of the domain of the function, which is obviously not a bounded set. The focus is on the range of the function, and the definition merely requires one to check whether the range is a bounded set. As the reader can see, a sequence $\{a_n\}$ is unbounded above if for any given $K > 0$, there exists $n \in \mathbf{N}$ satisfying $a_n > K$.   □

EXAMPLE 1 _____

Graph the sequence whose nth term is given by $a_n = \dfrac{1}{n}$. Show that this sequence is bounded.

Solution.

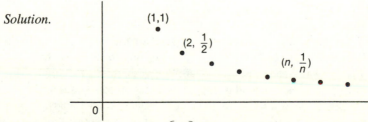

Figure 1.1.1   Graph of the sequence $\left\{\dfrac{1}{n}\right\}$ (two-dimensional).

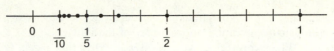

Figure 1.1.2 Graph of a few points of the sequence $\left\{\dfrac{1}{n}\right\}$ (one-dimensional).

Alternately, we may draw a one-dimensional graph of the sequence as shown in Figure 1.1.2.

Let $x \in \{a_n\}$. Then for some $n \in \mathbf{N}$, $x = \dfrac{1}{n}$. From the facts established in Chapter 0, we have $0 < \dfrac{1}{n} \leqslant 1$, whence $\{a_n\}$ is bounded. □

Discussion. Consider Figure 1.1.1. If we allow our eye to move consecutively from $(1,1)$ to $\left[2, \dfrac{1}{2}\right]$ to $\left[3, \dfrac{1}{3}\right]$ to $\cdots$, it becomes apparent that the points of the graph are getting closer and closer to the x-axis. Alternatively, consider the one-dimensional graph of the values of the sequence (Figure 1.1.2 is simply the y-axis of Figure 1.1.1). It we let our eye travel along the axis following the natural order in which the values of the sequence are formed, that is, $1, \dfrac{1}{2}, \dfrac{1}{3}, \dfrac{1}{4}, \cdots$, it is again apparent that the values of the sequence are approaching 0. Intuitively, we might think of the values of the sequence as a collection of stepping-stones forming a path which we are required to trace in a certain order. The issue is: is there a fixed number to which this path leads? For the case above, our intuition tells us that the path leads to 0; it seems reasonable to call this number the limit of the sequence, especially since no value of the sequence is in fact 0. It is also obvious from the picture why this sequence is bounded. □

The struggle to capture this notion of 'approaching to the limit' occupied many mathematicians in the nineteenth century. One result of their struggle was the following:

Definition. Let $\{a_n\}$ be a sequence of real numbers. We say that $\{a_n\}$ **has a limit** in case there exists a real number A such that for every positive real number ϵ, there exists a real number M such that

$$\text{if } n > M, \text{ then } |a_n - A| < \epsilon.$$

The number A is called the **limit** of the sequence $\{a_n\}$.

Discussion. The first thing that this definition does is to assert the existence of a number A. This number remains fixed for the rest of the definition. Thus, if a particular sequence is to satisfy the definition, one must try to find an appropriate candidate for A. The reader is likely familiar with many techniques for finding A from his earlier courses in calculus and should feel free to employ these techniques to find the A's required. The most obvious such technique is simply to calculate various terms of the sequence and to see if they appear to be approaching a fixed number. Having found A, the goal becomes one of proving that the likely candidate does indeed satisfy the definition. The next number mentioned in the definition is ϵ (epsilon). Epsilon is an arbitrary positive real number. The purpose of ϵ is to test whether the sequence is eventually close to A, and further to see if the sequence stays close to A. For a_n to be close to A, we would expect that $|a_n - A|$, which measures the distance from a_n to A, to be a small number; thus, if ϵ is going to be our test number, we would want ϵ to be small, in fact, very small. The way that ϵ tests whether a_n is close to A is by requiring us to find an M such that all the terms whose subscript is larger than M are within a distance of ϵ from A. Since terms with small subscripts are not likely to be very close to A, we would expect M to be a large number, and this will in general be the case. Just how large M will have to be, of course, depends on how small ϵ is. As a general rule, we can say that the smaller ϵ is, the larger an appropriate M will have to be for the definition to be satisfied. Finally, we have allowed M to be any real number; there would be no loss of generality if M were required to be a positive integer (**WHY?**).

Figure 1.1.3 illustrates the limit concept graphically. Consider the horizontal strip of width 2ϵ generated by the lines, $y = A - \epsilon$ and $y = A + \epsilon$. A given term, a_n, of the sequence, $\{a_n\}$, lies inside this strip exactly if the inequality $|a_n - A| < \epsilon$. Thus, for the number, A, to be the limit of the sequence, $\{a_n\}$, we must be able to specify a point, M, on the x-axis, such that for all n lying to the right of M, the corresponding term, a_n, gets trapped within the horizontal strip.   □

Notation.   If $\{a_n\}$ is a sequence having the number A as a limit, we write

$$\lim_{n \to \infty} a_n = A$$

(or simply $\lim a_n = A$) and say **the limit as n tends to infinity** of a_n is A (or, the sequence $\{a_n\}$ **converges** to the limit A).

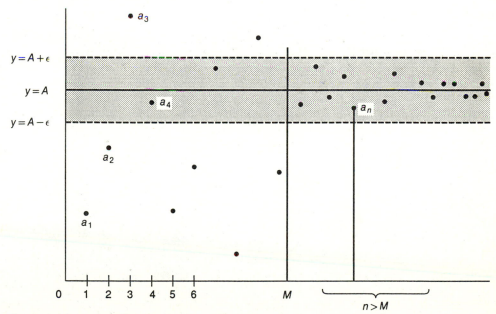

Figure 1.1.3   Geometrical illustration of $\lim_{n \to \infty} a_n = A$.

EXAMPLE 2 _____

Show that $\lim\limits_{n \to \infty} \dfrac{n}{n + 1} = 1$.

Solution. Let $\epsilon > 0$ be fixed, but arbitrary. Now,

$$\left| \frac{n}{n + 1} - 1 \right| = \left| \frac{n - (n + 1)}{n + 1} \right|$$

$$= \left| \frac{-1}{n + 1} \right|$$

$$= \frac{1}{n + 1}$$

by definition of the absolute value. Now, there is a positive integer M, such that $0 < \dfrac{1}{M} < \epsilon$ **(WHY?)**. Fix M with this property. If $n > M$, then

$$\left| \frac{n}{n + 1} - 1 \right| = \frac{1}{n + 1} < \frac{1}{n} < \frac{1}{M} < \epsilon. \qquad \square$$

Discussion. The heart of the computation is finding M, once ϵ has been given. That an M with the desired properties exists was the subject of Exercise 0.4.33. This exercise states a fundamental property about the structure of the real numbers, namely, that for any positive x, there is a positive integer N such that $0 < \dfrac{1}{N} < x$. Further, all the computations, together with the inequalities have also been established in the various exercises of Chapter 0. The example above is highly simplistic; however, it does illustrate the strategy involved in this type of problem. To begin with, the expression $|a_n - A|$ is simplified by algebraic means. The simplified expression is then replaced by other larger expressions, until one is found which can easily be made less than ϵ, provided only that n is sufficiently large. Figure 1.1.4 captures the geometry behind this example.

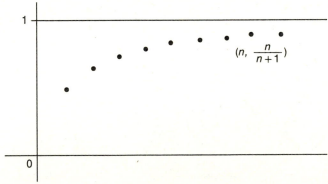

Figure 1.1.4 Graph of the sequence $\left\{ \dfrac{n}{n + 1} \right\}$ illustrating that the limit $= 1$.

In this example, the number A, which is the limit of the sequence, was given. Had it not been, it would have to be found. One way of doing this is to calculate various terms of the sequence. For example, $a_{10} = \dfrac{10}{11}$, while $a_{100} = \dfrac{100}{101}$, and so forth. Alternatively, a little judicious algebra is also a useful tool, as we will continually reiterate throughout this book. In the present case, one observes that

$$\frac{n}{n+1} = \frac{\dfrac{n}{n}}{\dfrac{n}{n} + \dfrac{1}{n}} = \frac{1}{1 + \dfrac{1}{n}}.$$

Since it is a well-known fact that the quantity $\dfrac{1}{n}$ becomes arbitrarily small as n becomes arbitrarily large, it is clear that the limit must be 1. □

EXAMPLE 3

Show that $\lim\limits_{n \to \infty} (\sqrt{n+1} - \sqrt{n}) = 0$.

Solution.   Fix $\epsilon > 0$. Then,

$$|\sqrt{n+1} - \sqrt{n}| = (\sqrt{n+1} - \sqrt{n}) \cdot \left[\frac{\sqrt{n+1} + \sqrt{n}}{\sqrt{n+1} + \sqrt{n}} \right]$$

$$= \frac{1}{\sqrt{n+1} + \sqrt{n}},$$

where the absolute value signs may be dispensed with, since n is a positive integer, whence all quantities are positive. It is straightforward that the last quantity is in fact less than $\dfrac{1}{2\sqrt{n}}$. Let $M = \dfrac{1}{\epsilon^2}$. Evidently, if $n > M$, then

$$\frac{1}{\epsilon} = \sqrt{M} < \sqrt{n} < 2\sqrt{n}.$$

Thus, for such an M and n, $|\sqrt{n+1} - \sqrt{n}| < \epsilon$, as desired. □

Discussion.   Again, note the strategy: use algebra to simplify the absolute value of the difference; replace the simplified quantity by another, larger quantity, which can easily be seen to be less than ϵ when n is sufficiently large. Evidently, the heart of the matter is an algebraic calculation; namely, we rationalize the numerator to get rid of the square roots, a technique which should have long since been part of the reader's algebraic tools.

The reader may wonder about the use of ϵ^2. The problem is that we must determine how large to choose M. If we start with

$$\frac{1}{2\sqrt{M}} < \epsilon,$$

this is equivalent to

$$\frac{1}{\epsilon} < 2\sqrt{M}$$

which in turn is equivalent to

$$\frac{1}{\epsilon^2} < 4M.$$

In the argument above, we have omitted the 4 since if the inequality is satisfied without the term 4, it will be all the more satisfied when the term 4 is present.

This same calculation, rationalizing, also finds the limit, had it not been given, since it is intuitively clear that $\dfrac{1}{\sqrt{n+1} + \sqrt{n}}$ must have 0 as a limit. □

One might think that all sequences have limits. However, a little thought will convince one that a sequence which gets large without bound cannot possibly have a limit. Once one knows that some sequences have limits while others do not, it becomes clear that it would be a good idea to understand how a sequence can fail to have a limit, or **diverge.** As a first step in the process, we take the definition of **convergent** sequence (one having a limit) and form its negation.

Negation of the Limit Definition

A sequence $\{a_n\}$ does not have a limit if for every real number A, there exists a positive ϵ such that for every M there exists an $n > M$ with $|a_n - A| \geq \epsilon$.

Discussion. The negation tells us that we must show that no real number can be the limit. Thus, an argument showing a sequence does not have a limit will start by picking an arbitrary real number which is then fixed and shown ultimately not to be the limit. Next an ϵ is found which will witness the fact that the sequence does not *stay* close to this previously picked A. We emphasize *stay*. Some terms of the sequence may get closer and closer to A, but they cannot all stay close to A after a certain point. Thus, no matter how large M is taken, we must always find terms with subscript exceeding M whose distance from A is at least as large as ϵ. It seems intuitively clear that a sequence such as $\{n^2\}$ will not have a limit, because no matter what our concept of infinity is, the terms of this sequence are clearly headed there in a hurry. We consider two examples, now, which illustrate the two reasons why a sequence can fail to have a limit. □

EXAMPLE 4 _____

Show that the sequence $\{n^2\}$ has no limit.

Solution. Let A be a fixed but arbitrary real number. Let $\epsilon = 1$, and set

$$K = |A| + 1.$$

If $n \geq K$, then

$$|n^2 - A| \geq ||n^2| - |A|| \quad \text{(by Theorem 0.6.3)}$$
$$\geq |(|A| + 1) - |A|| \qquad \textbf{(WHY?)}$$
$$= 1.$$

We have therefore shown that every term of sufficiently large subscript, $n \geq \max\{K,M\}$ for any choice of M, is not within ϵ distance of A. □

Discussion. The terms of the sequence $\{n^2\}$ obviously get large without bound, whence this sequence is unbounded. With this intuitive fact in our minds we set about trying to show that the negation of the limit definition is satisfied. From the negation, we see that the candidate for the limit, A, is arbitrary, which means that we can make no special assumptions about it. We can, however, choose ϵ, subject only to the requirement that ϵ is positive. In the solution, we have taken ϵ to be 1. It happens to be the case that for a sequence which gets large without bound, any positive real number will do as a choice for ϵ. (To see this, the reader should try carrying out the argument employing $\epsilon = 100$, or some other large number.) As stated, we have no control over A. This fact is accounted for in the argument by making the choice of M depend on the value of A, as well as the value of ϵ.

The argument for unbounded sequences is inherently simpler than an argument showing that a bounded sequence does not have a limit, and this example should be thoroughly understood as a prerequisite to the next case. To conclude this discussion, it seems apparent that we should expect convergent sequences to be bounded. □

EXAMPLE 5 _____

Show that the sequence $\left\{ (-1)^n \left[\dfrac{1}{2} - \dfrac{1}{n} \right] \right\}$ has no limit.

Solution. Fix A. Let $\epsilon = \dfrac{1}{3}$. For the given M, set $n \geq \max\{M,6\}$. There are two possibilities concerning A: that A is nonnegative, or that A is negative. Let us assume the former and also that $n = 2k + 1$ for some $k \in \mathbf{N}$. Then,

$$\left| (-1)^n \left[\frac{1}{2} - \frac{1}{n} \right] - A \right| = \left| (-1) \left[\left[\frac{1}{2} - \frac{1}{n} \right] + A \right] \right|$$

$$\geq \left| \frac{1}{2} - \frac{1}{n} \right| \qquad \textbf{(WHY?)}$$

$$\geq \left| \frac{1}{2} - \frac{1}{6} \right| = \frac{1}{3}.$$

The case when A is negative is treated similarly under the assumption that $n = 2k$ for some positive integer k. □

Discussion. This sequence is bounded. It is intuitively clear that an unbounded sequence cannot have a limit, since all the terms cannot eventually be close to a single fixed real number. To understand the intuitive reason this bounded sequence does not have a limit, we notice that there are two distinct numbers to which the terms of the sequence get close; namely, the odd terms are near $-\dfrac{1}{2}$ and the even terms are near

$\frac{1}{2}$ (see Figure 1.1.5). (As well, it would be instructive to the reader to create a table of the odd and even terms for this sequence.) Notice also that the odd terms get as close as we please to $-\frac{1}{2}$ and in fact stay that close, while the even terms get as close as we please to $\frac{1}{2}$ and also stay that close. Thus, this sequence seems to 'wander' or 'oscillate'. A bounded sequence which has no limit will always 'wander' or 'oscillate' in the sense that there will be at least two distinct numbers which its terms are sometimes close to, as in this example. Once these two numbers are known, a proof of divergence of the type given is easily constructed. We simply choose ϵ to be less than half the absolute value of the difference of the two numbers (in this case, $\frac{1}{3}$ is less than $\frac{1}{2} \cdot 1$) and use the fact that no matter what value of A is chosen, this value cannot be arbitrarily close to both the two numbers simultaneously. This permits us to find a suitably large M, which must exist, since some of the terms are eventually close to one of the two numbers, while other terms are eventually close to the other of the two numbers. The reader should study the example until he thoroughly understands how this strategy has been employed.   □

The problem of deciding whether or not a given sequence has a limit can be thought of as a game between two players, P1 and P2. The player P1 supplies A and M's, while the player P2 supplies ϵ's. To see how this game works, let us consider the sequences

$$\left\{ \frac{100}{n} \right\} \quad \text{and} \quad \left\{ \frac{(-1)^n}{2} \right\}.$$

The game starts by player P1 declaring A. In the case of the sequence $\left\{ \frac{100}{n} \right\}$ the smart player would set $A = 0$. P2 then names an ϵ and it is up to P1 to then find an M such that the definition is satisfied. Let us suppose that P2 sets $\epsilon = 1$. P1 would then set $M = 100$, and would note that if $n > 100$, then $\left| \frac{100}{n} - 0 \right| < 1$. P2 would then reply that 1 was pretty large for ϵ and set $\epsilon = \frac{1}{100}$. P1 now has to find a new M; in this case he might set $M = 10{,}000$, and would observe that if $n > M$, then $\left| \frac{100}{n} - 0 \right| < \frac{1}{100}$. It is clear that for this sequence no matter how small P2 chooses ϵ, P1 can always find an M such that $n > M$ implies $\left| \frac{100}{n} - 0 \right| < \epsilon$. So

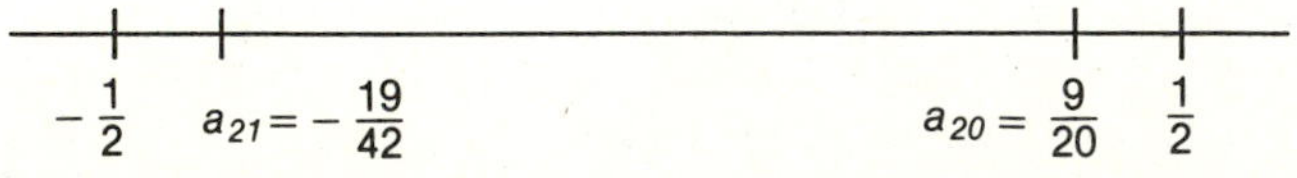

Figure on number line showing points: $-\frac{1}{2}$, $a_{21} = -\frac{19}{42}$, $a_{20} = \frac{9}{20}$, $\frac{1}{2}$.

Figure 1.1.5 In Example 4, odd terms get close to $-\frac{1}{2}$ and, even terms get close to $\frac{1}{2}$.

in this case we say P1 wins the game, for the simple reason that P1 has only to choose $M \geqslant \dfrac{100}{\epsilon}$.

For the second sequence, P1 might start off by declaring $A = \dfrac{1}{2}$. P2 sets $\epsilon = \dfrac{1}{2}$ as well. P1 then takes $M = 200$. P2 then points out that $a_{501} = -\dfrac{1}{2}$ and that $\left| -\dfrac{1}{2} - \dfrac{1}{2} \right| \geqslant \dfrac{1}{2}$. P1 then tries a new M, say $M = 1000$. But P2 can easily show, by using a_{1001}, that this choice does not work either. P1 then tries a new tack by changing A, say setting $A = -\dfrac{1}{2}$. P2 is happy with $\epsilon = \dfrac{1}{2}$. P1 tries $M = 10{,}000$. P2 then points out that $a_{20{,}000} = \dfrac{1}{2}$ and that $\left| \dfrac{1}{2} - \dfrac{-1}{2} \right| > \dfrac{1}{2}$. It should be clear that for the second sequence, no matter how P1 picks A, by sticking with $\epsilon = \dfrac{1}{2}$, P2 can prevent P1 from finding a suitable M so that the conclusion of the definition is satisfied. Thus, in this case we say that P2 wins the game. Of course there is a win for the first player exactly if the sequence has a limit, and a win for the second player exactly if the sequence does not have a limit.

In Exercise 2, we ask the reader to obtain limits using the definition. It is only by doing these exercises that you, the student, can hope to become comfortable with the limit definition. It is essential that you do so, since the various limit definitions are the fundamental tools of the subject.

EXERCISES

1. Complete the missing details in the solution to Example 5.

2. Use the definition of the limit to establish the existence or nonexistence of limits for the following sequences:

   (a) $\left\{ \dfrac{n^2 + 1}{n + 10} \right\};$ (b) $\left\{ \dfrac{n}{n^2 + 1} \right\};$

   (c) $\left\{ (-1)^n \left[\dfrac{1}{10} - \dfrac{1}{n} \right] \right\};$ (d) $\left\{ (-1)^n \left[\dfrac{1}{100} - \dfrac{1}{n} \right] \right\};$

   (e) $\left\{ \dfrac{1 + (-1)^n}{2} \right\};$ (f) $\left\{ (-1)^n n \right\};$

   (g) $\left\{ \dfrac{2n + 1}{n + 3} \right\};$ (h) $\left\{ \dfrac{1}{2n + 5} \right\};$

   (i) $\left\{ \dfrac{6n^2}{1 - 5n^2} \right\};$ (j) $\left\{ \dfrac{(-1)^n 6n^3}{1 + 4n^3} \right\};$

(k) $\{\sin n\pi\}$;

(l) $\left\{\sin\dfrac{n\pi}{2}\right\}$;

(m) $\left\{\dfrac{\sin n}{n^2}\right\}$;

(n) $\left\{\dfrac{1}{2}\left[1 - \left[-\dfrac{1}{2}\right]^n\right]\right\}$;

(o) $\left\{\dfrac{2^n}{n^5}\right\}$;

(p) $\left\{\dfrac{n^3}{2^n}\right\}$;

(q) $\left\{\dfrac{n^6}{3^n}\right\}$;

(r) $\left\{\dfrac{(-1)^n n^4}{2^n}\right\}$;

(s) $\left\{\sqrt{\dfrac{n}{2n+1}}\right\}$;

(t) $\left\{\dfrac{1}{(2n-9)^{\frac{1}{3}}}\right\}$;

(u) $\{\sqrt{n+3} - \sqrt{n}\}$;

(v) $\left\{\dfrac{2^n}{n!}\right\}$;

(w) $\{\sqrt{2n} - \sqrt{n}\}$;

(x) $\left\{\dfrac{100^n}{n!}\right\}$;

(y) $\left\{\dfrac{n!}{n^n}\right\}$;

(z) $\{(n+1)^{2/3} - n^{2/3}\}$;

(a′) $\left\{\dfrac{2^n - (-2)^n}{n}\right\}$;

(b′) $\{\sqrt{4n^2 + n} - 2n\}$;

(c′) $a_n = \begin{cases} \dfrac{n}{2n+1}, & \text{if } n \text{ is odd} \\[2mm] \dfrac{3n-5}{6n+1}, & \text{if } n \text{ is even;} \end{cases}$

(d′) $a_n = \begin{cases} 2, & \text{if } n = 3k, \ k \in \mathbf{N} \\[2mm] \dfrac{2}{n^2}, & \text{if } n = 3k - 1, k \in \mathbf{N} \\[2mm] 2^n, & \text{if } n = 3k - 2, k \in \mathbf{N}. \end{cases}$

3. Given $\epsilon = 0 \cdot 0000005$, find a suitable M such that for $n > M$,

$$\left| \frac{2n^3 + 5n}{3n^3 - 6} - \frac{2}{3} \right| < \epsilon.$$

Repeat the exercise with $\epsilon = 0 \cdot 005, 0 \cdot 5$, and 2.5.

4. Consider the two-player game described at the end of the section. For the sequence given by

$$a_n = \frac{(-1)^n(1 + n)}{4n},$$

show that P2 has a win. What is an upper bound on ϵ, so that if P2 chooses ϵ less than this upper bound, P2 will be guaranteed a win?

5. Evaluate $\lim_{n\to\infty} t_n$, where t_n is defined as follows:

(a) $t_n = \left[\dfrac{1}{n^2} + \dfrac{2}{n^2} + \cdots + \dfrac{n}{n^2} \right]$;

(b) $t_n = \left[1 - \dfrac{1}{2} \right]\left[1 - \dfrac{1}{3} \right]\left[1 - \dfrac{1}{4} \right] \cdots \left[1 - \dfrac{1}{n} \right]$;

(c) $t_n = \left[1 - \dfrac{1}{2^2} \right]\left[1 - \dfrac{1}{3^2} \right]\left[1 - \dfrac{1}{4^2} \right] \cdots \left[1 - \dfrac{1}{n^2} \right]$;

(d) $t_n = \left[\dfrac{1}{1 \cdot 2} + \dfrac{1}{2 \cdot 3} + \cdots + \dfrac{1}{n \cdot (n + 1)} \right]$;

(e) $t_n = \dfrac{1 - 2 + 3 - 4 + \cdots - 2n}{\sqrt{n^2 + 1}}$;

(f) $t_1 = \dfrac{1}{2}$, $t_{n+1} = t_n + \dfrac{1}{(n + 1)(n + 2)}$ $(n > 1)$;

(g) $t_n = \dfrac{r_n}{5}$ where r_n is the remainder when n is divided by 9.

6. If $a_n = a$ for all n, prove that the constant sequence $\{a_n\}$ converges to the limit a. Prove that $\lim a_n = A$ if and only if $\lim b_n = 0$, where $b_n = a_n - A$ for each $n \in \mathbf{N}$.

7. Let $\{a_n\}$ and $\{b_n\}$ be two sequences. If there exists an integer k such that $a_n = b_n$ for $n > k$, show that either $\{a_n\}$ and $\{b_n\}$ have the same limit, or else both fail to have limits.

8. Given a sequence $\{a_n\}$, define the sequence $\{b_n\}$ by setting $b_n = a_{n+k}$, where $k \in \mathbf{N}$ is fixed. Show that $\{b_n\}$ converges if and only if $\{a_n\}$ converges, and in that case, $\lim_{n\to\infty} b_n = \lim_{n\to\infty} a_n$.

9. If a real number b appears an infinite number of times as an element of a convergent sequence $\{a_n\}$, prove that $\lim_{n\to\infty} a_n = b$.

10. If $\{a_n\}$ is convergent, and if $a_n \leqslant A$ for all n (after a certain stage), show that $\lim a_n \leqslant A$.

11. If $\{a_n\}$ and $\{b_n\}$ are two convergent sequences satisfying $a_n < b_n$ for all n, can you conclude that $\lim a_n < \lim b_n$?

12. If $\{a_n\}$ converges to a limit $L > 0$, show that there exists $M > 0$ such that $|a_n| > \dfrac{L}{2}$ for $n > M$.

13. Give examples of
(a) a sequence of rational numbers having an irrational number as limit;
(b) a sequence of irrational numbers having a rational number as limit.

14. If the sequence $\{a_n\}$ is such that the two sequences $\{a_{2n}\}$ and $\{a_{2n+1}\}$ formed by the even and the odd terms of $\{a_n\}$ both converge to L, prove that $\lim_{n\to\infty} a_n = L$.

15. Let $f: \mathbf{N} \to \mathbf{N}$ be a one-to-one and onto function. Then the sequence $\{f(n)\}$ is a **rearrangement** of $\mathbf{N}$. A sequence $\{b_n\}$ is said to be a **rearrangement** of a sequence $\{a_n\}$ if there exists a rearrangement $\{f(n)\}$ of $\mathbf{N}$ such that $b_{f(n)} = a_n$. Prove that $\{a_n\}$ converges to a limit L if and only if any rearrangement $\{b_n\}$ has limit L.

16. Give a formal proof that for $b > 0$, $\lim_{n\to\infty} \dfrac{[\,bn\,]}{bn} = 1$, where $[x]$ denotes the greatest integer not exceeding x. Hence or otherwise, show that for $a > 0$, $b > 0$, $\lim\limits_{n \to \infty} \dfrac{[\,bn\,]}{an} =$

$\dfrac{b}{a}$, and $\lim\limits_{n \to \infty} \left[\dfrac{1}{an} \right] bn = 0$.

17. We say that the sequence $\{a_n\}$ **diverges to** $+\infty$ (written $\lim a_n = +\infty$) provided given $K \in \mathbf{R}$ there exists $M \in \mathbf{R}$ satisfying $n > M$ implies $a_n \geqslant K$.
    Define '**diverges to** $-\infty$'. Which of the nonconvergent sequences in Exercise 2 above diverge to $+\infty$ or $-\infty$?

18. If $\{a_n\}$ diverges to $+\infty$ and if there exists n_0 such that for $n > n_0$, $b_n \geqslant a_n$, prove that $\{b_n\}$ diverges to $+\infty$.

19. Let $\{a_n\}$ be a sequence with $a_n > 0$ for all n and $\lim \dfrac{a_{n+1}}{a_n} = A > 1$. Prove that $\lim a_n = +\infty$. What happens when $A = 1$?

20. Given an arbitrary sequence $\{a_n\}$, one can construct a new sequence $\{b_n\}$ by any of the following operations (to be made precise by the reader):
    (a) deleting a finite number of terms;
    (b) inserting a finite number of terms;
    (c) deleting an infinite number of terms;
    (d) deleting every second term;
    (e) inserting an infinite number of terms at random places;
    (f) inserting a 0 between every consecutive term;
    (g) altering a finite number of terms;
    (h) altering an infinite number of terms.
    Which of these operations will affect the convergence properties of the sequence $\{b_n\}$ in relation to the sequence $\{a_n\}$?

1.2 BASIC LIMIT THEOREMS

In this section we establish the basic theorems which govern the behavior of limits of sequences. The reader should begin looking for patterns, because, as we shall see, many of these results are repeated over again for the different types of limits, and also because the methods which are used to obtain the results are limited in number. We shall try to emphasize this internal structure as we proceed.

Theorem 1.2.1. The limit of a sequence, if it exists, is unique.

Proof. Let $\{a_n\}$ be an arbitrary convergent sequence. Let A and B be any two real numbers both of which are limits of the sequence $\{a_n\}$. We assume for the sake of argument that $A \neq B$. It follows that $|A - B| > 0$. Call this positive quantity d. Let $\epsilon = \dfrac{d}{3}$. Now since A is a limit, there is a real number M_A, depending on A, such that if $n \geqslant M_A$, then $|a_n - A| < \epsilon$. Further, since B is a limit, there is an $M_B \in \mathbf{R}$ such that if $n \geqslant M_B$, then $|a_n - B| < \epsilon$. Let M be the maximum of M_A and M_B. Then, if $n \geqslant M$,

$$|a_n - A| < \epsilon \quad \text{and} \quad |a_n - B| < \epsilon.$$

Now, without loss of generality, we may assume that $A < B$. Under this assumption, using Theorem 0.6.4 and observing that $B - A > 2\epsilon$, we have

$$a_n < A + \epsilon < B - \epsilon < a_n. \qquad \textbf{(WHY?)}$$

But this is clearly absurd. □

Discussion. In the solutions presented in the last section, we have seen that the calculations of arithmetic are the essential tools with which our arguments will be created. As can be seen above, these tools are also used in the creation of proofs. All of the necessary arithmetic was developed in Chapter 0. Moreover, a standard of proof was laid down there as well. In the arguments presented from this point forward, we shall employ the tools of arithmetic without explicit reference to which particular tool is required in a specific instance. Thus, for example, we have asserted above that $|A - B| > 0$; no reference is given as to which arithmetical fact would permit this conclusion; it is assumed that the reader can (and will) fill in the necessary arithmetical steps so that the arguments given can be brought to the standard of proof given in Chapter 0. All our arguments, whether as proofs for theorems or as solutions to examples must be able to meet this standard; this can be accomplished provided we are always able to supply the missing steps, which for the instance above means being able to show why the fact that $A - B \neq 0$ implies that $|A - B| > 0$. In this regard, no step may be taken as 'obvious' until the supporting justification is understood in its entirety!

Turning now to the details of the proof, notice the similarity of this proof to the technique employed in Example 1.1.5 shows that 'oscillating' sequences do not have limits. The reader should also compare this proof with the proof of Theorem 0.4.1 which asserts that the supremum is unique. The geometry of the situation is made clear in Figure 1.2.1. The reader should make clear to himself why there is no loss of generality involved in making the assumption that $A < B$. Also, the details leading to the set of inequalities at the end of the proof that force the contradiction $a_n < a_n$ should be fully worked out.

A contradiction could also be arrived at as follows: Note that $d = |A - B| = |(A - a_n) + (a_n - B)| \leqslant |a_n - A| + |a_n - B| < \epsilon + \epsilon = 2\epsilon < d$. The process of 'adding' and 'subtracting' an equal quantity, and using the triangle inequality is a standard technique, which the reader should grasp thoroughly. □

Theorem 1.2.2. Let $\{a_n\}$, $\{b_n\}$, and $\{c_n\}$ be sequences such that for every $n \in \mathbf{N}$,

$$a_n \leqslant b_n \leqslant c_n.$$

If $\{a_n\}$ and $\{c_n\}$ both converge to A, then $\{b_n\}$ also converges to A.

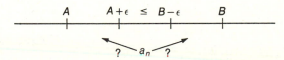

Figure 1.2.1 Contradiction resulting from the assumption that limit is not unique (Theorem 1.2.1).

Proof. Let $\epsilon > 0$ be fixed. By hypothesis there is an M_1 such that if $n \geqslant M_1$, then $|a_n - A| < \epsilon$. Similarly, there is an M_2 such that $n \geqslant M_2$ implies $|c_n - A| < \epsilon$. Let M be the larger of M_1 and M_2. Now, if $n \geqslant M$, then

$$A - \epsilon < a_n \leqslant b_n \leqslant c_n < A + \epsilon. \qquad \textbf{(WHY?)}$$

It follows that

$$|b_n - A| < \epsilon,$$

as desired. Since ϵ was arbitrary, we are done.   □

Discussion. Notice how the proof flows naturally from writing down the definition of convergence of a_n to A, followed by the definition of convergence of c_n to A, followed by choosing A so that the conditions are satisfied simultaneously. We then use Theorem 0.6.4 to manipulate the inequalities and obtain the desired form. Again, the geometry is clear and is shown in Figure 1.2.2. For obvious reasons, this theorem is often call the 'sandwich' theorem (or a 'squeeze' theorem) for sequences.   □

The next theorem spells out an important property possessed by all convergent sequences.

Theorem 1.2.3. Every convergent sequence is bounded.

Proof. Let $\{a_n\}$ be an arbitrary convergent sequence. We must find a real number B such that for every $n \in \mathbf{N}$,

$$|a_n| \leqslant B.$$

To find B, let $\epsilon = 1$, and find M such that if $n \geqslant M$, then

$$|a_n - A| < \epsilon,$$

where A is the limit of the sequence. We may suppose that M is in fact a positive integer (**WHY?**). Now the set

$$\{|a_n|: n \leqslant M\}$$

is a finite set and so has a maximum, say B_1. Let B be the maximum of B_1 and $|A| + 1$. Evidently, for $n \leqslant M$, $|a_n| \leqslant B_1 \leqslant B$. For $n > M$, $|a_n - A| < 1$, whence $|a_n| \leqslant |A| + 1 \leqslant B$. Thus, for all n, $|a_n| \leqslant B$.   □

Discussion. The intuition leading to this theorem is quite simple. First, the definition of limit states that for A to be the limit of a sequence, all the terms of the sequence having large subscript must be 'close to' A. Since there are only a finite number of terms having small subscript, and every finite set of real numbers is bounded, we ought to be able to construct a bound for all the terms of the sequence. The proof only formalizes these intuitive reasonable ideas.

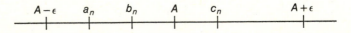

Figure 1.2.2 Geometrical illustration of 'sandwich theorem.'

The contrapositive equivalent of the above theorem asserts that a sequence that is not bounded can never converge. This is a useful tool in deciding the nonconvergence of certain sequences, where it might be a lot easier to check that the sequence is unbounded (for example, the sequence $\{n^3\}$).

The statement of the above theorem is an implication, where the hypothesis is that the sequence is convergent, and the conclusion is that it is bounded. The reader should ask the question: What about the converse? In this case, the converse turns out to be false. An easy counterexample would be the sequence discussed in Example 1.1.5. Then, the natural question would be: What additional conditions are needed to guarantee that the converse also holds? This is explored in the next section.

$\square$

Our next several theorems concern operations on sequences. Just as one can think of adding two real numbers, so one could imagine adding together two sequences:

$$\{a_n\} + \{b_n\}.$$

The quantity displayed makes clear our intent, namely, to combine two sequences by an additive process; it does not, however, give any indication how this process might be performed. For sequences, we have settled on performing operations 'term by term'. This yields a defining equation

$$\{a_n\} + \{b_n\} = \{a_n + b_n : n \in \mathbf{N}\}.$$

In this equation, the operation on the left, which has been denoted by a standard $+$ sign, is defined in terms of a computation which we know how to perform and which is given on the right. Namely, we know how to add two numbers, and this is what the $+$ sign on the right-hand side requires us to do. This definition extends our usual definition of addition of numbers. Also, it is merely an example of the usual definition for addition of functions, with which the reader is almost certainly familiar.

Having defined addition of two sequences, we can immediately think of multiplying or dividing sequence, or of taking the absolute value of a sequence. In all cases, standard usage requires these operations to be performed, term by term. Thus,

$$\{a_n\} \cdot \{b_n\} = \{a_n \cdot b_n\},$$

and if $b_n \neq 0$ for every $n \in \mathbf{N}$, then, we define

$$\frac{\{a_n\}}{\{b_n\}} = \left\{ \frac{a_n}{b_n} \right\}.$$

Also, the absolute value of the sequence $\{a_n\}$ is given by $|\{a_n\}| = \{|a_n|\}$.

Having specified operations on sequences, we are led to obvious questions. One such question is: If $\{a_n\}$ converges to A, and $\{b_n\}$ converges to B, to what, if anything, will $\{a_n + b_n\}$ converge? This type of question is addressed in the following theorems.

Theorem 1.2.4. Let $\{a_n\}$ and $\{b_n\}$ be sequences having A and B as limits, respectively. Then $\{a_n + b_n\}$ converges to $A + B$.

Proof. Fix $\epsilon > 0$. Let M_1 be chosen such that $n \geqslant M_1$ implies $|a_n - A| < \dfrac{\epsilon}{2}$. Let M_2 be chosen such that $n \geqslant M_2$ implies $|b_n - B| < \dfrac{\epsilon}{2}$. Set $M = \max \{M_1, M_2\}$. It follows that

$$\begin{aligned}
|(a_n + b_n) - (A + B)| &= |(a_n - A) + (b_n - B)| \\
&\leqslant |a_n - A| + |b_n - B| \\
&< \frac{\epsilon}{2} + \frac{\epsilon}{2} = \epsilon,
\end{aligned}$$

whenever $n \geqslant M$. $\square$

Discussion. From the sequence of statements in the proof, it appears as if one knows how to choose M_1 and M_2 before doing the calculation which splits the sum into its constituent parts by using the triangle inequality (Theorem 0.6.2). This is not the case. In fact, one experiments with the calculation first, and then having found out how to choose M_1 and M_2 in terms of $\dfrac{\epsilon}{2}$, we write down the proof accordingly. Thus, in the proof above, we preferred to choose M_1, M_2 such that the quantities $|a_n - A|$, $|b_n - B|$ are each less than $\dfrac{\epsilon}{2}$, rather than ϵ, because in the final calculation, we want $|(a_n + b_n) - (A + B)| < \epsilon$. The choice of $\dfrac{\epsilon}{2}$ is not obligatory, for if we choose $|a_n - A|$ and $|b_n - B|$ less that ϵ each, then in the final step, $|(a_n + b_n) - (A + B)| < 2\epsilon$, and the conclusion will still be valid (**WHY?**). The reader should note the use of Theorem 0.6.2, which will be a consistent feature of many of our elementary arguments. $\square$

Theorem 1.2.5. Let $\{a_n\}$ and $\{b_n\}$ be sequences converging to A and B, respectively. Then the sequence $\{a_n \cdot b_n\}$ converges to $A \cdot B$.

Proof. Fix $\epsilon > 0$. Consider,

$$\begin{aligned}
|a_n \cdot b_n - A \cdot B| &= |(a_n \cdot b_n - b_n \cdot A) + (b_n \cdot A - A \cdot B)| \\
&\leqslant |a_n \cdot b_n - b_n \cdot A| + |b_n \cdot A - A \cdot B| \\
&= |b_n| \cdot |a_n - A| + |A| \cdot |b_n - B|.
\end{aligned}$$

Now $\{b_n\}$ is a convergent sequence, so by Theorem 1.2.4, there is a positive real number K such that $|b_n| < K$ for all $n \in \mathbf{N}$. We may assume K is at least 1, so that we choose M_1 such that $n \geqslant M_1$ implies $|a_n - A| < \dfrac{\epsilon}{2K}$. Further, we may choose M_2 such that $n \geqslant M_2$ implies $|b_n - B| < \dfrac{\epsilon}{2(|A| + 1)}$. Let $M = \max \{M_1, M_2\}$, whence for $n \geqslant M$ we have, starting from the inequalities above,

$$\begin{aligned}
|a_n \cdot b_n - A \cdot B| &\leqslant |b_n| \cdot |a_n - A| + |A| \cdot |b_n - B| \\
&< K \cdot \frac{\epsilon}{2K} + |A| \cdot \frac{\epsilon}{2(|A| + 1)} \\
&< \frac{\epsilon}{2} + \frac{\epsilon}{2} = \epsilon.
\end{aligned}$$

$\square$

Discussion. As noted earlier in the comments following Theorem 0.6.4, a feature of many of these proofs is the addition and subtraction of the same quantity inside the absolute value signs. The purpose in this case, as it will usually be, is to obtain quantities which we know can be made as small as we please. In this case, the terms are $|a_n - A|$ and $|b_n - B|$. Of course, there are likely to be leftover terms, and here the leftover terms are $|b_n|$ and $|A|$. But leftover terms are of no consequence as long as these terms are bounded and multiplied by other terms which can be made arbitrarily small. For the case at hand, since $|b_n| < K$, we can replace it by K, and then make $|a_n - A|$ so small that its product with K will be less than $\dfrac{\epsilon}{2}$. (This is why we need to be able to make $|a_n - A|$ as small as we please, and not merely less than ϵ.) With this in mind, the reader should now make sure he understands how the other term is dealt with. The reason for using $\dfrac{\epsilon}{2(|A| + 1)}$, rather than $\dfrac{\epsilon}{2A}$ is to take care of the possibility that $A = 0$. Lastly, again note the use of Theorem 0.6.2. The importance of this type of computation can not be overemphasized. □

Theorem 1.2.6. Let $\{a_n\}$ be a sequence of nonzero terms which converges to A. If $A \neq 0$, then $\left\{ \dfrac{1}{a_n} \right\}$ converges to $\dfrac{1}{A}$.

    Proof. Fix $\epsilon > 0$. Since $A \neq 0$, there is an M_1 such that $n > M_1$ implies $\dfrac{|A|}{2} < |a_n|$ (**WHY?**). Then for $n > M_1$, we have

$$\left| \frac{1}{a_n} - \frac{1}{A} \right| = \frac{|A - a_n|}{|a_n| \cdot |A|}$$

$$< \frac{2|a_n - A|}{|A|^2}.$$

From this calculation, it is clear that we should choose M_2 so that $n > M_2$ implies $|a_n - A| < \epsilon \cdot \dfrac{A^2}{2}$. Let $M = \max \{M_1, M_2\}$, whence for $n > M$ we have

$$\left| \frac{1}{a_n} - \frac{1}{A} \right| < \frac{2}{A^2} \cdot \frac{A^2}{2} \cdot \epsilon = \epsilon.$$

□

Discussion. The requirement that each of the terms be nonzero can be relaxed. The essential fact is that the limit be different from zero, for then all the terms will eventually be nonzero (**WHY?**), and for those terms the limit of the inverses will be $\dfrac{1}{A}$. It is essential that the reader understand how and why we arrived at our choice of M_2. Respecting this, our comments following Theorem 1.2.5 should be reviewed. Note how we use the arithmetical fact that making the denominator of a fraction smaller increases the size of the fraction. Our calculations continually hinge on such basic elementary results from arithmetic! □

The proofs of the following are left to Exercises 1, 2, and 4.

Theorem 1.2.7. If $\{a_n\}$ converges to A, then $\{|a_n|\}$ converges to $|A|$.

Theorem 1.2.8. If $\{a_n\}$ and $\{b_n\}$ converge to A and B, respectively, and if $a_n \leqslant b_n$ for every $n \in \mathbf{N}$, then $A \leqslant B$.

Theorem 1.2.9. Let B and b denote the supremum and infimum, respectively, of $\{a_n\}$. If $\{a_n\}$ converges to A, then $b \leqslant A \leqslant B$.

EXERCISES

1. Prove Theorem 1.2.7. Supply an example to show that the converse of Theorem 1.2.7 is not in general true. However, if $\{|a_n|\}$ converges to 0, then prove that $\{a_n\}$ also converges to 0.

2. Prove Theorem 1.2.8. Give an example which shows that a_n may be strictly less than b_n for all n, but that A may equal B.

3. For the following sequences $\{a_n\}$, use the limit theorems to establish convergence.

   (a) $a_n = \dfrac{2n - 1}{3n + 4 - 5^{1/n}}$;

   (b) $a_n = \dfrac{n^2 + n - 1}{3n^2 - 4n}$;

   (c) $a_n = \dfrac{P(n + 1)}{P(n)}$ where $P(x) = ax^3 + bx^2 + cx + d,\ a, b, c, d \in \mathbf{R}$;

   (d) $a_n = \dfrac{1^2 + 2^2 + \cdots + n^2}{6n^3}$;

   (e) $a_n = \dfrac{1^3 + 2^3 + \cdots + n^3}{(2n + 1)^4}$;

   (f) $a_n = \dfrac{1}{(n + 1)^2} + \dfrac{1}{(n + 2)^2} + \cdots + \dfrac{1}{(n + n)^2}$;

   (g) $a_n = 1 + x + x^2 + \cdots + x^n$, where $|x| < 1$.

4. Prove Theorem 1.2.9.

5. State and prove an appropriate limit theorem involving subtraction.

6. State and prove an appropriate theorem concerning the convergence of the ratio of two convergent sequences.

7. Without using Theorem 1.2.5, formally prove that if $\lim\limits_{n \to \infty} a_n = L$, then $\lim\limits_{n \to \infty} a_n^2 = L^2$.

8. If $\left\{ \dfrac{a_n}{n} \right\}$ converges to $L \neq 0$, prove that the sequence $\{a_n\}$ must be unbounded. Is the converse true?

9. Theorems 1.2.4 and 1.2.5 require $\{a_n\}$ and $\{b_n\}$ to be convergent. What can be said if this condition is dropped? Give examples which elucidate the situation.

10. Let $\{a_n\}$ converge to 0 and $\{b_n\}$ be bounded. Show that $\{a_n \cdot b_n\}$ converges to 0.

11. Can $\{a_n \cdot b_n\}$ and $\{a_n\}$ be both convergent, and yet $\{b_n\}$ is divergent?

12. Prove the following:
    (a) if $\lim a_n = +\infty$, then $\lim ca_n = +\infty$ if $c > 0$ and if $c < 0$;
    (b) if $\lim a_n = +\infty$ and $\{b_n\}$ is bounded, then $\lim(a_n + b_n) = +\infty$;
    (c) if $\lim a_n = +\infty$, then $\lim(-a_n) = -\infty$;
    (d) if $a_n \neq 0$ for all n, $\{a_n\}$ diverges to $+\infty$ if and only if $\left\{\dfrac{1}{a_n}\right\}$ converges to 0.

13. Show that the term-by-term product of a bounded divergent sequence with a convergent sequence converges if and only if the limit of the convergent sequence is 0.

14. Prove or disprove:
    (a) if $\{a_n\}$ and $\{b_n\}$ diverge, $\{a_n + b_n\}$ diverges;
    (b) if $\{a_n\}$ converges and $\{b_n\}$ diverges, $\{a_n + b_n\}$ diverges;
    (c) if $\{a_n\}$ and $\{b_n\}$ diverge, $\{a_n - b_n\}$ diverges;
    (d) if $\{a_n\}$ and $\{b_n\}$ diverge, $\{a_n \cdot b_n\}$ diverges;
    (e) if $\{a_n\}$ and $\{a_n b_n\}$ converge, then $\{b_n\}$ converges;
    (f) if $\{a_n\}$ and $\{a_n b_n\}$ diverge, then $\{b_n\}$ diverges.

15. Let $\{a_n\}$ be a convergent sequence with limit A. Set

$$b_n = \frac{1}{n} \cdot \sum_{k=1}^{n} a_k,$$

that is, the **arithmetic average** of the first n terms of $\{a_n\}$. Prove that $\{b_n\}$ is a convergent sequence. Does the fact that $\{b_n\}$ converges tell us anything about the convergence of $\{a_n\}$?

16. Repeat Exercise 15 with $b_n = (a_1 \cdot a_2 \cdots a_n)^{1/n}$, the **geometric average** of the first n terms of $\{a_n\}$.

17. Let $\{a_n\}$ and $\{b_n\}$ be sequences converging to A and B, respectively. Define

$$t_n = \frac{1}{n} \cdot \sum_{k=1}^{n} a_k b_{n-k}.$$

Show that $\{t_n\}$ converges, and find its limit. What would happen if the term $\dfrac{1}{n}$ was omitted from the above expression for t_n?

18. Let $P(n)$ and $Q(n)$ be two nonzero polynomials in n. Let $\{a_n\}$ be the sequence obtained by forming the ratio of $P(n)$ over $Q(n)$. Show that $\{a_n\}$ converges if and only if the degree of $Q(n)$ is at least as large as the degree of $P(n)$.

19. Let $f: \mathbf{N} \to \mathbf{N}$ be a function with $f(k)$ denoted by n_k. Further, suppose that $f(k) < f(k+1)$ for every $k \in \mathbf{N}$. If $\{a_n\}$ is any sequence, then

$$\{a_{n_k} : k \in \mathbf{N}\}$$

is called a **subsequence** of $\{a_n\}$. Prove the following:
    (a) if $m \in \mathbf{N}$, then there is a $k \in \mathbf{N}$ such that $m \leqslant n_k$;
    (b) if $\{a_n\}$ converges, then $\{a_{n_k}\}$ converges to the same limit;
    What can you say about the converse of (b)?

20. For each of the bounded divergent sequences in Exercise 1.1.1, find a convergent subsequence.

21. Let $\{a_n\}$ converge to a, where all numbers are nonnegative. Show that $\{\sqrt{a_n}\}$ converges to $\sqrt{a}$.

22. Show that for any convergent sequence of real numbers, the sequence obtained by taking the cube root of each term is convergent.

23. Let $a > 0$. Show that $\{a^{1/n}\}$ converges to 1.

24. Show that $\{n^{1/n}\}$ converges to 1. [HINT: Use the Binomial Theorem.]

25. Show that $\lim\limits_{n\to\infty} \dfrac{a^n}{n!} = 0$.

26. Discuss the convergence or divergence of $\{(n!)^{1/n}\}$.

27. Discuss the convergence or divergence of the sequence $\{n^p a^n\}$ for various a and p.

28. Let

$$a_n = \sum_{k=1}^{n} \frac{1}{n^2 + k}.$$

Show that $\{a_n\}$ is convergent. [HINT: Use Theorem 1.2.2.]

29. Repeat Exercise 28, where the sum is up to $2n$, instead of n.

30. Let $0 < a < 1$. Show that the sequence having nth term $b_n = a^n$ converges to 0. What happens if $a > 1$?

31. If $0 < a \leqslant b \leqslant c$, show that $\lim\limits_{n\to\infty}(a^n + b^n + c^n)^{1/n} = c$.

32. If $\{(a_n + b_n)\}$ converges to A, and $\{(a_n - b_n)\}$ converges to B, find the limit of $\{a_n b_n\}$.

33. If $a_0 + a_1 + \cdots + a_k = 0$, show that

$$\lim_{n\to\infty} [a_0\sqrt{n} + a_1\sqrt{n+1} + \cdots + a_k\sqrt{n+k}] = 0.$$

34. Let $a_n > 0$ for all n and set $b_n = \dfrac{a_{n+1}}{a_n}$ and $c_n = a_n^{1/n}$. If $\lim b_n = L$, prove that $\lim c_n = L$. Is the converse true?

35. Let $\{a_n^{(i)}\}$ be a finite number of sequences, where $i = 1, 2, \ldots, k$. Generalize Theorems 1.2.4 and 1.2.5 for the sum (product) of these k sequences.

36. If $\lim b_n = 0$ and $|a_n - A| < Kb_n$ for some constant K, prove that $\lim a_n = A$.

37. If $a_n > 0$ and if $\lim \dfrac{a_{n+1}}{a_n} = A < 1$, prove that $\lim a_n = 0$. What happens when $A = 1$? Discuss the situation when $A > 1$. (See Exercise 1.1.19).

1.3 MONOTONICITY AND ITS CONSEQUENCES

We have defined the concept of limit for a sequence, but except for rather arduous calculations, as in the exercises at the end of section 1.1, we have no means of knowing whether a given sequence has a limit. In this section we shall remedy that and in doing so will provide the first example of power of the completeness axiom as a tool of analysis.

We have seen that a convergent sequence is always bounded, but not conversely. We are therefore led to look for conditions on a bounded sequence which would guarantee convergence. To this end, we study the following concept.

Definition. A sequence $\{a_n\}$ is said to be **monotone increasing** if for all $n, m \in \mathbf{N}$, $n \leqslant m$ .implies. $a_n \leqslant a_m$.

In a similar manner we can define **monotone decreasing** (the reader should do so). A sequence which is either monotone decreasing or increasing is said to be **monotone**. If the inequalities are strict ($n < m$ implies $a_n < a_m$), then the sequence is **strictly monotone** (increasing for the inequalities shown).

Discussion. The definition of a monotonic increasing (decreasing) sequence conveys the simple idea that each term of the sequence is larger (smaller) than or equal to the preceding term. Monotonicity is a very useful concept, as we shall see soon. Given a sequence $\{a_n\}$, there are several methods of testing whether it is monotonic increasing or not. One obvious way is to use the above definition. Sometimes, this can be hard. Other practical methods are:

(a) Check that the difference $(a_{n+1} - a_n) \geqslant 0$ for all n;

(b) Check that the ratio $\dfrac{a_{n+1}}{a_n} \geqslant 1$ for all n;

(c) Using tools from elementary calculus, decide whether the function $f(n) = a_n$ is increasing, by using the first derivative test, namely, $f'(x) > 0$. This is formally treated in Chapter 4, where we discuss differentiation.

One can write down similar conditions for monotonic decreasing sequences. Note that we need not require that the monotonicity definition is satisfied for all n. In many instances, it suffices to demand that the definition holds from a fixed $k \in \mathbf{N}$ onwards. $\square$

The following theorem shows that in the presence of monotonicity, a bounded sequence will converge. It further tells us to what limit does the sequence converge. It is a remarkable theorem on the convergence of sequences, and it employs the powerful tool of completeness of $\mathbf{R}$ for its proof.

Theorem 1.3.1. Let $\{a_n\}$ be a monotone sequence. If $\{a_n\}$ is bounded above, then $\{a_n\}$ converges to sup $\{a_n\}$. If $\{a_n\}$ is bounded below, then $\{a_n\}$ converges to inf $\{a_n\}$.

Proof. We will prove the statement for the case where $\{a_n\}$ is an increasing sequence. The decreasing case is left to Exercise 3. Since $\{a_n\}$ is bounded, let $A = \sup \{a_n\}$. Fix $\epsilon > 0$. By choice of A, there is a term of the sequence, say a_M, such that

$$A - \epsilon < a_M \leqslant A.$$

Let $n \geqslant M$, then by the monotonicity of $\{a_n\}$,

$$A - \epsilon < a_M \leqslant a_n \leqslant A,$$

whence,

$$|a_n - A| < \epsilon. \qquad \square$$

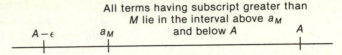

All terms having subscript greater than
M lie in the interval above a_M
and below A

$A - \epsilon$ a_M A

Figure 1.3.1   Graph illustrating monotonic, bounded sequence converges (one-dimensional).

Discussion.   The existence of the term of the sequence, a_M, having the desired properties is by virtue of Theorem 0.4.2, which characterizes the supremum. Once we have one term in the desired interval, monotonicity forces all the remaining terms to lie in the interval $(a_n, \sup \{a_n\})$, and so completes the proof. Lastly, boundedness forces the supremum to exist, and the supremum should appear to the reader to be a natural candidate for the limit. The geometry of the situation is summarized in Figures 1.3.1 and 1.3.2.   □

EXAMPLE 1 _____

Show that the sequence defined by $a_n = \left[1 + \dfrac{1}{n} \right]^n$ is convergent.

Solution.   We use the Binomial Theorem (Theorem 0.4.5) to obtain

$$a_n = \left[1 + \frac{1}{n} \right]^n = \sum_{k=0}^{n} \left[\begin{matrix} n \\ k \end{matrix} \right] \left[\frac{1}{n} \right]^k,$$

which is a sum of nonnegative terms. Now the $(k + 1)$th term of the binomial expansion of a_n is

$$\frac{n!}{k!(n - k)!} \left[\frac{1}{n} \right]^k.$$

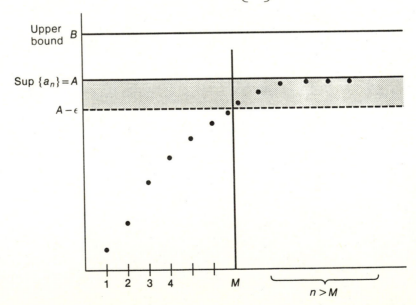

Figure 1.3.2   Graph illustrating monotonic, bounded sequence converges (two-dimensional).

We can compare the $(k + 1)$th term of a_n with the $(k + 1)$th term of a_{n+1} by computing the ratio. Since both are positive, the latter will be larger (or equal to) the former if and only if the ratio of the former over the latter is less than or equal to 1. Thus,

$$\frac{\dfrac{n!}{k!(n-k)!}\left[\dfrac{1}{n}\right]^k}{\dfrac{(n+1)!}{k!(n+1-k)!}\left[\dfrac{1}{n+1}\right]^k} = \left[\frac{n+1-k}{n+1}\right]\left[\frac{n+1}{n}\right]^k$$

and this quantity will be less than or equal to 1 if and only if

$$(n + 1 - k)(n + 1)^{k-1} \leqslant n^k$$

for each $k \in \{0, 1, \ldots, n\}$. To establish this, we induct on k. For $k = 0$,

$$(n + 1 - 0)(n + 1)^{0-1} \leqslant n^0,$$

which is obviously true. Thus, assume the inequality for $k = m$, where $0 \leqslant m \leqslant n$. If $m = n$, we are done, otherwise we have

$$(n + 1 - m)(n + 1)^{m-1} \leqslant n^m$$

whence

$$n^{m+1} = n \cdot n^m \geqslant n(n + 1 - m)(n + 1)^{m-1}$$

$$= [n \cdot (n + 1) - n \cdot m](n + 1)^{m-1}$$

$$> [(n + 1) \cdot n - (n + 1) \cdot m](n + 1)^{m-1} \quad (\textbf{WHY?})$$

$$= (n - m)(n + 1)^m$$

$$= [(n + 1) - (m + 1)](n + 1)^m ,$$

as desired. It is immediate that

$$\sum_{k=0}^{n} \binom{n}{k}\left[\frac{1}{n}\right]^k \leqslant \sum_{k=0}^{n+1} \binom{n+1}{k}\left[\frac{1}{n+1}\right]^k ,$$

since the $(k + 1)$th term of the first sum is less than or equal to the $(k + 1)$th term of the second. Thus, $\left[1 + \dfrac{1}{n}\right]^n$ is a monotone increasing sequence which will have a limit if we can show it is bounded above. Now, the reader can easily show by induction (Exercise 5) that

$$\frac{n!}{(n - k)!} \leqslant n^k ,$$

for any $k \in \{0, 1, \ldots, n\}$. It follows that

$$\sum_{k=0}^{n} \binom{n}{k}\left[\frac{1}{n}\right]^k \leqslant \sum_{k=0}^{n} \frac{1}{k!} \leqslant 1 + \sum_{k=0}^{n} \left[\frac{1}{2}\right]^k .$$

The last sum is a finite geometric series. It follows that 3 is an upper bound for the sum, and hence $\{a_n\}$ converges to a limit $A \leqslant 3$. $\qquad\square$

Discussion. We see again, as we have already seen in the exercises, that the Binomial Theorem is a highly useful tool for doing analysis, a comment which applies to proof by induction, as well. This proof also employs facts about geometric series, facts which should be well known, but if not, they can be found in the exercises at the end of section 0.4. At first glance, the computations perhaps seem arduous. While they are admittedly somewhat lengthy, they are completely straightforward and do not involve much more than the type of algebra learned in high school. The limit of the above sequence turns out to be the real number e (the base for the natural logarithm). It is formally developed in Chapter 10. $\qquad\square$

EXAMPLE 2 _____

Find the limit of the sequence whose nth term is

$$\left(1 + \frac{1}{2n}\right)^n.$$

Solution. The sequence given can be rewritten as

$$\left(1 + \frac{1}{2n}\right)^n = \left[\left(1 + \frac{1}{2n}\right)^{2n}\right]^{1/2}.$$

Now the sequence $\left(1 + \dfrac{1}{2n}\right)^{2n}$ is clearly a subsequence (recall the definition from Exercise 1.2.19) of the sequence $\left(1 + \dfrac{1}{n}\right)^n$ which was just treated. The limit of $\left(1 + \dfrac{1}{n}\right)^n$ happens to be e. Thus, since the limit of a subsequence is the limit of the sequence, we have that the limit of $\left(1 + \dfrac{1}{2n}\right)^n$ is $\sqrt{e}$. $\qquad\square$

EXAMPLE 3 _____

Find the limit of the sequence defined recursively by

$$a_1 = \sqrt{2}; \qquad a_{n+1} = \sqrt{2 + a_n} \qquad (n \geqslant 1).$$

Solution. This sequence has been shown to be monotone increasing with an upper bound of 2 (Exercise 0.4.16). If we consider the sequence $b_n = a_{n+1}$, we have

$$\lim b_n = \lim \sqrt{2 + a_n}$$
$$= \sqrt{2 + \lim a_n}. \qquad \textbf{(WHY?)}$$

Now the limit of a_n exists, call it A, and since b_n is a subsequence, it clearly has the same limit. We have then that

$$A = \sqrt{2 + A}.$$

This yields the equation $A^2 - A - 2 = 0$. The solutions to this equation are easily seen to be -1 and 2. It is clear from the initial conditions that the limit must be 2. □

Discussion. The values for the terms of this sequence are defined recursively: that is, an initial value is given for the first term of the sequence, and a rule is given so that the other terms may be calculated in increasing order from this first term. To find the limit of the sequence, we first show that the limit of the sequence exists. Then, having found the limit, we use the recursion formula to generate an algebraic equation in the unknown limit. The equation is then solved, and the limit found. For the case at hand, the equation produces several solutions, only one of which can be the limit. Thus, the procedure can yield numbers which have no relation to the original problem. The point is that the recursion formula can be used to generate an equation which the limit of the sequence, if it exists, must satisfy. Knowledge of the sequence allows us to select the solution of the equation which is, in fact, the limit. We note that a recursive formula can usually be used to generate an equation which can then be solved, even if the sequence being considered has no limit. For such a case, the calculations are nonsense. The generation of the equation which the limit must satisfy is only meaningful when it is known that the limit exists! □

EXERCISES

1. Decide whether the following sequences $\{a_n\}$ are (i) monotone, (ii) bounded, (iii) convergent. Where possible, compute the limit.

   (a) $a_n = n - \dfrac{1}{n}$;

   (b) $a_n = n^2 + (-1)^n$;

   (c) $a_n = n^{1-n}$;

   (d) $a_n = \sin \dfrac{\pi}{2n}$;

   (e) $a_n = n + \sqrt{a + \dfrac{1}{n^2}}, \ a > 0$;

   (f) $a_n = \sqrt{n+1} - \sqrt{n}$;

   (g) $a_n = 3^{1/n}$;

   (h) $a_n = n\sqrt{1 + \dfrac{1}{n^2}}$;

   (i) $a_n = \dfrac{2}{\sqrt{n^2 + 1} - n}$;

   (j) $a_n = \sqrt{2n^2 + 3n - 4}$;

   (k) $a_n = \left[\dfrac{100n}{n^2} \right]$;

(l) $a_n = \dfrac{n^3}{\dbinom{2n}{n}}$;

(m) $a_n = \left[1 + \dfrac{1}{2} + \dfrac{1}{3} + \cdots + \dfrac{1}{n}\right]$;

(n) $a_n = \left[1 + \dfrac{1}{2} + \dfrac{1}{4} + \cdots + \dfrac{1}{2^n}\right]$.

2. Find the limit of the following sequences $\{a_n\}$, where a_n is defined by:

(a) $\left[1 + \dfrac{2}{n}\right]^n$;

(b) $\left[1 + \dfrac{1}{n}\right]^{3n}$;

(c) $\left[1 + \dfrac{1}{(n+1)}\right]^n$;

(d) $\left[1 + \dfrac{1}{n^2}\right]^n$;

(e) $\left[1 + \dfrac{1}{(100+n)}\right]^n$;

(f) $\left[1 + \dfrac{1}{2^n}\right]^{2^{2^n}}$;

(g) $\left[\dfrac{99}{100} + \dfrac{1}{n}\right]^{\sqrt{n}}$;

(h) $(\alpha a^n + \beta b^n)^{1/n}$, $0 < a < b$, $\alpha, \beta > 0$.

3. Prove that a bounded decreasing sequence has a limit.

4. Must an unbounded sequence diverge to $+\infty$ or $-\infty$?

5. Fill in the missing induction argument in Example 1.

6. Define $\{a_n\}$ recursively by

$$a_1 = k,\ k \geqslant 0; \qquad a_{n+1} = \sqrt{k + a_n} \qquad (n \geqslant 1).$$

Show that $\{a_n\}$ has a limit, and find it.

7. Define $\{a_n\}$ recursively by

$$a_1 = k,\ k > 0; \qquad a_{n+1} = \dfrac{k}{1 + a_n} \qquad (n \geqslant 1).$$

Show that the sequence $\{a_n\}$ has a limit and find it.

8. Let x and y be positive real numbers. Define $\{a_n\}$ recursively by

$$a_0 = y, \qquad a_n = \dfrac{1}{2}\left[\dfrac{x}{a_{n-1}} + a_{n-1}\right] \qquad (n > 1).$$

Show that $\{a_n\}$ is decreasing and converges to $\sqrt{x}$. Estimate $\sqrt{2}$ using a_4.

9. The sequence $\{a_n\}$ is defined recursively by

$$a_2 > a_1 > 0, \qquad a_{n+1} = \frac{(a_n + a_{n-1})}{2} \qquad (n > 1).$$

Show that the subsequences $\{a_{2n}\}$ and $\{a_{2n-1}\}$ are both monotonic, and converge to a common limit. Show that $\lim a_n = \dfrac{2a_2 + a_1}{3}$.

10. Repeat Exercise 9 with $\{a_n\}$ defined by

$$a_2 > a_1 > 0, \qquad a_{n+1} = \sqrt{a_n \cdot a_{n-1}} \qquad (n > 1).$$

In this case, show that $\lim a_n = \sqrt{a_2^2 \cdot a_1}$.

11. Let $a > b > 0$, $a_1 = \dfrac{a + b}{2}$, $b_1 = \sqrt{ab}$, and for $n \geqslant 1$, $a_{n+1} = \dfrac{a_n + b_n}{2}$, $b_{n+1} = \sqrt{a_n \cdot b_n}$. Show that the sequences $\{a_n\}$ and $\{b_n\}$ converge to a common limit.

12. Let $\{a_n\}$ and $\{b_n\}$ be such that $a_1 > b_1 > 0$,

$$a_{n+1} = \frac{a_n + b_n}{2}, \qquad b_{n+1} = \frac{1}{2}\left[\frac{1}{a_n} + \frac{1}{b_n}\right] \qquad (n \geqslant 1).$$

Prove that $\{a_n\}$ and $\{b_n\}$ both converge to $\sqrt{a_1 b_1}$.

13. A sequence $\{s_n\}$ is defined as follows:

$$s_1 = a > 0, \qquad s_{n+1} = \sqrt{\frac{s_n^2 + ab^2}{a + 1}}, \ b > a \qquad (n \geqslant 1).$$

Show that $\{s_n\}$ is monotonic, and converges to b.

14. If $x_1 = 4$, $x_{n+1} = 3 - \dfrac{2}{x_n}$, $n \geqslant 1$, prove that $\{x_n\}$ converges to a limit. Find the limit.

15. Let p be any positive integer other than 1. Let $\{a_n\}$ be any sequence of nonnegative integers such that for every n, $0 \leqslant a_n < p$. Define the sequence $\{b_n\}$ by

$$b_n = \sum_{k=1}^{n} \frac{a_k}{p^k}.$$

(a) Show that the sequence $\{b_n\}$ converges to a real number in $[0,1]$.
(b) Show that if $x \in (0,1)$, then there is exactly one sequence $\{a_n\}$ such that the sequence $\{b_n\}$ converges to x, unless $x = \dfrac{q}{p^m}$, for some positive integers m and q. In the latter case, show that there are exactly two such sequences $\{a_n\}$.

16. A sequence $\{a_n\}$ is said to be **eventually monotone** if there is an M such that the subsequence consisting of all terms having subscript greater than or equal to M is monotone. Prove a convergence theorem about eventually monotone bounded sequences.

17. Let $\{a_n\}$ be a sequence having the property that there is an M and a q, where $0 < q < 1$, such that if $n \geqslant M$, then

$$\frac{|a_{n+1}|}{|a_n|} \leqslant q.$$

What can be said about the convergence of $\{a_n\}$?

18. Show that every bounded sequence has a monotonic subsequence.

19. Show that $\dfrac{n^n}{n! e^n}$ tends to a limit.

20. Let f be any function from **N** into the collection of all sequences of digits from the set $\{0, 1, 2\}$. Show that such a function can not be onto. Conclude that the real numbers are 'uncountable' (see Appendix). [HINT: Assume that an onto f exists and construct a new sequence by changing the nth term of $f(n)$. The argument required here is the famous diagonal argument due to Cantor!]

21. Let ω (little omega) denote the class of sequences of real numbers, and consider the following six mathematical sentences:

(a) $\exists A \; \forall \epsilon \; \exists M \; [\epsilon > 0 \text{ and } n > M \text{ .implies. } |a_n - A| < \epsilon]$;

(b) $\forall \epsilon \; \exists A \; \exists M \; [\epsilon > 0 \text{ and } n > M \text{ .implies. } |a_n - A| < \epsilon]$;

(c) $\forall \epsilon \; \exists M \; \exists A \; [\epsilon > 0 \text{ and } n > M \text{ .implies. } |a_n - A| < \epsilon]$;

(d) $\exists M \; \forall \epsilon \; \exists A \; [\epsilon > 0 \text{ and } n > M \text{ .implies. } |a_n - A| < \epsilon]$;

(e) $\exists A \; \exists M \; \forall \epsilon \; [\epsilon > 0 \text{ and } n > M \text{ .implies. } |a_n - A| < \epsilon]$;

(f) $\exists M \; \exists A \; \forall \epsilon \; [\epsilon > 0 \text{ and } n > M \text{ .implies. } |a_n - A| < \epsilon]$;

where $\{a_n\}$ is an arbitrary sequence. Each of these formulas defines a subset of ω. For example, the subset consisting of all sequences satisfying the first formula is the usual collection of convergent sequences. Call the classes $C_1, C_2, \ldots, C_6$, respectively. Find all set containment relations which hold between these classes. Where possible, give a 'nice' description of the classes defined. (The symbols $\forall$ (for all) and $\exists$ (there exists) are the universal and existential quantifiers, respectively.)

22. Repeat Exercise 21 with the change $|a_n - A| < 3\epsilon$, $|a_n - A| < \frac{3}{2}\epsilon$, and more generally, $|a_n - A| < k \cdot \epsilon$, ($k$, a positive constant).

23. Consider the following classes of sequences:

$$\omega = \text{the class of all real sequences,}$$
$$\mathbf{conv} = \text{the class of all convergent sequences,}$$
$$\mathbf{bdd} = \text{the class of all bounded sequences,}$$
$$\mathbf{div} = \text{the class of all divergent sequences,}$$
$$\mathbf{div_\infty} = \text{the class of all bounded sequences that diverge to } +\infty,$$
$$\mathbf{div_{-\infty}} = \text{the class of all sequences that diverge to } -\infty,$$
$$\mathbf{osc} = \text{the class of all sequences that oscillate,}$$
$$\mathbf{mon} = \text{the class of all monotonic sequences.}$$

Identify all possible containment relationships between these classes that you can think of from the development so far.

24. Consider the sequence defined by

$$a_n = \sum_{k=1}^{n} \frac{b_k}{10^{k!}},$$

where b_k is an arbitrary member of the set $\{1, 2, 3, \ldots, 9\}$. Show that $\{a_n\}$ converges to an irrational number.

25. Show that the convergence properties of a monotone sequence are completely determined by any of its subsequences.

26. Let $a_n = \left[\dfrac{n}{2}\right] - \dfrac{n^2}{2n + 1}$. Find sup $\{a_n\}$, inf $\{a_n\}$. Does $\{a_n\}$ converge?

Chapter 2

Limits of Functions

Our purpose in this chapter is to study the limit concept as applied to functions. The notion of 'limit as x tends to a of a function f' is fundamental to all further ideas in real analysis. We shall develop it here and then use it to define 'continuous function' and to obtain the elementary properties of continuous functions.

In the last chapter, we began the study of the limit concept as applied to sequences which are special types of functions having for a domain the set of all natural numbers, $\mathbf{N}$. In this chapter, we apply the concept to functions having as domains arbitrary subsets of the set $\mathbf{R}$ of real numbers.

2.1 FUNCTIONS, LIMITS AT INFINITY

The concept of function is central to the rest of this book, and so we discuss it at some length. As can be seen from the treatment in the Appendix, functions are collections of ordered pairs, where these collections satisfy certain constraints. Implicit in the definition is the notion of an **ordered pair**. These are defined in the Appendix, but the property which is important, in fact essential, is that *ordered pairs are equal if and only if they are equal coordinatewise*, namely,

$$(a,b) = (c,d) \text{ .if and only if. } a = c \text{ and } b = d.$$

Here, a is called the **first coordinate**, and b the **second coordinate**. Thus, we can use this to give the definition:

Definition. A **function** is a set f of ordered pairs such that if x is the first coordinate of an ordered pair in f, then there is exactly one y such that $(x, y) \in f$.

Discussion. The trouble with this definition is that it is too pat. The subtleties are hidden, and the motivation for the definition has long since disappeared. Analysis grew out of graphs and rules for computations and geometry, not out of rigorous discussions of ordered pairs. And so we should look to these for intuition (graphs, rules for computation, geometry). Let us examine these in turn.

Functions, as treated in the last century, were essentially rules for computation. By this we mean that for any given number which was a proper input, one could obtain a unique output by applying the rule. When thinking about functions in this way, we are really identifying the function with a computing machine. For a concrete example of this idea, the reader should think of a calculator which will compute the square root of nonnegative numbers. Obviously, not every number is suitable for computation purposes by all machines. This gives rise to the idea of **domain**. (The domain of the 'root x' machine is the nonnegative reals.) Also, we notice that not all numbers will appear as outputs, which gives rise to the idea of **range**. (The range of 'root x' is the nonnegative reals.) The main features of this discussion are that the rule is **single-valued** (that is, it produces a unique output for each accepted input), has a domain, and has a range. The trouble with the machine concept is that it is not suitable for mathematical analysis. But mathematicians realized that how the computation was accomplished was unimportant. The important fact is that with each element of the domain we associate a unique element of the range. This can be captured by considering sets of ordered pairs, and the machine in the middle can be dispensed with. The notion of 'rule' has not disappeared, however. We often specify functions by giving the rule for computation, together with the domain, for example,

$$f(x) = 2x + 5, x \in \mathbf{R}.$$

In set notation, this type of specification for functions takes the form

$$\{(x, 2x + 5) : x \in \mathbf{R}\}.$$

Either type of specification gives us immediate access to an algebraic rule for computation. It is through judicious manipulation of this rule that we will be able to establish the interesting properties of a particular function. For concrete examples of this, the reader should review our computations with particular sequences. Manipulation of the rule was the method by which limits were established. The student should also note that regardless of the notation, a function f is a set of ordered pairs and that '$f(x)$' does not denote a function, but a particular output of the function f, called the **value of the function at** x.

We shall consider only ordered pairs of real numbers, so our functions are real-valued functions of a real variable. We shall frequently use the arrow notation, namely $f: D \to \mathbf{R}$, where the domain is the subset D of $\mathbf{R}$, and the range is contained in $\mathbf{R}$. The abbreviations Dmn, Rng will be used throughout the book to denote the domain and the range. $\square$

Graphs provide us with pictures of functions. Pictures in turn lead naturally to questions about geometry. As such, pictures can be important aids to our intuition, and we should use them freely. To see how a graph can lead us to natural geometric questions, look at the graph of $f(x) = 2x,\ x \in \mathbf{R}$. The graph of this function (Figure 2.1.1) can be drawn by a single motion of the pencil across the page. The result is a

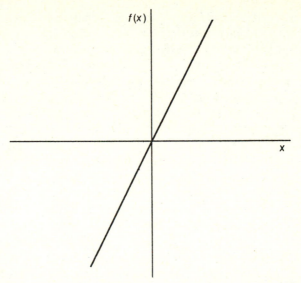

Figure 2.1.1   Graph of $f(x) = 2x$, $x \in \mathbf{R}$, showing that it can be drawn without lifting the pencil from paper.

continuous line segment, and mathematicians began to wonder what analytic properties of functions would lead to this property for their graphs. Other geometric ideas which arise are the fact that for some functions, if we input distinct x's which are close together, then the outputs will also be close together, while for others the outputs will be far apart. Graphs can be misleading. The graph of

$$f(x) = \begin{cases} x, & x \in \mathbf{Q} \\ 1 - x, & x \notin \mathbf{Q} \end{cases}$$

pictured in Figure 2.1.2 does not appear to represent a function because the rule

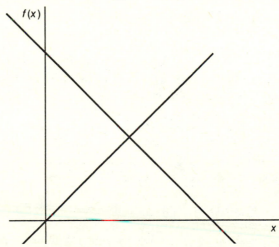

Figure 2.1.2   Intuitive graph of $f(x) = \begin{cases} x, & x \in \mathbf{Q} \\ 1 - x, & x \in \mathbf{R} \sim \mathbf{Q} \end{cases}$. Note: Both lines have infinitely many 'holes'.

appears to associate more than one y with a single value of x. However, examination of the rule shows that in fact there is a single unique y associated with each x, and so the rule is indeed single valued, even though the picture cannot make it seem so.

In summary, we will consistently emphasize functions from the point of view of a domain, D, and a rule $f(x) = \cdots , x \in D$. We will draw graphs whenever these will aid our intuition, but we will always test our intuition by using the algebraic and analytical tools we have developed. Once again we would state that pictures are absolutely essential to the generation of intuition, but they cannot form a part of any proof!

Unless explicitly stated otherwise, *all functions in this book will have both their domain and range contained in* **R**. With respect to domains, the reader should keep in mind the standard domains of the elementary calculus, namely open intervals (a,b); closed intervals $[a,b]$; and infinite intervals (a, ∞) or, $(-\infty, a]$ to illustrate the various possibilities. It is essential that the reader first understand the content of our theorems and definitions for functions having intervals for their domains, before attempting to deal with the subtleties which arise for functions having domains which are arbitrary subsets of the real numbers. For this reason, functions having interval domains will be emphasized and many of the subtleties left to the exercises.

For the rest of the book, the positive real numbers will be denoted by **R**$^+$.

Definition.   Let f be a function with domain D. We say that f **has a limit as x tends to** $+\infty$ provided there exists an $A \in$ **R** such that for every positive ϵ, there is an M such that

$$x \in D \text{ and } x > M \text{ .implies. } |f(x) - A| < \epsilon.$$

In the case that a number A satisfying the definition exists, we say that A is the **limit** of $f(x)$ as $x \to \infty$ and we write

$$\lim_{x \to \infty} f(x) = A.$$

Notation.   We will often use the symbol $+\infty$, instead of ∞, to emphasize we are looking at positive infinity, as opposed to negative infinity.

Discussion.   Let us compare this definition with that of the limit definition for sequences. Both require us to find a fixed real number A as a first step. Both use small values of ϵ as a test for closeness. Both require us to find an M, which depends on ϵ, such that the functional values (sequence values) are within a distance ϵ of A provided that x (or n, in the case of sequences) is at least as large as M. So what is the difference? Only that functions have a domain D which is an arbitrary subset of the real numbers, while for sequences the domain is the set of all natural numbers. In dealing with a sequence, we know that there are natural numbers—elements of the domain—which exceed any choice of M. For a function having an arbitrary domain, this is not necessarily the case, indeed, $(M, \infty) \cap D$ may very well be empty for some choices of M. Thus, we may expect that the differences between this definition of limit at $+\infty$ and the corresponding definition for sequences will arise for functions whose domain is bounded above. Such a difference is given in Exercise 3.

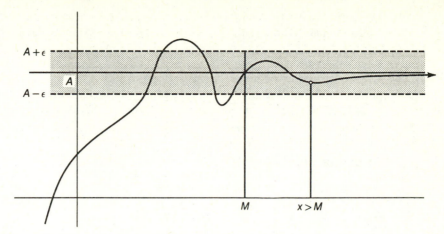

Figure 2.1.3 Graph illustrating $\lim_{x \to \infty} f(x) = A$.

Let us discuss the existence of limit at infinity geometrically. If the limit, A, exists, then, given $\epsilon > 0$, we can construct an infinite horizontal strip around the line $y = A$, of width 2ϵ, bounded by the lines $y = A - \epsilon$ and $y = A + \epsilon$. Then, we come up with a number M such that for all x in the domain of f, to the right of the point M, the values $f(x)$ lie in this strip. In other words, we can arrive at a stage (determined by M), from which point onwards, the graph of f lies entirely within this infinite strip. Figure 2.1.3 brings out these features, and is similar to Figure 1.1.3 for sequences. It is clear that if the limit at infinity did not exist, then for every number A, we can construct a horizontal strip of a suitable width, such that for every point M on the x-axis, we can always find points x to the right of M, where the graph shoots outside this strip.   □

EXAMPLE 1

Show that $f(x) = \dfrac{1}{x + 1}$; $x \in \mathbf{Q} \cap (0, \infty)$ has a limit as x tends to $+\infty$.

Solution.   It is clear that we should take $A = 0$. Now let ϵ be a fixed positive real number. We have

$$|f(x) - 0| = \left| \frac{1}{x + 1} - 0 \right|$$

$$= \frac{1}{x + 1} \quad \text{for } x \in \mathbf{Q} \cap (0, \infty).$$

Let $M = \dfrac{1}{\epsilon}$. Now if $x > M$, then $x + 1 > x > \dfrac{1}{\epsilon}$, whence

$$|f(x) - 0| < \frac{1}{x} < \epsilon.$$

Thus, the limit is 0 as claimed.   □

Discussion. A graph of f is shown in Figure 2.1.4 and makes the conclusion intuitively obvious. The calculations are essentially the same as those we would generate when considering the sequence $\left\{\dfrac{1}{n+1}\right\}$; indeed, it is these calculations which guided us in our choice of $A = 0$. Since the domain is unbounded, no special precautions need be taken beyond noting that all x's considered must come from the domain specified.   □

Negation of the Limit Definition

A function, f, having domain, D, will fail to have a limit as x tends to ∞ provided for every $A \in \mathbf{R}$, there exists $\epsilon > 0$ such that for every $M > 0$, there exists $x \in D$ such that $x > M$, and

$$|f(x) - A| \geqslant \epsilon.$$

Discussion. We compare this negation with that of the analogous statement for sequences. Both begin with the phrase 'for every real number A, there exists $\epsilon > 0$ such that for every $M > 0$', although in the sequence case there is no requirement that M be positive. The reader can check that the substance of the definition in the sequence case would not be changed by adding this requirement. Nor would the substance in the function case be changed if we did not require M to be positive. In the case of a function, we are then required to find an x which is in the domain of f and greater than the previously chosen M. This x acts to witness the fact that the particular A which was chosen at the beginning, cannot be the limit. Since this x is a witness, it must be in D, otherwise we could not apply f to it. This is contrasted with the case of sequences, since any positive integer n which is found will be in the domain of the sequence, due to the fact that a sequence is a function whose domain is the positive integers. Lastly, the two inequalities are identical. The level of similarity between the

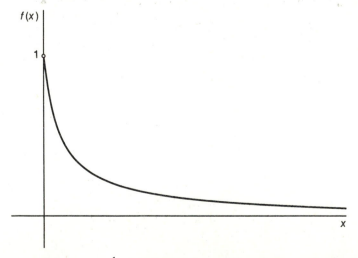

Figure 2.1.4   Graph of $f(x) = \dfrac{1}{x+1}$, $x \in \mathbf{Q} \cap (0, \infty)$. The graph has infinitely many holes.

two limit concepts is not remarkable given that, as the reader by now will have realized, the definition for functions is a generalization of the concept for sequences.

It is implicit in the above that if a function fails to have a limit as x tends to ∞, then the domain, D, cannot be bounded above. This is due to the fact that establishing a falsity generally requires a counterexample, which involves witnesses. In the above, a witness, x, must be found and three conditions must be satisfied:

    (i) $x \in D$;
   (ii) $x > M$;
  (iii) $|f(x) - A| \geqslant \epsilon$.

The first two conditions apply directly to x. By virtue of M being arbitrary they imply $\text{Dmn}\, f$ is unbounded. The third condition asserts that x witnesses the fact A cannot be the limit. The point is, since a witness must be found, that is, shown to exist, we could not expect to prove that a limit did not exist by a vacuous argument based on a domain which was bounded above.

Lastly, in the discussion following the definition of limit at infinity, we have already pointed out the geometrical meaning of the nonexistence of limit at infinity. That geometrical discussion captures, in an intuitive sense, all the analytical points which are made above. $\square$

EXAMPLE 2 _____

Using any standard definition of the function $f(x) = \cos x$, $x \in \mathbf{R}$, show that cos does not have a limit as x tends to ∞.

Solution. From any standard definition of $\cos x$ such as would appear in a calculus book, we have that $\cos 2n\pi = 1$, while $\cos (2n+1)\pi = -1$, where $n \in \mathbf{N}$. Now set $\epsilon = 1$ and let $M > 0$ be arbitrary, but fixed. Let $n > M$, $(n \in \mathbf{N})$ be chosen. Evidently, for any real number, A, whatsoever, the distance of A from one of $\cos n\pi$ and $\cos (n+1)\pi$ must be at least 1 (**WHY?**). Since $n\pi$ and $(n+1)\pi$ are both members of D, we are done. $\square$

Discussion. A comment on our use of trigonometric functions is useful. In the early stages of our development, trigonometric functions will be used mostly as sources of counterexamples. The reason for this is that the development of the analytic properties of the trigonometric functions, such as those associated with computing various limits, requires a tractable analytic definition of the function. The definition involving the wrapping function simply will not do. Suitable definitions will be developed later in Chapter 10, when an appropriate foundation has been laid. Until then, the reader, when asked to do problems involving trigonometric functions, should feel free to use any convenient definition and any properties which can be rigorously established from that definition. It is our belief that the properties employed above with respect to the cos function can be rigorously established from any of the usual definitions. To see this, the reader should take his favorite definition and go through the exercise of showing that $\cos 2n\pi = 1$, for all $n \in \mathbf{N}$. Similar remarks apply to the exponential and logarithmic functions.

Recalling our work with sequences, we found that a sequence failed to converge for one of two reasons, either it was unbounded, or it oscillated. Evidently, $\cos x$ oscillates as x tends to ∞, and this is the reason why it fails to converge to a limit as $x \to \infty$.

Lastly, we would reiterate that the definition of limits at infinity for functions is a generalization of the concept for sequences. Thus, each of the examples done for sequences can be reinterpreted in the context of limits of a function. To do this, one simply gives an analogous function definition based on the specification for the given sequence. The reader may obtain useful insights by reviewing the material on sequences in this light.   □

Given the relationship between the two limit definitions, we might expect that many theorems which are true about one type of limit are also true about the other type of limit. Indeed, this is one very good way of proceeding in mathematics. Namely: we know that certain things are true in a given situation; we ask which, if any, of these things remain true in the somewhat altered situation. For limits of functions, we might expect the following to be valid based on the results obtained for limits of sequences:

(a) the limit, if it exists, is unique;
(b) the existence of the limit implies a boundedness condition on Rng f;
(c) theorems relating limits of functions to arithmetic operations may be valid (sum, product, absolute value);
(d) monotonicity and boundedness conditions may imply the limit of a function exists.

The reader should stop here and try to formulate suitable statements for the theorems indicated above, based on our previous work and then try to prove those statements. In certain instances one will find that more hypotheses are needed to complete the proof. In other cases, the conclusion must be altered. By considering various examples, the industrious reader will be able to arrive at the correct statements of the theorems. It should be noted that the process of working out these statements will be empirical, and that proofs will be constructed only after this essentially experimental process has been completed.

Theorem 2.1.1. Let f be a function with domain D which is not bounded above. If f has a limit at $+\infty$ then this limit is unique.

Proof. By assertion, f has a limit as x tends to infinity, call it A. Let B be any other limit. If $B \neq A$, then without loss of generality, we may assume that $B < A$, whence $A - B$ is positive. Set $\epsilon = \dfrac{A - B}{2}$. Since A is a limit, we can find a real number M_A, depending on A, such that if $x > M_A$ and $x \in D$, then $|f(x) - A| < \epsilon$. Further, since B is also a limit, we can find M_B such that if $x > M_B$ and $x \in D$, then $|f(x) - B| < \epsilon$. Let $M = \max \{M_A, M_B\}$. Now D is not bounded above, so there is an $x_0 \in D$ with $x_0 > M$. For such an x_0 we have

$$f(x_0) < B + \epsilon = A - \epsilon < f(x_0), \qquad \textbf{(WHY?)}$$

which is absurd.   □

Discussion.   Compare this argument with that of Theorem 1.2.1. In essence the lines of reasoning, for both cases, are identical. The only significant difference between them is that at a key point we must use the fact that the domain of f is unbounded and contains members which are greater than M. This condition is automatically satisfied in the case of sequences. In Exercise 3 the reader will be asked to show that if a function has a bounded domain, then any real number will serve as a limit at infinity. In the proof, we could also force a contradiction by writing $A - B = (A - f(x)) + (f(x) - B)$, and applying the Triangle inequality.   □

Theorem 2.1.2.   Let f have a domain D which is not bounded above. If f has a limit at $+\infty$, then there is a real number B such that $\{f(x) : x \in D \text{ and } x > B\}$ is bounded.

   Proof.   Let A be the limit at $+\infty$ and $\epsilon = 1$. Then by definition there is an M such that if $x > M$ and $x \in D$, then $|f(x) - A| < 1$. It is immediate that if we set $B = M$, the conclusion will follow.   □

Discussion.   This theorem differs from the comparable theorem on sequences (Theorem 1.2.3) in a fundamental way related to the notion of bounded. A function, g, is **bounded,** if Rng g is a bounded set. Thus, for g to be bounded, there must be a fixed $K \in \mathbf{R}$ such that for all $x \in \text{Dmn } g$, $|g(x)| < K$. For the f of the theorem, f is bounded only on the subset $D \cap (M, \infty)$ for some M, not necessarily on the whole of D. In contrast, for sequences we found that the existence of the limit forces the whole of the sequence to be bounded, that is, the sequence is bounded as a function, whence for every n, $|a_n| < K$. In Exercise 4 the reader will be asked to carefully explore this difference.   □

Definition.   Let f be a function with domain D. We say that f is **monotone increasing on** D, provided that for every x and $y \in D$, $x < y$ implies $f(x) \leqslant f(y)$.

   In the obvious way, we can define **monotone decreasing on** D (the reader should do so). A function will be called **monotone** if it is either monotone increasing or decreasing on its domain. It is **strictly monotone** if $x < y$ implies the strict inequality $f(x) < f(y)$ (for the increasing case). A similar definition can be constructed for the decreasing case.

Discussion.   The definition of monotonicity for functions attempts to capture a basic property of graphs, namely, that some graphs go only up as they go from left to right across the page, while others go only down. The reader should ask himself what it means for a graph to go 'only up' and verify that the definition really does capture the intuitive ideas involved.   □

Theorem 2.1.3.   Let f be monotone on D. Then the limit at $+\infty$ exists, provided only that $\{f(x) : x \in D\}$ is bounded.

   Proof.   Without loss of generality, we may assume that f is monotone increasing. There are two cases, namely when D is bounded above, and when D has no upper bound. The former is left to Exercise 3. Thus, we assume that D is not bounded above. Since the set $S = \{f(x) : x \in D\}$ is bounded above, we may set $A = \sup S$. Fix $\epsilon > 0$. By Theorem 0.4.2, we can find $y \in S$ such that $A - \epsilon < y \leqslant A$. But $y = f(x_0)$ for some $x_0 \in D$. Let $M = x_0$. Thus, if $x > M$ with $x \in D$, we have,

$$A - \epsilon < y \leqslant f(x) \leqslant A,$$

whence $|f(x) - A| < \epsilon$. The decreasing case is left to Exercise 5. ☐

Discussion. Once again, we see that the crucial fact employed in the proof is the supremum principle. The reader should compare this theorem with Theorem 1.3.1. Note that the monotonicity was used in concluding $f(x) \geqslant f(x_0) = y$ from $x > M = x_0$. ☐

These theorems illustrate the results which can be obtained for limits at $+\infty$ and their similarity to those for sequences.

We conclude this section by defining the operations of addition, multiplication, and so on, as applied to functions. As in the case of sequences, this is done pointwise. Thus, for functions f and g with a common domain D, we define the **sum** $f + g$, the **product** $f \cdot g$, the **reciprocal** $\dfrac{1}{f}$, and the **absolute value function** $|f|$ as follows:

$$(f + g)(x) = f(x) + g(x), \; x \in D$$

$$(f \cdot g)(x) = f(x) \cdot g(x), \; x \in D$$

$$\left[\frac{1}{f} \right](x) = \frac{1}{f(x),} \; x \in D, \; f(x) \neq 0$$

$$|f|(x) = |f(x)|, \; x \in D$$

Obviously, $\dfrac{f}{g}$ stands for the function $f \cdot \dfrac{1}{g}$. The behavior of these functions as x approaching $\pm \infty$ are treated in Exercises 10–13.

EXERCISES

1. Define **limit as x tends to minus infinity** of f. Obtain a precise negation.

2. Prove theorems corresponding to Theorems 2.1.1 - 2.1.3, for limit as x tends to $-\infty$.

3. Let f have a bounded domain. Show that any real number will serve as a limit at infinity; use this result to complete the proof of Theorem 2.1.3.

4. Give an example of a function which is not bounded, that is, has unbounded range, but which has a limit at infinity. Why is it impossible to construct a sequence with this property?

5. Fill in the missing details in the proof of Theorem 2.1.3.

6. Prove or disprove that the following functions have limits at $+\infty$ $(-\infty)$; find $\lim\limits_{x \to \infty} f(x)$ ($\lim\limits_{x \to -\infty} f(x)$) whenever it exists.
   (a) $f(x) = \sin x, \qquad x \in \mathbf{R}$;

(b) $f(x) = \dfrac{1}{x^2}$, $x \in \mathbf{R}^+$;

(c) $f(x) = x^2$, $x \in [0,\, 10^{10000}]$;

(d) $f(x) = \dfrac{1 - x^2}{(1 + x)^2}$ $x \in \mathbf{R}^+$;

(e) $f(x) = \dfrac{x^3 + 1}{x^7 - 1}$, $x \in \mathbf{R} \sim \mathbf{Q}$;

(f) $f(x) = \dfrac{x - x^2}{1 + x^2}$;

(g) $f(x) = \dfrac{\cos x}{x}$, $x \in \mathbf{R}^+$;

(h) $f(x) = \dfrac{2^x}{e^x}$, $x \in \mathbf{Q}$;

(i) $f(x) = \sqrt{x + 10} - \sqrt{x + 2}$, $x \in \mathbf{R}^+$;

(j) $f(x) = \sqrt{2x} - \sqrt{x + 1}$, $x \in \mathbf{R}^+$;

(k) $f(x) = \dfrac{\sqrt{x} - x}{\sqrt{x} + x}$, $x \in \mathbf{R}^+$;

(l) $f(x) = \sqrt{x - \sqrt{x}} - \sqrt{x + \sqrt{x}}$, $x \in [1, \infty)$;

(m) $f(x) = \begin{cases} 1 - x, & x \leqslant 1 \\ 1 + x, & x > 1 \end{cases}$ $x \in \mathbf{R}$;

(n) $f(x) = \begin{cases} 1 - x, & x \in \mathbf{Q} \\ 1 + x, & x \notin \mathbf{Q} \end{cases}$ $x \in \mathbf{R}$;

(o) $f = \{(2,3),(3,4),(5,7),(9,11)\}$;

(p) $f(x) = \dfrac{3x - 2}{\sqrt{2x^2 + 1}}$, $x \in \mathbf{R}$;

(q) $f(x) = \dfrac{-3x + 1}{\sqrt{x^2 + x}}$, $x \in \mathbf{R}$.

7. Which of the following functions are monotone (strictly monotone) on their domains? Prove your answers.

(a) $f(x) = \cos x$, $x \in \mathbf{R}$;

(b) $f(x) = \cos x$, $x \in \bigcup_{n\in\mathbf{N}} [2n\pi,\, (2n+1)\pi]$;

(c) $f(x) = \dfrac{1}{x}$, $x \in \mathbf{R} \sim \mathbf{Q}$;

(d) $f(x) = \dfrac{1}{x^2}$, $x \in \mathbf{R} \sim \mathbf{Q}$;

(e) $f(x) = |x|$, $x \in [-25, 0]$;

(f) $f(x) = \sqrt{x}$, $x \in \mathbf{R}^+$;

(g) $f(x) = 0$, $x \in \mathbf{R}$;

(h) $f(x) = 0, \quad x \in \mathbf{Q}$;

(i) $f(x) = \begin{cases} 1 - 2x, & x < 1 \\ 2x, & x \geqslant 1; \end{cases}$

(j) $f(x) = \begin{cases} 1 - x, & x \in \mathbf{Q} \\ x, & x \notin \mathbf{Q}; \end{cases}$

(k) $f(x) = x^3, \quad x \in \mathbf{R}$;

(l) $f(x) = \dfrac{1}{x^2 + 1}, \quad x \in \mathbf{R}$;

(m) $f(x) = \dfrac{x}{x^2 + 1}, \quad x \in \mathbf{R}$;

(n) $f(x) = \dfrac{x^2}{x^2 - 1}, \quad x \in \mathbf{R} \sim \{-1,1\}$.

8. Which of the functions in Exercises 6 and 7 are bounded in their domains?

9. Let f and g be two functions that differ in value at a finite number of points in the common domain. Prove or disprove: $\lim_{x \to \infty} f(x) = \lim_{x \to \infty} g(x)$, provided it exists. What happens if f and g differ at an infinite number of points?

10. Let f and g be defined on D. Show that

$$\lim_{x \to \infty} (f + g)(x) = \lim_{x \to \infty} f(x) + \lim_{x \to \infty} g(x)$$

assuming that both limits on the right exist. Further, give an example to show that the limit on the left may exist even though the limits on the right fail to exist.

11. Discuss the equation

$$\lim_{x \to \infty} (f \cdot g)(x) = \lim_{x \to \infty} f(x) \cdot \lim_{x \to \infty} g(x).$$

12. Show that if $\lim_{x \to \infty} f(x) = A$, then $\lim_{x \to \infty} |f(x)| = |A|$, and $\lim_{x \to \infty} f^2(x) = A^2$. What about the converses?

13. Discuss $\lim_{x \to \infty} \dfrac{f(x)}{g(x)}$.

14. If f and g possess limits as x approaches $+\infty$, and if $f(x) \leqslant g(x)$ throughout $\mathbf{R}^+$, show that $\lim_{x \to \infty} f(x) \leqslant \lim_{x \to \infty} g(x)$. If $f(x) < g(x)$ throughout $\mathbf{R}^+$, can you conclude that $\lim_{x \to \infty} f(x) < \lim_{x \to \infty} g(x)$?

15. We say that f **diverges to** $+\infty$ as x tends to $+\infty$, provided for each $K > 0$, there exists a real number M such that $x \in \mathrm{Dmn}\, f$ and $x > M$ .implies. $f(x) > A$. Formulate the concept of '**diverges to** $-\infty$'. Prove that if $\lim_{x \to \infty} f = \infty$, then $\lim_{x \to \infty} \dfrac{1}{f} = 0$. Is the converse true?

16. Let $\lim_{x \to \infty} \dfrac{f(x)}{g(x)} = A \neq 0$, where f and g are defined for $x > a \in \mathbf{R}$, and further $g(x) > 0$ for $x > a$. Prove that
    (a) if $A > 0$, then $\lim_{x \to \infty} f(x) = \infty$ if and only if $\lim_{x \to \infty} g(x) = \infty$;
    (b) if $A < 0$, then $\lim_{x \to \infty} f(x) = -\infty$ if and only if $\lim_{x \to \infty} g(x) = \infty$.

17. A function defined on **R** of the form

$$f(x) = \sum_{i=0}^{n} a_i x^i$$

where $n \in \mathbf{N}$, and the $a_i \in \mathbf{R}$ is called a **polynomial function**; if $a_n \neq 0$, we say f is a **polynomial of degree** n. Let $P(x)$ and $Q(x)$ denote polynomials in x, and set $f(x) = \dfrac{P(x)}{Q(x)}$ for $x \in D$, where D does not contain any of the zeros of $Q(x)$. State and prove a theorem which completely describes the behavior of f at $+\infty$. Is this behavior eventually monotone? (You may use results from elementary calculus and the Fundamental Theorem of Algebra to settle the question of monotonicity.)

18. Let f be defined on D which is not bounded above. Show that $\lim\limits_{x \to \infty} f(x)$ exists, exactly if for every sequence, $\{a_n\}$ of elements of D which diverges to ∞, $\lim\limits_{n \to \infty} f(a_n)$ exists.

19. Show that the function

$$f(x) = \frac{x \tan x + 2x - 1}{x + 1}$$

does not possess a limit as x approaches $+\infty$, but if x ranges through a sequence of values $x = n\pi + \dfrac{\pi}{4}$ $(n = 0, 1, \ldots)$ then $f(x)$ approaches a limit.

20. If $f: (a,\infty) \to \mathbf{R}$ is such that $\lim\limits_{x \to \infty} x \cdot f(x) = L \in \mathbf{R}$, show that $\lim\limits_{x \to \infty} f(x) = 0$.

21. Obtain a set of sufficient conditions for the existence of $\lim\limits_{x \to \infty} (f \circ g)(x)$.

22. Show that the concept of limit at infinity can be regarded as a two-person game. Illustrate with examples.

2.2 LIMIT OF A FUNCTION AT A REAL NUMBER

The problem of formalizing the concept of limit was especially crucial for functions, since it is a prerequisite to any discussion of the geometry of the graphs of functions. We might expect that the definition of the limit of a function at a real number is quite similar to that for the limit at $+\infty$. To a degree this is the case. However, at $+\infty$ we must worry about the intuitive idea of 'x traveling off to $+\infty$' while now we want to capture the intuitive idea of 'x traveling toward some fixed real number'.

Definition. Let f be defined on D and let $a \in \mathbf{R}$. We say that f has a **limit as x tends to a** provided that there exists an $A \in \mathbf{R}$ such that for every $\epsilon > 0$, there exists δ such that for every $x \in D$,

$$0 < |x - a| < \delta \text{ .implies. } |f(x) - A| < \epsilon.$$

Further, in the case that such a number A exists, we shall say that A is the **limit as x tends to a of f**, or, more simply as the **limit at a of f** and write

$$\lim_{x \to a} f(x) = A.$$

Discussion.   If we compare the definition above with that of 'limit as x tends to $+\infty$', we find that they are the same until after the arbitrary ϵ is chosen. The definition above then requires us to find a positive δ, whereas the definition in the case of $+\infty$ required us to find an M. As was pointed out, M would generally be large since its purpose is to keep x close to $+\infty$. But δ will in general be very small since its purpose is to keep x close to a. It does this by requiring

$$|x - a| < \delta,$$

which restricts our attention to those members of the domain of f which are within a distance δ of a, if indeed there are any members of D which are close to a. In the case of x tending to ∞, x can travel only in one direction, while in the case of x tending to a real number a, the point a can be approached both from the left and the right sides. The observant reader will have noticed that we have omitted to write down a significant part of the δ inequality, namely,

$$0 < |x - a|.$$

This part of the inequality has the effect of preventing x from actually taking the value a. Perhaps this seems strange, but remember that in the definition of the limit at $+\infty$, x can never take the value $+\infty$, since $+\infty$ is not a number. Our interest is in what happens to the function values as x *tends to* $+\infty$. In the same way, our interest is not what actually happens when x takes the value a, rather what is happening when x *is close to a,* but different from a. That is why we require the distance from x to a to be positive.

The geometry of the situation can be made clear from a picture (see Figure 2.2.1). The picture has two parts, concerning a limit at a, and another limit at b. In both cases we look at A as the potential limit. First note that as soon as we are given an ϵ, this gives rise to an open interval, $(A - \epsilon, A + \epsilon)$, on the $f(x)$-axis (y-axis) (which we shall call the ϵ-interval). This interval cuts out a horizontal strip which runs parallel to the x-axis. Similarly, the open interval $(a - \delta, a + \delta)$ generates a vertical strip of width 2δ, parallel to the y-axis. These two strips intersect in a rectangle. Now for the limit to exist, we must be able to find a δ such that the rectangle generated by the intersection of the δ-strip with the ϵ-strip completely contains the graph for all the domain values which lie inside the δ-interval (see Figure 2.2.1). For the δ-interval about a, the graph associated with domain values in the δ-interval is completely contained in the generated rectangle. However, for the δ-interval about b, the graph is not contained in the associated rectangle, that is, there are domain values inside the δ-interval whose functional values lie outside the ϵ-interval. It can be seen from the figure that it is possible to choose a δ-interval about b which is small enough to ensure that the graph will lie in the generated rectangle. The reader should let ϵ shrink in his mind's eye, so that the interval about A shrinks. Notice that this will force the choice of δ to shrink if we are to generate a rectangle which will completely contain the graph. Thus, the δ we obtain depends on the ϵ, given in advance. If as ϵ shrinks to 0, there is always a choice for δ, then the limit will exist. For the examples below, the reader should draw the appropriate picture to verify the geometry of the situation.

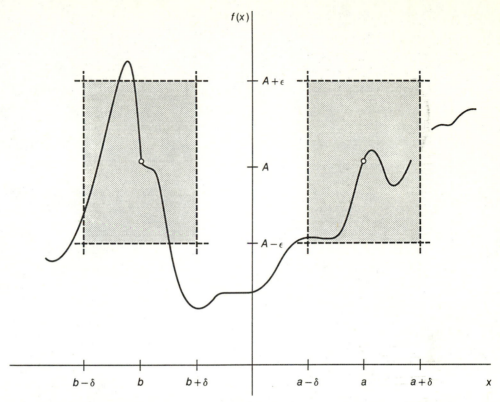

Figure 2.2.1 The figure depicting the geometry underlying the limit concept: $\lim\limits_{x \to a} f(x) = A$, but $\lim\limits_{x \to b} f(x) \neq A$.

The limit of $f(x)$ as x approaches a is not to be confused with the value of the function f at the member a. The reader will have noted that we do not require a to be a member of the domain of f. As we shall see, this has as a consequence that we must always be aware whether or not a is a member of the domain of f, which adds a degree of complexity to our work. However, this complexity is a result of the fact that there are many naturally arising situations in which we want to compute a limit where a is not in the domain of f. For example, if $f(x) = \dfrac{1}{x}$, $x > 0$, we may ask, what is the limit of f as x tends to 0. So that we may deal with this and other natural questions, such as arise if the domain is not an interval, we have permitted this complexity to exist. This does not deny the fact that our main interest is in the case when a belongs to the domain of f. □

EXAMPLE 1 _____

For $f(x) = x^2$, $x \in \mathbf{R}$, find the limit as x tends to 1.

Solution. We claim that $\lim\limits_{x \to 1} f(x) = 1$. To see this, let us fix $\epsilon > 0$ and consider the quantity $|f(x) - 1|$. Now,

$$|f(x) - 1| = |x^2 - 1| = |(x - 1)(x + 1)|$$
$$= |x - 1| \cdot |x + 1|.$$

Suppose $\delta \leqslant 1$. It is immediate that

$$|x - 1| < 1 \text{ .implies. } 0 < |x + 1| < 3, \qquad \textbf{(WHY?)} \quad (*)$$

and further, that

$$|x - 1| < 1 \text{ .implies. } |x + 1| \cdot |x - 1| < 3 \cdot |x - 1|.$$

Let us therefore set $\delta = \min \left\{ 1, \dfrac{\epsilon}{3} \right\}$. We then have that if $x \in D$ and $0 < |x - 1| < \delta$, then

$$|f(x) - 1| = |x^2 - 1|$$
$$< 3 \cdot |x - 1|$$
$$< 3 \cdot \delta$$
$$\leqslant 3 \cdot \frac{\epsilon}{3} = \epsilon,$$

which is the desired inequality. $\square$

Discussion.   The first thing to note is that the basic tool for manipulating the expression $|f(x) - A|$ is algebra. The second is that there is a basic strategy, namely to manipulate $|f(x) - A|$ into the form

$$|x - a| \cdot (\text{junk})$$

where the 'junk' has the property that it is bounded provided that δ is sufficiently small. This is why we refer to this term as 'junk', since once we know it is bounded, we can replace it by a single number and we don't have to worry about it anymore.

In the example above, we take $|x^2 - 1|$ and factor it to obtain

$$|x - 1| \cdot |x + 1|.$$

The term $|x - 1|$ is exactly the term that appears in the δ-inequality, and so it will be at least as small as δ. The 'junk' term, in this case is $|x + 1|$. This term is bounded above by 3 as long as we require $\delta \leqslant 1$ because the condition $|x - 1| < \delta$ is equivalent to

$$1 - \delta < x < 1 + \delta.$$

In other words, by restricting δ we force x to lie in the interval shown, and this permits us to assert $|x + 1| \leqslant 3$. Thus, if δ is small, that is, less than 1, then $3 \cdot \delta$ is also small, and in fact will be less than or equal to ϵ if δ is small enough.

The number 3 arises by virtue of the line marked with a (*) in the proof. If, alternatively, we had insisted that $\delta < 2$, then the reader can show that the 3 would be replaced by a 4, and the proof would be completed by setting $\delta = \min \{2, \frac{\epsilon}{4}\}$. Thus, there is nothing special about 3, other than it is determined by the restriction placed on δ which, in turn, is useful for generating a bound on the 'junk' term.

Finally, notice that in general δ *will depend on* ϵ and in fact δ will usually be much, much smaller than ϵ. The nature of this dependence of δ on ϵ will be determined by the bound on the junk term, and perhaps other factors as further examples will show.

It is suggested that the reader draw an appropriate graph of $f(x) = x^2$ containing analogous elements to those presented in Figure 2.2.1. This will supply geometric intuition regarding the computation of the limit.   □

EXAMPLE 2 _____

Let $f(x) = \dfrac{1}{x+2}$, $x \in \mathbf{R} \sim \{-2\}$. Show that $\displaystyle\lim_{x \to -3} \dfrac{1}{x+2}$ exists.

Solution. Let $\epsilon > 0$ be arbitrary but fixed. Moreover, let us take as a candidate for A the number -1, which happens to be the value of the function at $x = -3$. Let us now consider the quantity $|f(x) - A|$. Algebra yields

$$\left| \frac{1}{x+2} - (-1) \right| = \left| \frac{1 + (x+2)}{x+2} \right|$$

$$= \left| \frac{x - (-3)}{x+2} \right|$$

$$= |x - (-3)| \cdot \left| \frac{1}{x+2} \right|.$$

Further, if $\delta \leqslant \dfrac{1}{2}$, then

$$0 < |x - (-3)| < \frac{1}{2} \ \text{.implies.} \ x < -\frac{5}{2}$$

$$\text{.implies.} \ x + 2 < -\frac{1}{2}$$

$$\text{.implies.} \ \frac{1}{2} < |x+2|$$

$$\text{.implies.} \ \left| \frac{1}{x+2} \right| < 2.$$

We now set $\delta = \min\left\{ \dfrac{1}{2}, \dfrac{\epsilon}{2} \right\}$, whence

$$\left| \frac{1}{x+2} - (-1) \right| = |x - (-3)| \cdot \left| \frac{1}{x+2} \right|$$

$$< \delta \cdot \left| \frac{1}{x+2} \right|$$

$$< \delta \cdot 2 \leqslant \epsilon,$$

as desired.   □

Discussion. The geometry of this situation is captured in Figure 2.2.2. Notice that the function is defined everywhere except at $x = -2$. Close to this value, the graph shoots up, or down, suggesting that problems may arise if x is permitted to be too close to -2. By requiring that $\delta < \dfrac{1}{2}$, we prevent x from getting arbitrarily close to -2.

Algebraically, the problems at $x = -2$ show up in the term $\dfrac{1}{x+2}$, which is undefined when x takes -2 for a value. Moreover, since by using algebra, we have expressed $|f(x) - A|$ as a product of $|x - a|$ and $\left| \dfrac{1}{x+2} \right|$ $(a = -3)$, it is evident that we want to bound $\dfrac{1}{x+2}$ so that it can play the role of 'junk'. The restriction on δ is just what is required to accomplish this, and yields an upper bound of 2. The solution is completed by setting δ to be the minimum of $\left\{ \dfrac{1}{2}, \dfrac{\epsilon}{2} \right\}$. Note that $\dfrac{\epsilon}{2}$ was used instead of ϵ so that the added factor of 2 arising from the 'junk' term would disappear.

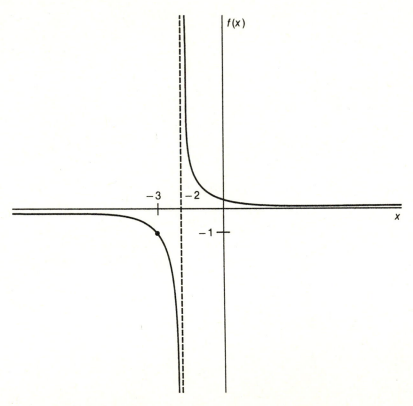

Figure 2.2.2   Graph of $f(x) = \dfrac{1}{x+1}$, $x \in \mathbf{R} \sim \{-2\}$ exhibiting $\lim\limits_{x \to -3} f(x) = -1$.

We have used a value of $\frac{1}{2}$ to prevent x from becoming arbitrarily close to -2. We could have used $\frac{3}{4}$, or any number which was less than 1. Had we used another number, an argument which was similar would have resulted. The reader would benefit from writing out one of these alternative arguments. In particular, it is essential that the reader understand why δ must be strictly less than 1. $\qquad\square$

EXAMPLE 3

Let $f(x) = \frac{1}{x}$, $x \in \left[0, \frac{1}{10}\right]$. Show that f has a limit as x tends to $\frac{1}{10}$.

Solution. Fix a positive ϵ. Let us now manipulate $|f(x) - A|$, where A has the value 10. Now

$$\left|\frac{1}{x} - 10\right| = \left|\frac{1 - 10x}{x}\right|$$

$$= \left|\frac{10}{x}\right| \cdot \left|x - \frac{1}{10}\right|.$$

Let $\delta = \min\left\{\frac{1}{20}, \frac{\epsilon}{200}\right\}$. It follows that

$$\left|\frac{1}{x} - 10\right| = \left|\frac{10}{x}\right| \cdot \left|x - \frac{1}{10}\right|$$

$$< 200 \cdot \left|x - \frac{1}{10}\right| \qquad\qquad \textbf{(WHY?)}$$

$$< 200 \cdot \frac{\epsilon}{200} = \epsilon$$

whenever $x \in \left[0, \frac{1}{10}\right]$ and $0 < \left|x - \frac{1}{10}\right| < \delta$. $\qquad\square$

Discussion. Again we follow the basic strategy of manipulating $|f(x) - A|$ to obtain a form $|x - a| \cdot (\text{junk})$, where there is a known bound on the size of 'junk'. In this case, the 'junk' turns out to be $\frac{10}{x}$, where $0 < x < \frac{1}{10}$. The problem with the quantity $\frac{10}{x}$ is that as x gets close to 0, the quantity gets very large (see Figure 2.2.3) and, unfortunately, is unbounded (the reader should try some values to see that this does happen). Notice that for $\frac{10}{x}$ to be really large, x must be really close to 0. Once we understand this fact, we see that the solution to our problems is to prevent x from getting too close to 0. Thus, we require $\delta < \frac{1}{20}$, whence $\left|x - \frac{1}{10}\right| < \frac{1}{20}$ will

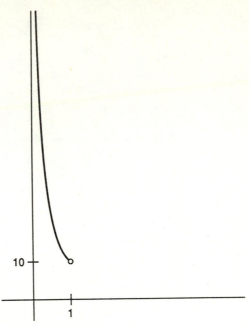

Figure 2.2.3 Graph of $f(x) = \dfrac{10}{x}$, $x \in (0, \dfrac{1}{10})$.

force $x > \dfrac{1}{20}$ **(WHY?)**. There is nothing special about $\dfrac{1}{20}$ other than the fact that it is less than $\dfrac{1}{10}$ and greater than 0. Any fixed number satisfying this requirement may be used as an upper bound for δ and will lead to a bound on the 'junk' term—the reader might try $\dfrac{1}{19}$ as an upper bound for δ to see the effect on the calculations. Observe that the larger we allow the upper bound on δ to be, the closer x is permitted to be to 0 and the smaller we will ultimately have to choose δ to be to make the calculation work out. Thus, the ultimate smallness of δ depends not only on the smallness of ϵ but also on the bound for the 'junk' term. Lastly, we emphasize that $\dfrac{1}{10}$ is not in the domain of f as defined, and indeed the function is defined only on the left-hand side of $\dfrac{1}{10}$.

The reader should compare the arguments in the previous two examples. Both deal with similar functions. One difference between the two examples is in the fact that $\dfrac{1}{10}$ is considerably closer to 0 than -3 is to -2. The reader should identify how this fact changes the computations. $\qquad\square$

We turn our attention now to the problem of why a function may fail to have a limit at a given real number. As in the case of sequences, the first step in solving the problem is to write down precisely what is meant by a function failing to have a limit. This means negating the limit definition.

Negation of the Limit Definition

Let f be a function with domain D and let $a \in \mathbf{R}$. The limit as x tends to a of f does not exist provided that for every $A \in \mathbf{R}$ there exists an $\epsilon > 0$ such that for every $\delta > 0$ there is an $x \in D$ such that

$$0 < |x - a| < \delta \text{ .and. } |f(x) - A| \geqslant \epsilon.$$

Discussion. What this is telling us is that no matter how we pick A, we must be able to find a single fixed ϵ (the choice of ϵ will likely depend on the choice of A) such that no matter how small we choose δ there will always be an x in the domain of the function which is within a distance of δ from a (but not equal to a) and for this x, the distance from $f(x)$ to A will be at least as large as ϵ. Notice that a key fact here is that we must always be able to find an x which is in the domain and which satisfies $0 < |x - a| < \delta$. This means that for every choice of δ,

$$[(a - \delta, a) \cup (a, a + \delta)] \cap D \neq \varnothing.$$

As we shall see in the next section, this requirement means that a is a **limit point** of D. It follows that if for some particular choice of δ the above intersection is empty, then the limit as x tends to a of f will automatically exist, a fact pursued further in Exercise 8. □

Our basic purpose is to understand why some functions should fail to have limits. Recall that we have already considered this question for sequences and we found that there were two fundamental reasons why a sequence should fail to have a limit. The first was that the sequence got large without bound as n approached ∞. The second was that the sequence 'wandered' or 'oscillated' as n tended to infinity without ever staying close to one fixed point. Thus, it seems reasonable that we might try these reasons, formulated in an appropriate manner, for functions.

EXAMPLE 4

Let $f(x) = \dfrac{1}{x - 2}$, $x \in D = \mathbf{R} \sim \mathbf{Q}$. Show that f does not have a limit as x tends to 2.

Solution. Let A be any fixed real number and set $\epsilon = 1$. Let $\delta < \dfrac{1}{2}$. Now every interval of real numbers contains irrational numbers, so there are members of the domain of f in $(2 - \delta, 2)$ and $(2, 2 + \delta)$. Let $x \in D \cap (2, 2 + \delta)$. An algebraic calculation will show $f(x) > 2$ (**HOW?**). Similarly, $x \in D \cap (2 - \delta, 2)$ implies that $f(x) < -2$. Thus, no matter what the choice of A, either $|f(x) - A| \geqslant 1$ for $x \in D \cap (2, 2 + \delta)$ or $|f(x) - A| \geqslant 1$ for $x \in D \cap (2 - \delta, 2)$ (**WHY?**). Thus, f has no limit at 2 as claimed. □

Discussion. The graph of f is shown in Figure 2.2.4. The picture illustrates the fact that if x is close to 2 on the right, then $f(x)$ is a very large positive number, while if x is close to 2 on the left, then $f(x)$ is a very large negative number. This fact is

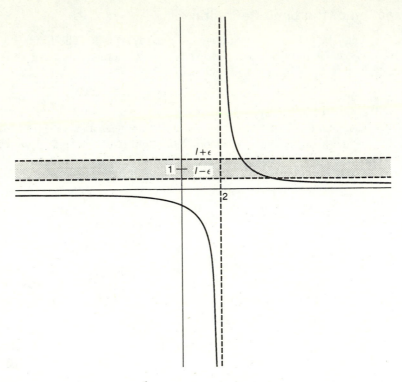

Figure 2.2.4   Graph of $f(x) = \dfrac{1}{x-2}$ showing nonexistence of limit at 2.

employed in the proof, since we use the fact that A is fixed, either nonnegative or negative, and choose an x on the appropriate side of 2 to witness that $|f(x) - A| \geqslant \epsilon$.   □

EXAMPLE 5 _____

Let $f(x) = \sin\dfrac{1}{x}$, $x \in \mathbf{R} \sim \{0\}$. Show that f does not have a limit as x tends to 0.

Solution.   Let A be any fixed real number, and let $\epsilon = 1$. We take it as an established fact that

$$\sin\frac{n\pi}{2} = \begin{cases} 1, & \text{if } n = 4k + 1, & k \in \mathbf{N} \\ 0, & \text{if } n = 2k, & k \in \mathbf{N} \\ -1, & \text{if } n = 4k + 3, & k \in \mathbf{N}. \end{cases}$$

Let $\delta > 0$ be chosen. We can find $k \in \mathbf{N}$ such that

$$\frac{2}{(4k + 1)\pi} < \delta \qquad\qquad \textbf{(WHY?)}$$

For such a value of k, we have either that

$$\left| \sin\frac{(4k + 1)\pi}{2} - A \right| \geqslant 1$$

or,

$$\left| \sin \frac{(4k + 3)\pi}{2} - A \right| \geqslant 1.$$

Since for any choice of k these numbers are in D, we are done.   ☐

Discussion.   The graph of $\sin \dfrac{1}{x}$ near 0 is shown in Figure 2.2.5. This is an example of a function which oscillates near a given point. In fact, as x moves in toward 0 from either side, the function moves up and down an infinite number of times. It is clear that a function with such a behavior at a given point can not have a limit at that point. Notice that the proof where the limit fails to exist does not use all the domain near 0, but only a small part of it. What has happened is that we have selected a sequence of domain points which converges to 0. We have then used the fact that the associated sequence of range points does not have a limit to show that the function does not have a limit. (The reader will have an opportunity to explore this idea further in Exercise 9.) It does not matter that if, for example, A were 0, the function would go through

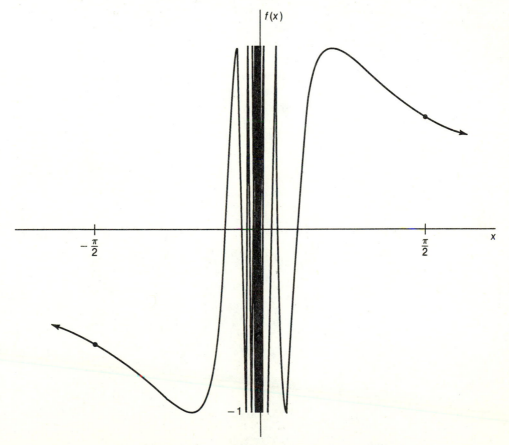

Figure 2.2.5   Graph of $f(x) = \sin \dfrac{1}{x}$, $x \in \mathbf{R} \sim \{0\}$ depicting near 0.

this point infinitely often. To have a limit the function values must get *close to a fixed A and stay there* as the domain points get close to *a*. The reader should carefully compare these remarks with those concerning why sequences fail to have limits. □

In summary, our previous two examples show that a function will fail to have a limit at $a \in \mathbf{R}$ if f is either unbounded near a, or if f oscillates near a. While we are not in a position now to show that these are the only reasons why a function can fail to have a limit at a, we will do so later.

EXERCISES

1. Given $0 < \delta < 1$, verify the following estimates:

(a) $|x - 2| < \delta$ .implies. $|x^2 - 4| < 5\delta$;

(b) $|x - 2| < \delta$ .implies. $\left|\dfrac{x - 2}{x + 3}\right| < \dfrac{1}{4}\delta$;

(c) $|x - 3| < \delta$ .implies. $|2x^2 - 11x + 15| < 3\delta$;

(d) $|x + 2| < \delta$ .implies. $|x^2 + 3x + 2| < 2\delta$;

(e) $|x + 1| < \delta$ .implies. $|x^3 + 1| < 7\delta$.

If in (a) $|x - 2|$ is replaced by $|x - 100|$, is the estimate still valid? What about analogous changes in (b)–(e)?

2. For each of the following functions with the given domains, use the definition to decide whether the limit exists at the point given.

(a) $f(x) = c; x \in \mathbf{R}, (c \in \mathbf{R}), a = 2$;

(b) $f(x) = c; x \in \mathbf{Q}, (c \in \mathbf{R}), a = 2$;

(c) $f(x) = 3x + 5; x \in \mathbf{R}, a = 2$;

(d) $f(x) = 4x - 3; x \in \mathbf{R}, a = -\dfrac{1}{2}$;

(e) $f(x) = \sqrt{x}; x \in \mathbf{R}^+, a = 0$;

(f) $f(x) = x^{1/3}; x \in \mathbf{R}, a = 2$;

(g) $f(x) = \dfrac{x + 3}{2x}; x \in \mathbf{R} \sim \{0\}, a = -2$;

(h) $f(x) = \dfrac{x^2 + 2x}{2x - 3}; x \in \mathbf{R} \sim \{0\}, a = 3$;

(i) $f(x) = \dfrac{1}{x^2}; x \in \mathbf{R} \sim \mathbf{Q}, a = 0$;

(j) $f(x) = \dfrac{1}{x^2}; x \in \mathbf{R} \sim \mathbf{Q}, a = \dfrac{1}{100}$;

(k) $f(x) = x^4 - 2x; x \in \mathbf{R}, a = 3$;

(l) $f(x) = \dfrac{1}{1 + x^2}; x \in \mathbf{Q}, a = 0$;

(m) $f(x) = \dfrac{1}{1 + x^3}; x \in [0, 1], a = 1$;

(n) $f(x) = \dfrac{x^2 + 2x}{x - 1}; x \in \mathbf{R} \sim \{1\}, a = 3$;

(o) $f(x) = \dfrac{x^2 - x - 2}{x^2 - 2x}$; $x \in \mathbf{R} \sim \{0,2\}$, $a = 2$;

(p) $f(x) = \dfrac{\sqrt{x - 2} - 2}{x - 6}$; $x \in \mathbf{R} \sim \{6\}$, $a = 6$;

(q) $f(x) = \dfrac{x^3 - 27}{x - 3}$; $x \in \mathbf{R} \sim \{3\}$, $a = 3$;

(r) $f(x) = \cos \dfrac{1}{x}$; $x \in (0, 1)$, $a = 0$;

(s) $f(x) = \sin \dfrac{1}{x^2}$; $x \in (-1, 0)$, $a = 0$;

(t) $f(x) = x \sin \dfrac{1}{x}$; $x \in (0, 1)$, $a = 0$;

(u) $f(x) = \dfrac{1}{x} \sin \dfrac{1}{x}$; $x \in (0, 1)$, $a = 0$;

(v) $f(x) = 2^x$; $x \in \mathbf{Q}$, $a = 0$;
(w) $f(x) = e^x$; $x \in \mathbf{Q}$, $a = 1$;
(x) $f(x) = [x]$; $x \in \mathbf{R}$, $a = 2$, $a \in \mathbf{Z}$, $a \notin \mathbf{Z}$;

(y) $f(x) = x \cdot \left[\dfrac{1}{x} \right]$; $x \in \mathbf{R} \sim \{0\}$, $a = 0$;

(z) $f(x) = x + \dfrac{x}{|x|}$; $x \in \mathbf{R} \sim \{0\}$, $a = 0$;

(a′) $f(x) = \begin{cases} 1, & x \geqslant 1 \\ \dfrac{1}{n}, & \dfrac{1}{n} \leqslant x \leqslant \dfrac{1}{n-1}; \\ 0, & x \leqslant 0 \end{cases}$ $a = 0$;

(b′) $f = \{(0,2), (2,3), (5,8), (6,6), (10,0)\}$, $a = 0$, $a = 3$;

(c′) $f(x) = \begin{cases} 3 + x, & x \leqslant 1 \\ 3 - x, & x > 1 \end{cases}$; $x \in \mathbf{R}$, $a = 1$;

(d′) $f(x) = \begin{cases} 2x, & x \in \mathbf{Q} \\ 1 - 2x, & x \notin \mathbf{Q} \end{cases}$; $a = \dfrac{1}{2}, \dfrac{1}{4}$;

(e′) $f(x) = \dfrac{\sqrt{1 + x} - \sqrt{1 + x^2}}{\sqrt{1 + x^2} - \sqrt{1 - x}}$; $x \in (-1, 1)$, $a = 0$;

(f′) $f(x) = \lim\limits_{n \to \infty} \dfrac{\ln(2 + x) - x^{2n} \sin x}{1 + x^{2n}}$; $x \in (-2, \infty)$, $a = 1$.

3. Let $f(x) = x^2$, $x \in (0, 1)$. Show that the limit exists as x tends to -1. Is this limit unique?

4. Prove that $\lim\limits_{x \to 0} \dfrac{x + 2}{x + 1} = 2$. Given $\epsilon = 5, 1, \dfrac{1}{10}, \dfrac{1}{100}$, find the corresponding δ for which $0 < |x| < \delta$ witnesses $\left| \dfrac{x + 2}{x + 1} - 2 \right| < \epsilon$.

5. Prove that $\lim\limits_{x \to a} f(x) = A$ if and only if $\lim\limits_{x \to a} g(x) = 0$, where $g(x) = f(x) - A$.

6. Let f be defined on D. We say that f is **unbounded** at $a \in \mathbf{R}$ provided that for every M and every positive δ there is an $x \in (a-\delta, \ a+\delta) \cap D$ such that $x \neq a$ and $|f(x)| \geq M$. Show that if f is unbounded at a, then the limit as x tends to a does not exist.

7. Let f be defined on D. We say that f **oscillates** at $a \in \mathbf{R}$ if there exist A, $B \in \mathbf{R}$ such that $A < B$ and for every positive δ there exist x, $y \in (a - \delta, \ a + \delta) \cap D$, but distinct from a, such that $f(x) \leq A$ and $f(y) \geq B$. Show that if f oscillates at a, then the limit as x tends to a of f does not exist.

8. Let f be defined on D and suppose for some $a \in \mathbf{R}$ and some $\delta > 0$ that $D \cap ((a - \delta, a) \cup (a, a + \delta))$ is empty. Show that any real number will serve as the limit as x tends to a of f.

9. Let f be defined on D. Suppose there is a sequence $\{a_n\} \subseteq D \sim \{a\}$ such that $\{a_n\}$ converges to a and that the sequence $\{f(a_n)\}$ has no limit. Show that the limit as x tends to a of f does not exist. Note that we have excluded a from the range of $\{a_n\}$. Give an example to show why this is necessary.

10. State the contrapositive of the result in Exercise 9.

11. Let f be defined on D such that every sequence of domain points which converges to a gives rise to a sequence of range points having the same limit, A. Show that the limit as x tends to a of f is A.

12. Give examples of functions f and g such that both f and g fail to possess limits as x approaches a, but $f + g$ (respectively $f \cdot g$) has a limit at $x = a$.

13. Let $f: \mathbf{R} \to \mathbf{R}$ satisfy the relationship $f(x + y) = f(x) + f(y)$ for all $x, y \in \mathbf{R}$. If f possesses a limit at $x = 0$, show that it must be 0. Further prove that f has a limit at every real number a.

14. Let f, g be defined on D and a be a limit point of D. Show that if both f and $f + g$ have limits at $x = a$, then g has a limit at $x = a$. Is the same conclusion valid if we consider $f \cdot g$ instead of $f + g$?

15. Show how the problem of whether $\lim\limits_{x \to a} f(x)$ exists can be interpreted as a two-person game. Illustrate with examples.

16. Prove that if $\lim\limits_{x \to a} f(x) = A > 0$, there exists a positive δ such that $f(x) > 0$ for $0 < |x - a| < \delta$. Is the result true when $A = 0$?

17. If $f(x) \leq g(x)$ for each x in their common domain, prove that $\lim\limits_{x \to a} f(x) \leq \lim\limits_{x \to a} g(x)$. If $f(x) < g(x)$ for each x, does it follow that $\lim\limits_{x \to a} f(x) < \lim\limits_{x \to a} g(x)$?

18. Prove the following 'squeeze theorem': If $f \leq h \leq g$, and if $\lim\limits_{x \to a} f = \lim\limits_{x \to a} g = L$, then $\lim\limits_{x \to a} h = L$.

19. Prove or disprove:
    (a) $\lim\limits_{x \to a} f(x) = A$ if and only if for each $c \in \mathbf{R}$, $\lim\limits_{x \to a-c} f(x + c) = A$;
    (b) $\lim\limits_{x \to a} f(x) = A$ if and only if for each $c \neq 0$, $\lim\limits_{x \to a/c} f(cx) = A$.

20. Formulate the concept of $\lim\limits_{x \to a} f = +\infty$ (respectively, $-\infty$). Prove that if $\lim\limits_{x \to a} f = +\infty$ and $\lim\limits_{x \to a} g = A$, then, $\lim\limits_{x \to a} (f + g) = +\infty$. Further, if $A \neq 0$, $\lim\limits_{x \to a} (f \cdot g) = +\infty$. Discuss the situation when $A = 0$.

21. Give examples of functions f and g such that both f and g have no limit at a, but $f + g$ (respectively, $f \cdot g$) has a limit at a.

22. Show that if $\lim\limits_{x \to a} f(x) = +\infty$, then $\lim\limits_{x \to a} \dfrac{1}{f(x)} = 0$. Also, prove that if $0 < f(x) < \infty$ for all $x \in \text{Dmn } f$ and $\lim\limits_{x \to a} \dfrac{1}{f(x)} = 0$, then $\lim\limits_{x \to a} f(x) = +\infty$.

2.3 BASIC LIMIT THEOREMS

As with the previous types of limits, we want to set down a collection of theorems which describe the fundamental relations governing the behavior of limits of functions at a, and also the consequences of the existence of the limit at a for the function f. Before proceeding, it will be useful to have one definition of a topological concept and the definition of bounded function.

Definition. Let $D \subseteq \mathbf{R}$ and $a \in D$. Then a is said to be a **limit point** of D provided that for every positive δ,

$$\{x : 0 < |x - a| < \delta\} \cap D \neq \varnothing.$$

Discussion. The effect of the assertion that a is a limit point of D is to ensure that every open interval which contains a also contains points of D other than a. In fact, it can be shown that every such open interval contains an infinite number of points of D (see Exercise 14). The concept of limit point arises in topology and will be explored in greater detail in Chapter 3. □

Definition. Let f be defined on D and $a \in D$. The f is said to be **bounded at** a provided for some $\delta > 0$, the set $\{f(x) : x \in (a - \delta, a + \delta)\}$ is bounded. We say that f is **bounded on** D provided f is bounded at every $a \in D$.

Discussion. It is important to notice the focus of this definition. It is on the range of f. This should be compared with the equivalent definition of a bounded sequence. □

Theorem 2.3.1. Let a be a limit point of D, the domain of f, and suppose that the limit as x tends to a of f exists. Then,

    (i) the limit at a is unique,
    (ii) f is bounded in the interval $(a - \delta, a + \delta)$ for some positive δ.

Proof. To establish (i), let us assume for the sake of argument that there are two distinct limits at a, say A and B, with $A < B$. Let us set $\epsilon = \dfrac{B - A}{2}$. Since the limit as x tends to a of f is A, we can find δ_A such that for all $x \in D$,

$$0 < |x - a| < \delta_A \text{ .implies. } |f(x) - A| < \epsilon.$$

Similarly, we can find δ_B such that for all $x \in D$,

$$0 < |x - a| < \delta_B \text{ .implies. } |f(x) - B| < \epsilon.$$

Let $\delta = \min\{\delta_A, \delta_B\}$. Since a is a limit point of D, there is an $x_0 \in D$ such that $0 < |x_0 - a| < \delta$. For such an x_0, we have

$$f(x_0) < A + \epsilon = B - \epsilon < f(x_0).$$ **(WHY?)**

But this is contradiction, whence $A = B$ as desired.

To prove (ii), let A be the limit as x tends to a of f and set $\epsilon = 1$. By assumption, there exists a positive δ such that

$$0 < |x - a| < \delta \text{ .implies. } |f(x) - A| < 1.$$

Evidently, this implies that for all $x \in D$,

$$0 < |x - a| < \delta \text{ .implies. } |f(x)| < |A| + 1.$$

Now if $a \notin D$ let $B = |A| + 1$. Otherwise, set $B = \max\{|f(a)|, |A| + 1\}$. In either case, we have found a bound, B, for f on $(a - \delta, a + \delta)$.   □

Discussion. Let us compare this theorem with our earlier results. For (i), the theorems of interest are 1.2.1 and 2.1.1. In all cases the problem is to establish the uniqueness of the limit. In each instance we proceed by assuming there are distinct limits A and B. And in every case the proof continues by forcing the existence of a number (sequence value or function value) which must be close to A and at the same time close to B. This is done by choosing ϵ to measure the closeness and then finding either M or δ to obtain the a_n or $f(x)$. Note that in the two earlier proofs we chose the maximum of M_A and M_B, while in this proof we choose the minimum of δ_A and δ_B. The reader can follow this thread even further by comparing the arguments to that for the uniqueness of the supremum (Theorem 0.4.1). Finally, notice that finding the required small value of δ is not enough. We must find a particular x_0 which satisfies

$$x_0 \in (a - \delta, a + \delta) \cap D,$$

since it is $f(x_0)$ which will act to witness the contradiction in the argument.

Turning to the second part of the theorem, we suggest that the reader compare this with the arguments in Theorems 1.2.3 and 2.1.2. We note that while the fact that a is a limit point of D is essential to the proof of (i) **(WHY?)**, it is unnecessary for the result in (ii). (See Exercise 8.)   □

EXAMPLE 1 _____

Let $f(x) = x, x \in [0,1]$. Show that the limit as x tends to 2 exists, but is not unique.

Solution. Let A be a fixed, but arbitrary real number. Let $\epsilon > 0$ be arbitrary and $\delta = 1$. Evidently, if $0 < |x - 2| < \delta$, then for each x, $x \in D$ implies $|f(x) - A| < \epsilon$. Since A was arbitrary, the limit cannot be unique.   □

Discussion. The essential fact on which the argument depends is that there are no x's in the domain which are within one unit of distance of 2. For this reason, the crucial implication is satisfied vacuously because its hypothesis is always false. Notice that the argument is still valid, even if 2 is added to the domain of f. The key fact is that it would still not be a limit point of the domain.   □

The theorem and example together suggest that as a general rule, we should require that the point at which we are computing a limit be a limit point of the domain of the function. In the future, unless otherwise stated, *we will assume the limits are computed only at limit points of the domain of the function in question.* This will ensure that if the limit exists, then we can discuss the limit as a unique real number.

As in the case of limits of sequence and limits at ∞, there are natural questions about how the arithmetic of functions interact with the limiting process for the case of limits at a. We present theorems dealing with products and reciprocals of functions, leaving other theorems to the exercises.

Theorem 2.3.2. Let f and g be defined on D, and let a be a limit point of D. If the limit of f and g both exist as x tends to a, then

$$\lim_{x \to a} (f \cdot g)(x) = \lim_{x \to a} f(x) \cdot \lim_{x \to a} g(x).$$

Proof. Let $\epsilon > 0$ be fixed and consider the quantity $|(f \cdot g)(x) - A \cdot B|$ where A and B are the limits at a of f and g, respectively. Now

$$|(f \cdot g)(x) - A \cdot B| = |f(x) \cdot g(x) - A \cdot B|$$

$$= |f(x) \cdot g(x) + (f(x) \cdot B - f(x) \cdot B) - A \cdot B|$$

$$= |(f(x) \cdot g(x) - f(x) \cdot B) + (f(x) \cdot B - A \cdot B)|$$

$$\leqslant |f(x) \cdot g(x) - f(x) \cdot B| + |f(x) \cdot B - A \cdot B|$$

$$= |f(x)| \cdot |g(x) - B| + |f(x) - A| \cdot |B|.$$

By Theorem 2.3.1, there is an $M > 0$ and a positive δ_1 such that if $x \in (a - \delta_1, a + \delta_1) \cap D$, then $|f(x)| < M$. Now, let $C = \max\{|B|, 1\}$. We choose δ_2 such that for all $x \in D$,

$$0 < |x - a| < \delta_2 \text{ .implies. } |g(x) - B| < \frac{\epsilon}{2M}.$$

Also, we choose δ_3 such that for all $x \in D$,

$$0 < |x - a| < \delta_3 \text{ .implies. } |f(x) - A| < \frac{\epsilon}{2C}.$$

It is immediate that if $\delta = \min\{\delta_1, \delta_2, \delta_3\}$, then for all $x \in D$,

$$0 < |x - a| < \delta \text{ .implies. } |(f \cdot g)(x) - A \cdot B| < \epsilon. \qquad \textbf{(WHY?)}$$

Thus, the limit of the product exists as claimed is the product of the limits. $\qquad \square$

Discussion. In the hypothesis of this theorem, we have required that a be a limit point of D. The reason for this is that we want

$$\lim_{x \to a} (f \cdot g)(x)$$

to be a unique quantity. For this to happen, the quantities on the right-hand side must be unique, and this requires that a be a limit point of D.

The reader should compare the argument here with that of Theorem 1.2.4. Especially, the reader should observe the similarities in the manipulation of the term $|(f \cdot g)(x) - A \cdot B|$ with $|a_n \cdot b_n - A \cdot B|$. In both cases, the first step consists of adding a form of 0, the precise form being determined by the context, followed by an application of the Triangle inequality. This sequence of steps is extremely common and should be thoroughly understood. The reader may wonder why we choose C as above. The purpose is to avoid any worry about the case $B = 0$. Lastly, note that we used Theorem 2.3.1 (ii), where the hypothesis contains no assumption regarding a being a limit point of D. See our remarks following Theorem 2.3.1. □

Theorem 2.3.3. Let f be defined on D. If the limit as x tends to a of f exists and is not zero, then the limit as x tends to a of $\dfrac{1}{f}$ exists, and equals $\dfrac{1}{\lim\limits_{x \to a} f}$.

Proof. The proof of the case when a is not a limit point of D is left to Exercise 8. Thus, we assume that a is a limit point of D and the limit as x tends to a of f is $A \neq 0$. It follows that $\dfrac{|A|}{2} > 0$. From the fact that the limit exists, we can find a positive δ_1 such that

$$0 < |x - a| < \delta_1 \text{ and } x \in D \text{ .implies. } \frac{|A|}{2} < |f(x)| \qquad \textbf{(WHY?)}$$

Now

$$\left| \frac{1}{f(x)} - \frac{1}{A} \right| = |f(x) - A| \cdot \frac{1}{|f(x)| \cdot |A|} \ .$$

As a consequence of the inequality containing δ_1, we have

$$\frac{1}{|f(x)| \cdot |A|} < \frac{2}{A^2}. \qquad \textbf{(WHY?)}$$

Now let $\epsilon > 0$ be fixed but arbitrary. Since the limit at a exists, choose δ_2 such that

$$0 < |x - a| < \delta_2 \quad \text{and} \quad x \in D \quad \text{.implies.} \quad |f(x) - A| < \frac{\epsilon \cdot A^2}{2}.$$

Let $\delta = \min \{\delta_1, \delta_2\}$. For such a choice of δ, we have that $x \in D$ and $0 < |x - a| < \delta$ imply that $\left| \dfrac{1}{f(x)} - \dfrac{1}{A} \right| < \epsilon$ **(WHY?)**. □

Discussion. The reader should compare the argument above with that for Theorem 1.2.6. They are almost identical. □

In the exercises at the end of the previous section, we had the reader use the limit definition to establish whether various functions had limits. The theorems generated in this section simplify many of those calculations, as the following example illustrates.

EXAMPLE 2 _____

Let $f(x) = x^3$, $x \in \mathbf{R}$. Show that $\lim\limits_{x \to 2} x^3$ exists.

Solution. We first check that 2 is a limit point of D. To do this, first let $\delta > 0$ be arbitrary. Since $\dfrac{2 + (2 + \delta)}{2} \in D$ (**WHY?**), and δ is arbitrary, 2 is a limit point of D as required. Now,

$$\lim_{x \to 2} x^3 = \lim_{x \to 2} x \times \lim_{x \to 2} x \times \lim_{x \to 2} x = 2 \times 2 \times 2 = 8$$

and the limit is computed.   □

Discussion. To make full use of these limit theorems, a set of basic functions whose limits are known must be established. Then a large class of new functions is constructed using the arithmetic of functions; new limits are then computed as applications of the theorems. For the algebraic functions, polynomials, and their ratios, this only requires that we be able to compute

$$\lim_{x \to a} x,$$

which has the effect of reducing the problem of computing limits for polynomials to trivialities.   □

EXERCISES

1. Discuss the equations:
   (a) $\lim\limits_{x \to a} (f \pm g)(x) = \lim\limits_{x \to a} f(x) \pm \lim\limits_{x \to a} g(x)$;
   (b) $\lim\limits_{x \to a} |f|(x) = \left|\lim\limits_{x \to a} f(x)\right|$;
   (c) $\lim\limits_{x \to a} f^2(x) = \left[\lim\limits_{x \to a} f(x)\right]^2$.

2. Where applicable, use the results of this section to do Exercise 2.2.1.

3. Some of the problems in Exercise 2.2.2 cannot be attacked using the theorems developed. Formulate limit theorems which would be useful for (e) and (f).

4. State and prove a general result which would be useful for computing limits as x tends to a of polynomial functions.

5. To what extent can the result of (4) be extended to rational forms of polynomials? State and prove a suitable result.

6. State and prove a result for functions comparable to Theorem 1.2.7.

7. State and prove a result for functions comparable to Theorem 1.2.8.

8. Show that Theorem 2.3.1(ii) remains true even if a is not a limit point of D.

9. Complete the proof of Theorem 2.3.3.

10. Let f be defined on D and have the property that the limit as x tends to a of f is A and further that $A > B$. Show that there is a δ-interval about a, $(a - \delta, a + \delta)$ such that if x is a domain point other than a which is in the interval, then $f(x) > A - \dfrac{A - B}{2}$.

11. Use examples to give a complete discussion of the outcome of the product of f with g when one or both of the limits on the right in the equation of Theorem 2.3.2 do not exist.

12. Let g be bounded in a δ-interval of a. Give a sufficient condition on f so that the product of f with g may have a limit at a.

13. Show that a is a limit point of D provided every open interval which contains a also contains an infinite number of points of D.

14. Let f and g be defined on $R+$. Discuss some sufficient conditions for the existence of $\lim_{x \to a} (f \circ g)(x)$ of the composite function $f \circ g$.

15. Let a be a limit point of the domain D of the function f. Prove or disprove: $\lim_{x \to a} f$ exists if and only if given $\epsilon > 0$, there exists $\delta > 0$ such that $|f(x_1) - f(x_2)| < \epsilon$ whenever x_1, $x_2 \in D$, $0 < |x_1 - a| < \delta$, and $0 < |x_2 - a| < \delta$.

2.4 MONOTONE FUNCTIONS

For sequences, we saw that the property of being monotone had a powerful effect on the existence of a limit. As well, with functions in the case of limits at infinity, we saw that monotonicity again played a role. We should therefore examine the effect of monotonicity on the problem of the existence of a limit for functions as x tends to a particular point, a. Recall the exact fact for sequences: every bounded monotonic sequence has a limit. Based on this, it would seem reasonable to try to prove if f is monotone on D and bounded in a δ-interval about a, then the limit as x tends to a exists. The reader who tries to prove this will encounter certain difficulties (Go ahead and try!) which stem from the fact that the statement is not a theorem. But more than that, they arise from the fact that we did not carefully model our earlier results. In the definition of limit at infinity for functions, x must approach $+\infty$ from values which are less than $+\infty$, since there are no real numbers which are greater than $+\infty$. Similarly, in the definition of limit at $-\infty$, x must approach through reals, all of which are greater than $-\infty$. In short, x can approach from only one side. With the definition of limit as x tends to a, x can approach from either direction (left or right), and this is the rub! The cure for this is simple: the notion of a **one-sided limit**.

Definition. Let f be defined on D. We say that the **limit as x tends to a from the left** exists if there exists $A \in \mathbf{R}$ such that for every positive ϵ there exists a positive δ such that $x \in D \cap (a - \delta, a)$ .implies. $|f(x) - A| < \epsilon$. If the limit exists, we write

$$\lim_{x \to a^-} f(x) = A.$$

This limit is often referred to as the **left-hand limit at** a. In a similar manner we invite the reader to define the **right-hand limit at** a (limit as x tends to a from the right, with the notation $\lim_{x \to a^+} f(x)$).

Discussion. If we compare this definition with the definition of 'limit as x tends to a of f', we see that the condition

$$x \in D \text{ and } 0 < |x - a| < \delta$$

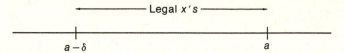

Figure 2.4.1   The δ-interval to be considered for left-hand limit.

has been replaced by

$$x \in D \cap (a - \delta, a).$$

It is clear that the effect of this change is to restrict the values of x which can be substituted into the term $|f(x) - A|$ to those which lie on the left-hand side of x, as shown in Figure 2.4.1. Since we are not allowed to use x's on the right-hand side of a to show that the definition does not hold, we would expect more functions to have a left-hand limit at a than have a limit at a, and this is indeed the case. Similar remarks apply to the right-hand limits. In Exercise 3, we ask the reader to show that limit at a exists if and only if both the left side limit and right side limits at a exist and are equal.

It is important that the reader distinguish between the concept being captured with one-sided limits and that of Example 2.2.3. In the case of one-sided limits, points of D may exist on both sides of the point a at which the one-sided limit is being computed. In the case of the example, the domain of the function is $\left[0, \dfrac{1}{10} \right]$, and the point of interest is $\dfrac{1}{10}$, which only has domain points on one side. In the former case, the restriction to consideration on only one side of a is by design, in the latter case it is merely fortuitous.   □

EXAMPLE 1 _____

Let

$$f(x) = \begin{cases} 1, & \text{if } x \in (-1,0) \\ \sin \dfrac{1}{x}, & \text{if } x \in (0,1). \end{cases}$$

Find the left-hand limit at 0.

Solution.   It seems likely that we should take $A = 1$ (**WHY?**). Let $\epsilon > 0$ be fixed. If we set $\delta = 1$, the desired inequalities will follow.   □

Discussion.   Functions, constant to the left of a point (such as f of this example on the left of 0), provide one of the few examples where the choice of δ is completely independent of the choice of ϵ. The reader can show that the limit at 0 does not exist, and further that the right-hand limit as x tends to 0 does not exist. The graph of this function is pictured in Figure 2.4.2. Other examples can be constructed which show that both one-sided limits can exist while the limit does not exist. Such examples appear in Exercise 1.   □

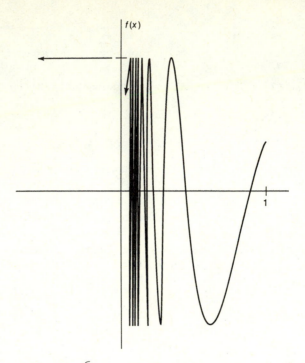

Figure 2.4.2   Graph of $f(x) = \begin{cases} 1, & x \in (-1, 0) \\ \sin\dfrac{1}{x}, & x \in (0, 1). \end{cases}$

EXAMPLE 2

Let

$$f(x) = \begin{cases} \dfrac{x}{2}, & x \leqslant 1 \\ 2x + 1, & x > 1. \end{cases}$$

Find the left and right side limits at $x = 1$.

Solution.   We shall show that the right side limit is 3. Let $\epsilon > 0$ be given, and set $\delta = \dfrac{\epsilon}{2}$. If $x \in (1, 1 + \delta)$, clearly, $|x - 1| < \delta$. Now,

$$|f(x) - 3| = |(2x + 1) - 3|$$
$$= 2|x - 1|$$
$$< 2\delta = \epsilon$$

proving our claim. Taking $\delta = 2\epsilon$, and repeating the above for the interval $(1 - \delta, 1)$, it is readily seen that the left side limit is $\dfrac{1}{2}$. $\square$

Discussion. The graph of $f(x)$ is shown in Figure 2.4.3. As can be seen from there, the graph is composed of two pieces, one on either side of the point 1. The left side branch is the part $f(x) = \dfrac{x}{2}$, which approaches the limit $\dfrac{1}{2}$ when x approaches 1 from the left side. The right side branch is the portion $f(x) = 2x + 1$, which approaches 3, as x approaches 1 from the right. Clearly, since these two limits are different, limit as x approaches 1 does not exist. The geometrical meaning of this situation is that there is a 'jump' of $\dfrac{5}{2}$ units in the graph at the point 1. Therefore, for any real number A, we can choose $\epsilon < \dfrac{5}{4}$ so that whatever $\delta > 0$ is, there will be points in the interval $(1 - \delta, 1 + \delta)$ at which the function values $f(x)$ will lie outside the horizontal strip generated by $y = A - \epsilon$ and $y = A + \epsilon$.

In the above example, the function considered was monotonic increasing, and it had both the one-sided limits. It is plausible that every monotonic function will have one-sided limits. The next theorem states the best possible monotonicity theorem for functions.

Theorem 2.4.1. Let f be monotone on D. If b, $c \in D$ with $b < c$, then for every a such that $b < a < c$, the one-sided limits as x tends to a of f exist.

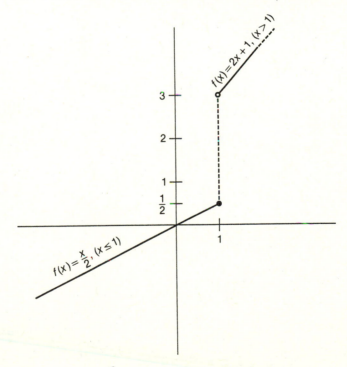

Figure 2.4.3 Graph of $f(x) = \begin{cases} \dfrac{x}{2}, & x \leqslant 1 \\ 2x + 1, & x > 1 \end{cases}$ showing left side limit and right side limits are different.

Proof. We will assume that f is monotone decreasing on D. Let a be given. We assume that a is a limit point of $D \cap (a - 1, a)$ and compute the left-hand limit at a. The remaining cases are left to Exercise 5. To continue, let

$$S = \{y: x < a \text{ and } y = f(x)\}.$$

Now, S is not empty since $b \in D$ and $b < a$. Further, since f is monotone decreasing and $a < c$ and $c \in D$, we have that $f(c)$ is a lower bound for S. Let $A = \inf S$, where the existence of A is obtained from the supremum principle. For a fixed $\epsilon > 0$, there is a $y \in S$ such that $A \leqslant y < A + \epsilon$ (**WHY?**). This $y = f(x)$ for some $x \in D$, whence we let $\delta = a - x$, and for this δ we have that $x \in D \cap (a - \delta, a)$ implies $|f(x) - A| < \epsilon$ (**WHY?**), as required. $\square$

Discussion. Even though this proof is written out for decreasing functions, it is easily seen to be similar in its basic structure to Theorem 2.1.3 and following the thread further, to Theorem 1.3.1. There is one item which the reader should note, namely, in the definition of S, we have required $x < a$. If it happened that f was defined at a, one would be tempted to use less than or equal, and thus permit $a \in S$. Had we proceeded in that manner, the proof would have broken down (**WHERE?**). It should be noted that for the proof above to really imitate those at infinity, the inequality must be strict. Also, the strictness of the inequality emphasizes the fact that we have no interest in the value of the function at a, or even if the function is defined at a.

Note that the theorem requires $b < a < c$. In the case $D = [b,c]$, it can also be shown that $\lim_{x \to b^+}$ and $\lim_{x \to c^-}$ exist. $\square$

EXERCISES

1. Graph the functions and find the one-sided limits indicated if they exist.

(a) $f(x) = \begin{cases} 3x, & x < 1 \\ x + 1, & x > 1 \end{cases}$ limit at 1^+ and 1^-;

(b) $f(x) = \begin{cases} x^2, & x > 0 \\ x^3, & x < 0 \end{cases}$ limit at 0^+ and 0^-;

(c) $f(x) = \begin{cases} \dfrac{1}{x}, & x > 0 \\ 0, & x < 0 \end{cases}$ limit at 0^+;

(d) $f(x) = \begin{cases} 1 - x, & x < 2 \\ 2x + 3, & x \geqslant 2 \end{cases}$ limit at 2^+;

(e) $f(x) = \begin{cases} x^2 + 3, & x < 0 \\ 3(x - 1), & x > 0 \end{cases}$ limit at 0^+;

(f) $f(x) = \begin{cases} \dfrac{1}{x^2}, & x \in \mathbf{Q}, \, x > 0 \\[2mm] \dfrac{1}{x^3}, & x \notin \mathbf{Q}, \, x > 0 \end{cases}$ limit at 2^-;

(g) $f(x) = \begin{cases} x, & x \in \mathbf{Q} \\ 1 - x, & x \notin \mathbf{Q} \end{cases}$ limit at 0^+;

(h) $f(x) = \begin{cases} x, & x \in \mathbf{Q} \\ 1 - x, & x \notin \mathbf{Q} \end{cases}$ limit at $\left[\dfrac{1}{2}\right]^-$;

(i) $f(x) = \begin{cases} x, & x \in \mathbf{Q} \\ -x, & x \notin \mathbf{Q} \end{cases}$ limit at 1^+;

(j) $f(x) = \left| \sin \dfrac{1}{x} \right|, \quad x \in \mathbf{R} \sim \mathbf{Q}$ limit at 0^-;

(k) $f(x) = \begin{cases} \dfrac{1}{x^2}, & x \in \mathbf{Q} \sim \{0\} \\[2mm] \dfrac{1}{x^3}, & x \notin \mathbf{Q} \end{cases}$ limit at 0^+;

(l) $f(x) = \begin{cases} x^2, & x \in \mathbf{Q} \\ 0, & x \in \mathbf{R} \sim \mathbf{Q} \end{cases}$ limit at 0^+;

(m) $f(x) = 2^x, \quad x \in \mathbf{Q}$ limit at 1^-;

(n) $f(x) = e^x, \quad x \in \mathbf{Q}$ limit at 0^+.

2. Show that $\displaystyle \lim_{x \to 0^+} \frac{x}{a} \left[\frac{b}{x} \right] = \frac{b}{a}$, where $[x] = $ greatest integer $\leqslant x$.

3. Show that if a is a limit point of D, the domain of f, and if the limit as x tends to a of f exists, then both one-sided limits at a exist and are equal.

4. Let a be a limit point of D, the domain of f. Find conditions on the one-sided limits which will guarantee the existence of the limit at a.

5. Fill in the missing details in the proof of Theorem 2.4.1.

6. Show that if f is strictly monotone on D, then f is one-to-one. Is the converse true?

7. Show that if f is strictly monotone on D, then f has an inverse, f^{-1}, which is also monotone.

8. Let f be strictly monotone on D and let the limit as x tends to a of f exist. What, if any, information does this give about the existence of limits for f^{-1} in each of the following cases?
   (a) D is an open interval and a is an interior point of D;
   (b) D is an arbitrary subset of the real numbers and a is any limit point of D.

9. Give an example of a monotone function for which the limit as x tends to 1 does not exist.

10. What can be said about the general shape of the graph of a monotone function?

11. Let I denote the interval $(-\infty,z]$ (or $(a,z]$ or $[a,z]$), and let J denote the interval $[z,\infty)$ (or $[z,b)$ or $[x,b]$). (Prove that if f is monotonic on I and J, f is monotonic on $I \cup J$).

12. Let f be defined on $[a,b]$. Suppose that for every $c \in [a,b]$ there is a δ-interval about c such that f is monotone increasing over this δ-interval (this is called **local monotonicity**). Show that f is monotone increasing on $[a,b]$.

13. In Exercise 12, can $[a,b]$ be replaced by an arbitrary subset of **R**? If not, describe the most general sets for which the theorem is true.

14. If f is locally monotone on D, what can be said about its one-sided limits?

15. Prove or disprove: If $g(x) = f(\frac{1}{x})$ where f is defined for $x > 0$, then, $\lim_{x \to \infty} f(x) = A$ if and only if $\lim_{x \to 0^+} g(x) = A$.

2.5 CONTINUITY

Let us suppose that we have a function which is defined on an interval, either open or closed. If we draw the graph of such functions we will observe that some can be drawn in one smooth 'continuous' sweep of our pen, while others have many breaks or jumps.

EXAMPLE 1

Sketch the graph of the following functions:

(a) $f(x) = x^2, x \in [-2, 2]$;

(b) $f(x) = \begin{cases} \dfrac{1}{x}, & x \in [-2, 2] \text{ and } x \neq 0 \\ \\ 0; & x = 0; \end{cases}$

(c) $f(x) = \begin{cases} x, & x \in [-2, 1] \\ -x, & x \in (1, 2]. \end{cases}$

Solution. The graphs are shown in Figure 2.5.1. ☐

Discussion. The reader will note that while the graph of the first function can be drawn in one 'continuous' motion, without lifting one's pen from the paper, the other graphs can not be drawn in this manner. This is a very striking property of the first graph, and it is natural to wonder if it can be captured by a suitable mathematical definition. In fact, mathematicians of the past several centuries did confront this question, namely:

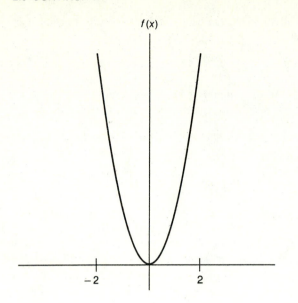

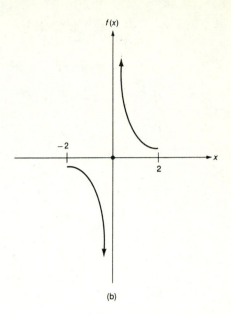

(b)

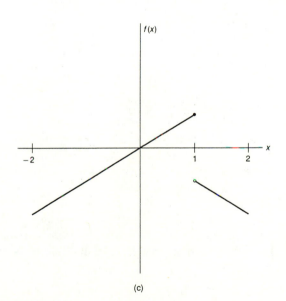

(c)

Figure 2.5.1 (a) Graph of $f(x) = x^2$.

(b) Graph of $f(x) = \begin{cases} \dfrac{1}{x}, & x \in [-2, 2], \quad x \neq 0 \\ 0, & x = 0. \end{cases}$

(c) Graph of $f(x) = \begin{cases} x, & x \in [-2, 1] \\ -x, & x \in [1, 2]. \end{cases}$

Is there a way to specify those curves which can be drawn with a single stroke of one's pen?

Their answer is our next definition. ☐

Definition. Let f be defined on D. We say that f is **continuous on** D provided that for every $y \in D$ and every positive ϵ, there is a positive δ such that for all $x \in D$

$$0 < |x - y| < \delta \text{ .implies. } |f(x) - f(y)| < \epsilon.$$

Further, in the event that for some $a \in D$ we have

$$\lim_{x \to a} f(x) = f(a),$$

we will say that f **is continuous at** a.

Discussion. First, the definition given above defines continuity for functions having arbitrary domains, not simply closed or open intervals. Second, the definition of continuity focuses entirely on points in the domain of f. This is in contrast to the case of computing a general limit where the point of interest, a, could be outside the domain of f.

In checking for continuity at a, the following three items must be established:

1. f must be defined at a;
2. the limit as x tends to a must exist (i.e., $\lim_{x \to a^+} f = \lim_{x \to a^-} f$;)
3. the limit must be $f(a)$.

If all three are satisfied, then the function is indeed continuous at a. If any one of the above fails, the function is not continuous at a. Evidently then, a function is continuous on its domain exactly if it is continuous at each point of its domain (**WHY?**).

There is another feature of the definition which should be emphasized. Recall that in the definition of limit, the value of δ was dependent on the choice of ϵ. Quite obviously δ still depends on ϵ. However, there is an additional dependence. Notice that y is chosen before δ, that is, an argument will proceed by fixing an arbitrary $y \in D$. It seems plausible that the value which is finally arrived at for δ will depend on the value of y, or more generally, where in the domain of f we happen to be working. To further clarify this point, consider Example 2.2.1. Notice that the final choice of δ arises out of the line

$$|x - 1| < 1 \text{ .implies. } 0 < |x + 1| < 3. \tag{*}$$

Thus, δ generally depends on the value of a in problems related to finding a limit. (Similar dependencies arise in Examples 2.2.2 and 2.2.3 and should be reviewed by the reader.) As a result, we can expect that the dependence of δ on y will introduce additional complexities for which our proofs must account.

The thrust of the discussion above relates to the analytic properties of the definition. Our initial impetus grew out of geometry. Thus, the question of how well this definition captures the intuitive idea 'single stroke of the pen' remains to be seen. This will be studied in further examples. ☐

EXAMPLE 2 _____

Let $f(x) = x^2$, $x \in [-2, 2]$. Show that f is continuous on this interval.

Solution. Let $y \in [-2, 2]$ be arbitrary but fixed. We show that f is continuous at y. Applying algebra to $|f(x) - f(y)|$, we get

$$|x^2 - y^2| = |x - y| \cdot |x + y|$$
$$\leqslant |x - y| \cdot 2 \cdot \max\{|x|, |y|\}$$
$$\leqslant |x - y| \cdot 4. \qquad (*)$$

Fix a positive ϵ, and let $\delta = \dfrac{\epsilon}{4}$. It is immediate that for all $x \in [-2, 2]$

$$0 < |x - y| < \delta \text{ .implies. } |f(x) - f(y)| < \epsilon.$$

Since y was an arbitrary member of D, the function is continuous on D. $\qquad \square$

Discussion. The reader should compare this with the computations in Example 2.2.1. It should be realized that continuity arguments are a generalization of limit arguments. Indeed, it may be said that a continuity argument merely establishes that for every $a \in D$,

$$\lim_{x \to a} f(x) = f(a).$$

For this reason, the similarities should be substantial. This can be seen from the fact that in its broad outline the argument is the same as that for Example 2.2.1. In particular, the main feature is to express $|f(x) - f(y)|$ as a product, one factor of which is $|x - y|$ and the other factor of which is 'junk', that is, is bounded. Once this is accomplished, the argument follows.

As mentioned in the discussion after the definition, the value of δ will depend on the value of y, or the part of the domain in which we are interested. In the present case, the key inequality is established in the line marked with an asterisk (*). It appears that we have eliminated the dependence on y, but the dependence is only hidden. To see this, the reader should work out this example again, but this time assuming that $D = [-10, 10]$. The point is to fully understand the way in which the nature of the domain affects the formulation of the argument.

As a last remark, we note that the graph of this function can be drawn with a single stroke of the pen, as shown in Figure 2.5.1(a). So, we see that for the first case, the definition agrees with the concept we were trying to capture. $\qquad \square$

EXAMPLE 3 _____

Let $f(x) = \dfrac{1}{x}$, $x \in [-2, 0) \cup (0, 2]$. Show that f is continuous on its domain D.

Solution. Let $y \in D$ be fixed, and a positive ϵ given. Then, $y \neq 0$, whence $0 < \dfrac{|y|}{2}$. We may assume that any choice of δ will satisfy $\delta < \dfrac{|y|}{2}$.

Under this assumption, if $|x - y| < \delta$, then

$$\left| \frac{1}{x} - \frac{1}{y} \right| = |x - y| \cdot \frac{1}{|x| \cdot |y|}$$

$$\leqslant |x - y| \cdot \frac{2}{y^2}. \qquad \textbf{(WHY?)} \quad (*)$$

Let us therefore set $\delta = \min \left\{ \dfrac{|y|}{2}, \; y^2 \cdot \dfrac{\epsilon}{2} \right\}$. It is immediate that $x \in D$ and

$$0 < |x - y| < \delta \text{ .implies. } \left| \frac{1}{x} - \frac{1}{y} \right| < \epsilon,$$

as desired. Thus, $f(x) = \dfrac{1}{x}$ is continuous on $[-2, 0) \cup (0, 2]$. $\quad\square$

Discussion. The calculations in this example are essentially the same as those done in Examples 2.2.2 and 2.2.3, as the reader should verify by direct comparison. In the present example, the reader should carefully note the role of y in obtaining the value of δ. The critical inequality which delineates this dependence is marked with an asterisk. As well, there is another source of dependence in the assumption that $\delta < \dfrac{y}{2}$, which acts to prevent y from being arbitrarily close to 0.

The example has additional interest. Looking back at our initial comments regarding geometry, this example seems in direct conflict to our intuition, or else our claim that we have really captured the 'heart and soul' of continuity is false. The reason for the seeming conflict is the fact that the graph cannot be drawn with a single strike of the pen. To see this, the reader should observe that the graph of this function coincides with the graph presented in Figure 2.5.1(b), except that no point would be plotted at $x = 0$, since f is not defined at 0 in the present example. Since the function graphed in Figure 2.5.1(b) was used as an example of a function which was not continuous, we appear to have something of a problem. However, there is a resolution.

Let us consider the function $g(x) = x^2$ with $D = [-2, -1) \cup (1, 2]$. The graph of the function g is in two pieces (see Figure 2.5.2), but this is due to the fact that the domain is in two pieces! Moreover, the break in the graph, where we are forced to pick up our pen, occurs at the points which are missing from the domain, that is, the interval $[-1, 1]$. Since we cannot move our pen across the domain without lifting it from the paper, it seems reasonable to believe that we should not be able to draw the graph at a single stroke of the pen. For this reason, it would seem that the function, g, which is the same as that presented in Example 2 except for the missing point in the domain, should be considered to be continuous, and this is the tack that mathematicians have taken. The method that they have adopted for pursuing this tack is to restrict continuity considerations to points which are in the domain of the function. Points not belonging to the domain are of no relevance.

Returning now to the present example, the function is continuous exactly because the point $x = 0$ is missing from its domain. Notice that any attempt to add $x = 0$ to D will force us to define $f(0)$, and this will immediately cause the new function,

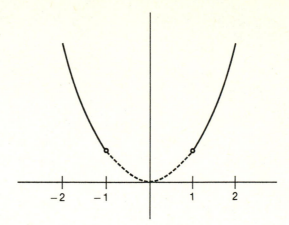

Figure 2.5.2   Graph $f(x) = x^2$, $x \in [-2, -1) \cup (1, 2]$.

which is now defined on the whole of $[-2, 2]$, to be discontinuous. In summary, we expect our geometric intuition to be borne out in full only for continuous functions whose domain is composed of a single interval.

There is still one other important fact to be gleaned from these examples. The function, $g(x) = x^2$, $x \in [-2, -1) \cup (1, 2]$ can be extended to a continuous function whose domain is all of $[-2, 2]$. (The function h with domain D' **extends** the function f with domain D, if $D \subseteq D'$ and for all $x \in D$, $f(x) = h(x)$.) As mentioned above, the function $f(x) = \dfrac{1}{x}$, which is defined on $[-2, 0) \cup (0, 2]$ does not have a continuous extension to all of $[-2, 2]$. The reason that no such extension exists is that the one-sided limits at 0 do not exist, and in consequence there is no way to choose a value for $f(0)$ which will lead to a continuous function. These ideas are explored further in the next example. □

Definition.   A function g is said to be an **extension** of a function f provided Dmn $f \subset$ Dmn g and for all $x \in$ Dmn f, $f(x) = g(x)$. If g is continuous, then the extension is said to be a **continuous extension**.

EXAMPLE 4 _____

Let

$$f(x) = \begin{cases} x^2, & x \in [-2, 0) \\ 1, & x \in (0, 2] \end{cases} .$$

Show that this function is continuous, but has no continuous extension to $[-2, 2]$.

Solution.   We first deal with the problem of establishing continuity. Fix $y \in D$ and a positive ϵ. Now $y \neq 0$, whence we may assume that any choice of δ satisfies $\delta < \dfrac{|y|}{2}$. The reader can check that $\delta = \min \left\{ \dfrac{|y|}{2}, \dfrac{\epsilon}{4} \right\}$ will do the job. (**WHY** is the restriction of δ absolutely essential to the argument?)

To see that no continuous extension exists, we observe (the reader can show) that

$$\lim_{x \to 0^+} f(x) = 1,$$

while

$$\lim_{x \to 0^-} f(x) = 0.$$

Thus, as shown in Exercise 2.4.3, the limit as x tends to 0 of f does not exist and so could not be equal to $g(0)$, for any extension g of f.   □

Discussion.   There are several important points here. The first is that 0 is a limit point of the domain of f. The second is that if there is a continuous extension of f to $[-2,2]$, then the value of the extension, g, at 0 will have to be given by

$$g(0) = \lim_{x \to 0} g(x) = \lim_{x \to 0} f(x).$$

Since this limit does not exist in the present case, as graphically illustrated in Figure 2.5.3, no extension is possible. However, if the limit had existed, then the value assigned to $g(0)$ would be determined by this limit. In particular, if the value of the limit exists and is unique, the only one possible extension is available. These ideas are explored further in the exercises.   □

The notion of extension is an important tool. Consider the computation indicated by 2^x, for x an arbitrary nonnegative real number. Work in Chapter 0 established the existence of real numbers corresponding to $2^{1/n}$, for $n \in \mathbf{N}$ (or $\mathbf{Z}$). For this reason, we can carry out the computation for $2^{p/q}$, $p,q \in \mathbf{N}$. However, we are left to wonder about the outcome of computations such as that indicated by 2^π, or other computations involving irrational exponents. The way around this problem is to use continuity. It can be established, with the tools developed, that the function $f(x) = 2^x$ such that

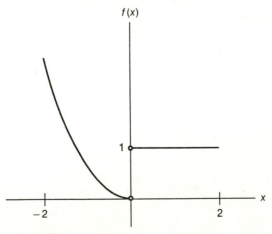

Figure 2.5.3   Graph $f(x) = \begin{cases} x^2, & x \in [-2, 0) \\ 1, & x \in (0, 2] \end{cases}$

$x \in \mathbf{Q}$ is continuous. It is reasonable to believe that any extension of 2^x to all of $\mathbf{R}$ which purports to capture exponentiation should also be continuous. Thus, the solution to the problem is to extend 2^x to all of $\mathbf{R}$ by continuity. This is a simple example of the use of extension by continuity. The general power x^y is formally done in Chapter 10. Other examples occur throughout mathematics.

We turn now to the question of why a function fails to be continuous. As always, the first step is to write down the negation of the definition of continuity.

Negation of the Definition of Continuity

A function f is **not continuous** on its domain D, if there exists a $y \in D$ such that for some $\epsilon > 0$ and every $\delta > 0$, there exists an $x \in D$ such that

$$|x - y| < \delta \quad \text{and} \quad |f(x) - f(y)| \geq \epsilon.$$

Discussion. Thus, f is not continuous on D if it is not continuous at some particular point of D. This means we are required to find $a \in D$ such that either

(i) $\lim_{x \to a} f(x)$ does not exist; or

(ii) $\lim_{x \to a} f(x)$ does exist, but is not equal to $f(a)$.

In either case, to be a candidate to witness the discontinuity of f, the point a must be a limit point of D. ☐

A function f which is not continuous at $a \in D$ is said to be **discontinuous at** a, or to have a **discontinuity at** a. If for every $y \in D$, f is discontinuous at y, we say that f is **totally discontinuous on** D.

Functions which are totally discontinuous are not often encountered but are by no means rare. We give an example.

EXAMPLE 5 _____

Show that the function given by

$$f(x) = \begin{cases} 1, & x \in \mathbf{R} \sim \mathbf{Q} \\ 0, & x \in \mathbf{Q} \end{cases}$$

is totally discontinuous.

Solution. Let y be an arbitrary, but fixed member of $\mathbf{R}$. Let $\epsilon = \dfrac{1}{2}$, and let $\delta > 0$ be fixed. Now the interval defined by $|x - y| < \delta$ contains both rationals and irrationals (**WHY?**). If y is rational, pick x in the interval to be irrational. If y is irrational pick x in the interval to be rational. In either case,

$$0 < |x - y| < \delta \quad \text{and} \quad |f(x) - f(y)| \geq \epsilon = \frac{1}{2}.$$

Thus, f is not continuous at y. Since y was an arbitrary member of D, we are done. ☐

Discussion. The graph of the function in Example 5 looks like two horizontal lines, one passing through $y = 1$, and the other being the x-axis. The reason for this is that the points on both parts of the graph are so close together that it is impossible to detect any holes. The reader should settle in his own mind how to picture this function.

It is instructive to think about how a function can get to be so discontinuous, as the one in Example 5. For example, suppose you wanted to build a really ill-behaved function, how would you do it? You might start with a function like $f(x) = x$, $x \in \mathbf{R}$ and change values of the function at various domain points. Very quickly, you would find that this is a very inefficient way of producing discontinuities. To really produce discontinuities, you have to get your hands on lots of points in the domain, as in the above example which can be thought of as arising from a constant function whose functional value was shifted on the rationals. This type of thinking suggests trying to classify the various types of discontinuities which may arise as discussed below.

□

If we think of discontinuities of functions as representing 'pathology', then we can classify discontinuities in terms of the degree of pathology they represent. The least pathological of all the discontinuities are the **removable discontinuities**. We say that the discontinuity at a is **removable** provided that the limit as x tends to a exists and that

$$\lim_{x \to a} f(x) \neq f(a).$$

Removable discontinuities can, indeed, be 'removed' simply by changing the functional value at a to make it agree with the limit as x tends to a. For this reason, a function with removable discontinuities can be thought of as being 'almost' continuous. A simple example of a function having a removable discontinuity is

$$f(x) = \begin{cases} x^2, & x \in [-2, 0) \cup (0,2] \\ 1, & x = 0 \end{cases}.$$

To remove this discontinuity, we merely set $f(0) = 0$. Thus, the 'repair' can be accomplished by moving only one point on the graph. The graph of the function in this example, is presented in Figure 2.5.4.

All other types of discontinuities require that

$$\lim_{x \to a} f(x) \text{ does not exist.}$$

Recall that even though this limit does not exist, both one-sided limits as x tends to a of f may exist. An example of this type was given in Example 4 and its graph is presented in Figure 2.5.3. Such a situation, where both one-sided limits exist but are different, represents the next step on the scale of ill behavior. If f is discontinuous at a, but both one-sided limits at a exist, we say that f has a **simple discontinuity at** a. Simple discontinuities include removable discontinuities. However, they are not limited to removable discontinuities. Inspection of Figure 2.5.3 shows that the discontinuity is of a much more serious nature than a removable discontinuity. It cannot be fixed by changing the value of the function at a single point, since there is a big 'jump' in the graph. For this reason, discontinuities where the one-sided limits exist but disagree are referred to as **jump** discontinuities.

Simple discontinuities are often referred to as discontinuities of the **first kind**, whence we may refer to all other types of discontinuities as **discontinuities of the second kind**. Discontinuities of the second kind involve the greatest degree of pathology, since they require the nonexistence of a one-sided limit at some point in the domain. As we have already remarked, this means that the function is unbounded or that it oscillates in a 'bad way'. Figure 2.5.1(b), which presents the graph of $f(x) = \dfrac{1}{x}$, with $f(0) = 0$, contains an example of a discontinuity of the second kind, due to the function being unbounded near 0. The ultimate in 'gross' behavior is perhaps contained in Example 2.4.1, which employs $\sin\dfrac{1}{x}$. The problem is that the function oscillates an infinite number of times in any neighborhood of 0, as can be seen from inspection of Figure 2.4.2.

The classification scheme presented above is not the only possible scheme for studying the behavior of functions. The importance of such schemes lies in the fact that they provide a methodological base for dealing with generic questions of the form

How bad can a function be and still be integrable?

'Integrable' can of course be replaced by 'differentiable', or any other suitable property of interest. We will from time to time approach questions of this type in the remainder of this text. Needless to say, continuity will play a major role in the discussions.

Natural questions arise concerning the arithmetic of continuous functions. The basic arithmetical properties of continuous functions are summarized in the following theorem.

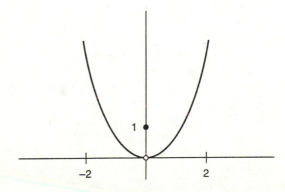

Figure 2.5.4 Graph of $f(x) = \begin{cases} x^2, \\ 1, x = 0 \end{cases}$ $x \in [-2, 0) \cup (0, 2]$.

Theorem 2.5.1. Let f and g be continuous on D, then

(i) $f \pm g$ is continuous;
(ii) $f \cdot g$ is continuous;
(iii) if $g(x) \neq 0$ for all $x \in D$, then $\dfrac{f}{g}$ is continuous;
(iv) $|f|$ is continuous.

The proof of this theorem is left to Exercise 4.

Theorem 2.5.2. Let f be continuous on D with $Rng\, f \subseteq D'$. If g is continuous on D', then $g \circ f$ is continuous on D.

Proof. Let $y \in D$ and let $\epsilon > 0$ be fixed. Set $w = f(y)$, then $w \in D'$. Since g is continuous on D', there is a $\delta_1 > 0$ such that $u \in D'$ and $|u - w| < \delta_1$ imply $|g(u) - g(w)| < \epsilon$. Since f is continuous on D and $\delta_1 > 0$, we can find $\delta > 0$ such that $x \in D$ and $|x - y| < \delta$ imply $|f(x) - f(y)| < \delta_1$. But this means that

$$|(g \circ f)(x) - (g \circ f)(y)| < \epsilon \qquad \textbf{(WHY?)}$$

whenever $x \in D$ and $|x - y| < \delta$. $\square$

Discussion. The intuition of the proof is really quite simple. Once we fix our y, we follow it out to the range of g by computing $(g \circ f)(y) = g(w)$, where w is in the range of f. Since g is continuous, the positive ϵ-interval centered at $g(w)$ gives rise to a positive δ_1-interval centered at w. This δ_1-interval about w is interpreted as an ϵ-interval; we then apply the continuity of f to obtain the required δ-interval about y.

It is important to recognize the utility of this theorem. Many times we are interested in computing the limits of sequences of various types. Some of these involve operations which are of a continuous nature. For example, even though we have not yet developed the properties of $f(x) = \ln x$ we can accept for the moment that it is a continuous function on the positive reals. Thus, if we have a sequence of the form $a_n = \ln b_n$, then by virtue of this theorem, we know that the convergence properties of a_n are completely determined by the convergence properties of b_n. This idea is more fully explored in Exercise 13. $\square$

Before proceeding to the exercises we want to draw the reader's attention to the function that appears in Exercise 1(h). This function is known as the **ruler function**. It has rather odd continuity properties; indeed, its behavior could only be termed pathological. We toyed with the idea of including this as an example. We decided not to include it on the grounds that this function provides an essential test of the student's understanding of many of the ideas which have been developed in the text. In short, if you, the student, can do this exercise, then you have gone a long way on the road to understanding analysis. If you cannot do it straightaway, then never fear, neither could we. The point is, keep trying until you can!

EXERCISES

1. Give a complete discussion of the continuity properties of the following functions, including types of discontinuities. Prove your answer, using definitions only.

   (a) $f(x) = x^3, x \in \mathbf{R}$;

   (b) $f(x) = 1 - x^2, x \in \mathbf{Q}$;

   (c) $f(x) = \dfrac{1}{x^2}, x \in [-3, 0) \cup (0, 2]$;

   (d) $f(x) = \dfrac{1}{1 + x^2}, x \in \mathbf{R}$;

   (e) $f(x) = \begin{cases} x^2, & x \in [0, 1] \\ x^3, & x \in (1, 5]; \end{cases}$

   (f) $f(x) = \begin{cases} x^2, & x \in \mathbf{Q} \\ -x^2, & x \in \mathbf{R} \sim \mathbf{Q}; \end{cases}$

   (g) $f(x) = \begin{cases} x^4, & x \in [0, 1] \\ x + 1, & x \in (1, 3); \end{cases}$

   (h) $f(x) = \begin{cases} 0, & x \in \mathbf{R} \sim \mathbf{Q} \\ \dfrac{1}{q}, & x \in \mathbf{Q} \text{ and } x = \dfrac{p}{q} \text{ in lowest terms}; \end{cases}$

   (i) $f(x) = \begin{cases} x, & x \in \{\dfrac{1}{n} : n \in \mathbf{N}\} \\ 0, & x \in [-1, 0); \end{cases}$

   (j) $f(x) = 2^x, x \in \mathbf{Q}$;

   (k) $f(x) = e^x, x \in \mathbf{Q}$;

   (l) $f(x) = x - [x], x \in \mathbf{R}$;

   (m) $f(x) = \dfrac{1}{2} - x + \dfrac{1}{2}[2x] - \dfrac{1}{2}[1 - 2x], x \in [0, 1]$;

   (n) $f(x) = \begin{cases} x, & x \in \mathbf{Q} \\ 1-x, & x \in \mathbf{R} \sim \mathbf{Q}; \end{cases}$

   (o) $f(x) = \begin{cases} 0, & x \in \mathbf{R} \sim \mathbf{Q} \\ (-1)^p \cdot q, & x \in \mathbf{Q}. \end{cases}$

   For the remaining problems, only consider continuity at the indicated point. You may assume knowledge of the domains and ranges of the sin, log, and exp functions.

   (p) $f(x) = \begin{cases} x \sin\dfrac{1}{x}, & x \neq 0 \\ 0, & x = 0 \end{cases}, x \in \mathbf{R}$;

(q) $f(x) = \begin{cases} e^{1/x}, & x \neq 0 \\ 0, & x = 0 \end{cases}$ at $y = 0$;

(r) $f(x) = \begin{cases} x^2 \sin^2 \dfrac{1}{x}, & x \neq 0 \\ 0, & x = 0 \end{cases}$ at $y = 0$;

(s) $f(x) = \lim\limits_{n \to \infty} \dfrac{\ln(2+x) - x^{2n}\sin x}{1 + x^{2n}}, \quad x \in (-2, \infty)$ at $y = 1$;

(t) $f(x) = \lim\limits_{n \to \infty} \dfrac{x^n \left[A + \sin\dfrac{1}{x-1} \right] + B + \sin\dfrac{1}{x-1}}{x^n} + 1; \ x \notin \{0, 1\}, A, B \in \mathbf{R}$, at $y = 1$.

2. Discuss, from the definition, the continuity, or lack thereof, and properties at 0 for the following functions:

     (a) $f(x) = \begin{cases} \sin \dfrac{1}{x^2}, & x \neq 0, x \in \mathbf{R} \\ 0, & x = 0; \end{cases}$

     (b) $f(x) = \begin{cases} x \sin \dfrac{1}{x}, & x \neq 0, x \in \mathbf{R} \\ 1, & x = 0. \end{cases}$

3. Define $f(0)$ so as to make the following functions continuous at the point $x = 0$:

     (a) $f(x) = \dfrac{\sin(\sin x)}{x}$;

     (b) $f(x) = \dfrac{\sin(\sin(x^2))}{x}$;

     (c) $f(x) = \dfrac{\sin(\sin(\sin x))}{x}$.

4. Prove Theorem 2.5.1.

5. Let $f: D \to \mathbf{R}$ be continuous at c and $f(c) > 0$. Show that there exists an $\epsilon > 0$ such that $f(x) > 0$ for $x \in D \cap (c - \epsilon, c + \epsilon)$.

6. Let $f: D \to \mathbf{R}$ be continuous at c. Prove that there exist $\epsilon, K > 0$ such that $|f(x)| < K$, for $x \in D \cap (c - \epsilon, c + \epsilon)$.

7. Let f be continuous on $[a, b] \cup [c, d]$ where $b < c$. Show that if y is an arbitrary real number, and e is any fixed element of (b, c), then there is a continuous function g with domain $[a, d]$ which extends f such that $f(e) = y$.

8. Let f be continuous on D, and let $a \notin D$ be a limit point of D. Show that if g is a continuous extension of f to $D \cup a$, then g is unique. Further, find conditions on f which guarantee that such a g will exist.

9. Let f be continuous on $\mathbf{Q}$ and g be a continuous extension of f to $\mathbf{R}$. Is g unique?

10. Develop the basic properties of the function $f(x) = e^x$ on $\mathbf{R}$, including the extension of the laws of exponents to arbitrary real exponents.

11. Let f be a polynomial function on $\mathbf{R}$. Show that f is continuous on all of $\mathbf{R}$.

12. Let f and g be polynomial functions on $\mathbf{R}$. Consider the rational function defined by $\dfrac{f}{g}$ and having domain $D = \{x : g(x) \neq 0\}$. Give a complete discussion of the continuity properties for $\dfrac{f}{g}$.

13. Let f be continuous on D and $\{a_n\}$ be a sequence of elements of D which converges to $a \in D$. Show that $\{f(a_n)\}$ is a convergent sequence. Can we drop the restriction that $a \in D$? What about the converse?

14. Let f and g be continuous on D. Show that max $\{f,g\}$ defined by

$$\text{max } \{f,g\}(x) = \text{max } \{f(x), g(x)\}$$

is continuous on D. Do the same for min $\{f, g\}$, defined in the obvious way.

15. A function f is said to be **linear** provided $f(x+y) = f(x) + f(y)$ for each x and y in its domain. Show that if f is linear and continuous on $\mathbf{R}$, then f is defined by $f(x) = cx$ for some $c \in \mathbf{R}$. (It can be shown that not every linear function from $\mathbf{R}$ into $\mathbf{R}$ is continuous.)

16. Let f be defined on $\mathbf{R}$ and continuous. Suppose that $f(x) = x^2$ whenever x is rational. What can be said about $f(x)$ for x irrational?

17. Suppose f is defined and continuous on $[0, 1]$. If $f(x)$ is always rational and $f(1) = 2$, what is $f(0)$?

18. Let f be monotone on $[a, b]$ and suppose the image of $[a, b]$ under f is an interval, that is, $f([a, b])$ is an interval. Show that f is continuous on $[a, b]$.

19. A function f is **subadditive** if $f(x + y) \leqslant f(x) + f(y)$ for $x, y \in \mathbf{R}$. Show that if f is subadditive, $f(0) = 0$, and f is continuous at 0, then, f is continuous on $\mathbf{R}$. Is the condition $f(0) = 0$ necessary?

20. If f and g are continuous on $\mathbf{R}$, and if $f(x) = g(x)$ for each $x \in \mathbf{Q}$, show that f and g are identical. What crucial property of $\mathbf{Q}$ is needed in the proof?

21. If $f: \mathbf{R} \to \mathbf{R}$ is continuous and $f\left[\dfrac{m}{2^n}\right] = 0$ for each $m \in \mathbf{Z}$, $n \in \mathbf{N}$, prove that $f = 0$.

22. Identify and classify the discontinuities of the functions in Exercise 1.

23. A function g is said to be the **restriction** of the function f to a domain D' provided $D' \subset \text{Dmn} f$ and $f = g$ on D'. Prove that if f is continuous on D, and $D' \subset D$, then the restriction of f to D' is also continuous. Show by an example that the converse need not be true.

24. Give an example of a function f, which is strictly increasing on D, but f^{-1} is not continuous on $f(D)$.

25. Let f be increasing in the interval $[a,b]$. Show that:

$$\lim_{x \to b^-} f(x) - \lim_{x \to a^+} f(x) \geqslant \sum_{k=1}^{n} [\lim_{x \to x_k^+} f(x) - \lim_{x \to x_k^-} f(x)]$$

where $a < x_1 < \cdots < x_n < b$. Hence, conclude that
(a) the set of discontinuities of a monotonic function is at most countable;
(b) there is a point of continuity of f in every open subinterval of $[a,b]$.

2.6 PROPERTIES OF CONTINUOUS FUNCTIONS

Let us return now to our model continuous function, namely, a function defined on an interval whose graph can be drawn with a single continuous sweep of the pen. With this in mind, consider the following situation:

The function f is defined on an interval I, a, $b \in I$ with $a < b$ and $f(a) < f(b)$.

This situation is pictured in Figure 2.6.1. Since f is continuous, the points $(a, f(a))$ and $(b, f(b))$ can apparently be connected by a single unbroken curve. This process will generate a set of y values, namely $\{y :$ there is an $x \in [a, b]$ such that $f(x) = y\}$. A little experimentation should quickly convince the reader that every real number in the interval $[f(a), f(b)]$ should belong to the set of generated y values. Since what we have just asserted is so obviously 'true', we should try to formalize it as a theorem.

Theorem 2.6.1. Let f be continuous on an interval I with $a < b$ and a, $b \in I$. If $f(a) < c < f(b)$, then there is an $x \in (a, b)$ such that $f(x) = c$.

Proof. Consider the set

$$A = \{x : x \in [a,b] \text{ and } f(x) < c\}.$$

This set is nonempty, since $a \in A$; it is bounded above, since $x \in A$ implies $x \leqslant b$. Thus, it has a supremum which we call d. We claim that $f(d) = c$. To establish the claim, we eliminate the other possibilities. First, suppose $c > f(d)$; this would imply

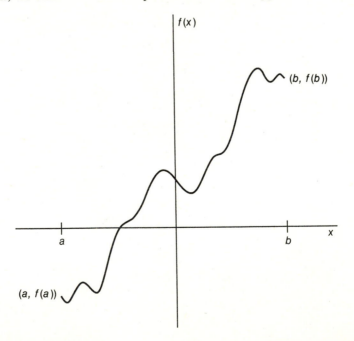

Figure 2.6.1 f defined in an interval $[a, b]$ with $a < b$ and $f(a) < f(b)$.

$d < b$ (**WHY?**). Let $\epsilon = c - f(d)$. By continuity of f at d, there is a $\delta > 0$ such that

$$d < x < d + \delta \text{ .implies. } f(x) < f(d) + \epsilon = c.$$

Since $(d, d + \delta) \cap [a, b] \neq \varnothing$, this contradicts our choice of d as sup A (**WHY?**); moreover, it follows that $d \neq a$. On the other hand, suppose $f(d) > c$. Let $\epsilon = f(d) - c$. Since f is continuous at d, there is a $\delta > 0$ such that

$$d - \delta < x < d \text{ .implies. } c = f(d) - \epsilon < f(x).$$

But such an x cannot be a member of A. This again contradicts our choice of $d = \sup A$. It follows that $f(d) = c$ as desired. ☐

Corollary. Let f be continuous on I, an interval. Then the range of f is an interval.

Proof. Let $a, b \in$ Rng f, with $a < b$. We must show (see Exercise 0.6.10) that if $c \in (a, b)$, then $c \in$ Rng f. But this is the content of Theorem 2.6.1. ☐

Discussion. Theorem 2.6.1 is often referred to as the **Intermediate Value Theorem**. This is a good name, since it describes what the theorem does. An alternative way to think of the theorem is in terms of the corollary, which spells out the fact that continuous functions map intervals to intervals. A portion of the hypothesis of Theorem 2.6.1 is that the domain of f is an interval. This requirement on the domain cannot be relaxed, as can be seen from the examples of the last section. Thus, this theorem is not simply a theorem about continuous functions, rather it is a theorem about continuous functions and intervals.

With respect to the proof, the reader should pay close attention to the employment of the supremum principle. Its use is the heart of the argument, and any attempt to prove the result without using this principle, in some form or other, must fail. The main thing here is the definition of the set to which we apply the principle, namely,

$$\{x : x \in [a, b] \text{ and } f(x) < c\}.$$

The choice of this set should appear natural in the sense that if we apply f to d, the supremum, then it should be intuitively obvious that $f(d) = c$. We emphasize that this basic intuition can only come about by sitting down and experimenting with examples in the presence of the question: How could one generate an x such that $f(x) = c$? Lastly, note that while the Supremum Principle generates the candidate value, d, for us, it is continuity which forces d to have the desired properties. ☐

Theorem 2.6.1 results from an interaction between the notion of continuity and a property of the domain of the function. The reader may wonder whether other such interactions exist. Such interactions do exist, and we study them in the next two theorems.

Theorem 2.6.2. Let f be continuous on a closed interval $[a, b]$. Then the range of f is bounded.

Proof. Define the set S by

$$S = \{c : c \in D \text{ and } f \text{ is bounded on } [a, c]\}.$$

S is not empty since $a \in S$. Further, if $b \in S$, we are through; otherwise, S is bounded above by b. Thus, S has a supremum. Call it d. We claim that $d = b$. Suppose not. Then $d < b$. Evidently, since f is continuous, there is a $\delta > 0$ such that $|d - x| < \delta$ implies $|f(x)| < f(d) + 1$. Since δ is positive, this contradicts that d is the supremum of S (**WHY?**). Thus, f is bounded on $[a,b]$, as claimed. $\square$

Theorem 2.6.3. Let f be defined and continuous on $[a,b]$. Then f attains the supremum of its range.

Proof. Let C denote the range of f. By the preceding theorem, C is bounded above. Since C is nonempty, C has a supremum which we denote by c. We claim that $c = f(x)$ for some $x \in [a,b]$. To see this, let

$$S = \{z : z \in [a,b] \text{ .and. } x \leqslant z \text{ implies } f(x) < c\}.$$

If S is empty, then $f(a) = c$ (**WHY?**). Thus, we may assume that S is nonempty. Since S is bounded above by b, S has a supremum, which we denote by x_0. We leave it to the reader to complete the argument (Exercise 1) by showing that $f(x_0) = c$. $\square$

Corollary 1. Let f be defined and continuous on $[a,b]$. Then the range of f is a closed interval.

Corollary 2. Let f be defined and continuous on $[a,b]$. Then there is a point $x_0 \in [a,b]$ such that for all $x \in [a,b]$, $f(x) \leqslant f(x_0)$.

Discussion. These theorems should be thought of as being about what continuous functions do to various types of domains. Theorem 2.6.1 says that if we apply a continuous function to an interval, the result will be an interval. Theorems 2.6.2 and 2.6.3 together say that if the interval is closed, then the result will also be a closed interval. Thus, continuous functions have the property that they preserve certain properties of subsets of **R**. This fact suggests all kinds of questions, such as exactly what properties are preserved by continuous functions, or, are there other classes of functions which preserve other properties of domain sets, and so on. Such questions have obviously been asked by mathematicians. We will provide some of the answers in later chapters. Nevertheless, the reader should begin exploring some of the possibilities, or at least trying to formulate additional questions.

Again, the reader should study the use of the Supremum Principle as the fundamental tool used in generating the proofs of these theorems. The simplicity of these proofs is due to the power of this principle. $\square$

Theorem 2.6.4. Let f be continuous and strictly increasing on an interval I. Then f^{-1} is continuous and strictly increasing on Rng f.

Proof. It has already been shown in Exercise 2.4.7 that f^{-1} exists and is strictly increasing. Hence, let $y \in$ Rng f, and $\epsilon > 0$ be fixed. Let $w = f^{-1}(y)$. There are several possibilities regarding where w is in I. If, for example, $I = [w, w]$, then we are done since $f^{-1} = \{(y, w)\}$, which is continuous (**WHY?**). We will treat in detail the case where w is the left-hand endpoint of I. With no loss of generality, we may assume that $w + \epsilon \in I$. Let $\delta = f(w + \epsilon) - y$. It is immediate from the monotonicity conditions that if $x \in$ Rng f and $|x - y| < \delta$, then $|f^{-1}(x) - f^{-1}(y)| < \epsilon$, as desired. The proof of the other cases is analogous and left to Exercise 2. $\square$

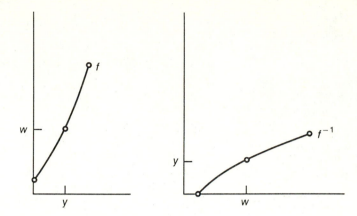

Figure 2.6.2 Figure illustrating Theorem 2.6.4.

Discussion. The intuition of the situation is best obtained from a picture (Figure 2.6.2). The reader should study how the condition that the domain is an interval is used, since the theorem fails without this condition. A prime example of a pair of functions which satisfy the conditions of the theorem are the logarithmic and exponential functions; these functions are developed in Chapter 10. □

EXERCISES

1. Complete the proof of Theorem 2.6.3.

2. Complete the proof of Theorem 2.6.4.

3. Find an example of a strictly increasing function which is continuous on $[0, 2] \cup (3, 5]$ whose inverse is not continuous.

4. Let f be strictly increasing and continuous on A. What can be said about f^{-1}?

5. Show that $f(x) = x^8 - 17x^6 + x^3 + 1$ has a root between 0 and 1.

6. Give an example of a continuous function with domain $\mathbf{Q}$ which does not satisfy the Intermediate Value Theorem. (In this problem and the next, the intervals being discussed are intervals on $\mathbf{Q}$.)

7. Let f be continuous on $\mathbf{Q}$ and suppose that f does satisfy the Intermediate Value Theorem. What can be said about f?

8. Let f be continuous on $[a, b]$ with $x_1, x_2, \ldots, x_n \in [a, b]$ and $g_1, g_2, \ldots, g_n$ real numbers all of one sign. Show that

$$\sum_{i=1}^{n} f(x_i)\, g_i = f(c) \sum_{i=1}^{n} g_i$$

for some $c \in [a, b]$.

9. Let f be defined on $[0, 2]$ and have at most one point of discontinuity on this interval. If $f(x)$ is rational for each $x \in [0, 1)$ and irrational for each $x \in (1, 2]$, prove that f has exactly one point of discontinuity. What is that point?

10. Let f and g be continuous on $\mathbf{R}$ and suppose that $f(x) = g(x)$ for each $x \in \mathbf{Q}$. What conclusion can be drawn about f and g?

11. Let f be one-to-one and continuous on $[a, b]$. Show that f is strictly monotone there.

12. Let $f(x) = a_0 + a_1x + \dots + a_nx^n$, where n is odd and $x \in \mathbf{R}$. Show that the range of f is all of $\mathbf{R}$, whence f must have a real root.

13. Let f be as in Exercise 12, except that n is even. Show that if $a_0a_n < 0$, then f has at least two real roots.

14. Let f be increasing and have the intermediate value property on $[a, b]$. Show that f is continuous.

15. Let $f: [a,b] \to [a,b]$ be continuous. Prove that there exists $c \in [a,b]$ such that $f(c) = c$. (Such a point is called a **fixed point** for the function f.) Does this result hold if we replace $[a,b]$ by either $[0,\infty)$ or $(0,1]$?

16. Let $f: \mathbf{Q} \to \mathbf{R}$ be continuous and satisfy the condition that for each $M > 0$ there exist $x, y \in \mathbf{Q}$ such that $f(x) < -M$ and $f(y) > M$. Show that the extension of f to $\mathbf{R}$ by continuity is onto $\mathbf{R}$.

17. If f is continuous in $[a, b]$, show that for some $\xi \in [a, b]$

$$f(\xi) = \frac{\lambda f(a) + \mu f(b)}{\lambda + \mu}$$

where $\dfrac{\lambda}{\mu}$ is positive.

18. Given

$$f(x) = \lim_{n \to \infty} \frac{\ln(2+x) - x^{2n}\sin x}{1 + x^{2n}}$$

explain why $f(x)$ does not vanish in $\left[0, \dfrac{\pi}{2}\right]$ even though $f(0)$ and $f\left(\dfrac{\pi}{2}\right)$ differ in sign.

19. Let f be defined on $[a,b]$. f is said to be **locally monotone increasing** on $[a,b]$ if for each x there is a $\delta > 0$ such that f is monotone increasing on $(x - \delta, x + \delta)$. Show that if f is locally monotone on $[a,b]$, then f is monotone on $[a,b]$.

20. Give an example of a continuous, strictly increasing function f, in $[0,1] \cup [2,3]$, whose inverse is not continuous.

21. Let $f: [a,b] \to \mathbf{R}$ be continuous, and $f(x) > 0$ for all $x \in [a,b]$. Show that there exists a constant $C > 0$ such that $f(x) \geqslant C > 0$ for $x \in [a,b]$. Give an example to show that the result need not be true if $[a,b]$ is replaced by either $[0,\infty)$ or $(0,1]$.

22. Let $f: [a,b] \to \mathbf{R}$ be continuous, and $g(x) = \sup \{f(t): a \leqslant t \leqslant x\}$. Show that $g(a) = f(a)$, g is increasing and continuous at a.

23. Use Theorem 2.6.1 to show that for each real number $y > 0$, there exists a positive mth-root for $m \in \mathbf{N}$. [HINT: Consider x^m.]

24. If f and g are continuous on $[a,b]$, $f(a) \geqslant g(a)$, and $f(b) \leqslant g(b)$, prove that there exists $c \in [a,b]$ such that $f(c) = g(c)$.

25. If f is continuous on $\mathbf{R}$ and for some $a,b \in \mathbf{R}$, $f(a) \cdot f(b) < 0$, prove that there exists $x \in (a,b)$ such that $f(x) = 0$.

26. Give examples of functions which are not continuous, but still possess the intermediate value property.

27. Construct a two-to-one function from $[0,1]$ to $\mathbf{R}$ (that is, $\{x: f(x) = y\}$ is either empty, or consists of exactly two members). Show that such a function can not be continuous.

Chapter 3

A Little Topology

In this chapter, we develop the basic topological properties of the real line. The reader might wonder: what is topology? One answer is that it is the study of those properties of spaces which are invariant under homeomorphisms. True as the last statement may be, it is hardly an answer for the uninitiate. To understand what this answer means, we must come to grips with the notion of 'topological property'.

Consider for a moment the concept of function. One way to think of functions is to focus on collections of ordered pairs, and to consider what properties such collections might have. Evidently, the function concept itself can be treated this way, as in the definition of function which appears in the Appendix on Set Theory. This approach is abstract and elegant. However, it loses much of the *raison d'être* of functions. Functions exist to 'get you from one place to another place'. This is probably why one of the synonyms for function is 'map'. If you are in a given place and have a map, the map tells you how to get to other places. If you have a given element of a domain, and you have a function on that domain, the function tells you how to find a given element of the range. Thinking of functions in this way makes one focus on three things: domain, transfer process, and range.

Now let us think of our domain and range as being arbitrary sets. As sets, they have no internal structure. We would not care, for example, what type of entities make up the members of the set. However, if we know something about the nature of the transfer process between the two sets, we can say something about the relationship of the sets to one another. For example, suppose that the domain set consists of ten marbles. If the transfer process satisfies the conditions of a function, we know that the range of the function can contain at most ten elements, although we cannot say what type of items these elements might be. If as well, we know that the function is one-to-one, while again we cannot say what the range set is composed of, we can say it includes ten items.

Evidently then, transfer processes that are one-to-one functions have a very interesting property. They guarantee that an attribute of the domain is also present in the range. The attribute to which we refer is that of 'size' of the domain set. The key fact that we want to highlight is that a select group of functions, namely one-to-one functions, can guarantee to preserve certain attributes of their domains. Indeed, in the case of one-to-one functions and the size attribute, the preservation is in both directions, that is, the domain has ten members if and only if the range has ten members.

Consider now the case of continuous functions. The motivation for defining this class of functions was an attempt to collect together all those functions whose graphs could be drawn with a single stroke of the pen. After a definition of continuity was given, it was discovered that for the graph of the continuous function to have the required property, the domain to which the function was applied also had to have a certain property. Further, work with the continuity concept led to several theorems of the form

If f is continuous on D and D has property **P**, then the range of f has property **P**.

Obviously then, continuous functions are special in that they preserve attributes, or structure, of their domains as one uses the function to move to the range.

Still another way of looking at these ideas is the following. Consider the interval $A = [0,1]$ and the set $B = [0,1] \cup [2,3]$. It is impossible to find a continuous function which maps A onto B. This follows directly from the fact that the image of a closed bounded interval under a continuous function must be a closed bounded interval, and B is not an interval. Thus, even though there are many functions which will map A onto B, none of these functions will be continuous. What this means is that a continuous function must somehow be inextricably wedded to its domain, and that the very notion of continuity must be tied up with the structure of **R**.

On the other hand, if we consider B as the domain, and A as the range, we see that there are continuous functions mapping B onto A (the reader should construct one). Thus, the property of being continuous for a function is not enough to guarantee that the domain and range will have equivalent properties. To ensure this, we will need more, namely, that both the function and its inverse are continuous.

In topology, a one-to-one, continuous function, whose inverse is also continuous, is called a **homeomorphism**. In the remainder of this chapter, we will be looking for **topological properties**, namely those properties of **R**, or of subsets of **R**, which are **invariant** (do not change) upon application of such a map.

In seeking such properties, the focus will be on a comparison of the attributes of the domain of a continuous function with that of the range of the function. The function itself, will be of little interest, other than to specify its continuity properties. The identification process will consist of showing that a given property, **P**, is preserved by one-to-one continuous functions, since if continuity guarantees that an attribute passes from the domain to the range of a function, the continuity of the inverse, for the case of homeomorphisms, will reverse the passage.

The identification of topological properties will tell us a great deal about the internal structure of **R**, providing information about questions like: how closely the points of **R** are packed together; is **R** connected, or does it have holes? With this in mind, let us begin.

3.1 BASIC TOPOLOGICAL CONCEPTS

The basic objects for study in topology are 'spaces' (or topological spaces). Exactly what a space should be was a matter of contention for a goodly length of time during the latter part of the last century and the first part of this century. The end result of these deliberations was that a space was a nonempty set with a certain collection of subsets selected out and termed 'open sets'. For us, our set is **R**, the set of all real numbers. We already have a concept of 'open interval', and with a little thought we can generalize it to 'open set'.

Think for a moment about the open interval (a, b), with $a < b$. For any fixed $c \in (a, b)$, there is an open interval containing c which is completely contained in (a, b). This is an utter triviality, since we may choose this interval to be (a, b). To see that this is not true for any arbitrary subset X of **R**, note that $a \in [a, b]$, but there is no open interval contained in $[a, b]$ which also has a as a member. Similarly, $(a, b) \cap \mathbf{Q}$ does not have this property, as the reader can show.

Definition. A subset S of **R** is **open** provided that for every $c \in S$, there is an open interval (a, b) such that $c \in (a, b) \subseteq S$.

Discussion. It is immediate from the definition that each of the sets of the form (x, y), $x, y \in \mathbf{R}$, which we have been calling open intervals is, in fact, an open subset of **R**. It might be thought that the only open sets are the open intervals; however, this is not the case since the following subsets of **R** are all open: $\mathbf{R}$, $\varnothing$, $(2, \infty)$, $(3, 5) \cup (7, 10)$, $(-\infty, -1) \cup (1, 4)$ (**WHY?**). On the other hand, while the last two examples show that the open subsets of **R** consist of more than the open intervals, the definition suggests that the open subsets must be very closely related to intervals. The reason for this is that whenever a point c is in an open set, the set must also include an open interval surrounding c. Thus, it can be seen that every open subset is in fact a union of open intervals (**WHY?**). Recall, that in section 2.6 we showed that the property of being an interval was a topological property, although it was not stated in this way. This suggests that the property of being an open set might also be a topological property. Before stating the appropriate theorem, we will need a definition.

Definition. Let f be a function having domain, D, and let $A \subseteq D$. The **image** of A under f (denoted by $f(A)$) is defined by

$$f(A) = \{y : \text{there exists } x \in A \text{ and } y = f(x)\}.$$

Theorem 3.1.1. Let f be a one-to-one continuous function having domain D, and suppose $A \subseteq D$ is an open subset of **R**. Then $f(A)$ is an open subset of R.

Proof. Let $y \in f(A)$. We must find an open interval about y which is a subset of $f(A)$. Now $y = f(x)$ for some $x \in A$. Since A is open, there exists an open interval (c, d) such that $x \in (c, d) \subseteq A$. We may assume that $c, d \in A$ (**WHY?**). Since f is one-to-one, $f(c)$, $f(d)$, and $f(x)$ are three distinct points in $f(A)$. Without loss of generality, we may assume that $f(c) < f(x)$. Since f is continuous and one-to-one, $f(d) \leqslant f(x)$ would yield a contradiction. To see this, first note that $f(d) = f(x)$

contradicts the fact that f is one-to-one. Thus, suppose $f(c) < f(d) < f(x)$. Evidently, by the Intermediate Value Theorem, there exists $z \in (c,x)$ such that $f(z) = f(d)$, whence f is again not one-to-one. A similar argument takes care of the case when $f(d) \leqslant f(c)$. Thus by the Intermediate Value Theorem and its consequences,

$$y = f(x) \in (f(c), f(d)) \subseteq f(A)$$

follows. Thus, $f(A)$ is open.   □

Discussion. The proof that the attribute of being an open set is a topological property employs two essential facts, namely, that the function is one-to-one, and that the image of an interval is again an interval.

To see that the condition 'f must be one-to-one' can not be relaxed, consider $f(x) = x^2$, where $x \in \mathbf{R}$. It is easily seen that $f((-1,1)) = [0,1)$, which is not an open interval, and is not an open set since $0 \in [0,1)$, but there is no open interval containing 0 which is a subset of $[0,1)$.   □

EXAMPLE 1 _____

Show that the attribute of being bounded is not a topological property.

Solution. Let $f(x) = \dfrac{1}{x}$ be defined on $D = (0,1)$. Since f is strictly decreasing on D, it is one-to-one. That it is continuous follows from Example 2.5.3. But, Rng $f = (1,\infty)$, which is an unbounded set.   □

Discussion. The proof that a particular attribute of a set is not topological requires a counterexample. In this case the function $f(x) = \dfrac{1}{x}$ together with its domain serve to show that the image of a bounded set is not necessarily bounded. The reader should compare this result with Theorem 2.6.3 and its corollaries.   □

Definition. Let S be a subset of $\mathbf{R}$ and $c \in S$. Then c is an **interior point** of S provided that there is an open interval (a, b) such that $c \in (a, b) \subseteq S$. If c is not an interior point of S, c is said to be a **boundary point**.

Discussion. If the reader thinks of what an interior point should be, according to the usual meaning of interior, then this usage is completely consistent with the intuitive meaning. One significant fact here is that any set can have interior points, not just open sets. Another fact is that a set is open if and only if all of its points are interior points (see Exercise 11).

If $c \in S$ is not an interior point, we have called c a boundary point of S. This should make sense intuitively, since the boundary usually refers to an edge. Thus, if c is not surrounded by points of S, then there must be points which are not in S which are close to c. If one thinks about this further, one sees that there may also be points which are not in S which one would want to call boundary points. This idea will be discussed further in Example 3 and Exercises 31 and 32.   □

EXAMPLE 2

Find the interior and boundary points of $\bigcap \left\{ \left[-\dfrac{1}{n}, 1 + \dfrac{1}{n} \right] : n \in \mathbf{N} \right\}$.

Solution. Since $-\dfrac{1}{n} < 0$ and $1 < 1 + \dfrac{1}{n}$ for every $n \in \mathbf{N}$, it follows that $[0,1]$ is contained in the intersection. On the other hand, if $a \notin [0,1]$, two cases ensue. First assume $a < 0$. By the Archimedean property, there exists $N \in \mathbf{N}$ such that $a < -\dfrac{1}{N}$, whence a does not belong to the intersection. On the other hand, if $a > 1$, a similar argument shows that at least one member of the intersection misses the point a. Hence, we conclude that the intersection is precisely the closed interval $[0,1]$. If $c \in (0,1)$, then c is clearly an interior point of $[0,1]$. Since there is no open interval containing 0 and contained in $[0,1]$, we see that 0 is not an interior point. Similarly, 1 is also not an interior point. Thus, the set of interior points of the given set is $(0,1)$. This argument also tells us what the boundary points are, namely, all points in $[0,1]$ which are not interior points. Thus, the set of boundary points is $\{0,1\}$. $\qquad\square$

Discussion. Note that the completeness of the real numbers is used in the computation of the intersection in the form of the Archimedean property. Here, 0 is indeed a point belonging to the set $[0,1]$, but is not qualified to be an interior point, since if an open interval (a, b) satisfies the relation: $0 \in (a, b) \subseteq [0,1]$, then simultaneously, $a < 0$ and $a \geqslant 0$, a contradiction. A similar consideration proves that 1 is not an interior point. $\qquad\square$

EXAMPLE 3

Find all interior and boundary points of $A = \left\{ \dfrac{1}{n} : n \in \mathbf{N} \right\}$ and its complement.

Solution. The set, A, contains no open interval (**WHY?**), whence it can have no interior points. Thus, every point of A is a boundary point of A. Now, consider A', the complement of A. The reader can verify

$$A' = (-\infty, 0] \cup (1, \infty) \cup \left[\bigcup \left\{ \left[\dfrac{1}{n+1}, \dfrac{1}{n} \right] : n \in \mathbf{N} \right\} \right].$$

Every point of A', except 0, is an interior point. Thus, 0 is a boundary point of A'. $\qquad\square$

Discussion. The two key facts in this example are first that for a set to have interior points, it must contain an open interval and second, the complement of a set can have boundary points which do not belong to the original set. The latter fact suggests that the boundary of a set should consist of the boundary points of the given set together with the boundary points of the complement (see Exercises 31 and 32). $\qquad\square$

Theorem 3.1.2. Let A be a collection of open sets. Then $\bigcup A$ is open. If A is a finite collection, then $\bigcap A$ is open.

Proof. Let $c \in \bigcup A$. Then there exists $B \in A$ such that $c \in B$. Now B is open, so there is an open interval (a, b) such that $c \in (a, b) \subseteq B \subseteq \bigcup A$ and we are done. Now to complete the proof, assume that A is finite, say $\{A_1, \ldots, A_n\}$. Let $c \in \bigcap A$. For each $i = 1, 2, \ldots, n$, we can choose a positive δ_i such that

$$(c - \delta_i, c + \delta_i) \subseteq A_i. \qquad \textbf{(WHY?)}$$

Let $\delta = \min\{\delta_1, \ldots, \delta_n\}$, whence $(c - \delta, c + \delta) \subseteq \bigcap A$. $\qquad \square$

Discussion. The attribute of being open is a property of some subsets of **R**. Mathematicians have developed various ways of manipulating sets, for example, taking intersections or forming unions. This theorem addresses the question of the degree to which the attribute of being open will be preserved by these natural operations on sets.

With respect to the proof, the only significant feature of the argument is the use of finiteness for the intersection part. Note that the minimum of a finite collection of nonzero numbers is always nonzero. But, it is quite possible that the infimum of an infinite collection of nonzero real numbers is zero. For example, $\inf \left\{ \dfrac{1}{n} : n \in \mathbf{N} \right\} = 0$. The reader should note this carefully and create an example of an infinite collection of open sets whose intersection is not open (see Exercise 7).

On a more general note, the branch of mathematics known as set-theoretic topology (general topology) begins by defining a **topology** on a nonempty set X as a collection of subsets (called **open sets**) which have the property that arbitrary unions of members of the collection and finite intersections of members of the collection belong to the collection, as well as the empty set and X. As the reader can readily see by a comparison of the general definition with the content of the theorem above, such a definition is not abstractly and artificially coined, but stems from basic properties of open sets on the real line. Similarly, many of the abstract definitions and ideas in mathematics are carved out of well-known elementary properties of the real numbers, and motivated by a desire to obtain deeper insight into the nature of the real number system. $\qquad \square$

We have seen that the concept of open interval can be generalized to that of open set. The reader may be wondering whether the concept of closed interval also has a generalization. The answer is yes. Again, the generalization is obtained by looking at the relationship of the set as a whole to particular points. Recall the definition of a limit point of a set: a is a **limit point** of $A \subseteq \mathbf{R}$ if for every positive δ, $[(a - \delta, a) \cup (a, a + \delta)] \cap A \neq \varnothing$.

Definition. A subset S of **R** is **closed** if S contains all its limit points.

Discussion. It is easily checked that every closed interval is closed. The following are also examples of closed subsets of **R**: **R**, $\varnothing$, $[2, 3] \cup [-1, 0]$, $[1, 1]$,

$\{0\} \cup \left\{ \dfrac{1}{n} : n \in \mathbf{N} \right\}$. The fact that arbitrary intersections and finite unions of closed sets are again closed is pursued in Exercises 12 and 13. The reader is invited to supply appropriate examples demonstrating that an arbitrary union of closed sets need not be closed.

The next theorem expresses the fundamental relationship between open and closed sets. It could also be used as the definition of a closed set, from which one could arrive at the above definition of a closed set as a theorem.

Theorem 3.1.3. Let $A \subseteq \mathbf{R}$. Then A is open if and only if the complement, A', of A is closed.

Proof. Let A be open. Fix $a \in \mathbf{R}$, such that a is a limit point of A'. If $a \in A'$, then we are done; hence for the sake of argument we assume that $a \in A$. But then, there is a neighborhood of a (any open set containing a), say $(a - \delta, a + \delta)$, which is completely contained in A. Since $A \cap A' = \varnothing$, a cannot be a limit point of A' (**WHY?**). Thus, we have a contradiction, whence $a \in A'$. It follows that A' is closed. Conversely, suppose that A' is closed for a fixed A. Let $a \in A$, and so not in A'. Thus, a is not a limit point of A', whence there is a neighborhood of a, say $(a - \delta, a + \delta)$, such that the intersection of this neighborhood with A' is empty. It is immediate that $(a - \delta, a + \delta) \subseteq A$, as desired, whence A is open. $\square$

Discussion. Note the use of an indirect argument to show that the complement of an open set is closed. This type of reasoning is often very useful in elementary topological proofs. Also, both proofs involve little more than manipulation of the relevant definitions. What is essential is that the reader have these at the 'tip of the tongue', since otherwise it is impossible to draw together the relevant facts.

Theorem 3.1.3 also tells us that by taking set-theoretic complements, any statement which we know is true about open sets can be translated into a statement about closed sets which will also be true. For example, we have shown that the union of an arbitrary collection of open sets is open. Taking the union of a collection of open sets corresponds to taking the intersection of the complements of these same sets. Thus, the intersection of an arbitrary collection of closed sets must be closed. The reader will be asked to give a direct proof of this fact in Exercise 13. $\square$

One of the interesting features of the topology of the reals is that it can be obtained from open intervals having rational end points, as shown in the next theorem.

Theorem 3.1.4. Let A be open. Then A is a countable union of open intervals with rational end points.

Proof. Fix $c \in A$. Then there is an interval (a,b) such that $c \in (a,b) \subseteq A$ with a and b both rational (**WHY?**). If we label the interval as $(a,b)_c$, then $A = \cup \{(a,b)_c : c \in A\}$. Since $\mathbf{Q}$ is countable, this collection of such intervals must be countable. $\square$

Discussion. As defined in the Appendix, a set is countable if it can be put in one-to-one correspondence with $\mathbf{N}$. A critical fact required for this proof is that $\mathbf{Q}$ is countable. This fact is shown in the Appendix. The reader should give a detailed explanation as to why an interval with rational end points exists. This should be followed by a detailed explanation as to why the collection of intervals is countable, since A in general will be uncountable.   □

Theorem 3.1.5.   Let A be open. Then A is a countable disjoint union of open intervals.

Proof.   For x, $y \in A$, we write $x \cong y$ if and only if x, $y \in (a, b) \subseteq A$ for some a, $b \in \mathbf{R}$. It is a straightforward matter to check that $\cong$ defines an equivalence relation (see Appendix) on A. It follows that the equivalence classes are a collection of disjoint intervals (**WHY?**). Further, each equivalence class contains at least two points (**WHY?**) and so, since it is an interval, contains a rational number. Thus, the collection of intervals is countable. To complete the proof, we need only check that an interval bounded above does not contain its end points (**WHY?**). This will certainly be true if the interval is not bounded. Thus, consider an interval, I, which is bounded above, and call its supremum b. If $b \in A'$, we are done. To see why $b \in A'$ must be so, consider $b < c$, where c is arbitrary. Then there is a c' such that

$$b < c' \leqslant c \text{ and } c' \in A',$$

since otherwise b could not be an upper bound for I. It follows that b is a limit point of A' (**WHY?**), and so is a member of A', since A' is the complement of an open set. Thus, $b \in A'$ as claimed.   □

Discussion.   The use of equivalence relations to get a decomposition of A into intervals is a nice application of equivalence relations as a tool. Since what we are trying to establish is that A is a union of a collection of disjoint open intervals, the properties of equivalence classes make the proof a triviality. However, the proof based on equivalence relations is not nearly so self-motivating as a direct construction of the required intervals. The constructive process also acts to motivate the definition of $\cong$, since the interval $I \subseteq A$ which contains $a \in A$ is obtained by

$$I_a = \bigcup \{(b, c) : a \in (b, c) \subseteq A \text{ and } b, c \in \mathbf{R}\}.$$

Once one has the collection of intervals I_a one must deal with the problem that many of the intervals are the same. The natural way to deal with problems of this type is to generate a suitable equivalence relation which identifies all those objects which are the same except for their name.   □

The development above establishes that all the basic topological properties of the real numbers have at their heart the order and completeness axioms. Indeed, the very definition of open set has as its foundation the concept of 'open interval' which itself arises out of the order properties of $\mathbf{R}$. It is clear then why this topology (collection of open sets) is called the **order topology** on $\mathbf{R}$.

The focus of the topological development has been on open sets, although we have defined closed sets and interior points as well. The thrust of these definitions is to capture properties which mathematicians recognized as being related to the structure of **R**. One would therefore expect that other definitions might play an important role as well. In the exercises we shall present a number of these definitions. We complete this section by defining one further set-theoretic operation and exploring some of its properties.

Definition. Let A be a subset of **R**. Set

$$A_{lm} = \{x : x \text{ is a limit point of } A\}.$$

A_{lm} is referred to as the **derived set** of A. $\qquad\qquad\qquad\qquad\qquad\qquad\square$

Theorem 3.1.6. Let $A \subseteq \mathbf{R}$. Then the derived set of A is closed; that is, $(A_{lm})_{lm} \subseteq A_{lm}$.

Proof. Let x be a limit point of A_{lm}. We must show that x is a limit point of A. Thus, fix $\delta > 0$. Since x is a limit point of A_{lm}, there exists $y \in A_{lm}$ such that $0 < |y - x| < \dfrac{\delta}{2}$ **(WHY?)**. Since y is a limit point of A, there exists $z \in A$ such that $0 < |y - z| < \dfrac{\delta}{2}$. It follows that

$$0 < |x - z| \leqslant |x - y| + |y - z| < \delta.$$

Since δ was arbitrary, x is a limit point of A. $\qquad\qquad\qquad\qquad\qquad\square$

Discussion. This proof should be reminiscent of many of our earlier proofs with limits. In essence, it makes the following points. To be a limit point of A_{lm}, a point x must have points of A_{lm} arbitrarily close to it. These points in turn, by virtue of the fact that they belong to A_{lm} must have points of A which are arbitrarily close to them. Thus, some points of A must end up being close to the point x, which makes x a limit point of A. The proof simply formalizes this intuition. $\qquad\qquad\qquad\qquad\qquad\square$

Theorem 3.1.7. Let $A \subseteq \mathbf{R}$. Then $A \cup A_{lm}$ is closed. Moreover, if $B \subseteq \mathbf{R}$ is closed and $A \subseteq B$, then $A \cup A_{lm} \subseteq B$.

Proof. Let x be a limit point of $A \cup A_{lm}$. Then either x is a limit point of A, or x is a limit point of A_{lm}. In the latter case, x is a limit point of A by our last theorem. Thus $A \cup A_{lm}$ is closed. The remainder of the proof is left to Exercise 14. $\qquad\square$

EXAMPLE 4 _____

Find the set of limit points of **Q**.

Solution. Let x be an arbitrary member of **R** and fix $\delta > 0$. Then there is a rational number q such that $0 < |q - x| < \delta$ **(WHY?)**. Thus, every real number is a limit point of **Q**. Thus, $\mathbf{Q}_{lm} = \mathbf{R}$. $\qquad\qquad\qquad\qquad\square$

Discussion. This example shows that the rationals are distributed throughout all the real numbers, and that no matter how we might try, we can never find a real number which is very far from all rational numbers. It also tells us that every real number can be obtained as a limit of a sequence of rational numbers. A set, A, with this property, that is, every member of **R** can be obtained as a limit point of A, is said to be **dense** in **R**. □

The main thrust of this section has been to develop criteria for distinguishing various types of sets of real numbers. The principal type among these is the collection of open sets. If the reader thinks about it, it will be clear that there are connections between the concept of open set, and that of continuous function. One reason for suggesting this is the fact that the open interval concept plays such an important role in the definitions of limit and continuity. The next two theorems delineate the connection between the concept of continuous function and the concepts of open and closed set.

Theorem 3.1.8.   Let f be defined on **R**. Then f is continuous on **R** if and only if for every open set $O \subseteq \mathbf{R}$, $f^{-1}(O)$ is an open subset of **R**.

Proof.   Let f be continuous, $O \subseteq \mathbf{R}$ be open, and $x \in f^{-1}(O)$. Now $f(x) = y \in O$, whence there is a positive ϵ such that $|y - z| < \epsilon$ implies $z \in O$. Since f is continuous on **R**, f is continuous at x, so there is a $\delta > 0$ such that $|x - w| < \delta$ implies $|f(x) - f(w)| < \epsilon$. But this means that $f(w) \in O$, whence $w \in f^{-1}(O)$. Thus, $f^{-1}(O)$ is open as desired.

Conversely, suppose that for every open set $O \subseteq \mathbf{R}$, $f^{-1}(O)$ is open, and fix $x \in \mathbf{R}$. We must show that f is continuous at x. Set $y = f(x)$ and fix $\epsilon > 0$. Evidently, $O = (y - \epsilon, y + \epsilon)$ is an open set. Thus, by hypothesis, $f^{-1}(O)$ is open. Since $x \in f^{-1}(O)$, we can choose $\delta > 0$ such that $|x - z| < \delta$ implies $z \in f^{-1}(O)$ which in turn implies $|f(x) - f(z)| < \epsilon$. Since ϵ was arbitrary, f is continuous at x. Since x was arbitrary, we are done. □

Discussion.   This theorem is very useful since it provides us with a means for characterizing continuous functions which is independent of the context of real numbers. Moreover, the proof is relatively straightforward; however, there are some subtleties as discussed below.

The reader may wonder why we have required the domain of the function to be the totality of the real numbers. The reason is most simply explained by considering an example. Let $f(x) = x + 3$, $x \in [0,1]$. Evidently, this is a continuous function having $[3,4]$ for its range. If we let $O = (2,5)$, we can ask about the nature of $f^{-1}(O)$, that is, is this set open? In answering this question, consider the point $4 \in O$. We know that $f(1) = 4$, and that $|z - 1| < \frac{1}{2}$ and $z \in [0,1]$ will imply that $f(z) \in O$. Thus, the argument presented as the proof of the theorem still has validity. But, on the other hand, we know that $f^{-1}(O) = [0,1]$ which is a closed subset of **R**. The reason for the breakdown is that not every z which satisfies $|z - 1| < \frac{1}{2}$ also satisfies $z \in [0,1]$.

The resolution of this problem relates to the fact that we want to characterize continuous functions *on a domain*. The flaw arises because we consider $D = [0,1]$ as a subset of **R**, relating the definition of open and closed sets to **R** instead of to D. Once this problem is recognized, the solution is easy. We simply define the concept of an open set **relative to** D (see Exercises 36 and 37). □

We close this section with the following theorem which establishes the relationship between closed sets and continuous functions. Given that this theorem is completely analogous to Theorem 3.1.8 and that a set is closed exactly if its complement is open, the reader may wonder about an analog to Theorem 3.1.1 which states that open sets are preserved by one-to-one continuous functions. The reader is asked to find a counterexample in Exercise 18. A more limited version of the analogous theorem is proved in section 3.6.

Theorem 3.1.9. Let f be defined on **R**. Then f is continuous on **R** if and only if for every closed set $C \subseteq \mathbf{R}$, $f^{-1}(C)$ is a closed subset of **R**.

Proof. Exercise 17. □

EXERCISES

1. Find the interior and the limit points of each of the following sets:
   (a) $\varnothing$;
   (b) **R**;
   (c) $(0,1)$;
   (d) **N**;
   (e) $\left\{ \dfrac{1}{n} : n \in \mathbf{N} \right\}$;
   (f) $(-1,3) \cap \mathbf{Q}$;
   (g) $\left\{ \dfrac{1}{m} + \dfrac{1}{n} : m,n \in \mathbf{N} \right\}$;
   (h) $(-2,4) \cap (\mathbf{R} \sim \mathbf{Q})$;
   (i) $\left\{ \dfrac{1}{n} : n \in \mathbf{N} \right\} \cup (2,3) \cup (3,4) \cup \{5\} \cup [6,7] \cup (\mathbf{Q} \cap [8,9])$.

2. Which of the sets in Exercise 1 are open? Which are closed?

3. Let A be an open subset of R. If one point is deleted, is A still open? If a finite number of points are deleted is A still open? A countably infinite set? A set which in its entirety constitutes a strictly monotone sequence?

4. Let A be a closed subset of R. If one point is deleted, is A still closed? If a finite number of points are deleted is A still closed? A countably infinite set? A set which in its entirety constitutes a strictly monotone sequence?

5. Let A be an open subset of R. If one point is added, is A still open? If a finite number of points are added is A still open? A countably infinite set? A set which in its entirety constitutes a strictly monotone sequence?

6. Let A be a closed subset of R. If one point is added, is A still closed? If a finite number of points are added is A still closed? A countably infinite set? A set which in its entirety constitutes a strictly monotone sequence?

7. Give an example of a collection of open sets whose intersection is not open.

8. Show that every finite set is closed and has no limit points.

9. Let $A \subseteq \mathbf{R}$ be a nonempty, closed bounded set. Show that $\sup A \in A$.

10. (a) Construct a set of real numbers with exactly three limit points.
    (b) Construct a subset of $[0,1]$ with a countably infinite number of limit points.

11. Show that a set is open if and only if it is composed entirely of interior points.

12. Show that a finite union of closed subsets of $\mathbf{R}$ is closed. Show that this can not be extended to infinite unions.

13. Give a direct proof of the fact that an arbitrary intersection of closed sets is closed.

14. Let $A \subseteq \mathbf{R}$. Show there is a unique smallest closed set, $\bar{A}$, which contains A. Show also $\bar{A} = A \cup A_{lm}$. This set is called the **closure** of A.

15. Establish the following properties of closure:
    (a) A is closed if and only if $A = \bar{A}$;
    (b) $\bar{\varnothing} = \varnothing$;
    (c) for every $A \subseteq \mathbf{R}$, $\bar{A} = \bar{\bar{A}}$;
    (d) for every $A, B \subseteq \mathbf{R}$, $\bar{A} \cup \bar{B} = \overline{(A \cup B)}$.

16. Prove or disprove:
    (a) $\overline{\bigcap A} = \bigcap \bar{A}$;
    (b) $\overline{\bigcup A} = \bigcup \bar{A}$
    where A is a family of arbitrary subsets of $\mathbf{R}$.

17. Let $f: \mathbf{R} \to \mathbf{R}$. Show that the inverse image of every closed set (under f) is closed if and only if f is continuous.

18. Give an example of a one-to-one continuous function from $\mathbf{R}$ into $\mathbf{R}$ for which there is a closed set A such that $f(A)$ is not closed.

19. Let $A \subseteq \mathbf{R}$. Then, $a \in A$ is called an **isolated point** of A provided there is an open interval (b, c) such that $(b, c) \cap A = \{a\}$. Find the set of isolated points of the subsets in Exercise 1.

20. Show that:
    (a) if A is open, then A has no isolated points;
    (b) if A is closed, then for each $a \in A$, a is either an isolated point of A or a limit point of A. Prove or disprove: If every point of A is isolated, then A is closed.

21. Is it true that if every point of A is a limit point of A, then A is closed? What about if no point of A is a limit point?

22. A set $A \subseteq \mathbf{R}$ is **clopen** if it is both open and closed. Give an example of a clopen subset of $\mathbf{R}$. Find all clopen subsets of $\mathbf{R}$.

23. Let $f: \mathbf{R} \to \mathbf{R}$ be $1-1$ (one-to-one) and continuous. Let (a, b) be an open interval. Show that $f((a, b))$ is also an open interval and give a precise description of the image interval. What can be said about the image of a closed interval?

24. Let $f: \mathbf{R} \to \mathbf{R}$ be $1-1$, continuous. Show that f must either be strictly increasing or strictly decreasing. Does this still hold if the domain of f is an arbitrary interval? What about if Dmn f is an arbitrary subset of $\mathbf{R}$?

25. Let $f: \mathbf{R} \to \mathbf{R}$ be a homeomorphism (i.e., f is one-to-one, and continuous and f^{-1} is also continuous). Let $A \subseteq \mathbf{R}$. Show that each of the following statements is true about A if and only if it is also true about $f(A)$.

(a) A has an isolated point;

(b) A is clopen;

(c) A is an interval;

(d) A is a union of two disjoint intervals;

(e) A has exactly two limit points;

(f) A has a nonempty interior.

26. Show that $A = \mathbf{R}$ is not a topological property.

27. Show that there is a continuous one-to-one function which maps $[0,1] \cup (2,3)$ onto $[0,1)$. Does there exist a function which will do the same job for $[0,1] \cup [2,3)$? Interpret these results in the context of Exercise 25(d).

28. Let $A°$, $\bar{A}$, and A' denote, respectively, the interior, the closure, and the complement of A. Show that for any $A \subseteq \mathbf{R}$:

(a) $A°° = A°$;

(b) $(A \cap B)° = A° \cap B°$ (can $\cap$ be replaced by $\cup$?);

(c) $(A')° = (\bar{A})'$.

29. Let A be a subset of $\mathbf{R}$. Show there is a unique largest open set which is a subset of A. Show that this set is in fact $A°$.

30. For a fixed $A \subseteq \mathbf{R}$, show that there are at most fourteen distinct sets which can be obtained from A by successive applications of the operations of $°$, $^-$, and $'$. Further, show that there is in fact a set which will yield fourteen distinct sets via these operations.

31. For a subset $A \subseteq \mathbf{R}$, define the **boundary,** $b(A) = \bar{A} \cap \overline{(A')}$. Prove the following:

(a) $\bar{A} = A \cup b(A)$;

(b) $A° = A \sim b(A)$;

(c) $\mathbf{R} = A° \cup b(A) \cup A'°$.

Compute the boundary of the sets described in Exercise 1.

32. Show that the boundary of A as defined in Exercise 31 consists of the union of the boundary points of A and the boundary points of A'.

33. Define the **exterior** of A, Ext(A), to be the complement of the closure of A. Prove or disprove: Ext($A \cup B$) = Ext(A) $\cap$ Ext(B).

34. Find necessary and sufficient conditions such that $(A_{lm})_{lm} = A_{lm}$. Give an example showing $(A_{lm})_{lm} \neq A_{lm}$.

35. Theorem 3.1.5 provides a powerful characterization of open subsets of $\mathbf{R}$ in terms of a countable union of disjoint open intervals. Does a similar characterization of closed subsets of $\mathbf{R}$ exist?

36. Let $D \subseteq \mathbf{R}$. We define the **relative topology** on D by calling a subset $U \subseteq D$ open (relative to D) if and only if $U = A \cap D$ for some open subset $A \subseteq \mathbf{R}$. We also say that U is **relatively open** in D. Prove the following results for $A \subseteq D$:

(a) A point $c \in D$ is a limit point of A with respect to the relative topology on D if and only if it is a limit point of A in $\mathbf{R}$;

(b) The closure of a subset $A \subseteq D$ with respect to the relative topology on D is the set $\bar{A} \cap D$;

(c) The set $A \subseteq D$ is closed in the relative topology on D if and only if $A = X \cap D$, where X is a closed set in $\mathbf{R}$.

37. Let f map D into $\mathbf{R}$. Show f is continuous on D if and only if for every open set $O \subseteq \mathbf{R}$, $f^{-1}(O)$ is open in the relative topology on D.

38. Let f map D into $\mathbf{R}$. Show f is continuous on D if and only if for every closed set $C \subseteq \mathbf{R}$, $f^{-1}(C)$ is closed in the relative topology on D.

39. A subset S of **R** is **connected** provided there do not exist open sets O_1 and O_2 such that $O_1 \cap O_2 = \emptyset$, $O_i \cap S \neq \emptyset$, $(i = 1, 2)$ and $S \subset O_1 \cup O_2$. Show that S is connected if and only if S is an interval. Can a set which consists entirely of isolated points ever be connected?

40. A set, A, is called **path connected** if for every $x, y \in A$, there exists a continuous function, ϕ from $[0,1]$ into A such that $\phi(0) = x$ and $\phi(1) = y$. Show that every connected subset of **R** is path connected.

3.2 PROPERTIES OF R ASSOCIATED WITH CLOSED BOUNDED SETS

In sections 2.6 and 3.1, we developed several facts about the images of subsets of **R** under one-to-one, continuous functions. It was shown that the image of an interval was an interval, and the image of a closed bounded interval was again a closed bounded interval. It was also demonstrated that the image of a bounded subset of **R** was not necessarily bounded. Thus, closed bounded intervals behave nicely under continuous functions. Since we have generalized the notion of a closed interval, we may wonder to what extent the above mentioned theorem about the image of a closed bounded interval under a continuous function can be generalized. The complete answer to this question will be given in section 3.6. In this section we develop the important properties of closed bounded subsets of **R**.

Since the generalized definition of a closed set is based on the notion of limit point, it is natural to expect that limit points must play a key role. Thus, the first result in this section is the Bolzano–Weierstrass Theorem on the existence of limit points for infinite bounded sets. The reader should not be surprised by the fact that all the results of this section have the completeness of **R** at the heart of their proofs.

Theorem 3.2.1 (Bolzano–Weierstrass). Let A be an infinite subset of **R**, which is bounded. Then A has a limit point.

Proof. Since A is bounded, there is an $M > 0$ such that for all $a \in A$, $-M < a < M$. We now define a collection of closed intervals for each $n \in \mathbf{N}$:

$$I_0 = [-M, M];$$

$$I_n^i = \left[-M + 2M\frac{(i-1)}{2^n}, -M + 2M\frac{i}{2^n} \right] \text{ for } 1 \leqslant i \leqslant 2^n.$$

It is clear that the collection I_n^i has union $[-M, M]$ and divides this interval into 2^n subintervals of equal length. From each collection, we will pick a subinterval which we will call J_n and which has the property that $J_n \cap A$ is infinite. We define J_n inductively as follows:

$$J_0 = I_0$$

Further, suppose that $J_1, J_2, \ldots, J_m$ have been defined so that

$$J_m \subseteq J_{m-1} \subseteq \ldots \subseteq J_0; \qquad J_k \cap A \text{ is infinite for } 0 \leqslant k \leqslant m$$

and each J_k is chosen from the collection I_k^i where $1 \leqslant i \leqslant 2^k$. By assumption there is a fixed s such that

$$J_m = \left[-M + \frac{2M(s-1)}{2^m}, \; -M + \frac{2Ms}{2^m} \right].$$

If $I_{m+1}^{2s-1} \cap A$ is infinite, set $J_{m+1} = I_{m+1}^{2s-1}$. Otherwise, set $J_{m+1} = I_{m+1}^{2s}$. It is clear that $J_{m+1} \subseteq J_m$ and that $J_{m+1} \cap A$ is infinite. Lastly, J_{m+1} is chosen from among the I_{m+1}^i as required. Let a_n denote the left-hand end point of J_n, b_n the right-hand end point. Then $\{a_n\}$ is monotone increasing and $\{b_n\}$ is monotone decreasing. Further, $a_{n+k} \leqslant b_n$ for all $k \in \mathbf{N}$. It is immediate that $\{a_n\}$ has a limit, call it b. To see that b is a limit point of the set A, let a positive ϵ be given and choose n so that

$$J_n \subseteq [b - \epsilon, b + \epsilon].$$

Such a choice is possible since $b_n - a_n = \dfrac{1}{2^n}$, for any given n. Since $J_n \cap A$ is infinite, we have that every deleted interval about b will contain points of A. Thus, b is the required limit point of A. $\qquad\square$

Discussion. The intuitive idea behind this proof is simple. We simply start with an interval which contains an infinite number of points of A. We divide it into two equal parts. Surely one of the halves must contain an infinite number of points of A. If the lower half has an infinite number of points from A, we select it for attention, if not, we select the upper half. But now we are looking at an interval which has half the length, and we repeat the procedure. This process generates a sequence of intervals, each of which is contained in its predecessor and which has half the length of its predecessor. From this we see that the end points of the intervals form two monotone sequences. At the appropriate moment we haul out the supremum principle in the form of the theorem on bounded monotone sequences, and use it to generate a limit point. The reader will note that without the Completeness Axiom, the proof could not be accomplished. The reader will be asked to discuss this fact further in Exercise 12. $\quad\square$

Theorem 3.2.1 has an immediate corollary which states the first important property of closed bounded subsets of **R**.

Corollary. Let A be a closed bounded subset of **R**. Then every infinite subset of A has a limit point in A.

Discussion. This corollary is in the form of an implication. Evidently, an immediate question of interest would be whether the converse is true. What would be particularly interesting about this question is that the condition—'every infinite subset of A has a limit point in A'—makes no mention of 'bounded'. The problem with the concept of boundedness is that it requires a notion of distance as a prerequisite. Thus, a converse could supply an important tool for generalizing the notion of 'closed and bounded' to situations where no distance function was available, provided we could obtain a definition of limit point which did not depend on distance. Such a definition exists (see Exercise 4), whence a converse would supply a more general notion of closed bounded sets.

Of course, all of the above is a mere pipe dream, unless a proof of the converse could be generated. It seems apparent that the condition at least guarantees that A is closed (**WHY?**). However, to show that A is also bounded is a horse of a different color. The industrious reader may wish to try. Otherwise, read on, Macduff. $\square$

Theorem 3.2.2. Let A be a subset of $\mathbf{R}$. Then A is closed and bounded exactly if every infinite subset of A has a limit point in A.

Proof. Let A satisfy the condition that every infinite subset of A has a limit point in A. Let x be an arbitrary limit point of A. Let $O_n = \left(x - \dfrac{1}{n}, x + \dfrac{1}{n} \right)$. Evidently, $\bigcap O_n = \{x\}$. Since x is a limit point of A, there is a sequence of distinct points $\{a_n\}$, such that $a_n \in A \cap O_n$. This sequence has a limit which, not surprisingly, is x. Now the points of the sequence constitute an infinite collection of points of A. Such a set has a limit point. Since a convergent sequence has only one limit point, and that limit point is x, we conclude that $x \in A$ as required. Thus, A is closed. Now, consider the collection of sets $[-n, n]$, where $n \in \mathbf{N}$. If A is unbounded, we may pick points $\{a_n\}$ such that $a_n \notin [-n, n]$. Such a sequence does not have a limit point in $\mathbf{R}$, much less A. Thus, A must be bounded. The reverse implication is contained in the corollary above. $\square$

Definition. A sequence $\{J_n\}$ of intervals is called **nested** provided that $J_{n+1} \subseteq J_n$ for each $n \in \mathbf{N}$.

Discussion. If one thinks of what 'nested' should mean, then a sequence of nested intervals has the right properties, in that each successive interval is found inside its successor. Note that if the length of the first interval is finite, then the lengths of a sequence of nested intervals form a monotonic decreasing sequence. $\square$

Theorem 3.2.3. Let $\{J_n : n \in \mathbf{N}\}$, denote a sequence of closed, bounded, nonempty, nested intervals. Then $\bigcap J_n \neq \varnothing$. Further, if the length of the intervals has limit 0 as n tends to ∞, then the intersection consists exactly of a single point.

Proof. Following the ideas developed in Theorem 3.2.1, let $\{a_n\}$ and $\{b_n\}$ be sequences of the left- and right-hand end points of J_n, respectively. As noted above, $\{a_n\}$ is monotone increasing and $\{b_n\}$ is monotone decreasing. If a and b denote the respective limits of a_n and b_n, then $a \leqslant b$ (**WHY?**). It is immediate that $[a, b] \subseteq J_n$ for each n. Further, if $c < a$, then there is an n such that $c < a_n$, and so $c \notin J_n$ and so not in the intersection. Thus,

$$\bigcap J_n = [a, b] \neq \varnothing,$$

the last since $a \leqslant b$. To complete the proof, we note that if the limit of the lengths of the J_n's is 0, then $b_n - a_n$ must tend to 0 as n tends to infinity. This forces $a = b$ (**WHY?**). $\square$

Discussion. Again note that the ultimate force which takes care of the argument is the Completeness Axiom. We can not overemphasize the importance of this axiom for the structural properties of the reals. $\square$

EXAMPLE 1 _____

Show by example that an analogous theorem about a nested sequence of open intervals is not valid.

Solution.   Let $O_n = \left[0, \dfrac{1}{n}\right)$. If $x \in \bigcap O_n$, then $x > 0$. On the other hand,

it is also the case that $x < \dfrac{1}{n}$ for every $n \in \mathbf{N}$, whence $x \leqslant 0$. Thus, $\bigcap O_n$ is

empty.   □

Discussion.   The point which one would like to have in $\bigcap O_n$ is 0. It is not there because it is the 'missing' limit point from all the sets. This is why the sets must all be closed in the hypothesis of Theorem 3.2.3. In Exercise 3 we ask the reader to show that bounded is also a necessary part of the hypothesis.   □

The next theorem is also sometimes referred to as the Bolzano–Weierstrass Theorem.

Theorem 3.2.4.   Let $\{a_n\}$ denote a bounded sequence of real numbers. Then $\{a_n\}$ contains a convergent subsequence.

Proof.   There are two cases, namely that $\{a_n\}$ takes finitely many distinct values and that $\{a_n\}$ takes infinitely many distinct values. For the first case, we note that there must be a subset $M \subseteq \mathbf{N}$ such that M is infinite and such that $m, n \in M$ implies $a_n = a_m$. But now $\{a_m : m \in M\}$ is a convergent subsequence since it is a constant sequence. Thus, the first case is established. For the second, $\{a_n\}$ denotes an infinite bounded set of real numbers. It follows that we can apply Theorem 3.2.1 to obtain a limit point. It is left to Exercise 5 to show that there is a subsequence which converges to the limit point.   □

Discussion.   The basic fact being employed in the proof of the first case is that if we divide up an infinite set, in this case $\mathbf{N}$, into a finite number of disjoint subsets, then at least one of the subsets must be infinite. Another way of stating this fact is to say that the union of a finite collection of finite sets is finite, which is a basic theorem of 'cardinal arithmetic', although a nontrivial one. In any case, it is the heart of the argument for the first case. For the second, we employ Theorem 3.2.1 which hides the use of the Completeness Axiom, but the reader should not forget its presence or its necessity to the argument.

Consider for a moment what these theorems are telling us about the convergence of sequences in $\mathbf{R}$. Specifically, suppose we want to construct a sequence of real numbers which has no limit. In past discussions we have asserted that such a sequence must either be unbounded, or it must oscillate in the sense that there are at least two distinct real numbers to which terms of the sequence are close to infinitely often. Theorem 3.2.4 supplies the means to prove this assertion. Thus, suppose $\{a_n\}$ is any bounded nonconvergent sequence. We claim that $\{a_n\}$ contains two convergent subsequences having distinct limits. The proof of this fact is left as Exercise 7. But what this means is the reason all of our examples of nonconvergent sequences failed to converge for one of the two named reasons is not that we carefully selected the examples to support this assertion, but rather because these are the only two possible reasons by which a sequence of real numbers can fail to be convergent. □

Definition. Let $S \subseteq \mathbf{R}$. A collection U of open sets is called an **open cover** of S provided $S \subseteq \bigcup U$.

Theorem 3.2.5 (Heine–Borel). Let $S \subseteq \mathbf{R}$. Then S is closed and bounded if and only if every open cover of S contains a finite subcollection which is also an open cover of S.

Proof. Let us assume that S is closed and bounded. Then there is an M, $0 \leqslant M$, such that $S \subseteq [-M, M]$. With this in mind, we can define the collection of intervals I_n^i, $1 \leqslant i \leqslant 2^n$, as in Theorem 3.2.1. Let U be any fixed open cover of S, and let us suppose for the sake of argument that no finite subcollection of U will cover S. Then we can choose a sequence of intervals, $\{J_n\}$, $n \in \mathbf{N} \cup \{0\}$, such that:

(i) J_n is chosen from among I_n^i, $1 \leqslant i \leqslant 2^n$;
(ii) $J_{n+1} \subseteq J_n$ for each $n \in \mathbf{N}$;
(iii) no finite subcollection of U will cover $J_n \cap S$ for each $n \in \mathbf{N}$.

Let a denote the unique member of $\cap \{J_n : n \in \mathbf{N}\}$. Then a is a limit point of S. Since S is closed, $a \in S$, whence there is a $P \in U$ such that $a \in P$. Since P is open, there is an interval about a of positive length, say $(a - c, a + c)$, such that this interval is completely contained in P. But now we can choose n sufficiently large that $J_n \subseteq (a - c, a + c)$. For this n, J_n is covered by a finite subcollection of U, since $J_n \subseteq P$. This contradicts our choice of J_n, whence our assumption that no finite subcollection of U covers S must be false.

To complete the proof we must show that the requirement that S be closed and bounded is necessary. We prove the contrapositive. Thus, let us assume that S is not closed and bounded, whence either S is not closed or S is not bounded. If S is not closed, then S has a limit point a which is not an element of S. Consider the sets U_n, defined by

$$U_n = \left\{ x : \left[x < a - \frac{1}{n} \text{ .or. } a + \frac{1}{n} < x \right] \quad \text{and } n \in \mathbf{N} \right\}.$$

Let U consist of the sets U_n, $n \in \mathbf{N}$. Then U is an open cover of S, but no finite subcollection will cover S. **(WHY?)** If, on the other hand, S is not bounded, then consider the collection of open intervals $(-n, n)$, for $n \in \mathbf{N}$. Clearly this collection covers S, but no finite subcollection will cover S. This completes the proof. □

Discussion. The proofs given are really sketches of the proof, and many important details have been left out. In Exercise 6, the reader will be asked to completely flesh out the details of these arguments. It should be clear that the same technique has been used to obtain each of the results in this section. A nested sequence of sets J_n with certain properties is constructed. The main feature is that the length of the intervals shrinks to 0 and so by completeness we can find a single point on which to focus our attention. The properties of this point are in part determined by constraints on the J_n's, and once we have this point to fix upon, we can get a contradiction as in the last argument or use its properties directly as in Theorem 3.2.1. ☐

Recall that Theorem 3.2.2 supplied us with a characterization of closed bounded sets which did not depend on the notion of bounded. Similarly, Theorem 3.2.5 tells us that closed bounded subsets of **R** can be characterized in terms of the property that every open cover has a finite **subcover** (a subcollection which is also a cover). Thus, the concept of closed and bounded can be rephrased in terms relating only to the concept of open set. While the notion of open set as it relates to **R** is intimately related to the notion of distance, the theorem above permits us to develop a more general notion of closed and bounded where the basic concept is that of open set unrelated to distance. This leads us to make the following definition.

Definition. Let $A \subseteq \mathbf{R}$. Then A is **compact** provided every open cover of A contains a finite subcover.

Discussion. Examination shows that this definition does not contain any features which are dependent upon **R**, whence it can be generalized to arbitrary topological spaces, which as we have mentioned are composed of a nonempty set, X, together with a collection of distinguished subsets of X which are called the open sets. The notion of open cover remains identical to the existing notion. The generalized notion quite clearly reduces to the present notion for **R**. Thus, in those more general situations where a concept of boundedness makes sense, it is natural to ask for an analog of Theorem 3.2.5, and such theorems will in almost all cases exist.

A finite set is obviously compact, but there exist infinite sets that are not compact. Theorem 3.2.5 lists all compact subsets of **R**, namely, they are precisely all the sets which are both closed and bounded. The word compact conveys a notion of small and its meaning led Hermann Weyl to quip: A city is 'compact' if it can be guarded by a finite number of arbitrarily nearsighted policemen. ☐

The theorems discussed in this section were all proven during the height of the study of elementary analysis which took place in the last century and many are the names of some of the most eminent mathematicians of the period, for example, Bolzano, Borel, Heine, and Weierstrass.

EXERCISES

1. Show that the sets I_n^i generated in Theorem 3.2.1 have all the properties claimed.
2. Show that the infinite sequence generated in the proof of Theorem 3.2.2 which is asserted not to have a limit point, in fact has no limit point.
3. Show that at least one of the intervals mentioned in Theorem 3.2.3 must be bounded in order for the conclusion to hold.
4. We will say that x is a **limit point** of A provided every open set O for which $x \in O$ contains points of A other than x. Show that this definition of limit point is equivalent to our previous definition of limit point.

5. Complete the details of Theorem 3.2.4.

6. Complete the details of Theorem 3.2.5.

7. Let $\{a_n\}$ be a bounded, nonconvergent sequence of distinct real numbers. Show that $\{a_n\}$ has at least two distinct limit points. Further show that any bounded, nonconvergent sequence must have at least two subsequences which converge to distinct limits.

8. Let f be defined on $[a, b]$, but unbounded there. Show that there is a $c \in [a, b]$ such that f is unbounded on $(c - \delta, c + \delta) \cap [a, b]$ for every positive δ.

9. A function f defined on $[a, b]$ is said to be **locally bounded** provided for every $c \in [a, b]$ there is a positive δ such that f is bounded on $(c - \delta, c + \delta)$. Show that a function which is locally bounded on $[a, b]$ is bounded on $[a, b]$.

10. Consider the field $\mathbf{Q}$ of rational numbers. A subset S of $\mathbf{Q}$ is open if there exists an open subset, O, of $\mathbf{R}$ that $S = O \cap \mathbf{Q}$. A subset C of $\mathbf{Q}$ is closed provided it is the complement of an open subset of $\mathbf{Q}$. (This is just the relative topology on $\mathbf{Q}$ of Exercise 3.1.36.) Show that the open subsets of $\mathbf{Q}$ satisfy the basic theorems on open sets contained in Section 3.1.

11. Show that $[0,1] \cap \mathbf{Q}$ is not compact in the topology of Exercise 10. Find an infinite subset of $\mathbf{Q}$ which is compact in this topology.

12. Prove or disprove Theorem 3.2.1 for $\mathbf{Q}$.

13. Prove or disprove Theorem 3.2.2 for $\mathbf{Q}$.

14. Prove or disprove Theorem 3.2.3 for $\mathbf{Q}$.

15. Can you characterize the compact subsets of $\mathbf{Q}$?

16. Let $\{a_n\}$ be a sequence having a subsequence which converges to a. Then a is called a **cluster point** or **cluster value** for the sequence. Show that every bounded nonconvergent sequence has at least two cluster points. What is the relationship between cluster points and limit points of a sequence?

17. Find all cluster points for the following sequences whose nth term is given by a_n. Which of the cluster points are limit points?

(a) $a_n = 1 + \dfrac{(-1)^n}{n}$;

(b) $a_n = (-1)^n$;

(c) $a_n = \sin\dfrac{n\pi}{16}$;

(d) $a_n = (-1)^n n$;

(e) $a_n = \dfrac{1}{n}\cos\dfrac{n\pi}{5}$.

18. Let $\{a_n\}$ be any sequence having $\mathbf{Q} \cap [0,1]$ for its range. Find all the limit points for such a sequence.

19. Let f be a function and a a limit point of the domain of f. Suppose f is bounded on an open set containing a, but the limit as x tends to a of f does not exist. Show that f oscillates at a (see Exercise 2.2.7).

20. Let f be a function defined on (a, b) and which is not continuous at $c \in (a, b)$. Show that either f is unbounded on an open set containing c or f oscillates at c.

21. Let $\{a_n\}$ be a sequence. Show that it has a limit a if and only if every subsequence has a as a cluster point.

22. Give an example of a sequence having:
    (a) no limit points;
    (b) exactly one limit point;
    (c) exactly two limit points;
    (d) exactly five limit points;
    (e) a countably infinite collection of limit points.
    Is it possible for a sequence of real numbers to have an uncountable collection of limit points?

23. Let $A \subseteq \mathbf{R}$. Then A is compact if and only if every sequence of points from A has a cluster point in A.

24. If $\{a_n\}$ has at least one limit point, can we conclude that it is bounded?

25. Let $A \subseteq \mathbf{R}$ and let $\mathbf{C}$ be a collection of closed subsets of A. $\mathbf{C}$ is said to satisfy the **finite intersection property** if every finite subcollection of $\mathbf{C}$ has a nonempty intersection. Prove that A is compact if and only if for each collection $\mathbf{C}$ of closed subsets of A that satisfies the finite intersection property, $\bigcap \mathbf{C} \neq \varnothing$.

26. Let A be an infinite closed bounded subset of $\mathbf{Q}$, say $[0,1] \cap \mathbf{Q}$. Find a collection $\mathbf{C}$ of subsets of A such that the intersection of any finite subcollection of subsets of $\mathbf{C}$ is nonempty, but $\bigcap C = \varnothing$.

27. We say that X is **dense in** Y if every point of Y is a member of X or a limit point of X. Which of the following are true?
    (a) $\mathbf{R} \sim \mathbf{Q}$ is dense in $\mathbf{R}$;
    (b) $\mathbf{R} \sim \mathbf{Q}$ is dense in $\mathbf{Q}$;
    (c) $\mathbf{Q}$ is dense in $\mathbf{Q}$;
    (d) $\mathbf{N}$ is dense in $\mathbf{R}$;
    (e) $\mathbf{N}$ is dense in $\mathbf{N}$;
    (f) $\mathbf{Q}$ is dense in $\mathbf{N}$;
    (g) $\mathbf{Q}$ is dense in $\mathbf{R}$;
    (h) (a, b) is dense in $\mathbf{R}$;
    (i) $\mathbf{R}$ is dense in $\mathbf{Q}$;
    (j) (a, b) is dense in $[a, b]$;
    (k) $[a, b]$ is dense in (a, b);
    (l) $\{\frac{1}{n} : n \in \mathbf{N}\}$ is dense in $(0,1)$.

28. Show that Y is dense in X exactly if $X \subseteq \bar{Y}$.

29. Let $f : \mathbf{Q} \rightarrow [0,1]$, such that $f(\mathbf{Q})$ is dense in $[0,1]$. Show that $f(\mathbf{Q})$ is not closed.

30. If $f : A \rightarrow \mathbf{R}$ is continuous, and A is compact, prove $f(A)$ is compact. Show that the result is no longer true if the word 'compact' is replaced by 'closed' or 'open'.

31. Show that the following subsets of $\mathbf{R}$ are not compact, by actually exhibiting an open cover that fails to produce a finite subcover:
    (a) $\mathbf{N}$;
    (b) $(0,1)$;
    (c) $\mathbf{R} \sim \mathbf{Q}$;
    (d) $\left\{ \frac{1}{n} : n \in \mathbf{N} \right\}$.

32. Show that a compact subset of $\mathbf{R}$ is closed. What about the converse?

33. Show that compactness is a topological property.

34. Let f and g be two functions which agree on a dense subset of $\operatorname{Dmn} f = \operatorname{Dmn} g$. Find a condition which will guarantee $f = g$.

3.3 THE CAUCHY CRITERION

In the last two sections we have seen the importance of the concept of 'limit point'. First, we saw how this concept was used as the foundation of the definition of a closed set. Second we saw that limit points play an essential role in the characterization of closed bounded sets. This suggests that limit points, and related topics, may be worthy of further investigation, and it is to this investigation that we devote this section.

The focus of the phrase, 'limit point', is on a point. However, limit points do not exist by themselves. Rather, they occur only in the context of an infinite collection of other points, and it is by virtue of these other points that a limit point achieves its existence. Within the context of $\mathbf{R}$, the Bolzano–Weierstrass Theorem characterizes the requirements for a set to have a limit point, namely, a set has a limit point exactly if it contains an infinite bounded subset. This characterization is particularly nice because to apply it to a given set, S, we do not need to actually find points of $\mathbf{R}$ that are limit points of S. Rather, we need only examine S to see if it has an infinite bounded subset.

The connection between limit points and limits of sequences are many. One connection is the alternate form of the Bolzano–Weierstrass Theorem asserting that a bounded sequence must have a cluster point. Another is that a is a limit point of S exactly if there is a sequence of distinct points from S which converges to a. Going the other way, we notice that a sequence of distinct points has a limit exactly if, when considered as a set, it has a unique limit point. Given this close relationship between limit points and limits of sequences, we may wonder whether it is also possible to characterize convergent sequences purely in terms of the sequence and with no reference to the limit. That there is hope is suggested by the fact that a bounded monotone sequence must have a limit, a statement which refers only to properties of the sequence.

The discussion above suggests that we should develop a notion of convergence which depends only on the properties of the particular sequence under consideration and not on any other considerations. This is the purpose underlying the concept of Cauchy convergence.

Definition. Let $\{a_n\}$ be a sequence of real numbers. We say that $\{a_n\}$ **converges in the sense of Cauchy** (is **Cauchy convergent** or, simply, is a **Cauchy sequence**) provided for every $\epsilon > 0$, there is an $N(\epsilon)$ such that

$$n > N(\epsilon) \text{ and } m > N(\epsilon) \text{ .implies. } |a_n - a_m| < \epsilon.$$

Discussion. If we compare this definition with the usual definition of convergence given in section 1.1, we see that the basic change is to replace A by a_m in the expression

$$|a_n - a_m| < \epsilon.$$

As in the original definition, $N = N(\epsilon)$, depends on the value of ϵ, which is given in advance. The intuition behind this change is simple. For sequences converging in the usual sense, we notice that as soon as $n > N$, we have

$$|a_n - A| < \epsilon$$

and that this means that *all* the terms with subscript larger than M must be close to A. If all are close to A, then all must be close together; in fact we get

$$|a_n - a_m| < |a_n - A| + |a_m - A| < 2\epsilon.$$

Further, it is intuitively reasonable that if all the terms of a sequence with sufficiently large subscript can be forced into an arbitrarily small interval, then the sequence should be convergent in the usual sense. $\square$

The intuitive discussion given above is formalized in the following theorem.

Theorem 3.3.1. Let $\{a_n\}$ be a sequence of real numbers. Then $\{a_n\}$ has a limit if and only if $\{a_n\}$ is Cauchy convergent.

Proof. We first assume that $\{a_n\}$ has a limit. Call it A. Let $\epsilon > 0$ be given, and find N such that $n \geqslant N$ implies $|a_n - A| < \dfrac{\epsilon}{2}$. If $m, n > N$, then

$$|a_n - a_m| \leqslant |a_n - A| + |a_m - A| < \frac{\epsilon}{2} + \frac{\epsilon}{2} = \epsilon.$$

Thus, $\{a_n\}$ is Cauchy convergent as claimed.

Conversely, suppose that $\{a_n\}$ is a Cauchy convergent sequence. Choosing $\epsilon = 1$, find $N(1)$. Fix $n > N(1)$, and let $M = |a_n| + 2$. Since there are only a finite number of terms whose subscript does not exceed $N(1)$, and since $m > N(1)$ implies $|a_m| < M$, we have that $\{a_n\}$ is bounded (**WHY?**). It follows from Theorem 3.2.4 that $\{a_n\}$ has a convergent subsequence. Let the limit be denoted by A. Fix $N(\epsilon)$, where ϵ is an arbitrary positive number. We can find an $n > N(\epsilon)$, such that $a_n \in (A - \epsilon, A + \epsilon)$ (**WHY?**). Now for any $m > N(\epsilon)$, we have

$$|a_m - A| \leqslant |a_m - a_n| + |a_n - A| < 2\epsilon.$$

Since ϵ was arbitrary, $\{a_n\}$ converges to A. $\square$

Discussion. Observe that the heart of the argument that every convergent sequence is Cauchy convergent is the straightforward implementation of the Triangle inequality. The proof of the converse can be summarized in three steps. First, it was shown that a Cauchy sequence is bounded. Second, the completeness of the underlying field was used to guarantee the existence of a subsequence converging to a limit. Third, the Cauchy property was used to show that the limit of the convergent subsequence had to be the limit of the sequence.

The use of the Completeness Axiom in the second step is vital. For example, if **R** is replaced by **Q** in the statement of the theorem, the result is no longer true. $\square$

A principal use of the Cauchy criterion is in establishing that a given sequence has a limit without having to find the limit.

EXAMPLE 1 _____

Consider the sequence $\{a_n\}$ defined by $a_n = \sum_{i=1}^{n} \frac{1}{i^2}$. Show that $\{a_n\}$ is a convergent sequence.

> *Solution.* To apply the Cauchy criterion, we must show that provided n,m are sufficiently large, the quantity $|a_n - a_m|$ will be arbitrarily small. Thus, consider the quantity A_n defined by
>
> $$A_k = \sum_{i=2^k}^{2^{k+1}-1} \frac{1}{i^2}.$$
>
> Direct computation establishes that $A_k \leqslant 2^{-k}$ (see Exercise 1). Now, fix $\epsilon > 0$. Since the A_k's are bounded by terms in a geometric series, as an application of the formula established in Exercise 0.4.21, we get that for all $s,t \in \mathbf{N}$ such that $s \leqslant t$
>
> $$\sum_{k=s}^{t} A_k \leqslant 2^{-(s-1)}.$$
>
> To complete the argument, let s be chosen so that $2^{-s} < \epsilon$. Now for any $n,m \geqslant s$, there exists a $j \in \mathbf{N}$ such that
>
> $$|a_n - a_m| \leqslant \sum_{k=s}^{s+j} A_k < \epsilon.$$
>
> Thus, $\{a_n\}$ is indeed a Cauchy sequence, and so converges. □

Discussion. It happens to be a fact that the limit of the sequence given in Example 1 is $\frac{\pi^2}{6}$. We suggest that even given this information, the reader would find it a difficult task to prove this sequence has a limit using the definition of Chapter 1. This is not to suggest inadequacy on the part of the reader. Rather, it is to suggest that establishing that a particular real number is the limit of an arbitrary sequence can be extremely difficult. One reason for this is that it is impossible to know the true value of most real numbers. For example, most of us think we know what π is. But this is only because we have given π a name, and not because we know the value of all its decimal places. Suffice it to say that most real numbers do not have names and thus are totally unknown.

Example 1 and the discussion provide evidence of the utility of the Cauchy convergence concept. However, these are not the only values of Cauchy convergence. To expand on this idea, consider a sequence $\{q_n\}$ of rational numbers which converges to $\sqrt{2}$. Viewed as a sequence of real numbers, we have a real number, $\sqrt{2}$, which is the limit of this sequence, and so the sequence satisfies the definition of convergence. However, if we think of the sequence as a sequence of rational numbers, and if our definition of convergence requires us to find a rational number which is the limit, then $\{q_n\}$ is no longer convergent since $\sqrt{2} \notin \mathbf{Q}$. This lack of convergence is particularly disturbing, since we have not altered the sequence, itself, in any way. We have merely changed the context in which we are considering the sequence by changing the under-lying field in which the sequence is found. But changing the context in which the sequence is considered has no effect on whether the sequence is Cauchy, since the property of being Cauchy refers only to properties of the sequence. It is this fact that makes the Cauchy concept a tool of such power that it can even serve as the heart of a replacement for the Supremum Principle (see Exercise 29).

EXERCISES

1. Let $\{A_k\}$ be defined as in Example 1. Show that $A_k \leqslant 2^{-k}$.

2. Show directly from the definition of a Cauchy sequence that the sum of two Cauchy sequences must again be a Cauchy sequence.

3. Show directly from the definition of a Cauchy sequence that the product of two Cauchy sequences must again be a Cauchy sequence.

4. Give a direct proof that every Cauchy sequence is bounded. Is the converse true?

5. Give examples of sequences that are monotone but not Cauchy, and Cauchy but not mono-tone.

6. Show that every subsequence of a Cauchy sequence is Cauchy. Now consider sequences of elements of $\mathbf{Q}$. Suppose a subsequence of a Cauchy sequence has a limit in $\mathbf{Q}$. What can be said about the original sequence?

7. Show if $\{a_n\}$ is Cauchy, then $\{|a_n|\}$ is Cauchy. Is the converse true?

8. If $\{a_n\}$ is Cauchy and for all n, $a_n > 0$, will $\left\{\dfrac{1}{a_n}\right\}$ be Cauchy?

9. Let $I_n = [a_n, b_n]$ be such that $I_{n+1} \subseteq I_n$ and $\lim_{n \to \infty} (a_n - b_n) = 0$. Show $\{a_n\}$ and $\{b_n\}$ are Cauchy and conclude $\bigcap I_n$ contains exactly one point.

10. Let $\{a_n\}$ be any sequence. Which of the following statements about $\{a_n\}$ are equivalent to the assertion that $\{a_n\}$ is a Cauchy sequence?
    (a) for every $\epsilon > 0$, there is an $N \in \mathbf{N}$ such that for every $p, q \in \mathbf{N}$, $|a_{N+p} - a_{N+q}| < \epsilon$;
    (b) for every $\epsilon > 0$, there is an $N \in \mathbf{N}$, such that for every $n \in \mathbf{N}$, $|a_N - a_{N+n}| < \epsilon$;
    (c) for every $\epsilon > 0$ and $p \in \mathbf{N}$, there is an $N \in \mathbf{N}$, such that $|a_N - a_{N+p}| < \epsilon$;
    (d) for every $\epsilon > 0$ and $p \in \mathbf{N}$, there is an $N \in \mathbf{N}$, such that $|a_N - a_{Np}| < \epsilon$;
    (e) for every $p \in \mathbf{N}$, $\lim_{n \to \infty} (a_n - a_{n+p}) = 0$.

11. Can there exist a function $f: \mathbf{N} \to \mathbf{N}$ such that for an arbitrary sequence $\{a_n\}$, $\{a_n\}$ is Cauchy if and only if for every positive ϵ there is an $N \in \mathbf{N}$ such that $n > N$ implies
$$|a_n - a_{f(n)}| < \epsilon?$$

12. Let f map $\mathbf{N} \times \mathbf{N}$ into $\mathbf{N}$ and suppose the sequence $\{a_n\}$ satisfies $|a_n - a_m| < f(n, m)$. Will any of the following f's guarantee that $\{a_n\}$ is Cauchy?
    (a) $f(n, m) = \dfrac{1}{n + m}$;
    (b) $f(n, m) = \dfrac{mn}{n + m}$;
    (c) $f(n, m) = \dfrac{mn}{n^2 + m^2}$.

13. Let $x_1 < x_2$ be any two real numbers. For $n > 2$, set $x_n = w_1 x_{n-1} + w_2 x_{n-2}$, where w_1, w_2 are nonnegative real numbers whose sum is 1. Show that $\{x_n\}$ is Cauchy. Find its limit.

14. Let $a_n = \sqrt{n}$. Show for n sufficiently large $|a_{n+k} - a_n| < \dfrac{k}{2\sqrt{n}}$. Why does this not establish that $\{a_n\}$ is Cauchy?

15. Let $\{x_n\}$ be a Cauchy sequence such that for all n, $x_n \in \mathbf{N}$. Show that $\{x_n\}$ must eventually be constant.

16. Let $\{x_n\}$ be a Cauchy sequence whose values all lie in A. If A is an infinite collection of isolated points, must $\{x_n\}$ eventually become constant?

17. Suppose $\{a_n\}$ satisfies the condition $|a_{n+1} - a_n| \leqslant \dfrac{1}{2^n}$. Show that $\{a_n\}$ is Cauchy.

18. Let $\{a_n\}$ be a sequence for which there exist constants r and c, $0 < r < 1$, $c > 0$ such that $|a_n - a_{n+1}| < cr^n$. What can be said about the convergence of $\{a_n\}$? Will your conclusions be altered if instead, you assume the condition that $\lim (a_{n+1} - a_n) = 0$?

19. Let $\{a_n\}$ be any sequence and set

$$s_n = \sum_{i=1}^{n} a_i, \qquad t_n = \sum_{i=1}^{n} |a_i|.$$

Show that if $\{t_n\}$ is Cauchy, then $\{s_n\}$ will also be Cauchy. Is the converse true?

20. Which of the following sequences $\{s_n\}$ is Cauchy?

(a) $s_n = \displaystyle\sum_{i=1}^{n} \left[\frac{1}{i!} \right]$;

(b) $s_n = \displaystyle\sum_{i=1}^{n} \left[\frac{1}{i} \right]$;

(c) $s_n = 1 + \dfrac{(-1)^n}{5} + \dfrac{1}{n}$;

(d) $s_n = \displaystyle\sum_{i=1}^{n} \frac{(-1)^i}{i}$;

(e) $s_n = \displaystyle\sum_{i=1}^{n} (-1)^i$;

(f) $s_n = \displaystyle\sum_{i=1}^{n} \frac{(-1)^i}{i!}$.

21. Let $\{x_n\}$, $\{y_n\}$, and $\{z_n\}$ be three sequences of real numbers such that $z_n = x_n$ if n is odd, and y_n otherwise. Under what conditions will $\{z_n\}$ be Cauchy?

22. Let f be continuous on D, and suppose that $\{a_n\}$ is a Cauchy sequence of elements of D. Show that if $\{a_n\}$ has a limit in D, then the sequence $\{f(a_n)\}$ will also be Cauchy, but that if $\{a_n\}$ has a limit which is not in D, then the sequence $\{f(a_n)\}$ need not be Cauchy.

23. Let f be continuous on $D \subseteq \mathbf{R}$ and let $\{a_n\}$ be a Cauchy sequence of elements of D. If $D = \mathbf{R}$ must $\{f(a_n)\}$ be Cauchy? If D is open, must $\{f(a_n)\}$ be Cauchy? If D is closed, must $\{f(a_n)\}$ be Cauchy?

24. Suppose f is defined on $[a, b]$ and f maps Cauchy sequences to Cauchy sequences. Must f be continuous?

25. A sequence $\{a_n\}$ is **contractive** if there exists a constant k, $0 < k < 1$, such that

$$|a_{n+2} - a_{n+1}| \leqslant k\,|a_{n+1} - a_n|.$$

Show that every contractive sequence is Cauchy. Further, show that if a is the limit of such a sequence, then

$$|a - a_n| \leqslant \frac{k}{1-k}|a_n - a_{n-1}|.$$

What can be said when $k = 1$?

26. The polynomial equation $x^3 - 5x + 1 = 0$ has a root, r, with $0 < r < 1$. Use an appropriate contractive sequence to compute r to within 10^{-4}.

27. A function $f: \mathbf{R} \to \mathbf{R}$ is a **contraction map** if there is k, $0 < k < 1$, such that for all $x, y \in \mathbf{R}$,

$$|f(x) - f(y)| \leqslant k|x - y|.$$

Show that a contraction map, f, always has a unique fixed point, that is, a point t satisfying the equation $f(t) = t$.

28. State and prove a theorem for $\mathbf{Q}$ analogous to 3.2.4.

29. Let $\mathbf{Q}^*$ denote the collection of all Cauchy convergent sequences of elements of $\mathbf{Q}$. For $\{a_n\}$, $\{b_n\} \in \mathbf{Q}^*$, define $\{a_n\} \cong \{b_n\}$ if and only if $\lim_{n \to \infty} \{a_n - b_n\} = 0$. Show that $\cong$ is an equivalence relation on $\mathbf{Q}^*$. Show that the equivalence classes so obtained form an ordered field under suitable field operations. Further show that this field is complete and can be identified with $\mathbf{R}$.

30. A set S is **linearly ordered** by $\leqslant$ if $\leqslant$ $\subseteq S \times S$, $\leqslant$ is reflexive, antisymmetric (see Appendix), transitive, and has the property that for all x, y either $(x, y) \in S$ or $(y, x) \in S$. A linear order of S is **dense** if for all x, y such that $x < y$ there exists z such that $x < z < y$. Show if S is countable and $\leqslant_1$ and $\leqslant_2$ are two dense linear orders of S having no upper or lower bounds, then there is a mapping $f: S \to S$ such that f is one-to-one and onto and for all $x, y \in S$, $x \leqslant y$ if and only if $f(x) \leqslant f(y)$.

31. A function, $\sigma(n, m)$, mapping $\mathbf{N} \times \mathbf{N}$ into $\mathbf{R}$ is called a **double sequence**. A double sequence, $\{\sigma(n, m)\}$ is said to have a **limit** provided there exists $A \in \mathbf{R}$ such that for every positive ϵ there exists $N \in \mathbf{N}$ such that

$$|\sigma(n, m) - A| < \epsilon \quad \text{whenever} \quad n, m > N.$$

In the event the limit A exists, we write

$$\lim_{n,m \to \infty} \sigma(n, m) = A.$$

Develop a Cauchy criterion for double sequences.

32. Let $\{\sigma_{(n,m)}\}$ be a double sequence having a limit, A. Further, suppose that for each fixed M, $\lim_{n \to \infty} \sigma(n, M)$ exists and for each fixed N, $\lim_{m \to \infty} \sigma(N, m)$ exists. These limits are called **partial limits**. Show that the two **iterated limits** satisfy

$$\lim_{M \to \infty} \lim_{n \to \infty} \sigma(n, M) = \lim_{N \to \infty} \lim_{m \to \infty} \sigma(n, M) = A.$$

Show by an example that there is a convergent double sequence such that none of the individual partial limits, $\lim_{n \to \infty} \sigma(n, M)$, or $\lim_{m \to \infty} \sigma(N, m)$, exists.

33. Let $\sigma(n, m) = \dfrac{n}{n+m}$ and consider the double sequence $\{\sigma(n,m)\}$. Show that all partial limits exist, that the two iterated limits exist, but that the double sequence does not have a limit.

3.4 LIMIT SUPERIOR AND LIMIT INFERIOR

In the last section we saw that it was possible to specify the class of convergent sequences of real numbers by focusing entirely on properties of the sequence, and omitting any reference to the limit. In this section, we further investigate the properties of sequences, but the focus is on a more general concept related to limit points.

Definition.   Let $\{a_n\}$ be a sequence. A number $x \in \mathbf{R}$ is called a **cluster point** of the sequence, provided that there is a subsequence $\{a_{n_k}\}$ of $\{a_n\}$ which converges to x.

Discussion.   Cluster points and limit points are obviously related. This is a conclusion of the version of the Bolzano–Weierstrass Theorem for sequences. That they are not the same can be seen from an examination of the proof of the Bolzano–Weierstrass Theorem (Theorem 3.2.4), which falls into two cases. The first case assumes that the sequence only assumes a finite number of distinct values. Thus, as a set of real numbers, $\{a_n : n \in \mathbf{N}\}$ is finite, and a finite set has no limit points (see Exercise 3.1.8). On the other hand, if the sequence takes on infinitely many distinct values, then the sequence forms an infinite bounded set of real numbers which has a limit point. This limit point must in turn be the limit of a subsequence converging to it. From this, it is easy to see that every limit point of a sequence is a cluster point, but not the other way around. And indeed, it is also clear why cluster point is a right concept, if we want the analogous concept to limit point in the context of sequences.   □

By the Bolzano–Weierstrass Theorem, we know that a bounded sequence will have cluster points. In general, then, an arbitrary sequence is likely to have lots of cluster points. The problem is always one of being able to get one's hands on a particular cluster point. Thus, one would like a mechanical process for manipulating a sequence which will be guaranteed to produce a cluster point.

Consider then the collection of cluster points of a sequence. A given real number can become a cluster point in one of two ways. Either it is a limit point of the sequence, or it is a value for a term of the sequence which is repeated an infinite number of times. Now we know that the collection of limit points of a set is closed (see Theorem 3.1.6). It therefore seems plausible that the collection of cluster points of a sequence is closed, and indeed this is the case (see Exercise 1). It follows that if the collection of cluster points of a sequence is bounded above, then the supremum of this collection will be a cluster point of the sequence (see Exercise 3.1.9). Thus, there are two natural cluster points to try to find, the least cluster point and the greatest cluster point. What we would like is a method for picking out these cluster points which depends only on the terms of the sequence and not on the set of cluster points. This leads to the following definition.

Definition. Let $\{a_n\}$ be a sequence and for each $n \in \mathbf{N}$, set $b_n = \sup\{a_k : k \geqslant n\}$. The **limit superior** of $\{a_n\}$ (denoted by $\overline{\lim}\{a_n\}$) is defined to be $\inf\{b_n\}$, provided it exists. Thus,

$$\overline{\lim}\{a_n\} = \inf\{x : x = \sup\{a_k : k \geqslant n\} \text{ for some } n \in \mathbf{N}\}.$$

Similarly, we define the **limit inferior** by

$$\underline{\lim}\{a_n\} = \sup\{x : x = \inf\{a_k : k \geqslant n\} \text{ for some } n \in \mathbf{N}\}.$$

We will usually simplify the notation by writing

$$\overline{\lim}\, a_n \quad \text{and} \quad \underline{\lim}\, a_n$$

to denote the limit superior and inferior, respectively. (We may also use the terminology **lim sup, lim inf,** respectively.)

Discussion. Let us determine the conditions under which the limit superior will, or will not, exist. The first thing to notice about the limit superior is that it is an infimum. Thus, using the axiom of completeness, we can guarantee the existence of the limit superior provided that the set of real numbers over which this infimum is calculated is nonempty and bounded below. If either of these conditions fails, the limit superior will not exist. Specifically, the limit superior will fail to exist if

$$A = \{x : x = \sup\{a_k : k \geqslant n\} \text{ for some } n \in \mathbf{N}\}$$

is either empty or not bounded below.

Let us consider how A could be empty. To become a member of A, an element must be a supremum of a set, A_n, of the form

$$A_n = \{a_k : k \geqslant n\}.$$

For all values of n, the sets A_n are never empty, since each A_n consists of a tail of the sequence. For example, for the sequence whose mth term is given by $\dfrac{1}{m}$, we have

$$A_n = \left\{\frac{1}{n}, \frac{1}{n+1}, \frac{1}{n+2}, \cdots\right\}.$$

Thus, for a particular value of n, the supremum of A_n can fail to exist only if A_n is not bounded above. This can happen only if the sequence $\{a_n\}$ is itself not bounded above as would happen if the mth term of the sequence were m^2, to take another example. But, whether any particular tail of a sequence is bounded is now a general property of the sequence. That is, if the supremum of a single A_n fails to exist, then for every value of n the supremum of A_n will fail to exist, and A will be empty. In summary, A will be empty exactly if $\{a_n\}$ is not bounded above.

The second reason that A can fail to have an infimum is that it is not bounded below. Under this assumption, A must be nonempty, whence $\{a_n\}$ is bounded above. As in the definition, set $b_n = \sup A_n$. The sequence $\{b_n\}$ can be shown to be monotone decreasing (see Exercise 4). Since $b_n \in A$, and these are the only members of A, we see that A is not bounded below exactly if the sequence $\{b_n\}$ diverges to $-\infty$. But this implies that $\{a_n\}$ satisfies the condition that for all $m \in \mathbf{N}$, there is an $N \in \mathbf{N}$ such that $n > N$ implies $a_n < -m$. Evidently, this is a strong condition since it requires that all remaining terms of the sequence are below any potential lower bound, and hence that the sequence diverges to $-\infty$.

In summary then, we see that the limit superior of a sequence will fail to exist for sequences which are not bounded above, and those which diverge to $-\infty$. As well, for a sequence which is bounded above, if the limit superior does not exist, then the sequence will not be bounded below, whence the limit inferior will not exist either.

□

EXAMPLE 1

Find the limit superior and the limit inferior of the sequence $\{a_n\}$, where $a_n = 1 + (-1)^n + \dfrac{1}{2^n}$.

Solution. For any fixed n, $a_n = 1 + 1 + \dfrac{1}{2^n}$ if n is even, and $1 - 1 + \dfrac{1}{2^n}$ when n is odd. Thus, $b_n = \sup\{a_k : k \geq n\} = 1 + 1 + \dfrac{1}{2^n}$ if n is even, and $1 + 1 + \dfrac{1}{2^{n+1}}$ when n is odd. Hence, $\overline{\lim}\,\{a_n\} = \inf\{b_n : n \in \mathbf{N}\} = 2$ (**WHY?**). A similar calculation shows that $\underline{\lim}\,\{a_n\} = 0$. □

Discussion. The calculations are straightforward from the definition. The reader should sketch a graph of the sequence. From this she will discover that the sequence oscillates between small intervals around 0 and 2. □

EXAMPLE 2

Find the limit superior and limit inferior of $\{a_n\}$, where $a_n = 2^n$.

Solution. Consider

$$c_n = \inf\{a_k : k \geq n\}.$$

Evidently, $c_n = a_n = 2^n$, since $\{a_n\}$ is monotone increasing. Moreover, c_n diverges to $+\infty$. Thus, it is clear that the supremum over $\{c_n : n \in \mathbf{N}\}$ does not exist, whence the limit inferior does not exist, even though the sequence, $\{a_n\}$, is bounded below. It follows that the limit superior also fails to exist. □

Discussion. The argument presented is merely a direct application of the ideas presented in the discussion following the definition of limit superior. □

Let us recall the motivation for the limit superior notion. The definition arose as a suggested means for finding the greatest cluster point of a sequence. The next theorem shows that we have succeeded.

Theorem 3.4.1. The limit superior of a sequence is the greatest cluster point of the sequence.

Proof. Let $\{a_n\}$ be a sequence having a as its limit superior. We want to generate a subsequence which converges to a. We denote the kth term of the subsequence by a_{n_k}, and define it by $a_{n_k} = a_m$ where a_m is the term of least subscript satisfying $m > n_{k-1}$ and $|a_m - a| < \dfrac{1}{k}$. It is clear that the subsequence as defined above will converge to a, provided we can generate terms for this subsequence. To see that the required terms exist, we proceed by induction on k. Thus, we assume that we have generated a_{n_j}, for each $j < k$. Now, we must find an a_m such that $|a_m - a| < \dfrac{1}{k}$ and also $m > N$, where N is some natural number which exceeds the subscript of any term which has been used in generating a_{n_j}, for $j < k$. Let $b_n = \sup \{a_k : k \geqslant n\}$. Observe that we can find a b_n such that $n > N$, and $|b_n - a| < \dfrac{1}{k}$ (**WHY?**). In fact, $b_n \geqslant a$, whence

$$a + \frac{1}{k} > b_n \geqslant a.$$

By definition of b_n, there is $a_p \in \{a_k : k \geqslant n\}$ such that

$$b_n \geqslant a_p > b_n - \frac{1}{k}.$$

Now p exceeds N and $|a_p - a| < \dfrac{1}{k}$, whence we have shown that a choice for a_{n_k} exists, since we have only to choose a term of the sequence with a minimal subscript which is within the prescribed distance of a. Thus, a is a cluster point as claimed.

To complete the proof, we must show that a is the greatest cluster point. To see this, consider the sequence $\{a_{n+m}\}$, for a fixed $m \in \mathbf{N}$. Evidently this is a subsequence of $\{a_n\}$. Moreover, $\{a_{n+m}\}$ has the same set of cluster points as the original sequence (see Exercise 2). Now, for each fixed m and for all $n \in \mathbf{N}$, $a_{n+m} \leqslant b_m$ (**WHY?**). It follows that every cluster point of $\{a_n\}$ must also be less than or equal to b_m. But since m was arbitrary, it follows that every cluster point must be less than or equal to the infimum of the b_m's, which is a. Thus, a is the greatest cluster point. $\square$

Discussion. This proof makes use of the simple idea that if we have numbers from a set A which are close to a, and for any number in A, say t_n, we can find numbers among the sequence which are close to t_n, then these latter numbers will be close to a, provided t_n is close to a. The property which allows us to find the numbers which are 'close to' is the basic property of the supremum and the infimum, which is contained in Theorem 0.4.2.

The main feature of the second part of the proof is that the tail of a sequence has the same set of cluster points as the original sequence. The reader is asked to produce a proof of this as Exercise 2, but it should be obvious.

Note that a similar proof reveals that the limit inferior of a sequence is the least cluster point of the sequence. The reader is asked to write out a detailed proof of this fact as Exercise 6. Thus, the sequence $\{a_n\}$ converges to a limit if and only if $\overline{\lim}\, a_n = \underline{\lim}\, a_n$.

The reader should note that the proof and statement of the theorem assume the existence of the limit superior. Thus, the theorem does not assert that the greatest cluster point will always be the limit superior. Examples of sequences having a greatest cluster point but no limit superior may be found in the exercises. $\square$

Theorem 3.4.2. Let $\{a_n\}$ be a sequence for which either the limit superior or the limit inferior exists. Then $\{a_n\}$ has a cluster point.

Proof. Immediate from Theorem 3.4.1. □

Discussion. As shall be made clear in the exercises, this result generalizes that of Theorem 3.2.4. Moreover, the cluster point generated by the argument given in Theorem 3.2.1 is due to the nonconstructive argument found in Theorem 3.2.1. This last argument is completely constructive, provided of course that we view the supremum of a set as an essentially 'constructed' number. □

In previous cases where we have formulated a limiting process, we have immediately raised questions about its behavior with respect to the usual operations of arithmetic. Similar questions can be asked about the limit superior and inferior. One relationship which is known to exist is that

$$\overline{\lim}\{a_n + b_n\} \leqslant \overline{\lim}\, a_n + \overline{\lim}\, b_n.$$

The reader is asked to explore and develop these types of relationships in Exercise 17.

EXERCISES

1. Show that the collection of cluster points of a sequence is a closed set.

2. Let $\{a_n\}$ be a sequence and consider the subsequence defined by $\{a_{n+m}\}$ for a fixed $m \in \mathbf{N}$. Show that the subsequence has the same set of cluster points as the original sequence.

3. Show that $\underline{\lim}\, a_n \leqslant \overline{\lim}\, a_n$.

4. Recall the sequence $\{b_n\}$ as given in the definition of limit superior. Show $\{b_n\}$ is monotone decreasing. Find $b_1, \ldots, b_6$ inclusive for each of the following sequences:
   (a) $(-1)^n n$;

   (b) $\left[\dfrac{n^4 + 5}{3^n}\right]$;

   (c) $-n^2$.

5. Find the limit inferior, the limit superior, and all cluster points for each of the sequences, $\{a_n\}$, where a_n is given below:
   (a) $(-1)^n$;

   (b) $\dfrac{n + (-1)^n(2n + 1)}{n}$;

   (c) $(-1)^n\left[1 - \dfrac{1}{n}\right] + (-1)^{n+1}\left[1 + \dfrac{1}{n}\right]$;

   (d) $(-1)^{n+1} + \sin\dfrac{n\pi}{4}$;

   (e) $\dfrac{1 + \cos\dfrac{n\pi}{2}}{(-1)^n n^2}$;

(f) $n^{\sin(n\pi/2)}$;

(g) $3 \sin \dfrac{n\pi}{2} + (-1)^n \left[2 + \dfrac{1}{n} \right]$;

(h) $\dfrac{1}{2^n} + (-1)^n \cos \dfrac{n\pi}{4} + \sin \dfrac{n\pi}{2}$;

(i) $\left[1 + \dfrac{1}{n} \right] \left[1 + \sin \dfrac{n\pi}{2} \right]^{1/n}$;

(j) $\left[1 + \dfrac{2^n}{e^n} \right] \sin \dfrac{n\pi}{2}$;

(k) $2^{(-1)^n} \left[1 + \dfrac{1}{n^2} \right] + 3^{(-1)^{n+1}}$;

(l) $(-1)^n \left[1 - e^n \left| \cos \dfrac{n\pi}{2} \right| \right]$;

(m) $n \cos n \dfrac{\pi}{2}$;

(n) $\dfrac{2}{3}, \dfrac{1}{3}, \dfrac{3}{4}, \dfrac{1}{4}, \dfrac{4}{5}, \dfrac{1}{5}, \dfrac{5}{6}, \ldots$;

(o) $\dfrac{3}{2}, \dfrac{-1}{2}, \dfrac{4}{3}, \dfrac{-1}{3}, \dfrac{5}{4}, \dfrac{-1}{4}, \dfrac{6}{5}, \ldots$;

(p) $-\dfrac{n}{4} + \left[\dfrac{n}{4} \right] + (-1)^n$, where $[x]$ is the greatest integer function;

(q) $(1 + (-1)^n) n^{(-1)^{n+1}} + \cos \dfrac{n\pi}{6}$;

(r) $r_n + r_{9n} + (-1)^n$, where r_n is the remainder when n is divided by 3;

(s) $\dfrac{r_{2n+1}}{3} + r_{4n} + \dfrac{1}{2^{n+1}}$, where r_n is the remainder when n is divided by 9;

(t) $a_1 = 0$, $a_{2n} = \dfrac{a_{2n-1}}{2}$, $a_{2n+1} = \dfrac{1}{2} + a_{2n}$;

(u) $\left[1 + \dfrac{(-1)^n}{n} \right]^n$;

(v) $a_k = \dfrac{j}{k+1}$, for $n = k^2 + j$, $j = 1, 2, \ldots, 2k + 1$, $k = 0, 1, \ldots$.

6. Show that the limit inferior is the least cluster point of a sequence.

7. Discuss the limit inferior, with particular reference to the conditions for its nonexistence.

8. Let $\{a_n\}$ be a sequence. Show $\{a_n\}$ has a limit a if and only if every subsequence has a as a cluster point.

9. Give an example of a sequence having:
   (a) no cluster points;
   (b) exactly one cluster point;
   (c) exactly two cluster points;
   (d) exactly five cluster points;

(e) a countably infinite collection of cluster points.

Is it possible for a sequence of real numbers to have an uncountable collection of cluster points?

10. Recall the distinction between cluster points and limit points. Give an example of a sequence having
    (a) exactly one cluster point and no limit points;
    (b) exactly two cluster points and no limit points;
    (c) exactly five cluster points and no limit points;
    (d) a countably infinite collection of cluster points and no limits.
    Is it possible for a sequence of real numbers to have an uncountable collection of cluster points and no limit points?

11. Let $A \subseteq \mathbf{R}$. Then A is compact if and only if every sequence of points from A has a cluster point in A.

12. Suppose $\{a_n\}$ has a cluster point. What can be said about the existence of the limit superior and the limit inferior?

13. Find a simple condition on a sequence which is equivalent to the existence of both the limit superior and the limit inferior.

14. Let $f: \mathbf{N} \rightarrow \mathbf{Q} \cap (0,1)$ be an onto function. Thinking of f as the sequence defined by $a_n = f(n)$, find the limit superior, the limit inferior, and all the cluster points.

15. Suppose $\overline{\lim} \, a_n = a$. Show that for every positive ϵ there is an $N \in \mathbf{N}$ such that $n > N$ implies $a_n < a + \epsilon$. Formulate a similar result for the limit inferior.

16. Find a condition on the limit superior and inferior which is equivalent to the existence of a limit for a sequence.

17. Prove or disprove; where a counterexample is obtained find the strongest possible relationship, or show that none can hold.
    (a) $\overline{\lim}(s_n + t_n) = \overline{\lim} \, s_n + \overline{\lim} \, t_n$;
    (b) $\underline{\lim}(s_n + t_n) = \underline{\lim} \, s_n + \underline{\lim} \, t_n$;
    (c) $\overline{\lim}(s_n \cdot t_n) = \overline{\lim} \, s_n \cdot \overline{\lim} \, t_n$;
    (d) $\underline{\lim}(s_n \cdot t_n) = \underline{\lim} \, s_n \cdot \underline{\lim} \, t_n$.

18. If $\{a_n\}$ converges to a, and $\{b_n\}$ is bounded, show that
$$\overline{\lim} \, a_n b_n = a \cdot \overline{\lim} \, b_n.$$

19. Show $a = \overline{\lim} \, a_n$ if and only if the following two conditions hold:
    (a) for every $\epsilon > 0$, there is an $N \in \mathbf{N}$ such that $n > N$ implies $a_n < a + \epsilon$;
    (b) for every $\epsilon > 0$ and every $N \in \mathbf{N}$, there is an $n \in \mathbf{N}$ such that $n > N$ and $a - \epsilon < a_n$.

20. State a result (similar to Exercise 19) for limit inferiors and prove it.

21. Let s_n be any sequence and define t_n by
$$t_n = \sum_{i=1}^{n} \frac{s_i}{n}.$$

Find any order relations ($\leqslant$) between
$$\overline{\lim} \, s_n, \; \overline{\lim} \, t_n, \; \underline{\lim} \, s_n \text{ and } \underline{\lim} \, t_n.$$

22. Let $\{a_n\}$ be a sequence of nonnegative reals. Define $s_n = \dfrac{a_{n+1}}{a_n}$ and $t_n = (a_n)^{1/n}$. Show
$$\underline{\lim} \, s_n \leqslant \underline{\lim} \, t_n \leqslant \overline{\lim} \, t_n \leqslant \overline{\lim} \, s_n.$$

Moreover, give examples to show that these inequalities may be strict.

3.5 **UNIFORM CONTINUITY**

We began this chapter by pointing out that the study of topology had to do with properties of sets which were preserved by one-to-one continuous functions. In section 3.2 we focused on closed bounded subsets of **R** and showed that such sets had very nice properties. The reader may already suspect that the image of a closed bounded set under a continuous function is again a closed bounded set. A limited version of this result was already established in section 2.6 where it was shown that the image of a closed interval was again a closed interval. Thus, the question of whether a continuous function takes closed bounded sets to closed bounded sets begs for an answer.

We can, however, approach things from another point of view. Let us consider the class of continuous functions having a given domain, $D \subseteq \mathbf{R}$. We might wonder whether the fact that D was a closed bounded subset of **R** would have any effect on the properties of the function, f. Looking at things from this direction provides a totally different perspective and quite conceivably could lead to new and interesting results. Not surprisingly, this approach is fruitful and it will be explored in this section. Of course, our ultimate aim will be to establish that continuous functions do indeed preserve closed bounded sets, but our route will be mildly circuitous.

We want to give the definition of the concept of uniform continuity. As a lead-in to this definition, recall the definition of continuity. Consider then a function, f, which is defined on an open interval, (a, b). (While we could deal with a more general domain, this setting is sufficiently rich to meet our requirements.) Now pick a particular $c \in (a, b)$ and ask whether f is continuous at c. To answer yes to this question, we must compute $\lim_{x \to c} f(x)$. This computation involves first setting a value for ϵ and then finding δ, meeting the requirements of the definition of continuity.

Recall that the value of δ in general depends both on the value of ϵ and also on the value of c. This dependence could be expressed functionally by

$$\delta = \delta(\epsilon, c).$$

The nature of dependence of δ on c can best be understood by considering some examples. Thus, consider the open interval $(0,10)$. For the function defined by $f(x) = x$, there is no dependence, that is, no matter what value of $c \in (0,10)$ is selected, setting $\delta = \epsilon$ will ensure

$$|f(x) - f(c)| = |x - c| < \epsilon \text{ whenever } |x - c| < \delta.$$

This is because the only occurrence of c in the expression $|f(x) - f(c)|$ is in the quantity, $x - c$.

As a second example, consider the function $f(x) = x^2$. The computation that arises requires working with the quantity

$$|x^2 - c^2| = |x + c| \cdot |x - c|$$

which must be made less than ϵ merely by making δ small (see Example 2.5.2 for further discussion of this function). The size of the term $|x + c|$ depends on where in the interval the point c resides. If it is near 0, then this term could almost be ignored in the calculation. If this term is near 10, then $|x + c|$ must be accounted for by making δ smaller. Because $|x + c|$ is bounded by 20 on the interval $(0,10)$, if we take $\delta = \dfrac{\epsilon}{20}$, this will guarantee

$$|x^2 - c^2| < \epsilon \quad \text{whenever} \quad |x - c| < \delta$$

irrespective of the value of c. For this example, a functional dependence of δ which will ensure the continuity requirement can be written as $\delta(\epsilon, c) = \min\{\epsilon, \dfrac{\epsilon}{c + 10}\}$ (**WHY?**). But the dependence of this expression on c can be eliminated because c is required to lie in the interval, $(0,10)$; this is what led to $\delta = \dfrac{\epsilon}{20}$.

As a third example, consider $f(x) = \dfrac{1}{x}$. If we pick $c \in (0,10)$, we end up working with

$$\left| \frac{1}{x} - \frac{1}{c} \right| = \left| \frac{c - x}{c \cdot x} \right| \leqslant \left| \frac{\delta}{c \cdot x} \right|.$$

No matter what we do, we cannot avoid the dependence of δ on c because as c gets close to 0, the quantity $\dfrac{1}{c \cdot x}$ becomes arbitrarily large. To cope with this, we must take δ much smaller than c, as well as being smaller than ϵ (see Example 2.5.3 for previous discussion).

Quite obviously a concept of continuity which avoided the dependence of δ on the choice of c would have utility. Such a concept exists, and we now present its definition.

Definition. A function f on $D \subseteq \mathbf{R}$ is said to be **uniformly continuous** on D provided for every $\epsilon > 0$ there is a $\delta > 0$ such that for every x, $y \in D$,

$$|f(x) - f(y)| < \epsilon \quad \text{whenever} \quad |x - y| < \delta.$$

Discussion. The first thing to note about the definition of uniform continuity is that its frame of reference is the entire domain of the function. Thus, functions are uniformly continuous on domains, not at single points. Recall that a function was continuous on its domain if it was continuous at each point of its domain. With this in mind, let us compare the definition of continuity of D with that of uniform continuity on D.

The definition of continuity on D asserts that for every $y \in D$ and every $\epsilon > 0$, there is a $\delta > 0$ such that for all $x \in D$, $|x - y| < \delta$ implies that $|f(x) - f(y)| < \epsilon$.

Observe that to change the continuity definition into the uniform continuity definition, one merely changes the order of quantification of the variables! Specifically, one moves the 'for all y' quantification inside of (to the right of) the 'there exists δ'. While the change itself is small, the effect of this change is substantial.

In the usual definition of continuity, we are first handed a y and an ϵ and then told to look for a δ. As discussed above, the choice of δ depends on both the size of ϵ and the particular value of y which we have been given.

In the uniform continuity definition, we are first handed an ϵ. No mention is made of any members of the domain. Instead, we are immediately asked to start a search for δ. Further, after we have a candidate for δ, this candidate must be checked against every $y \in D$ before it can be accepted. In other words, it must be the case that for every pair $x, y \in D$,

$$|f(x) - f(y)| < \epsilon \text{ whenever } |x - y| < \delta.$$

All that is required to reject a candidate δ is that we be able to find one single y with an x sufficiently close to it such that $x, y \in D$, $|x - y| < \delta$, and $|f(x) - f(y)| \geq \epsilon$. Thus, the choice of δ can depend only on the choice of ϵ. It must be independent of where we choose x and y from the domain.

To summarize, for continuity at a point y, given ϵ, we search for a δ, depending on both ϵ and the point y in question, whereas for uniform continuity on a domain, we look for a single δ that serves the purpose for all points in that domain. Thus, while continuity is a local property arising from a focus at points, the notion of uniform continuity is a global property arising from considerations related to the entire domain of a function. □

EXAMPLE 1 _____

Let $f(x) = \sqrt{x}$, $x \in [0, \infty)$. Show that f is uniformly continuous.

Solution. Let $\epsilon > 0$ be given. Choose $\delta = \epsilon^2$. If $x, y \in [0, \infty)$, then either both $x, y \in [0, \delta)$ or at least one of x, y is greater or equal to δ. In the first case, we have $\sqrt{x}, \sqrt{y} \in [0, \epsilon)$, and therefore,

$$|f(x) - f(y)| = |\sqrt{x} - \sqrt{y}| < |\epsilon - 0| = \epsilon.$$

In the latter case, $\sqrt{x} + \sqrt{y} \geq \sqrt{\delta} = \epsilon$, whence

$$|f(x) - f(y)| = |\sqrt{x} - \sqrt{y}|$$

$$= \frac{|x - y|}{\sqrt{x} + \sqrt{y}} \leq \frac{|x - y|}{\epsilon} < \frac{\delta}{\epsilon} = \frac{\epsilon^2}{\epsilon} = \epsilon$$

whenever $|x - y| < \delta$. Hence, for every $x, y \in [0, \infty)$, we have

$$|x - y| < \delta \text{ implies } |f(x) - f(y)| < \epsilon.$$

Since δ depends only on ϵ, the function $f(x) = \sqrt{x}$ is indeed uniformly continuous on $[0, \infty)$. □

Discussion. Let us compare the solution above with that of Example 2.5.3 which shows that $g(x) = \dfrac{1}{x}$ is continuous on $[-2,0) \cup (0,2]$. (Note we have renamed the function for the purpose of discussion.)

The first step in showing that g is continuous is to pick a $y \in \text{Dmn } g$ followed by an ϵ. For the remainder of that argument, the value of y is kept fixed. The argument then proceeds by restricting the choice of δ. Note that this restriction is based on the choice of y which had been previously fixed. The quantity $|g(x) - g(y)|$ is then examined and a final choice for δ made. Again we note that the final form of the choice of δ depends both on y and δ. Contrast this with our argument above for f.

First an ϵ is chosen. The quantity $|f(x) - f(y)|$ is then manipulated with no assumptions as to where in the domain the quantities x and y might reside. Out of this examination, after considerable experimentation, a choice for δ is made which depends only on ε. Actually, we have mildly overstated our case. In fact we did use information about the position of y, but since we had only two cases (any finite number would do), we were able to find one value of δ which would work independently of where y was located in the domain. We referred to experimentation. What we mean is that we rewrote $f(x) - f(y)$ and then made two key observations. The first was that as long as $x, y < \epsilon^2$, we could see directly that

$$|f(x) - f(y)| < \epsilon \quad \text{whenever} \quad |x - y| < \delta = \epsilon.$$

On the other hand, if $x, y > \epsilon^2$, only simple algebra is needed to achieve the desired conclusion. Thus, the problem is resolved by recognizing that only two computational situations need be treated and performing the required algebra.

Still, this does not fully explain the intuition used in constructing the argument. Consider the graph of f which is presented in Figure 3.5.1. Starting from (0,0), the graph rises sharply at first and then ever more slowly. Consider what this geometry means computationally. Let us suppose that x and y are a fixed distance apart, that is, that the value of $|x - y|$ is fixed, although x and y are allowed to slide along the horizontal axis. As x, y slide to the right, what happens to $|f(x) - f(y)|$? It gets smaller. Indeed, it goes to 0 as is evident from the computations presented in the example. But what is really important is that if we slide x, y to the left, there is a maximum value for $|f(x) - f(y)|$. In fact, the maximum is $\sqrt{|x - y|}$, which accounts for the computations presented.

On the other hand, if we repeat these geometric considerations for g, we come to rather different conclusions. Again, let $|x - y|$ be fixed. If we slide x, y to the right toward the point, 2, $|g(x) - g(y)|$ gets smaller, and if we could slide it far enough, by extending the domain, the difference would become arbitrarily small. However, as we slide x, y to the left, bringing them close to 0, the quantity $|g(x) - g(y)|$ becomes arbitrarily large. This is the heart of the problem, and why for g it is impossible to find a δ which is independent of the position of y in the domain of g. □

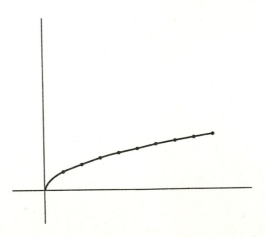

Figure 3.5.1 $\sqrt{x}$ is uniformly continuous in $[0, \infty)$.

EXAMPLE 2 _____

Show that $f(x) = x^2$ is uniformly continuous on $[0,8]$.

Solution.   Let $\epsilon > 0$ be fixed. Let $x,\ y \in [0,8]$ and consider

$$|x^2 - y^2| = |x - y||x + y|$$

$$\leqslant |x - y| \cdot 16. \qquad \textbf{(WHY?)}$$

Let $\delta = \dfrac{\epsilon}{16}$. For this choice of δ, we have that

$$|x - y| < \delta \ \text{ implies } \ |x^2 - y^2| < \epsilon,$$

as desired. Of course, x and y must belong to the stated interval for the inequality to be valid, as we shall discuss further in a later example.   □

Discussion.   Observe that computationally, the argument is similar to previous arguments for continuity (see Example 2.5.2). The key point is that a bound of 16 for the term $|x + y|$ can be found which is completely independent of where x and y are in the given interval.

The intuition behind the argument lies in the following. Consider x, y which are a fixed distance apart, and again ask what happens to $|x^2 - y^2|$ as we slide x, y along the interval comprising the domain of the function. Slide it to the left and the functional difference becomes smaller. Slide it to the right, and the functional difference becomes larger. However, it cannot become arbitrarily large. Now to find the required dependence on δ, we consider that part of the domain where the difference in functional values can be largest. In this case, this is over near 8 which yields the factor of 16.   □

To further illustrate the concept of uniform continuity, we turn to the question of how a function on a given domain can fail to be uniformly continuous. By now it should be clear that the first step in this process is to negate the definition, and we suggest that the reader do this before reading further.

Negation of the Definition of Uniform Continuity

A function f is not uniformly continuous on a domain D if there exists an $\epsilon > 0$ such that for every $\delta > 0$ there exist $x,\ y \in D$ such that

$$|x - y| < \delta \ \text{.and.} \ |f(x) - f(y)| \geqslant \epsilon.$$

Discussion.   To satisfy this statement for a function defined on D, we must be able to find a single fixed value for ϵ such that no matter how small we choose δ there will always exist a pair of points in D having the property that the δ-inequality holds while the ϵ-inequality fails for this pair of points. A little thought should convince the reader that a function which is not continuous on its domain can not be uniformly continuous on that domain. Since we have already detailed the reasons why a function may fail to be continuous on a domain, our interest here should focus on the question of why a function which is continuous on a domain D can fail to be uniformly continuous there.

It is a remarkable fact, which we will prove later, that if the domain for the function is closed and bounded, then continuity is enough to ensure uniform continuity. Thus, we are interested in functions which are continuous on sets which are not closed and bounded (compact). Our next three examples will cover all the possibilities. However, we already have the key intuition.

Suppose we fix $|x - y|$. If we can find a place in the domain which has the property that when we slide x, y close to this place, the change in $|f(x) - f(y)|$ becomes arbitrarily large, then there will be no hope that f could be uniformly continuous on its domain. Evidently, such a situation arises whenever the function is unbounded at a point. It would be nice if this type of situation were the only situation where uniform continuity cannot be achieved. However, two other situations also arise as the examples below show.   □

EXAMPLE 3 _____

Show that the function $f(x) = \dfrac{1}{x}$, $x \in (0,1]$ is not uniformly continuous.

Solution. Let $\epsilon = 1$, and $\delta > 0$ be fixed. Let $x, y \in D$, where $|x - y| = \dfrac{\delta}{2}$, and $0 < x, y < \delta$ (we assume $\delta \leqslant 1$). Clearly, such an x and y exist. For this choice, we have

$$\left| \frac{1}{x} - \frac{1}{y} \right| = |x - y| \cdot \left(\frac{1}{xy} \right) \geqslant \left(\frac{\delta}{2} \right) \left(\frac{2}{\delta^2} \right) \qquad \textbf{(WHY?)}$$

$$\geqslant 1,$$

as required.   □

Discussion. The reader should not be surprised that this function is not uniformly continuous on the interval mentioned. After all, this function has been continually referred to in previous discussion as a function for which we cannot eliminate the dependence of δ on the choice of y.

It is important to note that the value taken for ϵ was one of convenience. Any value would have worked, although the larger the value for ϵ, the closer to 0 we may have to choose y in order to ensure $\left| \dfrac{1}{x} - \dfrac{1}{y} \right|$ is greater than ϵ.   □

EXAMPLE 4 _____

Let $f(x) = x^2$, $x \in [0, \infty)$. Show f is not uniformly continuous.

Solution. Let $\epsilon = 1$ and let $1 \geqslant \delta > 0$ be fixed. Clearly, we can choose an x and y satisfying $|x - y| = \dfrac{\delta}{2}$ and $x, y > \dfrac{2}{\delta}$. For such a choice of x and y, we have $x, y \in D$, $|x - y| < \delta$ and

$$|x^2 - y^2| = |x - y| \cdot |x + y| \geqslant \left(\frac{\delta}{2} \right) \left(\frac{2}{\delta} + \frac{2}{\delta} \right) \qquad \textbf{(WHY?)}$$

$$= 2,$$

as desired.   □

Discussion. In the example above, the domain of the function is closed but unbounded. Further, the function is continuous on its entire domain and, in consequence, has no point at which the function is unbounded.

In the argument, the choice of ϵ appears magical. Actually it is not; any value for ϵ would have done. To see why, consider the computations with $|x^2 - y^2|$. Notice that the factor $|x + y|$ depends only on the values of x and y and not on the distance between x and y. Thus, as x and y get large without bound, the term $|x + y|$ also gets large without bound. As a result, to make the product small, the term $|x - y|$ (which measures the closeness of x and y) must be small enough to compensate for the growth of $|x + y|$. It is clear that no fixed amount of 'smallness' can do the job for the ever increasing values of x and y which are permitted by the domain $[0, \infty)$. Thus, we must choose ever smaller values for δ as we choose larger values for x and y, and it is this bit of intuition which is the heart of the argument.

To see the geometric intuition, consider a fixed value for $|x - y|$. As we slide x, y to the right, the value of $|x^2 - y^2|$ grows without bound. The reason we were able to establish uniform continuity in the case of Example 2 is that the domain was bounded above, preventing us from sliding x, y arbitrarily far to the right. ☐

In Examples 3 and 4, it is possible, by moving x,y, to make the value of $|f(x) - f(y)|$ as large as we please. One might think that this is a requirement for uniform continuity to fail, and if we could show, for example, that for each value of δ, the value of $|f(x) - f(y)|$ was bounded, provided only that $|x - y| < \delta$, the uniform continuity would hold. Such is not the case, as an oscillating example below shows.

EXAMPLE 5 _____

Let $f(x) = \sin \dfrac{1}{x}$, $x \in (0,1)$. Show that f is not uniformly continuous on $(0,1)$.

Solution. Again, let $\epsilon = 1$ and $1 > \delta > 0$ be fixed. We can choose $n \in \mathbf{N}$ such that $n > \dfrac{1}{\delta}$. If we let $x = \dfrac{2}{\pi(2n + 1)}$ and $y = \dfrac{2}{\pi(2n + 3)}$, then $0 < x, y < \delta$, whence

$$|x - y| < \frac{1}{n^2} < \delta \text{ .and. } \left| \sin \frac{1}{x} - \sin \frac{1}{y} \right| = 2 \geqslant 1,$$

as required. ☐

Discussion. The properties of the sine function required for this example are no more than those presented in Example 2.2.5 in which it was shown that the function $\sin \dfrac{1}{x}$ had no limit as x tended to 0. The intuition behind the argument can be grasped by thinking of the graph of the sine function stretching out to minus infinity. Now take this graph and push it in from left to right starting at minus infinity and keeping the point $(1, \sin 1)$ fixed. We could think of this as compressing a spring which had been infinitely long to a finite length (see Figure 3.5.2). Thus, we trap an infinite number of oscillations between 0 and 1. Since these oscillations reach a uniform height of 1 on each side of the line $y = 0$, and a complete oscillation exists in any δ-interval about

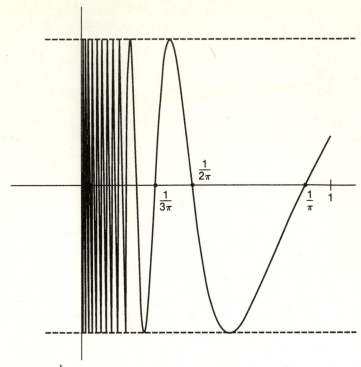

Figure 3.5.2 $\sin\dfrac{1}{x}$, $x \in (0, 1)$ is not uniformly continuous.

0, we have all that we need to destroy any hope for uniform continuity. Lastly, to see that $\sin\dfrac{1}{x}$ is continuous, apply Theorem 2.5.2 to the functions $\sin x$ and $\dfrac{1}{x}$. That the former is continuous will be established in Chapter 10.

In terms of the intuitive approach we have been developing, consider a fixed value for $|x - y|$. If we slide x, y along the axis of the independent variable, then we see that $|f(x) - f(y)|$ never exceeds 2. However, no matter how small we take δ, we see that we can always find values for x, y such that $|f(x) - f(y)|$ will be close to 2. Thus, even though $|f(x) - f(y)|$ does not become arbitrarily large, as in the previous examples, we still do not have uniform continuity. □

To complete this section, let us review the main points of our intuitive approach to uniform continuity. First, suppose that f is continuous on D, which we may assume is an interval. If we fix a $y \in D$ and a $\delta > 0$, then we can define the set

$$A_\delta^y = \{z : \text{there exists } x \in (y - \delta, y + \delta) \cap D \text{ and } |f(x) - f(y)| = z\}.$$

Intuitively, numbers get into A_δ^y provided they are obtainable as a distance between $f(x)$ and $f(y)$ for an x in the δ-interval about y. Now, if A_δ is the union of all the A_δ^y's, for $y \in D$, then the supremum of A_δ will be the smallest ϵ (assuming the supremum exists) which for this choice of δ will yield a valid implication of the form

$$|x - y| < \delta \quad \text{implies} \quad |f(x) - f(y)| \leqslant \epsilon.$$

The formation of the set A_δ amounts to looking at the possible values of $|f(x) - f(y)|$ which can be obtained by sliding x, y around in D. What we have observed is that the supremum of A_δ must exist for each choice of δ if we are to have any hope of achieving uniform continuity. Further, if we are to avoid the type of misbehavior displayed in Example 5, it must be the case that by making δ small, we can make the supremum over A_δ small.

Still another way of phrasing the question being posed here is: For a given size change in the independent variable, what is the largest change in the dependent variable which can result? Uniform continuity tells us that small changes will produce small changes. A more complete treatment of this approach is spelled out in Exercise 4. □

EXERCISES

1. Use the definition of uniform continuity to show which of the following functions are uniformly continuous. You may assume that sin and cos are continuous with the usual domains and ranges.

(a) $f(x) = 2x + 1, x \in \mathbf{R}$;

(b) $f(x) = 1 - x, x \in \mathbf{Q}$;

(c) $f(x) = x^2, x \in \mathbf{N}$;

(d) $f(x) = x^3, x \in \mathbf{Q}$;

(e) $f(x) = \dfrac{1}{x^2}, x \in (0.0001, 1]$;

(f) $f(x) = \dfrac{1}{x^2}, x \in (0, 1)$;

(g) $f(x) = \dfrac{1}{1 + x^2}, x \in \mathbf{R}$;

(h) $f(x) = \dfrac{10}{(1 + x^2)}, x \in \mathbf{Q}$;

(i) $f(x) = x^{1/3}, x \in \mathbf{R}$;

(j) $f(x) = \begin{cases} 1, & x > 0 \\ 0, & x < 0; \end{cases}$

(k) $f(x) = \sqrt{x + 1}, x \geqslant -1$;

(l) $f(x) = \dfrac{x^2 + 1}{x - 3}, x \in \mathbf{R} \sim \{3\}$;

(m) $f(x) = \dfrac{x^2 + 1}{x^2 - 3}, x \in [-2, 1]\ x \neq \pm\sqrt{3}$;

(n) $f(x) = \begin{cases} \dfrac{1 - \cos x}{x}, & x \in [-\pi, 0) \cup (0, 2] \\ 0, & x = 0 \end{cases} \quad x \in [-\pi, 2]$;

(o) $f(x) = \dfrac{x}{x^2 + 1}, x \in \mathbf{R}$;

(p) $f(x) = \sin x^2, x \in \mathbf{R}$;

(q) $f(x) = x \sin \dfrac{1}{x}, x \in (0, \pi)$;

(r) $f(x) = \sqrt{x} \sin \dfrac{1}{x}$, $x \in (0,\pi)$;

(s) $f(x) = x \sin \dfrac{1}{x^2}$, $x \in (0,\pi)$.

2. Let $P(x)$ and $Q(x)$ be two polynomials with integer coefficients. Let $f(x) = \dfrac{P(x)}{Q(x)}$, and have as its domain all real numbers which are not zeros for $Q(x)$. Find necessary and sufficient conditions for f to be uniformly continuous on its domain.

3. Discuss the uniform continuity properties of $f(x) = x^{1/n}$, $n \in \mathbf{N}$, on its domain.

4. Let f be defined on an interval I. Define A_δ^y and A_δ as at the end of the section. Define the functions g and h by

$$g(y,\delta) = \begin{cases} \sup A_\delta^y, & \text{if this exists} \\ \text{undefined}, & \text{otherwise;} \end{cases}$$

$$h(\delta) = \begin{cases} \sup A_\delta, & \text{if this exists} \\ \text{undefined}, & \text{otherwise.} \end{cases}$$

   (a) Show f is continuous on D if and only if for every $y \in D$, $\lim\limits_{\delta \to 0} g(y,\delta) = 0$ for every $\delta > 0$.

   (b) Show f is uniformly continuous on D if and only if $\lim\limits_{\delta \to 0} h(\delta) = 0$ for every $\delta > 0$.

5. Let $f(x) = x^2$, $x \in \mathbf{R}$, with g and h as in Exercise 4. Give explicit descriptions for g and h. Do the same for $f(x) = 1 - 2x$, $x \in \mathbf{R}$, and $f(x) = \dfrac{1}{x}$, $x \in (0.1,1)$.

6. Let f and g be uniformly continuous on a bounded set, D. What can be said about the sum $f + g$ and product fg? Do your conclusions alter if D is an arbitrary interval, in particular, $D = \mathbf{R}$?

7. Let f be uniformly continuous on (a, b). Show that f is bounded on (a, b).

8. Prove the Cauchy criterion for functions: $\lim\limits_{x \to a} f(x)$ exists and is finite if and only if for every $\epsilon > 0$ there exists $\delta > 0$ such that for every $x, y \in \operatorname{Dmn} f$, $0\,|x-a| < \delta$ and $0 < |y-a| < \delta$ imply $|f(x)-f(y)| < \epsilon$.

9. Let f be uniformly continuous on (a, b). Show that the left-hand limit at b exists.

10. Give examples which show that the results in Exercises 7 and 9 are not true if uniformly continuous is replaced by continuous.

11. Suppose f is defined on (a, b) and that for each $x \in (a, b)$ there is a $\delta > 0$ such that f is uniformly continuous on $(x - \delta, x + \delta)$, that is, f is locally uniformly continuous. Is f uniformly continuous on (a, b)? Would the answer change if the δ intervals were closed?

12. Let $f(x) = \sqrt{1 - x^2}$, $|x| < 1$. Is f uniformly continuous?

13. Let f be uniformly continuous on an interval I. Show f is uniformly continuous on every subinterval of I.

14. Let f be monotone increasing, continuous, and bounded on an interval I. Show that f is uniformly continuous on I.

15. Let I_1 and I_2 be two closed intervals. Show that if f is uniformly continuous on I_1 and I_2, then f is uniformly continuous on $I_1 \cup I_2$.

16. Can the result of Exercise 14 be extended to countably infinite collections of closed intervals?

17. Let D be bounded, a be a limit point of D which is not in D, and f be continuous on D but not having a continuous extension to $D \cup \{a\}$. Is it true that f is not uniformly continuous?

18. Show that the function $f: \mathbf{Q} \to \mathbf{Q}$ defined by $f(x) = \dfrac{1}{2 - x^2}$ is continuous but not uniformly continuous on its domain.

19. Suppose that f is uniformly continuous on a domain $D \subseteq \mathbf{R}$, and $\{x_n\}$ is a Cauchy sequence in D. Show that $\{f(x_n)\}$ is a Cauchy sequence in $\mathbf{R}$.

20. If $f: D \to \mathbf{R}$ is uniformly continuous, and for sequences $\{a_n\}$, $\{b_n\}$, if $\lim\limits_{n \to \infty}(a_n - b_n) = 0$, show that $\lim\limits_{n \to \infty}(f(a_n) - f(b_n)) = 0$. Give an example to show that mere continuity is not enough to ensure the validity of this result.

21. A function $f: D \to \mathbf{R}$ is **Lipschitz**, provided there is a constant $K > 0$ such that
$$|f(x) - f(y)| \leq K|x - y|$$
for $x, y \in D$. Show that a Lipschitz map is uniformly continuous.

22. For each of the functions given below either find a value of K proving the function to be Lipschitz on its domain, or show that no such K can exist.
    (a) $f(x) = 2x + 1$, $x \in \mathbf{R}$;
    (b) $f(x) = x^2$, $x \in [-2,2]$;
    (c) $f(x) = x^3$, $x \in [-8,8]$;
    (d) $f(x) = x^2$, $x \in \mathbf{R}$;
    (e) $f(x) = x^3$, $x \in \mathbf{R}$;
    (f) $f(x) = \dfrac{1}{x^2}$, $x \in (0.0001,1]$;
    (g) $f(x) = \dfrac{1}{x^2}$, $x \in (0,1)$;
    (h) $f(x) = \dfrac{1}{1+x^2}$, $x \in \mathbf{R}$;
    (i) $f(x) = \sqrt{x}$, $x \in [0,\infty)$;
    (j) $f(x) = x^{1/3}$, $x \in \mathbf{R}$;
    (k) $f(x) = \sin x$, $x \in \mathbf{R}$;
    (l) $f(x) = \sqrt{x + 1}$, $x \geq -1$;
    (m) $f(x) = \sin \dfrac{1}{x}$, $x \in (0,\pi)$;
    (n) $f(x) = x \sin \dfrac{1}{x}$, $x \in (0,\pi)$.

23. Let $f(x) = x^{p/q}$ where $p/q \in \mathbf{Q}$ and f is defined on D. Find conditions under which f will be Lipschitz and explicitly describe the dependence of these conditions on D.

24. Let f be defined on (a, b) and $y \in (a, b)$. Define the **limit superior of f at y** by
$$\varlimsup_{x \to y} f(x) = \inf_{\delta > 0} \ \sup_{0 < |x-y| < \delta} f(x).$$

    (a) Define the limit inferior, $\varliminf$, analogously.
    (b) Show $\varlimsup\limits_{x \to y} f(x) \leq A$ if and only if for every positive ϵ there exists a positive δ such that for every x with $0 < |x-y| < \delta$ we have $f(x) \leq A + \epsilon$.
    (c) Show $\varlimsup\limits_{x \to y} f(x) \geq A$ if and only if for every positive ϵ and positive δ there exists x such that $0 < |x-y| < \delta$ and $f(x) \geq A - \epsilon$.

(d) Show $\varliminf_{x \to y} f(x) \leqslant \varlimsup_{x \to y} f(x)$ with equality if and only if the limit exists.

25. Find the $\varlimsup$ and $\varliminf$ for each of the following functions at 0.

(a) $f(x) = x^{1/3}$, $x \in \mathbf{R}$;

(b) $f(x) = \begin{cases} 1, & x \geqslant 0 \\ 0, & x < 0; \end{cases}$

(c) $f(x) = \begin{cases} \dfrac{1}{x}, & x \neq 0 \\ 0, & x = 0; \end{cases}$

(d) $f(x) = \begin{cases} \dfrac{1 - \cos x}{x}, & x \in [-\pi, 0) \cup (0, 2] \\ 0, & x = 0; \end{cases}$

(e) $f(x) = \sin x^2$, $x \in \mathbf{R}$;

(f) $f(x) = x \sin \dfrac{1}{x}$, $x \in (0, \pi)$;

(g) $f(x) = \sqrt{x} \, \sin \dfrac{1}{x}$, $x \in (0, \pi)$.

26. Let f be defined on (a, b) and $y \in (a, b)$; f is said to be **lower semicontinuous at** y provided $f(y) \leqslant \varliminf_{x \to y} f(x)$. Similarly one can define upper semicontinuous at y. A function is said to be **(upper) lower semicontinuous on** (a, b) if it is (upper) lower semicontinuous for each $y \in (a, b)$.

(a) Show f is lower semicontinuous at y if and only if for each positive ϵ there exists a positive δ such that $f(y) \leqslant f(x) + \epsilon$ whenever $|x - y| < \delta$.

(b) Show f is continuous at y exactly if it is both upper and lower semicontinuous at y.

(c) Show f is lower semicontinuous on (a, b) if and only if the set $\{x : f(x) > a\}$ is open for each $a \in \mathbf{R}$.

(d) Suppose f has a jump discontinuity at y. Under what conditions will f be lower semi%continuous at y?

27. Determine the semicontinuity properties at 0 for each of the functions in Exercise 25.

3.6 CONTINUOUS FUNCTIONS DEFINED ON CLOSED BOUNDED SETS

At the beginning of the last section, we stated that it was our intention to answer the question of whether the attribute of being closed and bounded was a topological property. We have already answered this question for the case of closed bounded intervals in section 2.6. The first theorem of this section produces a proof for the general case.

Theorem 3.6.1. Let f be defined and continuous on a closed bounded subset of $\mathbf{R}$. Then the range of f is a closed bounded subset of $\mathbf{R}$.

Proof. Let D be the domain of f. Equivalently, it suffices to show that $f(D)$ is closed and bounded. To establish this, it is sufficient to show that $f(D)$ is compact.

Thus, let $\{O_\alpha\}$ be an arbitrary collection of open sets covering $f(D)$ and fix $y \in f(D)$. Then $y \in O_{\alpha(y)}$ for some $\alpha(y)$ which we fix. Since $O_{\alpha(y)}$ is open, there is an $\epsilon_{y,\alpha(y)} > 0$ such that if $|z - y| < \epsilon_{y,\alpha(y)}$, then $z \in O_{\alpha(y)}$. Also, since f is continuous, for each $x \in D$ such that $f(x) = y$, there is a $\delta_{x,\alpha(y)}$ such that $|x - w| < \delta_{x,\alpha(y)}$ and $w \in D$ imply $|f(w) - f(y)| < \epsilon_{y,\alpha(y)}$. Now set

$$S_{x,\alpha(y)} = \{w : |w - x| < \delta_{x,\alpha(y)}\}.$$

Evidently, if $w \in S_{x,\alpha(y)} \cap D$ then $f(z) \in O_\alpha(y)$. Further, the collection of $S_{x,\alpha(y)}$'s forms an open cover of D. Thus, since by the Heine–Borel Theorem D is compact, there is a finite subcollection which covers D. We can identify this finite subcollection as $S_{x_1,\alpha(y)}, \ldots, S_{x_n,\alpha(y)}$. These in turn identify a finite subcollection of the $O_{\alpha(y)}$'s, $O_{\alpha(y_1)}, \ldots, O_{\alpha(y_n)}$, where $y_i = f(x_i)$. The reader can easily show (see Exercise 1) that this finite subcollection covers $f(D)$. Since the $O_{\alpha(y)}$'s were an arbitrary open cover, it follows that $f(D)$ is compact. By the Heine–Borel Theorem, $f(D)$ is closed and bounded. $\qquad\square$

Discussion. The proof above shows the real power and utility of the compactness concept. With one punch, we are able to show that $f(D)$ was both closed and bounded. An alternative approach would first directly establish that $f(D)$ was closed, and then that it was bounded. Since D does not have to be an interval, the proof can be very complicated (see Exercise 2).

In concept, the proof above is easily described. Take an open cover of the image. Use the fact that the inverse image of an open set under a continuous function is open to generate an open cover of the domain. (In going from the range to the domain, we have to be aware of the comments following Theorem 3.1.8, which was why this theorem was not applied directly. Only the ideas in the proof of Theorem 3.1.8 were used.) Once an open cover of the domain was obtained, we applied the Heine–Borel Theorem to the domain to obtain a finite cover of the domain. But the images of the sets in this finite cover must comprise all of $f(D)$ and thus enable us to find a finite subcover of the original cover. $\qquad\square$

We have seen from the above theorems that continuous functions applied to closed bounded sets generate closed bounded sets. Closed bounded sets are very 'nice' subsets of **R**. It seems plausible then that the class of functions which can be continuous on a closed bounded set should be somewhat restrictive. Thus, one is led to asking whether a function which is continuous on a closed bounded set has any special properties. The answer turns out to be yes, and so we see that closed bounded sets actually make demands on the functions which are continuous on them.

Theorem 3.6.2. If f be continuous on a closed bounded subset $D \subseteq \mathbf{R}$, then f is uniformly continuous on D.

Proof. Let $\epsilon > 0$ be given. By continuity, for each $x \in D$, there exists $\delta_x > 0$ such that $|x - y| < \delta_x$ implies $|f(x) - f(y)| < \dfrac{\epsilon}{3}$. Note that the intervals $S_x = \left[x - \dfrac{\delta_x}{2}, \ x + \dfrac{\delta_x}{2}\right]$, $x \in D$, form an open covering of D. By the Heine–Borel

Theorem there is a finite collection of the x's, say, $x_1, \ldots, x_n$, such that the intervals S_{x_i}, $1 \leq i \leq n$, still cover D. Now set

$$\delta = \frac{1}{2} \min \{\delta_{x_1}, \ldots, \delta_{x_n}\}$$

and consider $u, v \in D$ such that $|u - v| < \delta$. Since the finite collection of intervals S_{x_i} covers D, we can find integers j, k such that $1 \leq j, k \leq n$, $u \in S_{x_j}$, and $v \in S_{x_k}$, whence

$$|u - x_j| < \frac{1}{2} \cdot \delta_{x_j} \quad \text{and} \quad |v - x_k| < \frac{1}{2} \cdot \delta_{x_k}.$$

By the definition of δ, we have that $|x_j - x_k| < \delta$, whence $|x_j - x_k| < \delta_{x_j}$. It follows that

$$\begin{aligned}
|f(u) - f(v)| &= |f(u) - f(x_k) + f(x_k) - f(x_j) + f(x_j) - f(v)| \\
&\leq |f(u) - f(x_k)| + |f(x_k) - f(x_j)| + |f(x_j) - f(v)| \\
&\leq \frac{\epsilon}{3} + \frac{\epsilon}{3} + \frac{\epsilon}{3} = \epsilon.
\end{aligned}$$

Since ϵ was arbitrary, f is uniformly continuous on D. $\qquad\square$

Discussion. As with the previous theorem, the use of the compactness concept simplifies the proof. Conceptually, the argument runs as follows.

Fix ϵ. For this ϵ, about each $x \in D$, find a δ_x interval which witnesses continuity at x. We use these subintervals to form a cover of D which is composed of the S_x's. The critical fact about the S_x's is that each has a total length which is half that of δ_x. By compactness, we generate a finite subcover of D. Since the list of covering intervals is finite, we know we can find a positive δ which yields an interval less than half the length of any of the intervals in the finite list. We now select two points, u, v, which are within a distance δ of one another. Each one of these points must be close to one of the special points which define the finite subcover. Thus, the points x_k, x_j are determined. We next observe that x_k and x_j cannot be very far apart. This is guaranteed by the definition of S_x. We now use the fact that u is close to x_k and that f is known to be continuous at x_k to obtain the fact that $|f(u) - f(x_k)|$ is small. Similarly, we get that $|f(x_j) - f(v)|$ and $|f(x_j) - f(x_k)|$ are small, whence the sum of the three terms taken together must also be small. This completes the argument. In Exercise 9, the reader is asked to supply all the details related to the inequalities employed in the proof. $\qquad\square$

EXERCISES

1. Show that the subcover generated in the proof of Theorem 3.6.1 actually covers $f(D)$.

2. Give a proof of Theorem 3.6.1 which does not resort to compactness.

3. Let $f(x) = \dfrac{1}{x - \pi}$, $x \in \mathbf{Q}$. Show f is continuous on $[0,6]$, but has an unbounded range.

4. Let f be defined and continuous on a closed interval of $\mathbf{Q}$. Show that the range of f is not necessarily bounded, and even if it is bounded it does not have to be closed.

5. Show that there are uniformly continuous functions defined on closed bounded subsets of **Q** and having range in **R** whose range is not closed in **R**. Can you do the same with **R** replaced by **Q**?

6. Let f be continuous on (a, b) and suppose that the right-hand limit at a exists and likewise the left-hand limit at b. Show f is uniformly continuous on (a, b).

7. A function $f: \mathbf{R} \to \mathbf{R}$ is said to be **periodic** on **R** if there exists a number $p > 0$ such that $f(x + p) = f(x)$ for all $x \in \mathbf{R}$. Prove that a continuous periodic function on **R** is uniformly continuous and bounded on **R**.

8. Recall the Lipschitz condition explored Exercise 3.5.21. Give an example of a uniformly continuous function defined on a closed interval, $[a, b]$, which is not Lipschitz.

9. Write out all the details concerning the inequalities used to complete the proof of Theorem 3.6.2.

10. Give an alternative proof of Theorem 3.6.2 for functions defined on closed intervals which runs along the following lines. Suppose f is not uniformly continuous. Then there is an exceptional epsilon, say ϵ_0. Consider $\delta_n = \dfrac{1}{n}$. For each choice δ_n, there must be an x_n such that for some x, $|x - x_n| < \delta_n$, but $|f(x) - f(x_n)| \geqslant \epsilon_0$. By pushing this reasoning to the limit, f can be shown to be discontinuous at a particular $x \in I$, resulting in a contradiction. Complete the details.

11. Let A be a noncompact subset of **R**. Show:
    (a) there exists a continuous function on A which is unbounded;
    (b) there exists a continuous, bounded function on A which has no maximum;
    (c) if, in addition, A is bounded, then there exists a continuous function on A which is not uniformly continuous.

12. Let D be a bounded set and suppose that f is continuous but not uniformly continuous on D. Show that D has a limit point a, such that $a \notin D$ and no extension of f to $D \cup \{a\}$ is continuous.

13. Let D be closed, and suppose f is continuous on D. Show f has a continuous extension to all of **R**. Note, this extension may not be unique. Show that if D is not closed, this result is not generally true.

14. Let f be uniformly continuous on a bounded set D. Then for every limit point a of D such that $a \notin D$, there is a continuous extension of f to $D \cup \{a\}$.

15. Let f be continuous on a bounded set D. Then f is uniformly continuous on D if and only if f has a continuous extension to all of $\bar{D}$.

16. Let f and g be uniformly continuous on D.
    (a) Show for any constant a, af is uniformly continuous on D.
    (b) Show if D is compact, fg is uniformly continuous on D.
    (c) Suppose D is merely bounded. Will the product be uniformly continuous?
    (d) What can be said about the composition of two uniformly continuous functions? Explore the possibilities.

17. Let $f(x) = \sqrt{1 - x^2}$, $|x| \leqslant 1$. Discuss the uniform continuity properties of f.

18. Let f be continuous on **R**. What can be concluded if both limits at infinity exist? Can anything be said if f is bounded?

19. Let f be upper semicontinuous (Exercise 3.5.26) on a compact set, D. Show $\mathrm{Rng}\,f$ is bounded above.

20. Let f be upper semicontinuous (Exercise 3.5.26) on a compact set, D. Show f assumes its maximum.

Chapter 4

Differentiation

In this chapter, we will consider a somewhat more complicated type of limit than those of the preceding chapters. One might think that our order reflected the historical development. However, this is not the case as the differential calculus was laid down long before the real numbers had been put on the firm foundation which we have so carefully sketched. Moreover, the concept of limit, as we have framed it, did not exist. The reason for our development is that it is only with the precision of expression of the nineteenth and twentieth centuries that today's mathematicians can really work with any form of limit. But if one is prepared to work on a completely intuitive level, then certain problems lead on naturally to the development of the derivative of a function. Such problems as

(1) given a function describing the position of a moving object with respect to time, find its velocity, and
(2) given a curved surface of a lens, find the tangent plane to the surface at a given point,

were at the center of the scientific thrust of the seventeenth century and their solution not only demanded the differential calculus, but also led naturally to its development on an intuitive level. It is not surprising in view of this that the two problems which are always treated in every elementary calculus book are:

(1) using the derivative to obtain the velocity and acceleration functions, and
(2) finding the tangent to a curve at a given point.

As is usually the case with creations, once conceived, they have a life of their own. And so is it with the derivative. Its achievements have far surpassed the expectations of Newton and Leibnitz and it is these achievements which are the subject of this chapter.

4.1 DEFINITION AND BASIC FACTS

As we have already mentioned, one problem which is always considered as motivation for the definition of derivative is that of finding the equation of the tangent line to a curve. We shall employ this same problem as the basis for our discussion of the derivative because so many of the important insights about the nature of the derivative are present in this example.

The notion of tangency arises in the geometry of the ancient Greeks long before the existence of analysis. In this context, one considers the problem of finding a straight line which passes through "exactly one point" on a curve. The earliest recognition of tangents appears to be with respect to circles where a tangent line was a straight line passing through one and only one point on the circle. Another form of this definition includes the assertion that the tangent line must lie on the same side as that of the curve (Kline, 1972).† In any event, for circles, there is a unique straight line which passes through a given point P on the circle and only through that given point. This straight line is referred to as the **tangent line to the circle** at P. It was known to the Greeks that the tangent line to a circle had many other properties. For example, it was known that the tangent at P was perpendicular to the diameter of the circle through P.

The fact that tangents to circles existed suggested that tangent to other curves might exist as well, and the Greeks searched, and indeed found, tangents to other curves such as various spirals and conic sections.

As soon as one has developed a theory of functions and coordinate geometry, one is practically forced to wonder about which curves will have tangents, and at a more basic level, just what would be a suitable analytic definition for the tangent concept. More precisely, let us suppose that we have a function f which is continuous on an open interval I, and that a is a fixed member of I. We want to know under what condition there will be a straight line passing through the point $P = (a, f(a))$, which can reasonably be said to be the tangent line to the graph of f at P.

To answer this question consider Figure 4.1.1. In this figure, we have pictured a curve defined by the graph of f, and a tangent line passing through the point $(a, f(a))$. Let us ignore for a moment the problem of whether, or under what conditions, the tangent to the curve at $(a, f(a))$ will exist, and suppose that it does. We can then ask: How can we find the tangent to the curve at $(a, f(a))$?

To answer the question of how to find the tangent, consider that the tangent line is a straight line. Thus, it is completely determined by a point on that line, and the angle γ between the straight line and the x-axis. Because the line we require is to be tangent to the curve at the point $(a, f(a))$, a point on the tangent line is handed to us as a condition of the problem. Thus, to find the tangent line, we need only find the angle γ. The key fact to be noticed here is that γ is completely determined by its tangent (that is, its inclination), and that this can be found from

$$\tan \gamma = \frac{y_2 - y_1}{x_2 - x_1}$$

where (x_1, y_1) and (x_2, y_2) are any two points on the tangent line. The fact that the

† M. Kline, *Mathematical Thought from Ancient to Modern Times*, Oxford University Press, New York, 1972.

ratio $\dfrac{y_2 - y_1}{x_2 - x_1}$ is a constant which can be calculated from any pair of points on the straight line, led to the realization that this ratio could be used as part of the description of a straight line. For this reason, the ratio was given a name, **slope**, a quantity which should be well familiar to any student of calculus. It was also realized that the slope of a straight line could be employed as part of the analytic description of a straight line. Thus, in our usual functional notation, we have the point-slope description of a straight line,

$$y = g(x) = m(x - x_1) + y_1$$

where (x_1, y_1) is any point on the line, and m is the slope of the straight line. Again, these are concepts which are dealt with in the early chapters of almost any calculus book.

With this characterization of a straight line in mind, let us assume that the tangent to the curve exists. We might then think of finding an approximation to it. Given that we already have one point on the line, namely, $(a, f(a))$ it seems obvious that any approximation to the tangent line should include this point. If we had another point, we would be done, since any second point will completely determine the line. The only possible source for a second point is the curve itself. Thus, we can pick any point $b \in I$ and take the straight line passing through $(a, f(a))$ and $(b, f(b))$ as an approximation to the tangent line. By employing the point-slope form of the straight line, we see that the approximation to the tangent line is

$$g_b(x) = \frac{f(b) - f(a)}{b - a}(x - a) + f(a),$$

where we employ the notation g_b to denote the approximation to the tangent line determined by $(b, f(b))$ as shown in Figure 4.1.1. This line is referred to as a **secant**

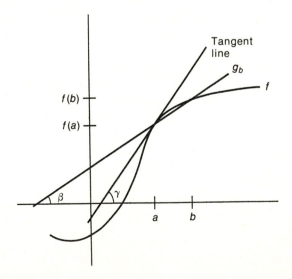

Figure 4.1.1 g_b is the approximation to the tangent line determined by $(b, f(b))$.

to the curve. Evidently, a better approximation to the tangent line can be obtained by employing the point $(c, f(c))$ for $a < c < b$. If we compare the analytic form of g_c,

$$g_c(x) = \frac{f(c) - f(a)}{c - a}(x - a) + f(a),$$

with that of g_b, we see that the only thing that has changed is the slope of the line. Thus, all the approximation process is doing is finding estimates of the slope of the tangent line. This leads ever so naturally to looking at the quantity

$$\frac{f(b) - f(a)}{b - a}$$

and asking what happens to this for a fixed a if we let b tend to a. Evidently, this is a question about limits, and although somewhat different in form, should be no different in substance.

Definition. Let $f: D \to \mathbf{R}$ be defined in a neighborhood about a; that is, $(a - c, a + c) \subseteq D$ for some $c > 0$. We will say that f is **differentiable** at a, provided there is an $L \in \mathbf{R}$ such that for every $\epsilon > 0$, there exists $\delta > 0$ such that if $0 < |h| < \delta$, then

$$\left| \frac{f(a + h) - f(a)}{h} - L \right| < \epsilon.$$

In the case that f is differentiable at a, we will write

$$f'(a) = \lim_{h \to 0} \frac{f(a + h) - f(a)}{h} = L,$$

and say that the **derivative of** f at a is L.

Discussion. Initially, the quantity

$$\frac{f(a + h) - f(a)}{h}$$

which is referred to as the **difference quotient**, looks completely different from something of the form

$$\frac{f(b) - f(a)}{b - a}.$$

To see that they are really the same, let $b = a + h$. It is immediate that

$$\frac{f(b) - f(a)}{b - a} = \frac{f(a + h) - f(a)}{h},$$

whence the two forms are merely two ways of looking at the same thing. Since the numerator of this expression is the change, or **increment**, in the function values calculated at the points a and $a + h$, while the denominator, h, is the distance between a and $a + h$, the value of the difference quotient can always be interpreted as a slope. Specifically, it is the slope of the straight line joining the two points $(a, f(a))$ and $(a + h, f(a + h))$.

A detail which should be noted is the use of $|h|$ in the definition. This ensures that h is permitted to be both positive and negative, or equivalently, that h is permitted to approach 0 from both directions. Thus, in Figure 4.1.1, we could as easily have selected a point b which lay to the left of a on the x-axis as one which lay to the right.

In the event that the limit L exists as h tends to 0, in line with the discussion above, we would interpret the number L to be a slope. Namely, we take it to be the slope of the tangent line to the curve at the point $(a, f(a))$. Analytically, this means that the tangent to the curve at $(a, f(a))$ is given by

$$g(x) = f'(a)(x - a) + f(a).$$

The reader should understand that this is essentially a definition. The notion of tangent is a geometric notion which provides motivation for the definition of the derivative. However, the limit as defined above, which is analytic in nature, does not necessarily have to produce a tangent, in the geometric sense, to the curve at the point $(a, f(a))$. For one thing, prior to defining the derivative, we don't have tangents to most types of curves. In such a case, where no geometric tangent is available, how are we to decide that the straight line passing through $(a, f(a))$ and having slope $f'(a)$ really is the correct tangent line? We can not decide, so when we assert that it is, we are essentially making a definition. What we can do is check that the analytic specification for a tangent line agrees with, or has the same properties as, the geometric tangent line in cases for which the latter exists. This type of check will be illustrated in Example 5. □

We have stressed that whenever a new limit definition arises, a number of natural questions arise. For example, is the limit unique, how does it behave with respect to numerical operations, and so on. Since these results are essential to the remaining development, we state two summary theorems.

Theorem 4.1.1.   Let f be defined in a neighborhood about a and differentiable at a. Then $f'(a)$ is unique.

Proof.   We offer a sketch; details are left to Exercise 20.

Assume for the sake of argument that $f'(a)$ is not unique, and that both L and M satisfy the definition. Then set $\epsilon = \dfrac{|L - M|}{3}$. A contradiction is now easily obtained. □

Theorem 4.1.2.   Let f and g be defined in a neighborhood about a and differentiable at a. Then

   (i) for any $c \in \mathbf{R}$ $(cf)'$ exists, and $(cf)' = cf'$;
   (ii) $(f + g)'(a)$ exists and $(f + g)'(a) = f'(a) + g'(a)$;
   (iii) $(fg)'(a)$ exists and $(fg)'(a) = f'(a)g(a) + f(a)g'(a)$;
   (iv) *if* $g'(a) \neq 0$, $\left[\dfrac{f}{g}\right]'(a)$ exists, and

$$\left[\frac{f}{g}\right]'(a) = \frac{f'(a)g(a) - f(a)g'(a)}{[g(a)]^2}.$$

Proof. We prove (iii) and leave the rest to Exercises 21–24. Thus, assume f and g are defined on (c,b) and differentiable at $a \in (c,b)$. Then

$$\left| \frac{(fg)(a+h) - (fg)(a)}{h} \right| = \left| \frac{f(a+h)\,g(a+h) - f(a)\,g(a)}{h} \right|$$

$$= \left| \frac{[f(a+h)\,g(a+h) - f(a)\,g(a+h)] + [f(a)\,g(a+h) - f(a)\,g(a)]}{h} \right|$$

$$= \left| \frac{f(a+h)\,g(a+h) - f(a)\,g(a+h)}{h} + \frac{f(a)\,g(a+h) - f(a)\,g(a)}{h} \right|. \tag{1}$$

It follows that

$$\left| \frac{(fg)(a+h) - (fg)(a)}{h} - [f'(a)g(a) + f(a)g'(a)] \right|$$

$$\leq \left| \frac{f(a+h)\,g(a+h) - f(a)\,g(a+h)}{h} - f'(a)g(a) \right|$$

$$+ \left| \frac{f(a)\,g(a+h) - f(a)\,g(a)}{h} - f(a)g'(a) \right|. \tag{2}$$

To complete the proof, we must show that each term on the right-hand side of Eq. 2 can be made arbitrarily small merely by taking h small. Consider the second term first.

$$\left| \frac{f(a)\,g(a+h) - f(a)\,g(a)}{h} - f(a)g'(a) \right| = \left| \frac{g(a+h) - g(a)}{h} - g'(a) \right| |f(a)|.$$

Since $g'(a)$ exists, the quantity, $\left| \dfrac{g(a+h) - g(a)}{h} - g'(a) \right|$, can be made arbitrarily small by taking h sufficiently small. Since $f(a)$ is a constant, the product of this quantity with $f(a)$ can also be made arbitrarily small by taking h small (**HOW?**). Now consider the first term on the left-hand side of Eq. 2. Set $g(a+h) = g(a) + \psi$. Then

$$\left| \frac{f(a+h)\,g(a+h) - f(a)\,g(a+h)}{h} - f'(a)\,g(a) \right|$$

$$= \left| \frac{f(a+h)\,(g(a) + \psi) - f(a)\,(g(a) + \psi)}{h} - f'(a)\,g(a) \right|$$

$$\leq \left| \frac{f(a+h)\,g(a) - f(a)\,g(a)}{h} - f'(a)\,g(a) \right| + \left| \frac{f(a+h) - f(a)}{h} \psi \right|$$

$$= \left| \frac{f(a+h) - f(a)}{h} - f'(a) \right| |g(a)| + \left| \frac{f(a+h) - f(a)}{h} \right| |\psi|. \qquad (3)$$

We must show that both terms in Eq. 3 can be made arbitrarily small by taking h to be small. The argument for the first term is essentially the same as the argument for the second term in Eq. 2, and is left to the reader. This leaves us to consider the product, $\left| \frac{f(a+h) - f(a)}{h} \right| |\psi|$. Since $f'(a)$ exists, we may assume the first term satisfies

$$\left| \frac{f(a+h) - f(a)}{h} \right| \leqslant |f'(a)| + 1$$

which may not be small, but is bounded. If we assume g is continuous at a, then, given $\epsilon > 0$, we can find a $\delta(\epsilon) > 0$ such that

$$|\psi| = |g(a+h) - g(a)| < \epsilon$$

whenever $|h| < \delta(\epsilon)$. Thus, the continuity of g at a would be enough to guarantee that $|\psi|$ can be made arbitrarily small by taking h small and hence, that the product will be small. Thus, the required conclusion is achieved, provided g is continuous at a. We will prove this fact in the next section (Theorem 4.2.1).   □

Discussion.   As an aid to understanding the proof, let us review the proof of Theorem 2.3.2 in which the product of the limits is shown to be the limit of the product. In that proof, the basic inequality is

$$|(fg)(x) - AB| \leqslant |f(x)| \, |g(x) - B| + |f(x) - A| \, |B|. \qquad (4)$$

The object is to show both terms on the left-hand side of (4) become small as $x \to a$. The second term, like the second term in Eq. 2, is easy to deal with because it is the product of a constant and something which can be made arbitrarily small. On the other hand, the first term on the left of Eq. 4 is difficult to handle because it is the product of two variable terms. However, it is tractable because the term $|f(x)|$ is bounded, whence it can be replaced by a constant, for example, any upper bound on $|f(x)|$.

If one attempts to repeat this argument with the two terms on the left-hand side of Eq. 2, one succeeds with the second term. The first term is particularly difficult to deal with because there is no common factor. Specifically, one has to deal with

$$\left| \frac{f(a + h) \, g(a + h) - f(a) \, g(a + h)}{h} - f'(a) \, g(a) \right|.$$

The source of the problem is that two of the terms involve $g(a+h)$ while the third involves $g(a)$. The way around this difficulty is to force the issue by rewriting $g(a + h)$ as $g(a) + \psi$ and performing the manipulations leading to Eq. 3. Both terms on the left-hand side of Eq. 3 are products. The first is tractable because it is the product of a constant and something which can be made to be arbitrarily small. The second does not obviously satisfy either of these conditions, that is, both terms are variable, and it is not clear why either term can be made small. If one examines $\left| \dfrac{f(a+h) - f(a)}{h} \right|$, one concludes that in general it cannot be made small, since its limiting value is $f'(a)$. Thus, the only hope lies with ψ. Since $\psi = g(a + h) - g(a)$, we observe that ψ will become small as $h \to 0$ exactly if $\lim\limits_{h\to0} g(a + h) = g(a)$, which is another way of saying that g is continuous at a.

If the reader wants to understand why one might think of this proof, she should consider the computations leading to Eq. 1 in the context of the preceding arguments for 'limit of the product is the product of the limits'. The computations attempt to apply the same technique. Because the situation with derivatives is more complex, the final argument takes on greater complexity. But the basic idea is, nevertheless, correct. $\square$

EXAMPLE 1 _____

Let $f(x) = x^2$, $x \in \mathbf{R}$. Show that $f'(a)$ exists for each $a \in \mathbf{R}$.

Solution. Let $a \in \mathbf{R}$ be fixed, and let us examine the difference quotient

$$
\begin{aligned}
\frac{f(a + h) - f(a)}{h} &= \frac{(a + h)^2 - a^2}{h} \\
&= \frac{a^2 + 2ah + h^2 - a^2}{h} \\
&= \frac{2ah + h^2}{h} = 2a + h.
\end{aligned}
$$

Evidently we should set $L = 2a$. Now let $\epsilon > 0$ and $\delta = \epsilon$. Then if $0 < |h| < \delta$, we have that

$$
\left| \frac{f(a + h) - f(a)}{h} - 2a \right| = |2a + h - 2a| = |h| < \delta = \epsilon.
$$

Thus, $f'(a) = 2a$ is the limit. Since a was arbitrary, we are done. $\square$

Discussion. We note only that the heart of computations for this type of function is the algebraic manipulations which the reader should be able to carry out with ease. The force of these computations is to eliminate h from the denominator of the difference quotient. As long as it is in the denominator, we cannot take the limit. Once we have reduced the difference quotient to the form $|2a + h|$ we can compute the limit by simply letting h tend to 0. This can be done by applying basic limit theorems, such as were developed in Chapter 2, or as a direct computation from the definition, as in the present example.

The definition of the derivative is based on a computation at a particular point. However, as the example illustrates, a function may have a derivative at each point of its domain. This is similar to the situation with respect to continuity, where we began by discussing continuity at a point and ended up with the concept of a continuous func-tion on a domain. This leads to the following definition. $\square$

Definition. Let f be defined on an open interval I. We say that f is **differentiable on** I provided that for each $a \in I$, f is differentiable at a. In the event that f is differentiable on I, we set

$$f' = \{(a, f'(a)) : a \in I\},$$

and refer to f' as the **derivative** of f on I.

Discussion. By Theorem 4.1.1, $f'(a)$ is unique for each $a \in I$. Thus, f' is a function, which by assumption has domain I. We have used a to denote the independent variable in the construction of f', however, we will generally use x in the sequel, as in $f'(x)$. □

EXAMPLE 2

Discuss the differentiability of $f(x) = x^{1/3}$.

Solution. By definition, f is differentiable at $x \in \mathbf{R}$ exactly if $f'(x)$ exists. Now,

$$f'(x) = \lim_{h \to 0} \frac{(x+h)^{1/3} - x^{1/3}}{h} = \lim_{h \to 0} \frac{(x+h)^{1/3} - x^{1/3}}{(x+h) - x}$$

$$= \lim_{h \to 0} \frac{1}{(x+h)^{2/3} + (x+h)^{1/3}x^{1/3} + x^{2/3}} \qquad \textbf{(WHY?)}$$

$$= \frac{1}{3x^{2/3}}.$$

The sequence of computations above is meaningful only if $x \neq 0$. Hence f is differentiable at all points except $x = 0$, and the derivative is given by $f'(x) = 1/3x^{-2/3}$, $x \neq 0$. □

Discussion. In the computations above, we have made full use of the limit theorems. Again the reader will perceive that the bulk of the calculations are algebraic.

The graph of the function $f(x) = x^{1/3}$ is presented in Figure 4.1.2. The graph is smooth, and it would appear that a tangent to the curve at each point should exist in the geometric sense of the definition (a few tangents have been drawn in to illustrate this). However, the computations above fail to produce a tangent to the curve at $(0,0)$. The reason for this failure is not that the tangent doesn't exist, since the y-axis would appear to satisfy the requirement of intersecting the curve only at the point $(0,0)$. Rather it is because of the fact that the analytic definition cannot capture this situation which would involve a vertical tangent line. Specifically, in a situation where the tangent line to a curve is vertical, the difference quotient leads to a limiting form which involves a 0 in the denominator which cannot be eliminated.

In a case where the derivative fails to exist because of a vertical tangent line, the problem can be eliminated by changing the coordinate system. Thus, in the present case, if we were to rotate the axis slightly in a counterclockwise direction, the derivative would then exist everywhere.

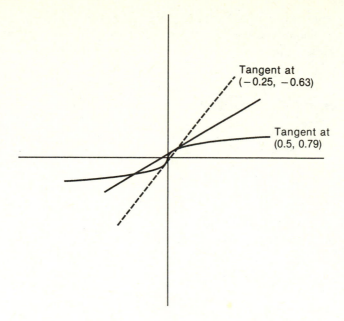

Figure 4.1.2   Analytic tangent cuts the graph in more than one point.

Examination of Figure 4.1.2 also illustrates that a tangent line, in the analytic sense, may cut the graph at more than one place. This is contrary to the geometric definition. The reason for this is that the original definition was developed based on figures such as circles. Such figures 'curve' in only one direction, while the graph for which we are finding tangent lines curves in two directions. To see what we are getting at, consider a point P which moves from left to right along the graph of f starting at $(-8, -2)$. At first, the path that P follows turns from right to left. As soon as P passes through $(0,0)$, the path reverses and begins turning from left to right. Circles do not behave in this manner. As long as a point moves in the same direction along a circle, the direction of turning is the same. In conclusion, the problem is not that a tangent to f should not exist, but rather that the geometric requirement of cutting the curve in only one point must be replaced by an alternative property. This is what the analytic definition supplies and thus permits us to find tangents to a wider variety of curves.   □

The example above illustrates a situation in which we have a curve for which the geometric tangent exists everywhere, but for which the analytic tangent fails to exist at certain points. This brings up the obvious problem of identifying those situations in which the derivative fails to exist. If the reader again considers Figure 4.1.1, and the related comments, it should seem plausible that if a function failed to be continuous at a, it would be unreasonable to expect it to be differentiable at a. In other words, differentiability at a should imply continuity at a. This fact is the first theorem of the next section, so we will not pursue it, although the ambitious reader may wish to generate the proof at this stage. But it suggests that what we want to find are examples of functions which are continuous but for which the derivatives do not exist at some point of their domain. As well, we want to understand why the derivatives fail to exist.

EXAMPLE 3

Discuss the differentiability of the function $f(x) = |x|$.

Solution. From the definition of absolute value, if $x > 0$, then $f(x) = x$, whereas if $x < 0$, then $f(x) = -x$. In both cases, a simple calculation shows that the derivative f' exists, and that $f'(x) = 1$ for $x > 0$, and $f'(x) = -1$ for $x < 0$. Thus, we only need worry about $x = 0$.

For the case $x = 0$,

$$\frac{f(x + h) - f(x)}{h} = \frac{|0 + h| - |0|}{h} = \frac{|h|}{h}.$$

As $h \to 0$, $\lim\limits_{h \to 0} \dfrac{|h|}{h}$ does not exist, since the expression is 1 for $h > 0$ and -1 for $h < 0$. Hence the function is not differentiable at $x = 0$. $\square$

Discussion. Figure 4.1.3 presents the graph of $|x|$ which is composed of two straight half-lines. Both emanate from $(0,0)$, with one rising at an angle of $45°$ with respect to the positive x-axis, and the other at an angle of $135°$ with respect to the positive x-axis. The slope of the first straight half-line is 1; the slope of the second straight half-line is -1. Thus, for $x \neq 0$ tangents to the curve exist. (In this context we are considering that a straight line is tangent to itself, although the Greeks would never have done this.)

The difficulty exists at $x = 0$. The problem is not that there does not exist a straight line which intersects the graph of $f(x) = |x|$ only at the point $(0,0)$. Rather the problem is that there are too many straight lines which have this property. Thus the geometric definition has broken down because of the fact that there is no unique straight line intersecting the curve in one and only one point.

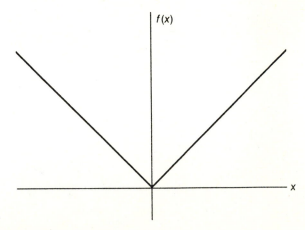

Figure 4.1.3 $f(x) = |x|$ is not differentiable at $x = 0$.

One solution to the problem posed by this example is to restrict the type of curve to which one seeks tangents. It seems plausible that this would have been the tack taken by the Greeks. They would have considered $f(x) = |x|$ to be an inappropriate example for two reasons. First, the graph consists of straight lines, and a straight line which cuts another straight line at one and only one point is obviously not a tangent. Second, to try and find a tangent to a corner of a geometric figure such as a triangle or a square would have seemed nonsensical for the obvious reason that no unique tangent line could exist. The difficulty with an approach based on an examination of the individual curve is that it leaves too much to the eye of the beholder.

The analytic approach deals with the problems posed by the example as follows. First, it makes straight lines tangent to themselves. Second it provides an analytic test which restricts the situations in which we can discuss tangency. Both are accomplished with a single definition by appealing to the idea of limit, which is clearly the appropriate tool for the job.

With respect to the limit, the situation presented is similar to that of a jump discontinuity. Namely, the derivative on each side of 0 exists, and is constant. Since the constants on the two sides are different, where the sides join together, a problem is bound to arise. ☐

We have generated situations where the derivative is infinite, and where the derivative fails to exist because the computation yields one value as h approaches 0^+, and another as h approaches 0^-. When we considered limits of functions, another case existed which involved an infinity of oscillations. This leads us to wonder whether such an example exists in the context of the derivative. Our next example illustrates this point.

EXAMPLE 4
_____

Show that

$$f(x) = x \sin \frac{1}{x}, \ x \in \mathbf{R} \sim \{0\}; \text{ and } f(0) = 0$$

is not differentiable at $x = 0$.

Solution. As shown in Example 2.2.5, the function $g(x) = \sin \frac{1}{x}$ assumes the values 1 and -1 in any interval of the form $(-\delta, \delta)$. It follows that the difference quotient $(h \sin \frac{1}{h} - 0)/h$ must also assume the value 1 and the value -1 (infinitely often) in any interval containing 0. Hence, the limit of the difference quotient cannot exist as $|h|$ tends to 0. ☐

Discussion. A graph of this function is presented in Figure 4.1.4. The graph also includes the two straight lines $y = x$ and $y = -x$. The reader will notice that the graph of f oscillates between these two straight lines, and that an infinite number of oscillations occur in any neighborhood of 0. This is why the difference quotient cannot have a limit.

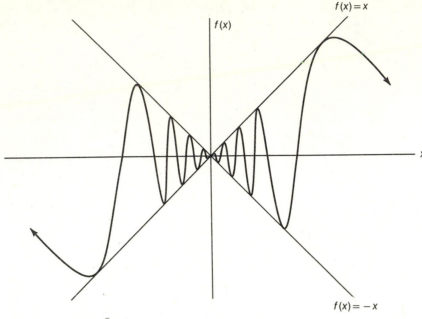

Figure 4.1.4 $f(x) = \begin{cases} x \sin \dfrac{1}{x}, & x \neq 0 \\ 0, & x = 0. \end{cases}$

Another way of thinking about this is to consider a point P on the graph of f. It is a fact that the tangent to f at P exists provided P is not $(0,0)$. As the point P slides in toward $(0,0)$, we obtain a series of tangent lines. The slopes of these tangent lines also oscillate, although in this case, they oscillate without bound. (To see that this is the case, the reader has only to apply the usual rules for differentiating the trigonometric functions to these functions.) Since the tangent lines near $(0,0)$ are also oscillating, it is apparent that the derivative could not exist at $(0,0)$. $\qquad\square$

The discussion thus far has presented examples of functions which are continuous on an interval but which fail to be differentiable at some point of the interval. Obviously, it is possible to have an example of a continuous function with a finite number of points in an interval for which it is not differentiable. But a really ugly function would be continuous on an interval but not differentiable anywhere on the interval. Such functions do indeed exist and an example will be outlined in Chapter 9. The reader may wish to try and construct such a beast in the interim.

The reader will also have noticed that in all cases where a derivative failed to exist at a point a, the derivative f' did not have a continuous extension which included the point a. For example, the derivative of $f(x) = |x|$ is $f'(x) = \text{sgn}(x)$ for $x \in \mathbf{R} \sim \{0\}$ and there is no way to include 0 in the domain of f' in such a way that a continuous function results. This leads to the question: If f is differentiable on I, must f' be continuous on I? The answer is no (Exercise 37).

We conclude this section by illustrating that a tangent constructed via the analytic methodology satisfies the geometric definition.

EXAMPLE 5 _____

Show that the analytic tangent to the parabola given by $f(x) = x^2$, $x \in \mathbf{R}$ satisfies the geometric properties required of a tangent, namely, that it includes only one point on the curve.

Solution.   In Example 1 we showed that for any $a \in \mathbf{R}$, $f'(a) = 2a$. Thus, the analytic tangent line to the parabola at $(a, f(a))$ is given by

$$g(x) = 2a(x - a) + a^2.$$

Now, the point P having first coordinate x is common to both the parabola and the tangent exactly if $g(x) = f(x)$. This yields

$$2a(x - a) + a^2 = x^2 \quad \text{if and only if} \quad 2a(x - a) + a^2 - x^2 = 0$$
$$\text{if and only if} \quad 2a(x - a) + (a + x)(a - x) = 0$$
$$\text{if and only if} \quad (x - a)(2a - (a + x)) = 0$$
$$\text{if and only if} \quad (x - a)(a - x) = 0.$$

The last equality is satisfied exactly if $x = a$, whence the only point common to both the parabola and the tangent line is $(a, f(a))$. $\square$

Discussion.   It would be nice if the tangent line was the unique straight line cutting the parabola at $(a, f(a))$. There is one other, namely the vertical straight line determined by the condition $x = a$. Nevertheless, the analytic tangent line, which is obtained as a limit of secants, has all the properties one would wish of a tangent line. More specifically, in all cases where a geometric tangent line is known to exist and is not vertical, the analytic tangent line also exists and has the same properties. For this reason, the analytic tangent line can reasonably be referred to as the tangent line. $\square$

The reader may well feel that we have placed undue emphasis on the notion of tangency in the development of the derivative. We would argue that the essence of the derivative notion is present in Figure 4.1.1, and it is this picture which the student should fully understand. Indeed, it is our feeling that the intuition required to correctly develop applications of the derivative is inherent in the tangency concept. For this reason we urge the reader to fully come to terms with the ideas contained in Figure 4.1.1 and the material related to it.

EXERCISES

1. Show that the derivative of f at the point a is given by the formula

$$f'(a) = \lim_{x \to a} \frac{f(x) - f(a)}{x - a}$$

provided the limit exists.

2. Use the definition of derivative to find derivative for the following functions on the indicated domain:
   (a) $f(x) = c$, $x \in \mathbf{R}$, c a constant;
   (b) $f(x) = x^3$, $x \in \mathbf{R}$;
   (c) $f(x) = \dfrac{1}{x}$, $x \in \mathbf{R} \sim \{0\}$;
   (d) $f(x) = \sqrt{x}$, $x \in \mathbf{R}^+ \cup \{0\}$;
   (e) $f(x) = \dfrac{1}{x^2}$, $x \in \mathbf{R} \sim \{0\}$;
   (f) $f(x) = \dfrac{1}{\sqrt{x}}$, $x \in \mathbf{R}^+$;
   (g) $f(x) = x^{2/3}$, $x \in \mathbf{R}$;
   (h) $f(x) = \begin{cases} \dfrac{x^3}{3}, & x \leqslant 0 \\ \dfrac{5}{2}x^2 - 4x, & x > 0, \end{cases}$ $x \in \mathbf{R}$;
   (i) $f(x) = \begin{cases} 0, & -2 \leqslant x \leqslant -1 \\ 1 - x^2, & -1 < x \leqslant 1, \end{cases}$ $x \in \mathbf{R}$.

3. Let
$$f(x) = \begin{cases} x^2, & x \leqslant 1 \\ x^3, & x > 1. \end{cases}$$

Show that f is not differentiable at $x = 1$.

4. Let
$$f(x) = \begin{cases} x^2, & x \leqslant 1 \\ \sqrt{x}, & x > 1. \end{cases}$$

Is f differentiable at $x = 1$?

5. Let
$$f(x) = \begin{cases} x^2, & x \leqslant 1 \\ 2x - 1, & x > 1. \end{cases}$$

Is f differentiable at $x = 1$?

6. Let
$$f(x) = \begin{cases} x^2, & x \in \mathbf{Q}, \\ 0, & x \notin \mathbf{Q}. \end{cases}$$

Is f differentiable at $x = 0$?

7. Let
$$f(x) = \begin{cases} 3x + 2, & x \in \mathbf{Q} \\ x^2 - 3x + 5, & x \notin \mathbf{Q}. \end{cases}$$

Is f differentiable at $x = 3$?

8. Let f be defined on $[-1,1]$ by

$$f(x) = \begin{cases} x^2, & x \text{ rational} \\ x^4, & x \text{ irrational.} \end{cases}$$

Show that f is differentiable at exactly one point of its domain and find its derivative there.

9. Given $f(x) = \sin\dfrac{1}{x}$, $g(x) = x\sin\dfrac{1}{x}$, and $h(x) = x^2\sin\dfrac{1}{x}$, with $f(0) = g(0) = h(0) = 0$, prove the following:

   (a) f is neither continuous nor differentiable at 0;
   (b) g is continuous, but not differentiable at 0;
   (c) h is differentiable at 0, but h' is not continuous at 0;
   (d) f' is unbounded near 0.

10. Let $f: \mathbf{R} \to \mathbf{R}$ be such that $f'(c)$ exists for some $c \in \mathbf{R}$. Prove that the sequence

$$\left\{ \frac{f(b_n) - f(a_n)}{b_n - a_n} \right\}$$ converges to $f'(c)$, where $\{a_n\}$ and $\{b_n\}$ are two sequences converging to c, where $a_n \neq b_n$.

11. Let f be defined on an interval I, and let $a \in I$. Prove that f is differentiable at a if and only if for each sequence $\{x_n\}$ in $I \sim \{a\}$ that converges to a, $\left\{ \dfrac{f(x_n) - f(a)}{x_n - a} \right\}$ converges.

Show that the latter sequence converges to $f'(a)$ in case f is differentiable at a.

12. Show that f is differentiable at a if and only if there exists a function $\alpha(h)$ defined in an open interval $(-\delta, \delta)$ and a constant k such that

$$f(a + h) = f(a) + kh + \alpha(h)$$

where $\dfrac{\alpha(h)}{h}$ tends to 0 as h tends to 0. If f is differentiable at a, prove that $k = f'(a)$.

13. Give examples to illustrate that not every function is the derivative of some other function.

14. Consider the graphs of $f(x) = x^2$ and $f(x) = x^3$. Can pieces of the two graphs be 'patched together' in such a way that a function which is differentiable on $\mathbf{R}$ results?

15. Let $f(x) = x^2$, $x \in \mathbf{R}$. Show that there are exactly two straight lines which intersect the curve at (a, a^2) and only at that point.

16. **Left-side** and **right-side derivatives** of f are defined by letting $h \to 0^-$ and $h \to 0^+$, respectively, in the definition of the derivative. Show that f is differentiable at x if and only if both the right- and left-side derivatives exist and are equal. Further, find a function for which both the one-sided derivatives exist at x, but which is not differentiable there.

17. Let f be defined at all points in an open interval I, except possibly at the point $a \in I$. We define the **generalized derivative** of f **from the left** at the point a by

$$\lim_{x \to a^-} \frac{f(x) - \lim\limits_{x \to a^-} f}{x - a}$$

if it exists. Similarly, define the generalized derivative from the right at the point a. Prove that if f has a one-sided derivative at a (Exercise 16), the corresponding generalized derivative also exists and the two are equal. Give an example to show that the converse need not be true.

18. Obtain the derivatives of $f(x) = \sin x$, $x \in \mathbf{R}$, and $f(x) = \cos x$, $x \in \mathbf{R}$; [HINT: Use the limits: $\lim_{h \to 0} \dfrac{\sin h}{h} = 1$ and $\lim_{h \to 0} \dfrac{1 - \cos h}{h} = 0$, in addition to familiar properties of trigonometric functions.]

19. Discuss the differentiability of the following functions:
    (a) $f(x) = |x| + |x + 1|$, $x \in \mathbf{R}$;
    (b) $f(x) = x \cdot |x|$, $x \in \mathbf{R}$.

20. Complete the proof of Theorem 4.1.1.

21. Prove Theorem 4.1.2 (i).

22. Prove Theorem 4.1.2 (ii).

23. Complete the missing details in the proof of Theorem 4.1.2 (iii).

24. Prove Theorem 4.1.2 (iv).

25. Establish a formula for differentiating the following functions:

$$f(x) = x^n \ (n \in \mathbf{N}), \ \sqrt{x}, \ \frac{1}{x^2}, \ \frac{1}{\sqrt{x}}, \ \frac{1}{x\sqrt{x}}.$$

26. Let $f(x) = x^{1/n}$, $x > 0$ and n a fixed member of $\mathbf{N}$. Show that f is differentiable for each $x > 0$, and find a formula for f'.

27. If $f: \mathbf{R} \to \mathbf{R}$ is differentiable at a, show that

$$f'(a) = \lim_{n \to \infty} \left(n\left\{ f\left(a + \frac{1}{n}\right) - f(a) \right\} \right).$$

Show by an example, that the existence of the limit on the right-hand side does not imply the existence of the derivative.

28. Let f be differentiable at x. Show that

$$\lim_{h \to 0} \frac{f(x + h) - f(x - h)}{2h} = f'(x).$$

29. Let $\alpha(h)$ be a nonzero function of h having limit 0 as $h \to 0$. Show that if f is differentiable at x, then

$$\lim_{h \to 0} \frac{f(x + \alpha(h)) - f(x)}{\alpha(h)} = f'(x).$$

30. Let f be differentiable at x and $\alpha, \beta \in \mathbf{R}$. Show that

$$\lim_{h \to 0} \frac{f(x - \alpha h) - f(x - \beta h)}{h} = (\alpha + \beta) f'(x).$$

31. Let $x(t)$ and $y(t)$, $t \in [0,1]$ be two functions from $[0,1]$ to $\mathbf{R}$. The set

$$C = \{(x(t), y(t)) : t \in [0,1]\}$$

will generate a graph in the plane which we will refer to as the **plane curve** C with **parameterization** $x(t)$, $y(t)$ whenever x and y are continuous on $[0,1]$. Define the concept of derivative at a point on a plane curve C in such a way that when this derivative exists, it will be the slope of the tangent to the curve at that point.

32. Let C be a plane curve and suppose that $x(t)$ and $y(t)$ are differentiable functions of t with $x'(t) \neq 0$ for $t \in [0,1]$. Show that the tangent to C exists at each point. Moreover, show that if $\dfrac{y'(t)}{x'(t)}$ is a constant, then C is a straight line.

33. Consider $f(x) = \sqrt{1 - x^2}$, $x \in [0,1]$. Show that $f'(x)$, $x \in [0,1]$ is the slope of a line perpendicular to the radius joining $(0,0)$ and $(x, f(x))$. What can you conclude from this computation?

34. The derivative of f' is called the **second-order derivative** of f (denoted by f''). Similarly all the **higher order derivatives** f''', f'''', $f^{(v)}$, ..., $f^{(n)}$ are defined. If f and g have second-order derivatives at a point a, prove that

    $$(f \cdot g)''(a) = f''(a)g(a) + 2f'(a)g'(a) + f(a)g''(a).$$

    More generally (stating the conditions needed) prove **Leibnitz's Formula** for the nth order derivative of the product $f \cdot g$:

    $$(f \cdot g)^{(n)}(a) = \sum_{k=0}^{k=n} \binom{n}{k} f^{(k)}(a)g^{(n-k)}(a)$$

    (where $f^{(0)} = f$, $g^{(0)} = g$).

35. Obtain the nth-derivative $f^{(n)}$ for the following functions: (You may use the fact that $(\ln x)' = \dfrac{1}{x}$ and $(e^x)' = e^x$.)

    (a) $f(x) = x^m$, $m > n$;

    (b) $f(x) = \dfrac{1}{x}$;

    (c) $f(x) = \ln x$;

    (d) $f(x) = x^m \ln x$, $m > n$;

    (e) $e^x \cos x$.

36. Sketch the graph of the following function and discuss its differentiability at the point $x = 0$:

    $$f(x) = \begin{cases} 0, & x = 0 \\ \dfrac{1}{4^{n-1}} - x, & \dfrac{1}{2 \cdot 4^{n-1}} \leqslant x \leqslant \dfrac{1}{4^{n-1}} \\ 2\left(x - \dfrac{1}{4^n}\right), & \dfrac{1}{4^n} \leqslant x \leqslant \dfrac{1}{2 \cdot 4^{n-1}} \\ f(-x), & -1 \leqslant x < 0 \end{cases} \quad , \quad n \in \mathbf{N}.$$

37. If f is differentiable on an interval I, must f' be continuous on I?

38. If f' exists and is bounded on A, prove that f is uniformly continuous on A.

39. Prove that if f is differentiable on an interval I and f' is bounded on I, then f satisfies Lipschitz condition (see Exercise 3.5.21) on I.

40. We say that f satisfies **Lipschitz's condition of order** α at $c \in \mathrm{Dmn}\, f$ if there exists a constant $K > 0$ such that $|f(x) - f(c)| \leqslant K|x - c|^\alpha$ for all x in a neighborhood of c, $x \neq c$. If $\alpha > 0$ and f satisfies Lipschitz's condition of order α at c, f is continuous at c, and if $\alpha > 1$, show that f is also differentiable at c. Give an example where f is Lipschitz's condition of order 1, but f' does not exist.

41. Let f and g be thrice differentiable in $\mathbf{R}$, and satisfy the identity $f(x)g(x) = 1$ throughout $\mathbf{R}$. Prove the following (whenever the denominator is nonzero):

    (a) $\dfrac{f'(x)}{f(x)} + \dfrac{g'(x)}{g(x)} = 0;$

    (b) $\dfrac{f''(x)}{f'(x)} - \dfrac{g''(x)}{g'(x)} = 2\dfrac{f'(x)}{f(x)};$

    (c) $\dfrac{f'''(x)}{f'(x)} - \dfrac{g'''(x)}{g'(x)} = 3\dfrac{f''(x)}{f(x)} - \dfrac{g''(x)}{g'(x)} + 3\dfrac{f'(x)g''(x)}{f(x)g'(x)}.$

4.2 CONTINUITY OF THE DERIVATIVE, THE DIFFERENTIAL, AND THE CHAIN RULE

Once we have settled on the derivative as a useful tool, the problem becomes one of finding the derivative of an arbitrary function. Merely applying the definition is not particularly satisfactory. Certain general methods were developed in Exercises 20 through 26 of the last section, but these do not generate derivatives for much more than the polynomials and rational functions. The most powerful single tool we have for obtaining derivatives rests in the Chain Rule, and the purpose of this section is to develop this result.

Our first result in this section relates the two familiar notions, namely continuity and differentiability:

Theorem 4.2.1. If f is differentiable at x, then f is continuous at x.

Proof. Let f be differentiable at x. Then, given $\epsilon > 0$, there exists $\delta > 0$ such that $|h| < \delta$ implies $|\alpha(h)| < \epsilon$, where

$$\alpha(h) = \frac{f(x + h) - f(x)}{h} - f'(x).$$

Let h be small enough to guarantee that $\alpha(h) < 1$. For such an h, we have

$$|f(x + h) - f(x)| < |f'(x)h + \alpha(h) h|$$
$$< |f'(x) + 1| \cdot |h|.$$

As $h \to 0$, the right-hand side must also approach the limit 0 (**WHY?**). Thus,

$$\lim_{h \to 0} f(x+h) = f(x),$$

which is another way of expressing the fact that f is continuous at x. $\square$

Discussion. The proof is a straightforward application of the two definitions. The theorem implies that the condition for differentiability is much more stringent than that for continuity. The example of the function $f(x) = |x|$ at $x = 0$, considered in section 4.1 reveals that a continuous function need not be differentiable. Thus, differentiable functions form a proper subclass of the class of all continuous functions. Geometrically speaking, for differentiability the graph of the function should not only be continuous, but, it must also be 'smooth'. While the absolute value function possesses only one point of nondifferentiability, there exist real-valued functions which are continuous everywhere on the real line but differentiable not even at a single point. One such example, due to Weierstrass, is discussed in Chapter 9 (Example 9.1.8).

There are two details contained in the proof worthy of further consideration. First, we examine the defining equation for $\alpha(h)$. This equation can be rewritten in the form

$$\alpha(h) = \frac{f(x+h) - f(x)}{h} - \frac{f'(x)h}{h}.$$

Written in this form, it is clear that the two denominators represent a change, or **increment** in the independent variable, that is, $h = (x+h) - x = \Delta x$ (we shall denote the change in a quantity x by Δx). The numerator of the first term also represents an increment, $f(x+h) - f(x) = \Delta f$. It is not so obvious, but the second term, $f'(x)h$, is an increment as well. To see this we define $g_x(h)$ by

$$g_x(h) = f'(x)h + f(x) = f'(x)((x+h) - x) + f(x).$$

Now $f'(x)h$ is seen to be given by

$$f'(x)h = g_x(h) - g_x(0) = f'(x)((x+h) - x) + f(x) - f(x).$$

As shown in Figure 4.2.1, this latter increment, associated with the function g_x, amounts to an increment determined by the tangent to the graph of f at the point $(x, f(x))$. Since the graph of g_x is a straight line, the increment in the numerator, Δg_x, is linear. Thus, we see that $\alpha(x)$ is composed of two terms, both of which are ratios of increments. The first, $\dfrac{\Delta f}{\Delta x}$, is the ratio of the change in the function for a given change in the independent variable. The second, $\dfrac{\Delta g_x}{\Delta x}$, is the ratio of the same change in the independent variable, to a change determined by the linear function g_x. Since g_x is a linear function, this latter ratio is a constant, independent of h. We see then, that $\alpha(h)$ is simply the difference between these two ratios of increments.

The second point concerns the following inequality

$$|f(x+h) - f(x)| < |f'(x) + 1| \cdot |h|.$$

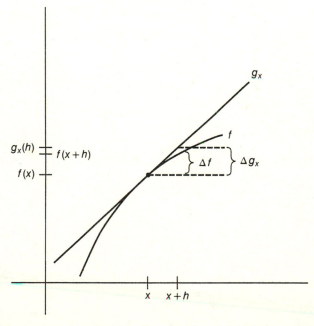

Figure 4.2.1 Increment associated with g_x is approximately the increment determined by the tangent line.

Observe that the right-hand side is linear in h. (Recall that x is fixed.) What this is saying is that Δf is approximately linear. Another way of saying this is that near x, f is approximately a straight line. What straight line? Why, the tangent line to the graph at $(x, f(x))$! These ideas are made precise in the corollary which follows. □

Corollary 1. Let f be differentiable at x. Then there is a function $\alpha(h)$, with limit 0 as $h \to 0$, defined in a neighborhood of 0 such that

$$f(x+h) - f(x) = f'(x)h + \alpha(h)h.$$

Proof. Obvious from Theorem 4.2.1. □

Discussion. Consider the following form of the equality, which is the subject of the corollary

$$f(x+h) = f'(x)h + f(x) + \alpha(h)h.$$

If we drop the term $\alpha(h)h$, which is negligible when h is sufficiently small due to the fact that both h and $\alpha(h)$ are tending to 0, we get

$$f(x+h) \approx f'(x)h + f(x),$$

[the symbol $\approx$ means 'approximately equal to'] which expresses the fact that if h is small, then $f(x+h)$ is almost a linear function of the increment $h = (x + h) - x$. This is essentially the same point as made above, except that we have specifically developed an approximate linear formulation for $f(x+h)$. □

The idea of using the derivative at x to provide a linear approximation to f near x permits us to obtain approximate values for functions near known values for these same functions. These ideas form the basis for our next definition.

Definition. If f is differentiable at x, the **differential** of f at x is the function $d_x f : \mathbf{R} \to \mathbf{R}$ defined by $d_x f(h) = f'(x)h$ for $h \in \mathbf{R}$.

Discussion. Note that in the above definition, if we take the function, $f(x) = x$, then $f'(x) = 1$, so that $d_x f(h) = 1 \cdot h = h$, showing that the differential of the function x at the point x is the identity function. Since h is the increment in x, we can say that the differential of x is just the increment Δx. By abbreviating $d_x x$ simply as dx, we are stating that $dx = h$. Then, for $y = f(x)$, what is $d_x y$ (or dy for short)? The definition tells us that this quantity is precisely $f'(x)h = f'(x)\,dx$ since $h = dx$. In other words, we obtain the identity $dy = f'(x)\,dx$ or restated, $\dfrac{dy}{dx} = f'(x)$. In this formula, $\dfrac{dy}{dx}$ is a true fraction, which is just the quotient of two differentials. Hence, it is not surprising that $\dfrac{dy}{dx}$ is alternate notation for the derivative $f'(x)$ of the function, $y = f(x)$, with respect to x. In the sequel, we will often use df instead of dy to denote the differential of the dependent variable.

While the increment h in x is the differential dx itself, the increment, $\Delta f = f(x+h) - f(x)$, in the function f is not the differential, df, but the quantity $f'(x)h + \alpha(h)h = df + \alpha(h)h$. Since for small enough increments h, the quantity $\alpha(h)h$

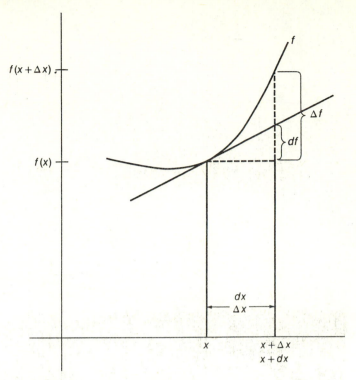

Figure 4.2.2   Graph illustrating the differential df and the increment Δf.

is negligibly small, we see that $f(x+h) - f(x) \approx df$, provided h is very small. This is most clearly seen in a picture, as in Figure 4.2.2. In summary then, the differential enables us to find approximate values for the expression $f(x+h) - f(x)$, for any differentiable function, for sufficiently small values of the increment h.   □

Before continuing toward our goal we want to give a concrete application of the use of the tangent line (differential) as a method of approximation.

EXAMPLE 1
_____

Develop a method for finding approximate solutions to an equation $f(x) = 0$ which can be applied to functions differentiable on **R** for which it is known that solutions to the equation exist.

Solution.   Let us suppose that we have an approximate solution and ask how we could find a better approximate solution. Consider the picture presented in Figure 4.2.3. If x_n is our present solution, and $x = a$ is an actual solution, it is apparent that if we merely slide down the tangent line to x_{n+1} we will have an even better approximation to a.

Recall that the tangent line to f is given by

$$g_{x_n}(x) = f'(x_n)(x - x_n) + f(x_n).$$

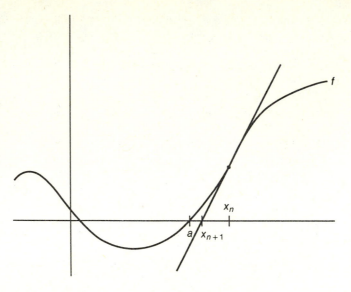

Figure 4.2.3   Approximate solution of $f(x) = 0$ (Newton's method).

Since x_{n+1} is defined by the fact that $g_{x_n}(x_{n+1}) = 0$, our task is to solve a linear equation. Thus, we set

$$f'(x_n)(x_{n+1} - x_n) + f(x_n) = 0,$$

which leads to

$$x_{n+1} = x_n - \frac{f(x_n)}{f'(x_n)}.$$

Evidently, this method can be applied repetitively to find an even better solution to the problem.   □

Discussion.   The method for solving equations presented above is known as Newton's method, after its inventor, Sir Isaac Newton. While it is impossible to reconstruct the precise reasoning which led him to the method, it is likely that it was based on consideration of a picture similar to that presented in Figure 4.2.2.

To illustrate how the method works, consider the polynomial function given by $f(x) = x^5 + 2x + 1$. It is easily checked that this has a root. If we take $x_0 = 0$ as the first approximate solution (0 is really easy to compute with) we see that $f(0) = 1$ and $f'(0) = 2$. But $x_1 = -\frac{1}{2}$ and $f(x_1) = -\frac{1}{32}$, which is a considerably better solution. Additional iterations yield even better results as the reader will find from Exercise 1.

The reader may well wonder to what degree the method depends on the fact that the function of interest yields a picture similar to that presented in Figure 4.2.2. An example of an unsuitable function is presented in Exercise 3, although no sensible mathematician would ever use Newton's method for this equation. In general, the effectiveness of the procedure depends on both the nature of the function and the given point at which an approximation is being computed. Much interesting and illustrative mathematics arises from Newton's method and we refer the interested reader to Saari and Urenko (1984)† for a survey of this area. ☐

We now turn to the task of proving the most important result of this section, namely the Chain Rule for differentiating composite functions.

Theorem 4.2.2 (Chain Rule). Let g be differentiable at x and f differentiable at $y = g(x)$. Then, $f \circ g$ is differentiable at x and

$$(f \circ g)'(x) = f'(g(x))g'(x).$$

Proof. Since g is differentiable, setting $k = g(x + h) - g(x)$, we observe that $k = g'(x)h + \alpha(h)$, where $\alpha(h)$ approaches 0 with h. Now, letting $y = g(x)$, consider the numerator of the difference quotient:

$$(f \circ g)(x+h) - (f \circ g)(x) = f(g(x+h)) - f(g(x))$$
$$= f(y+k) - f(y)$$
$$= f'(y)k + \alpha_1(k)k$$

where $\alpha_1(k)$ is found by the corollary and $\alpha_1(k) \to 0$ as $k \to 0$. Now, substituting the expression for k, we have

$$(f \circ g)(x+h) - (f \circ g)(x) = f'(y)(g(x+h) - g(x)) + \alpha_1(k)(g(x+h) - g(x)).$$

We have then that

$$\frac{(f \circ g)(x+h) - (f \circ g)(x)}{h} = f'(y)\frac{g(x+h) - g(x)}{h} + \alpha_1(k)\frac{g(x+h) - g(x)}{h}.$$

If we let $h \to 0$, then the first quantity on the right-hand side tends to $f'(y)g'(x) = f'(g(x))g'(x)$ and the second quantity tends to 0 since $\alpha_1(k) \to 0$ and $\frac{g(x+h) - g(x)}{h}$ tends to $g'(x)$. It is immediate that $f \circ g$ is differentiable at x with the derivative shown. ☐

Discussion. We have not formulated the argument above in terms of $\epsilon - \delta$. Rather we have adopted a looser approach which can be turned into an $\epsilon - \delta$ argument with little difficulty. Note that the argument uses continuity in two ways: first, we use the fact that the composition of continuous functions is again continuous, and second, we use the corollary to the fact that differentiability implies continuity. To write out an $\epsilon - \delta$ proof, one would have to spell out the application of these facts clearly, and we ask the reader to do so in Exercise 5.

The main use of the Chain Rule is in finding derivatives for composite functions which look very complex. Several applications appear in the exercises. ☐

A theorem which is useful in connection with the Chain Rule is:

† Saari, Donald G., and John B. Urenko. Newton's method, circle maps, and chaotic motion. *The American Math. Monthly*, **91**, No. 1, 3–17 (1984).

Theorem 4.2.3. Let f be strictly increasing on (a, b) with inverse g. If f is differentiable at $x \in (a, b)$, $f'(x) \neq 0$, and $y = f(x)$, then g is differentiable at y and $g'(y) = \dfrac{1}{f'(x)}$.

Proof. For small h, consider the difference quotient

$$\frac{g(y+h) - g(y)}{h} = \frac{g(y+h) - g(y)}{(y+h) - y}$$

$$= \frac{(x+k) - x}{f(x+k) - f(x)}$$

$$= \frac{1}{\dfrac{f(x+k) - f(x)}{(x+k) - x}}$$

for some k which depends on h. Now as $k \to 0$, $h \to 0$ also. Since $f'(x) \neq 0$, the result follows by allowing $k \to 0$.   □

Discussion. One would like to obtain this result by a direct application of the Chain Rule; however, not all the hypotheses for that theorem are met. Again, we shall ask the reader to rewrite the proof in terms of ϵ, δ in Exercise 6. Lastly, note that the theorem gives us the equation

$$g'(y) = \frac{1}{f'(x)}$$

which expresses the derivative of g as a function of x, the range variable, rather than as a function of y, the domain variable. To correct this, we can use the fact that $x = g(y)$, to obtain

$$g'(y) = \frac{1}{f'(g(y))}.$$

Loosely stated, this amounts to the equation $\dfrac{dx}{dy} = \dfrac{1}{\dfrac{dy}{dx}}$, where $x = g(y)$ and $y = f(x)$.   □

EXERCISES

1. For the function $f(x) = x^5 + 2x + 1$, continue the process begun in the discussion following Example 1 to find x_2 and x_3.

2. Find an approximate solution to $x^5 + x^3 + x + 1 = 0$.

3. Show that Newton's method fails to produce better approximate solutions to the equation $x^{1/3} = 0$ for any value of $x_n \neq 0$.

4. Formalize the proof of Theorem 4.2.1 in terms of $\epsilon - \delta$.

5. Formalize the proof of the Chain Rule (Theorem 4.2.2) in terms of $\epsilon - \delta$.

6. Formalize the proof of Theorem 4.2.3 in terms of $\epsilon - \delta$

7. Give an example of functions f and g such that $f \circ g$ is differentiable at x, g is differentiable at x, but f is not differentiable at $y = g(x)$.

8. Use the formula for inverses to find the derivative of $f(x) = x^{1/4}$, $x > 0$.

9. Use the formula for inverses to find the derivative of $f(x) = x^{1/n}$, $n \neq 0$ and $n \in \mathbf{Z}$ on an appropriate domain.

10. Find the derivative of $f(x) = x^q$, $q \in \mathbf{Q}$ on $x \in \mathbf{R}^+$.

11. Show that the function $f(x)$ defined by

$$f(x) = \begin{cases} x^2 \sin \dfrac{1}{x}, & x \in \mathbf{R} \sim 0 \\ 0, & x = 0 \end{cases}$$

is differentiable everywhere but does not have a continuous derivative.

12. If $t > 0$ is a rational number, and $f: \mathbf{R} \to \mathbf{R}$ is defined by

$$f(x) = \begin{cases} x^t \sin \dfrac{1}{x}, & x \neq 0 \\ 0, & x = 0 \end{cases}$$

determine the values of t for which $f'(0)$ exists.

13. Let f be defined on $\mathbf{R}$ by

$$f(x) = \begin{cases} x^3, & x < 2 \\ ax + b, & 2 \leqslant x \end{cases}$$

for some choice of $a, b \in \mathbf{R}$. Show that a and b can be chosen so that f has a continuous derivative on $\mathbf{R}$.

14. Let $f: D \to E$, $g: E \to F$, and $h: F \to \mathbf{R}$ be such that f is differentiable at $a \in D$, g is differentiable at $f(a) \in E$, and h is differentiable at $(g \circ f)(a) \in F$. Prove that $h \circ (g \circ f)$ is differentiable at a. Find the derivative $(h \circ (g \circ f))'$.

15. Obtain a formula for the second derivative of $(f \circ g)$, stating the conditions needed.

16. If f and g are differentiable, obtain the derivatives of the following (stating the conditions required):
    (a) f^n;
    (b) $\dfrac{1}{f}$;
    (c) $\sin f$;
    (d) $\ln f$;
    (e) e^f;
    (f) $f^m g^n$;
    (g) $\left[\dfrac{f}{g}\right]^{p/q}$, $\left(\dfrac{p}{q} \in \mathbf{Q}\right)$.

17. If f is differentiable, what can you say about the differentiability of $|f|$?

18. Use mathematical induction to extend the Chain Rule to differentiate $f_1 \circ f_2 \circ \dots \circ f_n$.

19. Suppose that f has a left-hand derivative at x. Show that f must exhibit left-hand continuity at x.

20. Assuming that there exists a function $L: (0, \infty) \to \mathbf{R}$ such that $L'(x) = \dfrac{1}{x}$, calculate the derivative of the following:

(a) $L(3x + 5)$;

(b) $[L(x^3)]^5$;

(c) $L(\alpha x)$, $\alpha > 0$;

(d) $L(L(L(x)))$, where $L(x) > 0$, $L(L(x)) > 0$.

21. Let $t: \left[-\dfrac{\pi}{2}, \dfrac{\pi}{2}\right] \to \mathbf{R}$ be such that $t'(x) = \dfrac{1}{1 + x^2}$. Find the derivatives of the following:

(a) $t(1 + x^2)$;

(b) $t(t(t(3x + 4)))$;

(c) $\dfrac{1}{t\left(\dfrac{1}{x}\right)} + t\left(\dfrac{1}{x}\right)$.

22. Let $s: (-1, 1) \to \left[-\dfrac{\pi}{2}, \dfrac{\pi}{2}\right]$ be such that $s'(x) = \dfrac{1}{\sqrt{1 - x^2}}$. Find the derivatives of the following:

(a) $\sin s(x^2)$;

(b) $\dfrac{1}{s(s(s(x)))}$;

(c) $\ln \tan s\left(\dfrac{1}{1 + x^2}\right)$.

23. Denoting $f''(x)$ by $\dfrac{d^2 y}{dx^2}$, show that Theorem 4.2.3 does not hold for second derivatives, that is, $\dfrac{d^2 x}{dy^2} \neq \dfrac{1}{\dfrac{d^2 y}{dx^2}}$.

4.3 THE MEAN VALUE THEOREM

One of the most useful results in the theory of differentiation is the Mean Value Theorem. Its consequences are many, as we shall see throughout the remainder of this book. Moreover, the result is essentially intuitive. The essentials to this theorem stem from the idea of local maximum and minimum points on a graph. We begin by studying these concepts.

Let f be defined on $[a, b]$ and $x_0 \in [a, b]$. The point x_0 is called a **maximum point** if $f(x_0) \geq f(x)$ for all $x \in [a, b]$. Such a maximum can be **strict** or **weak** depending on whether the inequality can be made strict or not. The value $f(x_0)$ is called a **maximum** for f on $[a, b]$ provided x_0 is a maximum point. Again, we can have strict or weak maxima. The point $x_0 \in [a, b]$ is called a **local maximum point** if there is a neighborhood $(x_0 - c, x_0 + c)$, $c > 0$, around x_0 such that $f(x_0) \geq f(x)$ for each $x \in (x_0 - c, x_0 + c)$. Similarly, the concepts of **minimum** and **local minimum** can be defined. These ideas are illustrated in Figure 4.3.1.

Theorem 4.3.1. Let f be defined and continuous on $[a, b]$. If f has a local maximum (minimum) at $x_0 \in (a, b)$ and if f is differentiable at x_0, then $f'(x_0) = 0$.

Proof. Let us suppose that f has a local maximum at x_0. Then, if $h < 0$,

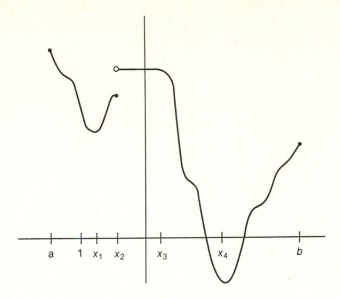

Figure 4.3.1 Note that a is both a maximum and a local maximum point; x_1 is a local minimum point; every point in (x_2, x_3) is both a local minimum and a local maximum; x_4 is a minimum and a local minimum; and b is a local maximum.

Proof. Let us suppose that f has a local maximum at x_0. Then, if $h < 0$,

$$\frac{f(x_0 + h) - f(x_0)}{h} \geqslant 0$$

since the numerator and the denominator are both negative. On the other hand, for $h > 0$, the numerator is still negative while the denominator is now positive, whence the difference quotient is now negative. By the result on one-sided derivatives (Exercise 4.1.16), we conclude that $f'(x_0) = 0$. The corresponding result for local minimum is left to the reader (Exercise 1). □

Discussion. The result is truly simple in nature. All one has to do is to write down the difference quotients on each side of the point x_0 and look at the sign. Since they have opposite signs, the left and the right side derivatives of f at x_0 are of opposite sign. But f being differentiable, the two one-sided derivatives must coincide. This can happen only if $f'(x_0) = 0$. Note that there is no requirement of continuity, except at x_0. The function in Exercise 4.1.8 shows that x_0 may be the only point of continuity or differentiability in the domain of the function. □

Our next theorem is the precursor to the so-called Mean Value Theorem and is known as **Rolle's Theorem**.

Theorem 4.3.2. Let f be continuous on $[a, b]$, $a < b$ and differentiable on (a, b). If $f(a) = f(b)$, there is a point $x_0 \in (a, b)$ such that $f'(x_0) = 0$.

Proof.   Since f is continuous on $[a, b]$, by Theorem 3.6.1, f attains both its maximum and its minimum. If both of these values coincide with $f(a)$, then f reduces to the constant function $f(x) = f(a)$ throughout $[a, b]$ and the result is immediate. If one of them, say the minimum, is different from $f(a)$, then there exists $x_0 \in (a, b)$ such that $f(x_0) \leqslant f(x)$ for all $x \in (a, b)$ (**WHY?**). Since x_0 is a local minimum point and since by hypothesis, f is differentiable at x_0, we must have $f'(x_0) = 0$ by our last result.   □

Discussion.   Rolle's Theorem, proved above is simply an application of Theorem 4.3.1 and the fact that a function that is continuous on a closed bounded interval must attain both its maximum and its minimum. Of course, this latter result has at its heart the Supremum Principle. The reader should make note of the hypothesis of the theorem: continuity on the closed interval with differentiability on the interior of that interval, since this will be the hypothesis required in all our applications of the Mean Value Theorem. Lastly, we note the geometry of Rolle's Theorem. Observe that the difference quotient evaluated between a and b satisfies

$$\frac{f(b) - f(a)}{b - a} = 0.$$

Thus, if we draw a secant line joining $(a, f(a))$ with $(b, f(b))$ we get a line whose slope is 0. The theorem then asserts that there ought to be a point in between, where this slope is actually achieved as a value for the derivative, and in this particular case, the tangent is horizontal (see Figure 4.3.2). The existence of this point is in fact guaranteed, but only if all the hypotheses of the theorem are satisfied, as our exercises make clear.

The point x_0 can be thought as providing a 'mean value' for the derivative in this special situation. The idea extends naturally to the **Mean Value Theorem** which is our next result.   □

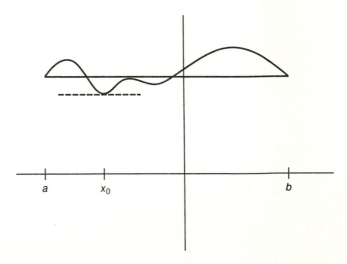

Figure 4.3.2   Graph illustrating Theorem 4.3.2 (Rolle's Theorem).

Theorem 4.3.3. Let f be continuous on $[a, b]$ where $a < b$ and differentiable in (a, b). Then there exists $x_0 \in (a, b)$ such that

$$f'(x_0) = \frac{f(b) - f(a)}{b - a}.$$

Proof. Define a function F on $[a, b]$ by

$$F(x) = f(x) - \frac{f(b) - f(a)}{b - a}(x - a) - f(a).$$

It is immediate that F is continuous on $[a, b]$, differentiable on (a, b) (**WHY?**) and further, $F(a) = F(b) = 0$. Thus, by Theorem 4.3.2, there exists an $x_0 \in (a, b)$ such that $F'(x_0) = 0$. But, a simple calculation shows that

$$F'(x_0) = f'(x_0) - \frac{f(b) - f(a)}{b - a}.$$

Hence, the number x_0 satisfies the conclusion of the theorem. $\qquad\qquad \square$

Discussion. The proof given above is completely trivial, once we have the function F. In fact, the construction of F is not mere trickery. Consider Figure 4.3.3. We have f together with the straight line corresponding to the secant joining $(a, f(a))$ with $(b, f(b))$. Let g denote the function whose graph is this indicated straight line. From the picture, we see that $(f - g)$ must satisfy $(f - g)(a) = (f - g)(b)$, since $f(a) = g(a)$ and $f(b) = g(b)$. Moreover, $f - g$ is continuous on $[a, b]$, differentiable on (a, b) whence we can apply Rolle's Theorem. Lastly, when $(f - g)'$ equals 0, the value of the derivative of f must equal the value of the derivative of g which is the slope of the straight line and is given by evaluating the difference quotient

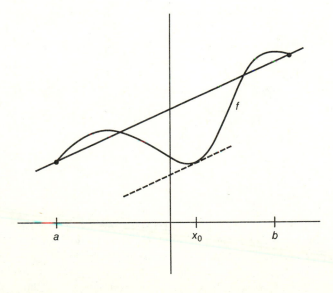

Figure 4.3.3 Graph illustrating Theorem 4.3.3 (Mean Value Theorem).

at a and b! If we now write out g and $f - g$, we get, using the secant form of the equation of a line

$$\frac{y - f(a)}{x - a} = \frac{f(b) - f(a)}{b - a}$$

whence

$$g(x) = y = \frac{f(b) - f(a)}{b - a}(x - a) + f(a)$$

and

$$(f - g)(x) = f(x) - \frac{f(b) - f(a)}{b - a}(x - a) - f(a) = F(x).$$

From the figure, we see that at x_0, the slope of the tangent to the curve is the same as that of the secant line, which makes the two lines parallel. The tangent line to the curve is indicated by the dashed line. To conclude, if we set out to find a function which naturally incorporates the function, f, together with the linear function defined by the secant joining $(a, f(a))$ with $(b, f(b))$ and which in addition satisfies the hypotheses of Rolle's Theorem, we are led to F and the proof of the theorem follows.

The principle contained in this theorem can be adopted to manufacture many interesting and useful Mean Value Theorems. The strategy is very simple. If a 'nice' (i.e., continuous in a closed interval, and differentiable in its interior) function vanishes at two points, then the derivative must vanish somewhere in between. Using this technique, we ask the reader to arrive at several Mean Value Theorems, a project that we pursue in the exercises. □

EXAMPLE 1

Use the Mean Value Theorem to estimate the sixth root of 65.

Solution. If f is differentiable on (a, b), then for some x_0

$$f(b) = f(a) + f'(x_0)(b - a).$$

In the present instance we let $f(x) = x^{1/6}$. This function is differentiable on $(64,65)$ and its derivative is given by $f'(x) = \dfrac{1}{6x^{5/6}}$. Since f' achieves an absolute maximum at $x = 64$, we have

$$2 < 65^{1/6} < 2 + \frac{1}{192}.$$

□

Discussion. The reader may well wonder about the relevance of this type of calculation in an age when a programmable calculator can be purchased for no more than 50 dollars. The answer lies not in the fact that the reader will be likely to avail himself of this calculation, instead of employing the calculator on the desk. Rather it lets in the fact that the use of this type of approximation is at the root of a great deal of numerical mathematics. We have already seen this in Newton's method. We will see it again in a more general form in Taylor's Theorem which also goes by the name of the Generalized Mean Value Theorem. And we remark that these approximation methods are at the heart of many other numerical methods which occur in differential equations and other branches of applied mathematics. Thus, we are dealing with a simple, but extremely important idea whose time has not passed.   □

The following form of the Mean Value Theorem, known as Cauchy's Mean Value Theorem, is an instance of this kind of argument. This theorem is indeed a generalization of the Mean Value Theorem.

Theorem 4.3.4 (Cauchy's Mean Value Theorem).   Let f and g be both continuous in $[a, b]$ with $a < b$, and differentiable in (a, b). If $g'(x) \neq 0$ for all $x \in (a, b)$, then $g(a) \neq g(b)$ and there exists $x_0 \in (a, b)$ such that

$$\frac{f(b) - f(a)}{g(b) - g(a)} = \frac{f'(x_0)}{g'(x_0)}.$$

Proof.   First note that $g(a) = g(b)$ contradicts Rolle's Theorem. Now, define F on $[a, b]$ by

$$F(x) = f(x) - f(a) - \frac{f(b) - f(a)}{g(b) - g(a)}(g(x) - g(a)).$$

It is immediate that F satisfies the hypotheses of Rolle's Theorem. Thus, there exists $x_0 \in (a, b)$ such that $F'(x_0) = 0$. The reader may now check that x_0 has the required property.   □

Discussion.   The proof given here is similar to that of the Mean Value Theorem 4.3.3. Once we specify the 'magic function' F which satisfies the hypothesis of Rolle's Theorem, the proof follows immediately. The reader should understand clearly how to construct such a function. Exercises 29, 30, and 32 are such instances.   □

EXERCISES

1. Complete the proof of Theorem 4.3.1.

2. Let $f(x) = x^3 - 2x$, $x \in \mathbf{R}$. Find all local extrema for f.

3. Let $f(x) = x^3 - 3x^2 - x + 3$, $x \in [-1, 3]$. Find the value of x_0 which will satisfy Rolle's Theorem.

4. Let $f(x) = x^3 - 4x^2 + 3x + 1$, $x \in [0, 2]$. Find the value of x_0 which will satisfy Mean Value Theorem.

5. Let $f(x) = 4x^2$, $g(x) = x^3 + 1$, $x \in [0, 2]$. Find the value of x_0 which will satisfy Cauchy's Mean Value Theorem.

6. If f is continuous on $[a, b]$, differentiable on (a, b), and if $f'(x) = 0$ throughout (a, b), prove that f is a constant on $[a, b]$.

7. Let f and g satisfy the hypothesis of the Mean Value Theorem on $[a, b]$, $a < b$. Show that if $f'(x) = g'(x)$ for all $x \in (a, b)$, then there is a constant C such that $f(x) = g(x) + C$ for all $x \in (a, b)$.

8. If f is twice differentiable on an interval I, and if $f''(x) = 0$ throughout the interval, show that $f(x) = kx + l$ for suitable constants k and l. If f is thrice differentiable on I and if $f'''(x) = 0$ on I, what is the form of f in the interval I?

9. Let $f: \mathbf{R} \to \mathbf{R}$ be such that $|f(x) - f(y)| \leq (x - y)^2$ for all x, $y \in \mathbf{R}$. Must f reduce to a constant?

10. Let f be continuous on $[a, b]$ and let $y \in (a, b)$. If $f'(y)$ exists for each $y \in (a, b)$, $y \neq x$, and if $\lim_{y \to x} f'(y)$ exists, prove that $f'(x)$ exists.

11. Give an example of a function f that is differentiable on all of $\mathbf{R}$ but having a point x_0 such that $\lim_{x \to x_0} f'(x) \neq f'(x_0)$.

12. Suppose f is differentiable on $[a, b]$. Show that f' must assume every value between its extremes on this interval. Deduce that if f is differentiable on $[a, b]$, then f' can not have discontinuities of the first kind.

13. Let f be defined by

$$f(x) = \begin{cases} x^2 \left| \sin \dfrac{1}{x^2} \right|, & x \neq 0 \\[2mm] 0, & x = 0. \end{cases}$$

Show that f has an absolute minimum at $x = 0$, that f is differentiable at $x = 0$, but that f' does not have a simple change of sign at $x = 0$.

14. Let f be continuous on $[0,a]$ with $f(0) = 0$. Show that if f is differentiable on $(0,a)$ and f' is positive and increasing, then $\dfrac{f(x)}{x}$ is also increasing.

15. Give an example of a bounded, monotonically increasing, differentiable function having the property that $\lim_{x \to \infty} f'(x) \neq 0$.

16. As shown in Example 1 the Mean Value Theorem can be used to form estimates for quantities like $28^{1/3}$, $17^{1/4}$, and $\sin 61°$. Find estimates for these quantities.

17. Let f be increasing on $[a, b]$. Show that if f is differentiable at $x_0 \in [a, b]$, then $f'(x_0) \geq 0$. If f is strictly increasing, can we conclude that $f'(x_0) > 0$?

18. Give an example of a function which is continuous on $[0,2]$, differentiable on $(0,1) \cup (1,2)$, and takes the same value at 0 and 2, but which does not satisfy Rolle's Theorem.

19. Give an example of a function which is differentiable on $(0,1)$ and such that $f(0) = f(1)$, but which does not satisfy Rolle's Theorem.

20. Give a careful definition of minimum and local minimum. Write out a rigorous proof of Theorem 4.3.1 assuming a local minimum.

21. Fill in the missing details in the proofs of Theorems 4.3.3 and 4.3.4.

22. Let f satisfy the hypothesis of the Mean Value Theorem on $[a, b]$ and suppose that $f'(x) > 0$ for all $x \in (a, b)$. Prove that f is strictly increasing.

23. Let f and g satisfy the hypothesis of the Mean Value Theorem on $[a, b]$. Show that if $g(a) \neq g(b)$ and f' and g' are not simultaneously zero, then there exists $x_0 \in (a, b)$ such that

$$\frac{f'(x_0)}{g'(x_0)} = \frac{f(b) - f(a)}{g(b) - g(a)}.$$

24. Explain the fallacy involved in the following proof of Theorem 4.3.4:

$$\frac{f(b) - f(a)}{g(b) - g(a)} = \frac{\dfrac{f(b) - f(a)}{b - a}}{\dfrac{g(b) - g(a)}{b - a}} = \frac{f'(x_0)}{g'(x_0)}$$

invoking Theorem 4.3.3.

25. If $a_i \in \mathbf{R}$, $0 \leqslant i \leqslant n$, and if

$$a_0 + \frac{a_1}{2} + \cdots + \frac{a_{n-1}}{n} + \frac{a_n}{n+1} = 0,$$

show that the polynomial $a_n x^n + a_{n-1} x^{n-1} + \cdots + a_1 x + a_0$ has at least one root in $(0,1)$.

26. Let f be defined in $(0,1]$ and possess a bounded derivative in that interval. Show that the sequence $\{a_n\}$ where $a_n = f\left(\dfrac{1}{n}\right)$ converges.

27. Let f be thrice differentiable in $[a, b]$. If $f(a) = f(b) = f'(a) = f'(b)$, prove that there exists $\xi \in (a, b)$ such that $f'''(\xi) = 0$.

28. Let C be a curve in the plane with derivatives at all $t \in (0,1)$. Show that if $x(a) \neq x(b)$, then for some $t \in (a, b)$, the tangent to C at $(x(t), y(t))$ is parallel to the secant joining $((x(a), y(a))$ with $((x(b), y(b))$.

29. Let

$$F(x) = \begin{vmatrix} f(x) & f(a) & f(b) \\ g(x) & g(a) & g(b) \\ h(x) & h(a) & h(b) \end{vmatrix}$$

where f, g, h satisfy the hypothesis of Mean Value Theorem in $[a, b]$, $a < b$. Prove that there exists $\xi \in (a, b)$ such that

$$F'(\xi) = \begin{vmatrix} f'(\xi) & f(a) & f(b) \\ g'(\xi) & g(a) & g(b) \\ h'(\xi) & h(a) & h(b) \end{vmatrix} = 0.$$

Choosing the functions f, g, and h appropriately, derive Rolle's, Mean Value, and Cauchy's Mean Value Theorems as particular cases of this example.

30. If f and g satisfy the hypothesis of Cauchy's Mean Value Theorem in $[a, b]$, $a < b$, prove that there exists $\xi \in (a, b)$ such that

$$\frac{f(\xi) - f(a)}{g(b) - g(\xi)} = \frac{f'(\xi)}{g'(\xi)}.$$

31. Suppose that f and g satisfy the hypothesis of Cauchy's Mean Value Theorem on (a, ∞). Moreover, suppose that $\lim\limits_{x \to \infty} f(x) = \lim\limits_{x \to \infty} g(x) = 0$. Show that for any $x \in (a, \infty)$, there exists $x_0 \in (a, \infty)$ such that $\dfrac{f(x)}{g(x)} = \dfrac{f'(x_0)}{g'(x_0)}$.

32. If ϕ and ψ are twice differentiable functions in (a, b), prove that there exists $\xi \in (a, b)$ satisfying

$$\frac{\begin{vmatrix} \phi(x) & x & 1 \\ \phi(a) & a & 1 \\ \phi(b) & b & 1 \end{vmatrix}}{\begin{vmatrix} \psi(x) & x & 1 \\ \psi(a) & a & 1 \\ \psi(b) & b & 1 \end{vmatrix}} = \frac{\phi''(\xi)}{\psi''(\xi)}.$$

33. Let f and g be n times differentiable in (a, b) and simultaneously vanish at n distinct points in (a, b). Show that there exists $\xi \in (a, b)$ such that $\dfrac{f(x)}{g(x)} = \dfrac{f^{(n)}(\xi)}{g^{(n)}(\xi)}$.

34. Let f be as in Theorem 4.3.3 and $a, b > 0$. Use Cauchy's Mean Value Theorem to show that there exists $\xi \in (a, b)$ where $f(b) - f(a) = \xi f'(\xi) \ln \dfrac{b}{a}$. Deduce that the sequence $a_n = n[a^{1/n} - 1]$ converges to $\ln a$.

35. Give a geometrical interpretation of Cauchy's Mean Value Theorem.

36. Let f be k times continuously differentiable in (a, b). Prove **Taylor Formula**: there exists $x_0 \in (a, b)$ such that
$$f(b) = f(a) + (b - a)f'(x) + \frac{(b - a)^2}{2}f''(a) + \cdots + \frac{(b - a)^{(k)}}{k!}f^{(k)}(x_0).$$

37. Prove (stating carefully the conditions needed) the following generalization of Cauchy's Mean Value Theorem which guarantees the existence of $\xi \in (a, b)$ such that
$$\frac{f(b) - f(a) - \displaystyle\sum_{k=1}^{n-1} \frac{(b-a)^k}{k!} f^{(k)}(a)}{g(b) - g(a) - \displaystyle\sum_{k=1}^{n-1} \frac{(b-a)^k}{k!} g^{(k)}(a)} = \frac{f^{(n)}(\xi)}{g^{(n)}(\xi)}.$$

38. Let f satisfy conditions of Rolle's Theorem in $[a-h, a+h]$ $(h > 0)$.

    (a) Prove that there exists θ $(0 < \theta < 1)$ such that
    $$\frac{f(a+h) - f(a-h)}{h} = f'(a+\theta h) + f'(a-\theta h).$$

    (b) Prove that there exists ξ $(0 < \xi < 1)$ such that
    $$\frac{f(a+h) - 2f(a) + f(a-h)}{h} = f'(a+\xi h) + f'(a-\xi h).$$

    If $f''(a)$ exists, prove that
    $$f''(a) = \lim_{h \to 0} \frac{f(a+h) - 2f(a) + f(a-h)}{h^2}.$$

39. Show that if f satisfies the hypotheses of the Mean Value Theorem in the interval $[a, a+h]$, then there exists θ, $0 < \theta < 1$ such that $f(a+h) = f(a) + hf'(a+\theta h)$. Obtain a similar statement for Cauchy's Mean Value Theorem in $[a, a+h]$.

40. If f is twice differentiable in $[a, a+h]$, show that there exists θ $(0 < \theta < 1)$ such that
$$f(a+h) = f(a) + hf'(a) + \frac{h^2}{2}f''(a+\theta h).$$

41. If f'' is continuous in $[a, a+h]$ and differentiable in $(a, a+h)$, prove that there exists θ $(0 < \theta < 1)$ satisfying
$$f(a+h) = f(a) + \frac{h}{2}[f'(a) + f'(a+h)] - \frac{h^3}{12}f'''(a+\theta h).$$

42. Assuming f'' is continuous on $[a, b]$, and $a < c < b$, prove that there exists $\xi \in (a, b)$ satisfying
$$(b-a)f(c) - (c-a)f(b) - (b-c)f(a) = \frac{1}{2}(b-a)(c-a)(c-b)f''(\xi).$$

43. P, Q, R are points on the curve $y = f(x)$, whose x-coordinates are x_P, x_Q, x_R, respectively. Assuming that f' exists at all points on the curve, prove that there exists

$z \in (x_P, x_Q) \cup (x_Q, x_R)$ such that

$$\pm \frac{1}{4} f''(z) = \frac{\text{area of triangle } PQR}{(x_P - x_Q)(x_Q - x_R)(x_R - x_P)}.$$

44. The **difference operators** with spacing $h > 0$ are defined by

$$\Delta^0 f(x) = f(x);$$
$$\Delta^1 f(x) = \Delta f(x) = f(x+h)) - f(x);$$
$$\Delta^{n+1} f(x) = \Delta(\Delta^n f(x))], n \geqslant 1.$$

(a) Show that $\Delta^n f(x) = \displaystyle\sum_{k=0}^{n} (-1)^{n-k} \binom{n}{k} f(x+kh);$

(b) If $P(x) = a_0 + a_1(x - t) + \cdots + a_n(x - t)^n$; show that $\Delta^n P(x) = n! h^n a_n$;

(c) If f is continuous on $[a, b]$ and n-times differentiable on (a, b) and if $x + nh \in [a, b]$ for $x \in [a, b]$, $h \neq 0$, show that there exists θ $(0 < \theta < 1)$ such that $\Delta^n f(x) = f^{(n)}(x + n\theta h)h^n$.

4.4 L'HOSPITAL'S RULE

We conclude this chapter with the first major application of the Mean Value Theorem. In practice, one often encounters a problem of evaluating a limit of the form $\displaystyle\lim_{x \to c} \frac{f(x)}{g(x)}$, where the expression reduces to the form $\dfrac{0}{0}$, when $x = c$. Since $\dfrac{0}{0}$ is a meaningless quantity, we simply cannot substitute c for x in the expression. In such situations, the following theorem (often called **L'Hospital's Rule**) enables us to compute the limit.

Theorem 4.4.1. Let f and g be defined on (a, b) with $a < b$. Suppose that f' and g' exist on (a, b) with $g'(x) \neq 0$ on (a, b). If $\displaystyle\lim_{x \to a^+} f(x) = \lim_{x \to a^+} g(x) = 0$, and $\displaystyle\lim_{x \to a^+} \frac{f'(x)}{g'(x)} = A$, then $\displaystyle\lim_{x \to a^+} \frac{f(x)}{g(x)} = A$.

Proof. Let us define f and g at a by $f(a) = g(a) = 0$. By Cauchy's Mean Value Theorem applied to f and g on the interval (a, x) (where $x < b$), there exists $x_0 \in (a, x)$ such that

$$\frac{f(x) - f(a)}{g(x) - g(a)} = \frac{f'(x_0)}{g'(x_0)}.$$

By hypothesis, there is a $\delta > 0$ such that $x_0 \in (a, a + \delta)$ will imply that

$$\left| \frac{f'(x_0)}{g'(x_0)} - A \right| < \epsilon$$

where ϵ has been prescribed. It is immediate, if $x \in (a, a + \delta)$, consideration of the interval (a, x) will have the same effect, and the proof follows. $\square$

Discussion. The reader should carefully verify the hypothesis of Cauchy's Mean Value Theorem. Moreover, in the exercises, we ask the reader to formalize this argument into strict $\epsilon - \delta$ reasoning. The force of this statement is that we are allowed, in the special circumstance of the hypothesis, to replace the functional values with those of the derivative of the functions. As the reader well knows, it is an extremely useful technique for finding limits. This form of L'Hospital's Rule is often referred to as the $\dfrac{0}{0}$ form. Various other forms, such as $\dfrac{\infty}{\infty}$, $\infty \cdot 0$, $\infty - \infty$, will be explored in the exercises. $\square$

EXAMPLE 1

Evaluate $\lim\limits_{x \to 0} \dfrac{\sin 4x}{\sin 3x}$.

Solution. Based on facts from elementary calculus (details presented formally in Chapter 9), both $\sin 4x$ and $\sin 3x$ are differentiable in an open interval about 0. Further, $[\sin x]' = \cos x$, and with no loss in generality we may assume that the interval chosen about 0 does not include a zero of $\cos x$. Thus, the hypothesis of Theorem 4.4.1 is satisfied. It follows that

$$\lim_{x \to 0} \frac{\sin 4x}{\sin 3x} = \lim_{x \to 0} \frac{4 \cos 4x}{3 \cos 3x}.$$

Since $\lim\limits_{x \to 0} \cos x = 1$, it follows that the limit of the right-hand side is $\dfrac{4}{3}$. $\square$

Discussion. The reader will note that Theorem 4.4.1 is based on right-hand limits at a. We have applied this theorem in a situation where we want to compute a limit. What this requires us to do is to first apply the theorem to the calculation of the right-hand limit, and then the left-hand limit. We must then check that the left- and right-hand limits are the same. $\square$

EXAMPLE 2

Let f be twice differentiable in a neighborhood of a. Evaluate

$$\lim_{h \to 0} \frac{f(a+h) - (f(a) + f'(a)h)}{h^2}.$$

Solution. Since the hypothesis of Theorem 4.4.1 is satisfied,

$$\lim_{h \to 0} \frac{f(a+h) - (f(a) + f'(a)h)}{h^2} = \lim_{h \to 0} \frac{f'(a+h) - f'(a)}{2h} = \frac{1}{2} f''(a).$$

$\square$

Discussion. This example has a certain look of artificiality to it. However, to dismiss it as such would be a mistake.

The required limit is in the form of a ratio as h tends to 0. Since both the numerator and the denominator have the limit 0, the force of the computation is to compare the rate at which the numerator is tending to 0 with the rate at which the denominator is tending to 0. There are several possible outcomes. For example, if the numerator approaches 0 much, much faster than the denominator, the final limit will be 0. If the numerator goes to 0 much, much slower than the denominator, the result will be ∞, or $-\infty$. Other cases will yield a real number other than 0. Thus the force of the computation is to compare one rate with another.

Now consider the numerator, $f(a+h) - (f(a) + f'(a)h)$. The first term is the value of the function near a. The second quantity, $f(a) + f'(a)h$, is the linear approximation to f obtained from the tangent line to the graph of f at $(a, f(a))$. Recall that the difference between these two quantities is given by $\alpha(h)h$, where $\alpha(h)$ has the property that it approaches 0 as h goes to 0. It is natural to ask about how rapidly $\alpha(h)$ tends to 0 as h tends to 0. This accounts for why one would consider a limit having $f(a+h) - (f(a) + f'(a)h)$ as its numerator.

What about the denominator? Obviously, the denominator should look like $\alpha(h)h$. One could therefore, in an experimental way, simply postulate a possible form for $\alpha(h)$. The simplest possible form would have us set $\alpha(h) = h$, which then gives rise to a denominator consisting of h^2.

Having decided to perform this computation, the outcome is almost like finding nirvana, because it leads immediately to an approximation of f near a of the form

$$f(a+h) \approx f(a) + f'(a)h + \frac{1}{2}f''(a)h^2$$

which contains the second derivative of f evaluated at a multiplied by h^2. Indeed, it is starting to look like f might be approximately a polynomial function. Given that polynomials are so easy to deal with, this result is just fraught with possibilities and certainly must have created a great deal of excitement in its initial discoverer. We shall pursue a few of these below. $\square$

The example above suggests that a function which is twice differentiable in a neighborhood of a can be represented as a quadratic polynomial involving derivatives evaluated at a. There are a number of ways to pursue this result. First, one could attempt to find a representation for f as a cubic polynomial involving three derivatives. This idea is explored in Exercise 2. Second, we could take the approach of the Mean Value Theorem. Under this approach, consider $f(b)$ for b near a as a linear function of the form

$$f(b) = f(a) + K(b-a).$$

Under these circumstances, what could be said about K? It turned out that $K = f'(x_0)$ for some $x_0 \in (a, b)$.

We can ask exactly the same question about the quadratic approximation suggested by Example 2. Namely, if we set

$$f(b) = f(a) + f'(a)(b-a) + \frac{1}{2}K(b-a)^2,$$

What can be said about K? In this case, we have included the factor $\frac{1}{2}$ precisely because it turned up in the computation performed in Example 2.

EXAMPLE 3

Let f be twice differentiable in the interval (a, b), and continuous on $[a, b]$. If we represent $f(b)$ by

$$f(b) = f(a) + f'(a)(b-a) + \frac{1}{2}K(b-a)^2,$$

what can be said about the value of K?

Solution. Consider the function of t defined by

$$F(t) = f(b) - f(t) - f'(t)(b-t) - \frac{1}{2}K(b-t)^2.$$

Observe that F is continuous on $[a, b]$ and differentiable on (a, b). Further, substitution shows that $F(b) = 0$, while the equation which defines K forces $F(a) = 0$. Thus the hypothesis of Rolle's Theorem is satisfied. Differentiation yields

$$\begin{aligned} F'(t) &= -f'(t) - f''(t)(b-t) + f'(t) + K(b-t) \\ &= K(b-t) - f''(t)(b-t). \end{aligned}$$

By Rolle's Theorem, there is a $t_0 \in (a, b)$ such that $F'(t_0) = 0$, whence $K = f''(t_0)$.   □

Discussion. Consider the quantity $f(b) - \left(f(a) + f'(a)(b-a) + \frac{1}{2}K(b-a)^2 \right)$.

There are two possible substitutions into this expression to obtain a function $F(t)$ to which one could apply Rolle's Theorem. The most natural substitution is to replace each occurrence of b by t to obtain

$$G(t) = f(t) - \left(f(a) + f'(a)(t-a) + \frac{1}{2}K(t-a)^2 \right).$$

This looks promising since $G(b) = 0 = G(a)$, and the remainder of the hypothesis of Rolle's Theorem holds as well. However, the approach falls apart when $G'(t)$ is computed as the reader will show in Exercise 3. Thus, one is forced to the other alternative, namely substituting $t = a$, which leads to our $F(t)$.

Once K has been determined, we have established the existence of $x_0 \in (a, b)$ such that

$$\frac{1}{2}f''(x_0)(b-a)^2 = f(a) + f'(a)(b-a).$$

From this equation it is easily seen why the term, $\frac{1}{2}f''(x_0)(b-a)^2$, is thought of as an error term. Namely, it gives the error between the linear approximation to f near a evaluated at b, and the function value at b, $f(b)$. What is especially important to notice is that this error depends on $(b-a)^2$. Thus if $f''(x)$ is bounded near a, this error term is likely to be small when $b-a$ is small. An example of the use of this idea will be given in Exercise 4.   □

EXERCISES

In the exercises below, you may use whatever facts are required concerning the derivatives of special functions.

1. Evaluate the following limits:

(a) $\lim\limits_{x\to 0} \dfrac{6\sin x - 6x + x^3}{2x^2 \ln(1+x) - 2x^3 + x^4}$;

(b) $\lim\limits_{x\to 0} \left[\ln\dfrac{1}{x}\right]^{\ln(1-x)}$;

(c) $\lim\limits_{x\to 0} \dfrac{\sin \ln(1+x)}{\ln(1+\sin x)}$;

(d) $\lim\limits_{x\to 0} \left(\dfrac{x}{e^x - 1}\right)^{1/x}$;

(e) $\lim\limits_{x\to 0} \dfrac{\sin(x\sin x) - (x\cos x)^2}{x^2}$;

(f) $\lim\limits_{x\to 1} \tan^2\left(\dfrac{\pi x^2}{2}\right)(1 + \sec \pi x)$;

(g) $\lim\limits_{x\to\infty} [(x+1)^\alpha - x^\alpha]$, $\alpha > 0$;

(h) $\lim\limits_{x\to 1} \left[\dfrac{x}{x-1} - \dfrac{1}{\ln x}\right]$;

(i) $\lim\limits_{x\to 0^+} \left(\dfrac{1}{x}\right)^{\sin x}$;

(j) $\lim\limits_{x\to 1^-} x^{1/(1-x)}$;

(k) $\lim\limits_{x\to 0^+} x^x$;

(l) $\lim\limits_{x\to(\pi/2)^-} (\tan x)^{\cos x}$;

(m) $\lim\limits_{t\to 1}(1 - t)\ln(1 - t^3)$;

(n) $\lim\limits_{x\to 0}\dfrac{\sinh(\sin x) - \sin(\sinh x)}{x^7}$;

(o) $\lim\limits_{x\to 0}(1 - \cos x)\cot(x^2)$;

(p) $\lim\limits_{x\to 0} \left[\dfrac{1}{e^x - 1} - \dfrac{1}{\sin x}\right]$;

(q) $\lim\limits_{x\to 0}\dfrac{1 - \cos x^2}{x^3 \sin x}$.

2. Suppose f is thrice differentiable in a neighborhood of a. Repeat the analysis of Example 2 to find an approximation to f which employs $f'''(a)$. In the process, evaluate

$$\lim_{h \to 0} \frac{f(a+h) - (f(a) + f'(a)h + \frac{1}{2}f''(a)h^2)}{h^3}.$$

3. Show that the remainder of the argument in Example 3 falls apart if one tries to use $G(t)$ as formulated in the Discussion following the Example.

4. Let $f(x) = \ln x$, $x > 0$. Find a linear estimate to $\ln 1.5$. Estimate the error involved in this estimate. Find an $x_0 \in (1, 1.5)$ which will determine the actual error in the estimate.

5. Let f be thrice differentiable on (c, d) and suppose $a, b \in (c, d)$ with $a < b$. Show that there is an $x_0 \in (a, b)$ such that

$$f(b) = f(a) + f'(a)(b-a) + \frac{1}{2}f''(a)(b-a)^2 + \frac{1}{6}f'''(x_0)(b-a)^3.$$

6. Let $f(x) = \ln x$, $x > 0$. Find a quadratic estimate to $\ln 1.5$. Estimate the error involved in this estimate. Find an $x_0 \in (1, 1.5)$ which will determine the actual error in the estimate.

7. Suppose f is four times differentiable in a neighborhood about a. What sort of approximation to f near a can be developed?

8. State and prove a formulation of the result in Exercise 5 for a function having four derivatives.

9. Let f and g satisfy the hypothesis of Cauchy's Mean Value Theorem on (a, ∞). Show that if $\lim_{x \to \infty} f(x) = \lim_{x \to \infty} g(x) = 0$, then

$$\lim_{x \to \infty} \frac{f(x)}{g(x)} = \lim_{x \to \infty} \frac{f'(x_0)}{g'(x_0)}.$$

10. What is the fallacy in the following computation?

$$\lim_{x \to 2} \frac{3x^2 - 4x - 4}{x^2 - 2x} = \lim_{x \to 2} \frac{6x - 4}{2x - 2} = \lim_{x \to 2} \frac{6}{2} = 3.$$

11. Show that $\lim_{x \to 0} \dfrac{x^2 \sin \frac{1}{x}}{\sin x} = 0$. Explain why L'Hospital's Rule does not apply.

12. Fill in all the missing details in Theorem 4.4.1, so as to put it into proper $\epsilon - \delta$ form of proof.

13. State and prove a form of Theorem 4.4.1 which involves infinite limits, that is, the $\dfrac{\infty}{\infty}$ form of L'Hospital's Rule.

14. Give an example where $\dfrac{f(x)}{g(x)}$ has a limit as $x \to a$, but $\dfrac{f'(x)}{g'(x)}$ fails to have a limit as x tends to a.

15. Determine A and B such that $\lim_{x \to 0} \dfrac{A \sin x - x(1 + B \cos x)}{x^3} = 1$.

16. Let

$$f(x) = \begin{cases} e^{-1/x^2}, & x \neq 0 \\ 0, & x = 0. \end{cases}$$

Prove that f possesses derivatives of all orders, and show further that for each $n \in \mathbf{N}$, the nth derivative at the point $x = 0$, $f^{(n)}(0) = 0$.

17. Find $\displaystyle\lim_{x\to\infty} \frac{xf'(x)}{f(x)}$, given that $\displaystyle\lim_{x\to\infty} f(x) = \lim_{x\to\infty} f'(x) = \lim_{x\to\infty} f''(x) = \infty$ and $\displaystyle\lim_{x\to\infty} \frac{xf'''(x)}{f''(x)} = k.$

18. Given a circle, center O, radius r, and a tangent line AT, P any point on the circle, M any point on the tangent at A such that $AM = AP$, and let MP meet AO at B. Find the limiting position of B as A approaches A.

19. Prove the following version of L'Hospital's Rule for sequences: If $\{a_n\}$, $\{b_n\}$ are sequences of real numbers such that $\{b_n\}$ increases and diverges to $+\infty$, then

$$\lim_{n\to\infty} \frac{a_{n+1} - a_n}{b_{n+1} - b_n} = L \quad \text{implies} \quad \lim_{n\to\infty} \frac{a_n}{b_n} = L.$$

20. Let $f(x) = x + \sin x \cos x$ and $g(x) = e^{\sin x} f(x)$. Show that:

(a) $\displaystyle\lim_{x\to\infty} f(x) = \lim_{x\to\infty} g(x) = +\infty;$

(b) $\displaystyle\lim_{x\to\infty} \frac{f'(x)}{g'(x)} = 0;$

(c) $\displaystyle\lim_{x\to\infty} \frac{f(x)}{g(x)}$ fails to exist.

Does this contradict L'Hospital's Rule?

21. Suppose f is defined on $[a,b]$, $c \in (a,b)$, and $f''(c)$ exists. Prove that

$$\lim_{h\to 0} \frac{f(c+h) - 2f(c) + f(c-h)}{h^2} = f''(c).$$

Give an example where the limit exists, but $f''(c)$ fails to exist.

22. Let $\{r_n\}$ denote the sequence of all rational numbers in the interval $(0,1)$. Show that $\underline{\lim} \{r_n^{r_n}\} = e^{-1/e}$ and $\overline{\lim} \{r_n^{r_n}\} = 1$.

23. Suppose f has two continuous derivatives and $f(0) = 0$. If g is defined by

$$g(x) = \begin{cases} \dfrac{f(x)}{x}, & x \neq 0 \\ f'(0), & x = 0 \end{cases}$$

prove that g has a continuous derivative.

24. Let f be differentiable in (a,∞). Prove the following:

(a) if $\displaystyle\lim_{x\to\infty} f(x) = 1$, $\displaystyle\lim_{x\to\infty} f'(x) = k$, then $k = 0$;

(b) if $\displaystyle\lim_{x\to\infty} f'(x) = 1$, then $\displaystyle\lim_{x\to\infty} \frac{f(x)}{x} = 1$;

(c) if $\displaystyle\lim_{x\to\infty} f'(x) = 0$, then $\displaystyle\lim_{x\to\infty} \frac{f(x)}{x} = 0.$

25. Show that there does not exist a polynomial $p(x)$ with coefficients from $\mathbf{R}$ such that for each $n \in \mathbf{N}$, $p(n) = n \ln n$.

Chapter 5

Integration

In this chapter, another fundamental notion called the **integral** of a function is introduced in a formal manner. After discussing the basic properties of integrable functions and various criteria for integrability of a function, we will indicate in Chapter 6 different directions in which the notion can be fruitfully generalized. The integral is defined using the Supremum Principle, and is realized as the limit of a set of suitable sums, thus ruling out the common misconception that integration is always a reverse process of differentiation. **The Fundamental Theorem of Integral Calculus** is then established, which brings forth the relationship between differential and integral calculus, namely for a certain class of functions, it turns out that integration is indeed a reverse process of differentiation, in a sense to be made precise later.

The earliest evidences of the so-called integral calculus are to be found in the works of Greek geometers who employed the **Method of Exhaustion** to give a meaning to, and to calculate areas of plane regions† with circular or parabolic boundaries. Centuries later, subsequent to the invention of calculus by Newton and Leibnitz, attention was focused on the inverse character of differentiation and techniques of evaluating both definite and indefinite integrals. But a rigorous and systematic mathematical formulation was first attempted by Riemann for the notion of the definite integral, and this together with Cauchy's extension to unbounded functions resulted in a complete and formal expression of the concept of the integral as the limit of a certain sum which incidentally justifies the literary meaning of the word. Toward the close of the last century, Stieltjes introduced a broader concept of integration replacing certain linear functions crucial to Riemann's definition by functions of a more general character. The beginning of this century saw the development of the notion of **measure** of a set of real numbers, which paved the way to the foundations of the modern theory of Lebesgue integral, now accepted as a beautiful and inevitable generalization of the Riemann integral.

† As we use the word 'region' in this text, it refers to any set of points in the plane.

5.1 MOTIVATION FOR DEFINITION OF THE RIEMANN–DARBOUX INTEGRAL

Since the study of the integral began with the geometrical considerations of calculating areas of plane figures, we begin our deliberations with a discussion of area.

One of the prime reasons for developing a notion of area is to provide a means of comparing plane figures. Simply stated, by assigning a number to each plane figure, the notion of area provides an answer to the question: Which is bigger? Quite obviously, not just any number will do. The number chosen for area must have certain properties. For example, it should be well-defined, which means that two competent mathematicians will assign the same number to the same figure in all cases. As well, if figure F_1 fits inside figure F_2, then the number assigned as the area of F_1 should be smaller than the number assigned as the area of F_2. (The industrious reader might want to make a list of other important properties which a notion of area should satisfy.) The point of this is that it is by no means a trivial task to come up with a means for assigning a number to each plane figure in such a way that a consistent answer to the question 'Which is bigger' is provided.

If one thinks about this problem, and we encourage the reader to do so, one sees that a simple first cut might consist of creating a small standard figure, perhaps a square, and then counting the number of these which one could fit inside a given figure of unknown area without overlap. Approaching the area in this manner would very quickly convince one that a good solution for the problem of assigning a number to plane figures existed for figures which were rectangles. Indeed, it seems likely that the well-known formula for computing the area of a rectangle would arise from this approach almost immediately. This formula,

$$\text{area of a rectangle} = \text{length} \times \text{width}$$

amounts to a definition. It is a definition in which we have great confidence, in the sense that if we apply it to calculate the number of square tiles required to lay a floor in a rectangular room, we know it will provide us with the correct number. The problem that follows from this is that of finding the correct generalization of this definition which we can apply to other plane figures.

Thus, our point of departure is the familiar concept of the area of a rectangular region, namely the product of its length and breadth. This concept is abstracted by considering a function defined on the closed interval $[a, b]$ of the real line and which assumes a constant value $k \geqslant 0$, throughout the interval. In this situation the graph of the function gives rise to a rectangular region bounded by the x-axis and the ordinates $x = a$ and $x = b$. Obviously, the area enclosed is $k(b - a)$. If further, $[a, b]$ is broken up into smaller intervals by inserting points of division between a and b, say

$$a = x_0 \leqslant x_1 \leqslant \cdots \leqslant x_{n-1} \leqslant x_n = b,$$

and if the function f is defined so as to take a constant value at each of the resulting subintervals, say (as for example in Figure 5.1.1)

$$f(x) = k_i \geqslant 0, \ \text{if } x \in [x_{i-1}, x_i), \ i = 1, 2, \dots, n, \ \text{and } f(b) = k_n,$$

and if d_i denoted the length $(x_i - x_{i-1})$ of the ith subinterval, then we get n rectangular regions and the total area enclosed by them above the x-axis is the finite sum of the various rectangles, namely

$$\text{area} = k_1 d_1 + k_2 d_2 + \cdots + k_n d_n.$$

Notice that in this last equation, we have generalized the notion of area. That is, we now are able to compute the area of a figure (see Figure 5.1.1) which is not a rectangle. How? By breaking up the figure into a series of nonoverlapping rectangles which include the totality of the figure, and summing their respective areas. This is merely the natural abstraction of the same process which was used by the early geometers.

Since the graph of the function above consists of n different **steps,** such a function is usually called a **step function** and what we just saw was that the area of a region bounded by a nonnegative step function, the vertical lines defined by $x = a$ and $x = b$, and the x-axis (see Figure 5.1.1) is just the sum of the areas of a finite number of rectangles resulting from the graph.

The analytic task which we have set for ourselves is to introduce the notion of an **integral** of a function. This integral will be a mapping from a subcollection of the class of all functions defined on an interval $[a, b]$ into **R**. As well, when the integral is applied to a function which is nonnegative on $[a, b]$, we will require that the real number which results from applying the function will be the area of the region bounded by the graph of f, the vertical lines $x = a$ and $x = b$ and the x-axis. This task will be achieved by approximating the given function by suitable step functions. The area of the region will then be approximated by the areas enclosed by these step functions, which in turn are obtained as a sum of the areas of nonoverlapping rectangles as described in the computations above. This, then, precisely summarizes the main ideas behind the formal treatment of the integral in the next section.

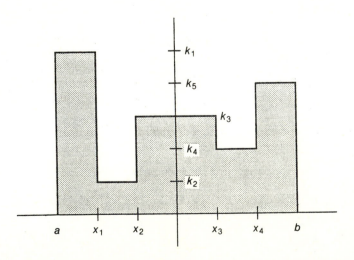

Figure 5.1.1   Area under a step function.

5.2 DEFINITION OF THE RIEMANN–DARBOUX INTEGRAL

We begin by introducing some terminology and basic notions which will be standard throughout this section.

Definition.   Let $a, b \in \mathbf{R}$ with $a \leqslant b$. By a **partition** of the interval $[a, b]$ we mean a finite collection of points $P = \{x_0, x_1, \ldots, x_n\}$ where

$$a = x_0 \leqslant x_1 \leqslant \cdots \leqslant x_n = b.$$

If P and Q are two partitions of $[a, b]$, we call Q a **refinement** of P provided $P \subseteq Q$.

Discussion.   The basic idea of a partition is to divide the interval $[a, b]$ into a finite collection of subintervals. Specifically, we have $n + 1$ points of division, with the first point being $x_0 = a$, and the last point being $x_n = b$. The result is to divide $[a, b]$ into n subintervals $[x_{i-1}, x_i]$, where $i = 1, 2, \ldots, n$. In terms of our goal, which as stated above, is to approximate functions with step functions, partitions will play an essential role by delineating the subintervals associated with each given step.

On the technical side, we have allowed a subinterval to consist of only one point, since it is quite possible that $x_{i-1} = x_i$. This amounts to permitting points to be repeated, although as we shall see, this makes no difference to the computations. For a given partition, P, we can produce a refinement Q by adding a finite number of additional points of $[a, b]$ to P. This will in general produce more divisions of the interval, whence the name. Lastly, given two partitions P and Q, it is not in general the case that one is a refinement of the other. The reader should produce an example. □

Definition.   For a given partition $P = \{x_0, x_1, \ldots, x_n\}$ of $[a, b]$ we let

$$d_i = x_i - x_{i-1}, \quad i = 1, 2, \ldots, n$$

be the **length** of the ith subinterval. Further, we set

$$\|P\| = \max \{d_1, d_2, \ldots, d_n\},$$

and call this quantity the **norm** of the partition P.

Discussion.   It is immediate from the definition of length of a subinterval (Exercise 1) that

$$d_1 + d_2 + \cdots + d_n = b - a.$$

If we refine a partition, P, to obtain a partition, Q, then, clearly,

$$\|Q\| \leqslant \|P\|.$$

As a general rule, the intent of forming a refinement of P will be to obtain a Q with a strictly smaller norm. However, it is definitely not the case that refining a partition will of necessity result in a reduced norm. On the other hand, it is the case that by taking refinements we can produce a partition of any interval with a norm which is less than any previously assigned positive number δ (**WHY?**). These ideas are illustrated in the following example. □

EXAMPLE 1 _____

Find a partition of $I = [-3, 4]$ having norm $\frac{1}{10}$.

Solution. The length of this interval is $4 - (-3) = 7$. Hence, a partition of I having norm $\frac{1}{10}$ must have at least 71 members. Fix δ such that $0 < \delta \leqslant \frac{1}{10}$. Set $x_0 = -3$ and $x_1 = -2.9$. For $i \geqslant 2$ set

$$x_i = \begin{cases} x_{i-1} + \delta, & \text{if } x_{i-1} + \delta < 4 \\ 4, & \text{otherwise.} \end{cases}$$

Let n be the least i such that $x_i = 4$, and set $P = \{x_0, x_1, \ldots, x_n\}$. It is easily checked that $\|P\| = \frac{1}{10}$. $\qquad \square$

Discussion. There are minor details which have been left to the reader. These should be completed. The reader should notice that the simplest possible partition satisfying the requirement is one in which the subintervals are of equal length. This partition would result from setting $\delta = \frac{1}{10}$. $\qquad \square$

The motivation which we have used as the foundation on which to develop the integral concept is the problem of finding the area of a region bounded by the graph of a nonnegative function, f, defined on $[a, b]$, the vertical lines given by $x = a$ and $x = b$, and the x-axis; formally, this region is the set of points given by

$$\{(x, y) : a \leqslant x \leqslant b \text{ and } 0 \leqslant y \leqslant f(x)\}$$

and pictured in Figure 5.2.1. However, as stated in the outline of our program, it is intended that we be able to compute an integral for other functions as well. In these cases, we will simply not be able to interpret the numerical result as measuring an area. Hence, we proceed by making a definition which for nonnegative functions yields area, but which can be applied to functions taking negative values as well. Thus, we will assume that when area is mentioned in the discussion below, the function being considered is nonnegative.

Let f be a real-valued function defined on $[a, b]$ and let us further assume that f is bounded. By the Supremum Principle, then, the set of values of f admit a supremum and an infimum. Let

$$M = \sup \{f(x) : x \in [a, b]\}$$

and

$$m = \inf \{f(x) : x \in [a, b]\}.$$

If $P = \{x_0, x_1, \ldots, x_n\}$ is any partition of $[a, b]$, since f is bounded on $[a, b]$, f is also bounded on each of the subintervals $[x_{i-1}, x_i]$, $i = 1, 2, \ldots, n$. Let M_i, m_i, respectively denote the supremum and the infimum of $f(x)$ in the ith subinterval $[x_{i-1}, x_i]$ (see Figure 5.2.1). These quantities exist by the completeness of **R** and they

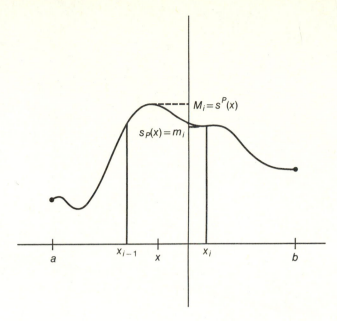

Figure 5.2.1 $s^P(x) = M_i$, $s_P = m_i (f > 0)$.

are unique by Theorem 0.4.1. This enables us to define two step functions, s^P and s_P, on $[a, b]$ as follows:

$$s^P(x) = M_i, \text{ if } x \in [x_{i-1}, x_i), i = 1, 2, \ldots, n$$

and

$$s_P(x) = m_i, \text{ if } x \in [x_{i-1}, x_i), i = 1, 2, \ldots, n,$$

with $s^P(b) = M_n$ and $s_P(b) = m_n$. Evidently the step functions, s^P and s_P, satisfy the fundamental inequality

$$s_P(x) \leqslant f(x) \leqslant s^P(x)$$

for all x in $[a, b]$ (see Exercise 3). Thus, the graph of the function, f, has now been 'sandwiched' between the graphs of two step functions, s_P and s^P, as can be seen from inspection of the ith subinterval in Figure 5.2.1. From this picture, it is intuitively obvious that any value we might want to assign as the area of the region under the function, f, (see Figure 5.2.1) must lie between the areas obtained from the step functions. (Values for the areas under the step function are known, since we can calculate them as a finite sum of the areas of nonoverlapping rectangles.)

Figure 5.2.1 relates to a nonnegative function. In the general case, the function of interest may take both positive and negative values. In Figures 5.2.2 and 5.2.3, graphs are presented which illustrate how a more general f is sandwiched between the step functions, s_P and s^P. Specifically, in Figure 5.2.2 the function f takes only negative values. Thus, on the ith subinterval we have $s_P(x) = m_i \leqslant f(x) \leqslant M_i = s^P(x) \leqslant 0$. In Figure 5.2.3 we illustrate a subinterval in which the graph of f crosses the x-axis. For such a case, M_i will be positive and m_i will be negative.

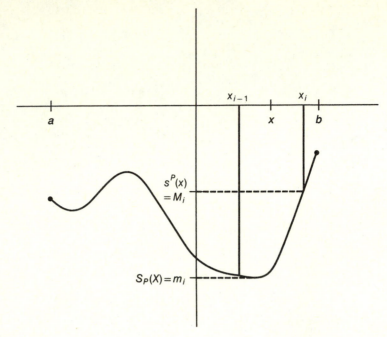

Figure 5.2.2 $s^P(x) = M_i$, $s_P(x) = m_i$ $(f < 0)$.

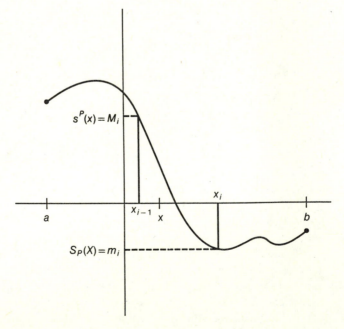

Figure 5.2.3 $s^P(x) = M_i$, $s_P(x) = m_i$ (f assumes positive and negative values).

Returning now to our main theme, the aim of our program is to associate a real number with each bounded function defined on $[a, b]$. In the discussion related to a nonnegative f, we suggested computing the area determined by each step function. Let us make this notion precise. Thus, in what follows, $P = \{x_0, \ldots, x_n\}$ is a partition of $[a, b]$, f is a bounded function on $[a, b]$, and M_i and m_i are the supremum and infimum on the ith subinterval, respectively.

Definition. By the **upper (Darboux) sum**, of the function, f, corresponding to the partition, P, we mean the number, $\bar{S}(P, f)$, given by

$$\bar{S}(P, f) = M_1 d_1 + M_2 d_2 + \cdots + M_n d_n.$$

Similarly, the **lower (Darboux) sum** of the function, f, corresponding to the partition, P, is given by

$$\underline{S}(P, f) = m_1 d_1 + m_2 d_1 + \cdots + m_n d_n.$$

Discussion. First and foremost, the reader should observe that a Darboux sum is exactly that, a *sum*. We emphasize this point, even though it is so patently obvious. Second, since every partition generates a finite collection of subintervals, every Darboux sum is *finite*. For this reason, a Darboux sum should be thought of as a *finite approximating sum*.

In the case of a general function, there is no universal interpretation which motivates this approximation. However, if f is nonnegative, the numbers which arise as Darboux sums corresponding to a partition, P, are nothing but the areas enclosed by the step functions s^P, s_P respectively, $x = a$ and $x = b$, and the x-axis. As such, they represent finite approximations to the area of the region determined by f (once again, see Figure 5.2.1).

The dependence of the Darboux sums on the particular partition, P, is clearly indicated. Because of the uniqueness of the supremum and infimum of a bounded set of real numbers and the fact that we are dealing with a finite sum, for a particular partition, P, and a fixed bounded function, f, the two numbers $\bar{S}(P, f)$ and $\underline{S}(P, f)$ are unique. This means that $\underline{S}$ and $\bar{S}$ are functions. The domains of these functions are the collection of pairs (P, f) where P is a partition of $[a, b]$ and f is bounded on $[a, b]$. While it is important to be able to think about $\underline{S}$ and $\bar{S}$ as functions, and to ask questions about them as functions, all of the intuition about them arises from one's understanding of what these functions do. In this sense, what is important is not the function aspect, but rather that each value returned by the function is an approximating sum over a finite partition.

As a matter of notation, when we are dealing with only one bounded function f we can dispense with the dependence on f and simply write $\bar{S}(P)$ and $\underline{S}(P)$ for the upper and lower sums given by P. $\square$

Upper and lower Darboux sums serve as the cornerstone of our development. As such it will be useful to establish some pertinent facts about them. This we do in the following lemmas which will assume that f and g are bounded functions on $[a, b]$, and that P is a partition of that interval.

Lemma 5.2.1. If $P = \{a, b\}$, then, $\bar{S}(P) = M(b - a)$ and $\underline{S}(P) = m(b - a)$. Further, if P is an arbitrary partition of $[a, b]$, then

$$m(b - a) \leqslant \underline{S}(P) \leqslant \bar{S}(P) \leqslant M(b - a).$$

Proof. The first statement is left to Exercise 4. Thus, let P be an arbitrary partition of $[a, b]$. Then

$$m \leqslant m_i \leqslant M_i \leqslant M,$$

for $i = 1, \ldots, n$. It follows that

$$md_i \leqslant m_i d_i \leqslant M_i d_i \leqslant Md_i,$$

for each i. If we now sum the n inequalities for $i = 1, \ldots, n$, we obtain

$$m(b - a) \leqslant \underline{S}(P) \leqslant \bar{S}(P) \leqslant M(b - a)$$

as desired. $\square$

Discussion. This lemma establishes that for a fixed bounded function, f, the collection of all upper sums as well as the collection of all lower sums over f is bounded below by $m(b - a)$, and bounded above by $M(b - a)$. This fact is essential to the development, and it is the reason why f is required to be bounded on $[a,b]$. $\square$

Lemma 5.2.2. Let f and g be defined on $[a, b]$ and P be a partition of $[a, b]$. Then

(a) $\bar{S}(P, cf) = c\bar{S}(P,f)$, for any real constant $c \geqslant 0$;
(b) $\bar{S}(P, cf) = c\underline{S}(P,f)$, for any real constant $c < 0$;
(c) $|\bar{S}(P, f)| \leqslant \bar{S}(P, |f|)$;
(d) $\bar{S}(P, f) + \bar{S}(P, g) \geqslant \bar{S}(P, f + g)$.

Proof. We prove (c) and leave the rest to Exercise 5. Consider the ith subinterval. If $x \in [x_{i-1}, x_i]$, then $-|f(x)| \leqslant f(x) \leqslant |f(x)|$, simply by definition of $|f|$. It follows that

$$-M_{i,|f|} \leqslant M_i = \sup \{f(x) : x \in [x_{i-1},x_i]\}$$
$$\leqslant \sup \{|f(x)| : x \in [x_{i-1},x_i]\} = M_{i,|f|}$$

where $M_{i,|f|}$ is the supremum of $|f|$ over the ith subinterval, whence,

$$-M_{i,|f|} \times d_i \leqslant M_i \times d_i \leqslant M_{i,|f|} \times d_i.$$

But this means that

$$|\bar{S}(P,f)| = |\sum_{i=1}^{n} M_i \times d_i| \leqslant \sum_{i=1}^{n} |M_i \times d_i|$$
$$\leqslant \sum_{i=1}^{n} M_{i,|f|} \times d_i = \bar{S}(P,|f|)$$

which is the desired inequality. $\square$

Discussion. This proof works because we are dealing with finite sums. Thus, the basic manipulations all reduce to versions of theorems proved in Chapter 0. For example, the final inequality, whose primary content is

$$|\bar{S}(P,f)| = |\sum_{i=1}^{n} M_i \times d_i| \leqslant \sum_{i=1}^{n} |M_i \times d_i|,$$

is merely a version of the Triangle inequality.

The only infinite process involved in the computation is the use of the Supremum Principle to obtain the various M_i's. However, this does not affect the computations, since it acts merely to produce the finite list of numbers which are to be manipulated.

It is critical that the reader understand that it is only by keeping the approximating sums finite that we are able to perform these computations. This requirement is the reason why we insist that a partition be a finite list of numbers from $[a, b]$. □

For various partitions P of $[a, b]$, and a fixed bounded function, f, on $[a, b]$, we set

$$\{\bar{S}(P)\} = \{\bar{S}(P, f)\} = \{\bar{S}(P, f) : P \text{ is a partition of } [a, b]\}$$

and

$$\{\underline{S}(P)\} = \{\underline{S}(P, f)\} = \{\underline{S}(P, f) : P \text{ is a partition of } [a, b]\}$$

and note that these sets of real numbers are both bounded above by $M(b - a)$ and below by $m(b - a)$. Hence, by the Supremum Principle, we may make the following definition.

Definition. The number given by inf $\{\bar{S}(P)\}$ is called the **upper Darboux integral** of f on $[a, b]$, and is denoted by $\overline{\int_a^b} f$. Similarly, the number given by sup $\{\underline{S}(P)\}$ is called the **lower Darboux integral** of f, on $[a, b]$, and is denoted by $\underline{\int_a^b} f$. Further, if

$$\overline{\int_a^b} f = \underline{\int_a^b} f,$$

then the common value is called the **Riemann–Darboux integral** of the function f on the interval $[a, b]$ and is denoted by $\int_a^b f$. Moreover, when the Riemann–Darboux integral of f exists, we will say that f is **Riemann–Darboux integrable** (or **R–D integrable**) on $[a, b]$.

Discussion. Let us review the development leading to this definition. First, the function f is assumed to be bounded, so that we are able to invoke the Supremum Principle over any subset of the range of f. Second, we produce two step functions by using the bounds on f over various subintervals; these step functions sandwich the function, f, between them. Third, we associate with each step function a number which can be thought of as the value of an approximating sum. For the step function above f, this number is referred to as the upper sum. For the step function below f, this number is referred to as the lower sum. Fourth, we find the infimum of all the upper sums and the supremum of all the lower sums. This step defines the upper and lower Darboux integrals. Finally, we observe that in some cases the upper and lower Darboux integrals generate the same number. In this last case, we say that the function is Riemann–Darboux integrable on $[a, b]$.

The reader will observe that this achieves our intent of developing a process which associates a real number with some subclass of the functions defined on $[a, b]$. We have generated such a process, but a number of questions are outstanding. The most obvious of these is related to characterizing, in a simple manner, those functions which are Riemann–Darboux integrable.

The other portion of our intent relates to the concept of area. Thus, consider a nonnegative function, f, on $[a, b]$, such as that shown in Figure 5.2.1. As we have already noted, for each partition, P, any number which we might choose to assign as the area under f must satisfy

$$\underline{S}(P) \leqslant \text{the area under } f \leqslant \bar{S}(P).$$

The argument for this assertion is *geometric*, not analytic. It is based on our belief that any sensible notion of area must satisfy the condition that if a plane figure, F_1, is enclosed in a plane figure F_2, then the areal measure of F_1 should be no more than the measure of F_2. In this case, the region defined by s^P on $[a, b]$ encloses the region determined by f, as shown in Figure 5.2.1. Moreover, we know from sound geometric principles how to obtain the number which is the area under s^P, namely calculate $\bar{S}(P)$. Similar reasoning establishes the left-hand side of inequality. Since this argument holds for every partition, we can assert that the area under f must satisfy

$$\inf \{\underline{S}(P)\} \leqslant \text{the area under } f \leqslant \sup \{\bar{S}(P)\}.$$

For this reason, under the assumption that the supremum and infimum are the same, we would be confident in *defining* the value produced by the integral to be the area under f. In making this definition, we would certainly want to perform a variety of checks to ensure that the definition was consistent with what we had been trying to achieve. Thus, we would want to verify that all the important features of our intrinsic notion of area had been captured. Suffice it to say that all such checks validate this approach to the problem of defining area.

Most importantly, the reader should come to grips with the way the notion of integral takes our knowledge of how to solve a problem in a very simple case, namely finding the area of a rectangle, and extends it to more general situations by forming finite approximating sums followed by applying a limiting process to the collection of approximations. This idea is the essence of all applications of the integral to real situations.   □

NOTE: The notations introduced so far will be standard for the remainder of this section.

We now generate some of the basic facts about the integration process.

Theorem 5.2.1.   If f is a bounded function defined on $[a, b]$ and Q is a refinement of a partition P of $[a, b]$, then $\underline{S}(P) \leqslant \underline{S}(Q) \leqslant \bar{S}(Q) \leqslant \bar{S}(P)$. Moreover, if Q was obtained by adjoining at most k more points to the partition P, then

$$|\bar{S}(P) - \bar{S}(Q)| \leqslant 2kM\|P\| \quad \text{and} \quad |\underline{S}(Q) - \underline{S}(P)| \leqslant 2kM\|P\|$$

where $M = \sup\{|f(x)| : x \in [a, b]\}$.

Proof. Let $P = \{x_0, x_1, \ldots, x_n\}$ and let us first assume that Q is obtained by adjoining one more point y to P, say, between x_{r-1} and x_r. Let d' and d'' denote the lengths of the new subintervals $[x_{r-1}, y]$ and $[y, x_r]$ so generated, and let M' and M'' be the suprema of f in these subintervals, respectively. Then M_r is never less than M' or M''. Now,

$$\bar{S}(Q) - \bar{S}(P) = M'd + M''d'' - M_r d_r \quad \text{(since all other terms cancel)}$$

$$= (M' - M_r)d' + (M'' - M_r)d'' \quad \text{(since } d_r = d' + d'')$$

$$\leqslant 0,$$

proving that $\bar{S}(Q) \leqslant \bar{S}(P)$. Similarly, considering the infima of f in these subintervals, the reader can prove that $\underline{S}(P) \leqslant \underline{S}(Q)$.

Next, if Q is *any* refinement of P, obtained by adding k more points, we construct a succession of k partitions $Q_1, Q_2, \ldots, Q_k = Q$, where each refinement Q_i contains just one more point than the preceding. It now follows that

$$\bar{S}(Q) \leqslant \bar{S}(Q_{k-1}) \leqslant \cdots \leqslant \bar{S}(Q_1) \leqslant \bar{S}(P)$$

and a similar result for lower sums.

The second assertion follows by an easy induction on the number k of points adjoined to obtain Q from the partition P. For $k = 1$,

$$|\bar{S}(P) - \bar{S}(Q)| = |(M' - M_r)d' + (M'' - M_r)d''|$$

$$\leqslant (M + M)d' + (M + M)d''$$

$$= 2M(d' + d'') \leqslant 2M\|P\|.$$

We leave the reader to complete this induction argument (Exercise 6). $\square$

Discussion. Only two basic facts are used in this proof. First, if an interval is dissected into two pieces by an intermediate point, the sum of the lengths of the two subintervals generated is exactly equal to the length of the original interval. Secondly, we have used the fact that the supremum of a larger set is larger or equal to that of a smaller set. The above theorem shows that the replacement of a partition by a finer one tends to increase the lower sums, and to lessen the upper sums by a quantity which is at most $2kM$ times the original norm. $\square$

In the next theorem it is shown that regardless of the partition involved, no lower sum can exceed any upper sum of any partition whatsoever.

Theorem 5.2.2. If f is a function bounded in $[a, b]$ and if P and Q are any two partitions of $[a, b]$, then $\underline{S}(Q) \leqslant \bar{S}(P)$.

Proof. We consider the partition $R = P \cup Q$ which is clearly a refinement of P, as well as Q. By Theorem 5.2.1, we have

$$\underline{S}(Q) \leqslant \underline{S}(R) \leqslant \bar{S}(R) \leqslant \bar{S}(P). \quad \square$$

Theorem 5.2.3. Let f be a bounded function defined on $[a, b]$. Then

$$\underline{\int_a^b} f \leqslant \overline{\int_a^b} f.$$

Proof. Let P be an arbitrary partition of $[a, b]$. Then for all partitions Q, $\underline{S}(Q) \leqslant \overline{S}(P)$, whence $\underline{\int_a^b} f \leqslant \overline{S}(P)$. Since P was an arbitrary partition of $[a, b]$, we have $\underline{\int_a^b} f \leqslant \overline{\int_a^b} f$ as desired. $\quad\square$

Discussion. The content of these two results merely spells out in analytic form what is obvious from Figures 5.2.1 through 5.2.3, namely that every lower sum is less than or equal to every upper sum, regardless of the partitions involved. After all, f sits between the two types of step functions, s_P and s^Q.

The simplicity of the arguments above is another illustration of the essential power of the supremum concept. $\quad\square$

Let us now turn to some examples to illustrate the nature of integrability.

EXAMPLE 2 _____

Discuss the Riemann–Darboux integrability of the function f defined on $[a, b]$ by $f(x) = k$ (a constant) for all x.

Solution. Note that whatever partition, P, is used, $M_r = m_r = k$ on any subinterval; hence

$$\overline{S}(P) = kd_1 + kd_2 + \ldots + kd_n = k(b - a).$$

Similarly, $\underline{S}(P) = k(b - a)$. Since P was arbitrary, it follows that

$$\underline{\int_a^b} f = \overline{\int_a^b} f = k(b - a),$$

whence f is R–D integrable on $[a, b]$ and $\int_a^b f = k(b - a)$. $\quad\square$

Discussion. The computations are straightforward. If k is positive, the region bounded by the graph of f, the vertical lines $x = a$ and $x = b$, and the x-axis is a rectangle. We have asserted that for nonnegative functions, integration produces area. For this function, we already know how to calculate the area, that is, length times width, which analytically is $k(b - a)$. $\quad\square$

EXAMPLE 3 _____

Discuss the Riemann-Darboux integrability of f defined on $[a, b]$ by

$$f(x) = \begin{cases} k > 0, & \text{if } x \in [a, b] \text{ and } x \neq c \in [a, b] \\ 0, & \text{if } x = c. \end{cases}$$

Solution. Let us show that f is integrable. For any partition P, we will have that the components of the upper sum agree with the components of the lower sum except on the interval(s) which contain c (there can be at most two of these with nonzero lengths). Suppose that $c \in [x_{i-1}, x_i]$. Then the contribution arising from this subinterval to $\underline{S}(P)$ will be 0, whereas the contribution to $\overline{S}(P)$ will be kd_i, since $k > 0$. It follows that

$$\overline{S}(P) \leqslant \underline{S}(P) + 2k\|P\|.$$

Since $\|P\|$ can be made as small as we want (**HOW?**), we conclude that for any positive ϵ we can choose a partition, P, such that

$$|\overline{S}(P) - \underline{S}(P)| \leqslant \epsilon.$$

Evidently, this forces $\int_{\underline{a}}^{b} f = \int_{a}^{\overline{b}} f$, whence f is R–D integrable (**WHY?**).   □

Discussion. The purpose of these examples is to develop some intuition about how and why functions are integrable. Consider the present example in relation to the approximation process. This process works by sandwiching f between the two step functions, s_P and s^P. Integrability is achieved when we can sandwich so closely that

$$\overline{S}(P) - \underline{S}(P) \quad \text{can be made as small as we please.}$$

In the present example, the sandwiching is perfect on all subintervals which do not have c as a member. For any partition, there are at most two of these, which we identify by the subscripts i, $i+1$. On any other subinterval, say $[x_{j-1}, x_j]$, we have that $m_j = M_j = k$. It follows that the contribution to the jth subinterval is the same for both the upper and lower sum. Equivalently, we have

$$(M_j - m_j) \times d_j = 0.$$

Now,

$$\overline{S}(P) - \underline{S}(P) = \sum_{k=0}^{n} (M_k - m_k) \times d_k.$$

Thus, the contribution to $\overline{S}(P) - \underline{S}(P)$ from the jth subinterval is small precisely because $M_j - m_j$ is small, in fact 0.

On the other hand, if we turn to either of the remaining two subintervals, the contribution to $\overline{S}(P) - \underline{S}(P)$ from either will be small exactly if d_i and/or d_{i+1} is small. These can be made arbitrarily small by choosing the norm of P to be small, and this is the method used to conclude the argument. The essential features of this discussion are pictured in Figure 5.2.4.

We did not compute the value of the integral. However, it is straightforward to see that $\int_{a}^{b} f = k(b - a)$, which is the same as that for the function in Example 2, even though the functions differ by changing the value of the first function at a single point. This suggests that by altering the value of the function at a point in $[a, b]$ (or even at a finite number of points), the value of the integral and the integrability of the function are unchanged. These facts are dealt with later in this section.

Implicit in the suggestions above is the idea that to be integrable, a function does not necessarily have to be continuous. This example demonstrates that fact, and the reader should study carefully the methods used to deal with the lack of continuity. At a deeper level, the reader should try to come to grips with what this suggests. Specifically, what functions are integrable?   □

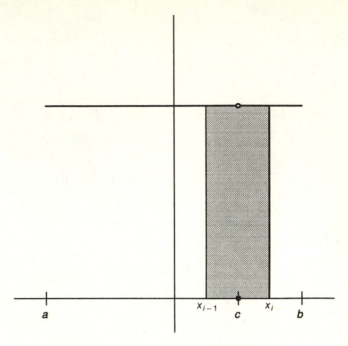

Figure 5.2.4 Only the shaded area contributes to $\bar{S}(P) - \underline{S}(P)$.

EXAMPLE 4 _____

Discuss the integrability of the function f defined on $[0,1]$ by

$$f(x) = \begin{cases} 0, & \text{if } x \text{ is irrational} \\ 1, & \text{if } x \text{ is rational.} \end{cases}$$

Solution.   Let P be an arbitrary partition of $[0,1]$. Evidently, the ith subinterval of this partition must contain an infinite number of rational and irrational points (**WHY?**). So $M_i = 1$ and $m_i = 0$. But this holds for every i. Thus, for any partition P of $[0,1]$, $\bar{S}(P) = b - a$ and $\underline{S}(P) = 0$. In consequence,

$$\underline{\int_a^b} f = 0, \quad \text{while} \quad \overline{\int_a^b} f = b - a,$$

whence f is not R–D integrable in $[0,1]$.   □

Discussion.   First and foremost, this example establishes that not all functions which are bounded on $[a, b]$ are integrable there. Further, it is apparent that continuity, or its lack, should play a role in the characterization of R–D integrable functions.

     Given this comment, it is essential that the reader understand the difference in the situation of Example 3 versus Example 4. As suggested in the discussion following Example 3, a function will be integrable exactly if we can make the quantity $\bar{S}(P, f) - \underline{S}(P, f)$ as small as we please by a careful selection of the partition. The basic tool which we have available for manipulation in arguments concerning the integral is the norm of P. This is the quantity which we adjust and it plays the same role as the δ in arguments concerning limit and continuity. In Example 3, we were able to establish the integrability of f precisely because we were able to use the norm of P to bound the difference between the upper and the lower integrals. This was accomplished by using the fact that there was only one point at which we had a problem, namely c, and that this resulted in a difference between the sums of at most $2k\|P\|$. Further, this quantity 'approached' 0 as the norm of P 'approached' 0. The question which arises is why we cannot do the same thing in the present case.

Consider now the situation of Example 4. We would like to construct an argument of the type given in Example 3 to show that f (of Example 4) is integrable. But this time, no matter how small the norm of P, each subinterval will still contain points of discontinuity of the function. Thus, no matter how small we choose the norm of the partition, on the ith subinterval the difference between M_i and m_i will not be small. Indeed, it will be constant and will contribute

$$(M_i - m_i) \times d_i = d_i$$

to the quantity $\overline{S}(P, f) - \underline{S}(P, f)$. Thus, the resulting difference between an upper sum and a lower sum will also be constant, indeed it will be $b - a$. As a result, the upper and lower integrals differ and f is not integrable.

The essential point here is that since the d_i's always sum to $b - a$, we cannot use the length as the factor which makes $(M_i - m_i) \times d_i$ small in all instances. Geometrically, the reader should observe that no matter what the choice of P, s^P and s_P do not closely sandwich the function of this example. $\quad\square$

Our next theorem formalizes some of the points made in the discussion above.

Theorem 5.2.4. A bounded function f defined on $[a, b]$ is Riemann–Darboux integrable on $[a, b]$ if and only if for every $\epsilon > 0$, there is a partition P of $[a, b]$ such that $\overline{S}(P) - \underline{S}(P) < \epsilon$.

Proof. Let f be integrable. Then given $\epsilon > 0$, there is a partition P of $[a, b]$ such that

$$\int_a^b f - \frac{\epsilon}{2} < \underline{S}(P) < \overline{S}(P) < \overline{\int_a^b} f + \frac{\epsilon}{2}. \qquad \textbf{(WHY?)}$$

The desired inequality now follows. Conversely, suppose for each $\epsilon > 0$ there is a partition P such that $\overline{S}(P) - \underline{S}(P) < \epsilon$. Since $\underline{S}(P) \leqslant \int_a^b f \leqslant \overline{\int_a^b} f \leqslant \overline{S}(P)$, the result follows. $\quad\square$

Discussion. This is the theorem which we will often apply to check the integrability of a function. Note that the tool for obtaining the desired partition will be the clever manipulation of the norm, specifically, we will make the norm small, as in Example 3. In general, if ϵ is small, the norm of P will have to be small as well to guarantee that the difference $\overline{S}(P) - \underline{S}(P) < \epsilon$. $\quad\square$

As we have suggested, it is of real importance to identify the class of integrable functions on a given interval $[a, b]$. By our basic assumption, they must all be bounded, but as Example 4 shows, this is by no means sufficient. Our next theorem shows that a continuous function will be integrable, but again as Example 3 shows, this is not a necessary condition.

Theorem 5.2.5. If f is continuous on $[a, b]$, then f is Riemann–Darboux integrable on $[a, b]$.

    Proof. By Theorem 3.6.2 f is uniformly continuous on $[a, b]$. Thus, given $\epsilon > 0$, we can find a $\delta > 0$ such that for all $x, y \in [a, b]$, with $|x - y| < \delta$, it is true that $|f(x) - f(y)| < \dfrac{\epsilon}{(b-a)}$. Now, choose a partition, P, with norm less than δ. The continuity of f guarantees that on each subinterval, $[x_{i-1}, x_i]$, of P, the infimum, m_i, and the supremum, M_i, of f are actually attained at points, say, y_i, z_i, in that subinterval. Since $|y_i - z_i| < \delta$, we have $M_i - m_i < \dfrac{\epsilon}{(b-a)}$. This being the case for $i = 1, 2, \ldots, n$, we get

$$\overline{S}(P) - \underline{S}(P) = \sum_{i=1}^{n} M_i d_i - \sum_{i=1}^{n} m_i d_i$$

$$= \sum_{i=1}^{n} (M_i - m_i) d_i$$

$$\leqslant \frac{\epsilon}{(b - a)} (b - a) \qquad\qquad \textbf{(WHY?)}$$

$$= \epsilon$$

whence Theorem 5.2.4 guarantees that f is R–D integrable. $\square$

Discussion. We urge the reader to observe the way continuity and Theorem 5.2.4 have been melded in this argument. The key is the fact that a function which is continuous on a closed interval, $[a, b]$, is uniformly continuous there. For this reason, we obtain a uniform bound, on $|f(y_i) - f(z_i)|$. This bound has the extraordinary property that it can be made as small as we please. In addition, we can ensure that the bound is satisfied for each i by the single step of making the norm of P sufficiently small. It is the existence of this uniform, arbitrarily small, bound which permits us to replace $M_i - m_i$ by a fixed, arbitrarily small, quantity which may then be factored out of the sum, as in the following line from the proof,

$$\sum_{i=1}^{n} (M_i - m_i) d_i \leqslant \frac{\epsilon}{(b - a)} (b - a).$$

Notice that if the uniform bound could not be made arbitrarily small, we would be forced back into the situation of Example 4, a situation where R–D integrability failed. $\square$

EXAMPLE 5 _____

Discuss the integrability of the function f on the interval $[0, 1]$ defined by

$$f(x) = \begin{cases} 0, & \text{if } x \in \mathbf{R} \sim \mathbf{Q} \\ \dfrac{1}{q}, & \text{if } x = \dfrac{p}{q} \in \mathbf{Q}, \text{ in its lowest terms.} \end{cases}$$

Solution. We will show that f is integrable. Let $\epsilon > 0$ be given and let N be the least integer such that $\dfrac{1}{N} < \dfrac{\epsilon}{2}$. Let k denote the number of rationals $\dfrac{p}{q} \in [0, 1]$ with denominator q less than N. We can enclose these finite number of points in subintervals of total length less than $\dfrac{\epsilon}{2}$ by choosing a partition, P, such that $\|P\| < \dfrac{\epsilon}{4k}$. Since f is bounded by 1, for such a partition, the total contribution to the difference $\bar{S}(P) - \underline{S}(P)$ from the subintervals containing these k points cannot exceed $\dfrac{\epsilon}{2}$. Further, on the intervals not containing any of these k points, $m_i = 0$, while $M_i \leqslant \dfrac{1}{N} < \dfrac{\epsilon}{2}$, whence the total contribution to $\bar{S}(P) - \underline{S}(P)$ from these subintervals is less than $\dfrac{\epsilon}{2}$. It is now immediate that

$$\bar{S}(P) - \underline{S}(P) < \frac{\epsilon}{2} + \frac{\epsilon}{2} = \epsilon$$

as desired. □

Discussion. In Exercise 2.5.1(h), the reader was asked to discuss the continuity properties of the above function. The conclusion of that exercise is that f is continuous on the irrationals and discontinuous on the rationals. Thus this function possesses a countable dense set of discontinuities, in the sense that the closure of the set containing the points of discontinuity consists of the entire domain, $[0, 1]$. With this in mind, and recalling our earlier remarks after Example 4, it seems remarkable that f should be integrable. We should find out why.

There is a fundamental intuitive difference between the Examples 4 and 5 which can be seen from Figure 5.2.5. If we draw a horizontal line given by $y = c > 0$ across the graph of f (dashed line in Figure 5.2.5b), we see that only a finite number of points of the graph lie above this line (see Exercise 10). On the other hand, this is not the case for the function of Example 4 as Figure 5.2.5a shows (provided the line crosses the y-axis between 0 and 1). This difference is the key. Here's why.

Our problem is to make $\bar{S}(P) - \underline{S}(P)$ small, in either case. To achieve this goal, we must make the contribution from each subinterval, $(M_i - m_i) \times d_i$ small. For the function of Example 4, we saw that $M_i - m_i$ had a fixed value of 1. Thus the only way to make the product small, was to have d_i small. However, this could not suffice to solve the problem because the sum of the d_i's was always the length of the interval $[a, b]$.

In the present example, every subinterval contains points of discontinuity. Now suppose we choose a partition where $\|P\|$ is very small. The only way this can happen is if n is very large, where $P = \{x_0, \ldots, x_n\}$. Relatively speaking, there will only be a few points, and hence a few subintervals, for which M_i, and hence $M_i - m_i$, is

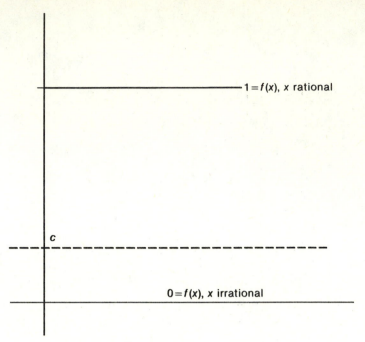

Figure 5.2.5(a)   Graph of $f(x) = \begin{cases} 1, & x \in \mathbf{Q} \\ 0, & x \notin \mathbf{Q} \end{cases}$ (Example 4).

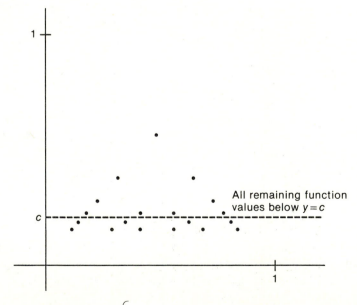

Figure 5.2.5(b)   Graph of $f(x) = \begin{cases} \dfrac{1}{q}, & x = \dfrac{p}{q} \in \mathbf{Q} \\ 0, & x \notin \mathbf{Q} \end{cases}$ (Example 5).

large. Thus, the contribution of most subintervals to the sum $\overline{S}(P) - \underline{S}(P)$ will be small, not because $\|P\|$ is small, but because $M_i - m_i$ is small! Since we can make the norm arbitrarily small, the contribution to the sum from the few subintervals where M_i is large can be made arbitrarily small.

The argument can also be approached geometrically, as follows. First observe that for any partition, P, $s_P = 0$ on $[0, 1]$, whence $\underline{S}(P) = 0$. Next we observe that the area under a line of constant height, $\dfrac{1}{N}$, in the unit square is exactly $\dfrac{1}{N}$. Thus, if we have all the functional values (or all but a finite number) trapped in the strip of height $\dfrac{1}{N}$, then $\overline{S}(P)$ should be near $\dfrac{1}{N}$ provided that P is suitably chosen. This is the intuition which the argument implements and similar intuitions are the heart of many arguments concerning integration. $\qquad\square$

The following theorem yields another rich class of integrable functions.

Theorem 5.2.6. A monotonic function defined on an interval $[a, b]$ is R–D integrable.

Proof. Let us assume that f is monotonically increasing and fix $\epsilon > 0$. Choose a partition P such that $\|P\| < \dfrac{\epsilon}{f(b) - f(a)}$ (the case where $f(b) - f(a) = 0$ is trivial). By monotonicity, we have that $M_{i-1} = m_i$ so that $\displaystyle\sum_{i=1}^{n} (M_i - m_i) = f(b) - f(a)$. Now,

$$\overline{S}(P) - \underline{S}(P) = \sum_{i=1}^{n} (M_i - m_i)\, d_i$$

$$< \left(\sum_{i=1}^{n} (M_i - m_i) \right) \frac{\epsilon}{f(b) - f(a)}$$

$$= \epsilon, \qquad\qquad\qquad\textbf{(WHY?)}$$

whence f is integrable. $\qquad\square$

Discussion. As in Theorem 5.2.5 and Example 5, the strategy here is to come up with a partition P which satisfies the condition of Theorem 5.2.4. The monotonicity of the function f guarantees that the maximum and the minimum values occur at the two endpoints of each subinterval. So, if we choose a partition with all subintervals having an equal length, say d, then since $\sum (M_i - m_i) = f(b) - f(a)$ (see Exercise 11), it turns out that $\overline{S}(P) - \underline{S}(P) = d \times [f(b) - f(a)]$. This justifies our choice of the quantity d to be less than $\dfrac{\epsilon}{f(b) - f(a)}$. $\qquad\square$

Theorems 5.1.5 and 5.1.6 together generate large class of integrable functions. They do not, however, characterize the class of all integrable functions. It might seem that there is no connection between the two theorems; however, this is not the case. It is a fact that a monotone function can have at most a countable set of discontinuities, thus a theorem which showed that functions having at most a countable set of discontinuities were integrable would subsume Theorem 5.2.6. Such a theorem is plausible and is in fact the case. However, at this moment, we do not have techniques of sufficient delicacy to deal with this situation. To substantially improve on the results in this section requires consideration of the nature of the set of discontinuities of the function in question. Such considerations are the subject of Lebesgue integration.

We close this section with a few more improvements on the class of integrable functions, the proofs of which are left as exercises.

Theorem 5.2.7. If f is R–D integrable on $[a, b]$ and g is obtained by altering the values of f at a finite number of points, then g is R–D integrable in $[a, b]$; furthermore, $\int_a^b f = \int_a^b g$.

Corollary. A bounded function on a closed interval $[a, b]$ whose set of discontinuities is finite is R–D integrable on $[a, b]$.

EXERCISES

1. Verify that for an arbitrary partition, P, of $[a, b]$,

$$\sum_{i=1}^{n} d_i = b - a,$$

where d_i denotes the length of the ith subinterval of P.

2. Find a partition of $[-e, \pi]$ such that $\|P\|$ is less than
   (a) $\dfrac{1}{20000}$;
   (b) $\dfrac{1}{\pi}$;
   (c) $\dfrac{1}{e^5}$;
   where e and π have their usual meanings.

3. Let f be bounded on $[a, b]$ and P be an arbitrary partition of $[a, b]$. Verify that $s_P(x) \leqslant f(x) \leqslant s^P(x)$ for all $x \in [a, b]$.

4. Supply a proof for the first part of Lemma 5.2.1.

5. Establish the relations stated in parts (a), (b), and (d) of Lemma 5.2.2.

6. Supply the missing proof for $\underline{S}(P) \leqslant \underline{S}(Q)$ in Theorem 5.2.1. Also, complete the induction argument in the latter half of the proof, for $\bar{S}(P)$ as well as $\underline{S}(P)$.

7. State and prove results corresponding to those in Lemma 5.2.2 (a), (c), and (d) for $\bar{S}(P)$.

8. Give an example of a function defined on $[0, 1]$ and a partition, P, such that $|\bar{S}(P, f)| < \bar{S}(P, |f|)$.

9. Give an example of functions, f and g defined on $[0, 1]$ and a partition, P, such that $\bar{S}(P, f+g) < \bar{S}(P, f) + \bar{S}(P, g)$.

10. Consider the function of Example 5, and let k denote the number of rationals in lowest terms in $[0, 1]$ having denominator less than N. Show that $k \leqslant \left(\dfrac{N^2 - 3N + 6}{2} \right)$.

11. Let f be monotone increasing on $[a, b]$. Show that

$$\sum_{n=1}^{n} (M_i - m_i) = f(b) - f(a).$$

How will this result change if f is monotone decreasing?

12. Show that $\int_a^a f = 0$, where a is in the domain of f.

13. Evaluate $\int_0^a [x]$.

14. Evaluate $\int_0^n f$, where $f(x) = \dfrac{(-1)^i}{i}$, if $x \in [i - 1, i)$ $(i = 1, 2, \ldots, n)$.

15. Evaluate $\int_{-1}^{1}$ sgn.

16. Evaluate $\int_0^1 \dfrac{1}{n}[nx^2]$.

17. Evaluate $\int_0^1 \dfrac{1}{n^2}[nx^2]$.

18. Prove that a function which is constant except at a finite number of points of a closed interval is R–D integrable in that interval. What is the value of the integral?

19. Discuss the integrability of the following functions in the intervals indicated, using Theorem 5.2.4. Also evaluate the integral of those functions which are R–D integrable.

(a) $f(x) = \begin{cases} a, & x \in \mathbf{Z} \\ b, & \text{otherwise} \end{cases}$ in $[-M, M]$;

(b) $f(x) = \begin{cases} 2^{-n}, & x \in (2^{-n-1}, 2^{-n}], n \in \mathbf{N}, \\ 0, & x = 0 \end{cases}$ in $[0, 1]$;

(c) $f(x) = \begin{cases} a^{1-n}, & x \in (a^{-n}, a^{1-n}], n \in \mathbf{N}, \\ 0, & x = 0 \end{cases}$ in $[0, 1]$, $a \in \mathbf{N}$, $a \geqslant 2$;

(d) $f(x) = \begin{cases} x, & x \in \mathbf{Q} \cap [0, 1] \\ 1-x, & x \in (\mathbf{R} \sim \mathbf{Q}) \cap [0, 1], \end{cases}$ in $[0, 1]$;

(e) $f(x) = \begin{cases} (-1)^{n-1}, & \dfrac{1}{n+1} < x \leqslant \dfrac{1}{n}, n \in \mathbf{N} \\ 0, & x = 0 \end{cases}$ in $[0, 1]$;

(f) $f(x) = \begin{cases} \dfrac{1}{n}, & \dfrac{1}{n+1} < x \leqslant \dfrac{1}{n}, n \in \mathbf{N} \\ 0, & x = 0 \end{cases}$ in $[0, 1]$;

(g) $f(x) = \begin{cases} 2nx, & \dfrac{1}{n+1} < x \leqslant \dfrac{1}{n}, n \in \mathbf{N} \\ 0, & x = 0 \end{cases}$ in $[0, 1]$;

(h) $f(x) = \begin{cases} 1, & x \in (\mathbf{R} \sim \mathbf{Q}) \cap [0, 1] \\ \dfrac{(q-2)}{q}, & x = \dfrac{p}{q} \text{ in its lowest terms}, x \in \mathbf{Q} \cap [0, 1]. \end{cases}$ in $[0, 1]$;

(i) $f(x) = \begin{cases} x, & x \in \mathbf{Q} \\ -x, & x \notin \mathbf{Q} \end{cases}$ in $[0, 4]$;

(j) $f(x) = \begin{cases} 0, & x = \dfrac{n}{n+1} \text{ or } \dfrac{n+1}{n}, \ n \in \mathbf{N} \\ 1, & \text{otherwise} \end{cases}$ in $[0, 2]$.

20. Discuss the integrability of the function f in $[0, 1]$ where

$$f(x) = \begin{cases} \sin\dfrac{1}{x}, & x \in (0, 1] \\ 0, & x = 0. \end{cases}$$

21. Prove Theorem 5.2.7 and its corollary.

22. If the word 'finite' is replaced by 'countable' in the statement of Theorem 5.2.7, do we get a theorem? Prove or give a counterexample.

23. Show that a bounded function in $[a, b]$, whose set of discontinuities has a single limit point, is integrable.

24. Show f is R–D integrable in $[a, b]$ if and only if there exists $I \in \mathbf{R}$ with the property that given $\epsilon > 0$, there exists a partition P of $[a, b]$ such that $|\bar{S}(P) - I| < \epsilon$, $|I - \underline{S}(P)| < \epsilon$.

25. In the proof of the necessity of Theorem 5.2.4, we claimed that there is a single partition P satisfying $\int_a^b f - \dfrac{\epsilon}{2} < \underline{S}(P) \leqslant \bar{S}(P) < \int_a^b f + \dfrac{\epsilon}{2}$. Show that such a single partition must exist.

26. Let f be continuous and bounded on (a, b). Show that f is integrable in $[a, b]$.

27. Let f be defined on $[0, 1]$ by:

$$f(x) = \begin{cases} \dfrac{1}{\sqrt{x}}, & x \neq 0 \\ 0, & x = 0. \end{cases}$$

Let P be any partition of $[0, 1]$ and M be an arbitrary positive real number. Show there is a set $\{c_i : i \in \mathbf{N}\}$ such that $x_i \leqslant c_i \leqslant x_{i+1}$ and $\sum f(c_i) d_i \geqslant M$. Note that f is 'improperly' Riemann–Darboux integrable over this interval.

28. Let f be unbounded on $[a, b]$, but defined there. Show for any partition P of $[a, b]$ there is a set $\{c_1\}$ as in Exercise 27, such that $\sum |f(c_i)| d_i$ exceeds any arbitrary positive real number M.

29. Let f be integrable on $[a, b]$ and $[c, d] \subseteq [a, b]$. Show that f is integrable on $[c, d]$.

30. Let f be continuous and nonnegative on $[a, b]$. If $f(x) > 0$ for some $x \in [a, b]$, can the same be said for $\int_a^b f$? What about if continuity is replaced by mere integrability?

31. Let f and g be defined and integrable on $[a, b]$ and satisfy $f \leqslant g$, that is, $f(x) \leqslant g(x)$ for each $x \in [a, b]$. Show for any partition P, $\bar{S}(P, f) \leqslant \bar{S}(P, g)$ and $\underline{S}(P, f) \leqslant \underline{S}(P, g)$. Conclude that $\int_a^b f \leqslant \int_a^b g$.

32. Let f be continuous on the range of g and g be continuous on $[a, b]$. Show $f \circ g$ is integrable on $[a, b]$.

33. Let f be continuous on the range of g, and g be monotone on $[a, b]$. Show that $f \circ g$ is integrable on $[a, b]$.

5.3 THE PROBLEM OF COMPUTING AN INTEGRAL

At this stage in our development, we have proven several theorems for testing whether a given function is integrable on an interval $[a, b]$. For example, we can see from the fact that $f(x) = x^2$, $x \in [0, 2]$ is continuous (or monotone) on the given interval, that it is integrable there. Unfortunately, this fact does not give us a method for finding the value of the integral. In practice, this is a difficult procedure, even given the so-called Fundamental Theorem of Calculus. One reason is that there are unpleasant functions, which have no elementary function for an antiderivative. The elementary functions (see Chapter 10) are those which are commonly treated in calculus books. An example of a function which is not elementary is e^{x^2}, and we leave it to the reader to try to find a simple antiderivative for this function!! In these situations, if one wants to find an integral, one is left with using the definition to evaluate the integral. Indeed, it is the definition of the integral as a limit of an approximating sum which underlies the sophisticated techniques of numerical integration explored at the end of section 5.4.

EXAMPLE 1 _____

Find the value of $\int_0^2 x^2$.

Solution.   We shall proceed numerically. First, we partition $[0, 2]$ into n equal subdivisions of length $\dfrac{2}{n}$ each, to obtain a partition

$$P_n = \left\{ 0, \frac{2}{n}, \frac{4}{n}, \ldots, \frac{2i}{n}, \ldots, \frac{2n}{n} = 2 \right\}.$$

For this partition,

$$\bar{S}(P_n) = \sum_{i=1}^{n} \left[\frac{2i}{n} \right]^2 \left[\frac{2}{n} \right]$$

$$= \frac{8}{n^3} \sum_{i=1}^{n} i^2$$

$$= \frac{8}{n^3} \frac{n(n + 1)(2n + 1)}{6},$$

where the last inequality is obtained by applying the formula for the sum of squares up to n. The sequence $\{\bar{S}(P_n)\}$ is monotonically decreasing and bounded below (**WHY?**). By taking the limit as n tends to infinity, we get

$$\inf \{\bar{S}(P_n)\} = \lim_{n \to \infty} \bar{S}(P_n) = \frac{16}{6} = \frac{8}{3}.$$

On the other hand, evaluating $\underline{S}(P_n)$ leads to

$$\underline{S}(P_n) = \sum_{i=0}^{n-1} \left[\frac{2i}{n}\right]^2 \left[\frac{2}{n}\right]$$

$$= \frac{8}{n^3} \sum_{i=1}^{n-1} i^2$$

$$= \frac{8}{n^3} \frac{(n-1)(n)(2n-1)}{6}.$$

On taking the limit of $\underline{S}(P_n)$ as n tends to infinity we again get quantity $\frac{8}{3} = \sup \underline{S}(P_n)$, a calculation which the reader should verify. Now, $\frac{8}{3} = \inf \overline{S}(P_n) \geqslant \int_0^2 x^2$ and $\frac{8}{3} = \sup \underline{S}(P_n) \leqslant \underline{\int_0^2} x^2$. Hence, $\underline{\int_0^2} x^2 = \frac{8}{3} = \overline{\int_0^2} x^2$ (**WHY?**), and we conclude that $\int_0^2 x^2 = \frac{8}{3}$. $\qquad\square$

Discussion. In the calculation above, we used a rather special collection of partitions, namely partitions where each subdivision was of equal length. Partitions of this type are exceedingly useful for calculation purposes, but as of this juncture, there is no guarantee that calculations involving only this type of partition will always generate either the upper or lower integral. Thus we did not write

$$\lim_{n\to\infty} \overline{S}(P_n) = \overline{\int_0^2} x^2.$$

Technically speaking, we should have computed the supremum of $\underline{S}(P)$ and the infimum of $\overline{S}(P)$ for *all possible* partitions, P, of $[0, 2]$, and identified both these quantities with the number $\frac{8}{3}$. Instead, we only used the special subcollection $\{P_n\}$ consisting of all partitions which generated subintervals of equal length, $d = \frac{2}{n}$. For these special partitions, we were able to show that

$$\inf\{\overline{S}(P_n)\} = \sup\{\underline{S}(P_n)\} = \frac{8}{3}.$$

This fact, together with Theorem 5.2.1, is sufficient to guarantee that x^2 is not only integrable, but to establish the value of the integral on $[0, 2]$.

While it is the case that if f is integrable on $[a, b]$, that calculations using equally spaced intervals will yield the value of the integral, it is not obviously the case that the equivalent statement can be made if f is not integrable. Even so, the calculations above are worth studying because of their ease. They exhibit two features of importance.

1. The partitions used consist of $(n + 1)$ equally spaced points.
2. The components of the upper and lower sums associated with suprema and infima over subintervals have been replaced by values obtained by evaluating the function at the endpoints of the subintervals.

The second item is a result of the fact that the function being integrated is monotone on the intervals in question. This may not hold for other functions. Indeed, the supremum and/or infimum may not be attained on a given subinterval (see Exercise 1).

In conclusion it is clear that a computation which involves equal length subintervals and evaluation of the function only at the endpoints of these subintervals, or other convenient places, is exceptionally nice. Thus it would behoove us to find out under what conditions such a calculation gives a complete answer to the question of whether a function is integrable, and if so, what the value of the integral is. □

To answer the question raised above, we will return to the approach originally taken by Riemann to the development of the integral which bears his name.

Definition. Let $P = \{x_0, \ldots, x_n\}$ be a partition of $[a, b]$. A finite sequence, c_i, such that $1 \leqslant i \leqslant n$ and $c_i \in [x_{i-i}, x_i]$ is called an **intermediate partition** for P.

Discussion. The intent of this definition is to generate a collection of points, with one point being a member of each of the subintervals generated by the partition, P. Some special choices of the c_i's are the left endpoint x_{i-1}, or the right endpoint x_i, or even the midpoint $\dfrac{x_{i-1} + x_i}{2}$.

In our previous calculations of the upper and lower Riemann–Darboux sums, we have used some special choices. Specifically, if f is continuous on $[a, b]$, then both M_i, m_i are attained on the ith interval. Thus, we can find $c_{i,M}$ and $c_{i,m}$ such that $f(c_{i,M}) = M_i$ and $f(c_{i,m}) = m_i$, respectively. These choices enter the calculations via $\overline{S}(P) = \sum f(c_{i,M})d_i$, and $\underline{S}(P) = \sum f(c_{i,m})d_i$, where $d_i = x_i - x_{i-1}$.

Thus, an intermediate partition should be thought of as a set of choices c_i which will enter the calculation $\sum\limits_{i=1}^{n} f(c_i)d_i$. This sum resembles an upper or lower sum over a partition except that we are no longer requiring that $f(c_i)$ be either M_i or m_i. Calculations of this general type, that is, $\sum f(c_i)d_i$ where $\{c_i\}$ is an intermediate partition, will be used in the next definition. This more general approach leads to the concept of a Riemann integral. □

Definition. Let f be defined on $[a, b]$, P be a partition of $[a, b]$, and $Q = \{c_i\}$ an intermediate partition for P. The **Riemann sum**, $R(f, P, Q)$, of the function f over the partition P, and the intermediate partition Q is defined by

$$R(f, P, Q) = \sum_{P} f(c_i)d_i$$

where the P under the summation sign indicates summation extends over all the subintervals generated by P, and the c_i's are the members of Q.

Discussion. It should be emphasized that $R(f, P, Q)$ is a real number, and for a given partition P there will be many different numbers $R(f, P, Q)$, in fact, one for each distinct intermediate partition Q. Two obvious candidates for Riemann sums are the upper and the lower Riemann–Darboux sums $\overline{S}(P)$, $\underline{S}(P)$ defined in section 5.2,

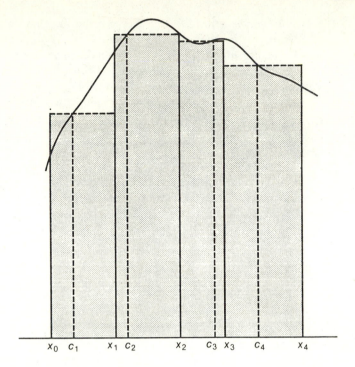

Figure 5.3.1   A typical Riemann sum $R(f, P, Q)$.

although these may not exist, since f is not required to be bounded on $[a, b]$; rather it is merely required to be defined on the total interval. For this reason, the Riemann sum is a generalization of the Riemann–Darboux sum. In the event that f is bounded, for any partition, P, and any intermediate partition, Q, of P, we have

$$\underline{S}(P) \leqslant R(f, P, Q) \leqslant \overline{S}(P).$$

As shown in Figure 5.3.1, the Riemann sum is also an approximating sum associated with a step function. However, for a given intermediate partition, Q, the associated step function neither lies above the function, f, as is the case with s^P, nor does it lie completely below the function as is the case with s_P. Instead, it lies somewhere in the middle, and as a result should more closely conform to f than either s^P or s_P. For the case of a nonnegative function, as shown in Figure 5.3.1, the Riemann sum also generates area. By virtue of the inequality above, this area must always lie between the area given by s_P and that given by s^P.   □

Definition.   Let f be defined on $[a,b]$. We say that f is **Riemann integrable (R-integrable)** on $[a, b]$ provided there is an $L \in \mathbf{R}$ such that for every $\epsilon > 0$ there exists $\delta > 0$ such that for every partition P and intermediate partition Q of P,

$$\|P\| < \delta \text{ implies } |R(f, P, Q) - L| < \epsilon.$$

The real number L is called the **Riemann integral** of the function f over the interval $[a, b]$, and we write $R\int_a^b f = L$.

Discussion. The definition must be viewed as a limit definition in the sense of our previous limit definitions. The number L is clearly the limit of the quantity $R(f, P, Q)$, a functional entity which 'approaches' L. The distinction between this and our previous definitions is in the variable quantity P (or more appropriately $\|P\|$) which is being made less than δ. In the earlier versions, the variable quantity, x, to be manipulated was constrained to move along the real line, and associated with each x was a unique real number, $f(x)$. In this case, the norm of P is also constrained to be a real number, but there are an infinity of partitions associated with this real number. Moreover, given a particular partition, P, there are infinitely many choices for Q and in consequence, there are many numbers of the form $R(f, P, Q)$ for this particular P. The result is that we are dealing with a much more complex form of limit.

The thrust of this definition is to isolate out the quantities $\|P\|$ and L as being those of interest. Thus, we must find a single L such that it is enough to have knowledge only about $\|P\|$ to ensure that $R(f, P, Q)$ is close to L. Note that for the definition to be satisfied, this must happen in spite of the fact that there are infinitely many partitions having a fixed small norm, and infinitely many intermediate partitions associated with a given one of these partitions.

While this definition contains all we need to know about integration, it suffers from the fact that it is difficult to work with. One may ask why then introduce it. Suppose for a minute that we were able to show that Riemann integrability and R–D integrability were equivalent concepts and further that the L of the definition above was $\int_a^b f$ whenever f was integrable on $[a, b]$. It would solve the problem suggested at the end of Example 1, since the L arrived at is independent of the choice of P and Q. Thus, if f is known to be integrable, the limits obtained using the methods of Example 1 must be the value of the integral! In other words, for integrable functions, we could compute our sums by evaluating the function at any point of convenience within each subinterval, and use subintervals of any type that was convenient, so long as the norm goes to 0.

Finally, the reader will realize that since we are dealing with a limit, there are some rather standard questions which must be asked, such as, is this limit unique, and so on. The problem of uniqueness is dealt with below. Answers to many of the other standard questions are presented in section 5.4. $\square$

Theorem 5.3.1. If f is Riemann Integrable on $[a, b]$, then $R\int_a^b f$ is unique.

Proof. The proof is left to Exercise 2. $\square$

The next theorem constitutes the first step in establishing an equivalence between the two types of integrals.

Theorem 5.3.2. If f is Riemann integrable on $[a, b]$, then f is bounded.

Proof. Let $\epsilon > 0$ be given, and let $\delta > 0$ be chosen satisfying the definition, with L the limit. For any P such that $\|P\| < \delta$, and any two intermediate partitions Q and Q' we have

$$|R(f, P, Q) - R(f, P, Q')| \leqslant |R(f, P, Q) - L| + |R(f, P, Q') - L| < 2\epsilon.$$

Thus, let P be a fixed partition having $\|P\| < \delta$ and let $Q = \{c_i\}$ be a fixed intermediate partition for P.

Now, if f is not bounded on $[a, b]$ then f is unbounded over a subinterval, say the subinterval $[x_{j-1}, x_j]$. Hence, we can choose a point $x \in [x_{j-1}, x_j]$ such that $|f(x) \times d_j|$ is as large as we please. In particular, we can find c'_j such that

$$|[f(c_j) - f(c'_j)] \times d_j| \geqslant 2\epsilon.$$

Now, if Q' is obtained from Q by replacing c_j by c'_j, then

$$|R(f, P, Q) - R(f, P, Q')| \geqslant 2\epsilon,$$

contrary to our initial inequality. It follows that f is bounded. □

Discussion.   The proof hinges on the fact that we can tie down the unboundedness of f to a single subinterval. This, of course is due to the fact that there are only finitely many subintervals to deal with. Had there been an infinite number, the situation would have been different. Once we have found an interval on which to focus, we use the fact that the function must assume arbitrarily large values to produce a contradiction.

The essential fact contained in this theorem is that there is no loss of generality in restricting our attention to bounded functions only, as we were forced to do in section 5.2. Without this result we could not hope to develop a general equivalence between the two results.

Lastly, the reader should compare this result with those in Exercises 5.2.27 and 5.2.28. □

The following result is known as **Darboux's Theorem.** It links the two definitions of integral by establishing that as the norm of the partition, $\|P\|$, approaches 0, the upper and lower Riemann–Darboux sums, $\bar{S}(P)$ and $\underline{S}(P)$, of a partition P indeed 'approach' the upper and lower R–D integrals $\overline{\int_a^b} f$ and $\underline{\int_a^b} f$, respectively.

Theorem 5.3.3. (Darboux's Theorem).   If f is bounded on $[a, b]$, then given $\epsilon > 0$, there exists a $\delta > 0$ such that if P is any partition of $[a, b]$ with $\|P\| < \delta$, then

$$\bar{S}(P) < \overline{\int_a^b} f + \epsilon \quad \text{and} \quad \underline{S}(P) > \underline{\int_a^b} f - \epsilon.$$

Proof.   Let $\epsilon > 0$ be given. By the property of the infimum, there exists a partition P_1 of $[a, b]$ satisfying

$$\bar{S}(P_1) < \overline{\int_a^b} f + \frac{\epsilon}{2}.$$

Suppose P_1 consists of k points other than a and b and set $\delta = \dfrac{\epsilon}{4kM}$, where M is the supremum of f in $[a, b]$. If we let P be any partition such that $\|P\| < \delta$ and $P_2 = P_1 \cup P$, then by Theorem 5.2.1 we have

$$|\bar{S}(P) - \bar{S}(P_2)| \leqslant 2kM\|P\| \leqslant 2kM\frac{\epsilon}{4kM} = \frac{\epsilon}{2}.$$

Hence,

$$\bar{S}(P) \leqslant \bar{S}(P_2) + \frac{\epsilon}{2} \leqslant \bar{S}(P_1) + \frac{\epsilon}{2}$$

$$\leqslant \overline{\int_a^b} f + \frac{\epsilon}{2} + \frac{\epsilon}{2}$$

$$= \overline{\int_a^b} f + \epsilon.$$

The assertion for the lower sums is left to Exercise 6. □

Discussion. This is a remarkable theorem because it manages to establish the connection between two apparently unconnected notions. Specifically, it takes the fact that the infimum of a set must have points of that set close to it, and replaces it by the fact that we can find partitions of small norm. The proof is extremely simple, but so clever. It is clever, because it takes a theorem, namely Theorem 5.2.1, and applies it in an unexpected way. Let us see how.

Theorem 5.2.1 tells us that if we obtain Q from P by adding n points to P, then

$$|\bar{S}(P) - \bar{S}(Q)| \leqslant 2nM \|P\|.$$

In the present case, we find the partition P_1 which has the property that $\bar{S}(P_1)$ is close to the upper integral. The obvious way to proceed is to take the norm of P_1, and start adding points. This approach fails because the number of points which we must add to P_1 to obtain an arbitrary partition, P, having norm less than δ, is unbounded. Thus the n in $2nM \|P_1\|$ can be arbitrarily large, making this a meaningless bound. The clever application of Theorem 5.2.1 comes in turning this situation around by thinking of adding P_1 to P. The key to this idea is that we notice that a common refinement of P_1 and P differs from P by at most k points. On the other hand, a common refinement of P and P_1 must yield an upper sum which is even closer to the upper integral than the upper sum over P_1. Moreover, the application of Theorem 5.2.1 is meaningful because k is fixed, while $\|P\|$ can be as small as we like.

The reader will note that the vital force behind this theorem is the basic properties of the supremum and infimum which enabled us to write the first inequality in the proof.

Roughly speaking, this theorem asserts that as the norm of P decreases, the upper sums 'approach' the value of the upper integral, and the lower sums 'approach' the lower integral. Since the collection $\{\bar{S}(P) : P$ is a partition of $[a, b]\}$ do not form a sequence (the domain is not $\mathbf{N}$, and there are uncountably many partitions of $[a, b]$), we can not speak of $\lim_{\|P\| \to 0} \{\bar{S}(P)\}$ in our usual sense. But if we agree to define this quantity as a real number L, provided given $\epsilon > 0$, there exists a $\delta > 0$ such that if P is any partition with $\|P\| < \delta$, we have $|\bar{S}(P) - L| < \epsilon$, then the above theorem states that

$$\lim_{\|P\| \to 0} \{\bar{S}(P)\} = \overline{\int_a^b} f$$

and

$$\lim_{\|P\| \to 0} \{\underline{S}(P)\} = \underline{\int_a^b} f.$$

We ask the reader to calculate the upper and lower R–D integrals in Example 1 above, using this theorem.   □

Theorem 5.3.4. Let f be Riemann integrable on $[a, b]$ with L as the Riemann integral. Then f is Riemann–Darboux integrable on $[a, b]$ and $\int_a^b f = L$.

Proof. By Theorem 5.3.2, f is bounded on $[a, b]$ whence both the upper and the lower integrals exist. Let $\epsilon > 0$ be given. Then there is a partition, P_1 of $[a, b]$, such that

$$\underline{\int_a^b} f - \frac{\epsilon}{2} \leqslant \underline{S}(P_1) \leqslant \bar{S}(P_1) \leqslant \overline{\int_a^b} f + \frac{\epsilon}{2}. \qquad \textbf{(WHY?)}$$

Let $\delta > 0$ be chosen which satisfies the definition of the Riemann integral for ϵ and L. Choose P to be any refinement of P_1 which satisfies $\|P\| < \delta$. For this partition, we have

$$\bar{S}(P) - \frac{\epsilon}{2} < \overline{\int_a^b} f \leqslant \bar{S}(P) + \frac{\epsilon}{2} \qquad \textbf{(WHY?)}$$

and

$$\bar{S}(P) - \frac{\epsilon}{2} < L < \bar{S}(P) + \frac{\epsilon}{2}$$

whence

$$\left| \overline{\int_a^b} f - L \right| < \epsilon.$$

Since ϵ was arbitrary, we have $\overline{\int_a^b} f = L$. Similarly, we can show that $\underline{\int_a^b} f = L$, whence the conclusion follows.   □

Discussion. The basic intuition on which the proof is based is simple. The definition of Riemann integrability allows us to choose partitions such that $R(f, P, Q)$ will be close to L, in particular, $\bar{S}(P)$ will be close to L. Further, we can choose partitions so that $\bar{S}(P)$ is close to $\overline{\int_a^b} f$. But taking common refinements allows us to come up with a single partition P such that $\bar{S}(P)$ is simultaneously close to L and also to $\overline{\int_a^b} f$. Thus, L must be close to $\overline{\int_a^b} f$, in fact as close as we please!   □

Next, we want to prove the converse of Theorem 5.3.4 which will then establish the equivalence of the two approaches to integration.

Theorem 5.3.5. If f is Riemann–Darboux integrable on $[a, b]$, then f is Riemann integrable on $[a, b]$, and $\int_a^b f = R \int_a^b f$.

Proof. Clearly, f is bounded. Let $\epsilon > 0$ be given. By Theorem 5.3.3, there exists $\delta > 0$ such that if $\|P\| < \delta$, we have

$$\underline{\int_a^b} f - \frac{\epsilon}{2} < \underline{S}(P) \leqslant \bar{S}(P) < \overline{\int_a^b} f + \frac{\epsilon}{2}.$$

Since f is Riemann–Darboux integrable, we have

$$\underline{\int_a^b} f = \overline{\int_a^b} f = L.$$

Thus,

$$L - \frac{\epsilon}{2} < \underline{S}(P) \leqslant R(f, P, Q) \leqslant \bar{S}(P) < L + \frac{\epsilon}{2}$$

for any Riemann sum $R(f, P, Q)$ obtained from the partition P. Thus,

$$|R(f, P, Q) - L| < \epsilon$$

proving that f is Riemann integrable, with L as the Riemann integral. $\square$

Discussion. The bulk of this proof is already contained in the proof of Darboux's Theorem. The only other fact needed to complete the proof is that a Riemann sum $R(f, P, Q)$ lies between the numbers $\underline{S}(P)$ and $\bar{S}(P)$. Note that the equality of the Riemann–Darboux integral and the Riemann integral is obtained automatically in this proof without much hard work. $\square$

We began this section with a problem of finding the value of a particular integral, $\int_0^2 x^2$. Our method was to obtain a formula for $R(f, P, Q)$ where

1. P was a partition of $[a, b]$ into n equal subintervals;
2. Q consists of the endpoints of the subintervals, either left hand or right hand.

Having found such a formula, we then proceeded to find the limit as n tended to infinity. Based on the results above, we know that for any function that is integrable (in either sense) on the interval $[a, b]$, this procedure will yield the correct value of the integral.

EXAMPLE 2

Evaluate $\int_{-1}^{3} 3x + 4$.

Solution. The function defined by $f(x) = 3x + 4$ is continuous on $[-1, 3]$, whence it is integrable there. If we subdivide $[-1, 3]$ into n subintervals of equal length, each subinterval has length $\dfrac{3 - (-1)}{n} = \dfrac{4}{n}$. The endpoints of these intervals are given by $c_i = -1 + i \times \dfrac{4}{n}$, where $i = 0, 1, \ldots, n$. If we use the right-hand endpoint of each subinterval to define the intermediate partition, then the Riemann sum is given by

$$R(3x + 4, P, Q) = \sum_{i=1}^{n} (3c_i + 4) \cdot \frac{4}{n}$$

$$= \frac{4}{n} \cdot \sum_{i=1}^{n} (3c_i + 4)$$

$$= \frac{4}{n} \cdot \sum_{i=1}^{n} \left[3 \left[-1 + i \cdot \frac{4}{n} \right] + 4 \right]$$

$$= \frac{4}{n} \cdot \sum_{i=1}^{n} \left[1 + \frac{12i}{n} \right]$$

$$= \frac{4}{n} \cdot \left[\sum_{i=1}^{n} 1 + \sum_{i=1}^{n} \frac{12i}{n} \right]$$

$$= \frac{4}{n} \cdot \left[n + \frac{12}{n} \cdot \sum_{i=1}^{n} i \right]$$

$$= 4 + \frac{48}{n^2} \cdot \frac{n(n+1)}{2}.$$

The limit as $n \to \infty$, of the last expression is 28, whence we see that the value of the integral is also 28.   □

Discussion. The computation above illustrates the utility of the formula for evaluating $\sum_{i=1}^{n} i$. Other examples require other formulae. This may have been the motivation behind the search for polynomials in n which would evaluate $\sum_{i=1}^{n} i^k$. Such formulae exist and can be found by solving a series of simultaneous equations which are generated under the assumption that such a formula does exist. The degree of the polynomial in n is always $k+1$.   □

The method of defining the integral has been based on the use of step functions to approximate the function. Approximating a function with a step function amounts to suggesting that a given function is locally constant, that is, around every x there is an interval on which the function is constant. This assumption is not likely to be true for most functions. Even so, as we have seen, the procedure still yields the correct value for the integral. The effect of this 'bad' assumption is felt in the rate of convergence. That is, we must generally work with partitions having very small norms if we want the approximate value to be close to the true value. Evidently, if one is going to use approximating sums to evaluate integrals, one would like to have a procedure which converged more quickly. As well, for a given approximation, one would like to be able to estimate the error. Further exploration of these questions must await development of some of the basic theory in the next section.

EXERCISES

1. Give an example of a function on [0, 1] for which there are infinitely many distinct subintervals such that f neither achieves its maximum nor its minimum on the subinterval.

2. Let f be Riemann integrable on $[a, b]$. Show the value of the integral is unique.

3. Use the methods developed to evaluate:

   (a) $\int_0^a x^2$;

   (b) $\int_2^3 x$;

   (c) $\int_{-3}^{-1} x$;

   (d) $\int_1^4 x^3$;

   (e) $\int_{-1}^1 (1 - x^2)$;

   (f) $\int_0^2 (2 - 3x + x^3)$.

4. Give an example of a function which is not Riemann integrable.

5. Fill in the missing details in Example 1.

6. Complete the missing proof for lower sums in Theorem 5.3.3.

7. Complete the proof of the fact that $\int_a^b f = L$ in Theorem 5.3.4.

8. Let f be a function which is defined on $[0, 1]$. If f takes one fixed value on the rationals and another on the irrationals, will f be integrable?

9. Let f be defined on $[a, b]$ but discontinuous at every point of the interval. Show f is not integrable there.

10. In earlier chapters we have discussed why limits fail to exist. Let f be a function defined on an interval $[a, b]$ but which is not integrable there. What, if any, conclusions can be drawn about f?

11. Let f and g be defined and bounded on $[a, b]$. For $c, d \in \mathbf{R}$ show

$$cS(f, P, Q) + dS(g, P, Q) = S(cf + dg, P, Q).$$

where P is an arbitrary partition of $[a, b]$ and Q is an intermediate partition of P. Use this result to show

$$c\int_a^b f + d\int_a^b g = \int_a^b (cf + dg).$$

12. Let $a > 0$. Use the partition $\{a, ar, ar^2, \ldots, ar^n = b\}$ of $[a, b]$ to compute $\int_a^b \frac{1}{x}$.

13. Show $\int_0^a \sin = 1 - \cos a$, where $0 < a \leqslant 1$. [HINT: Use the following:

$$\sum_{k=1}^n \sin kx = \frac{\sin \dfrac{(n+1)x}{2} \sin \dfrac{nx}{2}}{\sin \dfrac{x}{2}}, \quad x \neq 2m\pi, \ m \in \mathbf{Z}.]$$

14. Given f is integrable on $[a, b]$, show for every $\epsilon > 0$, there exist step functions g, h defined on $[a, b]$ such that $g \leqslant f \leqslant h$ and

$$\int_a^b(f - g) < \epsilon, \quad \int_a^b(h - f) < \epsilon.$$

15. Show f is integrable on $[a, b]$ if for every positive ϵ there exist step functions g, h such that $g \leqslant f \leqslant h$ and $\int_a^b (h - g) < \epsilon$.

16. Let f be bounded on $[a, b]$. If there exist a sequence of partitions, P_n, such that $\lim_{n \to \infty} (\bar{S}(f, P_n) - \underline{S}(f, P_n)) = (\bar{S}(f, P_n) - \underline{S}(f, P_n)) = 0$, prove f is integrable. Conversely,

show if f is integrable, there exists a sequence of partitions, P_n, such that

$$\int_a^b f = \lim_{n\to\infty} \bar{S}(f, P_n) = \lim_{n\to\infty} \underline{S}(f, P_n).$$

[NOTE: This justifies our approach to Example 1.]

17. If f is continuous on $[a, b]$, prove

$$\int_a^b f = \lim_{n\to\infty} \frac{b-a}{n+1} \sum_{k=0}^n f\left[a + \frac{k(b-a)}{n+1}\right] = \lim_{n\to\infty} \frac{b-a}{n+1} \sum_{k=0}^n f\left[a + \frac{(k+1)(b-a)}{n+1}\right].$$

18. Prove the following Cauchy's criterion for Riemann integrability: f is integrable in $[a, b]$ if and only if given $\epsilon > 0$, there exists $\delta > 0$ such that for all partitions P_1, P_2 such that $\|P_i\| < \delta$ $(i = 1, 2)$, and for all intermediate partitions Q_1, Q_2 of P_1, P_2, $|R(f, P_1, Q_1) - R(f, P_2, Q_2)| < \epsilon$.

19. Let $g : [0, 1] \to [0, 1]$ be a one-to-one, onto, continuous function. Show geometrically $\int_0^1 g(x)dx + \int_0^1 g^{-1}(x) = 1$.

20. If f is Riemann integrable in $[0, 1]$, and if $a_n = \frac{1}{n}\sum_{k=1}^n f\left[\frac{k}{n}\right]$, prove a_n converges to

$\int_0^1 f$. Show also if f is not Riemann integrable, $\{a_n\}$ may fail to converge. Give an example where $\{a_n\}$ converges, but f is not integrable.

21. If f satisfies Lipschitz's condition of order 1 in $[0, 1]$, with Lipschitz's constant M, prove

$$\left|\int_0^1 f - \frac{1}{n}\sum_{k=1}^n f\left[\frac{k}{n}\right]\right| < \frac{M}{2n}.$$

5.4. PROPERTIES OF THE INTEGRAL

In the previous sections, we considered methods which enable us to associate with each integrable function f defined on $[a, b]$, a unique real number called the integral (in the sense of Riemann–Darboux, as well as Riemann), and denoted by the symbol $\int_a^b f$. This passage from integrable functions to the value of the integral is a limiting process and as such, should exhibit certain nice properties. We have already established uniqueness. Additional properties are presented in the following set of theorems. Our first result proves that the integral is additive.

Theorem 5.4.1. If f and g are both integrable on $[a, b]$, then $f + g$ is integrable on $[a, b]$, and moreover,

$$\int_a^b f + g = \int_a^b f + \int_a^b g.$$

Proof. Let $\epsilon > 0$ be given. Since f and g are both integrable on $[a, b]$, we can choose a partition P such that

$$\int_a^b f - \frac{\epsilon}{2} < \underline{S}(f, P) \leqslant \bar{S}(f, P) < \int_a^b f + \frac{\epsilon}{2}$$

and

$$\int_a^b g - \frac{\epsilon}{2} < \underline{S}(g, P) \leq \bar{S}(g, P) < \int_a^b g + \frac{\epsilon}{2}.$$

Adding these two inequalities yields

$$\int_a^b f + \int_a^b g - \epsilon < \underline{S}(f, P) + \underline{S}(g, P) \leq \bar{S}(f, P) + \bar{S}(g, P) < \int_a^b f + \int_a^b g + \epsilon.$$

By Lemma 5.2.2(d), $\bar{S}(f + g, P) \leq \bar{S}(f, P) + \bar{S}(f, P)$. Since a similar statement is valid for lower sums, we have

$$\int_a^b f + \int_a^b g - \epsilon < \underline{S}(f + g, P) \leq \bar{S}(f + g, P) < \int_a^b f + \int_a^b g + \epsilon.$$

It is immediate from Theorem 5.2.4 that $f + g$ is integrable and further that

$$\int_a^b (f + g) = \int_a^b f + \int_a^b g. \qquad \textbf{(WHY?)}$$

$\square$

Discussion. Observe that the heart of this argument is the calculation implicit in Lemma 5.2.2(d). The proof of this lemma depends only on our ability to manipulate finite sums.

This theorem is analogous to our previous theorems which relate limiting processes to the operation of addition. In essence, it tells us that the integral (limit of a sum process) is well behaved with respect to addition. $\square$

Theorem 5.4.2. If f is integrable on $[a, b]$ and c is any constant, then cf is integrable on $[a, b]$ and

$$\int_a^b cf = c\int_a^b f.$$

Proof. There are two cases, namely, $c \geq 0$ and $c < 0$. We treat the latter and leave the former as an exercise. Let $\epsilon > 0$ be fixed, and let $\epsilon_1 = \min\left\{\epsilon, \dfrac{\epsilon}{|c|}\right\}$. Then there is a partition P, such that

$$\int_a^b f - \epsilon_1 < \underline{S}(f, P) \leq \bar{S}(f, P) < \int_a^b f + \epsilon_1. \qquad \textbf{(WHY?)}$$

Since $c < 0$, we obtain

$$c\int_a^b f + c\epsilon_1 < \bar{S}(cf, P) \leq \underline{S}(cf, P) < c\int_a^b f - c\epsilon_1.$$

Since $0 < |c\epsilon_1| \leq \epsilon$, it is immediate that

$$\int_a^b cf = c\int_a^b f.$$

$\square$

Discussion. The reader should note the implicit use of Theorem 5.2.4 in the arguments we have given. $\square$

Theorem 5.4.3. If f is integrable on $[a, b]$, then so is f^2.

Proof. Let $\epsilon > 0$ be fixed and M be a positive bound for $|f|$. Set $\epsilon_1 = \dfrac{\epsilon}{2M}$. Let P be a partition of $[a, b]$ satisfying $\overline{S}(P) - \underline{S}(P) < \epsilon_1$. For this partition, let M_i, m_i and d_i have their usual meanings (as in section 5.2). We want to calculate $\overline{S}(f^2, P) - \underline{S}(f^2, P)$. We claim that the contribution to the difference arising from the interval $[x_{i-1}, x_i]$ is $|M_i^2 - m_i^2| d_i$. To see this, note that one of M_i^2 and m_i^2 will be the supremum for f^2 while the other will be the infimum for f^2 on this subinterval, unless m_i is negative, M_i is positive, and $f(x) = 0$ for some x in the interval. Thus, there are two cases to be considered. In the former,

$$|M_i^2 - m_i^2| d_i = |M_i + m_i| (M_i - m_i) d_i$$
$$\leqslant 2M(M_i - m_i) d_i.$$

In the latter, one of the quantities M_i^2 and m_i^2 will be replaced by 0 to obtain either $M_i^2 d_i$ or $m_i^2 d_i$. Using the former quantity, we get

$$M_i^2 d_i = M_i (M_i - 0) d_i$$
$$< M_i (M_i - m_i) d_i$$
$$< 2M (M_i - m_i) d_i.$$

The latter quantity yields a similar inequality. Thus,

$$\overline{S}(f^2, P) - \underline{S}(f^2, P) < 2M(\overline{S}(f, P) - \underline{S}(f, P))$$
$$< 2M\epsilon_1 = \epsilon. \qquad \square$$

Discussion. The proof is simple. The only algebra used there is the identity $M_i^2 - m_i^2 = (M_i + m_i)(M_i - m_i)$. The quantity $M_i + m_i$ is less than or equal to twice the maximum value of the function in $[a, b]$. We are not readily concluding that M_i^2 and m_i^2 are the maxima and minima of f^2 in the ith subinterval. We have to take into consideration the points where the function $f(x) = 0$, and simultaneously m_i is negative. In such cases, the minimum value of f^2 in the subinterval is 0 and not m_i^2. $\qquad \square$

Theorem 5.4.4. If f and g are integrable on $[a, b]$, so is their product fg.

Proof. By our previous results, $(f - g)^2$, f^2, and g^2 are all integrable on $[a, b]$. The observation that

$$fg = \frac{f^2 + g^2 - (f - g)^2}{2}$$

completes the proof. $\qquad \square$

The results of this section have dealt with the relationship of the integral to the various algebraic operations which have been defined on functions. It is reasonable to ask about the interaction of the integral with the various other properties defined on functions, and we now turn to this direction.

Theorem 5.4.5. If f is nonnegative and integrable on $[a, b]$, then $\int_a^b f$ is nonnegative.

Proof. Observe that every lower sum is nonnegative. □

Corollary. If f and g are integrable on $[a, b]$, and $f \geqslant g$ throughout $[a, b]$, then $\int_a^b f \geqslant \int_a^b g$.

Theorem 5.4.6. If f is integrable on $[a, b]$, then $|f|$ is integrable on $[a, b]$, and further,

$$\left| \int_a^b f \right| \leqslant \int_a^b |f|.$$

Proof. Let $\epsilon > 0$ be fixed, and choose a partition, P, such that $\overline{S}(P) - \underline{S}(P) < \epsilon$. For a given subinterval of this partition, $[x_{i-1}, x_i]$, let M'_i and m'_i denote the supremum and infimum of $|f|$, respectively. The reader can check that $M_i - m_i \geqslant M'_i - m'_i$, whence we have

$$\overline{S}(|f|, P) - \underline{S}(|f|, P) \leqslant \overline{S}(P) - \underline{S}(P) < \epsilon.$$

Thus, $|f|$ is integrable on $[a, b]$. The last inequality follows from Lemma 5.2.2(c) which establishes the analogous result for upper sums. □

Discussion. The inequality established in Theorem 5.4.6 may be thought of as the ultimate generalization of the triangle inequality, $|a + b| \leqslant |a| + |b|$, that is, absolute value of the limit of a sum never exceeds the limit of the sum of the absolute values. □

Let us summarize our work in this section so far. Consider a fixed interval, say $[a, b]$. Let $\mathcal{R}[a, b]$ denote the class of all Riemann integrable functions on this interval. We have shown that if $f, g \in \mathcal{R}[a, b]$, then $f + g$, $f \cdot g$ and λf ($\lambda \in \mathbf{R}$) and $|f|$ belong to $\mathcal{R}[a, b]$. In other words, we say that this class is 'closed' under addition and multiplication, scalar multiplication, and the formation of the absolute value. Moreover, if we think of the integral as a function

$$\text{Int}: \mathcal{R}[a, b] \rightarrow \mathbf{R}$$

defined by $\text{Int}(f) = \int_a^b f$, with domain $\mathcal{R}[a, b]$ and range contained in $\mathbf{R}$, then this function has the properties $\text{Int}(f + g) = \text{Int}(f) + \text{Int}(g)$ and $\text{Int}(\lambda f) = \lambda \text{Int}(f)$. In other words, the function Int preserves 'vector sums' and 'scalar products'. In the language of linear algebra, the function Int acts as a linear mapping in the usual sense of vector spaces. This function also enjoys some additional properties such as $\text{Int}(f) \geqslant \text{Int}(g)$ whenever $f \geqslant g$. □

The last theorem in this section shows that the integral is additive on an interval.

Theorem 5.4.7. If f is integrable on $[a, b]$ and $c \in [a, b]$, then f is integrable on

$[a, c]$ and $[c, b]$ and further,

$$\int_a^b f = \int_a^c f + \int_c^b f.$$

Proof. Let P be any partition of $[a, b]$ which contains c. Let P' be the points of P which lie to the left of c, including c, and P'' be the points of P to the right of c, including c. Thus, $P = P'' \cup P'$. It is immediate that

$$\bar{S}(P') - \underline{S}(P') \leqslant \bar{S}(P) - \underline{S}(P)$$

and

$$\bar{S}(P'') - \underline{S}(P'') \leqslant \bar{S}(P) - \underline{S}(P).$$

Since all differences are nonnegative, and may be made less than any prescribed positive number, we obtain integrability in $[a, c]$ and $[c, b]$. The rest of the proof is left to the reader (Exercise 3). □

Discussion. This particular theorem has an important interpretation for nonnegative functions. Namely, it tells us that if we split the interval over which we are integrating into two parts, the value of the integral over the whole will be the sum of the two integrals over the subintervals. This amounts to dividing the region whose area must be found into two separate parts and observing that the total area is the sum of the areas of the separate portions. □

We conclude this section by applying some of the theory just developed. As we have already noted, when one approximates an integral via the limit of a sum process, one would like information on two aspects of the approximation. First one would like to know how good a given approximation is. Second one would like information on how rapidly one is approaching the limit.

Various techniques for approximating integrals have been developed. These techniques vary according to the entry corresponding to $f(c_i)$ in the Riemann sum. (Recall that we have already used M_i, m_i, and $f(x_i)$ as choices for this entry in an approximating sum.) The point is that by shrewdly choosing these values, one can force a more rapid convergence. Our next example illustrates this for the case of $f(x_i)$, which amounts to assuming the function is locally constant.

EXAMPLE 1 _____

Let f be defined on $[a, b]$ and have a continuous derivative there, with M being a bound for f' on $[a, b]$. Let $[a, b]$ be divided into n subintervals of equal width, $h = \dfrac{(b - a)}{n}$, with right-hand endpoints $x_0, x_1, \ldots, x_{n-1}$ and let

$$y_i = f(x_i), 0 \leqslant i \leqslant n-1.$$

Establish the **rectangular rule**:

$$\int_a^b f = \lim_{n \to \infty} (y_0 + y_1 + \cdots + y_{n-1})h.$$

Moreover, show that

$$\left| \int_a^b f - (y_0 + y_1 + \cdots + y_{n-1})h \right| \leqslant Mh(b-a),$$

where M is any bound on f'.

Solution. The first statement follows from Theorems 5.2.5 and 5.3.3. We prove the second statement. To this end, consider the ith subinterval, $[x_{i-1}, x_i]$. By Theorem 5.4.7,

$$\int_a^b f = \sum_{i=0}^{n-1} \int_{x_i}^{x_{i+1}} f.$$

Thus the problem reduces to estimating

$$\left| \int_{x_i}^{x_{i+1}} (f - y_i) \right| = \left| \int_{x_i}^{x_{i+1}} (f - f(x_i)) \right|.$$

The function $f - f(x_i)$ satisfies the hypothesis of the Mean Value Theorem on $[x_i, x_{i+1}]$, whence for each $x \in [x_i, x_{i+1}]$, we can choose c_x such that

$$|f(x) - f(x_i)| = |f'(c_x)|(x - x_i) \leqslant Mh,$$

where the last inequality follows from the fact that $x - x_i \leqslant h$. It is immediate that

$$\int_{x_i}^{x_{i+1}} |(f - f(x_i))| \leqslant Mh^2.$$

If we now sum over i, we get

$$\int_a^b f - \sum_{i=0}^{n-1} y_i \leqslant \sum_{i=0}^{n-1} Mh^2 = Mh \times \sum_{i=0}^{n-1} h$$

$$= Mh(b-a). \qquad \square$$

Discussion. The important feature of the argument in this example is the application of the Mean Value Theorem. It derives from the fact that we are approximating $f(x)$ on $[x_i, x_{i+1}]$ by $f(x_i)$, which is the function evaluated at the left-hand endpoint of the subinterval. This sets up the direct application of the theorem as in Example 4.3.1. The trick is to realize that we can apply it in each interval from x_i to x which yields

$$|f(x) - f(x_i)| = |f'(c_x)|(x - x_i).$$

Completing the proof is then merely a matter of completing the calculation. This application will undoubtedly give the reader further insight into why the Mean Value Theorem and its generalization are such powerful tools in analysis and its applications.

The reader should also look at the bound, $Mh(b - a)$. Evidently, rapid convergence will be achieved if M is small, which means that the function is flat. If the reader thinks about it, it should seem reasonable that $(b - a)$ appears in the bound. Clearly, the longer the interval over which we are integrating, the greater the error for a given number of subdivisions, n. These are the two unchanging parts of the bound. What is used to make them small is decreasing h, which is accomplished by increasing n. Quite obviously, we would like a term which gets small more rapidly than h in the bound.

It would seem obvious that the assumption that f is locally a constant is not a good one. A more tenable assumption would be that f is piecewise linear, that is, a series of straight lines not necessarily having slope 0. If one thinks about this idea, one quickly realizes that the best piecewise linear approximation to f on $[x_i, x_{i+1}]$ is the one which connects the points $(x_i, f(x_i))$ and $(x_{i+1}, f(x_{i+1}))$. This leads to the trapezoidal rule (Exercise 24). Evidently, one can also use more complicated approximations, say by requiring the approximating function to go through more points on each subinterval. These topics are treated in the discipline of Numerical Analysis. We suggest that the interested reader consult Conte and de Boor (1972)†.   □

EXERCISES

1. Fill in the missing details in the proof of Theorem 5.4.1.

2. Give a proof for the case not treated in Theorem 5.4.2.

3. Fill in the missing details of Theorem 5.4.6, and complete the proof for the equality of the two integrals in Theorem 5.4.7.

4. Give an example of a function f which is not integrable on $[0, 1]$ but such that f^2 is integrable there.

5. If f and g are integrable in $[a, b]$, prove that $f - g$ is integrable in $[a, b]$ and $\int_a^b (f - g) = \int_a^b f - \int_a^b g$.

6. Generalize Theorem 5.4.1 to the case of the sum of n integrable functions.

7. Let f be integrable on $[a, b]$, and let $P = \{a = x_0 < x_1 < \cdots < x_n = b\}$ be any partition of $[a, b]$. Show f is integrable in each subinterval, $[x_{i-1}, x_i]$, $(i = 1, 2, \ldots, n)$, and further,

$$\int_a^b f = \sum_{k=1}^n \int_{x_{k-1}}^{x_k} f.$$

8. If f is integrable on $[a, b]$ and $g: [a + c, b + c] \to \mathbf{R}$ is defined by $g(x) = f(x - c)$, for $x \in [a, b]$, prove that g is integrable on $[a + c, b + c]$ and

$$\int_{a+c}^{b+c} g = \int_a^b f.$$

9. If $\int_a^b f > 0$, must f be nonnegative on $[a, b]$? If $\int_a^b f = 0$, must $f = 0$ on $[a, b]$?

10. Is there any relationship between $\int_a^b f$ and $\int_a^b f^2$?

11. Let f be defined and integrable on $[a, b]$. Show that f^+ and f^- are integrable on $[a, b]$.

12. Use (11) above to show that the integrability of f on $[a, b]$ implies the integrability of $|f|$. Give an example to show that the converse need not hold.

13. If f and g are both integrable in $[a, b]$, what can you say about the integrability of $\max (f, g)$ and $\min (f, g)$?

14. If f is integrable, and if there exists m, M satisfying $0 < m \leqslant f \leqslant M$ in $[a, b]$, prove that $\dfrac{1}{f}$ is integrable in $[a, b]$.

† Conte, S. D., and Carl de Boor, 1972. *Elementary numerical analysis: an algorithmic approach.* McGraw-Hill, New York.

15. Prove or disprove: If f is continuous on $[a, b]$ and $\int_a^b fg = 0$ for every integrable function g on $[a, b]$, then $f(x) = 0$ on $[a, b]$.

16. Let $g \leqslant f \leqslant h$ on $[a, b]$, where g and h are integrable, and $\int_a^b g = \int_a^b h = A$, prove that f is integrable and $\int_a^b f = A$.

17. Is there any relationship between the value of $\int_a^b fg$ and $\left(\int_a^b f \right) \left(\int_a^b g \right)$, assuming that all integrals exist?

18. Show that $\int_a^b fg$ can exist while neither of the separate integrals in Exercise 17 exist.

19. Let $\int_a^b fg$ exist along with $\int_a^b f$. Can we draw any conclusions about $\int_a^b g$? Suppose we assume f is continuous, or monotone, or strictly monotone. Are your conclusions going to be changed?

20. If f is continuous and nonnegative on $[a, b]$ and if $M = \max f(x)$ in $[a, b]$, show that
$$\lim_{n \to \infty} \left[\int_a^b (f(x))^n \right]^{1/n} = M.$$

21. If f is periodic on $\mathbf{R}$ with period $\alpha > 0$, and integrable on $[0, \alpha]$, show f is integrable on $[t, t + \alpha]$ for any $t \in \mathbf{R}$, and $\int_t^{t+\alpha} f = \int_0^\alpha f$.

22. Let f be strictly monotone on $[a, b]$. Show that if f is nonnegative on $[a, b]$ then $\int_a^b f$ is positive.

23. Let f be positive on $[a, b]$ and integrable there. Must the value of the integral be positive (assuming that $a < b$)?

24. Let f be nonnegative on $[a, b]$. Show that
$$\int_a^b f \geqslant \int_c^d f$$
for any subinterval $[c, d]$ of $[a, b]$.

25. Let f be integrable on $[a, b]$ and define $F(x) = \int_a^x f$. Find a condition on f that will ensure that F is nondecreasing; strictly increasing; monotone.

26. Let g be the function of Example 5.2.4 and f be defined by
$$f(x) = \begin{cases} 1, & x > 0 \\ 0, & x = 0. \end{cases}$$
Show $f \circ g$ is not integrable on $[0, 1]$ even though both f and g are integrable.

27. A function is **even** on the interval $[-a, a]$, $a > 0$, provided $f(-x) = f(x)$ for each $x \in [-a, a]$. It is **odd** provided $f(-x) = -f(x)$ in that interval. Show that if f is even on $[-a, a]$, then $\int_{-a}^a f = 2 \int_0^a f$. Show that if f is odd, then $\int_{-a}^a f = 0$.

28. Let f and g be integrable on $[a, b]$. Establish the **Cauchy–Schwarz inequality**:
$$\left[\int_a^b fg \right]^2 \leqslant \left[\int_a^b f^2 \right] \left[\int_a^b g^2 \right].$$

29. Give a suitable definition of $\int_a^b f$ where $b < a$. For this definition, establish the formula:
$$\int_a^b f = -\int_b^a f.$$

30. Let $f \leqslant M$ (a constant) throughout $[a, b]$ and integrable there. Show that $\int_a^b f \leqslant M(b - a)$.

In the following exercises, 31–34, let f be defined on $[a, b]$ and have an appropriate number of derivatives. Let $[a, b]$ be divided into n subintervals of equal width, $h = \dfrac{b - a}{n}$, with right-hand endpoints $x_0, x_1, \ldots, x_n$ and let

$$y_i = f(x_i),\ 0 \leqslant i \leqslant n-1;\ y_n = f(b).$$

31. Establish the following for this **forward rectangular rule**: there exists $\psi \in (a, b)$ such that

$$\int_a^b f = (b - a)f(a) + \frac{(b - a)^2}{2} f'(\psi).$$

More generally, show if $x_0 \in [a, b]$ then there exists $\psi \in (a, b)$ such that

$$\int_a^b f = (b - a)f(x_0) + \frac{(b + a - 2x_0)^2}{2} f'(\psi),$$

which is the general **rectangular rule**.

32. Establish the **trapezoidal rule**:

$$\int_a^b f = \lim_{n \to \infty} \left(\frac{y_0}{2} + y_1 + \cdots + y_{n-1} + \frac{y_n}{2} \right) h.$$

Moreover, show that for any n there is a $c \in [a, b]$ such that

$$\int_a^b f - \left(\frac{y_0}{2} + y_1 + \cdots + y_{n-1} + \cdots + \frac{y_n}{2} \right) = -(b - a)h^2 \frac{f''(c)}{12}.$$

Why is this referred to as the trapezoidal rule?

33. Establish **Simpson's rule**:

$$\int_a^b f = \lim_{n \to \infty} S_n$$

where $S_n = \dfrac{1}{3}(y_0 + 4y_1 + 2y_2 + 4y_3 + 2y_4 + \cdots + 4y_{n-1} + y_n)h$, where n is even. Moreover, show that for some $c \in [a, b]$

$$\int_a^b f - S_n = - \frac{(b - a)h^4 f''''(c)}{180}.$$

34. Establish **midpoint rule**: $\int_a^b f = \lim_{n \to \infty} M_n$, where

$$M_n = h \sum_{k=1}^{n} f(a + (k - \tfrac{1}{2})h).$$

34. Why is Simpson's rule a generally more effective method for numerical integration than the rectangular rule?

35. For a polynomial $P(x)$ of degree at most 3, show that Simpson's rule yields the exact value.

36. Take $n = 4, 8$, respectively, and obtain approximations for $\int_0^1 f$, (where f is given below) using
    (a) Simpson's rule;
    (b) trapezoidal rule.
    Compare the two results.

$$\frac{1}{x}, \quad \frac{1}{1 + x^2}, \quad e^{-x^2}.$$

37. If $|f''(x)| < M$ in $[0, 1]$, show that the error in calculating $\int_0^1 f$ by Simpson's rule is less than $\dfrac{M}{2880 n^4}$ where the interval $[0, 1]$ is divided into $2n$ equal parts.

5.5 THE RELATIONSHIP BETWEEN INTEGRATION AND DIFFERENTIATION

The preceding sections saw the development of the notion of integral as a limit of approximating sums which have no apparent relationship to the process of differentiation. In this section, we bring forth the intimate connection between the notions of differentiation and integration for a certain class of functions, and show that in the case of continuous functions, the so-called Fundamental Theorem of Integral Calculus is true, namely integration is the reverse process of differentiation. To begin our discussion, we associate with a function f defined on the interval $[a, b]$, a new function which has the role of an 'antiderivative'. More precisely:

Definition.   If f is a function defined on $[a, b]$, a function F is called a **primitive** (or an **antiderivative**) of f on $[a, b]$, provided F is differentiable and $F'(x) = f(x)$ for all x in (a, b).

Discussion.   The essential point about antiderivatives is that they are not unique. Rather, if a function has an antiderivative, then it has infinitely many antiderivatives. The key additional fact regarding primitives is that two functions which are primitives for the same function must differ by a constant, as shown below. $\square$

Theorem 5.5.1.   Let F and G be primitives for f on $[a, b]$. Then $F - G$ is a constant on $[a, b]$.

   Proof.   Let $H = F - G$ on $[a, b]$. The reader can check that H satisfies the hypothesis of the Mean Value Theorem on $[a, b]$. Suppose, for the sake of argument, that H is not constant of $[a, b]$. Then there exist $c, d \in [a, b]$ such that $c < d$ and $H(c) \neq H(d)$. By the Mean Value Theorem, we can find $x \in (a, b)$ such that

$$H'(x) = \frac{H(d) - H(c)}{d - c} \neq 0.$$

However, $H'(x) = 0$ for all $x \in (c, d)$, whence we have a contradiction. $\square$

Discussion.   The proof of this theorem is another of the many applications we have seen for the Mean Value Theorem. The reader should come to an understanding of why the Mean Value Theorem is the natural tool to apply in this context. An attempt to construct a more direct proof from the definition of derivative might aid in developing this appreciation.
   The converse of this theorem is left as Exercise 1. It together with the theorem, implies that if a function has a primitive, it has in fact an infinite number of primitives. $\square$

   The next result which brings forth the relationship between integrals and primitives enables us to evaluate a Riemann integral easily, provided we have the knowledge and access to a primitive of that function. However, not all functions possess primitives, and the theorem is applicable only if the primitive is already available in advance.

Theorem 5.5.2 (Fundamental Theorem of Calculus). If f is integrable on $[a, b]$ and F is any primitive for f on $[a, b]$, then

$$\int_a^b f = F(b) - F(a).$$

Proof. Let $P = \{a = x_0, x_1, \ldots, x_n = b\}$ be any partition of $[a, b]$. Consider the interval $[x_{i-1}, x_i]$. By the Mean Value Theorem (Theorem 4.3.3), we have that for some $c_i \in (x_{i-1}, x_i)$,

$$F(x_i) - F(x_{i-1}) = F'(c_i) (x_i - x_{i-1}) = f(c_i)d_i$$

where $d_i = x_i - x_{i-1}$. Let Q be the intermediate partition of P consisting of the c_i's. It is immediate that

$$F(b) - F(a) = \sum_{i=1}^{n} [F(x_i) - F(x_{i-1})]$$

$$= \sum f(c_i) \, d_i = R(f, P, Q),$$

a Riemann sum. Thus, for every partition, P, regardless of norm, there is an intermediate partition, Q, such that $R(f, P, Q) = F(b) - F(a)$. Hence, we conclude that

$$\int_a^b f = F(b) - F(a). \qquad\qquad\textbf{(WHY?)}$$

□

Corollary. If the derivative, f', of f is integrable on $[a, b]$, then

$$\int_a^b f' = f(b) - f(a).$$

Discussion. Theorem 5.5.2 is known as the Fundamental Theorem of Calculus. Its purpose is to make the process of integration easier. Specifically, to obtain the integral of f on $[a, b]$, find *any* primitive, F, of f, evaluate this primitive at a and b, and finally, compute $F(b) - F(a)$. We emphasize that any primitive will do. It is clear that when a primitive is known, the process described above is much simpler than trying to use the methods suggested in the previous section. However, as the reader well knows from his previous studies, the work involved in finding a primitive for a given function is substantial, and as we have already remarked, a simple primitive may not exist. It is clear then that we should try to elucidate the conditions which will guarantee the existence of a primitive, F, although mere existence will not guarantee that we can produce a primitive in any kind of a usable form. Moreover, simply because a function has a primitive on a given closed interval does not ensure that it is integrable there.

Let us turn now to the proof of the theorem. As with the previous theorem, it is an application of the Mean Value Theorem, and a beautifully simple one at that. The key line of the proof is

$$F(x_i) - F(x_{i-1}) = F'(c_i)(x_i - x_{i-1}) = f(c_i)(x_i - x_{i-1}).$$

The essential fact which must be understood is that if we sum over i, the left-hand side sums to $F(b) - F(a)$, while the right-hand side is a Riemann sum. Once this is realized, letting the norm of the partition go to 0 completes the proof.

The Mean Value Theorem also provides possible insight about the original thinking which led to the Fundamental Theorem. Consider the problem of finding the area under a curve, as shown in Figure 5.5.1. Suppose the function, F, evaluated at c yields the area bounded by the graph of f, the x-axis, the lines $x = a$, and $x = c$ for any $c \in [a, b]$. The shaded portion of the figure has an area which is given by

$$F(c + \Delta x) - F(c) = F(c_0) \cdot \Delta x,$$

where $c_0 \in [c, c + \Delta x]$. One could supply a variety of arguments for this position, but the initial one was probably that it was 'intuitively obvious'. In any case, if one supposes that F is differentiable, then division by Δx yields

$$\frac{F(c + \Delta x) - F(c)}{\Delta x} = f(c_0).$$

Since the left-hand side contains a quantity which in the limit becomes the derivative of F, one concludes that f must be the derivative of F.

The Fundamental Theorem also gives rise to the more standard notation for integrals. If we set $\Delta x_i = x_i - x_{i-1}$, then

$$\int_a^b f = \lim_{\|P\| \to 0} R(f, P, Q) = \lim_{\|P\| \to 0} \sum_{i=1}^{n} f(c_i) \Delta x_i.$$

In the limit, $\Delta x \to dx$, which may be thought of as an infinitesimally small number. This forces $f(c_i) \to f(x)$, where $x \in [c_i, c_i + dx]$. Thus, we have the notational form

$$\int_a^b f(x)\, dx = \int_a^b f. \qquad \square$$

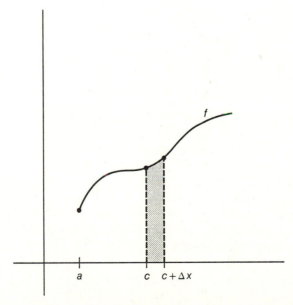

Figure 5.5.1 An increment of area under the graph of f; numerical value given by $F(c + \Delta x) - F(c)$.

Our aim now is to find a condition on an **integrand** (function to be integrated) which will guarantee the existence of a primitive.

Theorem 5.5.3.   Let f be integrable on $[a, b]$, and define

$$F(x) = \int_a^x f, \ x \in [a, b],$$

then F is a continuous function with domain $[a, b]$. Further, if $c \in (a, b)$ and f is continuous at c, then F is differentiable at c and $F'(c) = f(c)$.

Proof.   The fact that $F(x)$ is defined for each $x \in [a, b]$ follows from Theorem 5.4.7. That F is a function follows from the fact that the limit of a Riemann sum is unique. The continuity of F is left as Exercise 2.

To establish differentiability, consider the quantity $\dfrac{F(c + h) - F(c)}{h}$, where h is small enough to satisfy $c + h \in (a, b)$. From the definition of F, we have

$$\frac{F(c + h) - F(c)}{h} = \frac{1}{h} \int_c^{c+h} f. \qquad \textbf{(WHY?)}$$

Let M_h and m_h denote the maximum and the minimum of f, respectively, on the interval $[c, c + h]$ (the specification for this interval would be reversed if $h < 0$). It is immediate that

$$m_h h \leqslant \int_c^{c+h} f \leqslant M_h h.$$

Thus,

$$m_h \leqslant \frac{F(c + h) - F(c)}{h} < M_h.$$

Now, since f is continuous at c, we can find a $\delta > 0$ such that if $|h| < \delta$, we have

$$f(c) - \epsilon < m_h \leqslant \frac{F(c + h) - F(c)}{h} \leqslant M_h < f(c) + \epsilon.$$

But this means that

$$\left| \frac{F(c + h) - F(c)}{h} - f(c) \right| < \epsilon$$

whenever $|h| < \delta$, whence $F'(c) = f(c)$, as claimed. $\square$

Discussion.   This theorem makes four important points. First, it tells us that if f is integrable on $[a, b]$, then there is a function, F, which is naturally associated with f via the integration process. The domain of F is the same as the interval over which f is integrated, namely, $[a, b]$.   Second, F is continuous. Thus, the process of integration generates continuous functions. Third, if the function, f, is continuous on $[a, b]$, then F is differentiable on $[a, b]$. Thus, the process of integration applied to continuous functions generates differentiable functions. Fourth, the theorem tells us that at any point of continuity of f, we will have $F'(c) = f(c)$. This means that if f is continuous on the whole of $[a, b]$, then F will be a member of the family of primitives of f on $[a, b]$.

For the case of continuous functions, this leads to the notation

$$\int f(x)\, dx$$

for the family of primitives of f. This collection of symbols is often given the name: **indefinite integral** of f. It does not denote a function, but a family of functions. Thus, a member of the indefinite integral of f will always be an antiderivative for f. More generally, we will refer to any function, F, which is obtained by integration of f on some interval $[a, x]$ as an **integral** of f.

Naturally the discussion above leaves us to wonder about cases where f is not continuous. Evidently, the integral of f is not of necessity differentiable at a particular point of $[a, b]$. An example illustrating this fact is contained in Exercise 4. Moreover, there are functions which when integrated generate functions which are not differentiable at any point of their domain. Worse yet, even when the integral of f is differentiable, the derivative may not coincide with f, that is, $F'(c) \neq f(c)$ for various values of c in that interval. Thus, the question of just what can happen when we first integrate f and then try to differentiate its integral, F, is exceedingly complex. Of course, there is also the reverse process: differentiate f and then try to integrate the derivative f'. Suffice it to say that the corollary to Theorem 5.5.1 notwithstanding, the situation is equally complex and we shall explore it further in the exercises. $\quad\square$

The theorems proved so far lead naturally to

Theorem 5.5.4. Let f be continuous on $[a, b]$. Then there is a point $c \in (a, b)$ such that

$$f(c) = \frac{1}{b - a} \int_a^b f.$$

Discussion. The straightforward proof of this theorem is left to the reader. For obvious reasons, it is usually referred to as the **Mean Value Theorem for Integrals**. Notice that one conclusion which can be drawn from this theorem is that for a nonnegative continuous function, f, the area between f, the lines $x = a$, and $x = b$ and the x-axis can be realized as the area of a rectangle having one side of length $(b - a)$ and the other $f(c)$ for some $c \in (a, b)$. With a little work, the result can be tracked back to its ultimate home, namely the Completeness Axiom. $\quad\square$

Since we have developed the Fundamental Theorem, we would not want to leave this section without looking at the two most important techniques for finding primitives. The first is the well-known formula for **integration by parts**, given below.

Theorem 5.5.5. If f and g are differentiable functions on $[a, b]$ such that the derivatives f' and g' are both integrable on $[a, b]$, then

$$\int_a^b fg' = f(b)g(b) - f(a)g(a) - \int_a^b f'g.$$

Proof. By hypothesis, f and g are both continuous, and hence Riemann integrable. Therefore, fg' as well as $f'g$ are integrable. Consequently, $fg' + f'g = (fg)'$ is also integrable and by Theorem 5.4.1,

$$\int_a^b (fg)' = \int_a^b fg' + \int_a^b f'g.$$

By the Fundamental Theorem, we may then write

$$\int_a^b (fg)' = f(b)g(b) - f(a)g(a).$$

The result is now obvious.   □

Discussion. The above theorem is a clever device by which we can write down the integral of the product of two functions. What we need to know is that the primitive of one of the two should be expressible in a simple form and that the derivative of the other should also be simple so that the product of these two is easily integrable. In many instances, the fact that the identity function $f(x) = x$ is the primitive of the constant function 1 is exploited to compute $\int f$, by invoking the integration by parts rule to the product $f \cdot 1$.

The source of this theorem is the product rule for differentiation. The reader should ascertain this relationship, as the proof will then become transparent.   □

The next theorem is another device by which we can perform integration by composing the given function with another function g so that the new function $f \circ g$, admits an easy integral. This procedure is known as **the change of variable formula**, or **simple substitution**.

Theorem 5.5.6. Let f be defined and continuous on the range of the function g. If g' is integrable on $[c, d]$, then

$$\int_a^b f = \int_c^d (f \circ g)g'$$

where $a = g(c)$ and $b = g(d)$.

Proof. Let $F(x) = \int_a^x f$ be a primitive of f. Note that F is defined on the range of g. Since f is continuous, F is differentiable by Theorem 5.5.3, and $F' = f$. Thus, $G = F \circ g$ is defined on $[c, d]$. Clearly G is differentiable (**WHY?**) and by the Chain Rule, $G' = (F' \circ g)g' = (f \circ g)g'$. Also $f \circ g$ is continuous since f and g are, and hence integrable. By hypothesis, g' is also Riemann integrable, thus $(f \circ g)g'$ is integrable. Hence,

$$\int_c^d (f \circ g)g' = \int_c^d G' = G(d) - G(c)$$
$$= F(g(d)) - F(g(c))$$
$$= F(b) - F(a) = \int_a^b f. \qquad □$$

Discussion. The reader should note that there is no requirement that the quantity a be less than b. In fact, the opposite may be true with no effect on the correctness of the theorem. The source of the proof is in the Chain Rule for differentiation, and it is in this connection that the reader should seek insight into the proof.

In fact, the theorem might be thought of as a chain rule for integration, except that it is used exactly the opposite way from the Chain Rule, that is, the Chain Rule tells us how to differentiate a composite function while the Change of Variable Theorem tells us how to simplify an integral by rewriting it as a composite function. Thus, we are using the equalities in the opposite directions. Suffice it to say that the value of this theorem depends on the user's skill at shrewdly rewriting the original function so as to come up with a simple integral. For a detailed treatment of the many uses of this theorem, see the section on techniques of integration in any calculus book. □

We conclude this section with a theorem which is known as the **Second Mean Value Theorem for Integrals** or **Bonnet's Mean Value Theorem.**

Theorem 5.5.7.   If f is continuous and increasing on $[a, b]$ and g is nonnegative and integrable there, then there exists a $z \in [a, b]$ such that

$$\int_a^b fg = f(a) \int_a^z g + f(b) \int_z^b g.$$

Proof. By an easily proved generalization of the First Mean Value Theorem (see Exercise 12), there exists $y \in [a, b]$ such that

$$\int_a^b fg = f(y) \int_a^b g.$$

Also, $f(a) \leq f(y) \leq f(b)$, since f is increasing. Now, consider the function G defined on $[a, b]$ by

$$G(x) = [f(b) - f(a)] \int_x^b g.$$

Since g is nonnegative, G is a decreasing function. Further,

$$G(a) = [f(b) - f(a)] \int_a^b g$$

$$\geq [f(y) - f(a)] \int_a^b g$$

$$\geq 0 = G(b).$$

Since G is continuous, we can apply the Intermediate Value Theorem to obtain $z \in [a, b]$ such that

$$G(z) = [f(y) - f(a)] \int_z^b g.$$

Now,

$$G(z) = [f(b) - f(a)] \int_z^b g = [f(y) - f(a)] \int_a^b g.$$

For this particular z, we have by expanding,

$$f(b) \int_z^b g - f(a) \int_z^b g = f(y) \int_a^b g - f(a) \int_a^b g,$$

$$= \int_a^b fg - f(a) \int_a^b g.$$

Rearranging yields

$$\int_a^b fg = f(a) \left[\int_a^b g - \int_z^b g \right] + f(b) \int_z^b g,$$

which simplifies to the desired result. □

Discussion. This theorem can best be understood in two steps. First, f is continuous and increasing, while g is nonnegative and integrable. It should seem obvious that there is a $y \in [a, b]$ such that

$$\int_a^b fg = f(y) \int_a^b g.$$

This is the first step. Since f is increasing, $f(a) \leqslant f(y) \leqslant f(b)$. Thus,

$$f(a) \int_a^b g \leqslant f(y) \int_a^b g \leqslant f(b) \int_a^b g.$$

It should therefore seem reasonable that a z should exist which will permit us to integrate $f(a) \int_a^z g$ and $f(b) \int_z^b g$ and sum to get the value in the middle. However, the reader will note that to achieve this 'reasonableness' requires the full power of the Intermediate Value Theorem. $\square$

There are many applications of the Mean Value Theorem as we shall see when we develop the trigonometric functions and their inverses in Chapter 10.

EXERCISES

1. Prove the converse of Theorem 5.5.1.

2. Complete the proof of Theorem 5.5.3. Specifically, show that the function F is continuous on $[a, b]$.

3. Find the primitives for the following functions. Use whatever formulas are necessary for elementary functions.

(a) $\int \dfrac{x}{\sqrt{x^2 + 5}}$;

(b) $\int (2x^3 + 1)^7 x^2$;

(c) $\int \dfrac{v^2}{(v^3 - 2)^2}$;

(d) $\int \dfrac{x + 1}{x^2 + 2x + 3}$;

(e) $\int \sin^4 x \cos x$;

(f) $\int \dfrac{e^x - e^{-x}}{e^x + e^{-x}}$;

(g) $\int \dfrac{\sec x \tan x}{\sqrt{1 + \sec x}}$;

(h) $\int \dfrac{x \ln (1 + x^2)}{(1 + x^2)}$;

(i) $\int x \ln x$;

(j) $\int x \tan^{-1} x$;

(k) $\int x^2 \sin x$;

(l) $\int x e^x$;

(m) $\int \sec^5 x$;

(n) $\int \dfrac{x \ln x}{(x^2 - 1)^{3/2}}$;

(o) $\int \ln(x^2 + 1)$;

(p) $\int \dfrac{x^3}{e^{x^2}}$;

(q) $\int e^{ax} \cos(bx + c)$;

(r) $\dfrac{x^5}{x + 1}$;

4. Let f be defined on $[-1, 1]$ by

$$f(x) = \begin{cases} 1, & \text{if } x > 0 \\ 0, & \text{if } x = 0 \\ -1, & \text{if } x < 0. \end{cases}$$

Show that the integral of f is not differentiable at 0.

5. Let f be monotone increasing on $[a, b]$ and suppose that f is discontinuous at $z \in (a, b)$. Show that the integral of f cannot be differentiable at z.

6. Let $g: \mathbf{N} \to \mathbf{Q} \cap [0, 1]$ be one-to-one and onto. Set

$$M_x = \{i : g(i) \leqslant x, i \in \mathbf{N}\}.$$

We define f on $[0, 1]$ by

$$f(x) = \sum \{2^{-i} : i \in M_x\}.$$

Using whatever fact from the theory of infinite series you need, show that f is monotone increasing and discontinuous at every rational, but is continuous at every irrational. Conclude that the integral of f is not differentiable at any rational.

7. Let f be differentiable on $[a, b]$ and suppose that f' is integrable there. Show that $\int_a^b f' = f(b) - f(a)$.

8. Define f on $[-1, 1]$ by

$$f(x) = \begin{cases} x^2 \sin \dfrac{1}{x^2}, & x \neq 0 \\ 0, & x = 0. \end{cases}$$

Show that

$$f'(x) = \begin{cases} 2x \sin \dfrac{1}{x^2} - \left(\dfrac{2}{x}\right) \cos \dfrac{1}{x^2}, & x \neq 0 \\ 0, & x = 0. \end{cases}$$

Conclude that f' is not integrable on $[-1, 1]$.

9. Consider the function f discussed in Example 5.2.4. Show that $F(x) = \int_0^x f$ is differentiable on $[0, 1]$ but that $F'(x) \neq f(x)$ at any rational other than 0.

10. For each of the integrals, find the mean value specified by Theorem 5.5.4:

    (a) $\int_0^2 x^2$;

(b) $\int_0^1 \sin x$;

(c) $\int_0^3 e^x$.

11. Suppose that g is nonnegative on $[a, b]$ and that both g and fg are integrable there. Show if $m < f(x) < M$ are bounds for f on this interval, then there exists $z \in (m, M)$ such that

$$z \int_a^b g = \int_a^b fg.$$

12. Show if f is continuous and g is integrable on $[a, b]$, then there exists $z \in [a, b]$ such that

$$\int_a^b fg = f(z) \int_a^b g.$$

13. Suppose f has a continuous derivative on $[a, b]$. Show that f can be represented as the difference of two nondecreasing functions.

14. Let f be continuous on $[a, b]$ and suppose that for every function g which is integrable on $[a, b]$, $\int_a^b fg = 0$. What conclusions can be drawn about f?

15. Let f be defined on $[0, 1]$ by

$$f(x) = \begin{cases} 1 - x, & \text{if } x \text{ is irrational} \\ \sqrt{1 - x^2}, & \text{if } x \text{ is rational}. \end{cases}$$

    Find the values of the upper and the lower integrals of f.

16. Let $a, b > 0$. Use the Change of Variable Theorem to show that

$$\int_a^{ab} \frac{1}{t} = \int_1^b \frac{1}{t}.$$

17. If f is continuous on $[a, b]$, and g and h are differentiable with range contained in $[a, b]$, show that

$$\left(\int_g^h f \right)' = (f \circ h)h' - (f \circ g)g'.$$

18. Let f be integrable in $[a, b]$ and $F(x) = \int_x^b f$ for $x \in [a, b]$. Prove that at each point of continuity of f, $F'(x) = -f(x)$.

19. For $x > 0$, set $L(x) = \int_1^x \frac{1}{t}$. Establish the following formulas:

    (a) $L(ab) = L(a) + L(b)$;

    (b) $L\left[\dfrac{a}{b} \right] = L(a) - L(b)$;

    (c) $L(1) = 0$;

    (d) $L(a^q) = qL(a), q \in \mathbf{Q}$;

    (e) $(L(x))' = \dfrac{1}{x}$;

    (f) $L(x)$ is increasing and continuous on $\mathbf{R}^+$.

    [NOTE: The function $L(x)$ is the familiar logarithmic function.]

20. Define $E(x)$ to be the inverse of the function $L(x)$ considered in Exercise 19 for $x \in \mathbf{R}$. Find the derivative of $E(x)$ and use this to evaluate $\int_0^a E(x)$ for $a \in \mathbf{R}$.

21. Let $f(x) = x^2$. Show every primitive of f is realizable as $\int_a^x t^2$ for some choice of a. Is the same true for $f(x) = \cos x$?

22. Use your knowledge of primitives to compute the following limits:

(a) $\lim\limits_{n\to\infty} \left[\dfrac{1}{n+1} + \dfrac{1}{n+2} + \cdots + \dfrac{1}{2n} \right]$;

(b) $\lim\limits_{n\to\infty} \sum\limits_{k=0}^{n-1} \dfrac{1}{\sqrt{n^2 - k^2}}$;

(c) $\lim\limits_{n\to\infty} \sum\limits_{i=1}^{n} \dfrac{i\sqrt{i^2 + n^2}}{n^3}$;

(d) $\lim\limits_{n\to\infty} \sum\limits_{k=1}^{n} \dfrac{k^p}{n^{p+1}}$;

(e) $\lim\limits_{n\to\infty} \sum\limits_{r=1}^{n} \dfrac{n^3}{n^2 + r^2}$.

23. Let

$$f(x) = \begin{cases} \dfrac{x^2 - 4}{x - 2}, & x \neq 2 \\ 0, & x = 2. \end{cases}$$

The primitive $F(x) = \dfrac{x^2}{2} + 2x$ is differentiable at $x = 2$, but $F'(2) = 4 \neq f(2)$. Does this contradict the Fundamental Theorem?

24. Let

$$f(t) = \begin{cases} t, & t < 0 \\ t^2 + 1, & 0 \leqslant t \leqslant 2 \\ 0, & t > 2. \end{cases}$$

Find a primitive $F(x)$. Is F differentiable?

25. Let $F(x) = \int_{x-1}^{x+1} f$, where f is continuous on $\mathbf{R}$. Show F is differentiable, and compute F'.

26. $f(x) = \begin{cases} 1, & 0 \leqslant x < 1 \\ 2, & 1 \leqslant x < 2 \end{cases}$ is discontinuous at $x = 1$, but a primitive of f, namely,

$F(x) = \begin{cases} x, & 0 \leqslant x < 1 \\ 2x - 1, & 1 \leqslant x \leqslant 2 \end{cases}$ is continuous on $[0, 2]$. Is there any contradiction?

27. Let f be continuous in $[0, a]$. Define $f_0(x) = f(x)$, and for $n > 0$, $f_{n+1}(x) = \dfrac{1}{n!} \int_0^x f(t)(x - t)^n dt$. Show that the nth derivative of $f_n(x)$ exists and coincides with $f(x)$.

Chapter 6

Applications of Integration

In this chapter we present a number of topics related to integration. To begin with, we consider applications of the integral to applied problems. The remaining two topics amount to generalizations of the integral. The first of these concerns attempts to deal with functions which are not bounded, or functions which are defined on infinite intervals. The reader will already be familiar with this extension from his elementary calculus courses in the form of improper Riemann integrals. The second extension, the Riemann–Stieltjes integral, is new and will be fully described in section 6.3.

6.1 APPLICATIONS OF THE INTEGRAL CONCEPT

Ordinarily, one thinks of calculus as a branch of mathematics developed by Newton and Leibnitz. This is relatively true about the differential calculus, but much less true about the integral calculus. The problem of developing techniques for determining the area of plane figures extends back in time to at least the early Egyptians, thousands of years before Christ. For example, by the time of Archimedes (287–216 B.C.) techniques were developed which are the precursors of both the 'limit' and the 'integral' concepts. These techniques were founded on very simple intuitive ideas related to a unit square having a fixed area of one square unit, such as:

(1A) If the unit square is divided into n nonoverlapping, equal parts, each part has an equal fraction of the area and the sum of the areas of these parts must add to unity.

(2A) If a plane figure is divided into nonoverlapping pieces, then the area of the whole must be the sum of the areas of the various parts.

(3A) Any plane figure can be filled (almost) with small figures of known area, and the area of the figure must be approximately the sum of the known areas.

(4A) In general, if smaller figures are used to approximate the area of a plane figure, a better approximation will result.

Statements 1A–3A contain the principles used in developing the integral at the beginning of Chapter 5. However, the reader should realize that statements 1A–4A are not mathematical statements, rather they are the embodiments of physical observations and as such they can be verified experimentally, and for this reason can be taken as valid in the real world. Thus, any mathematical device which is created to capture the concept of area must at least satisfy statements 1A–4A, or more precisely, the translations of these statements into a suitable mathematical language. In addition, the process of verifying that a given mathematical device satisfies the mathematical forms of 1A–4A can be subjected to the same level of rigor employed elsewhere in this book.

To return to the historical discussions, Archimedes refined the techniques for finding the areas to the point where he was in essence finding limits, which is what the 'almost' in parentheses in 3A above implies. Moreover, the type of reasoning which led Archimedes to formulae for the lengths, areas, and/or volumes of various geometric objects, for example, segments of parabolas, volumes of ellipses of revolution, and so on, is no less valid today! Thus, we would expect that the integral should at least be useful for problems of finding area (already established), volume, and perhaps length.

In the remainder of this section, we will explore the uses of the integral as a tool for solving various physical problems. The solutions to each problem will be accomplished by presenting a formula which will amount to making a definition. As each definition is presented, the reader should develop answers to the questions like the following:

(1) What is the basic physical insight which is being employed?
(2) How is this insight being translated into a term in an approximating sum?
(3) What general physical principles should the quantity satisfy?
(4) What mathematical statements can be written down which if proved would validate the correctness of the mathematical concept?

Problem 1. Let f and g be continuous on $[a, b]$ with $f \geqslant g$ except at a finite number of points. Find the area of the region bounded by $x = a$, $x = b$, the graph of f, and the graph of g (see Figure 6.1.1).

Solution. To begin thinking about this problem in a constructive way, the reader might draw two wavy lines on a piece of paper, one above the other. Since it is known how to find the area of a rectangle, we might think of approximating the required area with a series of vertical nonoverlapping rectangular strips. Indeed, we can bound the area in question by taking a series of strips of maximum length which lie completely inside the figure whose area is required and summing to obtain an approximation, followed by taking a series of strips of minimum length which completely enclose the figure and again summing to find an approximate value for the area. Assuming that the graph of f is 'above' the graph of g, it is evident from the figure that a strip of maximum length which lies completely inside the figure has length

$$l_i = m_i(f) - M_i(g)$$

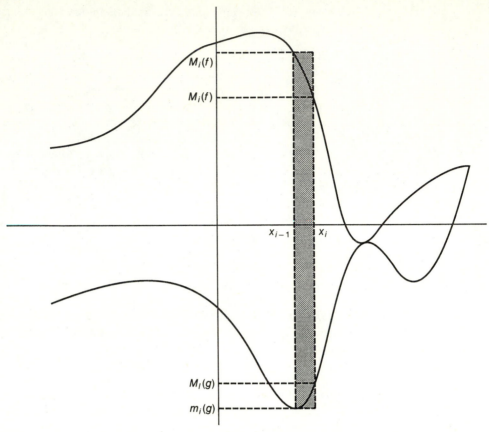

Figure 6.1.1   An entry for the Riemann sum in the interval $[\,|x^{i-1},\ x^i]$ (Problem 1)—area between two curves.

where $m_i(f)$ denotes the infimum of f on $[x_{i-1},\ x_i]$ and $M_i(g)$ is the supremum of g on the same interval. Similarly, the shortest length of the strip which encloses the analogous portion of area is

$$L_i = M_i(f) - m_i(g).$$

If we let $\Delta x_i = x_i - x_{i-1}$, then to obtain the contribution to the total approximation, we merely multiply L_i or l_i by Δx_i. Let us formalize these ideas.

Let P be a partition of $[a, b]$ and $m_i(f)$, $M_i(f)$, $m_i(g)$, and $M_i(g)$ have their usual meanings (see section 5.2). We will assume that P is chosen such that $l_i \geqslant 0$ for each i (see Exercise 2). It is easily established that

$$\sum_{i=1}^{n} [m_i(f) - M_i(g)]\,\Delta x_i \leqslant \sum_{i=1}^{n} [M_i(f) - m_i(g)]\,\Delta x_i.$$

Moreover, it is apparent from our initial comments that any number which we might want to identify as the area of the figure lies between the two numbers generated by these two approximating sums. Evidently, each of the approximations will be improved if we employ a partition having a smaller norm. Thus, what we want to do is to let $\|P\| \to 0$. If this process results in a common value, then we will be confident that we have generated a number which can be defined to be the area of the figure.

It can be shown, using the theorems established in section 5.3 that

$$\lim_{\|P\| \to 0} \left(\sum_{i=1}^{n} [m_i(f) - M_i(g)] \Delta x_i \right) = \lim_{\|P\| \to 0} \sum_{i=1}^{n} m_i(f) \Delta x_i - \lim_{\|P\| \to 0} M_i(g) \Delta x_i$$

$$= \int_a^b f \, dx - \int_a^b g \, dx$$

$$= \int_a^b (f - g) \, dx.$$

Similarly, we have

$$\lim_{\|P\| \to 0} \left(\sum_{i=1}^{n} [M_i(f) - m_i(g)] \Delta x_i \right) = \int_a^b (f - g) \, dx.$$

Hence, the formula for computing the required area is $\int_a^b (f - g) \, dx$. □

Discussion.   It is critical that the reader understand that the formula given for area amounts to a definition. Where this definition extends a previous definition, for example, for a region which is a rectangle, we could show that the value for area obtained with the extended method agrees with the old value. However, for new figures for which we had no previous means of assigning an area, we cannot hope to 'prove' that the value is correct, since we have no pre-existing value with which to compare. On the other hand, we can look for rigorous tests to apply to the computation which will show the formula has all the desired properties and satisfies various geometric truths. In Exercise 1 you will be asked to explore this issue.

The reader should see that the solution to the problem is an abstraction of a real physical process. To better understand this statement, the reader should take an ordinary piece of 8½ × 11 paper and cut a wavy bit off the top and another wavy bit off the bottom, so that a plane figure something like that in Figure 6.1.1 results. Now try to find the area. Evidently, one could not hope to find the exact value for the area. But one could find a good approximation. Indeed, one could do much better than we have done by using an approximation similar to that given by the trapezoidal rule. The point is to try it and in the process of coming up with a number which can reasonably be said to be area you will be forced into forming an approximating sum! Moreover, whatever type of approximation you use, it should be possible to formalize it and to show that as the approximation gets better, it leads directly to the integral shown.

It is critical that the reader understand that pictures can be misleading and that various apparent 'facts' must be checked. In the present case the obvious fact from the picture which must be checked is that each $l_i \geq 0$. For the region presented in Figure 6.1.1, a partition can be chosen for which at least one l_i is negative (**HOW?**). The reader should demonstrate this to himself. In any case, the fact that some l_i's may be negative is not a substantive issue (see Exercise 3).

A fourth point of importance for this problem is that we are able to bound the true area between two approximations. This bounding is based on common sense, that is, if one figure is enclosed by another, the area of the enclosed figure should be less than the area of the surrounding figure. Once we are able to show that both approximations lead to the same value in the limit, we are done. It would be nice if this were always possible, but such is not always the case. Where it is not possible, other tests should be developed to ensure the correctness of the solution.

Finally we remark on the notation adopted in this section. We are generating approximating sums of the form

$$\sum_{i=1}^{n} f(x_i)\, \Delta x_i. \tag{1}$$

This form is useful because as the norm of the underlying partition tends to 0, the sum naturally turns into $\int_a^b f(x)\, dx$, where $a = x_0$ and $b = x_n$. Thus, we would emphasize that in creating the approximation, one wants to be able to express the approximation in the form presented in (1), that is, as a finite sum, whose members consist of a function value times an increment of length.   □

Problem 2. Let f have a continuous derivative on $[a, b]$. Find the length of the graph of f joining the points $(a, f(a))$ and $(b, f(b))$.

Solution. Since f is differentiable on $[a, b]$, it is continuous there. Since the domain of interest is an interval, this means that the graph of f is a curve which can be drawn with one sweep of one's pen. Before reading further, we suggest that the reader draw such a graph, making sure that it has several wiggles. Now, using nothing more than a ruler and pencil, find a number which approximates the length of the graph.

In Figure 6.1.2, we present a curve, together with an approximation to it. The approximation was achieved by dividing the curve into segments and then

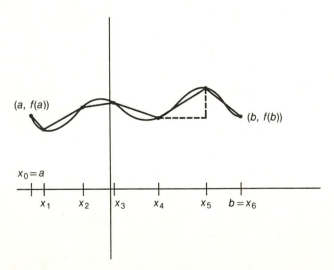

Figure 6.1.2 An entry for the Riemann sum (Problem 2)—length of a curve.

joining the endpoints of each segment of the curve with a straight line. The lengths of each straight line segment can be calculated, or measured, and then added together to obtain an approximate length of the graph.

These ideas are formalized as follows. Let P be any partition of $[a, b]$. The partition naturally divides the graph of f into n segments. The length of each segment is approximated by the length of the chord joining the endpoints of the segment. Thus, an approximation of the length of the graph is given by

$$\sum_{i=1}^{n} \sqrt{(x_i - x_{i-1})^2 + (f(x_i) - f(x_{i-1}))^2} = \sum_{i=1}^{n} \sqrt{\Delta x_i^2 + (f(x_i) - f(x_{i-1}))^2}.$$

The right-hand side can be manipulated by multiplying each term of the sum by the quantity $\dfrac{\Delta x_i}{\Delta x_i}$, to obtain

$$\left\{ \sqrt{\left[\frac{\Delta x_i}{\Delta x_i} \right]^2 + \left[\frac{f(x_i) - f(x_{i-1})}{\Delta x_i} \right]^2} \right\} \times \Delta x_i.$$

Observe that the first term under the radical sign is identically 1. If one ignores the square, the second term is a difference quotient and simply begs for an application of the Mean Value Theorem. The reader can verify that the Mean Value Theorem can be applied on the interval $[x_{i-1}, x_i]$ to obtain a point $c_i \in (x_{i-1}, x_i)$ such that

$$\frac{f(x_i) - f(x_{i-1})}{\Delta x_i} = f'(c_i).$$

This leads to

$$\sum_{i=1}^{n} \sqrt{(x_i - x_{i-1})^2 + (f(x_i) - f(x_{i-1}))^2} = \sum_{i=0}^{n} \sqrt{1 + f'(c_i)^2} \times \Delta x_i.$$

where each $c_i \in (x_{i-1}, x_i)$. By taking the limit as $\|P\| \to 0$, we have by results of section 5.4, that

$$\lim_{\|P\| \to 0} \sum_{i=0}^{n} \sqrt{1 + f'(c_i)^2} \times \Delta x_i = \int_a^b \sqrt{1 + [f'(x)]^2}\, dx, \tag{2}$$

which is the required formula for calculating length. $\qquad\qquad\qquad\qquad \square$

Discussion .   Consider again Figure 6.1.2 and the initial instructions at the beginning of the problem. It was hoped that these instructions would force you, the reader, into approximating your curve by dividing it into segments and approximating each segment with a straight line (chord). There are three important features of this approximation. The first is that it is natural in that it is a translation of a physical method for solving the problem. The second is that we know how to calculate the length of a straight line segment in the plane from the Pythagorean Theorem and this calculation can be checked against a measurement. The third is that as we divide the curve into more segments, the approximation by chords more closely represents the curve, and hence the associated sum of the lengths of the chords more closely approximates what we believe to be the length of the curve.

The length calculation results from the fact that each chord is naturally associated with a right triangle, as shown in Figure 6.1.2. The lengths of the three sides of the triangle are related by the Pythagorean Theorem and the lengths of sides other than the hypotenuse can be obtained as differences: $x_i - x_{i-1}$, and $f(x_i) - f(x_{i-1})$. Thus, the length of each chord (hypotenuse) is calculable and summing these lengths yields an approximation to the length of the curve.

It is very important that the reader understand that unless the length of the curve is known for some *a priori* reason, then the number which this process yields as length will essentially be a definition. A case where the length would be known in advance would be that of a curve which was a straight line; for a straight line, the length can be obtained by measurement. A case where the result would be a definition would be that of a portion of the graph of a parabola.

Unlike our solution to Problem 1 in which we had an upper and lower bound on what we believed was the true area, this argument is completely predicated on our intuitive belief that as we divide the curve into more segments of shorter length, the sum of the lengths of the chords will even more closely approximate the true length of the curve. In actual fact, what we believe should be the true length of the curve is an upper bound for each approximation to the length. This results from our belief that the shortest distance between two points is a straight line. Formally, it is a consequence of the Triangle inequality. Thus, if we accept that we can arbitrarily closely approximate the curve with straight line segments, then it is clear that the defined length should be the supremum of all lengths which can be obtained from approximating sums. This leads to the definition

$$\text{length} = \sup_{P} \left\{ \sum \sqrt{(x_i - x_{i-1})^2 + (f(x_i) - f(x_{i-1}))^2} : P \text{ is a partition of } [a, b] \right\}.$$

There are several things that we can do to check the intuition we have used in making this definition. The most important of these is to check that the formula developed will reproduce known correct answers for cases where some other methodology exists. For example, the formula should be checked immediately for straight lines and circles to see if the values generated will agree with values known to be correct (see Exercises 4 and 5).

The difficulty with the definition above is that it is next to impossible to use for purposes of calculation, unless of course one is going to use a digital computer. Thus, even though one has arrived at a suitable definition for the length of a curve, one is still left with the problem of generating a definition which is computationally tractable.

As it stands, this formula for the length of a curve does not look much like an integral. Yet it has features which are definitely related to the generation of an integral. Specifically, we started off by partitioning the interval $[a, b]$, and we followed this by computing a supremum as the norm of the partition shrinks to 0. The difficulty is that the terms being summed are not in the 'integral form'. At this point, we should clarify the concept of integral form.

When we sought to define the integral, we used approximating sums derived from a finite partition of an interval. Each individual entry into the sum is the product of two parts:

(1) A functional value in a given subinterval, or the supremum or infimum of the function on this subinterval;

(2) The length of the subinterval, or equivalently, the change in the independent variable over this subinterval, that is, $\Delta x_i = x_i - x_{i-1}$.

Finally, a limit was taken by letting the norm of the partition shrink to 0. This results in a limit of an approximating sum which looks like

$$\lim_{\|P\| \to 0} \left[\sum_{i=1}^{n} f(x_i) \, \Delta x_i \right]. \qquad \text{(integral form)}$$

For emphasis, we again stress that once this form has been achieved, the resultant integral drops right out, due to the fact that the interval of integration, $[a, b]$, satisfies $x_0 = a$ and $x_n = b$, whence the required integral is $\int_a^b f(x) \, dx$.

It is immediate from the discussion above that the difficulty with the length definition is how to put it into integral form. Specifically, the individual terms to be summed do not have a part which corresponds to a unit of length. The simplest way to introduce such a quantity into the formula is to multiply by $\dfrac{\Delta x_i}{\Delta x_i}$. Once this factor has been introduced into the sum, a bit of algebra follows. This leads to a term under the radical which is a difference quotient. Whenever one sees a difference quotient, one should at least ask the question whether the Mean Value Theorem can be usefully applied. In this case it can, and the final formula results.

There is still a question as to whether the function appearing in the integral is in fact integrable on $[a, b]$. The reader should satisfy himself that this is taken care of by our choice of hypothesis. Without this hypothesis, the computations would be to no avail, since the resulting function would not, in general, be integrable. Indeed, we would not in general even be able to progress beyond the second step unless f is differentiable. This would not change the validity of the initial setup, however; it would only mean that the conclusion could not be reached via an integral. $\qquad \square$

Prior to discussing our next problem we need to introduce the concept of solid of revolution.

Definition. An object is considered to be a **solid of revolution** provided it can be generated by rotating a region in the plane about a line in the plane which does not intersect the region. The line about which the region is rotated is referred to as the **axis of revolution**.

Discussion. Physically, solids of revolution are produced by two common and age-old processes. The first is a potter's wheel. The second is a carpenter's lathe. Both

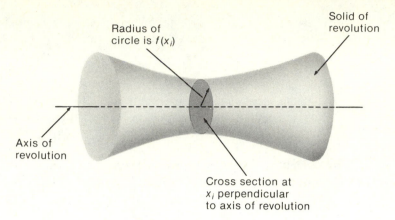

Figure 6.1.3   An entry for the Riemann sum (Problem 3)—volume of a solid of revolution.

processes take an irregular object, rotate it, and during the process of rotation shave off material so that the outer surface is smoothed by the shaving process. The result is that if a cross section is taken through the solid which is perpendicular to the axis of rotation, the outer edge of the surface generates a circle and the axis of rotation passes through its center, see Figure 6.1.3. For this reason, one could think of approximating a solid of rotation by stacking a series of disks, or coins, of various sizes one on top of the other and so that their centers fall on a straight line.   □

Problem 3.   Let f be a nonnegative continuous function defined on $[a, b]$. Find the volume of the surface obtained by rotating the region bounded by the graph of f, $x = a$, $x = b$, and the x-axis about the x-axis.

Solution.   Consider a partition, P, of $[a, b]$. Following our previously established notation, $m_i \leqslant f(x) \leqslant M_i$, for $x_{i-1} \leqslant x \leqslant x_i$. Further, let us denote by V_i, the volume obtained by rotating the region associated with the ith subinterval about the x-axis. Evidently, from our intuition about geometry and volume, it should be the case that the volume obtained by rotating the region associated with the ith subinterval but bounded above by m_i should be no larger than V_i; moreover, the solid of revolution generated by M_i generates an upper bound on V_i. Thus we should have

$$\pi m_i^2 \times \Delta x_i \leqslant V_i \leqslant \pi M_i^2 \times \Delta x_i.$$

This means that the total volume, V, of the solid should satisfy

$$\sum_{i=1}^{n} \pi m_i^2 \times \Delta x_i \leqslant V \leqslant \sum_{i=1}^{n} \pi M_i^2 \times \Delta x_i.$$

The left- and right-hand sides of this inequality are immediately recognizable as upper and lower Darboux sums. If we now replace m_i and/or M_i by $f(x)$ for some $x \in [x_{i-1}, x_i]$, say x_i, it is evident that V should be defined by

$$V = \lim_{\|P\| \to 0} \left[\sum_{i=1}^{n} \pi [f(x_i)]^2 \, \Delta x_i \right] = \pi \int_a^b [f(x)]^2 \, dx,$$

where we have replaced the Darboux sums by an equivalent Riemann sum by virtue of the theory developed in the last chapter. □

Discussion. The reader should be well aware by this time that the quantity, V, being calculated represents volume by definition. As such, there are various geometric truths which it should satisfy. For example, the volume of one object which can be fit inside a second should be smaller. The reader is asked to establish this and other properties in the exercises.

The critical intuition which leads to the solution of this problem is the fact that if we slice through a solid of revolution in a plane which is perpendicular to the axis of revolution, the resultant surface will be a circle, as shown in Figure 6.1.3. (To make this really concrete, think of a right cylinder, for example, a can of soup. The top of the cylinder is a circle, as is any cut through the cylinder which is perpendicular to the axis of revolution.) Having noticed that each cross section results in a circle, we proceed to think of the solid as being composed of thin disks. For the case of a cylinder, the disks will all have the same radius. For the general case, the radius of each disk will vary with x as is evident from Figure 6.1.3. The first disk has a radius $f(x_1)$ and a thickness Δx_1; the second a radius $f(x_2)$ and a thickness Δx_2; and so on. In this way we obtain a physical approximation to the given solid of revolution. But, and this is the key, we know how to find the volume of the approximation, since we have a formula for the volume of a disk. Specifically, the formula for the volume of a disk is $\pi \times r^2 \times h$, where the radius of the disk is r and the thickness is h. This formula is employed to obtain the lower bound on V, the upper bound on V, and again in the Riemann sum.

The ideas which lead to the calculation above are predicated on notions about area. At a much more primitive level, the very concept of volume and its basic properties can only arise from basic geometric principles which are obtained by experiment, for example, playing with building blocks to determine appropriate volume of a large cube in terms of the volume of a standard cube. It is the very basic physical ideas which the process of integration incorporates so powerfully to produce answers to such a wide variety of problems. □

Our last application of the integral is from physics and for this reason we will require two physical principles from hydrostatics.

H1 The pressure (force/unit area) exerted by a fluid of uniform density at any point below its surface is determined solely by the depth of the point below the surface of the fluid.

H2 (Pascal's Principle) The pressure exerted by a fluid at any point on its surface is the same in all directions.

The reader should realize that these are not mathematical statements, and as such are not subject to any mathematical test. For a mathematician to use these physical facts, they must first be turned into a mathematical form. Thus, we express pressure as a function of depth by

$$P(h) = \rho \times g \times h,$$

where ρ is the uniform density of the fluid, g is the acceleration of gravity, and h is the distance below the surface of the fluid.

Problem 4. Find the total force acting on a thin circular plate of diameter, $d = 4$, which is lowered into a fluid so that its top edge is level with the surface of the fluid.

Solution. Let us imagine that we set up a coordinate system with the point $(0,0)$ at the surface of the fluid and the negative y-axis extending vertically downward. One may then consider that the plate is positioned in the water with its center at $(0,-2)$, as shown in Figure 6.1.4. The plate is then given as the interior of the circle whose equation is

$$x^2 + (y + 2)^2 = 4.$$

Now imagine a narrow horizontal strip across the plate bounded below by y_{i-1} and above by y_i. An approximation to the total force acting on this strip, both front and back, is given by

$$2 \times (y_i \times \rho g) \times 2\sqrt{4 - (y_i + 2)^2}\, \Delta y_i.$$

It is evident then that an approximation to the total force can be obtained by summing over a finite number of such strips. Thus, if P is a partition of the y-axis from -4 to 0, then the total force on the plate, *TF*, is given by

$$TF = \lim_{\|P\| \to 0} \left[\sum_{i=1}^{n} 4\,(y_i \rho g) \times \sqrt{4 - (y_i + 2)^2}\, \Delta y_i \right]$$

$$= \int_{-4}^{0} 4\,(y\rho g)\sqrt{4 - (y + 2)^2}\, dy.$$

The evaluation of the integral is left to the reader.   □

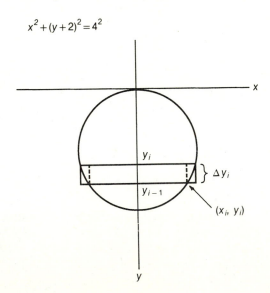

$$x^2 + (y + 2)^2 = 4^2$$

Figure 6.1.4   Circular plate positioned in water (Problem 4).

Discussion. The solution to this type of problem requires several steps. First, the relevant physical facts must be isolated. In this case, the physical facts required are the two principles H1 and H2, together with an understanding that to turn pressure into force, one simply multiplies by area. Second, one must express the physical information mathematically, which in this case means the equation

$$P(h) = \rho \times g \times h.$$

The third step involves thinking of the problem in the most concrete way possible. In the present case, the concrete thinking is developed by trying to obtain an approximate solution to the problem. The essential insight is that of noticing that the pressure is constant on a horizontal strip of plate. Thus, a natural, and particularly simple, approximation results from dividing the plate into horizontal strips.

To make clear the nature of the approximation, consider the product

$$2 \times (y_i \times \rho g) \times 2\sqrt{4 - (y_i + 2)^2}\, \Delta y_i.$$

The product has been subdivided by the use of '$\times$'. The first piece, 2, accounts for the front and back of the strip. The middle piece is the pressure term, while the last piece is the area of the strip. Notice that this product has exactly the required form for entry into an integral, that is, $f(y) \times \Delta y_i$, where $y \in [y_{i-1}, y_i]$.

Having said all this, one can still wonder about the correctness of the formula. This is explored in Exercises 14 and 15. $\square$

The exercises contain a variety of additional applications of the integral. Most, if not all, of these applications are treated in standard calculus texts. However, what the reader is being asked to do is concisely review the theory underlying each application. Indeed, in most cases, once the required facts are listed, you should be completely able to develop the required integral.

EXERCISES

1. Make a list of the geometric properties which any notion of area for plane figures should satisfy. Formulate these in terms of the area concept developed in Problem 1, and establish their truth. As an example of such a principle we have: if one plane figure is contained in a second, then the area of the former is less than or equal to the area of the latter.

2. Let f, g be continuous on $[a, b]$ and $f > g$ on $[a, b]$, except at a finite number of points. Show that there is a partition, P, of $[a, b]$ such that for each i, $l_i \geqslant 0$. Why does the hypothesis of this exercise imply that $f \geqslant g$ on $[a, b]$? What can be said if we weaken the hypothesis to $f \geqslant g$ on $[a, b]$?

3. Let f, g be continuous on $[a, b]$ with $f \geqslant g$. Show

$$\lim_{\|P\| \to 0} \left[\sum_{i=1}^{n} [m_i(f) - M_i(g)]\, \Delta x_i \right] \geqslant 0.$$

What can be said if this limit is 0?

4. Show that for the case of a straight line, the formula generated for length in Eq. 2 yields the correct length.

5. Show that the formula generated for length in Eq. 2 yields the correct circumference for a circle.

6. Let f satisfy the conditions of Problem 2 on $[a, b]$. If Q is a refinement of P on $[a, b]$, then the approximating length generated using Q is greater than or equal to the approximating length generated using P.

7. Make a list of other geometric properties which any definition of arc length should satisfy. Show that they are satisfied by the definition developed in Problem 2.

8. Let A and B be two solids of revolution. Suppose that B will fit inside A. State this notion in a suitable way, and prove that the volume of B is no more than the volume of A.

9. Check that the definition of volume given generates the correct value for cones and spheres.

10. State at least two geometric properties which any definition of volume should satisfy. State them in a manner suitable for application to the problem of finding the volume of a solid of revolution. Show that the given definition satisfies these properties.

11. Consider a solid figure. Give a definition of cross section. Suppose that for some axis a formula is known which gives the cross-sectional area at each point on the axis. What can be said about the volume of the figure? What tests could be applied to establish the correctness of your procedure for finding the volume? Prove your procedure satisfies these tests.

12. Consider a solid figure having a square base of side 8. Suppose further that if a cross section is taken through the figure which is perpendicular to both the base and an edge of the base, then the area of this cross section is proportional to the square of the distance from the center of the base to the line of intersection between the cross section and the base. Find an expression for the volume of the solid.

13. Consider a solid figure having a base which is an equilateral triangle of side 4. Suppose for a fixed altitude that any cross section which is perpendicular to both the base and the altitude is a square. Find an expression for the volume of the figure.

14. Find expressions for the maximum and minimum pressure on a horizontal strip of the plate in Problem 4. Both of these expressions involve a product of terms involving y times Δy_i. Consider the terms involving y. Show that the terms associated with the maximum must approach the terms associated with the minimum as Δy tends to 0. What does this mean about the solution given to the problem?

15. The solution to Problem 4 is numerical. To what extent does the solution depend on the coordinate system chosen for the solution? Prove your answer.

16. A particle moves from point a to point b on the x-axis, with $a < b$. If a variable force of $F(x)$ units acts on the particle at the point x in its travel, find an expression for the work done in moving the particle from a to b. Give a rigorous justification for the mathematical development.

17. Let f be continuous and monotone on $[a, b]$, $0 \leqslant a$. Find an expression for the volume of the solid obtained by revolving the graph of f about the y-axis. Specifically, develop the 'shell' method.

18. Consider a solid of revolution obtained by rotating a nonnegative function, f, about the x-axis. Find a formula for the surface area of this solid.

19. A student solved Exercise 18 by considering an increment of surface area associated with a disk. This led to an approximating sum of the form: $\sum_{i=1}^{n} 2\pi f(x_i) \Delta x_i$. The resultant integral for the surface area was $2\pi \int_{a}^{b} f(x) \, dx$. Give a rigorous argument showing this formula cannot be correct.

20. Consider a deck of ordinary playing cards, perhaps two or three decks stacked together. This stack of cards has a volume, that is, $l \times w \times h$, length times width times height. Suppose the cards are shifted so that the stack now leans to one side. What is the new volume? Suppose that the cards are stacked so that they rotate, or so that there is a wave, what is the volume? Is there a general principle here which can be formulated?

21. Let f and g be continuous on $[a, b]$, $0 \leqslant a$, with $f \geqslant g$. Find an expression for the volume of the solid of revolution obtained by rotating the plane figure generated by f and g about the y-axis.

22. Let $f(\theta)$, $0 \leqslant a \leqslant \theta \leqslant b \leqslant 2\pi$, be a function in polar coordinates, with f nonnegative. Find an expression for the area of that portion of the disk bounded by $\theta = a$, $\theta = b$, and the graph of f.

23. Let R be a region of the plane bounded by two continuous curves, f and g, and such that $f \geqslant g$, $f(a) = g(a)$ and $f(b) = g(b)$. Suppose that the region is filled with a thin metal plate whose density at any point (x, y) of the region is given by $\rho(x)$. Find an expression for the center of mass and the moment of inertia of the plate.

24. Let C be a curve in the plane having parametric form $x = x(t)$, $y = y(t)$, $0 \leqslant t \leqslant 1$. If x' and y' are continuous on $[0, 1]$ find an expression for the length of C.

25. Let C, $x(t)$, and $y(t)$ be as in Exercise 24. If $F(t)$ denotes a tangential force acting on a particle at the point $(x(t), y(t))$, find the work done in moving a particle along C from $(x(0), y(0))$ to $(x(1), y(1))$.

26. Let C be given as in Exercise 24, and suppose that C describes the position of a thin wire lying in the plane. If $\rho(t)$ denotes the density of the wire at the point $(x(t), y(t))$, find an expression for the mass of the wire.

6.2 IMPROPER RIEMANN INTEGRATION

Once we have developed the Riemann integral, a number of outstanding problems remain. The first of these is to find a simple characterization of the class of Riemann integrable functions on $[a, b]$. The second is to look for ways to extend the integral concept so that it can be applied to functions which are not Riemann integrable. The first of these problems is beyond the scope of this book, although, as we have remarked, the answer is directly related to the nature of the set of discontinuities of the function. One approach to the problem of extending the integral concept is the subject of this section.

All functions which are Riemann integrable have bounded domains and bounded ranges. That functions have bounded domains arises from the fact that each of the integral definitions required the function to be defined on a closed interval. That functions have bounded ranges arose as a prerequisite in the case of the Riemann–Darboux integral due to the fact that we required the supremum and infimum of the function to exist as a finite number on each subinterval. For the case of the Riemann integral, even though we dropped boundedness as a prerequisite, the fact that the function was bounded turned out to be a consequence of Riemann integrability (see Theorem 5.3.2). Thus, an obvious question which arises directly from the theory is whether the integral concept can be extended to include functions having unbounded domains, or unbounded ranges. In this section, we relax either or both of the bounded requirements, and consider integrals of functions which are either defined on unbounded intervals, or the interval is bounded, but the function itself is unbounded there. This leads to the idea of **improper integrals** and we discuss the convergence and divergence of such integrals. Two classical examples, namely the beta and the gamma integrals, will serve as appropriate illustrations.

Definition. Let f be a function defined on an interval $[a, b)$, $a,b \in \mathbf{R}$. (We also allow b to be $+\infty$.) If f is Riemann integrable on $[a, c]$ for each c such that $a \leqslant c < b$, but not Riemann integrable on $[a, b]$, then the integral, $\int_a^b f$, is said to be an **improper integral**. In particular, we say that the integral is **improper** at the point b, and b is a **singularity** for the integrand f. We then define the **improper integral**, $\int_a^b f$, by

$$\int_a^b f = \lim_{c \to b^-} \int_a^c f.$$

If this limit exists as a real number, A, then we say that the improper integral **converges** to A. If the limit is infinite, or fails to exist, the improper integral is said to **diverge**.

Discussion. We want to address the question of why this definition is a reasonable way to extend the integral concept. Thus, consider the fact that f is Riemann integrable on $[a, c]$ for each $a \leqslant c < b$. This fact forces f to be bounded on $[a, c]$, whence it means that f can fail to be integrable on $[a, b]$ only if one of the following two statements is true:

    1. f is unbounded in a neighborhood of $b < \infty$;
    2. $b = +\infty$.

Following the notation of section 5.5, let us define a function $F: [a, b) \to \mathbf{R}$ by

$$F(x) = \int_a^x f, \quad x \in [a, b).$$

For the former case, since f is Riemann integrable on $[a, c)$, by Theorem 5.5.2 F is continuous on $[a, b)$ for each $c \in [a, b)$. Indeed, if f is continuous on $[a, b)$, then F will be a primitive of f. Even so, we cannot guarantee that F is continuous at the point b. (The reader should be able to give many examples of functions which are continuous on an open interval but for which there is no continuous extension to a closed interval.) However, if it happens to be the case that F has a continuous extension at b, then it is clear that this extension must be given by

$$F(b) = \lim_{x \to b^-} F(x) = \lim_{x \to b^-} \int_a^x f.$$

Now, and this is the essential point, it may be the case that F has a continuous extension at b, *even though* f is unbounded at b. (Think of $f(x) = \dfrac{1}{x^{1/3}}$, $x \in [-1, 0)$.)

For such a case, the fact that F is continuous, or can be defined so as to be continuous, at b argues strongly that the integral of f should exist over the entire closed interval, $[a, b]$. Having said that the integral over the closed interval should exist, what should its value be? Evidently, the only possible sensible value would be $\lim_{x \to b^-} F(x)$, which is the value given by the definition.

In the case where $b = +\infty$, the definition reduces to

$$\int_a^\infty f = \lim_{N \to \infty} \int_a^N f$$

provided the latter limit exists. Expressing this in the language adopted above, we see that convergence of the improper integral implies $\lim_{x \to \infty} F(x)$ exists as a finite real number. Thus, it would appear reasonable to take this value as the value for the integral over the interval $[a, \infty)$. Again, the point is that there are functions for which this limit exists; $f(x) = \dfrac{1}{x^2}$ on $[1, \infty)$ is a good example.

Evidently a dual situation exists for intervals of the form $(a, b]$. Thus, if f is bounded in $(a, b]$ and integrable in $[c, b]$ for each $c > a$ (we allow c to be $-\infty$ also), then the improper integral $\int_a^b f$ is defined to be $\lim_{c \to a^+} \int_c^b f$. If the limit exists as a real number, then the improper integral converges. If the limit is either infinite, or does not exist, we then have a divergent improper integral. In case f is bounded and integrable in $(-\infty, b]$, then the limit $\lim_{N \to \infty} \int_{-N}^b f$ is defined to be the improper integral $\int_{-\infty}^b f$.

As in the case of Riemann integral, if $b < a$, we set $\int_b^a f = -\int_a^b f$.   □

Our next definition is a straightforward generalization of the initial definition.

Definition. Let $a < c < b$ (we allow $a = -\infty$, $b = +\infty$). If the integrals $\int_a^c f$ and $\int_c^b f$ are both improper, where either the first is improper at a and the second is improper at b, or both are improper at c, and if each is convergent, then we define $\int_a^b f = \int_a^c f + \int_c^b f$. We also say that the integral $\int_a^b f$ is convergent.

Discussion. The purpose of this definition is to extend the initial definition to cover cases where f is unbounded at a point c, $c \in (a, b)$, or where $a = -\infty$ and $b = +\infty$. These cases are handled by splitting the integral into two integrals at the point $c \in (a, b)$. If at least one of the integrals is divergent, the improper integral $\int_a^b f$ is divergent. We take this opportunity to warn the reader that if f is unbounded at a point c, and if $a = -\infty$ and $b = +\infty$, then the improper integral $\int_{-\infty}^{+\infty} f$ *should not be* evaluated as the limit $\lim_{N \to \infty} \int_{-N}^N f$. These two quantities are not the same. (The reader is asked in Exercise 1 to provide an example to illustrate this situation.) What we are demanding in this definition is that for an arbitrary c, the integral $\int_{-\infty}^c f$ as well as the integral $\int_{-c}^\infty f$ should separately converge.   □

EXAMPLE 1 _____

Discuss the convergence or divergence of the integrals

(a) $\displaystyle\int_0^1 \frac{1}{x^p}$;

(b) $\displaystyle\int_1^\infty \frac{1}{x^p}$;

(c) $\displaystyle\int_0^\infty \frac{1}{x^p}$.

Solution. The function $f(x) = \dfrac{1}{x^p}$ is continuous on $(0, 1]$, but is undefined at $x = 0$. If $p < 0$, it is bounded in $(0, 1]$, so we can extend the definition to $x = 0$ by setting the value to be 0 when $x = 0$. If $p = 0$, the function is identically 1 throughout $[0, 1]$. In both cases, f, itself has a continuous extension to the whole of $[0, 1]$, whence it is Riemann integrable there. For $p > 0$, $\dfrac{1}{x^p}$ is unbounded at 0, and an improper integral results and three cases must be treated.

If $0 < p < 1$, then $1 - p > 0$, and we then have

$$\int_0^1 \frac{1}{x^p} = \lim_{c \to 0^+} \int_c^1 \frac{1}{x^p} = \lim_{c \to 0^+} \int_c^1 x^{-p}$$

$$= \lim_{c \to 0^+} [F(1) - F(c)], \quad \text{where } F(x) = \frac{x^{1-p}}{1 - p}$$

$$= \lim_{c \to 0^+} \left(\frac{1}{1-p} - \frac{c^{1-p}}{1-p} \right)$$

$$= \frac{1}{1 - p}$$

whence the integral converges to $\dfrac{1}{1 - p}$.

For $p > 1$, $1 - p < 0$. If we repeat the computations above, we find that $F(c)$ is unbounded as c approaches 0^+. It follows that the above limit is $+\infty$, hence the improper integral diverges.

Finally, when $p = 1$, using facts (to be) developed in Chapter 10, we have

$$\int_0^1 \frac{1}{x} = \lim_{c \to 0^+} \int_{0'}^0 \frac{1}{x} = \lim_{c \to 0^+} (-\ln c) = +\infty$$

whence the integral diverges, concluding the third case.

For (b), if $p > 1$, since there is no discontinuity in $(1, \infty)$, we have

$$\int_1^\infty \frac{1}{x^p} = \lim_{N \to \infty} \int_1^N \frac{1}{x^p}$$

$$= \lim_{N \to \infty} \left[\frac{N^{1-p}}{1 - p} - \frac{1}{1 - p} \right]$$

$$= \frac{1}{p - 1}.$$

Hence the integral converges for $p > 1$. We leave it to Exercise 2, to show that the integral diverges to $+\infty$ when $p \leqslant 1$.

Finally, for (c), consider separately the intervals $(0, 1)$ and $(1, \infty)$. By the computations for the two previous cases, for any arbitrary p, one of the integrals converges and the other diverges. Hence, the integral diverges to $+\infty$ for all p. □

Discussion. This is a straightforward application of the definition of convergence, with the knowledge of a primitive of the function considered. The only fact that we have not yet developed is that $\ln x$ is a primitive of $\dfrac{1}{x}$. □

EXAMPLE 2
_____

Discuss the convergence of the improper integral $\displaystyle\int_0^5 \frac{1}{(x-2)^3}$.

Solution. Observe that the function is unbounded at $x = 2$. So we must separately consider the intervals $(0, 2)$ and $(2, 5)$, and the two associated improper integrals given by

$$\lim_{h \to 0^+} \int_0^{2-h} \frac{1}{(x-2)^3} + \lim_{k \to 0^+} \int_{2+k}^5 \frac{1}{(x-2)^3}.$$

A simple computation shows that both the integrals diverge, and hence we conclude that this integral is divergent. □

Discussion. The reader might be tempted to perform the above calculations as

$$\lim_{h \to 0^+} \left\{ \int_0^{2-h} \frac{1}{(x-2)^3} + \int_{2+h}^5 \frac{1}{(x-2)^3} \right\}$$

without taking care to evaluate the two separate limits, one for h and the other for k which are taken *independently*. The result, then, would be

$$\lim_{h \to 0^+} ((F(2-h) - F(0)) + (F(5) - F(2+h))), \quad \text{where } F(x) = \frac{-1}{2(x-2)^2}$$

$$= \lim_{h \to 0} \left(\left[\frac{-1}{2h^2} + \frac{1}{8} \right] + \left[\frac{-1}{18} + \frac{1}{2h^2} \right] \right)$$

$$= \frac{5}{72}$$

showing that the integral converges to the value $\dfrac{5}{72}$. This answer makes no apparent sense, in view of the fact that both the separate limit calculations are divergent. However, on reflection it suggests the following definition. □

Definition. If c is a point of discontinuity of the integral $\displaystyle\int_a^b f$, and $\displaystyle\lim_{h \to 0^+} \left(\int_a^{c-h} f + \int_{c+h}^b f \right) = A$ exists, while the improper integral $\displaystyle\int_a^b f$ is divergent, then the value A is called **Cauchy's Principal Value** of the divergent integral.

Discussion. The Cauchy Principal Value for an integral acts to extend the integral concept even further. To understand the rationale for this extension, consider Figure 6.2.1 which presents part of the graph of $f(x) = \dfrac{1}{(x-2)^3}$. From Example 2, we know that $\int_2^{2+h} f$ does not exist, even as an improper integral. This argues that the area of the region bounded by $x = 2$, $x = 2 + h$, $y = f(x)$, and $y = 0$ is infinite. However, what is apparent is that the area of this region should be identical to the area of the region bounded by $x = 2 - h$, $x = 2$, $y = f(x)$, and $y = 0$. The reason underlying this assertion is that the two regions are congruent in the usual geometrical sense. Moreover, in any evaluation of an integral, $\int_a^b f$, where $a < 2 - h$ and $2 + h < b$, these two infinite areas should exactly cancel one another due to having opposite signs in the computation. If one accepts that these infinities can, and should, cancel, then one immediately gets the Cauchy Principal Value.

Even if one accepts the reasoning above, it is clear that the existence of a Cauchy Principal Value in cases where the improper integrals do not exist is special and should be recognized as such. For this reason we avoid writing $\int_0^5 \dfrac{1}{(x-2)^3} = \dfrac{5}{72}$ and instead write

$$CPV \int_0^5 \frac{1}{(x-2)^3} = \frac{5}{72}$$

to indicate Cauchy's Principal Value of the divergent integral.

Two other forms of the Cauchy Principal Value are discussed in Exercises 4 and 5. □

Next, we consider functions which are nonnegative throughout the interval of integration, and obtain a test for deciding their convergence or divergence, by comparing them with an integral which is known to be convergent or divergent. Such a test is usually known as a **comparison test**. As a preliminary, we prove the following theorem, which resembles similar results on sequences and functions.

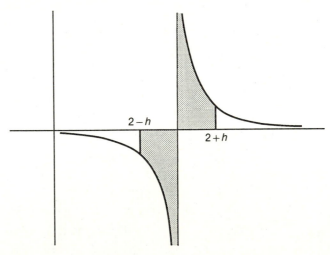

Figure 6.2.1 Cauchy's Principal Value for $\int_0^5 \dfrac{1}{(x-2)^3}$.

Theorem 6.2.1. If f is nonnegative and Riemann integrable in $[a, K]$, $K > a$, then the improper integral $\int_a^\infty f$ converges if and only if the function $F:[a, \infty) \to \mathbf{R}$ defined by $F(x) = \int_a^x f$ is bounded. If the hypothesis is satisfied, then

$$\int_a^\infty f = \sup\{F(x) : x > a\}.$$

Proof. Note that F is nonnegative and monotonically increasing. Hence $\lim_{x \to \infty} F(x)$ exists in $\mathbf{R} \cup \{\infty\}$, and further, $\sup\{F(x) : x > a\} = \lim_{x \to \infty} F(x) = \int_a^\infty f$. If F is bounded on $[a, \infty)$, say by M, then the above limit exists and is less or equal to M, whence the integral converges. On the other hand, if F is unbounded, by monotonicity, we conclude that $\lim_{x \to \infty} F(x) = \infty$, whence the integral diverges. $\square$

The following theorem is the so-called comparison test for convergence or divergence of the improper integral.

Theorem 6.2.2. Let $0 \leqslant f(x) \leqslant g(x)$ for $x \in [a, \infty)$ and let f and g be integrable in $[a, K]$, for every $K > a$. If the improper integral $\int_a^\infty g$ converges, then the improper integral $\int_a^\infty f$ also converges. If $\int_a^\infty f$ diverges, then the integral $\int_a^\infty g$ diverges.

Proof. If $\int_a^\infty g$ converges, then by Theorem 6.2.1, the function $G(x) = \int_a^x g$ is bounded. Also $0 \leqslant F(x) = \int_a^x f \leqslant G(x)$, proving that the integral $\int_a^\infty f$ converges. The divergence case is left to the exercises. $\square$

Discussion. The proof given is straightforward. Nevertheless, because comparison tests are so common, it is worth examining the intuition. Consider then Figure 6.2.2. Because g dominates f and both are nonnegative, it is evident that the region defined by the graph of f, $x = 0$, and the x-axis is included in the region defined by the graph of g, $x = 0$, and the x-axis. It seems evident that if the latter region has a finite area, then the former must also. Similarly, if the former has an infinite area, then the latter must also.

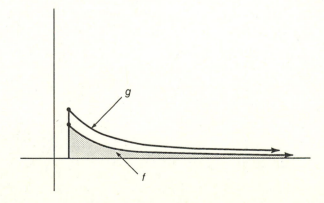

Figure 6.2.2 Illustration of the comparison test for improper integrals.

The utility of comparison tests rests on having a large collection of functions available with two properties. First, the convergence properties of the individual functions must be known. Second, the collection must contain enough functions so that an appropriate comparison can be made between some member of the collection and any given function for which the convergence properties are unknown. The class of functions whose convergence properties are discussed in Example 1(b) is one useful collection of functions which can be used in comparison tests. ☐

A practical way to use the above test is by a limit form of the comparison test. This is enunciated in the next theorem.

Theorem 6.2.3. Let f be nonnegative and bounded on $[a, \infty)$, g be positive on $[a, \infty)$, and $\lim_{x \to \infty} \dfrac{f(x)}{g(x)} = L$. Further, suppose that f and g are integrable on $[a, K]$, for each $K \in [a, \infty)$.

(a) If $L \neq 0$, then both the integrals either converge or both of them diverge;

(b) If $L = 0$, and the integral $\int_a^\infty g$ is convergent, $\int_a^\infty g$ is convergent;

(c) If $L = \infty$, and the integral $\int_a^\infty g$ is divergent, then $\int_a^\infty f$ is divergent.

Proof.   The proof is left to the reader as Exercise 7.   ☐

Discussion.   Theorem 6.2.3 is a typical reformulation of the comparison test. It results from the recognition that to compare two functions, for convergence or divergence purposes over the interval $[a, \infty)$, one real interest is that the behavior of the one closely reflects the behavior of the other only on the tail of the interval, that is, on $[b, \infty)$, where b can be very large. This can be completely captured by looking at the limit of the ratio of the two functions. For this reason, this type of test is referred to as **a ratio comparison test**.

The two tests given have been stated so as to apply to the problem of testing whether the improper integral over an interval of the form $[a, \infty)$ exists. In Exercise 8 we ask the reader to formulate an appropriate version of the ratio comparison test to apply in other situations. In the next example, such a test is applied.

The comments regarding the utility of the comparison test also apply to the ratio comparison test.   ☐

EXAMPLE 3 _____

Discuss the convergence or divergence of the following improper integrals:

(a) $\displaystyle\int_0^1 \frac{1}{\sqrt{x}\,(1 + x^2)}$;

(b) $\displaystyle\int_0^1 \frac{1}{x^2\,(1 + x)^2}$;

(c) $\displaystyle\int_0^1 \frac{1}{\sqrt{x}\,\sqrt{1 - x}}$.

Solution. (a) Here 0 is the only singularity of the integrand f. Compare the integral f with the integral of g on $(0, 1]$, where $g(x) = \dfrac{1}{\sqrt{x}}$. Since

$$\lim_{x \to 0^+} \frac{\dfrac{1}{\sqrt{x}(1 + x^2)}}{\dfrac{1}{\sqrt{x}}} = 1,$$

and the integral $\displaystyle\int_0^1 \frac{1}{\sqrt{x}}$ converges, we conclude that the given integral is convergent by Theorem 6.2.3.

(b) Again we form a ratio to make the comparison. This time, set $g(x) = \dfrac{1}{x^2}$ on $(0, 1]$. Since $\displaystyle\int_0^1 g$ is divergent, the integral of f is also divergent.

(c) In this case, both 0 and 1 are discontinuities of the integrand. So, we separately consider the integrals $\displaystyle\int_0^{1/2} f$ and $\displaystyle\int_{1/2}^1 f$. The former converges, by comparing it with $\displaystyle\int_0^{1/2} \frac{1}{\sqrt{x}}$. For the latter, we obtain convergence again, if we compare the integral with $\displaystyle\int_{1/2}^1 \frac{1}{\sqrt{(1 - x)}}$. Since both the integrals are convergent, we conclude that the given integral also converges. □

Discussion. The above examples illustrate our earlier remark that knowledge of the behavior of the improper integrals of the functions $\dfrac{1}{x^p}$ for various values of p is very useful. The reader should fill in all the missing details in parts (b) and (c), including checking that suitable hypotheses hold. □

Two important improper integrals, which have many practical applications are the **gamma** and the **beta** integrals. We study them in Examples 4 and 5. Some basic properties of the exponential function are assumed in what follows. These are formally developed in Chapter 10.

EXAMPLE 4 _____

Discuss the convergence or divergence of the integral $\displaystyle\int_0^\infty f$, where $f(x) = x^{a-1}e^{-x}dx$, $a > 0$.

Solution. Consider the intervals $(0,1]$ and $[1,\infty)$ separately and let $I_1 = \displaystyle\int_0^1 f$ and $I_2 = \displaystyle\int_1^\infty f$. Note that the improper integral $\displaystyle\int_1^\infty \frac{1}{x^2}$ converges by Example 1. Also, since $\dfrac{x^{a-1}e^{-x}}{x^{-2}}$ approaches 0 as $x \to \infty$ (**WHY?**), the integral I_2 converges for all a.

On the other hand, if $a < 1$, there is a discontinuity at $x = 0$. Comparing the integrand with $g(x) = x^{a-1}$, one readily sees that $\displaystyle\lim_{x \to 0^+} \frac{x^{a-1}e^{-x}}{x^{a-1}} = 1$.

Since $\int_0^1 x^{a-1}$ converges if $a - 1 > -1$, and diverges otherwise, we see that I_1 converges only if $a > 0$. Thus, the given integral converges for all $a > 0$.

□

Discussion. This integral is usually known as **Euler's second integral** or the **gamma integral**. The function $\Gamma: (0,\infty) \to \mathbf{R}$ defined by $\Gamma(a) = \int_0^\infty x^{a-1}e^{-x}$ is called the **gamma function**. The gamma function first appeared in 1729 in a correspondence between L. Euler and Goldbach. Euler was interested in a function f with the property that $f(n) = n!$ for each natural number n. If such a function could be found, it then makes sense to talk about factorials of real numbers such as 2.973. Euler discovered that the following 'infinite product' possesses this remarkable property:

$$\Gamma(n) = \left[\left(\frac{2}{1}\right)^n \frac{1}{n+1} \right] \left[\left(\frac{3}{2}\right)^n \frac{2}{n+2} \right] \left[\left(\frac{4}{3}\right)^n \frac{3}{n+3} \right] \cdots$$

and this expression can be obtained as the 'limit' of a finite product, resulting in the following definition of the gamma function:

$$\Gamma(x) = \lim_{n \to \infty} \frac{n!\,(n+1)^x}{(x+1)(x+2)\,\cdots\,(x+n)}$$

where x is any real number, except nonnegative integers. Euler also had an expression $n! = \int_0^1 (-\ln x)^n dx$, and he subsequently modified this expression to generate the gamma integral we have discussed above.

One of the important properties of gamma integral is that $\Gamma(x+1) = x\Gamma(x)$, which the reader can easily verify. Motivated by this identity, the gamma function can be extended to negative real numbers also. If $x \in (-1,0)$, one defines $\Gamma(x) = \frac{1}{x}\Gamma(x + 1)$, and more generally, if $x \in (-n, -n+1)$, we can define

$$\Gamma(x) = \frac{\Gamma(x + n)}{x(x + 1)(x + 2)\,\cdots\,(x + n - 1)}.$$

The graph of $f(x) = \Gamma(x)$ is given in Figure 6.2.3. Some properties of this function are explored in the exercises.

□

EXAMPLE 5 _____

Discuss the convergence of the integral $\int_0^1 x^{p-1}(1 - x)^{q-1}$.

Solution. If p and q are both greater than 1, this reduces to an ordinary Riemann integral, and hence trivially converges. If $p, q < 1$, there are discontinuities at $x = 0$ and $x = 1$. It is easy to see that the integral converges if both $1 - p < 1$ and $1 - q < 1$, that is, when $p > 0$ and $q > 0$. The reader is asked to complete the details of this example in Exercise 9.

□

Discussion. This integral is called **Euler's first integral** or the **beta integral**, and finds many interesting applications in statistics and applied mathematics. We define the beta function on the first quadrant of the Cartesian plane by $\beta(p, q) =$

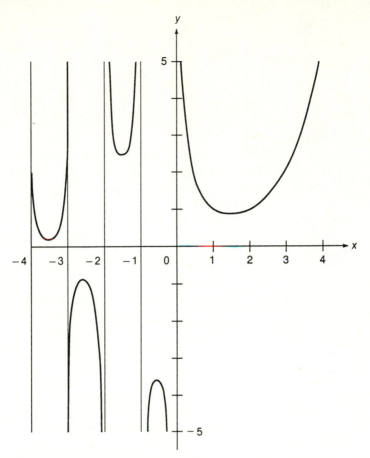

Figure 6.2.3   Graph of the gamma function $y = \Gamma(x)$.

$\int_0^1 x^{p-1}(1-x)^{q-1}$. There are interesting relationships between the gamma and the beta functions, which we explore in the exercises.   □

Now, we consider improper integrals of functions that are not necessarily positive. The following theorem is a 'Cauchy criterion' for the convergence of such types of improper integrals.

Theorem 6.2.4.   If f is integrable on $[a, K]$ for each K such that $a < K < \infty$, then the improper integral $\int_a^\infty f$ converges if and only if for each $\epsilon > 0$, there exists $X \geqslant a$ such that for all x_1, x_2, if $X < x_1 < x_2$, then

$$\left| \int_{x_1}^{x_2} f \right| < \epsilon.$$

Proof.   We prove the limit exists, that is, sufficiency. Necessity is left to the reader as Exercise 11. Following our usual tack, define $F(x) = \int_a^x f$, where $a \leqslant x$. The hypothesis guarantees that the sequence $\{F(n)\}$, $n \geqslant a$, is a Cauchy sequence

(**WHY?**), whence it has a limit, L. Now fix $\epsilon > 0$ and choose X such that, if $X < n < x_1 < x_2$, then $|F(n) - L| < \epsilon$ and $|F(x_1) - F(x_2)| < \epsilon$. It follows from the Triangle inequality that if $X < K$, then $|F(K) - L| < \epsilon$ (**WHY?**), whence

$$\int_a^\infty f = \lim_{K \to \infty} \int_a^K f = \lim_{K \to \infty} F(K) = L.$$

$\square$

Discussion. The reader should compare this theorem with the Cauchy criterion for sequences in section 3.3. Reflection should convince the reader that there is a natural generalization of the Cauchy criterion which deals with limits of functions at infinity. The reader is asked to consider this problem in Exercise 12. $\square$

Definition. The improper integral $\int_a^b f$ is said to be **absolutely convergent** provided $\int_a^b |f|$ is convergent. The integral is said to be **conditionally convergent** provided the improper integral $\int_a^b f$ converges and $\int_a^b |f|$ diverges.

Discussion. The requirement of absolute convergence is a strong one. It is easy to show that every absolutely convergent integral is convergent, but not conversely. We give an example of a convergent integral that fails to be absolutely convergent. $\square$

EXAMPLE 6 _____

Discuss the absolute convergence of the improper integral $\int_0^\infty \dfrac{\sin x}{x}$.

Solution. First, observe that, as will be seen from Chapter 10, $\lim_{x \to 0} \dfrac{\sin x}{x} = 1$. Thus, singularity is not at 0, but at the upper limit of integration. If $K > 0$, there exists $n \in \mathbf{N}$ and $t_n \in [0, \pi)$ such that $K = n\pi + t_n$. Hence,

$$\int_0^K \frac{\sin x}{x} = \int_0^{n\pi} \frac{\sin x}{x} + \int_{n\pi}^{n\pi + t_n} \frac{\sin x}{x}.$$

Let us call the first term A_n, and the second B_n. Now,

$$|B_n| = \left| \int_{n\pi}^{n\pi + t_n} \frac{\sin x}{x} \right| \leqslant \int_{n\pi}^{n\pi + t_n} \left| \frac{\sin x}{x} \right| \leqslant \int_{n\pi}^{n\pi + t_n} \frac{1}{n\pi} \leqslant \frac{\pi}{n\pi} = \frac{1}{n}$$

proving that the $\lim_{n \to \infty} B_n = 0$. Further,

$$A = \sum_{i=1}^n \left[\int_{(i-1)\pi}^{i\pi} \frac{\sin x}{x} \right],$$

where the term $a_i = \int_{(i-1)\pi}^{i\pi} \dfrac{\sin x}{x}$ has an alternating sign, is decreasing, and converges to 0. (This is easily checked based on computations from the calculus.) Hence, by Leibnitz's alternating series test (Theorem 7.4.1), $\sum a_i$ converges. Thus, we conclude that the improper integral also converges.

To see that this integral is not absolutely convergent, we consider $\int_0^\infty \frac{|\sin x|}{x}$.
We have

$$\int_0^{n\pi} \frac{|\sin x|}{x} = \sum_{k=1}^{n} \int_{(k-1)\pi}^{k\pi} \frac{|\sin x|}{x}$$

$$= \sum_{k=1}^{n} \int_0^{\pi} \frac{\sin t}{(k-1)\pi + t} \quad \text{(using } x = (k-1)\pi + t)$$

$$\geqslant \sum_{k=1}^{n} \frac{1}{k\pi} \int_0^{\pi} \sin t \, dt = \sum_{k=1}^{n} \frac{2}{k\pi}.$$

Since, as will be shown in Chapter 7, $\sum_{k=1}^{n} \frac{1}{k}$ approaches ∞ as n approaches ∞, we conclude that the integral diverges. Thus the given integral is conditionally convergent. $\square$

Discussion. In this example, we have employed several results from the theory of infinite series, which are proved later in Chapter 7. But this is not a disadvantage, since the student will already be familiar with the results, if not the proofs, from his elementary course in calculus. Moreover, the use of these results serves to establish the connection between certain types of improper integrals and infinite series. This connection is striking, and we explore further aspects in Chapter 7. $\square$

EXERCISES

1. Give an example of a function which illustrates the problem described following the definition of $\int_{-\infty}^{+\infty} f$.

2. Complete the proof of part (b) in Example 1.

3. Supply the missing details in Example 2.

4. Consider the problem of evaluating $\int_{-\infty}^{+\infty} f$. Define a Cauchy Principal Value for this type of integral and give an example of a function which is not improperly integrable on $[-\infty, \infty]$, but for which the Cauchy Principal Value exists.

5. Consider the problem of evaluating $\int_a^b f$ where for each u,v such that $a < u \leqslant v < b$, $\int_u^v f$ exists. Define a Cauchy Principal Value for this type of integral and give an example of a function which is not improperly integrable on $[a, b]$, but for which the Cauchy Principal Value exists.

6. Prove the divergence case in Theorem 6.2.2.

7. Supply a proof of Theorem 6.2.3.

8. Formulate and prove a version of Theorem 6.2.3 which can be used to test whether the improper integral over $[a, b]$ exists for functions unbounded at b.

9. Fill in the missing details in Example 5.

10. Supply an example to show that

$$\int_a^\infty f + g \neq \int_a^\infty f + \int_a^\infty g.$$

Are there conditions on f and g which will guarantee equality?

11. Complete the proof of Theorem 6.2.4.

12. Develop a Cauchy criterion for the existence of improper integrals of functions at infinity. Show that this criterion is equivalent to the original limit definition.

13. Discuss the convergence or divergence of the following integrals:

    (a) $\int_0^\infty xe^{-x}$;

    (b) $\int_2^\infty \dfrac{1}{x\sqrt{x^3 - 1}}$;

    (c) $\int_0^\infty \dfrac{1}{\sqrt{x}(1 + x)}$;

    (d) $\int_0^\infty \dfrac{\arctan x}{1 + x^2}$;

    (e) $\int_0^1 \dfrac{1}{x\sqrt{x}}$;

    (f) $\int_0^{1/e} \dfrac{1}{x(\ln x)^2}$

    (g) $\int_3^5 \dfrac{x^2}{\sqrt{(x - 3)(x - 5)}}$

    (h) $\int_a^b \dfrac{1}{(b - x)^n}$

    (i) $\int_{-\infty}^\infty \dfrac{1}{x^2 + 9x + 10}$;

    (j) $\int_0^{1/2} \dfrac{1}{x(\ln x)^2}$;

    (k) $\int_0^\infty e^{\alpha x} \sin \beta x$;

    (l) $\int_{-1}^1 \dfrac{1}{\sqrt{1 - x^2}}$;

    (m) $\int_{-3}^{-1} \dfrac{x^2 - 1}{x + 1}$;

    (n) $\int_{-3}^2 f$, where $f(x) = \begin{cases} \dfrac{1}{x^4}, & -3 \leqslant x < 0 \\[2mm] \dfrac{1}{\sqrt{x}}, & 0 < x \leqslant 2; \end{cases}$

    (o) $\int_{-\infty}^{+\infty} \dfrac{x}{\sqrt{2x^2 + 5}}$.

14. Find Cauchy's Principal Value of the following improper integrals:

    (a) $\int_{-1}^1 \dfrac{1}{x}$;

    (b) $\int_0^4 \dfrac{2}{(x - 2)^3}$;

(c) $\int_{-\infty}^{\infty} \sin x$;

(d) $\int_{-\infty}^{\infty} \cos x$;

(e) $\int_{-\infty}^{\infty} \frac{3}{x^3 + 2}$.

15. Show that $CPV \int_{-1}^{1} \frac{1}{|x|}$ does not exist.

16. If f is continuous on $\mathbf{R}$, and the integral $\int_{-\infty}^{\infty} f$ converges to A, show that $CPV \int_{-\infty}^{\infty} f = A$.

17. Prove that an absolutely convergent integral is convergent.

18. Discuss the convergence and absolute convergence of the following improper integrals:

(a) $\int_{0}^{\infty} \frac{\sin \alpha x}{x}$;

(b) $\int_{0}^{\infty} \frac{x^{\alpha - 1}}{1 + x}$;

(c) $\int_{0}^{\infty} \frac{\cos x}{\sqrt{x + x^2}}$;

(d) $\int_{0}^{\infty} \frac{x^{2m}}{1 + x^{2n}}$;

(e) $\int_{0}^{\infty} \frac{\cos ax - \cos bx}{x}$.

19. Give an example to show that the improper integral $\int_{a}^{b} f$ exists, while $\int_{a}^{b} f^2$ does not exist.

20. Prove that $\Gamma(x + 1) = x\Gamma(x)$.

21. Prove that $\Gamma(z) = \int_{0}^{1} \left[\ln \frac{1}{x} \right]^{z-1} dx$.

22. Prove the following properties of the beta integral:

(a) $\beta(x,1) = \frac{1}{x}$;

(b) $\beta(x+1,y) = \frac{x}{x+y}\beta(x, y)$;

(c) $\beta(x,y) = \frac{\Gamma(x)\Gamma(y)}{\Gamma(x+y)}$;

(d) $\beta(x,y) = 2\int_{0}^{\pi/2} \sin^{2x-1} t \cos^{2y-1} t\, dt$;

(e) $\beta\left[\frac{a+1}{2}, \frac{1}{2} \right] = 2\int_{0}^{\pi/2} \sin^a x$;

(f) $\beta(a,1 - a) = \int_{0}^{\infty} \frac{x^{a-1}}{1 + x} = \frac{\pi}{\sin \pi a}$;

(g) $\beta\left[\frac{19}{2}, \frac{1}{2} \right] = \int_{0}^{1} \frac{x^9}{\sqrt{x}\sqrt{(1 - x)}}$.

23. Show that $\int_{0}^{1} \frac{1}{\sqrt{1 - x^n}} = \frac{\sqrt{\pi}}{n} \frac{\Gamma\left[\dfrac{1}{n} \right]}{\Gamma\left[\dfrac{1}{n} + \dfrac{1}{2} \right]}$.

24. Use the following expression for π (**Wallis's product**)

$$2 \cdot \left[\frac{2 \cdot 2}{1 \cdot 3} \right] \left[\frac{4 \cdot 4}{3 \cdot 5} \right] \left[\frac{6 \cdot 6}{5 \cdot 7} \right] \left[\frac{8 \cdot 8}{7 \cdot 9} \right] \cdots$$

to show that $\Gamma \left[\frac{1}{2} \right] = \sqrt{\pi}$.

25. Find $\Gamma \left[-\frac{5}{2} \right]$.

26. Show that $\int_{-\infty}^{\infty} e^{-x^2} = \sqrt{\pi}$. [HINT: Use the fact that $\Gamma \left[\frac{1}{2} \right] = \sqrt{\pi}$.]

27. Let f be defined on $[a, b]$, $a, b \in \mathbf{R}$ and suppose that f is integrable on $[a, c]$, for each c such that $a \leqslant c < b$. Show that if f is not integrable on $[a, b]$, then f is unbounded in any neighborhood of b.

28. Is it possible that there could be a single nonnegative function f defined on $[0, \infty]$ such that for any bounded nonnegative function g, $\int_a^\infty g$ converges exactly if there is a c such that $g \leqslant f$ on $[c, \infty]$?

29. Could there be a single test function for the limit form of the comparison test?

30. Could there be a single positive function, g, defined on $[0, \infty)$ which would serve to determine the convergence or divergence of the improper integrals of all other bounded functions on $[a, \infty)$?

31. Let f be bounded in $[a, \infty)$ and integrable in $[a, t]$ for $t > a$, and let $\int_a^\infty g$ be absolutely convergent. Prove that $\int_a^\infty fg$ is absolutely convergent.

32. Prove **Abel's test**: Let f be bounded and monotonic in $[a, \infty)$, and let $\int_a^\infty g$ is convergent. Then, $\int_a^\infty fg$ is convergent.

33. Prove **Dirichlet's test**: Let f be bounded and monotonic in $[a, \infty)$, $\lim_{x \to \infty} f(x) = 0$, let $\int_a^t g$ be bounded for $t \geqslant a$. Then, $\int_a^\infty fg$ is convergent.

34. Test for convergence:

(a) $\int_0^\infty \sin x^2$;

(b) $\int_0^\infty e^{-ax} \cos x$;

(c) $\int_0^\infty e^{-ax} \frac{\sin x}{x}$;

(d) $\int_0^\infty \frac{\sin x}{x^p}$;

(e) $\int_e^\infty \frac{\ln x \sin x}{x}$.

6.3 RIEMANN–STIELTJES INTEGRATION

The theory of Riemann integration is based on limits of sums which take the form of

$$\lim_{\|P\| \to 0} \sum_{i=1}^n f(c_i) \times \Delta x_i.$$

In the special case that the partition, P, defines subintervals of equal length, then $\Delta x_i = \Delta x_j$, for all $i, j \leqslant n$. This remark is stated for Riemann sums, but the same holds true for Darboux sums. The truth of this remark is of course due to the fact that the quantity Δx_i is itself the length of the subinterval.

Having made these observations, one might look at sums of the form

$$\lim_{\|P\| \to 0} \sum_{i=1}^{n} f(c_i) \times \Delta g_i,$$

where P is a partition of $[a, b]$, f is a function defined on $[a, b]$, $c_i \in [x_{i-1}, x_i]$, g is a function defined on $[a, b]$, and $\Delta g_i = g(x_i) - g(x_{i-1})$. While the theory of such limits may seem artificial at first glance, in fact these limits arise in a natural way.

To motivate these ideas consider an urn filled with a thousand otherwise identical balls of ten different colors. If there are one hundred balls of each color, then the probability of picking a ball of a given color at random is simply $P(c_i) = 1/10$, where $P(c_i)$ stands for the probability of selecting a ball of color c_i. In probability theory, there may be values, V_i, attached to the selection of a ball of color, c_i, whence sums of the form

$$\sum_{i=1}^{n} V_i \times P(c_i)$$

arise. This sum is analogous to the familiar Riemann sum, since $P(c_i) = P(c_j)$.

Now suppose for contrast that the balls are not otherwise identical, so that the value of $P(c_i)$ depends on c_i, even though the number of balls of each color remains unchanged. The sum of interest is still

$$\sum_{i=1}^{n} V_i \times P(c_i)$$

but now $P(c_i) \neq P(c_j)$ for $i \neq j$, even though we still have one hundred of each type of ball. This situation corresponds to the more general type of sum discussed above. Although our example is finite in nature, it is apparent that similar sums could arise in situations involving continuous probability distributions. It is not our intent to discuss such situations here, but to mention them to illustrate the natural motivation underlying the considerations of this section.

In this section, then, we discuss a generalization of the concept of Riemann integral. The integrals considered are of the form $\int f \, dg$ rather than the conventional form $\int f$. Darboux–Stieltjes (Riemann–Stieltjes) integrals are generalizations of the concept of Darboux (Riemann) integral, in the sense that the integration is performed with respect to a function g. If we set $g(x) = x$, then the computation reduces to the ordinary Riemann integral. With respect to the nature of the function, g, a new class of functions called **functions of bounded variation** forms a satisfactory setting for this development. We conclude this section by studying some basic properties of such functions.

We shall now define the concept of Stieltjes integrals (both in the sense of Darboux and Riemann). First, we consider Darboux–Stieltjes integrals, which form a straightforward generalization of the concept of Riemann–Darboux integrals.

Definition. Let $f: [a, b] \to \mathbf{R}$ be bounded and $g: [a, b] \to \mathbf{R}$ be monotone increasing. Let $P = \{a = x_0 \leqslant x_1 \leqslant \cdots \leqslant x_n = b\}$ be a partition of $[a, b]$. We define the **upper** and **lower Darboux–Stieltjes sums** by

$$\bar{S}(f, g, P) = \sum_{i=1}^{n} M_i(g(x_i) - g(x_{i-1}))$$

$$\underline{S}(f, g, P) = \sum_{i=1}^{n} m_i(g(x_i) - g(x_{i-1}))$$

where M_i, m_i denote, respectively, the supremum and the infimum of f in the ith subinterval $[x_{i-1}, x_i]$. We also define the **upper Darboux–Stieltjes integral**

$$\overline{\int_a^b} f \, dg = \inf \{\bar{S}(f, g, P)\}$$

and the **lower Darboux–Stieltjes integral**

$$\underline{\int_a^b} f \, dg = \sup \underline{S}\{(f, g, P)\},$$

where the infima, suprema are taken over all possible partitions P of $[a, b]$. If

$$\overline{\int_a^b} f \, dg = \underline{\int_a^b} f \, dg,$$

we say that f is Darboux–Stieltjes integrable with respect to g in $[a, b]$, and the common value is the **Darboux–Stieltjes integral** D–S $\int_a^b f \, dg$.

Discussion. It is important that the reader understand the nature of the generalization being discussed. This is established by carefully comparing the present definition with that original definition of the upper and lower Darboux sums presented in section 5.2. Specifically, both definitions begin with a bounded function defined on a closed interval $[a, b]$. Both definitions take an arbitrary partition, P, of this interval. Both definitions employ the supremum and infimum of f, M_i, m_i on the ith subinterval. The distinction between the two is that the Stieltjes definition has a second function g defined and monotonically increasing on $[a, b]$. The original definition makes no mention of such a function. However, such a function is present in the original definition. This can be seen by considering how the function g is used in the extended definition. It appears as the multiplier in

$$M_i \times (g(x_i) - g(x_{i-1})) = M_i \times \Delta g_i.$$

If we ask whether an analogous function exists for the original definition, the answer is easily seen to be yes, since in that definition M_i is multiplied by Δx_i, the length of the ith subinterval. If one sets $g(x) = x$, which is a monotone increasing function on $[a, b]$, then the basic definition of Darboux integration is seen to be a special case of the more general situation. Moreover, this discussion also establishes the essential connection between the more usual notation for Riemann integrals and our present notation:

$$\int_a^b f \, dx, \quad \text{and} \quad \int_a^b f \, dg.$$

The close similarity between the two definitions suggest that the same techniques of proof used in the case of Darboux sums should also work in this generalized situation. This is indeed the case, and the reader can easily prove, for example, that if Q is a refinement of the partition, P, $\bar{S}(f, g, Q) \leqslant \bar{S}(f, g, P)$ and $\underline{S}(f, g, Q) \geqslant \underline{S}(f, g, P)$. In fact *any* upper sum exceeds *any* lower sum (Exercise 1), and therefore $\underline{\int_a^b} f \, dg \leqslant \overline{\int_a^b} f \, dg$.

Quite obviously, theorems about Darboux–Stieltjes integrals with respect to a monotonic increasing function g apply to the Riemann–Darboux integrals as particular cases. In many instances, theorems and proofs for Riemann–Darboux integrals apply almost word by word for the generalized situation of the Darboux–Stieltjes integral with respect to a monotonic increasing function. Three such instances are furnished in the following theorems. $\qquad\square$

Theorem 6.3.1. Let f be bounded and g be monotonic increasing in $[a, b]$. A necessary and sufficient condition for D–S $\int_a^b f \, dg$ to exist is that given $\epsilon > 0$, there exists a partition P of $[a, b]$ such that $\bar{S}(f, g, P) - \underline{S}(f, g, P) < \epsilon$.

Proof. Exercise 2. $\qquad\square$

Discussion. This theorem provides the essential tool for working with the Darboux–Stieltjes sums. $\qquad\square$

Theorem 6.3.2. If f is continuous, and g is monotonic increasing in $[a, b]$, then the Darboux–Stieltjes integral D–S $\int_a^b f \, dg$ exists.

Proof. By Theorem 3.6.2 f is uniformly continuous on $[a, b]$. Thus, given $\epsilon > 0$, we can find a $\delta > 0$ such that for all $x, y \in [a, b]$, with $|x - y| < \delta$, it is true that $|f(x) - f(y)| < \dfrac{\epsilon}{(g(b) - g(a))}$. (The case $g(a) = g(b)$ is trivial (**WHY?**).) Now, choose a partition, P, with norm less than δ. The continuity of f guarantees that on each subinterval, $[x_{i-1}, x_i]$, of P, the infimum, m_i, and the supremum, M_i, of f are actually attained at points, say, y_i, z_i, in that subinterval. Since $|y_i - z_i| < \delta$, we have $M_i - m_i < \dfrac{\epsilon}{(g(b) - g(a))}$. This being the case for $i = 1, 2, \ldots, n$, we get

$$\bar{S}(P) - \underline{S}(P) = \sum_{i=1}^n M_i \Delta g_i - \sum_{i=1}^n m_i \Delta g_i$$

$$= \sum_{i=1}^n (M_i - m_i) \, \Delta g_i$$

$$\leqslant \frac{\epsilon}{(g(b) - g(a))} \, (g(b) - g(a))$$

$$= \epsilon$$

whence Theorem 6.3.1 guarantees that f is D–S integrable. $\qquad\square$

Discussion. This proof amply illustrates the contention that many of the proofs of statements for Riemann–Stieltjes integration can be proven by adapting, with little or no change, the proof of the analogous statement for Darboux integrals. To see how the new proofs reflect the old, we urge the reader to inspect the proof of Theorem 5.2.4.

The reader should realize that the function g does not have to be continuous. In reality, g could have an infinite number of discontinuities. The beauty of this proof is that it completely avoids any discussion of the continuity, or lack thereof, of g. It is essential that the reader understand how this is accomplished.   □

Theorem 6.3.3. If f is monotonic, and g is monotonic increasing and continuous in $[a, b]$, the Darboux–Stieltjes integral D–S $\int_a^b f\, dg$ exists.

Proof.   Exercise 3.   □

EXAMPLE 1 _____

Discuss the Darboux–Stieltjes integrability of the function, $f(x) = x$, $x \in [0, 2]$, with respect to the function, $g: [0, 2] \to \mathbf{R}$ defined by

$$g(x) = \begin{cases} 0, & x \in [0, 1] \\ 1, & x \in (1, 2]. \end{cases}$$

Solution.   Given $\epsilon > 0$, choose a partition, P, of $[0, 2]$ such that $\|P\| < \epsilon$. Notice that if $\Delta g_k = g(x_k) - g(x_{k-1}) \neq 0$, then $[1, \delta) \subseteq [x_{k-1}, x_k]$, for some $\delta > 1$. It follows that there is exactly one k such that $\Delta g_k \neq 0$. For this k, we have

$$|\bar{S}(f, g, P) - \underline{S}(f, g, P)| = |\sum_{i=1}^{n} M_i \Delta g_i - \sum_{i=1}^{n} m_i \Delta g_i|$$

$$= M_k \Delta g_k - m_k \Delta g_k$$

$$= (M_k - m_k)(1 - 0) = x_{k+1} - x_k$$

$$\leqslant \|P\| < \epsilon.$$

Since ϵ was arbitrary, the existence of the integral follows, and its value is easily seen to be 1.   □

Discussion. This example illustrates one of the useful properties of Stieltjes integrals, namely their ability to assign different 'weights' to different values of f. In this case, the only point of f which is important for purposes of computing this integral is the value at 1. This is due to the fact that g is constant on any interval which does not include 1, while at 1, g undergoes rapid change.   □

EXAMPLE 2 _____

Discuss the Darboux–Stieltjes integrability of the function $f: [0, 2] \to \mathbf{R}$ defined by

$$f(x) = \begin{cases} 0, & x \in [0, 1] \\ 1, & x \in (1, 2] \end{cases}$$

with respect to the function $g(x) = f(x)$.

Solution. For any partition, Q, there exists a refinement $P = \{0 = x_0 \leqslant x_1 \leqslant \cdots \leqslant x_n = 2\}$ of $[0, 2]$, for which there exists a subinterval $[x_{k-1}, x_k]$ which contains the point 1 as well as a point greater than 1. As in the example above, we have $\Delta g_k = 1$ while $\Delta g_j = 0$ for $j \neq k$, whence,

$$\overline{S}(f, g, P) = \sum_{i=1}^{n} M_i \Delta g_i = M_k \Delta g_k = 1(1 - 0) = 1.$$

On the other hand,

$$\underline{S}(f, g, P) = \sum_{i=1}^{n} m_i \Delta g_i = m_k \Delta g_k = 0(1 - 0) = 0.$$

Consequently, $\overline{\int_0^1} f \, dg = 1$ and $\underline{\int_0^1} f \, dg = 0$. Hence, $\int_0^1 f \, dg$ does not exist. □

Discussion. As pointed out above, g does not have to be continuous. For this reason, Δg_i does not have to shrink to 0 as $\|P\| \to 0$. Now Theorem 6.3.2 uses the fact that $|f(x_i) - f(x_{i-1})|$ must shrink to 0 as the norm of P goes to 0 to avoid the problems with discontinuities in g. Theorem 6.3.3 uses the continuity of g, which forces Δg_i to shrink to 0 as the norm of P goes to 0 to avoid the difficulties with discontinuities in f. In this example, both f and g are discontinuous and the points of discontinuity match in such a way that the situation cannot be retrieved. □

Next, we consider the approach of Riemann, and discuss the Riemann–Stieltjes sums and integrals. The original definition of the Riemann integral is presented in section 5.3. Translation of that definition into the present context leads to:

Definition. Let f and g be defined on $[a, b]$ with g monotone increasing there. Let P be a partition of $[a, b]$ and $Q = \{c_i\}$ an intermediate partition for P. The **Riemann–Stieltjes sum** of f with respect to g over the partition, P, and intermediate partition, Q, is defined by the real number

$$R(f, g, P, Q)) = \sum_{i=1}^{n} f(c_i)(g(x_i) - g(x_{i-1})) = \sum_{i=1}^{n} f(c_i) \Delta g_i,$$

where the P under the summation sign indicates summation extends over all the subintervals generated by P, and the c_i's are the members of Q. We say that the function f is **Riemann–Stieltjes integrable** with respect to the function g in $[a, b]$, provided there exists a real number L with the property that given $\epsilon > 0$, there exists a $\delta > 0$ such that if $\|P\| < \delta$ and Q is any intermediate partition for P, we have

$$|R(f, g, P, Q) - L| < \epsilon.$$

In this case, we say that the **Riemann–Stieltjes integral** of f with respect to g is L and we write

$$\text{R-S} \int_a^b f\,dg = L.$$

Discussion. The reader can check that this definition is obtained from our earlier definition of Riemann integral by replacing Δx_i by Δg_i. Indeed, it is easily seen that this reduces to the Riemann integral if we set $g(x) = x$. As in the case of Riemann integrals, the upper and lower Darboux sums are special cases of Riemann sums for special choices of the points c_i.

A principal feature of the two treatments of the ordinary integral is their equivalence. One might suspect that like the standard Riemann–Darboux and Riemann integrals, the concepts of Darboux–Stieltjes and Riemann–Stieltjes integrals coincide. Unfortunately, this is not the case as the following example shows. □

EXAMPLE 3 _____

Discuss the Darboux–Stieltjes and Riemann–Stieltjes integrability of the function f with respect to the function g in $[0, 2]$, where

$$f(x) = \begin{cases} 0, & x \in [0, 1) \\ 1, & x \in [1, 2] \end{cases}$$

and

$$g(x) = \begin{cases} 0, & x \in [0, 1] \\ 1, & x \in (1, 2]. \end{cases}$$

Solution. Consider separately the intervals $[0, 1]$ and $[1, 2]$. Since g is constant, hence continuous, and f is monotone in $[0, 1]$, it follows that f is Darboux–Stieltjes integrable with respect to g in $[0, 1]$, and D-S $\int_0^1 f\,dg = 0$. On the other hand, f is constant, hence continuous, in $[1, 2]$ and g is monotonic increasing, whence D-S $\int_1^2 f\,dg$ exists and equals 1. To establish 1 as the value for the integral, one merely notices that all contributions to any approximating sum will be 0 except the contribution associated with the unique subinterval which contains $[0, \nu)$ for some $\nu > 1$. The contribution of this unique subinterval is 1. Thus, we conclude that D-S $\int_0^2 f\,dg = 1$. (This computation is explored in detail in Exercise 5.)

We now show that f is not Riemann–Stieltjes integrable with respect to g in $[0, 2]$. For each n, consider the partition P_n of $[0, 2]$ defined by

$$P_n = \left\{ 0, \frac{1}{n}, \frac{2}{n}, \ldots, 1 - \frac{1}{n}, 1 - \frac{1}{2n}, 1 + \frac{1}{2n}, 1 + \frac{1}{n}, \ldots, 2 - \frac{1}{n}, 2 \right\}$$

and choose b_i, c_i, respectively to be the left and right endpoints of the subintervals. Then $R(f, g, P_n, \{b_i\}) = 0$, whereas $R(f, g, P_n, \{c_i\}) = 1$. Since this holds for each n, we conclude that $\lim_{\|P\| \to 0} R(f, g, P, Q)$ does not exist. In other words, f is not Riemann–Stieltjes integrable with respect to g in $[0, 2]$. □

Discussion. In this example, as in Example 2, the functions f and g have a common point of discontinuity, namely $x = 1$. Nevertheless, f is D–S integrable with respect to g. While the reader may easily verify that we have correctly applied the relevant theorems, this verification will not lead to an essential understanding of difference between the two examples. Understanding requires going through the details of the calculation with the upper and lower sums. Specifically, the reader can check, by direct computation with the sums, that $\int_0^1 f\,dg = 0$. On the other hand, the reader should notice that for every subinterval of the form $[x_{i-1}, x_i] \subseteq [1, 2]$, $m_i = M_i = 1$. This ensures that the upper and lower sums generate the same value on the subinterval $[1, 2]$.

The key to the above argument establishing the integrability of f with respect to g is the fact that the computation is split at 1. This amounts to ensuring that $1 \in P$. We are permitted to use only partitions which include 1 because the process of taking the 'limit' in the Darboux case is based on finding the supremum for which there is a known upper bound, or an infimum for which there is a known lower bound. If some select subset of the numbers whose supremum is required will already generate the supremum (infimum), then including the remaining numbers will not change its value. That we have the supremum can be known, because we have a series of upper bounds available in the form of upper sums (lower sums in the case of infimum).

When considering Riemann–Stieltjes integration as defined above, we cannot ensure that any particular point belongs to every partition having a small norm. Indeed, the only points which are guaranteed to belong to every partition are a and b. However, the process of finding a limit requires us to produce a number, L, having the property that every partition having a small norm yields a Riemann–Stieltjes sum which is close to L. In the present example, every partition which fails to include 1 will have distinct intermediate partitions generating sums of 0 and 1, respectively. Quite obviously, this will destroy any possibility of having a limit.

It is easily checked that f is R–S integrable with respect to g on the two subintervals $[0, 1]$ and $[1, 2]$. This leads to the rather odd situation of a function which is not integrable on the interval $[0, 2]$, but which is integrable on $[0, 1]$ and $[1, 2]$. A slight change in the definition of R–S integrable permits us to rectify this situation. $\square$

Definition. We say that the function f is **revised Riemann–Stieltjes integrable** with respect to the function g in $[a, b]$, provided there exists a real number L with the property that given $\epsilon > 0$, there exists a partition P_ϵ of $[a, b]$ such that if P is any refinement of P_ϵ, we have

$$|R(f, g, P, Q) - L| < \epsilon,$$

for every intermediate partition Q of P. In this case, we say that the **revised Riemann–Stieltjes integral** of f with respect to g is L and we write

$$\text{rR–S} \int_a^b f\,dg = L.$$

Theorem 6.3.4. Let f be bounded and g be monotonic increasing in $[a, b]$. Then the revised Riemann–Stieltjes integral of f with respect to g exists if and only if the corresponding Darboux–Stieltjes integral exists, and if they exist, they are equal.

Proof.   Exercise 4.   □

Theorem 6.3.5.   Let f be bounded, and g be monotonically increasing in $[a, b]$. Then rR–S $\int_a^b f\,dg$ exists if and only if the collection $\bar{S}(f, g, P, Q)$ is Cauchy, in the sense that given $\epsilon > 0$, there exists a partition P_ϵ such that if P and R are refinements of P_ϵ, and Q and S are any intermediate partitions for P and R, respectively,

$$|\bar{S}(f, g, P, Q) - \bar{S}(f, g, R, S)| < \epsilon.$$

Proof.   Exercise 6.   □

A new class of functions, called **functions of bounded variation**, forms a more general setting for the discussion of Darboux (Riemann)–Stieltjes integrals. In what follows, we define these functions and we develop some of their elementary properties.

Definition.   Let f be a function defined on $[a, b]$. For each partition, $P = \{a_0, a_1, \ldots, a_n\}$, of $[a, b]$, let $V(f, P)$ denote the real number given by

$$V(f, P) = \sum_{i=1}^n |f(a_i) - f(a_{i-1})|.$$

The number $V(f, P)$ is called the **variation of f on $[a, b]$ for the partition P**.

Discussion.   The reader should recall our early discussions about why functions fail to be continuous. One reason was that the function values were oscillating. This definition is an attempt to quantify the degree to which a function is oscillating. It does so by looking for changes in the values of the function.

Clearly $V(f, P)$ is always bounded below by 0. We can sharpen this bound by noticing that

$$f(b) - f(a) = \sum_{i=1}^n f(a_i) - f(a_{i-1}),$$

whence by taking absolute values and using the Triangle inequality, we see that $|f(b) - f(a)| \leqslant V(f, P)$. If the function is monotone, then equality always holds (Exercise 18). However, for every function, there will be partitions for which $|f(b) - f(a)| = V(f, P)$. In general the collection, $V(f, P)$, may not be bounded above.

If one is thinking of the notion of the variation of a function as being a measure of its oscillatory behavior, it is evident that what is important is not a lower bound on the collection of numbers $V(f, P)$, but an upper bound. Moreover, this measure should be independent of the choice of partition.   □

Definition .   The function f is said to be of **bounded variation** on $[a, b]$ provided the set $\{V(f, P): P \text{ is a partition of } [a, b]\}$ is bounded above. If f is a function of bounded variation, then we set

$$V(f, [a, b]) = \sup \{V(f, P): P \text{ is a partition of } [a, b]\}.$$

We call this supremum, $V(f, [a, b])$ the **variation** of f on $[a, b]$.

Discussion. As indicated, the variation $V(f, P)$ corresponding to the partition, P, is an approximate measure of the 'vertical wiggle' of the graph of f which depends on the particular partition. The variation $V(f, [a, b])$ of f in $[a, b]$ is the total amount of vertical change in the graph of f throughout the interval, where the dependence on any particular partition has been eliminated by taking the supremum. We shall write $V(f)$ instead of $V(f, [a, b])$ when there is no confusion. $\square$

We briefly discuss some important properties of functions of bounded variation in the following set of theorems.

Theorem 6.3.6. If f is a function of bounded variation in $[a, b]$ and $a < c < b$, then f is a function of bounded variation in $[a, c]$ and $[c, b]$, and furthermore,

$$V(f, [a, c]) + V(f, [c, b]) = V(f, [a, b]).$$

Proof. Clearly, both $V(f, [a, c])$ and $V(f, [c, b])$ exist (**WHY?**). Let P be a partition of $[a, b]$ and $P*$ be obtained from P by adjoining the single point c. Let P' and P'' be the resulting partitions of $[a, c]$ and $[c, b]$, so that $P' \cup P'' = P*$. Now,

$$V(f, P) \leqslant V(P*, f) = V(P', f) + V(P'', f)$$

whence

$$V(f, P) \leqslant V(f, [a, c]) + V(f, [c, b]).$$

Taking supremum on the left-hand side, we obtain

$$V(f, [a, b]) \leqslant V(f, [a, c]) + V(f, [c, b]).$$

To prove the reverse inequality, if possible let $V(f, [a, b]) < V(f, [a, c]) + V(f, [c, b])$ and let $\epsilon = V(f, [a, c]) + V(f, [c, b]) - V(f, [a, b]) > 0$. There exist partitions P_1, P_2 of $[a, c]$ and $[c, b]$, respectively, such that $V(f, [a, c]) - \dfrac{\epsilon}{4} < V(P_1, f)$ and $V(f, [c, b]) - \dfrac{\epsilon}{4} < V(P_2, f)$. Therefore, adding the two, we get

$$V(f, [a, c]) + V(f, [c, b]) - \frac{\epsilon}{2} < V(P_1, f) + V(P_2, f) < V(f, [a, b]). \quad \textbf{(WHY?)}$$

Thus, since $V(f, [a, c]) + V(f, [c, b]) - V(f, [a, b]) < \dfrac{\epsilon}{2}$ we have a contradiction, proving the desired equality. $\square$

Theorem 6.3.7. If f and g are functions of bounded variation in $[a, b]$ then $f + g$ is a function of bounded variation in $[a, b]$ and furthermore, $V(f + g) \leqslant V(f) + V(g)$.

Proof. Exercise 19. $\square$

Theorem 6.3.8. If f and g are functions of bounded variation in $[a, b]$, then, fg is a function of bounded variation in $[a, b]$ and further, if M and N are the suprema of $|f|$ and $|g|$ in $[a, b]$, then $V(fg) \leqslant NV(g) + MV(f)$.

Proof. Exercise 20. $\square$

Theorem 6.3.9. If f is a function of bounded variation on $[a, b]$, then f is bounded in $[a, b]$.

Proof. For every the partition, $P = \{a, x, b\}$, the variation satisfies

$$V(f, P) \leq V(f, [a, b]).$$

$\square$

Theorem 6.3.10. If f is a monotonic function in $[a, b]$, then f is a function of bounded variation in $[a, b]$ and $V(f) = |f(b) - f(a)|$.

Proof. Exercise 21.

$\square$

It will be shown the in exercises that there exist continuous functions that are not functions of bounded variation; also there exist monotonic discontinuous functions, which are clearly (by Theorem 6.3.10) functions of bounded variation. Hence, the connection between continuity and bounded variation is not a pleasant one. However, monotonicity is intimately tied with this notion. We have seen that every monotonic function is a function of bounded variation. In the converse direction, while a function of bounded variation need not be monotonic, it always admits a decomposition as the difference of two monotonic increasing functions. This is the aim of our next few results.

Let f be a function of bounded variation in $[a, b]$ and let $x \in [a, b]$. Then we can consider a function F on $[a, b]$ defined by $F(x) = V(f, [a, x])$, $x \in [a, b]$. This function will be called the **variation function** for the function f in $[a, b]$. Clearly $F(a) = 0$ while $F(b) = V(f, [a, b])$. The following theorem relates the continuity of F to that of f.

Theorem 6.3.11. The variation function F, defined above, is continuous at $x \in [a, b]$ if and only if f is continuous at x.

Proof. Let F be continuous at x. Given $\epsilon > 0$ we can find $\delta > 0$ such that for all y in the domain, $|F(y) - F(x)| < \epsilon$ whenever $|y - x| < \delta$. Thus, $V(f, [x, y]) < \epsilon$. If $P = \{x, y\}$ is the trivial partition of $[x, y]$ then $V(f, P) = |f(y) - f(x)| \leq V(f, [x, y])$ and so $|f(y) - f(x)| \leq \epsilon$. Consequently, $\lim_{y \to x^+} f(y) = f(x)$. In a similar manner, we can prove left-continuity. The converse direction is left as an exercise to the reader.

$\square$

The next theorem yields a nice characterization of functions of bounded variation as the difference of two monotonic functions, and the result is proved by considering the auxiliary function F described earlier.

Theorem 6.3.12. If f is a function of bounded variation in $[a, b]$, then, f can be expressed as the difference $F - G$ of two nondecreasing functions.

Proof. Let $F(x) = V(f, [a, x])$, $x \in [a, b]$, and $G = f - F$. If $x < y$, then $F(y) - F(x) = V(f, [x, y]) > 0$ (**WHY?**) proving that F is nondecreasing.

Now, set $G = F - f$. Note that

$$G(y) - G(x) = F(y) - F(x) - [f(y) - f(x)]$$
$$= V(f, [x, y]) - [f(y) - f(x)]$$
$$\geqslant V(f, [x, y]) - [f(y) - f(x)] \geqslant 0$$

since, for $P = \{x, y\}$, we have $V(f, P) \leqslant V(f, [x, y])$.   □

We conclude this section with a final remark on the use of functions of bounded variation in the discussion of Riemann–Stieltjes integrals.

Let f be bounded and g be a function of bounded variation in $[a, b]$. By Theorem 6.3.12, there exist monotonic increasing functions g_1 and g_2 such that $g = g_1 - g_2$. If f is Riemann–Stieltjes integrable with respect to both g_1 and g_2, then we say that f is Riemann–Stieltjes integrable with respect to g in $[a, b]$ and we define

$$\text{R-S}\int_a^b f\,dg = \text{R-S}\int_a^b f\,dg_1 - \text{R-S}\int_a^b f\,dg_2.$$

Thus, we can extend all our earlier theorems where g is a monotonic increasing function to that of a function of bounded variation.

EXERCISES

1. Show that every upper Darboux–Stieltjes sum exceeds every Darboux–Stieltjes lower sum and conclude that $\underline{\int_a^b} f\,dg \leqslant \overline{\int_a^b} f\,dg$.

2. Prove Theorem 6.3.1.

3. Prove Theorem 6.3.3.

4. Prove Theorem 6.3.4.

5. Let f and g be as in Example 3. Let P be any partition of $[0,2]$ which includes 1, that is, $x_i = 1$ for some i. Show that every upper sum and every lower sum generate the same value for such a P.

6. Prove Theorem 6.3.5.

7. If g is monotonic increasing and bounded in $[a, b]$, and $f(x) = k$ in $[a, b]$, where k is any constant, show that $\text{D-S}\int_0^1 f\,dg$ exists and equals $k(g(b) - g(a))$.

8. Let f be bounded, and g be bounded monotonic increasing in $[a, b]$. Prove the following:

    (a) if $\text{D-S}\int_a^b f\,dg$ exists, then there exists α lying between the bounds of f in $[a, b]$ such that $\text{D-S}\int_a^b f\,dg = \alpha[g(b) - g(a)]$;

    (b) if f is continuous, there exists $\alpha \in [a, b]$ such that

    $$\text{D-S}\int_a^b f\,dg\ f(\alpha)[g(b) - g(a)];$$

    (c) if $|f(x)| < K$ throughout $[a, b]$, and if $\text{D-S}\int_a^b f\,dg$ exists, then

    $$\left| \text{D-S}\int_a^b f\,dg \right| \leqslant K[g(b) - g(a)].$$

9. Give an example to show that the value of the R–S integral may be affected, if we alter the value of the function at a single point.

10. Give an example where $|f|$ is R–S integrable with respect to g, but f is not R–S integrable with respect to g.

11. Evaluate the following Darboux–Stieltjes integrals:

   (a) D–S $\int_0^1 x^2 \, d(x^3)$;

   (b) D–S $\int_0^3 x \, d(x - [x])$;

   (c) D–S $\int_{-1}^1 x \, d(e^x)$;

   (d) D–S $\int_0^1 d([x^2])$;

   (e) D–S $\int_0^1 x \, dg$, where $g(x) = \begin{cases} -1, & x = 0 \\ x, & 0 < x < 1 \\ 2, & x = 1. \end{cases}$

12. Let f be bounded, g be increasing and differentiable in $[a, b]$, g' and f be both Riemann integrable in $[a, b]$. Prove that f is Riemann–Stieltjes integrable with respect to g in $[a, b]$ and further

$$\text{R–S} \int_a^b f \, dg = \int_a^b f(x) g'(x) \, dx.$$

[This exercise shows that sometimes a Riemann–Stieltjes integral reduces to an ordinary Riemann integral.]

13. Evaluate the following Riemann–Stieltjes integrals. You may use Exercise 12.

   (a) R–S $\int_\pi^{2\pi} \sin x \, d(\cos x)$;

   (b) R–S $\int_0^3 [x] \, d(e^x)$;

   (c) R–S $\int_{-\pi/2}^0 e^{|x|} \, d(\cos x)$;

   (d) R–S $\int_{-10}^{10} (x^2 + e^x) \, d(\text{sgn} \, x)$;

   (e) R–S $\int_0^1 x \, dg$ where $g(x) = \begin{cases} -1, & x = 0 \\ x, & 0 < x < 1 \\ 2, & x = 1. \end{cases}$

14. Let g_i ($i = 1, 2, 3$) be defined as follows:

$$g_1(x) = \begin{cases} 0, & x \le 0 \\ 1, & x > 0, \end{cases} \quad g_2(x) = \begin{cases} 0, & x < 0 \\ 1, & x \ge 0, \end{cases} \quad g_3(x) = \begin{cases} 0, & x \le 0 \\ \frac{1}{2}, & x = 0 \\ 1, & x > 0. \end{cases}$$

Discuss the D–S and R–S integrability of $\int_{-1}^1 g_i \, dg_j$ ($1 \le i, j \le 3$); also discuss $\int_{-1}^1 f \, dg_i$, where f is bounded in $[-1, 1]$ ($i = 1, 2, 3$).

15. If f is Darboux–Stieltjes integrable with respect to every monotonic increasing function g, must f be continuous? Prove or give a counterexample.

16. Let f be Riemann–Stieltjes integrable with respect to an increasing function g in $[a, b]$ and let

$$F(x) = \text{R-S} \int_a^x f \, dg, \; x \in [a, b].$$

Prove that F is continuous on $[a, b]$.

17. In Exercise 16, let g be a function of bounded variation in $[a, b]$. Prove the following:
   (a) F is a function of bounded variation in $[a, b]$;
   (b) every point of continuity of F is a point of continuity of g;
   (c) if g is increasing, g' exists, and f is continuous in $[a, b]$, then F is differentiable, and $F'(x) = f(x)g'(x)$.

18. Show that if f is monotone on $[a, b]$ that for any partition, P, $V(f, P) = |f(b) - f(a)|$. Further, show that even if f is not monotone on $[a, b]$ that there are partitions for which $V(f, P) = |f(b) - f(a)|$.

19. Prove Theorem 6.3.7.

20. Prove Theorem 6.3.8.

21. Prove Theorem 6.3.10.

22. Let g be an increasing continuous function on $[a, b]$, and f be Darboux–Stieltjes integrable with respect to g in $[a, b]$. Prove that f is Riemann–Stieltjes integrable with respect to g on $[a, b]$ and the two integrals are equal.

23. Show that if f possesses a bounded derivative in $[a, b]$, then f is a function of bounded variation in $[a, b]$.

24. Give an example of a function f that is of bounded variation, but f' is not bounded.

25. What is the relationship between Lipschitz's condition on f and the bounded variation of f?

26. Find the variation of the following functions on the indicated intervals:
   (a) $f(x) = \dfrac{10}{3}, \; x \in [0, 2]$;
   (b) $f(x) = |x|, \; x \in [0, 3]$;
   (c) $f(x) = 3x + 5, \; x \in [0, 1]$;
   (d) $f(x) = x^2, \; x \in [0, 2]$;
   (e) $f(x) = x^3, \; x \in [0, 2]$;
   (f) $f(x) = e^x, \; x \in [0, 1]$;
   (g) $f(x) = \cos x, \; x \in [0, 2\pi]$;
   (h) $f(x) = 2 \sin 3x, \; x \in [0, \pi]$;
   (i) $f(x) = \begin{cases} x^2, & 0 \leqslant x < 1 \\ x^3 + 1, & 1 \leqslant x \leqslant 2, \end{cases} \; x \in [0, 2]$;
   (j) $f(x) = \begin{cases} x, & 0 \leqslant x < 1 \\ 2, & x = 1 \\ 2 + x, & 1 < x \leqslant 2, \end{cases} \; x \in [0, 2]$;
   (k) $f(x) = x - [x], \; x \in [0, 3]$;
   (l) $f(x) = 2x^2 - 3x^3, \; x \in [-3, 4]$;
   (m) $f(x) = \begin{cases} 0, & x \notin \mathbf{Q} \\ \dfrac{1}{q}, & x = \dfrac{p}{q} \in \mathbf{Q} \; (p, q \in \mathbf{N}, \text{ relatively prime}), \end{cases} \; x \in [0, 1]$;
   (n) $f(x) = \begin{cases} x, & x \in \mathbf{Q} \\ 1 - x, & x \notin \mathbf{Q}, \end{cases} \; x \in [0, 1]$.

27. Give a example of a function of bounded variation that fails to be continuous.

28. Consider the function

$$f(x) = \begin{cases} \sin\dfrac{1}{x}, & x \in \left[0, \dfrac{2}{\pi}\right] \\ 0, & x = 0. \end{cases}$$

Using the partition $P = \left\{0, \dfrac{2}{(2n-1)\pi}, \ldots, \dfrac{2}{3\pi}, \dfrac{2}{\pi}\right\}$, show that f is continuous, but is not of bounded variation in $[0, 2/\pi]$.

29. Let

$$f(x) = \begin{cases} x\cos\dfrac{\pi}{2x}, & x \in (0, 1] \\ 0, & x = 0. \end{cases}$$

Show that f is continuous, but not a function of bounded variation in $[0, 1]$.

30. If f is a function of bounded variation in $[a, b]$, show that $|f|$ is also a function of bounded variation in $[a, b]$. What can you say about $V(f)$ as compared to $V(|f|)$?

31. Let f be defined on $[a, b]$ and let there exist a number k such that $|f(u) - f(v)| < k|u - v|$ for each u and v in $[a, b]$. Prove that f is a function of bounded variation in $[a, b]$ and $|V(f)[a, v] - V(f)[a, u]| < k|u - v|$.

32. If f is a function of bounded variation in $[a, b]$ and if there exists $k > 0$ satisfying $|f(x)| > k$ for all $x \in [a, b]$, then, show that $\dfrac{1}{f}$ is a function of bounded variation in $[a, b]$. Is there any relationship between $V(f)$ and $V\left(\dfrac{1}{f}\right)$?

33. Show that a polynomial $p(x)$ is a function of bounded variation in each closed interval $[a, b]$. Describe a method of finding the total variation of $p(x)$ on $[a, b]$, from the knowledge of the zeros of the derivative $p'(x)$.

34. If $V(x)$ denotes the variation function corresponding to a function f of bounded variation in $[a, b]$, set $P(x) = \dfrac{1}{2}(f(x) - f(a) + V(x))$, $N(x) = \dfrac{1}{2}(V(x) - f(x + f(a))$. ($P(x)$ and $N(x)$ are called the **positive variation, negative variation** of f in $[a, b]$.) Compute the positive and negative variations of the functions in Exercise 26.

35. Prove the following form of **integration by parts formula**: Let f and g be of bounded variation over $[a, b]$. Then f is Riemann–Stieltjes integrable with respect to g if and only if g is Riemann–Stieltjes integrable with respect to f on $[a, b]$. In either case,

$$\text{R--S} \int_a^b f\,dg = f(b)g(b) - f(a)g(a) - \int_a^b g\,df.$$

36. Prove the **first Mean Value Theorem** for Riemann–Stieltjes integrals: If f is continuous and g is strictly increasing in $[a, b]$, then there exists $c \in (a, b)$ satisfying

$$\text{R--S} \int_a^b f\,dg = f(c)[g(b) - g(a)].$$

Give an example to show that if g is not strictly increasing, the result need not be true.

37. Prove the **second Mean Value Theorem** for Riemann–Stieltjes integrals: If f is strictly increasing and g is continuous on $[a, b]$ then there exists $c \in (a, b)$ such that

$$\text{R-S}\int_a^b f\,dg = f(a)[g(c) - g(a)] + f(b)[g(b) - g(c)].$$

Can we drop the requirement that f is strictly increasing?

38. Let f be continuous on $[0, n]$, $n \in \mathbf{N}$. Prove that

$$\text{R-S}\int_0^n f\,d([x]) = \sum_{i=1}^n f(i).$$

[This exercise shows that Riemann–Stieltjes integral with respect to the function $f(x) = [x]$ reduces to ordinary summation.]

39. Let h be continuous and increasing on $[a, b]$, let $h(a) = c$, $h(b) = d$. If $\int_c^d f\,dg$ exists, prove that the integral $\int_a^b f(h(t))\,dg(h(t))$ exists, and the two integrals are equal. Give an example where the second integral exists, but not the first.

Chapter 7

Infinite Series of Constants

In Chapter 1, we discussed at length the notion of a sequence and the limit of a given sequence of real numbers. We are already familiar with the summation symbol, $\sum$ (sigma-notation), as applied to a finite number of terms of a sequence $\{a_n\}$ of real numbers (see Exercise 0.4.19). In Chapter 5, finite sums played an essential role in the definition of the integral. However, as the reader can recall, the treatment of the integral carefully avoided the problem of an infinite sum. The purpose of this chapter is to assign meaning to sums of the form

$$\frac{1}{2} + \frac{1}{4} + \frac{1}{8} + \frac{1}{16} + \frac{1}{32} + \cdots$$

where the '$\cdots$' is interpreted to indicate the remaining infinite number of additions which have to be performed. Our definition of this notion will lead to the conclusion that the 'addition' of an 'infinite number of real numbers', though it cannot be achieved physically, is made possible by applying the familiar limiting process to naturally associated sequences.

Infinite sums are not artificial. A simple example of an infinite sum is the infinite decimal expansion of the rational number ⅓. Another example concerns the infinite sum presented above.

Consider a line segment of unit length, $\overline{AB}$, as shown in Figure 7.0.1. Imagine that we mark the midpoint of this segment, and then the midpoint of its right-hand segment, and then the midpoint of the next right-hand segment and so forth. Now let us construct an infinite sum as follows: beginning at A, move to the first marked point to the right, that is, the midpoint of $\overline{AB}$, and take for the first entry to the sum the length of the segment from A to the midpoint; each additional entry to the sum is obtained by

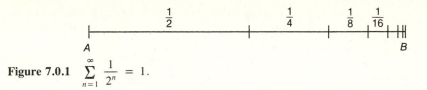

Figure 7.0.1 $\displaystyle\sum_{n=1}^{\infty} \frac{1}{2^n} = 1.$

moving to the midpoint adjacent and to the right of the point we are presently on, and the associated entry to the sum is length of the line segment traversed.

Several features of this process are evident. First, each succeeding term of the sum is exactly half of its predecessor. Second, the process is discrete, in the sense that if one thinks of actually physically performing the process, it would require an infinite number of discrete operations. Third, a fixed real number clearly exists which should be identified as the sum, namely, the length of $\overline{AB}$, which is 1.

The three features mentioned capture the essential difficulty associated with infinite sums with which mathematicians have struggled since the time of Zeno, indeed the example above in a somewhat different form is at the heart of Zeno's paradoxes. The difficulty revolves around assigning a suitable meaning to infinite sums. Clearly, such a meaning should exist, since the length of the line segment exists as a physical reality. Clearly also, the physical process of performing an infinite summation can never be realized. Thus, the problem for mathematicians was to create a suitable framework in which would incorporate an equation of the form:

$$\frac{1}{2} + \frac{1}{4} + \frac{1}{8} + \frac{1}{16} + \frac{1}{32} + \cdots = 1.$$

In summary, then, it is the purpose of this chapter to give a satisfactory meaning to the summation of an infinite number of terms of a sequence of real numbers, and to delineate those circumstances in which we can associate, in a meaningful way, a real number as a 'natural' **sum** of such an infinite series.

7.1 INFINITE SERIES AND ITS CONVERGENCE

Definition. Let p be an integer, $\{a_n : n \geq p\}$ be a sequence of real numbers, and let the sequence $\{s_n,\ n \geq p\}$ of numbers be defined by

$$s_n = \sum_{i=p}^{n} a_i,\ n = p,\ p + 1,\ \cdots.$$

The ordered pair $(\{a_n\}, \{s_n\})$ is formally called an **infinite series.**

Discussion. Let us see how this definition permits us to cope with the problem of assigning a meaning to expressions like

$$a_1 + a_2 + a_3 + a_4 + a_5 + a_6 + \cdots.$$

First, it requires us to have some method for specifying the individual terms of the series. Second, it replaces any notion involving an infinite summation process with that of a finite sum. This is exactly the technique which was employed in the definition of integral, and it is useful because it permits us to employ all our accumulated knowledge about the behavior of finite sums.

The reader will have noticed that we have described $\{a_n : n \geq p\}$ as a sequence. Strictly speaking, this is not true since the definition of sequence specifies functions having domain, the positive integers, and mapping into **R**. In this case, we have permitted our functions to have domains consisting of all integers greater than or equal to p. Nevertheless, it is easy to show (Exercise 1) that the above function is equivalent to a sequence. ☐

Notation. The definition above is necessary but cumbersome. (This is again amplified in the subsection on notation at the end of this section.) We shall abuse it by saying that the collection of symbols

$$\sum_{i=p}^{\infty} a_i, \quad p \text{ an arbitrary integer,}$$

is an infinite series.

For the special case of $p = 1$, we have notations of the form

$$a_1 + a_2 + \cdots + a_n + \cdots$$

or more simply $\sum a_n$ which represent infinite series. Attached to these convenient notations is the sequence $\{s_n\}$ which is referred to as the **sequence of partial sums** corresponding to the infinite series $\sum_{n=1}^{\infty} a_n$; specifically, the term s_n is the **nth partial sum** of the infinite series and a_n is referred to as the **nth term** of the infinite series.

Discussion. The above definition tells us that an infinite series is much more than the mere sequence of symbols

$$a_1 + a_2 + \cdots + a_n + \cdots .$$

Rather, we start with a sequence $\{a_n\}$ of numbers and immediately construct the associated sequence, $\{s_n\}$, its sequence of partial sums. It is this sequence, $\{s_n\}$, that will provide most of the information about the series, $\sum a_n$. Even though an infinite series can be simply written down from the sequence, $\{a_n\}$, by replacing the commas by $+$ signs, we emphasize that without the knowledge of the second sequence, $\{s_n\}$, we cannot further study the series. This is why we call the pair of these two sequences, together, the infinite series. In practice, we do not mention the sequence $\{s_n\}$, but merely say that $\sum a_n$ is an infinite series.

The definition of the series which we have given starts with the notion of sequence, which as we already know, is a function from **N** to **R**. As discussed above, this is easily generalized to the situation of

$$\sum_{n=p}^{\infty} a_n,$$

where the initial value of the index is the arbitrary integer p. Moreover, in the exercises at the end of section 0.4, we treated the problem of changing the index. Thus, we shall not be bound by the total formality of our definition of infinite series, but will feel free to consider the series of the form

$$\sum_{i=0}^{\infty} a_i, \quad \sum_{n=-3}^{\infty} a_{2n}$$

or, any other series which arises. As a further abuse of notation, some authors will use $\sum a_n$ as a generic notation for arbitrary infinite series, and even use it to denote specific series where the initial index value is other than 1. However, we agree that if there is no mention of the limits in the summation, $\sum a_n$ always means that the index n runs from 1 to ∞. $\qquad\square$

Next, we shall see how to realize a number, which can reasonably be called the **sum** of an infinite series. Naturally, this will be arrived at by using the sequence, $\{s_n\}$, which we constructed as an auxiliary sequence.

Definition. The series $\sum_{n=p}^{\infty} a_n$ is said to be **convergent** (or to **possess a sum**) if the associated sequence of partial sums, $\{s_n\}$, possesses a limit. Moreover, if $\lim_{n\to\infty} s_n = s$, then the number s is called the **sum** of the infinite series. We then write

$$\sum_{n=p}^{\infty} a_n = s.$$

The series $\sum_{n=p}^{\infty} a_n$ is said to be **divergent** provided it is not convergent, that is, if the sequence of partial sums fails to have a limit. Thus, we do not associate any 'sum' with a divergent series.

Discussion. It is quite clear that an infinite summation is a physical impossibility. Yet, by using the powerful tool of the limit concept, we are able to give an infinite sum a very concrete meaning. From the manner in which we constructed the sequence of partial sums, $\{s_n\}$, from the given series, $\sum_{n=p}^{\infty} a_n$, we observe that for the case $p = 1$,

$$s_1 = a_1,$$
$$s_2 = a_1 + a_1,$$
$$s_3 = a_1 + a_2 + a_3,$$
$$\cdots\cdots\cdots$$
$$s_n = a_1 + a_2 + \cdots + a_n$$

and so on. The natural 'termination' (if it were possible) would be to write

$$s_\infty = a_1 + a_2 + \cdots + a_n + \cdots .$$

However, to yield to this temptation would avoid any discussion of the conditions which make such an equality meaningful. For this reason, we are forced into exactly the type of considerations which led to the definition of the limit of a sequence. Such considerations, applied to the sequence of equalities given above, make it obvious that if a 'sum' of the series exists, it should be the limit of the sequence of its partial sums; this yields the definition which we have given above.

In addition to the benefits gained by looking at finite sums, for which a large body of knowledge has been developed, by specifying the existence of the infinite sum in terms of the limit of a sequence, we bring to bear on the summation problem the considerable body of theory which has already been developed for sequences. We would therefore encourage the ambitious reader to stop for a minute and consider the question: given my previous knowledge of sequences, how should the theory of series now be developed? What questions should be posed, and further, what are their answers?   □

The remainder of this chapter is devoted to the study of the limit as it occurs in the context of infinite series. One might think that we have already developed a fair amount of information about the topic from our study of sequences and the fact that the definition of this limit boils down to the definition of the limit of a sequence. Certainly, all of what we have learned about the theory of sequences must have application to the theory of infinite series. For example, we know why sequences fail to converge, thus we know why the sequence of partial sums $\{s_n\}$ of a series $\sum_{n=p}^{\infty} a_n$ will fail to converge. Our interest now becomes, what does this tell us about the sequence $\{a_n\}$? It is shown in Theorem 7.1.2 that for the sequence of partial sums to converge, the terms of the series must converge to 0. Of course, this observation is immediately followed by the question: Is the convergence of the sequence, $\{a_n\}$, to 0 enough to ensure the convergence of $\{s_n\}$? As we shall see, the answer is no, and this fact generates many of the interesting subtleties which differentiate the theory of series from the theory of sequences. Let us first begin with several examples.

EXAMPLE 1 _____

Examine the convergence properties of the series

$$1 + \frac{1}{2} + \frac{1}{4} + \cdots + \frac{1}{2^{n-1}} + \cdots = \sum_{n=1}^{\infty} \frac{1}{2^{n-1}}.$$

Solution.   For this series, we have

$$a_n = \frac{1}{2^{n-1}}.$$

Using the formula for the finite geometric series developed in Exercise 0.4.21, we have

$$s_n = \sum_{k=0}^{n-1} \left[\frac{1}{2} \right]^k$$

$$= \frac{1 - \frac{1}{2^n}}{1 - \frac{1}{2}} = 2 \left[1 - \frac{1}{2^n} \right].$$

It is immediate that $\{s_n\}$ converges to 2 (**WHY?**), whence the series converges with 2 as its sum. □

Discussion. The basic technique being employed here is to find an explicit formula for the nth term of the sequence of partial sums. Finding such an explicit formulation may not always be possible, and when it is, it may require the use of a variety of algebraic techniques for its accomplishment. However, if an explicit formula for s_n can be found, it is generally of real value, since it can be used as a tool for finding the sum as in the example above.

The formula developed above can be applied to the series generated from midpoints which was discussed in the Introduction. That series is given by $\sum_{n=2}^{\infty} \left(\dfrac{1}{2}\right)^{n-1}$. This series is almost the series specified above. The difference is in the initial value, $n = 2$ in the midpoint case, $n = 1$ in the case of the example. It is plausible (Exercise 2), that

$$\sum_{n=2}^{\infty} \left(\frac{1}{2}\right)^{n-1} = (-1) + \sum_{n=1}^{\infty} \left(\frac{1}{2}\right)^{n-1} = (-1) + \frac{1}{1 - \dfrac{1}{2}}. \tag{1}$$

This leads to a sum of 1 for the midpoint case, which is the value we know we should get for the reasons discussed in the Introduction. □

EXAMPLE 2 _____

Discuss the convergence or divergence of the series

$$1 - 1 + 1 - 1 + 1 - 1 + - \cdots = \sum_{n=1}^{\infty} (-1)^{n-1}.$$

Solution. It can be shown by induction that $s_{2n} = 0$, while $s_{2n+1} = 1$. Thus, the sequence $\{s_n\}$ of partial sums oscillates between 0 and 1, and so does not have a limit. As a result, the series cannot converge, whence it is divergent. □

Discussion. This series is a canonical example of an 'alternating series'. It is so-called because we alternate between adding a term followed by subtracting a term, or more precisely, adding a positive term followed by a negative term, and so on. If we write down the string

$$1 - 1 + 1 - 1 + \cdots ,$$

we might suspect that it is equal to

$$(1 - 1) + (1 - 1) + \cdots = 0 + 0 + \cdots = 0.$$

This calculation seems to be quite reasonable. However, the following is equally reasonable.

$$1 + (-1 + 1) + (-1 + 1) + \cdots = 1 + 0 + 0 + \cdots = 1.$$

The different values for the sum arise out of attempts to actually sum the entirety of the terms constituting the series and make clear why such attempts have inherent difficulties. Thus, it is evident that permitting imprecise calculations, such as those above, would have many undesirable consequences. In this case, the problems arose as a result of the introduction of parentheses into the summation process. For finite sums, we have seen that a generalized associative law holds, so that the introduction of parentheses cannot change the sum. However, in the calculation above, we are inserting an infinite number of parentheses simultaneously. Aside from the fact that the process would require very quick hands, it leads to nonsensical results; witness the above. (Still another introduction of parentheses can be used to sum the above series to $\frac{1}{2}$, a fact pursued in the exercises.) This example shows that we must view a series as a collection of numbers which are added together sequentially according to a fixed order. To change this order in many instances will change the sum, or produce a sum where none ought to exist. Lastly, the example shows why the notion of limit is essential to a proper definition of 'sum' for an infinite series.   □

EXAMPLE 3 _____

Discuss the convergence properties of the general **geometric series**

$$\sum_{n=1}^{\infty} x^{n-1} = 1 + x + x^2 + x^3 + \cdots$$

where x is a fixed real number.

Solution. If $x \neq 1$, we have the formula

$$s_n = \frac{1 - x^n}{1 - x}.$$

If $|x| < 1$, then the limit exists and we have

$$\sum_{n=1}^{\infty} x^{n-1} = \lim_{n \to \infty} \frac{1 - x^n}{1 - x} = \frac{1}{1 - x}.$$

If $|x| > 1$, then $\{s_n\}$ will diverge to $+\infty$, or will oscillate in an unbounded manner. The case $x = -1$ was treated in Example 2. For $x = 1$, $\{s_n\}$ clearly diverges to $+\infty$.   □

Discussion. This example is the general case for the series considered in Example 1. Infinite geometric series occur frequently in analysis and elsewhere in mathematics and science. The above solution shows that once the common ratio x has its absolute value less than 1, the series converges to the sum $\frac{1}{1-x}$. This is one of the more useful formulae in mathematics.   □

EXAMPLE 4 _____

Discuss the convergence of $\sum_{n=1}^{\infty} n^3$.

Solution. It can be shown by induction (Exercise 3, see also Exercise 0.4.47) that

$$s_n = \frac{n^2(n+1)^2}{4},$$

a fact which easily yields the divergence of the series.   □

Discussion. We have established far more than is required to show that this series is divergent. As we have already remarked, for a series to converge, the a_n's must converge to 0. This is not true in this example.   □

EXAMPLE 5 _____

Discuss the convergence of $\displaystyle\sum_{n=1}^{\infty} \frac{1}{n(n+1)}$.

Solution.   Using the pleasant fact that

$$\frac{1}{n(n+1)} = \frac{1}{n} - \frac{1}{n+1},$$

we have (by induction if necessary) that

$$s_n = \frac{1}{1 \cdot 2} + \frac{1}{2 \cdot 3} + \cdots + \frac{1}{n(n+1)}$$

$$= \left(1 - \frac{1}{2}\right) + \left(\frac{1}{2} - \frac{1}{3}\right) + \left(\frac{1}{3} - \frac{1}{4}\right) + \cdots + \left(\frac{1}{n} - \frac{1}{(n+1)}\right)$$

$$= 1 - \frac{1}{n+1},$$

whence it is immediate that this series sums to 1.   □

Discussion. This example makes really clear how useful it is to establish a formula for s_n. The method applied to split up the quantity $\dfrac{1}{n(n+1)}$ into two fractions is a familiar technique often encountered in integration, namely **the method of partial fractions.** (A description of this technique may be found in any elementary calculus book.) The formula for s_n is found by writing down several partial sums and noticing that cancellation takes place. A series which undergoes this type of cancellation is often referred to as a **telescoping** series.

We have not given a detailed proof of the formula for s_n but a simple inductive argument will suffice which is requested in Exercise 4.   □

From the examples above, the reader may get the impression that it is always possible to find a formula for s_n. Further, the reader may also believe that every convergent series has a 'sum' whose value we can know. Both of these ideas are wrong. It is always possible to *compute* a value for s_n for any n. However, it is not always possible to give a 'nice' formula for s_n of the type found in our previous examples and from which the sum can be found. Moreover, even if we have a series which is known to converge, we may not be able to 'know' what the limit is. To make this clear, consider the series of Example 5. Its sum is 1, and we 'know' very clearly what number has been identified as the sum. The series $\sum_{n=1}^{\infty} \frac{1}{n^2}$ is also known to converge, and the value of its sum is $\frac{\pi^2}{6}$. In this latter case, although the answer is irrational, we also feel that we 'know' the sum since there is a well-recognized constant which can be proven to be the limit of the partial sums. On the other hand, at present there is no identifiable constant which can be shown to be the sum of the series $\sum_{n=1}^{\infty} \frac{1}{n^3}$. Thus, in spite of the fact that we know that the series of inverse cubes has a sum, it cannot be said that we 'know' what that sum is.

The next example illustrates another situation where there is no known 'nice' formula for s_n although this should not deter the reader from trying to find one!

EXAMPLE 6 (Harmonic Series) _____

Discuss the convergence or divergence of the series $\sum_{n=1}^{\infty} \frac{1}{n}$.

Solution. We shall show that the series diverges. For this, we must prove that $\{s_n\}$ fails to have a limit. This is achieved by producing a suitable subsequence of $\{s_n\}$ which diverges. The desired candidate in this example is $\{s_{2^n}\}$. Now,

$$s_{2^n} = 1 + \frac{1}{2} + \cdots + \frac{1}{2^n}$$

$$= 1 + \frac{1}{2} + \left[\frac{1}{3} + \frac{1}{4}\right] + \left[\frac{1}{5} + \cdots + \frac{1}{8}\right]$$

$$+ \cdots + \left[\frac{1}{2^{n-1}+1} + \cdots + \frac{1}{2^n}\right]$$

where the introduction of this grouping is valid (**WHY?**). Further, note that the sum of the terms in each group is never less than $\frac{1}{2}$ (**WHY?**), whence,

$$s_{2^n} \geq \frac{1}{2} + \frac{1}{2} + \frac{1}{2} + \cdots + \frac{1}{2} = \frac{(n+1)}{2}.$$

Thus $\{s_{2^n}\}$ can be made as large as we please by choosing n sufficiently large, so the subsequence $\{s_{2^n}\}$ diverges; hence $\{s_n\}$ has no limit and consequently the harmonic series is divergent. $\square$

Discussion. As indicated above, there is no known formula for s_n which is simpler than the definition, that is, $\sum_{k=1}^{n} \frac{1}{k}$. Thus, we are forced to use a technique which does not depend on our finding an explicit formula for s_n. With no previous knowledge, it would require considerable effort to develop the convergence properties of this series. In the remainder of this chapter we will develop tests which enable the user to easily decide the basic issue of whether or not a given series converges.

The main insight is that if we can show that beyond any given n the remaining terms will sum to more than a fixed constant, then the series cannot converge. In our particular case, we have shown that for every n, $\sum_{k=n}^{\infty} \frac{1}{k} > \frac{1}{2}$. In fact, we have shown more than this, we have proven that $\sum_{k=n}^{m} \frac{1}{k} \geqslant \frac{1}{2}$, where $n = 2^i$ and $m = 2^{i+1}$.

This series has a very important feature. It is the canonical example of a divergent series which satisfies the condition that $\{a_n\} \to 0$. Initially, this is a startling result, yet not so startling when one recalls that not all improper Riemann integrals converge, even though the integrand may go to 0 as $x \to \infty$ (this comparison will later lead us to the integral test).

The fact that this series does not converge illustrates that for series the real issue, which determines the existence or nonexistence of a sum, is not whether $a_n \to 0$, but rather 'how fast' $a_n \to 0$. This idea gives rise to the notion of searching for a test series, that is, one whose terms approach 0 at the slowest possible rate, while still forming a convergent series. Such a series would be immensely valuable, since we could compare other series to it via some sort of comparison test and this comparison would then decide the issue of convergence.

The issues raised by the harmonic series stimulated a good deal of mathematical effort and it is worth looking at the historical method by which this series was shown to be divergent, a method used by Bernoulli.

Using Example 5,

$$1 = \frac{1}{1 \cdot 2} + \frac{1}{2 \cdot 3} + \cdots + \cdots$$

$$\frac{1}{2} = \frac{1}{2 \cdot 3} + \frac{1}{3 \cdot 4} + \cdots$$

$$\frac{1}{3} = \frac{1}{3 \cdot 4} + \cdots$$

and so on. Now adding by columns (can we ??),

$$1 + \frac{1}{2} + \frac{1}{3} + \cdots = \frac{1}{1 \cdot 2} + \frac{2}{2 \cdot 3} + \frac{3}{3 \cdot 4} + \cdots$$

$$= \frac{1}{2} + \frac{1}{3} + \frac{1}{4} + \cdots .$$

If the 'sum' on the right-hand side is A, then we are led to the paradoxical equation $A + 1 = A$, whence A must be infinite. In other words, we cannot associate a finite value to the series as a sum. The series must therefore diverge.

The argument of Bernoulli lends further substance to the difficulties involved in manipulating infinite sums. Just what does it mean to add an infinite number of infinite sums? These questions now have satisfactory answers, but they were not obtained without considerable mental struggle. $\qquad\square$

EXAMPLE 7

Discuss the convergence properties of the series $\sum\limits_{n=1}^{\infty} \dfrac{1}{n^2}$.

Solution. We shall not be concerned with determining the actual sum of this series, but merely deciding the issue of convergence. (It can be shown that the series sums to $\dfrac{\pi^2}{6}$.) Consider

$$A_n = \sum_{m}^{p} \frac{1}{k^2}, \quad \text{where } m = 2^{n-1} \text{ and } p = 2^n - 1, \ n \in \mathbf{N}.$$

We claim that $A_n < \left[\dfrac{1}{2}\right]^{n-1}$. To see this, note that A_n is a sum of 2^{n-1} terms, since by subtraction,

$$p - (m - 1) = [(2^n - 1) - 2^{n-1}] + 1 = 2^n - 2^{n-1} = 2^{n-1}.$$

Moreover, for each k such that $2^{n-1} \leqslant k \leqslant 2^n$,

$$\frac{1}{k^2} \leqslant \left[\frac{1}{2^{(n-1)}}\right]^2,$$

whence our claim about A_n follows. It seems plausible, and will be shown in the next section, that if we replace each A_n by $\dfrac{1}{2^{n-1}}$ and sum the series of replacements, the convergence of the replacement series should guarantee the convergence of $\sum\limits_{n=1}^{\infty} A_n$. The sequence, $\{s_n\}$, of partial sums associated with the original series is easily seen to be monotonically increasing, and as such, its convergence properties are completely determined by any subsequence, in this case, by the subsequence $\{t_n\}$, where $t_n = \sum\limits_{i=1}^{n} A_n$. It follows that $\sum\limits_{n=1}^{\infty} \dfrac{1}{n^2}$ is convergent. $\square$

Discussion. In both the Examples 6 and 7 the arguments were based on examining a subsequence of the sequence of partial sums. For the case of using a subsequence to establish the divergence, there is never any problem, since if one subsequence does not converge to a limit, the sequence *in toto* can not converge to a limit. However, this is not the case when we want to establish convergence. We well know that non-convergent sequences may possess convergent subsequences. Thus, when we start with the sequence $\sum a_n$ and convert to the series $\sum A_n$, we must be very sure that the sequence of partial sums associated with the new series has the same convergence properties as the sequence of partial sums associated with the old series. In Example 7, all difficulties are taken care of by the fact that the sequence $\{s_n\}$ is monotonic increasing. However, this will not generally be true and the reader should take care when formulating this type of argument.

Looking at a subsequence of the sequence of partial sums, $\{s_n\}$, is equivalent to introducing parentheses into the summation process. This can be seen in the definition of A_n which is the sum of 2^{n-1} consecutive terms of the series. Thus, A_1 is (the sum of) the first term of the series, A_2 is the sum of the second and third terms of the series, A_3 is the sum of the next four terms of the series, and so forth. In the latter part of this chapter, we will consider the problem of identifying those conditions under which parentheses can be introduced into the series without fear of altering the convergence properties of the original series. These considerations will lead to some of the more elegant results of the theory. $\square$

We will complete this section by proving several simple, but basic results. The first illustrates how results in the theory about finite summation carries over to the theory about infinite sums.

Theorem 7.1.1. If $\sum_{n=p}^{\infty} a_n$ converges, then the sum is unique. Further, if the sum is a, then $\sum_{n=p}^{\infty} ca_n$ is a convergent series for any real constant, c, and

$$\sum_{n=p}^{\infty} ca_n = ca.$$

In addition, if $\sum_{n=p}^{\infty} b_n = b$ is a convergent series, then $\sum_{n=p}^{\infty} (a_n \pm b_n)$ converges to $a \pm b$.

Proof. For uniqueness of the sum of a convergent series, recall that the limit of a sequence, when it exists, is unique. Thus, the sum, which is the limit of the sequence of partial sums, must be unique.

Let a be the limit of the sequence of partial sums of $\sum_{n=p}^{\infty} a_n$. The partial sum s_k is given by $\sum_{n=p}^{k} a_n$, where $k \geqslant p$. If we let t_k denote the partial sum $\sum_{n=p}^{k} ca_n$ where $k \geqslant p$, of the series whose terms are ca_n, then by the generalized distributive law, $cs_k = t_k$. By a special case of Theorem 1.2.5,

$$\lim_{k \to \infty} t_k = \lim_{k \to \infty} cs_k = ca.$$

Since this statement about the partial sums translates exactly into the required statement about the series, the proof is complete. The proof of the remainder of the theorem is left as Exercise 8. $\square$

Discussion. The proof completely illustrates the use of the previously developed theory of finite sums and sequences. While there are many additional subtleties associated with the theory of series, nevertheless, a substantial body of the theory can be obtained by direct analogy to the theory of sequences and finite series. $\square$

Theorem 7.1.2. If $\sum_{n=p}^{\infty} a_n$ is a convergent series, then $\lim_{n \to \infty} a_n = 0$.

Proof.   Let s_n denote the nth partial sum of the series so that

$$\sum_{n=p}^{\infty} a_n = \lim_{n \to \infty} s_n = s.$$

Note that $a_n = s_n - s_{n-1}$, whence

$$\lim_{n \to \infty} a_n = \lim_{n \to \infty} s_n - \lim_{n \to \infty} s_{n-1} = s - s = 0. \qquad \square$$

Discussion.   If the series is to have a sum, the theorem states that all the terms after some stage must become arbitrarily small. The contrapositive of the theorem states that if $\lim a_n \neq 0$, then the series cannot converge, and thus yields a simple first test for convergence, one which immediately takes care of the series in Examples 2 and 4. Unfortunately, or rather fortunately, as far as mathematicians are concerned, the result does not characterize convergent series, as the harmonic series of Example 6 shows. From this, we see that the main use of the theorem will be in its contrapositive form, that is, for establishing nonconvergence of series. We suggest that the reader write out a complete justification for the equalities which form the last line of the proof. $\square$

So far, we have stressed the similarities between infinite series and sequences, namely the series converges or diverges according as the associated sequence of partial sums converges or diverges. However, there is one important distinction. In studying sequences, it is essentially the behavior of the terms as n gets larger that is significant; thus, for sequences, for any fixed integer $p > 0$, we have the relation $\lim_{n \to \infty} a_n = \lim_{n \to \infty} a_{n+p}$ provided the limit in question exists. In other words, the convergence properties, *including the actual limit,* of a sequence are completely determined by any **tail** of the sequence.

But for a convergent series, every single term, and its position with respect to other terms in the sum, plays a vital role. If we omit a term a_i from the series $\sum_{n=p}^{\infty} a_n$, the sum will certainly diminish by that quantity. However, a moment's thought should convince the reader that the property of whether or not a series is convergent will be unaffected by the deletion of a 'finite' number of terms. Thus, we stress that the series $\sum a_n$ and the sequence $\{a_n\}$ are entirely different types of entities.

Notation.   We have defined series so as to permit an arbitrary initial value for the index. In Exercise 1, the reader will be asked to establish a result which will have the effect of obviating the necessity for this more general approach. That is, the content of Exercise 1 tells us that all the theorems which can be established for series having initial index 1 and which do not depend in some essential way on the initial value, can be translated into a form for series having any other integer as the initial value of the index. Since this is the case, throughout the remainder of this book we will discuss series of the form $\sum a_n$, where it is assumed that the initial index is 1. This not withstanding, we will take all theorems as being proven so that they may be applied in situations of other initial index values. In doing so there is the tacit assumption that the reader could reformulate any proof so as to make it apply in the more general case.

We conclude this section with a theorem which provides a necessary and sufficient condition for the convergence of a given series, and which is very similar to the Cauchy Criterion for the convergence of a sequence (see Theorem 3.3.1).

Theorem 7.1.3 (Cauchy Criterion). The series $\sum a_n$ is convergent if and only if given $\epsilon > 0$, there exists an $N \in \mathbf{N}$ such that

$$(n > N) \text{ and } (p \in \mathbf{N}) \text{ .implies. } |a_{n+1} + a_{n+2} + \cdots + a_{n+p}| < \epsilon.$$

Proof. Assume the series is convergent and let s_n denote the nth partial sum of the series. This sequence is convergent and so must satisfy the Cauchy criterion for sequences. Thus for any $\epsilon > 0$, there exists an $N \in \mathbf{N}$ such that if $n > N$ and $p \in \mathbf{N}$, then $|s_{n+p} - s_n| < \epsilon$. Now,

$$|s_{n+p} - s_n| = |\sum_{k=n}^{n+p} a_k|,$$

whence the desired conclusion follows. To establish the converse, assume the series is Cauchy. The sequence of partial sums is also Cauchy, whence it has a limit. Call this limit a. We leave it to the reader, Exercise 9, to show a is the sum of the series. □

Discussion. The above theorem asserts that if $\sum a_n$ is to have a sum, then 'blocks' of terms of arbitrary length must, after a certain stage, sum to a negligible quantity. For $p = 1$, this theorem is equivalent to the statement of Theorem 7.1.2. Moreover for each positive ϵ there is an $N \in \mathbf{N}$ such that $|\sum_{n>N} a_n| < \epsilon$. Of course, if ϵ is very small, N will have to be correspondingly very large. □

EXERCISES

1. Let $\{a_n : n \geqslant p\}$, p any integer, be a collection of real numbers. Show there is a function $\sigma : \mathbf{N} \to \{n : n \geqslant p\}$ such that:
   (a) $\sigma(1) = p$;
   (b) $\sigma(k+1) = \sigma(k) + 1$ for each $k \in \mathbf{N}$, $k > 1$.

2. Let $\{a_n\}$ be any sequence and let $p \in \mathbf{N}$ be fixed. Show $\sum_{n=1}^{\infty} a_n$ exists, exactly if $\sum_{n=p}^{\infty} a_n$ exists. Further show if either sum exists, then

$$\sum_{n=1}^{\infty} a_n = \sum_{n=1}^{p-1} a_n + \sum_{n=p}^{\infty} a_n.$$

   Use this result to establish the validity of Eq. 1 in the discussion following Example 1.

3. Give an inductive proof showing the formula for s_n given in Example 4 is correct.

4. Give an inductive proof showing the formula for s_n given in Example 5 is correct.

5. Show that the addition of a finite number of terms to a series cannot alter its convergence properties. Do the same for the deletion of a finite number of terms of a series.

6. Show if we add or delete an infinite number of terms from a series, then it will not, in general, have the same convergence properties as the original series. In particular, if we delete terms from a convergent series, will it still stay convergent?

7. If $\sum\limits_{n=1}^{\infty} a_n = s$, show that for $k \in \mathbf{N}$, $\sum\limits_{n=1}^{\infty} a_{n+k}$ converges to $s - \sum\limits_{i=1}^{k} a_i$.

8. Let $\sum a_n = a$ and $\sum b_n = b$. Show that $\sum (a_n \pm b_n) = a \pm b$.

9. Complete the proof of the Cauchy criterion for series.

10. Let a_n and b_n be two sequences such that $a_n = b_{n+1} - b_n$. Show that $\sum a_n$ converges if and only if $\lim\limits_{n\to\infty} b_n$ exists. Moreover, in the event of convergence, what relationship exists between these limits?

11. Let $p: \mathbf{N} \to \mathbf{N}$, be strictly increasing with $p(1) = 1$, and let $\sum a_n$ be an infinite series. Set $m = p(n)$, $m' = p(n+1) - 1$ and

$$b_n = \sum_m^{m'} a_k.$$

Show $\sum b_n$ will converge whenever $\sum a_n$ converges. Show the converse is false. (Note that this process amounts to introducing parentheses into the series $\sum a_n$.)

12. Let $\sum a_n$ and b_n be as in Exercise 11. Show if there is a constant $M > 0$ such that for all $n \in \mathbf{N}$, $p(n+1) - p(n) < M$ and $\lim\limits_{n\to\infty} a_n = 0$, then the convergence of $\sum a_n$ is equivalent to the convergence of $\sum b_n$.

13. Does the series $\sum \dfrac{(-1)^{n+1}}{n}$ converge?

14. Let $a_n = \sqrt{n+1} - \sqrt{n}$. Does the series $\sum a_n$ converge?

15. Discuss the convergence, and where possible find the sum of the following series:

(a) $\dfrac{1}{1\cdot 3} + \dfrac{1}{3\cdot 5} + \dfrac{1}{5\cdot 7} + \cdots$;

(b) $\dfrac{1}{1\cdot 4} + \dfrac{1}{2\cdot 5} + \dfrac{1}{3\cdot 6} + \dfrac{1}{4\cdot 7} + \cdots$;

(c) $\dfrac{1}{1\cdot 3\cdot 5} + \dfrac{1}{2\cdot 4\cdot 6} + \dfrac{1}{3\cdot 5\cdot 7} + \dfrac{1}{4\cdot 6\cdot 8} + \cdots$;

(d) $1 - \dfrac{1}{2\cdot 3} - \dfrac{1}{4\cdot 5} - \cdots$;

(e) $\sum\limits_{n=1}^{\infty} (-1)^{n+1}\dfrac{(2^n + 3^n)}{5\cdot 4^n}$;

(f) $\sum\limits_{n=1}^{\infty} \dfrac{(-1)^{n+1}}{n} \left[\sum\limits_{k=1}^{n} \dfrac{1}{k} \right]$;

(g) $\sum\limits_{n=1}^{\infty} a_n$ where $a_n = \begin{cases} \dfrac{-1}{n}, & \text{if } n \text{ is divisible by 3} \\ \dfrac{1}{n}, & \text{otherwise;} \end{cases}$

(h) $\sum\limits_{n=1}^{\infty} [nxe^{-nx^2} - (n-1)xe^{-(n-1)x^2}]$;

(i) $\sum\limits_{n=1}^{\infty} [a\tan n - a\tan (n-1)]$;

(j) $1 - 1 + 0 + 1 - 1 + 0 + 1 - 1 + 0 + \cdots$;

(k) $1 - 1 + \dfrac{1}{2} - \dfrac{1}{2} + \dfrac{1}{3} - \dfrac{1}{3} + \cdots\,;$

(l) $(1 - 1 + 1) - 1 + (1 - 1 + 1) - 1 + \cdots\,;$

(m) $\displaystyle\sum_{n=1}^{\infty} \sin\dfrac{\pi}{n}\,;$

(n) $\displaystyle\sum_{n=1}^{\infty} \dfrac{(-1)^n(2n + 1)}{(n + 1)(n + 2)}\,;$

(o) $\displaystyle\sum_{n=1}^{\infty} \dfrac{(-1)^{n+1}(n + 3)}{(n + 1)(n + 3)}\,;$

(p) $\displaystyle\sum_{n=1}^{\infty} \dfrac{(n - 2)}{(n^2 - 4)(n + 1)}\,.$

16. Consider the series of Example 2. Show the introduction of a finite number of parentheses will lead to the conclusion that the series must sum to $\dfrac{1}{2}$.

17. Consider $\displaystyle\sum_{n=1}^{\infty} \dfrac{(-1)^n}{n}$. In Exercise 13 you showed this series had a sum. Call this sum a. Find a bound on the quantity $|s_n - a|$, where s_n is the nth partial sum.

18. If $\displaystyle\sum_{n=1}^{\infty} a_n$ converges, show $\displaystyle\lim_{n \to \infty} t_n = 0$, where $t_n = \displaystyle\sum_{n+1}^{\infty} a_n$. ($t_n$ is usually referred to as the nth-**tail** of the series.)

19. If $a_1 = 1$, $a_{n+1} = a_n + \dfrac{b_n}{a_n}$, $(n > 1)$, where $b_n \geqslant 0$ is arbitrary, show $\lim a_n$ exists if $\sum b_n$ converges.

20. A sequence $\{b_n\}$ is said to be of **bounded variation** provided the series $\sum |b_n - b_{n+1}|$ converges. Prove every sequence of bounded variation is convergent, but not conversely.

21. Show every convergent monotone sequence is of bounded variation.

22. Which of the following sequences are of bounded variation?

(a) $\left\{\dfrac{(-1)^n}{n}\right\}\,;$

(b) $\left\{\dfrac{(-1)^n}{\sqrt{n}}\right\}\,;$

(c) $\left\{\dfrac{(-1)^n}{n^2}\right\}\,;$

(d) $\left\{\dfrac{\sin n}{n}\right\}\,.$

23. Show if the series $\sum a_n$ satisfies $\displaystyle\sum_{n=k}^{\infty} a_n > c$, for every $k \in \mathbf{N}$ where c is a fixed positive constant, then the series is divergent.

24. Let p, $\sum a_n$, and $\sum b_n$ be as in Exercise 11. Show if a_n is either nonnegative (or nonpositive) for all n, then the two series either both converge or both diverge.

25. Generalize the argument of Example 7 to show that if $1 < p < 2$, then $\sum \dfrac{1}{n^p}$ is convergent. Explain why the argument will not extend to the case $p = 1$.

26. Let $\{a_n\}$ be a monotonic decreasing sequence of positive terms such that $\sum a_n$ is convergent. Prove $\{na_n\} \to 0$. Is this condition sufficient for the convergence of $\sum a_n$?

27. Prove or disprove:

    (a) if $\sum a_n$ converges, then $\sum a_n^2$ converges;

    (b) if $\sum a_n$ converges, then $\sum \sqrt{a_n}$ converges;

    (c) if $\sum a_n$ converges, and b_n is bounded, then $\sum a_n b_n$ converges;

    (d) if $\sum a_n$ converges, then $|a_n - a_{n+1}|$ converges;

    (e) if $\sum a_n$ and $\sum b_n$ converge, then $\sum a_n b_n$ converges;

    (f) if $\sum a_n$ converges, then $\sum \dfrac{1}{1 + |a_n|}$ converges;

    (g) if $\sum a_n$ converges, then $\sum \dfrac{a_n}{n^2}$ converges;

    (h) if $\sum a_n$ converges, then the sequence $\left\{ \dfrac{a_1 + 2a_2 + \cdots + na_n}{n} \right\}$ converges to 0.

28. Consider the series $\sum a_n$. What is the effect of 'diluting' this series by inserting 0's into the series at random?

29. Let $\{a_n\}$ be a sequence and consider the series $\sum (a_n - a_{n-1})$. Give any conditions on $\{a_n\}$ which will guarantee the existence of a sum for the series.

30. Rewrite the series in Example 5, as $\sum \left(\dfrac{n}{n+1} - \dfrac{n-1}{n} \right)$. Show that if we remove the parentheses in each term, the resulting series is not convergent.

31. Consider an arbitrarily large deck of playing cards. Show these cards may be stacked in such a way that the lead edge of the top card is arbitrarily far, horizontally, from the lead edge of the bottom card, that is, a badly leaning tower is formed!

7.2. SERIES OF NONNEGATIVE TERMS AND TESTS FOR THEIR CONVERGENCE

The series $\sum a_n$ where all the terms a_n are nonnegative is called a **series of nonnegative terms.** Such a series is particularly well behaved, since the corresponding sequence $\{s_n\}$ of partial sums has the property that $s_n \leqslant s_{n+1}$ for all n. In other words, the sequence of partial sums is monotonically increasing, whence the sequence converges provided it is bounded above. If it is unbounded above, it diverges to $+\infty$. Thus, a series of nonnegative terms either converges or else diverges to $+\infty$. A series of nonnegative terms cannot 'wander' or 'oscillate' between two numbers. In this section we develop some simple tests to determine whether a series of nonnegative terms is convergent or divergent, where the knowledge of the actual sum is unimportant.

Theorem 7.2.1 (Comparison Test). Let $\sum a_n$, $\sum b_n$ be two series of nonnegative terms. If there exists a constant, $k > 0$, such that

(i) $a_n \leqslant kb_n$ for all n, and $\sum b_n$ converges, then, $\sum a_n$ converges;

(ii) $a_n \geqslant kb_n$ for all n, and $\sum b_n$ diverges, then $\sum a_n$ diverges.

Proof. Let s_n and t_n denote the nth partial sums of the series $\sum a_n$ and $\sum b_n$, respectively. If (i) holds, then, since $\sum b_n$ converges, and there exists $M > 0$ such that $t_n < M$ for all n. Thus,

$$s_n = \sum_{i=1}^{n} a_i \leqslant \sum_{i=1}^{n} kb_i = kt_n < kM,$$

whence $\{s_n\}$ is also bounded. Being monotonic increasing, $\{s_n\}$ converges, and consequently, $\sum a_n$ converges as well.

If (ii) holds, observe that $s_n \geqslant kt_n$, and the latter is unbounded, since $\{t_n\}$ diverges. Hence $\{s_n\}$ diverges. ☐

Discussion. In loose expression, the above test tells us that a nonnegative series whose terms are less than the corresponding terms of a known convergent series is convergent, while one whose terms always exceed those of a divergent series must diverge. The proof is very simple, but invokes great power, the Completeness Axiom, in the form of Theorem 1.3.1.

To apply these tests successfully, we need to have advance knowledge of some standard convergent and divergent series which are used as test series. We must then be able to relate the corresponding terms with the right type of inequality.

Lastly, it is not necessary to insist that the inequalities in (i) and (ii) hold for all n. It suffices to require that they hold from some stage $n = p$ onward. ☐

There is another form of the comparison test which involves limits and is somewhat more useful in actual practice that the previous test.

Corollary (Limit Form of Comparison Test). Let $\sum a_n$ and $\sum b_n$ be two series of positive terms such that

$$\lim_{n \to \infty} \frac{a_n}{b_n} = L.$$

(i) If $L \neq 0$, then both of the series either converge, or both of them diverge;

(ii) If $L = 0$, and $\sum b_n$ converges, then $\sum a_n$ converges;

(iii) If $L = \infty$, and if $\sum b_n$ diverges, then $\sum a_n$ also diverges.

Proof. To prove (i), given ϵ such that $L > \epsilon > 0$, we can find N satisfying

$$L - \epsilon < \frac{a_n}{b_n} < L + \epsilon$$

whenever $n > N$. Hence,

$$(L - \epsilon) b_n < a_n < (L + \epsilon) b_n.$$

The right-hand side of this inequality will establish convergence, while the left-hand side will establish divergence, simply by applying Theorem 7.2.1. The remainder of the proof is left as Exercise 2. ☐

Discussion. The limit form of the test is very useful. All we have to do is to compute the limit of the expression $\dfrac{a_n}{b_n}$. If the limit is nonzero, and one of the series is convergent (respectively divergent), the other is also convergent (respectively divergent), whence this is the ideal situation. If $\displaystyle\lim_{n \to \infty} \dfrac{a_n}{b_n} = 0$, we can only conclude the convergence of $\sum a_n$ from that of $\sum b_n$. No conclusion can be obtained for divergence. Similarly, case (iii) provides information about divergence only. These tests make it clear why a universal test series, to which all others could be compared, would be very useful. □

The use of these tests is illustrated with two examples.

EXAMPLE 1 _____

Discuss the convergence properties of the series $\sum \dfrac{1}{n^p}$ for $p > 0$, $p \in \mathbf{R}$.

> *Solution.* We claim that the series diverges for $0 < p \leqslant 1$ and converges for $p > 1$. For $p = 1$, the result in Example 7.1.6 gives divergence. Moreover, for $0 < p < 1$ we have $\dfrac{1}{n} \leqslant \dfrac{1}{n^p}$ for all $n \in \mathbf{N}$, whence $\sum \dfrac{1}{n^p}$ diverges by Theorem 7.2.1(ii). The case where $1 < p \leqslant 2$ was treated in Example 7.1.7 and Exercise 7.1.25. Finally, if $p > 2$, then $\dfrac{1}{n^p} < \dfrac{1}{n^2}$ and the series will converge by a direct application of Theorem 7.2.1(i). □

Discussion. The series $\sum \dfrac{1}{n^p}$, $p > 0$, are referred to as *p*-**series**, and provide a wealth of examples for use in the comparison and other tests. However, this is not what makes *p*-series fascinating to mathematicians. The fascination stems from the change from divergence to convergence as we go from $p = 1$ to $p > 1$. Surely, one thinks, there must be information contained in these results about just how fast the terms of the series must go to 0 in order to guarantee convergence. Another way of looking at this question is to ask: How many terms must we discard from the harmonic series $\sum \dfrac{1}{n}$ in order to get a convergent series? We know for example that if we toss out all the terms which do not have perfect square denominators, we are left with a convergent series. Other series generated in this way are the series with 'prime' denominators, and the series obtained by discarding all terms whose denominator contains the digit nine. We note that the former is divergent, while the latter is convergent! □

EXAMPLE 2 _____

Discuss the convergence or divergence of the series $\sum \dfrac{2n + 1}{n^3 + 3n + 4}$.

Solution. We apply the limit form of the comparison test with a_n as above and $b_n = \dfrac{1}{n^2}$. Evidently,

$$\lim_{n \to \infty} \frac{a_n}{b_n} = \lim_{n \to \infty} \frac{(2n + 1)n^2}{n^3 + 3n + 4} = 2 \neq 0,$$

whence the series converges by the corollary and Example 1. $\qquad \square$

Discussion. The strategy adopted here is very simple. We look for a series whose terms go to 0 at approximately the same rate as the series whose convergence we want to test. Recall that for ratios of integer polynomials of the form $\dfrac{P(n)}{Q(n)}$, as we have above in $\dfrac{(2n + 1)}{n^3 + 3n + 4}$, the limit as $n \to \infty$ is determined by the ratio of the term containing the highest power of n in the numerator and the term containing the highest power of n in the denominator. In the present case, this ratio is $\dfrac{2}{n^2}$, which converges to 0. However, if we introduce a factor of n^2 into the numerator, then a nonzero limit of 2 results. This is why we chose $\sum \dfrac{1}{n^2}$ as our test series. $\qquad \square$

The comparison test and the series generated so far enable us to deal with a fairly large collection of infinite series, including all series whose terms are ratios of integer polynomials of the form $\sum \dfrac{P(n)}{Q(n)}$. However, the scope is really quite limited and we are forced to look for tests of a substantially different character to handle other types of series. One such test is the condensation test due to Cauchy.

Theorem 7.2.2 (Cauchy's Condensation Test). Let $\sum a_n$ be a series of nonnegative terms such that for some $N \in \mathbf{N}$, $n > N$ implies $a_n \geqslant a_{n+1}$. The series $\sum a_n$ converges (diverges) if and only if the series $\sum 2^n a_{2^n}$ converges (diverges).

Proof. Let s_n, t_n, respectively, denote the nth partial sums of $\sum a_n$ and $\sum 2^n a_{2^n}$, respectively. Also, without loss of generality assume that $\{a_n\}$ is monotonically decreasing for $n \geqslant 1$. Given n there is a k satisfying $n < 2^k$, and hence

$s_n = a_1 + a_2 + \cdots + a_n$

$\qquad \leqslant a_1 + (a_2 + a_3) + (a_4 + \cdots + a_7) + \cdots + (a_{2^k} + \cdots + a_{2^{k+1}-1})$

$\qquad \leqslant a_1 + 2a_2 + 4a_4 + \cdots + 2^k a_{2^k} = t_k.$

Thus, if the second series converges, then $\{t_k\}$ is bounded. Consequently $\{s_n\}$ is bounded and $\sum a_n$ converges, since it is monotone increasing. Thus, the convergence of $\sum 2^n a_{2^n}$ implies the convergence of $\sum a_n$.

To see that the convergence of $\sum a_n$ implies the convergence of the condensed series, we treat the contrapositive. Thus, we assume that $\sum 2^n a_{2^n}$ diverges. Note that given any large n, there is a k such that n exceeds 2^k, and so

$$s_n \geqslant a_1 + a_2 + (a_3 + a_4) + (a_5 + \cdots + a_8) + \cdots + (a_{2^{k-1}+1} + \cdots + a_{2^k})$$

$$\geqslant \frac{a_1}{2} + a_2 + 2a_4 + 4a_8 + \cdots + 2^{k-1}a_{2^k} = \frac{t_k}{2}.$$

Hence, if the condensed series diverges, $\{t_n\}$ is unbounded whence $\{s_n\}$ is also unbounded and this forces the divergence of $\sum a_n$. ☐

Discussion. The theorem captures and generalizes the techniques employed in Examples 7.1.6 and 7.1.7 and the reader should review these examples to see that this is so. The hypothesis is that the terms of the series eventually become monotone decreasing, and nonnegative. Without either of these conditions, this approach would be impossible. The usefulness of this theorem lies in the fact that when we apply it to certain series, they are converted to forms whose convergence properties are easily checked. Finally, the convergence properties of $\sum a_n$ are derived from those of a 'condensed' series $\sum 2^n a_{2^n}$, hence the name 'condensation test'. ☐

EXAMPLE 3 _____

Discuss the convergence properties of $\sum \dfrac{1}{n^p}$, $p > 0$.

Solution. For $0 < p \leqslant 1$, we apply the condensation test to obtain the condensed series, $\sum 2^n \dfrac{1}{(2^n)^p}$. Manipulation yields

$$\sum 2^n \frac{1}{(2^n)^p} = \sum \frac{1}{2^{-n}} \frac{1}{2^{np}} = \sum \left(\frac{1}{2^{p-1}}\right)^n$$

which is a geometric series, and as such, converges exactly if $p - 1 > 0$, that is, $p > 1$. ☐

Discussion. This example contains no new information about the series. But it witnesses the ease with which the condensation test can be employed. ☐

EXAMPLE 4 _____

Discuss the convergence of $\sum \dfrac{1}{n (\ln n)^p}$, $p > 0$.

Solution. Again we apply the condensation test to obtain

$$\sum 2^n \frac{1}{2^n(\ln 2^n)^p} = \frac{1}{(\ln 2)^p} \sum \frac{1}{n^p}.$$

It is clear from Example 1 that the condensed series converges when $p > 1$ and diverges otherwise, whence the same is true of the original series. ☐

Discussion. The reader should note that there is nothing sacred about using groupings of length 2^n in generating this result. The principle is to use the largest term in a group multiplied by the number of terms in the group to estimate the contribution of the whole group to the final sum. This is a simple idea and yet it has wide applications. □

Another extremely useful test is the Maclaurin integral test, where we manufacture an improper integral from the terms of the series and then use the convergence or divergence of the integral to decide the issue of convergence for the series.

Theorem 7.2.3 (Integral Test). Let $f: \mathbf{R} \to \mathbf{R}$ be a nonnegative function which is monotonically decreasing. If $a_n = f(n)$ for $n \in \mathbf{N}$, then $\sum a_n$ converges if and only if the improper Riemann integral $\int_1^\infty f$ converges.

Proof. Let f be as required. It is immediate that for any $k \in \mathbf{N}$,

$$a_k \geqslant \overline{\int_k^{k+1}} f \geqslant \int_k^{k+1} f \geqslant \underline{\int_k^{k+1}} f \geqslant a_{k+1}. \qquad \textbf{(WHY?)}$$

It follows that

$$\sum_{k=1}^n a_k \geqslant \overline{\int_1^n} f \geqslant \int_1^n f \geqslant \underline{\int_1^n} f \geqslant \sum_{k=2}^{n+1} a_k.$$

From the left-hand inequalities, it follows that if the improper integral diverges, then the series must also diverge. On the other hand, the right-hand set of inequalities establish that if the integral converges, then the series must also converge. □

Discussion. The intuition underlying this theorem and its proof is completely captured in Figure 7.2.1. Although we have not made their invocation explicit, each of the conditions on the function f in the statement of the theorem is crucial for the proof and the reader should verify that there is no way to significantly weaken the hypothesis. The reader should convince himself that the stated inequalities are indeed true.

It should be pointed out that in the case where the series and the integral converge, it need not be the case that the sum of the series coincides with the value of the improper integral. The reader can easily construct suitable examples.

The relationship between series and improper integrals leads to many interesting results. One of these is explored in Exercise 24. □

EXAMPLE 5 _____

Discuss the convergence properties of $\sum n e^{-n}$.

Solution. Set $f(x) = xe^{-x}$, $x \in [0, \infty)$. Using properties of e^x established in calculus courses and proved in Chapter 10, f is decreasing and nonnegative and satisfies $f(n) = a_n$. Now, using the integration by parts formula, we see that

$$\int_1^n f = \frac{2}{e} - \frac{n+1}{e^n}.$$

This integral converges to $\dfrac{2}{e}$, whence the series must also converge. □

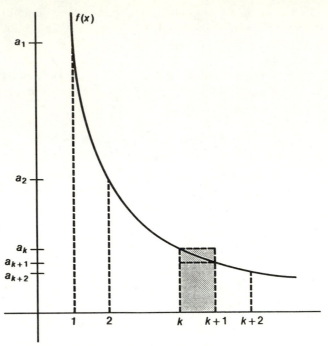

Figure 7.2.1   Graphical illustration of integral test.

Discussion.   The integral test employs the close relationship between integration and series of nonnegative terms. It is a simple test to apply. In a particular situation, we require only that the sequence of terms of the series be eventually monotonically decreasing and nonnegative. This is really all we need, although as the theorem is stated above, more is required.

As a general procedure for applying the theorem, we take the specification for a_n and use it to generate the specification for f. Thus, given ne^{-n}, we generated xe^{-x}. It must be checked that the function generated is also eventually monotone and non-negative, since it is quite possible that the function generated from a_n in the natural way will not in general be either nonnegative or decreasing. Lastly, the basic value of the test lies in the fact that the function, f, generated from a_n has an easily calculated indefinite integral. Unless this is the case, this test will have no practical value for the series under consideration. Again, we point out that the sum of the series need not be $\dfrac{2}{e}$.   □

EXERCISES

1. Give complete details of the proof of Theorem 7.2.1(ii).

2. Supply proofs for parts (ii) and (iii) of the limit form of the comparison test (corollary to Theorem 7.2.1).

3. Consider the series $\sum \dfrac{p(n)}{q(n)}$ where $p(n)$ and $q(n)$ are integer polynomials such that $q(n) \neq 0$ for all $n \in \mathbf{N}$. Find a necessary and sufficient condition for this series to converge.

4. State and prove a version of the condensation test which groups the terms of the series so that the nth group contains n terms.

5. Give an example of a series $\sum a_n$ whose terms are monotonically decreasing to 0 but for which the function f defined in the natural way, for example, $a_n = \dfrac{1}{n^2}$ and $f(x) = \dfrac{1}{x^2}$, does not share this property as $x \to \infty$.

6. Justify the string of inequalities which form the heart of the proof of the integral test.

7. Test the following series for convergence or divergence. You may assume that the trigonometric, exponential, and logarithmic functions have their usual properties.

   (a) $\sum \dfrac{\sqrt{n+1} - \sqrt{n}}{\sqrt{n}\,\sqrt{n+1}}$;

   (b) $\sum n^2 e^{-n}$;

   (c) $\sum n^q e^{-n}$, $q \in \mathbf{N}$;

   (d) $\sum n^n e^{-n}$;

   (e) $\sum \dfrac{1}{n!}$;

   (f) $\sum n^{-n}$;

   (g) $\sum a^n n^a$, where $a > 0$;

   (h) $\sum (n^{1/n} - 1)$;

   (i) $\sum (\sqrt{1 + n^2} - n)$;

   (j) $\sum \dfrac{1 + \sin n}{1 + n^2}$;

   (k) $\sum \ln \dfrac{n}{n^3 + 5}$;

   (l) $\sum \dfrac{\ln n^3}{n^3 + 2}$;

   (m) $\sum n^a(\sqrt{n+1} - 2\sqrt{n} + \sqrt{n-1})$, $a \in \mathbf{R}$;

   (n) $\sum \ln \dfrac{n^3}{n^3 + 2}$;

   (o) $\sum \dfrac{1}{n^{a + b/n}}$, $a, b \in \mathbf{R}$;

   (p) $\displaystyle\sum_{n=2} \dfrac{1}{n \ln n \ln \ln n}$;

   (q) $\displaystyle\sum_{n=2} \dfrac{1}{2^n \ln n \ln \ln n \ln \ln \ln n}$;

   (r) $\displaystyle\sum_{n=2} \dfrac{1}{n \ln n (\ln \ln n)^p}$;

   (s) $\displaystyle\sum_{n=2} \dfrac{1}{n \ln n \ln \ln n \ln \ln \ln n (\ln \ln \ln n)^p}$, $p > 1$;

   (t) $\displaystyle\sum_{n=0}^{\infty} \left[\dfrac{1}{3 + (-1)^n} \right]^n$.

8. Generalize the results in (r) and (s) of Exercise 7 to the case where the denominator is

$$n \ln n \ln \ln \ln n \ \cdots \ (\ln \ln \ln \ \cdots \ \ln n)^p$$

where $p \geqslant 1$ and the bracket consists of a string of k ln's.

9. Let $\sum a_n$ be a series with nonnegative terms and t_n its sequence of partial sums. Show $\sum a_n$ converges if and only if $\{t_n\}$ is bounded. Moreover if $\{t_n\}$ is bounded, then the supremum of $\{t_n\}$ is the sum of the series.

10. Let $a_n \geqslant 0$ for each n.

    (a) Let $\sum a_n$ converge, and let $b_n = \sum\limits_{i=n}^{\infty} a_i$. Prove that $\sum(\sqrt{b_n} - \sqrt{b_{n+1}})$ is convergent;

    (b) If $\sum a_n$ diverges, and $s_n = \sum\limits_{i=1}^{n} a_n$, prove that $\sum(\sqrt{s_{n+1}} - \sqrt{s_n})$ is divergent.

11. Let $\sum a_n$ be a series of nonnegative terms. Show if for some $k > 1$, the sequence $\{n^k a_n\}$ converges, then so does the series $\sum a_n$.

12. Is there a result similar to (11) which will establish divergence?

13. Let $\sum a_n$ be a convergent series of nonnegative terms. A nonnegative series $\sum b_n$ is said to **compare favorably** with $\sum a_n$ if there exists $M \in \mathbf{N}$ such that $n > M$ implies that $a_n \geqslant b_n$. Show there does not exist a series $\sum a_n$ such that every convergent series of nonnegative terms compares favorably with $\sum a_n$.

14. Show no finite list of nonnegative series will be such that every convergent series of nonnegative terms must compare favorably with at least one series in the list.

15. Show even if we take a countably infinite list of convergent series, it will still not be adequate to test every convergent series of nonnegative terms.

16. If $\sum a_n$, $\sum b_n$ $(b_n \neq 0)$ are both convergent, and if $\lim\limits_{n \to \infty} \dfrac{a_n}{b_n} = 0$, we say that $\sum b_n$ **converges more slowly** than $\sum a_n$. Prove given any convergent series $\sum a_n$, there always exists a series $\sum b_n$ which converges more slowly than $\sum a_n$.

17. If $\sum b_n$, $\sum a_n$ $(a_n \neq 0)$ are both divergent, and if $\lim\limits_{n \to \infty} \dfrac{b_n}{a_n} = 0$, we say that $\sum b_n$ **diverges more slowly** than $\sum a_n$. Prove no series exists that diverges more slowly than all others.

18. If $d_n > 0$ and $\sum d_n$ diverges, discuss the behavior of the following:

    (a) $\sum \dfrac{d_n}{1 + d_n}$;

    (b) $\sum \dfrac{d_n}{1 + n d_n}$;

    (c) $\sum \dfrac{d_n}{1 + n^2 d_n}$;

    (d) $\sum \dfrac{d_n}{1 + d_n^2}$.

19. Let $\sum a_n$ and $\sum b_n$ be two series of positive terms. Develop a comparison test based on the ratios, $\dfrac{a_{n+1}}{a_n}$ and $\dfrac{b_{n+1}}{b_n}$.

20. Using whatever results about $\ln x$ are required (see Chapter 10 for proofs) use the integral test to show the harmonic series, $\sum \dfrac{1}{n}$ is divergent. Further, set $h_n = \sum\limits_{i=1}^{n} \dfrac{1}{i}$. Show the sequence, $\{h_n - \ln n\}$, converges to a number in $(0,1)$. The value of the limit is approximately $.57722156649$, (correct to 10 decimal places) but it is not known whether the limit is rational. The limit of this sequence is generally denoted by the symbol, γ, and known as **Euler's constant**.

21. Let $a \geqslant b \geqslant 0$. If $[x]$ has its usual meaning, show the sequence, $\{h_{[na]} - h_{[nb]}\}$, converges and find an expression for its limit.

22. Prove the following generalization of the condensation test: Let $\{g_n\}$ be a sequence of positive integers such that for $k = 0, 1, \ldots$:
    (a) $g_k > g_{k-1} \geqslant 0$ and
    (b) $g_{k+1} - g_k \leqslant M(g_k - g_{k-1})$,
    where M is a positive constant. If $\sum a_n$ is a series of positive terms with the sequence a_n monotonically decreasing, then $\sum\limits_{n=0}^{\infty} a_n$ and $\sum\limits_{n=0}^{\infty} (g_{n+1} - g_n)a_{g_n}$ both converge or both diverge.

23. Let $\sum a_n$ be a convergent series of nonnegative terms, and consider the sequence $\{n^p a_n\}$. For what values of p can it always be said that the sequence converges to 0?

24. Consider the collection of functions, f, which are defined and nonnegative on $[0,\infty)$. Show that in general there is no relationship between the convergence of $\int_1^{\infty} f$ and $\sum\limits_{n=1}^{\infty} f(n)$, that is, give examples in which both converge, both diverge, and either one diverges while the other converges.

7.3 ABSOLUTE CONVERGENCE

In the last section, we developed tests for convergence which could be applied to series with nonnegative terms; moreover, this restriction was an essential hypothesis for the tests. In general, a series will have an infinite number of negative and an infinite number of positive terms. So it is important that we develop methods for dealing with such series.

Definition. A series, $\sum a_n$, is called **absolutely convergent** provided $\sum |a_n|$ is a convergent series. A series is called **conditionally convergent** if $\sum a_n$ is convergent, but $\sum |a_n|$ is divergent.

Discussion. The importance of this definition is that it focuses our attention on the possibility that there may be series which are convergent but which are not absolutely convergent. It is immediate that a convergent but not absolutely convergent series must have terms which are both positive and negative, since otherwise (for series whose terms are all of the one sign) the two types of convergence are equivalent. An example of a conditionally convergent series is $\sum \dfrac{(-1)^n}{n}$, while the series $\sum \dfrac{(-1)^n}{n^2}$ is an absolutely convergent series.

For a series to be absolutely convergent, the terms must get small at a rapid rate. This requirement that the terms become rapidly small is effectively illustrated by the collection of series discussed in Example 7.2.1.

On the other hand, a series which is conditionally convergent can have its terms approach 0 as slowly as we please. Thus, the reason why a conditionally convergent series converges must be due to the interaction of the positive terms with the negative terms. This will provide one focus for our investigations in this section. □

Theorem 7.3.1. If $\sum a_n$ is absolutely convergent, then it is convergent.

Proof.   Let s_n and t_n denote the nth partial sums of $\sum a_n$ and $\sum |a_n|$, respectively. Then,

$$
\begin{aligned}
|s_{n+p} - s_n| &= |a_n + a_{n+1} + \cdots + a_{n+p}| \\
&\leqslant |a_n| + |a_{n+1}| + \cdots + |a_{n+p}| \\
&= |t_{n+p} - t_n|.
\end{aligned}
$$

We now apply the Cauchy criterion and the hypothesis to complete the proof. □

Discussion.   The proof illustrates the utility of two basic principles. The first is the generalized Triangle inequality which is at the heart of the inequality string. The second is the Cauchy criterion for convergence (where the Completeness Axiom is hidden).

This theorem provides us with the means to apply all the theory which we developed for series with nonnegative terms to series with terms of both signs. There is, however, one restriction. If the series is 'absolutely' divergent, we can not in general conclude that the original series is also divergent. The canonical example in this regard is the series $\sum \dfrac{(-1)^{n+1}}{n}$ which was shown to be 'absolutely' divergent in Example 7.1.6 and convergent in Exercise 7.1.13. (The reader who has not done this exercise may wish to do so, or examine Theorem 7.4.1, which will effectively do the exercise for him.) Thus, the application of our previous results will generally be in the form of testing for absolute convergence, and concluding convergence of the original series when absolute convergence can be verified.

As noted before, a series will converge absolutely provided the rate at which its terms approach 0 is sufficiently rapid. The force of the tests which we have developed to date is to test whether the terms of a series approach 0 with the necessary rapidity, by comparing the terms of the unknown series against those of the known series. Thus, it is obvious that if the terms go to 0 fast enough, changing the sign of some of them can not affect the convergence properties, but if the terms go to 0 slowly then changing the sign of some terms most definitely will affect the convergence. □

Definition.   Let $\sum a_n$ be a series of arbitrary terms and set

$$
p_n = \frac{|a_n| + a_n}{2} \quad \text{and} \quad q_n = \frac{|a_n| - a_n}{2}.
$$

Then the series $\sum p_n$ is called the **positive part** of $\sum a_n$, and $\sum q_n$ is called the **negative part** of $\sum a_n$.

Discussion. The reader can verify that if $a_n \geqslant 0$, then $p_n = a_n$ and $q_n = 0$. On the other hand, if $a_n < 0$ then $p_n = 0$ and $q_n = |a_n|$. Thus, in essence, the series $\sum p_n$ collects together all the positive terms of the original series into a single sum. Similarly, the series $\sum q_n$ collects together all the negative terms, but with their signs changed so that the result is a series of positive terms. The motivation for doing this is that we think these two series may be of particular interest for conditionally convergent series. It is also important to notice that in the series, $\sum p_n$, the index values associated with terms in $\sum a_n$ which were negative now are associated with terms which are 0. A similar comment holds regarding $\sum q_n$. For this reason, the original series can be reconstructed from

$$a_n = p_n - q_n$$

(see Exercise 2). Lastly, since both the positive and negative parts of $\sum a_n$ are series with nonnegative terms, the theory developed in section 7.2 applies. $\qquad\square$

Theorem 7.3.2. If $\sum a_n$ is conditionally convergent, then both $\sum p_n$ and $\sum q_n$ are divergent; if $\sum a_n$ is absolutely convergent, then both $\sum p_n$ and $\sum q_n$ converge, and furthermore,

$$\sum a_n = \sum p_n - \sum q_n.$$

Proof. In the former case, $\sum a_n$ converges while $\sum |a_n|$ is divergent. We have

$$a_n = p_n - q_n \quad \text{and} \quad |a_n| = p_n + q_n.$$

Now, if $\sum q_n$ is convergent, since $p_n = a_n + q_n$, it follows that $\sum p_n$ is also convergent. But then, since $|a_n| = p_n + q_n$, it follows that $\sum |a_n|$ must converge as well (**WHY?**), which is a contradiction. So both the series must diverge. The second part is left to the reader as Exercise 3. $\qquad\square$

Discussion. In exercises of Section 7.1, we explored the effect of adding or deleting terms from a series. The basic fact employed here is that addition of an infinite number of terms to a series will not affect the convergence properties of the series, provided the infinite collection of terms added form an absolutely convergent series. $\qquad\square$

Next we explore the value of the concept of absolute convergence. In the next set of results we shall see that it is a remarkable property to demand from a series. The first result shows that the absolute convergence of a series permits us to rearrange the terms in any manner while not destroying the convergence properties or changing the sum. Before we state the result, we must make precise what we mean by the rearrangement of a given infinite series. Recall that the rearrangement of a finite series is nothing but a permutation, which is a one-to-one, onto function from the set to itself. We shall extend this notion to infinite sets as well.

Definition.   Let $f: \mathbf{N} \to \mathbf{N}$ be a one-to-one and onto function. Then $\sum\limits_{n=1}^{\infty} a_{f(n)}$ is called a **rearrangement** of the series $\sum a_n$.

Discussion.   If we think of what we ought to mean by 'rearrangement' of a series, then the motivation for this definition becomes very clear. Intuitively, a rearrangement of the terms of the series should take all the terms and mix them up and then add them in this different order. Thus, if we denote the rearranged series by $\sum b_n$, then each b_n should be identifiable as a particular a_n from the original series. Further, each a_n should be found exactly once among the b_n's. These two properties create a one-to-one and onto function from $\mathbf{N}$ to $\mathbf{N}$ for us in the following way: given n as a subscript for the a_n we know that $a_n = b_m$ for some term in the rearranged series, thus we get $f(n) = m$. Conversely, given a term b_n in the rearranged series, it is there only because it was an a_m for some m in the original series. Thus we see that the function f ought to be one-to-one and onto as required by the definition and that such functions are the tool required for creating a rearranged series.   □

Theorem 7.3.3.   Let $\sum a_n$ be an absolutely convergent series with sum, s. Then every rearrangement $\sum b_n$ of $\sum a_n$ converges (absolutely) to the sum, s.

   Proof.   Our first step is to reduce the problem to series with nonnegative terms. Let $\sum p_n$ and $\sum q_n$ be the positive and negative parts of $\sum a_n$, while $\sum p^*_n$ and $\sum q^*_n$ be the positive and negative parts of $\sum b_n$. Now,

$$a_n = p_n + q_n \qquad \text{and} \qquad b_n = p^*_n + q^*_n.$$

Thus, if $\sum p_n = \sum p^*_n$ and $\sum q_n = \sum q^*_n$, then $\sum a_n = \sum b_n$. Hence, it is enough to show that the positive and negative parts of the rearranged series preserve their original sum. To complete the reduction, we assert that the positive part of $\sum b_n$ is a rearrangement of the positive part of $\sum a_n$, and similarly for negative parts. (We leave the establishment of this claim to Exercise 4.)

   Since the positive and negative parts of a series are series with nonnegative terms, we have left to show that if $\sum b_n$ is a rearrangement of $\sum a_n$, a series with nonnegative terms, then the convergence of $\sum a_n$ to s implies the convergence of $\sum b_n$ to s. Since we are dealing with series of nonnegative terms, s is the least upper bound of the sequence of partial sums of $\sum a_n$. Let $\{t_n\}$ denote the sequence of partial sums of $\sum b_n$. We first claim that s is an upper bound for the t_n's. To see this, let f be the function which defines the rearrangement. Then given t_n, there is an $N \in \mathbf{N}$ such that if $m \leqslant n$, then $f^{-1}(m) \leqslant N$. Evidently, $t_n \leqslant s_N \leqslant s$, whence s is an upper bound for the collection of t_n's. Next, let $\epsilon > 0$ be fixed. Since s is the supremum of the set of s_n's, there exists an s_N such that $n \leqslant M$ implies $f(n) < M$. It follows that

$$s - \epsilon < s_N \leqslant t_M \leqslant s.$$

Thus s is the supremum of the collection of partial sums of the rearranged series, and so is the sum, since the rearranged series is also a series of nonnegative terms.   □

Discussion.   The argument given above is in two parts. The first part uses Theorem 7.3.2 to show that we need only prove the result for series which have nonnegative terms. The second half consists of proving the result for the reduced case. The reduction leads to considerable simplification, in fact the result is almost trivial for this special case, due to the fact that the sequence of partial sums is monotone and consequently, so tractable. Without this reduction, we would have to trap the partial sums inside the interval centered at s, a task of much greater delicacy. We will ask the reader to carry out this type of proof in the exercises. $\square$

The rearrangement property is one of the most elegant results on absolutely convergent series. For this reason, an absolutely convergent series is sometimes referred to as an **unconditionally convergent** series, in the sense that whatever rearrangement we adopt, we still preserve the absolute convergence as well as the original sum. This is in contrast to nonabsolutely convergent series which we have earlier agreed to call conditionally convergent series. The hypothesis of absolute convergence is vital to the conclusion, as the absence of it may very well affect the convergence and the sum of the rearrangement. Our next theorem of this section, usually known as Riemann's Theorem on the rearrangement of a conditionally convergent series, says that given any nonabsolutely convergent series, it can be suitably rearranged so as to yield any desired sum we want, or even divergence if we desire.

Theorem 7.3.4 (Riemann's Theorem).   Let $\sum a_n$ be a conditionally convergent series and let x and y be two given real numbers (including $\pm \infty$) with $x \leqslant y$. Then there exists a rearrangement $\sum b_n$ of $\sum a_n$ such that if t_n denotes the nth partial sum of $\sum b_n$, then

$$\underline{\lim}\, t_n = x \quad \text{and} \quad \overline{\lim}\, t_n = y.$$

Proof.   (Outline): We may safely assume that none of the a_n's is zero, since discarding those terms of a series which are zero does not affect the convergence or divergence (**WHY?**). As well, we assume that $x, y \in \mathbf{R}$, leaving the other cases to the reader as Exercise 7. Let $f: \mathbf{N} \to \mathbf{N}$ be a one-to-one function such that $a_{f(n)}$ is the nth positive term among the a_n's. Similarly, let $g: \mathbf{N} \to \mathbf{N}$ be a one-to-one function such that $a_{g(n)}$ is the nth negative term among the a_n's. It is a consequence of Theorem 7.3.2 that both $\sum a_{f(n)}$ and $\sum a_{g(n)}$ are divergent. Next, we define a third function $h: \mathbf{N} \to \mathbf{N}$ inductively as follows:

(i) $h(1)$ is the least n such that $y < \sum\limits_{i=1}^{h(1)} a_{f(n)}$;

(ii) $h(2)$ is the least n such that $\sum\limits_{i=1}^{h(1)} a_{f(n)} + \sum\limits_{i=1}^{h(2)} a_{g(n)} < x$;

(iii) $h(2n+1)$ is the least n such that $y < \sum\limits_{i=1}^{h(2n+1)} a_{f(n)} + \sum\limits_{i=1}^{h(2n)} a_{g(n)}$;

(iv) $h(2n+2)$ is the least n such that $\sum\limits_{i=1}^{h(2n+1)} a_{f(n)} + \sum\limits_{i=1}^{h(2n+2)} a_{g(n)} < x$.

It is straightforward to show that $h(2n) < h(2n+2)$, and $h(2n-1) < h(2n+1)$.
We now define the function $F: \mathbf{N} \to \mathbf{N}$ by

(a) $F(n) = f(n)$, if $1 \leqslant n \leqslant h(1)$;

(b) $F(n) = g(n)$, if $h(1) < n \leqslant h(1) + h(2)$;

(c) $F(n) = f(n)$, if
$$h(2j-1) + h(2j) < n \leqslant h(2j) + h(2j+1), \; 1 \leqslant j \in \mathbf{N};$$

(d) $F(n) = g(n)$, if
$$h(2j) + h(2j+1) < n \leqslant h(2j+1) + h(2j+2), \; 1 \leqslant j \in \mathbf{N}.$$

It is readily checked that F is one-to-one, and

$$\{a_n : n \in \mathbf{N}\} = \{a_{F(n)} : n \in \mathbf{N}\},$$

(Exercise 7). We claim that for any $n \in \mathbf{N}$, if $k = h(2n) + h(2n+1)$, then

$$\sum_{i=1}^{k-1} a_{F(n)} < y < \sum_{i=1}^{k} a_{F(n)},$$

and if $k = h(2n+1) + h(2n+2)$, then

$$\sum_{i=1}^{k} a_{F(n)} < x < \sum_{i=1}^{k-1} a_{F(n)}.$$

Since, $a_{F(i)} \to 0$ as $i \to \infty$, (Exercise 6) the result now follows (**WHY?**). $\qquad \square$

Discussion. The property of a conditionally convergent series to be rearranged to converge to any number whatever, or even to diverge to $\pm\infty$ is indeed remarkable; however, it is not really surprising once one has in hand the two significant facts which are employed in the proof of the theorem. These two facts are:

(1) to be convergent, the terms, a_n, must go to 0;

(2) to be conditionally convergent, both the positive and negative parts of a series must diverge.

To see how these two ideas are used, first consider the functions f and g. The positive integer, $f(n)$, is the subscript in the original series of the nth positive term. Similarly, $g(n)$ is the subscript of the nth negative term. Since both $\sum a_{f(n)}$ and $\sum a_{g(n)}$ are divergent, it follows that for every $k \in \mathbf{N}$,

$$\sum_{n=k}^{\infty} a_{f(n)} \quad \text{and} \quad \sum_{n=k}^{\infty} a_{g(n)}$$

are both divergent. Intuitively, the proof should generate a new series for which the sequence of partial sums oscillates from just below x to just above y. Suppose that a given partial sum is just below x. The fact that $\sum_{n=k}^{\infty} a_{f(n)}$ diverges guarantees that we will always have enough positive terms left unused to obtain a new sum, which includes all previously used terms and which is greater than y. Similarly, if we have a partial sum which is above y, there will always be enough negative terms unused to obtain a new sum which is less than x. This fact is employed formally in the definition of the function, h, which counts the number of positive (negative) terms required to take a finite partial sum from just below x to just above y (from just above y to just below x). Of course these terms have to be collected and added up in such a way as to accomplish this purpose. The definition of h also accounts for the order in which the terms must be added up, and the number of terms required to get from x to y, or vice versa. It does so by using the preestablished order on the positive (negative) terms, which is preserved by f (respectively g) and the four defining properties. In summary then, $h(2n - 1) - h(2n - 3)$, $(h(2n + 2) - h(2n))$ gives the number of additional positive (negative) terms which are required to complete half of the nth oscillation.

Once we have defined h, it is possible to define the permutation, F, which defines the rearrangement. The definition of F yields a sequence of partial sums which will oscillate from 'just above' y to 'just below' x. In this case, 'just above' means to exceed y by no more than the value of $a_{F(n)}$ for some n. It is at this point that we employ the fact that the terms of a convergent series must approach 0 to guarantee that x and y are the limit inferior and limit superior, respectively.

Many of the details of the proof have been left to the reader. These details can be proven by an appropriate induction. The reader who takes it upon himself to complete these details will find that a complete understanding of the proof results. $\square$

We give just one illustration of a rearrangement and show how the sum is altered.

EXAMPLE 1

Show

$$1 - \frac{1}{2} + \frac{1}{3} - \frac{1}{4} + \cdots = \ln 2$$

and further evaluate the sum of the rearranged series

$$1 + \frac{1}{3} - \frac{1}{2} + \frac{1}{5} + \frac{1}{7} - \frac{1}{4} + \cdots + + - \cdots$$

Solution. We shall briefly outline how we compute the sum of the given series. Set

$$g_n = \sum_{k=1}^{n} \frac{1}{k} - \ln n.$$

It is known (see Exercise 7.2.20) that the sequence $\{g_n\}$ converges to a limit, to which we assign the symbol, γ, and which is known as **Euler's constant**. If s_n and t_n denote the partial sums of the series and its rearrangement, then

$$s_{2n} = 1 - \frac{1}{2} + - \cdots + \frac{1}{2n - 1} - \frac{1}{2n}$$

$$= \left[1 + \frac{1}{2} + \cdots + \frac{1}{2n} \right] - 2 \left[\frac{1}{2} + \frac{1}{4} + \cdots + \frac{1}{2n} \right]$$

$$= \left[1 + \frac{1}{2} + \cdots + \frac{1}{2n} \right] - \left[1 + \frac{1}{2} + \cdots + \frac{1}{n} \right]$$

$$= (g_{2n} + \ln 2n) - (g_n + \ln n)$$
$$= g_{2n} - g_n + \ln 2.$$

Since g_n is Cauchy, we have $\lim s_{2n} = \ln 2$. It is left to the reader to show that $\lim s_n = \ln 2$ for any partial sum. For t_n we have

$$t_{3n} = \left[1 + \frac{1}{3} - \frac{1}{2} \right] + \left[\frac{1}{5} + \frac{1}{7} - \frac{1}{4} \right] + \cdots + \left[\frac{1}{4n-3} + \frac{1}{4n-1} - \frac{1}{2n} \right]$$

$$= \left[1 + \frac{1}{3} + \frac{1}{5} + \cdots + \frac{1}{4n-1} \right] - \frac{1}{2} \left[1 + \frac{1}{2} + \cdots + \frac{1}{n} \right]$$

$$= \left[1 + \frac{1}{2} + \cdots + \frac{1}{4n} \right] - \frac{1}{2} \left[1 + \frac{1}{2} + \cdots + \frac{1}{2n} \right]$$

$$- \frac{1}{2} \left[1 + \frac{1}{2} + \cdots + \frac{1}{n} \right]$$

so that

$$t_{3n} = (\ln 4n + g_{4n}) - \frac{1}{2}(\ln 2n + g_{2n}) - \frac{1}{2}(\ln n + g_n)$$

$$= \left[g_{4n} - \frac{1}{2}g_{2n} - \frac{1}{2}g_n \right] + \frac{3}{2}\ln 2,$$

whence, again since g_n is Cauchy,

$$\lim t_{3n} = \frac{3}{2}\ln 2.$$

Since

$$t_{3n+1} = t_{3n} + \frac{1}{4n+1} \quad \text{and} \quad t_{3n+2} = t_{3n} + \frac{1}{4n+1} + \frac{1}{4n+3},$$

it follows that $\lim t_n = \frac{3}{2}\ln 2$, as desired. $\square$

Discussion. The key to understanding this example is in coming to grips with the initial computations which establish the limit of $\{s_{2n}\}$. The easiest way to see what is going on in the string of equalities which begins $s_{2n} = \cdots$, is to replicate the string for some small value of n, say $n = 3$. This will elucidate the changes involved in the first three steps. The clever part is the introduction of a form of 0, that is, $\ln 2n - \ln 2n$ and $\ln n - \ln n$, which occurs in the fourth equality. The reader should recall the many previous occasions on which other forms of 0 have been introduced into equations. In any case, once this is done, the solution is apparent.

The rearrangement consisted of taking two positive terms followed by one negative term so that a grouping of three terms was obtained. This motivated us to compute the partial sum, t_{3n}, and since t_{3n+1} and t_{3n+2} differ from t_n only in terms with limit 0, it suffices to study the behavior of t_{3n}. The computations which evaluate $\lim_{n \to \infty} t_{3n}$ are similar to the computations for $\{s_{2n}\}$.

In the same vein, it is possible to show that if the above series for $\ln 2$ is rearranged so that p positive terms are followed by q negative terms each time, then the sum will be altered to $\ln 2 + \dfrac{1}{2} \ln \dfrac{p}{q}$. $\qquad \square$

To conclude this section, we introduce the notions of a subseries and subseries convergence and relate them to absolute convergence.

Definition. Let $f: \mathbf{N} \to \mathbf{N}$ be a one-to-one (but not necessarily onto) function. If $b_n = a_{f(n)}$, then the series $\sum b_n$ is called a **subseries** of the series $\sum a_n$.

Discussion. The reader can check that this definition is nothing more than the definition of a subsequence phrased appropriately for series. $\qquad \square$

Theorem 7.3.5. Let $\sum a_n$ be any series. Then $\sum a_n$ is absolutely convergent if and only if every subseries $\sum b_n$ of $\sum a_n$ is convergent. Moreover,

$$|\textstyle\sum b_n| \leqslant \sum |b_n| \leqslant \sum |a_n|.$$

Proof. We have already shown that a series which is not absolutely convergent has a divergent subseries. Thus, one-half of the theorem is already proved. To complete the proof, let $\sum a_n$ be an absolutely convergent series, and let $\sum b_n$ a subseries, defined by $b_n = a_{f(n)}$. Now, given n, we can find M such that $k < n$ exactly if $f^{-1}(k) < M$. Then

$$\left| \sum_{k=1}^{n} b_k \right| \leqslant \sum_{k=1}^{n} |b_k| \leqslant \sum_{k=1}^{M} |a_k| \leqslant \sum_{k=1}^{\infty} |a_k|.$$

All the required conclusions now follow. $\qquad \square$

Discussion. In this section we have studied three basic concepts related to an infinite series:

- **(i)** absolute convergence;
- **(ii)** rearrangement convergence, where every rearrangement of the series converges;
- **(iii)** subseries convergence; where every subseries of the original series converges.

We can summarize our results by saying that if a series possesses any one of the above properties, it must have the other two as well. Finally, the alternating form of the harmonic series, $\sum \dfrac{(-1)^{n+1}}{n}$, provides the canonical example of a conditionally convergent series where one and hence all the three conditions fail. $\qquad \square$

The reader may have noticed that Theorem 7.1.1, which discussed uniqueness and various arithmetic results for series avoided any discussion of the product of two series. The reason for this is multiplication of series requires one to assign a meaning to $(\sum a_n)(\sum b_n)$. If one reasons by analogy with sequences, the natural product is $\sum a_n b_n$, that is, term-by-term multiplication. There are three difficulties with this definition.

The first difficulty is illustrated by taking the series $\sum \dfrac{(-1)^n}{\sqrt{n}}$ and multiplying it by itself. While the initial series is convergent, its 'square' is not, as the reader can easily verify. The second difficulty relates to the harmonic series, $\sum \dfrac{1}{n}$. It is divergent, but its 'square' is convergent. Neither of these results is particularly satisfying, which suggests that an appropriate concept has not been realized. Moreover, the definition does not appear to be the natural extension of a finite product concept. The third difficulty relates to the case where all three series converge, say to a, b, and c, respectively. For this case, it is easily checked, using the alternating form of the harmonic series for example, that $a \cdot b \neq c$. Considerations such as these lead to:

Definition.   Let $\displaystyle\sum_{i=0}^{\infty} a_n$ and $\displaystyle\sum_{i=0}^{\infty} b_n$ be two infinite series. Set

$$c_n = a_0 b_n + a_1 b_{n-1} + \cdots + a_n b_0 = \sum_{k=0}^{n} a_k b_{n-k}$$

and define

$$\left[\sum_{n=0}^{\infty} a_n \right] \left[\sum_{n=0}^{\infty} b_n \right] = \sum_{n=0}^{\infty} c_n.$$

Discussion.   This definition is due to Cauchy and carries the name, **Cauchy product** or **convolution product**. We want to motivate the definition of c_n. Thus, consider the product of the two finite polynomials

$$\left[\sum_{k=0}^{n} a_k x^k \right] \times \left[\sum_{k=0}^{n} b_k x^k \right].$$

This product can be computed using the ordinary laws of arithmetic, since we are dealing with two finite sums. Let d_m denote the coefficient on x^m in the product and consider $m = i + j \leqslant n$. We claim (Exercise 20) $d_m = c_m$. We stress that $m \leqslant n$ is a requirement for this equality. The important point to notice here is that the coefficient on x^m involves only coefficients associated with powers of x for which the degree is less than or equal to m. For this reason, if we consider the various finite products from the series $\sum a_k$ and $\sum b_k$ as n tends to infinity,

$$\left[\sum_{k=0}^{n} a_k x^k \right] \times \left[\sum_{k=0}^{n} b_k x^k \right],$$

the coefficient, c_m on x^m after multiplication, becomes fixed as soon as $n \geqslant m$. For this reason, we may be confident of the formal assertion

$$\sum_{k=0}^{\infty} c_k x^k = \left[\sum_{k=0}^{\infty} a_k x^k \right] \times \left[\sum_{k=0}^{\infty} b_k x^k \right],$$

which illustrates the utility of the Cauchy product.

Given that $\sum a_n$, $\sum b_n$, and $\sum c_n$ converge to a, b, and c, respectively, one could hope that $ab = c$. We explore this and other questions below. $\square$

EXAMPLE 2 _____

Consider the series $\displaystyle\sum_{n=0}^{\infty} \frac{(-1)^n}{\sqrt{n+1}}$. What can be said about the convergence of the Cauchy product of this series with itself?

Solution. As noted above, the series is convergent. However,

$$c_n = (-1)^n \sum_{k=0}^{n} \frac{1}{\sqrt{(n-k+1)(k+1)}}.$$

Observe

$$(n - k + 1)(k + 1) = nk - k^2 + n + 1$$

$$\leqslant n^2 + n + 1 \leqslant (n + 1)^2.$$

Hence,

$$|c_n| \geqslant \frac{n+1}{\sqrt{(n+1)^2}} = 1.$$

Thus, c_n does not tend to zero, and the Cauchy product cannot converge. $\square$

Discussion. This example is due to Cauchy himself. It shows even this formulation of products for series will not satisfy the natural requirement that if one starts with two convergent series, the product series will converge and have sum which is the product of the sums of the factor series.

If one thinks about this example, one sees the difficulty is due to the fact that neither of the initial series is absolutely convergent. This suggests that a stronger hypothesis may be required to achieve the desired result. $\square$

Theorem 7.3.6 (Mertens). Suppose $\displaystyle\sum_{n=0}^{\infty} a_n$ converges absolutely to a, $\displaystyle\sum_{n=0}^{\infty} b_n$ converges to b. Then the Cauchy product converges to ab.

Proof. Let A_n, B_n, and C_n denote the partial sums up to n for the two series and the Cauchy product, respectively. Also, set $\beta_n = B_n - b$. Now,

$$C_n = \sum_{k=0}^{n} c_k = \sum_{k=0}^{n} \sum_{j=0}^{k} a_j b_{k-j}$$

$$= \sum_{k=0}^{n} a_k B_{n-k} \tag{*}$$

$$= \sum_{k=0}^{n} a_k (b + \beta_{n-k}) \tag{*}$$

$$= A_n b + \sum_{k=0}^{n} a_k \beta_{n-k}. \tag{*}$$

Evidently, $A_n b \to ab$ as $n \to \infty$. Thus, it suffices to show

$$\lim_{n \to \infty} \sum_{k=0}^{n} a_k \beta_{n-k} = 0.$$

To establish this claim, let $\epsilon > 0$ be given. Now, by hypothesis, $\sum |a_n|$ converges, and we call its sum α. Further, β_n converges to 0 and there exists β such that $|\beta_n| \leqslant \beta$ for all n. Choose $N \in \mathbf{N}$ such that $n > N$ implies $|\beta_n| < \dfrac{\epsilon}{\alpha}$, where we implicitly assume that $\alpha > 0$. For $n > N$ we have

$$\left| \sum_{k=0}^{n} a_k \beta_{n-k} \right| \leqslant \sum_{k=0}^{n} |a_{n-k} \beta_k|$$

$$= \sum_{k=0}^{N} |a_{n-k} \beta_k| + \sum_{k=N+1}^{n} |a_{n-k} \beta_k| \tag{*}$$

$$\leqslant \beta \sum_{k=0}^{N} |a_{n-k}| + \frac{\epsilon}{\alpha} \sum_{k=N+1}^{n} |a_{n-k}| \tag{*}$$

$$\leqslant \beta \sum_{k=0}^{N} |a_{n-k}| + \epsilon. \tag{*}$$

To complete the proof, notice that as $n \to \infty$, by the Cauchy criterion,

$$\beta \sum_{k=0}^{N} |a_{n-k}| \to 0. \tag{*}$$

Since ϵ was arbitrary, we are done. $\qquad\qquad\qquad\qquad\qquad\qquad\qquad\square$

Discussion. In Exercise 21, the reader is asked to supply justifications for all the statements in the above proof which are marked with (*).

There are two important steps in this argument. The first is the manipulation of C_n into a form involving $A_n b$ and other terms. The second key step in this argument is noticing that by splitting the sum of the other terms into two parts as follows,

$$\sum_{k=0}^{n} |a_{n-k} \beta_k| = \sum_{k=0}^{N} |a_{n-k} \beta_k| + \sum_{k=N+1}^{n} |a_{n-k} \beta_k|$$

that both parts can then be made arbitrarily small. Another example which requires this type of argument is given in Exercise 22 (see also Exercises 1.2.15 and 1.2.17).

This theorem provides a means for ensuring that the product of two series converge, and further, that the product series has the right sum. As has already been noted, if neither series is absolutely convergent, then the product does not have to converge. This leaves a small, but important, question. Suppose one starts with two convergent, but not absolutely convergent series. Could we have a situation in which the Cauchy product converges to other than the required sum? The next theorem deals with this question. $\square$

Theorem 7.3.7 (Abel). Suppose $\sum\limits_{n=0}^{\infty} a_n$ converges to a, $\sum\limits_{n=0}^{\infty} b_n$ converges to b, and the Cauchy product is convergent. Then the Cauchy product converges to ab.

Proof. Let A_n, B_n, and C_n be the partial sums of the three series. Observe

$$\sum_{k=0}^{n} C_n = \sum_{k=0}^{n} A_k B_{n-k}. \tag{*}$$

It follows that

$$\frac{1}{n}\sum_{k=0}^{n} C_n = \frac{1}{n}\sum_{k=0}^{n} A_k B_{n-k}. \tag{*}$$

Now $A_n \to a$ and $B_n \to b$ whence $\dfrac{1}{n}\sum\limits_{k=0}^{n} C_n \to ab$ (Exercise 24). $\square$

There remains one additional question, namely, if two series are absolutely convergent, what about their product?

Theorem 7.3.8. If two series are absolutely convergent, so is their Cauchy product, and the product of the sums is the sum of the products.

Proof. Exercise 25. $\square$

Cauchy products are a special example of double series. Recall that a double sequence, $\{\sigma(n, m)\}$, is a function from $\mathbf{N} \times \mathbf{N}$ into $\mathbf{R}$ and that a double sequence has a limit, a exactly if for every positive ϵ there exists $N \in \mathbf{N}$ such that

$$|\sigma(n, m) - a| < \epsilon \quad \text{whenever} \quad n, m > N$$

(see Exercises 3.3.31–3.3.33). We want to develop a notion of convergence for double series, $\sum\limits_{n,m=1}^{\infty} \sigma(n, m)$. As with ordinary series, the vehicle is the sequence of partial sums.

Definition. Let $\{\sigma(n, m)\}$ be a double sequence and consider the formal infinite series $\sum\limits_{n,m=1}^{\infty} \sigma(n, m)$. We define the sequence of partial sums of the double series by

$$s(n, m) = \sum_{k=1}^{n} \sum_{j=1}^{m} \sigma(k, j).$$

We will say that the double series **converges** to a sum, s, provided $\lim\limits_{n,m\to\infty} s(n, m) = s$.

If the limit of the sequence of partial sums does not exist, we say the series is **divergent**.

Discussion. This definition is completely consistent with previous definitions of convergence for series. The notions are based on the basic definition of double sequences and the convergence of same. If the reader has not completed Exercises 3.3.31–3.3.33, he would be well advised to do so before continuing with this material.

If we have two sequences $\{a_n\}$ and $\{b_m\}$ $n \geqslant 0$, we can define a double sequence (series) by setting $\sigma(n, m) = a_n b_m$. We can then ask about the convergence properties of the series, $\sum_{n,m=0}^{\infty} \sigma(n, m)$. Further, we can ask whether this double series bears any relation to the Cauchy product of the two series. $\quad\square$

Theorem 7.3.9. Let f be a one-to-one function from $\mathbf{N}$ onto $\mathbf{N} \times \mathbf{N}$ and let $\sum_{n,m=1}^{\infty} \sigma(n, m)$ be a double series. Then $\sum_{k=1}^{\infty} \sigma(f(k))$ converges absolutely exactly if $\sum_{n,m=1}^{\infty} \sigma(n, m)$ converges absolutely.

Proof. Exercise 31. $\quad\square$

EXERCISES

1. Verify directly that the alternating form of the harmonic series, $\sum \frac{(-1)^{n+1}}{n}$, fails the absolute convergence property, the rearrangement convergence property, and the subseries convergence property.

2. Let p_n and q_n be obtained from a_n as in the definition of positive and negative parts of a series. Prove all claims made about p_n and q_n in the discussion.

3. Complete the proof of Theorem 7.3.2.

4. Let $\sum b_n$ be a rearrangement of $\sum a_n$. Show the positive part of $\sum b_n$ is a rearrangement of the positive part of $\sum a_n$.

5. Give a direct proof of Theorem 7.3.3 which does not apply Theorem 7.3.2.

6. Let $\sum a_n$ be a convergent series and let $\sum a_{f(n)}$ be a rearrangement of same. Show $\lim_{n \to \infty} a_{f(n)} = 0$.

7. Complete the details of the proof of Theorem 7.3.4.

8. Rearrange the alternating form of the harmonic series to converge to 0; to 1; to -1.

9. Show the expression for the general term of t_{3n} which is given in Example 1 is correct.

10. Show if the alternating form of the harmonic series is rearranged so that each time p positive terms are followed by q negative terms, $p, q \in \mathbf{N}$, then the resultant series is convergent. Also find its sum.

11. Let $\{f_n\}$ be a sequence of functions satisfying:
    (i) $f_n : \mathbf{N} \to \mathbf{N}$ is one-to-one for all $n \in \mathbf{N}$;
    (ii) $A_n \subseteq \operatorname{Rng} f_n$ for each n;

(iii) if $i \neq j$, then $A_i \cap A_j = \varnothing$;

(iv) $\bigcup_j A_j = \mathbf{N}$.

Let $\sum a_n$ be an absolutely convergent series and set $b_n^k = a_{f_k(n)}$ for each n and k. Show

(a) for each fixed k, $\sum_{n=1}^{\infty} b_n^k$ is an absolutely convergent subseries of $\sum a_n$;

(b) if s_k is the sum of $\sum b_n^k$, then $\sum s_k$ is absolutely convergent and has the same sum as $\sum a_n$.

12. If $\sum a_n$ is absolutely convergent, which of the following are absolutely convergent?

(a) $\sum \dfrac{a_n}{1 + a_n}$;

(b) $\sum \dfrac{a_n^2}{1 + a_n^2}$;

(c) $\sum \sqrt{a_n a_{n+1}}$;

(d) $\sum \dfrac{|a_n a_{n+1}|}{|a_n| + |a_{n+1}|}$.

13. Let $\sum a_n$ be an absolutely convergent series and $\{b_n\}$ a bounded sequence. Is $\sum a_n b_n$ absolutely convergent?

14. Let a denote the sum of the alternating harmonic series. Rearrange the series by taking two positive terms followed by two negative terms and repeating indefinitely. Find an expression for the sum of the rearranged series.

15. Show it is possible to rearrange the series $\sum \dfrac{(-1)^{n+1}}{n}$ so that the resultant sequence of partial sums is bounded but does not converge.

16. Let $\sum a_n$ be a convergent series. Give a condition which will ensure that $\sum a_n^2$ will converge.

17. Suppose $\sum a_n^2$ and $\sum b_n^2$ are both convergent. Is the same true for $\sum a_n b_n$?

18. We have shown $\sum \dfrac{1}{n^2}$ is convergent. Let its sum be denoted by s. (In fact $s = \dfrac{\pi^2}{6}$.)

Show $\sum_{n=0}^{\infty} \dfrac{1}{(2n+1)^2} = \dfrac{3}{4} s$. Find the sums of the following series:

(a) $\dfrac{1}{2^2} + \dfrac{1}{4^2} + \dfrac{1}{6^2} + \cdots$;

(b) $1 + \dfrac{1}{5^2} + \dfrac{1}{7^2} + \dfrac{1}{11^2} + \dfrac{1}{13^2} + \cdots$;

(c) $1 - \dfrac{1}{2^2} - \dfrac{1}{4^2} + \dfrac{1}{5^2} + \dfrac{1}{7^2} - - + \cdots$.

19. Let $S = \sum_{j=1}^{\infty} (-1)^{j+1} a_j$, where $\{a_j\}$ is an eventually monotonically decreasing sequence of strictly positive terms, tending to 0. Define S^{pq} as the rearrangement (no signs changed) obtained from S by taking groups of p positive terms followed by a group of q negative terms. Prove if f is a continuous and eventually monotone function such that $f(2n-1) = a_{2n-1}$, and $p \geqslant q > 0$, then

$$S^{pq} = S + \dfrac{1}{2} \lim_{n \to \infty} \int_{qn}^{pn} f$$

(with the understanding that both sides may be infinite or may diverge by oscillation). Compute S^{pq} for the following series S:

(a) $1 - \dfrac{1}{2} + \dfrac{1}{3} - + - \cdots$;

(b) $1 - \dfrac{1}{2^k} + \dfrac{1}{3^k} - + \cdots$;

(c) $1 - \dfrac{1}{3} + \dfrac{1}{5} - + \cdots$;

(d) $\displaystyle\sum_{n=1}^{\infty} (-1)^{n+1} \dfrac{\cos(\ln n) + 2}{n}$.

20. Prove the definition of c_m in Cauchy product has the property of being the coefficient on x^m in the product of two finite polynomials of degree, n, where $n \geqslant m$.

21. Verify all equations marked with an (*) in Theorem 7.3.6.

22. Let $\{s_n\}$ be a sequence. Show if $s_n \to 0$, then $\dfrac{1}{n}\displaystyle\sum_{k=1}^{n} s_k$ converges to 0.

23. Verify the equations marked with an (*) in the proof of Theorem 7.3.7.

24. Let $\{a_n\}$ and $\{b_n\}$ be two sequences converging to a and b, respectively. Define $t_n = \dfrac{1}{n}\displaystyle\sum_{k=1}^{n} a_k b_{n-k}$. Show $\{t_n\}$ converges to ab.

25. Prove Theorem 7.3.8.

26. Consider $a_1 = 1$, $a_n = 2$ for $n \geqslant 2$ and $b_1 = 1$, $a_n = (-1)^{n+1}2$ for $n \geqslant 2$. Show the Cauchy product of $\sum a_n$ and $\sum b_n$ is convergent.

27. Let $\displaystyle\sum_{i=1}^{n} a_n$ be a series and $\{s_n\}$ its sequence of partial sums. Define σ_n by

$$\sigma_n = \frac{1}{n}\sum_{k=1}^{n} s_k.$$

Show if $\{s_n\}$ converges, then $\{\sigma_n\}$ converges to the same sum. Give a counterexample to show that the converse is not true.

28. Let s_n and σ_n be as in Exercise 27. Show if for every $M \in \mathbf{N}$, there exists $N \in \mathbf{N}$ such that $n > N$ implies $\sigma_n > M$, then s_n has the same property. Show the converse fails, namely, if s_n is unbounded, then σ_n may be bounded, or indeed, converge to 0.

29. For a series, $\displaystyle\sum_{n=1}^{\infty} a_n$, the sequence, $\{\sigma_n\}$ (see Exercise 27) is called the **sequence of arithmetic means**. A series is called **summable (Cesaro summable, or (C,1)-summable)** exactly if $\{\sigma_n\}$ is convergent. Show for series with nonnegative terms, convergence and summability are identical concepts. Discuss the Cesaro summability of the following series:

(a) $1 - 1 + 1 - 1 + \cdots$;

(b) $1 + 0 - 1 + 1 + 0 - 1 + \cdots$;

(c) $1 - 1 + 0 + 1 + 1 - 1 + 0 + 1 + \cdots$;

(d) $1 - 1 + 0 + 0 + 1 - 1 + 0 + 0 + \cdots$;

(e) $\dfrac{1}{2} - 1 + \dfrac{1}{2} + \dfrac{1}{2} + \dfrac{1}{2} - 1 + \dfrac{1}{2} + \dfrac{1}{2} + \cdots$;

(f) $\dfrac{1}{2} - \dfrac{1}{2} + \dfrac{1}{2} - \dfrac{1}{2} + \cdots$;

(g) $\dfrac{1}{k} - \dfrac{1}{k} + \dfrac{1}{k} - \dfrac{1}{k} + \cdots$ $(k \in \mathbf{N})$.

30. Establish the Cauchy-Schwarz and Minkowski inequalities for series. Let $\sum\limits_{n=1}^{\infty} a_n^2$ and $\sum\limits_{n=1}^{\infty} b_n^2$

converge. Show $\sum\limits_{n=1}^{\infty} a_n b_n$ and $\sum\limits_{n=1}^{\infty} (a_n + b_n)^2$ also converge and that

$$\left[\sum_{n=1}^{\infty} a_n b_n \right]^2 \leqslant \left[\sum_{n=1}^{\infty} a_n^2 \right] \left[\sum_{n=1}^{\infty} b_n^2 \right],$$

and

$$\left[\sum_{n=1}^{\infty} (a_n + b_n)^2 \right]^{1/2} \leqslant \left[\sum_{n=1}^{\infty} a_n^2 \right]^{1/2} + \left[\sum_{n=1}^{\infty} b_n^2 \right]^{1/2}.$$

31. Prove Theorem 7.3.9.

32. Show there is a one-to-one function f from $\mathbf{N} \cup \{0\}$ onto $(\mathbf{N} \cup \{0\}) \times (\mathbf{N} \cup \{0\})$ which will generate the Cauchy product of two series. What does this imply for absolutely convergent series?

33. Suppose that $\sum\limits_{n,m=1}^{\infty} \sigma(n, m)$ is a double series. Consider the associated partial sums $A_m =$

$\sum\limits_{n=1}^{\infty} \sigma(n, m)$ and $B_n = \sum\limits_{m=1}^{\infty} \sigma(n, m)$, as well as the iterated sums, $\sum\limits_{m=1}^{\infty} A_m$ and $\sum\limits_{n=1}^{\infty} B_n$. Under what conditions will these various series converge? Under what conditions will they all yield the same sums?

34. Prove a double series of positive terms converges if and only if its sequence of partial sums is bounded.

35. Show an absolutely convergent double series converges. What can you say about the converse?

36. Let $\sum\limits_{n,m} \sigma(n, m)$ be a double series. The series defined by A_m, B_n of Exercise 33 are called a

column series, a row series, respectively. Similarly a **diagonal series** is defined by $\sum\limits_{k=1}^{\infty} C_k$,

where $C_k = \sum\limits_{j=1}^{k} \sigma(j, k - j)$. There are various other ways (infinitely many, in fact) of form-

ing a single series from $\sum\limits_{n,m} \sigma(n, m)$. Prove if a double series of positive terms converges,

then any single series formed out of it converges. What can you say about the converse?

37. Discuss the convergence of the following double series. In particular, find the sums of each row series, column series, and diagonal series. Also discuss the two iterated sums $\sum\limits_{m=1}^{\infty} \sum\limits_{n=1}^{\infty} \sigma(m, n)$, $\sum\limits_{n=1}^{\infty} \sum\limits_{m=1}^{\infty} \sigma(m, n)$, in each case.

(a) $\sigma(1, m) = \sigma(n, 1) = 1$, $\sigma(2, m) = \sigma(n, 2) = -1$, $\sigma(n, m) = 0$ otherwise;

(b) $\sigma(n, n + 1) = 1$, $\sigma(m - 1, m) = -1$, $\sigma(n, m) = 0$ otherwise;

(c) $\quad 1 + 2 + 4 + 8 + \cdots$

$\quad -\dfrac{1}{2} - 1 - 2 - 4 - \cdots$

$\quad -\dfrac{1}{4} - \dfrac{1}{2} - 1 - 2 - \cdots$

$\quad -\dfrac{1}{8} - \dfrac{1}{4} - \dfrac{1}{2} - 1 - \cdots$

$\quad \cdots \quad \cdots \quad \cdots \quad \cdots \ ;$

(d) $\sigma(m, n) = \begin{cases} 1, & m = n+1, \ n = 1, 2, \ldots, \\ -1, & m = n-1, \ n = 1, 2, \ldots, \\ 0, & 0, \ \text{otherwise}; \end{cases}$

(e) $\sigma(n, n) = 2, \quad \sigma(n, n + 2) = -1, \quad \sigma(m + 2, m) = 1, \quad \sigma(n, m) = 0$ otherwise;

(f) $\sigma(n, n) = 2, \quad \sigma(n, n + 1) = -1, \quad \sigma(m + 1, m) = 1, \quad \sigma(n, m) = 0$ otherwise;

(g) (Cesaro's example)

$$\frac{1}{2} - \frac{1}{4} + \frac{1}{4} - \frac{1}{8} + \frac{1}{8} - \frac{1}{16} + \frac{1}{16} - \cdots$$

$$\frac{1}{2^2} - \frac{3}{4^2} + \frac{3}{4^2} - \frac{7}{8^2} + \frac{7}{8^2} - \frac{15}{16^2} + \frac{15}{16^2} - \cdots$$

$$\frac{1}{2^3} - \frac{3^2}{4^3} + \frac{3^2}{4^3} - \frac{7^2}{8^3} + \frac{7^2}{8^3} - \frac{15^2}{16^3} + \frac{15^2}{16^3} - \cdots$$

$$\frac{1}{2^4} - \frac{3^3}{4^4} + \frac{3^3}{4^2} - \frac{7^3}{8^3} + \frac{7^3}{8^3} - \frac{15^2}{16^4} + \frac{15^2}{16^4} - \cdots$$

$$\cdots \quad \cdots \quad \cdots \quad \cdots \quad \cdots \quad \cdots$$

38. Show any single series formed out of an absolutely convergent double series also converges absolutely. In particular, in an absolutely convergent double series, the sums by rows, by columns, and by diagonal are all equal.

39. Give examples to illustrate that the conclusions of Exercise 38 need not be true, if the double series is conditionally convergent.

40. Show the Cauchy product of two series can be obtained as the diagonal series of a suitable double series. Use this idea to give an alternate proof of Theorem 7.3.8.

7.4 SERIES WITH ARBITRARY TERMS

As pointed out in the last section, all the tests which we have developed so far require the series to be nonnegative. Actually, this can be weakened to a requirement that eventually the terms of the series be all of one sign, but this is not a significant addition to the power of the tool. The net result is that our tests may be used to decide whether an arbitrary series will converge absolutely, but none can detect conditional convergence. For this reason we would like to have some tests which can be applied to an arbitrary series.

One of the most easily dealt with forms of a series with both positive and negative terms is the one in which terms are alternately positive and negative. Such a series is called an **alternating series** for obvious reasons. Taking all the $a_n > 0$, an alternating series could be represented by $\sum_{n=1}^{\infty} (-1)^{n-1} a_n$. The following elegant test decides the convergence of such a series.

Theorem 7.4.1 (Leibnitz's Test). If $\{a_n\}$ is a nonincreasing sequence of positive terms converging to 0, then the alternating series $\sum_{n=1}^{\infty} (-1)^{n-1} a_n$ is convergent.

Proof. Consider the odd partial sums, namely those ending in positive terms. Since

$$s_{2n+1} - s_{2n-1} = a_{2n+1} - a_{2n} \leqslant 0$$

the odd partial sums form a monotonic decreasing sequence. The analogous computation for the even partial sums shows that $s_{2n+2} \geqslant s_{2n}$, whence the even partial sums form a monotonic increasing sequence. Now, $s_{2n+1} = s_{2n} + a_{2n+1}$, whence $s_{2n+1} \geqslant s_{2n} \geqslant a_2$. Consequently, the odd partial sums form a decreasing sequence bounded below, and so must converge, say to s. Similarly, the even partial sums form an increasing sequence bounded above and so must converge, say to t. But

$$0 = \lim_{n \to \infty} a_{n+1} = \lim_{n \to \infty} (s_{2n+1} - s_{2n}) = s - t$$

whence $s = t$. □

Discussion. This is a nice theorem because it is simple to apply and the proof is conceptually easy to understand. It does, however, require that the sequence, $\{a_n\}$, is monotonically decreasing, and that the associated series is alternating. Both are strong conditions, and so reduce the utility of the theorem. The condition that $\{a_n\}$ is monotone can be weakened to a requirement that the sequence be eventually monotonically decreasing to 0; however, this is not a significant weakening of the hypothesis. Finally, note that completeness in the form of Theorem 1.3.1 was vital for the proof. □

EXAMPLE 1 _____

Discuss the convergence of the series $\sum \dfrac{(-1)^{n-1}}{n}$.

Solution. The sequence $\left\{ \dfrac{1}{n} \right\}$ is monotonically decreasing to 0, whence we may apply Leibnitz's test to see that it converges. □

Our next two tests are similar to Leibnitz's test in that they consider situations where the terms of a series are composed of the term-by-term product of corresponding terms of two sequences. To establish these results, we shall require the following useful identity:

Lemma (Abel). Let $\{a_n\}$, $\{b_n\}$ be two arbitrary sequences and let $s_n = \sum\limits_{i=1}^{n} a_i$. Then,

$$\sum_{i=1}^{n} a_i b_i = s_n b_{n+1} - \sum_{i=1}^{n} s_i (b_{i+1} - b_i).$$

Discussion. The reader will be invited to check the above identity in Exercise 2. An immediate consequence of the identity is that the series $\sum a_i b_i$ converges exactly if both the sequence $\{s_n b_{n+1}\}$ and the infinite series $\sum s_n (b_{n+1} - b_n)$ converge. □

Theorem 7.4.2 (Dirichlet's Test). Let $\sum a_n$ be a series whose partial sums form a bounded sequence, and let $\{b_n\}$ be a sequence of decreasing terms converging to zero. Then $\sum a_n b_n$ is convergent.

Proof. It is given that for some M, the partial sums s_n of $\sum a_n$ satisfy the inequality $|s_n| < M$ for all n. Thus, $\lim s_n b_{n+1} = 0$ (**WHY?**). Also,

$$|s_n(b_{n+1} - b_n)| \leqslant M(b_n - b_{n+1})$$

whence

$$\sum_{i=1}^{n} s_i(b_{i+1} - b_i) \leqslant M \sum_{k=1}^{n}(b_i - b_{i+1}) = M(b_1 - b_{n+1}),$$

and consequently, $\sum a_n b_n$ converges (**WHY?**). ☐

Theorem 7.4.3 (Abel's Test). If $\sum a_n$ is convergent, and if $\{b_n\}$ is monotonic convergent sequence, then $\sum a_n b_n$ is convergent.

Proof. The existence of $\lim s_n b_{n+1}$ is guaranteed by the convergence of $\sum a_n$ and of $\{b_n\}$. An argument similar to the Dirichlet's test completes the proof (Exercise 3). ☐

Discussion. It is easy to see that Dirichlet's test is a generalization of Leibnitz's test, since we have only to note that the setting $a_n = (-1)^{n-1}$ will produce a series with a bounded sequence of partial sums.

Abel's test may be thought of in a somewhat different way. If we take the series $\sum a_n$ and multiply it term by term by a constant sequence $\{b_n\}$, then the resultant series $\sum a_n b_n$ will be convergent. We can ask: how can we generalize this result? There are several ways to go. We could require only that $\{b_n\}$ be bounded, or we could require only that $\sum b_n$ be convergent. It turns out that neither of these requirements is enough, and we will explore this further in the exercises. ☐

EXAMPLE 2 _____

Determine the convergence properties of $\sum_{n=2}^{\infty} \dfrac{(n^3+1)^{1/3} - n}{\ln n}$.

Solution. The sequence $\left\{ \dfrac{1}{\ln n} \right\}$ is monotone and convergent for $n \geqslant 2$. Thus, if $\sum (n^3+1)^{1/3} - n$ is convergent, we can use Abel's test to conclude convergence for the original series. Using algebra we have

$$\sum (n^3+1)^{1/3} - n = \sum \frac{1}{(n^3+1)^{2/3} + (n^3+1)^{1/3}n + n^2}.$$

The series on the right-hand side can now be shown to be convergent by an appropriate application of the comparison test. It is left to the reader to complete the details (Exercise 4). ☐

Discussion. The basic technique employed is to rationalize the numerator. We cannot overly stress the importance of algebra as a tool for attacking these problems. It is used implicitly throughout all the manipulations. □

Two of the very useful and frequently employed tests are given next. The first, called the ratio test and due to D'Alembert, draws conclusions about the behavior of a series by studying the sequence of ratios of consecutive terms of the series. The second, the root test, due to Cauchy, draws conclusions based on the behavior of the sequence formed by taking the nth root of the nth term of the given series.

Theorem 7.4.4 (Ratio Test). Given the series $\sum a_n$, let

$$r = \underline{\lim} \left| \frac{a_{n+1}}{a_n} \right| \quad \text{and} \quad R = \overline{\lim} \left| \frac{a_{n+1}}{a_n} \right|.$$

Then,

(i) the series $\sum a_n$ converges absolutely if $R < 1$;

(ii) the series diverges if $r > 1$;

(iii) the test gives no information if $r \leqslant 1 \leqslant R$.

Proof. For (i) assume that $R < 1$, and choose x such that $R < x < 1$. By definition of R, there exists an N such that $\left| \dfrac{a_{n+1}}{a_n} \right| < x$ whenever $n \geqslant N$. It is immediate that $|a_{n+1}| < |a_n| x$, which together with the above inequality can be used to show that

$$\sum_{k=N}^{N+p} |a_k| \leqslant \sum_{k=1}^{p} |a_N| \, |x^{k-N}|.$$

The sum on the right-hand side is geometric with ratio $x < 1$ and so is convergent as $p \to \infty$. Consequently, the sum on the left-hand side is also convergent, and so $\sum a_n$ converges as well.

For (ii), since $r > 1$, we have $|a_{n+1}| > |a_n|$ for all $n > N$. Evidently, this prevents the terms of the series from approaching 0, and so the series cannot converge.

For (iii), the series $\sum \dfrac{1}{n}$ is divergent, while the series $\sum \dfrac{1}{n^2}$ is convergent. Both satisfy $R = r = 1$ (Exercise 6). □

Discussion. The initial thrust of the argument in this theorem asserts that there is an x and an $N \in N$ such that $n \geqslant N$ implies

$$\left| \frac{a_{n+1}}{a_n} \right| < x < 1.$$

The truth of this inequality is derived from the basic properties of the limit inferior of a sequence. The reader should be able to supply all the reasons as to why this inequality is valid, or lacking this, review the basic properties of limit inferior (Exercise 5).

In the special case that the sequence $\left\{\left|\dfrac{a_{n+1}}{a_n}\right|\right\}$ converges, then $R = r$, whence we obtain convergence for $R < 1$, divergence for $R > 1$, and test fails when $R = 1$.

This test answers the question: Does a given series eventually have its terms go to 0 with the rapidity of a convergent geometric series, or on the other hand, diverge with the rapidity of a divergent geometric series? If the answer is 'yes' in the first instance, we conclude convergence; if 'yes' in the second, we conclude divergence. If the limiting ratio is 1, we get no conclusion.

While the test applies to all series, if we conclude convergence with this test, the series will converge absolutely, as well. If the series diverges by this test, no amount of changing signs of individual terms will ever generate a convergent series.

Finally, this test has particular utility, since it is totally self-contained. By this we mean that to apply this test, one need only consider the properties of the terms of the series whose convergence properties are required. No additional series are required for comparisons. The root test that is given below also has this feature.   □

EXAMPLE 3 _____

Discuss the convergence properties of the series $\displaystyle\sum_{n=0}^{\infty} \dfrac{x^n}{n!}$ ($x \in \mathbf{R}$).

Solution. Let x be fixed, we apply the ratio test as follows

$$\left|\dfrac{\dfrac{x^{n+1}}{(n+1)!}}{\dfrac{x^n}{n!}}\right| = \left|\dfrac{x^{n+1}}{(n+1)!}\dfrac{n!}{x^n}\right| = \left|\dfrac{x}{n+1}\right|.$$

Since x is fixed, it is immediate that $\left\{\dfrac{x}{n+1}\right\}$ converges to 0 for all x, whence the series converges (absolutely) for all values of x.   □

Discussion. The computations are straightforward, and illustrate the ease with which the ratio test may be applied.

The series to which we have applied the test may be well known to the reader. It sums to e^x, where e is the base for the natural logarithms. This series is tremendously useful and shows up in almost every branch of mathematics.   □

Theorem 7.4.5 (Root Test). Given the series $\sum a_n$, let

$$r = \overline{\lim} \, |a_n|^{1/n}.$$

Then,

(i) $\sum a_n$ converges absolutely if $r < 1$;
(ii) $\sum a_n$ diverges if $r > 1$;
(iii) no information is obtained if $r = 1$.

Proof. For (i), if $r < 1$, choose x such that $r < x < 1$. The definition of r guarantees the existence of an N such that $|a_n|^{1/n} < x$ for $n > N$ so that $|a_n| < x^n$ after a stage. By the comparison test, $\sum a_n$ converges (**WHY?**).

For (ii), notice that $a_n > 1$ infinitely often, since $r > 1$, so that $\lim a_n$ is different from zero. Hence, the series must diverge.

For (iii), the same examples which were used in the proof of the ratio test will also do the job here (Exercise 6). □

Discussion. As in the case of the ratio test, if the sequence $\{|a_n|^{1/n}\}$ converges to R, then we conclude that the series converges for $R < 1$, diverges for $R > 1$, and test fails for $R = 1$.

Since taking ratios and proceeding to limits is generally easier than a root extraction (of order n), the ratio test has the advantage that it is simpler to operate. On the other hand, the root test is certainly more powerful than the ratio test in the sense that whenever the ratio test succeeds, the root test also succeeds and delivers the same conclusions. But there are instances where the root test is decisive while the ratio test fails to give any conclusion whatsoever. The key to this remark is the simple inequality (see Exercise 3.4.22): if $a_n > 0$,

$$\underline{\lim} \frac{a_{n+1}}{a_n} \leqslant \underline{\lim} a_n^{1/n} \leqslant \overline{\lim} a_n^{1/n} \leqslant \overline{\lim} \frac{a_{n+1}}{a_n}.$$

The next example illustrates a situation where the ratio test fails but the root test prevails. □

EXAMPLE 4 _____

Under what conditions will the series defined by

$$1 + a + ab + a^2b + a^2b^2 + a^3b^2 + a^3b^3 + a^4b^3 + \cdots$$

converge?

Solution. It is easily seen that the ratio of any two consecutive terms alternate between a and b so that the ratio test will fail if $a < 1 < b$. However, the root test when applied yields

$$\lim (a^n b^n)^{1/2n} = \lim (a^{n+1} b^n)^{1/2n+1} = \sqrt{ab},$$

which is decisive provided $ab \neq 1$. The reader can complete the solution for the case where $ab = 1$ (Exercise 7). □

The question of whether a given series is convergent or divergent is in general a difficult one. There is no single, universal test that will deal with all possible cases. The foremost method is to verify the Cauchy criteria, but we have discussed several other useful tests above, including the popular ones like the ratio and the root tests, as well as the elegant test for an alternating series. Most of these have been derived in some fashion from one of the forms of the comparison test. We include here some more delicate tests which may be applied when all the earlier tests fail. In particular, some of these will be useful when the ratio and root tests fail, in other words, when the limit of $\dfrac{a_{n+1}}{a_n}$ and $a_n{}^{1/n}$ is equal to 1. The following criterion due to Kummer yields a large number of powerful tests, including the ratio and root tests, as special cases.

Theorem 7.4.6 (Kummer's Test). Let $\sum a_n$ be a series of positive terms, $\{D_n\}$ a sequence of positive terms, and set

$$p_n = D_n \frac{a_n}{a_{n+1}} - D_{n+1}.$$

Then $\sum a_n$ is convergent provided $\underline{\lim}\, p_n > 0$. Further, if $\sum \dfrac{1}{D_n}$ is divergent and $\overline{\lim}\, p_n < 0$, then $\sum a_n$ diverges.

Proof. We treat the case where $\underline{\lim}\, p_n > 0$ first. Fix $x > 0$ such that there exists $N \in \mathbf{N}$ such that $n > N$ implies $p_n > x$, and fix N with the asserted property. For $n = N, N + 1, N + 2, \ldots$, we have the following string of inequalities:

$$D_N a_N - D_{N+1} a_{N+1} > x\, a_{N+1}$$

$$D_{N+1} a_{N+1} - D_{N+2} a_{N+2} > x\, a_{N+2}$$

$$\cdots$$

$$\cdots$$

$$\cdots$$

$$D_{N+p-1} a_{N+p-1} - D_{N+p} a_{N+p} > x\, a_{N+p}.$$

If we let $\{s_n\}$ be the sequence of partial sums of $\sum a_n$ and add the inequalities, we obtain

$$x(s_{N+p} - s_N) < D_N a_N - D_{N+p} a_{N+p} < D_N a_N,$$

with the validity of the last inequality being due to the fact that we are dealing with sequences of positive terms. Mere manipulation of the last inequality yields

$$s_{N+p} < s_N + \frac{1}{x} D_N a_N,$$

whence $\{s_{N+p}\}$, $p \in \mathbf{N}$ is a bounded sequence. It now follows that $\sum a_n$ converges.

To complete the proof, let $\overline{\lim}\, p_n < 0$. It follows that there exists an $N \in \mathbf{N}$ such that for all $p \in \mathbf{N}$,

$$D_{N+p} a_{N+p} - D_{N+p+1} a_{N+p+1} \leqslant 0$$

which is equivalent to saying that $\{D_{N+p} a_{N+p}\}$ is monotone increasing. This yields

$$D_N a_N \frac{1}{D_{N+p}} \leqslant a_{N+p}.$$

Since the series $\sum \dfrac{1}{D_{N+p}}$ is divergent and $D_N a_N$ is a fixed, positive real number, the comparison test establishes the divergence of $\sum a_n$. $\qquad\square$

Discussion. Note that this is a test for series of nonnegative terms. To be valuable, we must have candidates for $\{D_n\}$. Some of the possible useful choices of the sequence $\{D_n\}$ are: $\{1\}$, $\{n\}$, $\{n \ln n\}$, $\{n \ln n \ln (\ln n)\}$, and so on.

If we set $D_n = 1$, it is easily seen that Kummer's test reduces to the ratio test, while the choice $D_n = n$ gives rise to Raabe's test given below. ☐

Corollary (Raabe's Test). Let $\sum a_n$ be a positive series. Then

(i) $\sum a_n$ is convergent if $\varliminf n \left(\dfrac{a_n}{a_{n+1}} - 1 \right) > 1$;

(ii) $\sum a_n$ is divergent if $\varlimsup n \left(\dfrac{a_n}{a_{n+1}} - 1 \right) < 1$.

Proof. The proof of this result is left as Exercise 8. ☐

EXAMPLE 5 _____

Test for convergence the series whose nth term is given by

$$a_n = \left[\frac{1 \cdot 4 \cdot 7 \, \cdots \, (3n-2)}{3 \cdot 6 \cdot 9 \, \cdots \, 3n} \right]^2.$$

Solution. We may apply Kummer's test directly by setting $D_n = n$, or we can apply Raabe's test. Using the latter, a simple computation shows that

$$n \left(\frac{a_n}{a_{n+1}} - 1 \right) = n \left(\left[\frac{3n + 3}{3n + 1} \right]^2 - 1 \right)$$

$$= \frac{12n^2 + 8n}{9n^2 + 6n + 1}.$$

Since the limit of this sequence exceeds 1, the series is convergent by Raabe's test. ☐

Discussion. In many instances, the nth term of a series involves powers, factorials, or huge products as above. Such series are particularly suited to tests which involve the ratio of successive terms since a good deal of cancellation can occur. One should always start with the ratio test, since this is by far the simplest to apply, and moreover, to apply any of the more delicate tests, such as Kummer's or Raabe's tests, the ratio $\dfrac{a_n}{a_{n+1}}$ must be calculated. In the instance above, it is easy to see that the ratio of successive terms of the series has limit 1, and so we are forced to use a test other than the ratio test. As with the ratio test, Raabe's test will not give any information if the generated sequence has limit 1. ☐

The last test presented is of even greater sensitivity than those already given. However, the list of such subtler tests is by no means exhaustive and the reader will be asked to establish additional tests in the exercises.

Theorem 7.4.7 (Gauss's Test).   Let $\sum a_n$ be a series of positive terms and suppose there is a bounded sequence $\{b_n\}$ and a constant k such that

$$\frac{a_n}{a_{n+1}} = 1 + \frac{k}{n} + \frac{b_n}{n^2}.$$

Then $\sum a_n$ is convergent if $k > 1$ and divergent if $k \leqslant 1$.

Proof.   We treat two cases, namely $k \neq 1$ and $k = 1$. For the former, observe that we may rewrite

$$\frac{a_n}{a_{n+1}} = 1 + \frac{k}{n} + \frac{b_n}{n^2}$$

as

$$n\left(\frac{a_n}{a_{n+1}} - 1\right) = k + \frac{b_n}{n}.$$

The sequence on the left, is exactly the expression in Raabe's test. Moreover, since k is a constant and $\{b_n\}$ is bounded, this sequence (on the left) has a limit, namely k. It is immediate that if $k > 1$ then $\sum a_n$ is convergent, whereas if $k < 1$, the series must diverge.

For the case where $k = 1$, we apply Kummer's test with $D_n = n \ln n$. Now, $\sum \dfrac{1}{D_n}$ is divergent (**WHY?**), hence we have only to show that

$$\underline{\lim}\left[D_n \frac{a_n}{a_{n+1}} - D_{n+1}\right] < 0.$$

Using the hypothesis regarding the ratio $\dfrac{a_n}{a_{n+1}}$, we can rewrite the expression above to be

$$n \ln n\left[1 + \frac{1}{n} + \frac{b_n}{n^2}\right] - (n+1)\ln(n+1).$$

We leave it to the reader to show (Exercise 9) that the limit of this expression is in fact, -1, whence the conclusion follows by Kummer's test. $\square$

Discussion.   Gauss's test is very useful in practice. Unlike the ratio, root, or Raabe's tests, this test gives conclusions even when the limit $k = 1$. Gauss's test should be tried whenever the ratio and Raabe's tests fail. This is particularly true when the expression $\dfrac{a_n}{a_{n+1}}$ is a ratio of polynomials since the required expression in $\dfrac{1}{n}$ may be very easy to obtain. This is illustrated in our last example. $\square$

EXAMPLE 6 _____

Test for convergence the series whose nth term is

$$a_n = \left[\frac{1.3.5.\ldots.(2n-1)}{2.4.6.\ldots.(2n)}\right]^2.$$

Solution. The reader may check that both Raabe's and ratio tests fail. We therefore apply Gauss's test. Now,

$$\frac{a_n}{a_{n+1}} = \left[\frac{2n+1}{2n+2}\right]^2$$

$$= 1 - \frac{1}{n} + \frac{1}{n^2}\left[\frac{5n^2 - 4n}{4n^2 + 8n + 4}\right]. \qquad \textbf{(WHY?)}$$

Since $k = -1$, the series diverges. ☐

Discussion. The reader may wonder how the expression on the right was generated. The answer is simple, long division, which once again reminds us of the power of simple algebraic techniques. ☐

EXERCISES

1. Let $\sum(-1)^{n-1}a_n$ be a series which satisfies the hypotheses of Leibnitz's test. Show that $s_{2n-1} \geqslant s_j \geqslant s_{2n}$ for $j > 2n \geqslant 2$.

2. Let $\{a_n\}$, $\{b_n\}$ be two arbitrary sequences with $s_n = \sum_{i=1}^{n} a_i$. Show for all n,

$$\sum_{i=1}^{n} a_i b_i = s_n b_{n+1} - \sum_{i=1}^{n} s_i(b_{i+1} - b_i).$$

3. Complete the details in the proof of Abel's test.

4. Complete the details of Example 2.

5. Give a careful derivation of the inequality which forms the basis of the proof of case (i) of the ratio test.

6. Check that the series $\sum\frac{1}{n}$ and $\sum\frac{1}{n^2}$ both have the property asserted in the proof of the ratio and root tests.

7. Complete the solution of Example 4.

8. Prove Raabe's test.

9. Complete the proof of Gauss's test.

10. Let $\sum a_n$ be a convergent series, and $\{b_n\}$ be a sequence.
    (a) Show that if $\{b_n\}$ is bounded, then $\sum a_n b_n$ will not necessarily converge;
    (b) Show that if $\{b_n\}$ is Cauchy, then $\sum a_n b_n$ will not necessarily converge;
    (c) Is there any condition other than monotonicity, which when added to the Cauchy condition will guarantee convergence?

11. Let $\sum a_n$ be a convergent series and $\{b_n\}$ a monotonic bounded sequence. Show $\sum a_n b_n$ is convergent.

12. Verify the inequalities which lead to the conclusion that the root test is a more sensitive test than the ratio test (see discussion following the root test).

13. Show if $\sum a_n^2$ is convergent, then $\sum\frac{|a_n|}{n}$ converges.

14. Give a careful proof (independent of Kummer's test) of Raabe's test.

15. Verify the calculations in Example 3.

16. Verify the calculations in Example 4.

17. Test for convergence and absolute convergence the series whose nth term is given by:

(a) $\dfrac{\ln n}{n}$;

(b) $\dfrac{\ln n}{n^2}$;

(c) $\ln \dfrac{n}{n+1}$;

(d) $\dfrac{(-1)^{n-1}}{n^{1+1/n}}$;

(e) $\dfrac{(-1)^n}{\ln(n+1)}$;

(f) $\dfrac{1}{\ln(n+1)^p}$, $p \geqslant 1$;

(g) $\dfrac{n^3 + 2^n}{2^n n^3}$;

(h) $\left[\dfrac{n}{1+n^2} \right]^n$;

(i) $\dfrac{\sqrt{n+1} - \sqrt{n}}{n^p}$, $p \geqslant 1$;

(j) $\dfrac{2^n + n^{1000}}{3^n + 1}$;

(k) $\dfrac{2.4.6. \ \cdots \ 2n}{1.3.5. \ \cdots \ (2n+1)}$;

(l) $\dfrac{n! e^n}{n^n}$;

(m) $(n^{1/n} - 1)^n$;

(n) $\dfrac{(-1)^n}{[\ln(n+1)]^{1/n}}$;

(o) $\dfrac{n^5(n+1)^n}{3n^n}$;

(p) $\dfrac{1.3.5. \ \cdots \ (2n-1)}{2.4.6. \ \cdots \ 2n} \ \dfrac{1}{n}$;

(q) $\dfrac{(n!)^2 100^n}{3^{n^2}}$;

(r) $\dfrac{n!}{3.5.7. \ \cdots \ (2n+1)}$;

(s) $\left[\dfrac{1.3.5. \ \cdots \ (2n-1)}{2.4.6. \ \cdots \ 2n} \right]^p$, $p \geqslant 1$;

(t) $(-1)^n \left[\dfrac{1.3.5. \ \cdots \ (2n-1)}{2.4.6. \ \cdots \ 2n} \right]^p$, $p \geqslant 1$;

(u) $\dfrac{e^n n!}{3.5.7. \ \cdots \ (2n-1)}$;

(v) $\dfrac{2^n + 1}{3^n + 2n}$;

(w) $\dfrac{1}{x^n - y^n}$, $x > y > 0$;

(x) $\dfrac{1}{a^n + 1}$, $a > -1$;

(y) $\dfrac{(-1)^{n-1}n^3}{2^n - 1}$;

(z) $\dfrac{(2n!)^3}{2^{6n}(n!)^6}$;

(a') $\dfrac{\sin n}{n}$;

(b') $(-1)^n \dfrac{|\sin n|}{n}$;

(c') $\dfrac{|\sin n|}{n}$;

(d') $(-1)^n \dfrac{\sin \dfrac{n\pi}{2}}{n}$.

18. Test for convergence the series defined by
$$1 + 2r + r^2 + 2r^3 + r^4 + 2r^5 + r^6 + 2r^7 + \cdots$$
where $r \in \mathbf{R}$ is arbitrary.

19. Discuss the convergence of the hypergeometric series given by
$$1 + \frac{ab}{cd} + \frac{a(a+1)b(b+1)}{c(c+1)d(d+1)} + \frac{a(a+1)(a+2)b(b+1)(b+2)}{c(c+1)(c+2)d(d+1)(d+2)} + \cdots$$
where $a, b, c, d \in \mathbf{R}$.

20. Let $a, b, c > 0$ with $b < a$. Test for convergence:
$$\frac{a}{b} + \frac{a(a+c)}{b(b+c)} + \frac{a(a+c)(a+2c)}{b(b+c)(b+2c)} + \cdots .$$

21. Test for convergence:

(a) $a + 1 + a^3 + a^2 + a^5 + a^4 + a^7 + \cdots$ $(a \in \mathbf{R})$;

(b) $1 - \dfrac{1}{3 \cdot 2^2} + \dfrac{1}{5 \cdot 3^2} - \dfrac{1}{7 \cdot 4^2} + \cdots$;

(c) $0 - \dfrac{1}{2} + \dfrac{1}{2^2} - \dfrac{1}{3} + \dfrac{2}{3^2} - \dfrac{1}{4} + \dfrac{3}{4^2} - \cdots$.

22. Let $\sum (-1)^{n-1}a_n$ satisfy the hypothesis of Leibnitz's test. If s_n denotes the nth partial sum of the series and s the sum, find a bound for $|s_n - s|$.

23. The series
$$1 - \frac{1}{2^2} + \frac{1}{3} - \frac{1}{4^2} + \frac{1}{5} - \frac{1}{6^2} + \cdots$$
is divergent. Does this contradict Leibnitz's test?

24. Consider the series $\sum \dfrac{(-1)^n}{n}$. For what values of n will s_n be accurate to 6 decimal places?

25. Let $\{a_n\}$ be a sequence of terms which alternate signs and such that $|a_n| \to 0$ monotonically. Let $\sum b_n$ be formed by taking p positive terms from a_n followed by q negative terms, and continuing this pattern. Is $\sum b_n$ convergent?

26. If the alternating series $\sum (-1)^{n-1} a_n$ converges by applying Leibnitz's test, with sum A, show there exists n_0 such that for $n \geqslant n_0$:

    (a) $|A - s_n| < |a_{n+1}|$,

    (b) $|A - s_n - \frac{1}{2} a_{n+1}| < \frac{1}{2} |a_{n+1}|$.

    Use this to compute the sum of $\sum\limits_{n=1}^{\infty} \frac{(-1)^{n+1}}{n^4}$ to 3 decimal places.

    Moreover, by considering the series

    $$1 - \frac{1}{2} + \frac{1}{3^2} - \frac{1}{2^2} + \frac{1}{3^4} - \frac{1}{2^4} + \cdots$$

    demonstrate that if the series converges, but Leibnitz's test does not work, then the above conclusions are not valid.

27. Prove **logarithmic test**: Let $\sum a_n$ be a series of nonnegative terms, and let $L_n = \dfrac{\ln \dfrac{1}{a_n}}{\ln n}$. The series converges if $\underline{\lim} L_n > 1$, and diverges if $L_n \leqslant 1$ for all n. Use this test to discuss the convergence or divergence of $\sum x^{\ln n}$ and $\sum x^{\ln \ln n}$.

28. Prove **second logarithmic test**: Let $\sum a_n$ be a series of nonnegative terms, and let $M_n = \dfrac{\ln \dfrac{1}{n a_n}}{\ln \ln n}$. The series converges if $\underline{\lim} M_n > 1$, and diverges if $M_n \leqslant 1$ for all n. Use this test to discuss the convergence of $\sum \dfrac{1}{n^{1 + (1/\ln n)}}$.

29. Prove **Bertrand's test**: If $a_n \geqslant 0$ and $B_n = (n-1) \ln n - \dfrac{a_{n+1}}{a_n} n \ln n$, then $\sum a_n$ converges if $\underline{\lim} B_n > 1$ and diverges if $\overline{\lim} B_n < 1$.

7.5 INFINITE PRODUCTS

This chapter has been concerned with assigning a meaning to infinite sums of real numbers and studying the notion of convergence of infinite series. The question naturally arises: Can we extend the meaning of 'product' to an infinite collection of real numbers? In this section, we will define the concept of an infinite product of real numbers and study the convergence properties of such products. Finally we draw some parallels between the convergence of infinite series and that of infinite products.

In order to make the notion of an infinite product precise, we begin by specifying what we mean by arbitrary finite products.

Definition. Let a_n be an arbitrary sequence of real numbers. We define the notation $\prod\limits_{n=1}^{k} a_n$ for each $k \in \mathbf{N}$ inductively by

(i) $\displaystyle\prod_{n=1}^{1} a_n = a_1$;

(ii) $\displaystyle\prod_{n=1}^{k} a_n = \left(\prod_{n=1}^{k-1} a_n \right) \times a_k$.

Discussion. The purpose of this definition is to provide a finite foundation on which we can build our edifice. The key fact which can be established is that finite products obey a generalized commutative and associative law. This law states that for any permutation, σ of the positive integers $n \in \{1, 2, \ldots, k\}$ we have

$$\prod_{n=1}^{k} a_n = \prod_{n=1}^{k} a_{\sigma(n)}.$$

The reader will be asked to establish this fact as Exercise 1 and we shall feel free to use it throughout the sequel. In essence, what it means is that so far as finite products are concerned, the order in which the terms are multiplied together is irrelevant to the answer. □

Definition. Let $\{a_n\}$ be a sequence of real numbers none of which is 0. The symbol $\displaystyle\prod_{i=1}^{\infty} a_i$ is called an **infinite product.** The term a_n is called the n**th factor** of the infinite product. Associated with the infinite product is the **sequence of partial products,** $\{P_n\}$, defined by $P_n = \displaystyle\prod_{i=1}^{n} a_i$.

Discussion. This definition is very similar to that for an infinite series except that we do not allow any term, a_n, to be zero. The reason is pretty obvious, a product in which one term is 0 will end up as 0 and this triviality is to be avoided.

As with infinite series, $\displaystyle\prod_{i=1}^{\infty} a_i$ is a formal symbol to which we must assign a suitable meaning. For series, this was accomplished by treating the pair $(\{a_n\}, \{s_n\})$ as the infinite series and then creating the infinite series notation, $\displaystyle\sum_{n=1}^{\infty} a_n$. In this way, infinite series were defined completely in terms of well-known concepts, namely, sequences. For products, we have the same problem. Formally, an infinite product should be, and is, the pair, $(\{a_n\}, \{P_n\})$. However, given the previous experience with series, we start directly from the symbol, $\displaystyle\prod_{i=1}^{\infty} a_i$, and then immediately associate the sequence of partial products. It is this sequence, the sequence of partial products, which we will use in obtaining all the theory. □

Definition. The infinite product $\displaystyle\prod_{i=1}^{\infty} a_i$ is said to **converge** to a real number P if $\displaystyle\lim_{n \to \infty} P_n = P$. If the sequence $\{P_n\}$ is divergent, we say that the infinite product **diverges.** If $\displaystyle\lim_{n \to \infty} P_n = 0$, we say that the infinite product **diverges to zero.**

Discussion. This definition is also similar to the analogous definition for series. However, there is a significant difference. If $a_k = 0$ was permitted, then it would follow that $P_n = 0$ for all $n > k$, and consequently, the sequence $\{P_n\}$ is eventually 0 whence the limit is 0. This triviality is ruled out, since we have assumed that none of the terms is 0. In consequence, all the terms of $\{P_n\}$ are different from 0. One might wonder why we have characterized the situation when $P_n \to 0$ as diverging to 0, rather than converging to 0. This will be clear, once we establish the connection between the convergence of an infinite series and of an infinite product, and demonstrate that whenever a product converges, (diverges, in particular, diverges to 0) the corresponding infinite series also must converge (diverge). $\square$

We begin by establishing a form of the Cauchy criterion for the convergence of the infinite product $\prod\limits_{i=1}^{\infty} a_i$, which is similar to Theorem 7.1.3.

Theorem 7.5.1 (Cauchy Criterion for Infinite Products). The infinite product $\prod\limits_{i=1}^{\infty} a_i$ converges if and only if given $\epsilon > 0$, there exists $N \in \mathbf{N}$ such that

$$\left| \frac{P_m}{P_n} - 1 \right| < \epsilon \quad \text{whenever} \quad m, n \geqslant N.$$

Proof. For necessity, we suppose the infinite product converges and let $P \neq 0$ be the product. Let $\epsilon > 0$. There exists N_1 such that $|P_n| > \dfrac{|P|}{2}$ for $n > N_1$ (**WHY?**). Also, we can find N_2 such that for $m, n > N_2$, we have $|P_m - P_n| < \dfrac{\epsilon |P|}{2}$. If $N = \max\{N_1, N_2\}$, on dividing by P_n, we conclude $\left| \dfrac{P_m}{P_n} - 1 \right| < \dfrac{\epsilon |P|}{2 |P_n|} < \epsilon$.

For sufficiency, there exists N_1 satisfying $\left| \dfrac{P_n}{P_{N_1}} - 1 \right| < \dfrac{1}{2}$ whenever $n \geqslant N_1$, or equivalently, $\dfrac{1}{2} < \left| \dfrac{P_n}{P_{N_1}} \right| < \dfrac{3}{2}$. From this it follows the sequence $\{P_n\}$ is bounded by the numbers $\dfrac{1}{2}| P_{N_1} |$ and $\dfrac{3}{2} |P_{N_1}|$. We now establish $\{P_n\}$ is convergent by proving it is a Cauchy sequence. If $\epsilon > 0$ is given, by hypothesis, there exists N_2 such that $\left| \dfrac{P_m}{P_n} - 1 \right| < \dfrac{2\epsilon}{3 |P_{N_1}|}$ whenever $n, m > N_2$. Finally, if $n > N = \max\{N_1, N_2\}$, then it follows

$$|P_m - P_n| = |P_n| \left| \frac{P_m}{P_n} - 1 \right| < \frac{3}{2} |P_{N_1}| \frac{2\epsilon}{3 |P_{N_1}|} = \epsilon$$

so that the sequence $\{P_n\}$ is a Cauchy sequence. Hence, it converges to a limit, which must be nonzero, whence the product also converges. $\square$

Discussion. The reader may wonder why we are claiming this is a Cauchy criterion. For series, the Cauchy criterion asserts

$$|s_n - s_m| < \epsilon$$

whenever n, m exceed a suitably chosen N. This has a substantially different appearance from the present criterion. However, let us put the criterion for series into words. It asserts that 'once n, m exceed N, the difference between s_n and s_m must be arbitrarily close to the the additive identity, 0'. If this idea is revised to account for the fact that P_n is a product, instead of a sum, then the revised criterion should read 'once n, m exceed N, the quotient of $\dfrac{P_n}{P_m}$ must be arbitrarily close to the the multiplicative identity, 1', or formally

$$\left| \frac{P_n}{P_m} - 1 \right| < \epsilon$$

whenever $n, m > N$, which is exactly the formulation given.

Theorems of this nature are extremely useful, if we are interested only in the convergence or divergence of a product, without caring for the actual value of the product itself. Moreover, this criterion is simple to apply. While the standard version of the Cauchy criterion for sequences must apply to the sequence, $\{P_n\}$, it is apparent that when dealing with two huge products, their difference will generally be hard to simplify, whereas the quotient may simplify easily. This is the practical advantage of the revised criterion.

The statement is an 'if and only if' condition, so we have proved both the necessity and sufficiency of the condition. Several well-known properties of sequences are used in the proof. The fact that $P \neq 0$ is vital to the proof. The sufficiency part used the Cauchy criteria for convergence of a sequence, which in turn depends on the Completeness Axiom for real numbers for its truth. □

Corollary. If $\displaystyle\prod_{i=1}^{\infty} a_i$ converges, then the sequence $\{a_n\}$ converges to 1.

Proof. Take $m = n + 1$ in Theorem 7.5.1. □

Discussion. This is similar to Theorem 7.1.2 for infinite series. In view of this corollary, if we write $a_n = 1 + u_n$, it follows that if the product $\displaystyle\prod_{i=1}^{\infty} a_i$ converges, then $u_n \to 0$. Since this resembles Theorem 7.1.3, it is customary to express the infinite product $\displaystyle\prod_{i=1}^{\infty} a_i$ as $\displaystyle\prod_{i=1}^{\infty}(1 + u_i)$, so that if $\displaystyle\prod_{i=1}^{\infty}(1 + u_i)$ converges, then u_n converges to 0. □

EXAMPLE 1 _____

Discuss the convergence properties of $\displaystyle\prod_{n=1}^{\infty} \left[1 - \frac{1}{(n + 1)^2} \right]$.

Solution. A direct computation shows

$$P_n = \left[1 - \frac{1}{2^2}\right]\left[1 - \frac{1}{3^2}\right] \cdots \left[1 - \frac{1}{(n+1)^2}\right]$$

$$= \frac{1 \cdot 3}{2^2}\, \frac{2 \cdot 4}{3^3} \cdots \frac{n(n+2)}{(n+1)^2}$$

$$= \frac{(n+2)}{2(n+1)}.$$

Thus, P_n converges to $\frac{1}{2}$, and so, the infinite product converges to $\frac{1}{2}$. □

Discussion. This is a straightforward application of the definition. However, the simplification of the expression for P_n needs some skill in algebra. □

Our next aim is to draw conclusions about the convergence or divergence of the infinite product $\prod_{i=1}^{\infty}(1 + u_i)$ from that of the infinite series $\sum u_n$. To study this parallelism, we need a few inequalities connecting products and sums of numbers.

Theorem 7.5.2 (Weierstrass's Inequalities). If $0 \leqslant u_n < 1$,

$$\prod_{i=1}^{n}(1 + u_i) > 1 + \sum_{i=1}^{n} u_i, \tag{1}$$

$$\prod_{i=1}^{n}(1 - u_i) > 1 - \sum_{i=1}^{n} u_i. \tag{2}$$

If in addition, $\sum_{i=1}^{n} u_i < 1$,

$$\prod_{i=1}^{n}(1 + u_i) < \frac{1}{\left[1 - \sum_{i=1}^{n} u_i\right]}, \tag{3}$$

$$\prod_{i=1}^{n}(1 - u_i) < \frac{1}{\left[1 + \sum_{i=1}^{n} u_i\right]}. \tag{4}$$

Proof. The proofs are straightforward applications of induction and are left as Exercise 3. □

We now consider infinite products, all of whose terms are greater or equal to 1. If we write the terms of the product as $(1 + u_n)$, then the condition amounts to asserting $u_n \geqslant 0$. In this case, the product behaves much like infinite series of positive terms, as the next theorem reveals.

Theorem 7.5.3. If $u_n \geqslant 0$, the infinite product $\prod_{i=1}^{\infty}(1 + u_i)$ converges or diverges exactly as the infinite series $\sum_{n=1}^{\infty} u_n$ converges or diverges.

Proof. Let $\sum u_n$ converge. There exists N such that $L = \sum_{N+1}^{\infty} u_n < 1$ (**WHY?**). Since $\{P_n\}$ is monotonically increasing, we have only to show it is bounded, to establish convergence. Now, for $n > N$,

$$\frac{P_n}{P_N} = \prod_{N+1}^{n}(1 + u_n)$$

$$< \frac{1}{\left[1 - \sum_{N+1}^{n} u_n\right]}$$

$$= \frac{1}{1 - L}.$$

Hence, $P_n < \dfrac{P_N}{1 - L}$ which is fixed, and the fact that $\{P_n\}$ is bounded follows.

If on the other hand, $\sum u_n$ diverges, given an arbitrary K, there exists M such that $\sum_1^N u_n > K - 1$ whenever $N > M$. Thus,

$$P_n > 1 + \sum_1^N u_n > K,$$

proving that the product diverges. $\qquad\square$

Corollary. If $u_n \geqslant 0$, then the infinite product $\prod_{i=1}^{\infty}(1 - u_i)$ converges or diverges with $\sum u_n$.

Discussion. Theorem 7.5.3 and its corollary are remarkable. They bring forth the intimate connection between infinite series and infinite products. If we rewrite the nth factor of the infinite product as $(1 + u_n)$, $u_n \geqslant 0$, we only have to test the convergence or divergence of the infinite series $\sum u_n$. The utility of this technique is obvious.

Consider the infinite product $\prod_{n=1}^{\infty}\left\{\dfrac{n}{n+1}\right\}$. The corresponding partial product is $P_n = \dfrac{1}{n+1}$, which has limit 0. Since $\dfrac{n}{n+1} = 1 - \dfrac{1}{n+1}$, the infinite series associated with this product is obviously $\sum \dfrac{1}{n+1}$ which diverges. This is the reason why, in the definition of convergence, a product diverges to 0, rather than converges to 0. In essence, 0 plays the role of $-\infty$ for products. If one recalls what one knows about logarithms, this may seem even more natural.

Finally, in order to apply these theorems, all the terms of the product must be greater than or equal to 1. □

Definition. The infinite product $\prod_{n=1}^{\infty} (1 + u_n)$, where u_n may be of either sign, is said to be **absolutely convergent** if the product $\prod_{n=1}^{\infty}(1 + |u_n|)$ is convergent. The product $\prod_{n=1}^{\infty}(1 + u_n)$ is **conditionally convergent** if $\prod_{n=1}^{\infty}(1 + u_n)$ converges, but $\prod_{n=1}^{\infty}(1 + |u_n|)$ diverges.

Theorem 7.5.4. Every absolutely convergent infinite product is convergent, but not conversely.

Proof. Use the inequality

$$\left| \prod_{i=1}^{i=p} (1 + u_{n+i}) - 1 \right| \leq \left| \prod_{i=1}^{i=p} (1 + |u_{n+i}|) - 1 \right|$$

to establish that absolute convergence implies convergence. We leave the reader to construct an example of a convergent product that does not converge absolutely. □

Corollary. The product $\prod_{n=1}^{\infty}(1 + u_n)$ converges absolutely if the corresponding infinite series $\sum_{n=1}^{\infty} u_n$ converges absolutely.

EXERCISES

1. Show that the generalized commutative and associative law holds for finite products of real numbers.
2. Supply an independent proof of corollary to Theorem 7.5.1.
3. Prove Weierstrass's inequalities (1) through (4).
4. Prove corollary under Theorem 7.5.2.
5. Complete the proof of Theorem 7.5.3 as well as its corollary.
6. Discuss the convergence or divergence of the following infinite products:

   (a) $\prod_{n=1}^{\infty} \left[1 + \dfrac{1}{n^p} \right]$;

   (b) $\prod_{n=1}^{\infty} \left[1 - \dfrac{1}{n^p} \right]$;

   (c) $\prod_{n=1}^{\infty} \left[1 - \dfrac{(-1)^{n-1}}{\sqrt{n}} \right]$;

(d) $\displaystyle\prod_{n=1}^{\infty}\left\{\left[1+\dfrac{1}{n}\right]e^{-\frac{1}{n}}\right\}$;

(e) $\displaystyle\prod_{n=1}^{\infty}n^{1/n}$;

(f) $\displaystyle\prod_{n=1}^{\infty}n^{1/n+k}$;

(g) $\left[1+\dfrac{1}{\sqrt{2}}\right]\left[1-\dfrac{1}{\sqrt{3}}\right]\left[1+\dfrac{1}{\sqrt{4}}\right]\left[1-\dfrac{1}{\sqrt{5}}\right]\cdots$;

(h) $\left[1-\dfrac{9}{3\cdot5}\right]\left[1-\dfrac{10}{4\cdot6}\right]\left[1-\dfrac{11}{5\cdot7}\right]\left[1-\dfrac{12}{6\cdot8}\right]\cdots$;

(i) $\left[1+\dfrac{1}{\sqrt{2}}\right]\left[1+\dfrac{1}{2}+\dfrac{1}{\sqrt{2}}\right]\left[1+\dfrac{1}{\sqrt{3}}\right]\left[1+\dfrac{1}{3}+\dfrac{1}{\sqrt{3}}\right]\cdots$;

(j) $\displaystyle\prod_{n=1}^{\infty}\left[\dfrac{x+n}{y+n}\right]$, $\quad 0<x<y$.

7. Given $a_1=1$, and for $n\geqslant1$, $a_n=n(a_{n-1}+1)$, show the product $\displaystyle\prod_{n=1}^{\infty}\left[1+\dfrac{1}{a_n}\right]$ converges to e.

8. Show that the product $\displaystyle\prod_{n=1}^{\infty}(1+u_n)$ converges absolutely or conditionally according as the infinite series $\displaystyle\sum_{n=1}^{\infty}\ln(1+u_n)$ converges absolutely or conditionally. If P is the value of the product, the sum of the infinite series is e^P.

9. Discuss the commutative and associative properties of an infinite product. Show a convergent infinite product will converge to the same number for every rearrangement of the factor if and only if the product converges absolutely. [HINT: Consider the series formed by logarithms of the terms.]

10. Prove if $\displaystyle\sum_{n=1}^{\infty}a_n^2$ converges, then the product $\displaystyle\prod_{n=1}^{\infty}(1+a_n)$:

    (a) converges if $\displaystyle\sum_{n=1}^{\infty}a_n$ converges;

    (b) diverges to $+\infty$ if $\displaystyle\sum_{n=1}^{\infty}a_n$ diverges to $+\infty$;

    (c) diverges to 0 if $\displaystyle\sum_{n=1}^{\infty}a_n$ diverges to $-\infty$;

    Is it possible for the product to converge, when both $\sum a_n$ and $\sum a_n^2$ diverge?

11. Discuss the absolute convergence of the product $\displaystyle\prod_{n=1}^{\infty}\left[1+\dfrac{\sin nx}{n^p}\right]$ for various values of p. What happens when $p=\dfrac{1}{2}$?

12. If $p_n=\dfrac{(n+a_1)(n+a_2)\cdots(n+a_n)}{(n+b_1)(n+b_2)\cdots(n+b_n)}$ and $\lambda=\displaystyle\sum_{i=1}^{n}(a_i-b_i)$, where all the b's are nonnegative, prove that the product, $\displaystyle\prod_{n=1}^{\infty}p_n$ converges absolutely when $\lambda=0$. What happens when $\lambda>0$ and $\lambda<0$?

13. Give an example where

   (a) $\prod_{i=1}^{\infty}(1 + u_i)$ converges, but $\sum u_n$ diverges;

   (b) $\prod_{i=1}^{\infty}(1 + u_i)$ diverges, but $\sum u_n$ converges.

14. Show every infinite product can be expressed as a suitable infinite series, and vice versa. In particular, the series $\sum \dfrac{1}{n(n+1)}$ is equivalent to the product $\dfrac{1}{2} \prod_{n=2}^{\infty} \left[1 + \dfrac{1}{n^2 - 1} \right]$.

15. Find the values of the following products by establishing the equivalence with the corresponding series:

   (a) $\displaystyle\prod_{n=2}^{\infty} \left[1 + \dfrac{1}{2^n - 2} \right] = 2 \sum_{n=1}^{\infty} 2^{-n}$;

   (b) $\displaystyle\prod_{n=2}^{\infty} \left[1 + \dfrac{1}{n^2 - 1} \right] = 2 \sum_{n=1}^{\infty} \dfrac{1}{n(n+1)}$.

16. If $s > 1$, consider the infinite product $\displaystyle\prod_{n=1}^{\infty} \dfrac{1}{1 - p_n^{-s}}$, where p_n is the nth prime number. Prove that the product converges absolutely. [NOTE: The product is the classical **Riemann zeta function** $\zeta(s) = \displaystyle\sum_{n=1}^{\infty} \dfrac{1}{n^s}$.]

17. If $I_n = \displaystyle\int_0^{\pi/2} \sin^n x\, dx$, $(n \geqslant 0)$, prove the following:

   (a) $I_{n+1} = \dfrac{n}{n + 1} I_{n-1}$ $(n \geqslant 1)$;

   (b) $1 \leqslant \dfrac{I_n}{I_{n+1}} < \left[1 + \dfrac{1}{n} \right]$ $(n \geqslant 1)$;

   (c) for $k \in \mathbf{N}$,

$$I_{2k+1} = \frac{2 \cdot 4 \cdot \ \cdots \ \cdot (2k-2) \cdot (2k)}{3 \cdot 5 \cdot \ \cdots \ \cdot (2k+1) \cdot (2k+1)},$$

$$I_{2k} = \frac{\pi}{2} \frac{1 \cdot 3 \cdot \ \cdots \ \cdot (2k-3) \cdot (2k-1)}{2 \cdot 4 \cdot \ \cdots \ \cdot (2k-2) \cdot (2k)};$$

   (d) $\dfrac{\pi}{2} \cdot \dfrac{I_{2k+1}}{I_{2k}} = \displaystyle\prod_{n=1}^{k} \dfrac{4n^2}{4n^2 - 1}$.

   Hence obtain **Wallis product**:

$$\frac{\pi}{2} = \lim_{k \to \infty} \left[\frac{2}{1} \right]^2 \left[\frac{4}{3} \right]^2 \cdots \left[\frac{2k}{2k-1} \right]^2 \frac{1}{2k+1}.$$

   Also show that $\sqrt{\pi} = \displaystyle\lim_{k \to \infty} \prod_{n=1}^{\infty} \dfrac{2n}{2n-1}$.

Chapter 8

Sequences of Functions

In the previous chapter, we studied the notion of the convergence of an infinite series whose terms are real numbers, and discussed the concept of the 'sum' of an infinite series of constant terms. In this chapter, we shall see that we can also consider infinite sequences and series whose terms are not mere constants, but real-valued functions defined on certain subsets of **R**. Thus, we shall study the behavior of a sequence $\{f_n\}$ or an infinite series $\sum f_n$ where the f_n's are functions defined on suitable subsets of real numbers. We shall discuss two types of convergence for sequences of functions, namely, 'pointwise convergence' and 'uniform convergence', respectively. Pointwise convergence is a natural extension of previous convergence concepts. But as we shall see, the pointwise limit function corresponding to a sequence of functions does not, in general, inherit the 'nice' properties of the individual functions comprising the sequence. We would like the limit function to share any nice properties common to the functions in the sequence, such as continuity, differentiability, and integrability. To achieve this end, pointwise convergence is not the answer and we are led instead to the notion of uniform convergence of a sequence of functions. We shall study both these properties in detail, and see how uniform convergence of sequences of functions guarantees that all the nice properties possessed by the individual members are also shared by the limit function. In the end, we shall see that in the presence of uniform convergence, certain limiting operations can be interchanged freely without affecting any of the limit properties. The chapter concludes with some consequences of uniform convergence.

8.1 POINTWISE CONVERGENCE OF A SEQUENCE OF FUNCTIONS

In Chapter 1, a thorough study of the convergence of sequences, $\{a_n\}$, of real numbers was presented. Such sequences, whose members are real numbers will be referred to as **sequences of constant terms** and it is essential that the reader be totally familiar with all the theory of such sequences prior to attempting this chapter.

Definition. A **sequence of functions defined on** A is a function f, having domain $\mathbf{N}$ and whose range is a subset of the collection of all functions having domain A and range a subset of $\mathbf{R}$. If f is a sequence of functions on A, we will denote $f(n)$ by f_n and denote the sequence itself by $\{f_n\}$.

Discussion. The definition of a sequence of functions as a function having domain $\mathbf{N}$ and range in the collection of functions from A into $\mathbf{R}$ is the formal concept. However, the focus of the concept is in the denotation of these sequences, $\{f_n\}$, which emphasizes the nature of the sequence as a collection of functions ordered by $\mathbf{N}$. Thus, each **term** of the sequence is a function having domain A and range a subset of $\mathbf{R}$.

As the reader may have guessed, our intention in discussing the convergence of such sequences is to build on previous concepts and knowledge. Thus, if we now fix x such that $x \in A$, this creates a sequence of constant terms, $\{f_n(x)\}$. Since $\{f_n(x)\}$ is a sequence of real numbers, we are in a position to apply all of our previously developed theories to the present task.

It should also be clear why we require the various functions, f_n, to have a common domain, A. Were this not the case, for a particular k, $x \in A$ might fail to be in the domain of f_k, whence some terms of the sequence, $\{f_n(x)\}$, would fail to exist. This would create needless difficulties and for this reason we have given a definition which avoids the problem. Thus, we stress that a sequence of functions defined on A refers to a collection of functions which all share the same domain, namely, A. □

Definition. The sequence $\{f_n\}$ of functions defined on $A \subseteq \mathbf{R}$ is said to **converge pointwise** on A, provided there exists a function f having domain A and for each $x \in A$ and every $\epsilon > 0$ there exists an $N(x) \in \mathbf{N}$ such that

$$|f_n(x) - f(x)| < \epsilon$$

whenever $n > N(x)$. In case a function, f, exists with the required properties, we say f is the **pointwise limit** of the sequence $\{f_n\}$ of functions on the set A, and we write $f_n \to f$ **(pointwise)** on A.

Discussion. The set A is a common domain for all the functions f_n in the sequence and each point x in this common domain, A, manufactures a sequence, $\{f_n(x)\}$, of constant terms. If for each $x \in A$ this sequence is a convergent sequence of real numbers in the usual sense, then a unique limit exists and it makes sense to call this limit, $f(x)$. Indeed, the function, f, whose existence is asserted in the definition is completely defined by the equation

$$f(x) = \lim_{n \to \infty} f_n(x).$$

This equation captures the essence of pointwise convergence, since it requires convergence of each of the individual sequences, $\{f_n(x)\}$, x fixed, and defines the limit function in terms of the pointwise limit at x. We use $N(x)$, rather than the simpler $N \in \mathbf{N}$, to emphasize that the value which will enable the definition to be satisfied depends on the point x. Since this value also depends on the given ϵ, we should have used $N(x,\epsilon)$. We refrained since all readers are well aware of the dependence of $N(x)$ on ϵ.

If the definition of pointwise convergence for a sequence of functions is compared with the definition of convergence for a sequence of constants, the similarities are striking. Specifically,

(i) convergent sequences of constants require the existence of a real number, L; convergent sequences of functions require the existence of a function, f, on the common domain A;

(ii) convergent sequences of constants require that to each positive ϵ there exists $N \in \mathbf{N}$; convergent sequences of functions require that to each positive ϵ and each $x \in A$ there exists $N(x) \in \mathbf{N}$;

(iii) convergent sequences of constants require that

$$|a_n - L| < \epsilon \text{ whenever } n > N,$$

convergent sequences of functions require that

$$|f_n(x) - f(x)| < \epsilon \text{ whenever } n > N(x).$$

The first key difference relates to the fact that $N(x)$ depends on the value of x as well as on the value of ϵ. The second difference is that convergence of the sequence $\{f_n(x)\}$ must be validated for each x in A. This is why the latter type of convergence is said to be pointwise on A. $\square$

We give one essential theorem and then illustrate pointwise convergence concept by means of some concrete examples.

Theorem 8.1.1. Let $\{f_n\}$ be a sequence of functions on A which converges pointwise on A. Then the pointwise limit, f, of the sequence is unique.

Proof. The proof of this theorem is implicit in the discussion above. We leave the generation of the formal details to the reader as Exercise 1. $\square$

EXAMPLE 1 _____

Discuss the pointwise convergence of the sequence of functions, $\{f_n\}$, where $f_n : (0, 1] \rightarrow \mathbf{R}$ is defined by

$$f_n(x) = \frac{1}{nx}, \quad x \in (0, 1], \ n \in \mathbf{N}.$$

Solution. Fix $\epsilon > 0$ and $x_0 \in (0, 1]$. Now, $f_n(x_0) = \dfrac{1}{nx_0}$, whence choose $N(x_0)$ such that $N(x_0) > \dfrac{1}{\epsilon x_0}$. It follows that if $n > N(x_0)$, then

$$|f_n(x_0) - 0| = \left| \frac{1}{nx_0} - 0 \right| < \left| \frac{1}{N(x_0)x_0} \right|$$

$$\leqslant \left| \frac{\epsilon x_0}{x_0} \right| = \epsilon.$$

Thus $\lim_{n\to\infty} f_n(x_0) = 0$ for each $x_0 \in (0, 1]$. We conclude that the sequence $\{f_n\}$ converges pointwise to the function, f, defined by $f(x) = 0$ for all $x \in (0, 1]$. $\square$

Discussion. The reader should study this argument from the point of view of examining the difficulty of constructing an argument which will deal with all of the various sequences which can arise for the different values of $x \in (0, 1]$. The difficulty is eliminated by picking an arbitrary $x_0 \in (0, 1]$, and then proceeding with the argument while keeping x_0 fixed. It is critical that the reader understand this technique, since all arguments in this chapter will employ it in some way. It should not be totally unfamiliar to the reader, since similar arguments were used when dealing with uniform continuity, and the reader may choose to review some of those arguments as an aid in understanding these.

The crucial fact used above is that no matter how close we take x_0 to 0, $\lim_{n\to\infty} \dfrac{1}{nx_0} = 0$. This is because x_0 is fixed, while n is increasing without bound. The existence of a unique limit for each x_0 permits the definition of f in terms of this limit. Thus, we set $f(x) = 0$ on $(0, 1]$ and write $f_n \to 0$ pointwise on $(0, 1]$. It is to be clearly understood that the 0 appearing on the right side of the arrow is not the number 0, but is to be interpreted as the function having domain $(0, 1]$ and satisfying $0(x) = 0$ for all $x \in (0, 1]$.

In Figure 8.1.1 we present the graphs of several of the f_n's. We have fixed x_0 and graphed the line $x = x_0$. Notice that the sequence $\{f_n(x_0)\}$ can be pictured as a

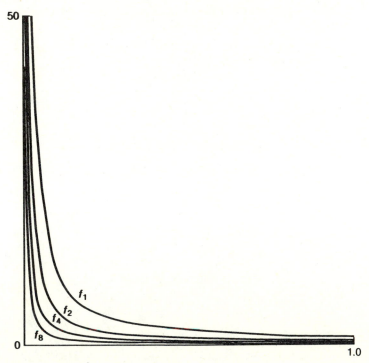

Figure 8.1.1 $f_n(x) = \dfrac{1}{nx}$ $(n = 1, 2, 3, 4, 8)$.

sequence of real numbers lying on the line determined by $x = x_0$. The individual members of the sequence are the points of intersection between the graph of particular f_n's and the graph of $x = x_0$. In this example, these points on the line $x = x_0$ clearly converge to a point on the x-axis. The reader may find that looking at pointwise convergence from this geometric perspective increases his insight into the topic. □

EXAMPLE 2

Discuss the pointwise convergence of the sequence of functions, $\{f_n\}$, where $f_n: [0, 1] \rightarrow \mathbf{R}$ is defined by

$$f_n(x) = \frac{x}{n}, \quad x \in [0, 1], \, n \in \mathbf{N}.$$

Solution. Fix $\epsilon > 0$ and $x_0 \in [0, 1]$. In this case $f_n(x_0) = \dfrac{x_0}{n}$, whence set $N(x_0) = \dfrac{1}{\epsilon}$. It follows that if $n > N(x_0)$, then

$$|f_n(x_0) - 0| = \left| \frac{x_0}{n} - 0 \right| = \left| \frac{x_0}{N(x_0)} \right|$$

$$\leqslant \left| \frac{1}{N(x_0)} \right| = \epsilon. \quad \textbf{(WHY?)}$$

Once again $\lim_{n \to \infty} f_n(x_0) = 0$ for each $x_0 \in [0, 1]$. We conclude that the sequence $\{f_n\}$ converges pointwise to the function, f, defined by $f(x) = 0$ for all $x \in [0, 1]$. □

Discussion. In this example, there is an apparent lack of dependence of $N(x)$ on the choice of x. It is important that the reader understand that this results from the fact that x occurs in the numerator of $f_n(x) = \dfrac{x}{n}$ and that $0 \leqslant x \leqslant 1$. For this reason, it is natural to make use of the inequality, $f_n(x) \leqslant \dfrac{1}{n}$, which eliminates the dependence on x. However, for a particular x, say $x = \dfrac{1}{2}$, this results in a choice of $N(x)$ which is larger than necessary. Lastly, the reader should compare the computations in Example 2 with those in Example 1 to see if it is possible to eliminate the dependence of $N(x)$, in Example 1, on x. □

EXAMPLE 3

Discuss the pointwise convergence of the sequence, $\{f_n\}$, where $f_n: [0, 1] \rightarrow \mathbf{R}$ is defined by $f_n(x) = x^n$, $x \in [0, 1]$, $n \in \mathbf{N}$.

Solution. If $x = 1$, then for each n, we have $f_n(1) = 1^n = 1$, so the sequence, $\{f_n(1)\}$, has all its terms equal to 1, and hence the limit is also 1. On the other hand, if $0 \leqslant x < 1$, we know that $f_n(x) = x^n$ which has limit 0 **(WHY?)**. Hence, for each $x < 1$, the sequence $\{f_n(x)\}$ converges to 0. Thus, in either case, we have that $\{f_n(x)\}$ is a convergent sequence of real numbers. We therefore conclude that the sequence, $\{f_n\}$, converges pointwise to the function f defined on $[0, 1]$ by

$$f(x) \;=\; \begin{cases} 1, & \text{if } 0 \leqslant x < 1 \\ 0, & \text{if } x = 1. \end{cases}$$

$\square$

Discussion. The most striking feature of this example is that each of the functions, f_n, is continuous, indeed, uniformly continuous, the sequence of functions converges pointwise to a limit, and yet the limit function is not continuous! It is one of the simplest examples demonstrating that pointwise convergence is the wrong tool for ensuring that a nice property, shared by all members of a sequence of functions, should be shared by the limit function, as well. Figure 8.1.2 presents the geometry of this example and should permit the reader to see why this sequence results in a discontinuous limit.

The fact that the limit f is discontinuous is evident in the argument for the existence of the limit. Its presence is in the fact that two arguments must be presented. The first is for the case $x = 1$, and the second for the case $0 \leqslant x < 1$. For these two cases, the limits of $\{x^n\}$ were respectively, 1 and 0. Thus, the resulting pointwise limit function, f, takes the value 0 throughout the interval $[0, 1)$ while at $x = 1$, $f(1) = 1$.

The argument presented was not an $\epsilon - N(x)$ argument, but depended heavily on previously established facts, which are presumed to be well known. Nevertheless, it is

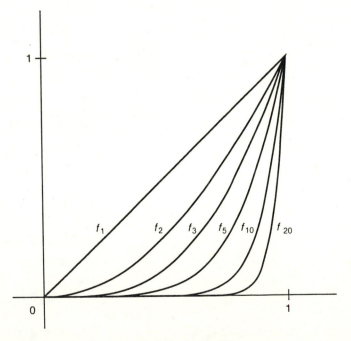

Figure 8.1.2 $f_n(x) = x^n$ $(n = 1, 2, 3, 5, 10, 20)$.

essential that the reader be able to write out $\epsilon - N(x)$ arguments, and we ask the reader to generate such an argument for this example in Exercise 2. $\square$

EXAMPLE 4

Discuss the pointwise convergence of the sequence $\{f_n\}$, where f_n is defined on **R** by

$$f_n(x) = \begin{cases} 1, & \text{if } -n \leqslant x \leqslant n \\ 0, & \text{otherwise.} \end{cases}$$

Solution. Define f on **R** by $f(x) = 1$ for all $x \in \mathbf{R}$. For any fixed x_0 and positive ϵ, let $N = N(x_0)$ be chosen such that $N > |x_0|$. If $n > N$, we have

$$|f_n(x_0) - f(x_0)| = |f_N(x_0) - 1| = |1 - 1| < \epsilon,$$

whence $\{f_n(x_0)\}$ converges to $f(x_0) = 1$. Thus, $f_n \to f$ pointwise on **R**. $\square$

Discussion. Note that f_N vanishes only outside $[-N, N]$ and takes the value 1 in that interval. Thus, the N manufactured in the above solution depends very much on the point x_0 in **R**. What we observe here intuitively is that as n gets larger, the functions, f_n, assume the value 1 over larger intervals, and so ultimately the pointwise limit becomes the function which is identically 1 on all of **R**.

Curiously enough, even though each f_n was a discontinuous function on **R**, the pointwise limit function is a continuous function, as shown in Figure 8.1.3. $\square$

EXAMPLE 5

Discuss the pointwise convergence of the sequence $f_n: [0, 1] \to \mathbf{R}$ defined by

$$f_n(x) = \begin{cases} n, & \text{if } x \in \left[0, \dfrac{1}{n}\right] \\ 0, & \text{otherwise.} \end{cases}$$

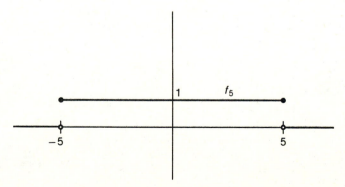

Figure 8.1.3 $f_n(x) = \begin{cases} 1, & -n \leqslant x \leqslant n \\ 0, & \text{otherwise} \end{cases} \quad (n = 5).$

Solution. Fix $x \in (0, 1]$. If $x = 0$, then $\{f_n(0)\}$ is a constant sequence consisting of 0's, and so converges. Thus, fix x such that $0 < x \leqslant 1$. Then there exists $N(x)$ such that $\dfrac{1}{N(x)} < x$. It is immediate that

$$f_{N(x)}(x) = f_{N(x)+1}(x) = \cdots = f_{N(x)+k}(x) = \cdots = 0 \quad (k \in \mathbf{N})$$

whence $\lim\limits_{n \to \infty} f_n(x) = 0$. Thus, for each $x \in [0, 1]$, $\{f_n(x)\}$ converges, hence $\{f_n\}$ converges pointwise to the function, f, which is identically 0 on $[0, 1]$. □

Discussion. Again we stress that the $N(x)$ which is chosen depends on the particular point x in $(0, 1]$. As a result, $f_k(x) = 0$ only for those subscripts, k, satisfying $x > \dfrac{1}{k}$.

An important feature of this example becomes evident if we compute $\int_0^1 f_n$ for each n. As the reader can check, the value of any of these integrals is 1, whereas the integral of the pointwise limit function is $\int_0^1 f = \int_0^1 0 = 0$. Consequently, we have the unpleasant situation that even though all limits exist,

$$\lim_{n \to \infty} \left(\int_0^1 f_n \right) \neq \int_0^1 (\lim_{n \to \infty} f_n),$$

where the limit on the right side refers to the pointwise limit. This example employs the canonical convergent sequence of integrable functions, for which it is impossible to interchange the order in which the limits are computed. That is, the limit of the integrals, as a convergent sequence of real numbers, is not equal to the integral of the limit function, as a real number.

The reader is urged to draw the graphs of the various f_n's and the limit function f on the same set of axes so as to more completely understand this example. □

Examples 3 and 5 illustrate major difficulties with the pointwise convergence concept. In the exercises there are additional examples where the pointwise limit fails to have some property which is shared by all the functions in the sequence. For this reason, we are forced to seek a more powerful notion of convergence for sequences of functions which will ensure that properties shared by all the members of a sequence will be shared by the limit function as well. This will be accomplished in section 8.2.

We close this section with a discussion of the negation of pointwise convergence.

Negation of the Definition of Pointwise Convergence

Let $\{f_n\}$ be a sequence of functions defined on A. Then $\{f_n\}$ **fails to converge (pointwise)** on A provided for every function, f having domain, A, there exists $x \in A$ and $\epsilon > 0$ such that for all $N \in \mathbf{N}$ there exists $n > N$ such that

$$|f_n(x) - f(x)| > \epsilon.$$

Discussion. We want to extract the essence of this negation. First consider that the negation requires that we examine every function f defined on A. Since if the limit of a given sequence exists, it is unique, a given convergent sequence of functions, $\{f_n\}$, can fail to converge to a given candidate, say, g, because g is not the unique limit function. Quite apparently, most candidate functions will not be the right limit function, and their failure will reflect this fact rather than the fact that the sequence doesn't converge. (To make this concrete, consider the sequence of Example 1, and the candidate limit function, g, on the interval $(0, 1]$ defined by $g(x) = 1$.) Thus, we want to make sure the failure to converge is due to the properties of $\{f_n\}$ and not due to a property of the candidate limit function.

Recall if the limit of the sequence of functions exists, then we have a sure fire method for finding the correct candidate for the limit, namely, the limit function is given by

$$f(x) = \lim_{n \to \infty} f_n(x).$$

From this we see the limit exists exactly if each of the sequences, $\{f_n(x)\}$, converges for each $x \in A$. Thus, the sequence, $\{f_n\}$, will fail to converge, exactly if we can find a particular $x \in A$ such that the sequence of real numbers, $\{f_n(x)\}$, fails to converge.

In Chapter 1, much effort was spent determining why a sequence of real numbers could fail to converge. Two reasons were found. First, the sequence was unbounded. Second the sequence oscillated. Thus, a sequence of functions will fail to converge pointwise on A, exactly if there is a particular $x \in A$ such that the sequence, $\{f_n(x)\}$, is either unbounded or oscillates. This is exactly what the above negation expresses. □

EXAMPLE 6 _____

Discuss the (pointwise) convergence properties of the sequence of functions defined on $[-1, 1]$ by

$$f_n(x) = \begin{cases} n, & \text{if } x \in \left[\dfrac{-1}{n}, \dfrac{1}{n} \right] \\ 0, & \text{otherwise.} \end{cases}$$

Solution. The reader can check, as shown in Example 5, that if $x \neq 0$, then $\lim_{n \to \infty} f_n(x) = 0$. However, $f_n(0) = n$, for every $n \in \mathbf{N}$, so that $\{f_n(0)\}$ is an unbounded sequence of real numbers and $\{f_n\}$ is not convergent on $[-1, 1]$ pointwise. □

Discussion. We have established lack of convergence by finding a divergent sequence of real numbers. We have not established the details as specified in the statement of negation above. The reader will be asked to do this as Exercise 4.

It is suggested that the reader carefully compare Examples 5 and 6. They employ very similar sequences, with rather different results. □

In previous chapters when a new notion of limiting process has been introduced, a number of standard questions have arisen. Basically, these questions related to how the limiting process behaved with respect to the standard arithmetic operations on the reals, or in those cases where the limiting process dealt with functions, the arithmetic of functions. Similar questions arise with respect to pointwise convergence of sequences of functions.

Consider then two sequences of functions, $\{f_n\}$ and $\{g_n\}$, which are defined on a common domain A. Clearly, we can create a new sequence of functions by employing one of the operations for combining functions, $\{f_n + g_n\}$, for example. Obviously, one would like to have some standard theorems which deal with these questions. The next theorem is one such. Because the proof is generally straightforward, it is left to the exercises. As well, in the exercises the reader will be asked to work out some of the theory.

Theorem 8.1.2. Let $\{f_n\}$ and $\{g_n\}$ be two sequences of functions defined and pointwise convergent on a common domain A. Show that $\{f_n \pm g_n\}$, $\{f_n \cdot g_n\}$, $\{|f_n|\}$ are pointwise convergent on A.

Proof.   Exercise 8. $\qquad\qquad\qquad\qquad\qquad\qquad\qquad\qquad\qquad\qquad\qquad\qquad$ $\square$

The reader should recall that bounded, monotone sequences have very nice properties, after all, we have invoked Theorem 1.3.1 with great frequency. As a result the reader may guess that bounded, monotone sequences of functions are also well behaved.

Theorem 8.1.3. Let $\{f_n\}$ be a sequence of functions on a common domain, A, and suppose that $f_n \le f_{n+1}$ for all $n \in \mathbf{N}$. If, for each $x \in A$, there exists $K_x \in \mathbf{R}$ such that $|f_n(x)| < K_x$, then $\{f_n\}$ converges pointwise on A.

Proof.   Exercise 15. $\qquad\qquad\qquad\qquad\qquad\qquad\qquad\qquad\qquad\qquad\qquad$ $\square$

EXERCISES

1. Write out the details of the proof of Theorem 8.1.1.

2. Give an $\epsilon - N(x)$ argument to establish the properties of the sequence of functions in Example 3.

3. Discuss the pointwise convergence of the following sequences $\{f_n\}$ of functions and illustrate graphically wherever possible:

(a) $f_n: (0, 1] \to \mathbf{R}$ defined by $f_n(x) = 1 - \dfrac{1}{nx}$;

(b) $f_n: [0, 1] \to \mathbf{R}$ defined by $f_n(x) = \dfrac{\sin nx}{\sqrt{n}}$;

(c) $f_n: [0, \pi] \to \mathbf{R}$ defined by $f_n(x) = (\sin x)^n$;

(d) $f_n: [0, \infty) \to \mathbf{R}$ defined by $f_n(x) = \dfrac{x}{n}$;

(e) $f_n: \mathbf{R} \to \mathbf{R}$ defined by $f_n(x) = \dfrac{nx}{1 + nx}$;

(f) $f_n: \mathbf{R} \to \mathbf{R}$ defined by $f_n(x) = \dfrac{nx}{1 + n^2 x^2}$;

(g) f_n: **R** $\rightarrow$ **R** defined by $f_n(x) = \dfrac{x^{2n}}{1 + x^{2n}}$;

(h) f_n: $[0, 1] \rightarrow$ **R** defined by $f_n(x) = n^2 x^n (1 - x)$;

(i) f_n: $(-1, 1) \rightarrow$ **R** defined by $f_n(x) = (1 - |x|)^n$;

(j) f_n: $[0, 1] \rightarrow$ **R** defined by

$$f_n(x) = \begin{cases} 1, & \text{if } x = \dfrac{p}{q}, \ (p, q) = 1 \text{ with } p + q = n \\ 0, & \text{otherwise;} \end{cases}$$

(k) f_n: $[0, \infty) \rightarrow$ **R** defined by $f_n(x) = \dfrac{xe^{-x/n}}{n}$;

(l) f_n: **R** $\rightarrow$ **R** defined by $f_n(x) = nxe^{-n^2x^2}$;

(m) χ_n: **R** $\rightarrow$ **R** defined by

$$\chi_n(x) = \begin{cases} 1, & x \in [-n, n] \\ 0, & |x| > n; \end{cases}$$

(The function χ_n is called the **characteristic function** of the closed interval, $[-n, n]$.)

(n) f_n: **R** $\rightarrow$ **R** defined by $f_n(x) = \dfrac{x^2 + nx}{n}$.

4. Give a detailed $\epsilon - N(x)$ argument showing that the sequence in Example 6 fails to converge on $[-1, 1]$.

5. Let $\{r_n\}$ be a sequence that contains each rational number in $[0,1]$ exactly once and let f_n: $[0, 1] \rightarrow$ **R** defined by

$$f_n(x) = \begin{cases} 0, & \text{if } x \text{ is irrational, or if } x = r_i, \ i > n \\ 1, & \text{if } x = r_i, \ i \leqslant n. \end{cases}$$

Discuss the pointwise convergence of the sequence $\{f_n\}$. For what values of x does the infinite series $\sum f_n(x)$ converge?

6. Give examples (different from the ones given in this section) in support of the following statements:

(a) each f_n is integrable, but the pointwise limit is not integrable;

(b) each f_n is bounded, but the pointwise limit is unbounded;

(c) each f_n is continuous on $[a, b]$ and differentiable on (a, b), and the pointwise limit is continuous on $[a, b]$ but not differentiable on (a, b);

(d) each f_n is uniformly continuous on A, but the pointwise limit is not uniformly continuous on A;

(e) $\displaystyle\int_a^b (\lim_{n \to \infty} f_n) \neq \lim_{n \to \infty} \int_a^b f_n$;

(f) $\lim f_n' \neq (\lim f_n)'$.

7. For each x in the domain A of a sequence $\{f_n\}$ of functions, the sequence $\{f_n(x)\}$ has an upper and lower limit point in **R*** $=$ **R** $\cup \{\infty\}$. Define $\overline{\lim} f_n$ to be the function defined by $\overline{\lim} f_n(x)$ and a similar definition for lower limits. Prove

(a) $\underline{\lim} f_n \leqslant \overline{\lim} f_n$;

(b) $-\underline{\lim} f_n = \overline{\lim} (-f_n)$;

(c) $\underline{\lim} f_n + \underline{\lim} g_n \leqslant \underline{\lim} (f_n + g_n)$.

What is the corresponding relation to that in (c) for upper limits? Prove it.

8. If $f_n \to f$ and $g_n \to g$ (pointwise on A), prove the following:
   (a) $f_n \pm g_n \to f \pm g$ (pointwise on A);
   (b) $f_n \cdot g_n \to f \cdot g$ (pointwise on A);
   (c) $|f_n| \to |f|$ (pointwise on A);
   (d) What can you say about $\dfrac{f_n}{g_n}$?

9. Give an example where $|f_n|$ converges pointwise, but f_n does not have a pointwise limit.

10. Obtain each of the following functions as a pointwise limit of a sequence of functions, each member of which is continuous and bounded (differentiable in the case of (c)):
   (a) $f(x) = x, \quad x \in \mathbf{R}$;
   (b) $f(x) = x^2, \quad x \in \mathbf{R}$;
   (c) $f(x) = |x|, \quad x \in [-1, 1]$;
   (d) $f(x) = \begin{cases} 0, & x \notin \mathbf{Q} \\ \dfrac{1}{q}, & x = \dfrac{p}{q}, \, p, q \in \mathbf{N}, \text{ relatively prime} \end{cases} \quad x \in [0, 1]$;
   (e) $f(x) = \begin{cases} x, & x \in \mathbf{Q} \\ 1 - x, & x \notin \mathbf{Q} \end{cases} \quad x \in [0, 1]$.

11. A sequence $\{f_n\}$ of functions is said to be **uniformly bounded** on a domain $D \subseteq \mathbf{R}$, provided there exists a positive number K such that $|f_n(x)| \leqslant K$ for each $n \in \mathbf{N}$ and for each $x \in D$. Determine whether each of the sequences in Example 3 is uniformly bounded.

12. Suppose $\{f_n\}$ is a sequence function which is uniformly bounded on D. What can be said about the limit function?

13. Give an example of a sequence of continuous functions that is not uniformly bounded, but converges to a bounded function.

14. Suppose $f_n \to f$ pointwise on A and $f_n, f\colon A \to B$. Further, suppose $g_n \to g$ pointwise on B. What can be said about $g \circ f$?

15. Prove Theorem 8.1.3.

16. Let $\{f_n\}$ satisfy the hypothesis of Theorem 8.1.3. Must the pointwise limit, f, be bounded above? Must the pointwise limit be bounded below? Must it be universally bounded?

17. State a Cauchy criterion for pointwise convergence of a sequence of functions. Prove that this criterion is equivalent to the original definition of pointwise convergence.

18. A sequence, $\{f_n\}$, defined on $[a, b]$ is said to converge **in the mean** to a function, f, provided
$$\lim_{n \to \infty} \left\{ \int_a^b [f_n(x) - f(x)]^2 \right\} = 0.$$

Which of the following functions converge in the mean?
   (a) $f_n\colon (0, 1] \to \mathbf{R}$ defined by $f_n(x) = 1 - \dfrac{1}{nx}$;
   (b) $f_n\colon [0, 1] \to \mathbf{R}$ defined by $f_n(x) = \dfrac{\sin nx}{\sqrt{n}}$;
   (c) $f_n\colon [0, \pi] \to \mathbf{R}$ defined by $f_n(x) = (\sin x)^n$;
   (d) $f_n\colon [0, 10] \to \mathbf{R}$ defined by $f_n(x) = \dfrac{x}{n}$;
   (e) $f_n\colon [0, 10] \to \mathbf{R}$ defined by $f_n(x) = \dfrac{nx}{1 + nx}$;

(f) $f_n: [0, 10] \rightarrow \mathbf{R}$ defined by $f_n(x) = \dfrac{nx}{1 + n^2x^2}$;

(g) $f_n: [0, 10] \rightarrow \mathbf{R}$ defined by $f_n(x) = \dfrac{x^{2n}}{1 + x^{2n}}$;

(h) $f_n: [0, 1] \rightarrow \mathbf{R}$ defined by $f_n(x) = n^2x^n(1 - x)$;

(i) $f_n: (-1, 1) \rightarrow \mathbf{R}$ defined by $f_n(x) = (1 - |x|)^n$;

(j) $f_n: [0, 8] \rightarrow \mathbf{R}$ defined by $f_n(x) = \dfrac{xe^{-x/n}}{n}$;

(k) $f_n: [0, 2] \rightarrow \mathbf{R}$ defined by $f_n(x) = nxe^{-n^2x^2}$;

(l) $f_n: \mathbf{R} \rightarrow \mathbf{R}$ defined by $f_n(x) = \dfrac{x^2 + nx}{n}$.

19. Give an example of a sequence of functions on $[0, 1]$ which converges in the mean to a function f, but converges pointwise to a different function, g.

20. Discuss and compare the pointwise and mean convergence of the following sequences of functions:

(a) $f_n(x) = \cos^n(x), \quad x \in [0, \pi]$;

(b) $f_n(x) = n^{3/2}xe^{-n^2x^2}, \quad x \in [-1, 1]$;

(c) $f_n(x) = \begin{cases} n, & \text{if } x \in \left[0, \dfrac{1}{n} \right] \\[4mm] 0, & \text{if } x \in [0, 1] \sim \left[0, \dfrac{1}{n} \right]. \end{cases}$

8.2 UNIFORM CONVERGENCE OF SEQUENCE OF FUNCTIONS

In the previous section, we studied the convergence of a sequence of functions by determining convergence at each point of the common domain. Thus, pointwise convergence could aptly be termed as a 'local property'. We also saw by means of several examples that this sort of convergence may destroy many pleasant properties possessed by all of the individual functions of the sequence. This defect will now be remedied by considering a new type of convergence, defined 'globally' on the entire domain under consideration and called uniform convergence over a set.

Recall that the sequence $\{f_n\}$ of functions converges pointwise to the function f provided for each x in the domain A, we have the relation: $\lim_{n \to \infty} f_n(x) = f(x)$. In other words, the necessary and sufficient condition for this to hold is that at each point, x, the constant sequence, $\{f_n(x)\}$, converges to the real number, $f(x)$, namely, given $\epsilon > 0$, at each point x, we can come up with an integer $N(x)$ (more precisely, $N(x, \epsilon)$), just to emphasize the fact that $N(x)$ depends on the ϵ given in advance, as well as the point x in question) such that for all $n > N(x)$, we have $|f_n(x) - f(x)| < \epsilon$. The important thing to note here, as was stressed in the last section, is that the integer $N(x)$ is a function of x as well as ϵ, and different points x in the domain may well yield different integers $N(x)$ satisfying this inequality.

It would be very nice, if instead of having to find an $N(x)$ for each x, one could find a single $N = N(\epsilon)$, depending on ϵ, which served the purpose 'uniformly' for all x in the domain. This is the property that we will insist on in generating the notion of uniform convergence. These observations lead to the following important definition.

Definition. A sequence $\{f_n\}$ of functions defined on a subset $A \subseteq \mathbf{R}$ is said to be **uniformly convergent on the set** A provided there exists a function, f, having domain A such that given $\epsilon > 0$ we can find an integer $N > 0$ such that

$$|f_n(x) - f(x)| < \epsilon, \quad \text{whenever} \quad n > N \text{ and for all } x \in A.$$

In the case where such a function exists, we will say that f is the **uniform limit of the sequence,** $\{f_n\}$**, on** A and write $f_n \to f$ **(uniformly)** on A.

Discussion. We want to explore the distinction between pointwise and uniform convergence very carefully:

  (i) pointwise convergent sequences of functions require the existence of a function, f, defined on A; uniformly convergent sequences of functions also require the existence of a function, f, on the common domain A;

  (ii) pointwise convergent sequences of functions require that to each positive ϵ and each $x \in A$ there exists $N(x) \in \mathbf{N}$; uniformly convergence sequences of functions require that to each positive ϵ, there exists an $N \in \mathbf{N}$, depending only on ϵ;

  (iii) pointwise convergent sequences of functions require that

$$|f_n(x) - f(x)| < \epsilon, \quad \text{whenever } n > N(x);$$

uniformly convergent sequences of functions require that

$$\text{for all } x \in A, \ |f_n(x) - f(x)| < \epsilon, \quad \text{whenever } n > N.$$

Examination of the three points of comparison reveals that the significant difference in the two concepts is completely related to the nature of $N(x)$ as opposed to N. $N(x)$ is permitted to depend on x; one for each x, whence pointwise. N, in the uniform case, must be independent of x, and must depend only on ϵ.

Within the definitions proper, this amounts to interchanging the order of quantification. Specifically, the 'pointwise' definition reads

'for each $\epsilon > 0$ and for each x, there exists $N(x)$.'

The 'uniform' definition reads

'for each $\epsilon > 0$, there exists $N \in \mathbf{N}$ such that for all x.'

The effect of interchanging the order of quantification in this manner is to eliminate the dependence of N on x. Thus, in the uniform case, once an ϵ has been given, one must search for an N which will force the inequality

$$|f_n(x) - f(x)| < \epsilon$$

to hold whenever $n > N$ and no matter what value of $x \in A$ is considered. There can be no exceptions!

As described, uniform convergence occurs in a 'global' way over an entire domain. Pointwise convergence occurs in a 'local' way, point by point throughout the domain. As a result, for some values of x, the rate of convergence can be arbitrarily slow, whereas for uniform convergence, there must be a minimum rate of convergence which holds globally over the whole domain.

It should be evident from the discussion above that a uniformly convergent sequence of functions will converge pointwise, as well. This fact, which we prove below, permits us to observe that if a sequence of functions converges uniformly, the natural candidate for the 'uniform' limit is none other than the 'pointwise-limit' function. In other words, the uniform limit, if it exists, cannot be different from the pointwise limit. □

Theorem 8.2.1. Let $\{f_n\}$ be a sequence of functions which converges uniformly on A. Then $\{f_n\}$ converges pointwise on A and the pointwise limit is the uniform limit.

Proof. Since $\{f_n\}$ converges uniformly on A, it has a limit on A, which we call f. Now let $\epsilon > 0$ be given, and fix $x_0 \in A$. By uniform convergence there exists $N \in \mathbf{N}$ such that for all $x \in A$, $|f_n(x) - f(x)| < \epsilon$ whenever $n > N$. This implies $|f_n(x_0) - f(x_0)| < \epsilon$ whenever $n > N$, whence $\{f_n(x_0)\}$ converges to $f(x_0)$. Since x_0 was arbitrary, $f_n \to f$ pointwise. Since the pointwise limit is unique, the uniform limit must also be unique, whence the uniform limit and the pointwise limit coincide. □

Discussion. All the details in the argument have been presented. The essence of the argument is in noticing that if N works for all the x's, it must work for each particular x. □

We illustrate the concept with a simple example.

EXAMPLE 1 _____

Show that the sequence of functions, $\{f_n\}$, where $f_n: [0,1] \to \mathbf{R}$ is defined by

$$f_n(x) = \frac{x}{n}, \quad x \in [0,1], \, n \in \mathbf{N}$$

is uniformly convergent on $[0,1]$.

Solution. Let f be the function which is identically 0 on $[0, 1]$. Fix $\epsilon > 0$ and set $N = \dfrac{1}{\epsilon}$. It follows that if $n > N$, then

$$|f_n(x) - 0| = \left| \frac{x}{n} - 0 \right| \leqslant \frac{1}{n} \leqslant \frac{1}{N} = \epsilon,$$

whence $f_n \to f$ uniformly on $[0,1]$. □

Discussion. The sequence of functions presented in this example was first discussed as Example 8.1.2. In the discussion, the essence of why the sequence is uniformly convergent was presented, and the reader who does not fully recall that discussion should review it now. □

Let us now consider the problem of why a sequence of functions on A can fail to converge uniformly.

Negation of Uniform Convergence

The sequence $\{f_n\}$ is **not uniformly convergent** on the set A, provided for every function, f, having domain A, there exists an $\epsilon > 0$ such that given any integer $N > 0$, there exists $x \in A$ and an $n > N$ such that $|f_n(x) - f(x)| \geqslant \epsilon$.

Discussion. Our intent is to identify the reasons why a sequence of functions can fail to converge uniformly. The contrapositive of Theorem 8.2.1 asserts that if a function fails to converge pointwise on A, then it cannot converge uniformly on A. We have already identified why a sequence of functions can fail to converge pointwise on A, namely, there must exist an $x \in A$ such that the sequence of real numbers, $\{f_n(x)\}$, fails to converge. These ideas, together with their meaning in terms of the $\epsilon - N$ definition, have been thoroughly discussed at the end of the last section, and the reader should review that discussion prior to continuing further with this one.

Given the above, in the remainder of this discussion we assume the sequence of functions converges pointwise on A. Thus, in denying that $\{f_n\}$ converges uniformly on A, we are asserting $\{f_n\}$ does not converge uniformly to its pointwise limit, f. To prove this assertion, we must once and for all declare a number, $\epsilon > 0$, which will universally witness the condition that whatever the choice of $N \in \mathbf{N}$ we will always be able to find a specific point x in the common domain A such that the distance between $f_n(x)$ and $f(x)$ is at least ϵ. Notice since $\{f_n\}$ converges pointwise, for a given fixed x, there will always be an $N = N(x)$ which will guarantee $|f_n(x) - f(x)| < \epsilon$. Thus, we see that each time we increase N, we will be required to find a new value of x to witness the failure of the uniform convergence inequality. In this sense, the choice of x depends on the choice of N, and no single x will do the job for all values of N.

Let us now examine the geometry of uniform convergence. Our aim will be to develop further intuition about these abstract definitions. It is evident from the discussions thus far that the sequence, $\{f_n\}$, converges uniformly to f on A provided for $\epsilon > 0$, we can find $N \in \mathbf{N}$ such that

$$\sup_{x \in A} |f_n(x) - f(x)| < \epsilon, \quad \text{whenever} \quad n > N.$$

This is an idea which can be clearly understood from a geometrical point of view. Given an arbitrary positive number, ϵ, consider two functions, $f + \epsilon$ and $f - \epsilon$ which are defined by

$$(f + \epsilon)(x) = f(x) + \epsilon \quad \text{and} \quad (f - \epsilon)(x) = f(x) - \epsilon.$$

The graphs of these functions run 'parallel' to the graph of the (pointwise-limit) function, f. This creates a 'tube-shaped' region of width 2ϵ centered around the graph of the function f (see Figure 8.2.1). The definition of uniform convergence demands that for this 2ϵ-tube, we must reach a certain stage (specified by a number $N \in \mathbf{N}$) such that the graphs of the functions, $f_{N+1}, f_{N+2}, f_{N+3}, \ldots$, must all be completely captured inside this tube. The significance of the number, N, is to tell us the maximum number of functions in the sequence which can (possibly) escape this tube.

Once the geometrical perspective on uniform convergence is grasped, then the negation of uniform convergence becomes very clear. Here the value of ϵ is declared

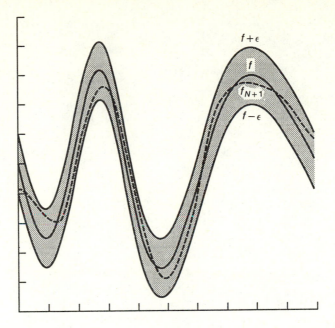

Figure 8.2.1 Graphical illustration of uniform convergence.

in advance around the pointwise limit function, f, and this defines a tube of width 2ϵ which remains fixed for the remainder of the discussion. We must then convince ourselves that no matter how large we choose N, the graph of some f_n, will escape the tube even though $n > N$! Again we stress that as N changes, the place in the domain, A, at which the graph of an f_n escapes the tube will change.

As a final note, one could view the definition and the negation of uniform convergence in terms of the two-person game discussed earlier in the context of limit of a sequence and limit of a function. The diligent reader may wish to do this as a further aid to understanding of the uniform convergence concept.   □

We illustrate the concept of uniform convergence as well as its negation by means of further examples.

EXAMPLE 2

Discuss the uniform convergence of the sequence of functions, $\{f_n\}$, where $f_n: (0, 1] \rightarrow \mathbf{R}$ is defined by

$$f_n(x) = \frac{1}{nx}, \quad x \in (0, 1], n \in \mathbf{N}.$$

Solution.   This sequence of functions was shown to be pointwise convergent to the limit function, f, which is identically 0, on $(0, 1]$ in Example 8.1.1. We show that this sequence is not uniformly convergent. Set $\epsilon = 1$, and fix N. Choose $x_0 \in (0, 1]$ such that $x_0 < \dfrac{1}{N+1}$, then

$$|f_{N+1}(x_0) - f(x_0)| = \left| \frac{1}{x_0(N+1)} - 0 \right| \geqslant 1,$$

whence f_n does not converge uniformly to f on $(0, 1]$.

Discussion. The basic reason why this sequence of functions cannot converge uniformly to f is that f is bounded on $(0, 1]$, whereas each f_n is unbounded on $(0, 1]$. Thus, no matter how large we had taken ϵ, we could always find a portion of the graph of f_n which escaped a 2ϵ-tube about f. The geometry of this situation is presented in Figure 8.1.1. ☐

EXAMPLE 3 _____

Discuss the uniform convergence of the sequence, $\{f_n\}$, where $f_n: [0, 1] \to \mathbf{R}$ is defined by $f_n(x) = 1 - \dfrac{x}{n}$, $n \in \mathbf{N}$.

Solution. As in Example 8.1.2, it is easy to see that f_n converges pointwise to the function f which is identically 1 on $[0, 1]$. We claim that this convergence is uniform as well. To this end, let $\epsilon > 0$ be given. We can find $N > 0$ satisfying $\dfrac{1}{N} < \epsilon$. Now, if $n > N$,

$$|f_n(x) - f(x)| = \left| \left[1 - \frac{x}{n} \right] - 1 \right|$$

$$= \left| \frac{x}{n} \right| < \frac{1}{n}, \quad \text{for all} \quad x \in [0, 1]$$

$$< \frac{1}{N} < \epsilon$$

by our choice of N. Thus, $\{f_n\}$ converges uniformly to 1 on $[0, 1]$. ☐

Discussion. Note the manner in which we came up with the magic number, N. First we compute $|f_n(x) - f(x)|$ which reduces to $\left| \dfrac{x}{n} \right|$, which, unfortunately still involves x. The key to making this expression less than ϵ for all x lies in the fact that x is in $[0, 1]$ so that $x \leqslant 1$. Thus, we simplify the problem to that of making $\dfrac{1}{n}$ smaller than ϵ, and we only have to invoke the Archimedean property of the real number system to find the N which will accomplish this. Note that what is really behind this argument is the powerful tool of the Completeness Axiom for the real numbers disguised as the Archimedean property!

The geometry of this example is presented in Figure 8.2.2. The pointwise limit is the graph of $y = 1$ from $x = 0$ to $x = 1$. Let us take a small strip around the x-axis (the limit function) of width ϵ on either side. The issue here is: can we capture the graphs of all the f_n's after a certain stage (say $n > N$) in this strip of width 2ϵ? That this can be done at each point of $[0, 1]$ is the notion of pointwise convergence. But we want the entire graph to be in this strip irrespective of which point in the domain is

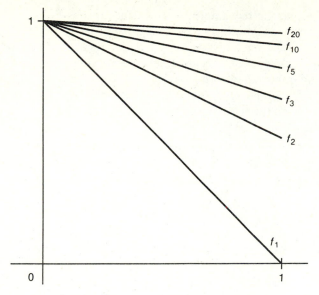

Figure 8.2.2 $f_n(x) = 1 - \dfrac{x}{n}$ ($n = 1, 2, 3, 5, 10, 20$).

considered. Clearly it is possible to find an N which ensures that the f_n's with $n > N$ have their graphs enclosed in the strip of width 2ϵ around the limit function. Of course, the stage N depends on the size of ϵ.

The reader should see that the sort of graphical considerations presented above can serve as an intuitive aid in deciding whether the convergence of a sequence of functions is uniform. □

EXAMPLE 4

Discuss the uniform convergence of $\{f_n\}$ where $f_n: [0, 1] \to [0,1]$ are defined by $f_n(x) = x^n$, $n = 1, 2, \ldots$.

Solution. The pointwise limit of this function was found in Example 8.1.3 and shown to be

$$f(x) = \begin{cases} 0, & \text{if } x < 1 \\ 1, & \text{if } x = 1. \end{cases}$$

Let us choose $\epsilon = \dfrac{1}{2}$ and let N be fixed. Consider the function f_{N+1}. The reader should have long since been aware of the fact that $\lim\limits_{x \to 1^-} x^{N+1} = 1$. Hence, there exists $x_0 \in (0,1)$ such that $x_0^{N+1} \geqslant \dfrac{1}{2}$. It is immediate that

$$|f_{N+1}(x_0) - f(x_0)| = |x^{N+1} - 0| \geqslant \epsilon,$$

whence f_n does not converge uniformly on $[0,1]$. □

Discussion. In Example 2, we remarked that any value of ϵ would have sufficed for the argument. In this example, not every positive number will do as a choice for ϵ.

Indeed, the requirement on the choice of ϵ is that $\epsilon < 1$. Any larger choice will not permit the construction of the argument (see Exercise 1).

The intuition behind this example can be seen from Figure 8.1.2. Specifically, the graph of each f_n must eventually curve upward, away from the x-axis, so as to attain the value 1 when $x = 1$. The argument simply builds on the fact that to get to 1, the graph of f_n must go outside of a 2ϵ-tube around the x-axis, provided ϵ is sufficiently small. ☐

EXAMPLE 5 _____

Discuss the uniform convergence of the sequence $\{f_n\}$ of functions where $f_n: [0, \infty) \to \mathbf{R}$ is defined by

$$f_n(x) = \frac{x}{1 + nx}.$$

Solution. The first step in the solution is to identify the pointwise limit, if it exists. This limit is easily computed for each x, and is the function which is identically zero on $[0, \infty)$. This will be confirmed by the argument that the convergence is uniform. Given $\epsilon > 0$, pick N satisfying $\frac{1}{N} < \epsilon$. If $n > N$, and $x > 0$, we have

$$|f_n(x) - f(x)| = \frac{x}{1 + nx} - 0 < \frac{x}{nx} = \frac{1}{n} < \frac{1}{N} < \epsilon,$$

and for $x = 0$, the inequality is obvious. Thus, $f_n \to f$ uniformly on $[0, \infty)$. ☐

Discussion. The crucial steps in the above reasoning are that from the given expression for f_n, we identify the pointwise limit and then simplify the expression, $|f_n(x) - f(x)|$. We must exploit our basic knowledge of inequalities to reduce this expression to one which is free of x, but depends on n, so that this quantity can be made small by choosing n large. The domain of the functions plays a very important role in this sort of calculation, which again illustrates the global nature of the concept of uniform convergence. ☐

EXAMPLE 6 _____

Discuss the uniform convergence of the sequence $\{f_n\}$ where $f_n: [0, \infty) \to \mathbf{R}$ is defined by
$$f_n(x) = \frac{nx}{1 + n^2x^2}.$$

Solution. For each fixed x, $f_n(x)$ clearly has the limit 0. Hence, for $x \geq 0$, $f_n \to f$ pointwise, where $f(x) = 0$ for all x. We claim that f_n cannot converge uniformly on $[0, \infty)$. To see this, note that $f_n\left(\frac{1}{n}\right) = \frac{1}{2}$ and take $\epsilon = \frac{1}{2}$. Then

$$\left| f_n\left(\frac{1}{n}\right) - 0 \right| = \frac{1}{2} \geq \epsilon, \quad \text{for all } n \in \mathbf{N}.$$ ☐

Discussion. How were the choice of ϵ and the point x, which were used to deny uniform convergence, obtained? The considerations are clear if we look at the graphs of members of the sequence of functions. Each f_n has a continuous graph commencing at the origin, and rising to a maximum height of $\frac{1}{2}$ at the point $x = \frac{1}{n}$ (use Theorem 4.3.1 to see this). The graph then falls rapidly and becomes asymptotic to the x-axis, that is, $\lim_{x \to \infty} f_n(x) = 0$ (see Figure 8.2.3). Thus, once the details of the graphs are available, the construction of the argument follows.

However, instead of $[0, \infty)$, if the common domain is taken to be $[a, \infty)$, for $a > 0$, the convergence becomes uniform. The reason is that the maximum height, $\frac{1}{2}$, is arrived at by each of the graphs at $\frac{1}{n}$, and as n gets larger this phenomenon occurs closer and closer to the origin. Thus, if n is sufficiently large, then $\frac{1}{n} < a$, whence the difficulty is eliminated. The reader should present an $\epsilon - N$ argument to show uniform convergence in $[a, \infty)$, $a > 0$. $\qquad\square$

The reader should by now be asking a number of questions regarding the notion of uniform convergence. Some of these questions are explored in the theorems below, and some in the exercises.

Theorem 8.2.2. Let $\{f_n\}$ and $\{g_n\}$ be uniformly convergent on A. Then $\{f_n \pm g_n\}$ is uniformly convergent on A.

Proof. Exercise 3. $\qquad\square$

Discussion. To construct this proof, the reader should examine the proof of the analogous result for sequences of real numbers. Then recognize that if an inequality holds for all $x \in A$, it must hold for each particular $x \in A$.

The shrewd reader will have noticed we have avoided mentioning certain other well-known arithmetic operations. Is this oversight, or is there a reason? $\qquad\square$

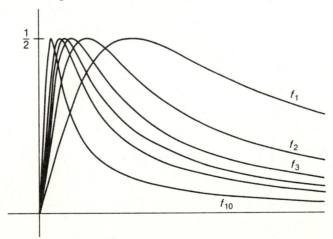

Figure 8.2.3 $f_n(x) = \dfrac{nx}{1 + n^2 x^2}$ $(n = 1, 2, 3, 4, 5, 10)$.

Theorem 8.2.3. Let $\{f_n\}$ be a monotone increasing sequence of functions on A, and suppose $\{f_n\}$ has a subsequence which is uniformly convergent on A. Then $\{f_n\}$ is uniformly convergent on A.

Proof. Let f be the limit of the subsequence. It can be checked (see Exercise 5) that for each n, $f_n \leqslant f$. It follows that $f_n \to f$ pointwise and uniformly. $\square$

The next theorem provides a useful test for uniform convergence of a sequence of functions.

Theorem 8.2.4. Let $\{f_n\}$ be pointwise convergent on A to a function, f. Define

$$M_n = \sup_{x \in A} |f_n(x) - f(x)|.$$

Then $f_n \to f$ uniformly on A if and only if $\lim_{n \to \infty} M_n = 0$.

Proof. Exercise 7. $\square$

Discussion. This theorem can be quite useful. For example, in Example 6, one would merely have had to note that $\frac{1}{2} \leqslant M_n$ to complete the argument. The difficulty in applying this result is in identifying the required supremum. But since many sequences comprise differentiable functions, the task is not insurmountable, as the next example shows.

EXAMPLE 7 _____

Discuss the pointwise and uniform convergence of the sequence $\{2nxe^{-nx^2}\}$ on $[a, \infty)$ where $a \geqslant 0$.

Solution. It can be checked (Exercise 8) that $f_n \to 0$ pointwise on $[0, \infty)$. It follows that $M_n = \sup_{x \in A} |f_n(x)|$. Further, each f_n is differentiable on $(0,\infty)$ and its derivative is given by

$$f'_n(x) = (2n - 4n^2x^2)e^{-nx^2}.$$

Theorem 4.3.1 establishes that the relative extrema of f_n on the interval $[0, \infty)$ occurs at $x = \dfrac{1}{\sqrt{2n}}$, whence $M_n = \sqrt{\dfrac{2n}{e}}$, provided that $a = 0$. Since M_n does not converge to 0, we have that f_n does not converge uniformly on $[0, \infty)$. It is left to the reader to show that the convergence is uniform on $[a, \infty)$ for $a > 0$. $\square$

Discussion. The functions in the sequence are presented graphically in Figure 8.2.4. It is obvious from the graphs of the individual functions that the convergence could not possibly be uniform on $[0, \infty)$. However, since the 'hump' gets squeezed in toward zero as n increases, the graphs demonstrate why the sequence can converge uniformly on the smaller domain. $\square$

The next theorem states the Cauchy criterion for the uniform convergence of a sequence of functions.

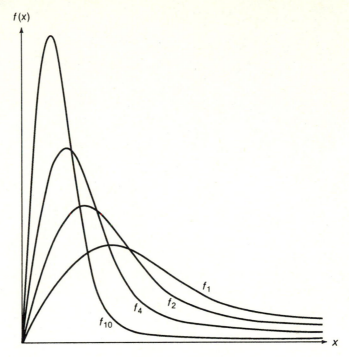

Figure 8.2.4 $f_n(x) = 2nxe^{-nx^2}$ $(n = 1, 2, 4, 10)$.

Theorem 8.2.5 (Cauchy Criterion).   Let $\{f_n\}$ be a sequence of functions defined on A. Then $\{f_n\}$ is uniformly convergent on A if and only if for positive ϵ, there exists an $N \in \mathbf{N}$ such that for all $x \in A$,

$$|f_n(x) - f_m(x)| < \epsilon, \quad \text{whenever} \quad n, m > N.$$

Proof.   Exercise 14.   □

Discussion.   Cauchy criteria have been discussed for sequences in section 3.3, for infinite series in section 7.1, and for infinite products in section 7.5. They are important tools for testing convergence, and if the reader does not feel totally able to construct the required proof, he should review the mentioned sections.   □

Theorem 8.2.6.   Let $\{f_n\}$ be a uniformly convergent sequence of functions defined on $[a, b]$. If each f_n is bounded on $[a, b]$, then the uniform limit, f is bounded on $[a, b]$.

Proof.   Exercise 20.   □

Discussion.   This is one of the many useful results which illustrate that a property shared by all the members of a uniformly convergent sequence of functions is retained by the limit function. We shall see several other results of the same nature in the next section.   □

EXERCISES

1. Show for the sequence of Example 4, an argument can be constructed for any value of ϵ which is less than 1.

2. Discuss the uniform convergence of the following sequences of functions on the domains mentioned against each. Where possible, describe the limit function.

   (a) $f_n(x) = 1 - nx$,   **R**;

   (b) $f_n(x) = 1 - \dfrac{x}{n}$, $[0, \infty)$;

   (c) $f_n(x) = \dfrac{n^2 x}{1 + n^3 x^2}$,   **R**;

   (d) $f_n(x) = \dfrac{e^{-nx}}{n}$, $x \geqslant 0$;

   (e) $f_n(x) = nxe^{-nx}$, $[0, 1]$;

   (f) $f_n(x) = \dfrac{x^n}{1 + x^n}$, $[0, 1]$;

   (g) $f_n = nx(1 - x^2)^n$, $[0, 1]$;

   (h) $f_n(x) = g\left(x + \dfrac{1}{n}\right)$,   where g is uniformly continuous on **R**;

   (i) $f_n(x) = \dfrac{nx}{1 + nx}$, $x \geqslant 0$;

   (j) $f_n(x) = \dfrac{\sin nx}{\sqrt{n}}$, $x \in [0, 2\pi]$;

   (k) $f_n(x) = (\sin x)^n$, $0 \leqslant x \leqslant \pi$;

   (l) $f_n(x) = n \ln\left(1 + \dfrac{x}{n}\right)$, $x \geqslant 0$;

   (m) $f_n(x) = n(x^{1/n} - 1)$, $x \geqslant a > 0$;

   (n) $f_n(x) = \dfrac{1}{n} \sin n^2 x$, $x \in \mathbf{R}$;

   (o) $f_n(x) = g(nx)$,   where $g(x) = \begin{cases} x, & 0 \leqslant x \leqslant \dfrac{1}{2} \\[2mm] 1 - x, & \dfrac{1}{2} \leqslant x \leqslant 1; \end{cases}$

   (p) $f_n(x) = \begin{cases} nx, & 0 \leqslant x \leqslant \dfrac{1}{n} \\[2mm] -nx + 2, & -\dfrac{1}{n} < x \leqslant \dfrac{2}{n} \\[2mm] 0, & \dfrac{2}{n} < x \leqslant 1 \end{cases}$ $[0, 1]$;

   (q) $f_n(x) = \begin{cases} 0, & \dfrac{2}{n} < x \leqslant 2 \\[2mm] n^2 x^2 - 2nx, & 0 \leqslant x \leqslant \dfrac{2}{n} \end{cases}$ $[0, 2]$;

   (r) $f_n(x) = x\left(1 + \dfrac{1}{n}\right)$, $x \in \mathbf{R}$;

$$(\text{s}) \ f_n(x) = \begin{cases} \dfrac{1}{n}, & \text{if } x = 0 \text{ or } x \in \mathbf{R} \sim \mathbf{Q} \\ q + \dfrac{1}{n}, & \text{if } x = \dfrac{p}{q}, \ q > 0, \text{ is rational in lowest terms} \end{cases} \quad x \in \mathbf{R}.$$

3. Prove if $\{f_n\}$ and $\{g_n\}$ are both uniformly convergent on a set A, so are $\{f_n \pm g_n\}$ (Theorem 8.2.2).

4. Suppose that in addition both sequences in Exercise 3 consist of functions which are bounded on A. Show $\{f_n g_n\}$ converges uniformly on A. What can be said if the boundedness condition fails?

5. Complete the proof of Theorem 8.2.3.

6. Let $\{f_n\}$ be a uniformly convergent sequence of functions on A. Show $\{f_n^+\}$ and $\{f_n^-\}$ are uniformly convergent sequences. What can be concluded about $\{|f_n|\}$?

7. Prove Theorem 8.2.4.

8. Show the sequence in Example 7 tends to 0 pointwise on $[0, \infty)$. Further show that the sequence converges uniformly on $[a, \infty)$ for $a > 0$.

9. Give an example of a uniformly convergent sequence $\{f_n\}$ such that the sequence of its derivatives fails to be uniformly convergent in the same domain.

10. Let $\{f_n\}$ be a sequence of continuous functions on $[0, 1]$ that converges uniformly. Show there exists $K > 0$ such that $|f_n(x)| < K$ for each $n \in \mathbf{N}$ and each $x \in [0, 1]$. Does the result still hold if we replace uniform convergence by pointwise convergence? What if we assume the limit function is bounded?

11. Prove if $\{f_n\}$ is uniformly convergent to a bounded function, then there exists $K, N > 0$ such that $|f_n(x)| < K$ for all $n > N$ and all x in the domain. Give an example to show why we cannot replace $n > N$ by 'for all $n \in \mathbf{N}$'.

12. If $\{f_n\}$ converges uniformly on an open interval (a, b) and converges at the points a and b, must it converge uniformly on $[a, b]$?

13. Give an example where $f_n \to f$ uniformly, but f_n^2 does not converge uniformly to f^2.

14. Prove the Cauchy criteria (Theorem 8.2.5) for uniform convergence.

15. Let $\{f_n\}$ converge uniformly on A. Show every subsequence of $\{f_n\}$ also converges uniformly on A. Is the converse true?

16. Let $\{f_n\}$ be uniformly convergent on A_i, $(i = 1, 2, \ldots, k)$. Show that $\{f_n\}$ is uniformly convergent on $\bigcup_{i=1}^{k} A_i$. Show that this result cannot be extended to the union of a countable number of sets.

17. Let each f_n be continuous on a set A, and B be a dense subset of A. If $\{f_n\}$ is uniformly convergent on A, is it true that $\{f_n\}$ is uniformly convergent on B? What can you say about the converse?

18. Let $\{f_n\}$ and f be defined on A. Then $\{f_n\}$ fails to converge uniformly to f on A if and only if there exists $\epsilon > 0$, a subsequence $\{f_{n_k}\}$ and a sequence $\{x_k\}$ of elements of A such that $|f_{n_k}(x_k) - f(x_k)| \geq \epsilon$ for all $k \in \mathbf{N}$.

19. Is it possible for a sequence of continuous functions to be uniformly convergent to a discontinuous limit function?

20. Prove Theorem 8.2.6. Is the result still valid, if we have only pointwise convergence?

21. If $\{f_n\}$ and $\{g_n\}$ converge uniformly to f and g, respectively, in $[a, b]$, prove the following:

(a) if each f_n is bounded, and f is bounded, then $\{f_n\}$ is uniformly bounded (Exercise 8.1.11);

(b) if $\{f_n\}$ and $\{g_n\}$ are both uniformly bounded, then $\{f_n \cdot g_n\}$ is uniformly convergent to fg.

22. If $\{f_n\}$ is a sequence of continuous functions on a compact set A such that for each x in A, $f_n(x)$ is monotonically increasing, and if $\{f_n\}$ converges pointwise to a continuous function f, show that the convergence is uniform on A (**Dini's Theorem**). Will the result still hold if we relax the compactness of A? What about if we drop the monotonicity condition?

23. For the functions in Exercise 8.1.10, is it possible to obtain a sequence $\{f_n\}$ of functions that converge uniformly to f in the indicated domains?

24. The sequence $\{f_n\}$ is defined for $x \geqslant 0$ as follows: set $f_1(x) = \sqrt{x}$, and for $n > 1$, $f_{n+1}(x) = \sqrt{x + f_n(x)}$. Show that if $0 < a < b < \infty$, then $\{f_n\}$ converges uniformly on $[a, b]$. Is the convergence uniform on $[0, 1]$?

25. The sequence $\{f_n\}$ is defined by $f_0(x) = 1$, and for $n \geqslant 1$, $f_n(x) = \sqrt{x \cdot f_{n-1}(x)}$. Prove that $\{f_n\}$ converges uniformly in $[0, 1]$. What is the limit?

26. Suppose that $f_n \to f$ uniformly on A and that it is uniformly bounded (Exercise 8.1.11) by K. If g is continuous on $[-K, K]$, then $\{(g \circ f_n)\}$ converges uniformly on A. What is the limit function?

27. Recall the sequence given by $f_n(x) = x^n$ was shown to converge pointwise, but not uniformly on $[0, 1]$. Let g be continuous on $[0, 1]$. Find a necessary and sufficient condition on g which will guarantee the product $\{g \circ f_n\}$ converges uniformly.

28. Suppose $f_n \to f$ uniformly on A, that each f_n is continuous, and that $\{x_n\}$ is a sequence of elements of A which tends to $x \in A$. Show $\{f_n(x_n)\}$ is convergent. What is its limit?

29. Let $\{f_n\}$ be a sequence of continuous functions which converges pointwise to a limit, f, on a compact set A. Show the convergence is uniform exactly if:

(a) f is continuous;

(b) for every $\epsilon > 0$, there exists $m \in \mathbf{N}$ and $\delta > 0$ such that $n > m$ and $|f_k(x) - f(x)| < \delta$ imply $|f_{k+n}(x) - f(x)| < \epsilon$ for all $x \in A$ and $k \in \mathbf{N}$.

30. Let $\{f_n\}$ and $\{g_n\}$ be the sequences of Exercises 2(r) and 2(s), respectively. Prove both sequences converge uniformly on every bounded interval. Prove $\{h_n = f_n g_n\}$ does not converge uniformly on any bounded interval.

31. A sequence of functions $\{f_n\}$ with a common domain D is **equicontinuous** on $A \subseteq D$ if and only if for each positive ϵ, there exists a $\delta = \delta(\epsilon) > 0$ such that $x, y \in A$, and $|x - y| < \delta$ implies that $|f_n(x) - f_n(y)| < \epsilon$ for each $n \in \mathbf{N}$. Let $\{f_n\}$ be a sequence of continuous functions on D which converges uniformly on a compact subset $A \subseteq D$. Prove $\{f_n\}$ is uniformly bounded, and equicontinuous on A.

32. Which of the following sequences of functions are (i) uniformly bounded, (ii) equicontinuous on the specified domains:

(a) $f_n(x) = \dfrac{x^n}{n}$, $[-1, 1]$;

(b) $f_n(x) = \sin nx$, $[0, 1]$;

(c) $f_n(x) = \dfrac{\sin nx}{x}$, $(0, 1)$.

33. Show a subsequence of an equicontinuous sequence is equicontinuous.

8.3 CONSEQUENCES OF UNIFORM CONVERGENCE

We have seen from earlier examples that if a sequence $\{f_n\}$ of functions has a point-wise limit function, f, we can not in general expect that the function, f, shares all the nice properties of each of the f_n's. Among the sequences considered were examples where each f_n is continuous, (respectively bounded, integrable, differentiable) but the pointwise limit function was not. What was lacking in these examples was precisely the uniform convergence property, as will be seen in the following set of results. We will thus conclude that the concept of uniform convergence is superior to that of point-wise convergence. We saw a result on uniform convergence and boundedness in Theorem 8.2.6 earlier. Our first theorem ensures that in the presence of uniform convergence, continuity is preserved.

Theorem 8.3.1.   If each f_n is continuous at a point, $a \in A$, and the sequence $\{f_n\}$ is uniformly convergent on the domain A to the function, f, then f is continuous at the point a.

Proof.   Let $\epsilon > 0$ be given. By uniform convergence, there exists $N \in \mathbf{N}$ such that for all $x \in A$ and $n \geqslant N$, we have

$$|f_n(x) - f(x)| < \frac{\epsilon}{3}.$$

Since f_N is continuous at the point a, we can find a $\delta > 0$ such that for each $x \in A$,

$$|f_N(x) - f_N(a)| < \frac{\epsilon}{3}, \quad \text{whenever} \quad |x - a| < \delta.$$

Finally, if $x \in A$ and $|x - a| < \delta$, we have

$$|f(x) - f(a)| \leqslant |f(x) - f_N(x)| + |f_N(x) - f_N(a)| + |f_N(a) - f(a)|$$

$$< \frac{\epsilon}{3} + \frac{\epsilon}{3} + \frac{\epsilon}{3} = \epsilon,$$

proving that f is continuous at the point a.   □

Discussion.   Note the technique adopted in the proof. Starting with the given ϵ we first arrive at the single N that satisfies the condition for uniform convergence for all x. We then use this N and consider f_N at a general point x close enough to the given point a, and employ the Triangle inequality by adding and subtracting the appropriate candidates. The reader should be well familiar with such techniques. This argument is the famous $\dfrac{\epsilon}{3}$ argument, which we have seen earlier.

Observe that the proof will break down if we had only pointwise convergence instead of uniform convergence. This is what happened in Example 8.1.3, and the reader would do well to attempt to construct the present argument for that sequence of functions to see exactly where and why the argument breaks down. Another noteworthy feature of this theorem is that it can profitably be used to negate uniform convergence of a sequence $\{f_n\}$ of continuous functions which has a discontinuous pointwise limit function. This is of great practical value as the next example shows.

However, the reader should be aware that the relationship is not one of equivalence. The fact that a sequence of continuous functions converges pointwise on A to a continuous limit does not ensure that the convergence is uniform.   □

Corollary. If $\{f_n\}$ is a sequence of continuous functions defined on a set A which converges uniformly to the function f on A, then f is continuous on the set A.

EXAMPLE 1 _____

Discuss the uniform convergence of the sequence of functions, $\{f_n\}$, where $f_n(x) =$ Arctan nx $(x \in \mathbf{R})$.

Solution. It is known that Arctan $0 = 0$, that for $y > 0$, we have $\lim_{y \to \infty}$ Arctan $y = \dfrac{\pi}{2}$, and that for $y < 0$, we have $\lim_{y \to -\infty}$ Arctan $y = -\dfrac{\pi}{2}$. Thus, fix $x \in \mathbf{R}$. It follows that

$$\lim_{n \to \infty} \text{Arctan } nx = \frac{\pi}{2} \text{ sgn } x,$$

whence $\{\text{Arctan } nx\}$ converges pointwise to a discontinuous function. Since Arctan x is continuous, the convergence is not uniform.   □

The next theorem presents a somewhat more general version of the previous theorem.

Theorem 8.3.2. Let $\{f_n\}$ be a sequence of continuous functions defined on a set A which converges uniformly to the function f on A. Further suppose that a is a limit point of A and that for each $n \in N$, $\lim_{x \to a} f_n(x) = a_n$, then

$$\lim_{x \to a} f(x) = \lim_{n \to \infty} a_n,$$

or equivalently,

$$\lim_{x \to a} \lim_{n \to \infty} f_n(x) = \lim_{n \to \infty} \lim_{x \to a} f_n(x).$$

Proof. Exercise 1.   □

Discussion. The proof of this form of the theorem is very similar to the proof of Theorem 8.3.1. The point of stating the theorem in this form is that it illustrates the fact that uniform convergence permits one to interchange the order in which limits are computed. This is particularly evident from

$$\lim_{x \to a} \lim_{n \to \infty} f_n(x) = \lim_{n \to \infty} \lim_{x \to a} f_n(x).$$

On the left-hand side, we first find the limit function, f, and then let $x \to a$ for the limit function. On the right-hand side, the individual limits, $\lim_{x \to a} f_n(x)$ are computed for each n thereby forming the sequence a_n. Finally, the limit of the sequence, $\{a_n\}$ is computed. Notice that in this computation, the requirement on a is that a is a limit point of A, not that $a \in A$.

Next we apply the uniform convergence concept to Riemann integrability. It was already established in Example 8.1.5 that pointwise convergence was insufficient to preserve the value of the limit of the integrals as the integral of the limit. However, as the next example shows, the total situation is even worse.

EXAMPLE 2

Let $\{r_n\}$ be an enumeration of the rationals in $[0, 1]$. Define $\{f_n\}$ on $[0,1]$ by

$$f_n(x) = \begin{cases} 0, & \text{if } x = r_m \text{ and } m \leqslant n \\ 1, & \text{otherwise.} \end{cases}$$

What can be said about the integration properties of the sequence and its pointwise limit?

Solution. The reader can verify that the pointwise limit on $[0,1]$ is given by

$$f(x) = \begin{cases} 0, & \text{if } x \text{ is irrational} \\ 1, & \text{otherwise.} \end{cases}$$

Since each f_n has a discontinuity only at a finite number of points, it is integrable on $[0,1]$ for each n. The pointwise limit function, f, is the canonical example of a function which is not Riemann integrable (Example 5.2.4). □

Discussion. The present example shows just how ugly the pointwise limit can be. It is nowhere continuous and fails to be integrable on any subinterval of its domain. Yet each of the functions, f_n, has only finitely many discontinuities, is integrable, and the integral of each f_n yields the same value, 1. The requirement of uniform convergence will turn this around. □

Theorem 8.3.3. If each f_n $(n \in \mathbf{N})$, is Riemann integrable on $[a, b]$ and the sequence $\{f_n\}$ converges uniformly to f on $[a, b]$, then f is Riemann integrable on $[a, b]$; furthermore,

$$\lim_{n \to \infty} \int_a^b f_n = \int_a^b \lim_{n \to \infty} f_n.$$

Proof. Let $\epsilon > 0$ be given. Since each f_n is integrable in $[a, b]$ there exists a partition, P_n, of $[a, b]$ such that

$$|\overline{S}(f_n, P_n) - \underline{S}(f_n, P_n)| < \frac{\epsilon}{3}.$$

Also by uniform convergence of the given sequence of functions, there exists $N \in \mathbf{N}$ such that for all $x \in [a, b]$ and for $n \geqslant N$, we have

$$|f_n(x) - f(x)| < \frac{\epsilon}{3(b - a)}.$$

Now if $m_{n,r}$, m_r denote the infima of f_n and f, respectively, in the rth subinterval of the partition, P_N, and d_r, the length of the rth subinterval, then, in particular, we have

$$m_{n,r} - m_r < \frac{\epsilon}{3(b - a)} \quad \text{for} \quad n \geqslant N.$$

Therefore,

$$\underline{S}(f_N, P_N) - \underline{S}(f, P_N) = \sum m_{N,r}d_r - \sum m_r d_r$$

$$= \sum (m_{N,r} - m_r)d_r < \frac{\epsilon}{3(b-a)} \sum d_r = \frac{\epsilon}{3}$$

so that

$$\underline{S}(f_N, P_N) \leqslant \underline{S}(f, P_N) + \frac{\epsilon}{3}.$$

Similarly considering the upper sums, we have the inequality

$$\bar{S}(f, P_N) \leqslant \bar{S}(f_N, P_N) + \frac{\epsilon}{3}.$$

Thus, we obtain

$$\bar{S}(f, P_N) - \underline{S}(f, P_N) < \bar{S}(f_N, P_N) - \underline{S}(f_N, P_N) + 2\frac{\epsilon}{3} \leqslant \epsilon.$$

Now, by Theorem 8.2.6, f is bounded, whence we apply Theorem 5.2.4 and the function f is integrable on $[a, b]$. Finally, note that

$$\left| \int_a^b f_n - \int_a^b f \right| \leqslant \int_a^b |f_n - f| < \frac{\epsilon}{(b-a)}(b-a) = \epsilon, \qquad \textbf{(WHY?)}$$

proving that the limit of the integral is the integral of the uniform limit.   □

Discussion.   The proof of this theorem is founded on the application of Theorem 5.2.4. The hypothesis of Theorem 5.2.4 requires that the function under discussion be bounded. Recall that for a function to be Riemann integrable, it must be bounded. Thus, each f_n is bounded. This permits the application of Theorem 8.2.6, to obtain that f is bounded, whence 5.2.4 applies.

To establish integrability of f, we have to produce a partition, P, of $[a, b]$ which satisfies the condition $\bar{S}(f, P) - \underline{S}(f, P) < \epsilon$ for any preassigned ϵ. The way we obtain this partition is by using the uniform convergence of the sequence to find a value of N which will guarantee that all f_n's having subscript exceeding N are inside a $\dfrac{2\epsilon}{3(b-a)}$-tube around f. This tube is then used in an extremely powerful way, namely, to conclude that

$$m_{n,r} - m_r < \frac{\epsilon}{3(b-a)} \quad \text{for} \quad n \geqslant N,$$

where $m_{n,r}$ and m_r are infima over various subintervals of arbitrary partitions for f_n and f, respectively. Notice that these infima do not have to occur at the same value of x for f_n and f; thus, it is not at all obvious why this inequality should hold. It is essential that the reader work this out (Exercise 2) so as to completely understand it. Once this inequality has been obtained, it becomes possible to replace statements about lower sums relative to f, by lower sums relative to f_N, leading to

$$\underline{S}(f_N, P_N) \leqslant \underline{S}(f, P_N) + \frac{\epsilon}{3}.$$

Obtaining the analogous inequalities for upper sums is straightforward, and the proof is essentially complete.

The theorem also asserts that in the presence of uniform convergence, we have the pleasant feature that we can interchange the integral and the limit, namely the limit of the integrals is equal to the integral of the (uniform) limit. Again, this theorem is useful for negating uniform convergence of a sequence of functions each of which is Riemann integrable, and for which the pointwise limit function is either not Riemann integrable, or takes a different value from the limit of the integrals.

Several other types of integrals exist, of which two have been developed elsewhere in this text. The obvious question arises as to whether it is possible to prove analogous results for Stieltjes integrals and improper Riemann integration. These ideas will be explored further in the exercises. $\square$

EXAMPLE 3

Is the sequence of functions, $\{2(n + 1)x(1 - x^2)^n\}$, uniformly convergent to its pointwise limit on $[0, 1]$?

Solution. It is left to the reader to verify that the pointwise limit of the f_n's is the zero function (Exercise 3). Further, the value of the integral of each f_n is quickly seen to be 1 by the Fundamental Theorem. Thus,

$$\int_0^1 f = 0 \neq \lim_{n \to \infty} \int_0^1 f_n = 1.$$

Thus, the convergence to the pointwise limit on $[0, 1]$ cannot be uniform. $\square$

Next, we consider the effect of uniform convergence on differentiation applied to each member of the sequence. Here again, the issue is obtaining the conditions under which the process of differentiation can be interchanged with the process of computing the limit of the sequence of functions. In thinking about this problem, it would seem that the conditions are likely to be restrictive since we are dealing with two sequences of functions, and two limit functions, that is, $f_n \to f$ and $f'_n \to f'$.

Theorem 8.3.4. Let $\{f_n\}$ be a sequence of functions defined on $[a, b]$. If each f_n has a continuous derivative on $[a, b]$ and the sequence of derivatives, $\{f'_n\}$, converges uniformly on $[a, b]$, and there exists $x_0 \in [a, b]$ such that $\{f_n(x_0)\}$ converges, then $f_n \to f$ uniformly on $[a, b]$ and

$$\lim_{n \to \infty} f'_n = f'.$$

Proof. We first show that $\{f_n\}$ satisfies the Cauchy criterion for uniform convergence. Thus, fix $\epsilon > 0$ to use the fact that f'_n converges uniformly to choose N such that $n,m > N$ imply

$$|f'_n(t) - f'_m(t)| < \frac{\epsilon}{2(b - a)} \quad \text{for all } t \in [0, 1].$$

Again, since $f_n(x_0)$ converges, we can choose N large enough, so that for $m,n > N$, we have

$$|f_n(x_0) - f_m(x_0)| < \frac{\epsilon}{2}.$$

Now we apply the Fundamental Theorem of Calculus in the form of Theorem 5.5.2 to observe that for each $x \in [0, 1]$,

$$f_n(x) = \int_{x_0}^{x} f_n'(t)\, dt + f_n(x_0).$$

It follows that

$$f_n(x) - f_m(x) = \int_{x_0}^{x} [f_n'(t) - f_m'(t)]\, dt + f_n(x_0) - f_m(x_0),$$

whence we obtain

$$|f_n(x) - f_m(x)| \leqslant \left|\int_{x_0}^{x} f_n'(t) - f_m'(t)\, dt\right| + |f_m(x_0) - f_n(x_0)|,$$

$$< \frac{\epsilon(b-a)}{2(b-a)} + \frac{\epsilon}{2} = \epsilon.$$

Thus, the sequence, $\{f_n\}$, converges uniformly on $[a, b]$, and we denote its uniform limit by f. To complete the proof, let $f_n' \rightarrow g$ on $[a, b]$. By Theorem 5.5.3, we have

$$f_n(x) - f_n(a) = \int_{a}^{x} f_n'(t)\, dt.$$

Since the convergence of $\{f_n'\}$ is uniform, Theorem 8.3.3 applies and letting n tend to infinity, we obtain

$$f(x) - f(a) = \int_{a}^{x} g(t)\, dt.$$

But g is continuous, whence for each $x \in (a, b)$ we have, by Theorem 5.5.3,

$$f'(x) = g(x).$$

$\square$

Discussion. The key to understanding the proof of this theorem begins with an understanding of how the Fundamental Theorem of Calculus is applied in this situation.

The first application is in the form of Theorem 5.5.2 to f_n', which is continuous on $[a, b]$, hence integrable there and for which f_n is a primitive. The distinctive feature of the application is that in the present situation we observe

$$f_n(x) = \int_{x_0}^{x} f_n'(t)\, dt + f_n(x_0)$$

where $x, x_0 \in [a, b]$. This application requires the introduction of a minus sign if $x < x_0$, but other than that it is straightforward. While this theorem could be applied using any member of $[a, b]$ as the lower limit of integration, we must use x_0 as the lower limit since subtraction of f_m from f_n leaves the quantity, $f_m(x_0) - f_n(x_0)$ as a residual, and the only way to eliminate it is by virtue of convergence of the sequence $\{f_n(x_0)\}$, whence it becomes arbitrarily small. The final outcome of this application of the Fundamental Theorem is the fact that $f_n \rightarrow f$ uniformly on $[a, b]$.

The second application of the Fundamental Theorem is in the form of Theorem 5.5.3 which states that for a continuous function, h, the function, H on $[a, b]$ defined by

$$H(x) = \int_{a}^{x} h(t)\, dt$$

satisfies $H' = h$ on $[a, b]$. In this case, the theorem can be applied with the lower limit on the integral being a, since it is known in advance that $f_n(a)$ converges to $f(a)$. Of course to complete this section of the proof, Theorem 8.3.3 must be applied, which is why the sequence of derivatives must be uniformly convergent. The use of Theorem 5.5.3 makes clear why each of the f_n''s must be continuous.

It is worth pointing out that the hypothesis requires convergence of f_n only at one point. One can construct examples to show that if any of the conditions in the hypothesis are dropped, the conclusion of the theorem may fail. These ideas are explored further in the exercises. $\qquad\qquad\qquad\qquad\qquad\qquad\qquad\qquad\qquad\qquad\quad$ □

EXERCISES

1. Prove Theorem 8.3.2.

2. Write out a complete argument establishing the truth of the inequality

$$m_{n,r} - m_r < \frac{\epsilon}{3(b-a)} \quad \text{for} \quad n \geqslant N$$

   of Theorem 8.3.3.

3. Verify the pointwise limit in Example 3 is the zero function.

4. Consider the sequence of functions, f_n, given by $f_n = \dfrac{\sin nx}{n}$ in $[0, 1]$. Show $\{f_n\}$ converges uniformly to 0, while f_n' does not converge even pointwise in $[0, 1]$. What do you conclude from this?

5. Show $f_n = nx(1 - x)^n$ is integrable in $[0, 1]$ for each n and $\lim \int_0^1 f_n = \int_0^1 \lim f_n$, yet the sequence is not uniformly convergent.

6. Compare $\displaystyle\lim_{n\to\infty} \int_0^1 f_n$ and $\displaystyle\int_0^1 \lim_{n\to\infty} f_n$, where $f_n = \dfrac{nx}{1 + nx}$ on $[0, 1]$.

7. Give an example of a non-uniformly convergent sequence $\{f_n\}$ in $[0, 1]$ with pointwise limit f, for which $\displaystyle\lim_{n\to\infty} \int_0^1 f_n$ and $\displaystyle\int_0^1 \lim_{n\to\infty} f_n$ are equal.

8. Show although $f_n(x) = xe^{-nx^2}$ is uniformly convergent in $[-1, 1]$ to a differentiable function, the limit and differentiation process cannot be interchanged.

9. Let g be continuous on $[a, b]$, and let $\{f_n\}$ be a sequence of continuous functions converging uniformly to f on $[a, b]$. Prove $\displaystyle\lim_{n\to\infty} \int_a^b f_n g = \int_a^b fg$.

10. Let f_n be such that f_n' is defined and continuous on $[a, b]$, $\{f_n'\}$ converges uniformly on $[a, b]$, and $\{f_n\}$ converges pointwise to f. Show

$$f' = \lim_{n\to\infty} f_n'.$$

11. Consider $f_n(x) = \dfrac{2x}{1 + n^2x^2}$ for $x \geqslant 0$, and limit f. Check whether the equation $\lim f_n'(x) = f'(x)$ is valid.

12. Let $f_n: [0, 1] \to \mathbf{R}$ be defined by $f_n = n$, if $x = \dfrac{1}{n}$ and 0 otherwise. Compare $\displaystyle\int_0^1 f_n$ with $\displaystyle\int_0^1 f$.

13. Discuss the pointwise and uniform convergence of $\{f_n\}$ where

$$f_n(x) = \begin{cases} -1, & x < \dfrac{\pi}{n} \\[2mm] \sin\dfrac{nx}{2}, & \dfrac{\pi}{n} \leqslant x \leqslant \dfrac{\pi}{n} \\[2mm] 1, & x > \dfrac{\pi}{n}. \end{cases}$$

14. Give an example showing $\{f_n\}$ may converge to f uniformly on $[a, b]$, f_n' may exist and be continuous on $[a, b]$, but $f'(x_0)$ fails to exist at some point $x_0 \in [a, b]$.

15. If $\{f_n\}$ is a sequence of functions which converge uniformly to a continuous function f on **R**, show

$$\lim_{n \to \infty} f_n\left(x + \frac{1}{n}\right) = f(x), \quad x \in \mathbf{R}.$$

16. Let $\{f_n\}$ be a uniformly bounded sequence of continuous functions on $[a, b]$ and suppose f to be a function on $[a, b]$ to which $\{f_n\}$ converges uniformly on $[a, c]$ for each $c \in (a, b)$. Prove that $\lim\limits_{n \to \infty} \left\{ \int_a^b f_n \right\} = \int_a^b f$.

17. Prove **Arzela's Theorem**: If $\{f_n\}$ is a uniformly bounded sequence of Riemann integrable functions converging pointwise to a Riemann integrable function f on $[a, b]$, then

$$\lim_{n \to \infty} \left\{ \int_a^b f_n \right\} = \int_a^b f.$$

18. Let $\{f_n\}$ be a sequence of functions which converges uniformly on $[a, b]$. If each f_n is improperly Riemann integrable on $[a, b]$, what can be said about f?

19. Repeat Exercise 18, except that the interval is $(0, \infty)$.

20. State and prove a suitable theorem about Stieltjes integration and uniformly convergent sequences of functions.

21. Let g and f_0 be continuous on $[a, b]$. Define the sequence, $\{f_n\}$, on $[a, b]$ by

$$f_n(x) = \int_a^x g(t) f_{n-1}(t)\, dt, \quad n \geqslant 1.$$

Show that $\{f_n\}$ converges uniformly to f, and that f satisfies $f'(x) = g(x)f(x)$. What can be said about the form of f?

22. Consider the sequence of functions defined by $f_n(x) = \dfrac{1}{n} e^{-n^2 x^2}$ defined on $[-1, 1]$. Give a complete discussion of the convergence properties of this sequence and its associated sequence of derivatives.

23. Let f be defined on $[0, 1]$ and define $S(f)$ by

$$S(f) = \lim_{n \to \infty} \frac{1}{n} \sum_{k=1}^{n} f\left(\frac{k}{n}\right) \quad \text{whenever this limit exists.}$$

Show that if $f_n \to f$ uniformly on $[0, 1]$ and that $S(f)$ and $S(f_n)$ exist, then the two limiting processes may be exchanged. Can this hypothesis be weakened?

24. Suppose that f and g are continuous on $[a, b]$ and that $f \geqslant 0$ and $g > 0$. Let M denote the maximum value of f on the interval and define M_n by

$$M_n = \int_a^b g(x)[f(x)]^n.$$

Show $(M_n)^{1/n} \rightarrow M$. Further show if $M > 0$, then $\dfrac{M_{n+1}}{M_n} \rightarrow M$.

25. Let g be a function of bounded variation in $[a, b]$. Let $\{f_n\}$ be a sequence of R–S integrable functions with respect to g on $[a, b]$, and let $\{f_n\}$ converge uniformly to f. Prove f is R–S integrable with respect to g on $[a, b]$, and $\left\{ \int_a^x f_n \, dg \right\}$ converges uniformly on $[a, b]$ to $\int_a^x f \, dg$.

26. Let $\sigma(n, m)$ be a double sequence. For each $n \in \mathbf{N}$, define $f_n : \mathbf{N} \rightarrow \mathbf{R}$ by $f_n(m) = \sigma(n, m)$. If $\{f_n\}$ converges uniformly to f on $\mathbf{N}$, and if the iterated limit $\lim_{m \to \infty} \lim_{n \to \infty} \sigma(n, m)$ exists, then the double sequence converges, and all three values coincide.

Chapter 9

Infinite Series of Functions

In the last chapter the concept of a sequence of functions was developed and various notions of convergence studied. In this chapter, the notion of an infinite series of functions is defined and analogous notions of convergence are developed. In thinking about this chapter, the reader should recall the previously established relationship between sequences and series of constants. Specifically, the basic theory of infinite series was developed by employing the sequence of partial sums as the foundation concept. This approach, which proved so successful in the earlier case, has obvious merit and should likely bear fruit in the present case. This then is the approach we will take, and with this in mind, the ambitious reader may want to try to develop some of the main ideas himself.

9.1 SERIES OF FUNCTIONS, POINTWISE AND UNIFORM CONVERGENCE

Recall the manner in which we constructed an infinite series $\sum a_n$ from a given sequence $\{a_n\}$ of real numbers, and discussed the convergence of such a series by using the auxiliary sequence, $\{s_n\}$, of its partial sums. We can imitate the same technique to consider infinite series whose members are functions defined on a subset A of **R**.

Definition. Let $\{f_n\}$ be a sequence of functions defined on a set $A \subseteq \mathbf{R}$. By the nth **partial sum** of this sequence, we mean the function, s_n, having domain A and defined by

$$s_n(x) = \sum_{i=1}^{n} f_i(x), \quad (x \in A).$$

The sequence of functions, $\{s_n\}$, is called the **associated sequence of partial sums**. By an **infinite series of functions** we mean the pair, $(\{f_n\}, \{s_n\})$, where $\{f_n\}$ is a sequence of functions on A and $\{s_n\}$ is its associated sequence of partial sums.

Notation. We abbreviate the infinite series by the symbol $\sum_{i=1}^{\infty} f_i$. This will generally be further abbreviated to $\sum f_n$.

Discussion. Infinite series of functions will always be specified in terms of the formal collection of symbols, $\sum f_n$. In order to be able to work with this concept, it must be replaced by previously defined terms which capture the intent of the underlying notion. Thus, the moment an infinite series $\sum f_n$ of functions is given, we immediately replace it with the sequence of partial sums, $\{s_n\}$. This sequence consists of functions which are defined on the same subset, A, as the f_n's and it is this sequence which will be the focus of our interest.

Once the series has been replaced by a sequence of functions, natural questions arise as to whether the sequence, $\{s_n\}$, of functions converges pointwise or uniformly on the subset A. These questions will occupy the remainder of this section. $\square$

Definition. The series $\sum f_n$ of functions defined on a set A is said to **converge pointwise** on A provided there exists a function, f, having domain, A, and the sequence, $\{s_n\}$, of associated partial sums converges pointwise to f on A. In this case, we write

$$\sum f_n = f \quad \text{(pointwise) on } A,$$

and refer to f as the pointwise limit of $\sum f_n$ on A.

Discussion. The statement $\sum f_n = f$ (pointwise) means that for each x in the common domain, A, we have the relationship

$$\lim_{n \to \infty} s_n(x) = f(x),$$

which in turn is equivalent to the statement that

$$\sum_{i=1}^{\infty} f_i(x) = f(x)$$

for each $x \in A$. This last assertion is a statement about an infinite series of constants. Thus, pointwise convergence of an infinite series of functions reduces to a statement about an infinite series of constants in the same way that pointwise convergence for a sequence of functions reduced to a statement about convergence of a sequence of constants. For this reason, we are able to bring to bear on questions of convergence for infinite series of functions, not only the previously developed theory for sequences of functions, but also the previously developed theory related to infinite series of constants.

We have not stated the definition of pointwise convergence for series as an $\epsilon - N$ definition, and this is left to the reader as Exercise 1. $\square$

The first concern with any limiting process is the uniqueness of the limit.

Theorem 9.1.1.   Let $\sum f_n$ converge pointwise on A. Then the limit, f, is unique.

Proof.   Exercise 2.   □

EXAMPLE 1

Discuss the pointwise convergence of the geometric series $\sum\limits_{n=1}^{\infty} x^{n-1}$.

Solution.   Here, $f_n(x) = x^{n-1}$ for each $x \in \mathbf{R}$ and so,

$$s_n(x) = 1 + x + x^2 + \cdots + x^{n-1}$$

$$= \begin{cases} \dfrac{1 - x^n}{1 - x}, & x \neq 1 \\[2mm] n, & x = 1. \end{cases}$$

If $|x| < 1$, we know that $x^n \to 0$ and so $\{s_n(x)\}$ converges pointwise to the function, $f(x) = \dfrac{1}{1 - x}$. For $|x| > 1$, it is clear that $\{x^n\}$ is divergent. Consequently, $\{s_n\}$ also diverges. For $x = 1$, $s_n(1) = n$, and hence the series diverges. Finally, if $x = -1$, we have the alternating series, $1 - 1 + 1 - 1 + \cdots$, which is also divergent. Thus, the above series converges pointwise to the function $\dfrac{1}{1 - x}$ if and only if $|x| < 1$.   □

Discussion.   Alternatively, the solution could proceed by fixing x, and applying the results of Example 7.1.3 for the infinite series of constants, $\sum\limits_{n=1}^{\infty} x^{n-1}$.

A noteworthy feature of this example is that each of the functions, f_n, is defined on the totality of $\mathbf{R}$. However, as is apparent from the solution, the series converges only on a portion of $\mathbf{R}$, namely, $(0,1)$. This is a very important feature of series of functions. Often the sequences of functions comprising the series will be defined on all of $\mathbf{R}$, but the series will converge only on a subset, or an interval, of $\mathbf{R}$. Indeed, it will often be the case that identifying the interval of convergence for a particular series is the crux of the problem.   □

EXAMPLE 2

Discuss the pointwise convergence of the series $\sum \dfrac{x^n}{n!}$, $x \in \mathbf{R}$.

Solution.   Fix $x \in \mathbf{R}$. Then $\sum \dfrac{x^n}{n!}$ is a series of constants and we can apply the ratio test (Theorem 7.4.4) with $a_n = \dfrac{x^n}{n!}$ to obtain

$$\lim \left| \frac{\dfrac{x^{n+1}}{(n+1)!}}{\dfrac{x^n}{n!}} \right| = \lim \left| \frac{x^{n+1}}{(n+1)!} \times \frac{n!}{x^n} \right| = \lim \left| \frac{x}{n+1} \right| = 0.$$

By Theorem 7.4.4 the series converges at x, and since x was arbitrary, the series converges pointwise on all of **R**. ☐

Discussion. The argument in this example illustrates how all of the previous theory developed for series of constants can be brought to bear on the issue of pointwise convergence of a series. All of the sophisticated tests for convergence are based on the behavior of the terms, and the rate at which the terms get small. As such, they can be applied to series of functions simply by holding x fixed.

The suggestion that the theory from series of constants has application to series of functions suggests a number of questions. Among them are: what analogies exist between the theory of series of constants and series of functions, and which definitions from the theory of series of constants have natural extensions to the theory of series of functions? ☐

EXAMPLE 3
_____

Discuss the pointwise convergence of the series, $\sum f_n$, of functions defined on **R** by:

$$f_1(x) = \frac{1}{x^2 + 1}, \text{ and for } n > 1,$$

$$f_n(x) = \left(\frac{x^{2n-2}}{x^{2n} + 1} - \frac{x^{2n-4}}{x^{2n-2} + 1} \right).$$

Solution. From the expression for f_n as a difference of two terms, we notice that this is an example of a telescoping series, whence, as the reader can easily verify (Exercise 3),

$$s_n(x) = \frac{x^{2n-2}}{x^{2n} + 1}.$$

The reader can check (Exercise 3) that if x satisfies the inequality $|x| < 1$, then $\{s_n(x)\}$ converges to 0, whereas for $|x| > 1$, $\{s_n(x)\}$ has the limit $\frac{1}{x^2}$. But for $x = \pm 1$, $\lim_{n \to \infty} s_n(x) = \frac{1}{2}$. Hence the pointwise limit function is given by

$$f(x) = \begin{cases} 0, & \text{if } |x| < 1 \\ \dfrac{1}{2}, & \text{if } x = \pm 1 \\ \dfrac{1}{x^2}, & \text{if } |x| > 1. \end{cases}$$

Thus, $\sum f_n = f$ (pointwise) for all $x \in$ **R**. ☐

Discussion. The manner in which we obtained the expression for $s_n(x)$, by virtue of the fact that the series telescopes, was first discussed in Example 7.1.5. Since the resultant expression for $s_n(x)$ involves powers of x, we have to treat various cases and employ the facts about the geometric series.

As with series of constants, this example and Example 1 both demonstrate the utility of obtaining an expression for the nth partial sum. Using the expression for the partial sum, we are able to obtain a functional specification for the limit function, f.

Unlike Example 1, the present series converges for all $x \in \mathbf{R}$. However, the limit function is not continuous, even though the individual f_n's are continuous, as are the s_n's. While this result should not be surprising given the theory for sequences of functions, it does suggest that the stronger form of convergence is required. □

Definition. Let $\{f_n\}$ is a sequence of functions defined on a subset $A \subseteq \mathbf{R}$. We say that the infinite series of functions, $\sum f_n$, **converges uniformly** on the set A provided for every $\epsilon > 0$ there exists a function, f, defined on A and an $N \in \mathbf{N}$ such that for all $x \in A$

$$\left| \sum_{i=1}^{n} f_i(x) - f(x) \right| = |s_n(x) - f(x)| < \epsilon \text{ whenever } n > N.$$

In the event that such an f exists, we say that $\sum f_n$ converges to f uniformly on A, and write $\sum f_n = f$ (uniformly) on A, or $\sum f_n \to f$ (uniformly) on A and refer to f as the uniform limit of $\sum f_n$ on A.

Discussion. We have given the $\epsilon - N$ definition of uniform convergence. We could as easily have given a definition of convergence by appealing to the concept $s_n \to f$ uniformly on A. Such a definition would have been completely equivalent to that given (Exercise 4).

The key concept underlying uniform convergence for series is the same as that for sequences. Namely, the idea is to create a tube of width 2ϵ, and require all partial sums having subscripts exceeding N to lie inside this tube. Notice that unlike the case for sequences, where the f_n's themselves had to lie inside the tube, for series it is the partial sums which must be contained inside the tube. Indeed, in almost all cases, the functions, f_n, will not lie inside the 2ϵ-tube for any value of n. □

Theorem 9.1.2. Let $\sum f_n$ be a series of functions defined on A. If $\sum f_n$ converges uniformly to f on A, then f is the pointwise limit on A and, as such, is unique.

Proof. Exercise 4. □

From this definition it is easy to frame the familiar Cauchy criterion for uniform convergence of an infinite series $\sum f_n$ as follows:

Theorem 9.1.3 (Cauchy Criterion). A necessary and sufficient condition for the series $\sum f_n$ to converge uniformly on the set A is that given $\epsilon > 0$, we can find an $n \in \mathbf{N}$ such that for all $m > n > N$ and all $x \in A$, we have

$$|s_m(x) - s_n(x)| < \epsilon;$$

or equivalently,

$$|f_{n+1}(x) + f_{n+2}(x) + \cdots + f_m(x)| < \epsilon.$$

Proof. Exercise 6. □

Discussion. The reader is already familiar with Cauchy criterion in several contexts. We again stress that the utility of this condition is that we do not have to know in advance the limit function, f, in order to test for uniform convergence. □

Theorem 9.1.4.   Let $\sum\limits_{n=1}^{\infty} f_n$ and $\sum\limits_{n=1}^{\infty} g_n$ be two infinite series which are uniformly convergent on A. If f and g are the respective limits, and a, b are two real constants, then

$$\sum_{n=1}^{\infty} af_n \pm \sum_{n=1}^{\infty} bg_n = af \pm bg \quad \text{(uniformly) on } A.$$

Proof.   Exercise 8.   □

Next we analyze the impact of uniform convergence on continuity.

Theorem 9.1.5.   If each f_n is continuous on A, and the series $\sum f_n$ converges uniformly to the function f on A, then f is continuous on A. Further, suppose that a is a limit point of A, and that for each $n \in N$, $\lim\limits_{x \to a} f_n(x) = a_n$. Then

$$\lim_{x \to a} \sum_{n=1}^{\infty} f_n(x) = \sum_{n=1}^{\infty} a_n.$$

Proof.   If each member, f_n, of the series, $\sum f_n$, is continuous, certainly s_n has to be continuous, being a finite sum of continuous functions. Now, if $\sum f_n$ converges uniformly to f on A, then $\{s_n\}$ converges uniformly to f on A. Thus, by Theorem 8.3.1, we know that f is necessarily continuous. The remainder of the theorem follows from Theorem 8.3.2.   □

Discussion.   The proof given above depends completely on the fact that $\sum f_n \to f$ uniformly on A exactly if the sequence of partial sums, s_n tends uniformly to f on A. While this is apparently true, still, it must be verified (Exercise 4).

We have avoided giving an $\epsilon - N$ proof of this theorem not because we dislike such proofs, but rather because we wanted to preserve that pleasure for the reader as Exercise 9. Generating such a proof is a useful exercise since it will force the reader to come to grips with many of the inequalities employed in these types of arguments.
                                                                       □

EXAMPLE 4 _____

Discuss the uniform convergence of the series, $\sum x(1 - x)^n$, on $[0, 1]$.

Solution.   A simple computation (Exercise 11) shows that

$$s_n(x) = \sum_{i=1}^{n} x(1 - x)^n = x \left[\frac{1 - (1 - x)^{n+1}}{1 - (1 - x)} \right].$$

Now, if $x \in (0,1)$, then

$$\lim_{n \to \infty} s_n(x) = x \left(\frac{1}{1 - 1 + x} \right) = 1.$$

For $x = 0, 1$, clearly $f_n(x) = 0$, whence $s_n(x) = 0$ for all $n \in \mathbf{N}$. Thus the pointwise limit function, f is defined by

$$f(x) = \begin{cases} 1, & \text{if } x \in (0, 1) \\ 0, & \text{if } x = 0, 1. \end{cases}$$

Consequently, we write $\sum x(1 - x)^n = f(x)$. Since the sum function f is discontinuous, while each component is continuous, by Theorem 9.1.5 the convergence cannot be uniform. $\quad\square$

Discussion. Note the ease with which we exploited Theorem 9.1.5 to negate uniform convergence, once we knew that the sum was a discontinuous function. This method should be tried before trying the definition using the $\epsilon - N$ technique. Because of its utility in this respect, Theorem 9.1.5 can be viewed as a test for the failure of uniform convergence of a series of functions. $\quad\square$

There is a very useful positive test for uniform convergence of a series of functions which arises by relating the terms of the series to those of a series with constant terms. This is known as Weierstrass's M-test, and is given in the next theorem.

Theorem 9.1.6 (Weierstrass's M-Test). If $\sum f_n$ is a series of functions defined on A and $\{M_n\}$ is a sequence of real numbers such that $\sum M_n$ is convergent, and the relation $|f_n(x)| < M_n$ holds for all $x \in A$, and for each $n \in \mathbf{N}$, then $\sum f_n$ converges uniformly and absolutely on the set A.

Proof. Let $\epsilon > 0$ be given. Since $\sum M_n$ converges we can find an $N \in \mathbf{N}$ such that for $m, n > N$, we have $\sum_{i=n+1}^{m} M_i < \epsilon$. Now for each $x \in A$,

$$\left| s_m(x) - s_n(x) \right| = \left| \sum_{i=n+1}^{m} f_i(x) \right|$$

$$\leqslant \sum_{i=n+1}^{m} |f_i(x)| \leqslant \sum_{i=n+1}^{m} M_i < \epsilon$$

whenever $m > n > N$. Hence by Cauchy criterion, we obtain uniform convergence on A. Absolute convergence is implicit in the inequalities generated. $\quad\square$

Discussion. The reader will have noticed that we have adopted a very relaxed style in the presentation of proofs. In the present argument we have not mentioned any of the basic elementary facts, such as the Triangle inequality, which are used in the proof. It is assumed that the reader is so familiar with these facts that they are by now second nature and that the reader will invoke them as required. This assumption may be incorrect. For this reason, the reader is invited to test its truth in Exercise 12.

As well, we did not define the notion of absolute convergence for series of functions. The original definition of absolute convergence is in section 7.3. If one thinks about how to generalize this definition, the natural generalization would appear to be that $\sum f_n$ converges **absolutely** on A provided $\sum |f_n|$ converges pointwise on A. This definition raises obvious questions. For example, if $\sum f_n$ converges absolutely and uniformly on A, will the absolute series converge uniformly? If a series converges absolutely, will the convergence be uniform? And so forth. Some of these questions are answered in the remaining examples of this section, others by examples in the exercises.

Weierstrass's M-test is one of the most practical methods for establishing uniform convergence in cases for which one does not have a specification for the pointwise limit. The only tool needed is a proper choice of a convergent series, $\sum M_n$, which dominates the terms f_n over the whole of A. Note also that it suffices that the condition $|f_n(x)| \leqslant M_n$ hold after a certain stage, and not necessarily for all n without exception. □

EXAMPLE 5

Discuss the uniform convergence of $\sum \dfrac{\sin nx}{n^2}$, $x \in \mathbf{R}$.

Solution. Here, $f_n(x) = \dfrac{\sin nx}{n^2}$. Since the maximum value of $\sin nx$ is 1, $\sum \dfrac{1}{n^2}$ converges, and $\left| \dfrac{\sin nx}{n^2} \right| \leqslant \dfrac{1}{n^2}$, by Weierstrass's M-test, we conclude that $\sum f_n$ converges uniformly and absolutely. □

Discussion. Weierstrass's test for uniform convergence automatically guarantees that the series is also absolutely convergent. Thus, if a series is uniformly but not absolutely convergent, then its uniform convergence cannot be derived by the application of the M-test. While this might suggest that an example of a series which converged uniformly, but not absolutely, was very ill-behaved, such is not the case. If the reader cannot create such an example on his own, an example can be found among the series in Exercise 13.

Note the manner in which we hit upon the candidate for the M_n series, namely, $\dfrac{1}{n^2}$ which converges. The success here is due to the fact that we can bound the sine function by a maximum value, 1, thus eliminating the variable x from the expression and obtaining a constant series. Finally, from the absolute convergence of $\sum f_n$ we conclude that $\sum f_n(x)$ converges for each x. □

EXAMPLE 6

Does the series $\sum\limits_{n=0}^{\infty} \dfrac{x^n}{n!}$ converge uniformly and/or absolutely on $\mathbf{R}$?

Solution. If Theorem 7.4.4 is applied to the computations in Example 7.4.3, it is seen that the series $\sum \dfrac{x^n}{n!}$ converges absolutely on $\mathbf{R}$. We claim that the convergence is not uniform. To see this, observe that $\sum\limits_{n=0}^{\infty} \dfrac{x^n}{n!}$ converges pointwise on $\mathbf{R}$ to the limit function e^x, as we will show in Chapter 10. Given this is the case, the reader can show that for any fixed n, we can find x such that $|e^x - s_n| \geqslant 1$ (Exercise 14). Thus, the convergence is not uniform on $\mathbf{R}$. □

Discussion.   This example shows that absolute convergence on **R** does not imply uniform convergence. Further examples can be constructed to show that absolute convergence on $[a, b]$ does not imply uniform convergence there (Exercise 15). It may be more surprising that uniform convergence does not imply absolute convergence. The reader can construct an example, or find an example in the exercises.

There are several other delicate tests, more powerful than the M-test, which are useful to test the uniform convergence of a conditionally convergent series of functions. Two such tests are appended below. We start with a definition.

Definition.   The infinite series, $\sum_{n=1}^{\infty} f_n$, is said to be **uniformly bounded** on a set A provided there exists a constant $K > 0$ such that $\sum_{k=1}^{n} |f_k(x)| < K$ for all $n \in \mathbf{N}$ and for all $x \in A$.

Discussion.   The uniformity of the boundedness concept is spelled out by the requirement that we need to produce a single constant K for which

$$\sum_{k=1}^{n} |f_k(x)| < K \quad \text{for all } x \text{ and for all } n.$$

The reader should note the difference between this concept and a concept of pointwise boundedness.

The definition of a uniformly bounded sequence of functions has previously appeared in Exercise 8.1.11. In essence the present definition asserts that the sequence of partial sums, $\{s_n\}$, is uniformly bounded on A. Both concepts will be required in the next several theorems. □

Theorem 9.1.7 (Abel's Test).   If $\sum f_n$ is uniformly convergent on a set A, $\{g_n\}$ is a uniformly bounded sequence on A such that for each $x \in A$, $\{g_n(x)\}$ is a monotonic (increasing or decreasing) sequence, then the series $\sum f_n g_n$ is uniformly convergent on A.

Proof.   If $s_n(x)$ denotes the partial sum function of $\sum f_n$, we can define $t_n = \sum_{n+1}^{\infty} f_n(x)$, so that $\sum f_n = s_n + t_n$ (**WHY?**). It is then easy to check that

$$f_n g_n = -t_n[g_n - g_{n+1}] + t_{n-1}g_n - t_n g_{n+1}.$$

Summing from $i = n + 1$ to $n + k$, this yields

$$\sum_{i=n+1}^{n+k} f_i g_i = \sum_{i=n+1}^{n+k} [-t_i(g_i - g_{i+1}) + t_n g_{n+1} - t_{n+k}g_{n+k+1}]$$

whence

$$\left| \sum_{i=n+1}^{n+k} f_i g_i \right| \leqslant \sum_{n+1}^{n+k} [|t_i| \, |g_i - g_{i+1}| + |t_n| \, |g_{n+1}| + |t_{n+k}| \, |g_{n+k+1}|].$$

Let $\epsilon > 0$ be given. By uniform boundedness of $\{g_n\}$ there is $K > 0$ such that $|g_n(x)| < K$ for all x in A and for all n. Also, there exists $N \in \mathbf{N}$ such that for all

$x \in A$ and all $n > N$, $|t_n(x)| < \dfrac{\epsilon}{4K}$ (**WHY?**). Again, by the monotonicity of the sequence $\{g_n\}$, we have

$$\sum_{n+1}^{n+k} |g_i(x) - g_{i+1}(x)| = |g_{n+1}(x) - g_{n+k+1}(x)| < 2K.$$

Putting all these facts together, we finally have for $k \geqslant 0$

$$|\sum_{n+1}^{n+k} f_i(x)g_i(x)| < |g_i(x) - g_{i+1}(x)| + 2K\frac{\epsilon}{4K}$$

$$< 2K\frac{\epsilon}{4K} + \frac{\epsilon}{2} = \epsilon.$$

The desired conclusion follows, once we invoke the Cauchy criterion. $\qquad\square$

Discussion. The proof of this theorem is quite complicated. One would like to construct a simple proof, which would be founded on the following string of inequalities:

$$|\sum_{k=n}^{m} f_n g_n| \leqslant \sum_{k=n}^{m} |f_n g_n| = \sum_{k=n}^{m} |f_n|\,|g_n| \leqslant \sum_{k=n}^{m} |f_n|K.$$

One would then apply the Cauchy criterion to the last series and be done. The difficulty with this argument is that the last series is not, in general, convergent. The canonical example of a resultant series, that is, at the far right, which would fail to converge is the series, $\sum \dfrac{x}{n}$ defined on $[0, 1]$. The reader may think that this situation is avoided because its occurrence requires the introduction of absolute values. Such is not the case, for $\{f_n\}$ and $\{g_n\}$ may be chosen so as to guarantee $f_n g_n \geqslant 0$.

The question therefore arises: what in the hypothesis prevents such a situation from arising. The answer is monotonicity of $\{g_n\}$. If this assumption is dropped then the divergent series $\sum \dfrac{x}{n}$ may result as the product, $f_n g_n$. $\qquad\square$

Theorem 9.1.8 (Dirichlet's Test). If $\{f_n\}$ and $\{g_n\}$ are such that $\sum f_n$ is uniformly bounded on A, the sequence $\{g_n\}$ is uniformly convergent on A, and for each $x \in A$, the sequence $\{g_n(x)\}$ is monotonic (increasing or decreasing) and tends to 0, then $\sum f_n g_n$ is uniformly convergent on A.

Proof. First note that we have the (easily checked) identity

$$f_i g_i = s_i[g_i - g_{i+1}] - s_{i-1}g_i + s_i g_{i+1}$$

where s_n has the usual meaning. Summing from $i = n + 1$ to $n + k$, we have

$$|\sum_{i=n+1}^{n+k} f_i g_i| \leqslant |s_i|\,|g_i - g_{i+1}| + |s_{n+k}|\,|g_{n+k+1}| + |s_n|\,|g_{n+1}|.$$

Let $\epsilon > 0$ be given. First, there is $K > 0$ satisfying $|s_n(x)| < K$ for all $x \in A$ and all $n > N$. By uniform convergence of $\{g_n\}$, there exists $N > 0$ such that for all $x \in A$, and $n > N$, we have $|g_n(x)| < \dfrac{\epsilon}{4K}$. Hence if $k > 0$, $n > N$, and $x \in A$, we have

$$\left| \sum_{i=n+1}^{n+k} f_i(x) g_i(x) \right| \leqslant K \sum_{i=n+1}^{n+k} |g_i(x) - g_{i+1}(x)| + 2K\frac{\epsilon}{4K}$$

$$< K\, |g_{n+1}(x) - g_{n+k+1}(x)| + \frac{\epsilon}{2} \quad \text{by monotonicity of } g_n$$

$$\leqslant \epsilon$$

proving the uniform convergence of $\sum f_n g_n$.   □

Discussion. Similar comments apply to the role of monotonicity in the hypothesis of Dirichlet's test.   □

EXAMPLE 7 _____

Discuss the uniform convergence of $\displaystyle\sum_{n=1}^{\infty} \frac{\sin nx}{n^p}$, $0 < p \in \mathbf{R}$.

> *Solution.* We can take $f_n(x) = \sin nx$, and by elementary trigonometry, it can be shown (Exercise 19, also see Exercise 5.3.13) if $x \neq \pm 2k\pi$, $k = 1, 2, \ldots$, then
>
> $$s_n(x) = \sum_{k=1}^{n} f_k(x) = \frac{\sin\dfrac{nx}{2} \sin\dfrac{(n+1)x}{2}}{\sin\dfrac{x}{2}}.$$
>
> If $x \in [d, 2\pi - d]$, then $|s_n(x)| < \dfrac{1}{\sin\dfrac{d}{2}}$ so that $\{s_n(x)\}$ is uniformly
>
> bounded in $[d, 2\pi - d]$. The sequence $\{g_n(x)\}$ is free of the variable x, and so is trivially uniformly convergent to 0 in the same interval, if $0 < k \leqslant 1$. So the conditions for Dirichlet's test are fulfilled, and by applying the test, we conclude that the given series is uniformly convergent in $[d, 2\pi - d]$.   □

Discussion. It is worth comparing the solution for this example to that for Example 5. The solution for Example 5 employed Weierstrass's M-test. Why not do the same in this case? The difficulty with the present example is the failure of $\sum \dfrac{1}{n^p}$ to converge for $p \leqslant 1$. Thus more subtle methods are required.   □

Next, we provide a short discussion of the term-by-term integration and term-by-term differentiation of an infinite series of functions. The considerations are very similar to those of sequences of functions discussed earlier. The following theorem justifies term-by-term integration in the presence of uniform convergence.

Theorem 9.1.9. If each f_n is Riemann integrable in $[a, b]$, and the series $\sum f_n$ converges uniformly in $[a, b]$ to f, then f is also Riemann integrable in $[a, b]$ and further $\sum \int_a^b f_n = \int_a^b f$. (In other words, the integral of the sum is the sum of the integrals.)

Proof. Let $\{s_n\}$ denote the sequence of partial sums of the series. Then, the sequence, $\{s_n\}$, converges uniformly in $[a, b]$ to f. Clearly, s_n is integrable, being a finite sum of integrable functions. Hence by Theorem 8.3.3, f is Riemann integrable in $[a, b]$ and

$$\int_a^b f = \lim \int_a^b s_n.$$

Using the fact that

$$\int_a^b s_n = \sum_{i=1}^n \int_a^b f_i,$$

and taking limit as n approaches infinity, we obtain

$$\int_a^b f = \sum_{n=1}^\infty \int_a^b f_n.$$

$\square$

The final theorem of this section gives conditions under which term-by-term differentiation of a series of function is valid.

Theorem 9.1.10. If each f_n possesses a derivative throughout $[a, b]$, f_n' is continuous on $[a, b]$ for each n, $\sum f_n$ converges to f on $[a, b]$, and $\sum f_n'$ converges uniformly on $[a, b]$, then

$$f'(x) = \sum f_n'(x)$$

for $x \in [a, b]$.

Proof. The partial sum s_n has a derivative throughout $[a, b]$, $\{s_n\}$ converges to f on $[a, b]$, and since $s_n' = f_1' + f_2' + \cdots + f_n'$, it is clear $\{s_n'\}$ converges uniformly to a function g on $[a, b]$. So Theorem 8.3.4 applies to guarantee that $f' = g$ throughout $[a, b]$, whence $f'(x) = \sum f_n'$ for each $x \in [a, b]$. $\square$

Discussion. The proofs of both of these theorems depend for their truth on finite additivity. That is, a finite sum of integrable (differentiable) functions is integrable (differentiable) and the sum of the integrals (derivative) is the integral (derivative) of the sum. These theorems delineate the circumstances in which this property, finite additivity, can be extended to infinite sums. $\square$

We conclude this section with an example of an everywhere continuous, nowhere differentiable function, which we promised in Chapter 4. The first example was constructed by Weierstrass in 1872, but it is believed that Bolzano knew of such a construction as early as 1830. The version we present here is essentially that of Van der Waerden (1930).

EXAMPLE 8 _____

There exists a function $f: \mathbf{R} \to \mathbf{R}$, which is continuous on $\mathbf{R}$, but does not possess a derivative at any point of $\mathbf{R}$.

Solution. We start with the function $g(x) = |x|$, $-2 \leqslant x \leqslant 2$, and extend it to the entire real line, periodically, by setting $g(x + 4p) = g(x)$, $x \in \mathbf{R}$, $p \in \mathbf{Z}$. If $S = \{4m : m \in \mathbf{Z}\}$, it is then clear that

$$g(x) = \inf \{ |x - s| : s \in S \}. \tag{1}$$

Also, note that if there is no even integer in the open interval (a, b), then $|g(a) - g(b)| = |a - b|$. For each n, set $f_n(x) = \dfrac{g(4^n x)}{4^n}$, $x \in \mathbf{R}$. Let $f(x) = \displaystyle\sum_{n=1}^{\infty} f_n(x)$. We claim that the function f has the desired properties.

Clearly, each f_n is continuous on $\mathbf{R}$ (**WHY?**). Also, $0 \leqslant f_n(x) \leqslant \dfrac{2}{4^n}$. Since $\sum \dfrac{2}{4^n}$ is a convergent series of constants, by Weierstrass's M-test, it follows that the series $\sum f_n$ is uniformly convergent to f on $\mathbf{R}$. Also, since each f_n is continuous on $\mathbf{R}$, we invoke Theorem 9.1.5 to conclude that f is continuous on $\mathbf{R}$.

We now show that f is not differentiable at any point on $\mathbf{R}$. Let $a \in \mathbf{R}$ be arbitrary, but fixed. We demonstrate that $f'(a)$ does not exist. To this end, for each $k \in \mathbf{N}$, define $\delta_k = +1$ or -1 (depending on k), such that there is no even integer in the open interval $(4^k a, 4^k a + \delta_k)$. In the ambiguous case where $4^k a$ happens to be an integer, either choice will do. For $1 \leqslant n \leqslant k$, we observe that there is no even integer between $4^n a$ and $4^n a + 4^{n-k}\delta_k$. For, if an even integer $2p$ were between them, then, $4^{k-n}2p$ would be between $4^k a$ and $4^k a + \delta_k$, which is a contradiction. Hence, by (1),

$$\left| f_n \left[1 + \frac{1}{4^k}\delta_k \right] - f_n(a) \right| = \frac{1}{4^n} \left| g(4^n a + 4^{n-k}\delta_k) - g(4^n a) \right| \tag{2}$$

$$= \frac{1}{4^k} \quad (1 \leqslant n \leqslant k).$$

On the other hand, if $n > k$, it is clear from (1) and the first equality in (2) that

$$f_n \left[a + \frac{1}{4^k}\delta_k \right] = f_n(a). \tag{3}$$

Call $h_k = \dfrac{\delta_k}{4^k}$, and use (2) and (3) to obtain

$$\frac{f(a + h_k) - f(a)}{h_k} = \sum_{n=1}^{k} \frac{f_n(a + h_k) - f_n(a)}{h_k} = \sum_{n=1}^{k} (\pm 1).$$

The last expression is an even integer if k is even, and an odd integer if k is odd. When $k \to \infty$, $h_k \to 0$, and so $\displaystyle\lim_{h_k \to 0} \frac{f(a + h_k) - f(a)}{h_k}$ does not exist. This proves that $f'(a)$ does not exist. $\qquad\square$

Discussion. The basic fact employed in this ingenious construction is that the absolute value function is not differentiable at its corner point, $x = 0$, even though it is continuous. The function, g, described above is composed of several of these graphs arrayed together on the real line, so as to form an infinite number of 'roofs', a roof constructed on each interval $(4m, 4m + 4)$, with height 2 at $4m + 2$, where $m \in \mathbf{Z}$. Such a graph is called a **saw-tooth** function. The function, f_1, has the same shape as that of g, except that each roof in the function g gets replaced by 4 smaller roofs, with $\frac{1}{4}$ times the width and height of the roofs in g. Thus, the graph of f_n consists of 4^n roofs in any interval of the form $(4m, 4m + 4)$, $m \in \mathbf{Z}$, and the height of each roof is $\frac{1}{4^n}$. Note that each roof contributes three points of nondifferentiability, one at its maximum, and two points at either end, common to the two adjacent roofs. So, as n increases, we have more and more points of nondifferentiability, since there are more and more sharp corners. Specifically, if $f_n(x) = 0$ for some x, it follows that $f_m(x) = 0$ for all $m > n$; also the 'peak point' of f_n reduces to a 'zero point' for f_{n+1}. Thus it is conceivable that when we take the sum of all these functions, and then take limit as n tends to infinity, we must have destroyed the differentiability at a huge collection of points. The above proof formalizes this intuition. The graphs of g and f_1 are drawn in Figure 9.1.1.

The continuity part of the proof is straightforward, and employs only the fact that uniform convergence preserves continuity. The differentiability part needs a delicate argument, which is not hard. Rather than proving $\lim_{h \to 0} \dfrac{f(a + h) - f(a)}{h}$ does not exist, we choose a sequence $\{h_k\}$ approaching 0, so that the corresponding difference quotient does not approach a limit. $\square$

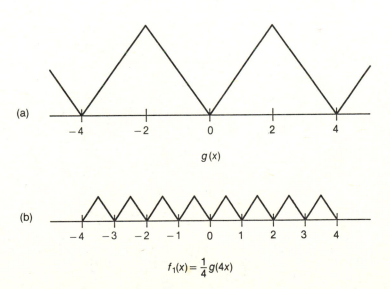

$$g(x)$$

$$f_1(x) = \tfrac{1}{4}g(4x)$$

Figure 9.1.1 (a) Graph of the function $g(x)$. (b) Graph of the function $f_1(x) = \dfrac{1}{4}g(4x)$.

EXERCISES

1. Give an $\epsilon - N$ type definition for the pointwise convergence of an infinite series of functions.

2. Prove Theorem 9.1.1.

3. Verify the formula $s_n(x)$ in Example 3. Verify the statements about the limit of the sequence.

4. Give a definition for the uniform convergence of a series of functions in terms of uniform convergence of the associated sequence of partial sums. Show this definition is completely equivalent to the definition given. Conclude the uniform limit must coincide with the pointwise limit, and hence must be unique.

5. Write a discussion of the geometric interpretation of uniform convergence for an infinite series of functions.

6. Prove Theorem 9.1.3.

7. Make a list of the various forms of Cauchy Criteria which have been developed in this text. Write a discussion which illustrates their essential similarities.

8. Prove Theorem 9.1.4. State and prove a similar theorem related to pointwise convergence.

9. Give an $\epsilon - N$ proof of Theorem 9.1.5.

10. Write a discussion of the proof of Theorem 9.1.5. What is the role of the Triangle inequality in the proof? What is the geometric intuition underlying the proof?

11. Verify the formula for s_n in Example 4.

12. What is the role of the Triangle inequality in Theorem 9.1.6? Why does the proof imply that the series converges absolutely?

13. Discuss the uniform and absolute convergence of the following series of functions in the domains noted against each:

(a) $\displaystyle\sum_{n=1}^{\infty} n^2 x^n, \quad \left[\dfrac{-1}{2}, \dfrac{1}{2}\right]$;

(b) $\displaystyle\sum_{n=1}^{\infty} \dfrac{x^n}{n^2(1 + x^n)}, \quad [0, 1]$;

(c) $\displaystyle\sum_{n=1}^{\infty} \dfrac{\cos nx}{5^n}, \quad \mathbf{R}$;

(d) $\displaystyle\sum_{n=1}^{\infty} \dfrac{(-1)^n}{n^x}, \quad x \geqslant 1$;

(e) $\displaystyle\sum_{n=1}^{\infty} n e^{-nx}, \ x \geqslant 2$;

(f) $\displaystyle\sum_{n=1}^{\infty} \dfrac{x}{n^{\alpha}(1 + nx^2)}, \ \alpha > \dfrac{1}{2}, \quad \mathbf{R}$;

(g) $\displaystyle\sum_{n=1}^{\infty} \dfrac{(-1)^n \sin\left[1 + \dfrac{x}{n}\right]}{\sqrt{n}}, \quad$ any compact subset of $\mathbf{R}$;

(h) $\displaystyle\sum_{n=1}^{\infty} \dfrac{x^2}{(1 + x^2)^n}, \quad \mathbf{R}$;

(i) $\displaystyle\sum_{n=1}^{\infty} e^{-nx}x^n, \quad x \in [0, 100];$

(j) $\displaystyle\sum_{n=1}^{\infty} \frac{(-1)^{n+1}x^2}{n}, \quad x \in [0, 5];$

(k) $\displaystyle\sum_{n=1}^{\infty} \frac{1}{n^2 + x^2}, \quad x \in \mathbf{R}^+;$

(l) $\displaystyle\sum_{n=1}^{\infty} \frac{nx^2}{n^3 + x^3}, \quad x \in [0, a], \quad a > 0;$

(m) $\displaystyle\sum_{n=1}^{\infty} \frac{(-1)^n}{x + n}, \quad x \in \mathbf{R}^+;$

(n) $\displaystyle\sum_{n=1}^{\infty} \frac{1}{x^n + 1}, \quad x \in \mathbf{R}^+;$

(o) $\displaystyle\sum_{n=1}^{\infty} \frac{x^{2n}}{(x + n)^2}, \quad x \in [0, 1];$

(p) $\displaystyle\sum_{n=1}^{\infty} \frac{x^n}{n^2}, \quad x \in [5, \infty);$

(q) $\displaystyle\sum_{n=1}^{\infty} \frac{1}{1 + n^2x^2}, \quad x \in [1, \infty);$

(r) $\displaystyle\sum_{n=1}^{\infty} n^{-x}, \quad x \in [\sqrt{3}, \infty);$

(s) $\displaystyle\sum_{n=1}^{\infty} \frac{1}{(nx)^2}, \quad x \neq 0;$

(t) $\displaystyle\sum_{n=1}^{\infty} \left[\frac{x^{2n+1}}{2n+1} - \frac{x^{n+1}}{2n+2} \right] \quad x \in [0, 1];$

(u) $\displaystyle\sum_{n=1}^{\infty} \frac{\sin nx}{n2^n}, \quad x \in \mathbf{R};$

(v) $\displaystyle\sum_{n=1}^{\infty} \frac{x^n}{1 + x^{n+1}}, \quad x \in [0, a], \quad 0 < a < 1 \text{ and } x \in [0, 1);$

(w) $\displaystyle\sum_{n=1}^{\infty} \sin^n x, \quad x \in \left[0, \frac{\pi}{2} - \delta \right], \quad \delta > 0;$

(x) $\displaystyle\sum_{n=1}^{\infty} \frac{1}{n}\sqrt{\frac{\sin nx}{n}}, \quad x \in \mathbf{R};$

(y) $\displaystyle\sum_{n=1}^{\infty} \frac{x^n}{n}e^{nx}, \quad x \in [0, 12];$

(z) $\displaystyle\sum_{n=1}^{\infty} f_n(x), \text{ where } f_n(x) = \begin{cases} 1, & x = \dfrac{m}{n}, \ m, n \in \mathbf{Z}, \ m, n \text{ relatively prime} \\ 0, & \text{otherwise} \end{cases}, \quad x \in \mathbf{R};$

(a′) $\displaystyle\sum_{n=1}^{\infty} ne^{-nx}, \quad x \in [a, \infty), \ a > 0;$

(b′) $\displaystyle\sum_{n=1}^{\infty} (1 - x^2)x^n, \quad [0, 1];$

(c′) $\displaystyle\sum_{n=1}^{\infty} \frac{x}{(1 + (n-1)x)(1 + nx)}$, $[a, b]$, $[0, b)$, $b > a > 0$;

(d′) $\displaystyle\sum_{n=1}^{\infty} n^{-x}$, $[1 + \delta, \infty)$, $\delta > 0$;

(e′) $\displaystyle\sum_{n=1}^{\infty} \frac{x}{1 + nx^p}$, $\mathbf{R}$;

(f′) $\displaystyle\sum_{n=1}^{\infty} \frac{1}{n^p + |x|^p}$, $\mathbf{R}$;

(g′) $\displaystyle\sum_{n=1}^{\infty} \frac{x}{n^p + x^2 n^q}$, $\mathbf{R}$;

(h′) $\displaystyle\sum_{n=1}^{\infty} \frac{(-1)^n x^{2n}}{n^p(1 + x^{2n})}$, $\mathbf{R}$.

14. Under the assumption that $\displaystyle\sum_{n=0}^{\infty} \frac{x^n}{n!}$ converges pointwise on $\mathbf{R}$ to $f(x) = e^x$, show the convergence cannot be uniform.

15. Construct an example of a series which is absolutely convergent on $[0, 1]$, but which fails to be uniformly convergent there.

16. If $\{f_n\}$, $\{g_n\}$ be such that $|f_n| \leqslant |g_n|$ on A, and if $\sum g_n$ is uniformly convergent on A, prove the same applies to $\sum f_n$.

17. If $\sum f_n$ converges uniformly on A, prove the sequence of functions $\{f_n\}$ converges uniformly to the zero function. Is the converse true?

18. If $\{f_n\}$ is a decreasing sequence of nonnegative functions that converge uniformly to 0 on A, prove the alternating series $\sum (-1)^n f_n$ converges uniformly on A.

19. Consider the trigonometric identity required for the solution of Example 7. Using any of the basic trigonometric identities which can be found in an elementary calculus book prove this identity for $n = 2$. Now prove it for arbitrary values of n.

20. If $\sum |a_n|$ converges, prove $\displaystyle\sum_{n=0}^{\infty} a_n \sin nx$ and $\displaystyle\sum_{n=0}^{\infty} a_n \cos nx$ are both uniformly convergent.

21. Let $\{a_n\}$ be a decreasing sequence of positive terms. Prove the series $\sum a_n \sin nx$ converges uniformly on $\mathbf{R}$ if and only if $na_n \to 0$ as $n \to 0$.

22. If $\{a_n\}$ is monotonic sequence converging to 0, discuss the uniform convergence of $\sum a_n \sin nx$ and $\sum a_n \cos nx$ in $[d, 2\pi - d]$.

23. Show $\sum \dfrac{\sin nx}{n^2}$ converges uniformly on $\mathbf{R}$ but the differentiated series $\sum \dfrac{\cos nx}{n}$ diverges for all x.

24. If $f(x) = \sum \dfrac{x^n}{n}$ on $[0, 1)$, show $\displaystyle\int_0^1 f = \sum_{n=1}^{\infty} \frac{1}{n(n + 1)}$.

25. Give examples in support of the following:
   (a) A series may converge uniformly, but not absolutely;
   (b) A series may converge to an integrable limit without being uniformly convergent;
   (c) A series of continuous functions with a continuous limit function need not be uniformly convergent;
   (d) $\sum f_n$ converges pointwise to f, term-by-term differentiation is valid, but the convergence is not uniform;

(e) $\sum f_n$ converges pointwise to f, term-by-term integration is valid, but the convergence is not uniform;

(f) The converse of Weierstrass's M-test is not true, that is, $\sum f_n$ converges uniformly and absolutely on A, but $\sum M_n$ diverges, where

$$M_n = \sup\{f_n(x): x \in A\}.$$

26. Comment on the effect of the following operations on a uniformly convergent series $\sum f_n$ on a domain A:

(a) adding a finite number of terms;

(b) deleting a finite number of terms;

(c) adding an infinite number of terms;

(d) deleting an infinite number of terms;

(e) adding an infinite number of terms, each of which is the zero function.

27. Prove **Dini's Theorem**: If each f_n is nonnegative and continuous on $[a, b]$, and $\sum f_n$ converges to a continuous function on $[a, b]$, then the convergence is uniform in $[a, b]$.

28. Prove the series $\zeta(s) = \sum_{n=1}^{\infty} \dfrac{1}{n^s}$ (see Exercise 7.5.15) converges uniformly on every interval of the form $1 + h \leqslant s < \infty$, where $h > 0$. Justify the validity of the equation

$$\zeta'(s) = -\sum_{n=1}^{\infty} \frac{\ln n}{n^s}$$

for $s > 1$. Obtain a similar series for the kth derivative $\zeta^{(k)}(s)$.

29. Given a convergent series $\sum a_n$, prove that the series, $\sum_{n=1}^{\infty} \dfrac{a_n}{n^x}$, converges uniformly on the interval $0 \leqslant x < \infty$. Use this to show

$$\lim_{x \to 0^+} \sum_{n=1}^{\infty} \frac{a_n}{n^x} = \sum_{n=1}^{\infty} a_n.$$

30. If $\sum |a_n|$ converges, prove

$$\int_0^1 \left[\sum_{n=1}^{\infty} a_n x^n \right] = \sum_{n=1}^{\infty} \frac{a_n}{n + 1}.$$

31. Given $f(x) = \sum_{n=1}^{\infty} \dfrac{1}{n^3 + n^4 x^2}$, justify the validity of the equation

$$f'(x) = -2x \sum_{n=1}^{\infty} \frac{1}{n^2(1 + nx^2)^2}.$$

32. Justify the equation

$$\lim_{x \to 1} \left[\sum_{n=1}^{\infty} \frac{nx^2}{n^3 + x^3} \right] = \sum_{n=1}^{\infty} \frac{n}{n^3 + 1}.$$

33. Find the derivative f' for the following functions:

(a) $f(x) = \displaystyle\sum_{n=-1}^{\infty} \frac{\sin nx}{e^{nx}}, \quad x > 0;$

(b) $f(x) = \displaystyle\sum_{n=1}^{\infty} \frac{\sin nx}{n^2}, \quad x \in [0, \pi];$

(c) $f(x) = \sum\limits_{n=1}^{\infty} \dfrac{n}{x^n}$, $|x| > 1$.

34. Compute the following:

(a) $\displaystyle\int_0^\pi \sum_{n=1}^{\infty} \dfrac{\sin nx}{n^2}$;

(b) $\displaystyle\int_1^2 \sum_{n=1}^{\infty} \dfrac{n}{e^{nx}}$;

(c) $\displaystyle\int_a^b \sum_{n=1}^{\infty} \dfrac{\sin nx}{e^{nx}}$, $(0 < a < b)$.

35. If $\sum |a_n|$ converges, prove that $\sum a_n f_n$ also converges uniformly, where f_n is any one of the following:

(a) $\cos nx$;

(b) $\sin nx$;

(c) $\cos a_n x$;

(d) $\sin a_n x$;

(e) $\dfrac{|x|^n}{1 + x^{2n}}$;

(f) $\dfrac{x^{2n}}{1 + x^{2n}}$.

36. If $\{f_n\}$ is bounded on A, and $\sum a_n$ is absolutely convergent, is it true that $\sum a_n f_n$ is uniformly convergent on A?

37. Develop a theory of uniform convergence for an infinite product of functions $\prod\limits_{n=1}^{\infty} f_n(x)$.

Relate the uniform convergence of the product $\prod\limits_{n=1}^{\infty} (1 + f_n(x))$ with that of the series $\sum f_n(x)$; derive a form of Weierstrass's M-test for infinite products.

38. Let $\sum f_n \to f$ uniformly on A, a be a limit point of the common domain, and for each $n \in \mathbf{N}$, $\lim\limits_{x \to a} f_n = a_n$. Prove $\sum a_n$ converges to $\lim\limits_{x \to a} f$.

39. Prove **du Bois-Reymond test**: If $\sum f_n$ and $\sum g_n$ are such that $\sum f_n$ and $\sum |g_n - g_{n+1}|$ are uniformly convergent on A, and $\{g_n\}$ is uniformly bounded on A, then $\sum f_n g_n$ is uniformly convergent on A.

40. Prove **Dedekind test**: If the sequence $\{s_n\}$ of partial sums of $\sum f_n$ is uniformly bounded, the sequence $\{g_n\}$ converges uniformly to 0, and if $\sum |g_n - g_{n+1}|$ is uniformly convergent, then $\sum f_n g_n$ converges.

41. If either (a) $\{a_n\}$ is monotonic and decreases to 0, or (b) $\{a_n\}$ tends to 0, and $\sum |a_n - a_{n+1}| < \infty$, prove that $\sum a_n \sin nx$ and $\sum a_n \cos nx$, both converge uniformly in $[\delta, 2\pi - \delta]$, $\delta > 0$.

42. Let $h: [0, 2] \to \mathbf{R}$ be defined by

$$h(t) = \begin{cases} 0, & t \in [0,1/3], \ [5/3,2] \\ 1, & t \in [2/3,4/3] \\ 3t - 1, & t \in [1/3,2/3] \\ 5 - 3t, & t \in [4/3,5/3] \end{cases}$$

and extend the definition of h to $\mathbf{R}$ by periodicity, by setting $h(t + 2) = h(t)$. Also set

$$f(t) = \sum_{n=1}^{\infty} \frac{h(3^{2n-2}t)}{2^n}, \quad g(t) = \sum_{n=1}^{\infty} \frac{h(3^{2n-1}t)}{2^n}.$$

Prove the following:

(a) f and g are continuous on $\mathbf{R}$;

(b) if $\Delta = \{(f(t), g(t)): t \in [0, 1]\}$, $\Delta \subseteq [0, 1] \times [0, 1]$;

(c) if $(a, b) \in [0, 1] \times [0, 1]$, let

$$a = \sum_{n=1}^{\infty} \frac{a_n}{2^n}, \quad b = \sum_{n=1}^{\infty} \frac{b_n}{2^n}, \quad c = 2 \sum_{n=1}^{\infty} \frac{c_n}{2^n},$$

where each a_n and each b_n is either 0 or 1, and $c_{2n-1} = a_n$, $c_{2n} = b_n$, $n \in \mathbf{N}$. Prove that $f(c) = a$, $g(c) = b$.

(d) $\phi : [0, 1] \rightarrow [0, 1] \times [0, 1]$ defined by $\phi(t) = (f(t), g(t))$ is continuous and onto. This is the classical example of a **space-filling curve** (that is, Δ 'fills' the unit square).

9.2 POWER SERIES

In the first section of this chapter we considered the basic properties of series of functions. Specifically, we considered many questions, for instance, when such a series could be integrated term-by-term, and so forth. The reason underlying our interest in these questions is that in many instances a given function can be represented by a series, and under suitable conditions, that is, requirements on uniform convergence, the series may be easy to deal with, whereas the original function is not. If one thinks about the type of functions which would make up a series representing a given unpleasant function, it is evident that if the series consisted of polynomials, then it would be easy to deal with in the extreme. This is the notion that motivates our discussion of power series.

Definition. Let $\{a_n\}$ be a sequence of real numbers for $n = 0, 1, \ldots$. The infinite series of functions $\sum_{n=0}^{\infty} a_n x^n$ is called a **power series** in x, centered at the origin. More generally one can consider power series of the form, $\sum a_n (x-a)^n$, and this will be known as a power series in x **centered at the point** a.

Discussion. We shall be concerned mainly with power series centered at origin, since the methodology for dealing with power series centered at a results from a minimal modification of the methodology for dealing with series centered at the origin. The questions which primarily interest us are: when does such a series converge, and moreover, when is the convergence uniform? Also, can we perform term-by-term operations such as differentiation and integration on such a series? The reason why we are interested in these questions is that many functions can be represented by power series and for the representation to be useful, we must have a complete understanding of its properties.

We want to adopt a convention for indices of power series. Namely, for power series, the notation, $\sum a_n x^n$, means $\sum_{n=0}^{\infty} a_n x^n$. The reason for this convention is that a power series includes the constant term $a_0 = a_0 x^0$.

Trivially, every power series $\sum a_n x^n$ converges for $x = 0$. It may happen that this is the only point at which it converges, as it happens in the case of $\sum (n!)x^n$. On the other extreme, it is possible that the power series converges for every value of x, as in the example of $\sum \dfrac{x^n}{n!}$. The third possibility is that for certain values we obtain convergence, and for certain others, we have divergence. This is illustrated by the geometric series $\sum x^n$. Our aim is to precisely nail down a stage which separates the values of x for which the series converges and those for which the series diverges. We approach this problem with a series of results, culminating in the precise formulation of what is known as the 'interval of convergence' of a power series.   □

Theorem 9.2.1.   If the power series $\sum a_n x^n$ converges for a value $x = x_0$, then it converges absolutely for all x satisfying the inequality $|x| < |x_0|$.

Proof. Since $\sum a_n x_0^n$ converges as a series of constant terms, the sequence $\{a_n x_0^n\}$ converges to 0, and hence is bounded, say by the real number M. Thus for any x, we have

$$|a_n x^n| = |a_n x_0^n| \left| \frac{x}{x_0} \right|^n \leqslant Mr^n$$

where $r = \left| \dfrac{x}{x_0} \right| < 1$. Since the geometric series $\sum Mr^n$ is convergent, the result follows by the comparison test.   □

Discussion.   The power of the theorem rests in the fact that by the mere knowledge that the series converges at a single point, x_0, we are able to conclude absolute convergence in an entire open interval $(-|x_0|, |x_0|)$. We stress that the theorem does not even require that the convergence at x_0 be absolute. The theorem says nothing at all about the behavior of the power series outside this interval (including the two endpoints). The series may or may not converge in this region.   □

For the divergence case, we have the following theorem:

Theorem 9.2.2.   If $\sum a_n x^n$ diverges for a value $x = x_0$, then it diverges for all x satisfying $|x| > |x_0|$.

Proof.   If for some x satisfying $|x| > |x_0|$, the series $\sum a_n x^n$ converges, then by the previous theorem, $\sum a_n x_0{}^n$ must converge, which is a contradiction.   □

Discussion.   As remarked in the previous discussion, divergence at a single point enables us to conclude divergence outside an entire open interval $(-|x_0|, |x_0|)$, but the theorem gives no information whatsoever as to what happens inside the interval. It may converge or diverge. We cannot obtain any conclusion about the behavior at the two endpoints.   □

As stated, a prime matter of concern for power series is delineating the points of convergence. Let us define A by

$$A = \{x: x \in \mathbf{R} \text{ and } \sum |a_n x^n| < \infty\}.$$

We have already noted that $0 \in A$ for every power series. Theorem 9.2.1 requires that A be connected, and exhibit a degree of symmetry about 0, that is, $a \in A$ implies $(-|a|, |a|) \subseteq A$. If A is not bounded, then A must be all of $\mathbf{R}$. Otherwise, A is bounded, whence it has a supremum. These considerations are summarized in the following possibilities about the power series $\sum a_n x^n$:

(i) it converges for all $x \in \mathbf{R}$;

(ii) it converges for no value of x other than $x = 0$;

(iii) there is a certain point, say $x = R$ so that for all x satisfying $|x| < R$, the series converges absolutely, and diverges for those x with $|x| > R$.

It is our aim to spell out precisely how to arrive at this magic number R. This brings us to our next theorem.

Theorem 9.2.3. Let $\sum\limits_{n=0}^{\infty} a_n x^n$ be a power series. If

$$A = \{x: x \in \mathbf{R} \text{ and } \sum a_n x^n < \infty\}$$

is bounded, and $R = \sup A$, then $\sum a_n x^n$ converges absolutely for $|x| < R$ and diverges for $|x| > R$. The series may converge or diverge for $x \pm R$.

Proof. If $|x| < R$, we can choose x_0 such that $|x| < |x_0| < R$ (**WHY?**). Thus $x_0 \in A$, and so by Theorem 9.2.1, the series converges (absolutely). If $|x| > R$, then $x \notin A$ and so $\sum a_n x^n$ diverges. $\square$

Discussion. The above theorem separates the real line into two parts, one an open interval, where we are guaranteed to have absolute convergence, and the other consisting of two half-rays where there is divergence. Both these regions have the points $x = \pm R$ as boundaries. The theorem draws no conclusion about the nature of the series at these endpoints. In fact all possibilities can occur at $\pm R$ (see Examples 1, 2, 3 below). $\square$

Definition. The number R, defined in Theorem 9.2.3 above, is called the **radius of convergence** of the power series $\sum a_n x^n$. The **interval of convergence** of the power series is the set of all values for which the power series converges.

Discussion. If R is defined as above, and $x \in (-R, R)$, then $|x| < R$, and hence by Theorem 7.5.3, we have (absolute) convergence. On the other hand, if $x \notin (-R, R)$, then $|x| > R$, so we have divergence. Thus the interval of convergence must certainly include the open interval $(-R, R)$. Since the results we have had so far do not tell us anything about the behavior of the series at $x = \pm R$, these two points may or may not belong to the interval of convergence.

If $R = 0$, then the set $A = \{0\}$ and so the radius of convergence is 0 and the interval of convergence is the singleton $\{0\}$. On the other hand, if A is unbounded, R becomes infinite and so the interval of convergence is the entire real line $\mathbf{R}$. $\square$

EXAMPLE 1 _____

Find the interval of convergence of $\sum x^n$.

Solution. We know that the geometric series converges for $|x| < 1$ diverges for $|x| > 1$, whence we see that $R = 1$. At $x = \pm 1$, by inspection, we have divergence, so we conclude that the interval of convergence is $(-1, 1)$. □

EXAMPLE 2 _____

Find the interval of convergence of $\sum \dfrac{x^{n+1}}{n+1}$.

Solution. Since for $x = 1$, $\sum \dfrac{1}{n+1}$ diverges, and for $x = -1$, $\sum \dfrac{(-1)^n}{n+1}$ converges, we conclude from the previous theorems that $R = 1$. It is immediate that the interval of convergence is $[-1, 1)$. □

Discussion. The solution was immediate, since substitution of ± 1 for x in the power series yielded the harmonic series, or its alternating form. We have used the properties of this series many times, and they should by now be completely familiar. In any case, the fact that the harmonic series diverges forces $R \leqslant 1$, while the fact that its alternating form converges forces $R \geqslant 1$. □

EXAMPLE 3 _____

Find the interval of convergence of $\sum \dfrac{x^n}{(n+1)^2}$.

Solution. Since $\sum \dfrac{1}{(n+1)^2}$ converges, $R \geqslant 1$. On the other hand, if we choose a value of x greater than 1, say, $1 + \delta$, $(\delta > 0,)$ we can use the ratio or root test to conclude that the series diverges for this value of x. So, R must be less than $1 + \delta$ for every $\delta > 0$. Thus, $R = 1$. Also, since $\sum \dfrac{1}{(n+1)^2}$ is absolutely convergent, we have convergence at $\pm R$, so the interval of convergence is $[-1, 1]$. □

Discussion. Once again, the strategy here is to look for some familiar points of convergence or divergence. In this example, both the points 1 and -1 are points of convergence. Luckily, for $x > 1$, we obtain divergence by using standard tests such as the ratio or root test. □

The next important question is: how can the interval of convergence be found? Equivalently, what is R? To obtain R as the supremum of a set of real numbers is, in general, not easy. Ideally, we require a formula which will enable us to write down the value of R directly from the coefficients a_n of the power series by simple computations. That such formulae might exist is plausible, since the distinguishing feature between two power series is the coefficients, a_n. The next two theorems provide methods for obtaining the radius of convergence.

Theorem 9.2.4. If $\sum a_n x^n$ is a power series with $a_n \neq 0$ for all n, and if $\rho = \lim \dfrac{a_{n+1}}{a_n}$ (finite or infinite), then the radius of convergence is given by $R = \dfrac{1}{\rho}$ (with $R = 0$ if $\rho = \infty$ and $R = \infty$ if $\rho = 0$).

Proof.   Using the ratio test, we have

$$\lim \left| \frac{a_{n+1} x^{n+1}}{a_n x^n} \right| = |x| \lim \left| \frac{a_{n+1}}{a_n} \right| = |x| \, \rho = \frac{|x|}{R}$$

so that if $\left| \dfrac{x}{R} \right| < 1$, we have (absolute) convergence, and for $\left| \dfrac{x}{R} \right| > 1$, we have divergence. In other words, R has the properties listed in Theorem 9.2.3, and since such a number is unique (**WHY?**) we get the desired expression for R.   □

The formula for R given above was obtained by using the ratio test. We can generate a second formula for the calculation of R, by using Cauchy's root test.

Theorem 9.2.5.   If $\sum a_n x^n$ is a power series and $\alpha = \overline{\lim} |a_n|^{1/n}$, then the radius of convergence is given by $R = \dfrac{1}{\alpha}$ (where $R = 0$ if $\alpha = \infty$ and $R = \infty$ if $\alpha = 0$).

Proof.   Since

$$\overline{\lim} |a_n x^n|^{1/n} = |x| \, \overline{\lim} |a_n|^{1/n} = |x| \, \alpha,$$

by the root test, $\sum |a_n x^n|$ converges for $|x| \, \alpha < 1$ and diverges for $|x| \, \alpha > 1$. If $|x| \, \alpha > 1$, then $|a_n x^n| > 1$ for infinitely many values of n, and $a_n x^n$ cannot tend to 0, so the series $\sum a_n x^n$ cannot converge. The remainder of the proof amounts to checking details for the various cases (Exercise 1).   □

Discussion.   These two theorems enable us to compute the radius of convergence directly in terms of the coefficients a_n. All we have to do is to compute the limit of either the ratio $\dfrac{a_{n+1}}{a_n}$ or the root $|a_n|^{1/n}$, whichever is easier to obtain, and the reciprocal of the number yields the radius of convergence. To obtain the interval of convergence, we have to check separately the convergence or divergence at the two endpoints of the interval in question.   □

EXAMPLE 4 _____

Find the interval of convergence of $\sum \dfrac{x^n}{n!}$.

Solution.   We have

$$\frac{a_{n+1}}{a_n} = \frac{n!}{(n+1)!} = \frac{1}{n+1} \to 0$$

showing that $R = \infty$ and hence the interval of convergence is **R**.   □

EXAMPLE 5 _____

Find the exact interval of convergence of $\sum a_n x^n$ where $a_{2n-1} = \dfrac{1}{2^n}$ and $a_{2n} = \dfrac{1}{4^n}$.

Solution. The reader should check that the ratio approach is undesirable in this case. Applying the root test yields

$$\overline{\lim} |a_n|^{1/n} = \frac{1}{\sqrt{2}} = \frac{1}{R}.$$

Further, the reader can check (Exercise 2) that the series converges at both endpoints so the interval of convergence is $\left[\dfrac{-1}{\sqrt{2}}, \dfrac{1}{\sqrt{2}} \right]$. □

Determination of the radius of convergence provides an open interval on which the power series is guaranteed to converge absolutely. Unfortunately, as we have seen from examples in the previous section, there is little relation between concepts of absolute and uniform convergence. Moreover, we know that the power which preserves important properties is uniform convergence, not absolute convergence. For this reason, the next task is to consider the uniform convergence of the power series, $\sum a_n x^n$. We have the following result:

Theorem 9.2.6. If R is the radius of convergence of the power series, $\sum a_n x^n$, then for every $\delta > 0$, the series converges uniformly in the interval $[-R + \delta, R - \delta]$.

Proof. If $x \in [-R + \delta, R - \delta]$, then $|a_n x^n| \leqslant a_n (R - \delta)^n$ and the series $\sum a_n (R - \delta)^n$ is convergent. By Weierstrass's M-test, we obtain uniform convergence in the interval $[-R + \delta, R - \delta]$. □

Discussion. This theorem establishes the utility of power series as a means of representing functions. Specifically, if the power series converges to f on an interval, we can almost be sure that the convergence will be uniform. The reason for this, which is employed in the proof, is the monotonicity of the various terms $|a_n x^n|$.

The above theorem asserts that the power series is uniformly convergent in any closed interval that is contained in the open interval $(-R, R)$. One might wonder whether this is enough to guarantee uniform convergence in the entire closed interval $[-R, R]$, or even on the open interval $(-R, R)$. Uniform convergence on either of the intervals does not follow from our results, and is not true in general.

Uniform convergence in $[-R + \delta, R + \delta]$ implies the existence of an integer, N, independent of x in that interval and with its usual properties. But the choice of N may very well depend on δ, whence if δ assumes a sequence of values which decrease to 0, the sequence of corresponding values of N need not be bounded. In such a case no value of N will exist that is independent of x in the entire open interval $(-R, R)$. The next example illustrates this point. □

EXAMPLE 6 _____

Discuss the uniform convergence properties of the power series, $\sum x^n$.

Solution.   Clearly, $R = 1$ and therefore the power series converges absolutely in $(-1, 1)$. By the above theorem, the convergence is uniform in $[-1 + \delta, 1 - \delta]$. We shall see that the convergence is not uniform in $(-1, 1)$. For, if it were, then the series would be uniformly Cauchy, so that given $\epsilon > 0$ there is N such that

$$|x^{n+1} + x^{n+2} + \cdots + x^{n+p}| < \epsilon$$

for $n > N$ and $p = 1, 2, \ldots$. Choosing $p = 1$, we get $|x^{n+1}| < \epsilon$ for $n > N$ and $x \in (-1, 1)$. But this is impossible since whatever be n, the function x^{n+1} on $(-1, 1)$ has the limit 1 as $x \to 1$, whence it follows that for some values of x, x^{n+1} must be closer to 1. Thus, the power series converges uniformly in all the intervals $[-1 + \delta, 1 - \delta]$, but not in $(-1, 1)$.   □

From the example given above, the question naturally arises as to when we can extend the interval of uniform convergence right up to either of the endpoints. A possible suggestion would be to insist that the series converge at each point (which was not the case in the example cited above). That this is sufficient is the content of the next theorem due to Abel.

Theorem 9.2.7 (Abel).   If $\sum a_n x^n$ has radius of convergence R, and if the series converges at $x = R$, then it converges uniformly in $[-R + \delta, R]$; also if it converges at $x = -R$, then the convergence is uniform in $[-R, R - \delta]$.

Proof.   Without loss of generality, we can assume that $R = 1$. To see this, observe that $\sum a_n x^n$ has radius of convergence R if and only if $\sum b_n x^n$ has radius of convergence 1, where $b_n = \dfrac{a_n}{R^n}$. Now let $\epsilon > 0$ be given. By the convergence of $\sum a_n$, there is N such that for $n > N$ and $p = 1, 2, \ldots$,

$$|a_{n+1} + a_{n+2} + \cdots + a_{n+p}| < \epsilon.$$

Now for any n and p, we have

$$|a_{n+1}x^{n+1} + a_{n+2}x^{n+2} + \cdots + a_{n+p}x^{n+p}|$$

$$= \left| a_{n+1}x^{n+1} + \sum_{j=n+2}^{n+p} \left(\sum_{i=n+1}^{j} a_i - \sum_{i=n+1}^{j-1} a^i \right)(x^j - x^{j+1}) \right| \qquad (*)$$

$$= \left| \sum_{j=n+1}^{n+p} \left[(x^j - x^{j+1}) \sum_{i=n+1}^{j} a_i \right] + x^{n+p} \sum_{i=n+1}^{n+p} a_i \right|. \qquad (*)$$

In $[0, 1]$ it is true that $x^j - x^{j+1} \geqslant 0$ so for all $n > N$, all $x \in [0,1]$ and $p = 1, 2, \ldots$, we have

$$\sum_{i=n+1}^{n+p} a_i x^i < \epsilon \sum_{j=n+1}^{n+p-1} (x^j - x^{j+1}) + \epsilon x^{n+p}$$

$$= \epsilon x^{n+1} < \epsilon. \qquad (*)$$

Since the N is independent of x, we obtain uniform convergence in $[0, 1]$. We already know that there is uniform convergence in $[-1 + \delta, 1 - \delta]$ for any $\delta > 0$. Thus we have uniform convergence in $[-1 + \delta, 1]$. The second statement is left to the reader as Exercise 3.   □

Discussion. This theorem is very useful. If R is the radius of convergence of a known power series and if $\sum a_n R^n$ converges then the series is uniformly convergent in $[-R + \delta, R]$ for any positive δ. Similarly, if $\sum (-1)^n a_n R^n$ is convergent, then the uniformity of convergence extends right up to $x = R$.   □

Corollary. Let $\sum_{n=0}^{\infty} a_n$ be any convergent series. Then the power series $\sum a_n x^n$ converges uniformly on $(-1, 1]$ to a limit function, f, and

$$\lim_{x \to 1} f(x) = \sum a_n.$$

Proof. Exercise 13.   □

As one might expect, the uniform convergence properties of power series mean that the limit function will share the nice features of the polynomials making up the power series. The next several theorems explore the effects of uniform convergence.

Theorem 9.2.8. Every power series represents a continuous function on its interval of convergence.

Proof. Let $\sum a_n x^n$ converge to f on A, the interval of convergence of the power series. Fix $x \in A$. If x is an interior point of A, then there is a positive δ such that $\sum a_n x^n$ converges uniformly on $[x - \delta, x + \delta]$. Since each $f_n(x) = a_n x^n$ is continuous and the series converges uniformly, f is continuous on $[x - \delta, x + \delta]$. On the other hand, if x is an endpoint of the interval there are two possibilities, namely, $x = 0$ or $x \neq 0$. If the former, then $f = \{(0, 0)\}$ and continuity follows trivially. If the latter, then we have uniform convergence on an interval of the form, $[x , x + \delta)$ or $(x - \delta, x]$. In either case, the continuity of f at x follows.   □

Discussion. The argument presented consists of assertions without reasons. Each of the assertions amounts to the application of a theorem. The reader should supply the required reasons (Exercise 4).   □

Theorem 9.2.9. A power series is term-by-term Riemann integrable on any interval included in its interval of convergence.

Proof. Exercise 5.   □

With respect to term-by-term differentiation, we have the following pleasant result:

Theorem 9.2.10. The power series $\sum a_n x^n$, and the series $\sum n a_n x^{n-1}$ obtained by term-by-term differentiation have the same interval of convergence.

Proof. If R denotes the radius of convergence of $\sum a_n x^n$, then the radius of convergence of $\sum n a_n x^{n-1}$ is computed using 9.2.5 by

$$\alpha_1 = \overline{\lim} |na_n|^{1/n} = \lim n^{1/n} \overline{\lim} |a_n|^{1/n} = \alpha,$$

whence $\dfrac{1}{\alpha_1} = \dfrac{1}{\alpha} = R$. The case for the endpoints is left to Exercise 6. □

Corollary. The power series $\sum a_n x^n$ and the term-by-term integrated series, $\sum \dfrac{a_n x^{n+1}}{(n+1)}$, have the same interval of convergence.

Proof. Exercise 6. □

The next result, which justifies term-by-term differentiation of a power series, is a consequence of Theorem 9.2.6.

Theorem 9.2.11. If $\sum a_n x^n$ has a nonzero radius of convergence, it can be differentiated term-by-term within its interval of convergence.

Proof. Let x belong to the interval of convergence. Then there is a closed interval, $[a, b]$, such that $x \in [a, b]$ and $\sum a_n x^n$ converges uniformly on $[a, b]$ (Exercise 7). The reader may check that the hypothesis of Theorem 9.1.10 applies (Exercise 8), and the result follows.

Discussion. Theorem 9.2.10 asserts that if

$$a_0 + a_1 x + a_2 x^2 + \cdots = f(x)$$

then

$$a_1 + 2a_2 x + \cdots = f'(x)$$

for each x in the interval of convergence. This theorem certainly hints at the fact that functions which can be represented by power series must have nice differentiation properties. □

An important consequence of this result, in conjunction with Theorems 9.2.7 and 9.2.9, is the following theorem which is concerned with the repeated term-by-term differentiation of a given power series any number of times.

Theorem 9.2.12. A power series, $\sum a_n x^n = f(x)$, possesses derivatives of all orders within the interval of convergence; each derivative may be obtained by term-by-term differentiation and all of them converge and are continuous on the common interval of convergence.

Proof. Exercise 9. □

Corollary. If the power series, $\sum a_n x^n$, has a nonzero radius of convergence, and if $f(x)$ denotes the sum function in the interval of convergence, then for each n,

$$a_n = \frac{f^{(n)}(0)}{n!}.$$

Proof. If

$$f(x) = a_0 + a_1 x + a_2 x^2 + \cdots$$

then by repeated application of Theorem 9.2.12, we have

$$f^{(n)}(x) = (n(n-1)(n-2) \cdots 3 \cdot 2 \cdot 1)(a_n + a_{n+1}x + \cdots).$$

Since $x = 0$ belongs to the interval of convergence, substituting $x = 0$, we obtain

$$\frac{f^n(0)}{n!} = a_n$$

as required.   □

The next result shows that the limit function $f(x)$ uniquely determines the coefficients of the power series $\sum a_n x^n$.

Theorem 9.2.13.   If $\sum a_n x^n$ and $\sum b_n x^n$ both converge to the same function $f(x)$ in some neighborhood of 0, then for all n, $a_n = b_n$; in other words the two series are identical.

Proof.   If in some open interval containing 0,

$$f(x) = \sum a_n x^n = \sum b_n x^n$$

then by Theorem 9.2.12,

$$\frac{f^n(0)}{n!} = a_n = b_n$$

for all n.   □

Discussion.   Theorem 9.2.13 is remarkable. To see why, consider an arbitrary function, f, which is defined on $[-1,1]$. It seems plausible that there would be many distinct series of functions which converge to f. If one adds the requirements that the given series must consist of continuous functions and that the convergence must be uniform, then these requirements will have two effects. First, the two requirements limit the choice of f to continuous functions on $[-1,1]$. Second, there will be fewer series which converge to f under these more stringent conditions. Nevertheless, there will still be an infinite number of such series.

Now consider the case of power series, and of a function, f, which is the sum of that power series, $\sum a_{n,}x^n$. Suppose, for the sake of argument, that we changed the value of a_0 to be b_0. The new power series $b_0 + \sum_{n=1}^{\infty} a_n x^n$ will no longer converge to f, although it will converge. While this is not surprising, what is surprising is the fact that there is no way to adjust the values of the coefficients, a_n, $n = 1, 2, \ldots$ so as to obtain a new series, $\sum b_n x^n$, which does converge to f. Thus, for a power series to converge to f, one must get all the coefficients right, so to speak. In summary then, given that f has a power series representation, f uniquely determines that representation.

The results contained in the last several theorems also impose rather strong conditions on f. Specifically, f must have derivatives of all orders on its interval of convergence. Thus, the class of functions which have power series representations must be restricted to very nice functions indeed.

This leaves us with several burning questions. What functions have power series representations? Given that a function has a power series representation, how can it be found? These questions will be considered in the next section.   □

We conclude with some results for combining power series.

Theorem 9.2.14. Let $\sum a_n x^n$ and $\sum b_n x^n$ be two power series having intervals of convergence, A_1 and A_2, respectively. Then, the formula,

$$\sum a_n x^n + \sum b_n x^n = \sum (a_n + b_n) x^n,$$

is valid on $A_1 \cap A_2$.

Proof. Exercise 10. □

In section 7.3 we defined the Cauchy product of two series, $\sum\limits_{n=0}^{\infty} a_n$ and $\sum\limits_{n=0}^{\infty} b_n$ by setting $c_n = \sum\limits_{k=0}^{n} a_n b_{n-k}$ and taking the product to be

$$\left(\sum_{n=0}^{\infty} a_n \right) \cdot \left(\sum_{n=0}^{\infty} b_n \right) = \sum_{n=0}^{\infty} c_n,$$

where on the left we have the formal product of the two infinite series. For two power series, $\sum a_n x^n$ and $\sum a_n x^n$, we define the **Cauchy product** by extension as

$$\left(\sum a_n x^n \right) \cdot \left(\sum b_n x^n \right) = \sum c_n x^n,$$

where on the left we have the formal product of the two infinite series. The reader can check that this definition is the correct extension, based on the discussion following the definition of the Cauchy product in section 7.3.

Theorem 9.2.15. Let $\sum a_n x^n$ and $\sum b_n x^n$ be two power series with a common radius of convergence, R, and limit functions, f and g, respectively. Then

$$\sum c_n x^n = f(x) \cdot g(x)$$

for each $x \in (-R, R)$.

Proof. Without loss of generality we may assume that the radius of convergence is nonzero. Fix $x \in (-R, R)$. Then $\sum a_n x^n$ converges absolutely to $f(x)$. Similarly, $\sum b_n x^n$ converges absolutely to $g(x)$. Now (Exercise 11), $\sum c_n x^n$ is the Cauchy product of the two power series evaluated at x and considered as series of real constants. By Theorem 7.3.8,

$$\sum c_n x^n = f(x) \cdot g(x)$$

as desired. □

Discussion. It would be really nice if the open interval, $(-R, R)$, could be replaced by the interval of convergence. Such a result seems very plausible given Theorems 9.2.6 and 9.2.7. The reader is invited to explore this suggestion in Exercise 12. □

It is also possible to treat division of two power series. This is explored in Exercise 32.

EXERCISES

1. Complete the proof of Theorem 9.2.5.

2. Complete the details of the solution to Example 5.

3. Complete the proof of Theorem 9.2.7. In the process, verify all equalities marked with an (*).

4. Supply all reasons to justify the assertions making up the proof of Theorem 9.2.8.

5. Prove Theorem 9.2.9.

6. Complete the proof of Theorem 9.2.10 and prove its corollary.

7. Suppose that $\sum a_n x^n$ has a nonzero radius of convergence. Show if x belongs to the interior of the interval of convergence, then there is a closed interval, $[a, b]$, such that $x \in [a, b]$ and the series converges uniformly on $[a, b]$.

8. Complete the details of Theorem 9.2.11.

9. Prove Theorem 9.2.12.

10. Prove Theorem 9.2.14.

11. Let $\sum a_n x^n$ and $\sum b_n x^n$ be two power series. Show for any fixed x, $\sum c_n x^n$, is the Cauchy product of the two series considered as series of real constants.

12. Can the interval, $(-R, R)$, mentioned in Theorem 9.2.15 be replaced by the interval of convergence?

13. Prove the corollary to Theorem 9.2.7. Use this corollary to give a simple proof of Theorem 7.3.7.

14. Determine the radius of convergence and the exact interval of convergence of the following power series:

(a) $\sum \dfrac{(-1)^n (nx)^n}{n!}$;

(b) $\sum (-1)^n \dfrac{(x-1)^n}{n!}$;

(c) $\sum \dfrac{(\ln n)(x-5)^n}{\sqrt{n}}$;

(d) $\sum (\sin n) x^n$;

(e) $\sum a^{n^2} x^n$, $a < 1$;

(f) $\sum (1 - (-2)^n) x^n$;

(g) $\sum \dfrac{(x+3)^n}{(n+2) 2^n}$;

(h) $\sum \dfrac{(-1)^n 2^{2n} x^{2n}}{2n}$;

(i) $\sum \dfrac{n(x-2)^n}{3^n (n+1)}$;

(j) $\sum \dfrac{(n!)^2 x^{n+1}}{(2n!)}$;

(k) $\sum \dfrac{(-1)^n (n+1)^n x^n}{n^2 + 1}$;

(l) $\sum (-1)^n \dfrac{x^{2n+1}}{(2n+1)!}$;

(m) $\sum \dfrac{(n!)(x+2)^n}{n^n}$;

(n) $\sum \dfrac{3^{\sqrt{n}}x^n}{\sqrt{n^2+1}}$;

(o) $\sum \dfrac{3^{\sqrt{n}}x^{2n+1}}{\sqrt{n}}$;

(p) $\sum \left[\dfrac{(4+(-1)^n)}{5}\right]^n x^n$;

(q) $\sum \dfrac{n^\alpha x^n}{n!}$;

(r) $\sum \dfrac{n^n x^n}{n!}$;

(s) $\sum \dfrac{x^n}{n\ln n}$;

(t) $\sum \dfrac{x^n}{\ln n}$;

(u) $\sum \dbinom{k}{n} x^n$;

(v) $\sum \dfrac{3^n x^{2n+1}}{\sqrt{x}}$;

(w) $\sum \dfrac{x^{2n+1}}{4^n}$;

(x) $\sum a_n x^n$, where $a_n = \begin{cases} 1, & n=m^2,\ m\in \mathbf{N} \\ 0, & \text{otherwise}; \end{cases}$

(y) $\sum a_n x^n$, where $a_n = \begin{cases} 1, & n=m!,\ m\in \mathbf{N} \\ 0, & \text{otherwise}; \end{cases}$

(z) $\sum \dfrac{(-1)^n 4^n x^{2n}}{(3n-4)}$;

(a′) $\sum \dfrac{(n!)^2 (2n+2)! x^n}{(2n!)[(n+1)!]^2}$;

(b′) $\sum \dfrac{(-1)^n x^{4n+1}}{(4n+1)!(2n)}$;

(c′) $\sum \dfrac{(-1)^n x^{2n}}{(n!)^2 4^n}$.

15. Prove if a_n is an integer for each n, and if infinitely many of them are 0, then the radius of convergence, R, of the power series $\sum a_n x^n$ can never exceed 1. Can the same conclusion be obtained if $\overline{\lim}|a_n| > 0$?

16. If R and S are the radii of convergence of $\sum a_n x^n$ and $\sum b_n x^n$, respectively, what can you say about the radius of convergence of the following power series?
    (a) $\sum a_n x^{kn}$;
    (b) $\sum (a_n \pm b_n)x^n$;
    (c) $\sum (a_n b_n)x^n$;
    (d) $\sum a_n^k x^n$;
    (e) $\sum a_n^k x^{2n}$;

(f) $\sum a_n x^{n^2}$;

(g) the Cauchy product series $\sum c_n x^n$, where $c_n = \sum_{j=1}^{n} a_n b_{n-j}$.

17. Does there exist a power series $\sum a_n x^n$ that represents $|x|$ for all $x \in \mathbf{R}$?

18. Show the series $\sum (n + 1)! x^n$ and $\sum n! x^n$ have the same interval of convergence and define the same function on the interval of convergence. Is there any contradiction to Theorem 9.2.13?

19. Construct a power series whose exact interval of convergence is $[-3, 5)$.

20. Given $a_0 = 1$, $a_n = 2$ for $n \geqslant 1$, $b_n = \dfrac{(-1)^n 8 - \dfrac{3}{4^n}}{5}$,

    (a) show that $\sum a_n$, $\sum b_n$ both diverge, but the Cauchy product $\sum c_n$ is absolutely convergent;

    (b) find the radii of convergence of $\sum a_n x^n$, $\sum b_n x^n$, $\sum c_n x^n$.

21. Find the Cauchy product of the power series $3 + \sum_{n=1}^{\infty} 3^n x^n$ and $-2 + \sum_{n=1}^{\infty} 2^n x^n$.

22. Prove, using the Cauchy product,

$$\sum_{n=1}^{\infty} n x^{n-1} = \frac{1}{(1 - x)^2}.$$

23. If $\sum a_n$ converges, but not absolutely, show the radius of convergence of $\sum a_n x^n$ is 1.

24. We say $\sum a_n$ is **Abel summable** to L, if $\lim_{x \to 1^-} f(x) = L$, where $f(x) = \sum a_n x^n$. In this case, we write $\sum a_n = L(A)$. Show the following series are Abel summable, and find their Abel sums.

    (a) $1 - 1 + 1 - 1 + \cdots$;

    (b) $1 - 2 + 3 - 4 + \cdots$;

    (c) $1 - 3 + 6 - 10 + \cdots$;

    (d) $1 - \dfrac{1}{3} + \dfrac{1}{5} - \dfrac{1}{7} + \cdots$.

25. If $\sum_{n=0}^{\infty} a_n = L(A)$ and $\sum_{n=0}^{\infty} b_n = M(A)$, show $\sum_{n=0}^{\infty} (a_n + b_n) = L + M(A)$. What can you say about the Abel sum of the following series?

$$0 + a_0 + 0 + a_1 + 0 + a_2 + \cdots + 0 + a_n + 0 + \cdots .$$

26. If $\sum a_n = L$, prove that $\sum a_n = L(A)$, but not conversely.

27. Justify the equation

$$\frac{\pi}{4} = 1 - \frac{1}{3} + \frac{1}{5} - \cdots .$$

[HINT: Consider $\int_0^x \dfrac{1}{1 + t^2} dt$ in $|t| < 1$, and use Abel's Theorem.]

28. By integrating the power series for $\dfrac{1}{1 + x + x^2}$, derive the identity:

$$\frac{\pi}{3^{3/2}} = 1 - \frac{1}{2} + \frac{1}{4} - \frac{1}{5} + \cdots .$$

29. Let $\sum a_n x^n$ have radius of convergence $R > 0$, and $\sum \dfrac{a_n R^{n+1}}{n + 1}$ be convergent. If

$\sum a_n x^n = f(x)$, $|x| < R$, show that f is integrable in $[0, R]$, and

$$\int_0^R f = \sum \frac{a_n R^{n+1}}{n+1}$$

irrespective of the way f is defined at R.

30. Starting from the geometric series $\sum x^{n-1}$, $-1 < x < 1$, derive the following:

(a) $\displaystyle\sum_{n=0}^{\infty} (n+1)x^n = \frac{1}{(1-x)^2}$;

(b) $\displaystyle\sum_{n=0}^{\infty} (n+1)x^{2n} = \frac{1}{(1-x^2)^2}$;

(c) $\displaystyle\sum_{n=0}^{\infty} (-1)^n (n+1)x^n = \frac{1}{(1+x)^2}$;

(d) $\displaystyle\sum_{n=0}^{\infty} (n+1)x^{n+2} = \frac{x^2}{(1-x)^2}$;

(e) $\displaystyle\sum_{n=0}^{\infty} \frac{n+1}{n+3}x^{n+3} = \int_0^x \frac{t^2}{(1-t^2)}\,dt$.

31. If $a_n + a_{n-1} + a_{n-2} = 0$, $n = 2, 3, \ldots$, show for each x for which the power series $\sum a_n x^n$ converges, the sum is $\dfrac{a_0 + (a_1 + a_0)x}{1 + x + x^2}$.

32. Let $\sum b_n x^n$ and $\sum c_n x^n$ be two power series which converge on $(-R, R)$ to f and g, respectively. Further suppose that $b_0 \neq 0$. Show there is an interval, $(-r, r) \subseteq (-R, R)$ such that $\dfrac{g}{f}$ is defined and bounded. Further show $\dfrac{g}{f}$ has a power series representation on this interval, and give an explicit method for finding the coefficients of this power series.

33. Suppose $f(x) = \displaystyle\sum_{n=0}^{\infty} a_n x^n$ on $(-R, R)$, $R > 0$ and $g(x) = \displaystyle\sum_{n=1}^{\infty} b_n x^n$ on $(-S, S)$ for $S > 0$. Show the composite function $h(x) = f(g(x))$ is represented by a power series having a positive radius of convergence, and this power series can be obtained by substituting the series for g into the series for f and rearranging terms.

9.3 TAYLOR SERIES

In section 9.2, we saw how a power series gives rise to a continuous function in its interval of convergence. In this section, the converse problem is investigated, namely, given an arbitrary function, $f(x)$, find a power series whose sum is precisely the given function.

The idea that a given function might be represented as a power series was introduced in section 4.4 where the formula

$$f(a + h) \approx f(a) + f'(a)h + \frac{1}{2}f''(a)h^2$$

was developed as part of Example 4.4.2. If one sets $a = 0$, and replaces h by x, the formula becomes

$$f(x) \approx f(0) + f'(0)x + \frac{1}{2}f''(0)x^2$$

which looks suspiciously like the first three terms of the power series for f, should such exist. This approach to approximating a function with a polynomial was known, in a very primitive form, to Newton, around 1676, and developed further by Taylor and Maclaurin in the 1700s. As such, this approach to the representation of functions predates any notion of power series, uniform convergence, and so forth.

Functions which can be represented as power series over an interval are very special. For example, to have a representation as a power series requires that the function have lots of derivatives, at least at $x = 0$. This suggests that as a class, this collection of function is worthy of study and leads to the following definition.

Definition. Let f be a function defined in a neighborhood of 0. We say f is **analytic at** 0 provided there is a power series, $\sum a_n x^n$, which converges to f on an interval, $(-R, R)$.

Discussion. We stress that for f to be analytic at 0, it must be representable by a power series over an open interval which includes $\{0\}$.

Having defined this class of functions, one would like to have a nice test for membership in the class. The elements of such a test must relate to requirements on f to have a power series. If f has such a power series, then by Theorem 9.2.13, the series must be unique and its coefficients, a_n, calculated by the formula

$$a_n = \frac{f^{(n)}(0)}{n!}.$$

Thus, one immediate test is whether f has derivatives of all orders at the origin. Unfortunately, as we shall see, this is not sufficient.   □

Given that f is a function which has derivatives of all orders at the origin, or indeed, at a, it makes sense to give the following definition:

Definition. If $f(x)$ possesses derivatives of all orders in some neighborhood of origin, then the (formal) power series,

$$\sum_{n=0}^{\infty} \frac{f^{(n)}(0)}{n!} x^n$$

is called the **Taylor series expansion** of f about the point 0. If $f(x)$ possesses derivatives of all orders in some neighborhood of a, then the (formal) power series,

$$\sum_{n=0}^{\infty} \frac{f^{(n)}(a)}{n!} (x - a)^n$$

is called the **Taylor series expansion** of f about the point a.

Discussion. The definition requires that we start with a function $f(x)$ which can be differentiated infinitely often at a fixed point, which for purposes of discussion we take to be 0. We then compute the value of the nth derivative $f^{(n)}(x)$ at the point $x = 0$ and write down the formal infinite series $\sum_{n=0}^{\infty} \frac{f^{(n)}(0)}{n!} x^n$ (with the constant term equal to $f(0)$) without worrying about the convergence properties of the series.

The moment one writes down such an infinite series, several questions naturally arise about its convergence properties. First of all, there is no guarantee that the series converges for any value of x other than 0, or $x = a$ in the general case. Second, even if it converges for some x, there is still no guarantee that the sum of the series is exactly the function value, $f(x)$, for the function which generated the series. Thus, at this stage, the Taylor series expansion of the infinitely differentiable function, f, is just a formal infinite series.

Given our previous definition, if the Taylor expansion for f at 0 actually converges to f on some open interval, then f is analytic at 0. More generally, if the Taylor expansion of f at a converges to f on an open interval which includes a, then f is said to be **analytic at** a. Thus, all the questions posed above relate to whether f is analytic.

As a matter of historical interest, the Taylor expansion for a function about 0 is referred to as the **Maclaurin series**, or **Maclaurin expansion**. One would think that this is due to the fact that Maclaurin's work preceded Taylor's. But this is not the case. Taylor's more general work preceded Maclaurin's by almost 50 years and in addition, it appears that Maclaurin was aware of Taylor's work. Nevertheless, Maclaurin's name stuck to the special case of Taylor's series! But as we have hinted, the basic theory of approximating a function by a polynomial having coefficients determined by the derivative of the functions was worked out in the late 1600s by Newton and others.

□

EXAMPLE 1 _____

Obtain the Taylor series generated by the function given below (usually referred to as **Cauchy's function**):

$$f(x) = \begin{cases} e^{-1/x^2}, & \text{if } x \neq 0 \\ 0, & \text{if } x = 0. \end{cases}$$

Solution. To write down the Taylor infinite series, one has to compute all the derivatives at origin. It is left as Exercise 1 to show that $f^{(n)}(0) = 0$ for each n. (The computations are not easy!). Thus the corresponding Taylor series is given by

$$\sum \frac{0}{n!} x^n = 0 + 0 \cdot x + 0 \cdot x^2 + \cdots .$$

Thus we see that the series (trivially) converges to the function, g, which is identically 0 for all $x \in \mathbf{R}$.

□

Discussion. In this example, the function, f, admits a nice Taylor series expansion, which certainly converges for each x, but unfortunately the sum function obtained is not the function, f, which we started with, except at the single point $x = 0$. The point of this example is that it shows that even though a function possesses all the derivatives one could want, it is not enough to guarantee that the function is analytic on even a minuscule interval.

The reader is advised to draw the graph of this function, and note that the graph has an 'infinite-order contact with x-axis at origin.

□

Next, we consider an alternate approach. Rather than writing an infinite power series corresponding to a given function let us begin by posing the question:

> Given a function, f, can we find a sequence of polynomials which approximate the function in some region, that is, near some point, a?

This is the historical approach which began with Newton, Taylor, and others. The polynomials employed were developed by extending the formula

$$f(a + h) \approx f(a) + f'(a)h + \frac{1}{2}f''(a)h^2$$

to include higher powers of h. Thus, a sequence of polynomials, $\{P_n\}$, is generated each of which is hoped to be a better approximation to f.

Definition. Let f be infinitely differentiable in an open interval about a. Then for each n, the polynomial

$$P_n(x) = \sum_{i=0}^{n} \frac{f^{(i)}(a)}{i!} (x - a)^i$$

is called the **Taylor polynomial of degree** n at a corresponding to the function, f. For $a = 0$, the Taylor polynomial of degree n at origin is given by $P_n(x) = \sum_{i=0}^{n} \frac{f^{(i)}(0)}{i!} x^i$.

Discussion. For each n, $P_n(x)$ is just a polynomial of degree n consisting of $n + 1$ terms, with the function value at a as the constant term. Indeed, this polynomial is just the nth partial sum of the Taylor series. However, Taylor polynomials do not arise from power series considerations. Rather, as shown in section 4.4, they arise from attempts to approximate differentiable functions near points for which functional values are known. Even so, the process obviously generates a sequence of functions which are intended to approximate a given function, so the natural questions related to convergence immediately appear.

In summary then, we have a sequence of polynomials, $P_0(x)$, $P_1(x)$, $P_n(x)$, and so on, and we want to know whether this sequence converges (uniformly) to some function, and if so, is the limit function the original function, f? In Example 1 above, all the Taylor polynomials of all degrees turned out to be the zero polynomial and hence the sequence, though convergent at each point, was not convergent to the parent function, except at origin. So the answer to these questions is in general 'no'. But if 'no' were the complete picture, Taylor series would not appear as a topic in every calculus course. □

Definition. If $P_n(x)$ denotes the nth Taylor polynomial corresponding to $f(x)$ about a, then the function, R_{n+1}, corresponding to the difference

$$R_{n+1}(x) = f(x) - P_n(x)$$

is called the $n + 1$st **Taylor remainder at** a.

Discussion. The $n + 1$st Taylor remainder at a when evaluated at x is precisely the value to be added to the value of the nth Taylor polynomial at x so as to equal the function value, $f(x)$. Thinking about Taylor polynomials in this way, via remainders, implies that the purpose of the nth Taylor polynomial is to approximate the function, f, on some interval. Thus, the remainder is, in effect, an error term. We stress that as an error term, its value depends on x. As a general rule, one would expect that the farther a particular x is from a, the point of expansion, the larger will be the magnitude of $R_{n+1}(x)$.

As a matter of notation, the reader may wonder why the subscript on the remainder is $n+1$, instead of n. If one writes the equation,

$$f(x) = P_n(x) + R_{n+1}(x),$$

then R_{n+1} is in fact the $n + 1$st term in the expression on the right-hand side (if we do not count the constant term), since $P_n(x)$ is a polynomial of degree n, whose last term is $\dfrac{f^{(n)}(a)}{n!}(x - a)^n$. For this reason, it is common practice to assign it a subscript of $n+1$ instead of n. So, it is obvious that when we refer to $R_n(x)$, we mean the Taylor remainder that corresponds to the Taylor polynomial $P_{n-1}(x)$ of degree $(n - 1)$. In what follows, we shall be frequently using $R_n(x)$, as a matter of convenience.

Evidently the sequence, $\{P_n\}$, converges (uniformly) to f on A, if and only if the Taylor remainder sequence of functions, $\{R_{n+1}\}$, converges (uniformly) to 0 (Exercise 2). Thus, adequate information about the nature of functions possessing a Taylor series (that converges precisely to the function at all points) can be obtained from the study of the sequence, $\{R_{n+1}\}$, of its Taylor remainders. For this reason different authors have studied different forms of the Taylor remainder function. The object of the study is not that different remainders are possible, rather, it is that one would like to bound the function, R_{n+1}, over an interval. In the next few results, we will illustrate some of the forms of Taylor remainders and their uses in determining the nature of Taylor series corresponding to a given function. However, for clarity, we begin with an example. □

EXAMPLE 2

Use graphical techniques to illustrate the nature of the convergence problem for the Taylor expansion of $f(x) = e^x$ at the origin.

Solution. The fifth degree Taylor polynomial for e^x is given by

$$P_5(x) = 1 + x + \frac{x^2}{2!} + \frac{x^3}{3!} + \frac{x^4}{4!} + \frac{x^5}{5!}.$$

The formula for $R_6(x)$ is given by

$$R_6(x) = e^x - \left[1 + x + \frac{x^2}{2!} + \frac{x^3}{3!} + \frac{x^4}{4!} + \frac{x^5}{5!} \right].$$

In Figure 9.3.1 we present a graph of e^x, P_1, P_3, P_5, and R_6 on $[-3, 3]$ to illustrate these concepts. □

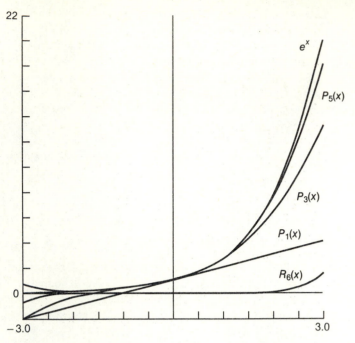

Figure 9.3.1   Taylor polynomials $P_1(x)$, $P_3(x)$, $P_5(x)$, $R_6(x)$, for $f(x) = e^x$.

Discussion.   In terms of the approximation of a function by a polynomial, the fifth Taylor polynomial does a remarkable job of approximating e^x. Indeed, in the interval, $[-2, 2]$, the magnitude of the remainder, $|R_6|$, is less than 0.1, and it is only 1.7 at $x = 3$.

In general terms, the remainder grows as x moves away from 0, the point about which the expansion is taken. If one is to understand this growth, it would be useful to have a formula for $R_{n+1}(x)$ which does not involve the original function, as does the defining equation for R_{n+1}. $\square$

Theorem 9.3.1 (Schlomlich–Roche's Form of Taylor Remainder).   Let f be defined and possess derivatives up to order n in some neighborhood U of 0. Then there exists a number θ such that $0 < \theta < 1$ and if $k < n$,

$$R_n(x) = \frac{f^{(n)}(\theta x)(1 - \theta)^k}{(n - k)(n - 1)!} x^n.$$

Proof.   Let $x_0 \neq 0$ be a member of U, and define the auxiliary function g by setting

$$g(t) = f(x_0) - f(t) - (x_0 - t)f'(t) - \cdots - \frac{(x_0 - t)^{n-1}}{(n - 1)!} f^{(n-1)}(t) - A(x_0 - t)^{n-k}$$

where the constant A is determined by the condition that $g(0) = 0$. Now the function g defined above is continuous and differentiable in $[0, x_0]$. Further, $g(0) = 0$ by the definition of A, and $g(x_0) = 0$ as the reader can check. Hence the Mean Value Theorem of differential calculus (Theorem 4.3.2) applies and there exists $\xi \in (0, x_0)$ satisfying $g'(\xi) = 0$. In fact, $\xi = \theta x_0$ for some θ satisfying $0 < \theta < 1$ (Exercise 3). A direct computation shows that

$$g'(t) = -\frac{(x_0 - t)^{n-1}}{(n-1)!}f^{(n)}(t) + A(n-k)(x_0 - t)^{n-k-1}$$

so that the requirement that $g'(\xi) = 0$ together with the fact that $\xi = \theta x_0$ yields

$$A = \frac{(x_0 - \theta x_0)^k f^{(n)}(\theta x_0)}{(n-1)!(n-k)} = \frac{x_0^k(1-\theta)^k f^{(n)}(\theta x_0)}{(n-1)!(n-k)}.$$

Substituting this value in the definition of A, we finally obtain

$$f(x_0) = f(0) + x_0 f'(0) + \frac{x_0^2 f''(0)}{2} + \cdots + \frac{x_0^{n-1}f^{(n-1)}(0)}{(n-1)!} + \frac{x_0^n(1-\theta)^k f^{(n)}(\theta x_0)}{(n-1)!(n-k)}.$$

Since x_0 is an arbitrary point in the neighborhood, U of 0, replacing it by a general point x, we get the desired expression for $R_n(x)$. $\qquad\square$

Discussion. The key to this theorem is the Mean Value Theorem. First, it is another in the long string of consequences of the Mean Value Theorem (see exercises in section 4.3). More importantly, the proof of the Mean Value Theorem supplies the critical ideas required for generating the proof of this theorem. If the reader does not see the reasons which support this last statement, he should review the proof of the Mean Value Theorem and the rest of the material presented in section 4.3. In Exercise 4 the reader will be asked to establish the general form of the Schlomlich–Roche remainder.

As we have stated, one purpose in obtaining expressions for the Taylor remainder is to obtain bounds on the error in $P_n(x)$. Ideally one wants an expression which does not involve the original function, f, in any way. This is too much to hope for, and inspection reveals that f has been replaced by $f^{(n)}$ in

$$R_n(x) = \frac{f^{(n)}(\theta x)(1 - \theta)^k}{(n-k)(n-1)!}x^n.$$

While this situation is less than the ideal, in many instances $f^{(n)}$ can be replaced by a maximum value, or by dint of cleverness something even better, and a formula not involving f in any form results. $\qquad\square$

The Schlomlich–Roche form of the Taylor remainder is one of the most general forms. More useful and simpler forms of the remainder can be obtained from this form as special cases. For example, setting $k = 0$ we have the following corollary:

Corollary (Lagrange's Form of Taylor Remainder). If the function f possesses derivatives up to order n in some neighborhood of 0, and if $x \neq 0$ is an arbitrary point in that neighborhood, there exists a number $\theta \in (0, 1)$ such that

$$R_n(x) = \frac{f^{(n)}(\theta x)}{n!}x^n.$$

Discussion. This is the form of the Taylor remainder that is most common and widely used. In essence, it states that a function f which is differentiable n times in some neighborhood of origin can be expanded as a polynomial of degree n together with an error term, namely, the Taylor remainder after n terms as follows:

$$f(x) = f(0) + f'(0) + \frac{f''(0)x^2}{2!} + \cdots + \frac{f^{(n-1)}(0)x^{n-1}}{(n-1)!} + \frac{f^{(n)}(\theta x)x^n}{n!}$$

for some number $\theta \in (0, 1)$. We stress that the number θ depends on the point x, as well as the stage, n, at which the expansion is terminated. Thus for each x and each n, we have a number $\theta(x, n)$. ☐

By setting $k = n - 1$ in Theorem 9.3.1 we obtain:

Corollary (Cauchy's Form of Taylor Remainder). Under the conditions of Theorem 9.3.1, there exists $\theta \in (0, 1)$ satisfying

$$R_n(x) = \frac{f^{(n)}(\theta x)(1 - \theta)^{n-1}x^n}{(n - 1)!}.$$

EXAMPLE 3

Estimate the error involved in using P_5 to approximate e.

Solution. The sixth Taylor remainder for e^x evaluated at 1 is given by

$$R_6(1) = \frac{e^\theta 1^6}{6!},$$

where $\theta \in (0,1)$. Since $e \leqslant 3$, it is immediate that the error is less than $\frac{1}{240}$. ☐

Theorem 9.3.2. If the function, f, admits derivatives of all orders in $(-b, b)$ and if there exists $K > 0$ such that $\frac{f^{(n)}(x)}{n!} < K^n$ for all n and all $x \in (-b, b)$, then the Taylor series, $\sum \frac{f^{(n)}(0)x^n}{n!}$, converges to the function, f, throughout $(-a, a)$ where $a = \min\left\{ b, \frac{1}{K} \right\}$.

Proof. Using Lagrange's form of Taylor remainder, we have $R_n(x) = \frac{f^{(n)}(\xi)x^n}{n!}$ for some $\xi \in (-b, b)$. Consequently by hypothesis,

$$|R_n(x)| < K^n|x|^n \quad \text{for all} \ \ x \in (-b, b).$$

If a is chosen as required in the statement of the theorem, and $x \in (-a, a)$ then, $|R_n(x)| < r^n$ where $r = \frac{x}{K} < 1$. Since r_n converges to 0, we have $R_n(x) \to 0$, so the Taylor series converges to $f(x)$ in $(-a, a)$. ☐

Discussion. In the light of the above theorem, let us further analyze Example 1. We have seen that all the derivatives vanish so that the Taylor remainder after n terms is still $f(x)$. Thus for any nonzero x, $R_n(x) = e^{-1/x^2}$ which never approaches zero. Again if $b > 0$, let $x_n = n^{-1/2}$. Then after a stage, say, $n > N$, $x_n \in (-b, b)$. Using Lagrange's form of remainder, now corresponding to each x_n we have

$$f^{(n)}(x_n) = e^{-1/x^2} \frac{n!}{x_n^2} = \left[\frac{n}{e^2}\right]^{n/2} n!$$

Since for sufficiently large n, we have $\dfrac{n}{e^2}$ arbitrarily large, Theorem 9.3.2. cannot apply for any value of b and K. $\square$

EXAMPLE 4

Obtain a Taylor expansion of the function $(1 + x)^m$ in a neighborhood of 0, where m is any real number. Deduce the **binomial series**

$$(1 + x)^m = \sum_{n=0}^{\infty} \binom{m}{n} x^n.$$

[Here, for an arbitrary real number m, the expression $\binom{m}{n}$ is the nth **binomial co-efficient** which is the fraction $\dfrac{m(m - 1)(m - 2) \cdots (m - n + 1)}{n!}$.]

Solution. The function $f(x) = (1 + x)^m$ is clearly defined in a neighborhood of 0 and it is readily seen that

$$f^{(n)}(x) = m(m - 1) \cdots (m - n + 1)(1 + x)^{m-n}.$$

So, the Taylor infinite series corresponding to the function, f, about origin is the formal series

$$\sum_{n=0}^{\infty} \frac{f^{(n)}(0)x^n}{n!} = \sum_{n=0}^{\infty} \binom{m}{n} x^n.$$

We first study the convergence of this series. If m is a nonnegative integer, then for $n > m$, the coefficients, $\binom{m}{n} = 0$, hence the series converges trivially for all real x. If $m \notin \mathbf{N}$, then the above is an infinite power series, whose radius of convergence is easily seen to be 1, so the infinite Taylor series converges for $|x| < 1$. However, we still do not know whether the sum is actually $(1 + x)^m$.

For $x \in (0, 1)$, we use Lagrange's form of Taylor remainder, and obtain the remainder

$$R_n(x) = \binom{m}{n}(1 + \xi)^{m-n} x^n,$$

where $0 < \xi < x$. If we choose $n > m$, then, $(1 + \xi)^{m-n} < 1$, so

$$\left| R_n(x) \right| \leq \left| \binom{m}{n} x^n \right|.$$

Now, $\displaystyle\sum_{n=0}^{\infty} \binom{m}{n} x^n$ converges (Exercise 6), so $\displaystyle\lim_{n \to \infty} \binom{m}{n} = 0$. Consequently, $R_n(x) \to 0$, proving that in $(0, 1)$, the infinite Taylor series actually converges to the sum $(1 + x)^m$.

For x in the interval $(-1, 0)$, we choose the Cauchy's form of Taylor remainder, and obtain

$$R_n(x) = n \begin{bmatrix} m \\ n \end{bmatrix} (1 + \xi)^{m-n}(x - \xi)^{n-1}$$

$$= n \begin{bmatrix} m \\ n \end{bmatrix} \frac{(1 + \xi)^m}{x - \xi} x^{n+1} \left[\frac{x - \xi}{x + x\xi} \right]^n$$

where ξ satisfies the inequality $-1 < x < \xi < 0$. Now, the function, $g(\xi) = \frac{x - \xi}{x + x\xi}$, is decreasing in the interval $(-1, 0)$ (**WHY?**), so $g(\xi) \leqslant g(0) = 1$. Thus, $0 < \frac{x - \xi}{x + x\xi} < 1$. It now follows that

$$|R_n(x)| \leqslant \left| \frac{(1 + \xi)^m x}{x - \xi} \right| \left| n \begin{bmatrix} m \\ n \end{bmatrix} x^n \right|.$$

Using the ratio test, we can conclude that the series, $\sum_{n=0}^{\infty} n \begin{bmatrix} m \\ n \end{bmatrix} x^n$, converges for $|x| < 1$, so that $\lim_{n \to \infty} n \begin{bmatrix} m \\ n \end{bmatrix} x^n = 0$. It is now immediate that $R_n(x) \to 0$ for $x \in (-1, 0)$.

Thus, for all x satisfying $|x| < 1$, the infinite series expansion

$$(1 + x)^m = \sum_{n=0}^{\infty} \begin{bmatrix} m \\ n \end{bmatrix} x^n$$

is valid.   □

Discussion. There are several important features to be noted in the above example. Since $(1 + x)^m$ can be differentiated any number of times in a neighborhood of 0, we could immediately write down the Taylor infinite series associated with the function about origin in an elegant form. We also show very easily, using either the ratio or the root test that the series converges for all x in $(-1, 1)$. But, the real problem here is to show that the infinite Taylor series converges *precisely* to the function from which it was generated. This is where the role of the Taylor remainder is important. In $(0, 1)$, we chose the Lagrange's form, which was quite easy to compute, and we could easily show that the remainder converges to 0, by looking at each component in the expression. But, in the interval $(-1, 0)$, we preferred to use the Cauchy's form, because the Lagrange's form will only provide a very poor estimate for $R_n(x)$ in $(-1, 0)$.   □

EXAMPLE 5 _____

Show that if $f^{(n+1)}$ exists and is continuous and if $f^{(n+1)}(0) \neq 0$, then $\lim_{x \to 0} \theta_n(x) = \frac{1}{n+1}$, where θ_n represents the θ occurring in the nth Taylor remainder.

Solution. Since f satisfies the hypothesis of the corollary to Theorem 9.3.1 (Lagrange's form), we can write the Taylor expansion about origin corresponding to $f(x)$ stopping at the nth, as well as the $(n + 1)$th stages, respectively, as follows, resulting in the Taylor remainders at these two stages:

$$f(x) = f(0) + \frac{f'(0)x}{1!} + \frac{f''(0)x^2}{2!} + \cdots + \frac{f^{(n)}(\theta_n x)x^n}{n!}$$

and

$$f(x) = f(0) + \frac{f'(0)x}{1!} + \frac{f''(0)x^2}{2!} + \cdots + \frac{f^{(n)}(\theta_n x)x^n}{n!} + \frac{f^{(n+1)}(\theta_{n+1}x)x^{n+1}}{n!}$$

where θ_n, θ_{n+1}, respectively, denote the θ occurring in the statement of the corollary at the nth and the $(n + 1)$th stages. Equating the above two expressions, we obtain

$$\frac{x^n}{n!} [f^{(n)}(\theta_n x) - f^{(n)}(0)] = \frac{x^{n+1}}{(n+1)!} f^{(n+1)}(\theta_{n+1}x)$$

whence

$$f^{(n)}(\theta_n x) - f^{(n)}(0) = \frac{x}{n+1} f^{(n+1)}(\theta_{n+1}x).$$

Now, $f^{(n)}$ satisfies the conditions for the Mean Value Theorem in differential calculus (Theorem 4.3.3), so there exists a ξ between 0 and $\theta_n x$ satisfying

$$\theta_n x f^{(n+1)}(\xi) = \frac{x}{n+1} f^{(n+1)}(\theta_{n+1}x),$$

hence,

$$\theta_n = \frac{1}{n+1} \frac{f^{(n+1)}(\theta_{n+1}x)}{f^{(n+1)}(\xi)}.$$

The continuity of $f^{(n+1)}$ guarantees that as x approaches 0, since ξ also approaches 0, the term $\dfrac{f^{(n+1)}(\theta_{n+1}x)}{f^{(n+1)}(\xi)}$ approaches 1, and we obtain

$$\lim_{x \to 0} \theta_n = \frac{1}{n+1}. \qquad \square$$

EXERCISES

1. Using the well-known formula for the derivative of e^x, show $f^{(n)}(0) = 0$ for all $n \in \mathbf{N}$, where f is as in Example 1.

2. Let f be infinitely differentiable on $(a - R, a + R)$. Show the sequence of Taylor polynomials for f at a converges uniformly on $(a - R, a + R)$ exactly if the sequence of remainders converges uniformly to zero on the same interval.

3. Establish the claim about ξ in the proof of Theorem 9.3.1, namely that $\xi = \theta x_0$ for some $\theta \in (0, 1)$.

4. State and prove a general form of the Schlomlich–Roche Theorem to cover the case of a Taylor expansion about a.

5. Supply an independent proof of the validity of Lagrange's and Cauchy's form of Taylor remainder, without using Theorem 9.3.1.

6. Show $\sum_{n=0}^{\infty} \binom{m}{n} x^n$ is convergent for $x \in (0, 1)$ and $m \in \mathbf{R}$.

7. Obtain the Taylor remainder (all the three forms) after three terms of the following functions in $[0, x]$. Use whatever formulas are required to find derivatives.
   (a) $x^3 + 4x^2 - 3x + 5$;
   (b) $\sqrt{1 + x}$, $x > 0$;
   (c) $\sqrt{1 - x^2}$, $-1 < x < 1$;
   (d) $(1 + x)^{1/3}$, $-1 < x$;
   (e) $f(x) = \ln \cos x$;
   (f) $f(x) = e^{\cos x}$;
   (g) $f(x) = \dfrac{x}{e^x - 1}$;
   (h) $f(x) = e^{\text{Arcsin} \, x}$;
   (i) $f(x) = \dfrac{1}{\sqrt{1 - x^2}}$.

8. Obtain a Taylor expansion of the following functions about origin. In each case, obtain the interval of convergence of the infinite Taylor series associated with the function. Prove (where possible) the series converges to the function in that interval:
   (a) $f(x) = \sin x + \cos x$;
   (b) $f(x) = \cosh x = \dfrac{e^x + e^{-x}}{2}$;
   (c) $f(x) = \tanh x = \dfrac{e^x - e^{-x}}{e^x + e^{-x}}$;
   (d) $f(x) = \ln (1 + x)$ [HINT: Use Cauchy's form of remainder in $(-1, 0)$];
   (e) $f(x) = \ln \dfrac{1 + x}{1 - x}$;
   (f) $f(x) = \text{Arctan} \, x$ [HINT: Consider the expansion of the derivative];
   (g) $f(x) = \text{Arcsin} \, x$;
   (h) $f(x) = \int_0^x e^{-t^2} dt$.

9. Obtain a Taylor expansion of the following functions about the point $a \in \mathbf{R}$:
   (a) e^{x+1};
   (b) $\sin x$;
   (c) $\cos x$;
   (d) $\ln (1 + x)$, $a > -1$.

10. Prove any power series is the Taylor series of its sum.

11. Let P be a polynomial on $[a, b]$. Show this polynomial is its own Taylor series.

12. Obtain a Taylor series expansion of $f(x) = x^6 + 14x^5 - 14x^3 + 21x^2 + x - 6$ about the point $x = 2$. Obtain $f(2.01)$ correct to four decimal places.

13. Expand $f(x) = \dfrac{1}{x}$ in a Taylor series about $a = 1$. What can be said about the convergence properties of this series?

14. If $a, h > 0$, $n \in \mathbf{N}$, prove the existence of θ, $0 < \theta < 1$ satisfying

$$\frac{1}{a + h} = \frac{1}{a} - \frac{h}{a^2} + \frac{h^2}{a^3} - \cdots + \frac{(-1)^{n-1} h^{n-1}}{a^n} + \frac{(-1)^n h^n}{(a + \theta h)^{n+1}}.$$

15. Show the power series, $\sum_{n=0}^{\infty} \dfrac{x^n}{n^n}$, is convergent to f for all $x \in \mathbf{R}$. What is the Taylor series for f expanded about 0?

16. Suppose there is known to be a function which is continuous and differentiable on $\mathbf{R}$ and satisfies $f'(x) = f(x)$ for all $x \in \mathbf{R}$. Given this function satisfies $f(0) = 1$, find the Taylor series expansion for f at 0.

17. Starting with the identity $\int_a^x f'(t)dt = f(x) - f(a)$, obtain the **integral form of the Taylor remainder**: If f has derivatives through order n in some neighborhood of x_0 and $f^{(n)}$ is Riemann integrable on any interval in that neighborhood, then for all x in that neighborhood, the Taylor remainder after n terms is given by the integral

$$R_n(x) = \frac{1}{(n-1)!} \int_{x_0}^x (x - t)^{n-1} f^{(n)}(t)\, dt.$$

Obtain also the Lagrange's and the Schlomlich Roche's forms of remainder in integral form.

18. If $f(x)$ possesses continuous derivatives up to order $(n + 2)$, and $f^{(n+1)}(0) \neq 0$, and θ_n is the term occurring in the nth Taylor remainder, prove

$$\theta_n(x) = \frac{1}{n+1} + \frac{n}{2(n+1)^2(n+2)}\left[\frac{f^{(n+2)}(0)}{f^{(n+1)}(0)} + \epsilon_x\right]x$$

where $\epsilon_x \to 0$ as $x \to 0$.

19. Let f be n times differentiable at c and let $P_n(x)$ be the nth Taylor polynomial at $x = c$. Show

$$\lim_{x \to c} \frac{f(x) - P_n(x)}{(x - c)^n} = 0.$$

20. Let $0 < a < 1$. Show the equation $\sin x = ax$ has a root near π. Further, show $\pi(1 - a)$ and $\pi(1 - a + a^2)$ are successively better approximations to this root. What about $\pi(1 - a + a^2 - a^3)$?

21. Expand $(1 - x)^{n+1/2}$ using Lagrange's form of remainder at the nth stage, and show θ converges to $\dfrac{4n+1}{(2n+1)^2}$ as x approaches 1. More generally, if $f(x) = (1 - x)^m$, where $m > 0$, then θ approaches $1 - \left[\dfrac{n}{m}\right]^{1/(m-n)}$ as x approaches 1.

22. Let f be an odd function, that is, $f(x) = f(-x)$, for all x and suppose f can be expanded in an infinite Taylor series at 0. Show the terms of this series all have odd degree. Prove an analogous result for even functions. Why are these functions called odd and even?

23. Prove the following form of Taylor's Theorem (**Young's form**): If $f(x)$ and its successive $n - 1$ derivatives are continuous at $x = a$, and $f^{(n)}(a)$ exists, then

$$f(a + h) = f(a) + \frac{hf'(a)}{1!} + \cdots + \frac{h^{n-1}f^{(n-1)}(a)}{(n-1)!} + \frac{h^n}{n!}M$$

where $M \to f^{(n)}(a)$ as $h \to 0$.

24. The numbers B_n in the expansion $\dfrac{x}{e^x - 1} = \sum_{n=0}^{\infty} \dfrac{B_n x^n}{n!}$ are called **Bernoulli's numbers**.

   (a) Prove $B_{2n+1} = 0$ for all $n \in \mathbf{N}$;
   (b) Obtain the first six Bernoulli's numbers;
   (c) Show $\sum_{k=0}^{n-1} \binom{n}{k} B_k = 0$ and use this identity to compute the first six even Bernoulli's numbers.

25. If $\dfrac{xe^{xt}}{e^x - 1}$ is expanded in a power series about 0 in the form $\sum\limits_{n=0}^{\infty} P_n(t)\dfrac{x^n}{n!}$, show

$$P_n(t) = \sum_{k=0}^{n} \binom{n}{k} P_k(0)t^{n-k}.$$

The $P_n(t)$ are called **Bernoulli polynomials**, and $P_n(0)$'s can be identified with the Bernuolli's numbers. Prove

(a) $P_n(t + 1) - P_n(t) = nt^{n-1}$, $n \in \mathbf{N}$;

(b) $\dfrac{P_{n+1}(k + 1) - P_{n+1}(0)}{n + 1} = \sum\limits_{i=1}^{k-1} i^n$, $(n = 2, 3, \ldots)$.

26. If f is a polynomial of degree n, show

$$\sum_{k=1}^{n} (-1)^{k-1} \binom{n}{k} f(x + kh) = \left[\sum_{k=1}^{n} \frac{1}{k} \right] f(x) + hf'(x).$$

27. Prove **Cauchy's Generalized Mean Value Theorem**. If f and g together with their successive $n - 1$ derivatives are continuous in $[a, b]$ and $f^{(n)}$, $g^{(n)}$ both exist in (a, b), then there exists a number $\xi \in (a, b)$ satisfying

$$\frac{f(b)-f(a)-\dfrac{(b-a)}{1!}f'(a)- \cdots -\dfrac{(b-a)^{n-1}}{(n-1)!}f^{(n-1)}(a)}{g(b)-g(a)-\dfrac{(b-a)}{1!}g'(a)- \cdots -\dfrac{(b-a)^{p-1}}{(p-1)!}g^{p-1}(a)} = \frac{(p-1)!}{(n-1)!}(b-\xi)^{n-p}\frac{f^{(n)}(\xi)}{g^p(\xi)}.$$

28. If $f(x + h) = f(x) + hf'(x) + \cdots + \dfrac{h^n}{n!}f^{(n)}(x + \theta h)$, where $0 < \theta < 1$, prove the following:

(a) $\theta \to \dfrac{1}{n+1}$ as $h \to 0$;

(b) θ is independent of x and h provided $f(x)$ is of the form $A + Bx + \cdots + Kx^{n+1}$.

9.4 WEIERSTRASS'S APPROXIMATION THEOREM

In the last section we defined an analytic function as being a function, f, which could be represented by a power series, specifically, a Taylor series, on an open interval. We saw that to even have a Taylor series, in a formal sense, the function, f, would have to be very well behaved on that interval, in the sense that it would have to possess an infinite number of derivatives, each of which was continuous on the interval. We followed this definition by presenting an example of a function which dashed our hopes that any function which admitted a Taylor series expansion would have to be represented by that Taylor series on at least some small open interval about the point of expansion.

The negative result that mere possession of derivatives in an interval is not enough to guarantee that a function is analytic is certainly disheartening and must have come as a rude shock to those studying the problem of representing functions by power series. In fact, Cauchy's function has so many nice properties that it hardly seems plausible that an arbitrary continuous function might be representable by a sequence or series of polynomials. Nevertheless, mathematicians did not give up the cause and continued to pursue the goal of being able to represent an arbitrary continuous function by polynomials.

In this section we present the realization of the goal in the form of Weierstrass's Approximation Theorem, which dates back to 1885. This remarkable theorem asserts that every continuous function defined on a closed interval is not only representable as a sequence of polynomials, indeed, it is uniformly representable as such a sequence! There are several constructive proofs of this statement due to various mathematicians, Bernstein, Laguerre, Tchebychev, Lebesgue, Fourier, to mention a few. These proofs provide an explicit construction which will witness the truth of the theorem by spelling out the sequence of polynomials. Our proof will adopt this approach using the Bernstein polynomials. We will define these polynomials and study their basic properties before proving the main theorem.

Definition. Let f be a real-valued function defined on $[0, 1]$. The nth **Bernstein polynomial associated with** f is defined by

$$B_{f,n}(x) = \sum_{k=0}^{n} \binom{n}{k} x^k (1-x)^{n-k} f\left(\frac{k}{n}\right), \quad n \in \mathbf{N}, \quad x \in \mathbf{R}.$$

Discussion. Recall from Section 0.4 that the numbers $\binom{n}{k}$ are the familiar Binomial coefficients, namely,

$$\binom{n}{k} = \frac{n!}{k!(n-k)!}, \quad n \in \mathbf{N}, \quad k = 0, 1, 2, \cdots.$$

There are several facts to be observed from this definition. First of all, each $B_{f,n}$ is a polynomial of degree n in the variable x. For example, $B_{f,3}$ is

$$B_{f,3}(x) = (1-x)^3 f(0) + 3x(1-x)^2 f\left(\frac{1}{3}\right) + 3x^2(1-x)f\left(\frac{2}{3}\right) + x^3 f(1).$$

As such, $B_{f,3}(0) = f(0)$ and $B_{f,3}(1) = f(1)$.

Secondly, each Bernstein polynomial depends on f. Indeed, the nth polynomial uses $n + 1$ functional values. Moreover, each functional value which is used, is used infinitely often in the sequence of polynomials, $\{B_{f,n}\}$. Thus, the polynomials depend ever more strongly on the given function, f.

As another example, consider f defined by $f(x) = 1$ for all x. Then the Bernstein polynomials reduce to the constant polynomial, 1, for each n, since from the Binomial Theorem we obtain

$$1 = (x + 1 - x)^n = \sum_{k=0}^{n} \binom{n}{k} x^{n-k}(1-x)^k = B_{1,n}(x).$$

This representation of the constant polynomial, 1, will prove useful in the proof of Theorem 9.4.1. □

Before beginning the proof of the Weierstrass Approximation Theorem, we present a further identity in the form of an example which will be useful in the proof of the theorem.

EXAMPLE 1

Show that $x = \sum_{k=0}^{n} \frac{k}{n} x^k (1-x)^{n-k}$.

Solution. We have

$$1 = B_{1,n-1} = \sum_{k=0}^{n-1} \binom{n-1}{k} x^k (1-x)^{n-1-k}.$$

Thus, if we simply multiply by x, we obtain

$$x = x B_{1,n-1} = \sum_{k=0}^{n-1} \binom{n-1}{k} x^{k+1} (1-x)^{n-1-k}.$$

Now, $\binom{n-1}{k} = \frac{k+1}{n} \times \binom{n}{k+1}$ (Exercise 1), whence

$$x = \sum_{k=0}^{n-1} \frac{k+1}{n} \binom{n}{k+1} x^{k+1} (1-x)^{n-(k+1)}$$

$$= \sum_{j=1}^{n} \frac{j}{n} \binom{n}{j} x^j (1-x)^{n-j}$$

$$= \sum_{j=0}^{n} \frac{j}{n} \binom{n}{j} x^j (1-x)^{n-j}$$

where we may include the term with $j = 0$ in the last sum since it is 0. Replacing j by k completes the proof. □

Discussion. The calculations presented, while not particularly difficult, are, nevertheless, neither obvious nor easily motivated. Yet it is calculations like these which are the foundation of the proof of Weierstrass's Theorem by means of Bernstein polynomials. In Exercises 1–3 there are further identities of a like nature which one should complete prior to reading the proof of Theorem 9.4.1.

Theorem 9.4.1 (Weierstrass). If f is continuous on $[0, 1]$, then the sequence of Bernstein polynomials $\{B_{f,n}\}$ associated with f converge uniformly to f in $[0,1]$.

Proof. Since f is continuous on $[0, 1]$, there exists a constant $K > 0$ such that $|f(x)| < K$, for all $x \in [0, 1]$. Since $[0, 1]$ is compact, the function, f, is uniformly continuous on $[0, 1]$. Hence, given $\epsilon > 0$, there exists $\delta > 0$ such that for all $x, y \in [0, 1]$, whenever $|x - y| < \delta$, we have

$$|f(x) - f(y)| < \frac{\epsilon}{2}.$$

Now, fix an arbitrary $x \in [0,1]$. For this fixed x we have

$$|f(x) - B_{f,n}(x)| = |f(x) \cdot 1 - B_{f,n}(x)|$$

$$= \left| \sum_{k=0}^{n} \binom{n}{k} x^k (1-x)^{n-k} \left(f(x) - f\left(\frac{k}{n}\right) \right) \right|$$

$$\leqslant \sum_{k=0}^{n} \binom{n}{k} x^k (1-x)^{n-k} \left| f(x) - f\left(\frac{k}{n}\right) \right|. \tag{1}$$

Recall that x is fixed. Thus, for each value of $k = 0, 1, \ldots, n$, the inequality, $\left| x - \dfrac{k}{n} \right| < \delta$, is either satisfied, or fails. Thus, we decompose the sum (1) into two parts, $\sum_1$ and $\sum_2$, where the first sum includes all terms from (1) for which the inequality, $\left| x - \dfrac{k}{n} \right| < \delta$, is satisfied and the second includes all terms from (1) for which the inequality fails. For $\sum_1$ we have,

$$\sum_1 = \sum_{k:\, \left| x-\frac{k}{n} \right| < \delta} \binom{n}{k} x^k (1-x)^{n-k} \left| f(x) - f\left(\frac{k}{n}\right) \right|$$

$$= \sum_{k:\, \left| x-\frac{k}{n} \right| < \delta} \binom{n}{k} x^k (1-x)^{n-k} \frac{\epsilon}{2}$$

$$= \left[\sum_{k:\, \left| x-\frac{k}{n} \right| < \delta} \binom{n}{k} x^k (1-x)^{n-k} \right] \frac{\epsilon}{2}$$

$$\leqslant \left[\sum_{k=0}^{n} \binom{n}{k} x^k (1-x)^{n-k} \right] \cdot \frac{\epsilon}{2}$$

$$= \frac{\epsilon}{2}, \tag{2}$$

where the last equality is by virtue of the identity for $B_{1,n}$. The second identity in Exercise 3 asserts that

$$\sum_{k=0}^{n} \binom{n}{k} x^k (1-x)^{n-k} \left(x - \frac{k}{n} \right)^2 = \frac{x(1-x)}{n}$$

$$\leqslant \frac{1}{4n}$$

since $x(1-x) \leqslant \dfrac{1}{4}$ for all $x \in [0,1]$ (Exercise 4). Now take $N \geqslant \dfrac{K}{\epsilon \delta^2}$, then

$$\sum_2 \leqslant \sum_{k=0}^{n} \left[\frac{\left(x - \frac{k}{n} \right)^2}{\left(x - \frac{k}{n} \right)^2} \right] \binom{n}{k} x^k (1-x)^{n-k} \left(|f(x)| + \left| f\left(\frac{k}{n}\right) \right| \right)$$

$$= \sum_{k=0}^{n} \left[x - \frac{k}{n} \right]^2 \binom{n}{k} x^k (1-x)^{n-k} \left[\frac{|f(x)| + \left| f\left[\frac{k}{n} \right] \right|}{\left[x - \frac{k}{n} \right]^2} \right]$$

$$\leqslant \sum_{k=0}^{n} \left[x - \frac{k}{n} \right]^2 \binom{n}{k} x^k (1-x)^{n-k} \left[\frac{2K}{\delta^2} \right]$$

$$< \frac{1}{4n} \cdot \frac{2K}{\delta^2}$$

$$< \frac{\epsilon}{2}, \quad \text{whenever} \quad n > N. \tag{3}$$

Thus, for the given ϵ, we have chosen $N \in \mathbf{N}$ such that if $n \geqslant N$, then

$$|f(x) - B_{f,n}| \leqslant \sum_1 + \sum_2 < \frac{\epsilon}{2} + \frac{\epsilon}{2} = \epsilon$$

proving that the sequence $\{B_{f,n}\}$ converges uniformly to f on $[0, 1]$. □

Discussion. This proof is difficult, and we review it step by step. To establish uniform convergence of the sequence, $\{B_{f,n}\}$, we have to show that for every positive ϵ there exists an $N \in \mathbf{N}$ such that $|f(x) - B_{f,n}(x)| < \epsilon$ for all $x \in [0, 1]$ whenever $n > N$. Let us see that the proof actually accomplishes this requirement.

Consider $|f(x) - B_{f,n}(x)|$. This quantity is bounded by the sum, (1). The computations leading to this bound are based on a fixed x, but in no way depend on that x. Thus, the result captured in (1) is valid for all $x \in [0, 1]$.

The next important step in the proof is the decomposition of the sum in (1) into $\sum_1$ and $\sum_2$. It is important to realize that the particular terms from the sum in (1) which end up as part of $\sum_1$ will depend on the value of x, the value of δ, and the value of n. Similarly, which particular terms end up as part of $\sum_2$ also depends on the value of x, the value of δ, and the value of n. For this reason, it is essential to make sure that the arguments which make up the remainder of the proof are not affected by changing which particular terms of the sum in (1) end up in $\sum_1$, and which end up in $\sum_2$.

Consider then the computations with $\sum_1$ leading to (2). The first step in this string depends on the fact that $\left| x - \frac{k}{n} \right| < \delta$ implies $\left| f(x) - f\left[\frac{k}{n} \right] \right| < \frac{\epsilon}{2}$. The remainder of these computations are algebraic in nature and do not depend on the value of x or the value of n or which terms are included in $\sum_1$. Thus, these computations will remain valid provided we do not change ϵ or δ. Indeed, the inequality captured in (2) holds for all the Bernstein polynomials, $B_{f,n}$, because in essence, it is not a statement about Bernstein polynomials at all, rather it is a statement which depends for its truth on the continuity of f. As a result of the computations leading to (2), we obtain an ϵ bound on $\sum_1$.

The next step in the proof amounts to generating an ϵ bound on $\sum_2$. This bound is generated from the identity

$$\sum_{k=0}^{n} \binom{n}{k} x^k (1-x)^{n-k} \left[x - \frac{k}{n} \right]^2 = \frac{1}{n} x(1-x) \qquad (4)$$

which is the second identity requested in Exercise 3. Arriving at such an identity would result only after considerable experimentation with Bernstein polynomials. In any case, once one has this identity, one can notice that by introducing a form of 1 into $\sum_2$ and an application of the Triangle inequality, it becomes possible to replace $\sum_2$ by the quantity on the left-hand side of (4) multiplied by the constant, $\frac{2K}{\delta^2}$. Since the quantity in (4) becomes arbitrarily small as n becomes large, we are done as long as the previous computations do not depend on the choice of n. Since they do not, we have the required bound on $\sum_2$.

Further insight into this proof can be gained from looking again at (1) which in summary form asserts that

$$|f(x) - B_{f,n}(x)| \leq \sum_{k=0}^{n} \binom{n}{k} x^k (1-x)^{n-k} \left| f(x) - f\left[\frac{k}{n} \right] \right|. \qquad (1)$$

If one poses the question as to why the sum on the right might be small, one concludes that the individual terms can be small for one of two reasons. First, $\left| f(x) - f\left[\frac{k}{n} \right] \right|$ can be small, whence its product with another term which is bounded would also be small. Second, $\binom{n}{k} x^k (1-x)^{n-k}$ could be small, whence its product with a term which is bounded would also be small. To obtain the first, we apply continuity. To obtain the second, we use the fact that f is bounded on $[0,1]$ and the identity in (4).

It is at this point that one sees how the function, f, is employed in the proof. Specifically, f determines the dependence of δ on ϵ and the value of K, the universal bound. The number, $\frac{K}{\epsilon \delta^2}$, then determines the value of N, or how many terms of the sequence must be taken to obtain the required approximation.

Finally, the crucial fact on which the proof rests is that a continuous function on a closed interval is uniformly continuous. It is uniform continuity which permits us to obtain a single δ which does not depend on x and a single bound over the entire interval. Without these very powerful theorems, there would be no hope of a result like this. $\qquad \square$

Corollary. Let f be a continuous function on $[a, b]$. Then there is a sequence of functions, $\{P_n\}$, such that P_n is a polynomial of degree, n, which converges uniformly to f on $[a, b]$.

Proof. Let g be defined on $[0, 1]$ by $g(x) = a + (b - a)x$. Then $f \circ g$ is a continuous function with domain $[0, 1]$. As such there is a sequence of Bernstein polynomials, $\{B_{f \circ g, n}\}$, which converges uniformly to $f \circ g$ on $[0,1]$. We claim, Exercise 5, that $\{B_{f \circ g, n}(a + (b - a)x)\}$ is a sequence of polynomials which converges uniformly to f on $[a, b]$.   □

Discussion.   Theorem 9.4.1 and its corollary assert that every continuous function is almost a polynomial. With this in mind, the reader must surely be wondering about how this result and Cauchy's function could both appear in the same book, much less be products of the same axiom scheme.

Cauchy's function reveals that not every function can be obtained as the sum of its power series. Weierstrass's Approximation Theorem says that even Cauchy's function can be uniformly obtained as a sequence of polynomials, and in consequence, as a series, each member of which is a polynomial. The point is that the series of polynomials which approximates the Cauchy function is not a power series. This seems a simple enough answer, but the situation is still a bit more complex.

Let us consider the Cauchy function, f, on the interval from $[-1, 1]$. For any fixed $\epsilon > 0$, there is a tube about f of width, ϵ, such that there is a polynomial, P, which lies completely inside this ϵ tube. By Exercise 9.3.10, this polynomial is a power series! Thus, there is a power series which approximates the Cauchy function arbitrarily closely. Why is this not a contradiction? The answer is that as ϵ is made smaller, the power series changes. In particular, each smaller ϵ will, in general, generate a new value for the constant term, the coefficient on x, and the other terms in the power series approximation to f. (If Bernstein polynomials are used, the constant term will be fixed.) This is completely different from the Taylor series approach where each addition to the approximation has no effect on the coefficients of terms of lower degree. Indeed, this fact about the Taylor series coefficients is at the heart of the properties of Taylor series.   □

We leave the reader with a final example.

EXAMPLE 2 _____

Find the first five Bernstein polynomials for $\cos 6x$. Illustrate how these polynomials approximate $\cos 6x$.

Solution.   The polynomials in order are:

$$B_{f,1} = (1 - x)\cos 0 + x\cos 6,$$

$$B_{f,2} = (1 - x)^2 \cos 0 + 2x(1 - x)\cos 3 + x^2 \cos 6,$$

$$B_{f,3} = (1 - x)^3 \cos 0 + 3x(1 - x)^2 \cos 2 + 3x^2(1 - x)\cos 4 + x^3 \cos 6,$$

$$B_{f,4} = (1 - x)^4 \cos 0 + 4x(1 - x)^3 \cos \frac{6}{4} + 6x^2(1 - x)^2 \cos 3$$
$$+ 4x^3(1 - x)\cos \frac{18}{4} + x^4 \cos 6,$$

$$B_{f,5} = (1 - x)^5 \cos 0 + 5x(1 - x)^4 \cos \frac{6}{5} + 10x^2(1 - x)^3 \cos \frac{12}{5}$$
$$+ 10x^3(1 - x)^2 \cos \frac{18}{5} + 5x^4(1 - x)\cos \frac{24}{5} + x^5 \cos 6,$$

where $f(x) = \cos 6x$. Figure 9.4.1 presents graphs of the Bernstein polynomials together with that of $\cos 6x$. As can be seen from inspection, the convergence is not nearly so rapid as for the power series for e^x. But $\cos 6x$ is a more complicated function. □

Discussion. In relation to the previous discussion the reader can check the following. First, the constant term of each of the Bernstein polynomials for $\cos 6x$ will be $\cos 0 = 1$. Second, the coefficients on all positive powers of x change as n changes. For example the first coefficient on x is $\cos 6 - \cos 0$, while the second coefficient on x is $2(\cos 3 - \cos 0)$, and so forth. Thus, it is easy to see that the sequence of polynomials cannot possibly be part of a single power series. □

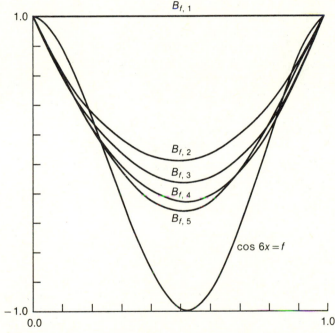

Figure 9.4.1 Bernstein polynomials $B_{f,1}$, $B_{f,2}$, $B_{f,3}$, $B_{f,4}$, $B_{f,5}$ for $\cos 6x$.

EXERCISES

1. Show $\dbinom{n-1}{k-1} = \dfrac{k}{n} \times \dbinom{n}{k}$ and $\dbinom{n-2}{k-2} = \dfrac{k(k-1)}{n(n-1)} \times \dbinom{n}{k}$.

2. Show $(n^2 - n)x^2 = \displaystyle\sum_{k=0}^{n} (k^2 - k) \dbinom{n}{k} x^k (1-x)^{n-k}$.

3. Show $\left(1 - \dfrac{1}{n}\right)x^2 + \dfrac{1}{n}x = \displaystyle\sum_{k=0}^{n} \left(\dfrac{k}{n}\right)^2 \dbinom{n}{k} x^k (1-x)^{n-k}$. Use this to show

$$\dfrac{1}{n}x(1-x) = \sum_{k=0}^{n} \left(x - \dfrac{k}{n}\right)^2 \dbinom{n}{k} x^k (1-x)^{n-k}.$$

4. Show $x(1-x) \leqslant \dfrac{1}{4}$ for all $x \in [0, 1]$.

5. Complete the proof of the corollary to Theorem 9.4.1.

6. Obtain the first six Bernstein polynomials for the following functions in the indicated interval:

    (a) $f(x) = x$, $[0, 1]$;

    (b) $f(x) = x^2$, $[0, 1]$;

    (c) $f(x) = x^3 + 2x^2$, $[0, 1]$;

    (d) $f(x) = |x|$, $[-1, 1]$;

    (e) $f(x) = \sin x$, $[0, \pi]$;

    (f) $f(x) = e^x$, $[-1, 1]$.

7. In view of Exercise 6 and the results in sections 9.3 and 9.4, discuss the relative merits of Taylor and Bernstein polynomials as methods for approximating functions.

8. Let $\epsilon = 0.2$ and $f(x) = \cos 6x$. Find a Bernstein polynomial which approximates f to within ϵ.

9. If f is continuous on $[a, b]$ such that $\displaystyle\int_a^b x^n f(x)\, dx = 0$ for all nonnegative integers n, prove f is the zero function on $[a, b]$.

10. How large must n be, so that the nth Bernstein polynomial, B_n, associated with x^2 satisfies $|f(x) - B_n(x)| \leqslant 0.001$ for all $x \in [0, 1]$?

11. Let f be a bounded function on $[0, 1]$, say $|f(x)| \leqslant K$ for all $x \in [0, 1]$. Show all the Bernstein polynomials, $B_n(f)$, are bounded by K.

12. Let f be continuous on $[a, b]$. Show there exists a sequence, $\{p_n\}$, of polynomials converging to f uniformly on $[a, b]$, and such that $p_n(a) = f(a)$ for all n.

13. Show there does not exist a sequence of polynomials converging uniformly on $\mathbf{R}$ to f, where

    (a) $f(x) = e^x$;

    (b) $f(x) = \sin x$.

14. Show if f is continuous on $\mathbf{R}$, then there exists a sequence $\{p_n\}$ of polynomials converging uniformly to f on each bounded subset of $\mathbf{R}$.

15. If $f\colon [a, b] \to \mathbf{R}$ is continuous, show that f can be uniformly approximated on $[a, b]$ by a sequence $\{s_n\}$ of step-functions.

16. A function $h\colon [a, b] \to \mathbf{R}$ is **piecewise linear** on $[a, b]$ if there exist points $\{t_i\}$ and real numbers $\{a_i\}$, $\{b_i\}$ $(i = 0, 1, \ldots, n)$ with $t_0 = a$, $t_n = b$ and such that

$$h(x) = a_k x + b_k, \quad x \in [t_{k-1}, t_k], \quad 0 \leqslant k \leqslant n - 1.$$

Prove that every continuous function on $[a, b]$ can be uniformly approximated by a sequence of piecewise linear functions.

17. Give another proof of the Weierstrass Approximation Theorem using the sequence of **Legendre's polynomials**, $\{P_n\}$, where $P_0(t) = 0$ and

$$P_{n+1}(t) = P_n(t) + \frac{1}{2}\left[t - (P_n(t))^2 \right], \quad (n \geqslant 0).$$

[HINT: Show by induction

$$0 \leqslant \sqrt{t} - P_n(t) \leqslant \frac{2\sqrt{t}}{2 + n\sqrt{t}}$$

whence $\{P_n\}$ approaches $\sqrt{t}$ uniformly on $[0, 1]$.]

18. Let $D_n(x) = \alpha_n(1 - x^2)^n$, $n \in \mathbf{N}$, where α_n is defined by $\int_{-1}^{1} D_n = 1$ for each $n \in \mathbf{N}$. Let $f: [0, 1] \to \mathbf{R}$ be continuous. Prove the following:
    (a) $\alpha_n < \sqrt{n}$;
    (b) $D_n(x) \leq \sqrt{n}(1 - \delta^2)^n$ for $\delta \leq |x| \leq 1$;
    (c) $D_n(x)$ converges to 0 uniformly for $\delta \leq |x| \leq 1$;
    (d) The polynomials $P_n(x)$ defined by

$$P_n(x) = \int_{-1}^{1} f(x + t)D_n(t)\, dt = \int_{0}^{1} f(t)D_n(t - x)dt,$$

    converge uniformly to f in $[0, 1]$.
    (This is Landau's proof of Theorem 9.4.1. and D_n is called **Landau's kernel**.)

19. A **Dirac sequence** is a sequence, $\{K_n\}$, of functions on $\mathbf{R}$ satisfying:
    (a) $K_n(x) \geq 0$ for all n and all x;
    (b) each K_n is continuous;
    (c) $\int_{-\infty}^{\infty} K_n(t)dt = 1$;
    (d) Given ϵ and δ, there exists n such that if $n \geq N$,

$$\int_{-\infty}^{-\delta} K_n + \int_{\delta}^{\infty} K_n < \epsilon.$$

    If f is a piecewise linear and bounded function, we define the **convolution** to be

$$f_n(x) = K_n * f(x) = \int_{-\infty}^{\infty} f(t)K_n(x - t)\, dt.$$

    Prove the sequence, $\{f_n\}$, converges to f uniformly on each compact subset, $S \subseteq \mathbf{R}$.

20. If f is continuous on $[0, \pi]$, prove that given $\epsilon > 0$, there exists an even trigonometric polynomial T such that

$$|f(x) - T(x)| < \epsilon \quad \text{for all } x \in [0, \pi].$$

    [HINT: Set $g(y) = f(\text{Arccos } y)$, $y \in [-1, 1]$. Approximate $g(y)$ as a polynomial in y, and substitute back $y = \cos x$.]

Chapter 10

Transcendental Functions

The analysis which we have developed so far enables us to perform operations such as evaluating the limit of a function as x approaches some real number, finding the integral of a given function, or differentiating a function. Even though we have used several types of functions, for example, the trigonometric, logarithmic, and exponential functions, to furnish appropriate examples or in the exercises, we have up to this point only defined integral powers of the function $f(x) = x$ in a completely formal way. Of course, we have frequently used polynomial functions, which are of the form

$$f(x) = a_0 + a_1 x + \cdots + a_n x^n = \sum_{k=0}^{n} a_k x^k$$

where the a_i's are real numbers and $n \in \mathbf{N}$. Starting with the polynomials and applying standard algebraic manipulations such as addition, subtraction, multiplication, division, and root-extraction lead to a huge collection of functions, which are called **algebraic functions**. But there are lots of functions which cannot be manufactured by this procedure commencing with the polynomials, many of which are in common use in mathematics and science.

In this chapter, we will formally introduce some of the so-called **transcendental functions**, by which we mean those functions which cannot be obtained by standard algebraic procedures (addition, subtraction, multiplication, division, root-extraction, etc.) applied to polynomials. Explicitly, we shall define the exponential and logarithmic functions, the trigonometric functions, and the hyperbolic functions. There are several possible methods for introducing these new functions. For example, we could use the concept of uniform convergence and define new functions by means of power series or as uniform limits of certain sequences of functions. Alternatively, we could introduce the new functions as indefinite integrals of some known functions. Or, we could seek a function satisfying certain functional equations such as $f(xy) = f(x) + f(y)$, or

$f(xy) = f(x) + f(y)$, or $f(x + y) = f(x)f(y)$. Still another possibility is to create the new functions as solutions to some differential equations. In this chapter, we will employ this last method, to arrive at the exponential and trigonometric functions.

10.1 EXPONENTIAL FUNCTION

In this section, we establish the existence of a unique function which answers the demand that it be its own derivative. Then we will establish the basic properties of such a function and finally recognize this new function as the familiar exponential function.

Definition.   The sequence, $\{E_n\}$, of functions, $E_n: \mathbf{R} \to \mathbf{R}$ is defined inductively by

$$E_0(x) = 1,$$

$$E_{n+1}(x) = 1 + \int_0^x E_n(t)dt, \quad n \in \mathbf{N}, \quad x \in \mathbf{R}.$$

Discussion.   The above definition is inductive. It is easily seen that $E_1(x) = 1 + x$, and more generally, using induction, one can prove (Exercise 1) that

$$E_n(x) = 1 + \frac{x}{1!} + \frac{x^2}{2!} + \cdots + \frac{x^n}{n!}, \quad x \in \mathbf{R}.$$

Thus, for each n, $E_n(x)$ is a polynomial of degree n in the variable x. Evidently, E_n is continuous for each n and satisfies $E_n(0) = 1$. Moreover, for a fixed $x > 0$, the sequence of real numbers, $\{E_n(x)\}$, is monotonically increasing and the polynomial, E_n, is strictly increasing on $[0,\infty)$. As well, these polynomials enjoy the property that the derivative of E_{n+1} is E_n, for all $n \in \mathbf{N}$, as can be checked readily. Thus, this sequence consists of functions which are the natural candidates from which to create the ultimate function with the property that it is its own derivative. $\square$

Our aim now is to use this sequence to obtain a unique function, $E(x)$, which has the property that $E'(x) = E(x)$ for all $x \in \mathbf{R}$. This is the purpose of our first theorem in this section.

Theorem 10.1.1.   There exists a function $E: \mathbf{R} \to \mathbf{R}$ satisfying the following properties:

  (i) $E(0) = 1$;
  (ii) $E'(x) = E(x)$ for all $x \in \mathbf{R}$.

Proof.   First, we show that the sequence, $\{E_n\}$, defined above, converges uniformly on each interval, $[-a, a]$, $a > 0$. For $m \geqslant n > 2a$ and $|x| \leqslant a$, we have

$$|E_n(x) - E_m(x)| = \left| \frac{x^{n+1}}{(n+1)!} + \cdots + \frac{x^m}{m!} \right|$$

$$\leqslant \frac{a^{n+1}}{(n+1)!} + \cdots + \frac{a^m}{m!}$$

$$\leqslant \frac{a^{n+1}}{(n+1)!} \left[1 + \frac{a}{n} + \cdots + \left(\frac{a}{n} \right)^{m-n} \right]$$

$$< 2 \frac{a^{n+1}}{(n+1)!}. \qquad\qquad\qquad\qquad\qquad \textbf{(WHY?)}$$

Since the last expression converges to 0 (**WHY?**), we can apply Theorem 8.2.5 to conclude that the sequence, $\{E_n\}$, converges uniformly on each interval, $[-a, a]$, $a > 0$. In particular, it follows that for each $x \in \mathbf{R}$, the sequence, $\{E_n(x)\}$, converges. We may therefore define $E: \mathbf{R} \to \mathbf{R}$, by

$$E(x) = \lim_{n \to \infty} E_n(x), \quad x \in \mathbf{R}.$$

The fact that E is continuous follows from the corollary to Theorem 8.3.1, since for each x, there is an $a > 0$ satisfying $x \in [-a, a]$. Moreover, $E_n(0) = 1$ for all n (Exercise 1), and hence $E(0) = 1$. Again applying Theorem 8.3.4, we see that E is differentiable and for all $x \in [-a, a]$,

$$E'(x) = \lim_{n \to \infty} E_n'(x).$$

Since $a > 0$ is arbitrary, this equality is satisfied for all $x \in \mathbf{R}$. Lastly, since $E_{n+1}'(x) = E_n(x)$, it follows that

$$E'(x) = \lim_{n \to \infty} E_n'(x) = \lim_{n-1 \to \infty} E_{n-1}(x) = E(x).$$

$\square$

Discussion. The polynomial functions, E_n's, serve as natural approximations to the desired function. They have the key property that $E_n' = E_{n-1}$. This fact, together with the differentiability of each of the polynomials in the sequence and the powerful tool of uniform convergence enable us to invoke Theorem 8.3.4 and arrive at the conclusion that

$$\lim_{n \to \infty} E_n'(x) = \lim_{n-1 \to \infty} E_{n-1}(x).$$

Even though the sequence on the left side of the equality has one term less than the one on the right, this distinction disappears by taking the limits. This idea is the heart and soul of the proof.

It is almost an anticlimax that one finally obtains that the function, $E(x)$, is defined for all $x \in \mathbf{R}$, is continuous, and differentiable with the property that $E' = E$.

The definition of the sequence, $\{E_n\}$, makes it almost trivial to establish additional facts, for example, for $x > 0$, $E(x) > E_n(x)$ for all $n \in \mathbf{N}$. $\square$

Corollary 1. For all $x \in \mathbf{R}$,

$$E(x) = 1 + \frac{x}{1!} + \frac{x^2}{2!} + \cdots + \frac{x^n}{n!} + \cdots = \sum_{n=0}^{\infty} \frac{x^n}{n!}.$$

Proof. Exercise 2. $\square$

Corollary 2. The function $E(x)$ possesses derivatives of all orders and $E^{(n)}(x) = E(x)$ for all $n \in \mathbf{N}$, $x \in \mathbf{R}$.

Proof. Exercise 3. □

Next, we address ourselves to the question: Are there functions other than $E(x)$, which possess properties (i) and (ii) of Theorem 10.1.1? In other words, we are interested in determining whether these two properties characterize a function. Our next theorem will provide the answer by proving the uniqueness of the function, $E(x)$.

Theorem 10.1.2. If $F: \mathbf{R} \rightarrow \mathbf{R}$ is a function with the properties

(i) $F(0) = 1$, and
(ii) $F'(x) = F(x)$ for all $x \in \mathbf{R}$,

then $F(x) = E(x)$ for all $x \in \mathbf{R}$.

Proof. Set $G = E - F$. Then

$$G' = E' - F' = E - F = G,$$

so $G'(x) = G(x)$ for all $x \in \mathbf{R}$. Further,

$$G(0) = E(0) - F(0) = 1 - 1 = 0.$$

It is clear then (**WHY?**) that G possesses derivatives of all orders and that $G^{(n)}(x) = G(x)$ for all $x \in \mathbf{R}$. Hence, we can expand G in a Taylor series about the point 0 with a Lagrange remainder, and for any fixed $x \in \mathbf{R}$ we obtain

$$G(x) = G(0) + \frac{G'(0)}{1!} x + \cdots + \frac{G^{(n-1)}(0)}{(n-1)!} x^{n-1} + \frac{G^{(n)}(\xi_n)}{n!} x^n,$$

where $\xi_n \in (0, x)$ or $(x, 0)$. Since $G^{(k)}(0) = 0$ for all k, it follows that $G(x) = \frac{G^{(n)}(\xi_n)x^n}{n!}$. Since x is fixed, there exists a constant K such that

$$|G^{(n)}(x)| = |G(x)| < K.$$

Successively integrating both sides of $|G^{(n)}(x)| \leqslant K$ n times yields $|G(x)| \leqslant K\frac{|x|^n}{n!}$. But this inequality is valid for all $n \in \mathbf{N}$. Since $\lim\limits_{n \to \infty} \frac{|x|^n}{n!} = 0$, it follows that $G(x) = 0$, or equivalently that, $E(x) - F(x) = 0$. Since x was arbitrary, we have $E(x) = F(x)$, $x \in \mathbf{R}$. □

Discussion. Theorems of this nature are characterization theorems. In essence they establish the fact that there can be only one function with the specified properties. In the present case this means that there is exactly one function, f, such that

(i) $f = f'$;
(ii) $f(0) = 1$.

This function is none other than the exponential function, although we have yet to establish that the function, E, has the required properties to identify it as the exponential function.

It is really quite surprising that the two conditions are enough to totally determine a function, although this result should not surprise a reader familiar with differential equations who will recognize Theorems 10.1.1 and 10.1.2 as existence and uniqueness theorems. In any case, if either of conditions (i) or (ii) were omitted, then we might obtain many functions possessing the remaining properties, a fact pursued in the exercises. □

Definition. The real number e defined by $e = E(1)$ is called the **exponential constant**.

Discussion. From Corollary 1 to Theorem 10.1.1, we see that

$$e = \lim_{n \to \infty} \left[1 + \frac{1}{1!} + \frac{1}{2!} + \cdots + \frac{1}{n!} \right].$$

As we have long since known, by virtue of various convergence tests, the infinite series $\sum_{n=0}^{\infty} \frac{1}{n!}$ is convergent and this definition gives the sum a name, e. Since $E(x) > 1 + x$ for $x > 0$, we see that $e > 2$. On the other hand, $\sum_{n=0}^{k} \frac{1}{n!} < 1 + \sum_{n=0}^{k-1} \frac{1}{2^n}$. By the definition and careful analysis, we see

$$e = \sum_{n=0}^{\infty} \frac{1}{n!} < 1 + \sum_{n=0}^{\infty} \frac{1}{2^n} = 3.$$

Thus the real number, e, lies between 2 and 3 and can be computed to any degree of accuracy by using the partial sums of the infinite series for e. A reasonable approximation for e is 2.7182818846.

The series for e converges very rapidly as the reader can check by reviewing Example 9.3.2. Computationally, we can estimate the rate of convergence as follows. Let s_n denote the nth partial sum of the series, then

$$e - s_n = e - \sum_{k=0}^{n} \frac{1}{k!} = \sum_{k=n+1}^{\infty} \frac{1}{k!}$$

$$= \frac{1}{(n+1)!} + \frac{1}{(n+2)!} + \frac{1}{(n+3)!} + \cdots$$

$$= \frac{1}{(n+1)!} \left[1 + \frac{1}{n+2} + \frac{1}{(n+2)(n+3)} + \cdots \right]$$

$$< \frac{1}{(n+1)!} \left[1 + \frac{1}{n+1} + \frac{1}{(n+2)^2} + \cdots \right]$$

$$= \frac{1}{n!n},$$

where the last inequality is obtained by once again applying the formula for the sum of a geometric series.

This last inequality provides a very simple means for showing that e is irrational. Suppose for the sake of argument that e were rational, and $e = \dfrac{p}{q}$ for $p, q \in \mathbf{N}$. Then, by assumption and monotonicity for the series,

$$0 < q!(e - s_q) = q! \left[\frac{p}{q} - s_q \right] < \frac{1}{q}.$$

But this means that $q!(e - s_q)$ is a positive integer, which by virtue of the above must be between 0 and 1. It follows that e is irrational.

This argument, while it establishes that e is irrational, does not exclude the possibility that e is algebraic, that is, the solution to a polynomial equation where the polynomial has finite degree and the coefficients are integers. Numbers which are not algebraic are called transcendental, a term coined by Euler in the early 1700s.† Hermite established the transcendence of e in 1873, but this fact is more difficult to prove and is beyond the scope of this book. □

Our next theorem summarizes the properties of the function, $E(x)$, and in consequence identifies it as the exponential function.

Theorem 10.1.3. The function, E, defined on $\mathbf{R}$, has the following properties:

   (i) $E(x) > 0$ for all $x \in \mathbf{R}$;
   (ii) $E(x)$ is strictly increasing on $\mathbf{R}$;
   (iii) the range of $E(x)$ is the set $\mathbf{R}^+$;
   (iv) $\lim\limits_{x \to \infty} E(x) = \infty$; $\quad \lim\limits_{x \to -\infty} E(x) = 0$;
   (v) $E(x + y) = E(x)E(y)$ for all $x, y \in \mathbf{R}$;
   (vi) $E\left[\dfrac{m}{n} \right] = (e^m)^{1/n} = e^{m/n}$, for all $n, m \in \mathbf{Z}, n \neq 0$.

Proof. We shall prove (v) and (vi) leaving the rest as exercises. For a fixed y, $E(y) > 0$ (Exercise 9). Define a function $F: \mathbf{R} \to \mathbf{R}$ by setting $F(x) = \dfrac{E(x + y)}{E(y)}$, $x \in \mathbf{R}$. Now, $F(0) = 1$ and $F'(x) = F(x)$. Thus, by the uniqueness property of $E(x)$, we conclude that $F(x)$ must be $E(x)$ for all x. Thus, $E(x + y) = E(x)E(y)$ as desired.

To prove (vi), first note that $E(nx) = (E(x))^n$, for all $n \in \mathbf{N}$ (Exercise 10). It follows that

$$e = E(1) = E\left[n \cdot \frac{1}{n} \right] = E\left[\frac{1}{n} \right]^n.$$

---

† According to Kline [1972], p. 593, Euler asserted that numbers such as e 'transcended the power of algebra'. A proof that e is transcendental and not algebraic can be found in *Transcendental Number Theory* by A. Baker [1974].

Now $E\left(\dfrac{1}{n}\right) > 0$. Thus by definition of nth root, we see that $E\left(\dfrac{1}{n}\right) = e^{1/n}$. Next we observe that

$$E(n)E(-n) = E(n + (-n)) = E(0) = 1$$

which implies that

$$E(-n) = \frac{1}{E(n)} = \frac{1}{e^n} = e^{-n}.$$

In summary, these equations imply that if $m,\ n \in \mathbf{N}$,

$$E\left(\frac{m}{n}\right) = E\left(\frac{1}{n}\right)^m = (e^{1/n})^m = e^{m/n}$$

establishing (vi).   ☐

Discussion.   This theorem summarizes the familiar and essential properties of the function, $E(x)$, and relates them to the number e. In particular, the properties asserted in (v) and (vi) almost justify our referring to $E(x)$ as the **exponential** function.

  The reason underlying our reluctance to make the claim that E is the exponential function is that it is only for rational numbers, q, that we know that $E(q) = e^q$ is valid. Specifically, as noted in section 2.5, we have not even assigned a meaning to the expression, e^x where x is not rational. The next definition deals with this problem.   ☐

Definition.   If x is any real number, the xth **power of e** is defined by the equation

$$e^x = E(x).$$

Discussion.   If x is a rational number of the form $\dfrac{m}{n}$, for some $m,\ n \in \mathbf{N}$, this definition agrees with the definition of $e^{m/n}$ given in Theorem 10.1.3 (vi). To see this let us review the steps in the argument. First it was shown that for every $n \in \mathbf{N}$, $E\left(\dfrac{1}{n}\right)$, was an nth root of e. Since $e^{m/n} = (e^{1/n})^m$ is a definition (Exercise 0.5.13), to complete the argument, one has only to apply Theorem 10.1.3 (v) to $E\left(\dfrac{m}{n}\right)$. Thus, all positive rational powers of the number e are defined. It can easily be deduced that $E\left(\dfrac{p}{q}\right) = e^{p/q}$ holds for negative rationals $\dfrac{p}{q}$ as well.

  How should we go about defining an irrational power of e? For example, what is the meaning of $e^{\sqrt{2}}$? The definition supplies an answer, namely $E(\sqrt{2})$. But is it the right answer?

  Let us recall how powers were obtained. First, for any real number, x, and any positive integer n, x^n was defined (section 0.4). Next, the definition was extended to other integers by setting $x^{-n} = \dfrac{1}{x^n}$, for $x \neq 0$ and $x^0 = 1$, also for $x \neq 0$. As well, it was established that this extended definition satisfied the basic law of exponents expressed in Theorem 10.1.3 (v), see Exercise 0.4.23.

Once integral powers were defined, the next step was defining the nth root of a nonnegative real number. This step was taken in section 0.5 by obtaining the required root from

$$x^{1/n} = \sup \{y : y^n \leqslant x \text{ and } y \in \mathbf{R}\}.$$

Rational powers for all positive real numbers were then obtained via Exercise 0.5.13.

This suggest two tests for the definition of e^x. First, for all x, $y \in \mathbf{R}$ we should have $e^x e^y = e^{x+y}$, which the reader should note is implicit in what has already been established. Second, we should have that

$$e^x = \sup \{e^{m/n} : m, n \in \mathbf{Z} \text{ and } n \neq 0 \text{ and } \frac{m}{n} \leqslant x\}. \tag{1}$$

The verification of these two tests for the extended definition of e^x is left to Exercise 11.

A completely different approach to the development of the function, e^x, would have been to begin with the function e^q, for $q \in \mathbf{Q}$. One could then extend the definition via (1) above. While this would give rise to the same function, one would be left with having to establish the basic properties listed in Theorem 10.1.3, plus the fact that the derivative of e^x is e^x. To illustrate the difficulties of this approach, we explore it in the exercises.

Having managed to obtain e^x for all $x \in \mathbf{R}$, one now wonders about a^x where $a \in \mathbf{R}^+$. It would appear plausible that a^x could be defined in terms of e^x. This is indeed the case and will be explored in the next section. $\square$

EXERCISES

1. Verify all claims made in the discussion following the definition of the sequence of functions, $\{E_n\}$. In particular, show $E'_{n+1} = E_n$.

2. Prove Corollary 1 to Theorem 10.1.1.

3. Prove Corollary 2 to Theorem 10.1.1.

4. Let $f : \mathbf{R} \to \mathbf{R}$ be such that $f'(x) = f(x)$ for all $x \in \mathbf{R}$. Show $f(x) = \lambda E(x)$ for some constant, $\lambda \in \mathbf{R}$. Does this violate the uniqueness result in Theorem 10.1.2?

5. Show if $x \in [0, a]$ and $n \in \mathbf{N}$, then

$$\sum_{k=1}^{n} \frac{x^k}{k!} \leqslant e^x \leqslant \left[\sum_{k=1}^{n-1} \frac{x^k}{k!}\right] + \frac{x^n e^a}{n!}.$$

6. Prove if $n \geqslant 2$,

$$0 < en! - \left[\sum_{k=0}^{n} \frac{1}{k!}\right] n! < \frac{e}{n+1} < 1.$$

7. Calculate e accurate to seven decimal places and estimate the error involved.

8. If $x > 0$ and $x < \dfrac{n}{2}$, show

$$\left| \left(\sum_{k=0}^{n} \frac{x^k}{k!} \right) - e^x \right| < \frac{2}{(n+1)!} x^{n+1}.$$

Hence, deduce that $\dfrac{8}{3} < e < \dfrac{11}{4}$.

9. Prove parts (i), (ii), (iii) of Theorem 10.1.3.

10. Show that for all $n \in \mathbf{N}$, $E(nx) = (E(x))^n$. Extend this result to all $n \in \mathbf{Z}$.

11. Verify that the extended definition of e^x satisfies the two claims made for it in the discussion following the definition.

12. Let us suppose that the function e^q is defined for all $q \in \mathbf{Q}$. Extend this definition to all reals by using the supremum. Now prove a suitable version of Theorem 10.1.3.

13. Show that $\lim\limits_{n \to \infty} x^n e^{-x} = 0$ for all $n \in \mathbf{N}$.

14. Supply detailed reasons for all steps in the proof of Theorem 10.1.2.

15. Define the function, $\exp : \mathbf{R} \to \mathbf{R}$, directly by

$$\exp(x) = \sum_{n=0}^{\infty} \frac{x^n}{n!}.$$

Prove $\exp(x)$ is well defined and has all the properties claimed for $E(x)$. In short, develop the exponential function directly from the power series definition.

16. Show

$$e^x = \lim_{n \to \infty} \left(1 + \frac{x}{n} \right)^n, \quad x \in \mathbf{R}.$$

17. Consider the compound interest problem. Namely, let an amount of money, P, be invested for 1 year at an interest rate r. At simple interest, one is entitled to collect $P(1+r)$ at the end of the year. If the interest is compounded twice, at the end of $\dfrac{1}{2}$ year, an amount of interest equal to $\dfrac{Pr}{2}$ is added to the account. At the end of the year, a further amount of interest is paid, $\dfrac{r}{2}\left(P + \dfrac{Pr}{2} \right)$. Similarly, interest could be compounded thrice, four times, or n times. What rate of interest will result as $n \to \infty$?

18. If $f : \mathbf{R} \to \mathbf{R}$ is continuous and satisfies the identity $f(x + y) = f(x)f(y)$, $x, y \in \mathbf{R}$, prove that $f(x) = e^{kx}$, for some constant, k.

19. What can you say about f in Exercise 4 if it satisfies the condition $f'(x) = kf(x)$, where k is a constant?

20. If $f'(x) \geqslant xf(x)$, $x \in \mathbf{R}$, show there exists a constant k such that $f(x) \geqslant ke^x$.

21. Prove the following inequalities:

(a) $\left[1 + \dfrac{1}{n-1} \right]^{n-1} < e < \left[1 + \dfrac{1}{n-1} \right]^{n}$;

(b) $\dfrac{n^n}{n!} < e^{n-1} < \dfrac{n^{n+1}}{n!}$;

(c) $e\left[\dfrac{n^n}{e^n} \right] < n! < en\left[\dfrac{n^n}{e^n} \right]$;

(d) $0 < e - \left[1 + \dfrac{1}{1!} + \dfrac{1}{2!} + \cdots + \dfrac{1}{n!} \right] < \dfrac{3}{(n+1)!}$.

22. Let $n \geqslant 1$ and P_n be polynomials such that

$$P_n(x)e^{nx} + P_{n-1}(x)e^{(n-1)x} + \cdots + P_1(x)e^x + P_0(x) = 0$$

for arbitrarily large x. Show $P_n = 0$ for all n.

23. Let F be differentiable and such that $F'(x) = -2xF(x)$ for all x. Show $F(x) = e^{-x^2}$.

24. Show e^q is irrational for all $q \in \mathbf{Q}$, $q \neq 0$.

25. Evaluate $\displaystyle\lim_{x \to 2} \dfrac{1}{x - 2} \int_2^x e^{\sqrt{1 + t^2}}\, dt$.

26. Find a Taylor expansion of $\displaystyle\int_0^x e^{-t^2}\, dt$ in a neighborhood of 0.

27. Find the first four nonvanishing terms in the Taylor expansion for e^{e^x}.

28. Express the following functions $f(x)$ as a power series in x.

(a) $f(x) = \displaystyle\int_0^x e^{-t^2}$;

(b) $f(x) = e^{-x^2}$;

(c) $f(x) = \dfrac{1}{1 + e^x}$;

(d) $f(x) = \dfrac{e^{-x}}{1 + x^2}$.

29. Expand the following functions in a Taylor series about the point a:

(a) e^{2x};

(b) $e^{-x/3}$;

(c) e^{x^2}.

30. If $a > 1$, prove the sequence defined by

$$s_1 = a, \quad s_{n+1} = a^{s_n}, \quad n \geqslant 1$$

converges provided $a \leqslant e^{1/e}$.

10.2 LOGARITHMIC FUNCTION AND POWER FUNCTION

In the last section, we introduced the exponential function and studied its various remarkable properties. One nice fact about this function is that it is strictly increasing, is differentiable, and has the set $\{x: x \in \mathbf{R} \text{ and } x > 0\}$, for its range. These facts guarantee that the exponential function possesses an inverse function which is called the **logarithmic function**. We shall study the basic properties of this function and finally use it to define arbitrary powers of any real number. Note that we have already defined arbitrary powers of the unique real number e.

Definition. The **natural logarithmic function** is the function, $L: (0, \infty) \to \mathbf{R}$, which is the unique inverse of the exponential function, $E(x)$.

Discussion. It is clear that the function, L, exists, is unique, and has the specified domain and range. Also, since L and E are inverses of each other, we have

$$(L \circ E)(x) = x = (E \circ L)(x) \quad \text{for } x \in \text{Dmn } E \text{ or } x \in \text{Dmn } L.$$

Calling $E(x)$ by its standard name, e^x, and $L(x)$ by its standard name, $\ln x$, these equations take the form

$$\ln(e^x) = x \quad \text{and} \quad e^{\ln y} = y.$$

This equation captures the fundamental relationship between the logarithmic and exponential functions. Although the initial development of logarithms by Napier in 1594 was not as exponents of a fixed positive number base, this approach followed shortly thereafter (Briggs, 1615) and it is this equation, $e^{\ln y} = y$, that supplies the fundamental motivation for the logarithmic function. The utility of logarithms as a tool which aids the conduct of numerical computations arises from the fact that logarithms permit the substitution of addition for the operation of multiplication. While this use has all but disappeared with the introduction of calculators, the use of logarithmic transforms for data remains as important as ever.   ☐

The following theorem summarizes the basic properties of the logarithmic function:

Theorem 10.2.1.   The function, L, has the following properties:

(i) $L(x)$ is strictly increasing, has domain, $\{x : x \in \mathbf{R} \text{ and } x > 0\}$, and range, $\mathbf{R}$;

(ii) L is differentiable and $L'(x) = \dfrac{1}{x}$, $x \in \mathbf{R}^+$;

(iii) For $x, y > 0$, $L(xy) = L(x) + L(y)$;

(iv) $L(1) = 0$; $L(e) = 1$;

(v) $\lim\limits_{x \to 0^+} L(x) = -\infty$, and $\lim\limits_{x \to \infty} L(x) = \infty$.

Proof.   To prove (ii) note that the fact that L is differentiable follows from Theorem 4.2.3. Since $E(L(x)) = x$ for all $x \in \mathbf{R}^+$, it follows from differentiation using the Chain Rule that $E'(L(x)L'(x) = 1$, whence

$$L'(x) = \frac{1}{E'(L(x))} = \frac{1}{E(L(x))} = \frac{1}{x}.$$

To prove (iii), let $a = L(x)$ and $b = L(y)$ so that $E(a) = x$ and $E(b) = y$. Now $xy = E(a)E(b) = E(a+b)$ so that

$$L(xy) = a + b = L(x) + L(y).$$

The other parts are left as Exercise 1.   ☐

Discussion.   Compare this theorem with Theorem 10.1.3. These are simply the properties reflected from those of the exponential function by virtue of the fact that L is the inverse of E. The reader is advised to sketch the graphs of $E(x)$ and $L(x)$ on the same set of axes and compare them.

Part (iii) contains an extremely useful property of logarithms. Here the computation of L of a product $x \cdot y$ is rendered easy since it is just the addition of two numbers $L(x)$ and $L(y)$. This feature has been exploited in computational mathematics to multiply two numbers. Common logarithm and antilogarithm tables are available, and can be found as appendices to most university level introductory physics and chemistry texts published prior to 1970. This use has disappeared with the advent of hand-held calculators.

Property (ii) is equally remarkable. The simplest of all polynomials are the constant 1 and the function $f(x) = x$. Their ratio, $\frac{1}{x}$, is a rational function. As the reader will recall, while the function, $\frac{1}{x}$, $x > 0$ is continuous and bounded on any interval, $[a, b]$, where $a > 0$, and so is clearly integrable on $[a, b]$, it was impossible to evaluate this integral, other than numerically, for lack of an antiderivative. This situation is now remedied, and antiderivatives have been supplied for all functions of the form x^q, $q \in \mathbf{Q}$. This property also provides an alternate method of defining the function, $L(x)$, in terms of the definite integral $\int_1^x \frac{1}{t}\, dt$, a matter that is pursued in Exercise 13 (also see Exercise 5.5.19).   □

As discussed in the last section, for $x > 0$, a meaning has been assigned to x^r for all rational numbers, r, or for all real numbers, r, subject to the condition, $x = e$. We want now to complete the definition of x^r so that a unique real number is specified for all $r \in \mathbf{R}$ and all $x \in \mathbf{R}^+$. To accomplish this goal, we exploit the logarithmic function.

Definition.   If $\xi \in \mathbf{R}$ and $x > 0$, we define x^ξ by

$$x^\xi = E(\xi L(x)) = e^{\xi L(x)}.$$

The function $P_\xi : (0, \infty) \to \mathbf{R}$ defined by $P_\xi(x) = x^\xi$, is called the ξth **power function**.

Discussion.   Since $x > 0$, this definition makes sense. However, it requires further validation, as discussed following the definition of e^x. This validation will be provided in the next several theorems, the proofs of which are left to the reader.

As initial validation, the reader can show by induction that for each $n \in \mathbf{N}$, $n \cdot L(x) = L(x^n)$, so that the inverse nature of the function E reveals that $x^n = E(nL(x))$. Thus, the new definition extends the definition for powers which are natural numbers. This type of argument can be further extended to show that for all $q \in \mathbf{Q}$, $x^q = e^{qL(x)}$ (Exercise 2), whence the new definition extends the earlier ones for rational powers.

The question which remains is: Are we justified in using the definition for irrational powers? As in the case of e^ξ, what we want to verify is that

$$x^\xi = \sup \{x^q : q \in \mathbf{Q} \text{ and } q < \xi\}.$$

This problem will be explored below.   □

We now state some standard properties of the power function. Most of the facts are immediate from the well-known properties of the exponential and logarithmic functions and hence are left as exercises.

Theorem 10.2.2. If x, $y > 0$ and $\xi \in \mathbf{R}$, then

(i) $1^0 = 1$;

(ii) $x^\xi > 0$;

(iii) $(xy)^\xi = x^\xi y^\xi$;

(iv) $\left(\dfrac{x}{y}\right)^\xi = \dfrac{x^\xi}{y^\xi}$.

Proof. Exercise 3. □

Theorem 10.2.3. If ξ, $\eta \in \mathbf{R}$ and $x > 0$,

(i) $x^{\xi + \eta} = x^\xi x^\eta$;

(ii) $x^{-\xi} = \dfrac{1}{x^\xi}$;

(iii) $x^{\xi\eta} = x^{\xi\eta} = x^{\eta\xi}$;

(iv) $\xi < \eta$ implies $x^\xi < x^\eta$.

Proof. Exercise 4. □

Theorem 10.2.4. The function, $P_\xi: (0,\infty) \to \mathbf{R}$, defined by, $P_\xi(x) = x^\xi$, is differentiable and $P_\xi'(x) = \xi x^{\xi-1}$ for $x > 0$.

Proof. $P_\xi'(x)$ is the derivative of the function specified by $P_\xi(x) = e^{\xi L(x)}$. An application of the Chain Rule yields

$$P_\xi'(x) = e^{\xi L(x)} \cdot [\xi L(x)]' = x^\xi \left(\frac{\xi}{x}\right) = \xi x^{\xi-1}.$$

□

Discussion. These theorems summarize the properties of all functions of the form $f(x) = x^r$ where $r \in \mathbf{R}$ is fixed and $x \in \mathbf{R}^+$. While the properties presented go a long way toward justifying the definition of x^ξ, they do not quite address if the equation

$$x^\xi = \sup\{x^q : q \in \mathbf{Q} \text{ and } q < \xi\}$$

is satisfied. To address this question, we need to look at functions of the form $f(x) = a^x$, where $a > 0$ is fixed. □

Theorem 10.2.5. Let $a \in \mathbf{R}^+$ be fixed and consider the function, $f: \mathbf{R} \to \mathbf{R}^+$, defined by $f(x) = a^x$. Then f has the following properties:

(i) f is continuous and differentiable on $\mathbf{R}$;

(ii) if $a > 1$, f is strictly increasing, if $a < 1$, f is strictly decreasing, if $a = 1$, $f = 1$;

(iii) if $a > 0$ and h is defined on $\mathbf{Q}$ and $h(q) = a^q$, then f is the continuous extension of h to all of $\mathbf{R}$.

Proof. Exercise 5. □

Discussion.   Property (iii) has the effect of verifying the assertion that

$$x^\xi = \sup \{x^q : q \in \mathbf{Q} \text{ and } q < \xi\}.$$

□

EXERCISES

1. Complete the proof of Theorem 10.2.1.
2. Show for all $q \in \mathbf{Q}$, $x^q = e^{qL(x)}$.
3. Prove Theorem 10.2.2.
4. Prove Theorem 10.2.3.
5. Prove Theorem 10.2.5.
6. Evaluate $\lim\limits_{x \to \infty} \dfrac{(\ln x)^n}{x^\alpha}$ where α and n are positive real numbers.
7. If $a > 1$ and $a \neq 1$, define a function $\log_a : (0, \infty) \to \mathbf{R}$ by $\log_a(x) = \dfrac{L(x)}{L(a)}$, $x \in (0, \infty)$.
   This function is called the **logarithm of x to the base a**. Prove the following:
   (a) $\log_a$ is differentiable and $(\log_a)'(x) = \dfrac{1}{xL(a)}$;
   (b) $\log_a(xy) = \log_a(x) + \log_a(y)$;
   (c) $\log_a x = \dfrac{L(b)}{L(a)} \log_b x$, $x \in (0, \infty)$;
   (d) If $f(y) = a^y$ and $g(x) = \log_a x$, then f and g are inverses of each other;
   (e) $\log_{10} x = (\log_{10} e) L(x)$.
8. Show that $\lim\limits_{n \to \infty} (1 + \dfrac{1}{n})^n = e$. [HINT: Consider $L'(1)$.]
9. Show that

$$L(x+1) = x - \frac{x^2}{2} + \frac{x^3}{3} - \cdots + - \cdots + (-1)^{n-1}\frac{x^n}{n} + \int_0^x \frac{(-t)^n}{1+t}\, dt.$$

   [HINT: Expand $\dfrac{1}{1+x}$.]
   Hence evaluate $L(1.1)$ accurate to four decimal places.

10. Obtain a power series that represents the function $f(x) = \dfrac{1}{x+1}$ for $|x| < 1$ and use it to
    derive the fact that

$$\ln(1 + x) = \sum_{n=0}^{\infty} \frac{(-1)^n x^{n-1}}{n}.$$

    Hence, justify the equation

$$\ln 2 = 1 - \frac{1}{2} + \frac{1}{3} - \cdots .$$

11. Compute the limits, $\lim\limits_{x \to 0} x^\alpha$, $\alpha > 0$, and $\lim\limits_{x \to \infty} x^\alpha$, for $\alpha < 0$.
12. Obtain a Taylor expansion of $(1+x)^\alpha$ for various real numbers α.
13. Define $l(x) = \int_1^x \dfrac{1}{t}\, dt$, $x > 0$. Prove all the statements in Theorem 10.2.2 with $L(x)$
    replaced by $l(x)$ and also show that $l(x) = L(x)$ (cf., Exercise 5.5.19).

14. Evaluate the following limits:

(a) $\lim_{x\to 0^+} x^x$;

(b) $\lim_{x\to\infty} x^{1/x}$;

(c) $\lim_{x\to 0^+} x^{\ln x}$;

(d) $\lim_{x\to 0^+} \dfrac{10^x - 7^x}{x^2}$;

(e) $\lim_{x\to 0^+} (\ln x)^x$;

(f) $\lim_{x\to 0^+} (\ln x)^{\ln x}$;

(g) $\lim_{x\to 0^+} \dfrac{\ln x}{x^n}$;

(h) $\lim_{x\to\infty} \dfrac{\ln x}{x^n}$;

(i) $\lim_{x\to\infty} \dfrac{\ln x}{x^{0.00001}}$;

(j) $\lim_{x\to 0^+} x\ln x$;

(k) $\lim_{x\to\infty} x\left[\left(1 + \dfrac{1}{x}\right)^x - e\right]$;

(l) $\lim_{x\to\infty} x\left[\left(1 + \dfrac{1}{x}\right)^x - e\ln\left(1 + \dfrac{1}{x}\right)^x\right]$.

15. Derive the following inequalities:

(a) $1 - x < -\ln x < \dfrac{1}{x} - 1$, $0 < x < 1$;

(b) $\dfrac{x^2}{2} < x - \ln(1 + x) < \dfrac{x^2}{2(1 + x)}$, $-1 < x < 0$;

(c) $x - \dfrac{x^2}{2} + \dfrac{x^3}{3(1 + x)} < \ln(1 + x) < x - \dfrac{x^2}{2} + \dfrac{x^3}{3}$, $x > 0$;

(d) $x < -\ln(1 - x) < \dfrac{x}{1 - x}$, $0 < x < 1$;

(e) $\dfrac{1}{x} < \dfrac{1}{\ln(1 + x)} < 1 + \dfrac{1}{x}$, $x \in \mathbf{R}^+$;

(f) $\dfrac{\ln x}{x} \leqslant \dfrac{1}{\sqrt{x}}\int_1^x \dfrac{1}{t^{3/2}}\, dt$;

(g) $\dfrac{\ln x}{x} < \dfrac{2}{\sqrt{x}}$, $(x > 1)$.

16. Prove that the sequence $\{a_n\}$ defined by $a_n = n(a^{1/n} - 1)$, $a > 0$ is monotonic, and converges to $\ln a$. Obtain standard properties of $\ln x$ from this definition.

17. Let $g: \mathbf{R} \to \mathbf{R}$ be continuous, nonidentically zero and satisfy the identity $g(x + y) = g(x)g(y)$ for $x, y \in \mathbf{R}$. Show that $g(x) = a^x$ where $g(1) = a$.

18. Let $h: (0, \infty) \to \mathbf{R}$ be continuous and satisfy $h(xy) = h(x) + h(y)$ for $x, y \in \mathbf{R}$. What can you say about the function $h(x)$? What happens if, instead, h satisfies the identity $h(xy) = h(x)h(y)$?

19. Let $n \geqslant 1$, and f_n be polynomials such that

$$f_n(x)(\ln x)^n + f_{n-1}(x)(\ln x)^{n-1} + \cdots + f_0(x) = 0$$

for all $x > 0$. Show that all the f_n's are identically zero.

20. Derive the expansion

$$\ln 2 = 2 \sum_{k=1}^{\infty} \frac{1}{3^{2k-1}(2k-1)}.$$

Also estimate the error in taking the first six terms of the expansion for $\ln 2$.

21. In $-1 \leqslant x < 1$, prove that

$$-\ln(1-x) = x + \frac{x^2}{2} + \frac{x^3}{3} + \cdots.$$

Hence or otherwise, obtain the sum of the series $\sum_{n=0}^{\infty} \frac{1}{(n+1)(n+2)}$.

22. Obtain a power series expansion for $\ln \frac{1+x}{1-x}$, stating the range of validity of the expansion.

23. Derive the following expansions in $-1 < x \leqslant 1$:

(a) $\dfrac{\ln(1+x)}{1+x} = x - x^2 \left[1 + \dfrac{1}{2}\right] + x^3 \left[1 + \dfrac{1}{2} + \dfrac{1}{3}\right] - \cdots$;

(b) $[\ln(1+x)]^2 = 2 \left[\dfrac{x^2}{2} - \dfrac{x^3}{3}\left(1 + \dfrac{1}{2}\right) + \dfrac{x^4}{4}\left(1 + \dfrac{1}{2} + \dfrac{1}{3}\right) - \cdots \right.$

24. Prove that

$$\int_0^1 \frac{\ln(1+t)}{t}\,dt = \frac{\pi^2}{12}.$$

25. Express $\int_0^x \frac{\ln t}{1-t}\,dt$ as a power series in $x - 1$. Find its radius of convergence.

10.3 TRIGONOMETRIC FUNCTIONS

In this section, we shall introduce the familiar sine and cosine functions and from our definition, we shall derive all the well-known properties of these functions. Our approach will be in the same vein as that of the exponential functions, and we shall establish the uniqueness of these functions. During this process, we shall arrive at the unique real number, π, and study its role in relation to the trigonometric functions.

Definition. The sequences, $\{C_n\}$ and $\{S_n\}$, of functions mapping **R** into **R** are defined by

$$C_1(x) = 1, \quad S_1(x) = x,$$

and for $n > 1$,

$$C_{n+1}(x) = 1 - \int_0^x S_n(t)\,dt; \qquad S_n(x) = \int_0^x C_n(t)\,dt.$$

Discussion. As in the case of exponential functions, these definitions are simple and easy to understand, although the properties of the functions which result from these definitions are by no means obvious. A straightforward induction (Exercise 1) shows that for $n \geqslant 1$,

$$C_{n+1}(x) = 1 - \frac{x^2}{2!} + \frac{x^4}{4!} + - + \cdots + \frac{(-1)^n x^{2n}}{(2n)!} \qquad (1)$$

and

$$S_{n+1}(x) = x - \frac{x^3}{3!} + \frac{x^5}{5!} + - + \cdots + \frac{(-1)^n x^{2n+1}}{(2n+1)!}. \qquad (2)$$

For each n, these expressions are polynomials. So, they are differentiable (hence continuous) and integrable. As the reader can easily check by induction,

$$S_n'(x) = C_n(x); \text{ and } C_{n+1}'(x) = -S_n(x), \text{ for all } x \in \mathbf{R}, \ n \in \mathbf{N}. \qquad (3)$$

The reader can easily see the parallelism in the approach to the definition of these functions and the exponential function, $E_n(x)$, of section 10.1. In the present case, our aim is to create two new functions, S and C, with the properties that $S(0) = 0$, $C(0) = 1$, $S' = C$, and $C' = S$, which are the familiar properties of the sine and cosine functions. To obtain these functions, we will use the same type of approach and arguments as were used in the exponential case. With this in mind, the industrious reader may wish to proceed on his own at this point to see how much of the theory he can develop. $\qquad\square$

Definition. For $x \in \mathbf{R}$, we define the **trigonometric functions**, S and C, mapping $\mathbf{R}$ into $\mathbf{R}$ as follows:

$$S(x) = \lim_{n \to \infty} S_n(x);$$

$$C(x) = \lim_{n \to \infty} C_n(x).$$

Discussion. We must first make sure that these two limits exist at all points x, and hence that S and C are well defined. The key to this is the concept of uniform convergence.

In Figure 10.3.1 graphs of the function, C, C_2, C_4, and C_6 on the interval $[-2\pi, 2\pi]$ are presented. The function, C, is identified by its standard name, cos. The number, π, will be formally identified in Theorem 10.3.5. As can be seen, the approximation of C_6 to cos is very good on the interval from $-\pi$ to π. $\qquad\square$

Theorem 10.3.1. For each $x \in \mathbf{R}$ the sequences, $\{S_n(x)\}$ and $\{C_n(x)\}$, converge. Further, for each $K > 0$, the sequences $\{S_n\}$ and $\{C_n\}$ converge uniformly on $[-K, K]$. Further, the limit functions, S and C, respectively, are continuous on $[-K, K]$.

Proof. By arguments presented in section 10.1, the truth of the second assertion will imply the first. Thus, fix $K > 0$. If $|x| \leqslant K$, and $m > n > 2K$, then,

$$|C_m(x) - C_n(x)| = \left| \sum_{k=n}^{m-1} (-1)^k \frac{x^{2k}}{(2k)!} \right|$$

$$\leqslant \frac{K^{2n}}{(2n)!} \left[\sum_{k=0}^{m-n-1} \left[\frac{K}{2n} \right]^{2k} \right]$$

$$< \frac{16K^{2n}}{15(2n)!}. \qquad \textbf{(WHY?)}$$

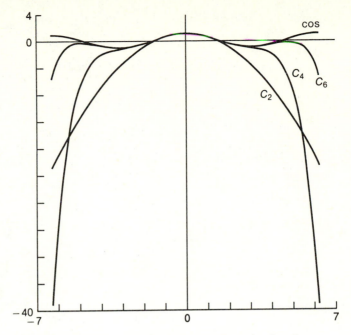

Figure 10.3.1 The polynomials C_2, C_4, C_6 generating the cosine function.

Since the last entry has limit 0 as n approaches infinity, we conclude that the sequence $\{C_n\}$ converges uniformly on each interval, $[-K, K]$. It follows immediately from the corollary to Theorem 8.3.1 that C is continuous on $[-K, K]$, for every $K > 0$.

The proof of this theorem for S is left to the reader as Exercise 2. □

Discussion. The techniques employed are completely analogous to those used in the development of the exponential function.

A further useful fact is that

$$C(0) = \lim_{n \to \infty} C_n(0) = 1.$$

This can be proved by induction. □

Theorem 10.3.2. The functions, C and S, possess derivatives of all orders; in particular, for all $x \in \mathbf{R}$,

$$C'(x) = -S(x) \quad \text{and} \quad S'(x) = C(x).$$

Proof. The uniform convergence of the sequence, $\{C_n\}$, coupled with Theorem 8.3.4 enable us to deduce that the limit function, C, is differentiable on $[-K, K]$. Further, if $x \in [-K, K]$,

$$C'(x) = \lim_{n \to \infty} C_n'(x) = \lim_{n \to \infty} (-S_{n+1}(x)) = -S(x).$$

Since $K > 0$ was arbitrary, it follows that $C'(x) = -S(x)$, $x \in \mathbf{R}$. The remainder of the proof is left as Exercise 3. □

Discussion. Evidently there are useful formulae which can be obtained for integrating C and S. These are left to the reader as Exercise 4. □

Next, we show that the functions, C and S, satisfy the so-called **Pythagorean identity**.

Corollary. The functions, C and S, satisfy the identity:

$$C^2(x) + S^2(x) = 1 \quad \text{for all} \quad x \in \mathbf{R}.$$

Proof.   Consider $F = C^2 + S^2$. Then, F is differentiable and further, for any $x \in \mathbf{R}$ we have,

$$F'(x) = 2C(x)C'(x) + 2S(x)S'(x) = -2S(x)C(x) + 2S(x)C(x) = 0.$$

So it follows that F must be a constant. But then, $F(0) = 1 + 0 = 1$ and we obtain the desired identity. □

Discussion. Instead of directly computing the expression, $C^2(x) + S^2(x)$, and checking that it simplifies to 1 for every choice of x, we have used an indirect approach. This avoids the direct computations which are not easy, and replaces them by the simple, but very clever, checking that the derivative is zero. Once this is known, it is trivial to find the constant to which F must be equal. We simply calculate $F(0)$!

The reader should note that we used the Chain Rule to differentiate the composite function. □

Our next aim is to establish the uniqueness of these functions. As in the case of exponential functions, the properties that characterize these functions are the form of the derivatives and the value of these functions at 0.

Theorem 10.3.3. If A and B are two functions from $\mathbf{R} \to \mathbf{R}$ such that $A' = -B$, $B' = A$, $A(0) = 1$, and $B(0) = 0$, then $A = C$ and $B = S$.

Proof.   Call $A - C = F$ and $B - D = G$. Then F and G are continuous, possess derivatives of all orders, $F(0) = 0$, $F''(0) = -F(0)$, and $F'(0) = 0$ for all $n \in \mathbf{N}$. If $x \in \mathbf{R}$ is arbitrary, we can expand F in a Taylor series about origin as follows:

$$F(x) = F(0) + \frac{F'(0)\,x}{1!} + \cdots + \frac{F^{(n-1)}(0)\,x^{n-1}}{(n-1)!} + \frac{F^{(n)}(\xi_n)\,x^n}{n!},$$

where $\xi_n \in [0, x]$ or $[x, 0]$, depending on the sign of x. By virtue of the fact that $A(0) = C(0)$ and $B(0) = S(0)$, it can be shown that $F(x) = \dfrac{F^{(n)}(\xi_n)}{n!}x^n$. Observe that $F^n(\xi_n)$ is either $\pm F(\xi_n)$ or $\pm G(\xi_n)$, whence in either case, by continuity there exists a $K > 0$ such that $|F^{(n)}(x)| \leqslant K|x|^n$ and we immediately conclude that $F(x) = 0$, that is, $A = C$.

A similar argument proves that $B = S$, Exercise 5. □

Discussion. The proof is very similar to the one used for the uniqueness of the exponential function (Theorem 10.1.2) and one may seek there for missing details, for example, the reason behind the last step.

Note that the above theorem shows that if F is any function mapping $\mathbf{R} \to \mathbf{R}$ with the three properties:

    (i) $F'' = -F$;
    (ii) $F(0) = 1$, and
    (iii) $F'(0) = 0$,

then F is identical with the function, C. A similar set of properties can be found to characterize S (Exercise 6). $\square$

Notation. Having established the uniqueness of these functions, we now call $C(x)$ the **cosine of** x. The name of the function associated with C will be **cos**. Similarly we call $S(x)$ the **sine of** x, and call S as **sin**.

Theorem 10.3.4. The functions, C and S, satisfy the following equations:

    (i) $C(-x) = C(x)$ and $S(-x) = -S(x)$ for all $x \in \mathbf{R}$;
    (ii) $C(x+y) = C(x)C(y) - S(x)S(y)$; $S(x+y) = S(x)C(y) + C(x)S(y)$,
        for all $x, y \in \mathbf{R}$.

Proof. Set $f(x) = C(-x)$. We see that $f'' = f$, $f(0) = 1$, $f''(0) = 0$; hence, by Theorem 10.3.3, $f = C$. A similar argument proves that $S(x) = -S(x)$ (Exercise 7).

For (ii), we first claim that if $f: \mathbf{R} \to \mathbf{R}$ satisfies the condition $f''(x) = -f(x)$, $x \in \mathbf{R}$, then there exist constants a, b such that $f = aC + bS$. To see this, consider $g(x) = f(0)C(x) + f'(0)S(x)$. Then it is readily seen that $g'' = -g$, $g(0) = f(0)$, and $g'(0) = f'(0)$ so that $f - g$ reduces to the zero function (Exercise 8). Thus, $a = f(0)$ and $b = f'(0)$. To complete the argument, fix $y \in \mathbf{R}$ and set $f(x) = C(x+y)$. One readily verifies that $f'' = -f$, so there exist $a,b \in \mathbf{R}$ such that

$$f(x) = C(x + y) = aC(x) + bS(x)$$

and in consequence,

$$f'(x) = -S(x + y) = -aS(x) + bC(x),$$

$x \in \mathbf{R}$. Letting $x = 0$, we obtain $a = C(y)$ and $b = -S(y)$, whence the first identity holds. The corresponding identity for $S(x + y)$ is proved similarly (Exercise 7). $\square$

Discussion. There are several features of the second part of the proof which are worthy of review. First, we employ the fact that if a function, f, satisfies the differential equation, $f'' = -f$, then f must be a scalar combination of the sine and cosine functions. It is not obvious that this should be true. But if one considers the content of Theorems 10.3.1–10.3.3, this result becomes more plausible, particularly when one thinks of other similar results such as the one for the exponential function.

Once the consequence of $f'' = -f$ is known, we have only to apply it in a clever way. Considering $C(x + y)$ as a function of x alone, that is, treating y as fixed for a moment, we verify that $C(x + y)$ has the property that $C''(x + y) = -C(x + y)$, when viewed as a function of x. Thus, it is a scalar combination of $S(x)$ and $C(x)$. These scalars cannot involve x, which is a variable, but can be expressed in terms of y, which is fixed. By setting $x = 0$, these constants are easily seen to be $C(y)$ and $S(y)$, respectively.

This type of proof is an indirect proof in the sense that we did not directly evaluate the combination $S(x)C(y) + C(x)S(y)$, nor did we try to expand $S(x + y)$. The differentiability properties of the functions, C and S, were the successful tools in this proof. As such, this argument, and the other similar arguments in this chapter—the argument for part (i) of this theorem is another example—illustrate one of the truly beautiful features of mathematics, namely, that ideas from completely different areas, for example, differential equations and trigonometry, can so fruitfully intermesh.

□

Next, we are going to identify a real number which is of fundamental importance to the theory of trigonometry. Once we have delineated its properties, we shall recognize it as the familiar number π.

Theorem 10.3.5. There exists a real number, $p \in [0, 2]$ such that $C(p) = 0$, $C(x) > 0$ for $x \in [0, p]$, and p is the smallest number with these properties.

Proof. We first claim that $C(2) < 0$. To see this, first note that $\dfrac{2^{2n}}{(2n)!} > \dfrac{2^{2n+2}}{(2n+2)!}$ for all $n > 1$. From Eq. 1 at the beginning of this section, we have that

$$C(2) = 1 - \frac{2^2}{2!} + \frac{2^4}{4!} - \frac{2^6}{6!} + \cdots$$

$$= (-1 + \frac{16}{24}) + (-\frac{2^6}{6!} + \frac{2^8}{8!}) + (- +) \cdots$$

$$< -1 + \frac{2}{3} < 0.$$

Since $C(0) = 1$ and C is continuous, there exists $y \in [0, 2]$ such that $C(y) = 0$. Let $p = \inf \{y: y \in [0, 2] \text{ and } C(y) = 0\}$. The reader can check (Exercise 9) that the requirements for the existence of p are met and that $C(p) = 0$.   □

Corollary. The real number, p, is the least positive real number such that $S(2p) = 0$.

Proof. From Theorem 10.3.4, $S(2x) = 2S(x)C(x)$, whence $S(2p) = 0$. From the same equation, $0 < y < p$, $S(2y) = 0$ implies $C(y) = 0$. **(WHY?)** Thus, $2p$ is the least positive real such that $S(2p) = 0$.   □

Discussion. The proof of this theorem invokes a very powerful theorem. As well the location of $2p$, somewhere in $[0, 2]$, is not particularly precise. An alternate proof, starting with the Pythagorean identity leads to $\sqrt{2} < p < \sqrt{3}$. The reader is asked to develop such a proof in Exercise 10. □

Definition. The real number $2p$ of the above theorem, which is the smallest positive zero for $\sin x$, is called **pi**, and is denoted by π.

Discussion. Our approach to the definition of π has been quite different than the historical approach. The number, π, was first identified geometrically as the ratio between the diameter and circumference of a circle, and values for π based on this approach are known from the Egyptian and Greek mathematics of 3000 years ago. The difficulty with the approach we have taken is that direct relationship of the trigonometric functions, S and C, with circles has to some degree been lost. Establishing this connection will be the reader's task in Exercises 11 and 12.

We shall show that π is irrational, although at this stage, we will not be able to decide whether it is transcendental. In fact, it is transcendental as was shown by Lindemann in 1882. The method used by Lindemann is conceptually simple. He showed that if p_k and x_k were all algebraic, and the p_k were not all zero, then

$$\sum_{k=1}^{n} p_k e^{x_k} \neq 0.$$

Since $e^{\pi i} + 1 = 0$, where $i^2 = -1$, π cannot be algebraic.

There are several methods to compute π to any number of decimal places, not all of which are equally effective. For example, we have already noted that $\frac{\pi^2}{6} = \sum \frac{1}{n^2}$. In 1674 Leibnitz obtained (see Exercises 26 and 27)

$$\frac{\pi}{4} = 1 - \frac{1}{3} + \frac{1}{5} - \frac{1}{7} + \frac{1}{9} - + \cdots$$

which after only 100,000 terms would yield an approximation of π as good as that known to Archimedes. In a paper in 1740, Euler developed several series approximations to powers of π, among them,

$$\sum_{n=1}^{\infty} \frac{1}{(2n-1)^2} = \frac{\pi^2}{8},$$

$$\sum_{n=1}^{\infty} \frac{(-1)^{n-1}}{(2n-1)^3} = \frac{\pi^3}{32},$$

and

$$\sum_{n=1}^{\infty} \frac{1}{(2n-1)^4} = \frac{\pi^4}{96}.$$

While these facts may not be of tremendous ultimate significance, it is surprising that this number, π, which has clear geometric importance, should also be the result of such diverse calculations. Is it any wonder then, that mathematicians have viewed it with continued interest and fascination? □

Theorem 10.3.6. The functions, C and S, satisfy the following identities:

(i) $C(x+2\pi) = C(x); S(x+2\pi) = S(x);$

(ii) $C(x) = S\left[\dfrac{\pi}{2} - x\right] = S\left[x + \dfrac{\pi}{2}\right];$

$$S(x) = C\left[\dfrac{\pi}{2} - x\right] = -C\left[\dfrac{\pi}{2} + x\right].$$

Proof. Observe that $S\left[\dfrac{\pi}{2}\right] = 1$. The rest follows by using the appropriate expansion formulas for $C(x + 2\pi)$ (Exercise 13). ☐

Discussion. Theorem 10.3.6 (i) asserts that S and C are **periodic functions** with **period**, 2π. This fact will prove useful in Exercise 11. ☐

Theorem 10.3.7. π is irrational.

Proof. We argue by contradiction. Thus, let $\pi = \dfrac{p}{q} \in \mathbf{Q}$. Next, for an arbitrary positive integer, n, set

$$f(x) = \frac{x^n(p-qx)^n}{n!}.$$

The reader can verify that for all $x \in \mathbf{R}$, $f\left[\dfrac{p}{q}-x\right] = f(x)$, Exercise 14. Further, we note that $n!f(x)$ is a polynomial with integer coefficients and each individual term of this polynomial has degree at least n. In consequence, $f^{(k)}(0) \in \mathbf{Z}$ for $k = 0, 1, 2, \ldots$; in other words, if f or one of its derivatives is evaluated at $x = 0$, the result is an integer. Using the property that $f\left[\dfrac{p}{q} - x\right] = f(x)$, it can be shown that if f or one of its derivatives is evaluated at $x = \dfrac{p}{q}$, the result is also an integer. Finally, note that on the interval $[0, 2\pi]$, f attains an absolute maximum at $x = \dfrac{p}{2q}$, whence it follows that if $0 < x < \pi = \dfrac{p}{q}$ and $n > 1$, then

$$0 < f(x)\sin x < f\left[\dfrac{p}{2q}\right] = \frac{(\pi p)^n}{2^{2n}n!} < \frac{1}{4}$$

provided n is sufficiently large.

Now we apply the properties of f in the following way. Define F by

$$F(x) = f(x) - f''(x) + f^{(4)}(x) - \cdots + (-1)^n f^{(2n)}(x).$$

Observe that $F(0)$ and $F(\pi)$ must be integers. A direct computation establishes that

$$[F'(x)\sin x - F(x)\cos x]' = f(x)\sin x.$$

Or, equivalently, $F'(x) \sin x - F(x) \cos x$ is an antiderivative for $f(x) \sin x$. It follows that since $f(x) \sin x$ is positive on $(0, \pi)$, then

$$0 < \int_0^\pi f(x) \sin x\, dx = F(\pi) - F(0) \in \mathbf{Z},$$

for any choice of n. But we can choose n such that $f(x) \sin x < \dfrac{1}{4}$ on $(0, \pi)$, whence

$$0 < \int_0^\pi f(x) \sin x\, dx = F(\pi) - F(0) \leqslant \frac{\pi}{4} < 1,$$

an evident contradiction. □

EXERCISES

1. Establish the formulae (1), (2), and (3) for C_{n+1} and S_{n+1}.
2. Prove the remaining assertions in Theorem 10.3.1. As well, show $S(0) = 0$.
3. Complete the proof of Theorem 10.3.2.
4. Prove a theorem about integrating C and S.
5. Complete the proof of Theorem 10.3.3 by showing in complete detail that $B = S$.
6. Find three properties which characterize the function, S, but which avoid any mention of C. Prove your answer.
7. Give detailed proofs of the identities in Theorem 10.3.4 for which no arguments have been given.
8. Give a detailed argument as to why the function, $f - g$, of Theorem 10.3.4 must be the zero function.
9. Verify that the p of Theorem 10.3.5 actually exists and has the required properties.
10. Use the Pythagorean identity to show that $\sqrt{2} < \pi/2 < \sqrt{3}$.
11. Consider the collection of points in the plane, A, defined by:
$$A = \{(x, y): x = r \cdot C(t), y = r \cdot S(t), r \in \mathbf{R}^+, r \text{ fixed, and } 0 \leqslant t \leqslant 2\pi\}.$$
Show A is a circle of radius, r. Use this fact to show that the functions, C and S, are the usual cosine and sine functions with their usual geometric interpretation relative to the unit circle.
12. Use the theory developed in Chapter 6 related to arc length to show that the number, π, has its usual geometric significance relating the diameter of a circle to its circumference.
13. Supply detailed arguments to complete the proof of Theorem 10.3.6.
14. Verify all the facts mentioned about the function, f, in Theorem 10.3.7.
15. Verify all the facts mentioned about the function, F, in Theorem 10.3.7.
16. Use the fact that $\cos(x+y) = \cos x \cos y - \sin x \sin y$, to derive the formulae
$$\sin x = \sqrt{\frac{1 - \cos 2x}{2}} \quad \text{and} \quad \cos x = \sqrt{\frac{1 + \cos 2x}{2}}.$$
17. Show that $\sin\left(\dfrac{\pi}{2}\right) = 1$. Obtain the values for $\sin\left(\dfrac{\pi}{4}\right)$ and $\cos\left(\dfrac{\pi}{4}\right)$.

18. Define $\tan x = \dfrac{\sin x}{\cos x}$, $\cos x \neq 0$. Obtain the following results:

(a) $\tan(\pi + x) = \tan x$;

(b) $[\tan x]' = \dfrac{1}{\cos^2 x}$, $x \neq \dfrac{(2n+1)\pi}{2}$;

(c) $\lim\limits_{x \to (\pi^-/2)} \tan x = \infty$, and $\lim\limits_{(x \to \pi^+/2)} \tan x = -\infty$.

19. Define $\sec x = \dfrac{1}{\cos x}$, $\cos x \neq 0$, $\operatorname{cosec} x = \dfrac{1}{\sin x}$, $\sin x \neq 0$, and $\cot x = \dfrac{\cos x}{\sin x}$, $\sin x \neq 0$.

(a) Prove $1 + \tan^2 x = \sec^2 x$;

(b) Prove $1 + \cot^2 x = \operatorname{cosec}^2 x$;

(c) Obtains results similar to Theorems 10.3.4 and 10.3.6 for $\tan x$, $\cot x$, $\sec x$ and $\operatorname{cosec} x$.

20. Show that $\lim\limits_{(x \to \pi/2)} \sin x = 1$ and $\lim\limits_{(x \to \pi/2)} \cos x = 0$.

21. Obtain the values of all the six trigonometric functions at the points (whenever it is defined):
$0, \dfrac{\pi}{9}, \dfrac{\pi}{6}, \dfrac{\pi}{5}, \dfrac{\pi}{4}, \dfrac{\pi}{3}, \dfrac{\pi}{2}$, and π.

22. Prove the following inequalities:

(a) $-1 \leqslant \sin x \leqslant 1$, $-1 \leqslant \cos x \leqslant 1$;

(b) $-x \leqslant \sin x \leqslant x$, $x \geqslant 0$;

(c) $1 - \dfrac{x^2}{2} \leqslant \cos x \leqslant 1$;

(d) $x - \dfrac{x^3}{6} \leqslant \sin x \leqslant x$;

(e) $1 - \dfrac{x^2}{2} \leqslant \cos x \leqslant 1 - \dfrac{x^2}{2} + \dfrac{x^4}{24}$;

(f) $1 - \dfrac{x^2}{2} + \dfrac{x^4}{24} - \dfrac{x^6}{720} \leqslant \cos x \leqslant 1 - \dfrac{x^2}{2} + \dfrac{x^4}{24}$;

(g) $\dfrac{2x}{\pi} \leqslant \sin x$ for $x \in [0, \dfrac{\pi}{2}]$;

(h) $\dfrac{2x}{\pi} < \sin x < x < \tan x$, $x \in \left(0, \dfrac{\pi}{2} \right)$.

23. Evaluate the following limits:

(a) $\lim\limits_{x \to 0} \dfrac{\sin x}{x}$; (b) $\lim\limits_{x \to 0} \dfrac{\tan x}{x}$; (c) $\lim\limits_{x \to 0} \left(\dfrac{\sin x}{x} \right)^{1/x^2}$; (d) $\lim\limits_{x \to \infty} \left(\dfrac{\sin x}{x} \right)^{1/x^2}$.

24. Evaluate the limits of the following sequences $\{a_n\}$ as $n \to \infty$:

(a) $a_0 = \sin x$, $x \in (0, 2\pi)$, $a_{n+1} = \sin a_n$;

(b) $a_0 = \cos x$, $x \in (0, 2\pi)$, $a_{n+1} = \cos a_n$;

(c) $a_0 = \tan x$, $x \in (0, \pi/2)$, $a_{n+1} = \tan a_n$;

(d) $a_0 = \sin x$, $x \in (0, 2\pi)$, $a_{2n+1} = \cos a_{2n}$, $a_{2n+2} = \sin a_{2n+1}$.

25. Let $S^{-1} : [-1, 1] \to \left[-\dfrac{\pi}{2}, \dfrac{\pi}{2} \right]$ be the inverse of the function $S(x)$. Show that S^{-1} is monotonic and differentiable in $(-1, 1)$ and

$$[S^{-1}(y)]' = \frac{1}{\sqrt{1 - y^2}}.$$

Deduce that

$$S^{-1}(y) = \int_0^y \frac{1}{\sqrt{1 - t^2}} \, dt$$

and hence conclude that

$$\pi = 2 \int_0^1 \frac{1}{\sqrt{1 - t^2}} \, dt$$

and obtain an infinite series expansion of π.

NOTE: S^{-1} is called the **arcsin** function.

26. As in Exercise 25, define the **arccos** and **arctan** functions, and obtain similar results for their representation.

27. Derive the expansion

$$\text{Arctan } x = \sum_{k=0}^{\infty} (-1)^k \frac{x^{2k+1}}{2k+1}, \qquad |x| < 1$$

and deduce the following infinite series expansion of π:

$$\pi = 4 \sum_{k=0}^{\infty} \frac{(-1)^k}{2k + 1}.$$

28. Derive the equation

$$\text{Arcsin } x = \sum_{n=0}^{\infty} \frac{1 \cdot 3 \cdot 5 \, \cdots \, (2n-1)}{2 \cdot 4 \, \cdots \, 2n} \cdot \frac{x^{2n+1}}{2n+1}.$$

State the range of validity of the above equality.

29. Starting with the trigonometrical identity,

$$\sin x = n \sin \frac{x}{n} \prod_{k=1}^{(n-1)/2} \left[1 - \frac{\sin^2 \frac{x}{n}}{\sin^2 \frac{k\pi}{n}} \right] \qquad n \text{ odd, } x \in \mathbf{R},$$

derive the following infinite product expansion of $\sin x$:

$$\sin x = x \prod_{k=1}^{\infty} \left[1 - \frac{x^2}{k^2 \pi^2} \right].$$

Also, obtain the infinite product:

$$\cos x = \prod_{k=1}^{\infty} \left[1 - \frac{4x^2}{(2k-1)^2 \pi^2} \right].$$

30. Define two sequences of functions from $\mathbf{R}$ into $\mathbf{R}$ as follows. Set $\text{ch}_1(x) = 1$, $\text{sh}_1(x) = x$ and for $n > 1$, set

$$\text{sh}_n(x) = \int_0^x \text{ch}_n(t) \, dt \quad \text{and} \quad \text{ch}_{n+1}(x) = 1 + \int_0^x \text{sh}_n(t) \, dt.$$

Show that there exist functions ch and sh from $\mathbf{R} \to \mathbf{R}$ satisfying $\text{ch}(0) = \text{sh}'(0) = 1$, $\text{sh}(0) = \text{ch}'(0) = 0$, $\text{ch}'' = \text{ch}$, and $\text{sh}'' = \text{sh}$. Moreover, $\text{ch}' = \text{sh}$ and $\text{sh}' = \text{ch}$. Show also that these functions are unique. [The functions sh and ch are, respectively, called **hyperbolic sine** and **hyperbolic cosine** functions, and are abbreviated as $\sinh x$, $\cosh x$.]

31. Show that

$$\sinh x = \frac{e^x - e^{-x}}{2}, \quad \cosh x = \frac{e^x + e^{-x}}{2} \qquad (x \in \mathbf{R}).$$

32. Define $\tanh x$, $\coth x$, $\operatorname{sech} x$, $\operatorname{cosech} x$ in an obvious manner. Obtain the derivatives of all six hyperbolic functions.

33. The inverse of $\sinh x$, $\cosh x$, and so on, are denoted by $\sinh^{-1} x$, $\cosh^{-1} x$, and so on. Derive the following formulae:

(a) $\sinh^{-1} x = \ln(x + \sqrt{(x^2 + 1)})$;

(b) $\cosh^{-1} x = \ln(x + \sqrt{(x^2 - 1)})$, $(x \geqslant 0)$;

(c) $\tanh^{-1} x = \dfrac{1}{2} \ln \dfrac{1 + x}{1 - x}$, $x \in (-1, 1)$.

34. Find the first four nonzero terms in the Taylor expansion of the following functions near origin:

$$\sqrt{\cos x}, \quad e^{\sin x}, \quad \sec x, \quad x \cot x, \quad (\text{Arcsin } x)^2, \quad \sinh^{-1} x, \quad \int_0^x \frac{\sin t}{t}\, dt.$$

35. The **gudermannian** is the function defined by $gd(x) = \text{Arctan}\sinh(x)$. Show that the derivative of $\operatorname{sech} x$ is $gd(x)$.

36. If a function $f: \mathbf{R} \to \mathbf{R}$ satisfies the conditions $f(0) = f(\pi) = 0$ and $f''(x) = -cf(x)$ for some $c > 0$, show that $c = \dfrac{1}{n^2}$ and $f(x) = k \sin nx$ for some $x \in \mathbf{R}$, $n \in \mathbf{N}$.

37. (**Wallis product**): Let $a_n = \displaystyle\int_0^{\pi/2} \sin^n x\, dx$, $n = 1, 2, \dots$. Prove the following:

(a) the sequence, $\{a_n\}$, is decreasing;

(b) the products below define the terms of the sequence

$$a_{2n} = \left[\frac{1 \cdot 3 \cdot 5 \;\cdots\; (2n-1)}{2 \cdot 4 \cdot 6 \;\cdots\; (2n)} \right] \cdot \frac{\pi}{2}$$

and

$$a_{2n-1} = \left[\frac{2 \cdot 4 \cdot 6 \;\cdots\; (2n-2)}{3 \cdot 5 \cdot 7 \;\cdots\; (2n-1)} \right];$$

(c) for all n,

$$\frac{2n}{2n+1} \cdot \frac{\pi}{2} < [2na_{2n-1}]^2 \cdot \frac{1}{2n+1} < \frac{\pi}{2};$$

(d) the Wallis' product for π is

$$\frac{\pi}{2} = \lim_{n \to \infty} \left[\frac{2 \cdot 4 \;\cdots\; (2n)}{1 \cdot 3 \cdot 5 \;\cdots\; (2n-1)} \right]^2 \cdot \frac{1}{2n+1}.$$

38. Use Wallis' product to obtain **Stirling's Formula**:

$$\sqrt{\pi} = \lim_{n \to \infty} \left[\frac{2^{2n}(n!)^2}{(2n)!\sqrt{n}} \right].$$

39. Prove the following special case of Stirling's approximation for $n!$:

$$n! \cong \sqrt{2\pi}\, e^{-n} n^{n + 1/2}.$$

40. Show that $\pi^e < e^\pi$.

41. Show

$$\pi = 16\,\text{Arctan}\frac{1}{5} - 4\,\text{Arctan}\frac{1}{239}$$

$$= 16 \sum_{n=0}^{\infty} \frac{(-1)^n}{(2n+1)5^{2n+1}} - 4 \sum_{n=0}^{\infty} \frac{(-1)^n}{(2n+1)(239)^{2n+1}}.$$

42. Let $a_1 = \dfrac{1}{\sqrt{2}}$, and $a_{n+1} = \sqrt{\dfrac{1 + a_n}{2}}$, $(n > 1)$. Show that the infinite product $\displaystyle\prod_{n=1}^{\infty} a_n$ converges to $\dfrac{2}{\pi}$.

43. Show that $\Gamma\left(\dfrac{1}{2}\right) = \sqrt{\pi}$.

44. Obtain the following expansions (stating the range of validity), where B_n denotes the nth Bernoulli's number:

(a) $\dfrac{x}{2}\dfrac{e^x + 1}{e^x - 1} = \dfrac{x}{2}\coth\dfrac{x}{2} = 1 + \displaystyle\sum_{n=2}^{\infty}\dfrac{B_n x^n}{n!}$;

(b) $x\coth x = \displaystyle\sum_{k=0}^{\infty}\dfrac{2^{2k}B_{2k}x^{2k}}{(2k)!}$;

(c) $\tanh x = \displaystyle\sum_{k=1}^{\infty}\dfrac{2^{2k}(2^{2k} - 1)B_{2k}x^{2k-1}}{(2k)!}$;

(d) $\dfrac{x}{\sinh x} = -\displaystyle\sum_{k=0}^{\infty}\dfrac{(2^{2k} - 2)B_{2k}x^{2k}}{(2k)!}$;

(e) $x\cot x = \displaystyle\sum_{k=0}^{\infty}(-1)^k\dfrac{2^{2k}B_{2k}x^{2k}}{(2k)!}$;

(f) $\tan x = \displaystyle\sum_{k=1}^{\infty}(-1)^{k+1}\dfrac{2^{2k}(2^{2k} - 1)B_{2k}x^{2k-1}}{(2k)!}$.

45. The **Euler's numbers**, E_n are defined by

$$\dfrac{1}{\cosh x} = \sum_{n=0}^{\infty}\dfrac{E_n x^n}{n!}.$$

Prove the following:

(a) $E_0 = 1$, $E_{2n-1} = 0$, $n \in \mathbf{N}$;

(b) $\displaystyle\sum_{k=0}^{n}\binom{2n}{2k}E_{2n-2k} = 0$, $n \geqslant 1$;

(c) $\sec x = \displaystyle\sum_{n=0}^{\infty}(-1)^n\dfrac{E_{2n}x^{2n}}{(2n)!}$.

Calculate the first ten Euler numbers.

46. Given $f(x) = \sin(p\,\mathrm{Arcsin}\,x)$, prove that

(a) $(1 - x^2)f''(x) - xf'(x) + p^2 f(x) = 0$;

(b) $(1 - x^2)f^{(n+2)}(x) - xf^{(n+1)}(x) + (p^2 - n^2)f^{(n)}(x) = 0$;

(c) use (b) to obtain the first four terms in the Taylor expansion of $\sin(p\,\mathrm{Arcsin}\,x)$ near 0.

47. Use the method suggested in Exercise 46 to obtain the Taylor expansion of the following functions near origin:

(a) $\dfrac{\mathrm{Arcsin}\,x}{\sqrt{1 - x^2}}$;

(b) $e^{\mathrm{Arctan}\,x}$;

(c) $\mathrm{Arctan}\,x$;

(d) $\sin\ln x$;

(e) $(\mathrm{Arcsin}\,x)^2$.

Chapter 11

Limits and Topology in the Plane

Previous work in this text has been concerned with various types of limiting processes where the underlying system which has contained the domain of all our functions has been the real numbers, $\mathbf{R}$. As has been emphasized, the real numbers are rather special due to the fact that they are the unique, complete ordered field. It might be expected that this fact in some way affects the results on limits. Thus, one naturally wonders whether the principal theorems on limits remain valid in other more general systems, or spaces. In this chapter the simplest possible system more general than the real line is considered, namely, the Cartesian plane. Quite apparently, one should expect substantial differences in the approach to limiting processes in the plane, as opposed to the real line. The reason for this is that a major tool for proving theorems on the real line has been the Completeness Axiom in the form of the Supremum Principle, and this will no longer be available for use in the same way, since the plane does not constitute a complete ordered field. Indeed, the plane cannot be made into an ordered field under any algebraic operations, nor can it be made into a field if the operations are to be performed componentwise. Thus, the tools which were derived from the interaction of order and algebra will have to be revised. It may be expected then that where analogous theorems to those proved before are valid, new techniques of proof will have to be developed to establish their truth. Developing suitable alternate techniques and generalizing old theorems to this new situation is the subject of the present chapter.

11.1 GEOMETRY OF FUNCTIONS OF TWO VARIABLES

We begin by defining the plane, $\mathbf{R}^2$, as the Cartesian product of $\mathbf{R}$ with itself:

$$\mathbf{R}^2 = \mathbf{R} \times \mathbf{R} = \{(x, y) : x, y \in \mathbf{R}\}.$$

Discussion. We have already made implicit use of the plane for drawing pictures of sequences and functions. However, our interest now is in the plane as a source of domains for functions. Formally, the plane is a collection of ordered pairs whose first and second coordinates are arbitrary real numbers. Thus, our domains will be collections of these ordered pairs. As before, we would like to develop geometric intuition as an aid to our reasoning. Thus, we may draw pictures of domains in the plane as shown in Figure 11.1.1. We would stress the usefulness of such pictures, but recall our injunctions that a picture can not be part of a proof. □

Having said that the domains for functions will be subsets of the plane, we must also specify where the ranges of such functions will lie. Perhaps the most natural place would be to say that the functions considered in this chapter will have their ranges in $\mathbf{R}^2$ as well. This is not the route we will take, although it is an interesting one. Rather, functions are required to have their ranges in $\mathbf{R}$. Thus, functions may be thought of as **real valued functions of two real variables**. (In these terms, the functions dealt with previously are **real valued functions of a single real variable**.) This phrase captures the sense of the notation which has been developed for dealing with functions from $\mathbf{R}^2$ into $\mathbf{R}$, for example; let

$$f = \{(w, z) : w = (x, y) \in \mathbf{R}^2 \text{ and } z = x + y\}.$$

This is a formally correct specification for a function of the type to be studied. However, such functions are usually specified by giving a rule for computation, and the domain. In this notation, one would write

$$f(x, y) = x + y, \quad (x, y) \in \mathbf{R}^2.$$

This notation abuses the definition of function; however, it does not lead to errors provided we are always aware of the correct interpretation of the notation and it is analogous to previous notations for functions of a single variable.

Having delineated the functions of interest, let us briefly review the principal issues on which to focus our attention. We are interested in the behavior of functions.

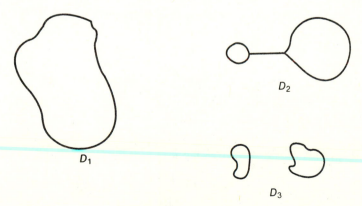

Figure 11.1.1 Some examples of domains in $\mathbf{R}^2$.

Specifically, we are interested in understanding what it means for a function from $\mathbf{R}^2$ into $\mathbf{R}$ to be continuous and the relationship, if any, between this type of continuity and continuity of functions of a single real variable. There are two distinct approaches to this problem which have been developed earlier in this text. One is to look at the limiting process:

$$\lim_{(x,y)\to(a,b)} f(x,\ y), \quad \text{where } (x,\ y),\ (a,\ b) \in \mathbf{R}^2.$$

This approach was taken in Chapters 1 and 2. The other is to approach the problem through the underlying topology of the domain space and the range space, an approach developed in Chapter 3. We shall develop both approaches in parallel in this chapter.

Before entering into a serious discussion of the analysis of the situation, we want to examine some of the methods which have been developed which help to generate an intuitive feeling for the type of functions under study. As stated above, we want to be able to use geometry, or pictures, to enhance our intuition. Unfortunately, the graph of an arbitrary function, $z = f(x,\ y)$, requires a three-dimensional space to contain it, two dimensions for the domain and one for the range. This leads to immediate problems, since our pictures are constructed on paper, confining us to two-dimensional representations. A number of techniques have been developed in the calculus for alleviating this problem, and we briefly review them.

Let us imagine then a domain, $D \subseteq \mathbf{R}^2$, and a collection of ordered triples $\{(x,\ y,\ z) : (x,\ y) \in D \text{ and } z = f(x,\ y)\}$. Since f is a function, to each ordered pair $(x_0,\ y_0) \in D$, there is a unique z such that $(x_0,\ y_0,\ z) \in f$. This means that if we construct the line parallel to the z-axis through the point $(x_0,\ y_0,\ 0)$, that is, $\{(x_0,\ y_0,\ z) : z \in \mathbf{R}\}$, then this line will contain exactly one ordered triple which is also a member of the graph of the function, f.

Thinking intuitively now, if the function is defined for all points which are 'near' some fixed point of D, say $(x',\ y')$, and the function is 'nice' in this region near $(x',\ y')$, then the graph of the function in this region will form a surface in three space, in the same way that the graph of a continuous function defined on an open interval generates a curve in the plane. Thus, to be able to think intuitively about the geometry of functions having domains in the plane, we need to be able to develop pictures of the surfaces generated by these functions.

To make these ideas concrete, the reader should imagine a three-dimensional coordinate system with x and y denoting the horizontal coordinates and z denoting the vertical coordinate. Further imagine a cone having its vertex at the point $(0, 0, 0)$, its main axis parallel to the z-axis, and opening upward, that is, in the positive z-direction. A precise mathematical description for such an object is

$$\{(x,\ y,\ z) : z = \sqrt{x^2 + y^2} \text{ and } \sqrt{x^2 + y^2} \leqslant 10\}.$$

This cone opens at $45°$ and has a height of 10 units. With this one in mind, we are ready to proceed.

The primary method for studying the geometry of a surface generated by a function of two variables is to intersect the surface with a sequence of planes, thereby generating a sequence of one or more curves and to study the properties of these curves.

Quite apparently, not all planes are of equal value for studying the properties of a given surface; indeed, an arbitrary plane will not even intersect the surface, so that some care must be taken in applying the technique. In applying this process, it is generally agreed that a plane which is perpendicular to one of the principal axes and passes through the surface will yield the most information.

Keeping the cone in mind, consider y_0, a fixed point on the y-axis, and the plane through the point $(0, y_0, 0)$ which is perpendicular to the y-axis. Such a plane will be parallel to the plane containing both the x- and the z-axes. For this reason, such a plane is called an $x - z$ **slice**. Now a given $x - z$ slice will not, in general intersect our cone. For this to happen, the plane must be close to the origin. Specifically, the requirement is that $|y_0| \leqslant 10$. For those y_0's for which the $x - z$ slice through y_0 intersects the cone, a family of curves is generated which are related by the fact that they all result from the intersection of a plane which is perpendicular to the y-axis and the specified cone.

EXAMPLE 1

Describe the family of curves determined by taking $x - z$ slices of the cone given by

$$\{(x, y, z) : z = \sqrt{x^2 + y^2} \text{ and } \sqrt{x^2 + y^2} \leqslant 10\}.$$

Solution. Let $0 \leqslant c \leqslant 10$. Then the curve of intersection between the $x - z$ slice through $y = c$ and the cone is given by

$$\{(x, z) : z^2 - x^2 = c^2 \text{ and } \sqrt{x^2 + c^2} \leqslant 10\}.$$

As is well known, for a particular value of c, we are looking at part of a hyperbola. This hyperbola opens upward, and has its minimum value at the point $(0, c, c)$. Thus, the family of curves is a sequence of hyperbolae, all opening upward and having their minimum points at $(0, c, c)$, where $c \leqslant 10$. This family is pictured in Figure 11.1.2. $\square$

Discussion. The surfaces which we are studying can be described in terms of a collection of points in three space. Such a description does not generally supply one with a concrete picture of the surface. It is this picture which is useful and which one must have if one is to be able to think about the surface in question. Slices provide information which can be used to construct a picture.

In the present case, the slices turn out to be familiar curves, namely, hyperbolae. In other cases, the resultant family may not be so familiar. However, there remains the fact that slices are curves and by looking at curves, the problem has been reduced to studying objects in two dimensions. As such, one can apply all the tools developed for studying the properties of curves.

Nevertheless, even though the family of curves turns out to be extremely simple and easy to describe, to fully understand or picture the surface, one must be able to visualize how the various curves sit in three space in relation to one another. This is often the hardest part. To develop this pictorial understanding, one must be able to describe the position and orientation of each curve in the family, and to say how the position and orientation depend on the value of c. In Figure 11.1.2, plots of $x - z$

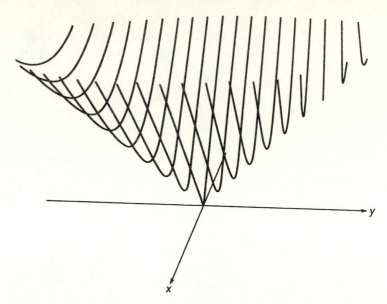

Figure 11.1.2 Perspective plots of a series of slices through the surface generated by $f(x, y) = \sqrt{x^2 + y^2}$. The eye of the viewer is above and in front of the surface at (40, 10, 15). In generating the slices, y is given a fixed value and x is permitted to vary so that each curve lies in a plane parallel to the $x - z$ plane. Each of the curves is a hyperbola, except when $y = c = 0$ when $z = |x|$.

slices for various values of c are presented. As can be seen, once the dependence of position and orientation is known, a picture of the surface can begin to be generated. □

In a similar manner, we define a $y - z$ **slice** as a plane through a fixed point $(x_0, 0, 0)$ and which is perpendicular to the x-axis. As above, when a $y - z$ slice intersects a surface generated by a real-valued function of two real variables, it generates the graph of a function of one variable. By considering a series of $x - z$ or $y - z$ slices, it is possible to develop a picture of the surface. This is the technique employed by most three-dimensional computer graphics programs. A program generates a series of $x - z$ ($y - z$) slices and these are plotted using standard perspective techniques. The programs are particularly simple due to the fact that the process of taking a slice generates a graph of a function. In Figure 11.1.3, we present the graph of the cone generated using both $x - z$ and $y - z$ slices.

Consider now the intersection of the surface with a plane perpendicular to the z-axis. Such a plane consists of the set of points given by

$$\{(x, y, z_0) : x, y \in \mathbf{R}\}$$

where z_0 is an arbitrary real number. As before, an arbitrary plane perpendicular to the z-axis may, or may not, intersect a given surface. When such a plane does intersect the surface, a curve is generated. Such curves are referred to as **level curves** or **contours**. Evidently, the collection of points which belong to the level curve generated by z_0 is given by

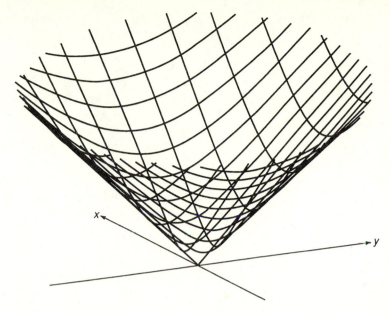

Figure 11.1.3 Perspective plots of a series of slices through the surface generated by $f(x,\ y) = \sqrt{x^2 + y^2}$. Both $x - z$ slices and $y - z$ slices are presented in the figure. In this figure the eye views the surface from below at $(40,\ 10,\ -15)$.

$$\{(x,\ y,\ z_0) : (x,\ y) \in \text{Dmn } f \text{ and } f(x,\ y) = z_0\}.$$

For a given surface and a given z_0, this collection of points may be empty, may be a curve which can be described by a single real-valued function of a real variable, or may comprise one, or more, whole regions of the plane through z_0.

To get a concrete feeling for the possibilities, the reader might imagine a soup bowl placed on a table, with the plane determined by the x and y axes as the top of the table and the z-axis passing through the center of the bowl. First note that if the bowl is composed of a 'suitably thin' material, then the points comprising the surface of the bowl can be given by a real-valued function of two real variables. Now imagine the result of passing a plane perpendicular to the z-axis through the bowl. If the bowl has a flat bottom, then a plane containing the bottom will yield a disk as the level curve. If the bowl has a flat rim, a plane containing the rim will produce a circular band. If the bowl is round, planes through the sides will produce circles as level curves. If one now imagines several bowls of differing shapes placed side by side, the possibilities for the level curves become endless.

An essential point in all this is that level curves are fundamentally different types of objects from slices, in that they cannot, in general be described by a collection of points which is a function. This means that they can be difficult to deal with. However, there is no denying the information which can be gleaned from level curves, as anyone who looked at a contour map prior to taking a hike well knows.

EXAMPLE 2 _____

Describe the level curves for the cone specified in Example 1.

Solution. Let $0 \leqslant c \leqslant 10$. Then, the level curve determined by the plane through c is the locus of points satisfying

$$c^2 = x^2 + y^2,$$

which is well known to be a circle of radius c. As c varies between 0 and 10, we obtain a family of circles. In Figure 11.1.4, various level curves are sketched. ☐

Discussion. As with slices, the family of level curves may turn out to be easy to describe. In this case they are a family of circles having a clearly determined dependence on the parameter c. However, as with slices, mere knowledge of the nature of the family of level curves is not enough. What is required is their spatial relationship to one another. In the present case, the spatial relationships are easily determined from the fact that the circle with radius c has the z-axis running through its center, lies in a plane which is perpendicular to the z-axis, and is at a height c above the $x - y$ plane. The amount of geometric information available from the level curves is apparent from Figure 11.1.4, which was sketched using a computer. It is important to note that unlike slices, which can always be represented by functions of a single variable, a parametric description of the level curve is generally required, for example, $(x(t), y(t), c)$ where $0 \leqslant t \leqslant 1$. ☐

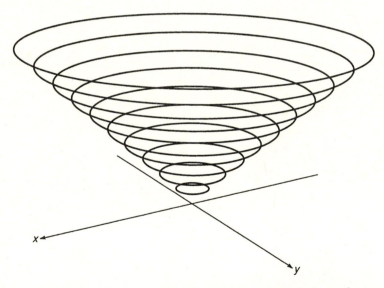

Figure 11.1.4 Perspective plots of a series of level curves through the surface generated by $f(x, y) = \sqrt{x^2 + y^2}$. The level curve defined by $z = c$ is a circle of radius c.

EXERCISES

1. For each of the following functions describe the various slices. Use this information to develop a description of the surface and a sketch. Where possible, try to come up with an

intuitive geometric description of the surface generated, for example, 'a bowl-shaped object with its base centered at $(0, 0, 0)$ and opening upward'. Where the domain of the function is not stated, assume it to be all pairs of real numbers which when input into the rule for computation yield a real number.

(a) $f(x, y) = 10$;

(b) $f(x, y) = 2x$;

(c) $f(x, y) = -3y$;

(d) $f(x, y) = \dfrac{x}{y}$, $y \neq 0$;

(e) $f(x, y) = xy$;

(f) $f(x, y) = x^2$;

(g) $f(x, y) = 2y^2$;

(h) $f(x, y) = \sqrt{10 - x^2 - y^2}$;

(i) $f(x, y) = x + y$, $-1 < x, y < 1$;

(j) $f(x, y) = x^2 + y^2$, $-10 \leqslant x, y \leqslant 10$;

(k) $f(x, y) = x^2 - y^2$, $-10 \leqslant x, y \leqslant 10$;

(l) $f(x, y) = 2x^2 - y^2$, $-10 \leqslant x, y \leqslant 10$;

(m) $f(x, y) = 2y^2 - x^2$, $-10 \leqslant x, y \leqslant 10$;

(n) $f(x, y) = \dfrac{1}{1 + x^2 + y^2}$, $-10 \leqslant x, y \leqslant 10$;

(o) $f(x, y) = \sin x + y$;

(p) $f(x, y) = x + \sin x + y$;

(q) $f(x, y) = x^4 - x^2 + y^4 - y^2$;

(r) $f(x, y) = \dfrac{x^2 + y^2}{1 + x^4 - y^4}$;

(s) $f(x, y) = \cos x - 2y$;

(t) $f(x, y) = \sin(x + y)$;

(u) $f(x, y) = \cos(x - 2y)$;

(v) $f(x, y) = \sin x + \sin y$;

(w) $f(x, y) = \sqrt{4 - x^2 - 4y^2}$;

(x) $f(x, y) = 4000 - 2x^2 - 3y^4$;

(y) $f(x, y) = e^{-(x^2 + y^2)}$;

(z) $f(x, y) = \dfrac{y^2 - x^2}{10}$.

2. Identify (and sketch) several level curves of the functions given in Exercise 1.

3. Let $z = g(x)$, $x \in [a, b]$ be a plane curve defined on the $x - z$-plane. The surface generated when this curve revolves around the z-axis is called a **surface of revolution** about z-axis. Express the surface so obtained in the form $z = f(x, y)$. Identify the level curves of the surface of revolution.

4. If $f(x, y)$ is of the form $f(x, y) = g(x) + h(y)$, then $z = f(x, y)$ is a **surface of translation**. Interpret this terminology by considering the $x - z$ and $y - z$ slices. If either g or h is a constant, the surface is called **cylindrical**. Interpret this geometrically.

5. Given the surface $z = f(x, y)$, how would you generate the surface $z = g(x, y)$, where $g(x, y)$ is as follows:

(a) $f(x, y) + 3$;

(b) $2 - 3f(x, y)$;

(c) $f(x + 2, y)$;

(d) $f(x, y - 5)$;

(e) $\dfrac{1}{3}f(x, y)$;

(f) $-f(x, y)$;

(g) $f(-x, -y)$;

(h) $f(x, -y)$;

(i) $f(-x, y)$;

(j) $f(2x, y)$;

(k) $f(x, 3y)$;

(l) $f(2x, 3y)$;

(m) $f(y, x)$;

(n) $-f(-y, -x)$;

(o) $-3f\left[\dfrac{1}{2}x, \dfrac{1}{3}y\right].$

11.2 DOUBLE SEQUENCES

The stated objective of this chapter is to develop the theory of limiting processes in the plane. Previously in this text, the theory of limiting processes was initiated via a study of sequences. We will adopt the same tack in this chapter, since sequences in two variables illustrate many of the complexities, yet their theory can be framed almost entirely in the language of functions of one variable.

Definition.   A **double sequence** is a function from $\mathbf{N} \times \mathbf{N}$ into $\mathbf{R}$. Individual terms of a double sequence will be denoted by $\sigma_{n,m}$ and the sequence itself by $\{\sigma_{n,m}\}$.

Discussion.   We want to try to develop some geometric intuition about double sequences. Thus imagine you are standing at the point $(0, 0)$ in the plane and looking out across the first quadrant. A double sequence could be thought of as a collection of sticks projecting above, or below, the plane and rising out of points in the plane which are associated with a pair of positive integers. In this analogy, the length of the stick at (n, m) would be $|\sigma_{n,m}|$, and it would project above the plane if $\sigma_{n,m}$ were positive, and below if $\sigma_{n,m}$ were negative.   □

EXAMPLE 1 _____

Describe the double sequence $\{\sigma_{n,m}\}$ where $\sigma_{n,m} = \sin\dfrac{mn\pi}{2}$.

Solution.   This sequence yields three possible values, 1, −1, and 0. Thus, using the analogy above, if one looks across the first quadrant, one would see some points with sticks projecting 1 unit above the plane, some with sticks projecting 1 unit below the plane, and some with no sticks showing whatsoever. But this doesn't tell us much.

Always when we thought about ordinary sequences, we had in mind the idea of n tending to infinity. With two variables, each of which can become large independently of the other, what is the appropriate concept? A natural approach to this problem would be to hold one of the variables fixed and to see what happened to the sequence as the other variable was allowed to go to infinity.

Let's try this for this example. First notice that $\sin\dfrac{nm\pi}{2}$ is symmetric in n and m, whence it does not matter if n is fixed and m permitted to increase, or vice-versa. Thus, fix m. There are two cases. Suppose m is odd. It can be shown (Exercise 1) that $\sin \dfrac{nm\pi}{2}$ produces the values $\ldots, 1, 0, -1, 0, 1, 0, -1, \ldots,$ consecutively, with the initial value being either ± 1. On the other hand, if m is even, then $\sin \dfrac{mn\pi}{2} = 0$ for all n. $\qquad\square$

Discussion. The description of $\sigma_{n,m}$ provides a more concrete way to think about this sequence. We can move along the positive y-axis (or m-axis) until the point $(0, m)$ is reached. We then look along the grid, parallel to the x-axis (or n-axis). Along this axis, we are looking at an ordinary sequence, and we can pose the usual questions about sequences. In this example, if m is odd, we would see a sequence which oscillates; if m is even, we see a constant sequence. Thus, we could picture the sequence as an array consisting of an infinite number of rows, each of which is infinite. The odd numbered rows in this array show the values $\ldots, 1, 0, -1, 0, 1, 0, -1, \ldots,$ consecutively, while the even numbered rows show only the value, 0.

On the other hand, if we fix n, this amounts to moving along the positive x-axis to the point $(n, 0)$ and then looking along the grid parallel to the y-axis. If n is odd, then we would see a sequence which oscillates in the same manner as if we had stopped at the point $(0, m = n)$ and looked along the grid parallel to the x-axis. Similarly, if n is even a sequence which is constantly zero is seen. In terms of the array, this amounts to moving out along the bottom of the array and looking up the columns. As with the rows, the odd numbered columns show an oscillating sequence, and the even numbered columns show a sequence which is constantly 0.

In the terms suggested in section 11.1, the method suggested amounts to looking at slices. By doing so, a much greater degree of intuition about the double sequence is obtained. $\qquad\square$

Definition. A double sequence, $\{\sigma_{n,m}\}$, is said to have a **limit as** n, m **tend to infinity** provided there exists an $A \in \mathbf{R}$ such that for every positive ϵ there exists $N \in \mathbf{N}$ such that

$$|\sigma_{n,m} - A| < \epsilon \text{ whenever } n, m > N.$$

If an A exists with these properties, A is called the **limit of the double sequence** $\{\sigma_{m,n}\}$. We write

$$\lim_{n,m \to \infty} \sigma_{n,m} = A$$

and say that the double sequence **converges** to the limit A.

Discussion. The difficulty in defining convergence for double sequences is that we are confronted with two independent variables, either of which could be very large. The notion that we are trying to capture is that eventually all terms of the sequence are close to some fixed number. In the case of one variable, it is clear that the substance of 'eventually' is captured by asserting that for all n sufficiently large, all terms of the sequence are close to the limit. For the case of two variables, we have said that having both n and m sufficiently large is the requirement which will ensure that the terms of the sequence are close to the limit. In general this means the choice of N must account for the way in which $\sigma_{n,m}$ depends on n and m.

In its other respects, this definition should look very much like other definitions of limits of which there are at least seven predecessors in this text, and we refer the reader to these for additional comments. In reviewing these comments, the reader will notice that there are a number of standard questions which arise whenever a limit has been defined, for example, is the limit unique, how does the limit relate to notions of addition and/or multiplication, and so on. These questions should be posed and answered for the present limit. While we will state the appropriate results, for the most part we will leave the proofs to the reader.

In the next several examples we shall demonstrate that this definition achieves our intent and captures what we wanted to capture. ◻

EXAMPLE 2 _____

Let $\{\sigma_{n,m}\}$ be given by $\sigma_{n,m} = \dfrac{1}{n+m}$. Show that this sequence has a limit.

Solution.   Let $A = 0$, and $\epsilon > 0$ be fixed. Now let $N > \dfrac{1}{\epsilon}$ be fixed. Then

$$\left| \frac{1}{n+m} - 0 \right| < \epsilon \quad \text{whenever } n, m > N. \qquad \textbf{(WHY?)}$$

◻

Discussion.   The fact that this sequence has limit (converges to) zero should hardly be surprising. The reader should notice that the proof given does not appear to make any use of the nature of the dependence of $\sigma_{n,m}$ on n and m. This is misleading, since we have made no attempt to choose a minimal value of N. To do this would require using all the information available (Exercise 2). ◻

EXAMPLE 3 _____

Discuss the convergence properties of the sequence $\{\sigma_{n,m}\}$ where $\sigma_{n,m} = \sin\dfrac{mn\pi}{2}$.

Solution.   Fix $\epsilon < 1$ and let $N \in \mathbf{N}$ be fixed. Take any odd m satisfying $m > N$. For this fixed m, the sequence, $\left\{ \sin\dfrac{mn\pi}{2} \right\}$, oscillates between ± 1 whence it has no limit as n tends to infinity. From this observation the reader can complete the proof (Exercise 3) by showing that whatever the choice of A, the inequality $|\sigma_{n,m} - A| < \epsilon$ whenever $n,m > N$ will not be universally satisfied. ◻

Discussion.   This sequence fails to converge for the classic reason that it exhibits essentially oscillatory behavior. Specifically, there are at least two distinct real numbers which a infinite number of terms of the sequence are close to. While this fact provided a sufficient reason for nonconvergence in the single variable case, the next example shows that the present context is more complicated. ◻

EXAMPLE 4 _____

Discuss the convergence properties of the sequence $\{\sigma_{n,m}\}$ where $\sigma_{n,m} = 2^{-m}\sin\dfrac{mn\pi}{2}$.

Solution. Let $A = 0$ and fix $\epsilon > 0$. Choose $N \in \mathbf{N}$ such that $N > \dfrac{1}{\epsilon}$. Now, if $n,m > N$, then

$$\left| 2^{-m}\sin\frac{mn\pi}{2} - 0 \right| < 2^{-m} < \epsilon \qquad \textbf{(WHY?)}$$

whence $\{\sigma_{n,m}\}$ converges to 0. $\square$

Discussion. The argument presented above is straightforward. But this sequence has further interest. Consider a fixed $M > N$, where N is as in the solution and M is odd. Then the sequence $\{\sigma_n = \sigma_{n,M}\}$ is an ordinary sequence. What are its convergence properties? From the arguments in Example 1, it takes the values $\dots, 2^{-M}, 0, -2^{-M}, 0, 2^{-M}, \dots$. This sequence is oscillatory, and so cannot converge. Yet the original sequence, $\{\sigma_{n,m}\}$, converges. The reason is that the factor, 2^{-m}, ensures that for large values of m, the product, $2^{-m}\sin\dfrac{mn\pi}{2}$, will be close to 0. $\square$

In the examples above, we have made substantial use of the idea of fixing one of the variables and letting the other variable become large without bound. This idea is directly analogous to the notion of a slice and its intent is to reduce a problem involving double sequences to one involving only ordinary sequences. The possibilities associated with exploiting this type of simplification lead to the following definition.

Definition. Let $\{\sigma_{n,m}\}$ be a double sequence. For each fixed M the sequence, $\{\sigma_{n,M}\}$ is called the Mth **partial sequence**. Similarly, for fixed N, $\{\sigma_{N,m}\}$ is called the Nth **partial sequence**. If the Mth partial sequence converges, we write

$$a_M = \lim_{n \to \infty} \sigma_{n,M}$$

and call a_M the Mth **partial limit**. If the Nth partial sequence converges, we write

$$b_N = \lim_{m \to \infty} \sigma_{N,m}$$

and call b_N the Nth **partial limit**. Finally, we refer to the two limits, when they exist,

$$\lim_{M \to \infty} a_M \quad \text{and} \quad \lim_{N \to \infty} b_N$$

as the **iterated limits** of the double sequence $\{\sigma_{n,m}\}$.

Discussion. The rationale which underlies this definition is simple. One can view double sequences as an infinite array of sequences of one variable laid out in the first quadrant. Individual sequences in this array are obtained in one of two ways. The first way is to move up the y-axis to a point $(0, M)$ and then consider the sequence

$\{\sigma_{n,M}\}$. This is equivalent to taking a slice parallel to the x-axis through the point $(0, y = M)$. The second is to move out on the x-axis, fix a point $(N, 0)$, and consider the sequence $\{\sigma_{N,m}\}$.

We can push the array concept further by adding the limits of each of the individual sequences of one variable at an appropriate position. Thus, if $\{\sigma_{n,M}\}$ has a limit, a_M, we think of a_M as being positioned in the row determined by M, that is, M units above the x-axis, at the far right. In other words, $\{a_M\}$ will be listed after all of the infinite number of $\sigma_{n,M}$'s, $n \in \mathbf{N}$ have been listed. If each of the limits, $\lim\limits_{n \to \infty} \sigma_{n,M}$, exists, then a new complete column can be added at the far right of the array; in general, since some of the limits may fail to exist, only a partial column will be added. In an analogous manner we can add a new row above all the other rows by placing b_N at the top of the column consisting of the $\sigma_{N,m}$'s. As before if each of the limits, $\lim\limits_{n \to \infty} \sigma_{N,m}$, exists, then each of the b_N's will exist and a complete top row will be generated. Otherwise, only a partial row will exist.

The central question in this approach is to determine the degree to which the convergence properties of the individual sequences, $\{\sigma_{n,M}\}$ and/or $\{\sigma_{N,m}\}$, and the two sequences of partial limits, $\{a_M\}$ and $\{b_N\}$, control the convergence properties of the double sequence. Intuitively, one believes that there should be a strong relationship. On the other hand, Example 4 shows that the relationship cannot be perfect, since for this example none of the Nth partial sequences is convergent, yet the double sequence itself is convergent.   □

EXAMPLE 5 _____

Let $\{\sigma_{n,m}\}$ be given by $\sigma_{n,m} = \dfrac{nm}{n^2 + m^2}$. Show that this sequence has no limit.

Solution. Fix M and consider the Mth partial sequence. The reader can show (Exercise 4) that

$$\lim_{n \to \infty} \frac{nM}{n^2 + M^2} = 0. \qquad \textbf{(WHY?)}$$

On the other hand, if we set $n = m$, then

$$\lim_{n \to \infty} \frac{nn}{n^2 + n^2} = \frac{1}{2}. \qquad \textbf{(WHY?)}$$

These two facts are incompatible with the double sequence having a limit.   □

Discussion. The reader can check that each of the Nth partial sequences also has a limit, and that this limit is also 0. It follows then that both of the iterated limits exist and also are equal to 0. But even this is not enough to guarantee that the double sequence has a limit.

The difficulty is that we can find a way of proceeding through the array which does not lead to a limit of 0. In short, all roads do not lead to Rome, and this is the reason why the sequence fails to converge. This idea is further explored in Exercise 5.   □

Theorem 11.2.1. The limit of a double convergent sequence is unique.

Proof. Exercise 6.   □

The next theorem gives the best possible result about the relationship between the convergence properties of a double sequence and its partial sequences.

Theorem 11.2.2. Let $\{\sigma_{n,m}\}$ be a convergent double sequence. Further suppose that each of the partial sequences is convergent. Then the two iterated limits exist and are equal to the limit of the double sequence.

Proof. Let A denote the limit of $\{\sigma_{n,m}\}$. We claim $\{a_M\}$ converges to A. To see this, fix $\epsilon > 0$ and choose $K \in \mathbf{N}$ such that $n,m > K$ implies $|\sigma_{n,m} - A| < \dfrac{\epsilon}{2}$. Now fix $M > K$. Since $\{\sigma_{n,M}\}$ converges to a_M, we can choose $J \in \mathbf{N}$ such that $n > J,K$ implies $|\sigma_{n,m} - a_M| < \dfrac{\epsilon}{2}$. It now follows that

$$|a_M - A| < \epsilon, \qquad\qquad \textbf{(WHY?)}$$

whence $\lim\limits_{n \to \infty} a_M = A$. The proof that $\{b_N\}$ converges to A is left to the reader (Exercise 7).   □

Discussion. The utility of this theorem is that it can provide candidates for the limit of a double sequence, and in some instances an easy means for identifying double sequences which do not converge.

For double sequences where an infinite number of the partial sequences converge, either an infinite number of a_M's, or an infinite number of b_N's must exist. In either case, one can find the limit of the resultant subsequence, if it exists, and this will be a candidate for the limit of the double sequence, in fact, it must be the limit, if the limit exists. For example, if an infinite number of the a_M exist and $A = \lim a_{M_k}$ for any subsequence, then if the limit of the double sequence exists, it must be A.

Suppose an infinite number of both the a_M's and the b_N's exist. An immediate consequence of the above is

$$\lim b_{N_k} = \lim a_{M_k}$$

for any subsequences. On the other hand, if either iterated limit fails to exist or equality fails, then the double sequence cannot have a limit.

While these results have positive utility in reducing questions about the convergence of double sequences to questions about the convergence of ordinary sequences, the results are not definitive. To see why, consider the analogy of a double sequence as an array. A path through the array is a move from $\sigma_{n,m}$ to $\sigma_{p,q}$ where $n \leqslant p$ and $m \leqslant q$; or a move to a_m or b_n; or a move from a_m to a_q; or from b_n to b_p. A double sequence converges if and only if all possible ways of proceeding (paths) through the array of points making up the sequence yield the same limit. The process of taking iterated limits amounts to selecting two paths through the array, namely by moving along the edges of the array. Unfortunately, there is simply not enough information about the totality of the double sequence in these two paths for this method to be successful in completely determining convergence properties. These ideas are explored precisely in Exercise 5. □

Theorem 11.2.3.   Let $\{\sigma_{n,m}\}$ be a double sequence. Then $\{\sigma_{n,m}\}$ is convergent if and only if for every $\epsilon > 0$ there exists $N \in \mathbf{N}$ such that

$$|\sigma_{n,m} - \sigma_{i,j}| < \epsilon$$

whenever $n,\ m > N$ and $i,\ j > N$.

   Proof.   Exercise 8.   □

Discussion.   This theorem states a typical Cauchy criterion. Its proof is similar to other Cauchy criteria and is left to the reader. As has been noted, the importance of Cauchy type results is they provide a means for establishing the convergence of a sequence which does not require that the value of the limit be known in advance.

   If we think about the Cauchy criterion in the context of the array analogy, it says that if we move to the point (N, N) in the plane and consider the quadrant of points, (n, m), satisfying $n,\ m > N$, then all the terms of the double sequence which lie in this quadrant must be within ϵ of one another.   □

   If one reviews the major results about sequences, one sees that the deeper results involve the notion of boundedness. There were two results of this type. First, a bounded monotone sequence must converge. Second, a bounded sequence must have a cluster point. Versions of both of these results are true for double sequences. Moreover, in both cases, the proofs are straightforward applications of the previous theory.

Theorem 11.2.4.   Let $\{\sigma_{n,m}\}$ be a double sequence such that all of its partial sequences are either monotone increasing or monotone decreasing. If $\{\sigma_{n,m}\}$ is bounded, then it is convergent.

   Proof.   Exercise 9.   □

Definition.   A number $a \in \mathbf{R}$ is said to be a **cluster point** for the double sequence, $\{\sigma_{n,m}\}$, provided for every $\epsilon > 0$ and every $N \in \mathbf{N}$ there exists $n,\ m > N$ such that $|a - \sigma_{n,m}| < \epsilon$.

Discussion.   The reader should notice that this definition avoids the possibility of using one of the partial sequences to generate a cluster point which was not a cluster point for any of the remaining terms of the double sequence.   □

Theorem 11.2.5.   A bounded double sequence $\{\sigma_{m,n}\}$ has a cluster point.

   Proof.   Consider the sequence $\{\sigma_{n,n}\}$. This sequence is bounded and so has a cluster point. This cluster point is a cluster point of the double sequence.   □

Discussion.   As the reader can see, both results are trivial extensions of previous theory and no new knowledge has really been gained. For the case of cluster points, this is because the values of the sequence are constrained to lie in **R**. It would be quite different if we took sequences, $\{\psi_n\}$, where $\psi: \mathbf{N} \rightarrow \mathbf{R}^2$. ☐

Theorem 11.2.6. Let $\{\sigma_{n,m}\}$ and $\{\tau_{n,m}\}$ be two double sequences which converge to s and t, respectively. Then

    (i) $\{\sigma_{n,m} + \tau_{n,m}\}$ converges to $s + t$.

    (ii) $\{\sigma_{n,m} \cdot \tau_{n,m}\}$ converges to $s \cdot t$.

    (iii) if in addition, $\{\tau_{n,m}\}$ consists of nonzero terms and $t \neq 0$, then $\left\{ \dfrac{\sigma_{n,m}}{\tau_{n,m}} \right\}$

    converges to $\dfrac{s}{t}$.

    Proof.   Exercise 10. ☐

Discussion.   Again there is nothing really new here and constructing the proof should consist of nothing more than review. ☐

EXERCISES

1. Consider the sequence, $\left\{ \sin \dfrac{nm\pi}{2} \right\}$. Show that if m is a fixed odd number, then $\sin \dfrac{nm\pi}{2}$ produces consecutively, $\dots, 1, 0, -1, 0, 1, 0, -1, \dots$, with the initial value being either ± 1.

2. Given $\epsilon > 0$ find the minimal N which will satisfy the definition of limit for $\left\{ \dfrac{1}{m+n} \right\}$.

3. Write out the complete analytic details showing that the sequence of Example 3 cannot converge.

4. Prove all claims made in the solution to Example 5.

5. Let ϕ be a one to one mapping of $\mathbf{N}$ into $\mathbf{N} \times \mathbf{N}$ such that for every $K \in \mathbf{N}$ there exists $n \in \mathbf{N}$, $\phi(n) = (i, j)$ and $i,j > K$ and such that for $n,m \in \mathbf{N}$, with $\phi(n) = (i, j)$, $\phi(m) = (p, q)$ and $n < m$, then $i \leqslant p$ and $j \leqslant q$. Such a function ϕ will be called a **path** through the double sequence. Show that a double sequence, $\{\sigma_{n,m}\}$ is convergent if and only if the family of sequences, $\{\sigma_{\phi(n)}\}$, where ϕ is a path, all have a common limit.

6. Prove Theorem 11.2.1.

7. Complete the proof of Theorem 11.2.2, filling in any missing details.

8. Prove Theorem 11.2.3.

9. Prove Theorem 11.2.4.

10. Prove Theorem 11.2.6.

11. Discuss the convergence properties of the following double sequences $\{\sigma_{n,m}\}$:

    (a) $\sigma_{n,m} = c$;

    (b) $\sigma_{n,m} = m$;

    (c) $\sigma_{n,m} = 1 + m + n$;

    (d) $\sigma_{n,m} = m^2 - n^2$;

    (e) $\sigma_{n,m} = \begin{cases} 1, & n = m \\ 0, & \text{otherwise}; \end{cases}$

(f) $\sigma_{n,m} = \begin{cases} 1, & n = m+1 \\ -1, & m = n+1 \\ 0, & \text{otherwise}; \end{cases}$

(g) $\sigma_{n,m} = (-1)^{n+m};$

(h) $\sigma_{n,m} = \dfrac{(-1)^{n+m}}{n};$

(i) $\sigma_{n,m} = \dfrac{\sin m}{n};$

(j) $\sigma_{n,m} = \dfrac{n^2 m^2}{n^4 + m^4}.$

(k) $\sigma_{n,m} = \dfrac{mn}{m^2 + n^2};$

(l) $\sigma_{n,m} = \dfrac{mn^2}{m^2 + n^3};$

(m) $\sigma_{n,m} = \dfrac{1}{m^2} + \dfrac{1}{n^2};$

(n) $\sigma_{n,m} = \dfrac{(-1)^m}{m} + \dfrac{1}{n};$

(o) $\sigma_{n,m} = (-1)^{n+m} \cos \dfrac{mn\pi}{4};$

(p) $\sigma_{n,m} = e^{-(m^2+n^2)};$

(q) $\sigma_{n,m} = \begin{cases} \dfrac{1}{1 + (m-n)^2}, & m \neq n \\ 0, & m = n; \end{cases}$

(r) $\sigma_{n,m} = \dfrac{(-1)^m m^2 n^2}{m^3 + n^6};$

(s) $\sigma_{n,m} = \dfrac{(-1)^m m^2 n^2}{m^3 + n^6};$

(t) $\sigma_{n,m} = \cos^{2n}(m!\pi x), \quad x \in [0,1];$

(u) $\sigma_{n,m} = (-1)^{m+n} \left[\dfrac{1}{n} + \dfrac{1}{m} \right];$

(v) $\sigma_{n,m} = \left[\dfrac{m+1}{m+2} \right]^{n+1} - \dfrac{m+1}{m+2} - \dfrac{1}{2^{n+1}} + \dfrac{1}{3}.$

12. Let $\{\sigma_{n,m}\}$ be a double sequence and define $g_m : \mathbf{N} \to \mathbf{R}$ by $g_m(n) = \sigma_{n,m}$. Suppose the sequence of functions, $\{g_m\}$ converges uniformly on $\mathbf{N}$ to a function, g, and that $\lim_{n \to \infty} g(n)$ exists. Show that $\{\sigma_{n,m}\}$ is convergent and find its limit.

13. Prove that every convergent double sequence is bounded. Give an example to show that the converse is not true.

11.3 PROPERTIES OF THE PLANE

Having developed some techniques for describing the geometry of real valued functions of two real variables and developed the theory of the simplest types of these functions, namely double sequences, we want to return to the principal theme of the chapter, which is the study of the continuity of these functions and begins with the limiting process:

$$\lim_{(x,y)\to(a,b)} f(x,\ y).$$

As with our earlier notions of limit, a notion of closeness must be developed and this quite obviously must be based on distance.

In section 0.6 we developed a measure of the distance between an arbitrary pair of real numbers; this measure was then used as a fundamental tool in all further considerations. Similarly, we must now develop a measure of the distance between arbitrary pairs of points in $\mathbf{R}^2$.

Definition. Let $(x,\ y)$, $(z,\ w) \in \mathbf{R}^2$. The distance, $\mathbf{d}((x,\ y),(w,\ z))$, between the pair of points is

$$\mathbf{d}((x,\ y),(z,\ w)) = \sqrt{(x-z)^2 + (y-w)^2}.$$

Discussion. The source of this definition is the **Pythagorean Theorem**. Essentially, our choice for the distance function reflects our beliefs about the inherent geometry of our world, namely, it is **Euclidean.** Having said this, one still wants to verify that this definition of distance satisfies the fundamental properties contained in Theorem 0.6.1.

$\square$

Theorem 11.3.1. Let $(x,\ y),(z,\ w),(u,\ v) \in \mathbf{R}^2$. Then

(i) $\mathbf{d}((x,\ y),(z,\ w)) = 0$ if and only if $(x,\ y) = (z,\ w)$,
   $\mathbf{d}((x,\ y),(z,\ w)) > 0$; otherwise
(ii) $\mathbf{d}((x,\ y),(z,\ w)) = \mathbf{d}((z,\ w),(x,\ y))$;
(iii) $\mathbf{d}((x,\ y),(z,\ w)) \leqslant \mathbf{d}((x,\ y),(u,\ v)) + \mathbf{d}((u,\ v),(z,\ w))$.

Proof. Statements (i) and (ii) are left as Exercise 1; we prove (iii). Consider the left-hand side of (iii), that is, the term $\mathbf{d}((x,\ y),(z,\ w))$, and notice it expands to

$$\mathbf{d}((x,\ y),(z,\ w)) = \sqrt{(x-z)^2 + (y-w)^2}$$
$$= \sqrt{((x-u) + (u-z))^2 + ((y-v) + (v-w))^2}.$$

Now set $a_1 = x-u$, $b_1 = u-z$, $a_2 = y-v$, and $b_2 = v-w$. It can be shown (Exercise 2) that what we want to prove is for a_i and b_i, $i = 1,\ 2$, as defined,

$$\left[\sum_{i=1}^{2} (a_i + b_i)^2 \right]^{1/2} \leqslant \left[\sum_{i=1}^{2} a_i^2 \right]^{1/2} + \left[\sum_{i=1}^{2} b_i^2 \right]^{1/2}. \qquad \textbf{(WHY?)}$$

Since both sides of this inequality are nonnegative, squaring both sides will preserve the inequality and results in the following equivalent inequality:

$$\sum_{i=1}^{2} (a_i + b_i)^2 \leqslant \sum_{i=1}^{2} a_i^2 + 2 \left[\sum_{i=1}^{2} a_i^2 \sum_{i=1}^{2} b_i^2 \right]^{1/2} + \sum_{i=1}^{2} b_i^2.$$

Expanding the left-hand side of this inequality yields

$$\sum_{i=1}^{2} (a_i + b_i)^2 = \sum_{i=1}^{2} a_i^2 + 2\sum_{i=1}^{2} a_i b_i + \sum_{i=1}^{2} b_i^2.$$

Application of algebra now reduces our problem to establishing

$$\sum_{i=1}^{2} a_i b_i \leqslant \left[\sum_{i=1}^{2} a_i^2 \sum_{i=1}^{2} b_i^2 \right]^{1/2}. \qquad \textbf{(WHY?)}$$

This last inequality is a consequence of the following lemma.   □

Lemma 11.3.1 (Cauchy–Schwarz Inequality).   Let a_i, b_i, $i = 1, 2$ be any four real numbers. Then,

$$\left[\sum_{i=1}^{2} a_i b_i \right]^2 \leqslant \sum_{i=1}^{2} a_i^2 \sum_{i=1}^{2} b_i^2.$$

Proof.   The inequality is valid exactly if

$$0 \leqslant \sum_{i=1}^{2} a_i^2 \sum_{i=1}^{2} b_i^2 - \left[\sum_{i=1}^{2} a_i b_i \right]^2.$$

Carrying out this calculation (Exercise 3) results in

$$\sum_{i=1}^{2} a_i^2 \sum_{i=1}^{2} b_i^2 - \left[\sum_{i=1}^{2} a_i b_i \right]^2 = (a_1 b_2 - b_1 a_2)^2. \qquad \textbf{(HOW?)}$$

Since the right-hand side is a square of some real number, it is nonnegative.   □

Discussion.   Evidently, even though the underlying geometry which we are studying has changed, the principal tool which we use to effect proofs remains the same: namely, the algebra. What has changed substantially is the complexity of the calculations which must be carried out. If we look back in section 0.6 at the proof of the equivalent result for points on the line, the proof was straightforward and the calculations simple. For the case at hand, the method is reasonably direct; indeed, there is a direct comparison between the arguments adopted in section 0.6 and the present argument, see Exercise 10. However, the calculations are an order of magnitude more difficult.

Let us review the steps in the argument. First we examine the quantity $\mathbf{d}((x, y),(z, w))$ as compared to $\mathbf{d}((x, y),(u, v)) + \mathbf{d}((u, v),(z, w))$. We notice that terms in $\mathbf{d}((x, y),(z, w))$ can be made similar to those on the right-hand side by addition and subtraction of u and v. Thus, $x - z$ becomes $x - u + u - z$, and $y - w$ becomes $y - v + v - z$. It is now possible to restate the problem in terms of four arbitrary real numbers, $x - u$, $y - v$, $u - z$, and $v - w$. Having made this substitution, the square root signs are removed and a new inequality developed. This inequality, the Cauchy–Schwarz inequality, has the property that it will yield the Triangle inequality as a consequence. The proof of the Cauchy–Schwarz inequality is a straightforward computation leading to

$$\sum_{1 \leqslant i < j \leqslant 2} (a_i b_j - a_j b_i)^2.$$

This formula is not apparently symmetric in a_i and b_j, although we would expect it to be. The student should resolve this matter as part of Exercise 3.

The reader may wonder why, in view of the fact that $n = 2$, we have employed the $\sum$ notation in the preceding calculations. We have used them to suggest a more general form of these inequalities may be valid with n arbitrary. $\square$

Once one has a proper notion of distance, it is possible to develop the limit concept without further ado. However, we delay that development to present some results on the topology of $\mathbf{R}^2$. The focus of this discussion will be on the underlying structure of the domain space, $\mathbf{R}^2$. Recall that from the point of view of topology (see Chapter 3), what we are interested in are the open sets.

Notation. In the remainder of this chapter, we shall use enlarged, boldface, lower-case letters to denote points of the plane, for example, $\mathbf{x}$, $\mathbf{y}$, $\mathbf{z}$, and so on.

Definition. Let $\mathbf{z} \in \mathbf{R}^2$ be a fixed point of the plane and $r \in \mathbf{R}$. The set

$$D_{\mathbf{z},r} = \{\mathbf{w} : \mathbf{d}(\mathbf{z}, \mathbf{w}) < r \text{ and } r > 0\}$$

will be called an **open disc of radius** r **centered at** $\mathbf{z}$. A set $A \subseteq \mathbf{R}^2$ is **open** if for every $\mathbf{z} \in A$ there is a positive real number r such that the open disc of radius r centered at $\mathbf{z}$, $D_{\mathbf{z},r}$, is a subset of A, that is, $D_{\mathbf{z},r} \subseteq A$.

Discussion. The concept of open disc of radius r centered at $\mathbf{z}$ has as a prerequisite the notion of distance. In simple English, the open disc of radius r centered at $\mathbf{z}$ is the collection of all points having a distance less than r from the point $\mathbf{z}$. The notion of open disc is used to define the more general notion of open subset of the plane. A subset, A, of the plane is open, provided for each $\mathbf{z} \in A$, we can always find an r such that the open disc of radius r centered at $\mathbf{z}$ is completely contained in A. Note for different points $\mathbf{z}$ and $\mathbf{w}$ belonging to A, we may be required to use different values of $r \in \mathbf{R}$. Indeed, the student can show that if $A \neq \mathbf{R}$, then it will be impossible to find a single value of r which will do for all points of A.

Let us compare the situation in the plane with the situation on the line. On the line, an open interval was a collection of points of the form $(a, b) = \{x : a < x < b\}$. Any such interval can be thought of as being centered at $a + \dfrac{b-a}{2}$. Thus, the open interval (a, b) is indeed a collection of all points whose distance from a fixed point is less than a prescribed amount, in this case, $\dfrac{b-a}{2}$. Consider the open disc of radius r centered at $(x, 0)$, for some x. If we consider the collection of points, $\{(x', 0) : \mathbf{d}((x, 0),(x', 0)) < r\}$, then this obviously generates an open interval on the x-axis. Thus, an open disc in the plane when intersected with the x-axis yields a subset of the line which turns out to be an open interval. More generally, if any open set $A \subset \mathbf{R}^2$ intersects a line, the subsets of the line which comprise the intersection will form an open set when considered as a subset of the line. However, the reverse is not true, namely, no nonempty subset of a line will constitute an open subset of the plane.

Recall in Chapter 3 we showed an arbitrary nonempty open set was the union of pairwise disjoint, open intervals. In the plane, we have an open set A satisfies

$$A = \bigcup \{D_\mathbf{z} : D_z \subset A\},$$

where $D_\mathbf{z}$ denotes an open disc of unspecified radius centered at $\mathbf{z}$. Thus, we have every open set is a union of open discs (Exercise 4). □

EXAMPLE 1 _____

Show that an open disc is an open subset of the plane.

Solution. Consider the open disc, $D_{\mathbf{z},r}$ and fix $\mathbf{w} \in D_{\mathbf{z},r}$. Let $d(\mathbf{z}, \mathbf{w}) = s$. Then $s < r$, whence $t = r - s > 0$. It follows if $\mathbf{u} \in D_{\mathbf{w},t}$, then $\mathbf{u} \in D_{\mathbf{z},r}$, as required. Thus, $D_{\mathbf{z},r}$ is open. □

Discussion. This example illustrates how with each point, $\mathbf{w}$, in an open set a different value for the radius of the open disc around $\mathbf{w}$ will be required to witness the property of the definition of open is satisfied. □

EXAMPLE 2 _____

Show no line is an open subset of the plane.

Solution. By a line we mean a set of points, L, of the form

$$L = \{(x(t), y(t)) : x(t) = at+b, \ y(t) = ct+d, \ \text{and} \ t \in \mathbf{R}\}.$$

(Here, a, b, c, d are constants, and t is the (real) variable.)

Now fix $\mathbf{z} \in L$ and let $r > 0$ be chosen. By definition of L, there is a $t \in \mathbf{R}$ such that $\mathbf{z} = (x(t), y(t))$. Fix this t. We claim (Exercise 5) that not both $\left[x(t) + \dfrac{r}{2}, y(t) \right]$ and $\left[x(t), y(t) + \dfrac{r}{2} \right]$ can be members of L. Since both are members of the open disc, $D_{\mathbf{z},r}$, and r was arbitrary, we conclude L cannot be open. □

Discussion. This example suggests that topologically, $\mathbf{R}$ and $\mathbf{R}^2$ are very different. One distinction is $\mathbf{R}^2$ has two dimensions, although we have not made this notion mathematically precise. Nevertheless, it is intuitively clear we can find lots of copies of $\mathbf{R}$ inside $\mathbf{R}^2$, for example, any line will serve as a copy, but no copies of $\mathbf{R}^2$ inside $\mathbf{R}$, although this last assertion is perhaps less clear. □

We turn now to developing the basic theorems which govern the topology of the plane.

Theorem 11.3.2. The collection of open subsets of $\mathbf{R}^2$ has the following properties:

(i) $\varnothing$ and $\mathbf{R}^2$ are open;
(ii) If X is any collection of open subsets of $\mathbf{R}^2$, then $\bigcup X$ is open;
(iii) If X is any finite collection of open subsets of the plane, then $\bigcap X$ is open.

Proof. Exercise 6. □

Discussion. In Chapter 3 we pointed out a topology on a set was a collection of special sets which as a collection had to satisfy the properties asserted for the open subsets of $\mathbf{R}^2$ in Theorem 11.3.2. Theorem 11.3.2 simply verifies that the definition of open set in terms of open discs yields a collection of sets with the required properties.

As is the case for $\mathbf{R}$, there are many possible topologies which could be put on $\mathbf{R}^2$; we have chosen the topology which is based on our ideas about the inherent structure of $\mathbf{R}^2$ as developed from the notion of distance. These ideas embody the fact that to all intents and purposes, our world is Euclidean. Thus our mathematics, which is a complete abstraction, yields results which agree with measurements made in the real world. □

The remainder of this section presents a series of definitions and theorems which explore the basic point set topology of the plane. The proofs of many of these theorems will be left as exercises, since for the most part they are straightforward. However, before proceeding further in this section, the reader should review the theorems and definitions presented in section 3.1. The purpose of this review is to focus on the question:

What theorems about $\mathbf{R}$ have analogies in $\mathbf{R}^2$?

Definition. Let $A \subseteq \mathbf{R}^2$.

   (i) $\mathbf{z} \in \mathbf{R}^2$ is a **limit point** of A, if for every $r > 0$, the open disc of radius r centered at $\mathbf{z}$ has a nonempty intersection with $A \sim \{\mathbf{z}\}$;
   (ii) A is **closed** if A contains all its limit points.
   (iii) $\mathbf{z} \in \mathbf{R}^2$ is an **interior point** of A, if for some $r > 0$, there is an open disc of radius r centered at $\mathbf{z}$ which is completely contained in A; otherwise, $\mathbf{z}$ is a **boundary point**. The boundary of A is denoted by bd A and defined by

$$\text{bd } A = \{\mathbf{w} : \mathbf{w} \in A \text{ and } \mathbf{w} \text{ is a boundary point of } A\}$$

$$\cup \{\mathbf{w} : \mathbf{w} \in \mathbf{R}^2 \sim A \text{ and } \mathbf{w} \text{ is a boundary point of } \mathbf{R}^2 \sim A\}.$$

Discussion. The key concept here is that of limit point. A definition for this concept has already been given for subsets of $\mathbf{R}$. Comparison of the definition for $\mathbf{R}$ with the definition for $\mathbf{R}^2$ reveals the former requires the intersection of $(a - \delta, a + \delta) \sim \{a\}$ with A be nonempty for every positive δ, while the latter requires $(D_{\mathbf{z},r} \sim \{\mathbf{z}\}) \cap A$ be nonempty for every positive r. Thus, in either case, the essential feature is to be a limit point; there must be points of A which are arbitrarily close to the candidate point, *other than the candidate point itself.* Thus, the candidate limit point cannot act as its own witness to the fact that there are points of A close to it. Having said this, we see the definition of limit point for $\mathbf{R}^2$ is the natural extension of the original definition in $\mathbf{R}$.

A point $\mathbf{w} \in A$ is a boundary point if it is not an interior point. As discussed in section 3.1, the boundary of A consists of the boundary points from A together with the boundary points from $\mathbf{R}^2 \sim A$. It is immediate that A and $\mathbf{R}^2 \sim A$ share the same boundary. □

EXAMPLE 3 _____

Find the limit points, boundary points, and interior points for the open disc, $D_{\mathbf{z},r}$.

Solution. Let $\mathbf{w} \in \mathbf{R}^2$ with $\mathbf{d}(\mathbf{w}, \mathbf{z}) = s$. We claim: if $s \leqslant r$, then $\mathbf{w}$ is a limit point of $D_{\mathbf{z},r}$; if $s < r$ then $\mathbf{w}$ is an interior point, whence $D_{\mathbf{z},r}$ contains no boundary points; if $s = r$, then $\mathbf{w}$ is a boundary point of the complement; if $s > r$, then $\mathbf{w}$ is neither a limit point, nor an interior point nor a boundary point. The proofs of these assertions are left to Exercise 7. In Figure 11.3.1 we picture these results.   □

EXAMPLE 4 _____

Show every finite subset of $\mathbf{R}^2$ is closed.

Solution. Let $A \subseteq \mathbf{R}^2$ be finite. Then $A = \{\mathbf{w}_1, \ldots, \mathbf{w}_n\}$ for some $n \in \mathbf{N}$. Now let $\mathbf{z} \in \mathbf{R}^2$ be fixed, and set $r_n = \mathbf{d}(\mathbf{z}, \mathbf{w}_n)$. Then at most one of the r_n's is 0. Let r be the minimum positive r_k, $k = 1, \ldots, n$. It follows if $r_k > 0$, then $\mathbf{w}_k \notin D_{\mathbf{z},r}$, whence $\mathbf{z}$ is not a limit point of A.   □

Theorem 11.3.3. Let $A \subseteq \mathbf{R}^2$. Then A is open exactly if the complement of A is closed.

Proof. Exercise 8.   □

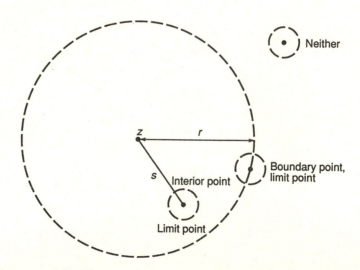

Figure 11.3.1 Schematic of the open disc, $D_{\mathbf{z},r}$. Points belong to $D_{\mathbf{z},r}$ provided they are inside, but not on, the dashed edge of the circle. A point whose distance to $\mathbf{z}$ is less than r is an interior point because we can construct a disc, as shown, centered on the point completely within $D_{\mathbf{z},r}$; such a point is also a limit point because every neighborhood contains points belonging to $D_{\mathbf{z},r}$. Boundary points have a distance r from $\mathbf{z}$, since as shown, every open disc centered on such a point must contain points in $D_{\mathbf{z},r}$, and points in the complement.

Discussion. The reader may want to consult Theorem 3.1.3 and realize that the proof of the present theorem merely requires a reformulation of the argument given there.

☐

One of the important properties of the topology on **R** is every open set can be realized as a countable union of open intervals, each of which has rational endpoints (Theorem 3.1.4). If one asks why this should be true, one realizes there are two essential facts required. The first is the collection of rationals is countable; the second is the collection of rationals is dense (see Exercise 3.2.27) in **R**. Since the collection of all pairs of rational numbers is also countable (Exercise 9), it is plausible that a version of this result may be true for the topology we have defined on $\mathbf{R}^2$.

Definition. Let A be a subset of $\mathbf{R}^2$. A is said to be **dense** in $\mathbf{R}^2$, provided every member of $\mathbf{R}^2$ is a limit point of A.

Discussion. Consider for a moment what the phrase 'A is dense in $\mathbf{R}^2$' should mean. It should mean near every point of $\mathbf{R}^2$, there is a point of A. The notion of 'near' is made precise by requiring each point of $\mathbf{R}^2$ to be a limit point of A. This has the effect of requiring each open disc centered at **z**, an arbitrary member of $\mathbf{R}^2$, to contain infinitely many points of A. Certainly this seems consistent with our usual meaning for 'dense'.

More importantly, the reader should consult Exercise 3.2.27 which contains the definition of 'dense' relative to **R**. It will then be clear the present definition is nothing more than a rephrasing of that definition.   ☐

Theorem 11.3.4. $\mathbf{Q} \times \mathbf{Q}$ is a dense subset of $\mathbf{R}^2$.

Proof. Fix $\mathbf{z} = (u, v) \in \mathbf{R}^2$ and $r > 0$. The interval $\left[u, u + \dfrac{r}{2} \right)$ contains a rational (**WHY?**), which we call p. Similarly, there is a rational, q, in the interval $\left[v, v + \dfrac{r}{2} \right)$. It follows $(p, q) \in \mathbf{Q} \times \mathbf{Q} \cap D_{\mathbf{z},r}$.

☐

Discussion. It is essential the reader recognize that the source of this proof is in the fundamental truths about **R**.   ☐

Theorem 11.3.5. Let A be an open subset of $\mathbf{R}^2$. Then A is a countable union of open discs $D_{\mathbf{z}}$, where **z** is a pair of rationals and where the radius of $D_{\mathbf{z}}$ is rational.

Proof. Let A be an open subset of $\mathbf{R}^2$ and let $\mathbf{X} \in A$ be arbitrary. Since A is open, we can find an open disc $D_{\mathbf{X},r} \subseteq A$. Moreover, we may assume the radius, r, of this disc is rational. By Theorem 11.3.4, we can find $\mathbf{z} \in \mathbf{Q} \times \mathbf{Q}$ such that $d(\mathbf{X}, \mathbf{z})$ is less than $\dfrac{r}{3}$. By the Triangle inequality,

$$\mathbf{X} \in D_{\mathbf{z}, 2r/3} \subset A.$$

Since **X** was arbitrary, the union over all the $D_{\mathbf{z}} \subseteq A$ contains A. Since there are only countably many such discs, the union is countable and we are done.   ☐

Discussion. The reader should compare this with the proof of Theorem 3.1.4. The reader should also consider Theorem 3.1.5 which is a sharpened version of Theorem 3.1.4, involving disjoint intervals. The obvious question is whether Theorem 11.3.5 can be similarly sharpened. The reader is asked to explore this possibility in Exercise 18. □

A notion which proved important in discussion of continuity was that of 'connectedness'. Specifically, we saw some functions which appeared not to be continuous from an intuitive point of view, suffered from this intuitive flaw due to the fact that their domains were not connected sets. Such an example was $f(x) = \dfrac{1}{x}$ defined on $(-\infty, 0) \cup (0, \infty)$. For this reason, it is useful to look at this property in the case of $\mathbf{R}^2$ and compare it with the connectedness properties of $\mathbf{R}$.

Definition. A nonempty set $A \subseteq \mathbf{R}^2$ is **connected** if there do not exist two open sets, O_1 and O_2 such that $A \subseteq O_1 \cup O_2$, $O_1 \cap O_2 = \varnothing$, and $A \cap O_i \neq \varnothing$ $(i = 1, 2)$. A is said to be **path-connected** provided for every $\mathbf{x}, \mathbf{y} \in A$ there exists a function, $\phi: [0,1] \rightarrow \mathbf{R}^2$ such that ϕ is one to one, $\phi(t) = (\phi_1(t), \phi_2(t))$, where ϕ_i is continuous for $i = 1, 2$, $(\phi_1(0), \phi_2(0)) = \mathbf{x}$, $(\phi_1(1), \phi_2(1)) = \mathbf{y}$, and $(\phi_1(t), \phi_2(t)) \in A$ for all $t \in [0, 1]$. The function ϕ will be called a **path** in A from $\mathbf{x}$ to $\mathbf{y}$.

Discussion. The idea which the definition of a connected set is trying to capture is that of a contiguous collection of points. Another way of expressing this idea is to say that the given set of points cannot be divided into two separate parts. Put precisely, this means if one takes various decompositions of A into nonempty sets, B and C, and if for every such decomposition,

$$(\bar{B} \cap C) \cup (B \cap \bar{C}) = \varnothing,$$

then A is connected (Exercise 19).

Connectedness is a property of certain subsets of $\mathbf{R}^2$. As such we can ask how it relates to the various set theoretic operations. For example, is the intersection of connected sets connected? The principal result in this direction is given in Exercise 20.

If A is not connected then A can be decomposed into a collection of subsets each of which is connected. The elements of this decomposition are called the **connected components** of A, or more simply, the components of A (see Exercise 21).

The idea behind path-connected is it is always possible to get from one place in the set to another place in the set by moving along a collection of 'pairwise adjacent' points (or path), which is completely contained in the set, A. Since mathematically, there is no such thing as a pair of adjacent points, we replace this with a mathematically precise notion which, not surprisingly, has continuity at its foundation.

Paths have nice properties. For one thing, as shown below, they are closed bounded subsets of $\mathbf{R}^2$. For another, they have finite length, as can be established using the techniques discussed in the applications of integration in Chapter 6 (Exercise 22).

The connected subsets of $\mathbf{R}$ are the intervals. As a consequence, every connected subset of $\mathbf{R}$ is path-connected. The next example shows this is not the case for $\mathbf{R}^2$. □

Before generating the example we prove:

Theorem 11.3.6. If $A \subseteq \mathbf{R}^2$ is path-connected, then A is connected.

Proof. Let $A \subseteq \mathbf{R}^2$ be path-connected. For the sake of argument, suppose A is not connected. Then there exist open sets, O_1 and O_2 such that $A \subseteq O_1 \cup O_2$, $O_1 \cap O_2 = \varnothing$, and $A \cap O_i \neq \varnothing$ for $i = 1, 2$. Thus, fix $\mathbf{u} \in A \cap O_1$ and $\mathbf{v} \in A \cap O_2$. Since A is path-connected, there is a path, ϕ, connecting $\mathbf{u}$ and $\mathbf{v}$. Now set

$$B = \{t : \phi(t) \in O_1\}.$$

By definition of a path, $B \subseteq [0, 1]$. By choice of $\mathbf{u}$, $B \neq \varnothing$. Thus, B has a supremum, t_0. We claim (Exercise 23) $\phi(t_0)$ will witness a contradiction, which completes the proof. □

Discussion. To complete the proof, the reader will have to employ the continuity properties of ϕ. However, the real power has already been exercised in the form of the Completeness Axiom. □

EXAMPLE 5 _____

Give an example of a connected but not path-connected subset of $\mathbf{R}^2$.

Solution. Consider the set, A, given by

$$A = \{(x, y) : x = 0 \text{ and } y \in [-1, 1]\} \cup \{(x, y) : y = \sin\frac{1}{x} \text{ and } x \in (0, 1]\}.$$

The reader can show (Exercise 24) $B = \{(x, y) : y = \sin\frac{1}{x} \text{ and } x \in (0, 1]\}$ is path-connected, and hence connected. It is also the case

$$\{(x, y) : x = 0 \text{ and } y \in [-1, 1]\}$$

is path-connected, and hence connected (**WHY?**). Finally, we claim any open set which contains $(0, 0)$ has a nonempty intersection with B (**WHY?**). It follows A is connected. It is also the case no path will connect any point in B to $(0, 0)$ (**WHY?**). □

Discussion. This example illustrates one of the key differences between $\mathbf{R}$ and $\mathbf{R}^2$. Again, it is intricately tied up with the fact $\mathbf{R}^2$ has two dimensions and $\mathbf{R}$ only one. □

Definition. A set, $A \subseteq \mathbf{R}^2$ is said to be **bounded** provided there exists $\mathbf{u} \in \mathbf{R}^2$ and $K \in \mathbf{R}$ such that for all $\mathbf{v} \in A$, $\mathbf{d}(\mathbf{u}, \mathbf{v}) < K$, equivalently, $A \subseteq D_{\mathbf{u},K}$.

Discussion. The reader should compare this definition of bounded with that for subsets of $\mathbf{R}$. The definition relative to $\mathbf{R}$ is essentially the same as the present definition, except that a fixed real number, 0, is used to play the role of $\mathbf{u}$. This suggests the definition above could be rephrased so that instead of $\mathbf{u}$, one always related things to the point $(0, 0)$ (Exercise 25). □

Theorem 11.3.7. Let $\mathbf{u}$, $\mathbf{v} \in \mathbf{R}^2$ and let ϕ be an arbitrary path from $\mathbf{u}$ to $\mathbf{v}$. Then Rng ϕ is closed and bounded in $\mathbf{R}^2$.

Proof. We first show Rng ϕ is bounded. Note that Rng ϕ_i is bounded for $i = 1, 2$ by Theorem 2.6.3. Thus, let K be a bound for both Rng ϕ_1 and Rng ϕ_2, then $\mathbf{d}((0, 0), \mathbf{v}) < 2K$ for all $\mathbf{v}$ in Rng ϕ (**WHY?**).

Now let $\mathbf{w}$ be a limit point of Rng ϕ. Let $\epsilon_n = \dfrac{1}{n}$ and $I_{n,k} = [k2^{-n}, (k+1)2^{-n}]$, for $k = 0, 1, \ldots, 2^n - 1$. We claim there is a nested sequence of intervals, $\cdots I_{n+1,j_{n+1}} \subseteq I_{n,j_n} \subseteq \cdots \subseteq I_{0,0}$ such that $D_{\mathbf{w},\epsilon_n} \cap \phi(I_{n,j_n})$ is infinite for every $n \in \mathbf{N}$. The proof of the claim is by induction. First note if $n = 0$, $I_{0,0} = [0, 1]$, and the result follows since $\mathbf{w}$ is a limit point of Rng ϕ (**WHY?**). Next suppose I_{m,k_m} has been obtained such that $D_{\mathbf{w},\epsilon_m} \cap \phi(I_{m,j_m})$ is infinite. The reader can show the intersection of $D_{\mathbf{w},\epsilon_{m+1}}$ and one of $\phi(I_{m+1,2j_m})$ and $\phi(I_{m+1,2j_m+1})$ must be infinite (Exercise 26) which implies the existence of the nested sequence. Having established that the sequence of intervals exists, we apply Theorem 3.2.3 to obtain t_0, the common point of intersection. We claim $\phi(t_0) = \mathbf{w} = (a, b)$. To see why, note if $\mathbf{v} \in D_{\mathbf{w},r}$ and $\mathbf{v} = (c, d)$, then $|a-c| < r$ and $|b-d| < r$. Thus, as $N \to \infty$ we can find $t \in I_{n,j_n}$ such that $\phi(t) \in D_{\mathbf{w},\epsilon_n}$. But now continuity of ϕ_1 and ϕ_2 will guarantee that $\phi(t_0)$ is also close to $\mathbf{w}$. It is left to the reader to completely spell out the remaining details of the argument (Exercise 27). $\square$

Discussion. The proof of this theorem makes use of a very general mathematical principle which is essentially hidden. In its most general form it is known as the **Fan Theorem.** In order to understand it, we shall briefly describe some ideas about trees. A **graph** is a collection of ordered pairs of members of a set, A, called the **field.** Consider then a graph, G, having field A. For x, $y \in A$, we say there is an **edge from x to y** provided $(x, y) \in G$. The cardinality of $\{x : (x, y) \in G\}$ is called the **in-degree of y.** The cardinality of $\{x : (y, x) \in G\}$ is called the **out-degree of y.** G is **connected** if for all x, $y \in A$, $x \neq y$ implies there exists a finite sequence $x = x_1, \ldots, x_n = y$ such that $(x_i, x_{i+1}) \in G$ for $i = 1, \ldots, n-1$. G **avoids cycles** if no x in A can be connected to itself. (In particular, $(x, x) \notin G$.) A **tree** is a connected graph which avoids cycles and which has a unique element in A having in-degree 0 and all other elements in A have in-degree 1. A tree is **binary** if every member of A has out-degree 2. A sequence $x_1, x_2, \ldots$, such that $(x_i, x_{i+1}) \in G$ for all i is called a **branch.** The Fan Theorem asserts that a binary tree in which every branch is finite must itself be finite.

We want to show how the Fan Theorem is applied in the proof of the present theorem. The reader can verify the sequence of sets, I_{n,k_n}, forms a binary tree, T, given by

$$T = \{(I_{n,k_n}, I_{n+1,j_{n+1}}) : j = 2k \text{ or } j = 2k+1\}.$$

Now consider $S \subseteq T$ defined by

$$S = \{(I_{n,k_n}, I_{n+1,k_{n+1}}) : (I_{n,k_n}, I_{n+1,k_{n+1}}) \in T \text{ and } \phi(I_{n+1,j_{n+1}}) \cap D_{\mathbf{w},\epsilon_{n+1}} \text{ is infinite}\}.$$

Note if I_{n,k_n} is in the field of S, then there is a branch of T, at least up to $I_{n,k}$ every member of which is in the field of S. Further, since

$$[0,1] = \bigcup \{I_{n,k} : k = 0, \ldots, 2^n - 1\},$$

there is a $j \leqslant 2^n - 1$ such that $\phi(I_{n,j}) \cap D_{\mathbf{w},\epsilon_n}$ is infinite. For this reason, S cannot be finite, whence S must have an infinite branch. This branch will be the required sequence of nested intervals. $\square$

Theorem 11.3.8. Let $\mathbf{u}, \mathbf{v} \in \mathbf{R}^2$. Then there is a path connecting $\mathbf{u}$ and $\mathbf{v}$. Further, if $\mathbf{u} \subseteq O \subseteq \mathbf{R}^2$ and O is open, then there is an open disc $D_{\mathbf{u}}$ such that $D_{\mathbf{u}} \subseteq O$ and $D_{\mathbf{u}}$ is path-connected.

Proof.   Exercise 28. $\square$

Discussion.   A general topological space which satisfies the first assertion is called a **path-connected space**. A space which satisfies the second is called a **locally path-connected space**. $\square$

Theorem 11.3.9.   Let O be a connected open subset of $\mathbf{R}^2$. Then O is path connected.

Proof.   Fix $\mathbf{u} \in O$. We first claim for every $\mathbf{v} \in O$, there is a path from $\mathbf{u}$ to $\mathbf{v}$. Let us suppose the claim is established, then for $\mathbf{x}$, $\mathbf{y} \in O$ we take a path from $\mathbf{x}$ to $\mathbf{u}$ and follow it by a path from $\mathbf{u}$ to $\mathbf{y}$. This yields a path from $\mathbf{x}$ to $\mathbf{y}$ (Exercise 29) and we are done. Now for the claim. Let

$$A = \{\mathbf{v} : \text{there is a path from } \mathbf{u} \text{ to } \mathbf{v}\}.$$

If $A = O$ we are done, whence suppose $A \neq O$. Let $B = \text{bd } A$. There are two possibilities. The first is that $B \cap O = \varnothing$. If this is the case, then it can be shown (Exercise 30) that O is not connected. Thus, the alternative, $B \cap O \neq \varnothing$, must hold. Fix $\mathbf{v} \in B \cap O$. We claim that $\mathbf{v} \in B \cap O$ implies $\mathbf{v} \in A$. To see this, note that since $\mathbf{R}^2$ is locally path-connected, there is a path-connected open disc, $D_{\mathbf{v}} \subseteq O$. This disc must contain points of A, since $\mathbf{v} \in B$. Fix any $\mathbf{w} \in A \cap D_{\mathbf{v}}$. Then $\mathbf{w}$ is path-connected to both $\mathbf{u}$ and $\mathbf{v}$. It follows from Exercise 29 that $\mathbf{u}$ is path-connected to $\mathbf{v}$, whence $\mathbf{v} \in A$. Further, since $\mathbf{v} \in \text{bd } A = B$, there exists $\mathbf{w} \in A' \cap D_{\mathbf{v}}$. By Exercise 29 there is a path in O from $\mathbf{u}$ to $\mathbf{w}$, which contradicts $\mathbf{w} \in A'$. Thus, in either event a contradiction is obtained. $\square$

Discussion.   This argument, while not a supremum argument, has its motivation in past uses of the supremum principle. Intuitively, we construct the largest possible set, A, and then show A must have the required property, that is, be O itself, or A can be enlarged.

The contents of this theorem are suggestive. One immediately wonders whether every closed connected subset of $\mathbf{R}^2$ is path-connected. The set of Example 5 provides a counterexample, but still leaves a question. Is every closed set which can be obtained as the closure of a connected, nonempty open set path-connected? The reader is invited to provide the answer in Exercise 33. $\square$

EXERCISES

1. Prove Theorem 11.3.1(i) and (ii).

2. Complete all the details in the proof of Theorem 11.3.1(iii).

3. Complete the proof of Lemma 11.3.1.

4. Show that every open subset of $\mathbf{R}^2$ is a union of open discs. Show further that there is an open set which cannot be obtained in a union of pairwise disjoint, open discs.

5. Complete the key details in Example 2.

6. Prove Theorem 11.3.2.

7. Complete the solution of Example 3.

8. Prove Theorem 11.3.3.

9. Show that if A is countable, then $A \times A$ is also countable.

10. For $a \in \mathbf{R}$, consider $|a| = \sqrt{a^2}$. Show that by using this formulation of the absolute value, there is a direct analogy between the proofs of the Triangle inequality for the one and two variablecase.

11. Determine whether the following subsets of $\mathbf{R}^2$ are open, closed, open and closed, or neither:
  (a) $\{(x, y): x = 4\}$;
  (b) $\{(x, y): x > y\}$;
  (c) $\{(x, y): x = y\}$;
  (d) $\{(x, y): x \neq y\}$;
  (e) $\{(x, y): x = 4 \text{ or } y = -3\}$;
  (f) $\{(x, y): 3x/2 = 2y/3\}$;
  (g) $\{(x, y): xy \neq 0\}$;
  (h) $\{(x, y): y > |x|\}$;
  (i) $\{(x, y): 2x + 3y > 7\}$;
  (j) $\{(x, y): x, y \in \mathbf{N}\}$;
  (k) $\{(x, y): x, y \in \mathbf{N} \text{ and } |x + y| < 5\}$;
  (l) $\{(x, y): x, y \in \mathbf{Q}\}$;
  (m) $\{(x, y): x, y \in \mathbf{Q} \text{ and } \mathbf{d}((x, y),(0, 0)) < \pi\}$;
  (n) $\{(x, y): 0 < x^2 + y^2 \leqslant 1 \}$;
  (o) $\{(x, y): 4 < x^2 \text{ and } y \in \mathbf{R} \}$;
  (p) $\{(x, y): 4 < x^2 \text{ and } y \in \mathbf{Q} \}$;
  (q) $\{(x, y): 4 < x^2 \text{ and } y \in \mathbf{N} \}$;
  (r) $\{(x, y): 4 \leqslant x^2 \text{ and } y \in \mathbf{R} \}$;
  (s) $\{(x, y): x^2 = y^2\}$;
  (t) $\{(x, y): x \geqslant 3 \text{ .or. } y < 2\}$;
  (u) $\{(x, y): |x - y| \neq 1\}$;
  (v) $\left\{ (x, y): x = 0 \text{ and } -1 \leqslant y \leqslant 1 \text{ .or. } 0 < x < 1 \text{ and } y = \sin\frac{1}{x} \right\}$;
  (w) $\left\{ (x, y): 0 < x < 1 \text{ .and. } \sin\frac{1}{x} - x < y < \sin\frac{1}{x} \right\}$.

12. Give appropriate examples in $\mathbf{R}^2$ to illustrate the following:
  (a) The intersection of an infinite collection of open sets need not be open;
  (b) The union of an infinite collection of closed sets need not be closed;
  (c) The intersection of an open set with a closed set can be open, closed, or neither;
  (d) The union of an open set with a closed set can be open, closed, or neither.

13. Determine the interior and boundary of each of the subsets in Exercise 11. Which of these sets is bounded?

14. Denoting the boundary of a set, A by bd (A), prove bd $(A) = \bar{A} \cap \overline{(\mathbf{R}^2 \sim A)}$. Prove further that bd (A) consists of all those points $\mathbf{W}$ such that each open disc centered at $\mathbf{W}$ intersects A as well as $\mathbf{R}^2 \sim A$.

15. Prove from the definition that the intersection of two open discs is nonempty, then it always contains an open disc.

16. If $\mathbf{W}, \mathbf{Z} \in \mathbf{R}^2$, $\mathbf{W} \neq \mathbf{Z}$, prove there exist two open discs $D_\mathbf{W}$, $D_\mathbf{Z}$ such that $D_\mathbf{Z} \cap D_\mathbf{W} = \varnothing$.

17. Find necessary and sufficient conditions for equality to hold in the Cauchy–Schwarz inequality.

18. Can Theorem 11.3.5 be sharpened so that a family of pairwise disjoint discs is employed?

19. Let $A \subseteq \mathbf{R}^2$. Show A is connected if and only if for every decomposition of A into nonempty sets, B and C,
$$(\overline{B} \cap C) \cup (B \cap \overline{C}) = \varnothing.$$

20. Let A and B be two connected subsets of $\mathbf{R}^2$ having nonempty intersection. Show $A \cup B$ is connected.

21. Let $A \subseteq \mathbf{R}^2$. For x, $y \in A$, define $x \sim y$ by there exists B such that $x, y \in B \subseteq A$ and B is connected. Show $\sim$ is an equivalence relation on A whose equivalence classes decompose A into maximal connected subsets.

22. Show that a path in $\mathbf{R}^2$ from $\mathbf{u}$ to $\mathbf{v}$ must have finite length.

23. Complete the proof of Theorem 11.3.6.

24. Complete the solution of Example 5.

25. Show $A \subseteq \mathbf{R}^2$ is bounded exactly if there is a $K \in \mathbf{R}$ such that for all $\mathbf{v} \in A$, $d(\mathbf{v}, (0, 0)) < K$.

26. Let $I_{n,k}$, $D_{\mathbf{W}, \epsilon_n}$ be as in the proof of Theorem 11.3.7. Show that if $I_{n,k} \cap D_{\mathbf{W}, \epsilon_n}$ is infinite, then one of $I_{n,2k} \cap D_{\mathbf{W}, \epsilon_n}$ and $I_{n,2k+1} \cap D_{\mathbf{W}, \epsilon_n}$ also must be infinite. Use this fact to show that the required nested sequence of intervals, $\{I_{n,j_n}\}$, exists.

27. Complete the proof of Theorem 11.3.7.

28. Prove Theorem 11.3.8.

29. Show that if there is a path from $\mathbf{x}$ to $\mathbf{u}$ in O and $\mathbf{u}$ to $\mathbf{y}$ in O, then there is a path from $\mathbf{x}$ to $\mathbf{y}$ in O.

30. Complete the details of Theorem 11.3.9.

31. Which of the sets in Exercise 11 are connected? Which are path-connected?

32. Find the maximal connected subsets of the various sets in Exercise 11 which are not connected.

33. Let A be the closure of a connected open subset of $\mathbf{R}^2$. Must A be path-connected?

34. Prove that an infinite binary tree must have an infinite branch.

35. A tree is $\mathbf{n}-\mathbf{ary}$ if the out-degree of each point is n. Prove that an infinite n-ary tree must have an infinite branch.

36. Let $A \subseteq \mathbf{R}^2$. Show that $\bigcap \{B : A \subseteq B\}$ is a closed subset of $\mathbf{R}^2$ which contains A.

37. Let $A \subseteq \mathbf{R}^2$. Show that there is a unique smallest closed set, $\overline{A}$, which contains A. The set $\overline{A}$ is called the **closure** of A.

38. Establish the following properties of closure:
    (a) if A is closed, then $A = \overline{A}$;
    (b) $\overline{\varnothing} = \varnothing$;
    (c) for every $A \subseteq \mathbf{R}^2$, $\overline{A} = \overline{\overline{A}}$;
    (d) for every $A, B \subseteq \mathbf{R}^2$, $\overline{A} \cup \overline{B} = \overline{(A \cup B)}$.
    Are the properties listed above in any way dependent on the nature (precise definition) of the topological space in which we are working? Could they, for example, be extended to $\mathbf{R}^3$?

39. Find the closures of the various sets listed in Exercise 11.

40. Prove or disprove:
(a) $\overline{\cap A} = \cap \overline{A}$;
(b) $\overline{\cup A} = \cup \overline{A}$.
where A is an arbitrary family of subsets of $\mathbf{R}^2$.

41. Let $A \subseteq \mathbf{R}^2$, and set $A_{lm} = \{x : x$ is a limit point of $A\}$. Show that $A \cup A_{lm}$ is closed. Is there a relation between $\overline{A}$ and $A \cup A_{lm}$?

42. Find A_{lm} for each of the sets in Exercise 11.

43. Let $A \subseteq \mathbf{R}^2$. Then, $\mathbf{z} \in A$ is called an **isolated point** of A provided there is an open disc $D_{\mathbf{z}}$ such that $D_{\mathbf{z}} \cap A = \{\mathbf{z}\}$. Show
(a) if A is open, then A has no isolated points;
(b) if A is closed, then for each $\mathbf{z} \in A$, $\mathbf{z}$ is either an isolated point of A or a limit point of A.
Prove or disprove: If every point of A is isolated, then A is closed.

44. Find the isolated points for each of the sets in Exercise 11.

45. Is it true that if every point of A is a limit point of A, that A is closed?

46. A set $A \subseteq \mathbf{R}^2$ is **clopen** if it is both open and closed. Give an example of a clopen subset of $\mathbf{R}^2$. Find all clopen subsets of $\mathbf{R}^2$.

47. Let A°, $\overline{A}$, and A' denote, respectively, the interior, the closure, and the complement of A. Show that for any $A \subseteq \mathbf{R}^2$,
(a) $A^{\circ\circ} = A^{\circ}$;
(b) $(A \cap B)^{\circ} = A^{\circ} \cap B^{\circ}$; (can $\cap$ be replaced by $\cup$?);
(c) $(A')^{\circ} = (\overline{A})'$.

48. Is the following (see Exercise 3.1.30) true in $\mathbf{R}^2$? For a fixed $A \subseteq \mathbf{R}^2$, there are at most fourteen distinct sets which can be obtained from A by successive applications of the operations of $^{\circ}$, $^{-}$, and $'$.

49. For $A \subseteq \mathbf{R}^2$, show bd $A = \overline{A} \cap \overline{(A')}$ and prove the following:
(a) $\overline{A} = A \cup$ bd (A);
(b) $A^{\circ} = A \sim$ bd (A);
(c) $\mathbf{R}^2 = A^{\circ} \cup$ bd $(A) \cup A'^{\circ}$.

50. Define the **exterior** of A, Ext (A), to be the complement of the closure of A. Prove or disprove: Ext $(A \cup B) =$ Ext $(A) \cap$ Ext (B).

51. Find the exterior of each of the sets in Exercise 11.

52. Let $D \subseteq \mathbf{R}^2$. We define the **relative topology** on D by calling a subset $U \subseteq D$ open (relative to D) if and only if $U = A \cap D$ for some open subset $A \subseteq \mathbf{R}^2$. We also say that U is **relatively open** in D. Prove the following results for $A \subseteq D$:
(a) A point $\mathbf{z} \in D$ is a limit point of $A \subseteq D$ with respect to the relative topology on D if and only if it is a limit point of A in $\mathbf{R}^2$;
(b) The closure of a subset $A \subseteq D$ with respect to the relative topology on D is the set $\overline{A} \cap D$;
(c) The set $A \subseteq D$ is closed in the relative topology on D if and only if $A = X \cap D$, where X is a closed set in $\mathbf{R}^2$.

11.4 CONVERGENCE OF SEQUENCES AND TOPOLOGY OF THE PLANE

The thrust of this section will be to study the convergence of a sequence of points in the plane. The properties of such sequences bear a strong relationship to various topological properties of the plane, and it is these relationships which are of particular interest. The properties which are being developed here are generalizations of the properties developed in section 3.2 for $\mathbf{R}$. Thus, the reader may find it useful to review that section as a prerequisite to the study of this one.

Definition. A **sequence in the plane** is a function whose domain is the set $\mathbf{N}$ of natural numbers and the range is a subset of $\mathbf{R}^2$.

Discussion. Sequences in any set are characterized as being functions from $\mathbf{N}$ into that set. In the present case the range is a subset of $\mathbf{R}^2$, whence we are dealing with sequences of points in the plane. The functions of immediate interest have the form $\mathbf{W}: \mathbf{N} \rightarrow \mathbf{R}^2$. Instead of $\mathbf{W}(n)$, we usually write $\mathbf{W}_n$ to denote values of the sequence. Since $\mathbf{W}_n$ is in $\mathbf{R}^2$, two ordinary sequences are required to generate the components, whence $\mathbf{W}_n = (x_n, y_n)$, where $x_n, y_n \in \mathbf{R}$. The sequence itself can be referred to as $\{\mathbf{W}_n\}$ or in component form, $\{(x_n, y_n)\}$.

In section 11.2, we have already considered a type of sequence, namely a function from $\mathbf{N} \times \mathbf{N}$ into $\mathbf{R}$, which we called double sequences. Double sequences added very little to the theory we had developed about the nature of the plane. This might seem surprising, since sequences were a tool for providing significant insight into the topology of $\mathbf{R}$. However, in the case of $\mathbf{R}$, the values of the usual sequences were in $\mathbf{R}$. For double sequences, the values were also in $\mathbf{R}$, not in $\mathbf{R}^2$. Thus, the behavior of double sequences could tell us little about the topology of $\mathbf{R}^2$. The sequences under study in this section, which have their range in $\mathbf{R}^2$, should offer more insight in the nature of $\mathbf{R}^2$.   □

Definition. Let $\{\mathbf{W}_n\} = \{(x_n, y_n)\}$ be a sequence. A point, $\mathbf{W}_0 = (x_0, y_0)$, is said to be the **limit** of the sequence, $\{\mathbf{W}_n\}$, provided for every $\epsilon > 0$, there exists $N \in \mathbf{N}$ such that

$$n \geqslant N \quad \text{implies} \quad \mathbf{d}(\mathbf{W}_n, \mathbf{W}_0) = \mathbf{d}((x_n, y_n), (x_0, y_0)) < \epsilon.$$

Discussion. This definition is almost identical to the definition of limit of a sequence given in Chapter 1. The only difference is that we are considering pairs of real numbers, instead of real numbers, and the distance function, $\mathbf{d}$, replaces the absolute value in the original definition. More precisely, the term, $|x_n - A|$, in the old definition now becomes $\mathbf{d}(\mathbf{W}_n, \mathbf{W}_0)$.

Examination of the present definition reveals the condition, $\mathbf{d}(\mathbf{W}_n, \mathbf{W}_0) < \epsilon$, translates into

$$\sqrt{(x_n - x_0)^2 + (y_n - y_0)^2} < \epsilon,$$

or equivalently,

$$(x_n - x_0)^2 + (y_n - y_0)^2 < \epsilon^2.$$

One immediately concludes that the inequality will eventually be satisfied if and only if the two sequences, $\{x_n\}$ and $\{y_n\}$, converge to x_0, and y_0, respectively (Exercise 1). In other words, the convergence of a sequence in $\mathbf{R}^2$ reduces to coordinatewise convergence, that is, each component sequence converges separately to the corresponding component of the limit. This is the reason why the convergence in a product space is usually referred to as coordinatewise convergence. $\square$

EXAMPLE 1 _____

Let $\{\mathbf{w}_n\}$ be given by $\mathbf{w}_n = \left[\dfrac{(-1)^n}{n}, \dfrac{1}{n} \right]$. Show that this sequence has a limit.

Solution. Let $\mathbf{w} = (0, 0)$ and fix $\epsilon > 0$. Let $N > \dfrac{2}{\epsilon}$, then for $n \geqslant N$,

$$\mathbf{d}(\mathbf{w}_n, \mathbf{w}) = \sqrt{\frac{1}{n^2} + \frac{1}{n^2}} = \frac{\sqrt{2}}{n} < \epsilon.$$

$\square$

Discussion. In view of Exercise 1, an alternative proof of convergence would simply observe that both of the component sequences converge. $\square$

Definition. A sequence $\{\mathbf{w}_n\}$ in $\mathbf{R}^2$ is said to be bounded, if there is a fixed $\mathbf{w}_0$ and an $M \in \mathbf{N}$ such that for all $n \in \mathbf{N}$,

$$\mathbf{d}(\mathbf{w}_n, \mathbf{w}_0) \leqslant M.$$

Discussion. This definition is completely equivalent to saying that the set, $\{\mathbf{w}_n : n \in \mathbf{N}\}$ is bounded. $\square$

Given that the convergence of a sequence $\{\mathbf{w}_n\}$ is completely determined by the convergence or nonconvergence of the two component sequences, $\{x_n\}$ and $\{y_n\}$, we would expect that there should be a strong relationship between convergence in $\mathbf{R}$ and convergence in $\mathbf{R}^2$. Indeed, we would expect that most of our earlier theorems on limits of a convergent sequence will hold in this situation as well.

Theorem 11.4.1. The limit of a convergent sequence of points in the plane is unique. Further, a convergent sequence of points in the plane is bounded.

Proof. Exercise 2. $\square$

Discussion. The contrapositive of the second part of this theorem asserts that an unbounded sequence cannot converge. This fact should seem completely obvious to the reader. It should also be transparent that if a sequence oscillates, in the sense that it has an infinite number of terms close to two distinct real numbers, it cannot converge. Of course, one wonders whether these are the only reasons why a sequence of points in the plane can fail to converge. The reader may wish to consider these questions in relation to the assertion that convergence in the plane is equivalent to componentwise convergence of the associated sequences. $\square$

Theorem 11.4.2. Let $\{\mathbf{u}_n\}$ and $\{\mathbf{v}_n\}$ be two convergent sequences of points in the plane having limits $\mathbf{u}$ and $\mathbf{v}$, respectively. Let addition and multiplication be performed coordinatewise. Then

$$\lim_{n \to \infty} (\mathbf{u}_n + \mathbf{v}_n) = \mathbf{u} + \mathbf{v} \quad \text{and} \quad \lim_{n \to \infty} (\mathbf{u}_n \cdot \mathbf{v}_n) = \mathbf{u} \cdot \mathbf{v}.$$

Proof. Exercise 3. $\square$

Discussion. One of the features of analysis which we have stressed in this text has been the force of the underlying algebraic structure as an analytical tool. For this reason, one would like to have an algebraic structure defined on $\mathbf{R}^2$ with which to work. Further, one would like to have the closest possible relationship between the algebraic structure on $\mathbf{R}$ and the extended structure on $\mathbf{R}^2$. The most natural and simplest way to extend the algebraic structure from $\mathbf{R}$ to $\mathbf{R}^2$ is to define the algebraic operations componentwise. After all, we have just finished remarking that the limit definition is essentially a componentwise definition, so why not do the same with algebra? The content of the present theorem would also serve to justify this approach. The difficulty is with the algebra.

If one asks what algebraic structure should result, one concludes that the desirable structure would be that $\{\mathbf{R}^2, \oplus, \otimes, (0, 0), (1, 1)\}$ constitutes a field, where $\oplus$ and $\otimes$ denote the additive and multiplicative operations on $\mathbf{R}^2$ and $(0, 0)$ and $(1, 1)$ denote the additive and multiplicative identities, respectively. The reader can verify that if $\oplus$ and $\otimes$ are componentwise addition and multiplication, then $\{\mathbf{R}^2, \oplus, \otimes, (0, 0), (1, 1)\}$ is not a field (Exercise 4). Of course there is a way to make $\mathbf{R}^2$ into a field and solve several other problems simultaneously, namely, one can define multiplication so that the result is the usual complex numbers. This process retains componentwise addition, changing only the multiplicative operation. Moreover, in the process, one still obtains a theorem similar to 11.4.2. However, further discussion of the complex numbers is beyond the scope of this book. $\square$

Definition. A sequence $\{\mathbf{w}_n\}$ is said to be a **Cauchy sequence** provided for every $\epsilon > 0$ there exists $N \in \mathbf{N}$ such that

$$|\mathbf{w}_n - \mathbf{w}_m| < \epsilon \quad \text{whenever} \quad n, m > N.$$

Discussion. The reader should recognize this as a typical Cauchy criterion. $\square$

EXAMPLE 2 _____

Let $\{\mathbf{w}_n\}$ be given by $\mathbf{w}_n = \left(\dfrac{k}{n}, \dfrac{k}{n} \right)$, where k is the largest integer such that $\dfrac{k}{n} < \sqrt{2}$. Show that this sequence is Cauchy.

Solution. Let $\epsilon > 0$ be given and let $N > \dfrac{2}{\epsilon}$ be fixed. Now suppose $\mathbf{w}_n =$

$$\left[\frac{k}{n}, \frac{k}{n} \right] \text{ and } \mathbf{W}_m = \left[\frac{j}{m}, \frac{j}{m} \right] \text{ with } m > n, \text{ then } \frac{k-1}{n} < \frac{j}{m} < \frac{k+1}{n}$$

(**WHY?**). Thus, if $n > N$, the Cauchy criterion is satisfied and the sequence is Cauchy. $\qquad\square$

Discussion. The first reason we are interested in Cauchy sequences is that they are convergent. The second is that one can identify Cauchy sequences with no reference to a limit. Indeed, the limit of a Cauchy sequence need not exist within the space in which the sequence resides.

In the present case, it is easily seen that the sequence converges to $(\sqrt{2}, \sqrt{2})$. However, considered as a sequence in $\mathbf{Q} \times \mathbf{Q}$, the sequence remains Cauchy, but is not convergent because one cannot find a limit for the sequence, since $(\sqrt{2}, \sqrt{2}) \notin \mathbf{Q} \times \mathbf{Q}$. If one thinks about this, one sees that one could identify the missing point $(\sqrt{2}, \sqrt{2})$ from within the space $\mathbf{Q} \times \mathbf{Q}$ by considering a Cauchy sequence which converged to it. This idea will be pursued in Exercises 32–35. $\qquad\square$

Theorem 11.4.3. A sequence of points in the plane is convergent exactly if it is Cauchy.

Proof. The proof that a convergent sequence is Cauchy is left to Exercise 5. We show that a Cauchy sequence has a limit, thus let $\{\mathbf{W}_n = (x_n, y_n)\}$ be a Cauchy sequence. Then each of the component sequences $\{x_n\}$ and $\{y_n\}$ is Cauchy, and so has a limit (**WHY?**). Let the respective limits be denoted by x and y and set $\mathbf{W} = (x, y)$. For any fixed $\epsilon > 0$, we can choose N such that $n > N$ implies

$$|x_n - x| < \frac{\epsilon}{2} \text{ and } |y_n - y| < \frac{\epsilon}{2}. \qquad \textbf{(WHY)}$$

It follows that $n > N$ implies $\mathbf{d}(\mathbf{W}_n, \mathbf{W}) < \epsilon$ (**WHY?**), whence $\mathbf{W}$ is the required limit. $\qquad\square$

Discussion. The fact that every Cauchy sequence in the plane has a limit means that the plane, like $\mathbf{R}$, is **complete**. This fact is a direct consequence of completeness in $\mathbf{R}$ and the fact that convergence in the plane is equivalent to convergence in each of the components. $\qquad\square$

Even though there are substantial similarities between $\mathbf{R}^2$ and $\mathbf{R}$, we may still expect that there will be differences due to the fact that we now have, from the coordinate point of view, two sequences of real numbers to keep track of instead of only one. And, as we have already pointed out, we no longer have a linearly ordered set with which to work. Let us digress for a moment to expand on this theme.

In the case of $\mathbf{R}$, the usual topology on $\mathbf{R}$ and the notion of order are intrinsically tied together. To see how, let us fix $x, y, z \in \mathbf{R}$ and related by the intuitive topological fact that y is closer to x than z is to x. Now this fact has all kinds of implications with respect to the mutual order relations, since it immediately leads to the inequality

$$|x - y| < |x - z|.$$

Similarly, we know that various things are forbidden, for example, we could not have $x < z < y$. As well, by Theorems 3.1.4 and 3.1.5, every open set can be obtained as a union of sets of the form, $\{x : a < x < b\}$. For this reason, the usual topology on $\mathbf{R}$ is referred to as the **order topology.**

Another obvious, but important, consequence of the relationship between topology and order on $\mathbf{R}$ is the fact that if we fix a positive distance, d_0, then there will be exactly two real numbers whose distance from x is d_0. Now consider the situation in $\mathbf{R}^2$. If we fix a distance, d_0, and for a fixed $\mathbf{w}$ ask how many $\mathbf{u}$'s are at this fixed distance from $\mathbf{w}$, the answer is uncountably many $\mathbf{u}$'s. Any attempt to remedy this situation would ignore the obvious geometric structure inherent in the real world which $\mathbf{R}^2$ is designed to capture.

Let us return now to our main theme. What we are interested in is looking at the deeper question of why sequences in $\mathbf{R}^2$ either do, or do not, converge. For sequences of real numbers, we found that divergence could be accounted for by one of two reasons, either the sequence was unbounded, or the sequence oscillated. In the latter case, if the sequence was bounded, then by the Bolzano-Weierstrass Theorem, we were guaranteed that the sequence at least had a cluster point. Quite obviously we would like to know whether analogous theorems are valid for $\mathbf{R}^2$. The most direct approach toward this goal is through additional results about the topology of $\mathbf{R}^2$. Our first item will be to consider the relationship of open sets in $\mathbf{R}^2$ to open sets in $\mathbf{R}$.

Theorem 11.4.4. Let A be an open subset of $\mathbf{R}^2$ and

$$A_1 = \{x : \text{for some } y \, ((x, y) \in A)\}.$$

Then A_1 is open. Similarly, if A is closed (bounded), A_1 will be closed (bounded).

Proof. Fix $x \in A_1$, then for some y, $(x, y) \in A$. But this means there is an $r > 0$ such that $D_{(x,y),r} \subseteq A$. It follows that the open interval $(x - r, x + r)$ is a subset of A_1, whence A_1 is open. The remaining parts are left as Exercise 6. □

Discussion. The set A_1 is usually called the **first projection** of A. It is the subset of $\mathbf{R}$ which is obtained by ignoring the second coordinates, or put another way, the set which results by retaining only the first coordinates. Similarly, we have a **second projection** formed by retaining only the second coordinates.

Looking at projections can be useful because one can use the properties of the resultant sets, to obtain clues about the original sets. The reader should note, however, that except for very special cases, $A \neq A_1 \times A_2$.

Given the previous assertions to the effect that convergence in $\mathbf{R}^2$ is equivalent to componentwise convergence in $\mathbf{R}$, it should not be surprising the topological properties of a set can be translated to properties about the projections. But the caveat above should suggest to the reader that what comes down will not always go up again. □

Definition. A collection of subsets of the plane, C, is said to **cover** a set, A, provided $A \subseteq \bigcup C$. C is an **open** cover if each member of C is an open set. A subset A of $\mathbf{R}^2$ is said to be **compact** if for every collection, C, of open sets which covers A there is a finite subcollection of C which also covers A.

Discussion.   There are several features of this definition of importance. First, C is not a subset of the plane. It is a collection of subsets of the plane. Thus, $B \in C$ implies $B \subseteq \mathbf{R}^2$. Second, C covers A provided to each $x \in A$ we can find a member of C, say B, such that $x \in B$. Finally, A will be compact provided for every open cover C of A there is a finite sequence, $C_1, \ldots, C_n$ such that each $C_i \in C$ and $A \subseteq \bigcup_{i=1}^{n} C_i$. Simply stated, A is compact if every open cover of A has a finite subcover. $\square$

The definitions of open cover and compact were discussed briefly in Chapter 3, principally in relation to the Heine–Borel Theorem. We want to discuss them more fully here, and develop the important relationship between compact and closed bounded subsets of the plane. We begin by proving a theorem on nests of closed bounded subsets of $\mathbf{R}^2$.

Theorem 11.4.5.   Let $A_n \subseteq \mathbf{R}^2$, $n \in \mathbf{N}$ be a collection of nonempty, closed, bounded sets such that $A_{n+1} \subset A_n$. Then $\bigcap_{n=1}^{\infty} A_n \neq \varnothing$.

Proof.   For $n \in \mathbf{N}$, define

$$I_{1,n} = \{x : \text{ for some } \mathbf{W}, (\mathbf{W} \in A_n \text{ and } \mathbf{W} = (x, y))\}.$$

The reader can show $I_{1,n+1} \subseteq I_{1,n}$ (**WHY?**). By Theorem 11.4.4, each of the $I_{1,n}$'s is closed and bounded, so by the theorem on nested systems of closed, bounded subsets of $\mathbf{R}$, the intersection is nonempty. Thus, fix $x^* \in \bigcap_{n=1}^{\infty} I_{1,n}$. Now $x^* \in I_n$ for all n, whence for each n we can find y_0 such that $(x^*, y_0) \in A_n$. It follows that

$$B_n = \{(x^*, y) : (x^*, y) \in A_n\}$$

is a nonempty, closed (**WHY?**) subset of A_n and further, $B_{n+1} \subseteq B_n$. Now set

$$I_{2,n} = \{y : (x^*, y) \in B_n\}$$

and it follows $I_{2,n} \neq \varnothing$. By Theorem 11.4.4, each $I_{2,n}$ is closed and bounded. We claim (Exercise 8) the sequence, $\{I_n\}$, is nested. By the result on nests we again see that the intersection is nonempty. Picking a y^* in the intersection yields the desired (x^*, y^*) in the intersection of the A_n's (**WHY?**). $\square$

Discussion.   In generating a proof for the above, one is tempted to simply generate $I_{1,n}$ and $I_{2,n}$ and use each to find an x^* and a y^*. Having done this, one is left with trying to show that (x^*, y^*) is indeed in the intersection of the A_n's. The reader should try this approach so that he can appreciate the difficulties which arise, and perhaps even generate an appropriate counterexample.

This proof illustrates both the power of projections, and the care with which this power must be applied. $\square$

EXAMPLE 3 _____

Show that the unit square, $A = \{(x, y) : 0 \leqslant x, y \leqslant 1\}$, is compact.

Solution. Let C be an open cover of A. Suppose that C has no finite subcover. Now for each n, consider the collection of rectangles, $A_{n,i,j}$, where i, $j = 0, \ldots, 2^n - 1$ is defined by

$$A_{n,i,j} = \{(x, y) : i2^{-n} \leqslant x \leqslant (i+1)2^{-n} \text{ and } j2^{-n} \leqslant y \leqslant (j+1)2^{-n}\}.$$

If each of these subsets has a finite subcover from C, then A itself can be covered by a finite collection of members of C. Thus, for some i and j, $A_{n,i,j}$ has no finite subcover from C. Now construct a tree, T, where $(A_{n,i,j}, A_{m,l,k}) \in T$ if and only if $n = m+1$ and $A_{n,i,j} \subseteq A_{m,l,k}$. It is easily checked that all ordered pairs in T such that the second coordinate has no finite subcover from C generate an infinite subtree, S. By the Fan Theorem for 4-ary trees, S has an infinite branch. We denote by S_n, the unique member of the field S of the form, $A_{n,i,j}$. Now the sequence, $\{S_n\}$, is a nested collection of nonempty, closed sets. It follows that $\bigcap_{n=1}^{\infty} S_n \neq \varnothing$, and in fact must consist of a single point, $\mathbf{w}$ (Exercise 10). But $\mathbf{w} \in A$, whence there exists $B \in C$ such that $\mathbf{w} \in B$. Since B is open, there is a disc, $D_{\mathbf{w},r}$, which is completely contained in B. But $r > 0$, whence for some n, $S_n \subseteq B$ (**WHY?**). This contradicts the choice of S_n (**HOW?**). Thus, C must have a finite subcover. □

Discussion. The critical idea in the solution to this example is to realize that if the square cannot be covered by a finite subcollection from C and we subdivide the square into a finite number of parts, then some one of these parts also must not be finitely coverable. Once this idea is understood, one simply pushes it to the limit by applying the Fan Theorem to construct a suitable nested sequence.

We stress that the ideas in this proof are key concepts in terms of the total understanding of compactness. They occur in more general form many times in topology. □

EXAMPLE 4 _____

Show the set $A = \left\{ \left[\dfrac{1}{n}, \dfrac{1}{n} \right] : n \in \mathbf{N} \right\}$ is not compact.

Solution. Let $r_n = \dfrac{1}{2n}$, $\mathbf{w}_n = (\dfrac{1}{n}, \dfrac{1}{n})$ and

$$C = \{D_{\mathbf{w}_n, r_n} : n \in \mathbf{N}\}.$$

Since $\mathbf{w}_n \in D_{\mathbf{w}_n, r_n}$, C covers A. But any finite collection of members of C must have a member with maximum subscript, say m, whence $\mathbf{w}_{3m}$ is not covered by this subcollection (**WHY?**). □

Discussion. This example illustrates why a set must be closed in order to be compact and how to construct a cover for which the finite subcover property fails. In the latter instance, the critical feature of the construction is that none of the elements comprising the cover contain the limit point which witnesses that A is not closed. □

One of our aims in this section was to prove the Bolzano–Weierstrass Theorem for $\mathbf{R}^2$. The next theorem yields the Bolzano–Weierstrass Theorem as a consequence.

Theorem 11.4.6. A bounded infinite set in the plane has a limit point.

Proof. Call the bounded infinite set B. If B has a limit point, we are done. Thus, assume B has no limit points, whence it is closed (**WHY?**). Since B is bounded, there exists M such that

$$B \subseteq A = \{(x, y) : -M \leqslant x, y \leqslant M\}. \qquad \textbf{(WHY?)}$$

Notice that $B \cap A$ is closed and bounded. Further, if C is a closed subset of A, then $B \cap C$ is closed and bounded. It is now possible to construct a nested sequence using the same ideas as in Example 3. The reader can then show that the intersection of this nested sequence is a single point, which must be a limit point of B (Exercise 12). $\square$

Discussion. In Exercise 13 the reader is asked to construct an alternate proof of this theorem using projections and appropriate theorems about **R**.

This theorem supplies us with the means to answer the question, why does a sequence of points in the plane fail to converge? As we shall see, that answer is the same as for **R**. $\square$

Definition. Let $\{\mathbf{w}_n\}$ be a sequence of points in the plane, and let $\{n_k\}$ denote an increasing sequence of members of **N**. The point **W** is a **cluster point** of $\{\mathbf{w}_n\}$ provided for some sequence, $\{n_k\}$, $\{\mathbf{w}_{n_k}\}$ converges to **W**.

Discussion. In straightforward terms, **W** is a cluster point for $\{\mathbf{w}_n\}$ exactly if there is a subsequence of $\{\mathbf{w}_n\}$ which converges to **W**. This is exactly analogous to the definition of cluster point given in Chapter 3 relative to **R**. $\square$

Corollary. A bounded sequence of points in the plane has a cluster point.

Proof. Exercise 14. $\square$

Discussion. By employing analogous arguments to those sketched in section 3.2 it is now possible to show that a nonconvergent sequence of points in the plane must either be unbounded, or must have at least two cluster points, that is, oscillate (Exercise 15).

Theorem 11.4.7. Let $\{\mathbf{w}_n\}$ be a sequence of points in $\mathbf{R}^2$ and let A denote its set of cluster points. Then,

  (i) $\{\mathbf{w}_n\}$ converges, if A has exactly one member, and $\{\mathbf{w}_n\}$ is bounded;
  (ii) $\{\mathbf{w}_n\}$ diverges, if A has more than one member;
  (iii) $\{\mathbf{w}_n\}$ diverges, if $A = \varnothing$.

Proof. We prove (i) and leave the others to Exercises 14 and 15. Let **W** be the unique cluster point of the sequence and let $\epsilon > 0$ be given. We claim that there exists $N \in \mathbf{N}$ such that $n > N$ implies $\mathbf{d}(\mathbf{W}, \mathbf{w}_n) < \epsilon$. Suppose this is not the case. Then there is an infinite subset of terms of the sequence none of which lie inside the disc, $D_{\mathbf{W}, \epsilon}$. This infinite collection constitutes a bounded subsequence which must have a cluster point. But this cluster point cannot be **w** (**WHY?**), whence the hypothesis is contradicted. $\qquad\square$

Discussion. The additional hypothesis in (i) to the effect that $\{\mathbf{w}_n\}$ is bounded is essential, since it is this fact which permits the generation of the additional cluster point. The reader can check that if $\mathbf{w}_n = (0, 2^{(-1)^n n})$, then $\{\mathbf{w}_n\}$ is an example of a nonconvergent sequence with exactly one cluster point. $\qquad\square$

Theorem 11.4.8. Let A be a subset of $\mathbf{R}^2$. The following are equivalent:

    (i) A is closed and bounded;
   (ii) A is compact;
  (iii) every infinite subset of A has a limit point in A.

Proof. Suppose (i) holds. Let $C = \{C_\alpha : \alpha \in I\}$, where I is an index set, be an arbitrary open cover of A. If some finite subset of C covers A, we are done. Thus, we suppose that no finite subcollection will cover A and seek a contradiction. Since A is bounded, there exists $M \in \mathbf{N}$ such that $-M \leqslant x, y \leqslant M$ for all $(x, y) \in A$. Then we define the rectangles, $A_{n,i,j}$, where $i, j = 0, \ldots, 2^n - 1$ by

$$A_{n,i,j} = \{(x, y) : Mi2^{-n+1} \leqslant x \leqslant M(i+1)2^{-n+1} \text{ .and. } Mj2^{-n+1} \leqslant y \leqslant M(j+1)2^{-n+1}\}.$$

The argument of Example 3 is now repeated to establish compactness, Exercise 16.

Suppose (ii) holds. We give an indirect argument to prove (iii). Thus, suppose that A has an infinite subset, B, which has no limit point in A. There are two possibilities, either B is unbounded, or B is bounded. The former case is left to the reader (Exercise 18). Thus, assume B is bounded. By Theorem 11.4.6, B must have a limit point, call it $\mathbf{b}$. Now for $\mathbf{w} \in A$ set $r_{\mathbf{w}} = \dfrac{d(\mathbf{w}, \mathbf{b})}{2}$ and let $C = \{D_{\mathbf{w}, r_{\mathbf{w}}} : \mathbf{w} \in A\}$. The reader can check that C covers A and $\mathbf{b} \notin \bigcup C$ (**WHY?**). Since $\mathbf{b}$ is a limit point of A it follows that no finite subcover of C can cover A (**WHY?**). This contradicts the assumption that A is compact.

The proof that (iii) implies (i) is left to Exercise 19. $\qquad\square$

Discussion. This theorem draws together three important properties. The first, closed and bounded, requires the set A to be the complement of an open set, and in addition to spatially small, that is, finite in extent. The former property of being closed is a classic topological property, and as such, can be discussed in any topological setting. The second, bounded, appears to require the concept of distance. Even though the present notion of open set was defined by using open discs which employed the notion of radius (distance), more general approaches to topology and open set do not require any notion of distance as a prerequisite for their definition. For this reason, it is not clear what role the concept of bounded has to play in a general topological setting.

The second notion, of being compact, belongs completely to the domain of topology, or so it would seem at first glance. Compactness relates to open covers of a set, and such covers can be discussed in any topological context, since the notion of open set is at the foundation of topology. The remainder of the definition talks about finite subcovers. Subcovers are clearly still completely in the domain of topology. The concept that is not purely topological, is that of being 'finite'. And it is this property that relates to 'bounded'. To see how, focus on the fact that the coverings are arbitrary. As such, we may expect that some particular coverings will consist only of spatially small sets, even if there is no concept of distance available in the space under study. Since even a covering which is composed of very small sets must satisfy the finite subcover property, we may expect that the union over a finite number of these small sets cannot be too large in extent. Thus, we see that in going from closed and bounded to compact, we have merely replaced one type of finiteness by another. As a last point, observe that the notion of compact is only interesting for sets, A, which are infinite. A finite set is automatically compact, and for that matter, closed and bounded.

Consider the third property, that every infinite subset of A has a limit point in A. Again two main properties are dealt with. The first, related to limit points, is completely topological in nature. The second relates to the cardinality of a set. In this case, the cardinality of the subset must be infinite. If one thinks about how a set can fail to be closed and bounded, it can either fail to be closed, or fail to be bounded. Recall that closed is equivalent to containing all its limit points. So why isn't closed enough? Again, notice that for there to be anything of interest happening at all, A must be infinite. The simplest case of an unbounded set which is also closed, is that given by an unbounded sequence $\{\mathbf{w}_n\}$. Evidently, (see Exercise 20 below), it is possible to construct such a sequence which has no limit points at all, and for this reason is closed. Thus, our third property is saying that the set in question cannot be closed for this reason, that is, lack of existence of limit points.   □

EXERCISES

1. Show that a sequence of points in the plane, $\{(x_n, y_n)\}$, converges exactly if the two associated component sequences converge.

2. Prove Theorem 11.4.1.

3. Prove Theorem 11.4.2.

4. Show that $\mathbf{R}^2$ is not a field under componentwise addition and multiplication.

5. Show that a convergent sequence of points in the plane is Cauchy. Show also that if $\{\mathbf{w}_n\}$ is Cauchy, then each of its component sequences is Cauchy.

6. Complete the proof of Theorem 11.4.4.

7. Consider the list of sets in Exercise 11.3.11. Find the first and second projections for all of these sets. In each case identify the topological properties shared by the projections and the parent set. In which cases can the parent set be obtained as the direct product of the projections?

8. Complete the proof of Theorem 11.4.5.

9. Give a proof of Theorem 11.4.6 using projections.

10. Complete all details of Example 3. In particular show that the intersection of the S_n's must be a single point.

11. For a bounded subset of the plane, A, define its **width** by

$$\text{width } A = \inf \{K : K \in \mathbf{R} \text{ and for all } \mathbf{u}, \mathbf{v} \in A \ \mathbf{d}(\mathbf{u}, \mathbf{v}) < K\}.$$

Show if $\{A_n\}$ is a nested sequence of nonempty, closed sets whose width shrinks to 0, then $\bigcap A_n$ is a single point.

12. Complete the proof of Theorem 11.4.6.

13. Construct a proof of Theorem 11.4.6 by using projections and appealing to the appropriate results about **R**.

14. Show every bounded sequence of points in the plane has a cluster point.

15. Show a nonconvergent sequence of points in the plane must either be unbounded, or oscillate.

16. Complete the argument that a closed bounded set of points in the plane is compact (Theorem 11.4.8).

17. Which of the sets in Exercise 11.3.11 are compact?

18. Show no unbounded subset of the plane is compact. Show that every finite subset of the plane is compact.

19. Complete the proof of Theorem 11.4.8 by showing that (iii) implies (i).

20. Give an example of an infinite sequence of points in the plane which has no limit points, and hence is closed.

21. Discuss the convergence or divergence of the following sequences $\{w_n\} = \{(x_n, y_n)\}$ in $\mathbf{R}^2$.

    (a) $\left[\dfrac{1}{n}, (-1)^n \right]$;

    (b) (x_n, y_n) where

$$ x_n = \frac{3n^2 - 2n + 6}{2n^2 + 4n - 2} \quad \text{and} \quad y_n = \begin{cases} \dfrac{1}{n}, & \text{if } n \text{ is odd} \\ 2 - \dfrac{1}{n}, & \text{otherwise.} \end{cases} $$

22. Let $\{\mathbf{w}_n\} = (x_n, y_n)$. Show if $\{x_n\}$ and $\{y_n\}$ are both monotonic and bounded, then $\{\mathbf{w}_n\}$ is convergent.

23. Prove or disprove: if a sequence, $\{\mathbf{w}_n\}$, in $\mathbf{R}^2$ has exactly one limit point, then it is convergent.

24. Prove or disprove: if a sequence, $\{\mathbf{w}_n\}$, in $\mathbf{R}^2$ has two or more limit points, then it is divergent.

25. Prove or disprove: if a sequence, $\{\mathbf{w}_n\}$, in $\mathbf{R}^2$ has no limit points then it can be either divergent or convergent.

26. Let A be a closed subset of $\mathbf{R}^2$. Show that $A_{1,x}$ is closed for all $x \in \mathbf{R}$, where

$$ A_{1,x} = \{y : (y, x) \in A\}. $$

27. Let A and B be open subsets of $\mathbf{R}$. Show $A \times B$ is an open subset of $\mathbf{R}^2$.

28. Let A be a bounded subset of $\mathbf{R}^2$. Show A is contained in a subset of $\mathbf{R}^2$ of the form $\{(x, y) : x_0 \leqslant x \leqslant x_1 \text{ and } y_0 \leqslant y \leqslant y_1\}$. Such a set is referred to as a **rectangle**.

29. Let $\mathbf{u}$ and $\mathbf{v}$ be any two points in the plane. Show there are two open discs, D_u and D_v centered at $\mathbf{u}$ and $\mathbf{v}$, respectively, and such that $D_u \cap D_v = \varnothing$.

30. Let $D \subseteq \mathbf{R}$ be compact and f be defined on D. Show f is continuous on D if and only if $\{(x, f(x)) : x \in D\}$ is compact, that is, the graph of f is a compact subset of the plane.

31. Let $\{\mathbf{w}_n\}$ be a sequence in $\mathbf{R}^2$. Suppose that for every $\epsilon > 0$ there exist $i, j \in \mathbf{N}$, $i \neq j$ such that $0 < \mathbf{d}(\mathbf{w}_i, \mathbf{w}_j) < \epsilon$. Is it true that $\{\mathbf{w}_n\}$ must have a limit point?

32. Consider the set $\mathbf{Q} \times \mathbf{Q}$, with the same distance function as is employed in $\mathbf{R}^2$. A sequence, $\{\mathbf{w}_n\}$, of elements of $\mathbf{Q} \times \mathbf{Q}$ is **Cauchy** if it is a Cauchy sequence in $\mathbf{R}^2$. Let $\mathbf{C}_{\mathbf{Q} \times \mathbf{Q}}$ denote the collection of all Cauchy sequences of members of $\mathbf{Q} \times \mathbf{Q}$. Define $\sim$ on $\mathbf{C}_{\mathbf{Q} \times \mathbf{Q}}$ by $\{\mathbf{w}_n\} \sim \{\mathbf{u}_n\}$ if and only if $d(\mathbf{w}_n, \mathbf{u}_n) \to 0$. Prove that $\sim$ is an equivalence relation with field $\mathbf{C}_{\mathbf{Q} \times \mathbf{Q}}$.

33. Let $\mathbf{C}_{\mathbf{Q} \times \mathbf{Q}/\sim}$ be the collection of equivalence classes of $\mathbf{C}_{\mathbf{Q} \times \mathbf{Q}}$ under the equivalence relation, $\sim$. Show $\mathbf{Q} \times \mathbf{Q}$ can be identified as a subset of $\mathbf{C}_{\mathbf{Q} \times \mathbf{Q}/\sim}$.

34. Define a distance function, $\mathbf{h}$, on $\mathbf{C}_{\mathbf{Q} \times \mathbf{Q}}$ by

$$\mathbf{h}(\{\mathbf{w}_n\}, \{\mathbf{u}_n\}) = \lim_{n \to \infty} \mathbf{d}(\mathbf{w}_n, \mathbf{u}_n).$$

Show first that for any pair of sequences in $\mathbf{C}_{\mathbf{Q} \times \mathbf{Q}}$ the limit on the right exists. Show second that the value is independent of the representative of the equivalence class used in its calculation and hence that $\mathbf{h}$ is **well defined.** Show third that $\mathbf{h}$ satisfies the properties for a distance function specified in Theorem 11.3.1. Finally, show the distance between any pair of equivalence classes associated with members of $\mathbf{Q} \times \mathbf{Q}$ as calculated with $\mathbf{h}$ is exactly the distance calculated with $\mathbf{d}$.

35. Define the concept of a Cauchy sequence of members of $\mathbf{C}_{\mathbf{Q} \times \mathbf{Q}/\sim}$. Define the concept of limit of a sequence. Show every Cauchy sequence has a limit, in other words, $\mathbf{C}_{\mathbf{Q} \times \mathbf{Q}/\sim}$ is complete. What does this mean about repeating the process specified in Exercises 32–34 with respect to $\mathbf{C}_{\mathbf{Q} \times \mathbf{Q}/\sim}$? Can $\mathbf{C}_{\mathbf{Q} \times \mathbf{Q}/\sim}$ be identified with any familiar space? If your answer is yes, can you make this identification mathematically precise?

36. Prove every sequence in $\mathbf{R}^2$ has a monotonic subsequence.

37. Prove $\mathbf{R}^2$ has the **Lindelöf property**, namely, each open cover of $\mathbf{R}^2$ can be reduced to a countable subcover.

11.5 LIMITS AND CONTINUITY OF REAL-VALUED FUNCTIONS OF TWO REAL VARIABLES

The main goal of this chapter is to develop the theory of limits for real-valued functions of two real variables. We are now ready to proceed with that task.

To set the stage for this discussion, we consider limits of functions $f: D \to \mathbf{R}$, where D is an arbitrary subset of the plane and recall that such functions assume a unique value at each point $(x, y) \in D$, which we denote by $f(x, y)$. The function itself can be specified by $w = f(x, y), (x, y) \in D$.

Definition. A real number L is said to be the **limit** of the function $w = f(x, y)$ as the point (x, y) approaches the point (a, b) provided given $\epsilon > 0$, there exists $\delta > 0$ such that for all points (x, y) in the domain D, we have

$$|f(x, y) - L| < \epsilon \quad \text{whenever} \quad 0 < \mathbf{d}((x, y), (a, b)) < \delta.$$

If the limit exists, we write

$$\lim_{(x,y) \to (a,b)} f(x, y) = L.$$

Discussion. The reader should immediately compare the present definition with the analogous definition for real-valued functions of a single real variable presented in section 2.2 to establish that there are no essential differences between the two definitions other than those associated with having the domain lie in $\mathbf{R}^2$, instead of in $\mathbf{R}$. As such, the discussion relative to that definition remains meaningful, and we shall not reproduce it here. Instead, we leave that task to the reader (Exercise 1). $\square$

EXAMPLE 1 _____

Let $f(x, y) = x^2 + y^2$, $(x, y) \in \mathbf{R}^2$. Show that f has a limit at each point of its domain, D.

Solution. Fix $(x_0, y_0) \in D$. Set $L = f(x_0, y_0)$ and fix $\epsilon > 0$. If we assume $\delta < 1$ there is an $M > 0$ such that $\mathbf{d}((x, y), (x_0, y_0) < \delta_1$ implies

$$
\begin{aligned}
|f(x, y) - L| &= |x^2 + y^2 - (x_0^2 + y_0^2)| \\
&= |(x^2 - x_0^2) + (y^2 - y_0^2)| \\
&\leqslant |x^2 - x_0^2| + |y^2 - y_0^2| \\
&= |x + x_0||x - x_0| + |y + y_0||y - y_0| \\
&\leqslant M(|x - x_0| + |y - y_0|). \quad \textbf{(WHY?)}
\end{aligned}
$$

Since we may assume that $M > 1$, let δ be the minimum of δ_1 and $\epsilon/2M$. For this choice of δ we have that $\mathbf{d}((x, y), (x_0, y_0)) < \delta_1$ implies

$$
|f(x, y) - L| = \epsilon
$$

as required. $\square$

Discussion. The reader should compare the argument above with analogous arguments in Chapter 2, Example 2.2.1. The basic flow of the argument is the same. The primary tool is still algebra, since the description of the function is algebraic. Differences in the details of the computation all relate to the fact that we must deal with $x - x_0$ and $y - y_0$ simultaneously. While it is true this introduces added difficulties, they are more computational than conceptual. $\square$

EXAMPLE 2 _____

Show that $\lim\limits_{(x,y) \to (0,0)} f(x, y) = 0$, where

$$
f(x, y) = \begin{cases} \dfrac{xy^2}{x^2 + y^2}, & (x, y) \neq (0,0) \\ 0, & (x, y) = (0,0). \end{cases}
$$

Solution. Let $\epsilon > 0$ be given and set $\delta = \epsilon$. If (x, y) is such that $\mathbf{d}((x, y), (0, 0)) < \delta$, since $|x| \leqslant \sqrt{x^2 + y^2} = d((x, y), (0, 0))$, we have

$$
\left| \frac{xy^2}{x^2 + y^2} - 0 \right| = |x| \left| \frac{y^2}{x^2 + y^2} \right| \leqslant |x| \cdot 1 < \delta = \epsilon. \quad \textbf{(WHY?)}
$$

Hence $\lim\limits_{(x,y) \to (0,0)} f(x, y) = 0$. $\square$

Discussion. Note the algebra involved in the proof. First, we recognize that the given expression is the product of x with $\dfrac{y^2}{x^2 + y^2}$, where the value of this fractional expression is nonnegative and at most equal to 1. Also, $|x| \leqslant \sqrt{x^2 + y^2} = \mathbf{d}((x, y), (0, 0))$. So if δ is chosen equal to ϵ, the result is

$$|f(x, y) - 0| \leqslant |x| \leqslant \delta = \epsilon.$$

Since x approaches 0 as $(x, y) \to (0,0)$, we see that the limit in question is 0.

As before, the basic strategy is to use algebra to decompose $|f(x, y) - f(a, b)|$ into a product of a term which is bounded and a term which approaches 0 as $(x, y) \to (a, b)$. This is the same strategy which has been employed throughout this text for dealing with this type of computation. □

We turn now to exploring the reasons why a function of two variables can fail to have a limit.

EXAMPLE 3 _____

Show that the function $f(x, y)$ given by

$$f(x, y) = \begin{cases} \dfrac{2xy}{x^2 + y^2}, & (x, y) \neq (0,0) \\ 0, & (x, y) = (0,0) \end{cases}$$

does not have a limit as $(x, y) \to (0, 0)$.

Solution. Let L be an arbitrary but fixed real number, and let $\delta > 0$ be fixed. Observe that we can find (x, y), with $x = y$ such that $0 < \mathbf{d}((x, y), (0, 0)) < \delta$. For such an (x, y), $f(x, y) = 1$. On the other hand, $f(x, 0) = 0$. Thus, in any disc centered at $(0, 0)$, there will be points (x, y) such that $|f(x, y) - L| \geqslant \dfrac{1}{2}$ (**WHY?**). This ensures that the limit can not exist. □

Discussion. As demonstrated for sequences, there are two essential reasons why limits fail to exist, unboundedness and oscillatory behavior. In the present instance, we have identified a form of oscillatory behavior as the reason for the lack of a limit.

The oscillatory behavior present in this example is essentially different from the analogous behavior in $\mathbf{R}$. To see why, consider $\sin\dfrac{1}{x}$ as $x \to 0$. In this case, x is constrained to move along a single path as it tends to 0. Thus, the function values must oscillate as x moves along this one path. For the two variable case above, as (x, y) moves toward $(0, 0)$ along the path determined by $x = y$, no oscillation in the function values is observed. Similarly, as (x, y) moves toward $(0, 0)$ on the path determined by $y = 0$, no oscillation is observed. However, the function values on the two paths are two distinct constants, whence the limit cannot exist. Thus, to observe the type of oscillatory behavior present in the example of $\sin\dfrac{1}{x}$, one must take a path which wiggles back and forth between the two straight line paths mentioned. □

The one situation where the uniqueness of a limit proved nontrivial was that of functions having domains which were arbitrary subsets of **R**.

Theorem 11.5.1. Let f be defined on $D \subseteq \mathbf{R}^2$ and $\mathbf{W}$ be a limit point of D. If the limit as $(x, y) \to \mathbf{W}$ of f exists, then it is unique.

Proof. Suppose L and M are two values for the limit as $(x, y) \to \mathbf{W}$ of f. Since the limit exists, we can find r_n such that $|f(x, y) - L| < \dfrac{1}{n}$ and $|f(x, y) - M| < \dfrac{1}{n}$ whenever $\mathbf{d}((x, y), \mathbf{W}) < r_n$ and $(x, y) \in D$ (**WHY?**). Since for each r_n, $D_{\mathbf{W}, r_n} \cap D \neq \varnothing$, we have $|L - M| < \dfrac{1}{n}$ for every $n \in \mathbf{N}$ (**WHY?**), whence $L = M$. $\qquad\square$

Discussion. If $\mathbf{W}$ is not a limit point of D, then the limit exists but is not unique (Exercise 2). $\qquad\square$

Mathematicians always look for theory that permits them to avoid the rigor of tedious computations. Thus, having accepted that the essential difference in taking limits of functions of two variables is computational, rather than substantial, effort was made to see if the computational difficulties could be avoided. The simplest way to reduce the computational difficulty would be to reduce the problem of finding the limit of a function of two variables to one of finding the limit of a function of a single variable. That such a reduction might be possible is certainly suggested by the fact that a sequence in the plane converges exactly if it converges componentwise.

Consider then the problem of finding the limit of $f(x, y)$ as (x, y) approaches (a, b). If an arbitrary line is drawn through (a, b) and (x, y) is permitted to approach (a, b) by moving along this line, then the goal of effectively reducing the problem to that of a single variable problem has been achieved. There are two obvious lines along which one might approach (a, b), namely

$$\{(x, b) : x \in \mathbf{R}\} \quad \text{and} \quad \{(a, y) : y \in \mathbf{R}\}.$$

The first of these lines is parallel to the x-axis, the second is parallel to the y-axis. Thinking of things in this manner leads to the concept of **iterated limits** which we now make precise.

Definition. Assume that $f(x, y)$ is defined on D and that the rectangle

$$S = \{(x, y) : 0 < |x - a| < r \text{ and } 0 < |y - b| < r\} \subseteq D$$

for some $r \in \mathbf{R}$. Further assume that for each x_0 with $0 < |x_0 - a| < r$, $\lim\limits_{y \to b} f(x_0, y)$ exists and defines a function $f^b(x_0)$. Similarly, we suppose that for each y_0 such that $0 < |y_0 - b| < r$, $\lim\limits_{x \to a} f(x, y_0)$ exists and defines a function $f^a(y_0)$. If $\lim\limits_{x_0 \to a} f^b(x_0)$ exists, we write

$$\lim\limits_{x \to a} \lim\limits_{y \to b} f(x, y) \quad \text{exists} \tag{1}$$

and say that the **iterated limit as** x **tends to** a **after** y **tends to** b **exists.** Similarly, if $\lim_{y_0 \to b} f^a(y_0)$ exists, we write

$$\lim_{y \to b} \lim_{x \to a} f(x, y) \quad \text{exists} \tag{2}$$

and say that the **iterated limit as** y **tends to** b **after** x **tends to** a **exists.** □

Discussion.   The definition above is cumbersome. The reason for this is that we must first make precise the meaning of the two **partial limits**

$$\lim_{x \to a} f(x, y) \quad \text{and} \quad \lim_{y \to b} f(x, y).$$

The problem with these limits is that rather than being a single limit, the notation denotes an infinity of limits, each of which must exist. If each does exist, then a function results. We have denoted the two functions by $f^a(y)$ and $f^b(x)$. To complete the process of computing an iterated limit, one lets y tend to b, in the former case, or lets x tend to a in the latter. The more standard notation for iterated limits does not refer to the functions f^a and f^b, but refers only to the iterated limit process as indicated in (1) and (2) above.

The process of taking iterated limits accomplishes the goal of reducing two variable limits to one variable limit. It does so by looking at a rectangle around the point of interest, and establishing that the function is well behaved on a bidirectional grid of lines in the rectangle. Unfortunately, there is a loss to the theory, as the following theorem makes clear. □

Theorem 11.5.2.   Let $f(x, y)$ be defined on D such that the limit as (x, y) tends to (a, b) exists. If f is defined on a rectangle surrounding (a, b) and each of the partial limits exist in this rectangle then,

$$\lim_{y \to b} \lim_{x \to a} f(x, y) = \lim_{x \to a} \lim_{y \to b} f(x, y) = \lim_{(x,y) \to (a,b)} f(x, y).$$

Proof.   We suppose that f is defined on

$$D = \{(x, y) : |x - a| < r \quad \text{and} \quad |y - b| < r\}$$

where $r > 0$. By assumption, the limit at (a, b) exists and we call it L. Also the two functions, f^a and f^b, exist on D. Now let $\epsilon > 0$ be given. We can choose $s > 0$ such that $(x, y) \in D_{(a,b),s}$ implies $|f(x, y) - L| < \dfrac{\epsilon}{2}$ whence

$$|f^a(y) - L| \leqslant \epsilon \quad \text{and} \quad |f^a(y) - L| \leqslant \epsilon. \qquad \textbf{(WHY?)}$$

Thus, all the limits must agree. □

Discussion.   The purpose of iterated limits is to reduce the problem of taking limits in the plane to one of taking limits on a line. As this theorem shows, if all the required limits exist, they must coalesce at the same value. Unfortunately, if any of the limits fail to exist, little can be said.

Example 3 is particularly instructive. The two functions, f^a and f^b, exist and are the constant function 0. Further, the value of the function at $(x, 0)$ or $(0, y)$ is 0 so f

agrees with f^a and f^b on the common portions of their respective domains. Even so, the limit does not exist. Other examples can be constructed in which any of the required limits fail to exist. The function of Exercise 3 is another good example.

These examples lead us to revise our questions concerning reduction. We may ask whether there is some special set of lines through the point (a, b) which has the property that if all limits taken on this special collection of lines exist and agree, then the limit in the plane will be forced to exist. The answer to this question is already available to us. Consider what we know about limits in **R**. In that situation, for a function to have a limit at the point a, it is required that for all sequences approaching a the limit of the function applied to the sequence must exist, and further all limits must agree. Evidently, an analogous theorem must be valid in $\mathbf{R}^2$ (Exercise 4). For this reason, it appears unlikely that any special collection of lines could do the job of guaranteeing the existence of limits in the plane.

The results on double sequences should be reviewed in the context of this theorem and the mentioned examples as they also lead to the conclusion that no special set of lines can exist.

In summary then, the most important use of Theorem 11.5.2 is in showing that a given limit does not exist. This is accomplished by checking that one or the other of the iterated limits do not exist, or, in the case both do exist, that they do not agree.

$\square$

The main conceptual outgrowth of the limit definition is the notion of continuity. For the case of functions of a single real variable, continuity extends the notion of limit from that of points, to one which encompasses the whole domain of a function. In cases of interest, this was generally an interval. From the discussion above, we see that the case of most interest would be that in which the function was defined on a disc, or rectangle. Actually, there is one other case of real interest, namely, when the function is defined on D and this set is a dense subset of a disc in $\mathbf{R}^2$. The reason for this case being of interest is that under these circumstances, the domain of the function can be extended to all of the disc, and the definition of the extended function is both natural and unique. However, to explore these questions fully requires the definition of continuity.

Definition. Let $(a, b) \in D \subseteq \mathbf{R}^2$. We say that the function $f(x, y)$ is **continuous** at the point (a, b) provided

$$\lim_{(x,y) \to (a,b)} f(x, y) = f(a, b).$$

If f is continuous at every point of its domain, we say f **is continuous on** D.

Discussion. If we spell this definition in terms of $\epsilon - \delta$ formalism, we have for each $(a, b) \in D$, and each $\epsilon > 0$, there exists a $\delta > 0$ such that for all $(x, y) \in D$

$$|f(x, y) - f(a, b)| < \epsilon \text{ whenever } \mathbf{d}((x, y), (a, b)) < \delta.$$

As with our previous definition of continuity, it is essential to note that the δ which solves the problem depends on both the value of ϵ, as expected, and also on the point of interest, (a, b).

Given the definition of continuity, we can now return to some of our earlier points related to iterated limits. Thus, suppose that f is defined on an open disc centered at (a, b), and that f is continuous on that disc, except possibly at (a, b). Suppose further that on all straight lines through (a, b), the limit as (x, y) approaches (a, b) along the straight line exists and further that all these limits agree. Must the limit at (a, b) exist? It would seem that enough conditions have been written down to force the limit to exist. However, this is not the case, and we challenge the reader to find a counterexample (Exercise 5)!   □

We now prove an important theorem which characterizes continuous functions. The content of this theorem serves as the basis for the general definition of continuous, however it requires one definition.

Definition.   Let D be an arbitrary subset of $\mathbf{R}^2$, and $B \subseteq D$. B is **open relative to** D if and only if there exists an open subset of $\mathbf{R}^2$, O, such that $B = O \cap D$.

Discussion.   This definition provides a means for taking the topology from a large set and relativizing it to a subset.   □

EXAMPLE 4 _____

Find the subsets of $D = \{(x, 0) : x \in \mathbf{R}\}$ which are open relative to D.

Solution.   We claim for every open set, $U \subseteq \mathbf{R}$, $B = \{(x, 0) : x \in U\}$ is open relative to D. To see this, observe $O = \{(x, y) : x \in U$ and $y \in \mathbf{R}\}$ is an open subset of $\mathbf{R}^2$ and $B = O \cap D$.   □

Discussion.   This example illustrates that the open subsets of the x-axis which are generated by taking open subsets of $\mathbf{R}^2$ and relativizing to the x-axis are exactly the subsets which we would hope to obtain.   □

Theorem 11.5.3.   Let f map $D \subseteq \mathbf{R}^2$ into $\mathbf{R}$. Then f is continuous on D if and only if the inverse image under f of every open subset of $\mathbf{R}$ is open relative to D.

Proof.   We leave the proof that the continuity of f implies that the inverse images of open sets are open relative to D as Exercise 6. Thus, we assume that f is defined on D and that the inverse image of every open subset of $\mathbf{R}$ is open relative to D. Now, fix $(a, b) \in D$ and $\epsilon > 0$. The interval, $I = (f(a, b) - \epsilon, f(a, b) + \epsilon)$ is an open subset of $\mathbf{R}$, whence $f^{-1}(I) = A$ is an open subset relative to D satisfying $(a, b) \in A$. Now $A = O \cap D$ for some open subset $O \subseteq \mathbf{R}^2$. Since $(a, b) \in O$, we can find a disc, centered at (a, b), of positive radius, δ, such that $D_\delta \subseteq O$ (**WHY?**). It follows $f(D_\delta \cap D) \subseteq I$, whence we are done (**WHY?**).   □

Discussion.   The main importance of this theorem is that it provides a means for defining the continuity concept in topological generality. The notion of distance does not appear. Only the notion of open set is needed.   □

Most of the standard theorems on continuity, for example, discussing the arithmetic of continuous functions, carry through word by word with only minor modifications. We ask the reader to prove some of these in the exercises. However, as we saw in Chapter 3, the real importance of continuity lies in the fact that continuous functions transfer topological properties of the domain to the range of the function. The following were important examples of transfers, or related consequences, where the domain was a subset of $\mathbf{R}$:

if the domain was an interval, then the range was an interval;

if the domain was closed and bounded, then the range was closed and bounded;

intermediate values were assumed;

if the domain was closed and bounded, then the function assumed both its supremum and its infimum.

The first of these involves the notion of interval, which appears to have no direct counterpart in the $\mathbf{R}^2$ setting. However, if one recalls that the intervals are the connected subsets of $\mathbf{R}$, then the property being preserved is that of being connected and quite clearly we can ask whether the image of a connected subset of $\mathbf{R}^2$ under a continuous function will be connected. More generally, we can ask what requirements can be put on the domain of a real-valued function of two real variables which would ensure that the range is connected. This and other questions are explored in the theorems below.

Theorem 11.5.4. Let f map $D \subseteq \mathbf{R}^2$ into $\mathbf{R}$. If D is connected, then the range of f is connected.

Proof. Let f and D satisfy the hypothesis of the theorem and suppose that A is the range of f and that A is not connected. Since connected subsets of $\mathbf{R}$ are intervals, we have that A is not an interval. It follows that there is an $a \in \mathbf{R}$ such that $A \subseteq (-\infty, a) \cup (a, \infty)$ and that neither $B_1 = A \cap (-\infty, a)$, nor $B_2 = A \cap (a, \infty)$ are empty. Now,

$$D = f^{-1}(B_1 \cup B_2) = f^{-1}(B_1) \cup f^{-1}(B_2)$$

which decomposes D as the union of two open sets neither of which is empty. This contradicts the assumption that D is connected. ☐

Discussion. It would appear that an essential feature of the proof is the fact that only connected subsets of $\mathbf{R}$ are the intervals. However, we could as easily have phrased the argument in more generality, simply taking an arbitrary decomposition of A as the union of two open sets.

Other questions naturally arise related to connectedness. For example, if A is path-connected, will its image be path-connected? Will the number of connected components remain the same? ☐

Theorem 11.5.5. Let f be a continuous function defined on a closed and bounded subset $D \subseteq \mathbf{R}^2$. Then the values of f form a bounded subset of $\mathbf{R}$.

Proof. Let f and D be as specified in the hypothesis. Since f is continuous, for each $\mathbf{X} \in D$, there exists a $\delta = \delta(\mathbf{X}) > 0$ such that $|f(\mathbf{X}) - f(\mathbf{y})| < 1$ whenever

$d(\mathbf{X}, \mathbf{y}) < \delta(xx)$ and $\mathbf{y} \in D$ (**WHY?**). The collection of open discs $D_{\mathbf{X}, \delta(\mathbf{X})}$ forms an open cover of D. Since closed and bounded is equivalent to compact, there is a finite subcollection of these open discs which also covers D. List these as $\{D_1, \ldots, D_n\}$ with associated centers $\{\mathbf{X}_1, \ldots, \mathbf{X}_n\}$. If we set

$$M = \max\{|f(\mathbf{X}_1)|, |f(\mathbf{X}_2)|, \ldots, |f(\mathbf{X}_n)|\},$$

then for all $\mathbf{y} \in D$, $|f(\mathbf{y})| < M + 1$ (**WHY?**). $\qquad\square$

Discussion. The important feature of this proof is that it illustrates the power of compactness as a tool for proving theorems. As well, the proof provides insight as to why the theorem is true. By this we mean that the use of compactness forces all points in the domain to be related to only a finite number of points in D, namely, the $\mathbf{X}_i$'s. Since we have reduced the problem to considering only a finite number of points, it is possible to generate the required bound.

The reader should compare this with the proof of Theorem 3.6.1 which employs the Supremum Principle. $\qquad\square$.

Theorem 11.5.6. Let f be continuous on a nonempty, closed bounded subset, D of $\mathbf{R}^2$ and let M, m be the supremum and infimum of f on D. Then there exist points $(a, b), (c, d) \in D$ such that $f(a, b) = M$ and $f(c, d) = m$.

Proof. We let f and D be as above. Since f is continuous and D is closed and bounded, $A = \text{Rng}\, f$ is bounded and nonempty. Thus, the supremum and infimum of A exist as real numbers, say M and m. There are two possibilities regarding M, namely, M is a limit point of A, or M is an isolated point of A (**WHY?**). Suppose M is a limit point of A. Let $\{a_i\}$ be a sequence of distinct points of A which converge to M. Since each $a_i \in A$, there exists a sequence $\{\mathbf{X}_i\}$ of members of D such that $f(\mathbf{X}_i) = a_i$ (**WHY?**). The sequence, $\{\mathbf{w}_i\}$, consists of an infinite number of distinct points (**WHY?**), whence compactness ensures the sequence has a limit point in D, which we call $\mathbf{X}$, and it can be shown $f(\mathbf{X}) = M$ (**HOW?**). On the other hand, if M is an isolated point of A, then $M \in A$ (**WHY?**), and the result follows. The proof for the infimum is similar. $\qquad\square$

Discussion. The proof of this theorem is a particularly nice illustration of the use of the third formulation of compactness present in Theorem 11.4.8. The proof is conceptually simple, in that we obtain the maximum, M, of the range as a limit point of the range and then go back to the domain and find a limit point which must map onto this point. The existence of this point mapping onto M completes the proof. The reader will find it useful to write out the proof for the minimum (Exercise 7). $\qquad\square$

One of the really important facts about continuous functions on compact subsets of $\mathbf{R}$ was that they were uniformly continuous.

Definition. Let f be defined on D. Then f is **uniformly continuous** on D, provided given $\epsilon > 0$ there exist $\delta > 0$ such that

$$|f(\mathbf{u}) - f(\mathbf{v})| < \epsilon \quad \text{whenever} \quad d(\mathbf{u}, \mathbf{v}) < \delta \quad \text{and} \quad \mathbf{u}, \mathbf{v} \in D.$$

Discussion. The reader can compare this definition with that presented in section 3.5. They are the same in all essential respects and the comments given there are relevant here. ☐

Theorem 11.5.7. Let D be a closed bounded subset of $\mathbf{R}^2$. If f is continuous on D, then f is uniformly continuous on D.

Proof. Let $\epsilon > 0$ be given. Then to each $\mathbf{w} \in D$ there exists a $\delta_{\mathbf{w}}$ such that $|f(\mathbf{w}) - f(\mathbf{u})| < \dfrac{\epsilon}{2}$ whenever $\mathbf{u} \in D_{\mathbf{w},\delta_w}$. The collection of open discs of the form, $D_{\mathbf{w},\delta_w}$, is an open cover of D (**WHY?**). Hence, it has a finite subcover. If we let δ be the minimum of the $\delta_{\mathbf{w}}$'s for this subcollection, the reader can show

$$|f(\mathbf{u}) - f(\mathbf{v})| < \epsilon \quad \text{whenever} \quad \mathbf{d}(\mathbf{u}, \mathbf{v}) < \delta.$$ ☐

Discussion. Again, this proof illustrates the power of compactness. The reader is invited to complete the details in Exercise 8. ☐

EXERCISES

1. Write a 'discussion' which would follow the definition of limit as $(x, y) \to (a, b)$ of $f(x, y)$. Include all the points which a student should come to grips with in terms of understanding this definition and the relationship between this definition and the analogous definition for $\mathbf{R}$.

2. Let $f(x, y)$ be defined on D. Show if (a, b) is not a limit point of D, then any real number L will serve as the limit of f as (x, y) tends to (a, b).

3. Consider f defined by

$$f(x, y) = \begin{cases} x \sin \dfrac{1}{y}, & \text{if } y \neq 0 \\ 0, & \text{otherwise.} \end{cases}$$

   Show the limit as $(x, y) \to (0, 0)$ exists but that the function, f^b fails to exist because the various partial limits fail to exist. On the other hand, show that f^a does exist.

4. Let f be defined on an open disc, D and let $(a, b) \in \bar{D}$. Show the limit as $(x, y) \to (a, b)$ exists exactly if there is a fixed $L \in \mathbf{R}$ such that for every sequence of elements of D, $\{\mathbf{w}_n\}$, which converges to (a, b), $\{f(\mathbf{w}_n)\}$ converges to L.

5. Find a function defined on $\mathbf{R}^2$ such that the limit as $(x, y) \to (0,0)$ along any straight line exists and further that all these limits agree, but such that the limit at $(0, 0)$ of f does not exist.

6. Let f map $D \subseteq \mathbf{R}^2$ into $\mathbf{R}$. Show if f is continuous then, the inverse image under f of every open set is open.

7. Write out a detailed proof that a continuous function on a closed bounded subset of $\mathbf{R}^2$ attains its minimum.

8. Complete the proof of Theorem 11.5.7.

9. Show rectangles are pathwise connected subsets of $\mathbf{R}^2$.

10. Let ϕ be a path in $\mathbf{R}^2$. Show that Rng ϕ is a closed bounded subset of $\mathbf{R}^2$.

11. Let f be continuous on $D \subseteq \mathbf{R}^2$. Show that if $A \subseteq D$ is closed, then $f(A)$ is a closed subset of Rng f.

12. Evaluate the following limits, if they exist:

(a) $\displaystyle\lim_{(x,y)\to(0,0)} \frac{x^2 - y^2}{x^2 + y^2}$;

(b) $\displaystyle\lim_{(x,y)\to(0,0)} \frac{xy}{x^2 + y^2}$;

(c) $\displaystyle\lim_{(x,y)\to(0,0)} \frac{x - y}{x^2 + y^2}$;

(d) $\displaystyle\lim_{(x,y)\to(0,0)} \frac{xy(x - y)}{x^2 + y^2}$;

(e) $\displaystyle\lim_{(x,y)\to(0,0)} \frac{x^2 + y}{\sqrt{x^2 + y^2}}$;

(f) $\displaystyle\lim_{(x,y)\to(0,0)} \frac{x^4 + 3x^2y^2 + 2xy^3}{(x^2 + y^2)^2}$;

(g) $\displaystyle\lim_{(x,y)\to(0,0)} xy\left[\frac{x^2 - y^2}{x^2 + y^2}\right]$;

(h) $\displaystyle\lim_{(x,y)\to(0,0)} \frac{2xy^2}{x^2 + y^4}$;

(i) $\displaystyle\lim_{(x,y)\to(0,0)} \frac{x^2y^2}{x^2y^2 + (x - y)^2}$;

(j) $\displaystyle\lim_{(x,y)\to(0,0)} \frac{x^4 + y^4}{x^2 + y^2}$;

(k) $\displaystyle\lim_{(x,y)\to(0,0)} \frac{1}{|x|} + \frac{1}{|y|}$;

(l) $\displaystyle\lim_{(x,y)\to(0,0)} \frac{x^2 y^2}{x^2 + y^2}$;

(m) $\displaystyle\lim_{(x,y)\to(0,0)} \frac{2x^5 + 2y^3(2x^2 - y^2)}{(x^2 + y^2)^2}$;

(n) $\displaystyle\lim_{(x,y)\to(2,1)} (2x + y^2)$;

(o) $\displaystyle\lim_{(x,y)\to(2,3)} 2xy$;

(p) $\displaystyle\lim_{(x,y)\to(0,0)} \frac{\sin xy}{x}$;

(q) $\displaystyle\lim_{(x,y)\to(0,0)} \frac{\sin xy}{xy}$;

(r) $\displaystyle\lim_{(x,y)\to(0,0)} (x + y) \sin\frac{1}{x} \sin\frac{1}{y}$;

(s) $\displaystyle\lim_{(x,y)\to(1,0)} \frac{x\sin(x^2 + y^2)}{x^2 + y^2}$;

(t) $\displaystyle\lim_{(x,y)\to(0,1)} \text{Arctan}\frac{x}{y}$;

(u) $\displaystyle\lim_{(x,y)\to(4,\pi)} x^2 \sin\frac{y}{x}$;

(v) $\displaystyle\lim_{(x,y)\to(0,1)} e^{1/x^2(y-1)^2}$.

13. For the following functions, discuss the existence of the two iterated limits, and the limit as (x, y) approaches $(0, 0)$.

(a) $f(x, y) = \dfrac{x - y}{x + y}$;

(b) $f(x, y) = \begin{cases} 1, & xy \neq 0 \\ 0, & xy = 0; \end{cases}$

(c) $f(x, y) = \begin{cases} \dfrac{x^3 + y^3}{x - y}, & x \neq y \\ 0, & x = y; \end{cases}$

(d) $f(x, y) = \begin{cases} x \sin \dfrac{1}{y} + y \sin \dfrac{1}{x}, & xy \neq 0 \\ 0, & xy = 0; \end{cases}$

(e) $f(x, y) = \begin{cases} \dfrac{xy}{x^2 + y^2} + y \sin \dfrac{1}{x}, & x \neq 0 \\ 0, & x = 0; \end{cases}$

(f) $f(x, y) = \begin{cases} xy\dfrac{x^2 - y^2}{x^2 + y^2}, & (x, y) \neq (0, 0) \\ 0, & (x, y) = (0, 0). \end{cases}$

14. Examine the behavior of $\dfrac{x^4 y^4}{(x^2 + y^4)^3}$ as $(x, y) \to (0, 0)$. In particular what is the limit as we approach origin along the parabola $y = x^2$?

15. Given
$$f(x, y) = \begin{cases} 0, & \text{if } y \leqslant 0 \text{ or } y \geqslant x^2 \\ 1, & \text{if } 0 < y < x^2. \end{cases}$$

Show $f(x, y)$ approaches the limit 0 along any straight line through origin, but the limit does not exist. Exhibit a curve through $(0, 0)$ along which $f(x, y)$ approaches the limit 1.

16. Discuss the continuity of the following functions at the points indicated against each:

(a) $f(x, y) = (1 + xy)^2$ at $(0, 1)$;

(b) $f(x, y) = \begin{cases} \dfrac{\sin (x^2 + y^2)}{x^2 + y^2}, & x^2 + y^2 \neq 0 \\ 0, & \text{otherwise} \end{cases}$ at $(0, 0)$;

(c) $f(x, y) = \begin{cases} \dfrac{xy^2}{x^2 + y^4}, & (x, y) \neq (0, 0) \\ 0, & (x, y) = (0, 0) \end{cases}$ at $(0, 0)$;

(d) $f(x, y) = \begin{cases} \dfrac{x^2 - y^2}{x^2 + y^2}, & (x, y) \neq (0, 0) \\ 0, & (x, y) = (0, 0) \end{cases}$ at $(0, 0)$ and $(0, 2)$;

(e) $f(x, y) = \begin{cases} x + y, & x \neq y \\ x^2 - 2y, & x = y \end{cases}$ at $(0, 0)$, $(1, 2)$, $(2, 2)$, and $(4, 4)$;

(f) $f(x, y) = \begin{cases} 10xy, & (x, y) \neq (2, 3) \\ 5, & (x, y) = (2, 3); \end{cases}$ at $(2, 3)$ and $(0, 0)$;

(g) $f(x, y) = \begin{cases} e^{\frac{|x-2y|}{x^2 - 4xy + 4y^2}}, & x \neq 2y \\ 0, & x = 2y. \end{cases}$

17. Find the points of discontinuity of the following functions:

(a) $f(x, y) = \begin{cases} xy \ln(xy), & xy > 0 \\ 0, & xy = 0; \end{cases}$

(b) $f(x, y) = \begin{cases} \dfrac{\sin(xy)}{x}, & x \neq 0 \\ y, & x = 0; \end{cases}$

(c) $f(x, y) = \dfrac{5x + y}{x - y}$;

(d) $f(x, y) = x^2 \ln(x^2 + y^2)$;

(e) $f(x, y) = \begin{cases} 0, & x \text{ or } y \notin \mathbf{Q} \\ \dfrac{1}{q} + \dfrac{1}{s}, & x = \dfrac{p}{q}, y = \dfrac{r}{s}, \text{ in their lowest terms;} \end{cases}$

(f) $f(x, y) = \begin{cases} x + y, & x + y \in \mathbf{Q} \\ 1 - x - y, & \text{otherwise;} \end{cases}$

(g) $f(x, y) = \begin{cases} x + y, & x \in \mathbf{Q} \text{ or } y \in \mathbf{Q} \\ 1 - x - y, & \text{otherwise;} \end{cases}$

(h) $f(x, y) = \begin{cases} x + y, & x \in \mathbf{Q} \text{ and } y \in \mathbf{Q} \\ 1 - x - y, & \text{otherwise.} \end{cases}$

18. Give an example of a function $f(x, y)$ which is discontinuous at $(0, 0)$, but the functions $g(x) = f(x, 0)$ and $h(y) = f(0, y)$ are separately continuous.

19. Given $f(x, y) = e^{-1/|x-y|}$ when $x \neq y$, how should you define the function when $x = y$, so as to make it continuous at all points in the plane?

20. Given

$$f(x, y) = \begin{cases} \dfrac{4y(x^2 - y)}{x^4}, & 0 < y < x^2 \\ 0, & y \leqslant 0 \text{ or } y \geqslant x^2, \end{cases}$$

discuss the possible discontinuities along the paths $y = 0$ and $y = x^2$. Is $f(x, y)$ continuous at $(0, 0)$?

21. Let

$$f(x, \ y) = \begin{cases} (x^2 + \ y^2) \operatorname{Arctan}\left[\dfrac{y}{x}\right], & x \neq 0 \\[2mm] \qquad\qquad 0, & \text{if } (x, \ y) = (0, \ 0) \end{cases}$$

but undefined when $x = 0$ and $y \neq 0$. Is $f(x, \ y)$ continuous at $(0, 0)$? Is it possible to define $f(0, \ 1)$ suitably so that it is continuous at $(0, 1)$?

22. Show the following functions are continuous from $\mathbf{R}^2$ to $\mathbf{R}$, where $(x, \ y) \in \mathbf{R}^2$:

   (a) $+ : \mathbf{R}^2 \to \mathbf{R}$ defined by $+(x, \ y) = x + y$;

   (b) $\cdot : \mathbf{R}^2 \to \mathbf{R}$ defined by $\cdot \, (x, \ y) = xy$;

   (c) $\| \cdot \| : \mathbf{R}^2 \to \mathbf{R}$ defined by $\| \cdot \|((x, \ y)) = \sqrt{x^2 + y^2}$;

   (d) $\max : \mathbf{R}^2 \to \mathbf{R}$ defined by $\max (x, \ y) = \max \{|x|, \ |y|\}$;

   (e) $\min : \mathbf{R}^2 \to \mathbf{R}$ defined by $\min (x, \ y) = \min \{|x|, \ |y|\}$;

   (f) $\| \cdot \|_1 : \mathbf{R}^2 \to \mathbf{R}$ defined by $\| \cdot \|_1((x, \ y)) = |x| + |y|$;

   (g) $P_1 : \mathbf{R}^2 \to \mathbf{R}$ defined by $P_1(x, \ y) = x$;

   (h) $P_2 : \mathbf{R}^2 \to \mathbf{R}$ defined by $P_2(x, \ y) = y$.

23. If f and g are two functions on $\mathbf{R}^2$ to $\mathbf{R}$ such that $f(x, \ y) = g(x, \ y)$ for all $(x, \ y) \in \mathbf{Q} \times \mathbf{Q}$, show that f and g must be identical. What property of $\mathbf{Q} \times \mathbf{Q}$ is used here?

24. Show that if $f : \mathbf{R}^2 \to \mathbf{R}$ is continuous, then, $\{(x, \ y) \in \mathbf{R} : f(x, \ y) = 0\}$ is a closed set.

Chapter 12

Metric Spaces

Analysis is primarily concerned with limiting processes and in this context we have studied convergent sequences and continuous functions associated with $\mathbf{R}$ and $\mathbf{R}^2$. If one recalls the various definitions from earlier chapters, it will be clear that the vital force behind these concepts is the notion of 'nearness' which, in the case of $\mathbf{R}$, was used in the disguised form of the absolute value of the difference between two numbers. Thus, $|x - y|$ denotes the **distance** between the real numbers x and y and the following familiar properties of the absolute value were frequently used in our discussions and proofs:

    (i) $|x - y| \geqslant 0$;
    (ii) $|x - y| = 0$ if and only if $x = y$;
    (iii) $|x - y| = |y - x|$ (**symmetry**);
    (iv) $|x - z| \leqslant |x - y| + |y - z|$ (**Triangle inequality**),
        where x, y, and z are any three real numbers.

In many areas of mathematics, it is useful to have a notion of 'distance' which can be applied to elements of an abstract set of objects, rather than the familiar real numbers. (The last chapter illustrates this in that the distance notion was developed for pairs of real numbers.) The development of a more general notion of distance satisfying the properties listed above leads to the concept of a metric space. The goal of this chapter is to define metric spaces and to explore limiting processes in this general setting.

12.1 DEFINITION AND EXAMPLES OF METRIC SPACES

Definition. Let X be a nonempty set. A **distance function (metric)** on X is a function $\rho: X \times X \to [0, \infty)$ which satisfies the following axioms:

  (i) $\rho(x, y) \geqslant 0$ for all $x, y \in X$;

 (ii) $\rho(x, y) = 0$ if and only if $x = y$;

(iii) $\rho(x, y) = \rho(y, x)$ for $x, y \in X$ (symmetry);

(iv) $\rho(x, z) \leqslant \rho(x, y) + \rho(y, z)$ for $x, y, z \in X$ (Triangle inequality).

The nonnegative real number $\rho(x, y)$ is called the **distance** between the members x and y of the set X and the pair (X, ρ) is called a **metric space**.

Discussion. In simplest terms, a metric space is a nonempty set together with a function which specifies the distance between any pair of points in the set. The set X can be any arbitrary nonempty set, such as the set of all books in the Library of Congress, or the set of all convergent sequences, or a finite set. It is important to note that the domain of the distance function, ρ, is not X itself, but the Cartesian product of X with itself, namely, $X \times X$.

Axiom (i) ensures that Rng ρ is contained in $[0, \infty)$, whence distance cannot be negative. Axiom (ii) asserts that the only occasion when $\rho(x, y) = 0$ is when x and y are the same element of X. Axiom (iii), often referred to as **symmetry** axiom, requires the distance between x and y to be the same as the distance between y and x, and is a familiar fact about distance which we would want any distance concept to capture. Axiom (iv) is appropriately called the **Triangle inequality**, since it also is designed to capture the analogous geometric idea about triangles in the plane. This last axiom is very important and we have seen earlier that the Triangle inequality was an indispensable tool in proving many (almost all) theorems about convergence on the real line and again in the plane.

To verify that a given nonempty set, X, together with a distance function, ρ, is a metric space, one must verify the four axioms. Of these, only the verification of the Triangle inequality is likely to present difficulties. The calculations presented in the proof of Theorem 11.3.1 are typical, particularly for **Euclidean spaces**, that is, spaces in which distance satisfies the Pythagorean Theorem. As in the proof of Theorem 11.3.1, an inequality such as the Cauchy–Schwartz inequality may be the key to a successful verification of the Triangle inequality. □

We shall provide some concrete examples to illustrate this concept.

EXAMPLE 1 _____

Let $X = \mathbf{R}$ and set $\rho(x, y) = |x - y|$. Show (X, ρ) is a metric space.

Solution. That (X, ρ) is a metric space follows from Theorem 0.6.1. (Exercise 1). □

EXAMPLE 2 _____

Let $X = \mathbf{R}$ and set $\rho(x, y) = 2|x - y|$. Show (X, ρ) is a metric space.

Solution. The verification of the metric space axioms for this example follows directly from Theorem 0.6.1 and is left to the reader as Exercise 2. □

Discussion. This example illustrates that the distance properties contained in the four axioms are not nearly strong enough to capture the relations between distances and numbers which we take for granted as part of the way we have approached mathematics. The reader might want to consider why early mathematicians decided to take the ρ of Example 1 as the means for measuring distance on **R** instead of the ρ of this example. □

EXAMPLE 3 _____

Let $X = \mathbf{R}^2$ and set $\rho((x, y), (z, w)) = \sqrt{(x - z)^2 + (y - w)^2}$. Show (X, ρ) is a metric space.

Solution. Apply Theorem 11.3.1. □

EXAMPLE 4 _____

Let $X = \mathbf{R}^2$ and set $\rho((x, y), (z, w)) = \sqrt{(x - z)^2 + 2(y - w)^2}$. Show (X, ρ) is a metric space.

Solution. Again apply Theorem 11.3.1 (Exercise 4). □

Discussion. This space fails to satisfy the Pythagorean Theorem. If one lived in a universe where distance satisfied this property, what would it mean for the laws of physics? □

EXAMPLE 5 _____

Let $X = \mathbf{R}^2$. For $1 < p \in \mathbf{N}$, set

$$\rho_p(\mathbf{X}, \mathbf{y}) = (|x_1 - y_1|^p + |x_2 - y_2|^p)^{1/p},$$

where $\mathbf{X} = (x_1, x_2)$ and $\mathbf{y} = (y_1, y_2)$. Show (X, ρ_p) is a metric space.

Solution. The reader can verify the first three axioms for a metric space. We therefore verify the Triangle inequality. Define

$$\|\mathbf{X}\|_p = (|x_1|^p + |x_2|^p)^{1/p}.$$

We need to show $\rho_p(\mathbf{X}, \mathbf{y}) \leqslant \rho_p(\mathbf{X}, \mathbf{z}) + \rho_p(\mathbf{z}, \mathbf{y})$. This is equivalent to showing

$$\|\mathbf{X} - \mathbf{y}\|_p \leqslant \|\mathbf{X} - \mathbf{z}\|_p + \|\mathbf{z} - \mathbf{y}\|_p$$

which is a consequence (**WHY?**) of the Minkowski's inequality which asserts

$$\|\mathbf{X} + \mathbf{y}\|_p \leqslant \|\mathbf{X}\|_p + \|\mathbf{y}\|_p.$$

Below we demonstrate the Minkowski's inequality to complete the solution to this example. □

Discussion. We have shown that ρ_p, as defined on $\mathbf{R}^2$, constitutes a metric. It is apparent that ρ_p could be defined on $\mathbf{R}^3$, or $\mathbf{R}^n$. It is left to the reader to make these generalizations and perform the computations to show the results are metric spaces.

In consistence with the more general definition used in linear analysis, the quantity, $\|\mathbf{X}\|_p$, is a typical example of the **norm** of the element $\mathbf{X}$. The norm of an element in $\mathbf{R}^2$ is analogous to the absolute value of an element of $\mathbf{R}$. The concept of a norm is tremendously useful in mathematics and generally is used as the tool which assigns a 'size' to each element in an abstract space, where the vector operations of addition and scalar multiplication are defined.

The reader should review Theorems 0.6.1 and 0.6.2 and observe the similarity in the use of the absolute value in proving the Triangle inequality. □

Lemma. Let $0 < \lambda < 1$ and $a, b > 0$. Then $a^\lambda b^{1-\lambda} \leqslant \lambda a + (1-\lambda)b$.

Proof. Consider

$$f(x) = (1 - \lambda) + \lambda x - x^\lambda.$$

Differentiation yields $f'(x) = \lambda(1 - x^{\lambda-1})$. Thus, f is decreasing if $x < 1$ and increasing if $x > 1$ (**WHY?**), whence $x = 1$ is a minimum and for all x, $f(x) \geqslant f(1) = 0$, or equivalently,

$$x^\lambda \leqslant \lambda x + (1 - \lambda).$$

Now if $b = 0$, then $a^\lambda b^{1-\lambda} \leqslant \lambda a + (1 - \lambda)b$ is trivial. Otherwise, the lemma is completed by setting $x = \dfrac{a}{b}$ (Exercise 6). □

Discussion. An alternate proof of the lemma based on Mean Value Theorem runs as follows. For $b > a > 0$,

$$b^{1-\lambda} - a^{1-\lambda} = (b - a)(1 - \lambda)c^{-\lambda},$$

where $c \in (a, b)$. Replacing $c^{-\lambda}$ by $a^{-\lambda}$ yields an inequality which when multiplied by a^λ will yield the required result (Exercise 7). These computations illustrate the use of the previously developed theory in this much more general setting.

The reader might wonder where the insight underlying these computations arose. If one sets $\lambda = \dfrac{1}{2}$, then the assertion, $\sqrt{ab} \leqslant \dfrac{a+b}{2}$, obtains. This is the well-known fact that the geometric mean of two numbers is less than the arithmetic mean. For other values of λ, one can rephrase this idea in terms of weighted means. □

Theorem 12.1.1 (Hölder). If $\mathbf{x}, \mathbf{y} \in \mathbf{R}^2$, $1 < p \in \mathbf{N}$ and $\dfrac{1}{p} + \dfrac{1}{q} = 1$, then

$$\sum_{i=1}^{2} |x_i y_i| \leqslant \|\mathbf{x}\|_p \|\mathbf{y}\|_q. \tag{1}$$

Proof. We may assume that both terms on the right-hand side of Eq. 1 are not zero (**WHY?**). Set $\lambda = \dfrac{1}{p}$ and $1 - \lambda = \dfrac{1}{q}$. For each i, $i = 1, 2$, we apply the lemma with

$$a = \frac{|x_i|^p}{\sum\limits_{n=1}^{2} |x_i|^p} \quad \text{and} \quad b = \frac{|y_i|^q}{\sum\limits_{n=1}^{2} |y_i|^q}.$$

Thus,

$$\frac{|x_i|\,|y_i|}{\|\mathbf{x}\|_p\,\|\mathbf{y}\|_q} \leqslant \frac{1}{p}\left[\frac{|x_i|^p}{\sum\limits_{n=1}^{2}|x_i|^p}\right] + \frac{1}{q}\left[\frac{|y_i|^q}{\sum\limits_{n=1}^{2}|y_i|^q}\right].$$

If the two resultant inequalities are summed, we obtain (**WHY?**)

$$\sum_{i=1}^{2}\left[\frac{|x_i|\,|y_i|}{\|\mathbf{x}\|_p\,\|\mathbf{y}\|_q}\right] \leqslant \frac{1}{p}(1) + \frac{1}{q}(1) = 1$$

whence

$$\sum_{i=1}^{2}|x_i y_i| \leqslant \|\mathbf{x}\|_p\,\|\mathbf{y}\|_q.$$

$\square$

Discussion. This inequality can be generalized in several ways. First, it can be extended to be valid in $\mathbf{R}^n$ (Exercise 8). Second, it can be revised to apply to other types of metric spaces which involve essentially different types of norms as discussed below. $\square$

Theorem 12.1.2 (Minkowski). Let $\mathbf{x}$, $\mathbf{y} \in \mathbf{R}^2$, $1 < p \in \mathbf{N}$, and then

$$\|\mathbf{x} + \mathbf{y}\|_p \leqslant \|\mathbf{x}\|_p + \|\mathbf{y}\|_p.$$

Proof. By algebra,

$$\sum_{n=1}^{2}|x_i + y_i|^p = \sum_{n=1}^{2}|x_i + y_i| \cdot |x_i + y_i|^{p-1}$$

$$\leqslant \sum_{n=1}^{2}|x_i| \cdot |x_i + y_i|^{p-1} + \sum_{n=1}^{2}|y_i| \cdot |x_i + y_i|^{p-1}.$$

Define q by $\dfrac{1}{q} = 1 - \dfrac{1}{p}$ and notice that $(p - 1)q = p$. We can apply the Hölder's inequality to each sum on the right-hand side of the above to obtain two inequalities:

$$\sum_{n=1}^{2}|x_i| \cdot |x_i + y_i|^{p-1} \leqslant \left[\sum_{n=1}^{2}|x_i|^p\right]^{1/p}\left[\sum_{n=1}^{2}|x_i + y_i|^{(p-1)q}\right]^{1/q}$$

and

$$\sum_{n=1}^{2}|y_i| \cdot |x_i + y_i|^{p-1} \leqslant \left[\sum_{n=1}^{2}|y_i|^p\right]^{1/p}\left[\sum_{n=1}^{2}|x_i + y_i|^{(p-1)q}\right]^{1/q}.$$

Combining these inequalities yields

$$\sum_{n=1}^{2}|x_i + y_i|^p \leqslant \left[\sum_{n=1}^{2}|x_i|^p\right]^{1/p}\left[\sum_{n=1}^{2}|x_i + y_i|^{(p-1)q}\right]^{1/q}$$

$$+ \left[\sum_{n=1}^{2} |y_i|^p \right]^{1/p} \left[\sum_{n=1}^{2} |x_i + y_i|^{(p-1)q} \right]^{1/q}$$

$$= \left[\left[\sum_{n=1}^{2} |x_i|^p \right]^{1/p} + \left[\sum_{n=1}^{2} |y_i|^p \right]^{1/p} \right] \left[\sum_{n=1}^{2} |x_i + y_i|^{(p-1)q} \right]^{1/q}.$$

Division by the last factor on the right yields (**WHY?**)

$$\left[\sum_{n=1}^{2} |x_i + y_i|^p \right]^{1-1/q} \leqslant \left[\sum_{n=1}^{2} |x_i|^p \right]^{1/p} + \left[\sum_{n=1}^{2} |y_i|^p \right]^{1/p}$$

which is equivalent to (**WHY?**)

$$\|\mathbf{x} + \mathbf{y}\|_p \leqslant \|\mathbf{x}\|_p + \|\mathbf{y}\|_p.$$

$\square$

Discussion. As with Hölder's inequality, Minkowski's inequality can also be generalized to other spaces. These ideas will be explored below and in the exercises. $\square$

EXAMPLE 6

Let $X = \mathbf{R}^2$ and set $\rho_\infty(\mathbf{x}, \mathbf{y}) = \max \{|x_1 - y_1|, |x_2 - y_2|\}$, where $\mathbf{x} = (x_1, x_2)$, $\mathbf{y} = (y_1, y_2)$. Show (X, ρ_∞) is a metric space.

Solution. Again, the only difficulty is the Triangle inequality. Thus, let $\mathbf{x}, \mathbf{y}, \mathbf{z} \in \mathbf{R}^2$. We claim (Exercise 11)

$$\max \{|x_1 - y_1|, |x_2 - y_2|\} \leqslant \max \{|x_1 - z_1|, |x_2 - z_2|\}$$
$$+ \max \{|z_1 - y_1|, |z_2 - y_2|\}$$

follows by inspection using the usual Triangle inequality in $\mathbf{R}$. $\square$

Discussion. It is an important fact that $\rho_\infty = \lim_{p \to \infty} \rho_p$, that is, $\rho_\infty(x, y) = \lim_{p \to \infty} \rho_p(x, y)$ for all x, y in the space. This fact is left as Exercise 13. $\square$

EXAMPLE 7

Let $\mathbf{C}[a, b]$ denote the collection of all continuous functions from $[a, b]$ into $\mathbf{R}$ and for $f, g \in \mathbf{C}[a, b]$, set $\rho_\infty(f, g) = \sup \{|f - g|(x) : x \in [a, b]\}$. Show (X, ρ_∞) is a metric space.

Solution. Again we treat the Triangle inequality. Thus, let $f, g, h \in \mathbf{C}[a, b]$. Now $\rho_\infty(f, g) \leqslant \rho_\infty(f, h) + \rho_\infty(h, g)$ is equivalent to

$$\sup \{|f - g|(x)\} \leqslant \sup \{|f - h|(x)\} + \sup \{|h - g|(x)\},$$

where $x \in [a, b]$. Since f, g, and h are continuous, the functions, $|f - g|$, $|f - h|$, and $|h - g|$ all achieve their supremums on the interval, $[a, b]$. The result now follows by inspection using the ordinary Triangle inequality in $\mathbf{R}$ (**WHY?**). $\square$

Discussion. This example creates a whole new class of spaces, namely, spaces in which the elements of the space are functions. Many interesting questions immediately arise. For example, how should we discuss convergence in this apparently new context? Are these spaces complete? And so forth.

The reader should notice that the metric, ρ_∞, on this space is the analog of the metric of the same name on $\mathbf{R}^2$. Its geometric interpretation is presented in Figure 12.1.1.   □

EXAMPLE 8
_____

Let $X = \mathbf{C}[a, b]$ and set $\rho(f, g) = \int_a^b |f - g|$. Show (X, ρ) is a metric space.

Solution. Once more, the heart of the matter is the Triangle inequality. Define $\|f\|$ by $\|f\| = \int_a^b |f|$. We claim the Triangle inequality will follow from an appropriate version of Minkowski's inequality (Exercise 16).   □

Discussion. This example illustrates that it is possible to define two totally different measures of closeness on the same underlying space of points. It suggests that when one considers issues related to convergence, the results obtained may depend on the way in which closeness is measured.

The geometric interpretation of this metric can also be seen from Figure 12.1.1. In this case, the measure of closeness is given by the area between the two curves. The reader will recall that we have already discussed convergence for sequences of functions. Implicitly, that discussion required a notion of closeness. It is useful to think about the present measures in terms of the notions developed for limits. How do the various notions relate? What are the important mathematical ideas?   □

EXAMPLE 9
_____

Let X denote the collection of all sequences, $\{x_n\}$, of real numbers such that $\sum_{n=1}^\infty |x_n| < \infty$ and set

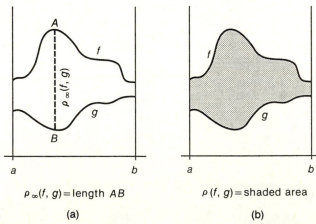

$\rho_\infty(f, g) = \text{length } AB$ $\rho(f, g) = \text{shaded area}$

(a)   (b)

Figure 12.1.1   (a) The ρ_∞ distance in $\mathbf{C}[a, b]$. (b) The ρ_1 distance in $\mathbf{C}[a, b]$.

$$\rho(\{x_n\}, \{y_n\}) = \sum_{n=1}^{\infty} |x_n - y_n|.$$

Show (X, ρ) is a metric space.

Solution.   One defines the norm of $\{x_n\}$ by

$$\|\{x_n\}\| = \sum_{n=1}^{\infty} |x_n|.$$

The Triangle inequality follows from Minkowski's inequality. It is left to the reader to develop an appropriate version of this inequality and to complete the proof (Exercises 19 and 20). □

Discussion.   An alternate metric on the collection of sequences having an absolutely convergent series is

$$\rho(\{x_n\}, \{y_n\}) = \sum_{n=1}^{\infty} \frac{1}{2^n} \left[\frac{|x_n - y_n|}{1 + |x_n - y_n|} \right].$$

Once again the same sorts of questions arise with respect to the space of sequences and its convergence properties under the various possible metrics. □

EXERCISES

1. Complete the verification that the space of Example 1 satisfies the metric space axioms.
2. Complete the verification that the space of Example 2 satisfies the metric space axioms.
3. Complete the verification that the space of Example 3 satisfies the metric space axioms.
4. Complete the verification that the space of Example 4 satisfies the metric space axioms.
5. Prove that in a metric space, (X, ρ), if $x, y, z \in X$, then

$$|\rho(x, z) - \rho(y, z)| \leq \rho(x, y).$$

6. Complete the proof of the lemma leading to Hölder's inequality.
7. Give an alternate proof of the lemma leading to Hölder's inequality using the Mean Value Theorem.
8. Let $\mathbf{X} = (x_1, \ldots, x_n) \in \mathbf{R}^n$. Define $\|\mathbf{X}\|_p$ for vectors in $\mathbf{R}^n$.
   (a) Extend Hölder's inequality to cover $\mathbf{R}^n$.
   (b) Is this inequality valid for $\rho \in [1, \infty) \sim \mathbf{N}$?
9. Extend Minkowski's inequality to $\mathbf{R}^n$.
10. Show if $X = \mathbf{R}^n$ and ρ_p is extended, then $(\mathbf{R}^n, \rho_p)$ is a metric space.
11. Complete the verification that the space of Example 6 satisfies the metric space axioms.
12. Show $(\mathbf{R}^n, \rho_\infty)$ is a metric space where ρ_∞ is the natural extension of the metric in Example 6.
13. For $X = \mathbf{R}^2$, show $\lim_{p \to \infty} \rho_p(\mathbf{X}, \mathbf{y}) = \rho_\infty(\mathbf{X}, \mathbf{y})$, $\mathbf{X}, \mathbf{y} \in \mathbf{R}^2$.
14. Extend the result of Exercise 12 to $\mathbf{R}^n$.
15. Complete the verification that the space of Example 7 satisfies the metric space axioms.

16. Develop an appropriate notion of norm and a version of Minkowski's inequality which will imply that the (X, ρ) of Example 8 is a metric space.

17. Prove Minkowski's inequality for the norm in Exercise 16.

18. Consider $C[0, 1]$ and the metrics ρ_∞ and ρ of Examples 7 and 8, respectively. For the following pairs of functions, compute the distance between them for each of the two metrics:
   (a) x and x^2;
   (b) x and x^3;
   (c) x and $\sin x$;
   (d) x and $\tan x$;
   (e) x and e^{x};
   (f) x and $\ln(x+1)$;
   (g) $\sin x$ and $\cos x$;
   (h) $\sqrt{x}$ and $\cos 2x$;
   (i) $1 - (x - 1)^2$ and $(2x + 3)^2$.

19. For the norm defined in Example 9, prove Minkowski's inequality.

20. Complete the demonstration that the space of Example 9 is a metric space.

21. Show that for X and ρ as given, the result is a metric space.

   (a) $X = \mathbf{R}^2$ and $\rho(\mathbf{x}, \mathbf{y}) = \begin{cases} |x_1 - y_1|, & \text{if } x_2 = y_2 \\ |x_1| + |x_2 - y_2| + |y_1|, & \text{otherwise}; \end{cases}$

   (b) X is any set and $\rho(x, y) = \begin{cases} 0, & \text{if } x = y \\ 1, & \text{otherwise}; \end{cases}$

   (This metric ρ is called the **trivial (discrete) metric** on X.)

   (c) $X = \mathbf{R}^2$ and $\rho(\mathbf{x}, \mathbf{y}) = \|\mathbf{x}\|_2 + \|\mathbf{y}\|_2$;

   (d) X is the collection of all sequences of real numbers and

   $$\rho(\{x_n\}, \{y_n\}) = \sum_{n=1}^{\infty} \frac{1}{2^n} \left[\frac{|x_n - y_n|}{1 + |x_n - y_n|} \right].$$

22. If $x_1, x_2, \ldots, x_n$ are points of a metric space, prove

$$\rho(x_1, x_n) \leq \sum_{i=1}^{n-1} d(x_i, x_{i+1}).$$

23. Which of the following could be metrics on $\mathbf{R}$:
   (a) $\rho(x, y) = |x^2 - y^2|$;
   (b) $\rho(x, y) = \dfrac{10}{7}|x - y|$;
   (c) $\rho(x, y) = \max\{2, |x - y|\}$;
   (d) $\rho(x, y) = \dfrac{1}{2} + \dfrac{x + y}{2} + |x|$;
   (e) $\rho(x, y) = \begin{cases} y - x, & x \leq y \\ 2(x - y), & y < x. \end{cases}$

24. Suppose ρ and ψ are metrics on the set, X. Decide which of the following functions are also metrics on the set, X:
   (a) $\lambda\rho$, $(\lambda \in \mathbf{R})$;
   (b) $\min(1, \rho)$;
   (c) $\dfrac{\rho}{\rho + 1}$;
   (d) ρ^2;

(e) $\sqrt{\rho}$;

(f) $\alpha\rho + \beta\psi$, $(\alpha, \beta \in \mathbf{R})$;

(g) $\rho\psi$;

(h) $\rho - \psi$;

(i) $\max\{\rho, \psi\}$.

25. Let f be a continuous monotone increasing function on the nonnegative reals satisfying $f(x) = 0$ implies $x = 0$. Show if ρ is any metric on X, then $f \circ \rho$ is also a metric on X.

26. Let X denote the collection of all integrable functions on $[a, b]$. Define $\rho(f, g)$ as in Example 8. Show that this is not a metric space. Show further that there is a natural way to turn it into a metric space.

27. Let $f \in \mathbf{C}[a, b]$. For $1 < p \in \mathbf{N}$, define $\|f\|_p = \left[\int_a^b |f|^p\right]^{1/p}$. Prove Hölder's inequality for this norm.

28. Prove Minkowski's inequality for the norm of Exercise 27.

29. Show $(\mathbf{C}[a, b], \rho_p)$ is a metric space, where $\rho_p = \|f - g\|_p$.

30. Show $\lim_{p \to \infty} \rho_p = \rho_\infty$ on $\mathbf{C}[a, b]$.

31. Which of the following pairs, (X, ρ), are metric spaces for the X and ρ given below?

(a) $X = \mathbf{N}$ and for $m, n \in \mathbf{N}$, $\rho(m, m) = 0$, and for $m \neq n$, $\rho(m, n) = \dfrac{1}{3^l}$, where $m - n = 3^l k$ and k is not a multiple of 3.

(b) $X = G$, a commutative group and let $p : X \to [0, \infty)$ be a function which satisfies: (i) $p(x) = 0$ if and only if x is the identity of G, (ii) $p(-x) = p(x)$, and (iii) $p(x + y) \leq p(x) + p(y)$ for $x, y \in G$. For $x, y \in G$ set $\rho(x, y) = p(x - y)$.

(c) X is the set of all bounded sequences of real numbers. Define $\rho(\{x_n\}, \{y_n\}) = \sup\{|x_i - y_i| : i = 1, 2, \ldots\}$.

(d) X is the collection of all sequences of reals whose terms are eventually zero. Define $\rho(\{x_n\}, \{y_n\}) = \sum_{i=1}^{\infty} |x_i - y_i|$.

(e) X is the collection of all convergent sequences of reals. Define
$$\rho(\{x_n\}, \{y_n\}) = \sum_{i=1}^{\infty} |x_i - y_i|.$$

(f) X is the collection of all sequences of reals which converge to 0. Define
$$\rho(\{x_n\}, \{y_n\}) = \sum_{i=1}^{\infty} |x_i - y_i|.$$

(g) X is the unit circle in the plane. Define $\rho(x, y) = 0$ if $x = y$, $\rho(x, y) = \pi$ if x and y are antipodal points and $\rho(x, y)$ is the length of the shortest arc of the circle joining x and y otherwise.

(h) $X = \mathbf{R}$ and $\rho(x, y) = 1 + |x - y|$ if exactly one of x and y is strictly positive, and $\rho(x, y) = |x - y|$, otherwise.

32. A **pseudometric** on a nonempty set, X, is a function, d, on $X \times X$ to the nonnegative reals which falls short of the definition of a metric in that $d(x, y) = 0$ need not imply $x = y$. Give an example of a pseudometric which is not a metric on X.

33. Let l_p denote the set of all real sequences $\{x_n\}$ such that $\sum_{i=1}^{\infty} |x_i|^p < \infty$. For $x = \{x_i\}$, $y = \{y_i\}$, define
$$\rho_p(x, y) = \left[\sum_{i=1}^{\infty} |x_i - y_i|^p\right]^{1/p}.$$

Verify that (l_p, ρ_p) is a metric space. For $p = 2$, the space, l_2, is usually known as a **Hilbert space**. If $p > q \geqslant 1$, show that $l_q \subseteq l_p$. Show also that for $p > 1$, $\bigcup\limits_{q > p} l_q$ is a proper subspace of l_p.

34. Let p be a fixed prime number (that is, $p \in \mathbf{N}$ and the only positive integers dividing p are 1 and p). For $x \in \mathbf{Q}$, we can express x in the form $x = p^k \dfrac{m}{n}$, where $k, m, n \in \mathbf{Z}$ and p divides neither m nor n. Set $v(x) = k$, and define $\rho_p: \mathbf{Q} \times \mathbf{Q} \to \mathbf{R}$ by

$$\rho_p(x, y) = \begin{cases} 0, & x = y \\ \dfrac{1}{p^{v(x-y)}}, & x \neq y. \end{cases}$$

Verify $(\mathbf{Q} \times \mathbf{Q}, \rho_p)$ is a metric space, and ρ_p satisfies the stronger inequality

$$\rho_p(x, z) \leqslant \max\{\rho_p(x, y), \rho_p(y, z)\}$$

[ρ_p is called the **p-adic metric** on $\mathbf{Q}$].

35. Let $L_2[-\pi, \pi]$ denote the set of all functions from $\mathbf{R}$ to $\mathbf{R}$, that are periodic, with period 2π (that is, $f(x + 2\pi) = f(x)$, $x \in \mathbf{R}$), and are integrable in $[-\pi, \pi]$. For $f, g \in L_2[-\pi, \pi]$, the **inner product** $<f, g>$ is defined by

$$<f, g> = \int_{-\pi}^{\pi} fg.$$

Prove the following:
(a) the inner product is well defined;
(b) $<\sum\limits_{i=1}^{n} a_i f_i, g> = \sum\limits_{i=1}^{n} a_i <f_i, g>$;
(c) $<f, \sum\limits_{i=1}^{n} a_i g_i> = \sum\limits_{i=1}^{n} a_i <f, g_i>$.

36. If in Exercise 35, we set $\|f\| = \sqrt{<f, f>} = \left\{\int_{-\pi}^{\pi} f^2\right\}^{1/2}$, then $\|\cdot\|$ has the following properties:

(a) $\|f\| \geqslant 0$; $\|0\| = 0$ for the zero function 0;
(b) $\|af\| = |a| \cdot \|f\|$, $(a \in \mathbf{R})$;
(c) $\|f + g\| \leqslant \|f\| + \|g\|$ for $f, g \in L_2[-\pi, \pi]$ (**Cauchy–Schwarz inequality**);
(d) $|<f, g>| \leqslant \|f\| \cdot \|g\|$, $f, g \in L_2[-\pi, \pi]$.
(e) $\|f - g\|^2 = \|f\|^2 + \|g\|^2 - 2\|f\| \|g\| < \dfrac{f}{\|f\|}, \dfrac{g}{\|g\|} >$ (**law of cosines**);
(f) $\|f + g\|^2 + \|f - g\|^2 = 2\|f\|^2 + 2\|g\|^2$ (**parallelogram law**).

37. In Example 36, prove that the function $\rho: L_2[-\pi, \pi] \to \mathbf{R}^+$ defined by $\rho(f, g) = \|f - g\|$ is a pseudometric on $L_2[-\pi, \pi]$.

38. We say that $f, g \in L_2[-\pi, \pi]$ are **orthogonal** if and only if $<f, g> = 0$. An **orthonormal family** of functions in $L_2[-\pi, \pi]$ is a collection of members which are pairwise orthogonal, such that $\|f\| = 1$ for each member f. Prove:
(a) if f and g are orthogonal, $\|f \pm g\|^2 = \|f\|^2 + \|g\|^2$ (**Pythagorean Theorem**);
(b) $\{1, \cos nx: n \in \mathbf{N}, \sin nx: n \in \mathbf{N}\}$ form an orthogonal family in $L_2[-\pi, \pi]$;
(c) $\{\dfrac{1}{\sqrt{2\pi}}, \dfrac{\cos nx}{\sqrt{\pi}} : n \in \mathbf{N}, \dfrac{\sin nx}{\sqrt{\pi}} : n \in \mathbf{N}\}$ form an orthonormal family of functions in $L_2[-\pi, \pi]$.

39. If $\Phi = \{\phi_i\}$ is an orthonormal family of functions in $L_2[-\pi, \pi]$, the **Fourier coefficients** of $f \in L_2[-\pi, \pi]$ are the numbers $\{\alpha_i\}$ defined by

$$\alpha_n = \langle f, \phi_n \rangle = \int_{-\pi}^{\pi} f\phi_n.$$

The Fourier series of f is the series whose generic term is $\alpha_n \phi_n$, and we write

$$f \sim \alpha_1 \phi_1 + \alpha_2 \phi_2 + \cdots .$$

For the orthonormal family in Exercise 38 (c), if

$$f \sim \frac{1}{2}a_0 + \sum_{n=1}^{\infty} (a_n \cos nx + b_n \sin nx)$$

prove that the Fourier coefficients are given by

$$a_n = \frac{1}{\pi} \int_{-\pi}^{\pi} f(x) \cos nx \, dx, \qquad b_n = \frac{1}{\pi} \int_{-\pi}^{\pi} f(x) \sin nx \, dx.$$

40. Let

$$S_n(x) = \frac{1}{2}c_0 + \sum_{n=1}^{\infty} (c_n \cos nx + d_n \sin nx)$$

and

$$\Delta(S_n(x)) = \int_{-\pi}^{\pi} [f(x) - S_n(x)]^2 \, dx.$$

Prove that the Fourier coefficients a_n's and b_n's have the property that they minimize $\Delta(S_n(x))$, that is, for $\Delta(S_n(x))$ to be least, we must choose $c_n = a_n$ and $d_n = b_n$ for all n.

41. For the series in Exercise 39, derive **Parseval's equation:**

$$\frac{1}{2}a_0^2 + \sum_{n=1}^{\infty} (a_n^2 + b_n^2) = \frac{1}{\pi} \int_{-\pi}^{\pi} f^2.$$

42. Let $\omega(x)$ be a nonnegative function, integrable in $[a, b]$. Then, the functions f and g, integrable in $[a, b]$ are **orthogonal with respect to the weight function** $\omega(x)$, provided

$$\langle f, g \rangle_\omega = \int_a^b f(x)g(x)\omega(x) = 0.$$

Similarly, one defines orthonormality with respect to the weight function. Prove the following: The **Legendre polynomials** are defined by

$$P_n(x) = \frac{1}{2^n n!} \frac{d^n}{dx^n} (x^2 - 1)^n, \quad n = 0, 1, 2, \ldots .$$

Establish the following:
(a) $(n+1)P_{n+1}(x) - (2n+1)xP_n(x) + nP_{n-1}(x) = 0$;
(b) $(1-x^2)P_n''(x) - 2xP_n'(x) + n(n+1)P_n(x) = 0$;
(c) The Legendre polynomials form an orthonormal system with weight function 1 in $L_2[-1, 1]$.

43. The **Hermite polynomials** are defined by

$$H_n(x) = (-1)^n e^{x^2} \frac{d^n}{dx^n} e^{-x^2}, \quad n = 0, 1, 2, \ldots .$$

Verify the **Hermite functions** ψ_n, defined by

$$\psi_n(x) = \frac{2^n n!}{\sqrt{\pi}} H_n(x) e^{-x^2/2}, \quad n = 0, 1, 2, \ldots$$

form an orthonormal system with weight function e^{-x^2} in $L_2(-\infty, \infty)$.

44. The **Laguerre polynomials** are defined by

$$L_n(x) = e^x \frac{d^n}{dx^n} x^n e^{-x}, \quad n = 0, 1, 2, \dots .$$

Show the **Laguerre functions** ϕ_n defined by

$$\phi_n(x) = \frac{1}{n!} e^{-x/2} L_n(x), \quad n = 0, 1, 2, \dots$$

form an orthonormal system with weight function e^{-x} in $L_2(0, \infty)$;

12.2 CONVERGENCE IN A METRIC SPACE

In section 12.1 we developed a concept of distance and applied it in the treatment of the notion of a metric space, (X, ρ). Numerous examples of metric spaces were given which ranged from the standard spaces having points in $\mathbf{R}^n$ and a distance function which was derived from the Pythagorean Theorem to spaces whose points were functions and whose distance function involved the computation of an integral. In the course of presenting these examples it was pointed out that a key question was the effect of the distance function on the convergence of sequences in the space. In this section we will study the role of the distance function, or metric, as it affects the notion of convergence of sequences in the space. To address this question we will have to define the notion of a sequence of points of a metric space and what it means for such a sequence to converge.

Unless otherwise specified, we let (X, ρ) be an arbitrary metric space and denote elements of the space by x, y, z, and so on. Previous considerations leading to convergence began with the idea of a neighborhood of a point, x, which for $\mathbf{R}$ took the form of an open interval, $(x - \epsilon, x + \epsilon)$. We generalize that idea as follows:

Definition.   Let (X, ρ) be a metric space, $x_0 \in X$ and $r > 0$ be a real number. The **open r-sphere (ball)** centered at x_0 and having radius, r, is the subset

$$S(x_0, r) = \{x : x \in X \text{ and } \rho(x, x_0) < r\}.$$

The corresponding **closed sphere** is the set

$$\bar{S}(x_0, r) = \{x : x \in X \text{ and } \rho(x, x_0) \leqslant r\}.$$

Discussion.   The definition of open sphere in a metric space is a straightforward generalization of the idea of an open neighborhood in $\mathbf{R}$, $(x_0 - r, x_0 + r)$, whose midpoint is x_0 and width is $2r$. Every open sphere is a subset of the corresponding closed sphere and an open sphere is never empty since it always contains its center.

The name 'sphere' arises from the geometrical picture of the circle in $\mathbf{R}^2$ or the sphere in $\mathbf{R}^3$. In the plane, viewed as a metric space with the usual distance, an open sphere is just a circle without its boundary, while a closed sphere is a circle with its boundary included. In $\mathbf{R}^3$, these assume the shape of the familiar solid spheres.

The open spheres determine the topology on the space. They are the basic open sets, and all other open sets are obtained as unions of these basic open sets. The reader

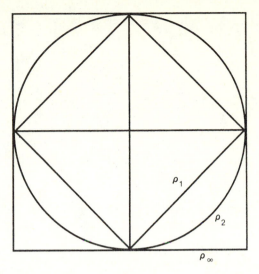

Figure 12.2.1 The unit spheres in $\mathbf{R}^2$ under the metrics ρ_1, ρ_2, and ρ_∞.

can review the development of these ideas in section 11.3 to further explore this approach.

The precise nature of an open sphere depends heavily on the definition of the metric, ρ, since it is the metric which determines exactly which members of a space get into an open sphere. Examples 1 and 2 illustrate this fact. □

EXAMPLE 1

Let $X = \mathbf{R}^2$ and consider the three metrics, ρ_1, ρ_2, and ρ_∞. Find $S((0, 0), 1)$ for each of these metrics.

Solution. The first two metrics mentioned are defined in Example 12.1.5. For ρ_1 we have $\rho_1((0, 0), (x, y)) < 1$ is equivalent to $|x| + |y| < 1$, and this results in the diamond-shaped area pictured in Figure 12.2.1 (**WHY?**). The metric, ρ_2, is the usual Euclidean metric, and the result is the circle, also indicated in Figure 12.2.1. The metric, ρ_∞, produces the largest set of all the three, based on the inequality, $\max\{|x|, |y|\} < 1$, and the result is again pictured in the figure. The reader is asked to verify the accuracy of the figure in Exercise 1. □

EXAMPLE 2

Let $X = \mathbf{C}[0, 1]$ and consider the metrics of Examples 12.1.7 and 12.1.8. Discuss the open sphere $S(f, 1)$, where f is the function which is identically zero on $[0, 1]$.

Solution. For the metric, ρ_∞, one simply takes a tube of radius, 1, about the x-axis as shown in Figure 12.2.2. Then $g \in S(f, 1)$ exactly if the graph of g lies completely inside the tube. The sphere associated with the metric, ρ, of Example

12.1.8 cannot be described so easily. The reason for this can be seen from the fact that

$$
g_n(x) = \begin{cases} n - n^2 x, & \text{if } x \leqslant \dfrac{1}{n} \\[2ex] 0, & \text{otherwise} \end{cases}
$$

satisfies $g_n \in S(f, 1)$ for all $n \in \mathbf{N}$ (**WHY?**). The graph of the function g_4 is presented in Figure 12.2.2 to illustrate the situation. In short, there is no simple graphical device which will serve to capture all the functions belonging to the sphere in this latter case. $\qquad\square$

Discussion. The key point which needs to be understood is that the definition of ρ has a substantial effect on the collection of points which end up in a given open sphere.

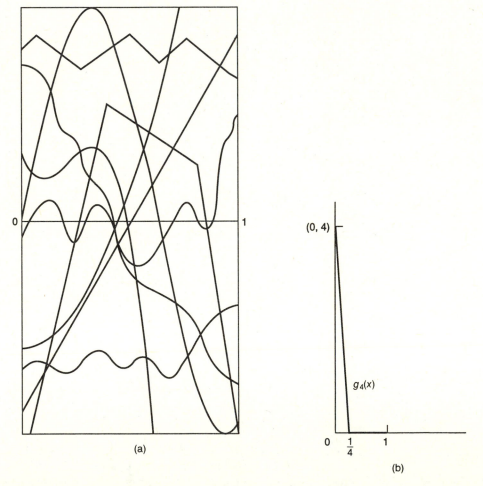

Figure 12.2.2   (a) Some members of the unit sphere in the space $\mathbf{C}[0, 1]$, ρ_∞). (b) Graph of $g_4(x)$.

This in turn is likely to affect whether a given sequence of point in a space is convergent. □

Definition. A **sequence** in a metric space, (X, ρ), is any function with domain, $\mathbf{N}$, and range a subset of X.

Discussion. If $X = \mathbf{R}$, this definition reduces to the familiar definition of a sequence of real numbers. If $f : \mathbf{N} \rightarrow X$ is a sequence in X, we shall use x_n to denote the value, $f(n)$, of the function at n and call it the nth **term** of the sequence. Consistent with standard practice, we specify the sequence by $\{x_n\}$. For some spaces we may choose an alternate notation which will emphasize the nature of the points in the space. For example, in $\mathbf{R}^2$ we will discuss sequences, $\{\mathbf{w}_n\}$, where $\mathbf{w}$ denotes an ordered pair, or in the case of $\mathbf{C}[a, b]$, sequences will be sequences of real-valued functions, $\{f_n\}$, each of which has domain, $[a, b]$. □

Definition. A sequence, $\{x_n\}$, of points in a metric space, (X, ρ), is said to **converge** to a point, $x \in X$, provided to every $\epsilon > 0$ there exists $N \in \mathbf{N}$ such that

$$\rho(x, x_n) < \epsilon \text{ whenever } n > N.$$

Discussion. In its basic form, this definition of a convergent sequence looks like every other definition of a convergent sequence given in this book. Like the others, it requires the existence of a **limit**, x. Like the others, it requires that all terms of the sequence eventually be close to the limit. The only difference is in the fact that the measure of closeness is in terms of the metric and the underlying space of points may be quite abstract.

In terms of open spheres, the definition requires that for any given positive ϵ, there must exist an N such that all terms of the sequence having a subscript exceeding N must lie inside the sphere of radius ϵ. Thus, the notion of convergence is intimately tied to the notion of open set. □

Theorem 12.2.1. The limit of a convergent sequence in a metric space is unique.

Proof. Exercise 3. □

Discussion. The proof of this theorem is a direct revision of the proof of the analogous theorem for sequences of $\mathbf{R}$ and the reader can produce it.

There are other standard questions which have always arisen about sequences. Of prime interest has always been the relationship between convergence and algebraic structure, as obtained from any operations defined on the space. The general theory of metric spaces is developed in the absence of algebraic structure. The reader will have noted that in the discussion so far, no mention of algebraic structure has been made. The reason for this is that the thrust of metric spaces is to study the interaction of a space and its possible metrics without the additional complexity of algebra. In this way one can hope to determine which results are essentially metric in nature and which depend in some essential way on the interaction between the algebraic structure and the topological structure resulting from the metric. Nevertheless, most of the concrete examples of metric spaces will have an algebraic structure residing somewhere in the background. The reader should be aware of this fact and always be wondering about the standard questions relating topology and algebra. □

EXAMPLE 3

Show the collection of convergent sequences in $\mathbf{R}^2$ is the same for the three metrics of Example 1.

Solution. Let $\{\mathbf{W}_n\}$ be a sequence of points in $\mathbf{R}^2$, where $\mathbf{W}_n = (w_{1,n}, w_{2,n})$. We need to show that convergence in $(\mathbf{R}^2, \rho_1)$ implies convergence in $(\mathbf{R}^2, \rho_2)$ implies convergence in $(\mathbf{R}^2, \rho_\infty)$ implies convergence in $(\mathbf{R}^2, \rho_1)$. We show convergence in $(\mathbf{R}^2, \rho_\infty)$ implies convergence in $(\mathbf{R}^2, \rho_1)$ and leave the rest to the reader as Exercise 4. Let $\mathbf{W}$ be the limit of $\{\mathbf{W}_n\}$ as a sequence in $(\mathbf{R}^2, \rho_\infty)$. Fix $\epsilon > 0$. By definition, there exists an $N \in \mathbf{N}$ such that $\rho_\infty(\mathbf{W}_n, \mathbf{W}) < \epsilon$ whenever $n \geqslant N$. But

$$\rho_1(\mathbf{W}_n, \mathbf{W}) = |w_{1,n} - w_1| + |w_{2,n} - w_2|$$
$$\leqslant \max\{|w_{1,n} - w_1|, |w_{2,n} - w_2|\} = \rho_\infty(\mathbf{W}_n, \mathbf{W}),$$

whence the convergence of $\{\mathbf{W}_n\}$ in the space, $(\mathbf{R}^2, \rho_1)$, follows (**WHY?**). □

EXAMPLE 4

Consider $g_n \in \mathbf{C}[0, 1]$, where

$$g_n(x) = \begin{cases} nx, & x \in [0, 1/n] \\ 2 - nx, & x \in (1/n, 2/n) \\ 0, & \text{otherwise.} \end{cases}$$

Discuss the convergence of the sequence, $\{g_n\}$, with respect to the metrics, ρ and ρ_∞, of Example 2 (see Examples 12.1.7 and 12.1.8).

Solution. Let $g(x) = 0$ for all $x \in [0, 1]$. Then

$$\rho(g_n, g) = \int_0^1 |g_n - g| = \int_0^1 |g_n| = \frac{1}{n},$$

whence $\{g_n\}$ converges to g in $(\mathbf{C}[0, 1], \rho)$ (**WHY?**). On the other hand, we claim that $\{g_n\}$ cannot converge in the space $(\mathbf{C}[0, 1], \rho_\infty)$. To see this, first note that if $\{g_n\}$ converges in $(\mathbf{C}[0, 1], \rho_\infty)$, then $\{g_n\}$ converges uniformly (Exercise 5) in the sense of Chapter 9, and hence pointwise. Since the pointwise limit of the sequence, $\{g_n\}$, is g, then the limit in $(\mathbf{C}[0, 1], \rho_\infty)$ would have to be g. But $\rho_\infty(\mathbf{W}_n, \mathbf{W}) = 1$ for all n (**WHY?**), whence the sequence cannot converge. □

Discussion. The first key point about this example is that as mentioned, convergence in $(\mathbf{C}[0, 1], \rho_\infty)$ implies uniform convergence, and in fact is equivalent to uniform convergence. This means that there is a metric which completely captures the notion of uniform convergence. Needless to say, one is immediately compelled to ask: Is there a metric which characterizes the notion of pointwise convergence?

The second key point is that the two notions of convergence are clearly different in that they identify different collections of convergent sequences. In general there will be relations between the collections of convergent sequences identified by different metrics on the same underlying space. For example, in the present case it can be shown if $\{g_n\}$ converges in $(\mathbf{C}[0, 1], \rho_\infty)$, then $\{g_n\}$ converges in $(\mathbf{C}[0, 1], \rho)$ (Exercise 6).

With respect to the problem of finding a metric which identifies the pointwise convergent sequences of $\mathbf{C}[0, 1]$, the metric ρ looks promising. However, this metric will not do the job since one can construct an example of a sequence of members of $\mathbf{C}[0, 1]$ which does not converge pointwise on $[0, 1]$, but which is convergent in $(\mathbf{C}[0, 1], \rho)$ (Exercise 7). □

Definition. A sequence, $\{x_n\}$, of elements of a metric space, (X, ρ), is said to be a **Cauchy sequence** provided for every positive ϵ there exists an $N \in \mathbf{N}$ such that

$$\rho(x_n, x_m) < \epsilon \quad \text{whenever} \quad n, m > N.$$

Discussion. This definition has the standard form for a Cauchy criterion. As with all Cauchy criteria for convergence, the important fact is that they do not require a limit to be found in order to identify convergent sequences. The reader can show (Exercise 8) that a convergent sequence in a metric space is Cauchy. □

EXAMPLE 5 _____

Let $f_n \in \mathbf{C}[-1, 1]$ be defined by

$$f_n(x) = \begin{cases} 0, & x \in \left[-1, -\dfrac{1}{n}\right] \\[2mm] \dfrac{nx + 1}{2}, & x \in \left(-\dfrac{1}{n}, \dfrac{1}{n}\right) \\[2mm] 1, & x \in \left[\dfrac{1}{n}, 1\right]. \end{cases}$$

Discuss the convergence properties of this sequence with respect to the two metrics, ρ and ρ_∞, of Example 4.

Solution. The reader can show that the sequence of functions, $\{f_n\}$, converges pointwise to the function, f, given by

$$f(x) = \begin{cases} 0, & \text{if } x \in [-1, 0) \\[2mm] \dfrac{1}{2}, & \text{if } x = 0 \\[2mm] 1, & \text{if } x \in (0, 1]. \end{cases}$$

On this basis, the reader can see that if $\{f_n\}$ is considered as a sequence in $(\mathbf{C}[-1, 1], \rho_\infty)$, then for any $N \in \mathbf{N}$ one can always find subscripts $n, m > N$ such that $\rho_\infty(f_n, f_m) > \dfrac{1}{4}$ (Exercise 9). For this reason, $\{f_n\}$ cannot be Cauchy in $(\mathbf{C}[-1, 1], \rho_\infty)$. However, the reader can also show that for $n < m$,

$$\rho(f_n, f_m) = \int_{-1}^{1} |f_n - f_m| < \frac{1}{2n},$$

whence $\{f_n\}$ is Cauchy in $(\mathbf{C}[-1, 1], \rho)$. On the other hand, it seems clear there is no function in $\mathbf{C}[-1, 1]$ which will serve as the limit for $\{f_n\}$ (**WHY?**).   □

Discussion.   This example illustrates the complex nature of the convergence notion in an abstract setting. First it shows that the choice of metric will determine whether a given sequence is, or is not, Cauchy. Second, it points out the essential utility of the Cauchy condition, since $\{f_n\}$ is Cauchy in $(\mathbf{C}[-1, 1], \rho)$, but it is not convergent because there is no function available in $\mathbf{C}[-1, 1]$ to serve as the limit. Third, it suggests the next definition.   □

Definition.   A metric space (X, ρ) is said to be **complete** provided every Cauchy sequence of elements of (X, ρ) is convergent.

Discussion.   The key to this definition is that in order for (X, ρ), to be complete, for every Cauchy sequence, $\{x_n\}$, of points of X, there must exist an $x \in X$ which will witness the fact that $\{x_n\}$ actually converges to x.

The canonical example of a complete metric space is the real numbers with the usual distance. Indeed, this definition seeks to generalize the essence of completeness as abstracted from the real numbers. The fundamental distinction is that since an abstract metric space is not linearly ordered, the supremum principle is not available for application. However, the equivalence between convergence of Cauchy sequences and the usual understanding of completeness for $\mathbf{R}$ serves as the basis for the abstracting process. Theorem 11.4.3 shows $\mathbf{R}^2$ is another example of a complete metric space.

The last example shows $(\mathbf{C}[-1, 1], \rho)$ is not complete (**WHY?**). Another example of a space which is not complete is $\mathbf{Q}$ with distance measured in the usual way. Similarly, $\mathbf{Q} \times \mathbf{Q}$ is not complete.   □

Theorem 12.2.2.   The metric space $(\mathbf{C}[a, b], \rho_\infty)$ is complete.

Proof.   Let $\{f_n\}$ be a Cauchy sequence in $\mathbf{C}[a, b]$. It can be checked that for each $x \in [a, b]$, the sequence, $\{f_n(x)\}$, is a Cauchy sequence of real numbers (**WHY?**), hence it has a limit which we call $f(x)$. It can further be shown $\{f_n\}$ converges uniformly to f on $[a, b]$, so f is continuous on $[a, b]$ (**WHY?**). Finally, it follows (Exercise 10) that $\{f_n\}$ converges to f in $(\mathbf{C}[a, b], \rho_\infty)$ which concludes the proof.   □

Discussion.   Initially one might think that completeness was an intrinsic property of a set. The last two examples make it abundantly clear that completeness depends on two things: the underlying set, and the way in which distance is measured on that set. To see the former, consider **R** and **Q** as metric spaces with the usual metric. **R** is complete, but **Q** is not, because various limits are missing. To see the latter, consider $(\mathbf{C}[-1, 1], \rho_\infty)$ and $(\mathbf{C}[-1, 1], \rho)$. $(\mathbf{C}[-1, 1], \rho_\infty)$ is complete because the metric is very tight in that for elements to be considered close, they must be very close everywhere on $[-1, 1]$. $(\mathbf{C}[-1, 1], \rho)$ is not complete because it permits a much greater slackness in deciding which functions are close to a given function. (This is best illustrated by calculations in Example 2.)

These considerations establish that the way in which distance is calculated determines how closely woven is the fabric of a given metric space. This in turn will have other important consequences for the type of analysis which can be performed on the space.   □

EXERCISES

1. Perform the calculations required to validate Figure 12.2.1.

2. Perform the calculations required to validate Figure 12.2.2 and the other assertions made in the solution of Example 2.

3. Prove Theorem 12.2.1.

4. Complete the proof that the various metrics mentioned in Example 3 all yield the same collection of convergent sequences in $\mathbf{R}^2$.

5. Let $\{f_n\}$ be a sequence in $(\mathbf{C}[a, b], \rho_\infty)$. Show $\{f_n\}$ converges in $(\mathbf{C}[a, b], \rho_\infty)$ exactly if it converges uniformly.

6. Let $\{f_n\}$ be a sequence in $(\mathbf{C}[a, b], \rho_\infty)$. Show $\{f_n\}$ converges in $(\mathbf{C}[a, b], \rho_\infty)$, then it converges in $(\mathbf{C}[a, b], \rho)$, where ρ is the integral measure of distance.

7. Give an example of a sequence which is convergent in $(\mathbf{C}[a, b], \rho)$, but which fails to converge pointwise on all of $[a, b]$.

8. Let (X, ρ) be an arbitrary metric space. Show that every convergent sequence is Cauchy.

9. Validate the computations of Example 5.

10. Complete the details in Theorem 12.2.2.

11. Describe the open spheres centered at the origin and having radius 1 in the various metric spaces of the Exercise 12.1.21. [The origin in this context refers to the natural candidate in the space which plays the role of 0.]

12. Describe the open spheres centered at the origin and having radius 1 in the various metric spaces of the Exercise 12.1.31.

13. Prove the intersection of two open spheres always contains a third open sphere.

14. Which spaces in Exercise 12.1.21 are complete? If a space is not complete, obtain a Cauchy sequence in that space which does not converge.

15. Consider the spaces of Exercise 12.1.21. In some of these spaces there are natural arithmetic operations. What, if any, relations hold between the arithmetic operations and convergent sequences in the space?

16. Let $\mathbf{B}[0,1]$ denote the set of all bounded real valued functions defined on $[0, 1]$, and define $\rho(f, g) = \int_0^1 |f - g|(t)\, dt$. Show the metric space $(\mathbf{B}([0, 1], \rho)$ is not complete.

17. If (X, ρ) is a complete metric space, is it true that (X, ρ_1) is complete, where:

    (a) $\rho_1(x, y) = \min(1, \rho(x, y))$;

    (b) $\rho_2(x, y) = \dfrac{\rho(x, y)}{1 + \rho(x, y)}$.

18. Consider the spaces of Exercise 12.1.31. In some of these spaces there are natural arithmetic operations. What, if any, relations hold between the arithmetic operations and convergent sequences in the space?

19. In the pseudometric space, (X, ρ), where X is an arbitrary set and $\rho(x, y) = 0$ for all $x, y \in X$, determine which sequences converge to which points. Is the space complete?

20. If $\{x_n\}$ and $\{y_n\}$ are sequences in a metric space (X, ρ) converging, respectively, to x and y, prove that $\lim\limits_{n \to \infty} \rho(x_n, y_n)$ converges to $\rho(x, y)$.

21. If $\{x_n\}$ is a Cauchy sequence in a metric space (X, ρ), prove that the sequence $\{\rho(x_n, x_1)\}$ is bounded.

22. A sequence $\{x_n\}$ in a metric space (X, ρ) is said to **cluster at** $x \in X$, provided given $\epsilon > 0$ and $m \in \mathbf{N}$, there exists $n \in \mathbf{N}$, $n \geq m$ such that $\rho(x_n, x) < \epsilon$. Decide which of the following statements are true:

    (a) if $\{x_n\}$ clusters at both x and y, then $x = y$;

    (b) if $\{x_n\}$ clusters at x and converges to y, then $x = y$;

    (c) if $\{x_n\}$ converges to x, then it clusters at x;

    (d) if $\{x_n\}$ clusters at x, and if X is complete, then $\{x_n\}$ converges to x;

    (e) if $\{x_n\}$ is Cauchy, and clusters to x, then it converges to x;

    (f) if A is closed, and $\{x_n\}$ is a sequence in A which clusters to x, then $x \in A$.

23. In the p-adic metric space $(\mathbf{Q}, \rho_p)$ (see Exercise 12.1.34), show two open spheres are either disjoint or one is completely contained in the other, and further, show that every triangle is isosceles.

24. Is the p-adic metric on $\mathbf{Q}$ complete?

25. Let (X, ρ) be a complete metric space, and S be a nonempty set. If $\mathbf{L}(S, X)$ denotes the set of all functions from S to X, then prove that $\mathbf{L}(S, X)$ is complete under the metric ρ_X defined by

$$\rho_X(f, g) = \sup\{\rho(f(x), g(x)) : x \in X\}, \quad f, g \in \mathbf{L}(S, X).$$

12.3 TOPOLOGY OF METRIC SPACES

In this section we describe the essential features of the topology of metric spaces. The main ideas are generalizations of ideas first discussed for $\mathbf{R}$ in Chapter 3 and later for $\mathbf{R}^2$ in Chapter 11. Due to the the variety of abstract metric spaces available, we would expect to obtain a rich theory.

Definition. A subset O of a metric space, (X, ρ), is said to be **open** provided for each $x \in O$ there is an open sphere, $B \subseteq X$, such that $x \in B \subseteq O$.

Discussion. This definition of open set is completely analogous to the definitions given in previous chapters. As the reader will see, analogous theorems hold as well.

$\square$

Theorem 12.3.1.   Let (X, ρ) be a metric space. Then

(i) every open sphere is an open subset of X;
(ii) $\varnothing$ and X are open;
(iii) if A is a collection of open subsets of X, then $\bigcup A$ is open;
(iv) if A is a finite collection of open subsets of X, then $\bigcap A$ is open.

Proof.   Exercise 1.   □

Definition.   Let (X, ρ) be a metric space with $A \subseteq X$, then

(i) $x \in X$ is a **limit point (accumulation point)** of A provided every open sphere centered at x contains points of A other than x;
(ii) A is **closed** if it contains all its limit points;
(iii) $x \in X$ is an **interior point** of A provided there is an open sphere, O, such that $x \in O \subseteq A$; otherwise, x is a **boundary point** of A; the **boundary** of A is denoted by bd A and given by

bd $A = \{x : x \in A$ and x is a boundary point of $A\}$

$\bigcup \{x : x \in X \sim A$ and x is a boundary point of $X \sim A\}.$

Discussion.   These definitions can be compared directly to the analogous definitions for $\mathbf{R}^2$, or for $\mathbf{R}$.   □

EXAMPLE 1 _____

Consider the sequence, $\{f_n\}$, where

$$f_n(x) = \begin{cases} n - n^3 x, & \text{if } x \leqslant \dfrac{1}{n^2} \\[2ex] 0, & \text{otherwise.} \end{cases}$$

Discuss the collection of limit points, interior points, and boundary points for this sequence considered as a set, A, in the spaces, $(\mathbf{C}[0, 1], \rho)$ and $(\mathbf{C}[0, 1], \rho_\infty)$.

Solution.   We consider $(\mathbf{C}[0, 1], \rho_\infty)$ first. Observe that for every n, f_n is not a limit point of A. To see this, one must check that for $m \neq n$,

$$0 < \rho_\infty(f_n, f_{n+1}) < \rho_\infty(f_n, f_m). \qquad \textbf{(WHY?)}$$

Next we note that the only function in $\mathbf{C}[0, 1]$ which could serve as a limit point of A is $f = 0$ (**WHY?**). But $\rho_\infty(f, f_n) > \dfrac{1}{2}$ for all n (**WHY?**), whence A has no limit points in $(\mathbf{C}[0, 1], \rho_\infty)$. With respect to the space, $(\mathbf{C}[0, 1], \rho)$, the reader can show (Exercise 2) the function f is the single limit point of the collection, A. For interior points, the reader can show that in both spaces A contains no open ball (sphere) (**WHY?**), and hence can have no interior points. Finally, every point of A in both spaces is a boundary point (**WHY?**). □

Discussion. Once again we see that by changing the metric one can change the topological properties of the space and of sets within the space. In the present example, the collection of functions, $\{f_n\}$, is a closed subset of $(\mathbf{C}[0, 1], \rho_\infty)$, but not of $(\mathbf{C}[0, 1], \rho)$. Since the complement of a closed set is an open set as the next theorem shows, changing the metric changes the collection of open sets.

This example is suggestive in another direction. Notice that the function specified by pointwise convergence of the sequence, $\{f_n\}$, is the zero function defined on $(0, 1]$. If the reader thinks about it, he will see that there are many other sequences which converge pointwise to a function not in $\mathbf{C}[0, 1]$, but which have the zero function as a limit point of the collection. Now pose the question, what properties must a function have in order to satisfy the condition that it can be obtained as a pointwise limit of a sequence of functions, $\{f_n\}$, in $\mathbf{C}[0, 1]$, and that $\{f_n\}$ have exactly the zero function of $\mathbf{C}[0, 1]$ as a limit point? The answer to this question requires that we be able to characterize those functions, f, which satisfy $\int_0^1 |f| = 0$. We will return to this idea later in the chapter. □

Theorem 12.3.2. A set O of a metric space (X, ρ) is open exactly if its complement is closed.

Proof. Let $O \subseteq X$ be open. Consider a limit point, x, of $X \sim O$. Every open ball centered at x contains a point of $X \sim O$ other than x. Thus, if $x \in O$, we would have a contradiction (**WHY?**), whence $x \in X \sim O$ and $X \sim O$ is closed. The converse is left to the reader (Exercise 3). □

Discussion. This proof is a straightforward application of the definitions and is given only to illustrate that the move to metric spaces has not made the development of the general theory more difficult. If anything, it has simplied it since one is not tempted to employ extraneous facts in the construction of proofs. □

The next theorem summarizes the properties of closed sets in a metric space.

Theorem 12.3.3. Let (X, ρ) be a metric space. Then

  (i) every closed sphere is a closed subset of X;
  (ii) $\varnothing$ and X are closed;
  (iii) if A is a collection of closed subsets of X, then $\bigcap A$ is closed;
  (iv) if A is a finite collection of closed subsets of X, then $\bigcup A$ is closed.

Proof. Exercise 4. □

Theorem 12.3.4. Let A be a subset of a metric space, (X, ρ). Then there is a smallest closed set, $\overline{A}$, which satisfies $A \subseteq \overline{A}$.

Proof. Fix A and let $Y \in C$ exactly if $A \subseteq Y$ and Y is closed in (X, ρ). $C \neq \varnothing$, since $X \in C$. It follows that $A \subseteq \bigcap C$ and that $\bigcap C$ is closed. Finally, if $A \subseteq Y$ and Y is closed, then $\bigcap A \subseteq Y$. Setting $\bar{A} = \bigcap A$ completes the proof. $\square$

Discussion.   The set $\bar{A}$ is called the **closure** of A; it is the generalization of the concept presented in Exercises 3.1.18 and 11.3.37. The reader can show it has the properties claimed in these exercises. $\square$

Definition.   A subset, D, of a metric space, (X, ρ), is **dense** provided every member of X is a limit point of D.

Discussion.   This is the same definition we gave in section 11.3.

One idea behind dense subsets is that we can view complex spaces, or sets, as being obtained from dense subsets by closure. In this context, we want to find a 'simple' dense subset inside the complex set or space. We then view the complex set as a completion of the simple set and believe that we have a better understanding of the complex set as a result.

As an illustration of these ideas, consider $\mathbf{R}$. Recall that one of the first facts obtained about $\mathbf{R}$ was that $\mathbf{Q}$ was a dense subset of $\mathbf{R}$. This fact was proved in Chapter 0, although it was not stated in this form. Now we think we understand what $\mathbf{Q}$ is, since it is composed of ratios of whole numbers and positive whole numbers are entities with which we have been dealing all of our lives. Thus, the full complexity of $\mathbf{R}$ can be understood in terms of some new points added to $\mathbf{Q}$ to fill in the holes.

One can pursue this same program with other spaces, and indeed, other types of mathematical objects. Thus, for example, we can understand groups in terms of permutation groups, which we think we understand. While this type of program has definite value, the reader should be aware that what the theory may be telling us is that what we have considered to be simple is in fact vastly more complicated than we had given it credit for. But if this were not the case, mathematics would hardly be worth the effort. In any case, the next example illustrates this idea. $\square$

EXAMPLE 2 _____

Find a countable dense subset of $(\mathbf{C}[0, 1], \rho_\infty)$.

Solution.   The polynomial functions with rational coefficients are a countable subset of the collection of all functions in $\mathbf{C}[0,1]$ (**WHY?**) We claim that the polynomial functions are dense. To see this, apply the Weierstrass's Approximation Theorem (Theorem 9.4.1). $\square$

Discussion.   Again, the idea is polynomials are simple. So continuous functions can't be too bad, can they??

The reader may wonder whether the polynomials are a dense subset of $(\mathbf{C}[0, 1], \rho)$. We leave the proof of this to Exercise 5. This leaves the question: Is there a subset of $\mathbf{C}[0, 1]$ which distinguishes the two metrics with respect to density? $\square$

In Theorem 11.3.5 it was shown that an arbitrary open subset, A, of $\mathbf{R}^2$ could be obtained as a union of open discs which had a pair of rationals for a center and a rational radius. Perforce, this implies that there is a countable collection of open sets, namely, those open discs centered at rationals and having a rational radius, from which all other open sets can be obtained as unions. The countable collection of open discs from which all other open sets can be obtained is referred to as a **countable base** for the topology. This situation, in which there is a countable base can be seen to hold in any of the Euclidean spaces, $\mathbf{R}^k$. There are three features of the Euclidean spaces required to obtain this result. The first is the collection of rational points (points in $\mathbf{R}^k$ having only rational coordinates) is countable. The second is the collection of rational points is dense in $\mathbf{R}^k$. And the third is that within each open disc, there is an open disc having a rational radius. Quite clearly, we may not expect all three of these properties to hold in an arbitrary metric space. Moreover, the first two properties arise from the fact that the underlying space, X, is $\mathbf{R}$, or one of its finite powers. Thus, one is led to look for the general result which applies to all metric spaces.

Definition. A metric space, (X, ρ), is called **separable** provided there is a countable subset, A, which is dense in X.

Theorem 12.3.5. A separable metric space has a countable base.

Proof. Let $A \subseteq X$ be a countable dense subset of X and let B be an arbitrary open set. The collection of all open spheres having a center in A and a rational radius is countable (Exercise 18). Now fix $x \in B$. By assumption, there is a sequence, $\{a_n\}$, of members of A which converges to x. Further, since B is open, there is an open sphere centered at x, S_x, such that $S_x \subseteq B$. Let $r > 0$ be the radius of S_x. Choose $q \in \mathbf{Q}$ such that $0 < q < \dfrac{r}{3}$ and pick a_N such that its distance from x is less than q (**HOW?**). Then the ball, D, centered at a_n of radius q satisfies $x \in D \subseteq B$. It follows (**WHY?**) that the collection of open spheres having a center in A and a rational radius is a countable base.   □

Discussion. The reader can see that the two elements required for the proof are first, that X contains a countable dense subset, and second, that the spheres having rational radii can be found inside any given open sphere.   □

Definition. A nonempty set $A \subseteq X$ is **connected** if there do not exist two opens sets, O_1 and O_2 such that $A \subseteq O_1 \cup O_2$, $O_1 \cap O_2 = \varnothing$, and $A \cap O_i \neq \varnothing$, $i = 1, 2$.

Discussion. This definition is essentially the same as that given in Chapter 11. However, in particular cases it is more difficult to apply than in either $\mathbf{R}$ or $\mathbf{R}^2$.   □

EXAMPLE 3 ——————————————————————————————————

Let
$$\mathbf{R}^n = \{\mathbf{x} = (x_1, x_2, \ldots, x_n) : x_i \in \mathbf{R}, \ 1 \leqslant i \leqslant n\},$$

and for $\mathbf{x}, \mathbf{y} \in \mathbf{R}^n$, let
$$\rho_\infty(\mathbf{x}, \mathbf{y}) = \max \{|x_i - y_i| : 1 \leqslant i \leqslant n\}.$$

Show $(\mathbf{R}^n, \rho_\infty)$ is connected.

    Solution. Suppose for the sake of argument that $(\mathbf{R}^n, \rho_\infty)$ is not connected. Then, there exist two nonempty open sets O_1 and O_2 such that $O_1 \cup O_2 = \mathbf{R}^n$ and $O_1 \cap O_2 = \varnothing$. We claim bd $O_1 \neq \varnothing$ (Exercise 6). For a fixed $x \in$ bd O_1, x cannot be in the interior of either O_1 or O_2, whence $O_1 \cup O_2 \neq X$. $\square$

Discussion. The key to this argument is that a nonempty, proper subset of $\mathbf{R}^n$ must have a nonempty boundary. The proof of this fact depends in an essential way on the completeness of $\mathbf{R}$. One method for obtaining the proof is by the type of argument presented in section 11.3 which established the path connectedness for $\mathbf{R}^2$. Other methods are more direct and it is left to the reader to develop one. $\square$

    There are many other aspects to elementary point set topology which could be developed. Some are presented in the exercises; others are left to other courses and other texts.

EXERCISES

1. Prove Theorem 12.3.1.

2. Perform the calculations necessary to validate the assertions made in Example 1.

3. Complete the proof of Theorem 12.3.2.

4. Prove the various assertions about closed sets in Theorem 12.3.3.

5. Show the polynomials are a dense subset of $(\mathbf{C}[0, 1], \rho)$.

6. Show if A is a nonempty, proper subset of $\mathbf{R}^n$, then bd $A \neq \varnothing$ in $(\mathbf{R}^n, \rho_\infty)$.

7. Let $f < g$ denote the usual order relation on functions in $\mathbf{C}[0, 1]$. For any fixed $f \in \mathbf{C}[0, 1]$ show $\{g : g \in \mathbf{C}[0, 1] \text{ and } g < f\}$ is open in $(\mathbf{C}[0, 1], \rho_\infty)$. Is it open in $(\mathbf{C}[0, 1], \rho)$ as well?

8. Prove the intersection of two open spheres always contains a third open sphere.

9. Give an example to show the closure of an open sphere in a metric space need not be the corresponding closed sphere.

10. Let A and B be subsets of a metric space, (X, ρ), and define

$$d(A, B) = \inf \{d(x, y) : x \in A, y \in B\}.$$

Prove $\overline{A} = \{x \in X : d(\{x\}, A) = 0\}$.

11. Let A_{lm} denote the set of accumulation points of A. Prove:
    (a) $\overline{A} = A \cup A_{lm}$;
    (b) A is closed if and only if $A_{lm} \subseteq A$;
    (c) A_{lm} is always a closed set.

12. Show that $\overline{A \cup B} = \overline{A} \cup \overline{B}$. Show that equality need not happen if $\cup$ is replaced by $\cap$. What can you say about the closures of an arbitrary union (intersection) of sets?

13. Let A be open and B be closed in (X, ρ). Show $A \sim B$ is open and $B \sim A$ is closed.

14. Let A° denote the set of all interior points of A. Show
    (a) A° is always an open set;
    (b) A is open if and only if $A = A^\circ$;

(c) $(A \cap B)^\circ = A^\circ \cap B^\circ$; can $\cap$ be replaced by $\cup$? What about arbitrary unions (intersections)?

(d) A° is the largest open subset of A;

(e) $X \sim \bar{A} = (X \sim A)^\circ$.

15. Start with an arbitrary set, A, in a metric space, (X, ρ), and repeatedly apply the operations of closure, interior, and complementation in any order. Show that at most 14 distinct sets can be produced by this process. Further, show there is a subset of **R** which actually generates 14 distinct sets. This is known as **Kuratowski problem**.

16. Let (X, ρ) be an arbitrary metric space with $A \subseteq X$. Show

(a) bd A is closed;

(b) A is open if and only if $A \cap$ bd $A = \emptyset$;

(c) A is closed if and only if bd $A \subseteq A$;

(d) bd $A = \emptyset$ if and only if A is both open and closed.

17. Show a subset, A, of a metric space is open if and only if it is a union of open spheres with rational radii.

18. Let (X, ρ) be a metric space and A be a countable dense subset. Show the collection of open spheres having a center in A and a rational radius is countable.

19. Let A be a subset of (X, ρ) and let ρ_A be the subspace metric on A induced by the metric, ρ. Show a subset, $H \subseteq A$ is open in (A, ρ_A) if and only if $H = K \cap A$, where K is an open set in (X, ρ). Give an example to show that in general there will be sets which are open in the subspace but not in the original space.

20. Prove the following are equivalent statements in any metric space, (X, ρ):

(a) A is dense;

(b) Each open sphere in the space intersects A;

(c) For each $x \in X$, there is a sequence of distinct points of A which converges to x.

21. By the **completion** of a metric space, (X, ρ), we mean a metric space, $(\tilde{X}, \tilde{\rho})$, together with an injection, $i: X \to \tilde{X}$, where $(\tilde{X}, \tilde{\rho})$ is a complete metric space, $i(X)$ is a dense subset of $\tilde{X}$, and $\tilde{\rho}|_{i(X) \times i(X)} = \rho$. Using arguments similar to those suggested in Exercises 11.4.31–11.4.39 prove every metric space can be embedded in a complete metric space.

22. A **contraction** in a metric space, (X, ρ), is a function, $f: X \to X$, satisfying $\rho(f(x), f(y)) \leq k\rho(x, y)$ for some k such that $0 < k < 1$ and for all distinct $x, y \in X$. Prove **Banach's Contraction Principle**: If (X, ρ) is a complete metric space and f is a contraction on X, there exists a unique $x_0 \in X$ such that $f(x_0) = x_0$. Such a point is called a **fixed point** of the function, f. [HINT: Show for any $x \in X$, the sequence, $\{x, f(x), ff(x), \ldots, f^n(x), \ldots\}$ is Cauchy, where $f^n = f \circ f \circ \cdots \circ f$ n times.]

23. Show by an example that completeness is vital for the conclusion in Exercise 22 above.

24. Prove the 'converse' of Banach's contraction principle: if for each nonempty closed subset A of a metric space X and for each contraction mapping $f: A \to A$, f has a fixed point, then X is a complete metric space.

25. In the metric space $(\mathbf{C}[0, 1/2], \rho_\infty)$, show that the function ϕ defined by $\phi(f)(x) = x^3 + 2x$, $x \in [0, 1/2]$, $f \in \mathbf{C}[0, 1/2]$ is a contraction map. Obtain the fixed point for ϕ guaranteed in Exercise 22.

26. If Y is a complete subspace of a metric space (X, ρ), prove that Y is closed. If (X, ρ) is a complete metric space, prove that a subset $Y \subseteq X$ is closed if and only if Y is complete. (A subset of a metric space is complete, if it is a complete metric space, in the relativized (metric) topology.)

27. If (X, ρ) is a complete metric space, and if $\{F_n\}$ is a decreasing sequence of closed sets, whose diameters tend to 0 as n tends to ∞, show that $\bigcap_{n=1}^{\infty} F_n$ is nonempty, and contains exactly one point.

28. Show the space l_∞ of all bounded sequences in **R** with the metric defined by

$$\rho_\infty(\{x_n\}, \{y_n\}) = \sup\{|x_n - y_n|\}, \quad \{x_n\}, \{y_n\} \in l_\infty$$

is not separable.
[HINT: Show that every dense subset is uncountable.]

12.4 CONTINUITY IN METRIC SPACES

In the first section of this chapter we presented a rich variety of metric spaces. These spaces consisted of an underlying set together with a metric which assigned a distance between any pair of points. It was seen, via the examples presented in sections 12.2 and 12.3, that by changing the metric one could change fundamental properties of the space. In this way it was demonstrated that to be different it was not necessary for two spaces to have different underlying sets, rather, changing the metric was enough.

Having demonstrated that there are many apparently different metric spaces, the question arises:

When are two metric spaces the same?

This type of question, when are two of something really the same, plays a central role in mathematics. In all cases, the tool which provides the answer is a function. Specifically, one uses a function to identify members of one object with members of another object in such a way as to establish that it is impossible to distinguish the 'before' behavior from the 'after' behavior. In topology, this would mean that we start with an $x \in X$ and identify it with a $y \in Y$, and show that the topological behavior of x within the space (X, ρ) cannot be distinguished from the topological behavior of $f(x) = y$ within the space (Y, ρ_1). The types of functions which perform this identification are the one-to-one functions which are continuous in both directions and they will be the focus of our interest in this section.

The reader may wonder why the question posed above was not emphasized in the previous treatment of continuous functions. The reason is simple. In going from **R** to **R** with no change in metric, one is still in the same space, whence it would hardly have made sense to consider the question. It is only now, with a rich variety of examples available for study, that it becomes important to be able to answer the question: Are these two given spaces really the same?

Definition. Let (X, ρ) and (Y, ρ_1) be two metric spaces. A function, $f: X \to Y$, is said to be **continuous** provided for every open set $O \subseteq Y$, $f^{-1}(O)$ is open in (X, ρ).

Discussion. The definition which we have given is the standard topological definition of continuous function. Moreover, given the preceding comments, it is easy to see the intuition behind the definition.

Continuous functions are to be used to tell when two metric spaces are really the same with respect to their topological properties. Topologies are characterized by their open sets. Thus, the class of functions which will identify when two metric spaces are topologically the same are functions which carry open subsets of one space into open subsets of another space. □

Theorem 12.4.1. Let (X, ρ) and (Y, ρ_1) be two metric spaces. Then a function, $f: X \to Y$, is continuous if and only if for every $\epsilon > 0$, and every $x \in X$ there exists $\delta > 0$ such that for all $x_1 \in X$

$$\rho_1(f(x), f(x_1)) < \epsilon \text{ whenever } \rho(x, x_1) < \delta.$$

Proof. Suppose f is continuous. Let $\epsilon > 0$ and $x \in X$ be given. The open sphere of radius ϵ centered at $f(x)$ is an open subset in (Y, ρ_1). Call this open sphere, O. By assumption, $f^{-1}(O)$ is open, whence there is an open sphere of radius δ centered at x, say O_x, such that $O_x \subseteq f^{-1}(O)$ (**WHY?**). But for all $x_1 \in O_x$, $f(x_1) \in O$, whence f satisfies the $\epsilon - \delta$ condition.

Conversely, suppose f satisfies the $\epsilon - \delta$ condition. Let O be an open subset of Y and consider $x \in f^{-1}(O)$. Fix $x \in f^{-1}(O)$, then there is a positive ϵ such that the open ball, $B_{f(x)}$ of radius, ϵ, is a subset of O (**WHY?**). Now, by the $\epsilon - \delta$ condition, we can choose $\delta > 0$ such that

$$\rho_1(f(x), f(x_1)) < \epsilon \text{ whenever } \rho(x, x_1) < \delta.$$

But this means that B_x, the open ball of radius δ centered at x, is a subset of $f^{-1}(O)$, whence $f^{-1}(O)$ is open, as required. □

Discussion. The reader can check that the $\epsilon - \delta$ condition specified above is completely equivalent to the condition used to define continuity on A for functions in Chapter 3.

The definition of continuous presented defines a global concept, namely, what it means for f to be a continuous function from one metric space into another metric space. In Chapter 3, we also had a local definition of continuity which specified what it means for a function to be continuous at a point. □

Definition. Let $x_0 \in X$ be fixed and $f: X \to Y$ where (X, ρ) and (Y, ρ_1) are metric spaces. Then f is said to be **continuous at** x_0 if for every open set, $O \subseteq Y$, such that $f(x) \in O$, there exists an open subset $O_x \subseteq X$ such that $x \in O_x \subseteq f^{-1}(O)$.

Discussion. This definition has a $\epsilon - \delta$ form. It is left to the reader to find it and prove the appropriate theorem (Exercise 1). □

The next theorem of this section describes continuity at a point in terms of convergent sequences.

Theorem 12.4.2. Let (X, ρ) and (Y, ρ_1) be metric spaces, $f: X \to Y$ and let $x_0 \in X$. Then the following statements are equivalent:

   (i) f is continuous at x_0;
   (ii) For every sequence, $\{x_n\}$, in X that converges to x_0, the sequence, $\{f(x_n)\}$, converges to $f(x_0)$.

   Proof. To see that (i) implies (ii), let $\{x_n\}$ be a sequence of points of X converging to x_0. Now consider an open ball, $B_{f(x_0)}$, of radius, ϵ, centered at $f(x_0)$. Since f is continuous at x_0, we can find an open ball, B_{x_0}, centered at x_0 having radius, δ, such that $B_{x_0} \subseteq f^{-1}(B_{x_0})$. But for this δ, we can find N such that $n > N$ implies $\rho(x_0, x_n) < \delta$. It follows that $n < N$ implies $\rho_1(f(x_0), f(x_n)) < \epsilon$ (**WHY?**). The converse is left to the reader as Exercise 2. □

   Discussion. This theorem reiterates the intimate relationship between the notions of continuity and convergence of a sequence. It says that continuous functions are precisely those functions which carry convergent sequences from the domain to convergent sequences in the range. Restated, this means that for a continuous function, f, the limit operation and the mapping process can be interchanged, that is, $\lim_{n \to \infty} f(x_n) = f(\lim_{n \to \infty} x_n)$.
   This theorem can profitably be used to negate continuity at a specified point. The function, f, will not be continuous at x_0 if we can find a convergent sequence in the domain with limit, x_0, whereas the image sequence, $\{f(x_n)\}$, fails to converge to $f(x_0)$. □

   The next theorem supplies other useful characterizations of continuous functions.

Theorem 12.4.3. Let (X, ρ) and (Y, ρ_1) be metric spaces and $f \colon X \to Y$ be a function. The following conditions are equivalent:

   (i) f is continuous;
   (ii) $f^{-1}[F]$ is closed for each closed set, $F \subseteq Y$;
   (iii) For each $A \subseteq X$, $f[\bar{A}] \subseteq \overline{f(A)}$.

   Proof. The reader can see that (i) and (ii) are equivalent by observing $f^{-1}[Y \sim A] = X \sim f^{-1}[A]$, and the complement of an open set is closed (**WHY?**).
   To see that (iii) is a consequence of (ii), observe $A \subseteq f^{-1}\overline{f(A)}$, whence $\bar{A} \subseteq f^{-1}\overline{f(A)}$ (**WHY?**). The proof that (iii) implies (i) is left as Exercise 3. □

   Discussion. The fact that the inverse image of a closed set under a continuous map is also closed should not surprise the reader. After all, closed sets are the complements of open sets, and topology may be viewed in terms of closed sets as easily as open sets. The third condition has a somewhat different flavor in that it starts with an $A \subseteq X$ and concludes with a statement about $\bar{A}$, which also resides in X. A similar condition can be formulated with respect to interiors (Exercise 4).
   In respect to the comment about condition (iii), we stress that the inverse image of an open (closed) set under a continuous map will be open (closed). It is not generally the case that the image of an open (closed) set under a continuous map will be open (closed). The reader is asked to provide examples in Exercise 5. □

Definition. Let (X, ρ) and (Y, ρ_1) be metric spaces. A one-to-one function, $f: X \to Y$, is a **homeomorphism** provided both f and f^{-1} are continuous functions. In that case, the spaces, (X, ρ) and (Y, ρ_1), are said to be **homeomorphic**.

Discussion. The existence of f^{-1} as a function from Y to X is guaranteed by the fact that f is one-to-one as well as onto. The effect of the bicontinuity of f (that is, both f and its inverse are continuous functions) is that both f and f^{-1} carry open (closed) sets to open (closed) sets, so that f faithfully maps open sets to open sets and closed sets to closed sets. As a consequence, there is a one-to-one correspondence between open sets of X and Y, and hence there is one-to-one correspondence between closed sets, closures, interiors, convergent sequences, and so on. In summary, homeomorphic spaces are topologically indistinguishable.

Properties that are preserved under a homeomorphism are called **topological invariants**. Open sets, closed sets, limit points of a set, interior, closure, and so on, are but a few examples of topological invariants. □

EXAMPLE 1 _____

Let $X = \mathbf{R}^2$ and consider the metrics, ρ_1 and ρ_∞ of Examples 12.1.5 and 12.1.6, respectively. Show (X, ρ_1) and (X, ρ_∞) are homeomorphic.

Solution. Let f be the identity function. Consider a ρ_∞-open set, O. Fix $\mathbf{x} \in O$. The there is a ρ_∞-open ball, $B_\mathbf{x}$, centered at $\mathbf{x}$ such that $B_\mathbf{x} \subseteq O$. Let δ denote the radius of $B_\mathbf{x}$ and let $C_\mathbf{x}$ denote the ρ_1-open ball of radius δ centered at $\mathbf{x}$. Then $\mathbf{x} \in C_\mathbf{x} \subseteq B_\mathbf{x} \subseteq O$ (**WHY?**), whence O is ρ_1-open. The reader can prove the reverse requirement (Exercise 6). □

Discussion. The reader can check that this example implies that all of the spaces, $(\mathbf{R}^2, \rho_p)$, are homeomorphic (Exercise 7).

The reader can also check that even though the spaces are homeomorphic, the distance between a pair of points in $\mathbf{R}^2$, $\mathbf{x}$ and $\mathbf{y}$, is not fixed. Thus, homeomorphisms do not preserve distance. They permit the fabric of a space to be distorted, while its topological properties remain unchanged. □

EXAMPLE 2 _____

Let $\{x_n\}$ be a sequence in a metric space. Show that the property of being Cauchy is not a topological property.

Solution. Let $X = (0, 1]$ and $Y = [1, \infty)$. Let ρ be the usual distance metric on X and Y. Define the function, f, by $f(x) = \dfrac{1}{x}$. Then f is continuous and one-to-one on X and maps X onto Y. The sequence, $\{\dfrac{1}{n}\}$, is Cauchy in (X, ρ) (**WHY?**). However, it is not Cauchy in (Y, ρ) (**WHY?**). □

Discussion. In view of Theorem 12.4.2, this result seems surprising. The key difference is that the sequence selected for study in the present example has no limit. If it had a limit, then Theorem 12.4.2 would guarantee that the image sequence was also Cauchy.   □

EXAMPLE 3

Show that the spaces, $(\mathbf{C}[0, 1], \rho)$ and $(\mathbf{C}[0, 1], \rho_\infty)$, are not homeomorphic.

> *Solution.* Example 12.3.1 presents a subset of $\mathbf{C}[0, 1]$ which has a limit point in $(\mathbf{C}[0, 1], \rho)$ but not in $(\mathbf{C}[0, 1], \rho_\infty)$. By Theorem 12.4.2, the spaces could not be homeomorphic no matter what function from X to X was taken as the candidate (**WHY?**).   □

Discussion. This example illustrates the fact that if we can find sets which are paired by the candidate homeomorphism, but topologically different, the spaces will not be homeomorphic to one another.

EXERCISES

1. Give a $\epsilon - \delta$ definition of continuity at a point for a function from one metric space to another and prove that the $\epsilon - \delta$ formulation is equivalent to the formulation given.

2. Complete the missing details in Theorem 12.4.2 and prove the converse.

3. Prove (iii) implies (i) in Theorem 12.4.3 and fill in any other missing details in the proof of the theorem.

4. Formulate a condition about interiors which can be used to characterize continuous functions. Prove this theorem.

5. Give an example of a continuous function from (X, ρ) to (Y, ρ_1) such that for some open $O \subseteq X$, $f(O)$ is not open.

6. Complete the solution of Example 1.

7. Show the set of all points where two continuous functions on (X, ρ) agree must be a closed set.

8. Let A be a dense subset of a metric space where two continuous functions, f and g, are equal. Prove f and g are identical on X.

9. Let $f: X \to Y$ be a function between metric spaces and let A and B be closed subsets of X such that $X = A \cup B$. If the restrictions of f to A and B are continuous, prove f is continuous.

10. Let (X, ρ), (Y, ρ_1) be metric spaces and $f: X \to Y$ be a function. For $x_0 \in X$, define the **oscillation** of f at x_0 to be g.l.b $\{\epsilon \in \mathbf{R}$: there exists an open sphere S in X with center x_0 such that for $a, b \in S$, $e(f(a), f(b)) \leqslant \epsilon\}$, if the bracketed set is nonempty and $+\infty$ otherwise. Show that the set of points where the oscillation of f is at least ϵ is a closed set; and f is continuous at a point if and only if the oscillation at that point is zero.

11. Let $f: X \to \mathbf{R}$ assume value 1 on a set, A, and 0 on its complement. Prove the set of points at which f is not continuous is precisely the boundary of S.

12. Let $x \in A \subseteq X$ be an interior point. Show x remains an interior point of A under any homeomorphism.

13. Show the metric space of Example 12.1.4 is homeomorphic to $\mathbf{R}^2$ with the usual metric.

14. Consider the closed unit disc, D, in $\mathbf{R}^2$ and the same disc with its center removed, C. Show that D and C are not homeomorphic when considered as metric spaces with the usual metric.

15. Let C be as in Exercise 14 and let $A = \mathbf{R}^2 \sim D$. Show C and A are not homeomorphic, but C and $\bar{A}$ are homeomorphic.

16. An **isometry** between two metric spaces (X, ρ) and (Y, ρ_1) is a function F satisfying

$$\rho_1(F(x), F(y)) = \rho(x, y), \quad x, y \in X.$$

Two spaces X and Y are **isometric** if there exists an isometry of X onto Y.
   (a) Show an isometry is necessarily one-to-one;
   (b) Show every isometry is a homeomorphism, but not conversely;
   (c) Show completeness is preserved under an isometry;
   (d) Construct a function $f: \mathbf{R}^+ \to \mathbf{R}^+$ which is not onto, but satisfies $|f(x) - f(y)| = |x - y|$ for all $x, y \in \mathbf{R}^+$.

17. Let f be a function from a metric space (X, ρ) to (Y, ρ_1). Prove or disprove: f is uniformly continuous if and only if for each pair of sequences $\{x_n\}$, $\{y_n\}$ in X, we have $\rho(x_n, y_n)$ converges to 0 implies $\rho_1(f(x_n), f(y_n))$ converges to 0.

18. A function f between two metric spaces (X, ρ) and (Y, ρ_1) is open (closed) if it maps open (closed) sets onto open (closed) sets. A function f between two metric spaces may be continuous or not continuous, open or not open, closed or not closed. Decide (with appropriate examples) which of the eight logical possibilities between these properties for f are possible.

19. A function $f: X \to \mathbf{R}$, where (X, ρ) is a metric space is **lower semicontinuous (upper semicontinuous)** provided for each $a \in \mathbf{R}$, $\{x \in X: f(x) > a\}$ ($\{x \in X: f(x) > a\}$) is an open set. Prove the following:
   (a) f is continuous if and only if it is both lower semicontinuous and upper semicontinuous;
   (b) f is lower semicontinuous if and only if for each $x \in X$ and each $a \in \mathbf{R}$, there is an open sphere S centered at x such that $a < f(s)$ for all $s \in S$;
   (c) f is lower semicontinuous if and only if $-f$ is upper semicontinuous;
   (d) If S is an open (a closed) subset of X, then the characteristic function $C_A: X \to \mathbf{R}$ is lower (upper) semicontinuous.

   [The **characteristic function** of the set A is defined by $C_A(x) = \begin{cases} 1, & x \in A \\ 0, & x \notin A. \end{cases}$]

12.5 COMPACT METRIC SPACES

In Chapter 3, we saw that subsets of the real line which were both closed and bounded were called compact sets and enjoyed very nice properties. These sets were characterized by the Heine–Borel covering property, namely, any covering of the set by open intervals can always be reduced to a finite subcover. In section 11.4 we proved that closed bounded subsets of $\mathbf{R}^2$ were also nice and discussed various properties of these sets in relation to the concept of being compact. In this section, we shall identify compact sets in an arbitrary metric space and investigate their properties. We will also show that continuous functions defined on compact metric spaces are nicely behaved, and exhibit the remarkable property of being uniformly continuous.

We begin by defining the notion of compactness using the familiar open cover property.

Definition. Let (X, ρ) be a metric space. A family, $\{G_\alpha : \alpha \in A\}$, of sets is said to **cover** X provided $X \subseteq \bigcup_{\alpha \in A} G_\alpha$. If each G_α is an open set, then the family, $\{G_\alpha\}$, is an **open cover** of X. A **subcover** of a cover $\{G_\alpha\}$ is a subcollection of the $\{G_\alpha\}$ which also forms a cover of X. If a subcover consists of a finite number of sets, then it is a **finite subcover** of the original cover.

Definition. A metric space, (X, ρ), is (**Heine–Borel**) **compact** if and only if every open cover of X contains a finite subcover.

Discussion. A thorough discussion of the compactness concept as it relates to $\mathbf{R}^2$ was presented in section 11.4. We suggest that the reader review that section, and we will not repeat the material presented. A particular focus of that review should be the content of Theorems 11.4.5–11.4.8. □

EXAMPLE 1
___

Let X be any infinite set and ρ the discrete metric. Is (X, ρ) a compact metric space?

Solution. Recall that the discrete metric on a set, X, is defined by

$$\rho(x, y) = \begin{cases} 0, & \text{if } x = y \\ 1, & \text{otherwise.} \end{cases}$$

Let B_x denote the open ball of radius, $\frac{1}{2}$, centered at x. Then $B_x = \{x\}$ (**WHY?**). It follows the family, $\{B_x : x \in X\}$, covers X. However, no finite subfamily covers X (**WHY?**), whence (X, ρ) is not compact. □

One feature which the reader will have gleaned from the review of section 11.4 is that many of the proofs related to compactness use nested collections of closed sets. This suggests that the compactness notion might have a formulation in terms of such collections. This insight is accurate, but to confirm it we need a definition.

Definition. A family, $\{F_\alpha\}$, of sets is said to have the **finite intersection property** if each finite subfamily of $\{F_\alpha\}$ has a nonempty intersection.

Discussion. Several instances of families of sets which satisfy the finite intersection property have already been studied in this book, although not under this name. In Chapter 3 we proved that a nested collection of nonempty closed intervals had a nonempty intersection, and in Chapter 11, we generalized that result to $\mathbf{R}^2$. In any case, the point is that a nested collection of sets satisfies the finite intersection property and serves as a motivating example.

Nested families are linearly ordered by inclusion. This is not the case with a general family satisfying the finite intersection property. All that is required is if we take any **finite** number of sets from the collection, then there must be at least one point common to all of them. The point may certainly differ for each finite collection. But we are not demanding that an arbitrary collection of sets from the family or, in particular the entire family of sets, should have some point in common.   □

EXAMPLE 2 _____

Let $A = \mathbf{N} \times \mathbf{N}$ and set

$$F_{(n,m)} = \{(x, y) : x, y \in \mathbf{R} \text{ and } |x| > n \text{ and } |y| > m\}.$$

Show $\{F_{(n,m)}\}$ has the finite intersection property. Further, show $\bigcap \{F_{(n,m)}\} = \varnothing$.

Solution. Let B be a finite subset of $\{F_{(n,m)}\}$. Let $C \subseteq A$ be the collection of subscripts of members of B. Then, C is finite, and there exists N such that if j is a coordinate of an ordered pair in C, then $j < N$ (**WHY?**). Now $(N, N) \in \bigcap B$ (**WHY?**), whence B is nonempty, as required. On the other hand, let $(x, y) \in \mathbf{R}^2$ and choose $N > |x|$ and $M > |y|$. Then $(x, y) \notin F_{(N,M)}$, whence $\bigcap \{F_{(n,m)}\} = \varnothing$ (**WHY?**).   □

Theorem 12.5.1. A metric space, (X, ρ), is compact if and only if each family of closed sets with finite intersection property has a nonempty intersection.

Proof. Let $\{F_\alpha\}$ be a family of closed sets with finite intersection property and suppose $\bigcap_\alpha F_\alpha = \varnothing$. Taking complements in X yields

$$X \sim (\bigcap F_\alpha) = \bigcup (X \sim F_\alpha) = X,$$

which means that the family, $\{X \sim F_\alpha\}$, is an open cover of the compact metric space, X. Hence a finite subfamily, say, $\{X \sim F_i\}$ $i = 1, 2, \ldots, k$, will still cover X. Taking complements once again results in $\bigcap_{i=1}^{k} F_i = \varnothing$, which is a contradiction (**WHY?**). The proof of the converse is left to the reader as Exercise 1.   □

Discussion. The intuition behind this proof is simple. It is known that closed sets are the complements of open sets. Thus, one simply takes the definition of compactness and uses the relationship between closed and open sets and De Morgan's Laws to obtain a property of families of closed sets which is equivalent to compactness.   □

It is possible, and useful, to consider the notion of compactness with respect to arbitrary subsets of X.

Definition. Let $A \subseteq X$, then A is said to be **compact** provided the metric space, (A, ρ_A), is compact, where ρ_A denotes the restriction of ρ to A.

Theorem 12.5.2. A closed subset of a compact set is compact.

Proof. Let A be a closed subset of the compact space, (X, ρ), and let $\{G_\alpha\}$ be an open cover of A. Then, since $B = X \sim A$ is also open, B together with $\{G_\alpha\}$ form an open cover of the compact space, X. So there exists a finite subcover, say, $\{B, G_1, G_2, \ldots, G_k\}$ which covers X. Consequently, $\{G_i\}$, $i = 1, \ldots, k$ forms a finite subcover of A (**WHY?**), proving that A is compact. $\square$

Discussion. The proof is straightforward. It employs the fact that $X \sim A$ is an open set to produce an open cover for the whole space, X, by adjoining this open set to the open cover of A. The open cover of X is reduced to a finite subcover using the compactness of X. One then notices that the finite cover of X must also be a finite cover of A, even without $X \sim A$. $\square$

Definition. A subset, A, of a metric space, (X, ρ), is **bounded** if there exists a sphere which contains A.

Discussion. The reader should compare this definition with the definition of bounded given in section 11.3 for subsets of the plane and check that the two definitions are equivalent.

From the above definition, if A is nonempty and is bounded, and $x, y \in A$, then $\rho(x, y) < \infty$. Define $\delta(A)$ by

$$\delta(A) = \sup \{\rho(x, y) : x, y \in A\}.$$

This number $\delta(A)$ is called the **diameter** of A, provided the supremum exists. Otherwise it is defined to be infinite. With this notion, we can check that A is bounded if and only if it possesses a finite diameter (Exercise 2). $\square$

In Chapter 3 and again in Chapter 11 it was demonstrated that closed bounded subsets were compact, and conversely. Thus, an important question is whether the analogous result holds for arbitrary metric spaces. The next theorem and example answer this question.

Theorem 12.5.3. A compact subset of a metric space is closed and bounded.

Proof. Let A be a compact subset in a metric space, (X, ρ) and fix $x \notin A$. For each $y \in A$, there exists a pair of disjoint spheres, $S(x, y)$ and $S(y)$, of radius r_y such that $x \in S(x, y)$ and $y \in S(y)$ (**WHY?**). The family, $\{S(y)\}$, forms an open cover of A, whence there is a finite subfamily which covers A. If r_{y_0} is the radius of smallest sphere in the subfamily, and such exists (**WHY?**), then $S(x, y_0)$ is disjoint from A. It follows A is closed (**WHY?**).

To prove A is bounded, observe the family, $\{S(x, 1) : x \in A\}$, is an open cover of A by spheres of radius 1 each. The compactness of A ensures that this open cover reduces to a finite subcover, so a finite collection of spheres of radius, 1, each will cover A, whence A is bounded (**WHY?**). $\square$

Discussion. The proof of the first part uses a very important property of metric spaces, namely, if $x, y \in X$ and $x \neq y$, then there exist spheres centered at x and y, respectively, which are mutually disjoint. This property is known as **Hausdorff property** and we ask the reader to establish it in Exercise 3.

The Hausdorff property has other important uses. For example, it is this property which enables us to show that the limit of a convergent sequence in a metric space is unique. In an arbitrary topological space which does not possess Hausdorff property, it can happen that a convergent sequence possesses several limits, even an infinite number of them. □

Corollary.   Let (X, ρ) be a compact metric space. Then X is bounded.

Proof. X is a compact subset, hence bounded. □

Discussion.   For arbitrary metric spaces, compact implies closed and bounded. The next example shows that a closed and bounded metric space need not be compact! □

EXAMPLE 3
_____

Give an example of a metric space in which there are closed bounded subsets which are not compact.

Solution.   Let $X = \{\mathbf{w} : 0 < \rho_2((0, 0), \mathbf{w}) \leqslant 1 \text{ and } \mathbf{w} \in \mathbf{R}^2\}$, where ρ_2 is usual metric. The space (X, ρ_2) is bounded, whence $A = X$ is a closed bounded subset. It is left to the reader to establish A is not compact (Exercise 4). □

Discussion.   If one thinks about this example, one sees that the difficulty lies in the fact that the space is not complete. In this context, the reader may want to review the contents of Theorem 11.3.4. □

Definition.   A metric space, (X, ρ), is said to be **countably compact**, provided every countable open cover (cover consisting of a countable number of open sets) has a finite subcover.

Discussion.   At first glance, the countably compact notion appears significantly weaker than the compactness notion. That is, it seems to demand much less to be able to reduce countable covers to finite covers, than to be able to reduce arbitrary covers to finite covers. □

Theorem 12.5.4.   A countably compact metric space is compact.

Proof.   Let (X, ρ) be a countably compact metric space and C be an arbitrary open cover of X. Let B be a countable base for (X, ρ) (**HOW?**). For each $x \in X$, choose $O_x \in B$ such that $x \in O_x$ and for some $O' \in C$, $O_x \subseteq O'$. Such a choice for O_x exists (**WHY?**). But the collection, $\{O_x : x \in X\}$, is a countable open cover for X, whence it has a finite subcover, $\{O_1, \ldots, O_n\}$. But for each O_i there is an O_i' such that $O_i \subseteq O_i' \in C$. Thus, C has been reduced to a finite subcover. □

Discussion.   Since compactness implies countable compactness, the two concepts are equivalent for metric spaces.

Theorem 12.5.1 shows compactness is equivalent to the condition that every family of closed sets with the finite intersection property has a nonempty intersection. But for metric spaces, this is equivalent to every countable family of nonempty closed sets which satisfies the finite intersection property has a nonempty intersection (Exercise 5). We can use this fact to discuss nests. □

Definition. Let (X, ρ) be a metric space and $\{F_n\}$ be a sequence of sets such that $n > m$ implies $F_n \subseteq F_m$. Such a sequence is called a **nest.**

Theorem 12.5.5. The following statements are equivalent:

  (i) (X, ρ) is a compact metric space;
  (ii) every nest of nonempty closed sets has a nonempty intersection;
  (iii) (Bolzano–Weierstrass compactness): every infinite subset of X has a limit point;
  (iv) (sequential compactness): every sequence in X has a convergent subsequence.

Proof. The equivalence of (i) and (ii) is left as Exercise 6. For (ii) implies (iii), let A be an infinite subset of X. If A does not have a limit point, then there is a countably infinite subset of A which does not have a limit point, whence we may assume $A = \{a_n\}$ is countable. Now for each $n \in \mathbf{N}$,

$$F_n = \{a_m : m \geqslant n\}$$

is closed (**WHY?**), whence the sequence, $\{F_n\}$, is a nest of nonempty closed sets. But $\bigcap \{F_n\} = \varnothing$ (**WHY?**), which contradicts the hypothesis. Thus, A must have a limit point.

For (iii) implies (iv), let $\{x_n\}$ be any sequence in X. If some member of $\{x_n\}$ repeats infinitely often, then the constant sequence comprising of this term is clearly a convergent subsequence. Otherwise the set, A, of distinct terms of this sequence is infinite and so by (iii) must admit a limit point, say x, whence there exists a subsequence which converges to x (**WHY?**).

For (iv) implies (ii), let $\{F_n\}$ be a nest of nonempty closed sets. From each F_n pick x_n, employing the Axiom of Choice, if necessary. The sequence, $\{x_n\}$ has a convergent subsequence. Let x be the limit of this sequence. It is left to the reader to show $x \in \bigcap \{F_n\}$ (Exercise 7). □

Corollary. A compact metric space is complete.

Proof. Let $\{x_n\}$ be a Cauchy sequence. Then $\{x_n\}$ has a convergent subsequence with limit, x. But the fact that $\{x_n\}$ is Cauchy guarantees that the sequence, itself, converges to x. □

Discussion. Given Theorem 12.5.5(iv), one is compelled to conjecture that a complete metric space must be compact. This turns out not to be the case. $\mathbf{R}$ provides a nice example. Nevertheless, one thinks that a complete metric space must be well on its way to compactness. The required additional property is given next. □

Definition. A subset, A, of a metric space, (X, ρ), is **precompact (totally bounded)** provided for every $\epsilon > 0$, there exist a finite number of points, $x_i \in X$, $i = 1, \ldots, k$ such that $X \subseteq \bigcup_{i=1}^{k} S(x_i, \epsilon)$, where $S(x_i, \epsilon)$ is the sphere of radius ϵ centered at x_i.

Discussion. The definition roughly states that finite number of translates of spheres of arbitrarily small radii will cover A. (Intuitively, this reminds us of the picture of an octopus.)

Every compact space, X, is precompact, since a cover of X by open spheres of radius, ϵ, each can be reduced to a finite covering, and this in turn gives us precompactness. Also, a precompact set must be bounded (**WHY?**). □

Theorem 12.5.6. A complete, totally bounded metric space X is compact.

Proof. Let A be an infinite subset of X. We show A has a limit point. For each $n \in \mathbf{N}$ let $\{x_{1,n}, \ldots, x_{m,n}\}$ be a finite collection of points such that

$$X = \bigcup_{i=1}^{m} S(x_{i,n}, \epsilon_n) \quad \text{where} \quad \epsilon_n = \frac{1}{3^n}.$$

We claim for every n there exists i such that $A \cap S(x_{i,n}, \epsilon_n)$ is infinite (**WHY?**). Further, we assert that if $A \cap S(x_{i,n}, \epsilon_n)$ is infinite, there exists j such that

$$A \cap S(x_{i,n+1}, \epsilon_{n+1}) \subseteq S(x_{i,n}, \epsilon_n)$$

and the intersection is infinite, as well. Thus, let S_1 be any one of the $S(x_{i,1}, \epsilon_1)$'s which has an infinite intersection with A. Choose S_2 to have an infinite intersection with $A \cap S_1$, and so forth. From each S_n, choose a point, $y_n \in A$. Such a choice exists (**WHY?**). The sequence, $\{y_n\}$, is Cauchy (**WHY?**), whence it has a limit, y. It can be shown y is a limit point of A (**HOW?**). The remainder of the details are left to Exercise 9. □

Discussion. This proof should bear a strong resemblance to every sequence in $\mathbf{R}$, or $\mathbf{R}^2$, has a cluster point. The insight which underlies the present result is the same, namely, if we divide up an infinite collection of points among a finite number of boxes, some box must contain an infinite number of points. □

We shall end this section with a study of continuous functions defined on a compact metric space. We shall see that such a function possesses remarkable properties, namely it is bounded, it attains its bounds and finally it is uniformly continuous. We begin with the following simple theorem.

Theorem 12.5.7. If $f: X \to Y$ is a continuous function between metric spaces, (X, ρ) and (Y, ρ_1) and $A \in X$ is compact, then $f(A)$ is compact.

Proof. Let $\{G_\alpha\}$ be a family of open sets which cover $B = f(A)$. Then, since f is continuous, the family, $f^{-1}(G_\alpha)$, forms an open cover (**WHY?**) of the compact space A, whence there is a finite subfamily, $\{f^{-1}(G_i)\}$, $i = 1, \ldots, k$, that covers A.

Consequently, the finite collection, $\{G_i\}$, $i = 1, \ldots, k$, covers $f(A)$. Thus, $f(A)$ is compact. $\square$

Discussion. Not surprisingly, the property of being compact is topological, that is, preserved by continuous functions. $\square$

Theorem 12.5.8. A continuous one-to-one function, f, of a compact metric space, (X, ρ), onto any metric space (Y, ρ_1) is a homeomorphism.

Proof. By the above theorem, $f[X]$ is compact, hence by Theorem 12.5.3 closed in Y. Now if $A \subseteq X$ is closed, A is compact, whence $f[A]$ is compact and hence closed in Y. In other words, $(f^{-1})^{-1}[A]$ is closed, showing f^{-1} is a continuous function, that is, f is a homeomorphism. $\square$

EXAMPLE 4 _____

Give an example of a metric space, (X, ρ), and a one-to-one continuous function, $f: X \to Y$, where (Y, ρ_1) is a metric space, which is not a homeomorphism. Show (X, ρ) is a metric space.

Solution. Consider the set $\mathbf{C}[0, 1]$ under the two metrics ρ and ρ_∞. The identity function is continuous in one direction but not the other. It is left to the reader to decide which (Exercise 8). $\square$

Definition. Let (X, ρ) and (Y, ρ_1) be metric spaces and $f: X \to Y$ be a function. We say that f is **uniformly continuous** on $A \subseteq X$ provided given $\epsilon > 0$, there exists a $\delta > 0$ such that for all $x, y \in A$

$$\rho_1(f(x), f(y)) < \epsilon \text{ whenever } \rho(x, y) < \delta.$$

Discussion. The reader can compare this definition of uniform continuity with those in Chapters 2 and 11. Only the context has changed. In all respects, the definition is the same and the previous discussion applies. $\square$

Theorem 12.5.9. Every continuous function defined on a compact metric space is uniformly continuous there.

Proof. Let $\epsilon > 0$ be given. For each $x_0 \in X$, by continuity of f at x_0, there exists a $\delta = \delta(x_0) > 0$ such that $\rho(x, x_0) < \delta(x_0)$ implies $\rho_1(f(x), f(x_0)) < \dfrac{\epsilon}{2}$. Now the family of spheres, $\left\{ S\left[x_0, \dfrac{\delta(x_0)}{2} \right] \right\}$, $x_0 \in X$ forms an open cover of the compact space, X, and hence reduces to a finite subcover, say, $\left\{ S(x_i, \dfrac{\delta_i}{2}) \right\}$, $i = 1, \ldots, k$. Let $\delta = \min \left[\dfrac{\delta_1}{2}, \dfrac{\delta_2}{2}, \ldots, \dfrac{\delta_k}{2} \right]$. Now fix $x, y \in X$, and let $\rho(x, y) < \delta$. For some j, $x, y \in S(x_j, \dfrac{\delta_j}{2})$, whence $\rho(x, x_j) < \dfrac{\delta_j}{2}$, and

$\rho(y, x_j) \leqslant \rho(y, x) + \rho(x, x_j) < \delta_j$. It follows that

$$\rho_1(x, y) \leqslant \rho_1(x, x_j) + \rho_1(y, x_j) = \frac{\epsilon}{2} + \frac{\epsilon}{2} = \epsilon.$$

This completes the proof.   □

Discussion.   The reader can compare this proof with that given in Theorem 11.5.7.

As the reader should recall, continuous functions on compact domains attain their maximums, at least when mapping from **R** into **R**. Unless the image space is linearly ordered, this property does not make sense. However, in the case when the image space is ordered, the result obtains as the reader can show in Exercise 11.   □

EXERCISES

1. Complete the proof of Theorem 12.5.1.

2. Formulate a definition of bounded for metric spaces which is analogous to that given for bounded subsets of $\mathbf{R}^2$ (section 11.3). Show the two formulations are equivalent. Further, show a subset of a metric space is bounded exactly if it has a finite diameter.

3. Let (X, ρ) be a metric space. Fix $x \neq y$ members of X. Show there exist two disjoint open spheres centered at x and y, respectively. Show these spheres can be chosen with the same radius.

4. Show the subset, A, of Example 3 is not compact.

5. Let (X, ρ) be a metric space. Show (X, ρ) is compact exactly if every countable family of closed sets with the finite intersection property has a nonempty intersection.

6. Show every countable family of closed sets with the finite intersection property has a nonempty intersection, exactly if every nest of closed sets has a nonempty intersection. Conclude that the latter property is equivalent to compactness for metric spaces.

7. Complete the proof of (iv) implies (ii) in Theorem 12.5.5.

8. Complete Example 4.

9. Complete the details of the proof that a totally bounded complete metric space is compact.

10. Show the metric space of Example 3 is not totally bounded.

11. Show a metric space X is compact if and only if every real-valued continuous function on X is bounded.

12. Let A and B be closed sets in a metric space (X, ρ). Show that there exists a continuous function $g: X \rightarrow \mathbf{R}$ such that $g(x) = 1$ on A, $g(x) = 0$ on B, $-1 < g(x) < 1$ outside $A \cup B$. [HINT: Consider

$$g(x) = \frac{d(x, A) - d(x, B)}{d(x, A) + d(x, B)}$$

13. Let A and B be disjoint closed subsets of a metric space (X, ρ). Prove there exist disjoint open sets U and V such that $A \subseteq U$, and $B \subseteq V$.

14. Let $\delta(A)$ denote the diameter of a subset A of a metric space (X, ρ). Prove the following:
    (a) $\delta(A) = 0$ exactly if A contains at most one point;
    (b) $A \subseteq B$ implies $\delta(A) \subseteq \delta(B)$;
    (c) $\delta(\overline{A}) = \delta(A)$;

(d) if A and B are disjoint, then $\delta(A \cup B) \leqslant \delta(A) + \delta(B)$;

(e) A is bounded if and only if $\delta(A) < \infty$.

15. For subsets A and B of a metric space (X, ρ), we define the **distance** between A and B by

$$\rho(A, B) = \inf \{\rho(x, y) : x \in A, y \in B\}$$

We abbreviate $\rho(\{x\}, B)$ as $\rho(x, B)$. Prove the following:

(a) $\bar{A} = \{x \in X : \rho(x, A) = 0\}$;

(b) $0 \leqslant \rho(A, B) \leqslant \rho(x, y) \leqslant \delta(A \cup B)$, $x, y \in X$;

(c) $\delta(A \cup B) \leqslant \delta(A) + \delta(B) + \rho(A, B)$.

16. A subset A of a metric space (X, ρ) is

(i) nowhere dense (meager) provided its closure $\bar{A}$ contains no open subset of X;

(ii) of first category (thin) in X if A can be expressed as a countable union of nowhere dense sets in X;

(iii) of second category (thick) in X if A is not of first category in X.

Prove that

(a) $\mathbf{Q}$ is of first category in $\mathbf{R}$;

(b) every countable subspace of $\mathbf{R}$ is of first category in $\mathbf{R}$;

(c) if X is of second category, and if $X = A \cup B$, then either A or B must be of second category;

(d) X is of second category in itself if and only if the intersection of every countable family of dense open sets in X is nonempty;

(e) if A is a dense subset of a complete metric space X, and if $A = \bigcap_{n=1}^{\infty} G_n$, where the G_n's are open in X, then $X \sim A$ is of first category.

17. A union of at most countable collection of closed sets is called an **F_σ-set,** and an intersection of at most countable collection of open sets is a **G_δ-set**. Prove:

(a) every closed set is an F_σ-set, but not conversely;

(b) every open set is a G_δ-set, but not conversely;

(c) the complement of an F_σ-set is a G_δ-set, and conversely;

(d) the irrationals in any proper interval can not be an F_σ-set;

(e) the rationals in any proper interval can not be a G_δ-set;

18. Show the set of points in $\mathbf{R}$ at which a real-valued function f is discontinuous, forms an F_σ-set.

19. Does there exist a real-valued function that is continuous only at rational numbers?

20. Prove **Baire's Category Theorem**: a complete metric space is of second category in itself.

21. Use Baire's Category Theorem to prove the existence of everywhere continuous, nowhere differentiable real-valued functions.

[HINT: Consider $E_n = \left\{ f \in \mathbf{C}[0, 1] : \text{there exists } x \in [0, 1 - 1/n], \text{ such that} \right.$

$\left| \dfrac{f(x + h) - f(x)}{h} \right| \leqslant n \text{ for } h \in (0, 1/n) \left. \right\}$. If $f \in \mathbf{C}[0, 1]$ has a derivative at some

point, then $f \in E_n$ for some n. Show that E_n is closed, and has empty interior.]

22. A real number $d > 0$ is called a **Lebesgue number** for a given open cover $\{G_i\}$ of a metric space X if each subset of X of diameter less than d is contained in at least one G_i. Prove that in a (sequentially) compact metric space, every open cover admits a Lebesgue number.

23. Let $\mathbf{C}_{00}(X)$ be the set of bounded real-valued continuous functions on X which have a **compact support**, that is, which vanish outside a compact subset of X. Show $\mathbf{C}_{00}(X)$, ρ_∞) is a metric space which is not complete. Show the completion is the space $\mathbf{C}_0(X)$ consisting of all functions f such that for every $\epsilon > 0$, there is a compact set $K_f \subseteq X$ such that $|f(x)| < \epsilon$ outside K_f.

24. The **Cantor set (Cantor's ternary set)** is defined to be the subset $K \subset [0, 1]$ consisting of those real numbers which can be expressed as $\sum\limits_{n=1}^{\infty} \dfrac{a_n}{3^n}$, where $a_n = 0$ or 2 (real numbers in $[0, 1]$ whose trecimal expansion avoids the digit 1). Prove the following properties of the Cantor set K:

(a) K is uncountable;

(b) K is a compact metric space;

(c) $[0, 1] \sim K$ consists of a countable disjoint union of open intervals of total length 1;

(d) K is nowhere dense in $[0, 1]$.

(e) K is **self-dense** (that is, each point of K is a limit point);

(f) K is totally disconnected.

25. Show the function ϕ defined by

$$\phi\left(\sum_{n=1}^{\infty} \frac{a_n}{3^n}\right) = \sum_{n=1}^{\infty} \frac{a_n}{2^{n+1}}$$

maps the Cantor set K continuously onto the interval $[0, 1]$.

26. Let ϕ be a map on the Cantor set K to $[0, 1] \times [0, 1]$ be defined by

$$\phi\left(\sum_{n=1}^{\infty} \frac{a_n}{3^n}\right) = \left(\sum_{n=1}^{\infty} \frac{a_{2n+1}}{2^{n+1}}, \sum_{n=1}^{\infty} \frac{a_{2n}}{2^{n+1}}\right)$$

Prove

(a) ϕ is well-defined;

(b) ϕ is continuous and onto the square $[0, 1] \times [0, 1]$;

(c) ϕ extends to a continuous function ϕ_1 on $[0, 1]$.

(This extension ϕ_1 is the **Peano curve**.)

Appendix on Set Theory

A.1 INTRODUCTION

This appendix contains only the briefest introduction to set theory. Any reader desiring a more thorough treatment should consult one of the texts mentioned in the references, for example, Monk [1969], which we heartily recommend.

The approach presented is axiomatic, and a complete set of axioms on which to develop set theory is presented. However, much of the theory is suppressed and mainly those items of interest and importance to the development of analysis are discussed.

A.2 AXIOMS FOR SET THEORY

The primitive notions of set theory are those of **class** and **membership.** Intuitively, classes are 'collections of objects'. Collecting objects into groups gives rise to the notion of 'being a member' of a group. Hence, the two primitive notions whose behavior is captured and defined by the axioms are class and membership.

Notationally, capital letters $A, B, C, \ldots, X, Y, Z$ will stand for classes while the membership relation is denoted by $\in$. The formula, $A \in B$, is read as 'the class, A, is a member of the class, B'. The negation, $A \notin B$, is read as 'the class, A, is not a member of the class, B'.

Axiom 1 (Extensionality).

$$\forall A \ \forall B \ [\forall C(C \in A \iff C \in B) \implies A = B].$$

Remark.   This axiom defines the conditions under which two classes are equal to one another, namely, when they have exactly the same members.   □

Definition.   A class X is a **set** if there is a class B such that $X \in B$. A class which is not a set is called a **proper class**.

Remark.   Lowercase letters are used to denote sets. Intuitively, sets are 'well-behaved classes'. They are well-behaved because they are small enough to be found as members of other classes. Note that for a class to be a set requires a witness, that is, to demonstrate A is a set, we must find a class, B, (the witness) such that $A \in B$.
                                                                                                                    □

Formally, we want to discuss classes, sets, and the relations between them in the same way which we have discussed numbers, functions, and so forth. To accomplish this, we specify certain expressions as being of particular importance. Expressions of the form $A = B$, $A = C$, and so on, are **set-theoretic formulas.** Expressions of the form $A \in A$, $X \in Y$, and so on, are also set-theoretic formulas. Formulas generated from the above set-theoretic formulas by use of logical connectives, for example, $\lor$ (or), $\land$ (and), and so on, or the universal ($\forall$) and existential ($\exists$) quantifiers are also set-theoretic.* In addition, in subjects such as analysis, one permits the symbols of analysis to appear, as shown below.

Axiom 2 (Class Building Axioms).   Let $\phi(X)$ be a set-theoretic formula not involving the letter A, then the following is an axiom:

$$\exists A \ \forall X[X \in A \iff X \text{ is a set } \land \ \phi(X)].$$

Remark.   This axiom permits the generation of classes of objects having specific properties. Such constructions occur continually in mathematics, for example, in forming the interval, $[0, 1]$.

The notation $\{X : \phi(X)\}$ is commonly used to stand for the class A obtained from $\phi(X)$ by Axiom 2. Thus,

$$[0, 1] = \{x : 0 \leqslant x \land x \leqslant 1\}.$$

It is implicit that within our set theory we can find sets which will play the role of 0, 1, and all the other 'real numbers'. This is the case; however, a full discussion of modeling the real numbers within set theory is beyond the scope of this appendix.

If $\phi(X)$ is a set-theoretic formula not involving either the letter A or the letter B and if

$$\forall X[X \in A \iff X \text{ is a set } \land \ \phi(X)]$$

and

$$\forall X[X \in B \iff X \text{ is a set } \land \ \phi(X)],$$

---

* For a thorough discussion of the language of set theory and its relationship to logic, we again refer the reader Monk [1969].

then $A = B$. In short, this means that the classes constructed using Axiom 2 are unique. □

Definition. $A \subseteq B \iff \forall C(C \in A \implies C \in B)$.

Remark.   The formula, $A \subseteq B$, is read 'A is **subclass of** B' (or A is **contained** in B for $A \subseteq B$). If a and b are sets, then we say a is a **subset** of b.

The relationship of 'being contained in' is the other important relation which can hold between classes. It is essential for the reader to differentiate between the membership relation, $\in$, and the relation, $\subseteq$. These two relationships are fundamentally different and they must not be confused. □

The first axiom defines equality, the second permits us to construct classes. However, we do not yet have any sets. Most of the rest of the axioms assert that certain constructions are guaranteed to yield sets, as opposed to classes.

Axiom 3 (Power Set). $\forall a \; \exists b \; \forall C(C \subseteq a \implies C \in b)$.

Remark.   This axiom asserts that if one starts with a set, a, then another set, b, is guaranteed to exist which has the property that every subclass of a is a member of b. Among the obvious, but important, consequences of this axiom are: the collection of all subclasses of a set is, itself, a set; and a subclass of a set is a set. □

Axiom 4 (Pairing). $\forall a \; \forall b \; \exists c(a \in c \wedge b \in c)$.

Remark.   This axiom guarantees that given two sets, a and b, a third set, c, can be found which has both these sets as members. Obviously this principal extends to any finite collection. □

Axiom 5 (Union). $\forall a \; \exists b \; \forall C(C \in a \implies C \subseteq b)$.

Remark.   This axiom will guarantee the existence, as a set, of arbitrary unions of families of sets, so long as the family, itself, is a set. To see this, think of the set, a, as being an index set. What is being indexed are the members of a, and each member of a acts as its own index. Then the axiom guarantees the existence of a set, b, which collects together the members of all of the sets which are indexed, that is, all members of the sets which are members of a. □

Definition. $\emptyset = \{x : x \neq x\}$.

Remark. $\emptyset$ is called the **empty class**. We cannot yet refer to it as the empty set, because, at this stage in the development, there is no way to prove $\emptyset$ is a set. That will follow from Axiom 7.

The empty class is particularly useful for demonstrating the difference between the membership relation, $\in$, and the subclass relation, $\subseteq$. $\emptyset$ is not a member of every class, since we can observe $\forall x (x \notin \emptyset)$ whence $\emptyset \notin \emptyset$. $\emptyset$ is a subclass of every class, (**WHY?**), and in particular, $\varnothing \subseteq \varnothing$. Thus, the two relations must be different.   □

Definition. $A \cap B = \{x : x \in A \wedge x \in B\}$. $A \cap B$ is called the **intersection** of A and B.

Remark. Since $A \cap B$ is a subclass of A and B, no axiom will be needed to guarantee that $a \cap b$ will be a set.   □

Axiom 6 (Regularity). $\forall A[A \neq \varnothing \Rightarrow \exists X(X \in A \wedge X \cap A = \varnothing)]$.

Remark. This axiom, unlike the others, is aimed at ensuring that the relation, $\in$, has no undesirable properties. One of the main properties being avoided is finite cyclical strings of classes of the form:

$$A = B_0 \in B_1 \cdots \in B_{n-1} \in B_n = A.$$

The reader can show, for example, $\forall A(A \notin A)$, and so forth.   □

Definition. $SA = \{x : x \in A \vee x = A\}$. SA is called the **successor** of A.

Remark. One should think of 'successor' as a unary operation. Given a set a, Sa will be a new set which is distinct from a.   □

Axiom 7 (Infinity). $\exists a[\varnothing \in a \wedge \forall X(X \in a \Rightarrow SX \in a)]$.

Remark. The axiom of infinity guarantees the existence of loads of sets. For example, $\varnothing$ is a set, $S\varnothing$ is a set, $SS\varnothing$ is a set, and so forth. With a little thought, the reader can see that any set with the property that is nonempty and closed under successor must be infinite.

   The reader should think about this axiom and the successor operation in the context of the positive integers and the Peano Axioms. The 'smallest' set which has $\varnothing$ as a member and is closed under successor should look very much like the positive integers, or, if one identifies 0 with $\varnothing$, the nonnegative integers. Indeed, this is how one can begin the process of modeling real analysis within set theory. That, however, is beyond the scope of this book. We will assume that all numbers can be represented as sets, and that there is a set which represents **R**.   □

Definition. $\{A, B\} = \{x : x = A \vee x = B\}$. $\{A, B\}$ is called the **unordered pair** A,B.

Definition. $\{A\} = \{A, A\}$. $\{A\}$ is called **singleton** A.

Remark. Of course if a and b are sets, then $\{a, b\}$ is a set. It follows that all finite collections of sets will also be sets. But the critical fact about unordered pairs is contained in the next theorem.   □

Theorem 1. If $\{a, b\} = \{c, d\}$, then either $a = c$ and $b = d$, or $a = d$ and $b = c$.

Remark.   The proof is a straightforward case analysis, but it is instructive.   □

Definition. $(A, B) = \{\{A\}, \{A, B\}\}$. (A, B) is called the **ordered pair** with **first coordinate** A and **second coordinate** B.

Remark.   If one thinks about ordered pairs, one sees that two things are critical: it must be possible to distinguish coordinates, and ordered pairs must have the equality property stated in the next theorem. The first is not possible without the second, so it is really the second which one must have.   □

Theorem 2.   If $(a, b) = (c, d)$, then $a = c$ and $b = d$.

Remark.   This is the property of ordered pairs which is used repetitively throughout mathematics. We could not have functions or relations without it.
The proof is case analysis and is instructive.   □

Definition.   Let R be a class. Then

(i) R is a **relation** if and only if $\forall A(A \in R \implies \exists c \exists d[A = (c, d)])$;
(ii) $\text{Dmn } R = \{x : \exists y[(x, y) \in R]\}$. $\text{Dmn } R$ is called the **domain** of R;
(iii) $\text{Rng } R = \{y : \exists x[(x, y) \in R]\}$. $\text{Rng } R$ is called the **range** of R;
(iv) F is a **function** if and only if F is a relation and

$$\forall x \forall y \forall z[(x, y) \in F \wedge (x, z) \in F . \implies . y = z].$$

Axiom 8 (Substitution).   If F is a function and $\text{Dmn } F$ is a set, then $\text{Rng } F$ is a set.

Remark.   This axiom again specifies that certain objects are sets. In this case the image of a set under a function must again be a set.   □

Axiom 9 (Relational Axiom of Choice).   If R is a relation, then there is a function F such that $F \subseteq R$ and $\text{Dmn } F = \text{Dmn } R$.

Remark.   This is a strong form of the Axiom of Choice which is discussed in section A.10. It is independent from the previous axioms and has many remarkable consequences. In analysis, one of these is the existence of a nonmeasurable set.   □

The axioms presented are generally sufficient to do most of mathematics. Exploring their deeper consequences is far beyond the scope of this book and again we recommend Monk [1969] for a concise and readable treatment.
Before continuing, we point out how the axioms permit the escape from Russell's paradox which results from considering the class

$$B = \{X : X \notin X\}.$$

The paradox results from asking whether $B \in B$. Ordinarily one obtains

$$B \in B \quad \text{if and only if} \quad B \notin B.$$

The paradox is avoided since for $B \in B$, it must be the case that B is a set. One concludes that B is not a set, but a proper class.

A.3 BOOLEAN ALGEBRA OF CLASSES

Of particular interest and use to working mathematicians are the Boolean operations and the associated relation of containment, or subset. In this section, we discuss the basic theory associated with the containment relation, together with theorems related to finite unions and intersections.

Theorem 3. Let A, B, and C be any classes. Then

     (i) $\varnothing \subseteq A$;
   (ii) if $A \subseteq \varnothing$, then $A = \varnothing$;
  (iii) $A \subseteq A$;
  (iv) if $A \subseteq B$ and $B \subseteq A$, then $A = B$;
   (v) if $A \subseteq B$ and $B \subseteq C$, then $A \subseteq C$.

Remark. The general method for showing equality of sets is specified in the extensionality axiom. The method is now refined to showing that containment goes in both directions, (iv). This, in fact, is a specification of an algorithm for showing equality between two sets, A, B. You must first show that $A \subseteq B$, and then show that $B \subseteq A$. *No method which does not establish these two facts is acceptable for establishing equality!*   ☐

Theorem 4. Let A, B, C, D, and X be classes. Then

      (i) $\varnothing \cap A = \varnothing$;
    (ii) $A \cap A = A$;
   (iii) $A \cap B = B \cap A$;
   (iv) $A \cap (B \cap C) = (A \cap B) \cap C$;
    (v) $A \cap B \subseteq A$;
   (vi) if $X \subseteq A$ and $X \subseteq B$, then $X \subseteq A \cap B$;
  (vii) $A = A \cap B$ if and only if $A \subseteq B$;
 (viii) if $A \subseteq C$ and $B \subseteq D$, then $A \cap B \subseteq C \cap D$.

Definition. Classes A and B are called **disjoint** if $A \cap B = \varnothing$. A class A is called a **family of pairwise disjoint sets** if every two distinct members of A are disjoint, that is,

$$\forall x \forall y[x \in A \land y \in A \land x \neq y . \Longrightarrow . x \cap y = \varnothing].$$

Theorem 5. Let A be a class and a and b be any sets. Then

    (i) $\varnothing$ and A are disjoint for any class A;
   (ii) if $a \notin A$, then A and $\{a\}$ are disjoint;
  (iii) $\varnothing$ and $\{a\}$ are families of pairwise disjoint sets;
  (iv) for $a \neq b$, $\{a, b\}$ is a family of pairwise disjoint sets if and only if $a \cap b = \varnothing$.

Definition. $A \cup B = \{x : x \in A \lor x \in B\}$. $A \cup B$ is called the **union** of A and B.

Theorem 6.   Let A, B, C, and D be classes, a, b, and x be sets.   Then

    (i) $A \cup \emptyset = A$;
    (ii) $A \cup A = A$;
    (iii) $A \cup (B \cup C) = (A \cup B) \cup C$;
    (iv) $A \subseteq A \cup B$;
    (v) $A \cup B = B \cup A$;
    (vi) $A \subseteq B$ if and only if $A \cup B = B$;
    (vii) $A \cup (B \cap C) = (A \cup B) \cap (A \cup C)$;
    (viii) $a \cup b$ is a set;
    (ix) $Sx = x \cup \{x\}$ and Sx is a set;
    (x) if $A \subseteq C$ and $B \subseteq D$, then $A \cup B \subseteq C \cup D$.

Remark.   The union operation provides a simple means for defining finite sets of any size and for defining n-tuples for any positive integer n.   □

Definition. $\{A, B, C\} = \{A\} \cup \{B, C\}$; $(A, B, C) = ((A, B), C)$.

Definition. $V^* = \{x : x = x\}$. V^* is called the **universe**.

Theorem 7.   Let x be any set and A be any class.   Then

    (i) $\forall x(x \in V^*)$;
    (ii) $\forall A(A \subseteq V^*)$;
    (iii) $\forall A(A \cap V^* = A)$;
    (iv) $\forall A(A \cup V^* = V^*)$;
    (v) V^* is a proper class.

Definition.
    (i) $A' = \{x : x \notin A\}$. A' is the **complement of** A.
    (ii) $A \sim B = \{x : x \in A \land x \notin B\}$. $A \sim B$ is called the **complement of** B **relative to** A.

Theorem 8.   Let A and B be any classes and a any set.   Then

    (i) $a \sim B$ is a set;
    (ii) $A' = V^* \sim A$;
    (iii) $A \sim B = A \cap B'$;
    (iv) $\emptyset' = V^*$;
    (v) $V^{*'} = \emptyset$;
    (vi) $A'' = A$;
    (vii) $A \sim A = \emptyset$;
    (viii) $A \subseteq B$ if and only if $B' \subseteq A'$;
    (ix) $A \subseteq B$ if and only if $A \sim B = \emptyset$;

(x) $(A \cap B)' = A' \cup B'$ and $(A \cup B)' = A' \cap B'$;

(xi) $A \cap A' = \varnothing$.

Remark.   The facts contained in (x) are known as **De Morgan's Laws** for sets.
□

A.4 INFINITE BOOLEAN OPERATIONS

Arbitrary unions and intersections of families of sets occur throughout mathematics. This section contains the essential facts related to these more general operations.

Definition. $\bigcup A = \{x : \exists y[y \in A \wedge x \in y]\}$. We call $\bigcup A$ the **union** of the family A.

Remark.   We often think of A as a function with domain I, called the index set. In such an instance, we set $A(i) = A_i$ and write

$$\bigcup \text{Rng } A = \bigcup \{A_i : i \in I\} = \bigcup_{i \in I} A_i.$$

For this case we say that A is an **indexed family of sets** with domain I.
□

Theorem 9.   Let A and B be any classes and a and b be sets. Then

 (i) $\bigcup \varnothing = \varnothing$;

 (ii) $\bigcup \{a\} = a$;

 (iii) $\bigcup \{a, b\} = a \cup b$;

 (iv) if $A \subseteq B$, then $\bigcup A \subseteq \bigcup B$;

 (v) $\bigcup A \cup \bigcup B = \bigcup (A \cup B)$;

 (vi) $\bigcup (A \cap B) \subseteq \bigcup A \cap \bigcup B$;

 (vii) $\bigcup a$ is a set.

Definition. $\bigcap A = \{x : \forall y(y \in A \Rightarrow x \in y)\}$. $\bigcap A$ is called the **intersection** of the family of sets, A.

Remark. $\bigcap A$ should be thought of as the intersection of all the sets which are members of the family A.
□

Theorem 10.   Let A and B be any classes and a and b be sets. Then

 (i) $\bigcap \varnothing = V^*$;

 (ii) $\bigcap \{a\} = a$;

 (iii) $\bigcap \{a, b\} = a \cap b$;

 (iv) $A \subseteq B$ implies $\bigcap B \subseteq \bigcap A$;

 (v) $\bigcap (A \cup B) = \bigcap A \cap \bigcap B$;

 (vi) $(\bigcap A) \cup (\bigcap B) \subseteq \bigcap (A \cap B)$.

Remark.   Most of the results for infinite unions and intersections are generalizations of analogous results for finite unions and intersections. There are notable exceptions, for example, 9(vi) and 10(vi); 10(i) is also surprising.
□

A.5 ALGEBRA OF RELATIONS

Recall that a relation is a class every member of which is an ordered pair. It is usually the case for a relation, R, that one writes xRy instead of $(x, y) \in R$. The canonical instance of this is the relation, $<$ on $\mathbf{R}$, where one writes $1 < x$, for example.

It is trivial that $\varnothing$ is a relation and that to check whether two relations, R and S are equal, one has only to show equivalence of membership for ordered pairs.

Below is a list of some of the more useful properties of relations. A more complete list can be found in Monk [1969].

Definition. $R^{-1} = \{(y, x) : (x, y) \in R\}$. R^{-1} is called the **inverse** of R.

Remark. This definition together with the Boolean operations permit us to notice $a = \bigcap\bigcap(a, b)$ and $b = \bigcap\bigcap\bigcap\{(a, b)\}^{-1}$. In consequence, there is a constructive method for obtaining the first and second coordinates of any ordered pair. $\square$

Theorem 11. Let R and S be relations. Then

    (i) $\mathrm{Dmn}(R \cup S) = \mathrm{Dmn}\,R \cup \mathrm{Dmn}\,S$ and $\mathrm{Rng}(R \cup S) = \mathrm{Rng}\,R \cup \mathrm{Rng}\,S$;

    (ii) $\mathrm{Dmn}(R \cap S) \subseteq \mathrm{Dmn}\,R \cap \mathrm{Dmn}\,S$ and similarly for Rng;

    (iii) $\mathrm{Dmn}\,R \sim \mathrm{Dmn}\,S \subseteq \mathrm{Dmn}(R \sim S)$ and similarly for Rng;

    (iv) if $R \subseteq S$, then $\mathrm{Dmn}\,R \subseteq \mathrm{Dmn}\,S$ and similarly for Rng;

    (v) $\mathrm{Dmn}\,\varnothing = \varnothing = \mathrm{Rng}\,\varnothing$;

    (vi) $\mathrm{Dmn}\,R^{-1} = \mathrm{Rng}\,R$ and $\mathrm{Dmn}\,R = \mathrm{Rng}\,R^{-1}$.

Definition. $\mathrm{Fld}\,R = \mathrm{Dmn}\,R \cup \mathrm{Rng}\,R$. $\mathrm{Fld}\,R$ is called the **field** of R. R is said to be **on** A if $A = \mathrm{Fld}\,R$.

Remark. It is straightforward that R and R^{-1} have the same field and trivial that R is on $\mathrm{Fld}\,R$. $\square$

Definition. $A \times B = \{(a, b) : a \in A \wedge b \in B\}$. $A \times B$ is called the **Cartesian product** of A and B. More generally, $A \times B \times C = (A \times B) \times C$.

Remark. A relation which can be viewed as being a subset of $A \times B$ is called a binary relation. We stress 'viewed', since the ternary relation, $(A \times B) \times C$ is also a subset of a Cartesian product. $\square$

Theorem 12. Let a and b be sets and A and B be classes. Then

    (i) $a \times b$ is a set;

    (ii) $A \times B$ is a relation;

    (iii) $A \times \varnothing = \varnothing = \varnothing \times A$;

    (iv) if A and B are both nonempty, then $A \times B$ is nonempty;

    (v) if $A \subseteq C$ and $B \subseteq D$, then $A \times B \subseteq C \times D$;

    (vi) $A \times (B \cup C) = (A \times B) \cup (A \times C)$;

    (vii) $(A \cap B) \times C = (A \times C) \cap (B \times C)$;

(viii) $A \times (B \sim C) = (A \times B) \sim (A \times C)$;

(ix) $(A \times B)^{-1} = B \times A$;

(x) if B is nonempty, then $\text{Dmn } A \times B = A$; similar statement holds for Rng .

Theorem 13. If r is a relation, then r^{-1}, Dmn r, Rng r, and Fld r are all sets.

A.6 FUNCTIONS

After ordered pairs, about the single most useful and prevalent entities in mathematics are functions. They are ubiquitous and their important properties and related definitions are listed below.

Definition. $F(A) = \{x : \forall y(A \text{ is a set} \wedge (A, y) \in F . \Rightarrow . x \in y)\}$. Read '$F$ of A' for $F(A)$. $F(A)$ is the value of the function, F, with input A.

Theorem 14. Let F be a function.

(i) If $x \in \text{Dmn } F$, then $F(x)$ is the unique y such that $(x, y) \in F$, and hence $(x, F(x)) \in F$; in particular, $F(x)$ is a set if $x \in \text{Dmn } F$;

(ii) If $A \notin \text{Dmn } F$, then $F(A) = V^*$.

Remark. This theorem gives the main properties of $F(A)$, namely, if A is in the domain of F, then $F(A)$ is the second coordinate of the ordered pair in F having first coordinate, A. In any other case, $F(A)$ is V^*, whence $F(A)$ is always defined. There is no possibility of confusion, since V^* cannot ever occur as a second coordinate of an ordered pair because it is a proper class. $\square$

Theorem 15. Let F and G be functions.

(i) $F = G$ if and only if $\text{Dmn } F = \text{Dmn } G$ and $F(x) = G(x)$ for all $x \in \text{Dmn } F$;

(ii) If $\text{Dmn } F \cap \text{Dmn } G = \varnothing$, then $F \cup G$ is a function.

Definition. Let F and G be functions and A and B be classes.

(i) $F \circ G = \{(x, z) : \exists y(x, y) \in G \wedge (y, z) \in F\}$. $F \circ G$ is called the **composition** of F and G;

(ii) F is **1–1** (**one-to-one, injection**) if and only if F and F^{-1} are both functions;

(iii) If $\text{Rng } F = A$, then F is said to be **onto** A, or a **surjection** on A;

(iv) If $\text{Rng } F \subseteq A$, then F is said to be **into** A.

(v) If $A = \text{Dmn } F$, F is said to be **from** A;

(vi) If F is 1–1 and $\text{Dmn } F = A$ and $\text{Rng } F = B$, then F is said to be a **1–1 correspondence** (**bijection**) from A to B;

(vii) $^A B = \{f : f \text{ is a function from } A \text{ into } B\}$;

(viii) A function, F, from A into A is called a **unary operation**;

(ix) A function, F, from $A \times A$ into A is called a **binary operation**.

Theorem 16. Let F and G be functions. Then

(i) $\text{Dmn}(F \circ G) = \{x : x \in \text{Dmn}\, G \wedge \exists y \in \text{Rng}\, G \cap \text{Dmn}\, F\}$;

(ii) if $x \in \text{Dmn}(F \circ G)$, then $(F \circ G)(x) = F(G(x))$;

(iii) the following three conditions are equivalent:

  (a) F is 1-1;

  (b) for all x, $y \in \text{Dmn}\, F$, if $F(x) = F(y)$, then $x = y$;

  (c) for all x, $y \in \text{Dmn}\, F$, if $x \neq y$, then $F(x) \neq F(y)$.

(iv) if F is a 1-1 function from A onto b, then A is a set;

(v) if F is a function, then $F*a$ is a set;

(vi) $^{\varnothing}B = \{\varnothing\}$; $\,^{A}\varnothing = \varnothing$;

(vii) ^{a}b is a set.

A.7 EQUIVALENCE RELATIONS

One of the most useful kinds of relations are equivalence relations. These occur in various forms throughout all branches of mathematics. Most of the important facts concerning equivalence relations are presented below.

Definition. Let R be a relation.

(i) R is **transitive** if and only if

$$\forall x,\ y,\ z[(x,\ y) \in R \text{ and } (y,\ z) \in R \implies (x,\ z) \in R];$$

(ii) R is **symmetric** if and only if $\forall x,\ y[(x,\ y) \in R \implies (y,\ x) \in R]$;

(iii) R is an **equivalence relation** if and only if R is transitive and symmetric;

(iv) R is **reflexive on** A if and only if $\forall x[x \in A \implies (x,\ x) \in R]$.

Remark. In the above definitions, R must be a relation, as stated in the preamble.

The canonical example of an equivalence relation is the equality relation, as the reader can easily check.

To be an equivalence relation, the definition given requires only that R must be transitive and symmetric. These two conditions imply that R will be reflexive on its field. Thus, the issue of whether R is reflexive never arises.

Often one starts with a set, or class, A, and constructs a relation, R, with the intention that R will be an equivalence relation on A. To verify this, one must show not only that R is transitive and symmetric, but also must show R is a relation on A. One way of accomplishing this is showing

$$\forall x\ [x \in A \implies (x,\ x) \in R],$$

in other words, R is reflexive on A. $\square$

Definition.   Let R be an equivalence relation.

  (i) $x/R = \{y : (x, y) \in R\}$. x/R is called the **equivalence class** of x under R;
  (ii) $\pi_R = \{(x, x/R) : x \in \text{Fld}\, R\}$.

Theorem 17.   Let R be an equivalence relation.

  (i) $\text{Dmn}\, R = \text{Rng}\, R = \text{Fld}\, R$;
  (ii) R is reflexive on $\text{Fld}\, R$;
  (iii) If $x \in \text{Fld}\, R$, then $x \in x/R$;
  (iv) For any x, $y \in \text{Fld}\, R$, xRy if and only if $x/R = y/R$;
  (v) For any x, $y \in \text{Fld}\, R$, if $x/R \cap y/R \neq \varnothing$, then $x/R = y/R$;
  (vi) π_R is a function;
  (vii) If R is a set, then π_R maps $\text{Fld}\, R$ onto $\{x/R : x \in \text{Fld}\, R\}$, and $\pi_R(x) = x/R$ for each $x \in \text{Fld}\, R$.

Remark.   This theorem contains the main properties of equivalence classes.

Part (iv) asserts x is related to y under **R** exactly if x and y belong to the same equivalence class. Part (v) asserts two equivalence classes are either disjoint or equal. These two facts mean that the nature of an equivalence class will be independent of any representative. It is for this reason that we can use x/R as a name for the equivalence class of x and realize that it refers not only to the equivalence class of x but also to the equivalence class of y, where y is any member of $\text{Fld}\, R$ such that xRy.

Finally, these facts imply π_R is a function, a fact which is found useful in many areas of mathematics.   □

Definition. P is a **partition** of A, if P is a family of pairwise disjoint nonempty sets and $\bigcup P = A$.

Theorem 18.   Let A be any set. Let

$$E(A) = \{R : R \text{ is an equivalence relation with field } A\}$$

and

$$P(A) = \{P : P \text{ is a partition of } A\}.$$

Then there is a natural 1–1 correspondence between $E(A)$ and $P(A)$.

Remark.   The important feature of this theorem is in the proof which is accomplished by noticing the equivalence classes form a partition. Once this has been observed, the details follow rather easily. But most importantly, the theorem tells us that we can usefully think of equivalence relations in terms of the partition generated by the equivalence classes.   □

A.8 ORDERING

Orderings also occur in all branches of mathematics. Orderings provide structure to sets. Perhaps the simplest example of such is the positive integers under $<$. Order provides not only structure to sets, but also a framework which can be used to establish proofs. Again the simplest example is induction on the positive integers.

Induction uses order in two ways to structure a proof. First the ordering supplies a place to start a proof. Second, the ordering is used to establish the truth of the required fact for x, a member of the underlying set, provided the fact is known for all members of the underlying set which are less than x. It is important to realize, although not used in this book, that forms of induction can be used on many different types of orderings.

Some of the definitions and theorems related to orderings are presented below.

Definition.   Let R be a relation.

   (i) R is **antisymmetric** if and only if xRy and yRx implies $x = y$;
  (ii) R is a **partial ordering** if and only if R is reflexive on Fld R, antisymmetric and transitive;
 (iii) A is **partially ordered** by R if and only if $(A \times A) \cap R$ is a partial ordering with Fld $R = A$.

Theorem 19.   If R is any partial ordering, then $(A \times A) \cap R$ is also a partial ordering.

Definition. F is an **isomorphism from R onto S**, if and only if R and S are relations, F is a function mapping Fld R onto Fld S, and xRy if and only if $F(x)SF(y)$ for all $x, y \in$ Fld R.

Remark.   The notion of isomorphism is intended to identify structures, relations, and so forth, which are the same except for their names. $\qquad \Box$

Theorem 20.

   (i) $\{(x,\ y) : x \subseteq y\}$ is a partial ordering;
  (ii) if $R \in V^*$ is any partial ordering, then there is a set A and an isomorphism F from R onto $(A \times A) \cap \{(x,\ y) : x \subseteq y\}$.

Remark.   This theorem asserts first, that the subset relation is a partial order, and second, that every partial ordering can be realized using the subset relation. $\qquad \Box$

Definition.   Let R be a partial ordering with field A and suppose that $X \subseteq A$ and $a \in A$.

   (i) a is an **R-upper bound** of X if and only if xRa for each $x \in X$;
  (ii) a is an **R-lower bound** for X if and only if aRx for each $x \in X$;
 (iii) a is an **R-greatest element** of X if and only if a is an R-upper bound for X and $a \in X$;
 (iv) a is an **R-least element** of X if and only if a is an R-lower bound for X and $a \in X$;
  (v) a is an **R-least upper bound** (R-**l.u.b**) for X if and only if a is an R-upper bound for X and a is a lower bound for the class of all R-upper bounds for X;

    (vi) a is an **R-greatest lower bound** (*R-g.l.b*) for X if and only if a is an R-lower bound for X and a is an upper bound for the class of all R-lower bounds for X;

   (vii) a is an **R-minimal element** for X if and only if $a \in X$ and for all $x \in X$, xRa implies $x = a$;

  (viii) a is an **R-maximal element** of X if and only if $a \in X$ and for all $x \in X$, aRx implies $x = a$.

Remark. All of these definitions occur in the context of real analysis in the discussions of suprema and infima. □

Theorem 21. Let R be a partial ordering with field A, and suppose that every subclass $B \subseteq A$ has an R-l.u.b. If F maps A into A, and for all x, $y \in A$, xRy implies $F(x)RF(y)$, then $F(x) = x$, for some $x \in A$.

Remark. This theorem asserts that if one has a partial ordering on A, then any order preserving map from A into A must have a fixed point, that is, a point x such that $F(x) = x$.

    Fixed points can be very useful objects because they may have associated properties not available for arbitrary points. Such properties can then be used in proofs. □

Definition. Let R be a relation.

    (i) R is a **simple ordering** or **linear ordering** if and only if R is a partial ordering and for all x, $y \in \operatorname{Fld} R$, xRy, or yRx;

   (ii) A is **simply ordered** by R if and only if $(A \times A) \cap R$ is a simple ordering with field A;

  (iii) A relation, R, is **well-founded** if and only if R is a relation and for every nonempty class, $A \subseteq \operatorname{Fld} R$, there is an $x \in A$ such that $A \cap \{y : yRx\} = \varnothing$;

  (iv) $\leqslant$ is a **well-ordering** if and only if $\leqslant$ is a simple ordering and $<$ is well-founded where, $< \, = \{(x, y) : (x, y) \in \, \leqslant \text{ and } x \neq y\}$.

Remark. The canonical well-founded relation is the membership relation, $\in$. The axiom which forces this is the regularity axiom.

    The symbols, $\leqslant$ and $<$, in (iv) refer to general orders, not to the standard orders on **R**.

    With respect to **R**, $\leqslant$ is a simple ordering, but it is not a well-ordering (**WHY?**). If one considers $\leqslant$ on **N**, it is a well-ordering (**WHY?**). □

Theorem 22. For any partial ordering $\leqslant$, the following are equivalent:

    (i) $\leqslant$ is a well-ordering;

   (ii) $\leqslant$ is a simple ordering and every nonempty class $A \subseteq \operatorname{Fld} \leqslant$ has a $\leqslant$-least element;

  (iii) every nonempty class $A \subseteq \operatorname{Fld} \leqslant$ has a $\leqslant$-least element.

Remark. Well-ordered sets are those on which there is a partial ordering satisfying every nonempty subset has a least element. In analysis, all subsets of the integers which are bounded below have this property, and so are well-ordered. If the reader studies the section on induction, he will realize that it is this fact which is at the heart of the method of proof by induction. □

As stated, one use of order is in providing structure for proofs. The following theorems, which involve order, are all equivalent to the Axiom of Choice and are useful from time to time in constructing proofs.

Theorem 23 (Well-Ordering Principle). Let A be a set. Then there is a well-ordering with field A.

Theorem 24 (Zorn's Lemma). Let R be a partial ordering of a set, A. If every simply ordered subset of A has an R-upper bound in A, then A has an R-maximal element.

Theorem 25 (Maximality Principle). Let $\subseteq$ be a partial ordering of a set, A. If every simply ordered subset of A has an $\subseteq$-upper bound in A, then A has an $\subseteq$-maximal element.

A.9 FINITE AND INFINITE SETS; COUNTABLE SETS

One of the main issues in set theory concerns the size of a set. For small sets, this issue can be settled by counting the elements. For large sets, counting, which amounts to well-ordering the elements of the set fails to provide a unique answer to the question. The solution is equipotence.

Definition. Two sets X and Y are **equipotent** if there exists a 1–1 correspondence between X and Y. If X and Y are equipotent, we write $X \cong Y$.

Remark. The intuition behind this solution to the problem can be seen by thinking of a large auditorium. If every seat is filled and there are people standing at the back, we know there are more people than seats. If every seat is filled and no one is standing, we know there are the same number of seats as people. If there are unfilled seats and no one is standing, we know there are more seats than people. In no case do we have to undertake a counting process to arrive at these conclusions. Thus, the notion of 1–1 correspondence is the perfect tool for addressing these questions.

The approach we are taking to cardinal numbers is straightforward, but has inherent difficulties. For an alternate approach which avoids these difficulties, see Monk [1969]. □

Theorem 26. $\cong$ is an equivalence relation on the class of all sets.

Definition. The equivalence classes corresponding to $\cong$ are called **cardinal numbers**.

Theorem 27 (Trichotomy Principle).   Let a and b be sets. Then there is a 1–1 function from a into b or a 1–1 function from b into a.

Remark.   As a result of the Trichotomy Principle, we can select a set from each of the equivalence classes determined by $\cong$ and this class will have a natural linear ordering on it determined by $a \leqslant b$ if and only if there is a 1–1 function from a into b.

In this context, the Trichotomy Principle is equivalent to the Axiom of Choice, which makes clear why the Axiom of Choice is essential to the development of the theory of cardinal numbers.   □

Theorem 28 (Schröder–Bernstein).   If X and Y are two sets such that X is equipotent with a subset of Y, and Y is equipotent with a subset of X, then X and Y are equipotent.

Definition. $P^*A = \{B : B \subseteq A\}$. P^*A is called the **power class** of A.

Theorem 29.   Let A and B be classes and a be any set.

    (i) $\varnothing \in P^*A$;
   (ii) $P^*\varnothing = \{\varnothing\}$;
  (iii) $A \subseteq B$ implies $P^*A \subseteq P^*B$;
  (iv) $P^*(A \cap B) = P^*A \cap P^*B$;
   (v) $P^*A \cup P^*B \subseteq P^*(A \cup B)$;
  (vi) P^*a is a set.

Remark.   This theorem gives some of the useful facts about power sets, the most important one being the power set of a set is again a set.   □

Theorem 30 (Cantor).   There does not exist a function mapping the set a onto P^*a.

   Proof.   Let a be a set and P^*a be its power set. Suppose, for the sake of argument, that F is a function mapping a onto P^*a. Set $B = \{x : x \in a \wedge x \notin F(x)\}$. Since F is onto and $B \subseteq a$, there exists $y \in a$ such that $F(y) = B$. The reader can check

$$y \in B \quad \text{if and only if} \quad y \notin B,$$

which is a contradiction.   □

Corollary.   If X is any set, then X is never equipotent with its power set P^*X.

Remark.   It is an important fact that a set always has smaller cardinality than its power set.   □

Definition.   A set is said to be **infinite** if it is equipotent with a proper subset of itself. A set is called **finite** if it is not infinite.

Remark.   For an alternative approach to the problem of finite versus infinite, see Monk [1969].   □

Theorem 31.

    (i) The set $\mathbf{N} = \{1, 2, \ldots, \}$ of natural numbers forms an infinite set;

    (ii) For each $n \in \mathbf{N}$, the set $I_n = \{1, 2, \ldots, n\}$ is a finite set;

    (iii) If A is finite, then there is an I_n equipotent with A, or $A = \varnothing$;

    (iv) For any set a, $P*a$ is equipotent with ${}^{a}I_2$, the set of all functions from a into I_2.

Proof. The mapping determined by $f(n) = n + 1$ takes $\mathbf{N}$ into a proper subset of itself, whence $\mathbf{N}$ is infinite.

We prove the second statement by induction. Consider I_1. The only subset of I_1 is $\varnothing$. Since any function, F, from I_1 into $\varnothing$ would have $F(1) \in \varnothing$, we would have a contradiction. Thus, I_1 is finite. Suppose I_{n+1} is finite. If I_{n+1} is equipotent with a proper subset of itself via F, then we claim that one can assume $F(i) \in I_n$ for all $i \in I_n$ (**WHY?**). But F restricted to I_n establishes that I_n is equipotent with a proper subset of itself (**HOW?**).   ☐

Remark. There are alternative and much more satisfactory approaches leading to these facts, see Monk [1969]. Unfortunately, they require considerably more machinery than is presently available.

The important fact here is the positive integers and 0 list the cardinalities of all the finite sets. The proof of this fact is beyond the scope of this book.   ☐

Definition. A set is said to be **countable (countably infinite)** if it is equipotent with the set $\mathbf{N}$. An infinite set that is not countable is said to be **uncountable**.

Theorem 32.

    (i) $\mathbf{N} \times \mathbf{N}$ is countable;

    (ii) If X is countable and Y is an infinite subset of X, then Y is countable;

    (iii) If X and Y are countable, so is $X \cup Y$;

    (iv) If A is a countable family of countable sets, $\bigcup A$ is countable;

    (v) If X and Y are countable, $X \times Y$ is countable;

    (vi) If X is uncountable and $X \subseteq Y$, then Y is uncountable.

Proof. We give an indication of how to prove (i). Consider Table 1 which presents a portion of $\mathbf{N} \times \mathbf{N}$.

Table 1

(1,1)	(1,2)	(1,3)	(1,4)	(1,5)	(1,6)	(1,7)	$\cdots$
(2,1)	(2,2)	(2,3)	(2,4)	(2,5)	(2,6)	(2,7)	$\cdots$
(3,1)	(3,2)	(3,3)	(3,4)	(3,5)	(3,6)	(3,7)	$\cdots$
(4,1)	(4,2)	(4,3)	(4,4)	(4,5)	(4,6)	(4,7)	$\cdots$
(5,1)	(5,2)	(5,3)	(5,4)	(5,5)	(5,6)	(5,7)	$\cdots$
(6,1)	(6,2)	(6,3)	(6,4)	(6,5)	(6,6)	(6,7)	$\cdots$
(7,1)	(7,2)	(7,3)	(7,4)	(7,5)	(7,6)	(7,7)	$\cdots$

We count the elements of $\mathbf{N} \times \mathbf{N}$ by indicating how they can be listed in order. The ordering is as follows: $(1, 1), (2, 1), (1, 2), (3, 1), (2, 2), (1, 3), (4, 1), (3, 2), (2, 3),$ $(1, 4), (5, 1), \ldots$. This ordering amounts to listing the diagonals as indicated by the arrows through the table. It is left to the reader to give a precise description of the function from $\mathbf{N}$ onto $\mathbf{N} \times \mathbf{N}$ which is determined by this process. $\qquad\square$

Remark. The indicated argument presented above can be recast to prove (ii)-(v).

$\qquad\square$

Theorem 33. The set $\mathbf{Q}$ of rational numbers is countable.

Remark. The reader can easily construct a mapping from $\mathbf{N} \times \mathbf{N}$ onto the positive rationals by observing that each positive rational can be thought of as an ordered pair in $\mathbf{N} \times \mathbf{N}$. The proof will follow.

A number is **algebraic** if it is the root of a polynomial of finite degree having integer coefficients. Clearly, every rational is algebraic. Using the results in Theorem 32, it can also be shown the algebraic numbers are countable as well. $\qquad\square$

Theorem 34. The set $\mathbf{R}$ of real numbers is uncountable.

Proof. For the sake of argument, we suppose the reals in $(0, 1)$ are countable. If this is the case, we can list them as a sequence, $\{a_n\}$. Each of these reals has a decimal expansion, $a_n = 0.a_{n,1}a_{n,2}a_{n,3}, \ldots$, each digit of which is one of 0, 1, $2, \ldots, 9$. On this basis we list the sequences of digits in the decimal expansions of the reals in $(0, 1)$ as in Table 2:

Table 2

$$
\begin{array}{ccccccccc}
a_{1,1} & a_{1,2} & a_{1,3} & a_{1,4} & a_{1,5} & a_{1,6} & a_{1,7} & \cdots \\
a_{2,1} & a_{2,2} & a_{2,3} & a_{2,4} & a_{2,5} & a_{2,6} & a_{2,7} & \cdots \\
a_{3,1} & a_{3,2} & a_{3,3} & a_{3,4} & a_{3,5} & a_{3,6} & a_{3,7} & \cdots \\
a_{4,1} & a_{4,2} & a_{4,3} & a_{4,4} & a_{4,5} & a_{4,6} & a_{4,7} & \cdots \\
a_{5,1} & a_{5,2} & a_{5,3} & a_{5,4} & a_{5,5} & a_{5,6} & a_{5,7} & \cdots \\
a_{6,1} & a_{6,2} & a_{6,3} & a_{6,4} & a_{6,5} & a_{6,6} & a_{6,7} & \cdots \\
a_{7,1} & a_{7,2} & a_{7,3} & a_{7,4} & a_{7,5} & a_{7,6} & a_{7,7} & \cdots \\
\vdots & \vdots & \vdots & \vdots & \vdots & \vdots & \vdots & \vdots
\end{array}
$$

We define the sequence, $\{b_n\}$, by

$$
b_n = \begin{cases} a_{n,n} + 1, & \text{if } a_{n,n} < 8 \\ 3, & \text{otherwise.} \end{cases}
$$

The real number, $b = 0.b_1b_2b_3, \ldots,$ is in $(0, 1)$, but cannot be among the numbers listed in the countable collection, whence the assumption that the reals in $(0, 1)$ are countable must be false. $\qquad\square$

Theorem 35. $\mathbf{R}$ and $P*\mathbf{N}$ are equipotent.

Proof. A real number a can be uniquely identified by

$$a = \sup\{x : x \in \mathbf{Q} \wedge x \leqslant a\}.$$

It follows that $\mathbf{R}$ is equipotent with a subset of the power set of $\mathbf{N}$. Finding a way to identify all subsets of $P*\mathbf{N}$ with a subset of $\mathbf{R}$ is left to the reader. ☐

A.10 DIRECT PRODUCTS AND THE AXIOM OF CHOICE

Product spaces appear regularly in many branches of mathematics. While finite products can be treated as generalizations of the Cartesian product, infinite dimensional spaces (not treated in this text) require more machinery.

Definition. Let A be a function with Dmn $A = I$.

$$\textstyle\prod A = \{f : f \text{ is a function, Dmn } f = I \text{ and } f_i \in A_i \text{ for each } i \in I\}.$$

$\prod A$ is called the **direct product** of the family A.

Remark. We emphasize the use of A_i, instead of $A(i)$ to denote the value of the function A at i. This approach is particularly fruitful if I is an ordered set. ☐

Theorem 36.

   (i) $\prod \varnothing = \{\varnothing\}$;
  (ii) If A is a function with Dmn $A = I$ and $A_i \neq \varnothing$ for each $i \in I$, then $\prod A$ is not empty;
 (iii) If A is a set, then so is $\prod A$.

Remark. The statement in (ii) is the Axiom of Choice for sets, which asserts that a product of nonempty sets is nonempty. This means that there will be a function, $f \in \prod A$ such that $f(i) \in A_i$ for each $i \in I$. The function, f, is called a choice function because it chooses an element out of each member of the infinite family of sets, A_i, $i \in I$.

The Axiom of Choice is known to be independent of the other axioms. Since it is a very powerful axiom with some disconcerting consequences, for example, the existence of a nonmeasurable set, some prefer not to assume its truth. Unfortunately, this also has consequences, for example, one can no longer prove such desirable and plausible results as the Hahn–Banach Theorem, or that every vector space has a Hamel basis. The examples mentioned all relate to analysis, but other examples can be given in almost any other branch of mathematics.

The Axiom of Choice has many equivalent forms. The simplest is perhaps the Trichotomy Principle. This statement, which asserts that for any pair of sets, a and b either there is a 1–1 function from a into b, or vice-versa, seems too plausible not to be true. For this reason, many would argue the Axiom of Choice is obviously true. For additional discussion of these ideas, see Monk [1969] or Rubin and Rubin [1963]. ☐

Suggested Readings

CALCULUS

1. Ellis, R., and Gulick, D., *Calculus with Analytic Geometry,* Harcourt Brace Jovanovich, 1982.
2. Hunt, R. A., *Calculus with Analytic Geometry,* Harper & Row, 1988.
3. Larsen, R. E., and Hostetler, R. P., *Calculus with Analytic Geometry,* Second Edition, D. C. Heath, 1982.
4. Leithold, L., *The Calculus with Analytic Geometry,* Fifth Edition, Harper & Row, 1986.

ELEMENTARY DEVELOPMENT

1. Binmore, K.G., *Mathematical Analysis: A Straightforward Approach,* Cambridge University Press, 1977.
2. Clark, C., *Elementary Mathematical Analysis,* Wadsworth, 1982.
3. Gaughan, E. D., *Introduction to Analysis,* Brooks/Cole, 1975.
4. Gemignani, M., *Introduction to Real Analysis,* W. B. Saunders, 1971.
5. Goffman, C., *Introduction to Real Analysis,* Harper & Row, 1966.
6. Hayes, C. A. Jr., *Concepts of Real Analysis,* John Wiley & Sons, 1964.
7. Lay, S. R., *Analysis—An Introduction to Proof,* Prentice-Hall, 1986.
8. Moss, R. M., and Roberts, G. T., *A Preliminary Course in Analysis,* Chapman & Hall, 1968.
9. Ramanujan, M. S., and Thomas, E. S., *Intermediate Analysis,* Collier-Macmillan, 1970.
10. Youse, B. K., *Introduction to Real Analysis,* Allyn & Bacon, 1972.

INTERMEDIATE ANALYSIS

1. Anderson, J. A., *Real Analysis,* Logos Press, 1969.
2. Apostol, T. M., *Mathematical Analysis,* Addison-Wesley, 1974.
3. Bartle, R. G., *The Elements of Real Analysis,* Second Edition, John Wiley & Sons, 1976.
4. Bartle, R. G., and Sherbert, D. R., *Introduction to Real Analysis,* John Wiley & Sons, 1982.
5. Burril, C. W., and Knusden, J. R., *Real Variables,* Holt, Reinhart and Winston, 1969.
6. Fulks, W., *Advanced Calculus,* John Wiley & Sons, 1978.
7. Goldberg, R. R., *Methods of Real Analysis,* John Wiley & Sons, 1976.
8. Johnsonbaugh, R., and Pfaffenberger, W. E., *Foundations of Mathematical Analysis,* Marcel Dekker, 1981.
9. Lang, S., *Analysis I,* Addison-Wesley, 1968.
10. Marsden, J. E., *Elementary Classical Analysis,* W. H. Freeman, 1974.
11. Olmstead, J. M. H., *Advanced Calculus,* Prentice-Hall, 1961.

12. Protter, M. H., and Morrey, C. C., *A First Course in Real Analysis,* Springer-Verlag, 1977.
13. Ross, K. A., *Elementary Analysis: The Theory of Calculus,* Springer-Verlag, 1980.
14. Rudin, W., *Principles of Mathematical Analysis,* McGraw-Hill, 1976.
15. Barner, M., and Flohr, F., *Analysis I,* Walter de Gruyter, 1982.
16. Rosentlicht, M., *Introduction to Analysis,* Scott, Foresman, 1968.
17. Sprecher, D. A., *Elements of Real Analysis,* Academic Press, 1970.
18. White, A. J., *Real Analysis, An Introduction,* Addison-Wesley, 1968.

ADVANCED ANALYSIS

1. Aliprantis, C. D., and Burkinshaw, O., *Principles of Real Analysis,* North-Holland, 1981.
2. Fischer, E., *Intermediate Real Analysis,* Springer-Verlag, 1983.
3. Folland, G. B., *Real Analysis,* Wiley Interscience, 1984.
4. Lang, S., *Analysis II,* Addison-Wesley, 1968.
5. Hewitt, E., and Stromberg, K., *Real and Abstract Analysis,* Springer-Verlag, 1955.
6. Phillip, E. R., *An Introduction to Analysis and Integration Theory,* Intext Educational Publishers, 1971.
7. Royden, H. L., *Real Analysis,* Third Edition, Macmillan, 1987.
8. Simmons, G. G., *Introduction to Topology and Modern Analysis,* McGraw-Hill, 1963.
9. Stromberg, K., *An Introduction to Classical Real Analysis,* PWS, 1980, Wadsworth, 1987.
10. Torchinsky, A., *Real Variables,* Addison-Wesley, 1988.

SET THEORY

1. Halmos, P. R., *Naive Set Theory,* Van Nostrand, 1960.
2. Monk, J. D., *Introduction to Set Theory,* McGraw-Hill, 1969.
3. Rubin, H. and Rubin, J., *Equivalents of the Axiom of Choice,* North-Holland, 1963.
4. Suppes, P., *Axiomatic Set Theory,* Van Nostrand, 1960.

HISTORY

1. Bell, E. T., *The Development of Mathematics,* McGraw-Hill, 1945.
2. Boyer, C. B., *A History of Mathematics,* John Wiley & Sons, 1968.
3. Eves, H., *An Introduction to the History of Mathematics,* Saunders, 1983.
4. Kline, M., *Mathematical Thought from Ancient to Modern Times,* Oxford University Press, 1972.
5. Priestley, W. M., *Calculus: A Historic Approach,* Springer-Verlag, 1979.

NUMBER SYSTEM

1. Cohen, L., and Ehrlich, L., *The Structure of the Real Number System,* Van-Nostrand, 1963.
2. Landau, E., *Foundations of Analysis,* Chelsea, 1951.
3. Niven, I., *Irrational Numbers,* Carus Mathematical Monographs, No. 11, Mathematical Association of America, 1956.
4. Thurston, H. A., *The Number System,* Blackie, 1956.

COUNTEREXAMPLES

1. Gelbaum, B. R., and Olmstead, J. M. H., *Counterexamples in Analysis,* Holden Day, 1964.
2. Steen, L. A., and Seebach, J. A., *Counterexamples in Topology,* Springer-Verlag, 1978.

PAPERS

1. Hewitt, E., *The Role of Compactness in Analysis,* American Math. Monthly 67, (1960), pp.499-516.
2. Saari, D. G., and Urenko, J. B., *Newton's Method, Circle Maps, and Chaotic Motion,* American Math. Monthly 91, No. 1, (1984), pp. 3-17.
3. Stone, M. H., *A Generalized Weierstrass Approximation Theorem,* Studies in Mathematics, Vol. 1, Mathematical Association of America, (1962), pp. 30-87.

OTHERS

1. Baker, A., *Transcendental Number Theory,* Cambridge University Press, 1972.
2. Conte, S. D., and de Boor, C., *Elementary Numerical Analysis: An Algorithmic Approach,* McGraw-Hill, 1972.
3. Corwin, L. J., and Szczarba, R. H., *Multivariable Calculus,* Marcel Dekker, 1982.
4. Dieudonne, J., *Foundations of Modern Analysis,* Academic Press, 1961.
5. Fleming, W., *Functions of Several Variables,* Springer-Verlag, 1977.
6. Hardy, G. H., *A Course in Pure Mathematics,* Tenth Edition, Cambridge University Press, 1952.
7. Hardy, G. H., and Wright, E. M., *An Introduction to the Theory of Numbers,* Third Edition, Oxford, Clarendon Press, 1954.
8. Hirschmann, I., *Infinite Series,* Holt, Reinhart and Winston, 1960.
9. Kelley, J. L., *General Topology,* Van Nostrand, 1955,
10. Knopp, K., *Theory and Applications of Infinite Series,* Second Edition, Hafner, 1951.
11. Wilder, R. L., *Introduction to Foundations of Mathematics,* Second Edition, John Wiley & Sons, 1965.

Index

Abel sum, 458
Abel's lemma, 372
Abel's test, 312
  series, 372
  series of functions, 434
Abel's theorem, 365
  power series, 451
Abel summable, 458
Absolute convergence (series of functions), 432
Absolutely convergent, 308
  product, 388
  series, 353
Absolute value, 48
  of a function, 92
  of sequences, 69
Accumulation point (metric space), 587
Addition, 13
  of functions, 92
  of sequences, 69
Additive
  identity, 13
  inverse, 14
Algebra of relations, 617
Algebraic, 42
  functions, 482
  number, 45, 626
Algebraically complete, 42
Alternating series, 370
Analytic (at a), 461
Analytic (at 0), 460
Analytic tangent, 192, 197

And (logical connective), 2
Antecedent, 6
Antiderivative, 273
Antisymmetric, 621
Arccos, 507
Archimedean Principle, 32
Archimedean Property, 40
Arcsin, 507
Arctan, 507
Arithmetic average, 73
Arzela's theorem, 424
Associative law, 13
Avoids cycles, 536
Axiom of choice, 613, 627
Axis of revolution, 291

Baire's category theorem, 607
Banach's contraction principle, 592
Bernoulli's Inequality, 38
Bernoulli's numbers, 471
Bernoulli's polynomials, 472
Bernstein's polynomial, 473
Bertrand's test, 382
Beta
  function, 306
  integral, 306
Bijection, 618
Binary operation, 13, 619
  tree, 536
Binomial
  coefficient, 34, 467

Binomial (*Continued*)
  series, 467
  Theorem, 34
Bolzano–Weierstrass
  compactness, 603
  Theorem, 152, 547
Bonnet's Mean Value Theorem, 279
Boolean algebra of classes, 614
Boundary, 151
  metric space, 587
  point, 142
    metric space, 587
    in $\mathbf{R}^2$, 531
    in $\mathbf{R}^2$, 531
Bounded, 26
  above, 26
  at a, 109
  metric space, 601
  $\mathbf{R}^2$, 535
  sequence, 55
  variation, 320
  variation (series), 343
Branch, 536

Cantor's ternary set, 608
  theorem, 624
Cardinal number, 623
Cartesian product, 617
Cauchy
  convergent, 160
  criterion (for improper integrals), 307
  criterion (series of functions), 430
  criterion for products, 384
  criterion for series, 341
  criterion for uniform convergence, 413
  product, 362, 455
  sequence, 160
  sequence (in $\mathbf{R}^2$), 543
  sequence in the plane, 543
  sequence (metric space), 583
Cauchy–Schwarz inequality, 271, 528, 576
Cauchy's condensation test, 347
Cauchy's form of Taylor remainder, 466
Cauchy's function, 461
Cauchy's generalized mean value theorem, 472
Cauchy's Mean value theorem, 219
Centered at a point (power series), 445
Cesaro summable, 368
Chain rule, 211
Change of variable formula, 278
Characteristic function, 401, 598
Class, 609
Class-building axioms, 610
Clopen, 150
  in $\mathbf{R}^2$, 540

Closed set, 144
  in $\mathbf{R}^2$, 531
Closed (in metric space), 587
Closed interval, 48
Closed r-sphere, 578
Closure, 150
  in $\mathbf{R}^2$, 539
  metric space, 589
Cluster at a point, 586
Cluster point, 158, 166
  of a double sequence, 524
Cluster value, 158
Column series, 369
Commensurable, 43
Commutative law, 13
Compact, 157, 545
  metric space, 599
  support, 608
Compares favorably, 352
Comparison test, 344
Complement, 615
  relative, 615
Complete, 29, 544
  metric space, 584
Completeness Axiom, 29
Completion, 592
Complex number, 20
Conclusion, 3
Conditionally convergent, 308
  product, 388
  series, 353
Conjunction, 2
Connected, 152, 534
  components, 534
  metric space, 590
Continuous
  at a, 122
  on D, 122
  extension, 125
  function on metric space, 593
  at a point in metric space, 594
  in $\mathbf{R}^2$, 557
Contours, 514
Contraction, 592
  map, 165
Contractive sequence, 165
Contradiction, 23
Contrapositive, 4
Convergent, 60
  double sequence, 519
  double series, 365
  integral, 298
  in the mean, 402
  metric space, 581
  product, 383

in the sense of Cauchy, 160
sequence in the plane, 541
series, 331
Converges, 57
    more slowly, 352
    pointwise, 392
        series, 427
    uniformly, 404
        series, 430
Converse, 3
Convolution, 481
    product, 362
Cos, 501
Cosec, 506
Cosech, 507
Cosh, 507
Cosine, 501
Cot, 506
Coth, 507
Countable, 625
    base, 590
Countably
    compact, 602
    infinite, 625
Counterexample, 6
Cover, 545, 599
Cut, 45
Cylindrical surface, 517

Darboux's theorem, 258
Darboux-Stieltjes integral, 314
De Morgan's Laws, 5, 616
Dedikind cut, 45
Dedikind's test, 444
Dense, 148
    metric space, 589
    in $\mathbf{R}^2$, 533
    in Y, 159
Derivative of a function
    on an interval, 196
    at a point, 191
Derived set, 147
Diagonal series, 369
Diameter, 601
Dictionary ordering, 25, 41
Difference
    operator, 223
    quotient, 191
Differentiable at a, 191
Differential, 208
Dini's theorem, 416, 443
Dirac sequence, 481
Direct product, 627
Dirichelt's test, 312
    for series, 372

for series of functions, 435
Discontinuity
    at a, 127
    of the first kind, 129
    of the second kind, 129
Discontinuous, 127
Discrete metric, 574
Disjoint, 614
Disjunction, 2
Distance, 49, 567
Distance between sets, 607
Distance function, 566
Distributive law, 14
Diverge, 60
Divergent
    double series, 366
    integral, 298
    product, 383
    series, 331
Diverges
    more slowly, 352
    to $+\infty$ (function), 94
    to $+\infty$ (sequence), 66
    to $-\infty$ (function), 94
    to $-\infty$ (sequence), 66
    to zero, 383
Division (of sequences), 69
Domain, 84, 613
Double
    Negative, 5
    sequence, 165, 518
Du Bois-Reymond test, 444

e, 486
Edge, 536
Empty class, 611
Equality Principles, 7
Equicontinuous, 416
Equipotent sets, 623
Equivalence
    class, 620
    relation, 619
Euclidean, 527
    spaces, 567
Euler's
    contrast, 353, 359
    first integral, 306
    numbers, 509
    second integral, 306
Eventually monotone, 81
Existential quantifier, 7
Exponential
    constant, 486
    function, 488
Extends, 125

Extension, 125
Extensionality axiom, 609
Exterior, 151
  in $\mathbf{R}^2$, 540

F_σ- set, 607
Factorial (n factorial), 34
Fails to converge pointwise, 398
Family of pairwise disjoint sets, 614
Fan theorem, 536
Fibonacci sequence, 40
Field, 13
Field
  of complex numbers over $\mathbf{F}$, 20
  of a graph, 536
  of a relation, 617
Finite, 624
  intersection property, 159, 599
First category, 607
First coordinate, 83, 613
First mean value theorem, 326
Fixed point, 138, 592
Forward rectangular rule, 272
Fourier coefficients, 577
Function, 83, 613
Functions of bounded variation, 313, 320
Fundamental Theorem
  of Calculus, 274
  of Integral Calculus, 230

G_δ- set, 607
Gamma function, 306
Gamma integral, 306
Gauss's test, 378
Generalized derivative
  from the left, 203
  from the right, 203
Geometric, 42
  average, 73
  series, 334
G.l.b., 26
Graph, 536
Greater than, 22
  or equal, 22
Greatest lower bound, 26
Greatest member, 26
Gudermannian, 508

Half-open interval, 48
Harmonic series, 336
Has a limit, 56
Hausdorff property, 601
Heine–Borel
  Theorem, 156
  compact, 599

Hermite
  functions, 577
  polynomials, 577
Higher order derivatives, 205
Hilbert
  Number, 45
  space, 576
Hölder's inequality, 569
Homeomorphic, 596
Homeomorphism, 140, 596
Hyperbolic cosine, 507
Hyperbolic sine, 507
Hypothesis, 3

If and only if (logical connective), 2
If . . . , then (logical connective), 2
Image of A under f, 141
Immediate successor, 33
Implication, 2
Implies, 2
Improper integral, 298
Increment, 191, 207
Indefinite in integral, 277
In-degree, 536
Indexed family of sets, 616
Indirect argument, 23
Induction hypothesis, 33
Inductively closed, 30
Inf, 26
Infimum, 26
Infinite, 624
  products, 383
  series, 329
  series of functions, 427
Infinity, 48
  axiom, 612
Injection, 618
Inner product, 576
Integers, 39
Integral, 230, 277
  form of Taylor remainder, 471
  part, 40
  test, 349
Integration
  by parts, 277
  by parts formula, 326
Interior point, 142
  metric space, 587
  in $\mathbf{R}^2$, 531
Intermediate partition, 255
Intermediate Value Theorem, 135
Intersection, 612
  of a family, 616
Interval, 52
  of convergence, 447

Invariant, 140
Inverse of a relation, 617
Irrational, 40
Isolated point, 150
  in $\mathbf{R}^2$, 540
Isometric, 598
Isometry, 598
Isomorphism, 621
Iterated limits, 165, 521, 555

Jump discontinuity, 129

Kummer's test, 376
Kuratowski's problem, 592

Lagrange's form of Taylor remainder, 465
Laguerre
  functions, 578
  polynomials, 578
Landau's kernel, 481
Law
  of cosines, 576
  of the excluded middle, 3
  of Trichotomy, 22
Least member, 26
Least upper bound, 26
Lebesgue number, 607
Left-hand limit at a, 114
Left-side derivative, 203
Legendre's polynomials, 480, 577
Leibnitz's formula, 205
Leibnitz's test, 370
Less than, 22
  or equal, 22
Level curves, 514
L'Hospital's Rule, 223
Lim inf, 167
Limit
  form of comparison test, 345
  as n tends to ∞ (sequences), 57
  as n, m tend to infinity, 519
  at a point (function), 95
  as x tends to a from the left, 114
  as x tends to a from the right, 114
  as x tends to a of f, 95
  as x tends to $+\infty$ (of a function), 86
  as x tends to $-\infty$ (of a function), 86, 92
  at $+\infty$ (of a function), 86
Limit inferior, 167
  of a double sequence, 519
  of a function, 95, 183
    in $\mathbf{R}^2$, 552
  in the plane, 541
  of a sequence, 56
    in metric space, 581

Limit point, 103, 109, 144
  of A, 157
  metric space, 587
  in $\mathbf{R}^2$, 531
Limit superior, 167
  of a function, 183
Lim sup, 167
Lindelöf property, 552
Linear function, 133
Linearly ordered, 165
Linear ordering, 622
Lipschitz, 183
Lipschitz's condition of order α, 205
Locally bounded, 158
Locally monotinic increasing, 138
Locally path-connected, 537
Local maximum point, 214
Local minimum point, 214
Local monotonicity, 120
Logarithm
  of x, 491
  of x to base a, 495
Logarithmic function, 491
Logarithmic test, 382
Logical equivalence, 2
Lower bound, 26
Lower Darboux integral, 239
Lower Darboux–Stieltjes sum, 314
Lower Darboux sum, 237
Lower semicontinuous, 184, 598
L.u.b., 26

Maclaurin
  expansion, 461
  series, 461
Maximality principle, 623
Maximum, 26, 52
  point, 214
Meager, 607
Mean Value theorem, 216
  for integrals, 277
Measure, 230
Membership, 609
Mertens theorem, 363
Method
  of Exhaustion, 230
  of partial fractions, 335
Metric, 567
  space, 567
Midpoint rule, 272
Minimum, 26, 52
  point, 214
Minkowski's inequality, 50, 570
Minus infinity, 48
Monotone, 75

Monotone (*Continued*)
  decreasing on a set (function), 91
  function, 91
  increasing on a set (function), 91
Monotonic
  decreasing, 75
  increasing, 74
Multiplication, 13
  of functions, 92
  of sequences, 69
Multiplicative
  identity, 13
  inverse, 14

n-ary tree, 539
n-plus-first binomial coefficient, 34
nth
  factor,383
  partial sum (function), 426
  root, 47
Natural
  logarithmic function, 491
  numbers, 30
Necessary, 2
Negation, 2
  of the definition of continuity, 127
  of the definition of uniform continuity, 177
  of the limit (at a) (function), 103
  of the limit definition (function), 88
  of the limit definition (sequences), 60
  of pointwise convergence, 398
  of uniform convergence, 406
Negative, 22
  part, 53
  of a series, 355
  variation, 326
Nest, 603
Nested, 154
Newton's method, 209
Nonnegative, 22
  integers, 34
Norm (of a partition), 233
Not (logical connective), 2
Not continuous, 127
Nowhere dense, 607
Number, 13

One, 14
One-sided limit at a, 114
One-to-one function, 618
Open r-sphere, 578
Open
  cover, 156, 545, 599
  disc (radius r centered at $\mathbf{z}$), 529
  interval, 48

relative to D, 149, 558
  set, 141, 144
    metric space, 586
    in $\mathbf{R}^2$, 529
Or (logical connective), 2
Order, 21
  topology, 146, 545
Order-complete, 29
Ordered
  field, 21
  pair, 83, 613
Orthogonal, 576
  with respect to a weight function, 577
Orthonormal family, 576
Oscillates at a, 108
Oscillation, 597
Out-degree, 536

p-adic metric, 576
p-series, 346
Pairing axiom, 611
Parallelogram law, 576
Parametrization, 204
Parseval's equation, 577
Partial
  limits, 165, 521, 556
  ordering, 621
  sequence, 521
  sum, 330, 426
Partially ordered, 621
Partition, 233, 620
Path, 525, 534
  connected, 152, 534
Path-connected space, 537
Peano curve, 608
Peano's Axioms, 32
Periodic function, 187, 504
Pi (π), 503
Piecewise linear, 480
Plane curve, 204
Pointwise, 392
  limit, 392
Polynomial
  of degree n, 95
  function, 95
Positive, 22
  elements, 25
  integers, 30
  part, 53
  part of a series, 355
  variation, 326
Possess a sum, 331
Power
  class, 624
  function, 493

series, 445
set, 611
set axiom, 611
Precompact, 604
Prime number, 46
Primitive, 273
Principle of Mathematical Induction, 30
Product (of two functions), 92
Proof by induction, 33
Proper class, 610
Pseudo-metric, 575
Pythagorean
theorem, 527, 576
identity, 500

Quantify, 7

Raabe's test, 377
Radius of convergence, 447
Range, 84, 613
Ratio
comparison test (integrals), 304
test, 373
Rational
functions, 25
numbers, 39
root theorem, 46
R–D integrable, 239
Real number line, 21
Real-valued
functions of a single real variable, 511
functions of two real variables, 511
Rearrangement
of N, 65
of a sequence, 65
Reciprocal (of a function), 92
Rectangle, 551
Rectangular rule, 268
Recursive definitions, 34
Refinement, 233
Reflexive relation, 619
Regularity axiom, 612
Relation, 613
Relational axiom of choice, 613
Relatively open, 149, 151
in $\mathbf{R}^2$, 540, 558
Relative topology, 151
in $\mathbf{R}^2$, 540
Removable discontinuity, 128
Restriction, 133
Revised Riemann–Stieltjes integrable, 319
Revised Riemann–Stieltjes integral, 319
R-g.l.b., 622
R-greatest element, 621
R-greater lower bound, 622

Riemann
integrable, 256
integral, 256
sum, 255
Riemann–Darboux
integrable, 239
integral, 238
Riemann's theorem, 357
Riemann–Stieltjes
integrable, 317
integral, 318
sum, 317
Riemann's zeta function, 390
Right-hand limit at a, 114
Right-side derivative, 203
R-integrable, 256
R-least element, 621
R-lower bound, 621
R-l.u.b., 621
R-maximal element, 622
R-minimal element, 622
Rolle's Theorem, 215
Root test, 374
Row series, 369
Ruler function, 130
R-upper bound, 621

Schlomlich–Roche's form of Taylor
remainder, 464
Schröder–Bernstein Theorem, 624
Sec, 506
Secant, 190
Sech, 507
Second category, 607
Second coordinate, 83, 613
Second logarithmic test, 382
Second mean value theorem, 327
for integrals, 279
Second-order derivative, 205
Second principle of mathematical induction, 40
Second projection, 545
Self-dense, 608
Separable, 590
Sequence, 54
of arithmetic means, 368
of constant terms, 392
of functions, 392
(in a metric space), 581
of partial products, 383
of partial sums, 330
in the plane, 541
Sequential compactness, 603
Series
of functions, 427
of nonnegative terms, 344

Set, 610
Set-theoretic formulas, 610
Sigma, 34
Signum, 53
Simple
   discontinuity, 128
   ordering, 622
   substitution, 278
Simply ordered, 622
Simpson's rule, 272
Sin, 501
Sine, 501
Single-valued, 84
Singleton, 612
Singularity, 298
Sinh, 507
Slice
   $(x-z)$, 513
   $(y-z)$, 514
Slope, 190
Solid of revolution, 291
Space-filling curve, 445
Step function, 232
Steps, 232
Stirling's formula, 508
Strictly monotone, 75
   function, 91
Strict maximum, 214
Subadditive function, 133
Subclass, 611
Subcover, 599
Subfield, 14
Subsequence, 73
Subseries, 361
Subset, 611
Substitution axiom, 613
Subtraction, 19
Successor operation, 30
Successor, 612
Sufficient, 2
Sum (of two functions), 92
Summable, 368
Sup, 26
Supremum, 26
Supremum Principle, 29
Surface
   of revolution, 517
   of translation, 517
Symmetric relation, 619
Symmetry, 567

Tail
   n th, 343
   of a series, 340
Tan, 506

Tangent line to a circle, 189
Tanh, 507
Taylor
   formula, 222
   polynomial of degree n, 462
   remainder, 462
      Cauchy's form, 466
      integral form, 471
      Lagrange's form, 465
      Schlomlich–Roche's form, 464
      Young's form, 471
   series expansion, 460
Telescoping, 335
Term, 392
   n th, 55, 330
Test for convergence
   Abel's, 312
      series, 372
      series of functions, 434
   Bertrand's, 382
   comparison, 344
      integrals, 304
   condensation, 347
   Dedikind's, 444
   Dirichlet's, 312
   Du Bois–Reymond, 444
   Gauss's, 378
   integral, 349
   Kummer's, 376
   Leibnitz's, 370
   limit form of comparison, 345
   logarithmic, 382
   Raabe's, 377
   ratio, 373
   root, 374
   Weierstrass's M-test, 432
Theorem
   Abel's, 365
      power series, 451
   Arzela's, 424
   Baire's category, 607
   Binomial, 34
   Bolzano–Weierstrass, 152
   Bonnet's mean value, 279
   Cantor's 624
   Darboux's, 358
   Dini's, 443
   Fan, 536
   (first) mean value, 326
   fundamental (of calculus), 230, 274
   generalized mean value, 472
   Heine–Borel, 156
   intermediate value, 135
   mean value, 216, 219
   Mertens, 363

Pythogorean, 527, 576
rational root, 46
Riemann's, 357
Rolle's, 215
Schröder–Bernstein, 624
second mean value, 327
  for integrals, 279
Weierstrass approximation, 474
Thick set, 607
Thin set, 607
Topological
  invariants, 140, 596
  properties, 140
Topology, 144
Totally bounded, 604
Totally discontinuous, 127
Transcendental
  functions, 482
  number, 45
Transitive, 22
  relation, 619
Trapezoidal rule, 272
Tree, 536
Triangle inequality, 50, 566
Trichotomy principle, 624
Trigonometric function, 498
Trivial metric, 574
Truth value, 3

Unary operator, 19, 619
Unbounded
  at a, 108
  sequence, 55
Unconditionally convergent series, 357
Uncountable, 625
Uniform limit of a sequence, 404
Uniformly bounded, 402, 434
Uniformly continuous (in $\mathbf{R}^2$), 560
Uniformly continuous function
    (on a metric space), 605

Uniformly continuous on D, 174
Uniformly convergent, 404
Union, 615
  of a family, 616
Union Axiom, 611
Universal quantifier, 7
Universe, 615
Unordered pair, 612
Upper bound, 26
Upper Darboux integral, 239
Upper Darboux–Stieltjes sum, 314
Upper Darboux sum, 237
Upper semicontinuous, 184, 598

Value of a function at x, 84
Variation
  of f (for a partition), 320
  function, 322
  of a function on an interval, 320

Wallis Product, 312, 390, 508
Weak maximum, 214
Weierstrass's approximation theorem, 474
Weierstrass's inequalities, 386
Weierstrass's M-test, 432
Well-defined, 552
Well-founded, 622
Well-ordering, 622
  principle, 623
  property, 32
Width, 550

xth power of e, 488
ξth power function, 493

Young's form of Taylor remainder, 471

Zero, 14
Zorn's lemma, 623

ISBN 0-06-044734-6

90000